THE OXFORD COMPANION TO

# Charles Dickens

## Anniversary Edition

Edited by Paul Schlicke

Foreword by Simon Callow

OXFORD
UNIVERSITY PRESS

# OXFORD
UNIVERSITY PRESS

Great Clarendon Street, Oxford OX2 6DP

Oxford University Press is a department of the University of Oxford.
It furthers the University's objective of excellence in research, scholarship,
and education by publishing worldwide in

Oxford  New York

Auckland  Cape Town  Dar es Salaam  Hong Kong  Karachi
Kuala Lumpur  Madrid  Melbourne  Mexico City  Nairobi
New Delhi  Shanghai  Taipei  Toronto

With offices in

Argentina  Austria  Brazil  Chile  Czech Republic  France  Greece
Guatemala  Hungary  Italy  Japan  Poland  Portugal  Singapore
South Korea  Switzerland  Thailand  Turkey  Ukraine  Vietnam

Oxford is a registered trade mark of Oxford University Press
in the UK and in certain other countries

Published in the United States
by Oxford University Press Inc., New York

© Oxford University Press 1999, 2000, 2011
Foreword © Simon Callow 2011

British Library Cataloguing in Publication Data
Data available

Library of Congress Cataloging in Publication Data
Data available

Printed in Great Britain
on acid-free paper by
Clays Ltd, St Ives plc

ISBN 978-0-19-964018-8

1 3 5 7 9 10 8 6 4 2

*for Judith and Franny*

# ACKNOWLEDGEMENTS

WITHOUT the encouragement and practical help of a great many people, this volume would have been quite impossible to produce. My thanks go, first of all, to the book's editorial team, for their invaluable support, and to the contributors, for the outstanding entries they have written. Planning and assembling this book has been an exhilarating experience, and I am as grateful for the graciousness and enthusiasm with which my collaborators have participated, as for the expertise which they have shared.

Formulating aims and objectives, establishing principles of organization, and drawing up lists of topics provided the first major challenge, and I am particularly grateful to Kathryn Chittick, Eric Evans, Susan Horton, David McGarvey, and David Paroissien for their help with this process. For consultation along the way and added assistance as the submission deadline loomed, I am indebted above all to Philip Collins, John Drew, Leon Litvack, Bill Long, Judith Napier, Leonee Ormond, David Parker, Bob Patten, Adam Roberts, Fred Schwarzbach, Grahame Smith, and Andrew Xavier.

I have had expert secretarial assistance from Jane Balme, Fiona Insch, Karen MacLachlan, and Maureen Wilkie, and huge amounts of technical support from David Bell, Fiona Cameron, Iain Cameron, David Hawley, John Lemon, Jim Mitchell, and Aenea Reid of the University of Aberdeen Computing Centre. I am grateful too to the staff of the University of Aberdeen Library, in particular Iain Beavan and Jennifer Beavan.

David Parker supplied meticulously expert information for the maps. The chronology was assembled by Michael Slater.

It has been a great pleasure working with staff from Oxford University Press. Pam Coote, Michael Cox, Alison Jones, and Wendy Tuckey have been unstinting in their help and unfailing in their patience and courtesy. Jeff New has been a most congenial and expert copy-editor.

Finally, and above all, I extend my heartfelt thanks to my friend and colleague Michael Slater, who has worked closely on the project at every step of the way. His nearly omniscient knowledge of and love for Dickens, and his generous support to me as General Editor, have been instrumental in creating *The Oxford Companion to Charles Dickens*.

PAUL SCHLICKE

# FOREWORD

THE term Dickensland was coined early on, a famous early commentary bearing the engaging title *A Week's Tramp in Dickens-Land*. It is a vast terrain, Dickensland, encompassing not only the uncommonly fertile work – novels, stories, plays, essays, reflections, autobiographical writings, histories, travel books, even a *Life of Christ* – and a uniquely eventful life, but a rich mass of commentary that commenced almost as soon as Dickens leaped into print. A guide to Dickensland is essential; there have been many, but none of them as useful or as stimulating as the present Oxford Companion, whose return to print is long overdue and constitutes a wonderful way of celebrating the coming bicentenary.

A companion is exactly what it is. To acquire it is to make friends with a whole host of brilliantly informed, probing, witty guides to the terrain, a whole learned society, in fact, whose individual members have hacked paths through the undergrowth and found unglimpsed wonders, or fascinating oddities, or yet more hidden depths. They have compiled statistics, analysed and elucidated texts, compared and contrasted documents, but all of them have found how to communicate their findings in lucid, engaging prose. In fact, the team Paul Schlicke assembled for the book is a roll-call of the great names of Dickens scholarship of the time (1999), many of them still vitally active in the field, others gone but, like Philip Collins, unforgotten and unsuperseded, still central to Dickensian discourse. Not for nothing did the original cover depict Samuel Pickwick addressing the Club, for the Schlickeans, every bit as much as the Pickwickians, and with equally inspired dedication, were, in Mr Pickwick's fine phrase, not content merely with examining the things that lay beyond them, but looked to truths 'which are hidden beyond'.

As with all the best companions, it is hard to tear oneself away. One thing leads to another, and there one is, an hour later, one's original enquiry effortlessly answered but a dozen new possibilities irresistibly opening up. It is a Dickensian Enquire Within, it is Dickensian Google, it is an accurate Dickensian Wikipedia. It is indispensable, inexhaustible, irreplaceable, and it is very good to have it back.

SIMON CALLOW

# PREFACE

THE first in Dickens's long line of memorable characters, the 'immortal' Samuel Pickwick, announces in the opening pages of the book which bears his name that he intends to travel with his companions for the purpose of 'enlarging his sphere of observation, to the advancement of knowledge, and the diffusion of learning'. Integral with the comic adventures for which he was conceived is the eager curiosity to observe and to learn which underlies his character. This trait reflects one primary aspect of his creator's achievement, which Walter Bagehot noted when he referred memorably to Dickens as 'a special correspondent for posterity'.

Throughout his life Dickens observed, recorded, and participated in a wide variety of issues and events which centrally occupied English men and women in the nineteenth century. A primary purpose of *The Oxford Companion to Charles Dickens* is to evoke that milieu in which he lived and wrote, as well as to provide detailed information about his life, works, and reputation. Above all, the *Companion* is designed to illuminate the active interrelation between the man, his writings and activities, and his time. Entries describe family, friends, and associates; literary and theatrical traditions which he inherited; institutions and ideas which he satirized; circumstances he responded to; houses he lived in and countries he visited; the cultural climate in which he moved. These are conceived not as inert background, but as integral components of his life and work. The book is organized to situate his public life and his private life within the dynamic context of the people, places, and activities which influenced him, even as he influenced them. In short (as Mr Micawber would say), the ambition of *The Oxford Companion to Charles Dickens* is to provide the most comprehensive of reference books on England's greatest novelist.

*The Oxford Companion to Charles Dickens* is also designed to reflect contemporary directions in literary study. Written by a international team of more than sixty scholars and specialists, it draws on recent work in areas such as publishing history, book illustration, periodical reviewing, women's studies, and cultural studies, and on challenging revaluations of readership and the canon. The *Companion* offers a composite picture of current approaches to scholarship, criticism, and theory, as they apply to Dickens. In so doing, it constitutes a synthesis of the state of the art of Dickens studies.

The *Companion* is organized to provide in one volume easily accessible, meticulously reliable information for the general reader and specialist alike. It offers breadth of scope allied to depth of detail, in order to serve both as a resource of first resort for the specialist, and as a source of accessible and dependable information for the general reader. An alphabetical ordering of crisply written entries, with extensive cross-referencing and a wide-ranging index, is presented to facilitate searching into specific topics and is intended to encourage exploration into related matters. It is a book to consult, to browse in, and to inspire further reading.

What the *Companion* does not do is to annotate Dickens's works. There are entries on authors he drew upon, but not on specific quotations and allusions. Similarly, it does not attempt to gloss his vocabulary or to itemize sartorial styles, culinary conventions, or vehicular varieties; readily available student editions provide such information. Instead, *The Oxford Companion to Charles Dickens* concentrates on the interaction of the author, his works, and the traditions and legacies of his age. It seeks to convey an overview of topics dealt with in entries which combine biographical, literary, and historical approaches. In doing so it aims to provide greater range, greater authority, and greater accessibility, than any other reference work devoted to Dickens.

As General Editor, I have found the planning, organizing, and editing of the book an exhilarating experience. I have been greatly impressed with the quality of the entries which contributors have submitted, even as I have been delighted by the good-humoured co-operation I have received from advisers, helpers, and contributors at every stage. I have greatly enlarged my sphere of observation during the compilation of this book, and it is my sincere hope that readers will find it the best of good companions.

PAUL SCHLICKE

*Aberdeen, February 1998*

# PREFACE TO ANNIVERSARY EDITION

WHEN Dickens inaugurated his hugely successful periodical *Household Words* in 1850, he announced his aspiration 'to live in the Household affections', and he promised that, in 'no mere utilitarian spirit', he would strive to 'tenderly cherish that light of Fancy which is inherent in the human breast.' In a like manner, when planning *The Oxford Companion to Charles Dickens* over a dozen years ago, the editorial team set out to create a work which would serve not only as a source of information but also as a stimulus to readers' imaginations, an engaging reference work which would immerse them in the rich texture of the Dickensian world.

Under a slightly variant title, *The Oxford Companion to Charles Dickens* was published in 1999 as the first title in a series of 'Oxford Reader's Companions'. Well received by reviewers, it sold gratifyingly well and was re-issued the next year (with minor corrections) in a paperback edition. Colleagues endorsed its usefulness for their students, and most pleasing of all, general readers frequently observed that when they opened the pages to look up a single detail, the cross referencing enticed them to proceed further, and before they knew it they had spent hours happily browsing through the volume. The *Oxford Reader's Companion to Dickens*, that is, proved itself to be no mere dry-as-dust compendium of Gradgrindian facts (although of course the facts had to be there, and they are there), but a most congenial companion.

The book has been unavailable for the past decade, but, in honour of the bicentenary of Dickens's birth in 1812, it now rises again like a phoenix, 'in all the glory of print', (as Dickens proudly described his first 'effusion', 'A Dinner at Poplar Walk'), with a brand new title, a brand new format, and a brand new (and most generous) foreword by Simon Callow. The bibliography has been brought up to date, and, with a handful of further emendations, the contents are the same as they were in the original printing, and the contributors are identified as they were when they wrote their entries. As general editor, I hope that this new edition of *The Oxford Companion to Charles Dickens* will stand as a living testament to the continuing stature of the greatest of English novelists, the 'Inimitable', Charles Dickens.

PAUL SCHLICKE

*Aberdeen, July 2011*

# CONTENTS

# MAPS

# EDITORIAL TEAM

## General Editor

PAUL SCHLICKE, Senior Lecturer in English, University of Aberdeen, and past President of the Dickens Society (1994). His works include *Dickens and Popular Entertainment* (1985) and *The Old Curiosity Shop: An Annotated Bibliography* (1988). He has edited three Dickens titles, and has written numerous essays and reviews on Dickensian topics.

## Consultant Editors

### Dickens

PHILIP COLLINS, Emeritus Professor of English, University of Leicester. His many works include *Dickens and Crime* (1962) and *Dickens and Education* (1963), and he is co-editor of *The Annotated Dickens* (1986).

MICHAEL SLATER, formerly Professor of Victorian Literature at Birkbeck College, University of London, former editor of the *Dickensian* (1968–77), and a past President of the Dickens Fellowship (1989–90). His writings on Dickens include *Dickens and Women* (1983), and he is editor of the Dent Uniform Edition of Dickens's journalism and series editor of the Everyman Dickens.

### History

ERIC J. EVANS, Professor of Social History at Lancaster University. His books include *The Forging of the Modern State: Early Industrial Britain, 1783–1870* (2nd edn., 1996), *The Birth of Modern Britain, 1780–1914* (1997), and *Social Policy, 1830–1914* (1978).

## Advisory Editors

MALCOLM ANDREWS, Professor of Victorian and Visual Studies at the University of Kent at Canterbury, and currently editor of the *Dickensian*. He is the author of *Dickens on England and the English* (1979) and *Dickens and the Grown-Up Child* (1994).

JOEL J. BRATTIN, Professor of English at Worcester Polytechnic Institute. President of the Dickens Society (2000), he is a specialist in 19th-century manuscripts. He has written extensively on Dickens, and serves on the editorial board of *Nineteenth-Century Prose*.

KATHRYN CHITTICK, Associate Professor of English at Trent University, Peterborough, Ontario. Her work on Dickens includes *Dickens and the 1830s* (1990) and *The Critical Reception of Charles Dickens, 1833–1841* (1989).

SUSAN HORTON, Professor of English at University of Massachusetts, Boston. Past President of the Dickens Society (1990), she is author of *Interpreting Interpreting: Dickens's Dombey* (1979) and *The Reader in the Dickens World: Style and Response* (1981).

MAC M. ANNE CROWTHER, Professor of Social History at the University of Glasgow. Her works include *The Workhouse System, 1834–1929* (1981).

HC HUGH CUNNINGHAM, Professor of Social History at the University of Kent at Canterbury. His books include *Leisure in the Industrial Revolution* (1980) and *Children and Childhood in Western Society since 1500* (1995).

JD JIM DAVIS, Associate Professor and Head of the School of Theatre, Film and Dance at the University of New South Wales. His works include *John Liston, Comedian* (1985) and *The Britannia Diaries* (1992), as well as a number of articles on Dickens and the theatre.

JMLD JOHN DREW, Lecturer at the University of Buckingham. He has published several articles on Dickens's essays and journalism, and is co-editor of volume 4 of the Dent Uniform Edition of Dickens's journalism.

IHD IAN DUNCAN, Barbara and Carlisle Moore Professor of English at the University of Oregon. He is author of *Modern Romance and Transformations of the Novel: The Gothic, Scott, Dickens* (1992).

AE ANGUS EASSON, formerly Professor of English at the University of Salford. He has edited Dickens's *The Old Curiosity Shop* (1972) and several of Elizabeth Gaskell's works. He is co-editor of Dickens's *Letters* (Pilgrim edn., vol. 7, 1993).

EME EDWIN EIGNER, Emeritus Professor of English Literature at the University of California at Riverside. His works include *The Metaphysical Novel in England and America: Dickens, Bulwer, Hawthorne, Melville* (1978) and *The Dickens Pantomime* (1989).

CE CLIVE EMSLEY, Professor of History at the Open University. His publications include *Crime and Society in England, 1750-1900* (2nd edn., 1996) and *The English Police: A Political and Social History* (2nd edn., 1996)

EJE ERIC J. EVANS, Consultant Editor, History.

KJF K. J. FIELDING, Emeritus Professor of English Literature, University of Edinburgh. He is editor of Dickens's *Speeches* (1960, rev. 1988), joint editor of Dickens's *Letters* (Pilgrim edn., vols. 1 and 5, 1965, 1981), and author of *Charles Dickens: A Critical Introduction* (1958, rev. 1965).

VG VIC GAMMON, Lecturer in Music Education, University of Leeds. His many articles on traditional and religious music and music education include 'The Musical Revolution of the Mid Nineteenth Century', in *Bands: The Brass Band Movement in the Nineteenth and Twentieth Centuries* (ed. Trevor Herbert, 1991).

RG ROBIN GILMOUR, late Reader in English at the University of Aberdeen. He has written *The Idea of the Gentleman in the Victorian Novel* (1981) and *The Victorian Period: The Intellectual and Cultural Context* (1993), and edited *Great Expectations* (Everyman, 1994).

RFG RUTH GLANCY, Assistant Professor of English at Concordia University College of Alberta. Her many books and articles on Dickens include editions of the *Christmas Books* (1988) and *Christmas Stories* (1996), and bibliographies of his Christmas writing and *A Tale of Two Cities* (1993).

MH MICHAEL HOLLINGTON, Professor of English at the Université de Toulon et du Var. He is author of *Dickens and the Grotesque* (1984) and *David Copperfield* (1996), and editor of *Charles Dickens: Critical Assessments* (4 vols., 1995).

AH ANNE HUMPHERYS, Professor of English, Lehman College and the Graduate School, City University of New York. Her works include *Travels into the Poor Man's Country: The Work of Henry Mayhew* (1977) plus articles and chapters on the work of Dickens, G. W. M. Reynolds, and Victorian popular culture and the press.

LJ LOUIS JAMES, formerly Professor of English at the University of Kent at Canterbury. His books include *Fiction for the Working Man, 1830–1850* (1963, 1975) and *Print and the People* (1976, 1978).

SL SALLY LEDGER, Reader in English at Birkbeck College, University of London. She is the author of *The New Woman: Fiction and Feminism at the Fin de Siècle* (1997), and edited *The Christmas Books* (Everyman, 1999).

LL LEON LITVACK, Senior Lecturer in English at the Queen's University of Belfast. His works include *Dombey and Son: An*

fiction, essays, and short stories in many publications.

SS    STELLA SWAIN, formerly Lecturer in English at the University of the West of England in Bristol. She has published in the field of Law and Literature, and her work includes an article on Dickens, 'Legal Fictions', in the journal *New Formations*.

BT    BEVERLY TAYLOR, Professor of English at the University of North Carolina at Chapel Hill. Her books include *The Return of King Arthur: British and American Arthurian Literature Since 1800* (1983), and she has published articles on a range of Victorian writers and artists.

DAT    DEBORAH A. THOMAS, Professor of English at Villanova University, Pennsylvania. She is the author of *Dickens and the Short Story* (1982), *Thackeray and Slavery* (1993), and *'Hard Times': A Fable of Fragmentation and Wholeness* (1997), and editor of *Charles Dickens: Selected Short Fiction* (1976).

MWT    MARK TURNER, Lecturer in English at Roehampton Institute, London. He is the author of *Trollope and the Magazines* (1998).

JDV    J. DON VANN, formerly Regent's Professor of English at the University of North Texas and founder and president of the Denton Dickens Fellowship. He is the author of *Victorian Novels in Serial* (1985) and co- editor of four volumes on Victorian periodicals.

ASW    ALAN S. WATTS, Honorary General Secretary of the Dickens Fellowship (1976–90) and President (1990–2). His works include *Dickens at Gadshill* (1989), *Life and Times of Charles Dickens* (1991), *The Confessions of Charles Dickens: A Very Factual Fiction* (1991).

EW    ELLA WESTLAND, Lecturer at the University of Exeter. Her publications on Dickens include a co-authored series of articles on his critical history, which appeared in *Dickens Quarterly*.

MW    MICHAEL WINSHIP, Professor of English at the University of Texas at Austin. He is author of *American Literary Publishing in the Mid-Nineteenth Century: The Business of Ticknor and Fields (1995)*.

AX    ANDREW XAVIER, Curator of the Dickens House Museum, London. He has published works on the portraits in the Dickens House collection and on museological matters.

Note: Biographical details given above were current in 1999 when the entries were written and the *Companion* was first published.

# CLASSIFIED CONTENTS LIST

*[entries are arranged alphabetically by headword beneath the topic headings]*

## Life of Dickens

*Private life and attitudes of Charles Dickens*
Dickens, Charles: private life
childhood
Christmas
Englishness, Dickens's
history, Dickens's attitudes
homes of Dickens
library of Dickens
pets belonging to Dickens

*Family of Charles Dickens*
Dickens, John
Dickens, Elizabeth
brothers and sisters of Dickens
Dickens, Catherine Hogarth
children of Dickens
relatives and descendants of Dickens

*Women in Dickens's life*
Beadnell, Maria (Mrs Winter)
Hogarth, Catherine, *see* Dickens, Catherine
Ternan, Ellen Lawless

*The Hogarth family*
Hogarth, Catherine, *see* Dickens, Catherine
Hogarth, George and Georgina
Hogarth, Georgina
Hogarth, Mary Scott

*The Dickens Circle*
Dickens circle, The
Ainsworth, William Harrison
Buckstone, John Baldwin
Bulwer-Lytton, Edward
Carlyle, Thomas
Clarke, Charles and Mary
Chorley, Henry
Collins, Charles Allston
Collins, Wilkie
Coutts, Angela Burdett
Dolby, George
Fechter, Charles
Fields, James and Annie
Fitzgerald, Percy
Forster, John
Horne, Richard Henry
Hullah, John

Jeffrey, Francis, Lord
Jerrold, Douglas William
Kent, Charles
Landor, Walter Savage
Lemon, Mark
Maclise, Daniel
Macready, William Charles
Morley, Henry
Russell, Lord John
Sala, George Augustus Henry
Stanfield, Clarkson
Stone, Frank
Stone, Marcus
Talfourd, Thomas Noon
Ternan family
Ternan, Ellen Lawless
Watson, the Hon. Richard and Lavinia
Webster, Benjamin
Yates, Edmund

*Public life of Charles Dickens*
Dickens, Charles: public life
amateur theatricals of Dickens
'Boz'
collaborations
editor, Dickens as: *see* Wills, William Henry
dedications
journalist, Dickens as
letters of Dickens
novelist and man of letters, Dickens as
playwright, Dickens as
poetry by Dickens
popularity of Dickens
portraits, busts, and photographs of
    Dickens
public readings
reputation of Dickens
speeches of Dickens

*Clubs, causes, organizations with which Dickens
was associated*
Athenaeum Club
Cerberus Club
charity and Dickens
Coutts, Angela Burdett
Garrick Club
Guild of Literature and Art

## The Literary and Theatrical Context

# Classified Contents List

# LIST OF ABBREVIATIONS

| | | | |
|---|---|---|---|
| AN | American Notes | LD | Little Dorrit |
| AYR | All the Year Round | LOL | Life of Our Lord, The |
| BH | Bleak House | LT | 'Lazy Tour of Two Idle |
| BL | Battle of Life, The | | Apprentices, The' |
| BM | Bentley's Miscellany | MED | Mystery of Edwin Drood, The |
| BR | Barnaby Rudge | MC | Martin Chuzzlewit |
| CB | Christmas Books | MHC | Master Humphrey's Clock |
| CC | Christmas Carol, A | MP | Miscellaneous Papers |
| CH | Cricket on the Hearth, The | NN | Nicholas Nickleby |
| CHE | Child's History of England, A | OCS | Old Curiosity Shop, The |
| CP | Collected Papers | OMF | Our Mutual Friend |
| CS | Christmas Stories | OT | Oliver Twist |
| DC | David Copperfield | Pilgrim | The Pilgrim Edition of The |
| DS | Dombey and Son | | Letters of Charles Dickens, ed. |
| Forster | John Forster, The Life of | | Madeline House, Graham |
| | Charles Dickens (1872–4), | | Storey, Kathleen Tillotson, et |
| | ed. J. W. T. Ley (1928) | | al. (1965– ) |
| GE | Great Expectations | PFI | Pictures from Italy |
| GSE | 'George Silverman's | PP | Pickwick Papers, The |
| | Explanation' | Readings | Charles Dickens: The Public |
| HD | 'Hunted Down' | | Readings, ed. Philip Collins |
| HM | Haunted Man | | (1975) |
| HR | 'Holiday Romance' | RP | Reprinted Pieces |
| HT | Hard Times | SB | Sketches by Boz |
| HW | Household Words | Speeches | The Speeches of Charles Dick- |
| Johnson | Edgar Johnson, Charles | | ens, ed. K. J. Fielding (1960) |
| | Dickens: His Tragedy and | SUTH | Sunday under Three Heads |
| | Triumph (1952) | SYC | Sketches of Young Couples |
| Journalism | Dickens' Journalism, ed. | SYG | Sketches of Young Gentlemen |
| | Michael Slater (4 vols., | TTC | Tale of Two Cities, A |
| | 1994– ) | UT | Uncommercial Traveller, The |

# DICKENS FAMILY TREE

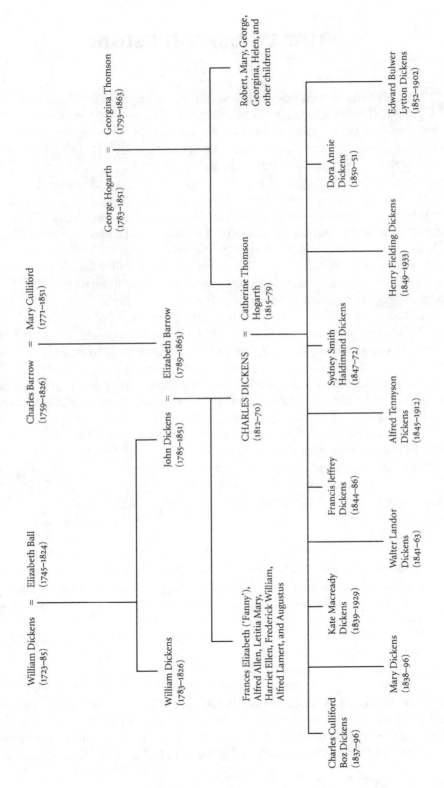

# HOW TO USE THIS BOOK

T HE organizing principle of the volume is an alphabetical listing of head-
words. These include names of people; titles of novels, stories, plays, collections, and of periodicals; aspects of authorship, publishing, readership, and
critical reception; events, institutions, movements, places, and a wide variety of
topics relating to the social, literary, theatrical, and artistic context in which Dickens lived and worked. Where related items fit conveniently together, they are
organized into comprehensive overview entries rather than being parcelled out
in bits; thus 'homes of Dickens' is a headword and not 'Lant Street', 'Tavistock
House', and so on; 'brothers and sisters of Dickens' is a headword and not 'Fanny
Dickens', 'Frederick Dickens', 'Augustus Dickens'.

Three topics—criticism and scholarship, editions, and London—are dealt
with in a series of interrelated, grouped entries. Each of these topics is headed by
a table of contents itemizing the relevant entries, as is the section entitled 'Dickens, Charles', which lists entries dealing with specific aspects of his life and work.
There is a classified contents list at the front of the volume, to aid searching by category of entry; and an index at the end, to direct readers to people and topics
which may not appear under a headword of their own.

Cross-references are indicated by the appearance of a headword in SMALL
CAPITALS, or by the use in brackets of 'see' or 'see also', followed by the headword.
As entries are provided for all of Dickens's novels, *Christmas Books, Household
Words* and *All the Year Round,* these are not cross-referenced. Cross-references are
given only where they are likely to amplify the entry in which they appear, and are
not used in every instance where a headword appears in the text. Similarly, index
listings direct readers only to those entries in which significant information
about a person or topic is given, and not to every entry in which they are mentioned.

Entries on individual novels are divided into sections dealing with inception
and composition; contract, text, and publication history; illustrations; sources
and context; plot, character, and theme; and reception. Details from novels are
cited by chapter number, or by book and chapter number when a novel is so
divided. Where significant differences between editions occur, these are discussed in the relevant entry.

Citations of Dickens's journalism normally refer readers both to the original
place of publication and (where available) to its appearance in later, more easily
accessible collections, such as *Reprinted Pieces* (*RP*), *Miscellaneous Papers* (*MP*),
ed. B. W. Matz, or to *Dickens' Journalism* (*Journalism*), ed. Michael Slater.

Letters are cited by recipient and date, from the Pilgrim edition wherever possible. Citations of editorial material in that edition are by volume and page number, separated by a full stop; thus 'Pilgrim 9.11 n' refers to a note on page 11 of
volume 9 of the Pilgrim edition of *The Letters of Charles Dickens*, ed. Madeline

**How to use this Book**

House, Graham Storey, Kathleen Tillotson, *et al.* (1965– ). Speeches are cited by page number from K. J. Fielding's edition (1960) as '*Speeches*'. Biographical material from John Forster's *Life of Charles Dickens* (1872–4) is cited from J. W. T. Ley's edition (1928) by book and chapter number, separated by a full stop; thus 'Forster 9.3' refers to book 9, chapter 3. Citations from Edgar Johnson's *Charles Dickens: His Tragedy and Triumph* (1952) are to 'Johnson' by volume and page number.

In addition to entries, there is a chronology of Dickens's life, works, and times on p. 641, and a Dickens family tree on p. xxvi. There is an appendix on p. 622 listing most of the named characters who appear in Dickens's imaginative writing.

Many entries have brief bibliographic references directing readers to further reading on a topic, and a general bibliography on p. 619 lists works which are frequently cited in the text. A list of abbreviations is given on p. xxv.

Entries are signed with initials, and a list of contributors appears on pp. xi–xv.

For a useful starting point for information about Dickens's career, readers are directed to the entry 'novelist and man of letters, Dickens as', which offers a succinct survey. As starting points for biographical information, it is suggested that readers consult 'Dickens, Charles: private life' and 'Dickens, Charles: public life'.

# A

**À Beckett, Gilbert Abbott** (1811–56), comic writer, playwright, and police magistrate. His 'burlesque ballad opera' *The Revolt of the Workhouse* (1834) influenced *Oliver Twist* (to William Mitchell, 16 February 1842), a favour À Beckett returned by adapting that novel for the St James Theatre (see DRAMATIZATIONS). He contributed an article, 'Authors and Actors', for the second number of BENTLEY'S MISCELLANY (February 1837). Two imitations of Dickens's works, *Oliver Twiss* and *The Posthumous Papers of the Wonderful Discovery Club*, both by 'Poz', were attributed to À Beckett, although he denied authorship (see PLAGIARISMS). He started a number of periodicals, the most important of which, *Figaro in London*, had Robert SEYMOUR as its principal illustrator. As one of the circle of writers who founded PUNCH, À Beckett was well known to Dickens and was invited to take on a small role in Dickens's AMATEUR THEATRICAL production of *Every Man In His Humour*—from which he withdrew on account of nervousness. Deeply moved by FORSTER's reading of *The CHIMES*, À Beckett was given advance copy and teamed with his *Punch* colleague Mark LEMON to write a dramatization authorized by Dickens. Dickens had great respect for À Beckett's conscientiousness as a police magistrate, and consulted with him about young women who might be suitable for admission to URANIA COTTAGE. À Beckett died suddenly of typhus while visiting Dickens's entourage on holiday at Boulogne-sur-Mer. PVWS

**abridgements of Dickens's works** were made by the author himself when preparing his PUBLIC READINGS. Since then most have been made either to introduce the novels to persons unfamiliar with them, or to make them suitable for a juvenile readership. Robert Graves's *The Real David Copperfield* (1933) had neither of these aims, but was primarily a criticism of Dickens's style. It reduced the size of that novel from 500,000 to 250,000 words to demonstrate that much of the text was superfluous. For this Graves was roundly con-demned by most critics, who pointed out how the Dickensian quality and most of the humour of the original were lost. Similar objections were made when the American Book of the Month Club issued as their free book for March 1943 a condensed version of no fewer than four Dickens novels, and in 1946 when Michael Harrison produced an abridged version of *Great Expectations*.

Typical of stories abridged for children was *Children's Stories from Dickens Re-Told by his Grand-Daughter and Others*, edited by Mary Angela Dickens. Like many other compilers, she concentrated on the pathetic and senti-mental characters. Her abridgements varied very much in length, and in faithfulness to the originals. Whereas she devoted only seven pages each to Jenny Wren (*OMF*), Trotty Veck (*The Chimes*), and the Blind Toymaker (*CH*), she gave 22 pages to Smike and Dotheboys Hall (*NN*), 33 to Barnaby Rudge, and the same number to Oliver Twist. The longer chapters contained a brief synopsis of the plot in which the character was involved, but many important episodes were omitted. Thus, in her version of *Barnaby Rudge* the Gordon Riots were dealt with very briefly, the emphasis being placed on Grip the Raven, and in dealing with *Oliver Twist*, the murder of Nancy was not mentioned at all.

Similar books were published in AMERICA. In 1868 TICKNOR AND FIELDS published a selection of abridged episodes, *Child Pictures from Dickens*, to which Dickens in a Preface gave his free consent. Such selections proved very popular. Most—Joyce Cobb's *Stories from Dickens* (1912), C. M. Courtney's *Tales from Dickens* (1917), and *Through Fairy Halls of My Book House* (1920), edited by Olive B. Miller—were compiled by women, Samuel M. Crothers's *The Children of Dickens* (1925), reprinted 33 times by 1950, being a notable exception. An abridgement of *Martin Chuzzle-wit* entitled *The Two Daughters* appeared in the New York magazine *Little Folks* (nd). In 1905 the *Children's Pickwick*, a bowdlerized version by Thomas Cartwright, omitted ex-pletives and all references to strong drink.

There were also abridgements for classroom use. In 1910 A. & C. Black included in their Supplementary Readers series *A Christmas Carol* and the *Story of Little Dombey*. McDougal published a 'Silent Reading Series' to encourage schoolchildren who hitherto had only read aloud in class to read silently to themselves. Publishers have since brought out textbooks which abridge the story, explain the action and the author's intentions, and add explanatory notes and questions (for example, the Penguin Masterstudies, Pan Study Aids, and Macmillan Master Guides series).

ASW

**actors, actresses, and other entertainers.** Dickens was an enthusiastic theatregoer who particularly admired good acting. As a shorthand writer at Doctors' Commons he went to the theatre nearly every night for at least three years, 'going to where there was the best acting: and always to see Mathews, whenever he played' (Forster 5.1; see MATHEWS, CHARLES, THE ELDER). Much impressed by Mathews's volatile comic style and his famous 'At Homes'—three or four of which he learnt by heart—Dickens continually drew on Mathews and other comic actors for inspiration. He admired the broad humour of J. B. BUCKSTONE, whose 'comicalities' he had gone home to dream of as a boy (*Speeches* p. 187), and the comic subtlety and pathos of Robert KEELEY (publishing an extensive account of his acting in *AYR* in 1869). For John Pritt HARLEY he wrote *The STRANGE GENTLEMAN*, and he was amongst the first to recognize J. L. Toole's talent and encourage him (Forster 7.2). In time comic actors such as Toole owed as much to stage adaptations of Dickens as Dickens had formerly owed to the influence of Mathews or the Surrey Theatre's low comedian Sam Vale, said to be a prototype of Sam Weller. Both Toole and the American actor Joseph Jefferson, for instance, significantly boosted their reputations through embodying Caleb Plummer (*CH*) on stage. Light comedians, such as the younger Charles MATHEWS, tended to play more dynamic and mercurial roles, like Jingle (*PP*), himself partly modelled upon the characters played by such actors as William Lewis and Richard Jones. Overall, as Earle Davis (1964) has demonstrated, Dickens's techniques of characterization owe much to the comic performances he saw in the contemporary theatre. Dickens also edited the MEMOIRS (1838) of the great clown Joseph Grimaldi, who regularly appeared at the patent theatres and at Sadler's Wells earlier in the century, and whose performances Dickens had seen when a small boy. In Dickens's lifetime clowns, with their often subversive humour, were associated with Harlequinades (later PANTOMIMES), particularly at Christmas. Dickens refers to his strong childhood 'veneration for Clowns', and also to his memories of Harlequin, Pantaloon, and Columbine (to marry the latter of whom 'would be to obtain the highest pitch of all human felicity'), in his evocative Preface to Grimaldi's *Memoirs*.

Although the impact of the comic stage is most evident in Dickens's work, he also enjoyed more serious forms of acting. In particular he admired William Charles MACREADY, the leading tragedian and actor-manager of his generation. Macready, who retired from the stage in 1851, was especially renowned for such roles as Macbeth, Lear, Virginius, and William Tell; as an actor he could be impassioned and terrifying, yet also suggest humanity and DOMESTICITY if necessary. Despite eccentricities of gesture and diction, he emphasized the sense of the words he spoke and the coherence of the characters he played. Dickens told Macready that, as 'a mere boy, I was one of your faithful and devoted adherents in the pit', becoming 'more earnest' in his study as he grew older (27 February 1851). He wrote enthusiastically about many of Macready's performances, including his 'fresh, distinct, vigorous and enjoyable' Benedick in *Much Ado About Nothing* (*Journalism* 2.55–9). Charles FECHTER was another tragedian much championed by Dickens, who encouraged him to come to England (he first performed in London in 1860). However, apart from his Hamlet and Iago, he was generally more revered for his romantically picturesque and passionate performances in melodrama. Dickens greatly admired French performers like Fechter and Rose Cheri, whose Clarissa Harlowe he described as 'a most charming, intelligent, modest, affecting piece of acting' (24 January 1847), whilst he had never seen anything 'in art, so exultedly horrific and awful' as Le Maître's portrayal of a murderous gambler in a melodrama at the Ambigu (February 1855).

Dickens has less to say about actresses than actors, although his Theatrical Young Gentleman demonstrates his familiarity with leading actresses, who are 'always designated by their surnames only, as Taylor, Nisbett, Faucit, Honey' (*SYG*). Yet he sometimes wrote enthusiastically of burlesque actresses such as Marie Wilton, whose performance as Pippo in *The Maid and the Magpie* he found 'astonishingly impudent . . . and so stupendously like a boy, and unlike a woman, that it is perfectly free from offence' (17 January 1858). He was also much taken by the French actress Mme Celeste (a notable Madame Defarge in 1860), and by Sara Woolgar's acting in J. B. Buckstone's melodrama *The Flowers of the Forest*. Another favourite was Mrs KEELEY, whose Smike at the Adelphi Theatre he much appreciated, whilst he recalled the acting of Elizabeth Yates as 'a beautiful part of my own youth' (23 September 1860). Professional actresses also appeared in his AMATEUR THEATRICALS, which was how he met Ellen TERNAN and her family (see TERNAN family). When Maria Ternan played opposite him in *The FROZEN DEEP*, he was touched by the distress and agitation in her face and by her 'natural emotion' as she knelt over the dying Wardour (5 September 1857); not long after he was writing to Buckstone concerning Ellen Ternan's engagement at the Haymarket. (13 October 1857).

Dickens's novels and journalism abound in references to actors and acting, and his characters themselves are often depicted as if they had just stepped off the stage. Jingle, who quotes Lord Grizzle's song 'In hurry, post-haste for a licence' from FIELDING's burlesque *Tom Thumb* after his elopement with the spinster aunt (*PP* 10), is a strolling player with a debt to Rover in O'Keefe's *Wild Oats*, Goldfinch in Holcroft's *Road to Ruin*, and with speech patterns traceable to Mathews's 'At Homes'. It was also as Jingle that Henry Irving scored one of his earliest successes in 1871. *The Old Curiosity Shop* introduces us to the Punch and Judy men Codlin and Short, and to Mrs Jarley and her waxworks, not to mention the equestrian performers of Astley's. *Little Dorrit* evokes the world of the ballet girl through Little Dorrit's sister Fanny; this milieu is also captured in 'Gaslight Fairies', where the 'fairies' range 'from an anxious woman of ten, learned in the prices of victual and fuel, up to a conceited young lady of five times that age,

who always persisted in standing on one leg longer than was necessary, with the determination (as I was informed), "to make a Part of it" ' (*HW* 2 February 1855). Central to *Hard Times* are Sleary and his circus, evoking not only memories of Astley's but also signifying the importance of the imagination within the thematic structure of the novel and the moral worth of theatrical folk. In *Great Expectations* Mr Wopsle's contribution to the decline of the drama in sundry roles provides not only comic relief, but also a satirical commentary on Pip's equivalent aspirations to become a gentleman. An aspirant Hamlet and George Barnwell, Wopsle ends up playing subsidiary roles in melodrama and pantomime in the minor theatres (*GE* 47). Most significant in its depiction of actors and actresses, through the Crummles family and company, is *Nicholas Nickleby*. Crummles, the actor-manager, employs Nicholas as an actor, commenting, 'There's genteel comedy in your walk and manner, juvenile tragedy in your eye, and touch-and-go farce in your laugh' (*NN* 22). Such versatility is also represented by Miss Snevellicci, 'who could do anything from a medley dance to Lady Macbeth, and always played some part in blue-silk knee-smalls at her benefit' (*NN* 23). Child performers (a frequent feature of the 19th-century stage) are satirized in the not-so-juvenile Infant Phenomenon (see INFANT PHENOMENA). Whilst the Crummles family represent a rather romanticized view of provincial actors, a harsher perspective is embodied in the poor Wedgingtons giving their ill-attended benefit in 'Out of Season' (*HW* 28 June 1856), or in the walking gentleman, who has 'to talk of his father's mansion in the country, with a dreary recollection of his own two-pair back, in the New Cut' ('Astley's', *SB*). Lower down the spectrum still are the strolling actors who set up their own makeshift theatres, such as RICHARDSON's, whose performers 'parading outside in all the dignity of wigs, spangles, red-ochre, and whitening' Dickens satirizes in his essay 'Greenwich Fair' (*SB*).

Dickens was acquainted with most of the leading actors of his time either socially or through charity work. Harley became a regular guest at Dickens's home from the late 1830s, whilst Macready, to whom Dickens was introduced by FORSTER, became one of his closest friends. Later in his life Dickens befriended the tragedian Charles Fechter, who was to present him with the gift of a Swiss chalet. Dickens's involvement with the profession was further enhanced by his support for the ROYAL GENERAL THEATRICAL FUND; his speeches, which reflect his passion for the theatre, his admiration for actors in general, and his concern for the welfare of the less prosperous members of the profession, were invariably a feature of the annual dinner held in aid of this charity. As a result, actor-managers such as Samuel Phelps, Benjamin WEBSTER, J. B. Buckstone (with whom he drank gin-slings after seeing the Spanish Dancers), and Charles KEAN (whom he cordially loathed), as well as melodramatic actors like T. P. Cooke, were all known to him. He was also no stranger to rehearsals, assisting Frederick YATES and the Keeleys with adaptations of his own work and later working with Fechter at the Lyceum.

Dickens had wanted to be a professional actor in his youth, but missed an audition at Covent Garden on account of illness. Even after his subsequent success as a writer he could not resist engaging in amateur theatricals: his acting in such performances and later in his public readings convinced many that he might have enjoyed an equally successful career on the stage. The *Leader* (20 January 1857) described Dickens, apropos his Richard Wardour in *The Frozen Deep*, as 'not only a great novelist, but a great actor also'. According to Forster, Dickens's strength was 'rather in the vividness and variety of his assumptions, than in the completeness, finish, or ideality he could give to any part of them', yet 'this was in itself so thoroughly genuine and enjoyable, and had in it such quickness and keenness of insight, that of its kind it was unrivalled' (Forster 5.1). (See THEATRE AND THEATRICALITY; THEATRES AND OTHER PLACES OF EXHIBITION.)    JD

Fawcett, F. Dubrez, *Dickens the Dramatist: On Stage, Screen, and Radio* (1952).

Fitzgerald, S. J. Adair, *Dickens and the Drama* (1910).

Johnson, Eleanor and Edgar (eds.), *The Dickens Theatrical Reader* (1964).

Lewes, G. H., *On Actors and the Art of Acting* (1875).

Marston, Westland, *Our Recent Actors* (1888).

Pemberton, Thomas E., *Charles Dickens and the Stage* (1888).

**adaptations of Dickens's works** (non-dramatic) introduce new situations, jokes, songs, etc. into the framework of one of Dickens's stories, without changing the main outline of the story or inventing new characters or plot developments (as opposed to a SEQUEL).

Most adaptations of Dickens's work were made in the early years of his career. They began immediately after *Pickwick*'s success. In 1837 and the following years there appeared about twenty parasitical publications—*The Penny Pickwick* (1837–9), *The Pickwick Gazette, a weekly register of Pickwickian proceedings* (1837), and the first of many song and joke books, with titles such as *Sam Weller's Favourite Song Book* and *Sam Weller's Pickwick Jest Book*. The popularity of such compilations waned from about 1845, but never entirely ceased. In 1927 Charles G. Harper published *Mr Pickwick's Second Time on Earth*, and as late as 1932 Stephen Leacock published *The Dry Pickwick*.

Several early adaptations were 'edited by Bos' (T. P. Prest). They included *The Sketch Book by 'Bos'* (1837), *Pickwick in America* (1838–9), *The Life and Adventures of Oliver Twist, the Workhouse Boy* (1839), *Nickelas Nickelbery. edited by 'Bos'* (1839), *Mister Humfries' Clock, 'Bos', Maker* (1840), and *Barnaby Budge* (1841). Having adapted *The Old Curiosity Shop* and *Barnaby Rudge*, Parley's Illuminated Library would have adapted the *Carol* had not Dickens obtained an injunction to prevent it.

In 1847 the newly founded satirical magazine *The Man in the Moon* criticized Dickens for his treatment of the death of Paul Dombey and published an *Inquest on the Late Master Paul Dombey* which concluded with a 'Requiem for Paul Dombey'. It referred to a pirated version of the novel, *Dombey and Daughter*, and subsequently published *Dombey and Son Finished*, which parodied Dickens's style, and his fondness for references to *The* ARABIAN NIGHTS and to sunshine and shadow (see PLAGIARISMS).

Robert B. Brough made two adaptations of *Hard Times*, the first in the magazine *Diogenes* in 1854, and a very similar work, entitled *Hard Times by Charles Diggins*, in 1856. An abridged version of these very funny parodies of Dickens's STYLE and SENTIMENT is reprinted in Collins (1971).

In an amusing article by J. H. McNulty, 'If Scrooge Had Died First', in the *Dickensian*, 31 (1935), the ghost of Scrooge upbraids a generous and charitable Marley for retaining redundant staff. 'But what would happen to them if I discharged them?' asks Marley. Scrooge replies: 'Are there no workhouses? Are there no prisons?'

The vogue for adaptations has not run its course even now. In 1982 Sue Roe's *Estella's Expectations* rewrote Pip's story from Estella's perspective, and Michael Noonan's *Magwitch*, also 1982, recounted the convict's adventures in Australia.      ASW

**Addison, Joseph** (1672–1719), ESSAYIST, classical scholar, and Whig statesman, whose writings Dickens knew from an early age. The periodicals he co-wrote with STEELE—*The Tatler* (1709–11) and *The Spectator* (1711–12, 1714)—were still popular in Regency England, and were among the 'Cooke's Pocket Library' collection owned by Dickens's father. They had an important influence on all Dickens's plans for founding a periodical, and a number of the essays are referred to in his writings. Speeches from his tragedy *Cato* (1713) are echoed in *David Copperfield* (17), 'Going into Society' (*CS*), and *Edwin Drood* (13).      JMLD

**advertising in and of Dickens's work.** Dickens lived in an era of brash and relentless advertising. Walls, fences, and hoardings in city and village were plastered with urgent bills and posters for all kinds of products and placebos. In 'Bill-sticking' (*HW* 22 March 1851; *RP*) Dickens describes the fights between rival groups of bill-stickers covering 'the hoarding of Trafalgar Square' with their offerings. The hoarding, bedecked with advertisements for theatres and fireworks, can be seen in Fox Talbot's famous photograph of 1844, which shows the construction of Nelson's Column, the 145 feet-high advertisement for Britain's naval greatness.

Most of Dickens's novels were issued in monthly shilling parts in green paper wrappers, with Dickens's text sandwiched between sections of copious and varied advertisements (see SERIAL LITERATURE). The novel's letterpress was preceded by a selection of advertisements taking their general title from that of the novel, such as 'The David Copper-field Advertiser'. This was printed with the text of the novel.

Sometimes further materials, called 'Inserts', were supplied ready-printed by advertisers themselves. These were stitched in at the end of the text. For instance, pamphlets from the National Anti-Corn Law League were sewn into various monthly parts of *Martin Chuzzlewit* (1843). A full prospectus for the Great EXHIBITION OF 1851 appeared as an Insert in April 1850.

What kind of goods and services were advertised? Countless pills and potions clamour for attention in the densely printed columns. There was Dr Locock's celebrated Pulmonary Wafers, Du Barry's Revalenta Arabica Food (which gets an amused mention in 'Bill-sticking'), and Taylor's Dietetic Cocoa. Morison's Pills were relentlessly advertised and universally swallowed. Their inventor, James Morison, the 'Hygeist' (1770–1840), earned himself an entry in *The Dictionary of National Biography*.

Third parties seized on the names of Dickens's characters to advertise their wares. New sheet music offered 'The Original Nicholas Nickleby Quadrilles, by Boz, Jun., author of the Pickwicks, danced at the Queen's balls' (October 1838). The following January a new comic song was advertised: 'The Ghost and the Baron of Grogswig, written and dedicated to the immortal Boz' by J. Major.

The Nickleby Pen, by Price & Co., of Birmingham, deserves mention for its elegant text: 'Like its original, it possesses uncommon flexibility of character with great powers of endurance.'

Deserving of notice, too, is Mr E. Moses, Tailor, whose advertisements appeared first in the *Dombey* Advertiser, and later took up the whole of the inside back cover of the nineteen numbers of *David Copperfield* (1849–50). His many flights of verse, lauding both his own and Dickens's products, are both ingenious and amusing, though his rhymes can be daringly dreadful. A typical offering will be found in the December 1849 Advertiser. It is called THE PROPER FIELD FOR COPPERFIELD. No wonder that Dickens complains: 'MOSES AND SON are on my track' in 'Bill-sticking'.

Advertising in these columns of fine print was not cheap. In 1838 an insertion of up to eight lines cost ten shillings and sixpence, half a column cost two guineas, a whole column three pounds ten. For a full page the fee was six guineas.

Dickens's publishers seemed content to accept advertisements from writers and artists wishing to cash in on the popularity of 'Boz'. In the *Nickleby* Advertisers (April 1838–October 1839), among the items on Patent Portable Water Closets and Eight-Keyed Cocoa Flutes, can be found 'Illustrations to the Pickwick Papers. By Samuel Weller' and 'Illustrations to Nicholas Nickleby. By Peter Palette'. Most of these illustrations were of good quality, and received encouraging reviews.

The prolific SENSATION NOVELIST G. W. M. Reynolds announced Part 14 of his pastiche *Pickwick Abroad* in the *Nickleby* Advertiser for March 1839. Like most of Reynolds's work it was not without merit. Far different were the wretched pirated works, poorly written, crudely illustrated, and sold for a penny a week. Examples are: *The Posthumourous Notes of the Pickwick Club, Oliver Twiss,* and *Nickelas Nickelbery*—all edited by 'Bos'. None of these crudities, of course, was advertised in the monthly numbers (see ADAPTATIONS; PLAGIARISMS).

Dickens's own works were continually promoted by his publishers, usually by the distribution of handbills and leaflets, and the inclusion of advertisements for the various editions and collections of his works as supplements bound in with his own or other authors' works. For instance, the complete *Pickwick*, and *Sketches by Boz* were advertised in the *Nickleby* Advertiser for May 1838. The following November Richard BENTLEY, Dickens's previous publisher, used the Advertiser to announce his three-volume *Oliver Twist* at 25 shillings. The *Dombey and Son* Advertiser for April 1848 announces not only the one-volume edition of *Dombey*, due on 12 April at one guinea, but editions of *Oliver Twist* (11 shillings), *Pictures from Italy* (6 shillings), and five-shilling editions of 'Mr Dickens's Christmas Books'.

Dickens's publishers engaged in a continuing promotion of his works. Thus, as *Nicholas Nickleby* neared its completion CHAPMAN AND HALL announced (August and September 1839) a 'New Work by Boz . . . ON AN ENTIRELY NEW PLAN'. This was the weekly MASTER HUMPHREY'S CLOCK, in which *The Old Curiosity Shop* and *Barnaby Rudge* ap-

peared. *Household Words* was announced as 'A New Weekly Miscellany' in the *Copperfield* Advertiser for February 1850. *Household Words* and its successor *All The Year Round* carried advertisements for Dickens's works from 1850 until his death.

Dickens himself was not above 'advertising' goods and services that pleased him. He recommends the George Inn at Grantham as 'one of the best inns in England' (*NN* 5), while Newman Noggs commends the ale at the King's Head in Barnard Castle (*NN* 7). Dickens gives Bramah's Patent Door Locks two free advertisements in *The Pickwick Papers* (*PP* 52 and 53). No doubt there are other 'advertisements' scattered throughout Dickens's works waiting to be discovered.      NR

Darwin, Bernard, *The Dickens Advertiser* (1930).

Dexter, Walter, 'The David Copperfield Advertiser', *Dickensian*, 41 (1945).

## Ainsworth, William Harrison (1805–82),

novelist, was successively for Dickens a literary model, mentor, friend, collaborator, successor, rival, and minor antagonist. Born in Manchester, Ainsworth was the son of a prominent solicitor who enthralled his child with stories of criminals. While still a schoolboy, Ainsworth wrote plays, poems, essays, and stories. After his father's death in 1824 he moved to London, where he practised law desultorily while devoting much of his energy to editing fancy ANNUALS and writing breathless novels. His second, *Rookwood* (1834), proved a great hit: Ainsworth was soon the darling of the young Tories publishing a wisecracking periodical, *Fraser's Magazine,* and of the brilliant social circles that gathered around the Countess of Blessington and Lord and Lady Holland. An elegant dandy with easy manners and genuine charm, Ainsworth became the literary lion of the day.

Sometime in 1834 or 1835 Ainsworth and Dickens became acquainted. Dickens was then a poor, struggling literary hack, producing news stories, Parliamentary reports, and supplementary literary sketches; he was surrounded, especially in the galleries of the House, by aspiring lawyers, while his own slender means and education foreclosed the possibility of a distinguished career at the bar. Ainsworth was everything Dickens wanted to be: a literary lion living in easy circumstances, on convivial terms with some of the brightest writers, wits, and social leaders of the day, and author of a phenomenally popular novel. Ainsworth, drawn to Dickens's irresistible vitality, quickly brought him into the company assembled at Ainsworth's home, Kensal Lodge, to which he removed in 1835 after separating from his wife and three daughters. Between 1835 and the early 1840s Ainsworth's guests included, besides his closest friend Dickens, such notables as John FORSTER, William Makepeace THACKERAY, Thomas CARLYLE, and George CRUIKSHANK.

Through these connections, and possibly at Ainsworth's instigation, John MACRONE purchased Dickens's periodical sketches and tales for republication in volumes, illustrated by Cruikshank. These became *Sketches by Boz*. Macrone also bought from Richard BENTLEY rights to *Rookwood*, which Ainsworth revised, Cruikshank illustrated, and Bentley republished. *Fraser's*, obligingly, gave it a premature puff. Despite this success, Macrone was struggling; and Ainsworth's next novel, *Crichton* (1837), did not sell well enough to pull the publisher out of debt. Ainsworth and Dickens between them promised continuing help, but Dickens became increasingly committed to other publishers and projects—to CHAPMAN AND HALL for the monthly serial *Pickwick Papers*, and to Richard Bentley for the monthly magazine BENTLEY'S MISCELLANY, which Dickens edited from January 1837 and to which he contributed *Oliver Twist*. Meanwhile, Ainsworth urged Macrone to sign up other 'gentlemanly' authors, at great cost but little benefit. Moreover, in the autumn of 1836 Ainsworth told Macrone that Dickens had contracted with Richard Bentley for two novels, and would therefore not produce for Macrone 'Gabriel Vardon, the Locksmith of London' (see BARNABY RUDGE). Macrone had expected the manuscript by the end of November; baulked, Macrone turned to Ainsworth for advice. Ainsworth replied that the sum Macrone had offered (£200) was 'preposterously small', and advised him to turn the matter over to his solicitor. Then Ainsworth proposed that, following *Crichton*, he write a monthly serial, imitating Dickens's format, entitled *The Lions of London: or Country Cousins in Town*. This would combine the appeal of Pierce EGAN's earlier *Tom and Jerry*, about young country squires visiting high and low life in contemporary London, with Dickens's evocation of old haunts in the intercalated *Pickwick* tales; the various stories, interspersed with songs, would be told by an old gentleman in his chambers to a company of listeners. To illustrate the serial, Ainsworth proposed Cruikshank for 'the modern comedy and manners' and John LEECH for 'the old—the romantic—the picturesque'. At one point Ainsworth asked Dickens to collaborate on the writing. However, nothing came of the project for Ainsworth, though Dickens attempted a very similar venture in MASTER HUMPHREY'S CLOCK, a weekly periodical illustrated by the antiquarian painter George CATTERMOLE and the modern comic artist Hablot Knight BROWNE ('Phiz').

*Crichton* was finally published in February 1837, by Bentley, to whom Macrone had been forced to sell the copyright. Ainsworth decided to return to fiction about criminals, and to write a 'full series of portraits of the robber', commencing with the young 18th-century thief Jack Sheppard, famous for his fabled escapes from old Newgate Prison. While engaged in research and writing, Ainsworth shared information with Cruikshank, who was to illustrate the book, and with Dickens, then composing *Oliver Twist*. Eventually, *Sheppard* succeeded *Twist* in the *Miscellany*. Whereas 18th-century plays celebrating Jack Sheppard enjoyed scant success, theatrical versions of Ainsworth's novel took London and later the provinces by storm. But the sympathy evoked for a rogue, and the potentially dangerous incitements caused by such marketing ploys as selling 'Shepherd bags' of house-breaking tools in the foyer of the theatre, provoked a reaction against 'NEWGATE NOVELS'. Had Dickens followed *Sheppard* with 'Gabriel Vardon', eventually published as *Barnaby Rudge*, he and Ainsworth would have issued HISTORICAL NOVELS about the new Newgate prison, where Fagin spends his last night in the condemned cell, about the old prison from which Sheppard made his amazing escapes, and about its destruction during the Gordon Riots (1780). So Ainsworth's decision to produce a series about robbers ended up, by 1840, associating Dickens with a type of fiction whose moral worth was vigorously debated by the press, and this unwanted association with Ainsworth's potboilers contributed to a cooling of their relations.

But though the seeds of that discord were sown in 1837, at the time Dickens and Ainsworth's friendship was at its peak. Dickens's phenomenal success with *Pickwick* put him on a more equal footing with Ainsworth, while Ainsworth's popularity increased with each novel he wrote. Equipoised at the top of the tree, the two friends went to Ainsworth's birthplace, Manchester, in January 1839, just after *Jack Sheppard* replaced the last instalments of *Oliver Twist* as the lead story in *Bentley's*. (In fact, Dickens edited the February instalment while in Manchester.) There they were courted and fêted by the town's leading citizens, among whom Dickens met the originals of *Nickleby's* Cheeryble brothers. Two months later Dickens broke definitively with Bentley, and Ainsworth took over as editor of the magazine. Ainsworth, Dickens, and Forster established a CERBERUS CLUB with themselves as the only members, but a dispute with Forster in 1839 temporarily estranged Ainsworth from Dickens; Daniel MACLISE increasingly replaced him as Dickens and Forster's mutual friend. Ainsworth made overtures to both Dickens and Forster in December 1840, inviting them to a dinner celebrating his completion of *The Tower of London*. Dickens reciprocated, inviting Ainsworth to a New Year's Eve party at Devonshire Terrace. There were occasional exchanges of letters and meals thereafter. Ainsworth joined Dickens in raising funds for the destitute families of several friends, and participated with Dickens and others in various professional and charitable activities. The 'unintelligible novelist', as Dickens called him, and his daughters visited Dickens at Lausanne in 1846, and he attended the *Dombey* dinner in 1848, though he hated the novel. But the old intimacy and reciprocal inspiration had passed, and the two authors drifted further and further apart, until years went by without their speaking to one another.

What Ainsworth brought to early Victorian fiction was the capacity to combine extensively researched historical fiction in the vein of SCOTT with the GOTHIC tradition of heightened drama, suspense, and mystery popularized by Mrs Radcliffe and with the demotic tradition of rogue literature. A fourth ingredient, especially evident in his novel about the brief reign of Lady Jane Grey, *The Tower of London*, was his use of settings surviving (often in dilapidated or ruined condition) in the present and redolent of historical associations. His fictions thus relocated the historically resonant scenes in Scott's novels to the midlands and London. In such locations Ainsworth set elaborate plots combining antiquarian learning with popular lore and Gothic inventions, producing novels freighted with undigested learning that nonetheless moved propulsively through famous events and gave a widening readership the sense that they lived amidst structures and traditions having a dramatic past and a significant influence even in the present.

In such ways, then, Ainsworth provided a model for Dickens's early fiction, especially *Oliver Twist* and the two novels appearing in *Master Humphrey's Clock*. Not only the fiction of the clock-case and Master Humphrey's tales, but also the mixture of Gothic and contemporary in *The Old Curiosity Shop*, the fusing of violent history with Gothic accessories and characters in *Barnaby Rudge*, and the combination of illustrators for the two novels all mark the influence of Ainsworth's practice. But when Dickens took up the mixture of Gothic and contemporary again, in *Bleak House*, and when he once again fused violent history with Gothic accessories and characters in *A Tale of Two Cities*, it was to be under the influence of Thomas Carlyle.

Ainsworth continued to edit periodicals—he started *Ainsworth's Magazine* in 1842 as a rival to *Bentley's*, hiring Cruikshank as illustrator, and bought the *New Monthly Magazine* in 1845. Terminating his own publication in 1854, he then purchased a much-reduced, lacklustre *Bentley's*, attempting to edit it from Brighton, to which he removed in 1853. A decade later Ainsworth was virtually a forgotten man. Robert BROWNING told Forster at a dinner party given by Dickens's publisher Frederic Chapman that 'a sad, forlorn-looking being stopped me to-day and reminded me of old times. He presently resolved himself into—whom do you think?—Harrison Ainsworth!' (Ellis 1911, 2.264). Less than four months before his death on 3 January 1882, Ainsworth attended a dinner given in his honour by the Lord Mayor of Manchester at the Town Hall. Few recognized, in the worn face framed by scraggy hair, the prime buck and literary lion of a half-century previously.

RLP

Ellis, S. M., *William Harrison Ainsworth and His Friends*, 2 vols. (1911).

Patten (1992, 1996).

Worth, George J., *William Harrison Ainsworth* (1972).

**Albert, Prince Consort.** See ROYALTY.

*All the Year Round* A weekly magazine (1859–93) of serial fiction, essays, poetry, topical journalism, and information which Dickens published and edited from 30 April 1859 (*see* SERIAL LITERATURE; PUBLISHING). Phoenix-like, it arose from the ashes of *Household Words* and the incendiary row in Dickens's private life which he felt compelled to spread to his professional relations, but although in many ways identical to its previous incarnation, *All the Year Round* differed in a number of important respects.

No established publishing house was now involved in the venture: Dickens and his sub-editor, W. H. WILLS, were joint proprietors, with interests of 75 per cent and 25 per cent respectively. The ownership of the name and goodwill attaching to the publication—which in the case of *Household Words* had been the cause of dispute with fellow proprietors BRADBURY AND EVANS—was to be exclusively Dickens's. In his determination to sever all connection with *Household Words*, a new office was set up at No. 26 Wellington Street North, only a few hundreds yards away from the old one. Here, a comfortable set of third-storey rooms was fitted up for Dickens when he chose to stay in his 'town tent' rather than make the long trip out to the family home at Gad's Hill, while—in an almost Scrooge-like touch—the working facilities for the staff were 'exceptionally plain', without 'a square yard of carpet of any kind . . . or a single article of furniture' save a table and two cane chairs (G. D. Carrow, 'Informal Call on Charles Dickens by a Philadelphia Clergyman', *Dickensian*, 63, 1967). The name of the new periodical was, like *Household Words*, linked to SHAKESPEARE, and stood beside an adapted quotation from *Othello* ('the story of [our] li[ves] | From year to year', 1.3); Dickens considered this an 'admirable' title, though only after accepting FORSTER's strong objection to his somewhat inappropriate previous choice, *Household Harmony* (Forster 8.5).

In terms of content, the most significant change was the reservation, in Dickens's

words, of 'the first place in these pages for a continuous original work of fiction . . . [which] . . . it is our hope and aim . . . may become a part of English literature' ('Note', *AYR* 26 November 1859). During the 1850s the reduction or abolition of the so-called 'taxes on knowledge' (stamp duty, paper and advertising taxes) made publishing periodicals a cheap and potentially profitable venture—aside from *All the Year Round*, 114 other magazines are known to have been founded in 1859 alone (W. J. Graham, *English Literary Periodicals*, 1966, 301)—and Dickens's policy was doubtless a wise response to fierce market competition. Nevertheless, in publishing *A Tale of Two Cities*, *Great Expectations*, and Wilkie COLLINS's *The Woman in White* all within the first 27 months of *All the Year Round*'s life, Dickens made a notable virtue of commercial necessity, and tripled circulation. Wilkie Collins's *The Moonstone* (January–August 1868), Charles READE's *Very Hard Cash* (March–December 1863; retitled *Hard Cash* for volume publication), and Mrs GASKELL's *A Dark Night's Work* (January–March 1863) were also successful speculations on Dickens's part which have arguably outlived their serialization to become 'part of English Literature'. Novels contributed by other writers such as BULWER-LYTTON, Percy FITZGERALD, Rosa Mullholland, Frances E. Trollope, and Edmund YATES, by contrast, are now by and large forgotten, but were nevertheless sufficiently popular as serials to sustain *All the Year Round*'s initial success.

The fact that sales of the first number had reached 125,000 copies owed much to the efficiency of the advance publicity for the new journal, masterminded by Dickens but orchestrated by Wills, who was now General Manager of the publication with control of the Commercial Department. On 26 March 1859 Wills authorized the distribution by W. H. Smith and Sons and others, of 300,000 handbills and 'double demy' posters (54 cm × 84 cm); advertising space was booked in numerous newspapers in the same month, while as late as May white or yellow showcards with black and red shaded letters were ADVERTISING the publication in towns throughout England, Wales, Scotland, and Ireland.

Thereafter, thanks to the continuing attraction of the weekly serials, subsequent circulation figures remained high, 'settling down to a steady sale of one hundred thousand' according to Wills (19 May 1859; *AYR* Letter Book, fo. 34), and 'several thousands higher' than that of *The TIMES*, according to Dickens in 1861 (to Bulwer-Lytton, 12 May 1861). Occasional dips did occur, usually as a result of serials such as Charles LEVER's *A Day's Ride: A Life's Romance* (September 1860–March 1861), and SALA's *Quite Alone* (February–November 1864), failing to appeal. On the first of these occasions Dickens was compelled to start publishing a serial himself—*Great Expectations*—to revive sales, while on the second, young staff writer Andrew Halliday (1830–77) was called upon to complete the story, following Sala's sudden departure to report on the American Civil War for the *Daily Telegraph*. However, such declines were more than compensated for by the massive annual sale of the 'Extra Christmas Numbers' (1860–7), which reached as high as 300,000 (E. E. Kellett, 'The Press', *Early Victorian England*, 1934: see CHRISTMAS STORIES). In the five years from April 1862 to April 1867, Dickens's profit-share from the publication averaged just over £2,750 per annum.

Even this success was dwarfed, however, by the popularity of *All the Year Round* in America, where J. Y. Emerson considered it had 'the largest circulation of any similar publication in the world', with an estimated 3 million readers (quoted in G. Grubb, 'Editorial Policies of Charles Dickens', *PMLA* 58, 1943). Nevertheless, Dickens's sale of US publishing rights, first to the entrepreneur Thomas Coke Evans (April–October 1859) and then to the more reliable J. M. Emerson and Co. of New York (1859–93) did not net more than £700 a year, and initially carried with it the disadvantage that in order to ship stereotype plates across the Atlantic in time for the American version to be published simultaneously with the British, copy for each issue had to be finalized a fortnight ahead of publication. Dickens later contracted with Emerson and Co. to supply a full set of plates for each month's numbers in advance of the London publication of the last in the set, but even this arrangement involved a loss of journalistic topicality in every fourth issue, and on at least one occasion Dickens missed the copy deadline for the US version with his own contri-

bution, leaving Wills to make up different editions (to Wills, 28 March 1860).

Instalments of serial novels occupied the space of two or three self-contained articles or essays, with the result that the average number of *All the Year Round* offered fewer items (five to seven) than a typical number of *Household Words* (eight to ten), particularly when the former contained two serials running concurrently. In addition, there was a marked increase of emphasis on foreign affairs in *All the Year Round*, partly due to Dickens's desire to support the cause of Giuseppe Garibaldi (1807–82) and Joseph Mazzini (1805–72) in the wars of Italian unification. Over a representative sample of seven volumes of each periodical, nearly 11 per cent of the non-fiction articles in *All the Year Round* dealt with some aspect of international affairs or cultures, as opposed to 4 per cent in *Household Words*. In most other popular subject areas—education, industry, emigration or science, for example—the trend is reversed.

Contributors to both *All the Year Round* and *Household Words*, as well as subsequent commentators, have judged the various changes in content and emphasis in the later publication to have been for the worse, in spite of its greater popularity with the public. Percy H. Fitzgerald, a prolific if uninspiring contributor to both periodicals, recalled that 'with the change in the form of the old journal [*Household Words*] there was now to be noted a change in the character of its contents. The new venture seemed to be less personal and to concede more to the humour of the times.' If *Household Words* had 'a quaintly old-fashioned air' and displayed Dickens's 'complete personality', *All the Year Round* was more 'up to date' and 'conventional' in approach (*Memories of Charles Dickens*, 1913). As John Hollingshead (1827–1904), one of Dickens's young protégés, later recollected, 'all the old "H.W." contributors regretted the merging of *Household Words* in *All the Year Round*. It was not the same journal, though we had the same chief' ('Fifty Years of *Household Words*', Jubilee Number, 1900). The leading scholar of Dickens's periodicals in the 20th century, meanwhile, has not only suggested that *All the Year Round* was 'inferior to its predecessor' but that it displays a noticeable 'deterioration' during the 1860s. The decrease in social and political content is read, moreover, as 'evidence of [Dickens's] declining interest in public affairs' (Philip Collins, 'The *AYR* Letter Book', *Victorian Periodicals Newsletter*, 10, 1970; 'The Significance of Dickens's Periodicals', *Review of English Literature*, 2, 1961).

One reason for the perceived decline in the quality of *All the Year Round* may be found in the boom in magazine publication in the 1860s, which made it harder for Dickens to attract and keep a talented stable of writers for the rates of pay he offered. Although there has been scholarly debate over the extent of Dickens's liberality as a paymaster, it would appear that the rate of 10s 6d per column for prose, or a guinea a page, was for the generality of contributors the standard Dickens adhered to, while rival publishers Bradbury and Evans and Smith, Elder and Co. are known to have offered as much as four and twelve guineas a page for work in *Once a Week* and *The Cornhill Magazine*. This may have influenced George ELIOT in her decision not to accept Dickens's repeated invitations to contribute a serial to *All the Year Round*, and to publish her novel *Romola* in the *Cornhill*, for an unprecedented rate per page of £26 14s 4d (to George Eliot of 28 April, 10 July and 14 November 1859; G. S. Haight, *George Eliot*, 1968). Comprehensive figures for Dickens's payment of contributors to *All the Year Round* are not available, however, as no 'office' or 'contributors' book similar to the one kept by Wills for *Household Words* has survived. An 'office set' of the journal, in which authors' names and other details were recorded, was available to editor B. W. MATZ at the turn of the century, but has since been lost sight of; aside from this, only a highly incomplete and illegible file of correspondence, known as the 'AYR Letter Book' (profiled by Collins 1970), exists to assist researchers.

Another explanation for *All the Year Round*'s decline may rest in the simple fact that, in quantitative terms, Dickens contributed far less of his own writing to it than he had to *Household Words*, and of that lesser quantity, over 70 per cent (120 items or instalments) was published between 1859 and 1863. Articles such as 'The Poor Man and His Beer' (in defence of a beer-brewing collective among the poor in Hertfordshire; *AYR* 30 April 1859; see DRINK AND TEMPERANCE), 'Leigh Hunt: A Remonstrance' (a posthumous apology to Leigh HUNT for Dickens's

portrayal of him as 'Skimpole' in *Bleak House*; *AYR* 24 December 1859; see CHARACTERS— ORIGINALS), and 'The Tattelsnivel Bleater' (a scalding satire on the inaccurate reporting of a provincial NEWSPAPER; *AYR* 31 December 1859) appeared during or shortly after the serialization of *A Tale of Two Cities* in 1859, as did the SENSATIONALIST short story 'HUNTED DOWN' (*AYR* 4 and 11 August 1860), first published for the unprecedented fee of £1,000 in the American journal the *New York Ledger* (20 and 27 August, 3 September 1859). Then in January 1860 Dickens inaugurated his first series of occasional articles in the guise of 'The UNCOMMERCIAL TRAVELLER' (1st series, January–October 1860), which was followed by *Great Expectations* (December 1860–August 1861), followed by a handful of journalistic items, and a second series of 'Uncommercial Traveller' papers (May–October 1863). It would be more accurate to say, therefore, that Dickens's involvement in his journal as an active contributor remained constant until 1863, but dwindled thereafter.

Nevertheless, the evidence of Dickens's correspondence suggests he still kept an extremely watchful eye over the publication even after 1863, making up numbers, suggesting, revising, pruning, censoring, issuing instructions to Wills, and through Wills, to contributors. Notable among his later contributions are a final series of seven essays by the 'Uncommercial Traveller' ('New Uncommercial Samples', December 1868–June 1869), the short story 'GEORGE SILVERMAN'S EXPLANATION' (1, 15, and 29 February 1868), and the four children's tales comprising 'A HOLIDAY ROMANCE' (25 January, 8 February, 14 March, and 4 April 1869). Like 'Hunted Down', these two pieces of fiction were written for the lucrative American market for £1,000 apiece, first appearing, respectively, in the *New York Ledger* (January–March 1867) and *Our Young Folks* (January, March, April, and May 1868). Following Wills's disabling hunting accident in the Spring of 1868, Dickens was left in charge not just of the literary side of *All the Year Round*, but also of the financial department, the latter being, as George DOLBY recalled, 'almost entirely foreign to his experiences' and constituting 'an extra source of worry and annoyance to him' (*Charles Dickens as I Knew Him*, 1885, p. 336). This did not prevent Dickens from planning a 'New Series' of the journal, however, to commence in December 1868, after deciding that an old series of twenty volumes was becoming irksome to subscribers (*AYR* 20. 337). Various improvements in paper and print quality were introduced, plus a decorative woodcut around the masthead on the cover, showing fruits and cereals to represent the yearly cycle of the seasons.

At the same time, Dickens seems to have decided to groom his eldest son Charley for an editorial role (see CHILDREN OF DICKENS). Charley undertook routine duties from September 1868, and in his father's opinion was 'evinc[ing] considerable aptitude in sub-editing work' by July 1869. He was officially designated sub-editor in April 1870, and became editor after Dickens's death two months later, vowing to readers that in the future the management of the journal 'shall be based on precisely the same principles as those on which it has, up to this time, been conducted' (*AYR* NS 4. 73). He inherited his father's 75 per-cent stake in the business, and in January 1871 bought Wills's 25 per-cent share, following the latter's understandable objection to Charley's decision to award himself both the editor's and the sub-editor's salary. The journal continued under Charles Dickens Jr.'s editorship for some time and finally ceased publication in 1895.            JMLD

Oppenlander, Ann Ella, *Dickens' All the Year Round: Descriptive Index and Contributor List* (1984).

**amateur theatricals of Dickens.** Dickens's first piece of writing, *Misnar, Sultan of India*, was a drama based very closely on his favourite childhood reading, The ARABIAN NIGHTS. Fairly certainly, its 9-year-old author wrote it not to be read but to be acted.

Later, as a schoolboy, Dickens formed a small dramatic company of his friends, he himself not only acting but undertaking the duties of director and stage manager. He continued throughout much of his life to gather companies together whenever he had time and opportunity, and he was always director, stage manager, prompter, and prime mover.

The Dickens family enjoyed presenting plays in their home. But when Dickens left school he apparently found other outlets for his histrionic talents. According to one of his first employers, he and a fellow clerk 'took every opportunity . . . of going together to a minor theatre where . . . they not unfrequently engaged in parts' (Forster 1.3). In his sketch 'Private Theatres' (*SB*) Dickens ridiculed such places and those who patronized them, but a few years prior to writing this sketch he might well have been one of the 'donkeys' he derided.

In 1833 he staged an operetta, *Clari, or the Maid of Milan*, in his parents' house in Bentinck Street. The parts were taken by members of the family and their friends, Dickens playing Clari's father. The programme included an interlude in which he played Sir Charles Courtall, and a concluding farce in which he assumed yet another character, that of Wing, a poor country actor. In the same year he wrote and produced (again in his parents' home) an operatic burlesque entitled O'THELLO, basing the lyrics on well-known tunes.

During the years when he was perfecting his shorthand skills in Doctors' Commons, Dickens was also assiduously learning the art of acting, modelling himself on the character ACTOR Charles MATHEWS the elder. He told FORSTER: 'I practised immensely (even such things as walking in and out, and sitting down in a chair) often four, five, six hours a day, shut up in my own room or walking about in the fields' (Forster 5.1). This letter shows that his theatrical expertise was not gained without a lot of hard work.

He might indeed have gone on the professional stage had he been able to attend the audition to which he was invited in the early 1830s. But by 1834 his *Sketches* were attracting attention. In 1836, after Sam Weller had appeared in *Pickwick*, Dickens found himself famous, so he put aside any idea of becoming a professional actor. 'I had never thought of the stage,' he remarked, 'save as a means of getting [money]' (Forster 1.4).

Nevertheless the hankering to be a second Mathews never left him. Not until he had completed the series of novels ending with *Barnaby Rudge* was there a real chance to show his abilities. This came in 1842 after visiting AMERICA and CANADA, when he agreed to assist the officers of the Montreal garrison in presenting the comedy *A Roland for an Oliver*. He had evidently been 'getting this up' since meeting one of the officers on the voyage from England, which shows how keen he was. He went to immense trouble to obtain the wig and side-whiskers needed for his part in the farce *Two O'Clock in the Morning* which was to follow the main item. Two other farces, *Deaf As a Post* and *High Life Below Stairs*, were also performed. His descriptions of himself conducting rehearsals give a vivid picture of how he appeared on that and many subsequent occasions. He wrote to Felton: 'See me with my coat off, the Stage Manager and Universal Director, urging impracticable ladies and impossible gentlemen on to the very confines of insanity—shouting and driving about, in my own person, to an extent which would justify any philanthropic stranger in clapping me into a strait waistcoat without further enquiry' (21 May 1842). And he wrote to Forster: 'Everybody was told they would have to submit to the most iron despotism; and didn't I come MACREADY over them? By no means. Certainly not. The pain I have taken with them, and the perspiration I have expended during the last ten days, exceed in amount anything you can imagine. I had regular plots of the scenery made out, and lists of the properties wanted; and had them nailed up by the prompter's chair. Every letter that had to be delivered, was written; every piece of money that had to be given, provided; and not a single thing lost sight of' (26 May 1842).

On returning to England he became so involved in writing AMERICAN NOTES and *Chuzzlewit*, that for the moment amateur theatricals were impossible. He also made a lengthy visit to ITALY. But as soon as he was back home, with no major novel to occupy him, he set about recruiting an amateur company. 'In less than three weeks after his return', Forster recorded, 'we had selected our play, cast our parts, and all but engaged our theatre' (Forster 5.1). *Every Man In His Humour* by Ben JONSON was the play selected. The actors included Dickens as Bobadil and Forster as Kitely. Other parts were taken by Douglas JERROLD, John LEECH, Mark LEMON, Henry Mayhew, Frank STONE, and Dickens's brother Fred. One of the reasons why Dickens's plays attracted such large audiences was that so many celebrities took part.

Dickens enjoyed his part hugely. He began to include Bobadil oaths in his letters—'By the foot of Pharaoh!' and 'By the body of Caesar!'—and to sign himself 'Bobadil' (8 and

10 August 1845). He made detailed arrangements with theatrical costumiers. 'Be very careful that the colours are bright; and that they will show well by Lamplight . . . I wish the tops of the boots, the gauntlets, and the hat-brim to be very large . . . I wish to see the red of which you propose to make Bobadil's breeches and hat. I want it to be a very gay, fierce, bright colour' (to Head, 13 August 1845). He submitted to the lengthy make-up needed for the part, each hair of his beard (and he was clean-shaven then) having to be affixed separately.

The play was presented on 20 September 1845 at Miss Kelly's Royalty Theatre in Dean Street, and although it was a private performance, reviews appeared in *The Times* and elsewhere. Also on the bill was Mrs Gore's farce *A Good Night's Rest*, in which Dickens and Mark Lemon displayed for the first time what a hilarious double-act they could be, departing widely from their script and adding their own outrageous inventions.

There were inevitably some adverse criticisms. Mrs Carlyle described Forster as imitating Macready without ever ceasing to be Forster, and her husband Thomas CARLYLE was even more outspoken. 'Poor little Dickens!' he declared, 'all painted in black and red, and affecting the voice of a man of six feet' (Carlyle, *Letters*, 23 September 1845).

If Dickens knew of these remarks, he ignored them. When Prince Albert made known his desire to see the play, rehearsals began again, and a private performance in aid of Southwood Smith's Sanatorium was given at the St James's Theatre on the 15th. It was a very distinguished audience, but somehow the play fell flat. Lord Melbourne was overheard to remark: 'I knew it would be dull, but not so damn dull as this' (Greville, *Diaries*, 1.566).

Such remarks had no effect on Dickens and his friends. In December they began rehearsing *The Elder Brother* by Fletcher and Massinger. It was presented on 3 January 1846 for Miss Kelly's benefit at her own little theatre. At that time Dickens was deeply involved with the DAILY NEWS. Once free of that and the play, he went to SWITZERLAND and did not resume theatricals until July 1847.

This next spell of theatricals continued with *The Merry Wives of Windsor*, first performed in May 1848 and then taken on tour to

Manchester, Liverpool, Birmingham, Edinburgh, and Glasgow. Altogether *Every Man In His Humour* was presented eight times (including three at Knebworth, BULWER-LYTTON's home), and *The Merry Wives* seven times. The principal plays were accompanied by various farces—*A Good Night's Rest, Love, Law, and Physic, Animal Magnetism*, and *A Day After the Wedding*, the titles giving broad hints of the plots. A programme of farces was also performed at the WATSONS' home Rockingham in January 1851.

At Knebworth, Bulwer-Lytton put forward the idea of a GUILD OF LITERATURE AND ART for which he wrote a new comedy, *Not So Bad As We Seem*. This was first presented on 16 May 1851 at Devonshire House in front of the Queen and then repeated at the request of the Duke of Devonshire eleven days later. On this occasion MR NIGHTINGALE'S DIARY, a farce written by Lemon and extensively revised by Dickens, was performed for the first time, Dickens playing six different characters, necessitating rapid changes of costume which bewildered and delighted the audience. The company then took this programme, plus Planché's *Charles XII* and *Used Up* by Boucicault and Mathews, on a tour of the provinces, finishing in Liverpool on 3 September 1852.

Then, mainly due to his work on *Bleak House* and *Hard Times*, there were no further theatricals until June 1855, apart from the children's plays presented on Twelfth Night. These were *Tom Thumb*, given in 1854, and *Fortunio, and His Seven Gifted Servants* in 1855, both performed in the schoolroom in Dickens's HOME, Tavistock House. Although the accommodation was limited—the audience could not exceed 25—Dickens felt it could be used for presenting more ambitious plays. He therefore began rehearsing Wilkie COLLINS's melodrama, *The Lighthouse*, which was presented in June 1855, Dickens himself playing Aaron Gurnock, the old lighthouse-keeper. To give more people the opportunity to see it, the play was given three times, each time with *Mr Nightingale's Diary*. Then on 10 July a repeat performance was given at Campden House, Kensington, in aid of the Bournemouth Sanatorium.

Two years later another of Collins's plays, *The* FROZEN DEEP, had its premiere in the same little theatre. Collins and Dickens took the leading roles and were supported by Lemon, Shirley Brooks, and members of the Dickens family. Four performances were given there during January 1857. Mrs Inchbald's farce *Animal Magnetism*, replaced from 8 January by BUCKSTONE's *Uncle John*, followed as an afterpiece. In June Dickens was invited by the Queen to perform the play at the Palace, but he begged to be excused on the grounds that he felt uneasy about the social position of his daughters having to act in such a situation. However, at his suggestion a private performance took place before the Queen and the royal family at the Gallery of Illustration in Regent Street on 4 July. On 8 July it had its first public performance in aid of a fund being raised to assist Douglas Jerrold's widow. Two more performances were given in London, and finally three in the Free Trade Hall, Manchester. Because the amateur actresses had difficulty making themselves heard there, three professionals—Mrs Ternan and two of her daughters (see TERNAN FAMILY)—were engaged. As it happened, this was the last occasion on which Dickens actually appeared in theatricals. Following his separation from his wife, he found himself estranged from several friends, such as Mark Lemon, who had been leading members of his amateur company; so it fell apart. It might have done so in any case, because by then Dickens was beginning to devote his energies to PUBLIC READINGS.

In 1870, however, he agreed to supervise the rehearsals of an amateur play in which both of his daughters were taking part. He would have been glad to have acted in it himself, but his lameness prevented him. Fortunately, he was able to act as stage-manager and prompter as of yore, demonstrating by acting out one part after another how the various characters should be portrayed. With his assistance the play was successfully presented on 2 June 1870, a week before his death.

ASW

**America, United States of.** For Dickens, America was at times a Utopian dream, at times an infernal pernicious nightmare of a place, at times every point on the scale in between. Dickens visited the country twice, once from 22 January to 7 June 1842 (including crossing into CANADA for nearly a month) and once from 19 November 1867 to 22 April

1868 (including a briefer visit to Canada). See map p. 616. Though both trips began in Boston and ended in New York, each had a character all its own. Washington IRVING seems to have planted some of the first seeds of interest for an American visit, and Dickens first mentions the possibility himself in a letter to the American publishers Wiley and Putnam, who had apparently suggested that Dickens make such a journey (31 August 1838; even at that early date, the rumour of a possible visit was puffed in the American newspapers). He became increasingly interested in the idea, overriding objections from FORSTER, Catherine DICKENS, and others, and persuading his English publishers CHAPMAN AND HALL to advance him money to pay for the trip, on the grounds that the trip would increase his value to them. In 1842 Dickens travelled with Catherine, but, after extensive discussion with friends and associates, left the children behind.

He arrived full of excitement after a difficult sea voyage on the steamer *Britannia*, bounding into the Tremont Hotel with Grimaldi's PANTOMIME greeting, 'Here we are' (see *MEMOIRS OF GRIMALDI*). Dickens knew he was on stage and seems initially to have welcomed the attention. The Dickenses were fêted at private and public banquets, balls, and evenings at the theatre to such an extent that he periodically attempted to refuse further public engagements. As one of his American critics noted about the 1842 tour, Dickens was honoured more enthusiastically and extravagantly than was the Marquis de Lafayette during his post-Revolutionary tours or George Washington during his entire lifetime. The most remarkable of these fêtes was doubtless the Boz Ball held 14 February 1842 in New York City. Many contemporary newspapers and diaries described it as probably the most magnificent such event of recent times. Over 3,000 persons turned out at the Park Theatre, which was decorated lavishly with flowers, wreaths, garlands, and representations of scenes from Dickens's works. The centre ornament of the second tier was a head of Dickens surmounted by an eagle clasping a laurel wreath in its talons. Dances alternated with *tableaux vivants* representing scenes and characters from his works. A special stage curtain was painted in imitation of the *Pickwick Papers'* frontispiece. Demand for tickets was so great that a repeat of the Boz

Ball was scheduled for two days later, but Dickens was unable to attend owing to a severe sore throat.

He met many of the country's finest writers and thinkers, often establishing strong, long-lasting friendships with them and later entertaining them in England. They included Washington Irving, Harriet Beecher STOWE, Henry Wadsworth Longfellow, Fitz-Greene Halleck, Cornelius Felton, Edgar Allan Poe, William Cullen Bryant, Horace Greeley, Henry Clay, John Quincy Adams, Oliver Wendell Holmes, Richard Henry Dana, Sr., and Jr., James Russell Lowell, and Daniel Webster. In Washington he was received by President John Tyler (as he also would be by Andrew Johnson on his second trip).

However, his initial excitement and positive feeling towards the country were soon transformed. On 31 January 1842 Dickens wrote to MACREADY with delight about his reception, remarking that Americans were 'as delicate, as considerate, as careful of giving the least offence, as the best Englishmen I ever saw.—I like their behaviour to Ladies infinitely better than that of my own countrymen; and their Institutions I reverence, love, and honour'. Dickens then surprised some of his first American audiences at banquets in Boston on 1 February and in Hartford, Connecticut, on 8 February with speeches that included a highly emotional description of the penurious dying Walter SCOTT as a victim of literary thieves who could have been stopped if an international COPYRIGHT agreement had been in place. Attacks on Dickens's views had appeared in American periodicals even before his arrival, but their intensity and number increased dramatically as soon as it became clear that he intended to use his popular credit to campaign in public appearances and in visits with congressmen and other influential figures for such an international agreement. As the controversy became more heated, he received a memorial in support of a copyright agreement between Britain and America from twelve eminent British authors, including CARLYLE and TENNYSON (Pilgrim 3.621–2).

By 22 February Dickens complained furiously to his friend Jonathan Chapman, the mayor of Boston, 'I have never in my life been so shocked and disgusted, or made so sick and sore at heart as I have been by the treatment I have received here . . . in reference to the International Copyright question. I,—the greatest loser by the existing Law alive,—say in perfect good humour and disinterestedness . . . that I hope the day will come when Writers will be justly treated; and straightway there fall upon me scores of your newspapers; imputing motives to me, the very suggestion of which turns my blood to gall; and attacking me in such terms of vagabond scurrility as they would denounce no murderer with. I vow to Heaven that the scorn and indignation I have felt under this unmanly and ungenerous treatment has been to me an amount of agony such as I never experienced since my birth.' The next month he wrote to Macready, 'I desire to be so honest and just to those who have so enthusiastically and earnestly welcomed me, that I burned the last letter I wrote to you . . . rather than let it come with anything that might seem like an ill-considered word of disappointment. I preferred that you should think me neglectful . . . Still it is of no use. I *am* disappointed. This is not the Republic I came to see. This is not the Republic of my imagination' (22 March 1842). Though Dickens was always ready for the rest of his life to say occasional good things about America, and especially about individual Americans, he never was able to return that Edenic republic to his imagination.

As Michael Slater has suggested, AUSTRALIA, which Dickens never visited, to some degree substituted as that imaginary state where Peggottys and Micawbers and even his own children might be sent with some sort of optimistic outlook (Slater 1978, p. 30). America, however, became to him primarily a place of self-delusion, unjustified arrogance, and hypocrisy. His response to American attack was the sort of bravado found in the letter to Chapman. After his return to England he wrote to his American secretary, George Washington PUTNAM, that he did not read the American newspapers sent him, but burned them unread as soon as they were received, 'according to my old custom' (18 October 1842). He repeatedly insisted that nothing would prevent his continued efforts to secure international copyright agreements and that nothing would stop him from denouncing slavery. But the American charges, though often outrageous and frequently complete fabrications, also rather often had some un-

questionably real foundation in Dickens's character and behaviour.

He had planned for a substantial period before his departure to write an account of his travels and had immersed himself in reading the accounts of previous visitors to America (Basil Hall, Frances TROLLOPE, Frederick MARRYAT, Harriet MARTINEAU, and others; see TRAVEL LITERATURE). The result, AMERICAN NOTES FOR GENERAL CIRCULATION (the title itself a dig at the instability and unreliability of American currency), was based in great part on the letters Dickens wrote during his travels, and appeared in England on 19 October 1842. To some degree he followed in the footsteps and opinions of former writer-visitors, but he was determined, especially at the start of his journey, to define a set of responses unique to himself, at least in degree.

*American Notes* dwells at length on what Dickens considered the great virtues of America and the American people, but the critical and public eye was more caught by his occasional attacks on certain institutions and characteristics, particularly spitting in public and the failure of the inhabitants to respect his privacy. But his strongest animosity was reserved for slavery, not international copyright. He was so repulsed by the sight of slaves that he cut short his visit to the American south, returning north from Richmond rather than continuing on to Charleston, South Carolina, as planned. Some of the American newspapers which had been critical of Dickens before his first visit had anticipated that his antipathy to slavery would emerge in his speaking engagements. However, he seems not to have uttered a public word on that issue during his visit, claiming merely that he would receive 'no public mark of respect in any place where slavery was;—and that's something' (to Forster, 24 February 1842), but reserving his expression of disgust at the institution for *American Notes, Martin Chuzzlewit*, and private correspondence and conversation.

Though a large number of Dickens's American audience were distressed by the tone of *American Notes*, the representation of the United States in *Martin Chuzzlewit* was many degrees more cynical and sarcastic. The chapters that take Martin Chuzzlewit and Mark Tapley to New York City on board the line-of-packet ship the *Screw*, and on to the settlement of 'Eden', a fictional version of the settlement of Cairo, Illinois, already denounced by Dickens (*AN* 12), are almost unrelentingly critical of American manners, politics, institutions, arts, and character. A Mr Bevan is the lone decent figure on the infernal landscape who receives any significant attention at all, with the exception of brief encounters with a group of amiable men on the steamboat journey to Eden, and with a couple who offer them crucial life-saving aid when they fall seriously ill in Eden (and who are themselves in turn taken in by Mark and Martin after a chance meeting on the streets of London near the end of the novel). Dickens's attitude towards America in *Chuzzlewit* seems to have intensified into something like Tom Pinch's when Martin first tells him he is thinking of going there: ' "No, no," cried Tom, in a kind of agony. "Don't go there. Pray don't. Think better of it. Don't be so dreadfully regardless of yourself. Don't go to America!"' (*MC* 12). The last words on America in the novel come as Martin and Mark sail from New York on their return journey to England. Mark Tapley explains how he would paint the likeness of an American eagle if so requested: 'I should like to draw it like a Bat, for its short-sightedness; like a Bantam, for its bragging; like a Magpie, for its honesty; like a Peacock, for its vanity, like a Ostrich, for its putting its head in the mud, and thinking nobody sees it—'. But Martin finishes for Mark: 'And like a Phoenix, for its power of springing from the ashes of its faults and vices, and soaring anew into the sky! . . . Well, Mark. Let us hope so' (*MC* 34). This combination of despair tempered by the least bit of optimism for the country's future remained Dickens's outlook until his death, though his public utterances before and during the second trip represent a much more positive view.

In 1867 Dickens made plans for a second visit to America. A key consideration (doubtless owing much to his father's improvidence, his own financial worries of the 1830s and 1840s, and the large family he had to provide for) was the opportunity it afforded for making a great deal of money there. In correspondence, particularly in the months before the PUBLIC READINGS tour of 1867–8, he often did write about America primarily as a potential source of income, and his American critics accused him of greed and an inflated

sense of self-importance. When Macready was considering an American tour in 1848, Dickens wrote to him, 'My sentiment is: Success to the United States as a golden campaigning ground, but blow the United States to 'tarnal smash as an Englishman's place of residence' (26 August 1848). In 1858 he estimated that he might make £10,000 from a reading tour in the United States, 'if I could resolve to go there' (to F. M. Evans, 16 March 1858). Eventually, over 100,000 persons heard him read, and he cleared a profit of £19,000 for seventy-six readings.

During this second visit Dickens was outspoken about his belief that the conditions and the behaviour he had complained about in *American Notes* and in *Martin Chuzzlewit* were vastly ameliorated. He consistently and frequently denied any plans to publish—and did not publish—any account of his second American visit, choosing instead to append to later editions of *American Notes* and *Martin Chuzzlewit* a statement of his sense of the great positive changes in the country, expressed in the words of his farewell speech given at the New York Press Club at a dinner held in his honour four days before his last departure from the United States. For the most part, he succeeded in this public-relations effort, and he continued to be inundated with gifts and positive attention of all kinds until he set sail for home. The most well-known American photographers, Mathew Brady and J. Gurney & Son, competed fiercely for the right to photograph him. On Samuel Clemens's (Mark Twain's) first date with his wife-to-be Olivia Langdon, they attended a reading in New York in late 1867, though Clemens later claimed he thought little of Dickens's performance. (He also claimed that he reread *A Tale of Two Cities* every two years and that he had used Dickens's grave-robbing scene from that novel when writing a similar scene for his *Tom Sawyer*.) Later, Clemens's September 1870 article, 'The Approaching Epidemic', predicted a frenzy of lecturers who would attempt to profit from Dickens's recent death. Still later, George DOLBY, Dickens's manager, organized lectures in London for Clemens.

But there were problems. Ticket speculators were rife and Dolby was forced to contrive all sorts of strategies to defeat them. Several public readings in Boston had to be cancelled in March 1868 because of the impeachment proceedings then under way in Washington against President Johnson. Because Dickens battled ill health for much of the second tour in a heroic attempt to complete his reading commitments, he refused a great number of engagements and callers, thus alienating some Americans previously friendly to him. Bryant, for instance, who in 1842 was the American, next to Irving, that Dickens most wanted to meet, was turned away from Dickens's hotel in New York, and subsequently refused to chair the New York Press Club farewell dinner.

Furthermore, Dickens failed to escape a renewal of the abuse of 1842. Before and during the reading tour, American periodicals relentlessly produced attacks on Dickens's greed ranging from the mildest remonstrance to the fiercest vitriol. Cartoons represented him surrounded by stacks of bills, but complaining about how little profit the tour had brought, or lugging immense moneybags as he boarded the ship for home. A typical poem sarcastically attributed to him, which accompanied one cartoon, read in part, 'Farewell Columbia! Land of soft delight; | Your shores will soon be lost unto my sight | But I will carry to my latest day | The sweet assurance of how well you pay. | . . . I hail you from the bottom of my purse | and beg your pardon for my former curse.'

But there was more vicious criticism on the second visit that had little to do with Dickens's avarice. His legal separation from Catherine in 1858 after 22 years of marriage and ten children had provoked a good deal of speculation in England and America about his private life. Remarkably, Dickens continued to hope that Ellen TERNAN might somehow travel with him or meet him in America, and he arranged with WILLS a code that would signal by telegram his final decision about the practicality of the idea. The idea was finally abandoned, and the code for 'don't come' was sent, perhaps because American newspapers had dredged up the story of the separation of a decade earlier and the role in it of a young mistress. The Chicago papers were especially persistent on this issue, probably because Dickens had cut Chicago from his original itinerary. The papers published the old 'Violated Letter' and also denounced Dickens for disloyalty to the 'widow' of his scapegrace bigamous youngest brother, Augustus, who had died in Chicago in 1866 after abandoning another family in England (in fact Dickens was caring for the family Augustus had left behind in England; see BROTHERS AND SISTERS OF DICKENS). These, for the most part unjust, charges would nevertheless have bruised sensitive areas of Dickens's psyche. Unfairly attacked for his refusal to go to Chicago, he must have been compelled to think often of the genuine difficulties of his personal and family life. Certainly, Dickens's encounters over the years with America and Americans and his written responses to those encounters led him more forcefully and insistently and over a longer stretch of time than any other relationship to confront his own real and potential failures—social, ethical, and literary. And no other individual or group responded as intensely or as publicly to his criticism as the Americans.

Because Dickens compared his desire to return to America for this final trip to Charles Darnay's return to 'the Loadstone Rock, Paris' in *A Tale of Two Cities*, many authors have explored the extent to which the American trip might be said to have killed him, and to which it might be described as suicidal. Undoubtedly the strain did not help his physical condition. But unlike Charles Darnay, who escapes death through Sydney Carton's substitution for him on the scaffold and then lives happily with Lucie Manette, Dickens may well have died in a final attempt to rescue a youthful Utopian dream that had turned into a nightmare.                    LDB

Meckier, Jerome, *Innocent Abroad: Charles Dickens's American Engagements* (1990).

Moss, Sidney P., *Charles Dickens's Quarrel with America* (1984).

—— and Moss, Carolyn J., *Charles Dickens and His Chicago Relatives: A Documentary Narrative* (1994).

Slater, Michael (ed.), *Dickens on America and the Americans* (1978).

### American Notes for General Circulation

As Dickens readied himself to set off for the United States aboard the steamship *Britannia* early in January 1842, he studied several recent accounts of travel in AMERICA—those of James Silk Buckingham, Frederick MARRYAT, and Harriet MARTINEAU (see TRAVEL; TRAVEL LITERATURE). No doubt, like any eager traveller, he was deciding what places to visit, preparing himself for new experiences, learning about local customs and manners, and so on. But almost as certainly he was thinking already about the travel book he himself would write.

Tony Weller suggested that Mr Pickwick escape his legal entanglements by setting off for the USA hidden in a piano, so he could 'write a book about the 'Merrikans as'll pay all his expenses and more, if he blows 'em up enough' (*PP* 45). Dickens had no lawsuit to flee, but he was hoping that his visit would be productive and remunerative. Having written five novels in as many years (simultaneously producing various lesser books and shorter works), he feared both the strain of overwork and the possibility of creative exhaustion. A travel book would be less taxing to write, and a change of scene might well provide material for his next novel (as, in fact, it was to do, for *Martin Chuzzlewit*).

Though Dickens had thought intermittently of an American journey for several years past, the decision to make the trip had come suddenly in September 1841. The timing was poor: North Atlantic weather is always uncertain, but in midwinter the only uncertainty is how bad it will be. The crossing was extraordinarily rough, but perhaps that only increased Dickens's pleasure at a reception that, in his own words, exceeded that of any 'King or Emperor upon the Earth' (to Thomas Mitton, 31 January 1842). This was only natural, since Dickens now was regarded as the leading writer of his generation on both sides of the Atlantic. Moreover, Dickens saw himself as a political radical, and so he was fully prepared to admire the young republic and its democratic institutions; on the other hand, the American public (and press) saw the young author as a kindred spirit who would counter what they saw as entrenched Old World bias against the USA that was reflected in many published accounts of European visitors.

Before long, both were greatly disillusioned. Dickens infuriated the press, if not the public, by broaching the issue of international COPYRIGHT. For his part, Dickens found the attacks of the press, and particularly their personal tone, infuriating. Many American habits grated on him as well, in particular spitting, the lack of personal hygiene, and crude table manners, but also the general in-

formality that made him subject to the ceaseless attentions of strangers. As he moved south toward the Mason–Dixon line, Dickens also encountered first-hand the 'peculiar institution' of slavery, from which he recoiled in horror. He sailed home in June as eager to leave the USA as he was to return home.

Dickens wrote many long letters from America, clearly planning to use them as *aides mémoires* as he set to work on his book. The strategy worked well: *American Notes* was completed early in October. Dickens relied mainly upon letters he had written to FORSTER, but reclaimed others from various correspondents as well. In several particular instances—his account of the EDUCATION of a deaf and dumb woman, Laura Bridgman, and his discussion of slavery—he also resorted quite literally (as the manuscript in the VICTORIA AND ALBERT MUSEUM demonstrates at a glance) to cutting and pasting printed materials he had gathered while still in the USA. Sections of the manuscript were set in type and corrected in proof as he wrote, and the book was published late in October.

The book divides rather neatly into two parts. The first, which recounts the voyage, the arrival, and Dickens's travels as far as Washington, DC, focuses mainly upon various American institutions—PRISONS, schools, and (in the capital) government. The second, mainly dealing with Dickens's travels in the West, dwells largely upon the rigours of travel by such means as train, canal and riverboat, and stagecoach, and, to a lesser extent, upon the scenery (much of which left Dickens singularly unimpressed). The general critical tone throughout is foreshadowed even in the full title—*American Notes for General Circulation*—alluding to recent banking crises and the widespread unreliability of private banknotes.

Dickens had written an introduction for the book in July, but acting on Forster's last-minute advice, he decided not to use it. This prefatory chapter might have made clearer the nature of his aims for *American Notes*: it was not meant to be an analysis of American life and institutions; nor would it dwell upon any of Dickens's purely personal experiences. Rather, it would simply catalogue his 'impressions' and his later thoughts about them. He also insistently proclaimed his right to report honestly abuses and foibles that he encountered in the USA, just as he had done and always would do at home. No doubt, as Forster evidently feared, had it been printed it would have antagonized American readers—who, in the event, were sufficiently antagonized by the book itself.

The book sold well (especially in the USA in pirated editions), but the notices even in England were disappointing: Dickens expected a vituperative response from the American press, yet the lukewarm and even a few negative English REVIEWS were the more stinging for having come as a surprise. English reviewers complained that the sights and places described, as well as the author's responses, were far from novel, and his impressions not sufficiently 'Dickensian'. But this was nothing compared to the American reviews, that saw the work as merely one more in a series of hostile and vengeful misrepresentations of republican virtues. Only the abolitionists responded positively, taking anti-slavery support wherever they might find it. Not only reviewers were incensed—Dickens also lost several personal friends as a result of this and the American portions of *Martin Chuzzlewit*, including Washington IRVING.

Perhaps the final 'chapter' of *American Notes* was written many years later, when Dickens returned to the USA in November 1867 to begin his hugely successful PUBLIC READING tour. At a public dinner in his honour in New York on 18 April 1868 he praised the great 'moral' and 'physical' changes he saw around him after an absence of twenty-five years, and noted that his remarks would from that time on be reprinted as an appendix to every subsequent edition of *American Notes* and *Martin Chuzzlewit*.                    FSS

Meckier, Jerome, *Innocent Abroad: Charles Dickens's American Engagements* (1990).
Moss, Sidney P., *Charles Dickens's Quarrel with America* (1984).
Slater, Michael (ed.), *Dickens on America and the Americans* (1978).
Welsh, Alexander (1987).

**amusements and recreation.** Dickens had a profound interest in popular recreation, and reference to it suffuses his early fiction and his journalism throughout his life. His basic philosophy can be found in the words he put into the mouth of Sleary, the CIRCUS owner in *Hard Times*: 'People must be amuthed' (*HT* 1.6). Believing the English to be 'the hardest worked people on whom the sun shines' (to Charles Knight, 17 March 1854), he was vociferous in arguing that they needed their amusements.

Dickens's frequent use of the word 'amusements' to describe what people did in their leisure hours itself helps to define his philosophy. In the anxious debates in much of the Victorian middle-class and religious world about the moral legitimacy of this or that form of leisure the underlying assumption was that leisure should reinvigorate you for work and be morally uplifting; recreation should re-create you. 'Amusements' carried none of this MORAL baggage; their function was to amuse, to make people laugh, and to facilitate the indulgence of fantasy within an overarching and enabling sociability.

In two ways Dickens himself contributed to the supply of amusements. In his early novels, one of his stated aims was quite specifically 'to amuse' (Schlicke 1985, p. 34), to entertain, and he was well aware (if not entirely pleased) that the amusement would carry over from the printed word of the novel to the plays and songs which were derived from them without his permission. And secondly, in his PUBLIC READINGS from 1853 onwards he became a public entertainer, deliberately drawing on his early and most explicitly entertaining novels and forging a close relationship with his audiences.

In defending amusements and in putting himself forward as an entertainer, Dickens was well aware that there were many who had a much sterner view of popular leisure. In his early writings in particular he pulled no punches in attacking those who wished to interfere with the way people passed their leisure hours. In the first version of 'London Recreations', published in the EVENING CHRONICLE on 17 March 1835, he concluded that 'Whatever be the class, or whatever the recreation, so long as it does not render a man absurd himself, or offensive to others, we hope it will never be interfered with, either by a misdirected feeling of propriety on the one hand, or detestable cant on the other' (Butt and Tillotson 1957, p. 45). The target he had in mind here was the group of EVANGELICALS who wanted to reform people's leisure by legislation. Led by Sir Andrew Agnew

(1793–1849), they focused their attention on Sunday observance, the Lord's Day Observance Society being formed in 1831. In SUNDAY UNDER THREE HEADS Dickens (under the pseudonym Timothy Sparks) painted a picture of Sunday as it would be under legislation proposed by SABBATARIANS—restricting the leisure of the poor while leaving that of the rich untouched—and as it might be in a more enlightened polity. Throughout his life he kept open a sharp eye on proposals to restrict what was legitimate on a Sunday, painting a famous picture of a dismal Sunday in *Little Dorrit* (1.3). But his concern stretched beyond specific proposals for control of leisure; he wanted more broadly to undermine a pervasive attitude within the churches which tended to induce guilt in those who enjoyed leisure occasions. In *The Old Curiosity Shop* Kit tries to persuade his mother, who is feeling guilty after an enjoyable night at Astley's, that there was something wrong with those who wanted to put down 'harmless cheerfulness and good-humour' (*OCS* 39, 41).

So strong was Dickens's sense that the legislature had hampered rather than enhanced the opportunities for recreation that even when he disapproved of the moral character of a form of popular entertainment, as with betting shops, he did not want to see 'a legislature which has always cared so little for the amusements of the people, in repressive action only' (*HW* 26 June 1852).

Part of the reason for this lifelong defence of popular entertainment against legislative interference was a sense which Dickens shared with many contemporaries (and to which he gave the most forceful articulation) that valued old customs and pastimes were under threat. 'We cling with peculiar fondness', he wrote in 'The First of May' (*SB*), 'to the custom of days gone by.' In part this can be interpreted as a romantic nostalgia for a merry England on the wane, of a piece with Dickens's love of CHRISTMAS. But the clinging to 'the custom of days gone by' was also an expression of something of fundamental importance to Dickens—the necessity of retaining links with CHILDHOOD. For Dickens childhood should be a time when the liberating forces of fancy and imagination could and should be allowed free play; hence his defence of FAIRY TALES ('Frauds on the Fairies', *HW* 1 October 1853), and his frequent invocation of the impact of reading on children. It was equally crucial that fancy and imagination, nourished by memories of childhood reading and events, should remain alive in adulthood. They were in a real sense what made life worth living; without fancy and imagination, you became a Scrooge. And it was through amusements and recreations that you could regain or maintain contact with childhood memories. Nostalgia was a powerful if ambiguous force in Dickens's own life, as he revealed in his reflections on how Rochester had changed since he left it as a child ('Dullborough Town', *UT*); he hated to see old customs and habits die out. But much more than this, the desire to keep old customs alive was a hearkening back to and attempt to re-enact the experiences of childhood.

In his descriptions of the recreational world of London in *Sketches by Boz* Dickens was drawing in large part on his memories of his own childhood and youth—of, for example, Astley's Circus or Greenwich FAIR. Seen from the adult perspective they lacked something of the glamour they had once possessed. It is easy to be carried along by Dickens's own tone of disillusionment and deduce that the world he was describing was in decline. Historians are in fact in some disagreement about the extent to which this was the case. The travelling theatres, jugglers, Punch and Judy men, acrobats, and circuses seem to eke out a precarious existence which is under threat from the forces of law and order, evangelicalism, the WORK ethic of INDUSTRIALISM, a grimly UTILITARIAN EDUCATION, and the pressures on space consequent on URBANIZATION. There was, for example, in the 1820s a concerted effort to rid London of its pleasure fairs, and a continuing and ultimately successful squeeze on the greatest of them, St Bartholomew's Fair. Greenwich Fair, too, described with so much gusto by Dickens, disappeared in the 1850s.

On the other hand, the central event at Greenwich Fair, as described by Dickens—and by many others—was the portable theatre of 'Muster' John RICHARDSON, a man who travelled a circuit through southern England, and who died in prosperity in 1837, leaving, it was said, some £20,000. It is possible that what Dickens and others tended to see as a world in decline was in fact adapting continually and with some success to new conditions. Theatre companies, circuses, and menageries were to be found throughout the length and breadth of Britain, most of them travelling well-worn circuits which enabled them to bring their entertainments to the remotest places on at least one occasion each year. More established but still popular theatrical companies had something of a stranglehold on the theatres of the capital, performing melodramas to huge audiences. New forms of entertainment were coming into being: circus in its modern form originated with Philip Astley (1742–1814) in the late 1760s, and entered a new phase of existence from 1823 under the impact of Andrew DUCROW (1793–1842); PANTOMIME, too, was transformed, the key figure being Joseph Grimaldi (1779–1837), whose MEMOIRS Dickens edited. Dickens's intimate knowledge of this exuberant world of entertainment ensured that, in his defending it, he was not simply or even mainly engaged in an indulgence of nostalgia.

In describing the circuses, fairs, boat-trips, theatres, and tea-gardens, Dickens's eye is focused as much on the audiences as on the entertainment, frequently isolating a family party for his attention—as in his account of Astley's in *Sketches by Boz*. His stance is that of the tolerant observer, amused by human foibles, but happy to see people enjoying themselves. But he also has in his vision those who want to restrict popular entertainments; there is a political edge to his assertions that what he is seeing are people 'disposed to be good-natured and sociable' ('London Recreations', *SB*), 'neat and clean, cheerful and contented' (*SUTH*); or, as he put it in 1850, again attacking the sabbatarians: 'The people in general are not gluttons, nor drunkards, nor gamblers, nor addicted to cruel sports, nor to the pushing of any amusement to furious and wild extremes. They are moderate, and easily pleased, and very sensible to all affectionate influences . . . Let us go into any place of Sunday enjoyment where any fair representation of the people resort, and we shall find them decent, orderly, quiet, sociable among their families and neighbours' ('The Sunday Screw', *HW* 22 June 1850).

Dickens was also able to describe the world of entertainment from the perspective of the suppliers—most notably the Crummleses in *Nicholas Nickleby*, Mrs Jarley and other showpeople in *The Old Curiosity Shop*, and Sleary's

circus in *Hard Times*. His descriptions in the first two of these novels themselves provide the historian with strong evidence that between the 1820s and 1840s there was a vibrant world of popular entertainment, and suggest that Dickens's fears of what the evangelicals and others might achieve were only very partially realized. Dickens was fascinated by the transformation—the magic—which occurred when these companies of performers, always on the edge of poverty or over it, often squabbling among themselves, took the stage. The reality—Vauxhall Gardens in daytime, the hangers-on outside Astley's (*SB*), or 'Gaslight Fairies' (*MP*)—was often dispiriting, but performance could provide both audiences and showpeople with the opportunity to escape from their workaday worlds and dismal surroundings. He was predisposed to sympathy with the lives and predicaments of 'those who minister to our amusement' ('Gaslight Fairies', *MP*, p. 14).

Dickens did not, however, bestow unqualified approval on the commercial entertainment which was on offer. In the two opening numbers of *Household Words* in 1850 he described the theatrical entertainment in the minor theatres and saloons of London, and did not disguise his sense that it would do little to raise the taste or improve the morals of the audiences—they deserved better ('The Amusements of the People', *HW* 30 March, 30 April 1850). It is true that in a later visit to the Britannia at Hoxton he was much more impressed both by the design of the theatre and by the drama itself, in which 'I was pleased to observe Virtue quite as triumphant as she usually is out of doors, and indeed I thought rather more so' ('Two Visits to a Cheap Theatre', *UT*). If this shows Dickens's willingness to respond to what was before him, there is nevertheless a trend towards increasing pessimism in his analysis of popular commercial entertainment. Even as early as *Nicholas Nickleby*, it is notable that the Crummleses exit from the novel to America with the intention of buying land—but they at least were 'a very happy little company' (*NN* 48). There is much more ambivalence about popular amusements in *The Old Curiosity Shop* where, first of all, the showpeople amongst whom Nell falls, with the exception of Mrs Jarley, are themselves morally less than scrupulous, and where in the figure of Quilp, Dickens has

created a monster who bears alarming resemblance to that staple of fairground and
street entertainment, Mr Punch; that is to say,
popular entertainment contained within it
forces of evil as well as good (Schlicke 1985,
p. 128).

After *The Old Curiosity Shop* show-people
play a much less prominent and significant
part in Dickens's fiction (*MC* 28; *DS* 22; *DC*
33; *BH* 24), and the image of popular entertainment as a whole is negative (*LD* 1.10; *OMF*
4.6; *MED* 14). The exception to this is *Hard
Times*, where Sleary's circus has a central role
to play. Significantly, however, we are not ourselves offered a view of the entertainment. We
know of what might be called the DOMESTIC
life of the members of the circus—and it is
sympathetically and realistically portrayed—
but fundamentally the role of the circus in
*Hard Times* is symbolic, standing for the imagination in contrast to the bombast of
Bounderby and the harsh utilitarianism of
Gradgrind.

One of the most striking aspects of Dickens's writings on amusements and recreations
is the dominant place taken by THEATRE. 'The
Amusements of the People' which Dickens
described in the opening numbers of *Household Words* were all theatrical. Dickens himself of course loved drama and acting (see
ACTORS, ACTRESSES; AMATEUR THEATRICALS),
and doubtless this has something to do with
the emphasis on theatre in his fiction. Equally
important is the fact that during his lifetime
theatre was popular in a way it has never been
since.

This emphasis, however, meant that some
other forms of recreation receive short shrift.
He gives little attention to SPORT, apart from
references to cricket as a symbolically uniting
occasion. Given the importance to Dickens of
sociability, it is not surprising that there is
little mention of entertainment in the home,
or of hobbies—the amusements and recreations Dickens describes are nearly all in public (Collins 1965, pp. 18–19), even though in
his own life home entertainment was a central
feature. Even within the world of public entertainment, the theatrical bias makes Dickens blind to the advance of MUSIC HALL,
which historians conventionally date from
mid-century, and which by the 1860s had
made a major impact on the entertainment
on offer in any town.

Even more striking is Dickens's neglect of
the great range of entertainment which historians have grouped together under the
heading of 'rational recreation'—mechanics'
institutes, libraries, parks, museums, concerts. This was not through ignorance.
Dickens approved of these forms of recreation, and worked on their behalf, but they
had no role to play in his fiction, and received
little attention in his journalism. The reason
is that Dickens was acutely aware of what was
missing from 'rational recreation': it gave no
scope for the imagination and it was too resolutely educational. A figure constantly in his
mind was 'Mr Barlow', the tutor in Thomas
Day's *Sandford and Merton* who represented
the dreariness and boredom of an education
without appeal to fancy (*UT*). He summed up
his reservations in writing that 'we think a
people formed *entirely* in their hours of
leisure by Polytechnic Institutions would be
an uncomfortable community' ('The Amusements of the People', *HW* 30 March 1850)—
uncomfortable because its members would
have no sympathy for one another. In his critical account of the Mechanics' Institute at
Rochester (Dullborough), he detected in its
activities 'a shyness in admitting that human
nature when at leisure has any desire whatever to be relieved and diverted; and a furtive
sliding in of any poor make-weight piece of
amusement, shamefacedly and edgewise'
(*UT*). In similar tone, he felt that the 1857
Manchester Exhibition of Art Treasures, admirable as it was in many ways, needed something animating, '*something in motion*', to
make an impact on 'the common people' (to
W. C. Macready, 3 August 1857). Dickens thus
distanced himself from the stricter rational
recreationists who emphasized the educational role of recreation—for Dickens, significantly, what people stood in need of
was 'sound rational amusement', the word
'amusement' as we have seen, carrying different overtones to 'recreation' (Schlicke 1985,
p. 212).

For Dickens amusements and recreation
had a function higher than education or the
instilling of good behaviour. This was, in a
world dominated by often soul-destroying
work, to restore people to their own humanity. There was, he believed, 'among the common people an innate love . . . for dramatic
entertainment in some form or other' ('The

Amusements of the People', *HW* 30 March 1850). That 'innate love' needed to be fostered and catered for, if need be by Dickens himself in his public readings. Amongst other benefits, good entertainment provided a bond between the generations and the sexes: 'Any knot of holiday-makers', he observed, 'without a large proportion of women and children among them, would be a perfect phenomenon' ('The Sunday Screw', *HW* 22 June 1850), and he delighted in depicting family parties at places of public entertainment ('Astley's', *SB*; *OCS* 39). Furthermore, good entertainment kept people in touch with their own childhoods, that vital ingredient of the happy person. In sum, any civilization without good amusements was doomed. Dickens felt in his own society that there were powerful groups who wanted to outlaw the kind of amusements of which he approved, and he worried about the lack of life-enhancing recreation; hence their centrality in his fiction and journalism. HC

Collins, P., 'Dickens and Popular Amusements', *The Dickensian*, 61 (1965).

Schlicke (1985).

**Andersen, Hans Christian** (1805–75), Danish writer and author of FAIRY TALES. Dickens had read Andersen's novel of Italy, *The Improvisatore* (translated 1845), his travel book *A Poet's Bazaar* (1846), and some of the tales before they first met at Lady Blessington's in July 1847. According to Andersen it was an emotional encounter, and he dedicated *A Christmas Greeting to my English Friends* to him (published in 1847, it included the tale 'The Old House' which Dickens particularly admired), as well as *A Poet's Day Dreams* (1853) and *To Be, or Not to Be?* (1857). Dickens's own story, 'A Child's Dream of a Star' (*HW* 6 April 1850) is in the bitter-sweet Andersen manner. In 1857 Andersen accepted an invitation to Gad's Hill, saying that he would be there 'for a week or a fortnight'. In fact he stayed for five weeks. Vain, lachrymose, morbidly self-pitying and introspective, with a gauche manner and minimal English, he severely tested the family's patience. Dickens's daughter Kate Perugini was later to write: 'He was a bony bore, and stayed on and on.' Dickens himself was able to simulate cordiality but the friendship waned and the two never met again. A contributory cause of the coolness may well have been the series of articles, 'A Visit to Charles Dickens in the Summer of 1857', which Andersen wrote for a Copenhagen paper; it was excerpted in a malicious manner, praising Catherine DICKENS fulsomely, in BENTLEY'S MISCELLANY in August 1860. GA

Bredsdorff, Elias, *Hans Christian Andersen* (1975).

**annuals and gift books.** Though reviewers and notable contributors disparaged the literary merit of annuals and gift books, Dickens did not escape the vogue for sumptuously bound collections of quality steel engravings and undistinguished poetry, tales, and travel sketches. Introduced to England by engraver Rudolph Ackermann, the 1823 *Forget Me Not* initiated enthusiasm for annuals that lasted over 30 years. Primarily addressed to young women and edited by fashionable ladies, annuals bore such titles as *Iris*, *Amulet*, and among the more successful, *Heath's Book of Beauty*, *Friendship's Offering*, and *The Keepsake*. As many as 63 annuals appeared on the market. Contributors, who acknowledged both low pay and the annuals' mediocrity and cliché (satirized by THACKERAY in *Fraser's Magazine* December 1837, p. 758), included Southey, LAMB, COLERIDGE, Elizabeth Barrett Browning, and TENNYSON. Dickens twice contributed to *The Keepsake*, published 1828–57 and edited 1841–50 by his friend the Countess of Blessington, who solicited work from celebrities frequenting her soirées. He provided the verses 'A Word in Season', and after her death he sent to her niece and successor, Marguerite Power (for whom Dickens raised money among Blessington's friends), the double story 'TO BE READ AT DUSK'. BT

***Arabian Nights, The.*** This collection of oriental tales, first recorded in their present form in 15th-century Cairo, was translated into French by Antoine Galland in 1704–8, and many English translations of his work appeared during the 18th and early 19th century, including Jonathan Scott's six-volume edition (1811), which was probably the version so avidly read by Dickens as a child, alongside *The Tales of the Genii, or The Delightful Lessons of Horam the Son of Asmar* (first published 1764). This latter book announced itself as 'translated from the Persian by Sir Charles

Morell, formerly Ambassador from the British Settlements in India to the Great Mogul', but was really written by the Revd James Ridley (1736–65). One of Dickens's earliest literary efforts, a drama called MISNAR, THE SULTAN OF INDIA, was based on one of Ridley's tales, the same one that serves to provide a powerful image at the climactic moment of *Great Expectations* (end of ch. 38).

The adult Dickens had in his library E. W. Lane's scholarly translation of *The Arabian Nights* (1839–41) which became the standard mid-Victorian edition, but pleads in the 1859 CHRISTMAS story 'The Haunted House' to continue using the old 'corrupted name' of Haroun Alraschid, 'so scented with sweet memories'. In the first Christmas story, 'A Christmas Tree' (*HW* 21 December 1850), he lovingly recalls how in reading *The Arabian Nights* as a child 'all common things [became] uncommon and enchanted to me. All lamps [were] wonderful; all rings [were] talismans . . .' He never lost his early delight in these stories and detailed allusions to them and their wonders appear frequently throughout his writings. He often uses such allusions to evoke a sense of wonder, glamour, or mystery in highly mundane surroundings, for example when Dick Swiveller, recovering from a fever, is bemused by the presence of the Marchioness in his room and thinks that he must be in 'an Arabian Night' and that the Marchioness must be a Genie—'Now for the two thousand black slaves with jars of jewels on their heads!' (*OCS* 44). Dickens also uses the *Nights* to evoke the imaginative joys of CHILDHOOD, as when Scrooge exuberantly recalls reading as a schoolboy about 'dear old honest Ali Baba' and about 'what's his name, who was put down in his drawers, asleep, at the Gate of Damascus' (*CC* 2); a less familiar but more elaborate example can be found in 'The Ghost in Master B's Room' in the 1859 Christmas number of *All The Year Round*.

A third use Dickens makes of allusions to the *Nights* is for satirical purposes. This can create a powerfully ironic effect, as at the beginning of *Hard Times* when the schoolmaster M'Choakumchild with his 'boiling store' of Fact is compared to Morgiana in the story of Ali Baba; or it can result in the brilliantly sustained lampooning of incompetent politicians in 'The Thousand and One Humbugs' (*HW* 21 and 28 April and 5 May 1855;

*MP*). In this parody we can also see Dickens's delight in the narrative form of *The Arabian Nights*, the embedding of stories within other stories, the 'framed-tales' device, something that strongly influenced his planning of MASTER HUMPHREY'S CLOCK and the Christmas Numbers of his later weekly journals. He was also fascinated by the figure of the storyteller Scheherezade (his nickname for Mrs GASKELL), explicitly recalled in his description of young David Copperfield's enforced feats of nocturnal storytelling (*DC* 7), and was undoubtedly conscious of a parallel between himself as a SERIAL NOVELIST favoured (granted continued life, as it were) by the public so long as he should be able to keep them wanting to read the next instalment of his constantly interrupted narratives.     MS

Caracciolo, Peter L. (ed.), *The Arabian Nights in English Literature* (1988), Editor's Introduction and M. Slater, 'Dickens in Wonderland'.

**art and artists.** Book ILLUSTRATIONS and prints provided the young Dickens with his earliest experiences of the fine arts. In early life he encountered two graphic artists who considerably influenced him, Hans Holbein, with his *Dance of Death* series, and William HOGARTH, with his satirical studies of 18th-century life. In the later 1830s Dickens began to visit art galleries: the Dulwich Picture Gallery with its remarkable holding of old masters, and Hampton Court Palace, which housed part of the royal reserve collection. Dickens's essay on Hampton Court, 'Please to Leave your Umbrella' (*HW* 1 May 1858; *MP*), refers to a characteristic Hampton Court painting as 'a stagnant pool of blacking in a frame', but he was a lifelong admirer of the Raphael tapestry cartoons which were then hanging there. An account of some of the portraits at Warwick Castle, which Dickens toured in 1838, is found in chapter 27 of *Dombey and Son*.

The watershed in Dickens's knowledge of the old masters came during his year in ITALY, 1844–5. In Genoa, where the Dickens family were living, he admired Van Dyck's Genoese portraits, but he was often unenthusiastic about the art galleries of other North Italian cities, particularly those in Verona and Mantua. Famous paintings sometimes drew an iconoclastic response from him. Leonardo da Vinci's *Last Supper*, in Milan, and Correggio's *Assumption of the Virgin*, in the dome of the Cathedral in Parma, both seemed to Dickens too damaged to be admired, while the violent scenes by Giulio Romano at the Palazzo del Te in Mantua provoked only dismay and horror. He was, however, appreciative of the art gallery in Bologna, dominated by the works of the Caraccis, Domenichino, Guido Reni, and Guercino, and he derived considerable pleasure from Andrea del Sarto's meditative *St Agnes* in the Cathedral at Pisa.

It was in Venice that Dickens saw two works which he recognized as of the highest quality, *The Assumption of the Virgin* by Titian and *Paradise* by Tintoretto. Dickens's admiration for Tintoretto, the most remarkable of his judgements on the fine arts, placed him ahead of the taste of his contemporaries.

In Rome, Dickens once again attacked famous works. He disliked the muscularity of Michelangelo's *Last Judgement* and of Raphael's *Fire in the Borgo*, although he was impressed by the latter's *Transfiguration*, at that time one of the most admired paintings in the world. The baroque statues of Bernini seemed to Dickens execrable, and he preferred the works of the neoclassical sculptor Canova. In his fiction, Dickens occasionally refers, to great satiric effect, to notable classical sculptures in the Capitoline and Vatican Museums, including the *Antinous*, the *Dying Gladiator*, and the *Laocoön*. Another particular favourite with visitors to Rome was the so-called portrait of *Beatrice Cenci*, then attributed to Guido Reni. The painting deeply impressed Dickens, moved by the story of Guido's sketching the head as Beatrice went to execution. A long passage on the painting is found in PICTURES FROM ITALY. In the book, as elsewhere, Dickens always makes it clear that he is speaking his mind about art, and not following convention. His daughter Kate Perugini (see CHILDREN OF DICKENS) believed that he followed his conception of 'nature' in arriving at his judgements (confirmed when he returned to Italy in 1853), and was impressed only by those works which expressed his ideal of 'truth'. Even so, *Pictures from Italy* reveals Dickens as very much a man of his time.

Among contemporary painters, Dickens had many artist friends, including David Wilkie, William Clarkson STANFIELD, Frank STONE, Edwin LANDSEER, W. P. FRITH, and Augustus Egg (1816–63). Daniel MACLISE was a very close friend of Dickens, particularly during the years 1839 to about 1845. The illustrators of his novels included men like George CATTERMOLE, Landseer, Maclise, Marcus STONE, and Luke FILDES, who were primarily painters rather than draughtsmen. Dickens was a regular attender at the Royal Academy exhibitions and was at the International Exhibition in Paris in 1855, when he noted the 'passion and action' of the French and Belgian paintings, comparing them favourably with the 'horrid respectability' of the British (October 1855). Dickens is known to have admired the work of a number of contemporary French painters, including Ary Scheffer, who painted his portrait in 1855, Paul Delaroche, whose *Hemicycle* in the École des Beaux Arts he described as 'the greatest work of art in the world' (18 March 1847), and Eugène Devéria, whose 'great brightness and brilliancy of colour' (22 July 1844) he noted in an account of the frescos in the Cathedral at Avignon.

By contrast, Dickens criticized the repetitive nature of most of the literary and historical genre scenes so popular in early Victorian Britain. His 'Ghost of Art' essay (*HW* 20 July 1850) and his comments on the 'Fancy Ball School' (*BH* 29) were attacks on unimaginative artists, who followed convention in both subject-matter and style. The famous onslaught on *Christ in the House of his Parents* by the PRE-RAPHAELITE painter John Everett Millais (*HW* 15 June 1850) sprang from a different source, Dickens's belief that it was almost blasphemous in its physical ugliness.

Among Dickens's few essays on the fine arts is his defence of Daniel Maclise's fresco design for the new Houses of Parliament, 'The Spirit of Chivalry' (*Shilling Magazine*, August 1845). Seeing a group of working men studying the painting in Westminster Hall, Dickens believed that this rough audience could sense the essential truth of the composition. Elsewhere he attacked the hypocrisy of artists who employed models of doubtful morality in order to represent noble characters. A related criticism is levelled at the portrait of Mr Casby (*LD* 1.13), where the sitter poses in an inappropriately pastoral setting.

Kate Perugini's belief that landscape was her father's favourite genre is confirmed by Dickens's expression of pleasure at certain works: some of Turner's watercolours, genre scenes by William Collins, and Venetian and marine paintings by Clarkson Stanfield.

Dickens owned many paintings, often gifts and frequently scenes from his novels. On occasion he purchased or commissioned works, including topographical watercolours by Samuel Prout and William Callow, a flower piece by William Henry Hunt, and *The Novel* and *The Play* by the Scottish artist Robert Hannah. Dickens bought *Waterfall at St Nighton's Keive, Near Tintagel* (1842) by Daniel Maclise, a painting of a country girl for which Dickens's sister-in-law, Georgina HOGARTH, was the model. At the end of his life he added two paintings by Philip Hermognes Calderon, showing young people in historical surroundings. Dickens's own collection is a good indication of his taste in contemporary British art. Most of the works at his Gad's Hill HOME were pleasing, brightly coloured, and often nostalgic in tone, surprisingly backward looking for the great novelist of the Victorian age.        LO

Lettis, R., 'Dickens and Art', *Dickens Studies Annual*, 14 (1985).

Ormond, Leonee, 'Dickens and Painting: The Old Masters', and 'Contemporary Art', *Dickensian*, 79 (1983), 80 (1984).

Perugini, Kate, 'Charles Dickens as a Lover of Art and Artists', *Magazine of Art* (1903).

**Athenaeum club,** a London club, founded in 1824 for men of intellectual distinction, to which Dickens was elected at the unusually early age of 26. Among the members were many, like Dickens, whose origins were hardly genteel, and many of extraordinary eminence—Macaulay, CARLYLE, THACKERAY, DISRAELI, RUSKIN, TROLLOPE, Arnold, BROWNING, Darwin, Faraday, Owen, Huxley, John Stuart MILL—as well as several of Dickens's oldest friends—John FORSTER, William MACREADY, Thomas Noon TALFOURD, Richard Monckton Milnes, and Daniel MACLISE. The membership of the club wonderfully demonstrates the smallness of the Victorian male intellectual's world. It was in the entrance hall to the Athenaeum that Thackeray reached out to Dickens to end the quarrel begun by Edmund YATES.        RN

**Australia.** Dickens was such a restless man that he often considered the 'convict run'—during the personal crisis of 1857–8, for instance, when, FORSTER tells us, he returned to 'his own old notion of having some slight idea

of going to settle in Australia'. In a letter of 3 July 1840 he had communicated to Lord Normanby a desire to write 'a vivid description of . . . Norfolk Island and such-like places'; on 14 April 1847 he told T. J. Serle, 'if you should have any commands for Australia after Dombey is finished, I think of making a little excursion there'; on 3 July 1850, likewise, to Mrs WATSON: 'I think of flying to Australia and taking to the Bush.' Between June and December 1862 he actively considered a firm offer for a PUBLIC READING tour from Spiers and Pond, who had just successfully organized the first English cricket tour of Australia, writing to Beard of how, 'constantly disturbed and dazzled by the great chance that seems to be waiting over there, I am restless' (4 November 1862). But in the end two of his sons, Alfred and Edward, were sent there instead, never to return (see EMIGRATION).

Though Australia perhaps 'dazzled' after the 1850 gold rush, before that it was an odd place to think of lighting out for: in Dickens's work, with the major exception of *David Copperfield*, where the Micawbers, Daniel Peggotty, Emily, Martha, and Mr Mell all make good there, it is considered a place for transportees rather than emigrants (see PRISONS AND PENAL TRANSPORTATION). Following Caroline Chisholm and her schemes to assist women to emigrate down under (see 'A Bundle of Emigrants' Letters', *HW* 30 March 1850), he sought to redeem 'fallen women' by persuading them to reform and go to Australia, but often met with frosty responses: the girls thought he meant as convicts rather than prospective brides (they 'make a fatal and decisive confusion between emigration and transportation', he writes in a letter of 12 April 1850; see PROSTITUTES). 'Willing Sophy' in 'Mrs Lirriper's Lodgings' helps explain the fascination (see CHRISTMAS STORIES). Like Dickens she 'took a great deal of black into me . . . when I was a small child being much neglected'; her face remains black from hard work until she is sent 'away to New South Wales where it might not be noticed'. She meets a 'Mulotter' on the voyage, marries him, and 'was *not* noticed in a new state of society to her dying day'. Such anonymity might have attracted Dickens.

In the novels, both transportation and emigration are connected with redemption—right from the start, in 'The Convict's Return'

(*PP* 6), where the 'prodigal son' returns 'truly contrite, penitent, and humbled, if ever man was'. The comic metamorphosis of Micawber, though, in Port Middlebay, 'that theer bald head of his, a perspiring in the sun', is finer, and the complex, tragicomic maturing of Magwitch finer still. A more astringent view of Australia emerges in *Great Expectations* ('it come flat to be there, for all I was growing rich'), and here the development of stoic calm is at issue—'he was the least anxious of any of us' during the last attempt at flight—rather than a pantomime transformation.

MH

Lansbury, Coral, *Arcady in Australia* (1970).
Lazarus, Mary, *A Tale of Two Brothers* (1973).

# B

**Bagehot, Walter** (1826–77), 'the most representative Victorian', one of Victorian Britain's most distinguished political writers and essayists, best known for *The English Constitution* (1867). His neoclassical judgement is representative of a view of Dickens still widespread well over a century after his famous essay of 1858, a review of the Cheap Edition ('Charles Dickens', *National Review*, October 1858; repr. [part] in Collins 1971). Accurately recognizing that 'his genius is essentially irregular and asymmetrical' and his world a 'disconnected' one, Bagehot deplores this as 'the overflow of a copious mind, though not the chastened expression of an harmonious one', and condemns Dickens's political opinions as 'sentimental radicalism'. He allows Dickens's POPULARITY—'There is no contemporary English writer whose works are read so generally through the whole house, who can give pleasure to the servants as well as to the mistress'—and praises both Dickens's STYLE—'descriptive, racy and flowing'—and its social range—'from quite the lowest to almost the highest'. He also notes Dickens's special facility in the 'delineating of city life'—particularly London's—and 'his marvellous power of observation', calling him, in a happy phrase, 'a special correspondent for posterity'. But he finds grievous faults: whenever Dickens 'attempted to make a long connected story . . . the result has been a complete failure'. Nor can he fashion a proper love story. Perhaps worse, he is 'utterly deficient in the faculty of reasoning . . . his abstract understanding is so far inferior to his picturesque imagination as to give even his best works the sense of jar and incompleteness'. Bagehot's is the judgement of a critic who sees clearly but disapproves of what he sees.                    EJE

**ballads.** See MUSIC, MUSICIANS, AND SONG.

**Barham, Richard Harris** (1788–1845), Anglican clergyman, novelist, humorist, and friend of Dickens from 1837. His macabre, grotesque, and humorous stories and verse, later collected as the *Ingoldsby Legends*, were first published in BENTLEY'S MISCELLANY under Dickens's editorship and were partly responsible for the initial success of the periodical. Barham had been a friend of BENTLEY's since their schooldays at St Paul's, and so he dealt more with the publisher than with the editor. In the dispute between Dickens and Bentley which eventually led to Dickens's resignation in 1838, Barham acted as mediator and advised the publisher to accept Dickens's suggestion of AINSWORTH as successor.

MWT

***Barnaby Rudge*** Dickens's fifth, much-delayed novel, initially published as a weekly SERIAL in 1841 in MASTER HUMPHREY'S CLOCK. The first of Dickens's two HISTORICAL novels (*A Tale of Two Cities* is the other), written in conscious emulation of SCOTT, it deals with the Gordon Riots of 1780.

### Inception and Composition

*Barnaby Rudge* had the longest and most troubled gestation of all of Dickens's novels. First conceived in 1836 as 'Gabriel Vardon, the Locksmith of London', it was intended to be a three-volume novel—unlike the 'low, cheap form of publication' of the serially produced *Pickwick*—involving 'the time, the labour, the casting about, in every direction' of a serious work of literature 'on which I might build my fame' (to Richard BENTLEY, 17 August 1836). Retitled *Barnaby Rudge* the following year, it was still not begun in 1838 (by which time *Nickleby* was under way), and although he then assured Bentley that 'I have recently been thinking a great deal about Barnaby Rudge' (10 February 1838), Dickens confided to FORSTER that he felt it 'hanging over him like a hideous nightmare' (February 1838).

On 3 January 1839 the writing at last commenced, only to break off less than three weeks later. 'It is no fiction to say that at present I *cannot* write this tale', he announced to Forster, complaining bitterly of 'the consciousness that my books are enriching everybody connected with them but myself, and that I, with such popularity as I have acquired, am struggling in old toils, and wasting my energies in the very height and freshness of my fame, and the best part of my life, to fill the pockets of others' (21 February 1839). The upshot was that he determined to hold over *Barnaby* for six more months. On 18 September he told Forster 'I have had a good notion for Barnaby', and on ?3 October he was again working 'tooth and nail at Barnaby', but he then discovered that it was being advertised as 'preparing for publication' and angrily instructed his lawyer to inform Bentley 'that I am not prepared to deliver the Manuscript of Barnaby Rudge to him on the First of January' (16 December 1839)—and indeed, the novel was never delivered to Bentley, with whom he severed all connection in July 1840.

Finally, in January 1841, having meantime completed *Pickwick, Oliver Twist, Nicholas Nickleby*, and *The Old Curiosity Shop*, Dickens turned for the last time to *Barnaby Rudge*, writing rapidly and expressing confidence as he took it to completion. He revised the previously written chapters on 21 January (to Forster, 22 January 1841) and on the 27th declared himself 'very busy'. Although he found himself 'cramped for room' at the short weekly instalments (16 March 1841) and 'fearfully hard at work, morning, noon, and night' (15 June 1841), he found time to spend four weeks touring SCOTLAND in June and July, to see The PIC-NIC PAPERS published in August, to convalesce from an operation in October for fistula, as well as to plan his trip to America. His letters to Forster indicate the zest with which he wrote the chapters describing the riots: 'I was always sure I could make a good thing of *Barnaby*, and I think you'll find it comes out strong to the last word' (11 August 1841); 'I have just burnt into Newgate, and am going in the next number to tear the prisoners out by the hair of their heads' (11 September 1841); 'I have let all the prisoners out of Newgate, burnt down Lord Mansfield's, and played the very devil . . . I feel quite smoky when I am at work. I want elbow-room terribly' (18 September 1841).

Revealing light on his conception of historical fiction is shed in a letter he wrote as the novel neared completion. John Landseer (1769–1852, father of Edwin LANDSEER), had written to him noting that the magistrate John Wilkes had been active in suppressing the riots. Dickens defended his decision not to notice it in the novel: 'It is almost indispensable in a work of fiction that the characters should belong to the Machinery of the Tale,—and the introduction towards the end of a story where there is always a great deal to do, of new actors until then unheard of, is a thing to be avoided, if possible, in every case' (5 November 1841).

Dickens finished the novel in November, and the final chapter was published on the 27th. (See also COMPOSITION, DICKENS'S METHODS.)

## Contracts, Text, and Publication History

The convoluted contractual history of *Barnaby Rudge*—there were eleven separate agreements bearing directly or indirectly on it—is testimony to the rapidity with which Dickens's fame took off. He broke one contract after another partly because of insensitive actions by his publishers, but primarily because the market value of his works rose, and continued to rise, faster than he, his publishers, or their respective advisers could possibly have foreseen.

On 9 May 1836 Dickens wrote to John MACRONE, publisher of *Sketches by Boz*, that he had 'great pleasure in accepting' £200 on delivery 'on or before the 30th day of November next' of the completed manuscript of 'Gabriel Vardon'. A mere three months later he told Bentley that 'some confidential friends' had advised him that he should have £500 for the COPYRIGHT of a novel in three volumes—the identical 'Gabriel Vardon' (17 August 1836)—and on 22 August he signed the first of six contracts with Bentley (Pilgrim 1.648–9). A year later, on 28 September 1837, the sum to be paid was raised to £700 (Pilgrim 1.654–5). On 22 September 1838, with writing still not begun, a new agreement again increased the payment, to £900, and released Dickens from the obligation to produce it as a three-volume novel, stipulating instead that *Barnaby Rudge* would follow *Oliver Twist* as Dickens's monthly contribution to BENTLEY'S MISCELLANY (Pilgrim 1.666–74). On 27 February 1839 Dickens resigned as editor of *Bentley's Miscellany* (Pilgrim 1.675–80) and in a separate agreement *Barnaby Rudge* reverted to a three-volume novel, to be delivered by January 1840, for which Dickens was to be paid £4,000 (Pilgrim 1.674–5). Finally, on

2 July 1840 Dickens gained formal release from all of his obligations to Bentley (Pilgrim 2.471–5).

Meanwhile Dickens had entered into contracts with CHAPMAN AND HALL, publishers of *Pickwick* and *Nickleby*, for a weekly serial to follow *Nickleby*, *Master Humphrey's Clock* (Pilgrim 1.681 and 2.464–71), and in July 1840 they advanced the money which enabled Dickens to buy out his contract with Bentley, with *Barnaby Rudge* now planned to follow *The Old Curiosity Shop* in *Master Humphrey's Clock* (Pilgrim 2.478–81), as in fact it did, appearing in weekly instalments from No. 46 (13 February 1841) to No. 88 (27 November 1841). By a further contract, with the Philadelphia publishers Lea and Blanchard, Dickens arranged for the first American publication of *Barnaby Rudge* (Pilgrim 1.652).

The novel's complete manuscript is held in the FORSTER COLLECTION. Its largely clean condition suggests that Dickens wrote easily, once he was finally under way. Only seven pages of proofs survive, also in the Forster Collection, but Butt and Tillotson observe that 'the considerable differences between manuscript and printed text show that much revision must have taken place in proof' (1957, p. 80).

*Barnaby Rudge* was published in a variety of formats. As part of *Master Humphrey's Clock* it appeared in weekly and in monthly parts, by 'BOZ', and within the three volumes of the completed miscellany, by 'Charles Dickens'. It was published concurrently in Philadelphia by Lea and Blanchard. With a subtitle, *A Tale of the Riots of 'Eighty*, it was published by Chapman and Hall in 1841 as a single separate volume from the plates of *Master Humphrey's Clock*, retaining their page numbering. A pirated edition, volume 1 of *Parley's Penny Library*, was published at once; it was published in Paris by Baudry in 1842 and, as part of *Master Humphrey's Clock*, by Tauchnitz in 1846. The Cheap Edition came out in weekly parts from November 1848 to April 1849 and as a single volume in 1849; the Library Edition, bound with *Hard Times*, in 1858, and the Charles Dickens Edition in 1868. There has been no authoritative edition among the many published since Dickens's death. Dickens wrote a Preface in November 1841, which he revised for the Cheap Edition and for the Charles Dickens Edition. There was no dedication. (See also EDITIONS; LEGAL DOCUMENTS; PUBLISHING.)

## Illustrations

Dickens's principal ILLUSTRATORS for *The Old Curiosity Shop*, Hablot BROWNE and George CATTERMOLE, shared the task of supplying plates for *Barnaby Rudge*. As for the rest of *Master Humphrey's Clock*, these were woodcuts 'dropped into the text' rather than the full-page steel engravings which more usually embellished Dickens's works—a process which added considerably to the production costs, but created closer integration of illustration with text. Browne drew 59 of the illustrations, depicting characters, and Cattermole seventeen, primarily of settings. There were two illustrations per weekly number, ornamental initial letters for the monthly issues, and occasional vignettes at the ends of chapters.

Thomas Sibson produced four plates each month for an extra-illustrated edition of *Master Humphrey's Clock* published by Robert Tyas (1840–2). In 1841 W. P. FRITH painted several portraits of Dolly Varden, and the following year Dickens commissioned him to paint 'two little companion pictures', of Dolly and of Kate Nickleby, for which he paid £40 (to Frith, 15 November 1842 and nn.). Browne drew a new frontispiece for the Cheap Edition, plus four new illustrations published in conjunction with that edition, which otherwise contains no illustration. Fred Barnard executed forty-six illustrations for Chapman and Hall's Household Edition of 1874.

## Sources and Context

Scott's precedent gave the historical novel enormous prestige, and it is unsurprising that the ambitious young Dickens aspired to that form at the very outset of his career as a writer of fiction. The subtitle which he added for volume publication, pointing to events some sixty years previously, pointedly emulates the stance which Scott indicated in his first novel, *Waverley, or 'Tis Sixty Years Since*, and a number of parallels with Scott's fiction are evident in *Barnaby*, notably the storming of Newgate, which recalls the attack on the Tolbooth in *The Heart of Mid-Lothian*, and the eponymous central character, who owes something to Scott's mad characters Davey Gellatley and Madge Wildfire. But, as critics have insisted, Dickens's view of history differs radically from Scott's, owing more to the apocalyptic vision of CARLYLE, as seen in particular in *The French Revolution* (1837), with its account of the fall of the Bastille. Dickens's engagement with pressing events of his own day (to say nothing of his abandonment of the three-volume form) meant, in Kathryn Chittick's words, that *Barnaby Rudge* confirmed Dickens not as 'the second Sir Walter Scott' but as 'a Victorian novelist . . . a novelist of contemporary life' (Chittick 1990, p. 166).

Dickens drew on written records of the events of 1780—the *Annual Register*, Holcroft's *Narrative of the Late Riots* (1780), and Watson's *Life of Lord George Gordon* (1795) were in his library—and offered what Butt and Tillotson conclude is 'a legitimate reading of the evidence' (1957, pp. 84–5). But recent events gave Dickens's concerns urgent topicality: the POOR LAW agitation of the late 1830s; the CHARTIST riots of 1839 (in Newport an attempt was made to release Chartist prisoners, and trials continued into 1840); the founding of the Anti-Corn Law League in 1839 and its agitation; the attempted assassination of Queen Victoria in June 1840 by Edward Oxford and his subsequent trial, in which he was found guilty but insane; the public hanging (which Dickens witnessed) in July 1840 of the convicted murderer Courvoisier; the harsh winters and trade depression—all these made the times seem parlous indeed, with chaos threatening from every side.

The novel was topical in another sense: the impact of the Oxford Movement had not yet made itself felt. Newman's *Tract 90* was published in March 1841, in May 1843 Pusey was suspended from preaching in the University, and in 1845 Newman converted to the ROMAN CATHOLIC church. By 1843 the Dickens who declared himself to be 'getting horribly bitter' about High Church attitudes, and who wrote a scathing attack on them in the EXAMINER, could not have presented the Catholics Haredale and Langdale with the tolerance accorded them in *Barnaby Rudge* (to Fonblanque, 13 March 1843; 'Report of the Commissioners . . . of Oxford', *Examiner*, 3 June 1843; *Journalism* 2.59–63).

Specific sources can be identified for various aspects of the novel. The character of Barnaby, the most prominent of Dickens's 'holy idiots', is a descendent of WORDS-WORTH's 'Idiot Boy' (see MADNESS). Sir John

Chester reflects Dickens's loathing of the worldly advice of Lord Chesterfield (1694–1773), found in his *Letters to His Son* (1774); he 'never compromised himself by an ungentlemanly action, and never was guilty of a manly one' (*BR* 25). And Barnaby's raven had a real-life prototype in a PET of Dickens, also known as Grip, whose death while the novel was in progress he described in comically grotesque detail (to Angus Fletcher, 15 June 1841).

### Plot, Character, and Theme

The opening chapters of *Barnaby Rudge* recount the private lives of several sets of characters, in a slow-moving narrative set in 1775, five years before the riots. The plot is set in motion by old cronies at the Maypole Inn, Chigwell, recounting to a stranger the story of an unsolved murder of many years previously. Two young men, Edward Chester and Joe Willett, are thwarted in romance, with Emma Haredale and Dolly Varden respectively, and rebellious against their unsympathetic fathers. The docile but fantastically imaginative idiot Barnaby lives alone with his mother, his father supposedly having been killed along with Reuben Haredale. The Varden household in London consists of Gabriel, a locksmith, long-suffering husband of a woman whose head is turned with religious enthusiasm, their coquettish daughter Dolly, the self-important apprentice Sim Tappertit, and the book's principal comic character, the shrewish and sycophantic maid Miggs.

In chapter 33, after a five-year gap, the somewhat demented Lord George Gordon and his villanous secretary Gashford are introduced, and private lives intersect with public events. Gordon's No-Popery activities foment a riot, described by Dickens with great vividness, which is joined by Barnaby, Hugh (the gipsy-like ostler at the Maypole), and Ned Dennis, the hangman. The Haredales' house, the Warren, is burned because its occupants are Catholics, and the Maypole is pillaged. Emma and Dolly are captured by the rioters, then rescued. Barnaby is arrested and placed in a cell with his father, who is revealed as the stranger of the early chapters and the long-sought murderer. The rioters storm Newgate and release the prisoners. Barnaby is pardoned, but his father, Hugh, and Dennis are hanged. Hugh is revealed to be the bastard son of the suave Sir John Chester, who is killed in a duel fighting his old enemy Geoffrey Haredale. Joe Willett, who has lost an arm fighting in the American revolution, marries Dolly; Edward and Emma marry and EMIGRATE to the West Indies. Sim's legs are crushed and Miggs becomes a prison turnkey.

### Reception

*Barnaby Rudge* met with little favour in its day, and (with notable exceptions) that judgement persists. Its modern bibliographer, Thomas Rice, calls it 'the least loved and the least read' of Dickens's books (Rice 1987, p. xv). Sales dropped from 70,000 per week at the outset to 30,000 by the close. Notices were down 40 per cent from 1839. Reviews ranged from the negative to the severe. Famously, Edgar Allan Poe saw an incongruity between the riots and the mystery which he claimed to have solved at once (*Graham's Magazine*, 20, 1842, repr. in Collins 1971). Even Dickens's closest friend and adviser, John Forster, allowed that the book was structurally flawed: 'The interest with which the tale begins, has ceased to be its interest before the close' (Forster 2.9; *Examiner*, 4 December 1841). In an unusually favourable notice Thomas HOOD admired the structure and perspicaciously saw contemporary relevance in Dickens's treatment of bigotry (*Athenaeum*, 22 January 1842).

On the other hand, *Barnaby Rudge* inspired a 'surprisingly large' number of DRAMATIZATIONS (Bolton 1987, p. 210), and Dolly Varden quickly established herself as a favourite with the Victorians, inspiring songs, dances, paintings, 'the Dolly Varden look' in ladies' fashion in the 1870s, and lending her name to a hat style, a spotted calico material, a species of trout, a variety of horse, and the buffer on a railway tender (Vanda Foster, 'The Dolly Varden', *Dickensian*, 73, 1977; Richard Dunn, 'In Pursuit of Dolly Varden', *Dickensian*, 74, 1978).

GISSING praised the book's construction (Introduction to the Rochester Edition, 1901), but A. C. Swinburne was perhaps the book's greatest admirer, praising it as 'a faultless work of creation' ('Charles Dickens', *Quarterly Review*, 196, 1902). Butt and Tillotson offered a meticulous demonstration of Dickens's planning of *Barnaby Rudge*, claiming that its 'long period of incubation' reveals not grudging fulfilment of an old obligation but

'tenacity of purpose and the grip of an original idea' (1957, p. 77). More recently, Harold Folland, James Gottshall, Steven Marcus (1965), Angus Wilson (1970), and Thomas Rice have written thoughtful defences of the novel's achievement.　　　　　　PVWS

Folland, Harold, 'The Doer and the Deed: Theme and Pattern in *Barnaby Rudge*', *PMLA* 74 (1959).

Gottshall, James, 'Devils Abroad: The Unity and Significance of *Barnaby Rudge*', *Nineteenth-Century Fiction*, 16 (1961).

Rice, Thomas, 'The End of Dickens's Apprenticeship: Variable Focus in *Barnaby Rudge*', *Nineteenth-Century Fiction*, 30 (1974).

**Battle of Life, The**　Dickens's fourth CHRISTMAS book, written in SWITZERLAND in 1846 while he was also at work on *Dombey*. He found great difficulty in writing it, and the result was, of all his works, 'with no argument at all, his most flawed and disliked' (Glancy 1985, p. xix). The story concerns the sacrifice by Marion Jeddler of her lover to her sister Grace. When the truth of her action emerges, their father is converted from cynicism. 'Exaggerated, absurd, impossible sentimentality', declared the MORNING CHRONICLE (24 December 1846).

The first reference to the story appears in a letter to FORSTER, mentioning 'an odd shadowy undefined idea . . . that I could connect a great battle-field somehow with my little Christmas story' (?22 June 1846). By 18 July he had decided on the title, but on 20 September confessed that he had cancelled the first scene, 'which I have never done before', and on 26 September he was 'sick, giddy and capriciously despondent' at the thought that 'there may be NO CHRISTMAS BOOK!' He reported that 'my soul sinks' at the constriction of space, the absence of supernatural machinery, and the need to be getting on with *Dombey*. He persevered nevertheless, and finished writing on 18 October, but without conviction: 'I really do not know what this story is worth', he told Forster.

He had 'that most delightful of all stories', *The Vicar of Wakefield*, in mind while he wrote, and considered that his story would have been better had it extended to the length of GOLDSMITH's book (to Forster, ?6 October and 26 September 1846). He was also working at the time on his children's version of the New Testament, The LIFE OF OUR LORD, which may account for the unusual amount of religious imagery in *The Battle of Life*.

The manuscript is in the Pierpont Morgan Library; no proofs survive. *The Battle of Life. A Love Story* was published on 19 December by BRADBURY AND EVANS with ILLUSTRATIONS by MACLISE, DOYLE, STANFIELD, and LEECH and a dedication to 'my English friends in Switzerland'. On seeing Leech's illustration of Marion with Alfred Warden, Dickens reacted 'with horror and agony not to be expressed', because in the story the rumour of an elopement is false. With unwonted consideration to an illustrator, however, Dickens let the plate stay rather than give pain to 'kind-hearted Leech' (to Forster, ?12 December 1846).

Reviews were generally hostile, but the book sold 23,000 copies on the day of publication. It was warmly reviewed in the EXAMINER (26 December 1846), probably by Forster, who, Philip Collins argues, 'helped arrest Dickens at immaturities he might have outgrown more quickly' ('Dickens's Self-Estimate', in Partlow 1970). There were few DRAMATIZATIONS, but KEELEY paid Dickens £100 to stage an authorized version at the Lyceum, adapted by Albert SMITH. Mrs Keeley's performance of Clemency, the cheerful clumsy servant, was hailed as 'one of her greatest triumphs on the stage' (Walter Goodman, *The Keeleys on the Stage and at Home*, 1895). PVWS

Carolan, Katherine, 'The Battle of Life, a Love Story', *Dickensian*, 69 (1973).

**Beadnell, Maria (Mrs Winter)** (1811–86), Dickens's first great love. It is not known how Dickens became acquainted with the City banker, George Beadnell, but by 1830 he had established himself as a devoted admirer of Beadnell's third and youngest daughter Maria. She was thirteen months older than he, small in stature and very pretty with dark ringlets. For four years Dickens was devotedly and obsessively in love with her. But Maria, who had several other admirers, was capricious and Dickens suffered torments of hope and jealousy and despair. The Beadnells disapproved of such a socially unacceptable suitor as Dickens and may have taken steps to separate the young people. Certainly in 1832 Dickens was having to communicate surreptitiously with Maria, using various go-betweens. In March 1833 he determined to bring the matter to a crisis. He returned her letters, explaining that he could no longer endure her 'heartless indifference' (18 March 1833). Her reply apparently offered him a crumb of comfort since he wrote again protesting undying devotion, but the situation had not really altered. After weeks more of anguish exacerbated by the meddling of Maria's friend Marianne Leigh, Dickens sent Maria a final appeal: 'I have never loved and I can never love any human creature breathing but yourself' (19 May 1833). He received an unsatisfactory reply and they went their separate ways. Dickens remained in occasional touch with Mr Beadnell, and according to a memorandum by Georgina HOGARTH may have once visited Maria after her 1845 marriage to Henry Louis Winter, manager of a sawmill in Finsbury.

In February 1855 Dickens, brooding on the 'one happiness [he had] missed in life, and one friend and companion he had never made' (Forster 8.2) suddenly received a letter from Maria. By now she had two daughters and was, she said, 'toothless, fat, old, and ugly'. About to leave for a short trip to Paris, Dickens responded in a series of passionate letters which convey how well he remembered his great love, and showing that he thought of her as unchanged: 'You are always the same in my remembrance.' He asks if she has read *David Copperfield* and seen in it 'a faithful reflection of the passion I had for you . . . and in little bits of "Dora" touches of your old self'. Perhaps she had read it and thought 'How dearly that boy must have loved me, and how vividly this man remembers it' (15 February 1855).

When he finally met her Dickens clearly found Maria Winter to be a shattering disappointment. Thereafter his few letters to her were short and formal in tone, and he avoided as far as possible any further contact with her. A few months after their meeting he wrote in *Little Dorrit* of Arthur Clennam's disillusionment at meeting again his old love of twenty-five years before. Flora Finching, once pretty and enchanting, had become fat, diffuse, and silly though kind-hearted. 'We have all had our Floras', wrote Dickens to the Duke of Devonshire, who particularly relished this character, adding 'mine is living, and extremely fat' (5 July 1856).

Winter became bankrupt in 1859 and next year went to Cambridge to read for Holy Orders, eventually becoming vicar of Alnmouth near Newcastle. He died in 1871 but Maria lived on for another sixteen years, keeping in touch with Georgina HOGARTH, collecting Dickens's books, and treasuring always romantic memories of her early association with the great novelist. By a Hardyesque coincidence, she is buried in the same Southsea cemetery as Ellen TERNAN.     MS

Suzannet, Comte Alain de, 'Maria Beadnell's Album', *Dickensian*, 31 (1935).

**Beard, Thomas.** See DICKENS CIRCLE, THE.

***Bell's Life in London*** (1822–86), a Regency Sunday sporting paper that printed Dickens's sketches 'Scenes and Characters' from September 1835 to January 1836. In April 1829 the *Westminster Review* said it had the largest circulation (estimated 22,000) of all the Sunday papers. Like most of the weeklies, it was politically liberal.

Dickens's sketches were printed under the pseudonym 'Tibbs'. These include 'Seven Dials' (27 September), 'Miss Evans and "The Eagle" ' (4 October), 'The Dancing Academy' (11 October), 'Making a Night of It' (18 October), 'Love and Oysters' (25 October), 'Some Account of an Omnibus Cad' (1 November), 'The Vocal Dressmaker' (22 November), 'The Prisoners' Van' (29 November), 'The Parlour' (13 December), 'Christmas Festivities' (27 December), 'The New Year' (3 January), and 'The Streets at Night' (17 January). Vincent George Dowling (1785–1852), editor of *Bell's Life in London* from 1824, was said to have been 'the first to discover the genius for sketching characters of Dickens' (Pilgrim 1.76–7 n.). Nonetheless, Dickens complained in the autumn of 1836 that the paper reprinted three of his new sketches from the MORNING CHRONICLE without permission, 'Scotland Yard', 'Doctors' Commons', and 'Vauxhall Gardens by Day'. *Sketches by Boz* was frequently excerpted in this paper from February 1836 and commended for its humour.     KC

***Bell's Weekly Magazine.*** This 'cheap' weekly periodical published by John Percival in quarto format, price 2d, from 18 January to 22 February 1834 (six numbers), is given as the source for the first publication of Dickens's sketch 'Sentiment' (7 June 1834) by Hilmer Nielsen in the *Dickensian*, 34 (1937/8). However, T. W. Hill, in the *Dickensian* (Autumn 1951), records that 'Sentiment' was not published until the book publication of *Sketches by Boz*, as do Butt and Tillotson (1964). Duane DeVries (1976) prints the *Bell's* attribution, with the note 'not seen'; and Michael Slater in the Dent *Sketches by Boz* (1994) and Dennis Walder in the Penguin (1996) also give *Bell's* as the original place of publication. The only extant run of the paper, in the British Library, contains nothing beyond February 1834.     KC

**Bentham, Jeremy** (1748–1832), philosopher, legal and penal reformer, political theorist, and somewhat Pickwickian chief of the circle variously known as Philosophical Radicals and UTILITARIANS, by whose ideas Dickens was both attracted and repelled. Dickens rejected what he took, mostly at second or third hand, to be utilitarian theory, but he shared Bentham's passion for legal REFORM and was closely allied in several reformist causes, especially involving PUBLIC HEALTH AND SANITATION, with members of Bentham's circle, like Edwin CHADWICK (a former private secretary) and Dr Southwood Smith (Bentham's physician and executor, in whose home Dickens very probably encountered Bentham's stuffed and mounted skeleton, currently on display at University College, London).     RN

**Bentley, Richard** (1794–1871), formerly a printer and co-publisher and founder in 1832 of Richard Bentley and Son, a prominent Victorian publisher. Between 22 August 1836 and 2 July 1840 Bentley signed nine agreements with Dickens. Eight related to Dickens's duties as editor of BENTLEY'S MIS-CELLANY and the publication of *Oliver Twist* and *Barnaby Rudge*; one (29 November 1837) detailed Dickens's payment for editing the MEMOIRS OF GRIMALDI. The 47 months of their contractual relationship were marked by tension and acrimony as each sought the upper hand in their negotiations. The practice of paying authors a fixed sum for the COPYRIGHT of books prompted their quarrel. This system was particularly inappropriate for Dickens, whose rapidly increasing popularity outpaced every fixed agreement he signed.

Dickens met Bentley in March 1836. Five months later, negotiations began for a three-volume novel Dickens had already promised to MACRONE. Bentley doubled the original copyright price. But following their discussion on 16 August 1836, Dickens wrote back to suggest £500 instead. The time and labour involved, Dickens explained, justified his proposal. As a further incentive, Dickens reminded Bentley of 'the great probability' of the book's having 'a very large sale . . . Recollect that you are dealing with an Author not quite unknown' (17 August 1836). Bentley consented but made the higher price payable only on condition of sales reaching 1,450 copies. This agreement of 22 August 1836 makes no reference to either the title or to a delivery date. But it did affirm that after its completion Dickens would also offer Bentley 'his next novel of three Volumes'.

On 4 November 1836 Bentley and Dickens drew closer. On this occasion, Dickens undertook to edit a projected humorous monthly publication called 'The Wits' Miscellany', retitled *Bentley's Miscellany* before publication began. This second agreement required Dickens to furnish 'an original article of his own writing', each month 'to consist of about a sheet of 16 pages'. In return, Bentley agreed to pay Dickens £20 a month for his editorial work and an additional 20 guineas for his contributions. Copyright of these pieces, like everything published in the journal, would belong exclusively to Bentley.

Dickens accepted Bentley's proposal with caution. Thinking it over, he was 'perfectly satisfied' that working for Bentley would not interfere with his ability to continue writing *Pickwick* for CHAPMAN AND HALL. But since the position would require his immediate resignation as a reporter from the MORNING CHRONICLE, he stipulated that his engagement should be for no less than a year. He also asked Bentley to specify his editorial duties and to stipulate 'the quantity of matter' he was to furnish monthly. 'The terms I leave to you to propose', he wrote, reminding Bentley that it was necessary to 'enlarge on the rapidly increasing value of my time and writings to myself' (2 November 1836).

Unexpected developments soon tested the apparent harmony between the two parties. It seems that Dickens underestimated Bentley's wish to retain some editorial control. Perhaps he also miscalculated the extent to which the publisher would go to accommodate his demands before offering resistance. In any event, the contract Dickens and Bentley signed on 4 November 1836 set the stage for a 'three-year duel' which ended in total rupture.

Within a month Dickens reported to Bentley with 'satisfaction' that he had finished his first 'MUDFOG' paper for the *Miscellany*. Editorial tasks, however, proceeded more slowly. The following week he spoke of being 'over head and ears in work'. Time spent revising and correcting the papers of others proved unrewarding. Rewriting the last half of one 'cost me three hours this morning' (?12 December 1836). Editing, he told Bentley, 'is hard work indeed' (?19 January 1837).

A second annoyance added to these early signs of tension. Language in the November contract refers specifically to Dickens's editorial duties. No clause in the agreement stipulated a comparable role for the publisher, beyond his exercising a right to veto 'the insertion of any article in the Miscellany.' Dickens evidently believed that the periodical's 'management' rested solely with him, an assumption he soon found challenged. 'I must beg you once again', he wrote to Bentley on ?18 January 1837, 'not to allow anybody but myself to interfere with the Miscellany.' Differences of opinion about the merit of submissions also fuelled Dickens's annoyance, some measure of which is conveyed in the letter he wrote on 16 September 1837 after discovering how all of the arrangements he had made for the next issue had been altered by Bentley: 'By these proceedings I have been actually superseded in my office as Editor . . . they are in direct violation of my agreement with you, and a gross insult to me.'

In a 'Retrospective Sketch' of their partnership, Bentley seems to have taken a calmer view of their disputes. He alleged that Dickens's 'inexperience' in conducting a monthly periodical warranted his active participation in procuring contributors and in arranging and choosing articles. Furthermore, claimed Bentley, Dickens 'gladly availed himself of' the guiding hand he offered. In September 1837, however, it took legal language to resolve their differences. In a separate clause of the agreement signed on 28 September—the third in the ten months since the idea originated—provisions for a co-operative effort were outlined. Although the conduct of the journal would remain with Dickens, the contents of each month would be arranged 'between him and Mr Bentley', while the publisher also acquired the right 'if he wishes of originating 3 Articles in every number'.

Frustration with this arrangement, however, was overshadowed by Dickens's resentment with the 'hard bargains' he thought Bentley drove over payment for his own writing. Bentley's original terms, under which Dickens received almost £500 a year for editing and contributing, were not ungenerous. And within ten months, Dickens won a 50 per-cent increase in editorial salary and extended his contract from one to three years. Rather, the problem lay with the copyright prices Bentley offered for *Oliver Twist* and *Barnaby Rudge*.

*Twist* was never part of the first two agreements with Bentley since the idea of writing a piece of continuous fiction occurred to Dickens *after* he agreed to edit the periodical. And while Dickens compelled Bentley to accept *Twist* as one of the two novels he promised him in August 1836, this compromise, together with payments for the copyright of it and *Rudge*, failed to convince him of the 'liberality' the publisher professed. Angered by Bentley's penny-pinching—deducting payments when instalments of *Twist* ran under the stipulated sixteen pages—his resentment simmered throughout 1838. On 21 January 1839 he expressed his frustration to FORSTER. Why should he accept 'the same journey-man terms' for *Rudge* that he had received for *Twist*? Why should his publisher amass 'immense profits' and he only a 'paltry' sum? Why should he continue to submit to Bentley's 'iron hand'?

Dickens's distress was such that he declared himself unable to begin *Rudge*, despite the agreement he signed on 28 September 1838 to publish it in the *Miscellany* as the sequel to *Twist*. Rather, it must 'stand over' for six months, he asserted. Dickens also sought release from his editorial duties and proposed AINSWORTH as his successor.

Initially, Bentley seemed unmoved but recognized that he had to give way. In two separate agreements signed on 27 February 1839 he accepted Dickens's resignation from the *Miscellany* and agreed to pay £2,000 (a tenfold increase of the novel's first copyright) on receipt of the manuscript of *Rudge*, promised for 1 January 1840. Dickens could also expect a further £1,000 for sales exceeding 10,000 copies.

Work on *Nickleby* delayed a start on *Rudge* until October 1839. The novel then progressed, but too slowly for the promised delivery date. Dickens considered asking for an extension until a false step by Bentley presented the opportunity he sought to 'burst the Bentleyean' bonds altogether. Angered by a premature announcement of the novel, he requested a release from the contract. Heated exchanges followed. 'War to the knife', Dickens exulted to Forster, who stepped in on Dickens's behalf to negotiate with Bentley. Under the terms of a settlement finally signed on 2 July 1840, Dickens agreed to pay Bentley £2,250 for the copyright and existing stock of *Twist* with money advanced to him by Chapman and Hall against the publication of *Rudge*. In return, Bentley surrendered all his claims on any of Dickens's writings.

After inviting Bentley to Gad's Hill in 1857, Dickens remarked how 'the old wound between us has quite healed up and left no mark' (5 October 1857). The publisher's son similarly claimed that 'the most cordial relations' existed between his father and Dickens, but blamed Forster for airing the dispute after their deaths. In his *Life* Forster agreed that Bentley had the law on his side in his disputes with Dickens. But 'the sale of brain-work', he added, 'can never be adjusted by agreement with the same exactness and certainty as that of ordinary goods and chattels' (8.5). DHP

Bentley, George, Letter to *The Times*, 8 December 1871.

***Bentley's Miscellany*** A monthly magazine (1837–68) was started in January 1837 by the publisher Richard BENTLEY, who asked Dickens to be its first editor. In October 1836 Bentley approached Dickens about becoming the editor of a new miscellany intended to rival Colburn's *New Monthly Magazine*, just a few months after he had signed a contract with the young author for his first two novels. On the verge of purchasing the 'old' MONTHLY MAGAZINE begun in 1796, Bentley had been persuaded by his clerk Edward S. Morgan (whose 'Brief Retrospect' of 4 July 1873 in the Bentley archive provides most of what is known about the origins of the *Miscellany*) to start an entirely new monthly publication, a 'Wits' Miscellany' of humorous papers. There was to be no mere reprinting of extracts: the miscellany was to consist entirely of original articles by commercial authors. It was to begin on 1 January 1837 and to be illustrated by George CRUIKSHANK, who had just done *Sketches by Boz*. Cruikshank's appeal as a satirist was established, and 'BOZ' was rising fast as a humorous commodity. Apparently, Dickens suggested the change from the 'Wits' miscellany to 'Bentley's' ('But why go to the other extreme?' quipped Richard Harris BARHAM). The style of the new name drew obviously upon a resemblance to other 'flash' magazines of the day, *Fraser's* and *Blackwood's*, and such a reputation was important to Bentley's designs for this new property. William MAGINN, the editor of *Fraser's*, was engaged to write the first half of the new magazine's introductory Prologue.

The second part of the Prologue, perhaps written by Dickens, represents the new post-Regency consciousness: the disavowal of political topics ('we have nothing to do with politics') and the attempt to conciliate both Tory and Whig is not in the early-19th-century style of magazine-writing. Dickens's journalism, unlike that of Maginn, never depended on party-political slanging, and *Bentley's* humour was to be gentle and without rancorous 'personality'—the precise ingredient *Fraser's* and *Blackwood's* were notorious for. The *Miscellany* was not a social gathering of tavern 'wits' but a commercial collection of all Bentley's most profitable authors, most of whom were only respectably talented. Bentley could not have coped with a wayward Maginn or LOCKHART, whose antics required strong nerves and deep pockets in a publisher.

If Bentley, in buying a new property and hiring a young editor, self-consciously tried to do the opposite of Colburn, still a number of their contributors overlapped. Theodore HOOK, appointed editor of the *New Monthly Magazine* by Colburn, was a 'Bentley author', and his piece on the playwright George Colman was the first article in the *Miscellany*. Frugal Bentley did not throw away so easily the contracts he had made while in partnership with Colburn: as such, the magazine was more of a publisher's list than a coterie of congenial authors. Seventeen of the 22 contributors advertised in December 1836 were Bentley authors, and so were ten of the fifteen contributors to the first issue. *Blackwood's* and *Fraser's* had been known for the outrageousness of their 'personality'; *Bentley's* had little or none of this: its contents for the first issues are merely a dilute solution of Regency facetiousness: approximately a hundred pages of comic verse, sentimental songs, travelogues, essays on topics from dentistry to theatre history, and short fiction.

Dickens's own contribution to the first issue of *Bentley's* (January 1837) consisted of a short satirical tale, 'The Public Life of Mr Tulrumble, Once Mayor of Mudfog', set in the village of Mudfog (later the 'MUDFOG PAPERS', satirizing scientific associations, appeared in October 1837 and September 1838, when *Oliver Twist* was not appearing). In March 1837 he also published 'The Pantomime of Life' (a satire of London street-life and parliamentary antics), and in May 1837 'Some Particulars Concerning a Lion' (literary lionism). In both issues, these articles were published under the general heading 'Stray Chapters by Boz', showing the humorous expectations still invoked by his pseudonym. *Oliver Twist* also began in February 1837 as a short satirical piece ('The Progress of a Parish Boy') set in the town of Mudfog—which by now represented an England where modern MALTHUSIAN and Whig reforms held sway. The success of the story's continuation showed what direction the readers preferred to see in a magazine. What the *Miscellany* began to offer was a very Victorian commodity: long runs of popular fiction like *Oliver Twist*, Samuel Lover's *Handy Andy*, and William Harrison AINSWORTH's *Jack Sheppard*. The successes of Bentley's *Standard Novels* list were redeployed in his magazine. But this economical recycling of publisher's property meant that Dickens's possibilities for shaping a new magazine were in fact limited. Most of the authors advertised were names now obscure: William Hamilton Maxwell, Charles Whitehead, Charles Ollier, Francis Mahony, John HARLEY, Thomas Haynes Bayly, Gilbert à BECKETT, James Sheridan KNOWLES, John Hamilton Reynolds, and Richard Harris Barham.

With some of these Dickens enjoyed a briefly convivial acquaintance of sociable outings; for others he had nothing but a young man's scorn. During the period of his editorship (January 1837–January 1839), he and Bentley did hold a number of dinners and small parties, but even before nine months had passed, Dickens had begun to leave the *Miscellany*'s affairs to Bentley. They had fallen out during the summer of 1837 over Bentley's refusal to accept *Oliver Twist*, then running as a serial in the magazine, in lieu of the 'second novel' of Dickens's personal contract with him. Dickens was also offended by Bentley's insertion of articles that he had never seen in the September 1837 issue, and he declared: 'By these proceedings I have been actually superseded in my office as Editor of the Miscellany' (16 September 1837).

In this month, when relations between publisher and writer were suspended, Dickens withheld the instalment of *Oliver Twist* (hence the 'Mudfog' satire on the British Association for the Advancement of Science, called 'Full Report of the First Meeting of the Mudfog Association for the Advancement of Everything' in October 1837), and threatened to resign but was persuaded to stay on, till the final break came in January 1839. In the short time between October 1836 and September 1837 Dickens had become too distinctive a commodity for Bentley's list, and in the development of his friendship with John FORSTER during this time also, he became aware of his commercial value to publishers.

Dickens bade farewell to his readers in his 'Familiar Epistle From a Parent to a Child Aged Two Years and Two Months' (February 1839), in which he hinted at his frustration with Bentley's interference. To Bentley, he recommended William Harrison Ainsworth as the next editor. Ainsworth was taken up by Bentley reluctantly, but in the same month his serial *Jack Sheppard*, widely seen as a second *Oliver Twist*, became the next great hit of the *Miscellany*. The sales of the magazine even rose to a high of 8,500 copies. But during 1841–2 they began to decline, and Ainsworth, who was as frustrated with Bentley as Dickens, resigned in December 1841. Bentley then became sole editor. Sales declined to a fraction of what they had been in 1839, and the lack of a strong serial at the front of the *Miscellany* in 1852 now made it seriously out of step with the trend that it had established. In November 1854 Bentley sold the magazine

to Ainsworth, who became editor and proprietor until December 1868. Under Ainsworth it jogged on respectably enough with a mixture of serial fiction and serious political articles. However, the final twist came when Bentley's son then repurchased it from Ainsworth (sales had fallen to 500) and extinguished it in his other property, *Temple Bar*.                KC

Gettmann, Royal A., *A Victorian Publisher: A Study of the Bentley Papers* (1960).
Morgan, Edward S., 'Brief Retrospect' (4 July 1873), in *Publishers' Archives: Richard Bentley & Son 1829–98* (1976; Microfilm).

**Bible.** Dickens was very familiar with the so-called 'Authorized Version' of the Bible, first published in 1611, the authoritative translation which was in common use throughout the English-speaking world (it is known as the 'King James Version' in the United States). His direction in his will that his children should 'humbly to try to guide themselves by the teaching of the New Testament in its broad spirit, and to put no faith in any man's narrow construction of its letter here or there' is indicative both of a liberal, non-sectarian personal faith and of a distinct preference for the teaching of the New over that of the Old Testament. His attitude can perhaps also be gauged from his description of the narrow Mrs Clennam's reading 'certain passages aloud from a book—sternly, fiercely, wrathfully—praying that her enemies . . . might be put to the edge of the sword, consumed by fire, smitten by plagues and leprosy, that their bones might be ground to dust, and that they might be utterly exterminated' (*LD* 1.3). The young Arthur Clennam, we are told in the same chapter, had had 'no more real knowledge of the beneficent history of the New Testament, than if he had been bred among idolaters'. Dickens's deep and personal response to the account of the life and ministry of Christ is evident in his retelling in simple language of the Gospel stories in his *The* LIFE OF OUR LORD written for his children in 1846. In 'Two Views of the Cheap Theatre' (*UT*) he insists that 'in the New Testament there is the most beautiful and affecting history conceivable by man, and there are terse models for all prayer and all preaching'.

Many of his citations of the Bible, particularly of the Ten Commandments and of phrases from the Book of Psalms, can be related to his familiarity with passages quoted in the rites of the BOOK OF COMMON PRAYER. Dickens appears to have been well aware of the stories in the Book of Genesis. He refers, for example, to the penalty of Adam (3: 17–19) (*MC* 19); to the story of Cain and Abel (*AN* 24; *CC* 1; *MC* 25 and 47; *LD* 1.11, 23, and 24; *GE* 15; *MED* 17). The story of Noah's flood is variously referred to (*MC* 23; *DS* 23; *OCS* 42). The description of Nimrod in Genesis 10 as 'a mighty hunter before the Lord' is echoed in chapters 11 and 12 of *Bleak House* (the latter chapter also contains a reference to Jacob's dream described in Genesis 31: 10). Mr Peggotty quotes the phrase 'darkness on the face of the deep' (Genesis 1: 2) (*DC* 32), and Slackbridge contortedly cites Esau's selling his birthright for a 'mess of pottage' (*HT* 2.4). Elsewhere in his work Dickens is inclined to use or paraphrase familiar echoes of the Old Testament such as 'flowing with milk and honey' (Exodus 3: 8) (*DS* 10), 'still, small voice' (1 Kings 19: 12) (*DS* 48; *OCS* 57), 'where the wicked cease from troubling' (Job 3: 17) (*DC* 51), or 'all flesh is grass' (Isaiah 40: 6) (*AN* 6; *OCS* 16 and *BH* 39).

Dickens's citations of the New Testament are too numerous, and often too fleeting, to be listed exhaustively. As both his novels and his letters to bereaved parents suggest, he was particularly affected by the Gospel accounts of Christ's references to children. He quoted Matthew 18: 2 to Dr F. H. Deane of Virginia (4 April 1842) and cited Matthew 19: 14 to Mark LEMON (31 January 1851), and expressed similar sentiments in Stave 4 of *A Christmas Carol* and in chapter 8 of *Bleak House*. Certain other passages also seem to have held a particular dramatic and moral significance for Dickens the novelist. Chapter 3 of *Bleak House* contains a memorable use of the story of the woman taken in adultery (John 8: 6) when Esther's unforgiving aunt is struck by paralysis. Miss Barbary has had the passage read to her, then suddenly cries out 'in an awful voice', 'Watch ye therefore . . . I say unto all, Watch!' (Mark 13: 35). At Jo's deathbed in the same novel Woodcourt is reciting the Lord's Prayer (Matthew 6: 9–13) (*BH* 47). When Magwitch dies (*GE* 56), Pip recalls the passage from Luke (18: 13) concerning the pharisee and the publican praying in the Temple and feels moved to repeat the words 'O Lord, be merciful to him, a sinner'. Carton echoes 'I am

the resurrection and the life' (John 11: 25) as he mounts the scaffold (*TTC* 3.15) and David Copperfield, remembering the same quotation at his mother's graveside, thinks of Peggotty in terms of 'the good and faithful servant' (Matthew 25: 23) (*DC* 9).

The implications of the story of the 'Good Samaritan' (Luke 10: 30–7) would appear to have rendered it a favourable parable of Dickens's, especially when he uses it ironically in connection with the 1834 POOR LAW. In chapter 4 of *Oliver Twist*, for example, a scene representing the story appears on both the parochial seal and on Bumble's official buttons. The workhouse in which Old Nandy is confined 'has been appointed by law to be the Good Samaritan of his district' (*LD* 1.31). Gradgrind is glimpsed 'proving . . . probably, in the main, that the Good Samaritan was a Bad Economist' (*HT* 2.12). When Betty Higden endeavours to escape from an uncomfortable death in the workhouse the narrator remarks of the Poor Law bureaucracy that 'It is a remarkable Christian improvement, to have made a pursuing Fury of the Good Samaritan' (*OMF* 3.8).

Dickens's quotations from the Epistles are less common than his references to the Gospels. He does, however, use both direct and indirect reference to the apocalyptic visions of the Book of Revelation throughout *Bleak House*. ALS

**Bildungsroman,** the German philosopher Wilhelm Dilthey's term for the 'novel of formation', whose classic exemplar is Goethe's *Wilhelm Meister's Apprenticeship* (1796), translated by CARLYLE in 1824: a 'great book' about personal development that influenced (besides Carlyle) BULWER-LYTTON, DISRAELI, and many more Victorian writers. Dickens possessed a copy by 1844. There may be some echoes in *David Copperfield* in such things as the hero's (rather colourless?) representativeness, or the David and Goliath and *Hamlet* motifs. Georg Lukács thought Goethe's novel could have 'no true artistic successors', but Jerome Buckley (*Season of Youth*, 1974) 'translates' the term into English literature, and treats both Dickens's first-person 'autobiographical' novels as *Bildungsromane*. MH

**biographies and biographers of Dickens.** Several hastily cobbled-together lives of Dickens, such as *Charles Dickens; the Story of* his *Life*, published and maybe also partly written by J. C. Hotten, appeared very soon after Dickens's death in 1870. These were completely eclipsed in 1872 by the appearance of the first volume of *The Life of Charles Dickens*, covering the years 1812–42, written by his life-long friend and chosen biographer John FORSTER. Here Dickens's vast and devoted public first learned of his 'hard experiences in boyhood', of his father's imprisonment and his own sufferings in the blacking factory, and they did so largely through his own account of these things in the so-called 'autobiographical fragment' printed by Forster (see WARREN'S BLACKING; DIARIES AND AUTOBIOGRAPHY). Two further volumes followed in 1873 and 1874 covering, respectively, 1842–52 and 1852–70, and in 1876 Forster published a revised edition in two volumes in which he divided his work, epic-style, into twelve books. CARLYLE gave memorable expression to his admiration: 'So long as Dickens is interesting to his fellow-men, here will be seen face to face, what Dickens's manner of existing was; his steady practicality, withal; the singularly solid business talent he continually had; and deeper than all, if one had the eye to see deep enough, dark, fateful, silent elements, tragical to look upon, and hiding amid dazzling radiances as of the sun, the elements of death itself' (Collins 1971, pp. 566–7).

Forster's *Dickens* has remained the classic, indispensable biography, despite all its inevitable reticences about DICKENS'S PRIVATE LIFE, the breakdown of his marriage, the relationship with Ellen TERNAN, and so on, and all its foregrounding of the Forster–Dickens friendship at the expense of other very important ones in Dickens's life, notably that with Wilkie COLLINS (see DICKENS, CATHERINE). For not only does Forster give us a vast amount of information about Dickens's professional, public, and social life but he gives us also 'the sense, as no other biographer does or now can, of being in the same room as Dickens, and . . . of being really inward with Dickens's personality and character' (Leavis 1970, p. x). Indeed, the sense of Dickens's extraordinary, super-dynamic personality is diffused throughout the work, mainly as a result of the frequent and extensive quotations from his LETTERS by which Forster sought to give to his book 'what was attainable of the value of autobiography' (11.3). The

two-volume version of his *Life of Dickens* was reprinted in Everyman's Library in 1927, but with the omission of all his footnotes, and again, in one large volume, by Cecil Palmer in 1928. The editor of the latter edition, J. W. T. LEY, stated that he had omitted as unimportant 'a very few' of Forster's footnotes and had restored one or two that Forster himself had omitted from the 1876 edition. At the end of each chapter Ley supplied extensive additional annotation, drawing freely on the mass of detailed information about various aspects of Dickens's life, particularly his early life, that had come to light since 1876—the story of the young Dickens's passionate love for Maria BEADNELL, Robert Langton's discoveries first published in his *The Childhood and Youth of Dickens* (1891), the indefatigable researches of F. G. KITTON and other early Dickens scholars, and so on. He was also able to utilize the various collections of Dickens's letters that had been published since Forster's *Life* as well as Mamie Dickens's *My Father As I Recall Him* (1897), with its now much-quoted description of Dickens at work (another family memoir, Sir Henry Dickens's *Memories of My Father*, appeared in the same year as Ley's edition of Forster). Ley's edition, though long out of print, remains the one most frequently cited for reference purposes by Dickens scholars.

It is significant that Ley did not attempt to write a new biography but contented himself with adding to Forster, because in 1928 the Dickens presented in biographies and memoirs was still essentially Forster's Dickens. A startlingly different one appeared the following year in a (very bad) novel called *This Side Idolatry* by 'Ephesian' (C. E. Bechhoffer Roberts). This showed a monster of vanity, ill-using his wife and finally abandoning her for a young actress Ellen Ternan. Roberts's fictional work was dismissed as mere irresponsible scandal-mongering, but five years later there appeared, in *The Daily Express* for 3 April 1934, an article entitled '98 Years Ago To-Day Charles Dickens Began His Honeymoon'. The writer was Thomas Wright, an elderly *litterateur* and an assiduous founder of literary societies, who was less concerned with Dickens's honeymoon than with claiming, on the authority of a dead clergyman to whom she had apparently 'confessed' some time after Dickens's death, that Ellen (by 1934 also safely dead) had been Dickens's reluctant mistress, and with calling for a reinterpretation of the later novels in the light of this 'fact'. That Wright's article had changed the face of Dickensian biography was at once manifested by Hugh Kingsmill's iconoclastic *The Sentimental Journey: A Life of Dickens* (1934). Wright himself elaborated on, and provided a certain amount of circumstantial evidence for, his assertions both in his *Life of Charles Dickens* (1935) and in his posthumously published autobiography *Thomas Wright of Olney* (1936).

In 1939 Gladys Storey, who had been a friend of Dickens's younger daughter Kate Perugini, published a book called *Dickens and Daughter*, based on many intimate conversations she had had with Mrs Perugini before the latter's death in 1929. The Ternan affair featured prominently in their talks, and Mrs Perugini's reported comments, which included describing her father as 'a wicked man', went beyond Wright in that she claimed Dickens and Ellen had had an illegitimate but short-lived infant, something for which no concrete evidence has ever been forthcoming.

The first Dickens biography to appear after the publication of *Dickens and Daughter* was Dame Una Pope-Hennessy's *Charles Dickens* (1945); it was far more balanced and scholarly than Kingsmill's book and was able to draw on the mass of new material presented in the Nonesuch Edition of Dickens's letters, as well as on Wright and Storey, whose claims regarding the Ternan relationship Pope-Hennessy broadly accepted. Hesketh Pearson's lively popular narrative *Dickens; his Character, Comedy and Career* (1949) added nothing to Pope-Hennessy, but Jack Lindsay's thoughtful Marxist and Freudian interpretation, *Dickens; a Biographical and Critical Study* (1950), is still well worth reading, as K. J. Fielding noted in his *Charles Dickens* ('Writers and Their Work', British Council, no. 37 [rev. edn. 1963], p. 35), 'for its examination of Dickens's fantasy, his creative impulses, and the themes and symbols into which they forced themselves . . .'

In 1952 came the most substantial and important biography since Forster's, Edgar Johnson's monumental two-volume *Charles Dickens: His Tragedy and Triumph*. Massively researched and documented, Johnson's book supplied a wealth of new details about almost every aspect of Dickens's crowded, multi-faceted life—his work with Miss COUTTS on the URANIA COTTAGE project, for example, and his MESMERIC experiments on Madame de la Rue. Johnson's technique resembles Forster's in that he quotes frequently and at length from Dickens's letters, both from those already published and from the 3,000 or so unpublished ones to which he had access. And just as Forster had included critical assessments of Dickens's books (interestingly discussed by Alec W. Brice in his 'The Compilation of the Critical Commentary in Forster's *Life of Dickens*', *Dickensian*, 70, 1974), so Johnson intersperses his, somewhat highly coloured, biographical narrative with a series of critical essays on the novels. These support his central thesis that Dickens gradually came to understand 'capitalist industrialism at least as well as most nineteenth-century political economists' (Johnson 2.1128) and understood it with an 'unwavering hostility' that was reflected in all his fiction—*Little Dorrit*, for example, is seen (2.903) as a 'revolutionary unmasking of finance capitalism'. Johnson's Dickens is a man who becomes steadily more disillusioned about contemporary society as well as experiencing increasing sadness in his private life, Ellen Ternan notwithstanding— 'All his fame had not brought him the things he most deeply wanted' (2.1104). This was his 'tragedy', his 'triumph' being that he never gave in to despair, never lost his faith in the people and in basic human decency, and continued to scale ever-greater heights in his art.

This interpretation of Dickens's life, together with the dual perspective on his character and personality first projected by Edmund WILSON, following the Ternan revelations, in his celebrated 'Two Scrooges' essay in *The Wound and the Bow* (1941), was to dominate the field of Dickensian biographical studies for many years, though a salutary corrective to it was to be found in K. J. Fielding's admirable *Charles Dickens. A Critical Introduction* (1958, rev. edn. 1965). Fielding, using his wide knowledge of Victorian reviews and journalism, illuminatingly places Dickens's literary career in its cultural-historical context and, as regards the Ternan affair, refrains from going a step beyond such factual evidence as exists (some more pieces for this particular jigsaw puzzle were supplied by Ada Nisbet in *Dickens and Ellen Ternan*, 1952, and by Felix Aylmer in *Dickens Incognito*, 1959, and more recently by Claire Tomalin in her *The Invisible Woman: Nelly Ternan and Charles Dickens*, 1990). A. G. Hoppé's annotation of the Everyman's Library reprints of the two-volume Forster (1966, 1969) added nothing new, and Christopher Hibbert's highly readable *The Making of Charles Dickens* (1967) distilled the Johnson/Edmund Wilson Dickens for a wider public. The Centenary Year of 1970 saw the publication of Angus Wilson's lavishly illustrated *The World of Charles Dickens*. Wilson, himself a major novelist whose own imaginative life had been richly nourished by Dickens, provides many brilliant insights into the interrelationship between Dickens's life and his art and the workings of what he calls 'the Dickens imaginative system' (p. 8). He probes that 'mixture of play and terror' which he sees as 'central to the whole of Dickens's world of fancy' (p. 11), and seeks to place him as fully as possible in the context of Victor ian popular culture, especially visual culture—the book's many carefully chosen illustrations are, of course, integral to this project. Wilson also usefully calls attention to something that does not much figure in Johnson's biography, the fact that Dickens was 'a devout and practising Christian' (p. 7), and he strongly rejects any 'death-wish' interpretation of Dickens's last strenuous years: 'Dickens "died in harness" because it was the nature of his eager, vital personality to explore and fight to the end . . .' (p. 297).

No other significant biography of Dickens appeared until Fred Kaplan's in 1988, though Johnson in 1977 brought out a one-volume revised edition of his biography which took into account scholarly work on Dickens during the preceding quarter-century and omitted some of the critical chapters. Noteworthy contributions to Dickensian biographical studies between 1970 and 1988 were made by Kaplan himself in his *Dickens and Mesmerism. The Hidden Springs of Fiction* (1975), which drew on many unpublished letters from Dickens to Emile de la Rue; by Philip Collins in his two-volume collection of contemporary reactions to Dickens as a man published in the Macmillan's 'Interviews and Recollections' series (1981); by Michael Slater in his *Dickens and Women* (1983); by Michael Allen through his detailed research into the subject of Dickens's homes during his childhood and early youth (Allen's work appeared first as a series of articles in the *Dickensian* and then in volume form as *Charles Dickens's Childhood*, 1988); and by George Curry in his *Charles Dickens and Annie Fields* (1988), based on a full study of the many passages about Dickens in the journals of his American publisher's wife, who became a much-loved and intimate friend (see FIELDS, JAMES AND ANNIE).

In his *Dickens. A Biography* Kaplan took account of all Dickensian biographical research since Johnson and, as in his *Mesmerism* book, made extensive use of unpublished letters. He builds up a detailed and lively picture of Dickens's quotidian existence and energetic engagement in a whole range of activities, is especially perceptive about Dickens's need to create around himself a 'supportive, protective community whose love for him would be unqualified' (p. 57), and judicious in his handling of the question of Dickens's relationship with Ellen, though making clear his conviction that they did become lovers. In Kaplan's narrative, however, Dickens the novelist gets somewhat overwhelmed by Dickens the psychologically scarred man, obsessed by his childhood sufferings and particularly by his mother's part in causing them. His great novels, products of what Forster called his 'healthy judgment and sleepless creative fancy', tend to appear primarily as a series of workings-out of this obsession.

In 1990 came Peter Ackroyd's massive *Dickens*, which might seem to give the lie to the Leavises' claim, quoted above, that no modern biographer could, like Forster, give the sense of 'being in the same room as Dickens'. Ackroyd's detail-packed narrative is, as Malcolm Andrews has put it, 'an intensive study of character in action' ('Charles Dickens, *Dickens* and Peter Ackroyd', in *Imitating Art: Essays in Biography*, ed. D. Ellis, 1993), solidly based on a formidable amount of research into both primary and secondary sources. His book is not presented like a conventional biography with its subject's life divided into clearly marked and dated sections or phases, informative chapter-titles, and elaborate footnote documentation. Ackroyd's 35 chapters (preceded by a 'Prologue' describing the public impact of Dickens's death, and followed by a brief 'Postscript' about seeing in Dickens the man and in his works 'the lineaments of the [Victorian] age itself') are designated only by numbers, and instead of the usual footnotes we have a series of bibliographical essays, 'Notes on Text and Sources', keyed to each chapter. These make it clear that Ackroyd has not only read every surviving word written *by* Dickens but also, amazingly, virtually everything ever written *about* Dickens. 'Surely it is from Dickens, of all writers', he remarks in his Prologue (p. xvi), 'that we learn that it is in details that the spirit fully lives', and he proceeds through his 'seamless' (Andrews's word), detail-packed narrative to make Dickens live for us in all his complexity and contradictoriness of character. Dickens the artist, Dickens the private man, Dickens the journalist and public figure—Ackroyd energetically carries forward the story of all of these together in his triumphant demonstration that Dickens's novels are 'not some separable entity to be extracted from his life and other works but rather part of the fabric of his existence'. His handling of the relationship with Ellen Ternan does not follow the Wright/ Storey line but persuasively argues that she fulfilled a deeper and more complex need in Dickens's life than has generally been understood. For an illuminating critical appreciation of Ackroyd's technique, in particular of the much-criticized interpolated 'visionary' passages in which he talks with Dickens, or Dickens converses with Oscar Wilde and other writers about whom Ackroyd has written (passages omitted from the 1994 abridged *Dickens*), see Malcolm Andrews's essay already cited.

In 1996 appeared Grahame Smith's *Charles Dickens. A Literary Life* which, as its title suggests (it forms part of the Macmillan series entitled 'Literary Lives') focuses primarily on Dickens's professional life both as novelist and as journalist, and thus resembles Fielding's book mentioned above. Smith takes Fielding's approach a stage further, however, in seeking to show that the forces operating on Dickens as a professional writer should be seen as 'not merely a background to the novels, but [as] actually shap[ing] them artistically through the mediating influence of Dickens's imagination' (p. 178).     MS

**biography of Dickens, fictional treatments of.** Dickens's life has been the subject of several novels ever since the rumours about his relationship with Ellen TERNAN began to gain wider currency. First in the field was 'Ephesian' (C. E. Bechhoffer Roberts) with *This Side Idolatry* (1928; reprinted 1946), which portrayed Dickens as monstrously egotistical and also cruel to his long-suffering wife, making no secret of his preference in the early days of their marriage for her sister Mary; eventually, after he has become infatuated with Ellen Ternan, Catherine denounces him—'Go to your actress! I know you through and through, and I despise you!' (see DICKENS, CATHERINE; HOGARTH, MARY). Later came W. Y. V. Dale's *I Rest My Claims* (1949), full of absurd blunders and more concerned with Catherine than with Dickens (who is here a very pallid creation), and Hebe Elsna's *Consider These Women* (1954), which presented Georgina HOGARTH as a sort of scheming Iago-figure, and elevated Catherine to an almost saintly level (Elsna also wrote *Unwanted Wife. A Defence of Mrs. Charles Dickens*, 1963; see Pansy Pakenham's severe review, *Dickensian*, 59, 1963). Ursula Bloom's *The Romance of Charles Dickens* (1961) is a vulgar travesty of Dickens's passion for Maria BEADNELL, with Maria presented as a hard-hearted little gold-digger. Victoria Lincoln's *Charles* (1963), strongly influenced by Edgar Johnson's biography of Dickens, was the first novel to attempt a more complex portrayal of the writer, very much following Johnson's 'triumph and tragedy' formula. In 1975 appeared Frederick Busch's altogether more sensational novel, *The Mutual Friend*, in which the story of Dickens's last years is luridly recalled by his former readings manager George DOLBY as he lies dying a pauper's death in a charity ward. Dolby ventriloquizes the voices of an imaginary former inmate of URANIA COTTAGE who sexually initiates Dickens's youngest son, of a forlornly dignified Catherine Dickens, and of a coldly calculating Ellen Ternan (who graphically recalls the one and only 'undistinguished' love-making that she permitted), and of the physically and emotionally agonized Dickens himself. Alan S. Watts's moving *Confessions of Charles Dickens* (1991) sticks much closer than Busch to the biographical facts, as his subtitle, *A Very Factual Fiction*, indicates; the only major departure from the historical record that he makes is to have Dickens refer to a child born to him by Ellen Ternan that died in infancy. Watts presents

Dickens as writing a troubled retrospective survey of his life during the early months of 1870 but affirming in the last entry (8 June) a joyful belief in the Divine 'grace and forgiveness' that awaits him (Watts skilfully interweaves here the famous passage from *Drood* about 'the Resurrection and the Life' that were almost the last words actually written by Dickens). MS

**Black, John** (1783–1855), editor of the MORNING CHRONICLE 1817–43, where Dickens found his first full-time employment as a reporter from 1834 to 1836, simultaneously with his publication of the pieces that were collected in *Sketches by Boz*. A temperamental Scot who is said to have delivered a dozen challenges to duels before he was 30, Black was revered by Dickens as his 'first hearty outand-out appreciator'. John Stuart MILL credited Black, who was an intimate friend of James Mill and others of BENTHAM'S inner circle, with being the first journalist to examine with a reformist's eye such hitherto sacred institutions as the law. RN

**Blackmore, Edward** (1799–1879). See ELLIS AND BLACKMORE.

**Blanchard, Samuel Laman** (1803–45), commonly known as Laman Blanchard and a member of the young Dickens's literary circle. Born at Great Yarmouth and educated at St Olave's School in Southwark. On leaving school he became a clerk at Doctor's Commons and began to publish dramatic sketches in *The Drama*. In 1822 he formed a close and enduring friendship with Douglas JERROLD and with him resolved first to fight alongside BYRON in Greece and then to embark on a theatrical career. The former scheme was rapidly abandoned; the latter proved a financial disaster. He subsequently worked for the MONTHLY MAGAZINE, to which he had already begun to contribute verse and prose. He married in 1823 and in 1828 his volume of poetry, *Lyric Offerings* was published by W. Harrison AINSWORTH. He then worked for a succession of liberal journals and newspapers, becoming editor of the short-lived *Constitutional* in 1836. From 1841 to 1845 he was closely associated with John FORSTER'S EXAMINER and he served as sub-editor of *Ainsworth's Magazine* 1842–3. In December 1844 he was present in Forster's rooms at Dickens's reading of *The*

*CHIMES* (he appears in MACLISE's sketch of the occasion). Following his wife's death he became acutely depressed and committed suicide at his home in Lambeth in February 1845. Blanchard's literary friends, including Dickens, Jerrold, Ainsworth, THACKERAY, BULWER-LYTTON, and CRUIKSHANK actively raised funds for the benefit of his orphaned children. Blanchard was the godfather, and subsequently father-in-law, to Jerrold's son, William Blanchard Jerrold. ALS

***Bleak House*** Dickens's ninth novel, published 1852–3. Structured with a daring double narrative and centred on institutional satire, it is technically his most ambitious novel and widely held to be his masterpiece.

### Inception and Composition
Between October 1850, when he finished *David Copperfield*, and November 1851, when he began writing *Bleak House*, Dickens was energetically pursuing his usual whirl of activities. He was routinely busy 'conducting' *Household Words*, launched 27 March 1850, and writing A CHILD'S HISTORY OF ENGLAND, which began serialization in the weekly from January 1851. He was more steadily involved in AMATEUR THEATRICALS than ever before or again, barnstorming the country with productions, including JONSON's *Every Man In His Humour* and BULWER-LYTTON'S *Not So Bad As We Seem*, to raise money for the GUILD OF LITERATURE AND ART—productions which continued to occupy his time even after *Bleak House* was under way. As the Pilgrim editors note (6. p.xi), 'his reforming zeal was at its height' at this time, as he worked indefatigably with Miss COUTTS to promote URANIA COTTAGE for fallen women, a model housing scheme, and the Ragged School movement (see CHARITY). He was active as a public speaker in support of reforming causes, and he wrote a stream of articles for *Household Words*, following on from those in the EXAMINER, on a variety of social abuses (see SPEECHES OF DICKENS; JOURNALIST, DICKENS AS). Inevitably, these interests found their way into the new book he was writing.

There was also a series of intimations of mortality, which darkened his life at the time. His wife Catherine DICKENS was so unwell that Dickens took her to Malvern in March 1851 for treatment. That month his father, John DICKENS, died after an excruciating operation, and two weeks later his infant daughter Dora, never robust, died suddenly, while Dickens was chairing a ROYAL GENERAL THEATRICAL FUND dinner. And after *Bleak House* was under way, his friends Richard WATSON, Alfred D'Orsay, and Catherine Macready—and the Duke of Wellington—died in quick succession. Meantime, the last of his children, Edward Bulwer Lytton Dickens ('Plorn'), was born on 13 March 1852 (although later a favourite child, 'on the whole I could have dispensed with him', Dickens commented acerbically to Miss Coutts on 16 March).

The first mention of the new novel appeared in a letter to Mary Boyle on 21 February 1851, when he described 'the first shadows of a new story hovering in a ghostly way about me'. On 17 August he wrote to Miss Coutts that he was 'pondering afar off, a new book. Violent restlessness, and vague ideas of going I don't know where, I don't know why, are the present symptoms of the disorder.' By 7 October he wrote to Henry Austin that the story was 'whirling' in his mind, creating a 'wild necessity of beginning to write', but the disruption of moving that autumn from his HOME in Devonshire Terrace to Tavistock House, with workmen engaged in major redecoration, prevented him from getting seriously to work until November. On the 21st he instructed Frederick Evans to advertise it for March publication, and the next day described himself to William Bradbury as 'a prisoner all day' at his writing desk (see BRADBURY AND EVANS). By 7 December he had 'only the short last chapter to do' to finish the first number.

As often, Dickens considered a number of options for a title. On 26 September he wrote to Frederick Evans, 'Wait, till I get rid of my workmen and get to my work, and see if we don't raise the (East) wind'—the 'East Wind' being part of two possible titles preserved in his memoranda. 'Tom-All-Alone's', the name used in the novel for the slum in which Jo lives, recurs nine times on the ten sheets of trial titles, with various subtitles, including 'The Solitary House' and 'The Ruined House'. 'Bleak House' apparently suited Dickens as soon as he thought of it; initially it was part of a longer title, 'Bleak House and The East Wind; how they both got into Chancery And never got out'; below that trial version on the same page Dickens wrote simply, as his final choice, 'Bleak House' (see George Ford, 'The Titles for *Bleak House*', *Dickensian*, 65, 1969).

CHANCERY was in his mind as subject-matter from the outset. On 8 December 1851 he wrote to WILLS thanking him for supplying information about Chancery cases, and expressing surprise at the sums to which court cases ran. 'I had modestly limited my costs to from forty to fifty thousand pounds', he noted (in Chapter 1 he raised this figure to 'SIX-TY to SEVEN-TY THOUSAND POUNDS'). A year later, responding to criticism that he was late in the day in calling for Chancery reform, he pointed out that as long ago as his first novel he had 'with all indignation and intensity' depicted 'the slow torture and death of a chancery prisoner' (*PP* 42, 44; to the Hon. Mrs Edward Cropper, 20 December 1852). Shortly after writing chapter 39, in which Mr Vholes is introduced, Dickens alluded to what he had written there in a letter to Miss Coutts, declaring his belief that 'the only intelligible and consistent principle of the English law' is 'the principle of making business for itself' (7 February 1853). Two months later he returned to the charge, telling her, 'I think the Giant who said Fie fi fo fum, must have been an impersonation of the Law. Grinding Jack's bones to make his bread, looks so like it!' (29 April 1853). And even as he was writing the final pages of the book, he asked Wills for more information about Chancery in order to remain '*within the facts*' when he came to write the Preface (7 August 1853). He retained a satirical view of Chancery after the novel was complete, as is evident in his article 'Legal and Equitable Jokes' (*HW* 23 September 1854).

Dickens was firmly in control of his materials throughout the nearly two years of composition, suffering no setbacks and making no important changes of plan. His letters from the time reveal his exhilaration. On 4 March 1852 he described himself to George HOGARTH as 'blazing away'; number 4, he declared to Frank STONE on 1 May, was 'rather a stunner'; a week later he could 'look forward to good things whereof the foundations are built' (to W. F. De Cerjat, 8 May 1852), and by 22 July he told Mary Boyle that he foresaw 'some very good things in Bleak House'. But it was also increasingly hard work. On 7 September he declined meeting the SILVER FORK novelist Catherine Gore, explaining that 'when I have a book to write I must give it the first place in my life'. The next month he told Wills that he was 'constantly occupied with Bleak House' (12 October 1852); in February he told FORSTER, overwork made him feel 'as if my head would split', and soon after he confessed, 'The spring does not seem to fly back again directly' (to Forster, ?March 1853). The next month, with Tulkinghorn's murder to compose, he barely made his mid-month deadline for submitting copy to the printers, and described himself as being in a 'frenzied state', rising at 5 a.m. to go 'furiously to work', with the result that by noon he was 'comparatively insensible' (to the Duke of Devonshire, 18 April 1853). After fighting off pressing social demands in May, he fell seriously ill in early June with a recurrence of his childhood kidney complaint, but after six days in bed he fled to Boulogne, where he recovered quickly. By 18 June he was able to report writing half of the current number 'with great ease' (to Wills) and, 'going tooth and nail' (to Wills, 1 August 1853), he finished the book 'very prettily indeed, I hope', in mid-August, writing the final pages in the *Household Words* office (to Miss Coutts, 27 August 1853; Pilgrim 7.131n.).

In February 1853 he became embroiled in controversy with George Henry LEWES, who wrote two open letters in the *Leader* (5 and 12 February) protesting that spontaneous combustion, which Dickens presented as the cause of Krook's death in chapter 32, was an impossibility. Dickens replied at length to Lewes in letters of 25 and 27 February, citing authorities in his defence; he referred to those authorities again in the next chapter of the novel, and he repeated his conviction of the reality of such a cause of death in the Preface published in September 1853. Dickens was faulty in his science, but most readers agree that Krook's death is 'one of the great imaginative events' in Dickens's works (See John B. West, 'Krook's Death by Spontaneous Combustion and the Controversy between Dickens and Lewes: A Physiologist's View', *Dickensian*, 90, 1994).

The writing of the novel called forth reflections on the nature of his art. 'I presume most writers of fiction write, partly from their imagination; and partly from their experience', he declared to Mrs S. J. Cumming (7 September 1852), and 'I have had recourse to both sources'. 'Pray do not suppose', he wrote to another correspondent, 'that I ever write merely to amuse, or without an object. I wish I were as clear of every offence before Heaven, as I am of that. I may try to insinuate it into people's hearts sometimes, in preference to knocking them down and breaking their heads with it . . . but I always have it. Without it, my pursuit—and the steadiness, patience, seclusion, regularity, hard work and self-concentration, it demands—would be utterly worthless to me' (to the Hon. Mrs Edward Cropper, 20 December 1852). And a year after he had completed the novel, he wrote to an American correspondent about 'the powers and purposes of Fiction': 'To interest and affect the general mind in behalf of anything that is clearly wrong—to stimulate and rouse the public soul to a compassionate or indignant feeling that it *must not be*—without obtruding any pet theory of cause or cure, and so throwing off allies as they spring up—I believe to be one of Fiction's highest uses. And this is the use to which I try to turn it' (to Henry Carey, 24 August 1854).

He celebrated the novel's conclusion with a banquet in Boulogne on 22 August, to which he invited his publishers Bradbury and Evans, and his intimate friends Mark LEMON and Wilkie COLLINS. His illustrator, Hablot BROWNE, was also invited but did not attend. 'The story has taken extraordinarily', he wrote to Mrs Watson a few days later; 'I have never had so many readers' (27 August 1853).

### Contract, Text, and Publication History

*Bleak House* was the last of Dickens's novels to be published by Bradbury and Evans under the agreement of 1 June 1844. That contract, which assigned to them a fourth share of profits, was limited to whatever Dickens might write 'during the next ensuing eight years' (Pilgrim 4.691). Relations were amicable, however, and soon after *Bleak House* was complete, on 28 December 1853, Dickens entered into a new agreement with his publishers for a shorter work (which was to become *Hard Times*), to appear serially in *Household Words* (Pilgrim 7.911).

The manuscript, trial titles, and corrected proofs, which are held in the FORSTER COLLECTION, were studied by George Ford and Sylvère Monod in preparing their edition of the novel, and Monod has written separately of the 'conscientious if not systematic' corrections which Dickens made at proof stage (' "When the Battle's Lost and Won...": Dickens v. the Compositors of *Bleak House*', *Dickensian*, 69, 1973). According to Monod, more than 40 different compositors prepared the text at great speed for publication from Dickens's heavily revised manuscript. Dickens restored 'over 700 manuscript readings', changed the proof without returning to manuscript a further 33 times, and made no correction 159 times, when proof differed from manuscript.

The novel appeared in four main editions during Dickens's lifetime: serially in twenty parts (as nineteen) between March 1852 and September 1853, published as one volume in September 1853; the Cheap Edition of 1858; the Library Edition of 1868; and the Charles Dickens Edition of 1869 (see EDITIONS OVER WHICH DICKENS HAD CONTROL). The authoritative modern text is Ford and Monod's Norton Critical Edition (1977).

*Bleak House* was dedicated 'As a remembrance of our friendly Union To My Companions in the Guild of Literature and Art'. His Preface, dated September 1853, defends the factuality of his depiction of Chancery and, in rebuttal to Lewes, the authenticity of spontaneous combustion. The Preface also contains perhaps his best-known public statement about the nature of his art: 'In Bleak House, I have purposely dwelt upon the romantic side of familiar things.'

### Illustrations
Dickens's principal ILLUSTRATOR, Hablot Browne, drew all the illustrations for *Bleak House*, including the frontispiece and title-page vignette. The cover wrapper—printed on blue paper rather than the green which covered the SERIAL parts of earlier novels—is tied closely to the novel's spirit and plot, making it clear that Dickens had thoroughly briefed Browne at an early stage. But Dickens's absence from London meant that a mistake in one of the plates for No. 9 could not be corrected in time (Browne had included a Smallweed who was not present in the text) and had to be cancelled, a corrected plate being included with the next number: Pilgrim 6.776n.). For the final plates, Dickens sent Browne instructions before he had written the relevant chapters (to Browne, 29 June

1853). Critics are divided as to the extent of Browne's achievement in illustrating *Bleak House*, but there is widespread admiration for the ten 'dark plates', specially executed to convey an appropriately gloomy atmosphere. All appear in the second half of the novel and, complementing the institutional focus of Dickens's satire, six contain no human figures at all. In *Bleak House*, Jane Rabb Cohen declares, Dickens and Browne 'reached the height—and the limits—of their collaboration' (Cohen 1980, p. 114).

### Sources and Context
Eighteen fifty-one was the year of the Great EXHIBITION, the opening of which was celebrated by *The TIMES* as a reminder 'of that day when all ages and climes shall be gathered round the throne of the MAKER' (2 May 1851). The Manchester *Guardian* looked back at the close of the year and concluded that there were 'good grounds for satisfaction, for hope, and for self-approval' (December 1851; quoted by Asa Briggs, *Victorian People*, 1965). Dickens took a less sanguine view, speculating on when there would be 'another Exhibition—for a great display of England's sins and negligences, to be, by a steady contemplation of all eyes, and a steady union of all hearts and hands, set right?' ('The Last Words of the Old Year', *HW* 4 January 1851). *Bleak House* picks up that bitter view of the age, opening with a vision of active uncreation, with London reverting to a primeval, inchoate mass of fog and mud, the directionless flux mirrored by the STYLE of the first two paragraphs, in which participles dangle without a main verb.

It is a novel quite unlike any which Dickens—or anyone else—had written before, placing institutional satire at the heart of the book's themes and structure. The primary focus of attack is on the Court of Chancery, originally established to expedite justice and defend the defenceless, but for over a century notorious for costs and delay. Dickens himself had sorry experience of Chancery justice in 1844, when he took the publishers of a pirated edition of *A Christmas Carol* to court, won, and found himself faced with costs of some £700, while the culprits walked away without losing a penny (see PLAGIARISMS). The Queen's Speech in 1851 promised Chancery reform, and *The Times* waged a vigorous campaign against inertia, vested interests, and antiquated and costly procedures—precisely the bases of Dickens's attack—but the eventual Bill was much watered down and brought little change. This disappointing result was due to the weakness of the GOVERNMENT, which, despite the 1832 REFORM act, remained in the hands of a coterie of aristocrats. Merely to list the sequence of Prime Ministers in mid-century gives point to Dickens's ridicule of Boodle and Coodle: Melbourne (July–November 1834), Peel (December 1834–April 1835), Melbourne (April 1835–August 1841), Peel (September 1841–June 1846), RUSSELL (July 1846–February 1852; resigned 22 February 1851; returned to office with cabinet unchanged 3 March 1851), Derby (February–December 1852), Aberdeen (December 1852–January 1855), Palmerston (February 1855–February 1858), Derby (February 1858–June 1859), Palmerston (June 1859–October 1865), Russell (October 1865–June 1866), Derby (June 1866–February 1868) …

Dickens's indictment of contemporary society ramifies widely. Satirical targets include not only the LAW but also 'telescopic philanthropy'—espousal of foreign charity while neglecting the poor at home; slum housing (see LONDON: SLUMS AND ROOKERIES); overcrowded urban graveyards (see PUBLIC HEALTH, SANITATION, AND HOUSING); neglect of contagious disease (see HEALTH, ILLNESS, AND DISABILITY); electoral corruption (see ELECTIONS AND THE FRANCHISE); DISSENTING preachers; CLASS divisions; and neglect of the EDUCATIONAL needs of the poor.

Specific individuals are clearly identifiable as CHARACTER ORIGINALS. Major examples include Boythorn, 'a most exact portrait of Walter Savage LANDOR' (to the Hon. Richard Watson, 6 May 1852); Inspector Bucket, derived from Detective Inspector Charles FIELD (although Dickens publicly denied this in a letter of 18 September 1853 to *The Times*); and notoriously, Harold Skimpole, modelled on Leigh HUNT. Dickens changed Skimpole's name from Leonard to Harold, and was pleased that Browne drew the character 'singularly unlike the great original' (to Forster, ?9 March 1852); nevertheless, the resemblance was evident to every reader who knew Hunt, and Dickens was later compelled to write a 'Remonstrance' directed towards Hunt's son for *All the Year Round* shortly after Hunt died (24 December 1859).

## Plot, Character, and Theme

The story's heroine, Esther Summerson, shares the narration of *Bleak House* with an omniscient narrator. Whereas her perspective is restrospective, considered, and compassionate (though sometimes quite sharp), his is highly rhetorical, witty, satiric, and immediate, told in the present tense. The omniscient narrator's impassioned language incites us to outrage at the world's wrongs; Esther, in sharp contrast, provides a moral lens on characters and events, and shows us how to live with Christian responsibility in an imperfect world.

The book's plot hinges on the Chancery case of Jarndyce and Jarndyce, the complications and costs of which make it a standing joke within the legal profession. Ada Clare and Richard Carstone, wards of Chancery, go to live in Bleak House, home of John Jarndyce, who refuses any involvement in the ruinous suit. Esther accompanies them as a companion for Ada, chosen by Mr Jarndyce. They pay a visit on the way to the philanthropist Mrs Jellyby, who neglects her family while devoting herself entirely to foreign charity.

Meanwhile, at Sir Leicester Dedlock's country estate, Chesney Wold, Lady Dedlock faints on seeing handwriting on a legal document. His interest roused, the family lawyer Tulkinghorn seeks out the scribe, known only as 'Nemo', and finds him dead in squalor of an opium overdose. The waif Jo shows a veiled lady Nemo's haunts in London; moved on by the police, Jo flees to Bleak House, where he infects first Esther's maid, then Esther herself, with smallpox. The hypocritical Harold Skimpole betrays Jo to Inspector Bucket.

The law clerk Guppy, rejected as a suitor by Esther, seeks independently to unravel the mystery, but on the night appointed to meet Nemo's landlord, Krook, is horrified to find that he has died of spontaneous combustion. Tulkinghorn, suspicious of Lady Dedlock, blackmails Trooper George into handing over copies of Nemo's writing. It is revealed that Esther is the illegitimate child of Lady Dedlock and Nemo. Jo dies at George's shooting gallery, attended by the young surgeon Allan Woodcourt. After a confrontation with Lady Dedlock, Tulkinghorn is murdered in his chambers. George is arrested for the murder, but the evidence seems to point to Lady Dedlock, who flees from Bleak House. Bucket proves that her fiery French maid Hortense is the murderess. Accompanied by Esther, he goes in search of Lady Dedlock and finds her dead at the gates of a squalid city churchyard where Nemo is buried.

Trooper George is reunited with his mother, Mrs Rouncewell, the Dedlocks' housekeeper. He refuses to work for his brother, a successful industrialist, and goes instead to Chesney Wold to tend Sir Leicester, who succumbed to a stroke when his wife ran away. Richard, whose fecklessness is fatally increased by his placing hopes on the outcome of the Chancery case, is estranged from Jarndyce, secretly marries Ada, and dies in despair when the Jarndyce and Jarndyce case is abandoned, all its assets consumed in court costs. Esther, having dutifully accepted an offer of marriage from Jarndyce, is given by him to her true love, Allan Woodcourt. Ada and her child are looked after by Jarndyce.

*Bleak House* is a novel full of secrets and of DETECTIVES, amateur and professional, trying to ferret them out. The detection uncovers a large number of surprising hidden connections between characters, thematically enforcing Dickens's point that the social malaise is the result of irresponsible denial of human relationships. The lowly Jo turns out to be the pivotal figure of the whole plot. The point is further made by Dickens's vision of society as a family, seen not only in the broken or dysfunctional families which populate the novel, but also in the metaphors which see the Lord Chancellor as a failed father figure, and Mrs Jellyby as illustrative of the maxim that charity should begin at home.

## Reception

*Bleak House* met with mixed REVIEWS, largely because some readers were disturbed by Dickens's outspoken attack on social issues. Forster was among those who disliked its 'didacticism'; he complained that, although the novel's construction was 'perhaps the best thing done by Dickens', nevertheless 'ingenuity is more apparent than freshness' (7.1). But sales of the serialized parts were impressively high. At an average of 34,000 copies of each monthly number, its circulation was 'half as large again as Copperfield!' (to the Hon. Mrs Richard Watson, 22 November 1852). Dick-

ens's personal profit was £11,000, making him (in the words of one contemporary) a 'literary Croesus' (quoted by Patten 1978, p. 233; see MONEY VALUES).

And whereas there had been a steady decline during the 1840s in the number of DRAMATIZATIONS of his works, *Bleak House* was 'among the half dozen most frequently dramatized of Dickens's novels and stories' (Bolton 1987, p. 349). Interestingly, there were few staged versions during his lifetime, but there was a 'burst' of productions in the 1870s and 1880s, notably one starring Jennie Lee in the role of Jo and another with Fanny Janauschek doubling as Lady Dedlock and Hortense.

The book's critical fortunes remained low with, for example, both George GISSING and G. K. CHESTERTON unimpressed, until Humphry HOUSE (1941) celebrated its vision of Victorian society, Lionel Stevenson identified *Bleak House* as the first of Dickens's 'dark' novels (1943), and John Butt and Kathleen Tillotson (1957) documented the topicality of the book's concerns. Since then *Bleak House* has attracted more critical attention than any other of Dickens's works, with particular interest shown in the character and narrative function of Esther (see CHARACTERIZATION). Hillis Miller's chapter on *Bleak House* in *Charles Dickens: The World of His Novels* (1958), later developed in his Introduction to the Penguin edition of the novel (1971), emphasized the book's symbolic evocation of the city, and more recently D. A. Miller's *The Novel and the Police* (1988), which draws on the theoretical work of Foucault to argue that the very form of the novel and its techniques 'systematically participate in a general economy of policing power', has been influential (p. 2; see CRITICISM AND SCHOLARSHIP: POST-STRUCTURALIST).

There have been several volumes of critical commentary devoted exclusively to *Bleak House*: collections of essays edited by Jacob Korg (*Twentieth Century Interpretations of Bleak House*, 1968), A. E. Dyson (*Dickens' Bleak House: A Casebook*, 1969), and Harold Bloom (*Charles Dickens's Bleak House*, 1987), and monographs by Philip Collins (*Dickens: Bleak House*, 1971), Grahame Smith (*Bleak House*, 1974), Graham Storey (*Bleak House*, 1987), and Jeremy Hawthorn (*Bleak House*, 1987). PVWS

Blount, Trevor, 'The Documentary Symbolism of Chancery in *Bleak House*', *Dickensian*, 62 (1966). (This three-part essay is the most important of ten essays on the topicality of *BH* which Blount published in various journals between 1963 and 1967.)
Butt and Tillotson (1957).
Harvey, W. J., *Character and the Novel* (1965).
House (1941).
Miller, D. A., *The Novel and the Police* (1988).
Newsom, Robert, *Dickens on the Romantic Side of Familiar Things: Bleak House and the Novel Tradition* (1977).
Stevenson, Lionel, 'Dickens' Dark Novels, 1851–7', *Sewanee Review*, 51 (1943).

**Book of Common Prayer.** Formerly the official service book of the CHURCH OF ENGLAND, containing the daily offices of Morning and Evening Prayer, the forms for administration of the sacraments, and other public and private rites. The book was originally compiled by Archbishop Cranmer and others in the reign of King Edward VI, condensing and translating certain of the Latin offices of the medieval Church and offering a single, comprehensive, and authoritative guide to the devotions of both priest and people ('common prayer' implied public and corporate worship). Its use was enforced by the first Act of Uniformity in 1549. The 1549 Prayer Book was revised with greater Protestant emphasis and reissued in 1552. Its use was abandoned during the reign of Queen Mary, but the use of a newly revised version was sanctioned and officially enforced early in the reign of Queen Elizabeth (1559). A final revision, which introduced readings from the Epistles and Gospels from the Authorized Version of the BIBLE (1611), was issued under the 1662 Act of Uniformity. It was this '1662' Prayer Book which remained in use until the twentieth century and which was familiar to Dickens.

Dickens knew the Prayer Book well. Perhaps his most striking use of one of its quotations from scripture is the brief citation of the first of the 'bidding sentences' from 'The Order for Evening Prayer' (Ezekiel 18: 27) as Jasper rushes to join the Cloisterham Cathedral choir for Evensong at the end of the opening chapter of *Edwin Drood*. Dickens had earlier used the opening quotation (John 11: 25–6, 'I am the resurrection and the life ...') of 'The Order for the Burial of the Dead' (*DC* 9 and *TTC* 3.9). The quotation is tellingly reused in the latter novel's final chapter. A further passage quoted in the service (1 Corinthians 15: 47–8) is glancingly cited in book 2, chapter 7. The burial service is also referred to (*OCS* 72; *DS* 58; *DC* 9; *HT* 2.9; *BH* 11, 39). The 'Form of the Solemnization of Matrimony' is glanced at (*DS* 4, 23, 50, and 60; *BH* 9 and 10; *OMF* 4.4). Dickens refers to the Litany ('The Curate—The Old Lady—The Schoolmaster' (*SB*); *AN* 6; *CC* 1; *The* CHIMES 1; *DS* 29; *BH* 12 and 26; *LD* 1.19; *MED* 17). The questions and answers of the Prayer Book Catechism are variously alluded to (*BR* 27; *DS* 4 and 9; *DC* 1 and 3; *BH* 28, 38, 45, and 49; *HT* 1.9; *GE* 7; *OMF* 3.8). David Copperfield confesses to inserting Miss Shepherd's name into the 'Prayer for the Royal Family' which appears in the Orders for Morning and Evening Prayer (*DC* 18). Miss Tox mistakenly recites the responses from the 'Gunpowder Treason' service (added 1605; removed 1859) which she is reading at Paul's christening (*DS* 5). Dickens refers briefly to the 'Table of Kindred and Affinity' (*GE* 10), and to the '39 Articles of Religion' (*DC* 29; *OMF* 2.10).

The Ten Commandments are formally repeated as part of the penitential rite at the opening of 'The Order of the Administration of the Lord's Supper or Holy Communion'. The second commandment is indirectly referred to (*LD* 2.16) and the phrase 'visit the sins of the father upon the children' is echoed (*BH* 3). Phrases from the translation of the Psalms contained in the Prayer Book psalter are to be found throughout Dickens's work.

ALS

**'Boz'**, the pseudonym most associated with Dickens's early reputation, was first used as a signature to the MONTHLY MAGAZINE sketch published in August 1834, 'The Boarding-House'. Coincidentally, 'Tibbs', the pseudonym Dickens later used in the BELL'S LIFE IN LONDON sketches between September 1835 and January 1836, is the name of the 'melancholy specimen of the story-teller' in this sketch. The use of 'Tibbs' suggests that he was not completely settled on 'Boz'. FORSTER attributes the inspiration for 'Boz' to 'the nickname of a pet child, his youngest brother Augustus, whom in honour of GOLDSMITH's *Vicar of Wakefield* he had dubbed Moses, which being facetiously pronounced through the nose became Boses, and being shortened became Boz. 'Boz was a very familiar house-hold name to me [Dickens], long before I was an author, and so I came to adopt it' (Forster 1.4). This account raises a question of pro-nunciation, dealt with in a *Dickensian* article of January 1925, which determined that the vowel sound corresponds to the pronunci-ation of the *o* in 'odd', not 'nose'.

In a letter to John MACRONE, the publisher of *Sketches by Boz* [?March 1836], Dickens writes, 'The Editor of "The Court Journal" [Samuel Laman BLANCHARD] told a friend of mine, as a mighty secret, that Boz was done by Leigh HUNT, and some one else, whose name my informant forgets.—Knowing fellow, is he not?' The identity of Boz was first revealed in the *Athenaeum* advertisement for *Sketches by Boz*, 2nd edn., appearing on 30 July 1836. In his diary entry for 8 January 1838, Dickens wrote that the pamphlet SUNDAY UNDER THREE HEADS (published 1836 under the pseu-donym 'Timothy Sparks') and SKETCHES OF YOUNG GENTLEMEN (1838 anonymously) were 'the only two things I have not done as Boz' (Pilgrim 1.630).

However light-hearted the adoption of 'Boz' may have been, Dickens was careful about its use, and, after becoming dissatisfied with the production of The VILLAGE CO-QUETTES in April 1837, requested J. P. HARLEY to remove 'Boz' from the play's advertising. And when, in the first rush of popularity, he negotiated a contract for a Christmas book tentatively titled 'SOLOMON BELL THE RAREE SHOWMAN' with Thomas Tegg, a fourth-rate publisher of remainders, he wrote to Tegg, 'For many reasons I should agree with you, in not wishing the name of "Boz" to be ap-pended to the Work' ([10 August 1836]). A couple of years later, when the Boz name was worth even more, he projected a Christmas book with CHAPMAN AND HALL, to be called 'Boz's Annual Register and Obituary of Blue Devils'.

In the period when Dickens was writing anonymity was the norm. In the quarterlies, Latin tags and Greek symbols were often used when signing off, while in the humorous monthlies silly pseudonyms were common-place. This was all part of the atmosphere of Regency clubbiness. THACKERAY at the same time was writing as Michael Angelo Titmarsh, Fitz-boodle, and Mr C. J. Yellowplush. 'Boz' was soon parodied by an imitator as 'Poz' (see

PLAGIARISMS) and 'Phiz' (Hablot K. BROWNE) as 'Quiz'.

The connotations of 'Boz' were comic: it was appropriate that BENTLEY'S facetious 'Wits' Miscellany' (BENTLEY'S MISCELLANY) should be edited by Boz and advertised as a Regency circle of wits. But apart from the smartness of this publisher's vehicle, there was also tremendous affection associated with the fun of Boz. This was especially ob-vious on the 1842 trip to AMERICA: 'everyone called him "Boz" in those days', recalled James T. FIELDS in *Yesterdays with Authors* (1871). There was a 'Boz Ball' given for him in New York in February 1842, to which 5,000 people came. A play, *Boz! A Masque Phrenological*, was staged in Boston in January 1842, and in March a parody of Dickens's reception in America called *Quozziana*, and another, in April 1842, called *Boz*, which ran successfully for 42 nights. All these productions featured various comic characters from his early works, especially Sam Weller; Dickens himself was included as a character.

At this period, Dickens would sign letters to his friends or talk about himself in the third person as 'Boz', usually in the context of a convivial outing or a comic point. His first son, born in the middle of *Pickwick*'s serial-ization (January 1837), was christened 'Charles Culliford Boz Dickens'. 'Bos' and 'Pos' imitations continued to appear up to at least 1842. Even as late as 1844, a reception in Birmingham welcomed him as 'Boz', and Elizabeth Barrett Browning called him 'Boz the Universal' (Pilgrim 4.438 n.) on the eve of his undertaking the editorship of the DAILY NEWS.

In fact, 'Boz' and 'Charles Dickens' co-existed for a few years. *Pickwick Papers* and *Nicholas Nickleby* in parts were described on their title-pages as being 'Edited by "Boz"'. But published in volume form, they were 'by Charles Dickens'—hence *Pickwick* is the first *book* (1837) to carry his name on the cover. *Oliver Twist* in its first edition was 'By "Boz"'—it had appeared serially in *Bentley's Mis-cellany*, which was 'edited by "Boz"'—but the advertisements at the back announced 'New Works of entertainment edited by Charles Dickens, Esq., (Boz.)'. The MEMOIRS OF JOSEPH GRIMALDI (1837) were edited by 'Boz', while The PIC-NIC PAPERS (1841) were edited by 'Charles Dickens'. In weekly parts, MASTER

*HUMPHREY'S CLOCK* (1840–1) was 'By "Boz" ';
in three volumes, it was 'by Charles Dickens'.
*AMERICAN NOTES* (1842) was 'by Charles Dickens', but in the same year, on the monthly
wrappers and with its original elaborate title,
*Martin Chuzzlewit* was still 'Edited by "Boz"
'—but one page in, on the title-page, it was 'by
Charles Dickens'. In the 1840s a new era in his
readers' affections began. The Christmas
books, beginning in 1843, were all 'by Charles
Dickens', and finally, with *Dombey and Son*
(1847–8), 'Boz' did not appear at all—both
wrappers and title-page announced the author as 'Charles Dickens'. Gradually, 'Charles
Dickens' had become its own identity, one
that indicated more of the serious reformer
than the comic 'Boz' would allow. The
significance of this last persona is acknowledged in *Household Words* (1850), where 'conducted by Charles Dickens' is printed across
the top of every page.　　　　　　　　　　KC

'Boz *versus* Dickens', *Parker's London Maga-
zine*, 1 (February 1845), 122–8.
Easson, Angus, 'Who is Boz? Dickens and His
Sketches', *Dickensian*, 81 (1985).

**Bradbury and Evans,** Dickens's printers
from 1836 and his publishers from 1845 to
1859. William Bradbury (1800–69), known as
a keen businessman, tall, imposing, and astute, started a print shop near St Paul's. In
1830 he was joined by Frederick Mullet Evans
(d. 1870), a jovial, Pickwickian figure known
around the office as 'Pater' and used by John
LEECH and William Makepeace THACKERAY as
a model for a Victorian paterfamilias. They
set up business in Bouverie Street, moving to
Lombard Street, Whitefriars, in July 1833.
Vigour coupled with geniality and competence proved a winning combination; soon
they were printers for several PUBLISHING
houses, and within a few decades they had
also established many periodicals that kept
the presses running between book orders (see
NEWSPAPERS, PERIODICALS, AND THE BRITISH
PRESS). The most successful of these was
*PUNCH*; the one with which Dickens was
closely associated was the *DAILY NEWS*.

Bradbury and Evans were picked by
Dickens's publishers, CHAPMAN AND HALL, to
be the printers for *Pickwick Papers*. Their
foreman, Charles Hicks, handled Dickens's
manuscript with dispatch and accuracy;
Dickens wrote him several friendly notes, in-

cluding one in the form of a rhyme commencing 'Oh Mr Hick I -S, I'm heartily sick I
Of this sixteenth Pickwick' (26 July 1837).
While Bradbury and Evans were invited to
the dinners celebrating the completion of
*Nicholas Nickleby* and *MASTER HUMPHREY'S
CLOCK*, they did not socialize with Dickens
much. They did present him, from some time
before 1839 onwards, with an annual Christmas turkey that may have suggested the one
Scrooge sends to Bob Cratchit (*CC* 5). Another sympathetic exchange was occasioned
by deaths: Dickens consoled Bradbury on
the death of his daughter in March of 1839
(3 March 1839), and Bradbury was deeply
affected by the death of Little Nell, one of
Dickens's many renderings of the May 1837
death of his sister-in-law Mary HOGARTH.

In the summer of 1843 Dickens turned to
his printers in hopes that they would supplant
Chapman and Hall as his publishers: 'A
printer is better than a bookseller', Dickens
told John FORSTER, 'and it is quite as much
the interest of one (if not more) to join me'
(28 June 1843). However, they were not ready
to do so. They had no experience of publishing serial novels or books in general, and no
expertise in advertising and retailing. Instead,
they suggested to Dickens that they could prepare an inexpensive collected edition of all his
previous writing. Dickens thought that idea
premature. Alternatively, as they had a few
years' experience with *Punch*, they offered to
venture any amount of money in a periodical
Dickens would edit. But Dickens, traumatized
by his labours on *Master Humphrey's Clock*,
vetoed that project. Things hung fire for a
year; but when the *Christmas Carol* accounts
came up shy, Dickens blamed his publishers
and determined to leave them.

Suppressing any indication that his recent
sales and profits were not strong, Dickens and
his agents negotiated a deal with Bradbury
and Evans, signed 1 June 1844. The complicated provisions of four related Agreements
essentially gave the printers nothing but a
quarter-share in anything Dickens might
write over the next eight years, in return for
which they advanced him several thousand
pounds so that he might take a year's break
from writing. These advances were not loans;
they were secured only by two Britannia Life
Assurance policies and the possibility of
future novels. This generosity contrasted

markedly with Hall's accountancy. A celebratory dinner ratifying the association included many of the foremost *Punch* contributors, who were to become Dickens's friends and fellow thespians over the next few years (see AMATEUR THEATRICALS).

When it came time to issue Dickens's first new work, *The* CHIMES, Bradbury and Evans lost their nerve. Though they printed the book, Chapman and Hall published it. Dickens was ecstatic about the result; he thought Bradbury and Evans earned more than half again what Chapman and Hall had produced on the *Carol* (which, with its coloured illustrations, was costlier to print). Soon Bradbury and Evans were charged with preparations for the 1845 Christmas offering, *The* CRICKET ON THE HEARTH. Simultaneously, Bradbury's friend Joseph Paxton, entrepreneurial gardener to the Duke of Devonshire, was preparing to found a newspaper on the liberal side, using Whitefriars as his printers. Bradbury consulted with the former journalist Dickens, and imperceptibly Dickens moved from assisting the publishers to editing the paper and contributing travel columns composed of rewrites of his letters from Italy. Concurrently, Bradbury and Evans reissued *Oliver Twist* in monthly parts, thereby gaining first-hand knowledge of the serial market. After only seventeen numbers of the *Daily News*, Dickens extricated himself from the editor's chair; he then decamped with his family to SWITZERLAND, where he planned to write a new twenty-part monthly, *Dombey and Son*.

Anxious lest the failing fortunes of the newspaper or its politics would be associated with his serial fiction, and fearful lest his printers mismanage its publication, Dickens considered returning to Chapman and Hall once again: 'the machinery is as familiar to them, as the ticking of their own watches' he told Forster (25 June 1846). But his new publishers wanted the business; this would be the first venture from which they might expect to go some way towards recouping their previous advances. And as it happened, Thackeray was also interested in having Bradbury and Evans—known to him through his association with *Punch*—publish his projected serial *Vanity Fair* in the same monthly format Dickens had popularized; indeed it had been scheduled to commence in May. So the two

novels came out neck and neck, Dickens's beginning in October 1846 and Thackeray's in January 1847. Bradbury and Evans conducted both serials well; they advertised extensively and kept a close eye on the ratio of stock to demand. As a result, both the sales and the profits of *Dombey* were excellent; the novel was 'a prodigious success' (to Thomas Beard, 21 October 1846; Pilgrim 6.639–40). Up to June of 1848 Dickens reaped over £9,000 and his new publishers made £5,500 from one-quarter of the profits plus commissions on sales. It was fortunate that Dickens's profits were so high, for Evans, like his predecessor Hall, had the awkward task of requesting from Dickens repayment of an advance, in this case £500 for PICTURES FROM ITALY. Given the prodigious results of his new partnership, Dickens repaid that advance without rancour.

During the succeeding decade Dickens's new works were all issued by Bradbury and Evans, though Chapman and Hall managed the quite lucrative Cheap Edition, a reprint, in numbers and volumes, of all the earlier fiction (see EDITIONS OVER WHICH DICKENS HAD CONTROL). There were few glitches. Dickens was too tired to write an 1847 Christmas book in the midst of *Dombey*, but upon its completion he indited a last offering in that form, *The* HAUNTED MAN. Despite Dickens's and Forster's claims that it sold well, in fact it sold 6,000 fewer copies than its predecessor and yielded nearly £500 less. But Dickens did not hold that decline against his publisher. *David Copperfield* was issued without difficulties. It too sold fewer copies than its predecessors: '*Dombey's* large sale has tumbled me down', Dickens told Forster (?22 Sept. 1849). Evans cheered Dickens, and as the novel drew to a close the large number of persons who communicated their enthusiasm to its author sustained and inspired him. Moreover, the back numbers sold more consistently in the years following initial publication than any other of the novels in parts.

Although Dickens's reputation took some buffeting from 1850 on, the 1850s ushered in a steady rise in his sales. Bradbury and Evans set the press run for *Bleak House*, Part 1, at 25,000, 3,000 more than the last parts of *Copperfield*. But the serial outran its printers' conservative projections. The presses ran night and day to furnish extra copies—within four months

38,500 copies were in print. And, unlike most serials, this one didn't lose subscribers in subsequent months; it held them, finishing at 34,000 copies of the last part. *Household Words* was also likely to become a '*good property*', Dickens told Angela Burdett COUTTS (12 April 1855). It produced a steady income and provided Dickens with an outlet for occasional writing, including A CHILD'S HISTORY OF ENGLAND (which sold poorly in volumes) and *Hard Times*. Dickens got half the profits; the other half was split between Bradbury and Evans (one-quarter of the whole), Dickens's sub-editor W. H. WILLS (one-eighth), and John Forster (one-eighth). Dickens's salary (£500) and Wills's (£416) were charged as expenses. One of the first twopenny weeklies to appeal to middle-class pocketbooks and provide original stories, *Household Words* sustained quality writing. And its predictable weekly production of twelve pages printed tightly in two columns kept Whitefriars' compositors, printers, and binders steadily at work.

There were, inevitably, crises. One of the most vexatious concerned the printers' estimates of how many printed columns the manuscript of Elizabeth GASKELL's *North and South* would fill. Worried about her prolixity and pace, Dickens estimated its length and asked Whitefriars to check him. They did, and they agreed. But when the instalments actually ran much longer than the estimate, Dickens blamed his partners: 'I am perfectly convinced there is not another house in the trade to which I could refer a question so vital to a periodical, who would lazily mislead me altogether' (to Wills, 24 August 1854). Still, somehow Bradbury's unpretentious hospitality and affection smoothed over the rough moments; Dickens, Forster, Evans, and the editor of *Punch*, Mark LEMON, spent a high-spirited evening at the Bradburys' in December 1855.

The last twenty-part serial Bradbury and Evans issued was *Little Dorrit* (December 1855 to June 1857). As usual, they mounted an extensive advertising campaign, and their efforts were roundly rewarded; the first part beat 'even *Bleak House* out of the field', a jubilant Dickens told Forster (?1 and 2 December 1855). It, too, continued to hold its initial circulation; Dickens could not resist crowing about his success to his readers in the final

part: 'In the Preface to Bleak House I remarked that I had never had so many readers. In the Preface to its next successor, Little Dorrit, I have still to repeat the same words.' Despite a few hitches over the always-contestable publishers' accounts, Dickens's relations with the printers remained very cordial throughout *Dorrit*. They also sustained amiable terms while coming to an agreement to publish a handsome new collected edition, the Library Edition, which Bradbury and Evans would print and which would be published both by them, for the properties in which they had an interest, and by Chapman and Hall, for their properties. The continuing presence of Chapman and Hall in Dickens's life, and in his publishers' lives, indicates how flexible all parties stayed with respect to their joint ventures.

But all that tolerance, restraint, good-feeling, and partnership vanished in an instant, as a result of Dickens's separation from his wife Catherine (see DICKENS, CATHERINE). In early June of 1858, to counteract injurious rumours, Dickens caused to be published in *The* TIMES and in *Household Words* a personal statement explaining his actions. He fully expected Mark Lemon, who had acted on behalf of Catherine in the negotiations, to print his defence in *Punch*. But Bradbury and Evans believed that inserting 'statements on a domestic and painful subject in the inappropriate columns of a comic miscellany' was wrong, and they refused to comply with Dickens's urgent request. That did it. As soon as he completed a reading tour, on 15 November 1858, Dickens had Forster and Wills move 'That the present partnership in Household Words be dissolved by the Cessation and discontinuance of that publication' (Pilgrim 8.758). It took time to wind up the partnerships, to kill off the periodical, and transfer copyrights and stock back to Chapman and Hall, but Dickens was determined, and he succeeded. The break was much more absolute than the 1844 one with Chapman and Hall. Bradbury and Evans never printed another work by Dickens. He believed they had been 'false' to his name by not supporting him when his personal reputation was at stake. He never spoke again to Bradbury, and swore he would not speak to Evans. Eventually his son Charley married Evans's daughter, Bessie; Dickens refused to attend because the reception would be at Evans's house. But when Bessie gave birth to a grandchild Dickens invited his granddaughter and her parents to Gad's Hill.                                                  RLP

Patten (1978).

Spielmann, M. H., *The History of 'Punch'* (1895).

**Braham, John** (1774–1856), a celebrated tenor, responsible for presenting several of Dickens's plays after he opened the St James's Theatre in December 1835. Dickens, who was introduced to him either by his sister Fanny or by George HOGARTH, wrote the libretto of HULLAH'S opera *The* VILLAGE COQUETTES (1836), in which Braham played Squire Norton (see BROTHERS AND SISTERS OF DICKENS). His two comic burlettas *The* STRANGE GENTLEMAN (1836) and IS SHE HIS WIFE? (1837) were also played under Braham's management. The St James's subsequently proved a financial failure and Braham returned to the concert-hall. According to Sir Walter SCOTT, Braham was a better singer than actor.     JD

**Brontë, Charlotte** (1816–55), novelist and poet, the third of five daughters of Patrick Brontë, a Yorkshire clergyman of Irish origin. Her first novel, *The Professor*, was published posthumously in 1857; her second, *Jane Eyre* (1847), was an immediate success. Dickens never read *Jane Eyre*, expressing a dislike of the 'school' out of which it grew; it seems likely that Brontë's passionate, rebellious heroines would not have appealed to him. He declined a biographical article submitted for publication in *Household Words* on the grounds that 'I could not reconcile it to my heart to publish these details so soon after Miss Brontë's death . . . It seems that she would have shrunk from this account of her trials . . .' (to Frank Smedley, 5 May 1855). For her part, Brontë disliked Dickens's ostentatious extravagance (Barker 1994, p. 660), and expressed contempt for Esther Summerson's narrative in *Bleak House*, finding it 'too often weak and twaddling; an amiable nature is caricatured, not faithfully rendered' (Gordon 1995, p. 247). Brontë's other novels are *Shirley* (1849) and *Villette* (1853).          SL

Barker, Juliet, *The Brontës* (1994).

Gordon, Lyndall, *Charlotte Brontë: A Passionate Life* (1995).

**brothers and sisters of Dickens.** Dickens had three sisters and four brothers. With his growing earning power, his talents, his connections, and his personality, his brothers and sisters looked to him for support, as did his parents, and at an early age he effectively became the head of the family. He helped his siblings with education, used influence to find them work, advised and castigated them; he entertained them, took them on holiday, helped them set up home; and in death he helped support their families. Death came early to all but one—only Letitia had a full life, reaching the age of 77; two, Alfred Allen and Harriet, died in childhood; Fanny, Alfred Lamert, and Augustus failed to reach 40, Fred died at 48. They had their talents, Fanny as an excellent musician and Alfred as a good watercolour artist, but these were greatly overshadowed by those of Dickens. There was depth of affection between them, and although Dickens gave much assistance, nevertheless they had to beware his anger, his tendency to organize them, and his sense of knowing what was best for them. If there was resentment and resistance to this, then that often worked against their own best interests.

Though they each shared troubles in early life, visited upon them by their parents (see DICKENS, JOHN), it was his elder sister Frances—known as Fanny—with whom Dickens, at that early age and later, could best communicate. There are many anecdotes and recollections of the two together—in the front garden at Portsmouth, attending school at Chatham, with their father on the Navy Pay Yacht, and performing songs together, at parties or standing on tables at The Mitre in Chatham; Fanny would also play the pianoforte. Such was her musical talent that she was chosen to pursue a career, attending the Royal Academy of Music from the age of 14, a move that caused some resentment in her brother. She married a fellow pupil from the academy, Henry Burnett, in 1837, and had two children, Henry, a weak and deformed child who died at the age of 9 (said to be the original of Paul Dombey), and Charles, born in 1841 (see CHARACTERS—ORIGINALS). Dickens stayed close to his sister all her life, which may have influenced the brother/ sister relationships in his novels. She enjoyed both humour and pathos in Dickens's writing, disliked affectation, was always frank and open, a cheerful companion, affectionate, as well as prompt and decided. Like her brother she was hard-working and energetic. Under her husband's influence she converted to EVANGELICAL Christianity. She died of consumption at the age of 38 and was buried at Highgate. Her husband, held in some ridicule by Dickens, lived for a further 45 years and contributed many reminiscences of his famous brother-in-law.

Letitia Dickens was born in London in 1816, and because of the age gap did not share closely with Fanny and Charles the pleasures of Chatham or the traumas of the Marshalsea. Nevertheless, his letters show great affection for her. Through her earlier years her health was poor. She was described as having a wearied expression, and as being less fun than the rest of the family. In 1837 she married Henry Austin, an architect and civil engineer, and though they had no children they did adopt a boy, a relation on her husband's side. Dickens knew Austin from his youth, and was on good terms with him throughout his life, seeking his professional advice on the houses he took, and constantly inviting him and Letitia to holidays and social occasions. Austin died in 1861, leaving no provision for Letitia, and Dickens mounted a lengthy campaign for a government pension for her, in recognition of her husband's extensive public service; though she eventually received £60 a year, Dickens continued to provide additional support. As if in defiance of her earlier poor health, she outlived Dickens by 23 years, and throughout remained a favourite with his children and with Georgina HOGARTH. Dickens's son Henry described her as 'a dear good soul, Betsy Trotwood all over', both in looks and manner. Her obituary in the *Illustrated London News*, somewhat in contradiction of earlier accounts, described her as having all the quickness and energy characteristic of the family, and a sense of humour that remained keen and bright throughout.

There was a gap of eight years between Dickens and his next-eldest brother Frederick (Fred). Dickens described him as his favourite when a child, and said he taught him as a boy. During a family crisis in 1834 Dickens moved into lodgings in Furnival's Inn and took Fred, then only 14, with him. He appears to have remained part of Dickens's household during the early years of his marriage at both Furnival's Inn and Doughty Street, though whether

he moved on to Devonshire Terrace is uncertain (see HOMES OF DICKENS). Dickens trusted the maturity of Fred sufficiently to leave him in charge of his children during his trip to America in 1842. He secured a post for him first with the publisher MACRONE, and then, in 1839, at the Treasury. In those early days, under Dickens's guidance, Fred made good progress—Dickens described him as quick and steady, a sharp young fellow. In 1845, though, the relationship began a spiral of disaffection when Fred met and fell in love with 15-year-old Anna Weller. Dickens disliked the family and considered Anna 'the most volatile little minx in existence' (31 March 1848). When Fred married her in December 1848 John Dickens was the only member of the family to attend the wedding. The whole episode was disastrous—Fred piled up debts of at least £600 in two years; his wife became ill and returned to her parents for proper medical care; in 1854 the couple separated for six months and in 1857 sued for judicial separation on the grounds of adultery. Fred refused to pay the alimony settlement of £60 a year and disappeared abroad to escape creditors, only to be arrested and imprisoned when he returned. After three months he was released from prison and declared bankrupt. Although Dickens wrote to him in February 1865, little is known of the last five years of his life, except that he died in Darlington in 1868, aged 48, staying at the home of a retired London innkeeper. SALA reported that Fred's habitual breakfast had been a penny bun and a glass of ginger-beer, the remainder of his diet being mainly gin. Dickens rejected his repeated demands to borrow money and after his death declared that Fred's had been a wasted life, 'but God forbid that one should be hard upon it, or upon anything in this world that is not deliberately and coldly wrong' (24 October 1868). He helped provide a decent funeral, but could not attend himself, sending instead his eldest son, Charles.

Alfred Lamert was the most reliable of Dickens's brothers. Born in 1822, he was too young to be greatly affected by the Marshalsea, but nevertheless grew up surrounded by his father's later difficulties. He gravitated towards his eldest brother in his teens, running errands for him, and then, in 1839, trained as an engineer at Tamworth near Birmingham, working on railway installation with George and Robert Stephenson until 1842. Dickens described him as extremely intelligent, active, and enterprising. From 1844 to 1854 he lived and worked in Yorkshire as a railway engineer, meeting there, and marrying in 1846, Helen Dobson—the wedding took place at Dickens's Devonshire Terrace home. In 1854 he moved back to London to become Superintendent Inspector for the Board of Health, and frequently spent time with Dickens, not just in London but also in Paris, Brighton, and Folkestone. Dickens was godfather to his first child, Alfred Charles Dickens—there were also four daughters. He died of pleurisy in Manchester in 1860 and was buried at Highgate. Dickens subsequently took responsibility for Alfred's wife and children.

Augustus Dickens, born 1827, was early in life given the nickname BOZ, arising from his mispronunciation of Moses (from GOLD-SMITH's *The Vicar of Wakefield*) as Bozes. In 1844 Dickens found work for him with a shipping merchant in the City of London, where he remained at least until 1850. Dickens stayed close to Augustus, involving him in social occasions, and providing the wedding breakfast for him at Devonshire Terrace in December 1848 when he married Harriet Lovell. But things went wrong in his marriage, just as they did for his two brothers—two years after their marriage his wife became blind and he separated from her. Little is known of him for the next eight years, but in 1858 he left the country for America, in company with Bertha Phillips, daughter of an Irish barrister. Augustus and Bertha lived together as man and wife in Chicago, from where he sought money from Dickens, who refused to reply, writing bitterly: 'It is a dreadful state of things that he should have fallen into this position, but I declare to you that I do not see how he is to be helped in it. He always has been, in a certain insupportable arrogance and presumption of character, so wrong, that, even when he had some prospects before him, I despaired of his ever being right . . . I have no hope of him (13 November 1859). The adventure lasted for eight years, until he died in Chicago in 1866 at the age of 39. Dickens had taken care of Harriet Dickens, the blind wife Augustus had left behind, but was attacked in the American press for refusing assistance to Bertha, although he did latterly give her an annuity shortly before she died.                    MA

Carlton, W. J., 'Fanny Dickens, Pianist and Vocalist', *Dickensian*, 53 (1957).

Moss, Sidney, and Moss, Carolyn, *Charles Dickens and His Chicago Relatives* (1994).

**Browne, Hablot Knight** (1815–82), Dickens's principal ILLUSTRATOR. Born in Kennington, Surrey, the ninth boy and thirteenth of fourteen children, Browne was apprenticed after his father's early death to a firm of line engravers. Exasperated by the tedium, he often etched amusing pictures in the margins of plates ('remarques'), or painted watercolours. In 1833 he won a medal from the Society of Arts; cancelling his indentures the next year, he set up at 3 Furnival's Inn with a fellow apprentice and lifelong friend, Robert Young (1816–1907), adept in etching. (Dickens, although unknown to Browne at the time, was a neighbour at 13, and later at 15, Furnival's Inn.) CHAPMAN AND HALL hired Browne to provide three wood engravings for the LIBRARY OF FICTION and to design three more, plus the paper cover, for Dickens's pamphlet SUNDAY UNDER THREE HEADS (both 1836). Consequently, when they and Dickens needed someone quickly to fill in as illustrator of *Pickwick* after June 1836, they preferred Browne to the other applicants, who included William Makepeace THACKERAY and, belatedly, John LEECH. Browne signed his first plates, for *Pickwick*, Part 4, 'N.E.M.O.', but thereafter he adopted 'Phiz', short for 'physiognomy'—the pseudo-science of inferring character from facial and cranial features. 'Phiz', Browne decided, would chime with Dickens's pseudonym 'BOZ'. Thenceforth, 'whether we like it or not', as Sir Angus Wilson says, Browne's depictions 'bit[e] deeply into the readers' vision of Dickens's world' (1970, p. 283). In all, according to Albert Johannsen, Browne drew 724 plates for Dickens, 567 etchings and 157 wood engravings.

From June 1836 until 1860 Browne illustrated most of Dickens's output. In his working relations with Dickens he was always quick and prompt; shrewdly observant, he caught Dickens's ideas and interpreted them fluently. They soon developed a routine for the two full-page pictures Browne supplied for each instalment of the monthly SERIALS: Dickens would write out the first portion to be illustrated, or summarize it on a scrap of paper, or talk it over with his artist, by the tenth of the month; then Browne would make preliminary drawings that, in design, faces and figures, settings, and details, expressed his understanding of Dickens's plot, characters, imagery, and themes. Dickens would approve or emend these sketches by mid-month; when the first design was settled, Browne would transfer the drawings to specially prepared metal plates and Robert Young would etch and print them while Browne repeated the routine for the second subject, completing both plates around the 25th. Since steel etchings only hold up for around 15,000 impressions, if the press run rose higher Browne had to produce two, and sometimes three, 'duplicate' steels of each design. Sometimes he and Young etched as many as four or even six steels in ten days. Each steel was independently etched; therefore Browne and Young could introduce corrections and changes in the second or third version. But as the plates, which appeared separate from the text at the front of each monthly part, were bound in with the letterpress in batches, the priority of the plate is no guarantee of the priority of the letterpress or part issue. However, when Dickens's novels were reprinted after initial serialization, Browne and Young sometimes improved their images in new copies, strengthening the design and modelling, and clarifying expressions, reactions, and interior accessories.

Browne was handsome, amiable, obliging, modest, and shy; he had a keen sense of humour, loved equestrian sports, enjoyed his family, and took delight in benign mishaps, benevolent spirits, and beautiful girls. Dickens's demands were exacting: no detail of a plate escaped his notice, especially early in their association, even though the time allowed for designing and etching all the plates was very short. Nonetheless, the illustrations brought out the geniality of Dickens's text, and were sufficiently well etched, for the most part, to make satisfactory accompaniments to the letterpress. Crucial to the collaboration, Browne's compliant temperament for twenty years absorbed Dickens's occasional outbursts and rebukes without flaring up.

Browne often, independently and intuitively, added elements to the design that commented on the scene. He might import political caricature or graphic symbolism, or deploy structural symmetries, props, pictures, and minor characters to further the humour, drama, or thematics of the scene. As Dickens's vision of society darkened, Browne adjusted his techniques, pioneering in the use of 'dark plates', where the plate was machine-ruled in parallel grooves which printed almost as a uniform tone either before or after the figures and background were hand drawn. These brooding, atmospheric designs harmonized with the gloomy, foggy world of *Bleak House* and *Little Dorrit*.

Browne's signature style was soon apparent in *Pickwick*, where an amiable cat and dog in the foreground reiterate the festive harmony of 'Christmas Eve at Mr. Wardle's' (plate 22), and where donkeys and pigs intimate stubbornness and sloth in 'Mr. Pickwick in the Pound' (plate 16). Browne produced 32 full-page illustrations, a frontispiece, and an illustrated title-page; for plates 22–39 he etched duplicate steels, and for the final double number (plates 40–1) he etched in triplicate. He also etched a new design to replace Robert BUSS's 'The Cricket Match' (Part 3), and copied all seven of SEYMOUR's plates and the second plate ('The Fat Boy Awake on This Occasion Only') by Buss. In addition, Browne redesigned many of the plates for the second volume edition in 1838.

Dickens so appreciated Browne's facility that he got the artist to design the scenery for his December 1836 operetta, *The VILLAGE COQUETTES*. Although George CRUIKSHANK was hired to illustrate the new periodical, *BENTLEY'S MISCELLANY*, that Dickens was to edit from January 1837, Dickens asked Browne to design the picture for the prospectus announcing the forthcoming publication. About the same time, Browne prepared the frontispiece for the publication of Dickens's play *The STRANGE GENTLEMAN* (December 1836 or January 1837). When Dickens's beloved sister-in-law, Mary HOGARTH, died suddenly in May 1837, Browne was asked to paint a posthumous portrait of her. Over the summer, while *Pickwick* was concluding, Browne took the first of several trips with Dickens, this one to France and Belgium. Later that autumn he produced six uninspired plates for Dickens's anonymous spoof, *SKETCHES OF YOUNG GENTLEMEN* (1838), a companion to Edward Caswall's earlier *Sketches of Young Ladies* (1837) to which Browne contributed six sprightly etchings and the wrapper design in a style modelled on Robert Seymour's. Two years later, Browne supplied six more etchings for Dickens's SKETCHES OF YOUNG COUPLES (1840). And he contributed a further six etchings to The PIC-NIC PAPERS (1841), which Dickens edited to benefit the widow and children of his first publisher, John MACRONE.

As soon as Pickwick was finished, Dickens and Browne plunged into preparations for the next twenty-monthly-part serial, Nicholas Nickleby (1838–9). In February 1838 they travelled into Yorkshire to view first-hand the infamous schools there that boarded neglected children, some of them illegitimate offspring who could never return home. The persons they met along the way were translated into the fiction and pictures, though Thackeray complained that Browne ought not always to draw from life, but 'think more and exaggerate less'. As Dickens's new serial was very successful, Browne and Young had to etch three and sometimes four versions of each illustration; in all, Browne made 39 full-page illustrations printed from more than a hundred original or duplicate steels, plus the design for the monthly wrapper.

Dickens's next publication, MASTER HUM-PHREY'S CLOCK (1840–1), was a weekly magazine. Dickens hired Browne and the antiquarian painter George CATTERMOLE to design wood engravings, which were cut in relief and printed with the letterpress. Although Dickens had hoped other authors might be commissioned to provide text, in the end he had to write all the copy himself, so the periodical changed into a vehicle for two successive weekly serials, The Old Curiosity Shop and Barnaby Rudge. For the most part, Cattermole depicted the quaint streets, picturesque interiors, and sentimental scenes, while Browne portrayed the grotesque characters and riotous energies that vitalize these novels. But the stylistic and subject differences between the two artists, clearer in Dickens's mind than on the page, are muted, partly because Browne transferred some of Cattermole's drawings on to the wood-blocks for the cutters. In all, Browne provided 132 of the 173 illustrations (Pilgrim 2.12 n.) and more than 20 initial letters; he also drew two of the three frontispieces for the bound volumes of the Clock. On the title-page of the first bound volume Phiz's identity as Browne was finally

revealed, a not-inappropriate moment, for as Michael Steig has argued, Browne by 1840 was metamorphosing from a caricaturist with a nom de crayon into a HOGARTHIAN moralist deploying many emblematic details (Steig 1978, p. 57).

When the Clock ran down, Dickens ran off to AMERICA. Browne married and, partly for his wife's health, moved in 1846 to Croydon, then in the country, thereby distancing himself from further social and professional interaction with Dickens. Browne also illustrated novels for other novelists, an activity about which Dickens never complained directly to his artist, even though by the end of Browne's life his approximately 1,500 designs for others doubled what he did for Dickens.

As soon as Dickens decided on a new twenty-monthly-part serial, Martin Chuzzlewit (1843–4), Browne returned as sole illustrator, having scotched Dickens's suggestion that John Leech be enlisted as a second artist. Browne made a total of 90 plates, etching duplicates and triplicates of some of the 38 full-page illustrations, the frontispiece, and the vignette title-page. He managed the visual complements to Dickens's social and ethical satire with great inventiveness, creating a variety of parallels, antitheses, and allusive details that reinforce and independently comment on Dickens's theme of 'selfishness'. Thereafter Browne was the only illustrator of Dombey and Son (1846–8), David Copperfield (1849–50), Bleak House (1852–3), and Little Dorrit (1855–7), all published in the twenty-monthly-part format. These serial parts were encased in a coloured paper wrapper; Robert Seymour had designed the one for Pickwick, which was printed on a blue-green paper stock. For the succeeding monthly serials Browne designed the wrappers, which were printed on a similarly tinted cover stock. Since the wrapper applied to all twenty parts, Dickens had to sketch out the whole of his story to the artist before he began to write; from Chuzzlewit—which was the first novel Dickens planned in advance—on, Browne's wrapper designs hint at the characters and events the plot will eventually unfold, 'shadowing out its drift and bearing', Dickens explained to Forster (26–9 October 1846). Moreover, these wrapper designs incorporate realistic figures and various kinds of symbolic imagery: playing-cards and games, suns and moons, a fool with cap and bells, buildings and animals. The combination inventively expresses the mimetic dimensions of Dickens's stories, the direction and contrasts of the plot and characters, and the metaphoric resonances of Dickens's vision.

Writing *Dombey* while in Switzerland, Dickens worried a great deal about whether the long-distance separation would affect the quality and character of Browne's plates. Anxious lest the portraits of Mr Dombey degenerate into caricature, Dickens was on the whole satisfied with Browne's efforts, though on occasion he was strongly provoked by a design. The novel was commercially successful; Browne had to etch copies of all 40 images. But since even these did not suffice for the demand, BRADBURY AND EVANS, Dickens's new publishers as well as printers, reproduced every plate by lithography, a process that yielded many more impressions than an etching. Browne's twelve independently published portraits of the main characters also sold briskly, as did his six 'extra' illustrations for *Pickwick* and four each for *The Old Curiosity Shop* and *Barnaby Rudge*. These supplementary sets of prints, suitable for framing, were executed in combinations of steel engraving and steel etching. They sometimes interpreted Dickens's texts even more extensively and inventively than the original plates.

The next collaboration, *Copperfield*, was perhaps the happiest blending of the two sensibilities; Dickens's gentle, somewhat melancholy reminiscences inspired Browne to exceptionally sensitive representations. The characters are lovingly depicted, unique but not grotesque, and the settings supply subtle shades of feeling and commentary. Sometimes Phiz anticipates events and attitudes only hinted at in the text because of David's undeveloped understanding—as when Mr Murdstone is shown in church before David becomes aware of his mother's suitor. And in shadowing David and Agnes with bad angels (Steerforth and Uriah Heep), both letterpress and plates structure an intricate interweaving of gender, CLASS, and MORAL antitheses (see also SEXUALITY). Each of the 40 images was duplicated, generally on paper of better quality than heretofore; however, the backgrounds are sometimes too deeply bitten in and too heavily inked—the first sign of a gradual breakdown in Browne's artistic control.

Browne etched two 'dark plates' prior to *Bleak House*: the pictures of Carker running away 'On the dark Road' in *Dombey*, Part 18, and of Martha standing by 'The River' in *Copperfield*, Part 16. He may have chosen to etch many more of these plates for *Bleak House* because of Dickens's increasingly sombre social analysis, but he may also, as Browne's son suggests, have wanted, 'as a sort of joke' (Browne 1914, p. 291), to etch plates that could not be reproduced by another means. By resorting to lithography, Bradbury and Evans would not have to pay Browne to etch copies of his own designs. To some extent Browne succeeded in foiling the publishers; all ten of the dark plates were etched in duplicates; the other 30 were lithographed before publication and mixed indiscriminately with the steels in binding. Dickens, who disliked the *Dombey* dark plate, approved of Browne's effects in *Bleak House*; the illustrations often depict scenes in which interior or exterior architecture overwhelms human beings. Moreover, while at times Browne's allusions to earlier graphic conventions are sharp and witty, in some of the streetscapes and interior scenes he develops a pattern of light and shadow that freights natural illumination with symbolic import. Q. D. Leavis thinks that these illustrations manifest 'a drying up or exhaustion of the artist's faculties and interests' (Leavis 1970, p. 360); on the contrary, Jane Rabb Cohen maintains that in this novel Dickens and Browne 'reached the height—and the limits—of their collaboration' (1980, p. 114). Michael Steig finds the plates 'uneven', but argues in response to Q. D. Leavis that *Bleak House* exhibits Browne's most complex Hogarthian satires (1978, p. 131).

Working-relations deteriorated during the production of *Little Dorrit*. Occasionally Browne seemed inattentive to Dickens's specifications sent from Paris. On 19 October 1855 Dickens asked W. H. WILLS to tell Bradbury and Evans 'that although I have communicated at full explanatory length with Browne, I have heard *nothing of or from* him' (19 October 1855). Some of Browne's portraits, such as those of the Clennams for Part 13, Dickens thought 'very good', 'capital' (to Browne, 8 November 1856), but in several other instances Dickens found fault with Browne's depictions. In February 1857 Dickens wrote directly to Browne requesting substantial changes in the preliminary drawings for Part 17, including a re-draughting of the overstrained and weeping Mr Dorrit, whom Browne had made 'too comic' (10 February 1857, Pilgrim 8.280).

By now Browne may have sensed that Dickens's prose, through its descriptive and abstractive powers, was usurping the usual role of illustrations: how could he depict the pervasive taint of the prison throughout society, or draw such characters as Physician and Chorus? Further, Browne was busy with other commissions and was tiring; he did not sign a single one of his *Little Dorrit* images. Even Browne's son admits that the drawings are 'very sketchy' (Browne 1914, p. 296). Whatever the causes, most critics think the plates for *Dorrit* inferior to Browne's immediately preceding work. Possibly because a horizontal format (where the plate image runs at right angles to the printed page) gave Browne more freedom and a certain independence from the adjoining letterpress, he designed 27 of the 40 plates horizontally. Most of the plates were duplicated by lithography, but two 'regular' etchings, and seven of the eight dark, machine-ruled plates, were re-etched. Whatever Dickens thought privately of Browne's capabilities, Browne was not replaced when it came time to designate an illustrator for another reprint series of Dickens's novels, the Library Edition: Browne executed 21 vignette title-pages (see EDITIONS OVER WHICH DICKENS HAD CONTROL).

*A Tale of Two Cities* was the last Dickens novel Browne illustrated, and its production was quite different from the preceding routine. The novel was published in weekly instalments in Dickens's new and unillustrated periodical *All the Year Round*; it was then republished in eight monthly parts with sixteen plates, none of them duplicated by any means. These parts did not sell particularly well. Dickens informed Browne in advance about the general design of the novel; the wrapper for the parts counterpoints the two cities, St Paul's at the top and Notre Dame at the bottom, with scenes in England running along the left side and counterpointed scenes in Paris (Lucie Manette versus Madame Defarge, for instance) running along the right side. But whereas for the riots in *Barnaby Rudge*, rendered in wood engravings, Browne had sketched very careful, dramatic designs in which each participant plays a clear role, for Dickens's later novel Browne's designs and execution slacken.

Browne never understood why he received no further commission from Dickens. He chewed over his rejection for the rest of his life, putting forth one reason after another. It is possible that Dickens resented Browne's working for *Once a Week*, the rival weekly that Bradbury and Evans initiated when Dickens deserted them to start *All the Year Round*. When Browne saw the announcement of Dickens's new monthly serial, *Our Mutual Friend*, he correctly guessed that Marcus STONE, son of Dickens's old friend and neighbour Frank STONE, would illustrate it. '*I* have been a "good boy" ', Browne complained to a friend, but 'Dickens probably thinks a new hand would give his old puppets a fresh look, or perhaps he does not like my illustrating Trollope neck-and-neck with him' (to Robert Young, undated, quoted in Kitton 1899, p. 113).

At the time Dickens was moving out of London to Gad's Hill, Browne moved back into town in order to be closer to the authors with whom he worked. However, his erratic and perfunctory drawings lost him patrons, and paralysis that struck in 1867 partially crippled his right hand. Frederic Cosens, an ardent Dickensian, commissioned Browne to make coloured replicas of all his Dickens plates. These were accomplished with great difficulty, as were 866 sketches for 57 wood engravings illustrating the Household Edition of Dickens's complete works (1873–4; see EDITIONS PUBLISHED AFTER DICKENS'S LIFETIME). Eventually Browne was unable to do any work; denied a government pension, he subsisted at Brighton from 1878 until his death 8 July 1882 on the income from the Royal Academy grant previously assigned to George Cruikshank. RLP

Browne, Edgar, *Phiz and Dickens* (1914).
Cohen (1980).
Hatton, Thomas, and Arthur H. Cleaver, *A Bibliography of The Periodical Works of Charles Dickens* (1933).
Johannsen, Albert, *Phiz: Illustrations from the Novels of Charles Dickens* (1956).
Kitton (1899).
Leavis, Q. D., 'The Dickens Illustrations: Their Function', Leavis (1970), ch. 7.
Steig (1978).

**Browning, Robert,** English poet and dramatist (1812–89). MACREADY, uncertain of the merit of Browning's blank-verse play *A Blot on the Scutcheon*, was swayed by Dickens's enthusiasm for it. 'Browning's play', he wrote to FORSTER (25 November 1842), 'has thrown me into a perfect passion of sorrow . . . I know nothing that is so affecting, nothing in any book I have ever read, as Mildred's recurrence to that "I was so young—I had no mother." ' The play was performed, but ran only three nights. A breach developed between Browning and Macready, although Dickens remained on cordial terms with both until the end of his life.                AR

**Buckstone, John Baldwin** (1802–79), comic ACTOR, actor-manager, and playwright. He was both a friend of Dickens and an influence on his acting style. For the Adelphi Theatre, which he joined in 1828, he wrote *The Green Bushes, Luke the Labourer, The Christening* (adapted from Dickens's 'The Bloomsbury Christening', *SB*), and *The Flowers of the Forest*. His farce *Uncle John* (Haymarket, 1833) was selected by Dickens as an afterpiece to *The* FROZEN DEEP in 1857. Buckstone subsequently performed at the Haymarket, becoming manager and lessee on Benjamin WEBSTER's retirement in 1853, and eliciting Dickens's thanks for engaging Ellen TERNAN there four years later. Dickens, on familiar terms with Buckstone through his charitable work with the ROYAL GENERAL THEATRICAL FUND, claimed that, as a boy, he had been so enchanted by Buckstone's acting that he had gone home afterwards 'to dream of his comicalities'. 'When at the Adelphi, Mr Buckstone was great in his most original boys, as he is excellent in everything. Who can forget at that time his leading home the inebriated Master Magog, the Beadle; or, in later days, his drunken man in *Presented at Court*; or his *Rough Diamond*, with his huge shirt collar and most natural account of his doings at his village home?' (*Speeches*, pp. 186–7). Buckstone retired in 1877; despite his popularity, his critics complained that he relied for effect on mannerisms, facial expressions, and vocal delivery at the expense of characterization.
                                                                    JD

**Bulwer-Lytton, Edward,** English novelist and man of letters (1803–73); more properly 'Edward Bulwer' before 1843, 'Edward Bulwer-Lytton' upon inheriting the family estate in that year, and Lord Lytton at the end of his days. He was a voluminous and (in his day) highly popular novelist, and if his works today read as often artificial, flabby, and overwritten—*Paul Clifford* (1830) opens with the memorable sentence: 'It was a dark and stormy night'—his influence was nonetheless widespread.

Dickens and Bulwer had a certain amount in common; they were both popular novelists who earned their living by their pen (Bulwer had published thirteen novels by the time *Pickwick* emerged), both professed liberal political sympathies, and both were friendly with John FORSTER, who probably introduced them in the late 1830s. Forster was engaged to be married to Letitia LANDON, but when scandal linked her name with Bulwer's (a married man) the engagement foundered. This affair does not seem to have affected Bulwer's friendship with Forster. His friendship with Dickens, however, did not really blossom until 1850 when the two men founded the GUILD OF LITERATURE AND ART together. This enterprise shows the extent to which they considered the career of the writer a serious vocation. As a means of contributing to the establishment of what they both called 'our Order', Bulwer wrote a play (*Not So Bad As We Seem*) which was produced (and acted in) by Dickens several times during 1851 (see AMATEUR THEATRICALS). The Guild may eventually have come to nothing, but the friendship between Bulwer-Lytton and Dickens blossomed; so much so, in fact, that Dickens's final child, born on 13 March 1852, was named Edward Bulwer Lytton Dickens. Bulwer-Lytton stood godfather.

The two men remained firm friends throughout the 1850s and 1860s; and, indeed, Dickens trusted Lytton's literary judgement in some cases over his own. 'You will be surprised to hear,' he wrote to Forster (1 July 1861), 'that I have changed the end of Great Expectations from and after Pip's return to Joe's . . . Bulwer (who has been, as I think I told you, extraordinarily taken by the book) so strongly urged it upon me, after reading the proofs, and supported his views with such good reasons, that I resolved to make the change.' This famous revision emphasizes traditional romantic conventions; originally Pip and Estella do not marry, and meet many years later ('It was two years more before I saw herself...') having lived very separate lives. In the revised version Pip and Estella come together, apparently to marry, under a starry sky. In many ways the revision stands as characteristic of Lytton's own aesthetic. Romantic sentiment is substituted for the sparser emotional tone Dickens originally intended, as if Dickens had his attention on the symbolic and thematic patterning of his novel, where Bulwer-Lytton had seen only the affective logic of the conclusion.

Dickens printed Lytton's *A Strange Story* in *All The Year Round* (1861–2), immediately following *Great Expectations*. This bizarre tale of occult goings-on was a product of Lytton's latter-day fascination with the supernatural. Dickens wrote to Forster that Lytton was 'a little weird occasionally regarding magic and spirits', though 'perfectly fair and frank under opposition' (1 July 1861).                    AR

> Eigner, Edwin M., *The Metaphysical Novel in England and America: Dickens, Bulwer, Melville and Hawthorne* (1978).
> Sadleir, Michael, *Bulwer: A Panorama* (1931).

**Bunyan, John** (1628–88), nonconformist minister and author of *The Pilgrim's Progress* (1678 and 1684) (see DISSENT). Along with the BIBLE, the *Pilgrim's Progress* was surely one of the few books which most 19th-century households had on their shelves. Part 1 is an allegory in which Christian, with a burden on his back, embarks on a pilgrimage from the City of Destruction to the Celestial City, encountering along the way such places as the Slough of Despond, the Valley of Humiliation, and Vanity Fair, and such people as Mr Worldly Wiseman, Giant Despair, and Hopeful. In Part 2 of the allegory, Christian's wife Christiana leads her children on the same pilgrimage. Little Nell in the *Old Curiosity Shop*, who 'seems to exist in a kind of allegory' (*OCS* 1), explicitly compares herself and her grandfather to Bunyan's Pilgrim, and young Martin Chuzzlewit is also reminiscent of Christian in his travels through the corrupt worldliness of America to spiritual regeneration in Eden. Among other allusions by Dickens to Bunyan's allegory, Lady Dedlock in her boredom is said to be in 'the clutch of the Giant Despair' (*BH* 12), Fanny Dorrit's marriage jolts her 'through a Slough of Despond' (*LD* 2.15), and Mrs Sparsit likewise falls 'from her pinnacle of exultation into the Slough of Despond' (*HT* 3.5). Mrs Gamp memorably describes life's sorrows as 'this Piljian's Projiss of a mortal wale' (*MC* 25).                    MWT

**Burdett-Coutts, Angela.** See COUTTS, ANGELA BURDETT.

**Buss, Robert William** (1804–75), ILLUSTRATOR and painter. CHAPMAN AND HALL hired the young portraitist to illustrate Dickens's story 'A Little Talk about Spring and the Sweeps' in their June 1836 number of the LIBRARY OF FICTION. When SEYMOUR's April suicide left the publishers without an illustrator for the third part of *Pickwick*, John Jackson, the wood engraver who had cut Buss's *Library of Fiction* plate, recommended the artist to Chapman and Hall. Buss did a trial plate from the second number, 'Mr Pickwick at the Review', and sketched pen-and-ink portraits of Seymour's Pickwickians (Morgan Library). Trained as an engraver, Buss tried to teach himself etching; although his trial plate was ineptly bitten in, the publishers announced that the illustrations for the third number would be done by Buss, 'a very humorous and talented artist'. Buss then drew two scenes, 'The Cricket Match' and 'The Fat Boy Awake', and after trying to prepare the plates himself, gave them over to a professional etcher whose faithful execution lacked the verve and spontaneity of the original artist's hand. Buss went ahead with drawings for the fourth number, 'Mr. Pickwick and his Friends under the Influence of "the Salmon" ' and 'The Break-down', designed a new title-page and an illustration of 'Mr Winkle's First Shot', and presumed that he was now the continuing illustrator for this project. However, the other partners agreed that the quality of the two published plates was inferior—although just exactly how much interest Dickens took in the whole affair is uncertain. Paying the artist what he termed 'the *wretchedly ridiculous sum*' of 30 shillings for his efforts, the publishers fired Buss and hired Hablot Knight BROWNE. Buss kept his outrage to himself, even when his *Library of Fiction* plate was scrapped in favour of a substitute by George CRUIKSHANK, and his two *Pickwick* plates were redesigned by Browne. However, prompted by FORSTER's slighting reference in the first volume of his *Life of Dickens* (1871), Buss wrote an explanation of his association for Forster (11 December 1871), and later elaborated it in 'My Connexion with *The Pickwick Papers*', completed 2 March 1872 but unpublished until Walter DEXTER and J. W. T. LEY printed it in *The Origin of Pickwick* (1936). Buss remained a great admirer of Dickens's humour and moral vision and painted or drew a number of subjects from Dickens's novels. After Dickens's death, Buss began a large watercolour of the writer at his Gad's Hill desk, surrounded by the creatures of his fancy. In poor health himself, Buss did not live to finish the picture, 'Dickens's Dream', now at DICKENS HOUSE.                   RLP

**Byron, Lord;** George Gordon (1788–1824), the most famous poet of Dickens's youth. The suddenness of Dickens's own fame was compared to Lord Byron's in the second *Quarterly Review* about him in June 1839. However, Dickens himself tends to make fun of the widespread infatuation with Byron that lingered in the 1830s. The young ladies in 'Horatio Sparkins' (*SB*) exclaim of the mysterious (otherwise Cockney) hero, 'How like Lord Byron!', and in the *Old Curiosity Shop* the young schoolgirls scream when they see Byron's representation in Jarley's waxworks (*OCS* 29). For these reasons, Dickens's young men find it useful to model themselves after Byron: Mr Septimus Hicks, one of the boarders in 'The Boarding House' (*SB*), perpetually quotes *Don Juan*, while Dick Swiveller looks 'gloomily' upon Miss Sophy and recites 'My boat is on the shore' ('To Thomas Moore'; *OCS* 8). Swiveller later bids goodbye to the Marchioness in a slight variation on Byron, 'fare thee well—and put up the chain, Marchioness, in case of accidents' (*OCS* 58). Martin Chuzzlewit, while in America, receives a letter from a young poet, enquiring about the possibilities of boat-fare to England and 'any critical observations that have ever presented themselves to your reflective faculties' on *Cain* (*MC* 22). Micawber, embarking for Australia, translates Byron into the familial plural with 'our Boat is on the shore, and our Bark is on the sea' (*DC* 54). It is part of Mrs Skewton's pretensions to quote Byron: 'as

your cousin Feenix says, the sword wears out the what's-its-name' ('So We'll Go No More A Roving'; *DS* 27). And Mr Turveydrop, also an image of faded seductive powers, croons 'Wooman, lovely Wooman' ('I would I were a careless child'; *BH* 14). Dickens's quotations from Byron in his letters include incidental phrases from *Don Juan* and *Childe Harold*, but again his making fun of Byronic angst is more common: he uses the phrase 'maudlin and Byronical' in a memorable description of a Cockney coal-heaver in his drunken moments (to Andrew Bell, 1 February 1843). He advises a young poetic aspirant to 'Leave Byron to his gloomy greatness' (25 November 1840).

Dickens does, however, use the Byronic image without irony in the depiction of some of his own heroes. Steerforth perhaps best stands for the type of the corrupt but troubled idler who envies the more Victorian David Copperfield his domestic peace and professional earnestness. Others of this type include James Harthouse (*HT*), Henry Gowan (*LD*), Sydney Carton (*TTC*), and Eugene Wrayburn (*OMF*). All are upper-class dilettantes and as such untrustworthy, but when they discover the capacity for self-sacrifice, as with Carton and Wrayburn, they suddenly become more prominent than the ostensible heroes of the novels in which they appear.

Dickens's Gad's Hill library contained editions of Byron's *Works* printed in 1829 (Murray) and 1837, and an 1859 edition of *Childe Harold*. Dickens was acquainted with a few writers who had known Byron, such as Bryan Waller Procter and the Countess of Blessington, and apparently considered renting Byron's former villa near Genoa in 1844. He later came to know Byron's daughter, Ada, Countess of Lovelace (1815–52), who on her deathbed asked to see Dickens, because of the impression made on her by the death of Paul in *Dombey and Son*.                   KC

Harvey, W. R., 'Charles Dickens and the Byronic Hero', *Nineteenth-Century Fiction*, 24 (1969).

# C

**Canada.** Dickens visited Canada in 1842 and described his impressions in chapters 14 and 15 of *American Notes for General Circulation*. After a month of exhausting travel in AMERICA, Dickens and his wife arrived at the Canadian side of Niagara Falls on 26 April. They rested there until 4 May, finding the falls awe-inspiring and the country more congenial in its English roots than the United States. After crossing Lake Ontario by steamboat, they spent two nights in Toronto. Dickens praises its buildings in AMERICAN NOTES, but deplores the violence of the politics. On 6 May they boarded the steamboat again for an overnight sail, calling at Port Hope and Coburg ('a cheerful, thriving little town'), and arriving at Kingston in the morning. Dickens found Kingston, at that time the capital of the Province of Canada, a 'very poor town', but he approved of the penitentiary. On 10 May the Dickenses travelled by steamboat down the St Lawrence River to Montreal, with an uncomfortable three-hour stagecoach portage around the rapids at Dickenson's Landing. Dickens was particularly impressed by the beauty of the Thousand Islands and the sight of a huge log raft with several dozen wooden houses on it, 'like a nautical street.' During his stay in Montreal he visited Quebec City via overnight steamboat and found it unforgettably picturesque. While in Montreal Dickens stage managed and acted in two evenings of plays with his friend the Earl of Mulgrave and an amateur company of officers from the local garrison (see AMATEUR THEATRICALS). The Garrison Amateurs played for a private audience on 25 May and in public at the Theatre Royal on 28 May. The Dickenses left for New York on 30 May. Dickens's son Francis served in the Canadian North West Mounted Police from 1874 to 1886 (see CHILDREN OF DICKENS). Articles on French, English, and native life in Canada by other writers appeared from time to time in Dickens's journals *Household Words* and *All the Year Round.*          RFG

**capital punishment** was, from the mid-16th to the end of the 18th century, the prin-

cipal punishment for treason or felony. Execution was in public, usually by hanging; and hanging meant slow strangulation on the end of a rope, since the drop was not developed until the end of the period. Of course, not everyone convicted of felony was executed, and a variety of expedients were employed to ensure that only a few such offenders died on the scaffold as an example to others. Most notable here was benefit of clergy, which originated in the special position of the Church during the Middle Ages and which enabled those capable of reading a verse from the Bible to escape the gallows on their first felony conviction. From the early eighteenth century transportation was seen increasingly as an option, and by the end of the century penal reformers were urging the use of incarceration so that the offender might be reformed (see CRIME; PRISONS AND PENAL TRANSPORTATION). Thus, while the number of capital statutes increased during the 18th century under the notorious 'Bloody Code', at the same time there was a considerable broadening of alternative punishments.

In the 1820s the criminal code was rationalized and the capital statutes were consolidated. On average during this decade there were between 60 and 70 executions a year in England and Wales; property offenders continued to be a majority of those executed, with murderers only accounting for around a quarter. Throughout the second quarter of the century the number of felonies carrying the death penalty was reduced; from the 1840s until the end of the century the annual average of executions in England and Wales was between 10 and 15. In 1861 the Offences Against the Person Act abolished the death sentence for all crimes other than murder and high treason. These developments can be, and have been, interpreted as the result of an increasing humanitarianism and a belief in progress; and if historians are now rather sceptical, that, certainly, was how contemporaries understood them. In the 1840s it was popular among writers and intellectuals to argue for the total abolition of capital punishment. Dickens was deeply involved in the debates. Profoundly moved by a visit to an execution in 1840, he wrote a gruesome description of the gallows in *Barnaby Rudge* (1841) and, early in 1846, four long letters to the DAILY NEWS advocating 'the total abolition of the Punishment of Death'. By the end of the decade, however, his position had become ambivalent and he perceived the greatest evil to be the degrading effect of the execution on the crowds which assembled to watch. This shift provoked a quarrel with Douglas JERROLD, who still argued for total abolition of the death penalty. Dickens's new attitude was a better reflection of that of the Victorian elite which, even though some of its members joined execution crowds, generally considered these to be objectionable, potentially dangerous, and the vestiges of a barbarous age. In May 1868 Parliament passed a bill ending public executions, but by this time Dickens himself no longer participated in the debates and had abandoned his opposition to hanging.　　　　　　　　　　　　CE

Cooper, D., *The Lesson of the Scaffold* (1974).
Gatrell, V. A. C., *The Hanging Tree: Execution and the English People, 1770–1868* (1994).

**Carlton Chronicle** (11 June 1836–13 May 1837). Dickens's sketch 'The Hospital Patient' was first published here, 6 August 1836. The editor, Percival Weldon Banks (1805–50), was a contributor to *Fraser's Magazine*. He asked Dickens to write a series of sketches, but the paper failed after less than a year. The only other sketch of Dickens's to appear was 'Hackney Cabs' (1 September 1836), a revised version of 'Some Account of an Omnibus Cad', which had appeared in BELL'S LIFE IN LONDON, 1 November 1835 (see DeVries 1976). To Dickens's chagrin, later sketches ('Scotland Yard', published here 8 October, and 'Doctors' Commons', 15 October) were simply lifted from the MORNING CHRONICLE without compensation. His work continued to receive regular notices, mainly in the form of excerpts. Dickens remained friendly with Banks, whom he later asked to contribute to BENTLEY'S MISCELLANY.　　　　　　　　KC

**Carlton, William J.** (1886–1973), Dickens scholar and authority on the history of shorthand. His *Charles Dickens Shorthand Writer* (1926) remains the fullest and most authoritative study of Dickens's career as a shorthand reporter. Between 1948 and 1972 he published, nearly all in the DICKENSIAN, a series of meticulously researched articles illuminating many aspects of Dickens's early life and including some important additions to our knowledge of his later years, such as 'Dickens's Forgotten Retreat in France' (*Dickensian*, 62, 1966). The Editors of the Pilgrim Edition of Dickens's LETTERS acknowledge a very great indebtedness to Carlton's work, particularly in their first volume.　　MS

**Carlyle, Thomas** (1795–1881), essayist, historian, biographer, the epitome of 'the Victorian sage', and the writer who had the greatest influence on Dickens of all his contemporaries. Dickens dedicated *Hard Times*, his most didactic and theoretical novel, to Carlyle, and once said of him, 'I would go at all times farther to see Carlyle than any man alive' (Forster 11.3).

Dickens and Carlyle first met at a dinner party in 1840, at which Carlyle sized BOZ up as 'a quiet, shrewd-looking little fellow, who seems to guess pretty well what he is and what others are' (quoted in Johnson 1.316). Carlyle was almost twenty years Dickens's senior, and was so much the younger man's idol—while he had deep doubts himself about the seriousness of what he called 'fictioneering'— that they were never to become what one would exactly call *close* friends. But they were frequently in one another's company. Indeed, in his latter years, and especially after the death of his beloved wife Jane in 1866, Carlyle rarely ventured out except for the occasional dinner with Dickens or FORSTER (Goldberg 1972, p. 18). Carlyle was chief among the select party Dickens assembled to hear him read *The* CHIMES—the most Carlylean of the Christmas books—before it was published. He attended several of Dickens's AMATEUR THEATRICALS and PUBLIC READINGS, including one of *Pickwick* that caused him to laugh so hard that, as one observer put it, 'I thought Carlyle would split . . . he sat on the front bench and he haw-hawed right out over and over till he fairly exhausted himself. Dickens would read and then he would stop in order to give Carlyle a chance to stop' (quoted in Johnson 2.1009). The Carlyles were frequent guests at Dickensian festivities, and Jane describes one lively New Year's Eve party in particular as 'the most agreeable party that I ever was at in London,' with Dickens proving himself to be 'the *best* conjuror I ever saw—and I have paid money to see several' (quoted in Goldberg 1972, p. 17). (There was much mutual admiration between Jane and Dickens; regarding her talents as a writer he confided to Forster that 'None of the writing women come near her at all': Forster 8.7.)

Dickens naturally turned to Carlyle for help with his research on *A Tale of Two Cities*, for Carlyle's *The French Revolution* was a work he never tired of reading. Carlyle responded—somewhat to Dickens's dismay—by sending two whole cartloads of books selected from the London Library. But wading through all that material only deepened Dickens's admiration for Carlyle's learning and insight (Johnson 2.947–8).

Carlyle's responses to Dickens were ambivalent. Jane records that reading *A Christmas Carol* produced in him 'a perfect convulsion of hospitality' (quoted in Goldberg 1972, p. 14). He writes in *Past and Present* at once disparagingly and with a hint of jealously of the great enthusiasm for Dickens in the United States, 'feeling that he, though small *is* something' (ed. Altick 1965, p. 60). In the same not entirely generous vein, he declined an invitation to a gala dinner sending Dickens off on his Italian journey in 1844, though he wrote at the time that, in Forster's account, he 'discerned in the inner man of him a real music of the genuine kind' (Forster 4.3).

If Carlyle for some years did not wholeheartedly reciprocate Dickens's high regard, seeing in him at least initially something too much of the dandy and entertainer, his respect steadily deepened. He wrote to Forster just after Dickens's death that 'No death since 1866 has fallen on me with such a stroke. No literary man's hitherto ever did. The good, the gentle, high-gifted, ever-friendly, noble Dickens—every inch of him an Honest Man' (Forster 11.3). And in Forster's *Life* he found, beyond the cheerful public exterior, evidence of seriousness of the highest kind—'deeper than all, if one had the eye to see deep enough, dark, fateful, silent elements, tragical to look upon, and hiding amid dazzling radiances as of the sun, the elements of death itself' (quoted in Collins 1971, p. 567).

Carlyle's work presents massive and fascinating contradictions representative of the great tensions besetting the Victorians and ourselves. Almost every one of the age's leading ideas finds expression in his work in some form. Pervaded by a sense of the divine, he was no Christian, had no religious affiliation, and nothing one could call a creed. So great was his dislike of the mechanical and of theorizing that he would characterize the divine or spiritual only negatively—as the silent, invisible, organic, unconscious. Fiercely independent and as suspicious of traditional institutions and 'quackery' as any BENTHAMITE, he detested democracy as the machinery of the ballot-box and idealized a sort of natural aristocracy in which the less able would freely follow the strong, divinely inspired leader who could by rightful might maintain the organic relations necessary to community. By any measure a thinker and an immensely self-conscious one at that, he decried self-consciousness and speculation and theory. As earnest as any Victorian, he was also famous for his explosive laughter.

Dickens shared most of these tensions, albeit in much less extreme or explicit form. What he may have revered most in Carlyle was his relentless attack on theories of human nature as essentially calculating and self-interested and Carlyle's practical ethics—the idea of duty derived from Goethe as attending to the self-evidently good: ' "Do the Duty *which lies nearest thee*", which thou knowest to be a Duty! Thy second duty will already have become clearer' ('The Everlasting Yea' in *Sartor Resartus*). As little as she resembles the Carlylean strongman, *Bleak House*'s Esther Summerson adopts just such an ethics when she proposes to let the immediate domestic 'circle of duty gradually and naturally expand itself' (*BH* 8) rather than follow the forced and mechanical prescriptions of the professional philanthropists like Mrs Pardiggle and Mrs Jellyby, who have lots of theories but no organic connection with the people they aim to help.                    RN

Goldberg, Michael K., *Carlyle and Dickens* (1972).

Oddie, William, *Dickens and Carlyle: The Question of Influence* (1972).

**Cattermole, George** (1800–68), antiquarian painter and Dickens ILLUSTRATOR. Youngest child of a Norfolk squire and trained as an architectural draughtsman, Cattermole achieved early fame as a contributor to John Britton's publications on Britain's historic architecture (1807–36) and to an illustrated edition of SCOTT's collected works (1833). In 1839 Cattermole refused a knighthood for his oils and watercolours of medieval subjects. On 20 August of that year he married a distant relative of Dickens's mother.

Cattermole and Dickens probably first met in 1836–7 at Gore House, the salon of the Countess of Blessington; the young artist was then a spirited, fun-loving bachelor, an excellent whip fond of driving stagecoaches. Dickens was warmly attracted to Cattermole, sought out his company many times, and by 1841 had nicknamed his tender and sentimental friend 'Kittenmoles'.

In 1840 Dickens cajoled him into providing drawings for wood engravings illustrating MASTER HUMPHREY'S CLOCK: Cattermole was to design those plates with architectural and antiquarian interest, while BROWNE did the modern scenes. But Dickens often let his senior artist pick or decline the subjects, and in general treated him with a reverence and deference rarely accorded to any other of Dickens's collaborators. Dickens was pleased with Cattermole's nostalgic evocations of old times and buildings, such as the Maypole Inn—the artist's Bedford Terrace studio contained tapestries, armour, weapons, and an escritoire with 'hideous, gaping "Old Curiosity Shop" faces' (Kitton 1890, 2.180). When the *Clock* ceased to be a series of disconnected tales and the narrative of *The Old Curiosity Shop* supervened, Cattermole designed the Shop interior, though his uncertainty about what the child looked like led Dickens to assign portraits of Nell in the early instalments to Browne or, in one case, to the engraver Samuel WILLIAMS. Only about a fifth of the *Clock*'s wood engravings are by Cattermole, but that number includes his most famous, 'Nell dead'. Although the artist draws faces rather crudely, reducing them and generalizing them in contrast to the lovingly detailed settings, Dickens told Cattermole 'that this is *the very first time*' any illustrations 'caused me to feel that they expressed the idea I had in my mind' (30 January 1841). Powerfully associated with Mary HOGARTH, Nell continued her grip on Dickens's imagination after the novel's conclusion. He commissioned Cattermole to paint watercolours of Nell's grave and

the Shop interior; the results, received when Dickens returned from America, 'charmed' him and gratified his 'inmost heart' (20 December 1842).

For the *Shop*'s successor, *Barnaby Rudge*, Cattermole once again drew the insides and outsides of buildings: 'John Willet's bar is *noble*', Dickens told him (19 August 1841). These were rendered so lifelike and distinct that, as Jane Cohen remarks, they 'acquire a status almost like that of characters' (Cohen 1980, p. 131). Less inspired by the mob scenes, and increasingly fatigued and ill as the novel came to its close, Cattermole chafed a bit under Dickens's more and more particular instructions and could not always incorporate the requested textual details. Dickens saw his scenes with a writer's eye, whereas Cattermole drew with a painter's hand and an antiquarian's fancy. Inevitably the two perspectives diverged; the somewhat perfunctory last engravings testify to a loosening of the collaborative vigour.

From 1837 to 1841 Dickens and Cattermole often celebrated 'convivial occasions' together at their homes, and with the members of the SHAKESPEARE CLUB (until it disbanded in December 1839) and the Portwiners (a group, including FORSTER, THACKERAY, BULWER-LYTTON, Charles and Edwin LANDSEER, MACREADY, LEMON, and MACLISE, who assembled in Cattermole's drawing-room). Cattermole gave sumptuous dinners in the elaborately decorated rooms of his house on Clapham Rise, and though increasingly reclusive and nervous, he could host such occasions splendidly. But during the 1840s his health and spirits deteriorated. There was a brief flare-up of conviviality when Cattermole consented to play Wellbred in Dickens's 1845 AMATEUR THEATRICAL production of Ben JONSON's *Every Man In His Humour*. A few other exchanges marked the long twilight of the friendship, which terminated when, profoundly depressed over the death of two of his beloved children five years earlier, Cattermole died on 24 July 1868. That was not quite the end. The Cattermoles had been in need for some years. Dickens helped petition for pensions from the Royal Academy and the government, and he made some effort to raise funds privately for the widow and her children. Not much came of any of these solicitations, but his distant cousin was nonetheless grateful for Dickens's magnanimity and practical sympathy. RLP

**Cerberus Club,** a convivial society named for the mythical three-headed dog who guards the Underworld, with Dickens, John FORSTER and Harrison AINSWORTH as sole members. Early in 1838 Dickens wrote a comic memorandum of club regulations regarding food and drink, and club goblets were specially designed and engraved (Pilgrim 1.637). Dickens's sketchy diary of the time records no meetings after 9 January 1839, the club presumably having disbanded soon thereafter as Dickens's relations with Ainsworth cooled.

PVWS

'The Cerberus Club', *Dickensian*, 46 (1949).
Schlicke, Paul, 'Glorious Apollers and Ancient Buffaloes', *Dickensian*, 90 (1994).

**Cervantes Saavedra, Miguel de** (1547–1616), Spanish novelist and dramatist whose great novel *Don Quixote de la Mancha* (1605 and 1615) was influential on Dickens. Part satire, part picaresque romance, *Don Quixote* is the story of an idealistic gentleman devoted to the chivalric tradition who travels the world with his down-to-earth squire, Sancho Panza, in search of noble adventures. Young David Copperfield read *Don Quixote* at the Murdstone's to alleviate the dreariness (*DC* 4), as young Dickens had done to escape his own troubles. Reviews of the *Pickwick Papers* compared Dickens's tale to Cervantes's: 'The renowned Mr Pickwick is, himself, the legitimate successor to Don Quixote; indeed, he is the cockney Quixote of the nineteenth century, and instead of armour of iron, he is encased in a good coating of aldermanic fur, and instead of spear and sword, has his own powers of declamation with which to go forth to do fearful battle upon the swindler, the wrong-doer, and the oppressor of the innocent' (*Monthly Magazine*, January 1837). FORSTER agreed that 'Sam Weller and Mr Pickwick are the Sancho and the Quixote of Londoners, and as little likely to pass away as the old city itself' (Forster 2.1). MWT

**Chadwick, Sir Edwin** (1800–90), civil servant and UTILITARIAN, chief architect of the new POOR LAW of 1834 so powerfully satirized by Dickens in *Oliver Twist*, but known especially and more favourably for his efforts on behalf of PUBLIC HEALTH AND SANITATION, in which ventures he and Dickens regularly joined forces, thanks in part to the mediation of Dickens's brother-in-law Henry Austin, a sanitary engineer and close associate of Chadwick's (see BROTHERS AND SISTERS OF DICKENS). The last of BENTHAM'S several private secretaries, Chadwick tended Bentham in his final illness and was chosen by the old man to be his official expounder after his death, an office Chadwick declined. He was elected to the ATHENAEUM in 1838, the same year as Dickens, although it was another ten years before they had much contact. Chadwick epitomized the stereotype of the utilitarian—relentlessly rational and energetic, the perfect writer of Blue Books, a devotee of efficiency and facts. His relationship with Dickens highlights Dickens's ambivalence about the utilitarians: on the one hand, Dickens vowed that he would differ with Chadwick over the new Poor Law 'to the death' (to Henry Austin, 25 September 1842); on the other, no one was more zealous than he in supporting and propagandizing for Chadwick's many sanitary proposals. Indeed, in their restless crusading for philanthropic causes, their unfailing confidence that they knew what was best for the objects of their concern, and their passion for order and cleanliness, Chadwick and Dickens much resembled one another.

RN

**Chancery.** For Dickens and his contemporaries, the Court of Chancery was emblematic of all that was wrong with the law. Ironically, the origins of Chancery's jurisdiction lay in the recognition during the 14th and 15th centuries that a special jurisdiction in equity (synonymous with fairness and natural justice) was needed to mitigate the inflexibility of the common law. By the early 17th century Chancery had become one of the major royal central courts for the adjudication of wide-ranging disputes over land-ownership, inheritance, trusts, debts, and business transactions, with its own distinctive procedures and remedies. In term time the Court sat at Westminster, out of term it sat in the old hall of Lincoln's Inn. Litigants found it more attractive than the common law courts because it was possible to initiate proceedings in English rather than in Latin; and it provided remedies otherwise unavailable, for example to widows and orphans. The opposition between equity and law eroded, however, and Chancery became synonymous with expense, technicality, delay, and inconclusiveness of outcome which blighted many innocent lives. Parliamentary inquiries in 1735, 1810–11, 1826, and 1836, failed to produce reforms.

Chancery's problems stemmed from its bureaucratic culture and the manifold officers and offices involved in the course of litigation. Litigants paid court fees to the official staff, and judges then sold these lucrative offices to court officials. Moreover, each stage in the proceedings imposed additional fees on litigants. Thus, officials had a vested interest in the perpetuation of litigation. Many cases were not heard until many years after they had been set down. The technicality and expense of going to law put a premium on tactics and the wearing down of one's opponents.

Dickens experienced the shortcomings of Chancery in 1844 when he successfully obtained an injunction to prevent breach of COPYRIGHT with respect to a pirated edition of *A Christmas Carol*. But the principal defendants, Lee and Haddock, declared themselves bankrupt, and instead of the public apology and damages that he had expected, Dickens found himself faced with costs of £700.

The reform of Chancery was highly topical in the 1850s. Dickens, who had previously depicted a Chancery prisoner imprisoned 'long enough to have lost friends, fortune, home and happiness' (*PP* 41–2), published two articles on 'The Martyrs of Chancery' (*HW* 7 December 1850 and 15 February 1851). The Queen's Speech of 1851 pledged to address Chancery abuses, but obstruction in the House of Lords and pressure from the legal profession watered down reforms. That same year *The* TIMES waged a vigorous campaign for Chancery reform, and Dickens's celebrated indictment of Chancery in *Bleak House* 'followed in almost every respect the charges already levelled in the columns of *The Times*' (Butt and Tillotson 1957). Like the fog and dirt that are its first symbols, the Chancery suit is omnipresent, insinuating itself into every aspect of life and every strata of society. The distinguished legal historian Sir William Holdsworth concluded that *Bleak House* was, in all essentials, correct.                    DS

Holdsworth, William S., *Charles Dickens as a Legal Historian* (1928).

**Chapman and Hall,** Dickens's publishers from 1836. In 1830 Edward Chapman (1804–80), the meditative, literary son of a Richmond solicitor, joined with William Hall (?1801–47), a brisk businessman with a knack for computation, in a bookselling and PUBLISHING shop at 186 Strand, London. In 1835 they issued a Christmas spoof, *The Squib Annual*, illustrated by Robert SEYMOUR. The artist then proposed that Chapman and Hall publish his comic etchings about cockney sportsmen, and that they hire a writer to compose letterpress leading up to the pictures. Having had some experience selling SERIALS, Chapman suggested that plates and text be issued in self-contained monthly parts. Seymour agreed. William Hall went looking for a hack writer, and after he had been turned down by Charles Whitehead and possibly others, he approached Dickens with this journeyman assignment. Eager for recognition and income, Dickens accepted; he thought it an especially good sign that Hall had been the bookseller who sold him a copy of the December 1833 MONTHLY MAGAZINE in which his first story appeared. After writing enough for two parts, Dickens went off to Chalk on his honeymoon, leaving his publishers to put together a first instalment that stops awkwardly two pages into chapter 3. *Pickwick Papers*, Part 1, appeared at the end of March 1836 and sold poorly. Chapman and Hall reduced the print run from 1,000 to 500 for Part 2. Just after etching a plate for that part, on 20 April, Seymour committed suicide. At this juncture Dickens persuaded Chapman and Hall to continue with the failing project by decreasing the number of illustrations per part from four to two, hiring a new illustrator, extending the letterpress from 24 to 36 pages, and increasing his stipend per instalment. The first successor to Seymour, Robert BUSS, could not etch his designs competently, so Chapman and Hall fired him, and sales of the third part did little to restore the publishers' confidence in the venture. But whether the hiring of Hablot Knight BROWNE as the third illustrator, the introduction of Sam Weller, word-of-mouth about earlier instalments, the efforts of vendors, or Dickens's increasing confidence and exuberance made the difference, the sales of the parts did begin thereafter to rise, until by November 1837 nearly 40,000 readers bought the final part.

Chapman and Hall were quick to seize on the other advantages of serial publication. The parts could be advertised and reviewed monthly; they were themselves excellent vehicles for other ADVERTISEMENTS; and by recycling revenues from preceding parts the publishers multiplied manyfold the power of a small capital investment. At first, as the serial caught fire during the autumn of 1836, they found that the costs of reprinting earlier parts and producing new ones exceeded income, but after the new year profits turned the corner. On the parts alone, Chapman and Hall said they cleared £14,000.

They were also quick to encourage and reward Dickens. On the first anniversary of *Pickwick* they gave the author a bonus of £500, a set of SHAKESPEARE, and a banquet; in July 1837, following the death of Mary HOGARTH, they presented Dickens with a set of six Pickwickian punch ladles; anticipating negotiations for a new periodical, in August they instructed counsel to draw up an agreement giving Dickens £2,000 for the whole of *Pickwick*, an increase to £100 per part from the original £14 3s 6d; on 18 November at a dinner at the Prince of Wales Hotel they presented Dickens with a set of silver spoons decorated with *Pickwick* characters on the handles; and on the same day they leased back for five years the one-third COPYRIGHT on *Pickwick* they assigned to Dickens. In these latter negotiations John FORSTER played a crucial role; and thenceforth Forster was 'the most influential' adviser the firm ever had (Waugh 1930, p. 27).

On this same Saturday Chapman and Hall contracted to pay Dickens £150 per part for a new serial identical in format to *Pickwick*. Dickens retained the copyright of *Nicholas Nickleby* in its entirety, although he agreed to lease it to his publishers for five years following serialization. From the first sales were strong, exceeding 50,000 copies on the opening part and sustaining interest among buyers to such an extent that the profits at least equalled those for *Pickwick*. At the conclusion of *Nickleby* the publishers organized another celebratory dinner, held at the Albion in Aldersgate Street on 5 October 1839. After a splendid meal and mediocre speeches, MACLISE's spirited oil PORTRAIT of the author, which had been commissioned by Chapman and Hall and engraved for the frontispiece of *Nickleby*, was presented as a tribute from what

a grateful Dickens called 'the best of booksellers past, present, or to come' (to Chapman, 14 November 1839).

Once again, at the conclusion of one profitable serial Chapman and Hall had to look forward to negotiations for the next Dickens production; their tributes to the success of the concluding title were always, therefore, part of a strategy of wooing the author for a new project. Dickens knew that. Towards the conclusion of *Nickleby*, he told Forster to remind the publishers that 'if they do something handsome—even handsomer perhaps than they dreamt of doing', they would find him 'tractable'. He also offered, as further inducement, 'rough notes of proposals for the New Work' (to Forster, 14 July 1839). Chapman and Hall chipped in another £1,500 for *Nickleby*. But the new work, somewhat to their dismay, was not to be another monthly-part novel; instead, Dickens wanted to produce an illustrated weekly serial, entitled MASTER HUMPHREY'S CLOCK, which would contain stories by assistants as well as himself. Proposals for an agreement, signed on 15 October 1839, specified that Dickens would be paid to supply twelve pages of original literary matter (by himself or others) each week, that Chapman and Hall would publish the serial in weekly and monthly instalments, and that Dickens and his publishers owned the copyright, and net profits, jointly. The publishers could cancel the periodical at any time after twelve months, and either party could quit at the end of five years. Hall's calculations based on a projected sale of 40,000 copies per week showed comfortable profits for everyone; when demand for the first number soared to 70,000 copies, Dickens was jubilant, estimating that the *Clock* would be worth £10,000 a year to him. However, sales quickly fell off; the public expected a continuing story by Dickens instead of unconnected short snippets. So, after consulting with his publishers, Dickens jettisoned the *Clock* machinery and commenced *The Old Curiosity Shop*, which reached 100,000 copies weekly by its conclusion.

From almost the beginning of his career, Dickens had received some revenue for his writings from American publishers. For the *Clock* he worked with Chapman and Hall to arrange shipment of stereotype plates to a Philadelphia firm, Lea and Blanchard, who published the two novels contained therein in monthly instalments (see EDITIONS: FOREIGN ENGLISH-LANGUAGE EDITIONS OF DICKENS). Chapman and Hall also sent out stereotypes to India, though that venture was unremunerative; and they posted advance proofs to Germany, where TRANSLATIONS of Dickens's earlier works had made him wildly popular. But the expense of hiring two artists and a relay of wood-engravers to prepare the illustrations, and other unexpected costs, absorbed much of the revenue; few of the thousands of pounds expected were actually gained. Moreover, Chapman and Hall had purchased the barely begun *Barnaby Rudge* from Richard BENTLEY for £3,000. To secure that debt, they wanted some formal security; after complex negotiations with Dickens and his representatives, the publishers emerged with a bittersweet contract. *Barnaby Rudge* would now appear as the second novel in the *Clock*; they would pay Dickens his weekly editorial fee and in effect give him half of the copyright in the novel, since he owned half the copyright and received half the profits of the *Clock*. They thus paid twice for the novel and surrendered half the rights in an unwritten text. When they suggested that some lien against Dickens's other literary properties might be effected to secure their debt, Dickens and his advisers were outraged. Eventually William Chapman, attorney for his son's firm, drafted a bond that attached certain of Dickens's literary rights and the proceeds of a £2,000 life insurance policy. Infuriated at this 'offensive way of putting me into double irons' (to Chapman and Hall, ?3 August 1841), Dickens demanded that Edward Chapman return an earlier letter of thanks for the original loan. Chapman and Hall backed down once again, pitching the bond into the fire, and amicable relations resumed.

By the end of *Barnaby*, however, the *Clock* was losing money and revenues from other sources were insufficient to redeem the bond, still a moral if not a legal obligation. William Hall hoped that the new undertaking Dickens planned to replace the *Clock* would be another 20-part novel. Instead, Dickens primed John Forster to propose, after a good dinner on 21 August 1841, that Chapman and Hall pay Dickens £2,000 to retire from public notice for a year. At the end of that time Dickens would burst forth with a new work, in three volumes, assigning half-profits and copyright to his publishers. Two weeks earlier they had nearly lost Dickens over the bond; now, having brought calculations on the profits of a new serial in their pockets, they were instead asked to forego publishing anything for twelve months while subventing Dickens's break, after which they had to risk an entirely new venture for them, a three-volume novel. Chapman and Hall put up a good front, gave in, and let a triumphant Dickens rest for a year.

Eventually the agreement for what would become *Martin Chuzzlewit* declared that the new work would be issued in monthly parts—Dickens realized that if he contracted for a whole novel due in a year he would in effect have to write it during his 'vacation'. Another clause in that agreement specified that the loans and advances from his publishers would be paid off out of his share of the net profits from the new serial. If returns were insufficient after the fifth instalment, Chapman and Hall could deduct £50 a month from Dickens's £200 monthly cheque, and if at the end of the serial the indebtedness was still unsettled, all Dickens's half of the profits would be applied until he cleared his account.

Unexpectedly, AMERICAN NOTES intervened. Dickens planned it as an inexpensive volume, a 'ten and sixpenny touch' (to Hall, 14 September 1841) composed of his American journals and letters home. It swelled into two volumes, sold hugely in AMERICA and substantially in Britain, and repaid a further advance of £800 which his ever-obliging publishers had provided when Dickens's vacation turned into an American tour.

But the interruption in the routine of serialized novels, or the downturn in publishing that hit both America and Britain hard in the early 1840s, or the quality of the writing, damped sales of *Chuzzlewit*. By the fifth instalment, it was not earning enough to repay any portion of Dickens's debt. When on 27 June 1843 William Hall invoked the clause specifying a reduction in Dickens's monthly stipend, Dickens exploded. 'I am bent upon paying Chapman and Hall *down*', Dickens told Forster. 'And when I have done that, Mr Hall shall have a piece of my mind' (28 June 1843). Dickens approached his printers, BRADBURY AND EVANS, but they had little experience publishing books and were consequently hesitant to make a commitment to an author who, while enormously successful in the past, was known for breaking contracts and was not earning his keep at present.

Dickens tried to earn extra by producing a little Christmas book, *A Christmas Carol*, which he had Chapman and Hall publish on commission. But once again his estimate of the profits was overly optimistic, so little could be put aside towards his debts. Other incidents amplified his anger towards his publishers, who he believed mismanaged his affairs and overcharged him. On 12 February 1844 Dickens wrote to his solicitor Thomas Mitton that Chapman and Hall were 'past and over'. As the year progressed, the accounts turned more favourable, but Dickens persisted in his determination to give all his business over to his printers. Eventually, and somewhat reluctantly, Bradbury and Evans assumed Dickens's debt and stock of back issues; on 1 June 1844 the transfer was effected. But even that change was quickly modified. Since Bradbury and Evans were unfamiliar with book distribution, Chapman and Hall obligingly agreed to handle Dickens's 1844 Christmas book, *The* CHIMES; title-page and advertisements carry their name, not Bradbury and Evans's. And of course Chapman and Hall continued to account for books on which they shared copyright with Dickens, including the reissue of the early novels in a Cheap Edition (1847–52), so in many senses the change of publishers was less absolute that it at first appeared (see EDITIONS OVER WHICH DICKENS HAD CONTROL). Nor did Dickens break emotionally with his first publishers. Moved by Hall's sudden death in March 1847, he told Edward Chapman he would attend the funeral; afterwards he wrote to Browne 'that I bought the Magazine in which the first thing I ever wrote was published—from poor Hall's hands[.]—I have been thinking all day of that' (15 March 1847).

When Dickens broke with Bradbury and Evans in 1857 because they refused to publish in their magazine PUNCH his explanation of the separation from Catherine, he resumed his relations with his former publishing house, now headed by Frederic Chapman, Edward's cousin (see DICKENS, CATHERINE). But Dickens was unable to complete the separation from his printers until, by a variety of manoeuvres, in May 1859 he ceased editing

*Household Words*, bought the name and back stock at auction, sold the stock to Chapman and Hall, and folded his former periodical into his new one, *All the Year Round*. Dickens owned his new weekly, which was published from its offices in Wellington Street, Strand; Chapman and Hall were not publishers, only receivers of accounts and exclusive agent for its distribution outside London. The firm of Charles Whiting undertook the printing. The venture was from the first a considerable hit, with *A Tale of Two Cities* running in instalments and garnering more than 100,000 customers weekly.

In other ways, Dickens's relations with his publishers changed. The firm to which he returned was no longer an intimate, familial enterprise mixing bookselling with bonhomie. It was a complex commercial enterprise that Frederic had purchased from Edward Chapman with the backing of wealthy friends. It claimed an impressive company of authors, including Thomas CARLYLE, the BROWNINGS, and Anthony TROLLOPE. Frederic was much more energetic and sociable than his country-bred cousin Edward; he gave Lucullan feasts at his Ovington Square house, and in the office he pushed out the product as fast as it came in, selling bulk orders at discount, expanding overseas distribution, remaindering inventory, and devising new ways of moving the wares. Dickens complained to Charles LEVER, half humorously, that Frederic 'is a Monstrous Humbug... [who] seems to me to be making holiday one half of his life, and making mistakes the other half, and making money (I suppose) in spite of himself, always' (2 January 1860). Despite occasional grumblings, however, Dickens grew to trust Chapman with more and more of his business.

In the spring of 1861 Dickens bought out Bradbury and Evans's copyrights and stock of all the publications they shared with him; he then sold to Chapman and Hall his former printer's share, so he and his publishers would henceforth be equal partners in back works. These included the Cheap Edition, still moving as many as 300,000 of its penny-halfpenny numbers each year, and the sluggish Library Edition, which Frederic unloaded in wholesale quantity to America by adding reprints of the original illustrations.

*Great Expectations* also reaped large rewards. It stabilized the circulation of *All*

the Year Round, dropping because Charles LEVER's novel was so tedious, and it reached more readers through its three-volume reprint, which was bought mainly by circulating libraries. The collected editions reached ever further afield, as Frederic Chapman exploited the benefits of newly enacted binational copyright agreements and pushed copies on to publishers in America and the colonies. He also steadily lowered the price on back stock and various reprintings, with the expected result that sales and profits increased.

In 1863 Dickens offered his terms for publishing a new twenty-part serial: if Chapman paid him £6,000 while he was writing it, paid all the expenses of publication, and took only a 5 per cent commission on gross sales, then Chapman could have half of any remaining profit from the serial run. But once the serial was finished the firm would own no portion of the copyright in the parts or in any future edition. Chapman agreed and contracted for printing with William Clowes, a huge firm used to stereotyping cold-type impositions for future reprintings. Dickens did well out of his bargain, although the novel, Our Mutual Friend, did not inspire enthusiasm or customers; Chapman lost about £700, but kept his most lucrative author and continued to profit from their other joint ventures. One other collected edition, suggested originally by the Boston firm of TICKNOR AND FIELDS, yielded satisfactory results for all concerned: the Charles Dickens Edition, each title a single volume bound in red cloth with Dickens's signature stamped in gold on the cover, became an immense undertaking. Chapman advertised hugely: he printed 1,350,000 prospectuses and placarded railway stations for months. He counted on volume discounts and bulk orders, and he was right; moreover, Dickens's second American tour, and the PUBLIC READINGS, further stimulated the public.

Concluding that the poor showing of Our Mutual Friend testified to the obsolescence of the twenty-part novel, Dickens offered Chapman two choices for the next serial: run it weekly in All the Year Round or publish it in twelve monthly parts. Since Chapman would have no share in the former arrangement, he opted for the latter, advancing £7,500 for all the profits on the first 25,000 copies. The agreement provided that if Dickens died before the serial was completely written, Chapman would be reimbursed a portion of his advance. Unhappily, that clause proved prophetic, and Dickens's estate repaid £1,500 because Dickens died before Edwin Drood was completed.

Throughout his life, Dickens considered his publishers to be partners in a very sensitive business, one that touched his literary and personal reputation, his professionalism, and his values. In his skyrocket ascent, he broke many promises and contracts; but no publisher emerged poorer for his association with Dickens, though several suffered a great loss at his departure. Although Dickens was furious when Hall tried to collect his debt, part of his anger was directed towards himself and towards the stinginess of the marketplace, which had yet to reward him, after ten years of exceptional acclaim, with any financial security. Within months of turning to Bradbury and Evans, Dickens's accounts with Chapman and Hall turned profitable; that good fortune, Hall's sudden death, Edward Chapman's complaisance, and Frederic Chapman's enterprise kept Dickens affiliated with the firm throughout the remainder of his lifetime.

After Dickens's death Chapman and Hall continued to publish the works in their previous editions as well as in new ones, such as the Household Edition (1871–80) illustrated with poor wood engravings from new designs by the partially incapacitated Browne, and by new plates commissioned from other artists (see EDITIONS PUBLISHED AFTER DICKENS'S LIFETIME). They also issued Forster's Life and the first edition of Dickens's LETTERS. Late in the 1870s Chapman concluded a complex agreement with Routledge to supply inexpensive copies in bulk, and the quantities sold in the home market, abroad, and in translation, or given away as a prize or incentive, grew decade by decade. In 1868 Anthony Trollope bought for £10,000 a third interest in the firm for his son Henry Merivale Trollope, so Dickens's sales thereafter enriched the family of another writer. The firm continued its association with Dickens in the new century. Arthur Waugh, managing director 1902–30, helped organize the Dickens Fellowship, and B. W. MATZ, who worked for Chapman and Hall for more than forty years, beginning at 15, identified many of Dickens's unsigned pieces and added them to the firm's principal editions of Dickens as the *Miscellaneous Papers*. In the 1930s the firm sold 877 steels and woodblocks —all that remained of the printing plates for the original illustrations—to the Nonesuch Press for their edition of Dickens's works. Chapman and Hall then merged with Methuen, and in 1955 further mergers created the Associated Book Publishers. But the Chapman and Hall imprint resurfaced one more time, as publisher of essays edited by Michael Slater commemorating the centenary of Dickens's death: *Dickens 1970*.　　RLP

Patten (1978).

Waugh, Arthur, *A Hundred Years of Publishing: Being the Story of Chapman & Hall, Ltd.* (1930).

**Chappell & Co.,** established 1811, were an important firm of MUSIC and musical instrument sellers and publishers based in New Bond Street in London where (at least nominally) the firm is still based. In the middle years of the 19th century Chappell & Co. extended its entrepreneurial activities into concert promotion, and it is as the promoters and organizers of his PUBLIC READINGS that the firm was connected to Dickens. For his part Dickens was well pleased to be free of the business side of his performances. Chappell appointed George DOLBY (whom Mark Twain described as 'a gladsome gorilla') to manage the tours, and after some initial tension he and Dickens seem to have got on well together. For thirty performances in 1866 Chappell paid Dickens £50 per performance plus all expenses.　　VG

**characterization.** Discussion of characters and characterization has dominated commentary on Dickens's fiction from the first enthusiastic responses to Sam Weller to the most recent studies of his art. Throughout, debate has remained intense, provoking quips from Oscar Wilde, scorn from Aldous Huxley ('Mentally drowned and blinded by the sticky overflowings of his heart, Dickens was incapable, when moved, of re-creating, in terms of art, the reality which had moved him'), and fervent defence. 'When people say Dickens exaggerates,' wrote George Santayana in 1921, referring to the rich gallery of characters the novelist created, 'it seems to me they can have no eyes and no ears.' The 'polite world', he

continued, is lying when it refuses to believe that individuals like Quilp, or Squeers, or Serjeant Buzfuz exist; 'there are such people', he asserted, reminding us that 'we are such people ourselves in our true moments, in our veritable impulses', though we take care to stifle and hide those moments by adopting conventional masks (1922, pp. 203–4).

Reference to some comparative statistics compiled by John R. Greenfield in his *Dictionary of British Literary Characters* helps account for the focus on character among Dickens's readers. Greenfield counts some 11,663 figures invented by novelists writing between the later 17th century and 1890, 989 (approximately 8 per-cent) of whom are Dickens's, a sum which puts him ahead of SCOTT (872), and gives him a commanding lead over all other Victorian novelists save TROLLOPE, whose 1,289 characters take first place. On a different scale, Dickens leads his contemporaries for citations in the 1996 *Oxford Dictionary of Quotations*: all fifteen of his novels win entries, and significantly the overwhelming majority of quotations included illustrate the distinctive spoken idioms of both minor and major characters (see STYLE). The assertion of Dickens's uniqueness through the individualized speech of his characters, in fact, is often said to constitute his genius, the test of greatness on which Dickens's fiction stands or falls. For command of 'word, phrase, rhythm and image' and in 'ease and range', wrote F. R. LEAVIS, 'there is surely no greater master of English except SHAKESPEARE' (1970, pp. 206–7).

What assumptions about character and the method of establishing different persons in narrative fiction shape this extraordinary achievement? Comments by Dickens himself on two different occasions provide significant clues. Toasting THACKERAY on the thirteenth anniversary of the ROYAL GENERAL THEATRICAL FUND on 29 March 1858, Dickens remarked: 'Every good actor plays direct to every good author, and every writer of fiction, though he may not adopt the dramatic form, writes in effect for the stage' (*Speeches*, p. 262). A second observation made as an aside to FORSTER reveals a similar conviction about the affinities Dickens saw between writing novels and writing plays. Nowhere was proof more evident than in his own career as a novelist, one, Dickens thought, that might easily have been as successful 'on the boards' as it had been 'between them' (5.1).

Forster recounts how Dickens went on to support this proposition by offering some 'interesting' revelations about attempts he made as a young man 'to get upon the stage', the most serious of which was an audition he requested with the stage-manager of Covent Garden Theatre in 1832. Offering himself for consideration, Dickens wrote to describe what he thought he could do and how he believed he had 'a strong perception of character and oddity, and a natural power of reproducing in my own person what I observed in others'. Additional disclosures to Forster about the businesslike way in which he set about preparing for an audition which, if it had been held, might have altered the course of English stage history to the detriment of the novel, further emphasize the theatrical components of Dickens's approach to character: the revelation of persons through voice, gesture, and movement (see THEATRE AND THEATRICALITY). Dickens recounts how, for at least three years, he went nightly to the theatre, seeking the best acting and always going to see Charles MATHEWS the elder when he played. He also practised 'immensely (even such things as walking in and out, and sitting down in a chair)', often from four to six hours a day. He shut himself in his room; he walked about in fields; he prescribed for himself a system for learning parts and he learned to impersonate a great number of different characters (Forster 1.4; 5.1).

The role played by the theatre in shaping Dickens's approach to character proved decisive because it fostered his two greatest natural gifts: his exceptionally acute powers of aural and visual observation, which, combined, produced something 'that is possibly unique in the English novel' (Wilson 1960, p. 379). Therefore, it is to the aural and to the visual one turns in an effort to isolate the means by which Dickens endowed his characters with 'life' and made them distinctive.

All of Dickens's most memorable characters define themselves through their speech and a distinctive private language. This method proves well suited to entertaining; it also serves as an effective way to distinguish one person from another in the crowded, panoramic novels typical of Dickens's fiction. Earliest among Dickens's favourite devices

is the speech tag, a particular exclamation, word, or expression made the sole property of a single character. Linguistic eccentricity at this level ranges from Miss Knag's dry 'hem' (*NN*), hangman Dennis's macabre wish 'to work people off' (*BR*), and Mark Tapley's repeated efforts to 'be jolly' (*MC*) in depressing circumstances, to Mr Micawber's 'difficulties' and belief in 'something turning up' and Mrs Micawber's repeated assertions that she 'never will desert Mr Micawber' (*DC*).

The same device also appears in later novels (Wemmick's 'portable property' and Joe Gargery's 'old chap' and 'I say, you know! Pip' in *Great Expectations*) and in a more extended and sophisticated form. Take the opening chapter of the second half of *Little Dorrit*, when eight characters arrive at the convent of the Great Saint Bernard. Dickens carefully avoids calling any one of them by name; he has no need to because the individualizing and typifying language-features of each are already familiar to the reader. Among the travellers we quickly recognize Rigaud's 'Holy blue' (a fictional Anglo-French speech habit, variants of which set apart Mlle Hortense as a foreigner in *Bleak House* and which were used again for French speakers in *A Tale of Two Cities*), Edward ('Tip') Dorrit's affected drawl ('d'ye') and employment of slang terms he imagines fashionable among gentlemen, and his sister Fanny's haughty refinement. Easiest of all to identify is the pompous gentility of William Dorrit, unchanged since his Marshalsea days when he announced: 'I have received—hem—Testimonials in many ways, and of many degrees of value, and they have always been—ha—unfortunately acceptable.'

Characters defined through their speech idiom number among Dickens's greatest triumphs in characterization. From the richly varied idiolects reserved for Sam and Tony Weller, both masters of the short, pithy comparison ('Dumb as a drum vith a hole in it, sir', says Sam when Mr Pickwick asks him to be quiet at the magistrate's court), to the jerky, staccato rhythms of Alfred Jingle's telegraphic speech, Dickens's gift for exploiting distinctive modes of speech took him to heights critics unanimously praise: Mrs Gamp and Mr Pecksniff. To the former belongs what is probably 'the most individual, certainly the most complex idiolect in the whole of Dickens' (Golding 1985, p. 109). Her irregular syntax, 'owldacious' lexical eccentricities, perverse reversals of normal word order, extra syllables, and most idiosyncratic non-standard pronunciations ('roge' for rose, 'parapidge' for parapets) endow her with an energy that tends to overshadow any structural role she plays in the novel. Critics comment on Mrs Nickleby's never-ending orations, Flora Finching's cheerful asides, and the aggressive outbursts fired by Mr F's Aunt (LD) on similar artistic grounds, noting simultaneously how these flowing monologues full of random associations mingled with conscious and half-conscious thoughts anticipate the stream of consciousness narration developed by Joyce and other moderns.

Significantly, in view of the consensus about the failure of some of Dickens's central male characters—Oliver Twist, Nicholas Nickleby, Martin Chuzzlewit, and equally undistinguished figures like Rose Maylie, Little Nell, Mary Graham, and Ruth Pinch— none of these 'straight' representations has an idiolect comparable with his most notable secondary characters. Important exceptions are the distinctive and flexible modes of voice which give depth to the portrayal of David Copperfield. Among the successful devices employed in this novel are the variations in tempo that occur when David slows the narration to present a series of impressions or writes his four 'Retrospective' chapters. Pip, Dickens's other male first-person narrator, illustrates another development: the use of a changing speech idiom to convey alterations in Pip's character as he records his growth and increasing maturity. Elsewhere in the same novel we see, in the depiction of Miss Havisham and Estella, how Dickens abandons speech idioms used as a series of variations on basic, unchanging linguistic grounds for those that suggest subtle modifications. Estella's adult idiom, for example, loses the aggressive coldness she displayed as a child reared by Miss Havisham, while her adopted mother's psychological development is conveyed by similar changes in speech as her harshly insistent imperatives gradually give way to a softened tone and a desperate plea to justify her manipulation of Estella. Her final words, repeated 'innumerable times', 'What have I done! . . . I forgive her!' aptly characterize her alteration.

Verbal exchanges between characters are another technique Dickens uses to imply complexity and inner life, all the more compellingly rendered when they occur in intense, claustrophobic settings. Two examples show pedagogues hoisted by their own petard: Gradgrind in his study questioned by his daughter (HT), when Louisa asks him, 'Father, . . . do you think I love Mr Bounderby?', and Riderhood, the interloper in Bradley Headstone's classroom (OMF), tormenting the schoolmaster with a series of questions of the kind Headstone himself would put. 'Wot's the diwisions of water, my lambs? Wot sorts of water is there on the land?' Riderhood asks, leading the 'lambs' to his grim climax, which he signals by producing the tell-tale bundle of clothes he has fished out of the river.

An almost equally marvellous eye combines with Dickens's genius for speech and helps shape the representations of people who came within the range of the author's unique vision. Mamie Dickens's account of her father's strange behaviour when at work on Hard Times points to the aural and visual aspects of a novelist evidently accustomed to talking rapidly in a low voice and then pulling a variety of faces in the mirror in the course of composing (see COMPOSITION); equally revealing is the metaphor Dickens used to describe how his mind's eye worked. Reporting to W. H. WILLS in September 1858 on the progress of his first provincial PUBLIC READING tour in the north of England, he commented how, walking from Durham to Sunderland, he 'made a little fanciful photograph' in his mind of the Pit Country suitable for use one day. 'I couldn't help looking upon my mind as I was doing it, as a sort of capitally prepared and highly sensitive plate. And I said, without the least conceit (as Watkins [a London photographer] might have said of a plate of his) "it really is a pleasure to work with you, you receive the impression so nicely" ' (24 September 1858).

Photographic impressions, presumably embodiments of accuracy, of course underwent highly imaginative treatment as they were later transformed into art. The comment, however, draws attention to the fact that Dickens saw the things and people he wrote about, that they were visual images that persisted in his mind with the retentiveness of a plate made specially sensitive and then exposed to light. Not surprisingly, visual signals like gesture and movement feature prominently as aids to characterization, second only to the use of distinctive modes of speech. Depicting emotion, temperament, and desire through action proved particularly suited to the *small* gesture to signify depth and passion beneath a surface over which the character tries hard to maintain absolute control. Mr Dombey and Honoraria Dedlock have this trait in common, allowing only occasional glimpses of their feelings when something unexpected catches them off guard. Although the narrator frequently tells us about the coolness of Mr Dombey's apparently frozen heart, the more effective scenes are those in which Dickens uses unspoken gestures to reveal it. Taken aback by his sister's hesitant observation that Paul could not be sent away to the seaside 'without Florence', the narrator brilliantly conveys the intensity of Mr Dombey's agitation, which he subordinates by 'going slowly to the bookcase', unlocking it, and returning with a book to read. ' "Anybody else, Louisa?", he said, without looking up and turning over the leaves' (*DS* 8).

Action or movement as a way of indicating inner feelings plays an equal role in an exchange between Sir Leicester Dedlock and his wife when they return from a visit to Paris, he complacent as he reviews his importance to society, having read his morning's correspondence, and she 'bored'—but not unvigilant, especially having noticed one of Tulkinghorn's 'long effusions'. Calling attention to it, she prompts her husband to reveal the lawyer's enigmatic postscript addressed to herself: 'I have seen him.' She immediately leans forward, looks out of the window, and surprises her husband by announcing that she would like 'to walk a little'. Alighting so quickly, she eludes her husband's ever-present polite hand, only to regain her self-possession within a minute or two, signalled by her willingness to smile, look handsome, take Sir Leicester's arm, lounge with him for a quarter of a mile, and then, very much bored, resume 'her seat in the carriage' (*BH* 12).

Success in scenes like this (Rosa Dartle's impulsive assault on the harp (*DC*), and Jaggers's masterful use of his handkerchief to gain poise (*GE*) are additional examples) indicates another strength of Dickens's characterization. Many of his more subtle effects occur when he probes states of repression, guilt, and fear. In this respect, villains such as Sikes, on the run and tormented by the image of Nancy's upturned eyes as he clubbed her to death, Fagin's mounting fear as the inevitability of his execution grows, or Jonas Chuzzlewit's increasing tension after bludgeoning Montague Tigg to death prove far more interesting than Dickens's bland good characters. Equally compelling are the later portraits of Headstone (*OMF*) and John Jasper (*MED*), murderers whose mental states Dickens conveys with convincing authenticity. Perhaps most notable is the experimental exploration of Jasper's 'scattered consciousness' suggested in his dreams and in the states of disjointed duality that beset him. Here, in this last, unfinished novel, the *doppelgänger* appears less as a GOTHIC and more as a realistic device, successfully integrated into the novel's theme of doubles (Miss Twinkleton's two phases, Durdles drunk and sober, the Landless twins) to suggest a general sense of life splitting up, of things coming apart.

Saintly children like Oliver, Nell, and Florence Dombey, and young women destined for marriage, like Rose Maylie, Ruth Pinch, Mary Graham, and Agnes Wickfield inevitably come in for critical attack, especially when complex villains serve as the benchmark of interest and success. Esther Summerson (*BH*) fared just as badly for many decades until perceptive explorations of her psychology successfully rehabilitated her. Equally faulted and found wanting are mere caricatures of badness, villains with no fullness or depth like Monks (*OT*) and Arthur Gride (*NN*), or aristocratic rakes and would-be seducers like Sir Mulberry Hawk or Lord Verisopht (*NN*), allegorical figures incapable of expansion beyond their one-dimensional names. Out of his social range as Dickens is when portraying members of the aristocracy, characters drawn from this stratum of society lack compelling detail and fail to convince, both in speech and in gesture. Sir Leicester Dedlock remains an exception. His syntax is stiff enough to convey the character's own personality and yet capable of reflecting a becoming dignity and genuine feeling for his wife, complications to his personality which save the portrait from caricature, despite his name.

Also problematic is Dickens's insistence on domestic happiness as a way either to redeem flawed male characters or to reward good ones (see DOMESTICITY). Love thus pressed into service accounts for dissatisfaction with Dickens's endings, doses of idealism many readers refuse. In response, two things deserve comment. Happy endings, or rather endings in which the author concludes the action following a peal of wedding bells, were a fictional convention to which Dickens assented, partly in agreement and partly as a necessity. More remarkable, therefore, are the occasions on which he flouts the historical limitations he accepted so that his books could be read aloud in family circles, and exploits Victorian novelistic censorship to advantage. One consequence of his not being able to write directly about human SEXUALITY is the appearance of female characters whose denial of a sexual self generates interest: women locked in passionless marriages like Edith Dombey, Louisa Bounderby, and Honoria Dedlock, and men and women like Uriah Heep, Rosa Dartle, and Bradley Headstone whose libidinal impulses find expression in forms of self-loathing and sadism. Equally unsettling depths are lightly hinted at in other curious marriages: the malevolent magnetism Quilp exerts over 'pretty . . . obedient, timid loving Mrs Quilp' (*OCS*) and Jonas Chuzzlewit's sinister dominion over Mercy Pecksniff, so 'sadly, strangely altered! So careworn and dejected' after her marriage. Even the 'moral man' Pecksniff, the embodiment of middle-class respectability, has a lascivious nature, one Dickens intimates when Pecksniff drinks too much in the company of Mrs Todgers, and later lays bare when the arch-hypocrite declares his love to Mary Graham.

Fondness for caricature and for presenting figures possessing only a single defining trait number among Dickens's limitations, a cause of unevenness some have disparaged. Objections to this feature, however, should take into account the literary tradition of the panoramic social novel Dickens inherited from SMOLLETT, FIELDING, and Scott, a form that has important links with the picaresque and which demands variety and even abundance. Viewed within this context, the multiplicity of Dickens's characters and his appetite for character-revealing names commands attention on the grounds of inventiveness. Against the

JONSONIAN Blaze and Sparkle (jewellers; *BH*), Sowerberry and Mould (undertakers: *OT*; *MC*), transparently significant names like Count Smorltalk, Dr Nockermorf, Lord Mutanhed, and Lady Snuphanuph (*PP*), and the farcical Americans Martin Chuzzlewit encounters abroad (Choke, Chollop, Hominy, La Fayette Kettle, and Brick), one must set Spottletoe and Sweedlepipe (*MC*) and the host of characters associated with vowels and consonants Dickens favoured. The consonants 'p', 'd' and 'k', and the 'le' ending all attracted him (Perker, Jinks, Wilkins, Wardle, Trundle, Jingle, Bardell), indicative of the delight in eccentric and ingenious sounds Dickens retained throughout his career. Another innovative naming device used to provide a shifting perspective on a single character, and hence to give a greater sense of depth, was the use of different appellations for a single character. Those used to address David Copperfield, for example, run through a variety of permutations from 'David' (Mr Murdstone) and 'Mas'r Davy bor' (Mr Peggotty and Ham) to 'Master Copperfield' (Heep) and even 'Mister Copperfull' (Mrs Crupp).

Assessments of the presentation of characters in Dickens's fiction have varied. Walter BAGEHOT, for example, who listed Dickens's 'power of observation in detail' as one of his 'special excellences' and pronounced 'the store of human detail' in his books 'endless and enormous', nevertheless assigned Dickens's 'exaggerated personifications' of people to 'an altogether lower range of intellectual achievements'. For all their charm, even Dickens's 'best specimens' fell short of depicting 'actual living men'. 'Who could compare the genius, marvellous as must be its fertility, which was needful to create a Falstaff with that shown in the higher productions of the same mind in Hamlet, Ophelia and Lear?' One feels, Bagehot maintained, an instantaneous difference 'between the aggregating incident which makes up from the externalities of life other accidents analogous to itself, and the central idea of a real character' which reveals itself not in 'accidents' but rather unfolds gradually 'in wide spheres of action' (1858).

The emphasis Dickens placed on the 'externalities' of his characters' lives also bothered G. H. LEWES, whose comparison in 1872 of his characters to 'frogs whose brains have been taken out for physiological purposes' signals a significant shift in taste. For Lewes, realism as it applied to characterization meant the ability to foreground change rather than certainty or predictability. 'It is this complexity of the organism which Dickens wholly fails to conceive; his characters have nothing fluctuating and incalculable in them, even when they embody true observations; and very often they are creations so fantastic that one is at a loss to understand how he could, without hallucination, believe them to be like reality'. Mantalini (*NN*), Rosa Dartle, Lady Dedlock, Esther Summerson, Mr Dick (*DC*), Arthur Gride (*NN*), Edith Dombey, and Mr Carker (*DS*) constitute Lewes's shortlist of Dickens's long list of mistakes, 'monstrous failures' on account of their lack of 'fluctuating spontaneity'. Even in Dickens's 'successful figures' Lewes discerned, after study, 'only touches of verisimilitude'.

Henry James added to a rising tide of hostile criticism by posing two influential questions in *The Art of Fiction* (1884): 'What is character but the determination of incident? What is incident but the illustration of character?' The answers James proposed introduced a new aesthetic concept: the interdependence of characters and the texts they inhabit and the assumption that characters should always serve a clear purpose in the plot and contribute to the novel's thematic framework. Acceptance of these proposals meant that many of Dickens's characters became liabilities, excrescences like Quilp, Mrs Gamp, Pecksniff, Mr F's Aunt, and others whose anarchic energy, speech, or actions threaten to detach them from their surrounding structures. Dickens's books, pronounced David Cecil in *Early Victorian Novelists* (1934), 'have no organic unity; they are full of characters who serve no purpose in furthering the plot'.

Such views can be countered in different ways. One option is to exempt Dickens from definitions of realistic fiction that value interiority and character development: Dickens's 'greatest figures' belong to poetry, states T. S. Eliot, 'like figures of Dante or Shakespeare', and betray 'no process or calculation'. Another is to recognize the voice of history in the strictures of James and Cecil and acknowledge their criticisms for what they are: the reformulation of an old preference for a kind of novelistic realism advocated by Dr JOHNSON.

For him, the novel of 'manners' remained an inferior achievement to the novel of 'nature': 'characters of manner', although 'very entertaining', he maintained, are to be seen as the work of 'a more superficial observer than the characters of nature', which required a man to dive into the 'recesses of the human heart'. This distinction serves as the basis for Johnson's memorable assessment of Richardson and Fielding, in whom he saw as great a difference as between 'a man who knew how a watch was made and a man who could tell the hour by looking on the dial plate'. The same idea in more invidious terms recurs in a statement of Johnson's reported by Mrs Thrale, that 'Richardson had picked at the kernel of life . . . while Fielding was contented with the husk'.

Forcing the taxonomy of husks and kernels on characters is about as helpful (and as misleading) as E. M. Forster's far-reaching distinction in his *Aspects of the Novel* (1927) between 'flat' and 'round', terms which are used to suggest that difference in method necessarily means inferiority in artistry. Better, therefore, to accept Dickens's characters on their own terms and to acknowledge the obvious: that while their internal lives are often less scrupulously represented than their external appearance, alternative ways exist to represent the riches and complexities of human personality. How scrutable are human beings? 'The only ways by which we come at any knowledge of what passes in the minds of others', wrote Henry Fielding, 'are their words and actions' (quoted in Miriam Allott, *Novelists on the Novel*, 1959, p. 275). On these 'the wiser part of mankind' chiefly depended as 'the surer and more infallible guide'. Dickens's art of characterization, with his gift for representing externalities, certainly allies him with Fielding, one of his earliest and most important fictional mentors. Yet for all Dickens's emphasis on words and actions and his sympathy with HOGARTH's axiom that faces are indexes to minds, he also shared the artist's warning in his *Analysis of Beauty* (1753) that *fronti nulla fides*, that appearances are not always reliable, that observers can be misled. It is a wonderful fact to reflect on, notes the narrator in *A Tale of Two Cities*, 'that every human creature is constituted to be that profound secret and mystery to every other'. Perhaps this 'solemn consideration' can serve as ground for future reassessments of Dickens's characterization along the lines recently suggested by Brian Rosenberg (1996): 'So much information seems available for apprehension—so many physical particulars, gestures, habits, words—yet, as with people in the world, so little proves to be definitive and unambiguous . . . Characters that seem initially to be thoroughly knowable prove in the end to be as present and absent, definite and indefinite, as shadows.' DHP

Golding (1985).

Greenfield, John R. (ed.), *Dictionary of British Literary Characters: 18th- and 19th-Century Novels* (1993).

Rosenberg, Brian, *Little Dorrit's Shadows: Character and Contradiction in Dickens* (1996).

Santayana, George, 'Dickens', *Soliloquies in England* (1922).

Wilson, Angus, 'Charles Dickens: A Haunting', in Ford and Lane (1960).

**characters—originals.** 'Everyone in writing must speak from points of his experience', Dickens commented to Leigh HUNT, 'and so I of mine with you' (?early November 1854). This explanation accompanies the apology Dickens offered Hunt, who was deeply mortified to find a version of himself paraded in *Bleak House* as Harold Skimpole and easily recognizable to CARLYLE as his neighbour in Cheyne Row, 'an airy, crotchety, most clever copious talker' (Pilgrim 1.341 n.). Dickens continued to explain how fictitious narratives necessarily also depart from reality: when he felt himself going too close to Hunt, his 'original', he wrote, 'I stopped myself, and the most blotted parts of my MS. are those in which I have been striving hard to make the impression I was writing from, *un*like you'.

The qualification Dickens offered as balm to Hunt's wounded feelings contains an important truth about the extent to which Dickens saw his art as a compromise between invention and representation of the world around him. What the letter fails to reveal is the delight Dickens took in his ability to capture people's defining idiosyncrasies as he observed them and reproduced them so as to make some individuals immediately identifiable. Speaking without constraint to another correspondent, Dickens stated of Skimpole as Hunt: 'I suppose he is the most exact portrait that ever was painted in words! . . . It is an

absolute reproduction of a real man' without 'an atom of exaggeration or suppression'. But Dickens did add one key concession: 'Of course I have been careful to keep the outward figure away from the fact' (to the Hon. Mrs Richard Watson, 21 September 1853)—and he *had* suppressed Hunt's intellectual achievement (see Roberts 1996).

'Facts', however, made their way into other characters despite bargains Dickens made with himself to avoid giving offence. Less willing than Hunt to settle for apologies was the diminutive Mrs Jane Seymour Hill, a London manicurist and chiropodist and earlier victim of Dickens's eye for exact detail. When she recognized herself with all her 'personal deformities' as Miss Mowcher in the December 1849 instalment of *David Copperfield*, she engaged a solicitor who informed Dickens that his client would sue for 'the great mental torture and agony' the portrait caused, unless Dickens undertook alterations he proposed on Mrs Hill's behalf (Pilgrim 5.676–7). Three months later, in the thirty-second chapter belonging to the eleventh monthly number, Dickens managed to undo the mischief he had created in the earlier chapter, albeit at the expense of artistic coherence. Beneath her lively manner, he discovers principles, makes Miss Mowcher responsible for the arrest of Littimer, and allows the dwarfish lady to lecture the reader about stature: 'Try not to associate bodily defects with mental, my friend, except for a solid reason.'

The instant recognizability of Mrs Hill has an amusing counterpart in the woman on whom Dickens modelled Mrs Nickleby's distinctive 'scatterbrained gabble': his mother (see DICKENS, ELIZABETH). Opinions differ among his contemporaries as to the resemblance: to Eleanor Christian, who met her in 1841, Mrs Dickens had 'a good stock of common sense, and a matter-of-fact manner'; to Thomas Powell, remembering her in 1888, she was 'incoherent' in her speech and vain about her 'wasp-waist'. To Dickens's incredulity, 'Mrs Nickleby herself [as he referred to his mother] once asked me . . . if I really believed there ever was such a woman' (to John Forster, 27 September 1842).

On rare occasions Dickens felt the pain rather than the real person behind the representation. Such was the case with Mary HOGARTH, whose emotional presence informs

Rose Maylie's sudden illness (*OT* 33) and the death of Little Nell, whose demise wrung Dickens's heart and made 'Old wounds bleed afresh' (to Forster, ?8 January 1841). While maintaining that Nell's 'wanderings' were 'quite imaginary and wholly fictitious', he admitted that the feelings this character's death evoked clearly had their origin in an attachment to his young sister-in-law who died in 1837. 'The grave has closed over a very deep affection and strong love of mine', Dickens confided to Joseph S. Smith on 12 February 1842.

More typically, the 'originals' supply traits and mannerisms Dickens observed which he then reproduced in a character developed from his imagination. Such portraits—composites of people known to Dickens and details drawn from fiction, the theatre, and other sources—frequently appear. The most elaborate, of whom Miss Havisham is a good example, combine details from several prototypes with traits from theatrical and literary characters, adding, in her case, to the complexity of a bitter, inward-looking woman secluded from life after meeting with disappointment in love (see Stone 1979). At the other extreme are minor characters like the mysterious stranger Pip meets at the Three Jolly Bargemen, who holds his head on one side, and keeps one of his eyes half shut, 'as if he were taking aim at something with an invisible gun', a trait Dickens copied from Thomas Henry Buckle, the historian, with whom he occasionally dined. Buckle, Dickens observed, was a man who had read every book that was ever written and was 'a perfect Gulf of information', who delighted in 'closing one eye' and taking aim at you before 'exploding a mine of knowledge' (to Frank Stone, 30 May 1854).

Real names such as Fagin (Bob Fagin was a workmate in WARREN'S BLACKING warehouse) and compelling eccentricities caught Dickens's eye. Mrs Gamp's habit of rubbing her nose along the top of a tall fender, her propensity for snuff, cucumbers, and curious sayings owe their origin to a nurse hired by Miss COUTTS to take charge of 'an invalid very dear to her' (Pilgrim 3.520 n.). The same nurse reappears elsewhere, adding further 'life' to the portrait of the intense and strange Rosa Dartle (*DC*). Inspector Bucket's 'horrible sharpness' and detective brilliance in *Bleak House* was transferred from Charles Frederick FIELD, chief inspector of the Metropolitan detective police, and first fictionalized as 'Wield' in two essays on detectives Dickens contributed to *Household Words* ('A Detective Police Party', *HW* 27 July and 10 August 1850; repr. *Journalism* 2.265–82). Guster and Jo had models based on press reports and were later worked into *Bleak House* via entries in the HOUSEHOLD NARRATIVE. Also in the news were Maria Manning (1821–49), a former lady's maid hanged for murdering her lover, on whom Dickens based Mlle Hortense, and John Sadleir (1814–56), financier and swindler whose suicide provided material for Merdle's death. Other portraits based on specific individuals or representative figures include Mr Micawber, whose ornate flourishes of speech resemble those characteristically delivered by Dickens's father (see DICKENS, JOHN); Mr Fang, the insolent and harsh police-magistrate based on Mr Laing of Hatton Garden (*OT*); and Wackford Squeers, the sadistic schoolmaster of an institution in Yorkshire Dickens had visited in order to obtain material for *Nicholas Nickleby*.

Defending the veracity of Nancy's loyalty to the brutal Sikes, Dickens asserted emphatically in the 1841 Preface to *Oliver Twist*, 'IT IS TRUE'. Exactness, precision, the ability to write convincing dialogue, and a reporter's eye for accuracy account for the frequency with which convincing cases can be made for the many prototypes of Dickens's characters. On occasions, he was happy to admit to them in public (the Preface to *Nickleby* names originals for the Cheerybles); frequently he rejoiced in confidence to friends—'Mr Boythorn is (between ourselves) a most exact portrait of Walter Savage LANDOR' (to the Hon. Mrs Richard Watson, 6 May 1852)—and throughout his career, he remained true to his conviction that art brought together truths which existed and truths which had never been told. Admitting the pleasure he took in Flora Finching, a fictionalized version of Maria BEADNELL Winters when she re-entered his life in 1855, he noted in a letter to the Duke of Devonshire dated 5 July 1856: 'It is a wonderful gratification to find that everybody knows her', testimony to the fact that 'we have all had our Floras (mine is living, and extremely fat).' It 'was a half serious half ridiculous truth' worth recording, he added.                    DHP

Alexander, Doris, *Creating Characters with Dickens* (1991).

Pugh, Edwin, *The Charles Dickens Originals* (1912).

Roberts, Adam, 'Skimpole, Leigh Hunt and Dickens's "Remonstrance"', *Dickensian*, 92 (1996).

**charity and Dickens.** 'There is hardly a woe or a misery', the Revd William Tuckniss wrote in the early 1860s, 'which has not been assuaged or mitigated by benevolent exertions.' England's charitable institutions, Tuckniss went on to say, were the 'highest glory of our land . . . and that which makes it pre-eminently the admiration and envy of all other countries' (Henry Mayhew, *London Labour and the London Poor*, vol. 4, 1861–2, p. xvii). Dickens's views of organized charity were more complex and less complacent, and they reflected his differing responses to the many different forms of charitable activity—activity with a wide range of purposes, motivations, social theories, and attitudes toward their intended recipients. Some charities were designed simply to alleviate poverty and other forms of suffering, whether temporary or long-term; others sought 'improvement' through EDUCATION, or through assistance conceived as 'help toward doing without help'; still others sought to 'rescue' the poor from MORAL failure, usually through RELIGIOUS instruction or through causes like the temperance movement (see DRINK AND TEMPERANCE). Finally, there was the hope of saving souls at home and abroad—most often through conversion to EVANGELICAL Christianity. Thus, while Victorian England could rightly claim an unparalleled array of philanthropic agencies—extraordinary for their scale, scope, and zeal—Dickens regarded a lot of charitable activity as misguided, ineffectual, and self-serving. Indeed, he was as shrewd a critic of organized charity as he was a sincere proponent of Cheeryble-style benevolence. Moreover, his views were informed by a considerable amount of direct observation, arising from his own involvement in a wide range of philanthropic causes—a 'grind of charitable business', as Humphry HOUSE put it, that 'would be astounding in any man', and was 'scarcely credible in the greatest English creative genius of his time' (*All in Due Time*, 1955, p. 235).

Dickens found aspects of this grind tiresome. 'For a good many years I have suffered a great deal from charities, but never anything like what I suffer now', Dickens wrote to Edmund YATES in 1858: 'The amount of correspondence they inflict upon me is really incredible. But this is nothing. Benevolent men get behind the piers of the gates, lying in wait for my going out . . . Benevolent bullies drive up in hansom cabs . . . and stay long at the door . . . My man has been heard to say (at The Burton Arms) "that if it wos a wicious place, well and good—that an't door work; but that wen all the Christian wirtues is always a-shoulderin' and a-helberin' on you in the 'all, a-tryin' to git past you and cut upstairs into Master's room, wy no wages as you couldn't name wouldn't make it up to you" ' (28 April 1858).

Part of this unwanted attention was inevitable for a public figure long associated with sympathy for the poor, but part of it was a result of Dickens's own charitable commitments. By Victorian standards, his charitable donations were not extraordinary. Charitable giving, after all, was often seen as a quasi-civic duty for prosperous members of the middle and upper classes, whose collective support of philanthropic undertakings far outweighed in monetary value, for example, the relief provided under the POOR LAW. The amount of time that Dickens devoted to charitable causes, however, was truly extraordinary. His most sustained philanthropic project was managing URANIA COTTAGE, the 'home for homeless women' that he had planned and set up on behalf of Angela Burdett COUTTS. In addition to this, Dickens acted as Miss Coutts's almoner from the early 1840s through the late 1850s, supplying her with advice about a host of philanthropic projects, ranging from individual assistance for people in need to the large model housing development that Miss Coutts built in Bethnal Green. (He also defended Miss Coutts from begging-letter writers, one of the banes of the charitable world.)

On his own initiative, Dickens provided support for many other Victorian philanthropies. Through SPEECHES, PUBLIC READINGS, subscriptions, and reform-minded journalism, he provided help for mechanics' institutes, adult education, soup kitchens, emigration schemes, health and sanitary bodies, model dwellings associations, prison reform, recreational societies, and thirteen separate hospitals and sanatoriums. He was an early friend of the Ragged Schools (discussed more fully later in this entry), and the schools quickly claimed him as an important ally. He was active in efforts to provide relief and pensions for disabled or retired actors, writers, artists, and their families—serving as a trustee of the ROYAL GENERAL THEATRICAL FUND, as an officer of the GUILD OF LITERATURE AND ART, and as chairman at anniversary meetings of both the Artists' Benevolent Fund and the Artists' General Benevolent Fund. His banking records show that he made at least 43 donations to benevolent and provident funds. And he agreed to be listed as an officer of such diverse voluntary bodies as the Metropolitan Drapers' Association, the Poor Man's Guardian Society, the Birmingham and Midland Institute, the Metropolitan Sanitary Association, the Orphan Working School, the Metropolitan Improvement Association, the Royal Hospital for Incurables, the Hospital for Sick Children, and the Newsvendors' Provident and Benevolent Institution.

Dickens was also generous outside the framework of established charities. When the actor Edward Elton died in 1843, Dickens chaired a committee to establish a fund for Elton's seven orphaned children. After Douglas JERROLD's death in 1857, Dickens organized a relief fund for the Jerrold family, for which he helped raise money through charitable readings and by performing in AMATEUR THEATRICALS. And these were not isolated cases, as shown by Dickens's kindnesses to the working-class writer John Overs, to Bertha White and her family, to John Poole, and to others less well known. Even Dickens's friends were sometimes astonished by his charitable zeal. Percy FITZGERALD found Dickens's 'well-organized *system*' of giving to the poor 'truly extraordinary', and 'without parallel in the case of any great writer' (*Memories of Charles Dickens*, 1913, pp. 178–9).

There is evidence to support this view in a broader context. 'He had already learned', G. H. LEWES recalled of Dickens's very early career, 'to look upon the world as a scene where it was the duty of each man in his own way to make the lot of the miserable Many a little less miserable.' In 1839 W. C. MACREADY offered a toast to Dickens 'as one who had

made the amelioration of his fellow-men the object of all his labours—and whose characteristic was philanthropy'. Dickens's most remarkable characteristic, Henrietta Ward recalled, 'was, undoubtedly, his extreme sympathy'. Thomas Adolphus Trollope thought that Dickens 'made a nearer approach to obeying the divine precept, "Love thy neighbour as thyself", than one man in a hundred thousand. His benevolence, his active, energising desire for good to all God's creatures, and restless anxiety to be in some way active for the achieving of it, were unceasing and busy in his heart ever and always' (Collins 1981, 1.26, 29, 73; 2.339).

Recollective testimony must be used with caution, but observers more remote from Dickens came to similar conclusions. Lord Shaftesbury, the greatest philanthropist of the age, saw Dickens as 'a phenomenon, an exception, a special production . . . God gave him . . . a general retainer against all suffering and oppression'. In a passage omitted by his biographer, however, Shaftesbury went on to comment, 'And yet, strange to say, he never gave me a helping hand—at least, I never heard of it' (Collins 1971, pp. 567–8).

Shaftesbury's private judgement is revealing. It points above all else to the gulf between evangelical and non-evangelical motivations in charitable work, but it also recalls the offence that Dickens gave to Gospel Christians. Dickens invariably recoiled from all repressive forms of puritanism, which made him, for example, an outspoken critic of SABBATARIANISM, a cause very dear to many serious Christians. But he also gave offence by his caricatures of religious enthusiasm. Indeed, in the eyes of 'vital Christians', conversion was essential for salvation. MISSIONARY hopes thus coloured a great many philanthropies, whether explicitly religious or not, and provided the backdrop for the predominantly evangelical ethos of Victorian charity. In Dickens's eyes, however, missionaries were 'perfect nuisances', who 'leave every place worse than they found it' (30 November 1865). He was particularly dismayed by overseas missionary work—work regarded by many as the leading philanthropic cause of the era.

Dickens first satirized the overseas missionary projects associated with Exeter Hall—the celebrated meeting hall in the Strand used for the annual meetings of all the major evangelical societies—in his 1835 sketch 'The Ladies' Societies' (*SB*), and he returned to the theme in *Pickwick Papers* (through the enthusiasms of the drunken deputy shepherd Stiggins and the citizens of Muggleton). Just over a decade later, Dickens bluntly declared in the EXAMINER that 'It might be laid down as a very good general rule of social and political guidance, that whatever Exeter Hall champions, is the thing by no means to be done' (*Journalism*, 2.108–26). This expostulation referred to the evangelical motivations behind the Niger expedition of 1841, an ill-advised and costly episode that formed part of the inspiration for Mrs Jellyby's later devotion to the improvement of Borrioboola-Gha, 'on the left bank of the Niger', in *Bleak House*. Although Dickens probably modelled Mrs Jellyby's domestic habits on Caroline Chisholm (whose Family Colonisation Loan Society he warmly praised), the folly of Borrioboola-Gha was intended as a comment on what Dickens and PUNCH both labelled 'telescopic philanthropy'.

Dickens made the point elsewhere in *Bleak House* by having the homeless orphan Jo sit to eat his crust of bread on the steps of the Society for the Propagation of the Gospel in Foreign Parts. When a clergyman connected with the London City Mission objected to this passage, Dickens argued forcibly that home missions and foreign missions were not conducted on an equal basis, and 'that the home claim is by far the stronger and more pressing of the two' (9 July 1852). Dickens's point was a good one: in 1847, for example, the three largest foreign missionary societies all enjoyed incomes in excess of £100,000, whereas the London City Mission, the best-known domestic missionary agency, had an income of only slightly over £14,000.

Dickens commended the London City Mission for some of its work in London slums (particularly in *Household Words*), and in 1860 he gave cautious praise to a theatre service at the Britannia in Hoxton, which was part of an evangelically sponsored series of services intended to reach out to the poor in their own environs (reprinted as 'Two Views of a Cheap Theatre', *UT*). At home or abroad, however, religious labours that smacked of hypocrisy or self-gratification were sure to arouse Dickens's anger—as shown most memorably by Chadband, the oily, canting

religionist in *Bleak House*. Without links to any particular church or chapel, Chadband invoked, in an implicitly nonconformist vein, the lower-middle-class and upper-working-class world of domestic missionary enterprise, both paid and voluntary. Like his spiritual predecessors Stiggins in *Pickwick* and Melchisedech Howler in *Dombey and Son*, Chadband trades in religious forms and professions strictly for his own benefit. And like Stiggins and Howler, he offended evangelical DISSENTERS. According to a review of *Bleak House* in the nonconformist *Eclectic Review*, 'There is an evident attempt to bring odium on the pastors of the *underprivileged* sects, and on the enterprises of world-wide philanthropy which form one of the chief glories of the age in which we live' (December 1853).

Mrs Pardiggle, again in *Bleak House*, shows that Dickens's objections to offensive and self-serving philanthropy were by no means confined to dissenters. Clearly an Anglican, Mrs Pardiggle is distinguished by her 'rapacious benevolence' and her self-appointed role as an 'inexorable moral policeman'—intrusive bullying that shows how far removed she is from any genuine sympathy and understanding for the poor. 'I am a School lady, I am a Visiting lady, I am a Reading lady, I am a Distributing lady; I am on the local Linen Box Committee, and many general committees; and my canvassing alone is very extensive', Mrs Pardiggle tells Esther and Ada, in her characteristic manner (*BH* 8). Though Dickens gave Mrs Pardiggle several traits associated with Puseyism (her children are named after saints of the early English church and she has an enthusiasm for matins), the charitable activities to which she lays claim are predominantly the products of evangelical zeal, and Dickens clearly intended her to ridicule abuses that extended throughout the charitable world. The same may be said for Honeythunder, the bullying professional philanthropist employed by the Haven of Philanthropy in *The Mystery of Edwin Drood*. The metaphor used to describe Honeythunder is professional boxing—diametrically opposed to what Dickens took to be the true spirit of charity.

Dickens was also an effective critic of two other aspects of Victorian philanthropy: 'ticket charity', which placed patronage in the hands of individual donors and led to arbitrary and unsystematic relief, and snobbery, which elicited charitable support for purely social reasons. Under the ticket system, common among Victorian charities, subscribers were given tickets in return for their support; they then gave the tickets to needy applicants, who in turn converted the tickets into assistance from the charity. This system was defended for its allegedly beneficial effects on donors, as well as for its effectiveness in distinguishing between the deserving and undeserving poor, but Dickens thought the system unnecessarily degrading for recipients and ultimately detrimental (as he argued forcibly, for example, in the case of the Governesses' Benevolent Institution).

Dickens was also quick to perceive (and condemn) the role of philanthropy in confirming genteel social status. 'There were men there—your City aristocracy', Dickens wrote of a hospital dinner in 1843, 'who made such speeches, and expressed such sentiments, as any moderately intelligent dustman would have blushed through his cindery bloom to have thought of. Sleek, slobbering, bow-paunched, overfed, apoplectic, snorting cattle—and the auditory leaping up in their delight! I never saw such an illustration of the Power of Purse, or felt so degraded and debased by its contemplation' (3 May 1843). The snobbery of fashionable subscription lists, noisy committee work, and annual dinners continued to dismay him, as *Our Mutual Friend* (1.17) makes clear—though of course he had to put up with a great deal of this. But as *Bleak House* shows (through Mrs Jellyby, Mrs Pardiggle, and Miss Wisk), Dickens also objected to what he saw as the self-important and narrow-minded world of ladies' auxiliaries, ladies' committees, and ladies' missions. This attitude, however, may strike modern readers differently from Dickens's objections to the snobbish and patronizing aspects of charitable work. Women performed charitable work of enormous value, and philanthropic activity opened up many important channels for women to act independently outside the home.

Dickens's attitude toward the Ragged Schools can serve as a final, more extended example of his response to organized charity. His reaction to the schools clearly illustrates not only the kind of charitable work that he found hopeful and urgent, but also what he took to be the limitations of approaching important issues of social reform within an exclusively voluntary and philanthropic context.

Ragged Schools were set up, as Dickens explained in a letter to the DAILY NEWS in 1846, to provide rudimentary instruction to 'the most miserable and neglected outcasts in London . . . to commence their recognition as immortal human creatures, before the Gaol Chaplain becomes their only schoolmaster' (4 February 1846). The Ragged School idea had roots in the Sunday School movement, although the supporters of the schools usually traced their efforts to a neighbourhood school set up in 1818 by the Portsmouth cobbler John Pounds. The idea began to attract wider support in the 1830s and early 1840s; in London, for example, early schools were established in places like the 'Devil's Acre' in Westminster and Field Lane in Saffron Hill by agents of the London City Mission, itself formed in 1835. In 1843, both Dickens and Shaftesbury became interested in Ragged School labours through the work of the Field Lane School. In 1844 the Ragged School Union was formed to give coherence and direction to London Ragged Schools, and Shaftesbury became the society's first president. Evangelical and non-denominational in character, the RSU proved highly successful: from around 20 schools in 1845, the society grew to include nearly 200 schools and refuges by 1870, the year of the Education Act (with enrollment growing to almost 37,000 day, evening, and industrial students, and almost 30,000 Sunday students).

In September 1843 Dickens visited the Field Lane School on behalf of Miss Coutts. 'In the prodigious misery and ignorance of the swarming masses of mankind in England', he wrote, 'the seeds of its certain ruin are sown.' 'Whether this effort will succeed', he added of the school, 'it is quite impossible to say. But that [the effort] is a great one, beginning at the right end, among thousands of immortal creatures, who cannot, in their present state, be held accountable for what they do, it is as impossible to doubt' (to Angela Burdett Coutts, 16 September 1843).

Though Dickens failed to write an article dealing with the schools that he had immediately proposed to the *Edinburgh Review*, he was clearly impressed by the schools and willing to assist them. He certainly encouraged Miss Coutts's support. He also tried to interest the government in providing an annual grant, in 1843 and again in 1846. His most important early contribution, however, was his signed letter to the *Daily News* in 1846. As the reformer and Ragged School advocate Mary Carpenter noted, 'The struggling efforts of a few individuals were brought into a striking and brilliant light by the magic pen of Charles Dickens who, by none of his writings, has reflected more true honour on himself, than by those simple but touching columns in the *Daily News*' (*Ragged Schools*, 1850, p. 4).

Dickens continued to have contact with the schools, often to consider candidates for Urania Cottage. He also continued his support. His 22 April 1848 *Examiner* article 'Ignorance in Crime', for example, argued for industrial education. His outcry about neglected and abandoned children in *The* HAUNTED MAN (1848) was reproduced at least seven times in Ragged School and reformatory literature by 1853. *Household Words* gave Dickens many further opportunities to support preventive education, particularly in the early and mid 1850s, when the journal ran a number of articles on Ragged Schools, industrial schools, ragged dormitories, emigration schemes, reformatory programmes, and initiatives such as the Ragged School Shoeblack Society. The most important of these was Dickens's own article, 'A Sleep to Startle Us' (*HW* 13 March 1852). Describing a visit to the Field Lane School to inspect a new dormitory, Dickens concluded with a strongly worded appeal for government support of Ragged Schools. Finally, Dickens's banking records show that he made donations to the schools in 1848, 1849, and 1853.

There are many reasons for Dickens's early enthusiasm for Ragged Schools. The schools were genuinely pioneering, and helped to bring an urgent social problem to light; they were based on the belief that prevention was better (and cheaper) than cure; they advanced a kind of practical environmentalism; they charged no fees; they developed a range of associated relief schemes (including dormitories and refuges, industrial-training programmes, clothing and sick funds, savings banks, EMIGRATION plans, and LIBRARIES and reading rooms); they were operated with little pomp and fanfare; they were firmly non-denominational; and they were intended to help children become better able to help themselves.

But Dickens also found much to criticize, and his criticisms are equally revealing. Whereas the Ragged Schools remained predominantly voluntarist, Dickens came increasingly to favour more powerful state solutions to the problems of juvenile ignorance and crime. He thus viewed the schools as an initial step, not as a permanent solution. Moreover, he was increasingly frustrated by the strongly evangelical character of the work. From the outset, he felt Ragged School education presented too many religious mysteries. Despite their good intentions, Ragged School teachers struck him as 'narrow-minded and odd' (12 August 1850); and the schools themselves rarely seemed 'free from injudicious and mistaken teaching' (*HW* 11 September 1852). These criticisms (and others) are familiar from Dickens's comic description of a ragged school in *Our Mutual Friend* (2.1), which provides almost no evidence of his early interest in the schools.

This comic account of a Ragged School underlines a final point. Dickens's fictional depictions of organized charity were almost always intended to attack abuses. There are exceptions—as, for example, the favourable treatment given to the Hospital for Sick Children (Great Ormond Street) in *Our Mutual Friend*. To understand Dickens's full view of Victorian philanthropy, however, readers need to go beyond the novels to Dickens's speeches, letters, and journalism, and to his direct involvement in a wide range of charitable endeavours.     NP

House (1941).

Pope (1978).

Prochaska, F. K., 'Philanthropy', in F. M. L. Thompson (ed.), *The Cambridge Social History of Britain, 1750–1950*, vol. 3 (1990).

**Charles Dickens Museum**. See DICKENS HOUSE MUSEUM.

**Chartism,** a political movement, largely supported by working people, which advocated radical democratic change in the political system (see CLASS; ELECTIONS). It was active between 1838 and 1848 and took its name from the People's Charter with six points: universal manhood suffrage; equal electoral districts; vote by secret ballot; payment of MPs; no property qualification for MPs; annual parliaments.

Dickens's radical political beliefs might have inclined him to support the objectives of Chartism, but he was no disciple. Chartism was included in the extravagantly ironic list of outrages he threatened when, Quilp-like, he assumed a passion for Queen Victoria on the eve of her marriage to Albert: 'The presence of my wife aggravates me. I loathe my parents. I begin to have thoughts of the Serpentine, of the regent's canal, of the razors upstairs, of the chemist's down the street . . . of turning Chartist [or] of heading some bloody assault on the palace and saving Her by my single hand' (to Forster, 12 February 1840). Dickens's letter followed extensive press coverage of trials of Chartists involved in the so-called Newport Rising of 1839 and other unrest. After the first Chartist Convention and the failure of the petition to Parliament, the political initiative within the movement passed to those who advocated (though they rarely practised) violence as the only means of obtaining their objectives. Dickens's horror of political violence was inveterate and probably instinctive. His sympathies for the working-classes were much more with their social disadvantages than with their political aspirations. He wanted FACTORY reform and a repeal of the hated new POOR LAW while the Chartist petition was concerned exclusively with political objectives. Thus, though extracts from *Nicholas Nickleby* might find their way into the Chartist *Penny Gazette of Variety and Amusement* (Ackroyd 1990, p. 326), it should not be inferred that Dickens was a Chartist sympathizer. Some of his friends were enrolled as special constables in London during the Chartist National Convention of April 1848, and he addressed some sardonic words to the prison governor who would shortly have charge of the leading Chartist, Ernest Jones (to Augustus Tracey, 8 April 1848). After a failed mass demonstration of Chartists that spring, he wrote an article attacking 'gross and palpable' misinformation from the Bench in the trials that followed, but added, 'It is unnecessary for us to observe that we have not the least sympathy with physical-force chartism in the abstract, or with the tried and convicted physical-force chartists in

particular' ('Judicial Special Pleading', *Examiner*, 23 December 1848; repr. *Journalism* 2.137–42).

*The Old Curiosity Shop* first appeared in 1840, during a brief lull in Chartist activity. Nell's journey takes her through 'a long suburb of red brick houses . . . where coal dust and factory smoke darkened the shrinking leaves' and 'struggling vegetation sickened and sank under the hot breath of kiln and furnace'. Dickens's sympathy for those who live in 'this mournful place' is evident, but his account of a Chartist torchlight parade is lurid, attacking those who urged on 'bands of unemployed labourers . . . to frightful cries and threats . . . Maddened men, armed with sword and firebrand, spurning the tears and prayers of women who would restrain them, rushed forth on errands of terror and destruction, to work no ruin half so surely as their own' (*OCS* 45). Later, Dickens much admired Elizabeth GASKELL's *Mary Barton* (1848) for its similarly sympathetic account of the sufferings of working people and its explanation of why workers were attracted to Chartism.

In *Barnaby Rudge* (1841) Dickens's account of the Gordon riots draws implicit parallels between historical and contemporary events. Like Chartist agitators, the anti-Catholic London mob runs amok. 'The disturbance had attained to such a formidable height, and the rioters had grown, with impunity, to be so audacious, that the sight of this great force, continually augmented by new arrivals, instead of operating as a check, stimulated them to outrages of greater hardihood than any they had yet committed; and helped kindle a flame in London, the like of which had never been beheld' (*BR* 63). Dickens's message was always one of social reform peacably achieved, not political change extorted under threat.                                          EJE

**Chesterton, G. K.** (1874–1936), considered by many Dickensians to be the finest of all Dickens critics. He first wrote on Dickens in *The Bookman* (1900, 1903) and published a full-length study, *Charles Dickens*, in 1906. This was in part a response to GISSING, whose 1898 study had, in Chesterton's view, over-emphasized the darker side of Dickens's work. Chesterton sets out to celebrate in his own exuberant style Dickens's supreme comic artistry and fecundity, and his glorification of the common man, most notably in the figure of Sam Weller. Despite occasional lapses into questionable assertions or a facile jokiness, Chesterton brilliantly succeeds in conveying the unique flavour of Dickens's art and offers many penetrating insights into the workings of his imagination. Between 1907 and 1909 he wrote individual prefaces for each of Dickens's books as they were reprinted by J. M. Dent in his Everyman's Library. These prefaces, collected under the title *Appreciations and Criticisms of the Works of Charles Dickens* in 1911 (reprinted 1933 with the first two nouns of the title reversed), naturally contain more detailed comment on individual novels than the 1906 book, and some of Chesterton's most interesting and stimulating discussion of Dickens's work can be found here, such as his fine analysis of the centripetal structure of *Bleak House*. In *The Victorian Age in Literature* (1913) Chesterton featured Dickens prominently, defining his as 'that most exquisite of arts ... the art of enjoying everybody', and for the rest of his career he continued to champion Dickens as a supremely great artist in a period when most academic critics regarded his achievement with indifference or downright disdain. T. S. Eliot declared (1932), 'There is no better critic of Dickens living than Mr Chesterton', and many distinguished later Dickens scholars and biographers, such as Sylvère Monod and Peter Ackroyd, have echoed such praise.                 MS

Chesterton on Dickens, ed. Alzina Stone Dale (vol. 15 of The Collected Works of . . . Chesterton, 1989).

Chesterton on Dickens, ed. M. Slater (1992).

The Chesterton Review, 11.4 (special Dickens number) (1985).

**childhood.** In 1863 a writer in one of the more popular Victorian magazines asked the rhetorical question: 'Is not our own time distinguished from all that have preceded it by the intensity of its interests in and regard for children?' Victorian literature, painting, and photography all bear witness to the fascination with childhood in this period. There is no doubting the intensity of this interest, but the reasons for it are complicated and elusive. The idea of childhood in Victorian culture is a knot of contradictory attitudes. The children in Dickens's novels, in all their vivid range and variety of types, reflect both the

cultural complexities inherent in the contemporary view of childhood as well as the effects on Dickens of his own troubled childhood experiences. We need to understand something of the cultural and historical status of childhood in this period as well as the nature of Dickens's perception of his own childhood in order to appreciate the kind of fictional children he created and the purposes they served in the larger design of those novels.

Walter Houghton, in *The Victorian Frame of Mind*, observed that 'Rousseau and Wesley can be thought of as the immediate fountainheads of the two great streams of Victorian MORALITY'. This is a useful pointer to what might be thought of as one of the primary complications in Victorian attitudes to the child: childhood viewed as a condition of innate depravity, and childhood as a period of natural innocence and purity. From Rousseau, and particularly from his influential treatise *Émile*, came, in popularized form, the view that the child possessed a natural integrity and moral nobility and that from its earliest days it was prey to the corrupting influence of civilization with its unnatural restraints and enervating luxuries. The system of 'negative EDUCATION' outlined in *Émile* was a prescription for allowing the child to learn by experience, by being allowed to develop his natural curiosity, rather than by formal instruction and indoctrination—'the art of controlling without precepts' (Book 2). Under this scheme as much attention was paid to physical recreation as to intellectual development. The premiss for this form of education was as follows: 'Let us lay it down as an incontrovertible rule that the first impulses of nature are always right; there is no original sin in the human heart, the how and the why of the entrance of every vice can be traced' (ibid.).

The reference to 'original sin' points to what Houghton considered the other 'fountainhead' of Victorian morality, Wesley and the Puritan revival. Under the harsher forms of this puritanism, the belief that the child was innately sinful (having helplessly inherited man's fallen condition) was accompanied by a conviction that the child should be brought up under an austere, unremitting discipline. Mr Murdstone's brutal treatment of the child David Copperfield is justified under such a regime: 'the gloomy theology of the Murdstones made all children out to be a swarm of little vipers' (*DC* 4). Arthur Clennam, in *Little Dorrit*, is a man whose will was systematically broken during the wretched childhood he lived out under his supposed mother's fanatical Calvinism. The child Pip in *Great Expectations* is made the subject of philosophical speculations by the pompous, selfish adults at the Gargery dinner-table: ' "Why is it that the young are never grateful?" This moral mystery seemed too much for the company until Mr Hubble tersely solved it by saying, "Naterally wicious". Everybody then murmured "True!" ' (*GE* 4).

The natural vice that children were allegedly born into was diametrically opposed to the natural innocence argued by Rousseau and celebrated by the British Romantic poets Blake, WORDSWORTH, and COLERIDGE in particular. Mr Hubble's 'Naterally wicious', issued as a kind of crude reflex verdict at the Gargery dinner party, suggests how ingrained such views had become. But equally conventional as an automatic response was the Wordsworthian formula: 'The Child is father of the Man.' Writing in Dickens's magazine *Household Words* in 1853, G. A. SALA remarks, 'as regards the child being father to the man: of men being but children of a larger growth . . . These are both very easy things to say; and we get them by heart pat, and somewhat in a parrot manner; and we go on repeating our pet phrase over and over . . . till we firmly believe it to be true'. So in their different ways both the Wesleyan and the Rousseauesque-Romantic views on the nature of childhood had by Dickens's time become popular clichés. These contradictory valuations constituted Dickens's ideological heritage in terms of his attitudes to childhood. Dickens is held to be the Victorian champion of the Rousseauesque-Romantic idealization of childhood, and there is plenty of evidence for this. For instance, one of his favourite poems was Wordsworth's 'We are Seven', which pits obstinate adult matter-of-factness against the equally obstinate, whimsically imaginative creeds of childhood. But he could also be caustic about its more sentimental manifestations, as in the case of Charlie Hexam's school in *Our Mutual Friend*, where 'the place was pervaded by a grimly ludicrous pretence that every pupil was childish and innocent'.

The education of children in the Victorian period was subject to further contradictions. *Hard Times* is the classic dramatization of apparently incompatible views on what was best for children in educational terms. Should they be taught knowledge in a regimented fashion so as to instil an intellectual sophistication and ensure that they would function efficiently as citizens and employees; or should they be allowed to follow their imaginative impulses and learn as their curiosity led them? Either view could be argued as being in the best interests of the child, but it was the former which was increasingly seen as of value to the nation and its empire. 'Don't you feel how naughty it is of you . . . to be a wax-work child, when you might have the proud consciousness of assisting . . . the manufactures of your country; of improving your mind by the constant contemplation of the steam-engine?' demands Miss Monflathers of Little Nell (*OCS* 31). Dickens is best known as the champion of Fancy in this debate, as the collapse of Mr Gradgrind's world in *Hard Times* makes clear. In private he was rather more lenient towards Gradgrind's ideals than that fable suggests: 'I often say to Mr Gradgrind that there is reason and good intention in much that he does . . . but that he over-does it. Perhaps by dint of his going his way and my going mine, we shall meet at last at some halfway house where there are flowers on the carpets and a little standing-room for Queen Mab's Chariot among the Steam Engines' (to Henry Cole, 17 June 1854). The point is that he felt the balance had swung too far towards UTILITARIAN priorities in the education of children, as he confided to Angela Burdett COUTTS: 'It would be a great thing for all of us, if more who are powerfully concerned with Education, thought as you do, of the imaginative faculty' (6 September 1850).

The dilemma between utilitarian and Romantic principles in the education of children was reflected in the CHILDREN'S LITERATURE produced in the early Victorian period. The moral-didactic tale, designed to sweeten the pill of knowledge or moral instruction by administering it in the form of an engaging story, flourished side by side with FAIRY TALES and a new kind of literature for children dedicated purely to entertaining the imagination. Dickens spoke out loudly, not only in his

# childhood

novels and stories but also in his journalism, for the protection and encouragement of fairy literature and romantic tales for children. He was indignant about the practice of appropriating fairy stories for moral-didactic purposes, as for example when George CRUIKSHANK rewrote *Cinderella* as a temperance tract. In response to this Dickens wrote an article in *Household Words*, 'Frauds on the Fairies', in which he made some of his most eloquent general remarks on childhood and its literature. According to him, fairy stories were 'nurseries of fancy', from which children might learn 'forbearance, courtesy, consideration for the poor and aged, kind treatment of animals, the love of nature, abhorrence of tyranny and brute force'. In other words, left in their pristine condition, fairy literature and romantic tales had a profound morally educative influence on the growing child; and this in turn would contribute to the cultural health of the nation: 'a nation without fancy, without some romance, never did, never can, never will, hold a great place under the sun.' The determination to sustain into adult life a childlike capacity for wonder and fancy is, in Dickens, expressed in his urging us not to outgrow childhood in certain important respects. 'Where We Stopped Growing' is the title of one of his most attractive essays for *Household Words*, and it almost offers a prescription for remodelling the adult into a species of grown-up child.

Dickens often uses the naive, spontaneously generous and affectionate child as an agent of resistance to the materialistic, utilitarian, and emotionally reticent culture of his day. He endows the child with an invincible purity—Oliver Twist and Dick (*OT* 7), Little Nell—or with an imperviousness to the more rebarbative values of the age; for example, the 'old-fashioned' Paul Dombey, who instinctively resists the harsh competitiveness and dismal cash-nexus basis on which his merchant father has built his own identity. Victorian fiction is crowded with such 'old-fashioned' children, and Dickens was credited with having inaugurated the use of the term. A writer in the 1890s affectionately reviewed some of the more prominent 'old-fashioned' children in Victorian fiction, including Paul, David Copperfield, Lewis Carroll's Alice, and little Lord Fauntleroy, and noted the characteristic as a peculiarly modern one (Frederick

Adye, 'Old Fashioned Children', *Macmillan's Magazine*, 68, 1893).

In what could be seen as a symptom of the age's disagreements about the proper institutional care for children, Dickens's fiction parades before us a wide variety of educational establishments, from the sadistic regimes of Dotheboys Hall and Salem House, through Blimber's forcing academy for young gentlemen and the school run by Gradgrind, to the benign paternalism of Dr Strong's school and Mr Marton's village school in *The Old Curiosity Shop*. The Ragged School movement, the corrective schools for young offenders, and the 'Schools of Industry' attracted Dickens's interest as places where the juvenile poor and outcast could be given rudimentary education. The Ragged Schools depended on voluntary help, often through church sponsorship, and for Dickens this sometimes meant a curriculum that was insufficiently secular, 'presenting too many religious mysteries and difficulties, to minds not sufficiently prepared for their reception'. His sensitivity to making history and scripture knowledge more accessible to children prompted him to produce his CHILD'S HISTORY OF ENGLAND and The LIFE OF OUR LORD for his own children.

Dickens's childhood experience in the WARREN'S BLACKING warehouse made him feel that his own childhood had come to an abrupt end and that he had been prematurely exposed to adult responsibilities and independence. This undoubtedly made him especially sensitive to the neglect and exploitation of children in Victorian England. In the 1830s and 1840s the issue of PUBLIC HEALTH was given prominence and was accompanied by reformist legislation which particularly concerned the condition of working children. An act of 1842 forbade the employment in mines of children under the age of 10. In 1847 a FACTORY ACT limited the working hours for children in textile factories to ten. The infant children of hard-pressed working families were left for the working day in care, if they were lucky. Otherwise they might be left alone all day, heavily sedated by near-lethal compounds of gin and opium, so as to allow the rest of the family to work their long hours. Dickens's *A Christmas Carol* germinated from his response to reading about such conditions in the report of a Parliamentary committee set up to enquire into the working circumstances of the poor. He thought initially of issuing a pamphlet 'Appeal on Behalf of the Poor Man's Child', but changed his mind in favour of a Christmas story of redemption: a hard-hearted man, who has deliberately forgotten what it was like to be a child, undergoes a change of heart (partly by being shown scenes of his own boyhood) and becomes a second father to his clerk's poor crippled child, Tiny Tim. The *Carol* also features, perhaps as a survival of that pamphlet idea, two emblematic children, Ignorance and Want: 'Yellow, meagre, ragged, scowling, wolfish; but prostrate, too, in their humility.' Another such child, equally appalling, appears in *The* HAUNTED MAN: 'A baby savage, a young monster, a child who had never been a child.'

Dickens, like many of the more liberalminded Victorians, feared for the consequences of social neglect, especially where it affected children. He supported a number of the growing institutions for the care of abandoned children, notably Coram's Foundling Hospital in London. His own childhood experiences reinforced his concern for these social victims, with whose predicament he was able to identify: 'the deep remembrance of the sense I had of being utterly neglected and hopeless [during the blacking factory months] ... but for the mercy of God, I might easily have been, for any care that was taken of me, a little robber or a little vagabond' (Forster 1.2). He later fictionalized these alternative futures in the fortunes of Oliver Twist and the Artful Dodger, with Oliver as the child's version of 'the principle of Good surviving every adverse circumstance', and the Dodger as the roistering, delinquent offspring of neglect. In mid-Victorian London an estimated 30,000 street children were at loose in the city, 'naked, filthy, roaming, lawless', a race of little savages populating the most advanced centre of civilization in the world. Jo the crossing-sweeper in *Bleak House* is a type of this juvenile vagrancy, on an evolutionary level more or less with the dogs and cattle that pass by him in the London streets: 'I am scarcely human', he reflects, in what is meant to be a terrible indictment of the dereliction of social responsibility in Victorian England.

Although he habitually blamed government or petty officialdom for the crime bred from neglect of children, Dickens was not consistent in his sense of the possibilities of rehabilitation of the criminal young. In his 'Visit to Newgate', in *Sketches by Boz*, he surveyed the area of the prison set aside for boys under 14 years of age, mainly pickpockets: 'fourteen such terrible little faces we never beheld.—There was not one redeeming feature among them ... we never saw fourteen such irreclaimable wretches, before.' In the Cheap Edition (1850) of the *Sketches* Dickens altered the last part of this to 'fourteen such hopeless creatures of neglect', a significant shift of emphasis.

Life could be appalling for the working child of poor parents; but there could be other forms of cruelty reserved for the children of middle-class Victorians. Little Paul Dombey is a good example of such a child. Born into a prosperous family, he is soon crushed by the weight of his father's dynastic ambitions and isolated from the sympathetic companionship of other children. Boy children of the middle classes were particularly subject to the social and professional ambitions of their parents. Conduct books of the period emphasize the extent to which genderspecific expectations are established early in a child's life. The girl was destined for marriage, dependency, and home-making: her 'natural' aptitude for a nurturing, domestic role would flourish in a private environment. The boy was destined to make his own way in the public, competitive world of the professions, and he should be prepared early for this role, according to Trevethan Spicer in *Masculine Education* (1855): 'With regard to girls there is little difficulty; they have their needlework, their Dolls, and are content. Not so boys; the boy is the father to the man, and as men have to rough it in the outer world, and fight their way to the post of honour that they may select for their goal, so the sports of boys must of necessity be rough, to prepare them for their future turbulent career' (p. 87). Such principles gave birth to the single-sex public schools of the 19th century, which, for boys, were the institutional means of weaning them from the mother, the home, and childhood. 'Men do not play like children', was the austere ideal; to which Dickens offered the view, in *A Christmas Carol*, that 'it is good to be children sometimes, and never better than at Christmas, when its mighty Founder was a child himself'.

Dickens is credited with many innovations as a writer, in terms of technique and of opening up new areas for the novelist to explore. But in no respect is he more innovative than in his capacity to represent the child's point of view in fiction, whether he does this through using a child as a narrator, as in his stories 'A HOLIDAY ROMANCE' (1868), or using an older first-person narrator to recapture his own childhood years, as in *David Copperfield* and *Great Expectations*, or by a sympathetic third-person narration which generates an intimacy with the child's viewpoint, as in the first sixteen chapters of *Dombey and Son* when we are shown the thoughts and feelings of little Paul Dombey. At its best, this assumption of the child's-eye view is managed without condescension and without resorting to stereotyped conventions in imitating childhood speech. The eccentricity of a child's thought processes, the impulse to make rapid associations between unlike things (e.g. David Copperfield's likening Peggotty's forefinger to a nutmeg grater), the craving for love and security, the comic-pathetic naivety—all these are registered with fine sensitivity and reproduced in some of Dickens's most naturally relaxed prose. It is as if he is at home in this vein of writing. No other Victorian writer offers us such a sympathetic insight into the condition of childhood.                                MYA

Adrian, Arthur, *Dickens and the Parent–Child Relationship* (1984).
Andrews (1994).
Coveney, Peter, *The Image of Childhood* (1967).
Cunningham, Hugh, *The Children of the Poor: Representations of Childhood since the Seventeenth Century* (1991).
Grylls, David, *Guardians and Angels: Parents and Children in Nineteenth-century Literature* (1978).
Wilson, Angus, 'Dickens on Children and Childhood', in Slater (1970).

**children of Dickens.** Dickens had ten children, who, on the whole, pleased him more as youngsters than they did as adults. The eldest was Charles (known as Charley), born 1837. Angela Burdett COUTTS showed a great deal of interest in Charley, paying for his education at Eton and then for two years in Leipzig, in preparation for a career in merchant banking. Early on his father had doubts about Charley's will to succeed, describing him, shortly after his seventeenth birthday, as very

gentle and affectionate, but with 'less fixed purpose and energy than he could have supposed possible in a child of mine' (to Coutts, 14 January 1854). At 18 he entered Barings Bank, where he stayed for four years, during that time getting caught up in the separation of his parents in 1858 (see DICKENS, CATHERINE). With encouragement from Dickens he lived with his mother for a year, but then gave up Barings and went to Hong Kong to gain experience in the tea trade. In 1861 he returned to London and, aged just 24, set up in business for himself. That same year he married Bessie Evans, daughter of one of the BRADBURY AND EVANS partners, but fierce disapproval of his son's father-in-law kept Dickens away from the wedding. One year later Charley presented Dickens with his first grandchild, Mary Angela. After seven years his business failed; then a printing partnership with his brother-in-law also failed and Charley was made bankrupt. Dickens then hired him to help on *All the Year Round* and, Charley proving adept at this work, appointed his son sub-editor, and in his will left Charley his share of the business. Charley took over as editor of *All the Year Round* after his father died, and continued for the next eighteen years. The magazine was, unsurprisingly, never as successful as it had been with his father's input, yet successful enough to stay in print until Charley decided, as sole owner, to end its publication in 1893. He had success, too, with the production of a guidebook, *Dickens's Dictionary of London*, which he followed up with similar guides to Paris, Oxford, Cambridge, and the Thames. Following his father's death he bought Gad's Hill Place, to the annoyance of other members of the family, only to find that he had to resell it in 1879. In 1887–8 he went to the United States, filling halls for readings from his father's books. There was interest, too, in articles he wrote about his father, and in his biographical and bibliographical introductions to a new edition of Dickens's works published by Macmillan (see EDITIONS PUBLISHED AFTER DICKENS'S LIFETIME). At the age of 59, just one year older than his father, he died of a similar apoplectic attack. He left one son and seven daughters.

Dickens had three daughters, one of whom, Dora, died aged eight months. The others were Mary (Mamie), born 1838, and

Katherine (Katey), born 1839. Of the two Katey was her father's favourite, nicknamed 'Lucifer-Box', yet she was the one most anxious to leave home, and she married the writer Charles COLLINS in 1860, said not to be a marriage made for love. After a long illness Collins died in 1873 and she remarried the following year, to the artist Carlo Perugini. She achieved some success herself as a painter, and though she wrote a few articles giving insights into her father, most information was given in her frequent conversations with Gladys Storey (see Storey 1939). She died in 1929. Mamie ('Mild Gloster') idolized her father and lived with him till his death in 1870. She never married, and with Georgina HOGARTH shared the task of editing the first edition of her father's LETTERS; she also wrote a book on him. She died in 1896, just three days after the death of her brother Charley.

Of the other children, Walter, born 1841, joined the army and went to INDIA at the age of 16, where he died six years later. Francis (Frank), born 1844, was said by his sister Kate and brother Henry to be the cleverest and best of them. At the age of 20 he joined the Bengal Mounted Police, and stayed in India for six years, returning the year after his father's death. Over three years he speculated with and lost his inheritance, and was finally found a post with Canada's Northwest Mounted Police, with whom he served for twelve years. He died in Moline, Illinois, in 1886. Alfred, born 1845, made a career for himself in AUSTRALIA, leaving at the age of 20 and not returning for 45 years. When he did come back he found great success lecturing on his father's life and reciting from his books, so much so that he sought to repeat the success in America. Unfortunately his health was poor, and after two months he collapsed and died in New York. He was married twice and had two children. Alfred was followed to Australia by his younger brother Edward, nicknamed Plorn, whom Dickens specially loved. Born in 1852, he was only 16 when he left England. He became a Member of Parliament in New South Wales and died there in 1902. The seventh child, Sydney, born 1847, progressed at the early age of 13 into a navy cadetship. He did well in his career, but failed miserably at handling his finances, and continually turned to his father for support. Frustrated at this, Dickens's last letter to him forbade him to

visit Gad's Hill on his next shore leave. His inheritance from his father helped clear his debts, but he died at sea two years later, aged only 25. Henry was born in 1849, and went on to become the most successful of Dickens's sons. At Cambridge University he won a scholarship for Trinity Hall and studied law. In 1873 he was called to the bar, and he married in 1876. Of all Dickens's children Henry was the steadiest and achieved most—he took Silk in 1892, became Common Serjeant in 1917, sitting as judge at the Old Bailey, and was knighted in 1922. He retired at the age of 80, in 1929. Henry was involved in the production of the first edition of his father's letters, he wrote his own books, and regularly performed readings from Dickens. In conversations with Gladys Storey in 1928 he was instrumental in confirming his father's relationship with Ellen TERNAN. He died in 1933, victim of a road accident, and the last of Dickens's children.                                                           MA

Adrian, Arthur A., *Georgina Hogarth and the Dickens Circle* (1957).

Bowen, W. H., *Charles Dickens and His Family* (1956).

Lazarus, Mary, *A Tale of Two Brothers* (1973).

Moss, Sidney P. and Moss, Carolyn J., *Charles Dickens and his Chicago Relatives* (1994).

Storey (1939).

**children's literature.** In the essay 'Mr Barlow' (*UT*) Dickens described himself 'as a great reader of good fiction at an unusually early age'. But he grew up before the days of good juvenile fiction, and the stories that formed him—FAIRY TALES, the ARABIAN NIGHTS, *Tales of the Genii*, and the works of the classic 18th-century NOVELISTS—had not been written for children. The first in particular were generally deplored by educationalists of the day. The ideal child then was a well-informed, rational being with a sensible contempt for the fantastic, and fairy tales were held to belong to the ignorant and superstitious. They did not become generally acceptable until Dickens had children of his own, but they had been the passion of his childhood; he was over 12 when he staged one of Mme d'Aulnoy's fairy-tales—'Cherry and Fair Star'—in the toy theatre with which the boys at Wellington House Academy amused themselves. (They also performed Isaac Pocock's lurid melodrama *The Miller and his Men.*)

The Mr Barlow of his essay, who infuriated him by 'always hinting doubts of the veracity of Sinbad the Sailor', is the pedagogue who purveys instruction in Thomas Day's *The History of Sandford and Merton* (1783–9), a work typical of its time with its plethora of factual information and moral reflection set in a clumsy framework of fiction. Dickens execrated this type of book. Mrs Pipchin, who feels that a child's mind should be opened by force like an oyster, uses moral tales 'of a violent and stunning character' to make her point with her young pupils (*DS* 8). *Hard Times* satirizes the Gradgrind philosophy, founded upon hard facts. 'This is the new discovery'; fancy must be totally discarded (*HT* 1.2). Whereas Mr Gradgrind denounces the tales of fairies and genies that Sissy Jupe reads to her father as 'destructive nonsense' (*HT* 1.7), Dickens passionately defends the special need for fairy tales in a UTILITARIAN age (see 'Frauds on the Fairies', *HW* 1 October 1853).

*Sandford and Merton* is one of the few children's books that Dickens actually names. He remembered learning his alphabet from rhymes such as 'A was an Archer' and 'The history of an apple pie' in books with 'deliciously smooth covers of bright red or green'. The 'evening hymn' with which his nursemaid sang him to sleep is probably that by Isaac Watts, whose *Divine and Moral Songs*, first published in 1715, were an inescapable part of childhood for well over 150 years. The nursemaid recalled that he used to recite Watts's 'The Sluggard' with great dramatic effect. He must have read *The History of Little Goody Two-Shoes* (1765), one of the most famous of John Newbery's publications, for there is a send-up of 'the Adventures of Little Margery' in *Our Mutual Friend* (*OMF* 2.1); and 'Thomas Twopence', whose philosophy was that you were to do good because a good thing would come of it, conveys the substance of many mid-18th-century books. (The pious lady-visitors of the Ragged School described in this chapter would, however, have probably insisted on more godly reading: see CHARITY.) The book with the crocodiles and alligators in it that the small David reads to Peggotty (*DC* 2) is unidentifiable; the tracts with the hiccuping Bible references that blighted the dreary Sundays of Arthur Clennam's childhood (*LD* 3) are typical of early 19th-century Religious Tract Society publica-tions. It is clear that young Dickens himself rapidly graduated from the meagre juvenile books of his day to fantasy and romance, and his father's DEFOE, SMOLLETT, FIELDING, and GOLDSMITH. But he did not have them for long; John DICKENS's desperate financial situation meant that in 1823 the boy was sent out to try to sell the volumes to a drunken bookseller in Hampstead Road.

Dickens himself wrote three books specifically for children. *The* LIFE OF OUR LORD was intended solely for his own family; though written in 1849, it was not published until 1934. It presents Christ as a humanitarian rather than as God Incarnate, and the emphasis is on the parables and works of charity. There was also *A* CHILD'S HISTORY OF ENGLAND, and 'A HOLIDAY ROMANCE'.          GA

Avery, Gillian (ed.), Introduction to Dickens, *A Holiday Romance and Other Writings for Children* (1995).

Hearn, Michael Patrick, 'Charles Dickens', in Jane Bingham (ed.), *Writers for Children* (1988).

**children's versions of Dickens's works.** A survey conducted by Edward Salmon in 1888 for his book *Juvenile Literature As It Is* found that Dickens was easily the favourite author of 790 boys, but in those days they would have read the full text. The first ABRIDGEMENTS of Dickens in the 1890s were school readers. In 1905 Amy Steedman's *Dickens for Boys and Girls* appeared, a children's biography with extracts from some novels, and from then retellings became popular. (Mamie Dickens also wrote a life for children, *Charles Dickens by his Eldest Daughter*, 1911, in which there is much about the Dickens CHILDREN and the family PETS.) Annie Douglas Severance introduced her reduction of *David Copperfield* and *Oliver Twist* in *The Child's Dickens* (1905) with the explanation that she had wished 'to simplify them by excluding the elements of unpleasantness and discursiveness which at times mar the original works'. In 1934 J. Walker McSpadden offered *Child Stories from Dickens*, 'in the reverent hope that it will serve as both introduction and incentive to the bulky volumes which so often alarm young people by their very size'. Both included original text, but several editors contented themselves with plot summaries; Russell Thorndike did many 32-page reductions in the 1940s. The fullest coverage is Hallie Erminie Rives's *Tales from Dickens* (Indianapolis, 1905), illustrated by Reginald Birch, which takes in all Dickens's novels, including *Martin Chuzzlewit, Hard Times, Our Mutual Friend*, and *Edwin Drood*, of which there are few if any other retellings.

The most general approach was through the child characters; David Copperfield was always the most popular, and there are versions of the novel illustrated by Edward Ardizzone (1959) and Faith Jaques (1971). Some books featured minor juveniles as well as the standard principals; Lucy Weedon's *Child Characters from Dickens* (1905), illustrated by Arthur Dixon, included children from the Christmas stories; Samuel McChord Crothers's *The Children of Dickens* (1925), illustrated by Jessie Wilcox Smith, takes in the Jellyby children, the Infant Phenomenon, the Kenwigs, Todgers' boy Bailey, Sissy Jupe, young Wilkins Micawber, and Joe the Fat Boy. Kate Dickinson Sweetser's *Ten Boys from Dickens* and *Ten Girls from Dickens* (1925) also included less obvious characters such as 'Deputy' from *Drood*, Kit Nubbles and the Marchioness from *The Old Curiosity Shop*, and Tilly Slowboy (*CH*). One of the most curious compilations was E. P. Woodcock's *Beautiful Bairns: Stories from Dickens by Uncle Reg* (1914), where, although the author affirms his devotion to Dickens ('Uncle Reg loves the chickabids sincerely but he has to give place to Charles Dickens'), the original text is submerged in a froth of personal anecdotes, reminiscences, and mini-sermons.

Interest in retellings seems to have waned in the last decades of the 20th century, but a picture book, Edward Blishen's *Stand up, Mr Dickens* (1995), illustrated by Jill Bennett, attempts to give the flavour of five novels in the style of a reading by Dickens himself.    GA

**Child's History of England, A** Dickens had contemplated such a nursery history since 1843. However, he seems to have put the project aside for some years; it was serialized in 39 episodes in *Household Words* between January 1851 and December 1853 and published in three volumes in 1852, 1853, and 1854. The history opens with a brief account of pre-Roman Britain, in which the Druids (hateful because of their human sacrifices and tax evasion) figure largely, but only goes as far as 1688: suc-

ceeding events 'would be neither easily related nor easily understood in such a book as this'.

Dickens was no historian and was certainly relying on other popular histories. The source usually given is Thomas Keightley's *History of England* (1837–9), which he is known to have possessed, but a more likely work, at least for the earlier chapters, is David Hume's very popular *History of Great Britain* (1754–61), which also starts with the Druids and finishes with the Glorious Revolution. However, Dickens did not share Hume's sympathy for the Stuarts, whom he cordially detested—as he did all other rulers except Alfred and Oliver Cromwell, reserving his particular hatred for Henry VIII and James I. He himself thought that the book was innovatory in its iconoclasm and its support of 'The People'. But the popular juvenile history books of the day, such as *Mrs Markham's History of England* by Elizabeth Penrose (1823) and *Little Arthur's History of England* by Maria Callcott (1835), were also severe on English sovereigns, and had more about the lives of ordinary people. His own work has very little to say about social and economic history and is almost entirely a record of kings and queens. As such it is often difficult to follow, and the reader has to struggle through a maze of dynastic marriages and claims to the throne without any help from genealogical tables, and very few dates.

Passionate in its partisanship, unbalanced in what it chooses to include, the book is mostly a record of bloodshed. There is hardly a page without macabre detail of torture, burnings, beheadings, massacre, and human cruelty. G. K. CHESTERTON felt that *A Child's History* represented 'the cock-sure, healthy-minded, essentially manly and essentially ungentlemanly view of history which characterised the Radicals of that particular Radical era'. This is certainly true of the book's jingoism, contempt for the past, and admiration of the present, but the savage emotion and the violence belong uniquely to Dickens.    GA

**Chimes, The** Dickens's second CHRISTMAS BOOK, written in 1844 while he was living in ITALY and published 16 December by BRADBURY AND EVANS, with illustrations by MACLISE, LEECH, DOYLE, and STANFIELD. (Because distribution was handled by CHAPMAN AND HALL, they are named as publishers on the title-page.) The manuscript and corrected proofs are in the FORSTER COLLECTION; additional proofs are in the DEXTER COLLECTION.

*The Chimes. A Goblin Story of Some Bells that Rang an Old Year Out and a New Year In*, like the *Carol*, concerns the conversion of the protagonist by supernatural agency. Trotty Veck, a good-hearted ticket porter, is convinced by figures of authority that the poor are 'born bad'. Falling asleep on Christmas Eve he is disabused by the spirits of the chimes, which show him a horrific vision of what the future might hold for those he loves. Having learned the lesson 'that we must trust and hope, and neither doubt ourselves, nor the good in one another', Trotty awakes to joyful wedding preparations of his daughter.

A successor to the *Carol* was part of Dickens's agreement with Bradbury and Evans (8 May 1844). Finding it difficult to start writing on account of the 'maddening' bells of Genoa, he used the disturbance as inspiration (to Forster, 6 and 8 October 1844). Although he missed the streets of London, by mid-October he was 'in regular, ferocious excitement with the *Chimes*', finishing on 3 November and celebrating with ' "a real good cry" '. He made a flying visit to London to correct proofs (having entrusted preliminary corrections to FORSTER) and to read the story to select groups of friends. Maclise reported 'shrieks of laughter . . . floods of tears', and Dickens marvelled to Catherine, 'If you could have seen MACREADY last night—undisguisedly sobbing, and crying on the sofa, as I read—you would have felt (as I did) what a thing it is to have Power' (Pilgrim 4.235 n.; Mrs Charles Dickens, 2 December 1844).

LEMON and À BECKETT, provided with advance copy, brought out a DRAMATIZED version at the Adelphi, with O. Smith as Trotty, two days after publication. But neither that production nor the small number of other stage versions achieved much popularity. Dickens adapted the story for a PUBLIC READING in 1858 for his second programme of readings, but it was not successful, and he delivered it only ten times.

Initial sales were good, and Dickens's net profit on the first edition of 20,000 copies was £1,065 8s 2d (Patten 1978, p. 161). Response was mixed, however, and *The Chimes* never achieved popularity remotely approaching that of the *Carol*. Its vigorous topical satire—

described by CHESTERTON (1906) as a 'war cry'—against heartless magistrates, smug politicians, and self-important political economists, robs it of the geniality which made the *Carol* so attractive. But it marks a decisive shift away from the spontaneous comedy of Dickens's early work and points to the careful planning and thematic seriousness of the work of his maturity.                            PVWS

Slater, Michael, 'Dickens (and Forster) at Work on *The Chimes*', *Dickens Studies*, 2 (1966).

**Chorley, Henry Fothergill** (1808–72), journalist, novelist, and close friend of Dickens. Unlike many contemporary reviewers, Chorley admired Dickens's later novels and reviewed them favourably. The two men became intimate around 1854 when, according to Dickens's daughter Mamie, they worked on a charitable project together. Since 1834 Chorley had written weekly reviews of musical performances and notices of new novels for the *Athenaeum*, and had become that influential journal's most prolific reviewer. Although his novels were unsuccessful, two books on MUSIC and musical performers were widely read and remain important sources of information on 19th-century performance practice: *Music and Manners in France and Germany* (1841, republished with substantial alterations as *Modern German Music* in 1854) and *Thirty Years' Musical Recollections* (1862), which chronicled operatic singers and performances in London.

Dickens often invited Chorley to Gad's Hill Place and Dickens and his daughters were frequent guests at Chorley's elegant suppers in his tiny house in Eaton Square, Belgravia. By his contemporaries Chorley was much ridiculed for his high voice and his love of dressing in bright colours (one acquaintance termed him the missing link between the chimpanzee and the cockatoo). He was irascible, and in the 1860s he drank too much and quarrelled with many acquaintances, but never with Dickens. Dickens printed several of Chorley's musical articles in *All the Year Round*, including several in which Chorley ridiculed Wagner's later operas, and he persuaded CHAPMAN AND HALL to publish Chorley's last novel, *A Prodigy: A Tale of Music* (3 vols., 1866). The novel's dedication is 'to Charles Dickens, Esq., as a poor expression of admiration, gratitude, and affection, on the part of the author'. In his will Chorley left £50 for a ring to be given Dickens 'in memory of one greatly helped by him'. When Dickens died first, Chorley was devastated and he asked Mamie for two cedar branches from Gad's Hill. He directed that these symbols of his friendship with Dickens be placed in his coffin, and they were buried with him. RTB

Hewlett, Henry G. (compiled), *Henry Fothergill Chorley: Autobiography, Memoir and Letters*, 2 vols. (1873).

Lehmann, R. C., *Memories of Half a Century: A Record of Friendships* (1908).

**Christmas** was Dickens's favourite celebration, and the one with which he is most often associated because of the abiding popularity of his 1843 CHRISTMAS BOOK, *A Christmas Carol*. So perfectly did the book express the moral teachings of Christ as well as the English celebration of the season that it became an inseparable part of the English-speaking Christmas. Dickens came to be associated with the season so completely that Theodore Watts-Dunton's famous story of the barrow girl in Covent Garden who, on hearing of Dickens's death, exclaimed, 'Then will Father Christmas die too?' has the ring of truth. For many readers the core of Dickens's social criticism can be found in his Christmas writings, what Louis Cazamian in *Le Roman social en Angleterre* (1903) calls his 'philosophie de Noël'.

Dickens describes the Christmases of his childhood in 'A Christmas Tree' (1850), the first of his CHRISTMAS STORIES written for his journal *Household Words*. His memories are far from idealized, however; the toys that he remembers receiving at Christmas are as frightening as they are entertaining, including a demoniacal jack-in-the-box that flies out at him even in dreams. The adult world is represented by the toys that terrify as well as entertain and by the GHOST STORIES that the young Dickens found both enthralling and horrifying. In the sketch the child is seen as highly imaginative but vulnerable, often the innocent victim of adult oppression and insensitivity. For Dickens, Christ's defence of the child was one of the most important tenets of his teaching; the need to nurture the child's imagination and innocence became central to all of Dickens's writings for Christmas, the season when Christ's own childhood was celebrated (see CHILDHOOD; LIFE OF OUR LORD, THE).

The nurturing of the imagination through toys, the THEATRE, and PANTOMIME, and storytelling (particularly fantasy-like FAIRY tales and THE ARABIAN NIGHTS) which Dickens describes in 'A Christmas Tree' was central to his own celebration of Christmas with his family. Every year the Dickens children would perform plays on Twelfth Night, the last night of the Christmas season. Family games, dancing, and other domestic entertainments made the celebration of Christmas cheerful and busy for Dickens, his friends and family (see AMUSEMENTS).

Dickens's first Christmas sketch appeared as 'Christmas Festivities' in BELL'S LIFE IN LONDON, 27 December 1835; it was republished as 'A Christmas Dinner' in the first series of *Sketches by Boz*, February 1836. Appearing in the 'Characters' section, the essay describes a merry family Christmas party where, because of the season, old resentments are forgotten and old wounds healed. That Dickens had the theme of *A Christmas Carol* in mind at this early date is evident in his opening line: 'Christmas time! That man must be a misanthrope indeed, in whose breast something like a jovial feeling is not roused—in whose mind some pleasant associations are not awakened—by the recurrence of Christmas.' *A Christmas Carol* was to tell the story of that misanthrope, as well as developing in Tiny Tim the essay's reference to a child who has died. In this early sketch such griefs are merely a reminder not to dwell on past losses but to enjoy present blessings.

The well-to-do Londoners of 'A Christmas Dinner' are an old middle-class family rather than the *nouveau riche* class that Dickens frequently satirizes in *Sketches by Boz* (see CLASS). He stresses the importance of stability through the grandparents, who are passing on the Christmas rituals that have been enjoyed in their family for generations. Tradition is also central to his next Christmas description, in *Pickwick Papers*. Here the setting is a large country house, Dingley Dell, where again the older generation is venerated as being the link to the past and the guardians of customs that Dickens recognizes as having been observed in Mr Wardle's family 'from time immemorial' (*PP* 28).

By the 1830s the celebration of Christmas in England had been altered radically by the Puritan ban on any type of Christmas festivities during the Interregnum (1649–60), and by the rise of the Industrial Revolution. In the Dingley Dell Christmas, Dickens was able to re-create an almost feudal celebration in which the squire ensures the happiness of his servants, house-guests, and family. It is a nostalgic portrait that harks back to pre-Puritan times in glorifying the ancient ceremonies and customs of medieval England, a portrait that was heavily influenced by Washington IRVING's description of Christmas at Bracebridge Hall in *The Sketch Book* (1820).

The Christmas episode in *Pickwick Papers* looked forward to *A Christmas Carol* in the story Mr Wardle tells to his guests. 'The Story of the Goblins who Stole a Sexton' concerns a misanthrope who is reformed through visions of happy family life forced on him by the goblins. The use of the supernatural to bring about a change of heart became the basis of Dickens's five Christmas books in the 1840s.

The deepening of Dickens's sense that he could use the Christmas season for moral purposes can be seen in MASTER HUMPHREY'S CLOCK, the serial publication he wrote in 1840–1. Master Humphrey is an elderly bachelor whose childhood deformity, rather than leading him into moroseness and self-pity, has instead been the source of his compassionate interest in others. He meets a deaf gentleman in a tavern one Christmas day, and sees that his mind too 'was wandering among old Christmas Days . . . many of them sprung up together, not with a long gap between each but in unbroken succession like days of the week' (*MHC* 2). Now the value of age is not merely the ability to pass on Christmas traditions; rather, these old men see Christmas as a time for personal introspection and spiritual growth, when old griefs are not so much forgotten in the merry rituals of the season, as welcomed as the source of greater compassion and understanding.

While writing *Martin Chuzzlewit* in 1843, Dickens conceived the idea of writing a story specifically for the Christmas season that would 'awaken some loving and forbearing thoughts, never out of season in a Christian land' (*CB*, Preface). In *A Christmas Carol* Dickens revolutionized the literary portrayal

of Christmas by describing, not the nostalgic traditional Christmas celebrated by the old families, but Christmas as it was celebrated by the working poor of early-Victorian England. *A Christmas Carol* was inspired by Dickens's knowledge that many of his contemporaries, including the new business classes, UTILITARIAN thinkers, and political economists, did not 'keep' Christmas at all. For employers like Scrooge it was just another working day. In his joyful 'carol' Dickens set out to show how selfishness and greed had become the dominant spirit of the age. Juxtaposed against Scrooge, the miser engaged in the lonely pursuit of gain, is his nephew Fred and his clerk Bob Cratchit: both celebrate Christmas, not just as the keeping alive of old rituals and entertainments (although party games and family activities do play a large part in *A Christmas Carol*), but as a reminder of Christ's teachings. For Fred Christmas is 'a kind, forgiving, charitable, pleasant time: the only time I know of, in the long calendar of the year, when men and women seem by one consent to open their shut-up hearts freely . . .' (*CC* 1).

The Christmas book was a reminder to Dickens's readers that although the tenets of Christianity were being eroded by the new society, the human heart is essentially compassionate, and business can coexist with kindness. Scrooge's story was hugely popular from the start, and it also inspired a wave of Christmas book publishing that included writers such as William Makepeace THACKERAY, Elizabeth GASKELL, and Anthony TROLLOPE.

The publication of *A Christmas Carol* coincided with other signs that Christmas was becoming more widely celebrated once again. In 1841 Prince Albert had made popular the German tradition of the Christmas tree, first introduced from the continent a few years earlier (see ROYALTY). In the 1840s Christmas cards were first designed, often with the intention of inspiring charitable thoughts in the manner of *A Christmas Carol*, although it was some years before they became commercially popular. Dickens wrote four more short books for the Christmas market in the 1840s: *The CHIMES* in 1844, another attack on utilitarianism and political economy; *The CRICKET ON THE HEARTH* in 1845, and *The BATTLE OF LIFE* in 1846, both domestic stories of simple heroism and family love; and *The HAUNTED MAN* in 1848, a parable about the moral power of memory. Acutely aware of the danger of describing Christmas festivities over and over again, he deliberately concentrated instead on what he came to call his 'Carol philosophy' (Forster 5.1): the value of the child, the power of memory to restore childhood innocence and moral sense, and the need for human contact and compassion. Several of these Christmas books did not take place at Christmas at all, but in *The Haunted Man* he explained why he wrote stories for that season: 'Christmas is a time in which, of all times in the year, the memory of every remediable sorrow, wrong, and trouble in the world around us, should be active with us, not less than our own experiences, for all good ...' (*HM* 3).

Dickens brought his '*Carol* philosophy' to Christmas hearths from 1850 to 1867 with his annual Christmas numbers for his journals *Household Words* (1850–8) and *All the Year Round* (1859–67). Only the first two numbers were about Christmas specifically; after that they became stories linked by a framework, written by Dickens, that exemplified in different ways the power of the human spirit to overcome adversity and be active for good. In requesting stories for the 1852 number, for example, he told a would-be contributor on 19 October that the stories should 'strike the chord of the season' but need not refer to Christmas at all. The celebration of the season, while still present in some of the stories, became secondary to the spiritual importance of Christ's birth and teaching.

This importance is clear in Dickens's use of Christmas celebrations in his later novels. In *Great Expectations* the Christmas dinner scene is neatly juxtaposed against the feeding of a convict on the marshes by the young hero, Pip. While that scene demonstrates true Christian compassion and hospitality, the formal Christmas dinner is its antithesis. The adults at the table, ill-mannered, self-serving, hypocritical, and greedy, accuse the child of being 'naterally wicious' (*GE* 4), and exclude him from the enjoyment of the meal. The two attitudes—one of generous compassion, the other of snobbish social hypocrisy—form the central conflict of the novel.

Dickens described Christmas for the last time in *The Mystery of Edwin Drood*, where the discrepancy between its spiritual significance and the hollowness of its celebration in Victorian England is even more striking. An intended marriage is broken off; an uncle appears to have murdered his nephew on Christmas day, although as the novel is unfinished this plot is not fully revealed. Dickens's description of Cloisterham's preparations is markedly unfestive: there is 'an unusual air of gallantry and dissipation . . . a poor little Twelfth Cake' and a pantomime advertised by the portrait of a clown saying ' "How do you do to-morrow?" quite as large as life, and almost as miserably' (*MED* 14). It is not surprising that Dickens, now a mature novelist, should have come to use Christmas for ironic purposes to reveal his growing sense of the lack of Christian behaviour in Victorian England. He refers earlier in the novel to the stoning of Christians as a 'custom of late years comfortably established among the police regulations of our English communities . . . as if the days of St Stephen were revived' (*MED* 5).

Despite his ironic depiction of Christmas in the later novels, Dickens's Christmas stories, concluding in 1867, continued to celebrate the season with the exuberance and sincerity of the earlier works. In his own life also he continued to 'keep Christmas well,' as Scrooge had taught the world to do so many years before; Dickens's Christmas writings have inspired the keeping of the season ever since.                                              RFG

Glancy (1985).

**Christmas books** The generic title of the collection of the five tales for Christmas which Dickens wrote in the 1840s: *A Christmas Carol* (1843), *The CHIMES* (1844), *The CRICKET ON THE HEARTH* (1845), *The BATTLE OF LIFE* (1846), and *The HAUNTED MAN* (1848). First published separately, they were collected in 1852 in a single volume of the Cheap Edition, published by CHAPMAN AND HALL (see EDITIONS OVER WHICH DICKENS HAD CONTROL). As Ruth Glancy observes, 'they changed the course of Christmas publishing', and, along with the CHRISTMAS STORIES of the 1850s and 1860s, 'occupied Dickens's time and attention for the twenty-five years of his career as a mature writer' (Glancy 1985, p. xix). They have permanently linked Dickens's name with CHRISTMAS, and are central to the widely held view that the essence of Dickens is what Louis Cazamian called the 'Philosophy of Christmas', cheerful, benevolent, and morally idealistic. Each of the stories was 'a whimsical kind of masque' (Preface), dealing with the moral benefits of memory and imagination, and later critics have examined them as experiments with structure and theme, important in the development of Dickens's art in his later novels. Of the five novellas, however, only the *Carol* has retained its popularity with the general reader and the admiration of critics.                                    PVWS

Cazamian, Louis, 'Dickens: The Philosophy of Christmas', in *The Social Novel in England 1830–1850* (1973; originally published in French in 1903).

**Christmas Carol, A** Dickens's first and best-loved CHRISTMAS BOOK, written and published in 1843, while *Martin Chuzzlewit* was in progress. The most perfect work Dickens ever wrote, it was an instant success (a 'national benefit', according to THACKERAY), and its popularity has never faded. The protagonist is probably better known than any other Dickens character, even to people who have never heard of Dickens.

The story concerns the miser Ebeneezer Scrooge, haunted on Christmas Eve by the ghost of his dead partner, Jacob Marley. His spectral visitor sends three Spirits to haunt Scrooge for his reclamation. The Ghost of Christmas Past takes Scrooge to revisit scenes of his childhood and youth; the Ghost of Christmas Present shows him the festivities at the home of his poor clerk, Bob Cratchit, and of his jovial nephew; the Ghost of Christmas Future presents a vision in which Cratchit's crippled son Tiny Tim and Scrooge himself are both dead. Moved by what he has seen, Scrooge sends a turkey to the Cratchits, gives money to charity, and celebrates the day at his nephew's party.

Dickens associated storytelling with CHRISTMAS, and had already written a fanciful story of the supernaturally induced conversion of a misanthrope, Gabriel Grub, for the Christmas number of *Pickwick*. FORSTER reported that Dickens took 'secret delight' in giving 'a higher form' to nursery tales (4.2), but the *Carol* is also underpinned by Dickens's passionate concern about social issues (see NURSERY RHYMES). The previous spring

he was 'perfectly stricken down' by the Second Report of the Children's Employment Commission and vowed to strike 'a Sledge hammer' blow 'on behalf of the Poor Man's Child' (to Southwood Smith, 6 and 10 March 1843). And in the autumn, having visited a Ragged School (see CHARITY), he reported to Miss COUTTS that 'My heart sinks within me when I go into these scenes' (16 September 1843). The tale's allegory warns against Man's children, Ignorance and Want, and urges Scrooge and the reader to 'open their shut-up hearts freely, and to think of people below them as if they really were fellow passengers to the grave'.

Dickens wrote the story in October and November of 1843. He confessed that writing it while also writing *Chuzzlewit* was 'pretty tight work', but he also saw it opening out implications for future full-length novels: 'When I see the effect of such a little *whole* as that . . . I have a strong sense of the immense effect I could produce with an entire book' (to Felton, 2 January 1844; to Mitton, 6 December 1843).

*A Christmas Carol in Prose. Being a Ghost Story of Christmas* was published by CHAPMAN AND HALL on 19 December 1843. The manuscript, which Dickens gave to his lawyer Thomas Mitton, is now in the Pierpont Morgan Library in New York. The initial printing of 6,000 copies was snapped up in days, and the book had sold out in its seventh printing by May (Patten 1978, p. 146). Dickens himself 'wept and laughed and wept again, and excited himself in a most extraordinary manner' over it (to Felton, 2 January 1844). He hoped it would clear his debt to Chapman and Hall, but lavish production, including four coloured plates and four woodcuts by John LEECH, meant that Dickens realized only £230 from the first printing (to Forster, 11 February 1844). To add insult to injury, a plagiarized version appeared on 6 January 1844. Dickens took the rival publishers, Lee and Haddock, to court and won the case, only to find himself liable to costs of around £700 when the pirates declared bankruptcy. His bitterness was permanent, and resurfaced in his depiction of CHANCERY in *Bleak House*.

DRAMATIZED versions of *A Christmas Carol* appeared at once; by February 1844 at least eight theatrical productions had been staged. Edward STIRLING's version at the Adelphi, with O. Smith as Scrooge, was advertised as 'sanctioned' by Dickens, who himself adapted the story for his first PUBLIC READINGS in Birmingham on 27 and 30 December 1853. In its original form the reading took three hours to perform, but he gradually revised it down to one and a half hours. It remained in his repertoire throughout his reading career, and was the principal reading in his final Farewell performance in 1870 (Collins 1975, p. 1). Interestingly, it is the only one of Dickens's works in which 'the vast majority' of adaptations have appeared in the 20th rather than the 19th century (Bolton 1987, p. 234).

There have been innumerable stage, radio, and film versions; Scrooge's name and his cry, 'Bah! Humbug!', are universally known. Philip Collins describes it as having 'institutional status' (' "Carol Philosophy, Cheerful Views" ', *Études anglaises*, 23, 1970). Paul Davis has written a book-length study of the *Carol* as a 'culture-text', exploring the range of British and American adaptations to show how they 'have reflected changing cultural perspectives of successive eras'.

*A Christmas Carol* has come to be seen as the quintessential Dickens work. For G. K. CHESTERTON the benevolent optimism of the converted Scrooge represents the central meaning of everything Dickens wrote (Chesterton 1906). Edmund WILSON, on the contrary, sees Scrooge's conversion as only temporary, and argues that Dickens's work reveals a man deeply divided against himself (Wilson 1941). A delightfully told tale, in which structure and content are 'coterminous' (John Butt, *Pope, Dickens and Others*, 1969, p. 137), it is also the work in which Dickens begins to explore what were to be among his foremost concerns, the power of memory and imagination to nurture moral growth (Kathleen Tillotson, *Dickens Memorial Lectures*, 1970). It is the supreme instance of Dickens's abiding POPULARITY, a miniature triumph of art.                    PVWS

Davis, Paul, *The Lives and Times of Ebenezer Scrooge* (1990).
Patten, Robert L., 'Dickens Time and Again', *Dickens Studies Annual*, 2 (1972).

**Christmas stories** Collective title of stories, sketches, and essays written by Dickens for Christmas numbers of *Household Words* (1850–8) and *All the Year Round* (1859–67), in a few cases in COLLABORATION with Wilkie COLLINS.

Dickens's CHRISTMAS offerings were enormously popular. As he said when reluctantly deciding not to write a CHRISTMAS BOOK in 1847, he was 'very loath to lose the money. And still more so to leave any gap at Christmas firesides which I ought to fill' (to FORSTER, 19 September 1847). But instead of writing novella-length stories as he had done in the 1840s, once he was conducting a weekly miscellaneous periodical he annually devoted one number to a collection of stories for Christmas. The first Christmas number of *Household Words* was part of the journal's normal run; thereafter it was an 'extra' number of 24 pages, expanded to 36 (later 48) in *All the Year Round*. Latterly Christmas numbers sold nearly 300,000 copies each (Forster 8.5; Patten 1978, p. 301).

They were first presented as rounds of stories told by the fireside, but from 1854 Dickens devised a framework (e.g. friends staying in a haunted house, with memories doing the haunting, 1859; an unclaimed piece of luggage containing manuscript stories, 1862). Twice (1857, 1867) he and Wilkie Collins collaborated alone. As Ruth Glancy observes, the stories are usually not *about* Christmas but *for* Christmas, embodying Dickens's conviction that storytelling, like memory, could be morally renewing (Introduction to Everyman Edition). Dickens was never entirely satisfied with the contributions from others, deploring their 'want of cohesion or originality', and finally, 'sick of the thing', he stopped publishing a Christmas number (to Wills, 26 July 1868).

Dickens's own stories were diverse (see SHORT-STORY AND SKETCH WRITER, DICKENS AS). His first offering, 'A Christmas Tree' (1850), was a reverie inspired by children round a tree, in which the narrator recalled past Christmases, especially in CHILDHOOD. 'What Christmas Is As We Grow Older' (1851) was another reminiscence, alluding to family and friends who had died. In 1852 he contributed two items to 'A Round of Stories by the Christmas Fire', 'The Poor Relation's Story', about an old bachelor who builds a 'castle in the air', and 'The Child's Story', an allegory of life's journey. For 'Another Round . . .' in 1853 he wrote 'The Schoolboy's Story', about an orphan tormented by pupils when he becomes

Latin master, who forgives all, and 'Nobody's Story', a stinging satire on government dereliction in EDUCATION, recreation, and PUBLIC HEALTH. 'Seven Poor Travellers' (1854), the first Christmas number with a framework, depicted travellers in a charity lodging telling stories, including Dickens's 'The Story of Richard Doubledick', about a soldier hoping to be killed but finding renewal. 'The Holly Tree' was the frame for 1855, in which travellers were snowed in at an inn of that name. For it Dickens wrote reminiscences of 'The Guest'; an account by 'The Boots' of two little children eloping to Gretna Green; and 'The Bill', in which the Guest is reunited with the girl he loved. 'The Wreck of the Golden Mary' (1856) recounts the adventures of survivors of a shipwreck, written partly in collaboration with Collins. They collaborated again in 1857 on 'Perils of Certain English Prisoners', a story inspired by the Indian Mutiny in which English colonists on a Caribbean island are set upon by pirates. 'Going Into Society', a story about the fairground dwarf Chops, who wins a fortune and is then cheated of it, was Dickens's portion of the last Christmas number of *Household Words*, 'A House to Let' (1858).

The first Christmas number of *All the Year Round* (1859) was 'The Haunted House', in which Master B. discovers that the ghost is his own childhood. 'A Message from the Sea' (1860), written in collaboration by Dickens and Collins, with interpolated tales by other hands, concerned disputed ownership of a sum of money. For 'Tom Tiddler's Ground' (1861; the name is from a children's game), a traveller's visit to the misanthropic hermit Mr Mopes provides the frame. 'Somebody's Luggage' (1862) recounts tales found in manuscript in an unclaimed bag, including 'His Boots', about a bachelor who comes to love a French orphan, and 'His Brown-Paper Parcel', about a pavement artist. 'Mrs Lirriper's Lodgings' (1863) is a monologue by a garrulous landlady bringing up an orphan. 'Mrs Lirriper's Legacy' (1864) tells of the landlady's daily life and of her taking the boy to his father's deathbed. 'Doctor Marigold's Prescriptions' (1865) is the monologue of a cheapjack who invents stories for his deaf-and-dumb adopted daughter. 'Mugby Junction' (1866) tells of a 'man from nowhere' whose adventures include the compelling GHOST STORY of 'The Signalman', troubled by

visions of terrible accidents which subsequently come to pass. The final Christmas number, 'No Thoroughfare' (1867), written in collaboration with Collins, has a complicated plot of mistaken identity, embezzlement, and attempted murder.

The first volume with the title *Christmas Stories*, published by CHAPMAN AND HALL in 1859, included the nine Christmas numbers from *Household Words* in their entirety, with authorship of individual items unattributed. There were no illustrations. Tauchnitz published three Christmas numbers in a single volume as *Christmas Stories*, in 1862, naming the authors (see COPYRIGHT). The first collection containing only Dickens's own writings was selected and arranged by him for the Diamond Edition, published in Boston by TICKNOR AND FIELDS in 1867, with eight illustrations by Sol EYTINGE. Entitled *The Uncommercial Traveller and Additional Christmas Stories*, it consisted of nine pieces only, omitting those of his Christmas writings which were separately published in REPRINTED PIECES. Chapman and Hall issued a one-volume edition of the Christmas numbers of *All the Year Round* (with attributions) in 1868. The Charles Dickens Edition published by Chapman and Hall in 1871 included writings solely by Dickens or by him in collaboration with Wilkie Collins. Containing eight illustrations by various hands, it restored items to their chronological order and added stories which Dickens had omitted for the Diamond Edition. Later EDITIONS generally follow the Gadshill Edition of 1898, which added further Christmas writings by Dickens, but there has never been a standard edition. Only fragments of manuscript survive, in various collections. See Glancy (1985) for details.

DRAMATIZATIONS were made of a few of the stories, none particularly successful (see Bolton 1987). Collins, with help from Dickens, adapted 'No Thoroughfare' for the stage, where it had an excellent run of around 200 performances. Dickens prepared several of his stories for PUBLIC READINGS; some were seldom performed, others never, but two SENTIMENTAL readings, 'Boots at the Holly Tree Inn' and 'Doctor Marigold's Prescriptions', were among the most popular in his repertoire, and a third, 'The Poor Traveller', although less admired, was performed regularly during his first season, 1858–9.

A complete list of Dickens's collaborators on the Christmas stories, with profiles of the authors, is given in Appendix A of Thomas (1982). PVWS

**Church of England.** The established Church of England (officially 'Protestant' after 1689, though even in Dickens's day some members objected to the term), into which Dickens was baptized and to which he belonged throughout his life, except for a brief interval in the 1840s when he attended UNITARIAN chapels.

The doctrines of the Church of England are defined by the Thirty-Nine Articles, which evolved over a period of years following Henry VIII's separation of the Church of England from the Church of Rome (see CHILD'S HISTORY OF ENGLAND, A; ROMAN CATHOLICISM). Because they were written to appeal to the widest possible audience, they admit of varying interpretations, both Protestant and Catholic. The more Protestant wing in the 19th century was referred to as Low Church (often closely resembling the beliefs of outright nonconformists or DISSENTERS), while the more Catholic wing was similarly identified as High Church or Anglo-Catholic. The liberal wing was identified as latitudinarian or Broad Church, and its character was generally influenced by Enlightenment ideas, stressing reason, common sense, progress, and tolerance.

Dickens hated doctrine and doctrinal disputes. His religious and moral beliefs were liberal and closely resembled those of the 18th-century UTILITARIAN divine William Paley (whose books stressed God's desire for human happiness and were required reading at Cambridge) and the Broad Church thought of Thomas Arnold of Rugby, father of Matthew. FORSTER reports that Arthur Stanley's *Life and Correspondence of Thomas Arnold* was a particular aid to Dickens in helping him through 'those trying regions of reflection which most men of thought and all men of genius have at some time to pass through' (Forster 4.6). He was equally contemptuous of Low and High Church enthusiasms, and his general dislike of powerful establishments led him briefly away from the Church of England altogether in the mid-1840s. But, as Forster writes, in the end 'he was able to accommodate all minor differences'

with the Church, and his will contains a highly orthodox profession of faith (Forster 4.1).

A piece written in 1843 for the EXAMINER ('Report of the Commissioners Appointed to Inquire into the Condition of the Persons Variously Engaged in the University of Oxford', *Journalism* 2) ridicules the High Church views of the Oxford Movement and is perhaps Dickens's most outspoken attack on conservative Anglicanism. Ironically likening the students of Oxford to the children employed in mines and factories, he finds them 'reduced to such a melancholy state of apathy and indifference as to be willing to sign anything, without asking what it is, or knowing what it means . . . to the extent of nine-and-thirty articles at once'. In the manuscript, Dickens had added after the reference to the Thirty-Nine Articles, 'every one of which shall contradict the other'. Dickens's attack here closely follows the lines of his even stronger anti-Roman Catholic sentiment: 'A vast number of witnesses being interrogated as to what they understood by the words Religion and Salvation, answered Lighted Candles. Some said water; some, bread; others, little boys . . .' And of course Dickens saw the Oxford Movement as inevitably tending Romeward (as in 'A Crisis in the Affairs of Mr John Bull', originally written for *Household Words* in 1850 on the occasion of the scare over 'Papal Agression', and reprinted in *Journalism* 2).

A more temperate but still strong attack against conservative Anglicanism appears in Dickens's portrayal of Mrs Pardiggle in *Bleak House*; her allegiance is signalled by the fact that her children bear the names of saints of the early English Church revered by the Oxford Movement (*BH* 8). The figure of Bishop in *Little Dorrit* (1.21) is notable chiefly for the absence of anything identifiably religious about him; he typifies the political power and secularization of the Established Church and is indistinguishable from any other member of the House of Lords or the other obsequious dinner guests of the Merdles.

The further an Anglican clergyman was from the seats of power, the more likely Dickens was to be sympathetic. The meek and kind Revd Frank Milvey in *Our Mutual Friend* is the most attractive clergyman in all of Dickens, and, perhaps not coincidentally, he is 'wretchedly paid' (*OMF* 1.9). Had Dickens lived to finish *Edwin Drood* we might have had his most interesting and sustained account of the Church. As it is, that novel contains a highly varied collection of churchmen and related types, from the smooth and cautious Dean of Cloisterham Cathedral, to the more attractive Revd Septimus Crisparkle (a minor canon who adheres to the brand of 'muscular Christianity' associated with Thomas Arnold and Charles Kingsley), to the mysterious John Jasper (very probably the murderer of Edwin Drood), who as choirmaster is technically a layman, though an agent of the Cathedral nonetheless.     RN

Walder, Dennis, *Dickens and Religion* (1981).

**circus,** one of Dickens's favourite forms of entertainment, which he enjoyed both as a child and as an adult (see AMUSEMENTS; CHILDHOOD). The modern circus, despite the classical name, owes nothing to the Roman circus, but emerged in the latter half of the 18th century as a variety show with equestrian exercises its primary feature. Philip Astley (1742–1814), a retired cavalry officer, began giving exhibitions of riding skill at his riding school in 1768, along with comic acts, such as 'The Tailor's Journey to Brentford', a skit of supposed bad riding which remained in the repertoire for decades (it is one of Signor Jupe's routines in *Hard Times*). Astley moved in 1770 to a permanent building in Westminster Bridge Road, across the Thames from the Houses of Parliament, and soon outstripped his competitors, adding tumbling, juggling, clowns, and animal acts to his shows. In addition to a ring, Astley's Amphitheatre in Lambeth had a stage (for many years the largest in London), a pit, gallery, and boxes; with a huge central chandelier and ornaments, it rivalled even the 'legitimate' theatres for elegance. Despite four disastrous fires in 1794, 1803, 1830, and 1841, Astley's remained the pinnacle of the English circus until it closed forever in 1893 (the fondest aspiration of Mr E. W. B. Childers in *Hard Times* is that his 3-year-old son might one day perform at Astley's).

Astley developed plays performed on horseback, or hippodramas, as his central attraction (Mr Sleary describes an equestrian dramatization of 'The Children in the Wood' to Sissy and Louisa, *HT* 3.7), and these, along with the 'scenes in the circle' (exhibitions of trick riding, performed in elegant costumes), remained the key to his success—a formula famously summed up by Andrew DUCROW (1793–1842), proprietor of Astley's (1830–42) and the most accomplished rider of his, or perhaps any, age: 'Cut the dialect and get to the 'osses!' For nearly 40 years two of these equestrian acts were quick-change routines in which the rider impersonated characters from *Pickwick Papers* or *Oliver Twist*. During the 1830s a performer named W. F. Wallett developed the role of clown into a 'Shakespearean jester' (Mr E. W. B. Childers is contemptuous of such a clown as a 'Cackler', *HT* 1.6), but it was not until after mid-century that artistes such as Charles Blondin (1824–97) and Jules Leotard (1830–70) developed daredevil acts on the high-wire and flying trapeze.

Circus troupes travelled from the earliest days, competing with itinerant individual showmen, theatre companies, and menageries (see FAIRS AND ITINERANT ENTERTAINERS). They performed not in the huge canvas tents of later years but, like Mr Sleary (*HT* 1.3), in temporary wooden pavilions, or 'booths'. One of the foremost spectacles of the travelling circus was the parade of the entire company through a town on the way to setting up the pavilion (as Mrs Jarley does daily with her waxworks exhibition, *OCS* 29), and the fact that Dickens does not mention a parade in *Hard Times* suggests that his image of Sleary's circus is drawn more from his acquaintance with Astley's than with a travelling show.

Dickens knew the circus well from an early age, although he turned to LEMON for advice on 'any slang terms among the tumblers and Circus-people, that you can call to mind' when he began writing *Hard Times* (20 February 1854). 'There is no other place which recalls so strongly our recollections of childhood than Astley's', he wrote in 'Astley's' (*SB*). Kit and Barbara take their families there on their half-holiday: 'Dear, dear, what a place it looked, that Astley's, with all the paint, gilding, and looking-glass; the vague smell of horses suggestive of coming wonders; the curtain that hid such gorgeous mysteries . . .' (*OCS* 39). And in *Bleak House* Trooper George seeks relief from his troubles by paying a visit there (*BH* 21). Dickens's fullest treatment of the circus, however, occurs in

*Hard Times*, in which Sleary's Horse-Riding represents carefree imagination, the 'more than one thing needful' which is so disastrously absent from Mr Gradgrind's philosophy of Fact.

Some of Dickens's most delightful letters are concerned with the circus, describing to Beard a female lion-tamer he saw at Margate (14 July 1847), to FORSTER a personal visit from William Cooke, then lessee of Astley's, to consult about stage properties for an amateur theatrical production (18 October 1856), and again to Forster, gleefully reporting a visit to see Adah Isaacs Menken (1835–68), who, 'ascending the fearful precipices not as hitherto done by a dummy', was taking the town by storm in her flesh-coloured bodystocking, tied to the back of a horse in the most famous of all hippodramas, *Mazeppa* (8 October 1864). In its variety, spectacle, skill, and comedy, its appeal to childlike delight, and its opportunity for release from everyday cares into a jocund world of fantasy, the circus above all other forms of entertainment embodied some of Dickens's most cherished values. (See also THEATRE AND THEATRICALITY.)                                                          PVWS

> Saxon, A. H., *Enter Foot and Horse: A History of Hippodrama in England and America* (1968).
> Schlicke (1985).
> —— ' "Delightful, Splendid and Surprising": The Theatre Dickens Knew', *Dutch Dickensian*, 11 (1990).
> —— 'Dickens in the Circus', *Theatre Notebook*, 47 (1993).
> Speaight, George, *A History of the Circus* (1980).

**Clarke, Charles** (1787–1877) and his wife **Mary** (1809–98) were prolific writers (and he a lecturer) on literary topics, sometimes in collaboration, as in their *Recollections of Writers* (1878) to which Mary contributed reminiscences of Dickens. Though moving in literary circles (Charles had been friendly with Lamb, Leigh HUNT, and Keats), they did not meet Dickens until 1848 when Mary, an accomplished amateur actress, participated in his AMATEUR THEATRICALS, which she recalled with enthusiasm, impressed by his managerial and histrionic skills, and basking in his 'bewitching winningness' and good humour. Later they lived in Italy, Mary contributing to *All the Year Round*.          PC

**class and status.** Dickens lived at a time of unprecedented social upheaval, when the impact of the industrial and democratic revolutions on English domestic life was profound and when writers became preoccupied with matters of social class as they had not been before and, arguably, were not to be with quite the same intensity again. There was a loosening of the boundaries of rank and a corresponding belief in the possibilities of self-improvement—it was the age of Samuel Smiles's *Self-Help* (1859)—with its often implicit assumptions about social advancement. An age of social aspiration is a time of pretension, snobbery, class assertion and class deference, and self-deception; and these are among the central subjects of Victorian fiction. In the early works, up to and including *Martin Chuzzlewit* (1843–4), social class is treated on the whole in a comic manner; from *Dombey and Son* (1846–8) onwards the treatment is more sombre.

Dickens liked to quote some lines from BULWER-LYTTON's play *The Lady of Lyons*, in which the hero speaks of raising himself above 'those twin jailers of the daring heart—low birth and iron fortune'. In fact his own birth was not low, relatively speaking. He came from the lower middle class: his paternal grandmother was Lord Crewe's housekeeper (reputedly the original for Mrs Rouncewell in *Bleak House*), his father, John DICKENS, a minor civil servant, his mother the daughter of a civil servant. In an age when only a tiny minority went on to university, and when there were only three universities in England to go to, there was no particular stigma in leaving school at 15, as he did, although there would have been if knowledge of his blacking-factory experience had emerged during his lifetime (see WARREN'S BLACKING). To what extent Dickens felt his interrupted schooling to have been a disadvantage it is difficult to say. There are signs of bitterness in the autobiographical fragment, where he speaks of his resentment at having his 'early hopes of growing up to be a learned and distinguished man, crushed in [his] breast' (see DIARIES). But the evidence of both the life and the fiction suggests that he was never greatly interested in learning. Socially, he was more at home in the new middle-class republic of letters represented by CARLYLE and FORSTER than with the grand Whig hostess Lady Holland, who inquired if Boz was 'presentable' before inviting him to one of her soirées at Holland House. It was through his friendship with Sir Edward Bulwer-Lytton (after whom he named one of his sons) that he came to know the less respectable Gore House circle of Lady Blessington and Count D'Orsay (after whom he named another), where he seems to have felt more comfortable.

Dickens's early success was built on his brilliant mimicry of cockney characters and speech, his command of the social underworld, his compassion for the downtrodden, and his eye for social pretension, which was particularly rife in the early Victorian period. It is well known that *Pickwick Papers* (1836–7) became a great popular success only after the introduction of the Wellers, and there is a kind of ideal balance of the classes at the end of that novel which Dickens was never to achieve again. In *Oliver Twist* (1837–9) they are violently separated, into a powerfully rendered underworld where something of Sam's eloquence survives in the pickpockets' gang, and an anaemic world of middle-class respectability. In *Nicholas Nickleby* (1838–9) respectability emerges as a central theme, and Nicholas himself is the first of Dickens's attempts at the young gentleman hero. He is caught, interestingly, between two classes: the unrespectable, represented at its worst by the schoolmaster Squeers and at its best by the actor-manager Vincent Crummles, and the aristocratic, seen at its least offensive in Lord Frederick Verisopht and at its most predatory in Sir Mulberry Hawk. Here the historical conflict seems sharpest. When Nicholas challenges Sir Mulberry with the assertion that 'I am the son of a country gentleman . . . your equal in birth and education, and your superior I trust in everything besides', one feels the raw edge of the early Victorian middle-class challenge to aristocratic leadership.

Nicholas's assertion of gentlemanliness is decidedly shaky, but it introduces a concept which is at the heart of Dickens's preoccupation with social class. The Victorians were endlessly fascinated by what it meant to be a gentleman (and to a lesser extent, a lady). The attraction of the concept is that it was a category from the older hierarchy of rank which was capable of making the transition to the

new society of class, and it could do so because it was open to penetration from below and held a unique status in British society. A baronet might hold a higher rank than a 'country gentleman', a wealthy mill-owner might be able to buy him out several times over, but (in theory) both would acknowledge the supremacy of the gentlemanly code. But what went to the making of a gentleman? How socially exclusive was the type (for without exclusion there would be no point)? And what was the relationship between social exclusion and MORALITY, always a difficult and shifting boundary? These questions exercised Dickens and his contemporaries, and he returned to them in successive novels.

Although not a Nickleby or a Copperfield, Mr Dombey in *Dombey and Son* (1846–8) shows a distinct advance into new and in some ways more original territory. As a merchant-prince of the expanding empire, Dombey embodies the patriarchal character of early Victorian capitalism; and Dickens shows his deadening influence reaching out from home to office to school to empire. And there are also the first signs of a more complex interaction between middle class and aristocracy in Major Bagstock's realization that Dombey is a coming man, and in his subsequent successful attempts to bring Dombey and his aristocratic friends together at Leamington. Mr Dombey is not a complex character, but the issues of class and social change are touched on with a subtlety new in Dickens.

'Despite their descents into the lowest class,' Mrs Oliphant wrote in 1855, 'and their occasional flights into the less familiar ground of fashion, it is the air and breath of middle-class respectability which fills the books of Mr Dickens.' This statement holds true of *David Copperfield*, which barely reaches the world of fashion and only touches the world of the poor when David is working in the Murdstone and Grinby warehouse, but it does not really fit the subsequent novels. *Copperfield* can be seen as Dickens's first sustained attempt to explore the making of a middle-class young man; it is a BILDUNGS-ROMAN which offers different models and parallels to David's progress: the BYRONIC Steerforth; decent, industrious Traddles; the self-helping Uriah Heep; the profligate Micawbers. Because it negotiates failure so easily, at least on the surface, *Copperfield* must be considered the most middle-class of his mature novels.

The same can hardly be said of *Bleak House* (1852–3), which encompasses the extremes of the aristocratic Dedlocks and the illiterate Jo, the crossing-sweeper, and asks us to see the relationship between them. The first-person narrator, Esther Summerson, could conceivably be called middle class and respectable, despite her illegitimacy, but the other, omniscient narrator is not: that voice is urgent, angry, impatient with class distinction, apocalyptic. Similarly with *Little Dorrit* (1855–7), which brings together the highest society in the land with the occupants of the Marshalsea Debtor's Prison. Here, as in *Hard Times* (1854), one sees an interesting development in Dickens's treatment of class. It is not just that—as in *Bleak House*—he has brought together the highest and the lowest, Society and the Marshalsea, but that he has shown Society adjusting to new wealth and indeed battening on it. In *Hard Times* it is the dandified James Harthouse who makes up to and nearly seduces Louisa Gradgrind, and in *Little Dorrit* the aristocratic Henry Gowan courts and marries Pet Meagles. A new phase of social development is taking place and, as one would expect, Dickens is there to observe it.

Of all Dickens's treatments of social class, *Great Expectations* (1860–1) is the most thorough and radical; indeed, it is the supreme treatment of the topic in Victorian literature. A return to the *Bildungsroman* form of *Copperfield*, it deprives the orphan hero of the kindly aunt who restored his genteel birthright in the earlier novel. Pip is a blacksmith's boy with coarse hands and thick boots, in love with a young lady, and Dickens shows what becoming a gentleman looks like from the other side of the fence. Then comes the anonymous gift and he is able to realize his dreams. We get both the realities of class and the hidden power of fantasy, and Pip's ability to realize that fantasy is brought down to its roots in a convict's gift. Dickens shows how much money and gentility, cash and culture, depend on one another. But Pip's painful enlightenment about the realities of class does not invalidate the moral lessons he has learned: he is a better person for his experiences. Dickens asks us to face the hard question: would Pip have been better staying at the forge? The answer is, probably not. There was, after all, a positive side to the Victorian preoccupation with manners, and it is to be seen in the character of Herbert Pocket.

Throughout his career Dickens had shown himself drawn to two contrasting types of gentlemanliness, the dandy and the self-made man. For most of the time he was a man of the middle class, preaching the virtues of hard work and earnestness, those 'steady, plain, hard-working qualities' which David Copperfield affirms. But there was a side to him which was fascinated by the figure of the dandy, and in his last completed novel, *Our Mutual Friend* (1864–5), the two types are at the centre of the book's treatment of class: Bradley Headstone, a schoolteacher who has made his way up from the ranks, and Eugene Wrayburn, a languid, briefless barrister. The struggle between them is one of the most powerful things Dickens ever did but also one of the most puzzling, in that his sympathies now go to the dandy and against the self-made man. It seems that he was disenchanted with the middle class, identifying it with Podsnap and the Veneerings, and saw new potential in the once *outré* figure of the dandy. There is no redemption for Headstone: there is for Wrayburn.

Dickens was a man of his time to the extent that he believed some social distinctions mattered. Pip in his illness does not bless Joe as a 'Christian gentleman' but as a 'gentle Christian man', and Dickens would have considered it humbug to call him a gentleman. But he valued gentlemanliness, just as he valued, even as he lightly mocked it, the best side of the English upper classes represented by Sir Leicester Dedlock. He was interested, as any novelist of his time inevitably was, in the relationship between manners and morals, and therefore in social class. He was also a mimic, and mimicry cannot flourish in a classless society, or at least a society where there are not differences of accent. On the other hand he was always clear that in the last analysis morality is more important than class. It is this that ensures that Dickens's major novels master the subject of class and are not, as are those of some of his contemporaries, mastered by it.                RG

Briggs, Asa, 'The Language of Class in Early Nineteenth-Century England', in A. Briggs and J. Saville (eds.), *Essays in Labour History* (1960).

Gilmour (1981).

Moers, Ellen, *The Dandy: Brummell to Beerbohm* (1960).

**classical myth and legend.** Like THACK-ERAY, TROLLOPE, and other Victorian writers, Dickens was fond of burlesque allusions to classical myth, legend, and history—he liked to mock his more unheroic contemporaries by holding them up against Greek and Roman gods, emperors, and heroes.

The habit begins in Dickens's earliest writing. In his first published story, 'Mr Minns and his Cousin' (*SB*), we meet middle-class people with pretentious classical Christian names and prosaic surnames: *Augustus* Minns, his cousins *Amelia* and *Octavius*, and nephew *Alexander Augustus* Budden, whose house is near 'Grogus's the great ironmonger's'. Elsewhere in *Sketches by Boz* are similar comic effects: in 'Sentiment', the Miss Crumptons inhabit 'Minerva House', and in 'Greenwich Fair' Boz overhears 'Oh do tickle him for me, Mary . . . and similar Lucretian ejaculations'. In other sketches, porters are 'Atlases', a waitress 'Hebe', and a bailiff 'the sheriff-officer's Mercury'. Modern counterparts of Damon and Pythias appear in 'Making a Night of It', but tellingly, 'Damons are rather hard to find in these days of imprisonment for debt (except the sham ones, and they cost half-a-crown)'.

A line of classical shams follows on in Dickens's novels. 'The Oracle' William Giles, who taught Dickens Latin as a child, nicknamed him 'The Inimitable', and earned in return that equally complimentary title, is often travestied, first in Chevy Slyme in *Martin Chuzzlewit*—'Might he not . . . have sat upon a tripod in the ancient times, and prophesied to a perfectly unlimited extent, if previously supplied with gin-and-water at the public cost?'—and later in such comic figures as 'the oracular Bunsby' in *Dombey and Son*. There are joke Venuses, both male and female, from the hilariously reluctant Miggs—'I wouldn't lay myself out as she does . . . I wouldn't seem to say to all male creeturs "Come and kiss me"—and here a shudder quite convulsed her frame—"for any earthly crowns as might be offered. Worlds", Miggs added solemnly, "should not reduce me. No. Not if I was

Wenis" ' (*BR* 70)—to the more tragicomic figure of the depressive Mr Venus, who appears to have been born in a teacup: 'blowing his tea, his head and face peering out of the darkness, over the smoke of it, as if he were modernizing the old original rise in his family' (*OMF* 1.7). There is also a sharply satiric Cupid in *Little Dorrit*—Mr Sparkler, in Venice, 'like Venus's son taking after his mother', his bottom in the air like Mrs Merdle's parrot (*LD* 2.6).

Though such later examples—particularly after the warning classical figure of Allegory on Tulkinghorn's ceiling in *Bleak House*, perhaps—sometimes exhibit darker tones, there is often a benevolent edge to the jokes, and some comic comparisons with ancient myth—Susan Nipper ('I may not be a Amazon, Miss Floy'—*DS* 23), or Boythorn defying the Dedlocks ('I am looked upon, about here, as a second Ajax defying the lightning'—*BH* 18)—even seem designed to emphasize the possibility of heroism in modern life. Dickens and some of his contemporaries—Daumier, for instance, with his affectionate caricatures of modern petit-bourgeois Penelopes and Odysseuses—in fact offer evidence of a continuity between the 18th-century mock-heroic figures of FIELDING and Pope and Joyce's definitively modern 'classical' hero, Leopold Bloom.                                    MH

**clothing** is an important feature of Dickens's work, used to describe his characters or illuminate their personalities, to set the social scene, and sometimes aid the plot.

Apart from his natural talents for observation and description, Dickens had a personal interest in clothes. Often described by his contemporaries as dapper and dressy, he shocked Americans with his flamboyant waistcoats in 1842. His taste tended towards the theatrical and responded to the fashions of his youth. The bright silk waistcoats and cravats of the 1830s, glossy velvet collars, gold rings, watch-chains, and shirt-pins are vividly described in early novels such as *Nicholas Nickleby* or those set in this period like *David Copperfield*. These contrast with the darker, duller, more uniform clothes fashionable for men by the time of Dickens's death.

Many of his works include fashions of the Regency and even the late 18th century, worn by elderly men and women. This can be comical, in the case of the ageing dandy Turveydrop, whose model was the Prince Regent (*BH* 14), or more sinister, in the ancient bridegroom Arthur Gride, whose outmoded clothes were bought cheap at a pawnbroker's and who still wears his long grey hair in an 18th-century pigtail (*NN* 47). Often, old-fashioned clothes portray an endearing eccentricity. Mr Pickwick's 'tights' were a type of long, close-fitting breeches known as pantaloons and these are also worn by Mr Micawber (*DC* 11). The Cheeryble brothers (*NN* 35) wear the earlier knee breeches (sometimes known as 'shorts' or 'smalls') and, like Mr Pickwick, gaiters which protected the lower part of the legs. Trousers had largely superseded breeches and pantaloons by the 1830s but Dickens makes fun of their genteel euphemisms: 'inexpressibles', 'unmentionables', and 'inexplicables' in *Sketches by Boz*.

Both Miss Tox (*NN*) and Miss Trotwood (*DC*) wear 'scanty' dresses which suggest the narrow skirts of their youth, rather than the more fashionable bell shape of the 1840s and 1850s, when Mrs Pardiggle's skirt is so wide it knocks down little chairs (*BH* 8). Dickens's heroines, as ideal women of their period, express their ladylike qualities in neat, quiet, and unassuming dress. This was the convention for young, unmarried girls. Married women like Mrs Merdle (*LD* 1.21) could wear precious jewellery and rich, expensive clothes, in effect as a showcase for a husband's wealth and status. When Edith Dombey leaves her detested husband she makes a dramatic statement by stamping on all the jewels and clothes he has given her (*DS* 47).

Edith's mother, Mrs Skewton, is one of several female characters parodied for dressing too young for their age. Louisa Chick (also *DS*), Mercy Pecksniff (*MC*), and Lady Tippins (*OMF*) are other examples. Dickens also mocks the unfeminine 'Bloomer' costume in his essay 'Sucking Pigs' (*HW* 8 November 1851).

One of the most graphic images of female clothing is Mrs Gamp, the midwife, with her second-hand, snuff-stained gowns, pattens (a type of overshoe), and oversized umbrella. Long usage had so moulded her gowns to the shape of her figure that a dress suspended from the bedpost led 'more than one impatient husband coming in precipitately at about the time of twilight' to think Mrs Gamp

had hanged herself (*MC* 49). Dickens delights in the idea of clothes which seem to have a life of their own, most memorably in 'Meditations in Monmouth Street' (*SB*); Mr Jaggers, the lawyer's boots which creaked 'as if *they* laughed in a dry and suspicious way' (*GE* 24); Miss Tox's small handbags which went off like little pistols when snapped shut (*DS* 1); and Miss Murdstone's, 'that shut up like a bite', her lips compressed in sympathy with the snap (*DC* 38).

The extraordinary variety and panoramic quality of the Victorian social scene is captured by Dickens's descriptions of how people looked. His range is enormous and remarkable for its depiction of every social CLASS and occupation. In 'Shabby-Genteel People' (*SB*) he charts the decaying state of failed men's clothes, such as 'an old rusty suit of threadbare black cloth which shines with constant wear as if it had been beeswaxed'. *Oliver Twist* reveals a detailed picture of poverty and low life, from Oliver's workhouse clothes to those of the young pickpockets, prostitutes, and housebreakers with whom he is forced to associate. Bill Sikes and other working-class men wear velveteen or corduroy coats and often dirty neck-handkerchiefs (in place of the middle-class shirt collar and necktie).

The importance of clothes as social identification is illustrated when Oliver escapes from this life; on acquiring new clothes it is immediately obvious that he looks 'like a gentleman's son' (*OT* 41). Similarly, Pip (in *GE*) feels the contrast of his new clothes with those of his blacksmith brother-in-law, Joe Gargery. Yet Joe has a simple dignity in his working clothes which is lost with his ill-fitting Sunday best. The way clothes are worn can be as important as the garments themselves. Pip also notices how Herbert Pocket carries off his old clothes much better than Pip does his new ones (*GE* 27, 22).

Dickens has a good understanding of how clothes were made, bought, and sold. He describes Madame Mantalini's, a typical fashionable London dressmaker's where Kate Nickleby is apprenticed (*NN*), and the more modest Mr Omer, draper and haberdasher, who makes David Copperfield's mourning. Mourning was strictly observed by everyone and prosperous households like the Dombey's provided it new for all the servants (*DS* 2). Some ready-made clothes were available by the 1830s, and Mr Pickwick was able to kit out his servant, Sam Weller, in an emporium selling both new and second-hand clothes (*PP* 12). The second-hand market, however, was widespread and extremely important at this time, both for the provision of less expensive clothing and a means of raising money. Mr Jingle pawned his clothes and 'lived for three weeks upon a pair of boots, and a silk umbrella with an ivory handle' (*PP* 42), while in *Oliver Twist* the pickpockets make a living selling silk pocket handkerchiefs stolen from fashionable gentlemen.

Dickens inspired one significant fashion: the 'Dolly Varden' hat and dress of 1871. A revival of an 18th-century style of straw hat and polonaise gown, this costume took its name from the character in *Barnaby Rudge*.     PB

Altick, R. D., 'The Way They Looked', in *The Presence of the Present* (1991).

Buck, Anne, *Victorian Costume and Costume Accessories* (2nd rev. edn., 1984).

**Cobbett, William** (1763–1835), the 'Poor Man's Friend' and best-selling journalist of the Regency period. Dickens told James T. FIELDS that Cobbett was one of his favourite authors, and Dickens himself has been compared to Cobbett as a master of a particularly 'plain, downright' English style (Collins 1981, 2.313, 203). Cobbett is part of the movement establishing public opinion as a political force; Francis JEFFREY considered him the most influential journalist of his day, and HAZLITT described him as 'a kind of fourth estate in the politics of this country' (*Spirit of the Age*, 1825). He became an MP (1832–5) in the new REFORM Parliament, where Dickens may have observed him towards the end of his life. Dickens had a copy of *Selections from Cobbett's Political Works* (1835) in his Gad's Hill library, and Dickens's jaunts as an observer in *Sketches by Boz* and the UNCOMMERCIAL TRAVELLER could be compared to Cobbett's *Rural Rides*, to which he refers in the EXAMINER (21 July 1849).     KC

Williams, Raymond, *Cobbett* (1983).

**Coleridge, Samuel Taylor** (1772–1834), Romantic poet and literary critic. Dickens showed respect for the work of Coleridge, noted in correspondence the reading of 'Christabel' (to Forster, ?2 November 1839), and owned a copy of his *Poetical Works* (Pilgrim 4.717). While the Romantic echoes in Dickens's work are WORDSWORTHIAN and BYRONIC, there is a Coleridgean strain evident in the novelist's anti-rationalist stance, and his trust in the spontaneous, untutored imagination, in such novels as *The Old Curiosity Shop*, *Hard Times*, and *Our Mutual Friend*.

LL

Stone, D. D., 'Death and Circuses: Charles Dickens and the Byroads of Romanticism', in *The Romantic Impulse in Victorian Fiction* (1980).

**collaborations.** Much of Dickens's work was illustrated, and this involved collaboration with his ILLUSTRATORS. His theatrical activities were inherently collaborative, as was his editing. Some of his journalistic writing, too, was collaborative, with Dickens sharing the composition with a colleague, but the only author with whom he collaborated on imaginative fiction was Wilkie COLLINS.

In his fiction he worked closely with his various illustrators to integrate plates and text, selecting subjects for illustration and giving detailed instructions about composition. The idea for *Pickwick* originated with Robert SEYMOUR as comic engravings accompanied by letterpress, and although Dickens quickly assumed a dominant role, especially after Seymour's suicide, Mrs Seymour claimed afterwards that her late husband, not Dickens, was the work's only begetter. George CRUIKSHANK likewise, after Dickens's death, claimed that the central ideas for *Oliver Twist* originated not with Dickens but with him. Dickens and FORSTER disputed both claims, and in all his other illustrated works there was no question but that the illustrators were subordinate to him.

Early in his career Dickens wrote several plays, working with actors and musicians, in particular with John Pritt HARLEY and John HULLAH (see PLAYWRIGHT, DICKENS AS). He contributed substantially to plays written by friends, in which he acted: MR NIGHTINGALE'S DIARY (1851) by Mark LEMON, *The Lighthouse* (1855) and *The FROZEN DEEP* (1857) by Collins. It is uncertain how great a contribution he made to the adaptation for the stage of 'No Thoroughfare' (1867), written initially as a Christmas story by himself and Collins. He also gave advance copy of some of his writings to theatres for DRAMATIZATIONS, occasionally offering advice for the production.

As an editor he kept firm control over the opinions expressed in, and the house style of, everything which appeared, without attribution, in journals which he edited, offering suggestions to contributors or unilaterally making emendations to articles. He also jointly wrote a considerable number of pieces in *Household Words* and *All the Year Round*, particularly with his sub-editor W. H. WILLS. Those from *Household Words* have been gathered in two volumes, edited by Harry Stone, as *The Uncollected Writings of Charles Dickens: Household Words 1850–59* (1969).

Starting in 1854, the Christmas stories in his journals consisted of contributions within a framework devised and written by himself. He and Wilkie Collins collaborated without outside help on 'Perils of Certain English Prisoners' (1857) and 'No Thoroughfare' (1867), and with additional contributions by others, on 'The Wreck of the Golden Mary' (1856). They also worked together in writing 'The LAZY TOUR OF TWO IDLE APPRENTICES' (*HW* 3–31 October 1857), based on an expedition which they took for the purpose.

PVWS

## collections of Dickens materials.

Printed editions of Dickens's works published in his lifetime, especially first editions in their original serial instalments, often command high prices from dealers. But for the most part such printed works cannot be considered extraordinarily rare, as they were usually published in large editions; therefore, the following discussion of key Dickens collections focuses on manuscripts, proofs, and letters, rather than on published materials.

The most important repositories for Dickens manuscripts are in England and the United States of America. Though scores of museums and libraries hold Dickens letters, there are only four essential collections of major Dickens manuscripts in England: the VICTORIA AND ALBERT MUSEUM, the British Library, the DICKENS HOUSE MUSEUM, and the Wisbech and Fenland Museum in Cambridgeshire. The most important collections in the United States include the Pierpont Morgan Library in New York, the Berg Collection of the New York Public Library, the Free Library of Philadelphia, the Rosenbach Museum and Library in Philadelphia, the

Huntington Library in San Marino, California, and the collections at Harvard and Yale Universities.

The Forster Collection in the Victoria and Albert Museum, National Art Library, London, undoubtedly holds the greatest treasures. Dickens left most of his literary manuscripts to his friend and biographer John FORSTER, and these now form the cornerstone of the Forster Collection. The complete manuscripts of all the novels from *The Old Curiosity Shop* (1840–1) to *A Tale of Two Cities* (1859), and major portions of *Oliver Twist* and *The Mystery of Edwin Drood*, are all here, along with those of AMERICAN NOTES, PICTURES FROM ITALY, The CHIMES, and SKETCHES OF YOUNG COUPLES. The collection is also rich in proofs: all the novels from *The Old Curiosity Shop* to *Edwin Drood* (with the exceptions of *A Tale of Two Cities* and *Our Mutual Friend*) are represented, as is *The Chimes*. The collection includes Dickens's DIARIES from 1838 to 1841, manuscripts and proofs of a number of articles, reviews, and letters contributed to the EXAMINER, the DAILY NEWS, and *Household Words*, fragments of *A CHILD'S HISTORY OF ENGLAND*, and the prefaces, dedications, and memoranda for various Dickens novels; it also has several hundred LETTERS, including 180 addressed to John Forster (see COMPOSITION, DICKENS'S METHODS OF).

The collection in the British Library, including materials in the J. F. Dexter Collection, includes several manuscript pages of *Pickwick Papers* and *Nicholas Nickleby*, as well as corrected proofs of *The Old Curiosity Shop*, *Martin Chuzzlewit*, *Hard Times*, and *Little Dorrit*. The British Library also owns several hundred letters, including 140 addressed to Dickens's wife Catherine (see DICKENS, CATHERINE).

The Dickens House Museum now holds the bulk of the Suzannet Collection. A page of *Pickwick Papers*, a part of a page of *Oliver Twist*, and chapter 9 of *Nicholas Nickleby* are among the most valuable items. The Dickens House also owns manuscripts of poems, a preface to *Dombey and Son*, an article for *Household Words*, and some memoranda and annotated proofs; it is particularly rich in annotated prompt-copies for Dickens's readings and for plays Dickens produced, and also holds nearly 450 letters, including 183 to

Dickens's friend Thomas Beard (see PUBLIC READING TEXTS).

The Wisbech and Fenland museum's treasure is the manuscript of *Great Expectations*.

Other noteworthy collections in England include the John Rylands University Library of Manchester, with the manuscript of 'A Child's Dream of a Star' (*HW*), a speech, a notebook in shorthand, and various letters, including 29 to the GASKELLS; and the Brotherton Collection at the University of Leeds, which holds 170 Dickens letters.

The richest collection of Dickens manuscripts in the United States is in the Pierpont Morgan Library in New York. The Morgan Library is the only institution in America to hold the manuscript of a Dickens novel: *Our Mutual Friend*. The Morgan also owns the manuscripts of *A Christmas Carol*, *The CRICKET ON THE HEARTH*, *The BATTLE OF LIFE*, and *SKETCHES OF YOUNG GENTLEMEN*, as well as pages of *Nicholas Nickleby* and *Pickwick Papers* and the manuscripts of articles published in *Household Words* and REPRINTED PIECES. The Morgan Library houses over 1,300 Dickens letters.

The Berg Collection of the New York Public Library includes a page of *Pickwick Papers*, some fragments of *Oliver Twist*, a page of *Martin Chuzzlewit*, and manuscripts of various articles and stories, as well as proofs of *Our Mutual Friend* and an 1867 diary. The Berg holds about 500 Dickens letters, and a rich collection of annotated prompt-copies for Dickens's readings; the book of memoranda Dickens kept from 1855–70 is another treasure.

The Free Library of Philadelphia houses the complete manuscript of *The LIFE OF OUR LORD*, half a page of *Nicholas Nickleby*, a poem, and some fragmentary proof of *Martin Chuzzlewit*, as well as five notebooks in shorthand and about 900 Dickens letters.

The Rosenbach Museum and Library, also in Philadelphia, holds substantial fragments of the *Pickwick Papers* manuscript, and nearly 100 pages of *Nicholas Nickleby*, as well as many Dickens letters.

The Huntington Library in San Marino, California, owns a number of manuscripts of short pieces by Dickens, including articles published in *Household Words*, a speech, a piece rejected by PUNCH, and a chapter of *A Child's History of England*, as well as about 1,000 letters.

Harvard University holds the manuscript to 'GEORGE SILVERMAN'S EXPLANATION', as well as some pieces reprinted in *The UNCOMMERCIAL TRAVELLER*. Harvard has fragments of corrected proof of both *A Child's History of England* and *David Copperfield*, and many Dickens letters.

The library at Yale University holds the manuscripts of the two MUDFOG PAPERS published in BENTLEY'S MISCELLANY and of a variety of other articles and sketches, including pieces published in the MORNING CHRONICLE and *Household Words*. Yale owns four pages of *Oliver Twist*, some corrected proofs of *Edwin Drood*, some manuscript prologues for plays, and hundreds of letters.

Many other private and public collections in the United States have notable Dickens materials: the Princeton University Library owns the manuscripts of several articles reprinted in *The Uncommercial Traveller*, and the University of Texas holds a few minor manuscripts and about 150 Dickens letters.          JJB

**Collins, Charles Allston** (1828–73), painter, writer, and younger brother of Wilkie COLLINS. He contributed to *Household Words* from 1858 and extensively to *All the Year Round*. Dickens particularly admired his 'Our Eye-Witness' sketches. In 1860 Dickens's daughter Kate married Collins, against her father's advice (see CHILDREN OF DICKENS). Dickens worried about Collins's ill health and doubted that Kate loved him. After the wedding, Mamie Dickens found her father on his knees sobbing. 'But for me,' he wept, 'Katie would not have left home' (Storey 1939, p. 106). Collins painted a portrait of Georgina HOGARTH (now in the DICKENS HOUSE MUSEUM), designed the cover for *The Mystery of Edwin Drood*, and died young.       PVWS

**Collins, Wilkie** (1824–89)—who characterized himself thus: 'personally (when I have my high-heeled boots on) I stand five feet, three inches high ... I have nothing great about me but my moustachios and my intellect', and whose head Dickens described as 'triangular, with a knob in the middle' —was Dickens's most important literary COLLABORATOR and interlocutor, and (after FORSTER) his most important friend. They first met in March 1851, when Collins accepted a small part in

BULWER-LYTTON's *Not So Bad as We Seem*, which Dickens's AMATEUR THEATRICAL company was then about to perform. Collins fitted well into what Dickens called the 'half-gypsy life of our theatricals'. Partly through such collaborations (which culminated in Collins's play *The* FROZEN DEEP), they soon developed a friendship which was to last, with only relatively minor and temporary difficulties, until Dickens's death.

The twelve-year age gap between the two is the most obvious fact about that friendship. In their relationship as writers, for instance, Dickens can be seen in an avuncular role, furthering the career of his gifted protégé: Eliza Lynn Linton described him as 'a literary Mentor to a younger Telemachus'. Collins was taken on as a member of the staff of *Household Words* in November 1856, clearly as a kind of favourite pupil. 'He and I might do something in Household Words together . . . have talked so much within the last 3 or 4 years about Fiction-Writing, and I see him so ready to catch at what I have tried to prove right, and to avoid what I thought wrong, and altogether to go at it in the spirit I have fired him with', Dickens wrote to WILLS (10 July 1856). Their first collaboration there, 'The Wreck of the Golden Mary', appeared that same Christmas, and regularly thereafter they worked together on the annual Christmas stories. Collins's career prospered under Dickens's tutelage, until in 1862 he was able to give up working for *All the Year Round*, where two of his most important novels—*The Woman in White* and *The Moonstone*—were first serialized.

Besides his relative youth, Collins had a thoroughly un-Victorian and even bohemian personality: he later became an opium addict, and maintained two separate *ménages* without ever marrying. Kaplan describes him as 'casually libertine'. The attraction of his company for Dickens was thus the opposite of that of Forster, who by contrast became more and more respectable and even pompous in the 1850s and 1860s, and married a woman with £36,000 (he would later be satirized as Podsnap in *Our Mutual Friend*). It is possible to consider the two major friends as expressions of two opposing aspects of Dickens's own character.

By 1856, in fact, in Collins's phrase, 'Dickens's domestic skeleton was becoming a pretty big one', and their frequent outings together may have offered momentary release from the continual effort of keeping up appearances in the midst of domestic unhappiness. They frequently travelled together: to ITALY in 1853, for instance ('he takes things easily and is not put out by small matters'—to Mrs Charles Dickens, 13 October 1853), and to PARIS at carnival time in 1855. Collins again visited the family in Paris during the carnival season of 1856, when there may have been masked visits to disreputable places, one of them described as 'much the same as our own National Argyll Rooms' (to Collins, 22 April 1856; the reference is to a high-class London ballroom). Their travels together culminate in 'The LAZY TOUR OF TWO IDLE APPRENTICES' of 1857, their joint account of a journey to Cumberland and Northern England during which Collins observed Dickens combining writing and sightseeing with the pursuit of his sudden infatuation with Ellen TERNAN.

The friendship with Wilkie Collins is the one close relationship that seems to have flourished and deepened after Dickens's separation from Catherine DICKENS. Some years later though, after about 1867, it too began to falter. In June of that year Dickens was impressed by the first three numbers of *The Moonstone*, proposing to Collins that they collaborate for the first time in six years on that year's Christmas story, 'No Thoroughfare', which Collins went on to turn into a play. But in 1868, when Dickens returned from America to find both *The Moonstone* and the play *No Thoroughfare* successes (in London and in Paris), the mood changes. There may be a hint of jealousy in his objection to 'a vein of obstinate conceit' in *The Moonstone*, its construction 'wearisome beyond endurance' (to Wills, 26 July 1868). Conversely, Collins may have been annoyed by Dickens's obvious dislike of his invalid son-in-law, Collins's brother; Charles FECHTER describes him looking across the table at Charles COLLINS as if to say 'Astonishing you should be here today, but tomorrow you will be in your chamber never to come out again' (see George Curry, *Dickens and Annie Fields*, 1988).

Some scholars think that these 'uncle–nephew' tensions are reflected in the relations between Jasper and Edwin in the unfinished

*Mystery of Edwin Drood*, a book which they construe as an attempt to outdo *The Moonstone*. Others regard some of the potentially subversive ingredients of Collins's SENSATION NOVELS—'in which incident took precedence over character, and criminal activity, particularly violent and sexual crime such as murder or bigamy, took place in a contemporary, domestic, middle-class setting' (Peters 1991)—as influences on Dickens's later work, altering the character of the last novel he wrote.

Yet, as T. S. Eliot (1932) remarks, Collins, as 'a master of plot and situation', was ultimately a different kind of writer from Dickens, with his poetic and myth-making powers, his capacity to create characters with 'that kind of reality which is almost supernatural'. Dickens in fact found Collins's technique and pre-occupation with plot-secrets somewhat self-conscious and obtrusive; he advised him to make his allusions to the secret of 'Sister Rose' 'a little less emphatic' (19 March 1855), and wrote of *The Woman in White* that 'the great pains you take express themselves a trifle too much, and you know that I always contest your disposition to give an audience credit for nothing' (7 January 1860). It is worth paying attention to these debates, for they provide clues to many of the subtleties of Dickens's mature art.                    MH

Eliot, T. S., 'Wilkie Collins and Dickens', *Selected Essays* (1932).

Lonoff, Sue, 'Charles Dickens and Wilkie Collins', *Nineteenth Century Fiction*, 35 (1980).

Peters, Catherine, *The King of Inventors* (1991).

**composition, Dickens's methods of.**
Dickens himself often described his compositional habits, and several of his friends and family members recorded observations of his practices when writing, but the most important documents revealing Dickens's methods of composition are the wealth of surviving manuscripts, corrected proofs, number plans, and memoranda of various sorts in Dickens's own hand.

Dickens often wrote in haste, sometimes (in the early stages of his career) beginning serial publication of one novel before the previous one was finished: *Oliver Twist*, for example, overlapped with both *Pickwick Papers* and *Nicholas Nickleby*, and Dickens conceived, wrote, and published *A Christmas Carol* while in the middle of writing *Martin Chuzzlewit* (see SERIAL LITERATURE). Furthermore, Dickens was invariably involved in a multitude of other activities while writing a novel. Yet despite the pressures of serial publication, Dickens was a careful, methodical, and painstaking artist, who was never, despite the insidious and persistent canard, 'paid by the word'.

Dickens published every one of his novels in serial form. Furthermore, Dickens *composed* serially, unlike some of his contemporaries, who published the first instalment only after writing the last one. Dickens told Constance Cross that his works 'are not written beyond the part that is to be published at a given time; but the plot, the motive of the book, is always perfected in my brain for a long time before I take up my pen. I add a great deal to the original idea as I work on, but, as I always know the end from the beginning, I can safely commit my work in parts to the press' (quoted in Collins 1981, 2.348). Despite the difficulties inherent in this form of composition, Dickens never missed a serial instalment, with one important exception: when his sister-in-law Mary HOGARTH died, he was 'so shaken and unnerved', as he wrote to Thomas Beard, that he was 'compelled to lay aside all thoughts of my usual monthly work, for once' (17 May 1837), missing serial instalments of both *Pickwick Papers* and *Oliver Twist*. In the 33 years of Dickens's remaining career, this happened only once more, under pressure of work in September 1838—until all the instalments stopped forever, midway through *Edwin Drood*.

Though later in his career Dickens sometimes had two or more monthly instalments completed before he began publication, by the time he was halfway through a novel he was generally working right up to his deadline; Dickens wrote to Carey, Lea, & Blanchard that he 'only completed each Number [of *Nicholas Nickleby*] a day or two before its publication' (18 July 1838). Dickens generally reserved the early part of the month for novel-writing, trying (sometimes with great difficulty) to complete his monthly portion by the middle of the month, in order to give his ILLUSTRATOR enough time to draw and etch the plates to accompany his text; Dickens's contract for *Nicholas Nickleby* stipulated that he deliver instalments of his manuscript by the 15th, though later contracts simply indicated that the instalments be 'in time' (Patten 1978, pp. 89 and 123).

Dickens wrote his fiction in the mornings primarily, though he occasionally wrote in the afternoons. He described his schedule in various letters, telling FORSTER early in his career that he went 'to work at half-past [eight]', and was 'commonly free by one o'clock or so' (2 September 1840). In 1867 Dickens told the Revd G. D. Carrow that his 'invariable habit of working' involved writing at his desk from 'ten precisely' until two or 'if particularly in the vein' until four in the afternoon; he told Carrow, 'so rigid is my conformity to this method of work that my family say I am a monomaniac on the subject' (quoted in *Dickensian*, 63, 1967). In the early years of his career, though, Dickens did sometimes work at night; when composing *Oliver Twist*, he 'often wrote till late at night, something he never did in later years' (Johnson 1.221).

Dickens's brother-in-law, Henry Burnett, recalled a 'night in Doughty Street' when he and his wife joined Mrs Charles Dickens in a fireside chat. Dickens, at work on *Oliver Twist*, joined them, seated himself at a little table, and 're-commenced' writing (see DICKENS, CATHERINE; BROTHERS AND SISTERS OF DICKENS). They continued talking, and Dickens 'every now and then (the feather of his pen still moving rapidly from side to side), put in a cheerful interlude. It was interesting to watch, upon the sly, the mind and the muscles working (or, if you please, *playing*) in company, as new thoughts were being dropped upon the paper' (quoted in Collins 1981, 2.22). Writing at night and writing in company were both, evidently, extremely rare occurrences, especially later in his career.

Under unusual circumstances, Dickens was capable of working extended hours; when writing *David Copperfield*, he told his wife, he worked 'nine hours at a stretch' (20 August 1850), for example. When Dickens was observing his usual schedule he found it essential to preserve the routine of his whole day, rejecting all invitations that threatened to disturb that routine.

Dickens usually wrote two to four manuscript pages a day, in his maturity, though sometimes significantly less. He told Forster that when planning *Barnaby Rudge* he 'sat and *thought* all day; not writing a line . . . I imaged

forth a good deal of *Barnaby* by keeping my mind steadily upon him' (29 January 1841). On some occasions, especially at the beginning of novels, he would report writing as little as a single page in a day. But if he was capable of very slow work, he was equally capable of prodigious output; he told W. H. WILLS that he wrote 'exactly 72 words' of *Hard Times* in five days (22 June 1854), but he completed the whole 100,000-word novel in substantially less than six months.

Dickens wrote many more pages a day as a young man, in large part because the pages had significantly fewer words on them: over time, his handwriting grew increasingly small and compact. Late in his career it took only about 27 manuscript pages to complete a 32-page monthly instalment, whereas he might easily write more than 90 for an instalment of his early novels. A sample page of *Nicholas Nickleby* manuscript corresponds to less than 175 words (approximately a third of a page) as published in the first edition. A fragment of *Edwin Drood* manuscript, which has been reproduced in facsimile, is incomplete, giving only the top half of the final page of Dickens's manuscript (and omitting Dickens's page number, 20, from the top line), but even so, it provides the text of over 350 words (about two-thirds of a page) as published in the first edition.

Dickens invariably used a goose-quill pen, and preferred black ink (often fading to brown in surviving manuscripts) through his early career, beginning to favour blue ink in the late 1840s, though black or brown ink appears at various times throughout the remainder of his writing career. He never used pencil, even for private memoranda. He usually wrote on a fairly standard-size sheet of paper: the surviving manuscripts of most of the novels are on paper measuring within a half-centimetre of 18.5 × 22.5 centimetres (roughly 7 × 9 inches).

Dickens preferred to write in a quiet study, near a window, with fresh flowers in a nearby vase. By the late 1840s he also needed a collection of familiar objects, including 'the bronze images of two toads duelling', close at hand (Ackroyd 1990, p. 503). In a letter to Wills he complained of barking dogs in the street keeping him from working on *Bleak House* (9 December 1852). Though he required solitude and silence, he also needed the stimulation of

London available to him; he found beginning work on his 1844 Christmas book when he was abroad most difficult (?6 October 1844 and ?mid-October 1844), and wrote to Forster that he needed the 'MAGIC LANTERN' of 'a day in London' (30 August 1846). Beginning *Dombey and Son*, he told Forster that 'Invention, thank God, seems the easiest thing in the world', but he found he could not work 'at what I call a rapid pace', saying his difficulty was partly 'the absence of streets and numbers of figures. I can't express how much I want these. It seems as if they supplied something to my brain, which it cannot bear, when busy, to lose' (30 August 1846).

Dickens generally worked at his desk, though he wrote *Barnaby Rudge* on his couch for a time after his painful fistula operation in early October of 1841.

Though Dickens almost always worked alone, his daughter Mamie joined him once when recovering from an illness, and her recollections are striking: 'I was lying on the sofa endeavouring to keep perfectly quiet, while my father wrote busily and rapidly at his desk, when he suddenly jumped from his chair and rushed to a mirror which hung near, and in which I could see the reflection of some extraordinary facial contortions which he was making. He returned rapidly to his desk, wrote furiously for a few moments, and then went back to the mirror. The facial pantomime was resumed, and then turning toward, but evidently not seeing, me, he began talking rapidly in a low voice[.] Ceasing this soon, however, he returned once more to his desk, where he remained silently writing until luncheon time' (quoted in Collins 1981, 1.121; see CHILDREN OF DICKENS).

Dickens's emotional involvement with his own creation was extraordinary; he laughed and wept over his own characters, and made the most eccentric faces when creating them, as Mamie noted. He felt great tension when writing of Nell's death in *The Old Curiosity Shop*, re-experiencing all the pain of Mary Hogarth's death; when he finished *The CHIMES*, he wrote to Forster that he had 'had what women call "a real good cry!" ' (3 and [4] November 1844).

The process of beginning a work of fiction was particularly emotionally involving: when beginning *The HAUNTED MAN*, he told Mrs WATSON that his 'state of inaccessibility and irascibility' 'utterly confounds and scares the House' (5 October 1848), and when he was 'planning and planning the story of Hard Times', he told W. H. Wills, he was 'in a dreary state' (18 April 1854). A letter to Miss COUTTS gives an idea of his mental state when in the throes of compositional agony: he told her 'Your note finds me settling myself to Little Dorrit again, and in the usual wretchedness of such settlement—which is unsettlement. Prowling about the rooms, sitting down, getting up, stirring the fire, looking out of window, tearing my hair, sitting down to write, writing nothing, writing something and tearing it up, going out, coming in, a Monster to my family, a dread Phenomenon to myself, &c &c &c' (19 February 1856).

Despite this emotional involvement, Dickens could also, in talking about his literary labours, sound quite emotionally cold, or even murderous: nearing the end of *David Copperfield*, he wrote to his wife 'I have still Dora to kill' (21 August 1850).

Dickens often felt frustration at constraints of space, particularly for those novels published in smaller weekly instalments; he bemoaned to Forster his lack of 'elbow room' in *Barnaby Rudge* (18 September 1841), and when writing *Hard Times* complained to Forster that 'The difficulty of the space is CRUSHING' (?February 1854), telling Mrs Richard Watson that 'the compression and close condensation necessary for that disjointed form of publication [of *Hard Times* in *Household Words*] gave me perpetual trouble' (1 November 1854). He also complained of this constraint when writing *Great Expectations*.

Dickens drew upon a variety of sources when composing his fiction. His reading and his experiences in the theatre played a part, as did, on comparatively rare occasions, research, but primarily Dickens drew on his own keen observation and life experiences, as well as his brilliant imagination. But for the most part Dickens's novels seem to have come to him relatively easily. He told Forster: 'when . . . I sit down to my book, some beneficent power shows it all to me . . . and I don't invent it—really do not—but see it, and write it down' (?October 1841). George Henry LEWES reported that Dickens 'once declared to me that every word said by his characters was distinctly heard by him' (quoted in Collins 1981,

1.25). But Dickens's writing was never automatic, and rarely (except in letters) unrevised. Nor was his writing unplanned. He disparaged the very notion in a letter to Peter Cunningham, saying that 'it encourages the public to believe in the impossibility that books are produced in [a] very sudden and Cavalier manner' (11 March 1854).

On occasion, Dickens conducted research for his fiction, modelling Fang, the magistrate in *Oliver Twist*, on the notorious magistrate Mr Laing, and visiting Yorkshire schools before writing about Dotheboys Hall in *Nicholas Nickleby*. When he was planning *A Tale of Two Cities* Thomas CARLYLE sent him cartloads of books on the French Revolution—though Dickens probably did not read them all.

Beginning in 1855, he occasionally made entries in a Memoranda Book, telling Angela Burdett-Coutts that he has noted 'new ideas for a story . . . in a little book I keep' (5 September 1857). This little book (Dickens wrote on just 25 of its 176 small pages, making fewer than 120 entries) included ideas for plots, characters, names, situations, titles, and even scraps of dialogue, many of which were never used. Fred Kaplan reproduces *Dickens' Book of Memoranda* with transcriptions and notes (1981).

Titles were particularly important to Dickens, and finding the right one was a vital part of the groundwork for a novel: Dickens needed to find a title he liked before he began writing in earnest. Trial titles for several of the novels exist. On one of the more than fifteen surviving pages of possibilities for *David Copperfield* is 'Mag's Diversions: Being the personal history, adventures, experience, and observation, of Mr David Copperfield the Younger And his Great-Aunt Margaret'; of the eleven surviving pages devoted to titles for *Bleak House*, all but the last one begin with 'Tom-All-Alone's'. Dickens made up number plans, or working notes, for most of his later novels. (Three pages of plans for *The Old Curiosity Shop* survive, and two for *Martin Chuzzlewit*, along with trial titles and some pages of character names; although there are only a few pages of notes for *Great Expectations*, and nothing at all for *A Tale of Two Cities*, plans exist for all the other novels beginning with *Dombey and Son*.) Dickens evidently began to draw these plans up some

time in advance: he drew up pages for each of the twelve instalments of *Edwin Drood*, though the plans for the final six numbers contain no more than the name of the novel and the number of the instalment.

These plans, including bits of plot, sketches of character, fragments of dialogue, and even notations about theme, often provide great insight into Dickens's imagination and craftsmanship; they are reproduced with transcriptions in Harry Stone's *Dickens's Working Notes for His Novels* (1987).

The plans evidently served both retrospective and prospective functions: they provided a reminder of what he had done, as well as a way of noting what he needed to do in the future. Dickens used these notes to organize his instalments, noting the contents of each chapter. He created, usually, a single page for each monthly instalment (or its equivalent, in the case of the weekly *Hard Times*), turning that page sideways, dividing it down the middle, making general notations and queries about the instalment (usually answered by himself) on the left half, and inscribing more specific notations about the essential events and characters of each chapter on the right half.

On the left side of the plans for the thirteenth instalment of *David Copperfield*, for example, Dickens considered what belongs in the instalment: he determined not to treat 'The Doctor, Annie, and Mr Jack Maldon' in this number, and to treat Traddles in the 'Next No.'; he decided he must 'carry on the thread of Uriah, carefully, and not obtrusively; also of David and Agnes'. On the right side, he treated elements of plot, and noted the characters he wished to deal with in each chapter, but he also quoted from Julia Mills's diary: 'Self and Young Gazelle. J. M'; he also noted, with respect to 'Uriah and his mother', that he must explain 'Why 'Umble'. Sometimes notations indicate how far in advance Dickens was plotting; the plans for the fifth instalment of *David Copperfield*, for example, include an allusion to Agnes as 'the real heroine'. At times Dickens was very explicit about thematic matters, as when he identified Sissy Jupe specifically with the 'Power of affection' in the plans for *Hard Times*. His notations about the deaths of important characters can seem surprisingly cold-blooded; when he determined, in the fifteenth number of *Bleak House*, that

Jo must die, his terse note reads simply 'Jo? Yes. Kill him', doubly underlined. Sometimes, the notes identify a historical source for a character, as when the notes about Frederick Dorrit mention 'the clarionet-player I saw at the Ambigu in Paris'. When Dickens planned his treatment of David at the Murdstone and Grinby warehouse in chapter 11 of *David Copperfield*, the notes are extraordinarily brief, but evocative: the words 'what I know so well' stand alone on the left-hand side of the page (see DICKENS: PRIVATE LIFE).

At times, Dickens worked out last-minute structural changes in the number plans, determining to provide four chapters rather than three in the tenth instalment of *David Copperfield*, or to replace the chapter treating 'A Marriage Contract' with one introducing Mr Venus in the second instalment of *Our Mutual Friend*, and deferring the Lammle marriage until the conclusion of the third instalment.

In addition to the usual form of number plans, Dickens sometimes drew up special notes: for *Great Expectations* he prepared a page about dates and ages, a table noting the tides for the conclusion of the novel, and a page of 'General Mems' about the strings he needs to pull together; for *Little Dorrit*, with its extraordinarily convoluted plot, he drew up two additional pages of what he called 'Mems: for working the story round', where he noted precisely what he had already committed himself to doing, and calculated in some detail just what needed to be in Arthur Clennam's father's uncle's mysterious will.

The most interesting and revealing sources of information about Dickens's habits of composition are the handwritten manuscripts themselves, increasingly heavily revised over the course of his career. Dickens never used an amanuensis for his fiction (though on rare occasions he dictated a letter, and he did dictate the MEMOIRS OF GRIMALDI to his father (see DICKENS, JOHN) and *A CHILD'S HISTORY OF ENGLAND* to Georgina HOGARTH. Dickens told Frau Alberti that he never dictated, saying 'I can as soon imagine a painter dictating his pictures'. He told her 'I write every word of my books with my own hand, and do not write them very quickly either. I write with great care and pains (being passionately fond of my art, and thinking it worth any trouble), and persevere, and work

hard' (30 April 1856). Dickens avoided most abbreviations (though he did use Mr for Mister), and invariably wrote out numbers—even dates—in long form; he only rarely availed himself of ditto marks.

Georgina Hogarth did not find Dickens's handwriting difficult, but she appears to be exceptional; Sylvère Monod speaks for the majority when he declares it 'excruciatingly difficult to read' (1968, p. 71). Dickens wrote to the child Francis Waugh that 'printers can read anything, and they have made me lazy about the shapes of my letters, and the clearness of my loops, and the roundness of my O's (there's a round one though), and all that' (30 June 1858). His capital letters are often particularly difficult to distinguish from lower-case ones—especially the letters 'a' and 'c', but often 's' and 'w' as well.

Dickens, who invariably began renumbering with each new monthly instalment, almost always wrote on one side of a page only—though in a few rare cases he added a passage on the verso of a page, to be inserted on the recto. Often, if he began a page and did not like what he had written, he simply turned the page over and began again, so false starts of a line or two (and occasionally a bit more) appear with some frequency on the back of his pages.

Dickens usually made deletions with thick swirls of ink, making the deleted words difficult (or impossible) to decipher. In *Pickwick Papers* and the early chapters of *Oliver Twist*, however, he sometimes deleted with a single line. On those occasions when he cut several lines, he usually marked them as a block, and deleted them with several diagonal lines through the passage.

When he added text, Dickens usually wrote it in above the original line. On rare occasions he added text below the line. His use of a caret to indicate placement of an interlineation was usual, but by no means constant. His revisions were plentiful and complex; secondary interlineations and deletions to his initial revisions indicate clearly that Dickens considered and reconsidered his words and the effect they would have on a reader.

Though Dickens rarely added material on the back of a page, the fourth chapter of *Great Expectations* provides a notable exception. At Christmas dinner, where Pip is tormented by the Hubbles, the Wopsles, Pumblechook, and

Mrs Joe, Pip receives his only succour from Joe, who gives him gravy. Dickens interlined the paragraphs in which Joe gives him gravy, and added the paragraph establishing the meaning of the gravy to the verso, with a note to the printer at the point where the paragraph should be added reading 'See back'.

Despite the difficulty of his handwriting and the complexity of Dickens's manuscript revisions, there is little evidence that he ever made a fair copy. Illustrator Marcus STONE wrote that Dickens advised him 'Never make a fair copy of a much corrected manuscript. A MS with few or no corrections is always given to the boy beginner to set up, and you will get a proof full of errors. The MS which is difficult to decipher is put into the hands of a first rate compositor whose proof will give very little trouble' (MS in Dickens House; quoted in Collins 1981, 2.188–9).

Over time, Dickens's revisions within his manuscripts grew increasingly complex. Though most of these were probably made at the time of original inscription or shortly thereafter, in some rare cases revisions were made with different colours of ink, suggesting at least a small gap in time. (Of course, serial publication meant that there was almost never a chance for more than a few weeks between initial inscription of the manuscript and submission of that manuscript to the printers.)

Examination of a representative page of the *Nicholas Nickleby* manuscript (part of chapter 15 in the published text) reveals no visible revisions in the final eleven lines of the page: the only changes are in Fanny's letter, and even these are for the most part decidedly minor. There are only six interlined words, and only seventeen deleted ones, most of comparatively little interest. Dickens alters 'taken' to 'took', in order to make Fanny's grammar more consistently weak; he changes 'must come to be hanged' to the slightly less formal 'is sure to be hanged' for similar reasons. Interlining 'much' before 'more' is typical; Dickens often intensifies effects in the manuscript. His fumblings with the word 'assassin' and 'and cetrer' could be mere pen slips.

The differences between this early manuscript and the final page of Dickens's manuscript of *Edwin Drood* are striking. The many revisions in the latter half of the first paragraph and in the second one are far more typical of his late (and even middle-period) manuscripts, with Dickens shaping many key phrases through revision. '[G]lorious light from moving boughs', 'Mrs Tope, and attendant sweeping sprites. Come, in due time', 'red curtains in the loft, fearlessly flapping', 'that remote elevation', and 'leading the line' are a few of the substantial phrases interlined here. Dickens created the simile 'like children shirking bed' through interlineation, and interlined several key verbs and modifiers, including 'subdue', 'preach', 'struggling', 'yawningly', 'sundry', 'of the sky', and 'small and straggling'. Dickens substituted 'enjoy' for 'delight in', and 'nightgowns' for 'gowns'; clearly, he deleted nearly as many words as he added here.

Dickens accomplished many things through his revisions within the manuscripts, often heightening or strengthening rhetorical effects, occasionally toning them down or making them more subtle, adjusting names, creating and emphasizing characteristic gestures, adjusting plot, correcting errors, revealing theme, creating humour, and even, at times, censoring himself: the famous first sentence of *A Tale of Two Cities* originally ended with 'direct to Hell', but Dickens crossed that phrase out, substituting 'direct the other way' through interlineation.

Usually, his revisions do not alter the fundamental direction of his work, and only rarely does he change the opening of a work substantially; when working on The BATTLE OF LIFE, he told Forster, 'I cancelled the beginning of a first scene—which I have never done before' (?20 September 1846). His rejection of a seven-page passage in the sixth chapter of *Martin Chuzzlewit* is exceptional. Significant alterations in plot are comparatively rare; Dickens was likely to work that sort of thing out in his head, and in the number plans, before he drafted chapters. Nevertheless, the opening paragraphs of the fourth chapter of *Little Dorrit* make it clear that it was originally to have been Jeremiah Flintwinch, and not Affery, who would have the peculiar 'dreams' that prove central to the mystery plot of that novel. Dickens clearly wanted to create a mystery and to develop the idea of dream and reality, but he was content to leave the details of the mystery (such as the contents of the mysterious iron box) to be worked out later.

Dickens rarely sought another's opinion of his works. Forster read many of the novels in manuscript, and Dickens revised a few passages on his recommendation; Dickens also altered the direction of *David Copperfield* by changing the essential character of Miss Mowcher, after receiving a letter of protest from Mrs Jane Seymour Hill, the real-life dwarf after whom Dickens all-too-evidently modelled the fictional character (see CHARACTERS—ORIGINALS). More notoriously, Dickens altered the original ending of *Great Expectations* at BULWER-LYTTON's suggestion.

An important (and sometimes overlooked) part of Dickens's process of composition was communication with his illustrators about what specifically should be illustrated and how. Often this was a hurried job: Dickens was sometimes unable to provide his illustrator with proofs of the text to be illustrated, so he would often simply tell him what he wanted, by letter or in person, usually as he neared completion of a number. In a letter to Forster he evinced great concern over the illustrations to *Dombey and Son*, providing hints for H. K. BROWNE with respect to the illustrations of Mr Dombey, Miss Tox, Susan Nipper, and others (18 July 1846).

The final pre-publication phase of composition was the correction of proof. Dickens did not, typically, read proof against his original manuscript; this led to some unfortunate mistakes. For example, in the fifth chapter of *Bleak House*, in the passage where Krook first meets Ada Clare, he remarks on her hair, saying 'Here's lovely hair!' In the manuscript, Dickens interlined the sentence 'I buy hair' just after this. The compositors misread the interlineation and printed 'Strong hair'; when Dickens found this in the proofs, he rightly understood this to be nonsense, and struck it out. Had he been able to read proofs against his manuscript, we would presumably still have 'I buy hair', but he did not—and no subsequent editor has restored Dickens's original phrase.

Dickens often read proof in some haste, and occasionally delegated this responsibility to Forster, inviting him to 'erase anything that seems to you too strong' in *Barnaby Rudge* (5 April 1841), and to make cuts in the first instalment of *Dombey and Son*: 'In case more cutting is wanted, I must ask you to try your hand. I shall agree to whatever you propose'

(13 and 14 August 1846). Even more surprising, perhaps, are those (rare) cases where Dickens asked Forster to add a bit to the proofs, as when he forgot to discuss the fate of the dog Diogenes in the final chapter of *Dombey and Son*. In his letter to Forster, he offered a couple of suggestions, and then exhorted him to add 'Just what you think best' (25 March 1848).

Still, Dickens generally took proof-reading seriously, making many changes and corrections in the details of spelling and punctuation, especially with respect to the dialect of such characters as Mrs Gamp and Flora Finching. Though his work in proof was often painstaking and extensive with respect to such details, he did not, typically, extensively rewrite his novels in proof (though the proofs of articles written by others for *Household Words* or *All the Year Round* were another matter entirely).

Dickens cared deeply about the presentation of his text. Enraged at a typographical error, Dickens complained to printer F. M. Evans 'your men are enough to drive me mad!' Dickens accused them of making 'a flagrant and unpardonable mistake' (the substitution of 'Dark' for 'Deep'), and described himself as 'so disgusted by it, that I throw down my pen in an absolute despair' (16 December 1851).

Because Dickens had rigid space constraints (precisely 32 pages for a standard monthly instalment), he usually preferred to write a little extra, and then trim the instalment down to size in proof. He would sometimes write significantly more than could fit, requiring substantial cuts; most often, he would trim dialogue, descriptive passages, or humorous observations. These passages deleted from proof, which would probably never have been cut had Dickens not chosen serial publication, are often of great interest: when Dick Swiveller first meets Sally Brass in *The Old Curiosity Shop*, Dick muses, in an unpublished paragraph, about whether or not she can be a 'dragon', a 'she-dragon', or a 'mermaid', finally settling on a 'dragon'; near the end of *Our Mutual Friend* there is a fascinating unpublished passage exploring the murderer Bradley Headstone's obsessions with his crime, and with the river, which 'ran in his thoughts distractingly' and 'seemed to call out to him'. Though most of Dickens's novels went through several different editions during his lifetime, he rarely made extensive or significant changes in his works at this time, unlike, say, Henry James; once a novel was in print, his creative interest in it was substantially diminished (see EDITIONS OVER WHICH DICKENS HAD CONTROL). He did, however, remove many references to 'The Jew' for the 1867 edition of *Oliver Twist*; he also revised several prefaces, most particularly to *American Notes* and *Martin Chuzzlewit*. Dickens also adjusted the phrasing of the final sentence of *Great Expectations* to heighten its ambiguity, and provided descriptive running headlines for the Charles Dickens Edition of his works, begun in 1867. But for the most part, the changes in later editions represent alterations in spelling and punctuation rather than in wording, and there is next to no evidence that those alterations represent Dickens's own preferences; his most creative compositional energies were most strongly engaged at the time of original inscription.

JJB

Butt and Tillotson (1957).

**copyright.** Copyright, of widespread concern only after the invention of printing from moveable type, developed around three related issues: (1) concerns about propriety, notably expressed in the Crown's right to control the publication of political and religious materials through censorship, customs and excise acts, and licensing of printing presses; (2) concerns about property and underwriting learning, expressed in many ways, one of which was the issuing of Crown privileges to print certain works for a term or in perpetuity in order to support education; and (3) concerns about promoting invention, which among other things made copyright terms multiples of the terms for royal patents, fourteen years.

In 1709 the first Copyright Act in the world received Queen Anne's royal assent. This Act recognized a statutory right for authors to share in their writings. Hitherto copyright had been a right asserted by printers, who after purchasing manuscripts outright from authors or other owners entered the titles in the Stationers' Company register to assert their exclusive right to print copies. Booksellers, commercial successors to 17th-century printers, wanted at the beginning of the 18th

century to reaffirm their permanent ownership of copying rights to lucrative properties, such as the plays of Shakespeare and the poems of Milton. But Queen Anne's Act granted vested copyright owners the right to publish for only 21 years from 10 April 1710. Queen Anne's Act also granted to authors producing new texts after 10 April 1710 the exclusive right to print for fourteen years, renewable for another fourteen years if at the expiration of the first term the author was still living. The Act extinguished the author's residual common-law right, although that implication was not fully established until the House of Lords heard a case on appeal in 1774. The outcome was that authors had no rights beyond a statutory copyright of defined extent, and booksellers could not claim that they owned 'perpetual copyright'. The proliferation of cheap editions of standard texts, some of which found their way into Dickens's small boyhood library, is partly a consequence of this extinguishing of booksellers' monopoly control.

One other important outcome of Queen Anne's Act, decided in the courts in 1741, was that authors retain copyright in their unpublished materials. In the subsequent elaboration of this right the concern for propriety became influential: if an author did not wish a manuscript to be printed, so that no statutory copyright term had been established for it, an author retained all rights, even if the manuscript of the unpublished work came to be owned by someone else. Dickens's unpublished correspondence and any other unpublished writings, no matter where they are located, are still 'in copyright', and cannot be printed without permission of Dickens's heirs.

The principal law affecting Dickens's copyright during his lifetime was 5 & 6 Vict. c. 45, the 1842 Copyright Amendment Act that secured to the author, heirs, and assigns copyright for 42 years or seven years after the author's death, whichever was longer. This statute, justified on the grounds that it encouraged 'the Production of Literary Works of lasting Benefit to the World', gave authors and their estates a much longer-term interest in their writings. (Whereas the copyright of the serial edition of *Pickwick*, 1836–7, expired in 1879, the copyright of *Drood* extended to 1912.) In time it shifted power away from booksellers and publishers and towards writers, who leased their copyrights for stipulated terms or numbers of printings, and who then had the opportunity to lease them out again for additional editions. It also made prosecution for infringement of copyright easier.

During Dickens's childhood and youth there were few successful actions for infringement of copyright. ADAPTATIONS, ABRIDGMENTS, digests of other journals ('parasytical Weekly Publications', John Murray called them), parodies, imitations, and SEQUELS were common theatrical, literary, and graphic genres; indeed, many commercial enterprises depended on constantly producing new variants of old favourites. At the start of his career Dickens himself borrowed and burlesqued preceding and contemporary materials; and some of his playwright friends continued to translate foreign—mainly French—drama for the English stage, without paying or even acknowledging the original author, until the 1850s. But when Dickens saw his own works being staged, as *Oliver Twist* was, months before he had even conceived of the novel's ending, and when cheap imitations of his stories flooded the market within days of his own publication, he launched both verbal and legal attacks (see DRAMATIZATIONS; PLAGIARISMS). In 1837 he also supported the efforts of his friend Thomas Noon TALFOURD (the 'original' of Tommy Traddles in *Copperfield* and the dedicatee of *Pickwick*) to have a bill passed strengthening authors' copyrights. That bill was finally passed through the efforts of Philip Henry Stanhope, Lord Mahon, Thomas Babington Macaulay, and Sir Robert Peel; it received the royal assent on 1 July 1842.

By that date Dickens had written and published six major works and a number of minor pieces. Almost all of them had been reprinted, some several times, in unauthorized versions—'piracies', Dickens called them, though the absence of specific statutory prohibitions against imitations and the contradictions of court decisions in equity made Wordsworth's term, 'moral piracy', a more accurate description of the practice. However, before 1842, and even afterwards, Dickens's legal efforts to stop the pirates were, for the most part, unavailing; even when he won, the defendants took bankruptcy, thus avoiding payment of damages and sticking Dickens, in

one instance, with all his 'expences, costs and charges' (to T. N. Talfourd, 5 May 1844; see CHANCERY).

Another deficiency in the earlier copyright acts was the absence of regulation about copies of British authors printed abroad, for sale in the colonies or other countries, and copies of titles by foreign nationals imported into Britain. When Dickens travelled to AMERICA in the winter and spring of 1842, he spoke out, frequently, in favour of an 'international'—by which he meant, at a minimum, a 'bi-national'—copyright agreement with America granting reciprocal privileges to subjects or citizens of other countries. Dickens's own books were for the most part published in the United States by agreement, various publishers securing from him, for a few pounds, proofs or advanced sheets or later stereotypes of his latest work, and then announcing in American papers that they were publishing that title (see EDITIONS: FOREIGN ENGLISH-LANGUAGE EDITIONS OF DICKENS'S WORKS). By 'trade courtesy', a long-standing practice, other publishers would not rush out competing editions—except when a severe depression, or a trade war, or some other exceptional event triggered frenzy and the collapse of orderly markets.

American authors, too, could be printed and sold in Britain without any copyright agreement. Some of them, like William Cullen Bryant and Washington IRVING, wanted revenue from their British sales and some protection for American writings against the flood of cheaper British imports, and therefore supported Dickens's position. But the American press, goaded by sensationalist publishers, protectionist printers, and politicians disingenuously rallying around the notion that cheap knowledge was a public benefit, hurled execrations upon Dickens's head. He returned home somewhat damaged in reputation and feelings, and in *Martin Chuzzlewit* he satirized cut-throat, 'piratical', and hypocritical American journalism. For the next ten years Dickens refused to 'enter into any negociation' for the transmission of early proofs to America, a resolution he ended when Harper's offered £360 to serialize *Bleak House* in their magazine simultaneously with its British issue.

Gradually the 1842 Act, though badly composed and subject to repeated amendment and judicial clarification, stabilized publishing within Britain. From 1844 on Dickens had comparatively little trouble establishing and defending his domestic copyrights. His later difficulties arose from his international renown: in the absence of international law, how could he control the publication abroad of his works in English or in translation, the importation into British colonies of cheaper, unauthorized editions printed abroad, and the importation into Britain itself of those cheap editions, challenging the authorized home products?

In the first year of Victoria's reign, 1838, legislation permitting copyright exchanges among nations was passed, but the first 'international' Copyright Act was 7 & 8 Vict. c. 12, an 1844 Act repealing its 1838 predecessor, which had never been used. The consequence to Dickens was that his works now could be circulated in English in signatory countries and be protected there by those countries' copyright laws, although he was not a citizen there and had not first published his books there—usual provisions for establishing copyright in a country, except in post-Revolutionary France, where Napoleon's imperial decree granted copyright to any living author, French or not (5 February 1810), and guaranteed a French author home copyright even if the title was first published abroad. Britain signed conventions with Prussia and Saxony almost immediately.

The principal publisher to take advantage of these conventions was Bernhard Christian Tauchnitz, apprenticed to his uncle, the Leipzig printer and publisher Karl Tauchnitz, who died in 1836. The young Tauchnitz, not yet 21, founded his own firm the following year; and in September 1841 he launched an ambitious 'Collection of British Authors', reprinting texts in English for continental distribution. Although Tauchnitz said that 'from the first' he required the written authority of his author, and 'he paid for it', no surviving records indicate that he paid Dickens for English-language editions of any book before he came to London in 1843 to sign up British writers, including Benjamin DISRAELI, Harrison AINSWORTH, Edward BULWER-LYTTON, and Dickens. With these agreements in hand, Tauchnitz acquired the right to sell British books in those German states participating, either directly or through the Prussian *Zoll-*verein, in the Anglo-German convention; when in 1852 France concluded a bi-national treaty with Britain, Tauchnitz extended his range, using his influence with British authors to secure protection for his editions in French markets.

From October 1843 until his death, Dickens maintained cordial relations with Tauchnitz. He sent his son Charley, at age 16, to the Tauchnitz family in 1853 to learn German, assuring Angela Burdett COUTTS, whose interest in his first-born Dickens had also solicited, that Tauchnitz 'is a gentleman of great honor and integrity' (9 December 1852). Tauchnitz paid Dickens a lump sum for each of his titles, and the Dickens volumes issued in the Tauchnitz series, which eventually numbered over 4,000 volumes, were a principal way Anglophone readers, whether British travellers or foreign nationals, read Dickens in Europe. For whatever reasons, there was never serious difficulty about stopping the importation into Britain or its dominions of these Tauchnitz editions: the publisher was scrupulous about his markets, and from 1844 importation even of personal copies obtained abroad was 'absolutely prohibited'. Dickens's own publishers, beginning in 1847, began marketing cheaper editions of his collected works for home consumption; some of these, in later years, made their way into overseas British markets. The situation was not clear or uniform throughout the royal dominions; for instance, Canada continued to import American editions of British authors instead of the higher-priced British printings, and Indian, Australian, and New Zealand booksellers marketed a variety of authorized British and unauthorized foreign editions, chiefly American, despite the efforts of John Murray and others to produce in Britain inexpensive libraries of popular works specifically for sale to colonial customers. Authorized editions sometimes, and unauthorized ones rarely, paid authors something.

One further copyright law affected Dickens: in 1852 the Anglo-French convention established Dickens's rights as an author in France, rights that, as in all the bi-national conventions, were defined by the home country, not the author's country. Thus, in France Dickens's copyrights passed to his widow for her life and to his children for another twenty years. These provisions applied primarily to

TRANSLATIONS; after 1852 Dickens's British publications specify that the right of translation is reserved—before that foreigners translated British novels with impunity. In January 1856 Dickens concluded an agreement with the Parisian publishing house Hachette for a uniform edition in translation of all his works; the publisher offered 500 francs per volume for titles published before the 1852 bi-national convention (which were essentially uncovered by any copyright law), and 1,000 francs per volumes for those published thereafter. Dickens forwarded the proposed terms to Tauchnitz; when he said they were fair (and would not infringe on his own rights), Dickens concluded the deal. Subsequently much better versions of early work that had hitherto been available only in hasty, careless translations, and equally good renditions of the later novels, were circulated throughout France and its colonies. Additional bi-national conventions reciprocally extending copyright protection were signed by Britain with Belgium, Spain, the remaining German states, and the States of Sardinia before Dickens's death. As late as 1869, however, Dickens refused to authorize a translation in any non-signatory state.

Dickens's largest foreign market was probably the United States, and there no bi-national convention existed. But there were laws protecting American publishers' printings, and statutes and court decisions in Britain that made it reasonably clear that British publication had to precede publication in a non-signatory country for British copyright to be established. (There was a period of time when non-nationals could obtain British copyright by residing anywhere in the realm on the day of publication; hence many American authors travelled to the British West Indies to secure British copyright on the same day they published in America.)

As Dickens and his publishers concluded more and more lucrative agreements with American agents and publishers for 'simultaneous publication' in both countries, all parties had to be punctilious about release dates so as not to jeopardize copyright. Dickens told Harold Ticknor in February 1870 that he 'was certain' of the English copyright being lost' on any portion of Drood published first in the United States (to Fields, Osgood & Co., 14 May 1870). During Dickens's lifetime the timing seems to have worked correctly almost all the time; but later in the century when authors' works were sold through syndicates as newspaper filler to journals all over the world, such niceties of dating were less reliably observed.

For the most part, American industry's protectionist laws prevented the importation of printed sheets from other countries; print had to be set, or stereotypes printed, in the United States. But in anticipation of Dickens's second American tour, Frederic Chapman managed to sell large quantities of the Library Edition, printed in Britain, to the American publishers TICKNOR AND FIELDS, Scribner's, Appleton, Little and Brown, and Lippincott, even though Ticknor and Fields were simultaneously preparing their own Diamond Edition in fourteen volumes with new illustrations by Sol EYTINGE Jr. If one adds to the sums Dickens cleared from American publishers for authorization to print or early copies of texts, the sums he made from collected editions and the reading editions marketed during and after his second American tour, Dickens received around £10,000 from a country with which Britain had no copyright agreement. That remuneration shows not only that Dickens was mistaken in asserting that in America his writings were worthless to him, but also that international copyright was a necessary and useful, but not absolute, precondition for authors to make money from overseas sales.

Throughout his lifetime Dickens entered into a wide variety of contracts with printers, publishers, and distribution agents. He obtained more and more control as laws, combined with his own reputation and marketing power and competent legal advice, enhanced his bargaining position. In 1861, as a result of the break with BRADBURY AND EVANS and his return to CHAPMAN AND HALL, Dickens decided to consolidate all his titles and rights with one publisher. He therefore purchased from Bradbury and Evans whatever share in their prior publications they still retained, and he then sold that share (at a profit) to Frederic Chapman. Thereafter Chapman and Hall held a half-interest in all Dickens's earlier copyrights; for future serials—there were only two—they obtained merely a short-term lease, and for All the Year Round they possessed no portion of the copyright. Given this stake in Dickens's previous titles and the young Frederic Chapman's zeal for disposing of large quantities at small mark-ups, the firm vastly enlarged its printings and sales during the final decade of Dickens's life. And thereafter, sharing copyright with Dickens's heirs, they expanded circulation even further. Dickens's copyrights not only eventually enriched himself and his family; they also provided a steady and dependable return for Chapman and Hall into the 20th century.                RLP

> Nowell-Smith, Simon, *International Copyright Law and the Publisher in the Reign of Queen Victoria* (1968).
> Patten (1978).
> Rose, Mark, *Authors and Owners* (1993).

**Coutts, Angela Burdett** (1814–1906), close friend of Dickens in the 1840s and 1850s, was daughter of Sir Francis Burdett, Bart., MP, and in 1837 unexpectedly inherited half the proceeds of Coutts' Bank, founded by her maternal grandfather (whose surname she thereupon adopted). Thus becoming Britain's richest woman save the Queen, she was probably its most munificent philanthropist, though she also lived splendidly in her Piccadilly mansion, entertaining a remarkable range of notabilities, to one of whom, the Duke of Wellington, she unsuccessfully proposed in 1847. Shy and physically unattractive, she inevitably attracted many suitors but remained single until 1881 when she made what Queen Victoria among others called a 'mad marriage' to a young American. She was pious, inclining to EVANGELICALISM, serious-minded and imbued with a sense of duty ('What is the use of my means but to try to do some good with them?'), and she gave enormous sums to a wide range of CHARITIES, taking the initiative in establishing sundry benevolent ventures. 'The nursing-mother of the CHURCH OF ENGLAND' for her church-building and endowment of colonial bishoprics, she was also 'God's Almoner', and 'The Queen of the Poor', of Costermongers, of Ireland, and of Baltimore (an Irish fishing-village she befriended). The Prince of Wales called her the most remarkable woman in the land, except his mother. She was the first woman to be raised to the peerage (1871), given the Freedom of the City of London, and buried in Westminster Abbey for charitable services.

She met Dickens in 1839, and later recalled her first impressions of him: 'his restlessness, vivacity, impetuosity, generous impulses, earnestness and frank sincerity' and 'rather overpoweringly energetic' personality. Soon they were close friends, an association he made public by dedicating *Chuzzlewit* to her (1844) 'with ... True and Earnest Regard'. (Mrs Gamp derived from a nurse employed in her household: see CHARACTERS—ORIGINALS.) He often sent her advance proofs of his serials and invited her to pre-publication readings of his latest writings. She interested herself in his eldest son Charley, sending him splendid birthday cakes and paying for his education at Eton, and also presenting Dickens's second son Walter with an East India Company Cadetship (see CHILDREN OF DICKENS). Dickens worked hard on some of her charitable ventures, and when she needed a secretary he offered his own services, with 'a daily messenger with a Dispatch Box' passing between them (16 November 1855), but instead his *Household Words* henchman W. H. WILLS was installed. Their friendship virtually ended, however, when he separated from his wife (see DICKENS, CATHERINE). He had elaborately explained his reasons for this in advance, hoping that she would 'hold me in the old place in your regard' (9 May 1858), but she strongly deprecated his decision, sided with Catherine, and then and later tried to effect a reconciliation. 'But nothing on earth', he replied (19 May 1858), '—no, not even you— no consideration, human or Divine, can move me from the resolution I have taken'. In the few later letters he wrote to her and her companion Mrs Brown, he keeps fondly recalling 'the old time' of their intimacy and reiterating his love for her—but now it was her turn to be immovable. From the preceding years over 500 letters to her survive, one of the longest and most informative series of Dickens's correspondence (see Edgar Johnson's selection, 1953).

From 1843 Dickens was soliciting her influence or financial help for various individuals and good causes, and offering to be 'a faithful steward of [her] bounty' (28 July 1843). The first prolonged effort concerned the new Field Lane Ragged School (in the Fagin area of Holborn), an Evangelical venture which spread under the presidency of Lord Ashley (later Shaftesbury). This provided evening classes taught by volunteers for the most destitute of the poor, offering them religious instruction, elementary EDU-CATION, trade training, and physical succour. He investigated it, largely on her behalf, and after a visit and further enquiries sent her a lengthy 'sledge-hammer account' (he told FORSTER, 24 September 1843), sure that 'she will do whatever I ask her in this matter. She is a most excellent creature . . . and I have a most perfect affection and respect for her.' He urged her to send money and use her influence to obtain government support: faulty and inadequate though the school was, it was making a heroic effort in grotesquely difficult circumstances where no other agencies operated. She sent a donation; he approached the government, unavailingly.

Their longest charitable collaboration was over URANIA COTTAGE, the home for homeless women which she established in 1847. In a 2,000-word letter (26 May 1846), he outlined a plan for this and offered to help direct it. Over the years, until 1858, he virtually ran it, chairing its committee, selecting staff and inmates, regularly visiting it to supervise arrangements and deal with crises, and the like, sometimes disagreeing with her when he thought her piety and austerity would damagingly restrict the regime—'a grind of charitable effort', remarked Humphry HOUSE, 'astounding in any man . . . scarcely credible in the greatest English creative genius of his time' (*All in Due Time*, 1955). He also helped her over housing projects, examining possible sites and suggesting operative principles.

PC

**Craik, Dinah Maria Mulock** (1826–87), prolific novelist. In the late 19th-century her books were more widely read than those of any other novelist except Dickens. Her most famous was *John Halifax, Gentleman* (1856). Dickens considered one of her stories 'the best Ghost story . . . that ever was written'. Doubting that its author could be female, he surmised that 'it must have been written by some wild Frenchman' (to Angela Burdett Coutts, 8 March 1855). Her only contribution to *Household Words*, 'A Ghost Story' was published in the 24 March 1855 issue.

SL

**Cricket on the Hearth, The** Dickens's third CHRISTMAS BOOK, written while he was helping to launch the DAILY NEWS and published by BRADBURY AND EVANS on 20 December 1845, with illustrations by LEECH, MACLISE, DOYLE, and STANFIELD (the ILLUSTRATORS for *The* CHIMES), plus an engraving of Boxer the dog by LANDSEER. Although FORSTER's claim (5.1) that its sales 'doubled' those of the *Carol* and *The Chimes* is incorrect, reviews were generally favourable and it quickly went through two editions, which brought Dickens profits of £1,022 5s 5d (Patten 1978, p. 168).

*The Cricket on the Hearth. A Fairy Tale of Home* concerns the allaying of suspicions which arise in the mind of the 'lumbering, slow, honest' carrier John Peerybingle when he sees his young wife, Dot, talking with a stranger. The story's supernatural agent, the cricket, reassures him that Dot is faithful, and the stranger is revealed to be the long-lost son of Caleb Plummer, a toymaker, who has carried out an innocent deception on his blind daughter Bertha. Dickens described the book to Miss COUTTS on the day he finished writing it as 'quiet and DOMESTIC . . . interesting and pretty' (1 December 1845).

In July 1845 Dickens had proposed starting a periodical to be called 'The Cricket': '*Carol* philosophy, cheerful views, sharp anatomisation of humbug, jolly good temper; papers always in season, pat to the time of year; and a vein of glowing, hearty, generous, mirthful beaming reference in everything to Home and Fireside'. When Forster objected, Dickens clung to the conception, as 'a delicate and beautiful fancy for a Christmas book, making the Cricket a little household god' (Forster 5.1). He wrote the *Cricket* that autumn, and although the previous Christmas books had not had dedications, he inscribed this one to Lord JEFFREY. The manuscript, with memoranda and variants, is in the Pierpont Morgan Library (see COLLECTIONS OF DICKENS MATERIALS).

A dramatization by Albert SMITH, authorized by Dickens, opened at the Lyceum on the date of publication, with KEELEY as Caleb and Mrs KEELEY as Dot. It ran for over 60 nights, and by mid-January there were at least seventeen productions of the *Cricket* in London. Dickens devised a PUBLIC READING which he used in his first charity performances in 1853 and in his first professional readings in 1858, but it was 'the least popular in the repertoire', given on only four occasions

(Collins 1975, p. 37). The real success story was the dramatization by Dion Boucicault, called *Dot*, with a framework derived from *A Midsummer Night's Dream*, which opened in New York in 1859 and was first seen in London in 1862. It was produced repeatedly in Britain and America for the remainder of the century, starring at various times John Toole, Henry Irving, and Jean Davenport (see INFANT PHENOMENA).

The *Cricket* has received little critical attention, but Andrew Sanders has argued that it has key similarities to SHAKESPEAREAN comedy and should be seen 'both as a significant indication of the tastes of the 1840s and of Dickens himself' (Introduction to the Genesis facsimile edition, 1981).                PVWS

## crime, crime prevention, and criminals.

Dickens's writing career spanned that period of the 19th century in Britain when crime was seen largely as the work of those characterized as the 'dangerous' or 'criminal' classes and when professional police forces were being introduced and developed across the country. Crime and criminals figure significantly in Dickens's novels and his journalistic work. He both drew upon, and helped to shape popular perceptions of these issues during his lifetime, while characters such as Bucket, Fagin, Magwitch, Merdle, and Sikes continued to be stereotypes long after his death.

The collection of national crime statistics for England and Wales began in 1810; the detail and categorization of these was greatly improved during the 1830s and again in the 1850s, but they still present many problems. Contemporaries were aware of what is now known as the 'dark figure' of crime, in other words, the unknown number of offences committed but never reported and, consequently, never listed. However, recognition of the 'dark figure' did not stop Victorian commentators from using and interpreting the statistics to back up their arguments about the direction and pattern of crime. Moreover, while historians argue over the merits and ultimate value of the statistics, for all their imperfections they present a picture which makes sense in the light of other social data from the 19th century.

The statistics suggest that crime, particularly theft, increased significantly in the first half of the century; this is what might be expected from a society experiencing the travails of industrialization and the capitalization of INDUSTRY, and when there was little mechanism for coping realistically with a dearth resulting from a harvest failure or a temporary collapse of the markets for the new industrial goods. From the 1850s the statistics suggest that theft began to level off and even decline—with the exception of burglary. Again, this is what might be expected given a general spread of prosperity, increasing social peace, the end of the threat of serious dearth and famine, and, perhaps, the presence of policemen on the streets.

The statistics also suggest that most theft was extremely petty, commonly involving clothing taken from employers or from washing-lines or hedges where it had been stretched out to dry, or bedding, furniture, cutlery, cups, and plates stolen from landlords. Most of the property stolen was sold or pawned, and much of the latter was done in dolly shops at the bottom end of the market. Such theft rarely involved violence, and the great panics over 'garotting'—as street robbery was termed—during the 1850s and again in 1862 rarely involved more than a few dozen offences. Violent crime, primarily assaults and homicides, followed a similar pattern to theft, but commonly involved people who were known to each other, indeed, who were often related; the major exception here were policemen who, from their first appearance in the late 1820s to the end of the century and beyond, were assaulted in disproportionate numbers.

There were some professional criminals, in the sense of individuals who sought to make a living, or a significant part of their living, from theft or from fencing the goods taken by others. It has been alleged that Dickens modelled Fagin on a notorious east London receiver, Isaac 'Ikey' Solomons, who was transported to Van Diemen's Land in 1827 (see PRISONS AND PENAL TRANSPORTATION). There is, however, no real evidence for this, and contemporary pictures of Solomons suggest a man with neither Fagin's physical characteristics nor his unkempt appearance. Solomons apart, there were plenty of stories in circulation in the second quarter of the century of 'kidsmen' training street children in the art of picking pockets, and then setting them to work for bed and board. Juvenile crime was perceived as a problem, and increasingly so from the early 19th century, yet few such offenders were cast in the mould of the Artful Dodger or seem to have worked for a 'kidsman'. A study of court records suggests that much—probably most—theft was opportunist. Moreover, few of the adult offenders brought before the courts fitted the image of the 'professional' criminal that might be inferred from contemplating Magwitch in his prime or reading the description of Sikes and his activities. Yet it was out of a fear of such offenders that reformers and journalists helped to shape the contemporary perception of the criminal class as a unified, anti-social group lurking within the lower reaches of the working class, and specifically the urban working class. The Victorians were proud of the wealth of their burgeoning cities, but these cities appeared also to offer both temptations to the criminal, and a myriad of shadowy places in which he might hide (see URBANIZATION).

The influential BENTHAMITE reformer Edwin CHADWICK, who played a key role in the development of the New Poor Law and the Royal Commission on a Rural Constabulary during the 1830s, believed that criminals were essentially those members of the working class who preferred idleness to a hard day's honest labour (see POOR RELIEF; CLASS). Similar ideas were deployed by Henry Mayhew in his massive survey of the poor of mid-century London; the fourth volume, published in its final, enlarged form in 1861–2, focused on 'the Non-Workers, or in other words, the Dangerous Classes of the Metropolis' (see LONDON: STREETS). Several of Dickens's minor criminal characters, like Gaffer Hexam, the 'half-savage' dredgerman of *Our Mutual Friend*, and Good Mrs Brown, who accosts and strips little Florence in *Dombey and Son*, are strongly reminiscent of characters interviewed and/or described by Mayhew and his collaborators. And like Mayhew and other journalists addressing the urban problems of Victorian Britain, Dickens himself made explorations into the London slums in company with police officers. The articles resulting from all of these forays tended to portray the poor as different, even exotic peoples; the descriptions were not unlike the TRAVEL LITERATURE of the time discussing the indigenous peoples of Africa, America, or Asia. Of course, the slum dwellers of the Victorian cities did look different from the middle-class and the respectable working-class readership of this literature (see LONDON: SLUMS). Their lodgings were crammed and malodorous; their diet was poor, and the casual labour by which most of them had to earn their living was often hard and physically demanding. To a society which believed that physiognomy revealed character, the sunken eyes, hollow cheeks, and shabby clothes of the labouring poor must have spoken volumes. Respectable people did not venture into districts like the St Giles Rookery in London or Angel Meadow in Manchester. They read about them; and the journalists doubtless embroidered their stories to titillate their readers. Yet for all the supposed threat from the 'dangerous classes' and from individuals like Sikes, there were probably as many, if not far more, Mrs Nubbleses in these districts striving for respectability and independence, and seeking to establish 'that air of comfort . . . which . . . cleanliness and order can always impart in some degree' (*OCS* 10). Dickens had a lifelong preoccupation with EDUCATION, sanitary reform, and housing as supremely important crime-prevention agents, especially as regards children (see PUBLIC HEALTH, SANITATION, AND HOUSING). The link between 'Ignorance and Crime' (the title of one of his *EXAMINER* pieces), was a constant theme with him in all his writings.

The fascination with the 'criminal' or 'dangerous classes' which were suspected to lurk in the slums, ready to sally forth and commit crimes against the respectable, led to the omission of the middle-class offender from categorization among 'criminals'. There were periodic scares about fraud and corruption, and classic literary fraudsters like Dickens's Merdle (*LD*) and Montague Tigg (*MC*) and TROLLOPE's Augustus Melmotte appear to have been constructed with a basis in real offenders; Merdle, for example, seems to have had his origins in John Sadleir MP, a Chairman of the London and County Bank and a director of the Tipperary Joint-Stock Bank, who committed suicide in January 1856 when it was revealed that he had embezzled £200,000 and issued £150,000 in fictitious Swedish Railway shares (see MONEY AND FINANCE). The spread of capitalist enterprise, the lack of information on where to invest and on the validity of ventures, together with a relatively lax system of regulation in the money market throughout the Victorian period, all contributed to opportunities for the unscrupulous. Yet the fraudster was not seen as a member of a criminal class; rather, he was the rotten apple in an otherwise sound barrel.

Crime was also seen as, essentially, male behaviour (see SEXUALITY AND GENDER). The statistics reveal the number of women brought before the major courts to have been significantly less than the number of men; moreover, the proportion of women brought before these courts had been in decline since the 17th century. This may reflect an actual decline given that the role of women was re-emphasized more and more as being focused in the private sphere of the home where other forms of control on their behaviour were present. Equally, it may have been the result of a form of male chivalry, with victims reluctant to prosecute women offenders, or bringing them before the lower courts where the penalties were less. Again, towards the close of the 19th century, it is at least arguable that women offenders were disappearing from the courts because they were seen as in need of psychiatric treatment rather than the penal sanction (see MADNESS). Victorian commentators recognized the smaller percentage of women brought before the courts, and it fitted well with their perceptions of femininity; women offenders, it was suspected, particularly towards the end of the century, were those who, by seeking employment in the labour market, were rejecting their femininity and acquiring male characteristics. But for mid-century commentators, with their fascination for the so-called criminal classes, the female equivalent—and associate—of the male criminal was the PROSTITUTE. The life of Sikes's Nancy, for example, had been 'squandered in the streets and among the most noisome stews and dens of London' (OT 40); but even relatively liberal analysts of prostitution, like Dr William Acton, could describe women as entering the profession for similar reasons to men becoming thieves—some driven to it by necessity, but others by a love of idleness and luxury. Dickens's philanthropic streak was profoundly moved by the 'fallen woman'. He was instrumental in the creation and development of URANIA COTTAGE where, at any one time, thirteen young

women rescued from a life on the streets were to be educated and prepared for a fresh start in the colonies. Martha Endell's new life in Australia (DC) was a fictional account of the opportunities that he hoped her flesh-and-blood equivalents would find.

The perception of criminality as a form of behaviour located within a section of the working class contributed significantly to developments in penal policy. The transportation of serious or supposedly incorrigible offenders was a widely used option from the end of the Napoleonic Wars until the 1850s. But there was always an ambivalence about the system. Official investigations revealed the brutality inflicted on convicts sent to Norfolk Island and the Blue Mountain chain gangs, but also the lenient treatment experienced by others. Rumours of the latter led to a belief that transportation was not a punishment but a golden opportunity to create a good life and accumulate wealth. Convinced that this was the predominant attitude among criminal offenders, on 2 July 1840 Dickens wrote to the Home Secretary offering to write a narrative about the terrors of Norfolk Island. In the event, however, he only ever produced one significant character with experience of penal Australia—Abel Magwitch, a transportee who has made his fortune and, interestingly, who uses it to make a London gentleman and thus revenge himself on colonial gentlemen. Furthermore, *Great Expectations* was published in 1861 when, under pressure from free settlers and native-born white Australians, transportation was all but ended.

The period from 1815 to 1857, when transportation was virtually ended, also witnessed considerable developments in the use of the prison. Drawing both upon Enlightenment ideas of how the human mind might be shaped and upon EVANGELICAL faith in the power of the Bible and contemplation, penal reformers experimented with systems which were expected to teach offenders the virtues of labour and to bring them to a personal recognition and admission of their wickedness. There were arguments about how best the reform of convicts might be achieved, notably between those who favoured the 'silent system', whereby prisoners were not allowed to speak or otherwise communicate with each other, and those who advocated the 'separate system', in which the convict was kept in solitude to contemplate his, or less commonly her, offences. In both systems reformers urged the need for vigorous labour, possibly on a treadmill, or alone with a hand crank. Dickens himself favoured the silent system, and his most celebrated participation in the debates on penal reform was his critical account of the separate system at Cherry Hill, Pennsylvania, published in AMERICAN NOTES.

The reformers appeared triumphant with the opening of Pentonville Prison in London in 1842. Here, initially, the offenders were stripped of their identity, given a number, made to wear a mask, kept in solitude, and required to maintain silence. Pentonville's architecture, and its routine, were urged as models for provincial prisons, but the triumph was relatively short-lived. Some among the public rapidly became cynical about the success of the reformation policies; was the penitent convict genuine, or simply behaving as the chaplain and prison officials wished? Dickens captured the mood with his portrait of the "umble' and penitent Number Twenty-Seven, as Uriah Heep became. But there was also criticism from the other direction; for some of the inmates the experience of such treatment brought psychological breakdown. Thus, the system appeared insufficiently severe since it enabled some to avoid reformation through chicanery, but it also seemed too severe since it drove others to insanity and even suicide.

By the mid-1850s, as transportation came to an end and concerns grew about serious offenders being released from prison, albeit on licence, in Britain rather than on the other side of the world, so the enthusiasm for the reformative powers of the penitentiary were on the wane. Nevertheless, prison had been accepted as the principal means of dealing with criminal offenders. Four large convict prisons were developed, Chatham, Dartmoor, Portland, and Portsmouth, where the offenders toiled on public works; while local prisons, which were not brought under a centralized, national control until 1877, continued to deploy a variety of strategies, though it seems they were not always clear as to whether the primary aim was to punish or reform.

For Dickens, in contrast, the problem was relatively straightforward. He had a generally bleak view of the adult criminal who, he feared, was incorrigible. The juvenile offender, however, could be reformed, and sending him to prison would only expose him to the corrupting influence of hardened offenders. For Dickens, as for others, ignorance was a major cause of crime and, as he became involved with Urania Cottage, so he also became involved with Ragged Schools which he saw as both preventive and reformative institutions.

Alongside the changes in the penal system came the development of the new police. Reformers like Chadwick insisted that the old system of parish constables and night watchmen was ineffective, and that what was required to keep the criminal classes in check and prevent crime was a new bureaucratic and regimented system of police. The first of the new forces was the Metropolitan Police of London, established in 1829; clauses in the Municipal Corporations Act of 1835 required town councils to establish watch committees which were to oversee police forces; legislation of 1839 and 1840 enabled county magistrates to establish constabularies for their jurisdictions if they so wished; the County and Borough Police Act of 1856 required all counties and boroughs which had not yet established police forces so to do. Dickens shared the reformers' enthusiasm for the new police; in both his journalistic work and his novels he was critical of the old watchmen, the parish constables, and the Bow Street Runners who, from the mid-18th century, had provided a kind of detective police for the metropolis. Recent historical research has thrown doubt on much of the reformers' case by noting the increasing efficiency of many night watches, the fact that watchmen were sometimes on the ground in London in much greater numbers than the new police constables, and that the kind of corruption present among some of the old thief-takers was also to be found among the new police. Nevertheless, there appears to have been a general desire for a new threshold of order on the streets in the early 19th century, and the new police went some way towards meeting this desire. Moreover, the imperturbable British Bobby, patrolling his beat at a steady regulation two-and-one-half miles an hour, was fairly rapidly absorbed into the list of institutions which respectable Victorians considered as models for other, less fortunate nations. The efficient, imperturbable, and significantly anonymous, constables who, in *Bleak House*, arrive on the scene of Nemo's dead body and require Jo, the crossing-sweeper, to 'move on', are important manifestations of this image of the Bobby.

Of course, the new police were not universally popular, especially when they were directed towards the domestication of working-class leisure pursuits and the enforcement of legislation to control working-class betting, drinking, and Sunday trading, or when they were employed to protect blackleg labour during strikes (see GAMBLING; DRINK AND TEMPERANCE; SABBATARIANISM). Detective police were regarded with particular suspicion, and not just by the working class. The policeman in plain clothes had the potential to be a spy. The Metropolitan Police had been given their distinctive blue uniform in 1829 deliberately to avoid them being mistaken for either soldiers (who generally wore scarlet coats) or spies; it was a common assumption among the 'freeborn Englishmen' that continental policing involved both, and that this was something to be avoided at all costs. It was concerns such as this which limited the numbers of police detectives, particularly in the Metropolitan Police; reformers put their faith in the preventive abilities of the patrolling, uniformed constable, and so did senior policemen, who recognized that the uniformed men could be much better controlled and supervised. Dickens, rather exceptionally, was fascinated by detectives; he glamorized them (particularly Inspector Charles Frederick FIELD) in articles and, perhaps most notably, in *Bleak House* with the character of Inspector Bucket, allegedly modelled on Field. Within a decade of Dickens's death, however, all the fears about the possible corruption of detective police appeared to be confirmed when, in 1877, four senior Metropolitan detectives were prosecuted for taking bribes from five men convicted of fraud and forgery in the 'Turf Fraud' scandal.

CE

Chesney, Kellow, *The Victorian Underworld* (1970).
Collins (1962).
Emsley, Clive, *Crime and English Society, 1750–1900* (2nd edn., 1996).

**Crimean War,** fought 1854–6 between an alliance of British and French forces against the Russians. Dickens strongly supported the need to go to war. He shared the prevalent Russophobia, thinking the country a threat to civilization. He made speeches on the war, notably to the Commercial Travellers' Schools on 30 December 1854, when he called the Tsar 'a rash and barbarian tyrant', and to the Administrative Reform Association on 27 June 1855 (*Speeches*, pp. 169–76, 197–208). He was horrified by the mismanagement of the war, writing to Mrs Richard WATSON a week after the Battle of Balaclava: 'I am full of mixed feelings about the War—admiration of our valiant men—burning desires to cut the Emperor of Russia's throat—and something like despair to see how the old cannon smoke and blood-mist obscure the wrongs and sufferings of the people at home' (1 November 1854). Two months later his focus was upon the 'melancholy . . . absorption of the English mind in the War . . . Every other subject of popular solicitude and sympathy goes down before it' (to de Cerjat, 3 January 1855). His concern that British military endeavour in a good cause was being negated by inefficiency and bumbling led to his joining the newly formed Administrative Reform Assocation in support of the campaigns of the MP Austen Layard. Between April and August 1855 he wrote several articles in *Household Words* attacking government incompetence. He assured Layard that he would be 'Damascus Steel to the core' on the issue (3 April 1855). He was as good as his word. Book 1, chapter 10 of *Little Dorrit*, 'Containing the Whole Science of Government', offers a justifiably famous attack on governmental inefficiency in all its guises: 'Whatever was required to be done, the Circumlocution Office was beforehand with all the public departments in the art of perceiving—HOW NOT TO DO IT.'

EJE

**criticism and scholarship:** *1. introduction; 2. the first 100 years; 3. biographical; 4. feminist; 5. Freudian; 6. historicist; 7. Marxist; 8. new critical; 9. poststructuralist; 10. textual scholarship.*

**1. Introduction** Literary criticism gives a useful indication of how Dickens's writing has been interpreted at different times. Once in print, it helps to shape other readers' responses and in some cases exerts a long-lasting influence over attitudes towards Dickens's work. Although he was well served before 1950 by a small number of distinguished admirers, there was initial reluctance within universities to accept Dickens into the pantheon of great authors, despite—or perhaps because of—his huge POPULARITY with the general reader. Once this barrier was breached, Dickens criticism written by academics flooded into publication, bearing the traces of the major intellectual movements that have transformed the practice of literary criticism in western universities over the past 50 years. At present, there is no sign of any decline in Dickens's high standing as a serious writer and a centrally important figure in Victorian Studies.                            EW

Collins (1971).

Ford (1955).

Ford and Lane (1961).

Hollington, Michael (ed.), *Charles Dickens: Critical Assessments*, 4 vols. (1995).

Slater, M. *et al.*, 'Dickens and Fame 1870–1970', *Dickensian*, 66 (1970).

Wall, Stephen (ed.), *Charles Dickens* (1970).

Westland, E., Trezise, S., *et al.*, 'Dickens and Critical Change', *Dickens Quarterly*, 9–12 (1992–5).

**2. The first 100 years** Dickens's imaginative writing was noticed as early as December 1833, the month in which his first sketch, 'A Dinner at Poplar Walk', appeared in the MONTHLY MAGAZINE (Chittick 1989, p. 88). When *Pickwick* began to attract attention, 'BOZ' was compared not only with established humorists and magazine writers of the day, but with the foremost novelists of the past—in the words of the *Athenaeum* reviewer, his formula was 'two pounds of SMOLLETT, three ounces of STERNE, a handful of HOOK, a dash of a grammatical Pierce EGAN' (3 December 1836, repr. Collins 1971). Although the serious quarterlies were suspicious that his POPULARITY as a writer on 'low' materials in a 'low' form of SERIAL PUBLICATION was ephemeral—a charge which was to be made repeatedly by highbrow critics—by 1838 Dickens was already being seriously discussed in comparison with CERVANTES, FIELDING, SCOTT, HOGARTH, and SHAKESPEARE (see Collins 1971).

By far the greatest bulk of critical assessment of Dickens's work during his lifetime

was carried out in REVIEWS, and whereas some notices did little more than reprint extracts, it was then routine practice for reviewers to consider the latest publication in relation to an author's previous work, with the result that Dickens's oeuvre was under constant revaluation. Overwhelmingly, early critics praised his humour (especially as seen in his characters), his pathos, and his eye for topical detail; his STYLE and his aesthetic achievement were hardly mentioned.

The first study of lasting importance, other than a review, was written by Richard Henry HORNE, who accorded Dickens pride of place as the first figure to be discussed in his *New Spirit of the Age* (1844). Conceived in conscious imitation of HAZLITT's *Spirit of the Age* (1825), Horne's project was to celebrate a new generation of talent, and he perspicaciously singled out Dickens as the representative figure of an emerging era, inexhaustible in his variety and morally uplifting in his depiction of mundane reality. For Horne, Dickens's chief achievement, like Hogarth's, was an ability to combine observation of particularized individuality with generalization, and thereby to portray the 'type and essence' of reality.

The single most insightful and influential critical assessment during Dickens's lifetime came from the French critic Hippolyte Taine. First published in the *Revue des deux mondes* (1856), it was incorporated into his *Histoire de la littérature anglaise* (1863) and appeared in an English translation in 1871–4. Although writing before Dickens had progressed beyond *Hard Times*, and although, as FORSTER vigorously complained in his *Life of Dickens* (9.1), neglecting Dickens's humour, Taine presented an extended analysis of Dickens as a major author. Dismissing his social concerns as merely SENTIMENTAL, Taine identified a 'lucid and energetic' poetic imagination as the source of his greatness, and responded with fascination to the 'hallucinatory' power which animates his world. 'The difference between a madman and a man of genius is not very great', Taine declared, in a sentence which might serve as the starting-point for a great deal of 20th-century interpretation of Dickens.

From mid-century, a growing chorus of critical dissent appeared among writers and critics, even as Dickens's popularity with the common reader consolidated his status as a classic (see READERSHIP). An emerging concern with the aesthetics of the novel as a legitimate art form, coupled with a narrowly realist conception of that form, led critics to decry his art as crude and implausible. George Henry LEWES was the foremost spokesman for this view, finding Dickens's characters 'unreal and impossible . . . speaking a language never heard in life, moving like pieces of simple mechanism . . . For the reader of cultivated taste', he concluded, 'there is little beyond the stirring of their emotions' ('Dickens in Relation to Criticism', *Fortnightly Review*, 27, 1872; repr. [part] in Collins 1971). An indication of the pervasiveness of the attitudes represented by Lewes is the case of George GISSING, who delighted in Dickens's humour and pathos, and found praiseworthy elements of realism in the novels, but whose theoretical conception of what the novel should be forced him to apologize for large portions of Dickens's art. A positive side of this literal-mindedness was the antiquarian interest of enthusiasts like F. G. KITTON, who explored the places Dickens wrote about and ferreted out 'originals' for his characters (see CHARACTERS—ORIGINALS). The negative side reached its nadir in Bloomsbury, with Virginia Woolf sneering that whereas she would 'cheerfully become Shakespeare's cat', she 'would not cross the road' to meet Dickens (*Nation*, 12 September 1925). E. M. Forster condemned Dickens's characters as 'flat' (*Aspects of the Novel*, 1927); in the same spirit, Aldous Huxley denigrated Dickens for 'vulgarity' (*Vulgarity in Literature*, 1930).

The greatest of all Dickens critics, G. K. CHESTERTON, emerged just after the turn of the century, in a number of writings, most notably in *Charles Dickens* (1906) and in introductions to the Everyman edition of the novels, collected as *Appreciations and Criticisms of the Works of Charles Dickens* (1911). Responsive to the humour, humanity, and fecundity of Dickens, Chesterton's exhilarating (and sometimes maddening) reliance on paradox sheds light on innumerable complexities of Dickens's art. Celebrating his characters as 'timeless gods' who inhabit not novels but a 'mythology', Chesterton overturns the narrow strictures of realism by insisting that Dickens's art makes things 'seem more actual than things really are'.

Further reaction against negative views of Dickens followed, in defence of (in George Ford's happy distinction: 1955, p. 242) both the 'fat man's Dickens' and the 'thin man's Dickens'. George Santayana ('Dickens', *The Dial*, 71, 1921; repr. Ford and Lane 1962) and J. B. Priestley (*The English Comic Characters*, 1925) wrote exuberantly on Dickens's comedy, while the Marxist critic T. A. Jackson, following RUSKIN's and G. B. Shaw's admiration of Dickens's social criticism, was a generation ahead of his time in his analysis of the novels' construction (*Charles Dickens: The Progress of a Radical*, 1937).

But modern criticism can be said to start (and this survey end) with three milestone studies published just over a century after Dickens first appeared in print: Edmund WILSON's 'Dickens: The Two Scrooges' (1940, 1941), George ORWELL's 'Charles Dickens' (1940), and Humphry HOUSE's *The Dickens World* (1941, 1942).                    PVWS

**3. Biographical** Dickens was so forceful a personality and achieved his unique celebrity so early in life, that virtually from the beginnings of his career criticism of the work has been intertwined with an interest in the man. Indeed, as has often been noticed, affection for the personality not uncommonly occludes criticism proper.

Dickens was profoundly ambivalent about personal publicity. In 1860 he burned most of the letters in his possession and expressed the wish that every letter he had ever written might end the same way (Johnson 2.963). He kept the secret of his father's imprisonment for debt and his own relegation as a 'labouring hind' to WARREN'S BLACKING a profound secret from almost everyone, including his children; the crucial exception, however, was John FORSTER—the friend to whom he happened to have entrusted not only the famous 'autobiographical fragment', but the task of writing his life (Forster 1.2) (see DICKENS: PRIVATE LIFE; DIARIES). His intense feelings of shame notwithstanding, Dickens incorporated details of these painful months into *David Copperfield* with the merest revision and into *Little Dorrit* rather less directly. And throughout the work there is a long, tell-tale trail of allusions to Warren's and blacking bottles.

The appearance of the first volume of John Forster's *Life of Charles Dickens* in 1871, with the publication for the first time of the auto-biographical fragment, of course marked an epoch (see BIOGRAPHIES AND BIOGRAPHERS). Both in Dickens's own account ('I know how all these things have worked together to make me what I am', he writes towards the fragment's end) and in Forster's handling of it ('In what way those strange experiences of his boyhood affected him afterwards, the narrative of his life must show', he writes), there is an explicit invitation to make a very great deal of these early influences, which much subsequent criticism either gladly accepts or pointedly declines. And many critics who escape the fascination of the Marshalsea and Warren's have found much other biographical material useful to their criticism. Indeed, the classically 'Dickensian' pleasure of locating the originals of characters and places assumes—with much reason—that there is very little in Dickens's life that did not manage to find its way into the work. In this the Dickensian differs, moreover, not a very great deal from the more broadly historical scholar who takes Dickens as opening a peculiarly clear and wide window into the Victorian past and especially the social history of London, about which Walter BAGEHOT in 1858 remarked that Dickens wrote 'like a special correspondent for posterity'. So good a correspondent is Dickens, and so prolific a contributor to the life of his times, in fact, that it is often difficult to know just where biographical criticism leaves off and literary or even social history begin.

G. K. CHESTERTON's *Charles Dickens* (1906) is heavily biographical in its early chapters and places great emphasis on both Warren's and John DICKENS; its insights are often eclipsed by more recent and theoretically explicit work. It was Edmund WILSON's classic essay 'Dickens: The Two Scrooges' (collected in *The Wound and the Bow*, 1941) that first brought psychoanalysis to bear on Dickens criticism, but the ground had been prepared by Dickens himself (see CRITICISM: FREUDIAN). For Dickens places as much emphasis as does Freud upon the illimitable importance of CHILDHOOD in the life of the grown-up, and Dickens was himself of great importance to Freud's own thought—*David Copperfield* was Freud's favourite novel: he rather portentously gave a copy of it to his fiancée during their engagement, and he gave

the subject of one of his most important case histories the name of 'Dora'. Wilson was also the first major critic to make extensive use of recent revelations about Dickens's relationship with Ellen TERNAN, as well as Walter DEXTER's edition of the letters for the Nonesuch Edition (1938). This new material contributed to a significantly darker view of Dickens than had been presented by previous criticism, one reflected also in Edgar Johnson's great biography, *Charles Dickens: His Tragedy and Triumph* (1952).

As Philip Collins noted in an essay in the *TLS* (18 April 1980), it was Wilson who first made much of the PRISON as central symbol in *Little Dorrit*, not only as standing for oppressive institutions, but for 'imprisoning states of mind'. Lionel Trilling in his essay on the same novel (collected in *The Opposing Self*, 1955) reminds us that the picture Freud chose for the frontispiece of his *Introductory Lectures* showed a man in prison dreaming that gnomes were sawing away his bars, and claims that Dickens has significantly anticipated Freud's theory of the neuroses in his portrayal of the self-imprisoned Mrs Clennam. It is probably not coincidental, therefore, that the 1930s and 1940s saw both a resurgence of scholarly interest in Dickens and the first wave of psychoanalytic literary criticism, and it would be a subtle task indeed to argue for the priority of the Freudian chicken or the Dickensian egg.

The dangers most often associated with biographical criticism include the displacement of the literary work by the life, the reduction of the work to a mere diagnosis—the last link in a mechanical causal chain—and the uncritical acceptance of the life or the author's expressed intentions as interpretive guides to the work where both life and intention may be quite misleading. For the last 30 years or so biographical criticism has further laboured under the cloud of 'the death of the author', announced by various theorists as part of the larger death of belief in the autonomous individual of classical liberalism, and as part too of the growing appreciation of the creative role that readers themselves necessarily play in the act of reading. Under the influence of contemporary theory, it has become conventional to think of persons or 'subjects' as being constituted or 'constructed' by texts and 'discourse', rather than the other way round, and no doubt there is in this a healthy corrective to uncritical accounts of genius (see CRITICISM: POST-STRUCTURALIST). The personality of Dickens, however, has proven remarkably hard to kill—no less so than the texts that bear his name—and excellent critics continue to draw upon the life as if that remained a perfectly natural part of doing criticism and literary history. Notable examples are Angus Wilson's *The World of Charles Dickens* (1970), Michael Slater's *Dickens and Women* (1983), and Alexander Welsh's *From Copyright to Copperfield* (1987), all of which, for different reasons, play up the experiences of the adult Dickens against those of the small boy.    RN

**4. Feminist** Since 1970, when the Women's Movement made its first major impact on literary studies with the publication of Kate Millett's *Sexual Politics*, feminist theories have had an important bearing on the development of Victorian Studies. By 1990 a significant amount of Dickens criticism could be considered feminist, at least in the broad sense that it shared feminist assumptions about the importance of patriarchy and gender in any serious analysis of 19th-century culture.

Millett's few lines on Dickens encapsulated two concerns that have remained central for a subsequent generation of feminist critics: she deplored his 'SENTIMENTAL version of women', but recognized in his work the Victorians' capacity 'to face the issue of patriarchy and the condition of women'. Feminists have maintained an interest in Dickens's female characters, particularly his idealized heroines, but they have tended to subordinate this, as Millett did, to a broader historical appreciation of the part played by fiction in creating, condoning, or challenging the Victorians' view of patriarchal power structures and gender roles.

Not all criticism that focuses on female characters is feminist, though it normally implies an awareness about gender as an issue and a belief that women are devalued by recourse to female stereotypes. Objections to the perceived one-dimensionality of Dickens's women, for example, may be based primarily on the realist criterion that characters in fiction should be 'rounded'. Out of such mixed motives, Dickens's heroines have been

rehabilitated by the close readings which have claimed that characters sometimes regarded as insipidly feminine, like Esther Summerson and Little Dorrit, are psychologically more subtle than they may at first appear. The fullest treatment of Dickens's female characters, alongside an account of Dickens's relationships with real women, can be found in Michael Slater's *Dickens and Women* (1983).

Feminist criticism of female characters, like Françoise Basch's *Relative Creatures* (1974), was informed in the 1970s by feminist historians' research on the Victorian polarization of women into sinners and saints. Dickens's PROSTITUTES were usually read as cultural stereotypes; his good wife-mothers, on the other hand, were interpreted as being more complicated than mere male idealizations. Alexander Welsh in *The City of Dickens* (1971) identified the supernatural strength of DOMESTIC women in their role as angels of death, and later feminist classics like Sandra M. Gilbert and Susan Gubar's *The Madwoman in the Attic* (1979) and Nina Auerbach's *Woman and the Demon* (1982) developed this view of Victorian women's possession of power away from the public arena.

Underlying the diversity of readings of Dickens's novels produced by feminist criticism, where theory is always evolving and inevitably influenced by developments in other critical methodologies, it is possible to identify certain themes and approaches that have proved to be of enduring interest. Narrative structures taken from romance and FAIRY TALE have been explored by writers like Laurie Langbauer (*Women and Romance*, 1990). 'Reading the body' is the structuring theme of Helena Michie's *The Flesh Made Word* (1987) and Gail Turley Houston's *Consuming Fictions: Gender, Class, and Hunger in Dickens's Novels* (1994). Writing and reading as gendered activities, and the construction of the domain of fiction as feminine or professional authorship as masculine, have been recurring preoccupations in Dickens criticism since the early 1980s (see SEXUALITY; WOMEN AND WOMEN'S ISSUES).

Above all, throughout its first thirty years feminist criticism has retained its close alliance with feminist history, giving it a bias towards cultural materialism and an affinity with the later interdisciplinary procedures of new historicism. The highly influential work of Mary Poovey, Nancy Armstrong, and Catherine Gallagher published from the mid-1980s onwards exposed the crucial ideological functions of Victorian representations of gender and identified sexual relations as a site for changing power relations between classes and cultures. A striking example of their procedures can be found in Mary Poovey's article 'Reading History in Literature' (in Janet Levarie Smarr, *Historical Criticism and the Challenge of Theory*, 1993), which has as its centre-piece an analysis of *Our Mutual Friend* in relation to topical debates on financial speculation, the economics of Empire, and women's rights. Poovey uses fiction *as* history to reveal the role of the imagined domesticated woman and explore underlying fears that the professed Victorian faith in essential sexual difference might be untenable.

Feminist readings of Dickens's fiction inevitably vary according to the specific historical and theoretical framework adopted by the critic. The significance of housekeeping in middle-class homes has been one such contested area. Where the housekeeping role is defined as bearing considerable social and ideological status, Esther Summerson's efficiency can be seen as conferring power on the heroine and Dora Copperfield's incompetence as threatening to undermine the middle-class social fabric. Where ideas about Victorian patriarchy are revised to give responsibility for the ideological construction of woman's domestic sphere to middle-class women rather than men, readings of Dickens are again deeply affected. Judith Newton has argued, drawing on this later cultural model, that a figure like Florence Dombey can be seen as threatening to a patriarch like her father and a male author like Dickens, because she represents the powerful ideal of the good domesticated woman ('Making—and Remaking—History: Another Look At "Patriarchy"', *Tulsa Studies in Women's Literature*, 3, 1984).

Although recent feminist criticism has converged with other historicist work, most feminist critics agree that their methodology is underpinned by a political commitment. Many subscribe to the view that all acts of criticism are intrinsically political, and that extending our comprehension of Victorian culture through a focus on gender, and uncovering plurality and ideological conflict in 19th-century texts like Dickens's novels, can be a liberating activity for the late 20th-century reader. EW

Flint, Kate, *Dickens* (1986), ch. 6.

**5. Freudian** Psychoanalytical approaches offer many suggestive explanations of the most distinctive aspects of Dickens's writing, and Freudian ideas provide an important if controversial ingredient in some of the most interesting criticism of his life and work. Dickens's depiction of dreamlike and haunted states of mind, his interest in divided and obsessional characters, in CHILDHOOD experience and its influence on later life: all these seem to relate to the unconscious workings of the mind that Freud found in dreams, jokes, and slips of the tongue. Dickens's love of contradictory and paradoxical forms of expression recalls the complex and over-determined nature of the Freudian symptom, and the frequent discovery in Dickens's novels of a hidden or repressed past behind a respectable façade, often involving sexual transgression (*Oliver Twist, Bleak House, A Tale of Two Cities, Little Dorrit, Great Expectations*), has close parallels with the stories that Freud uncovered in his patients.

Dickens's texts anticipate Freud's writing in important ways, and there are striking parallels between Dickens's use of MESMERISM to treat Augusta de la Rue in the 1840s and Freud's early experiments with hypnotism in the 1890s. Although Freud himself admired Dickens's work, in particular *David Copperfield*, he wrote relatively little literary criticism, and only incidental remarks on Dickens. His essay on 'The Uncanny' (1912), a study of the early 19th-century German writer of fantastic stories E. T. A. Hoffmann, is the most directly rewarding for the reader of Dickens. For Freud, the 'uncanny' occurs when unfamiliar things seem strangely familiar, and is marked by strange kinds of repetition, the presence of animism, and the doubling of characters. These represent for Freud signs of the resurfacing in the mind of traumatic knowledge or feelings that had been earlier repressed. Doubling is a frequent motif in Dickens's work, as is the presence of ghosts and spirits. The return, or the fear of the return, of those thought to be dead occurs in many novels, and is particularly important in *Barnaby Rudge, A Tale of Two Cities*, and the opening chapters of *David Copperfield*.

Freudian criticism is marked by its interest in sexual repression, the workings of the unconscious mind, and the strange intensities of desire within families. The most influential, if speculative, early use of Freud in Dickens criticism was that of Edmund WILSON in his essay 'The Two Scrooges' of 1941. Wilson argued that Dickens was an essentially divided character, whose outward respectability was matched by a strong but unconscious rebellion and rage, directed particularly against parent-figures. This is exemplified for Wilson by the dramatic contrast between the idyllic comedy of much of *The Pickwick Papers* and the violent family dramas of its interpolated stories such as 'The Convict's Return' and 'The Old Man's Tale of the Queer Client'. This splitting, he argues, appears throughout Dickens's work and culminates in the portrayal of John Jasper in *The Mystery of Edwin Drood*, effectively a self-portrait by Dickens of his own haunted and divided consciousness.

The relation of fathers to their children is at the heart both of Freudian theory and Dickens's fiction. Steven Marcus, in his *Dickens: from Pickwick to Dombey*, allies a Freudian idiom to literary analysis to explore the importance of father–son relationships and the importance of the many doubled, divided, idealized, and infantile father-figures in the early novels. More recent critics have shown how Dickens depicts the attempt to escape or master paternal authority in the novels through the simultaneous absence of fathers and multiplication of substitute figures, such as Magwitch in *Great Expectations* and Micawber in *David Copperfield*. Classically Oedipal feelings, such as guilt and aggression, characteristically mark the relations of fathers and sons in Dickens's work, most noticeably in *Barnaby Rudge*; daughters such as Amy Dorrit and Agnes Wickfield frequently appear in idealized and indeed quasi-incestuous relations with their fathers.

Freud's later meta-psychological writings, in particular his 1920 essay 'Beyond The Pleasure Principle', provide important tools for the analysis of Dickens's plots and underlie Peter Brooks's seminal essay on *Great Expectations* (1992). For Brooks, Pip is in search of a plot for his life, but is condemned in the book continually to misrecognize what that plot is. Instead of the dynamic progress that he hopes for, Pip in fact is forced constantly to repeat himself and return unconsciously to the repressed past represented by his substitute-father Magwitch and the frozen sexuality of Satis House. The plot-structure of the novel represents for Brooks a fictional version of the death instinct, Freud's term for the instincts which bring living beings back to an inorganic state. Pip (and thus the reader) suffers strange and uncanny repetitions of his past life, until Magwitch's return forces the repressed and guilt-inducing material—crime, violence, and sexual desire—to cause a wholesale revision of Pip's self-understanding.

Dickens and Freud share many interests: in the bodily expressiveness and linguistic creativity of human life; in the significance of apparently marginal and deviant forms of behaviour; in the power of obsessive, sadistic, and masochistic impulses; in the incestuous passions of family life and the force of jokes and humour in human culture. Above all, as recent post-structuralist readings have emphasized, Freud helps us to see how strange and unsettling Dickens's work is, and how often it touches on repressed or secret desires and wishes. But it is also true that Freud is deeply indebted to the insights and example of literature, and Dickens's novels articulate before Freud many of the central assumptions upon which psychoanalysis rests. Dickens has been compared to a psychologist engaged in a lifelong psychoanalysis, but it is also possible to see Freud's major work, *The Interpretation of Dreams* (1900), as a form of writing very akin to an autobiographical novel like *David Copperfield*.                                   JMB

Brooks, Peter, *Reading for the Plot* (2nd edn., 1992).

Lukacher, Ned, *Primal Scenes: Literature, Philosophy, Psychoanalysis* (1986).

Sadoff, Dianne F., *Monsters of Affection* (1982).

**6. Historicist and cultural** Critics of various theoretical persuasions with a common interest in the social history of Victorian Britain have been fascinated by Dickens's fiction. A high proportion of what is termed 'Dickens studies' has been based on historical research, often centring on issues foregrounded by Dickens himself such as EDUCATION and social reform. Scholars like Humphry HOUSE and Philip Collins are well-known practitioners of this traditional approach. In Britain there has also been a strong school of left-wing Dickens critics, notably George ORWELL, Arnold Kettle, and Raymond Williams, rooted in a critique of industrial capitalism and a commitment to understanding literature's material conditions. In his various wide-ranging studies of British culture and society Raymond Williams has attached special significance to Dickens, whose writing career coincided with the emergence of a new URBAN culture. Williams found modern ways of seeing embedded in the very form of Dickens's novels. A new morality is implied in Dickens's vision of the INDUSTRIAL world as man-made, since society has the power to mould its environment and hence its people; there is a moral point, too, in those characters presented from the outside, like passers-by in a crowded street, since the plot reveals their hidden connections with each other (*The English Novel from Dickens to Lawrence*, 1970). Later theorists like Terry Eagleton in *Criticism and Ideology* (1975) and Edward W. Said in *Culture and Imperialism* (1993)—works which have made their own distinctive contributions to understanding Dickens in his historical moment—have criticized Williams's limitations from Marxist and anti-imperialist perspectives. But they have also fully recognized the extent of Williams's influence on a generation of cultural critics from the late 1950s onwards.

The 1980s saw the development of a self-conscious methodology presented as 'new historicism' (in the United States) or a new version of 'cultural materialism' (in Britain). Although some of the key scholars in the vanguard of this movement specialized in earlier periods—notably the Renaissance critic Stephen Greenblatt—their effect on Victorian studies was swift and pervasive. The hallmark of this new phase of historicized criticism was its sophisticated awareness of the relationship between a literary text and its historical context. Rather than being defined as distinct artefacts against an historical background, novels were treated—like other published texts—as part of an ideological web of written and unwritten discourses, considered to be inextricable from the power structures of society. There are many variations on this powerful theoretical model, but they are all indebted, directly or indirectly, to the work of Marx and Foucault.

Few critics have gone to the extreme of using historicist theory as a justification for reading Dickens's novels in exactly the same way as non-literary documents. More often, non-literary documents are subjected to the same kind of rhetorical analysis as novels and compared with features of Dickens's fiction, particularly in their use of narrative, metaphor, and other structuring principles. Scientific thinking was the focus for a number of studies of the 1980s, including Gillian Beer's *Darwin's Plots* (1983) and George Levine's *Darwin and the Novelists* (1988), where the writing of Darwin and other contemporary scientists was analysed alongside Victorian fiction. Chris Baldick's study, *In Frankenstein's Shadow* (1987), examined a wide range of 19th-century political texts, from Marx's *Capital* to cartoons in PUNCH, highlighting the recurring metaphor of monstrosity and throwing new light on Dickens's bizarre vision. David Trotter's *Circulation* (1988) used the 1842 Sanitary Report of Edwin CHADWICK to define one discursive field that shaped Dickens's view of the regulation of society. The recent growth of interest in Dickens as JOURNALIST is partly due to such determination to locate his fiction in the wider web of Victorian writing.

Where novels are the focus of historicist study, the main aims are to show how works are constructed out of the ideological material to hand, how they are constrained by the socio-economic circumstances of their production, and how they play their own reciprocating roles in endorsing or interrogating the concepts and social structures of their time (see PUBLISHING). Historicism thus directs critics towards understanding Dickens in Victorian terms, not only in areas that Dickens himself saw as 'issues' but over a much broader ideological field. In Malcolm Andrews's *Dickens and the Grown-Up Child* (1994), for example, the well-worn topic of CHILDHOOD in Dickens's fiction is given fresh treatment by examining the assumptions about children that the Victorians adopted or disputed.

For historicists, personal identity and the politics of self-representation are as much constructions of their time as any characters and themes in fiction. Dickens's autobiographical writing and public image have therefore been a further focus of contextualization and analysis. The author's account of his own childhood experience at WARREN's Blacking warehouse has been revalued by Alexander Welsh in *From Copyright to Copperfield* (1987) and David Musselwhite in *Partings Welded Together* (1987); Dickens can be read differently when situated in that cultural flux out of which emerged both his midcentury fiction and, later, the thinking of Freud. Feminist critics, with their particular commitment to interdisciplinarity in gender studies, have gone further than most in the historicist project of analysing the politics of a period through its multifarious cultural forms. This approach identifies literature as only one strand making up the complicated ideological weave of Victorianism. Mary Poovey's *Uneven Developments* (1989) typically includes chapters on medical practice, legislation, and the public image of Florence Nightingale beside an examination of *David Copperfield* and professional writing. Such critical texts show Dickens studies apparently in the process of being subsumed in the wider field of Victorian studies, where intellectual borders are breaking down, allowing disciplines like law and economics to take their place alongside literature and history. However, this movement should not be construed as threatening the intrinsic interest of Dickens, whose novels continue to be viewed by most historicist critics as peculiarly complex sites of ideological construction and conflict. Even critics who emphasize the distinction between a work of art like a Dickens novel and other types of text, as Grahame Smith does in *Charles Dickens: A Literary Life* (1996), often show the effect of historicism in their work, problematizing the Dickens we thought we knew by revealing his place in a new range of Victorian cultural contexts.                    EW

7. **Marxist** Marx and Engels admired Dickens. Their respective paths came closest to crossing in London in the post-1848 years, when Dickens actively championed GERMAN exiles. But the figure *Household Words* took up first—Gottfried Kinkel—was regarded by Marx and Engels as an impostor who masqueraded as a bearded revolutionary and told sentimental stories about the harshness of his imprisonment in Germany, duping Dickens in the same way as the street-beggar who claimed to know Mazzini. Engels had praised Dickens first in 1844, listing 'G. Sand, E. Sue and Boz' as pre-eminent amongst writers who rejected kings and princes and made the 'despised class' and their joys and sorrows into fit subjects for novels. Marx, reviewing *Latter-Day Pamphlets* in 1850, mockingly distinguishes CARLYLE's style from the 'Pecksniff-style' of the modern English bourgeoisie, and in 1854 places Dickens first amongst 'the splendid brotherhood of fiction writers in England whose graphic and eloquent pages have issued to the world more political and social truths than have been uttered by all the professional politicians, publicists and moralists put together'. The list also includes THACKERAY, Charlotte BRONTË, and GASKELL; Marx praises them for their sharp vignettes of the ignorance, hypocrisy, and petty tyranny of the English middle classes (see Peter Demetz (ed.), *Marx, Engels and the Poets*, 1967).

Yet Marx and Engels are not the first socialist enthusiasts for Dickens; none of their points is new, and what they say simply reflects the warm reception accorded to Dickens by the Fourierists and Left Hegelians in Russia and Germany and elsewhere. So that when George Bernard Shaw appears in the 1880s, fresh from reading Marx in the British Museum, and writes the first overtly Marxist Dickens criticism in Britain (his 1889 essay 'From Dickens to Ibsen', not published until 1985 in Dan H. Lawrence and Martin Quinn, *Shaw on Dickens*), there is already the pressure of a tradition. Thus, his famous later assertion that '*Little Dorrit* is more seditious than *Das Kapital*' echoes Marx's own dialectical or paradoxical formula above—according to which Dickens's imaginative writing gives us 'more social and political truths than . . . [the social and political theorists].'

Shaw continued producing memorable paradoxical formulations—his remark, for instance, that *Hard Times* shows 'that it is not our disorder but our order that is horrible'— throughout his long and influential career as a Dickens critic, lasting to the late 1940s, when he finally saw his earlier heretical propaganda in favour of the later Dickens vindicated in critical orthodoxy. Their impact is still to be felt in Arnold Kettle's essay on *Oliver Twist* in

*An Introduction to the English Novel* (1951), which declares dialectically that 'what is so important about the Artful Dodger is not his oddity but his normality, not his inability to cope with the world but his very ability to cope with it on its own terms'.

Yet the finest English Marxist critic is perhaps T. A. Jackson. His pre-war book *Charles Dickens: The Progress of a Radical* (1937) was praised by the non-Marxist Michael Slater as containing 'some of the most intelligent and interesting criticism of Dickens published during this period' (*Dickensian*, 66, 1970). The key point about his work—as Trezise (1994) also sees—is that he nearly always links politics and society with aesthetic and stylistic questions, as in his most influential formulation, a kind of reply to E. M. Forster: 'he drew men "in the flat" because he saw them primarily "in the flat". And he saw them so because so they were—because the constitution of society had flattened them, past repair.'

But we should not limit ourselves either to orthodox Marxists, or to English-language critics. Besides relatively orthodox European Marxists like Lukács, Frankfurt School Critical Theorists such as Adorno and Benjamin have a great deal to offer the study of Dickens. Adorno's essay on *The Old Curiosity Shop* (*Dickens Quarterly*, 6, 1989) is major Benjamin-inspired work about the traces of a pre-capitalist popular allegorizing culture (with its roots in the Baroque period, according to Benjamin and Adorno) in Dickens's novels; and Benjamin's own scattered notes and remarks make clear how central Dickens is to the theory of oral narrative and the novel assembled in his essay 'The Story-Teller'.

In the 1990s one might say that exclusively Marxist critical approaches are now rare, and that Foucault has replaced Marx as the dominant influence on radical criticism of Dickens. But the fruitful mixing of Marx with other theorists (begun by Edmund WILSON in his famous 'Two Scrooges' essay, with its Freudian-Marxist approach, and continued by critics such as Jack Lindsay) is still very common, as in some of the essays in John Schad's recent anthology of theoretically informed Dickens criticism. However, the broader dialogue with earlier socialist and Marxist Dickens critics that would surely still be profitable is unfortunately not to be found in Schad's volume.                    MH

Hollington, Michael, 'Adorno, Benjamin and *The Old Curiosity Shop*', *Dickens Quarterly*, 6 (1989).
Schad, John (ed.), *Dickens Refigured: Bodies, Desires and Other Histories* (1996).
Trezise, Simon, 'The Making of Dickens: The Evolution of Marxist Criticism', *Dickens Quarterly*, 11 (1994).

**8. New critical** By the 1950s literary criticism was dominated by professional academics located in university English Departments. In this post-war period the school of 'new criticism' prominent before the war remained at the leading edge of the newly defined discipline of English Literature. The hallmark of this movement was close textual analysis, initiated by studies like I. A. Richards's *Practical Criticism* (1929). A classic demonstration of new critical values and techniques can be found in Cleanth Brooks's *The Well Wrought Urn* (1949), which placed a high value on textual density, especially featuring metaphorical complexity and the language of paradox. A work of literature was treated as an autonomous whole, exhibiting an imaginative unity and dealing with universal themes. The focus of critical attention was on aesthetic form rather than cultural context, and historical matters were left largely to the scholars.

This approach was better equipped to deal with poetry and drama than with large works of fiction. Where novels came under scrutiny, the carefully crafted work epitomized by the fiction of Henry James met with approval, as did the Jamesian novel's commitment to psychological realism, involving complex characterization and fine moral distinctions. Critics holding this rarefied view of the art of the novel were not generally predisposed to appreciate the big SERIALIZED works of a popular entertainer like Dickens. Indeed, the influential Cambridge critic F. R. LEAVIS famously omitted Dickens (with the exception of the compact and thematically coherent *Hard Times*) from his account of English fiction in *The Great Tradition* (1948), thus setting Dickens's defenders the task of justifying the inclusion of one of the greatest British authors in the university canon.

Fortunately, Dickens attracted many critics who did not allow Jamesian and Leavisite prejudices to obscure their understanding of Dickens's unique works. Among the more influential post-war publications were essays like Dorothy Van Ghent's 'The Dickens World: A View from Todgers" (*Sewanee Review*, 58, 1950), which explored the characteristic transposition of the animate and the inanimate in Dickens's fiction, and full-length studies like J. Hillis Miller's *Charles Dickens: The World of His Novels* (1958). Much of the best Dickens criticism of the period 1940–70 combined formidable new-critical skills of textual analysis with a regard for other dimensions of the novels. John Butt and Kathleen Tillotson's *Dickens at Work* (1957) and Sylvère Monod's *Dickens romancier* (1954; trans. 1968) drew on detailed research into Dickens's writing process. Steven Marcus's *Dickens: From Pickwick to Dombey* (1965) blended textual interpretation with insights from psychoanalysis. John Lucas's *The Melancholy Man* (1970) combined new-critical methods with a perspective on society derived from Marx. The diversity of Dickens criticism, and equally the pervasiveness of new-critical concerns, can be seen in Ada Nisbet's survey in *Victorian Fiction: A Guide to Research* (1964) and in anthologies like *Dickens and the Twentieth Century* (1962, ed. John Gross and Gabriel Pearson). Many of the essays collected by A. E. Dyson in *Dickens* (1969) and Michael Slater in *Dickens 1970*, for all their distinctiveness, reveal a shared preoccupation with thematic seriousness, symbolic complexity, and structural unity typical of new criticism.

A taste for Dickens's later novels, from *Dombey* onwards, developed over this period. This preference reflects not only a preoccupation with 'Dickens's Dark Novels' (the title of an article by Lionel Stevenson, *Sewanee Review*, 51, 1943)—a fascination shared by the essayist Edmund WILSON and the biographer Edgar Johnson—but also a commitment to new-critical tenets. Kathleen Tillotson in *Novels of the Eighteen Forties* (1954) praised the careful design of *Dombey*, which she saw as 'the first novel of Dickens to be dominated by a leading idea [Pride], embodied in a single character [Mr Dombey]'. Lionel Trilling's much-reprinted essay on *Little Dorrit* (*Kenyon Review* 15, 1953) foregrounded the organizing metaphor of the prison, while other critics pursued the patterns of fog and lawcourts, or river and dustheaps, through *Bleak House* and *Our Mutual Friend*.

New-critical ideas were still prevalent in the productions of the Dickens Centenary in 1970, such as H. M. Daleski's *Dickens and the Art of Analogy* and Barbara Hardy's *The Moral Art of Dickens*. Indeed, formalist approaches to Dickens have never disappeared, and some excellent post-1970 work was carried out on larger structural forms. Peter Garrett's *The Victorian Multiplot Novel: Studies in Dialogical Form* (1980) explored the dynamics of Dickens's longer novels, and Susan Horton's *The Reader in the Dickens World* (1981), focusing on reader response, showed a sensitivity to genre and form characteristic of new criticism.

By 1970 Dickens's place in the academic canon was unquestioned. He had survived the rigours of new criticism, and was now declared by F. R. and Q. D. Leavis to be 'the SHAKESPEARE of the novel' (Leavis 1970). Indeed, recognition of his moral seriousness and technical brilliance was beginning to screen his comic and anarchic qualities, prompting a corrective shift in emphasis in later studies like James Kincaid's *Dickens and the Rhetoric of Laughter* (1971) and John Carey's *The Violent Effigy* (1973). On the wider intellectual scene more far-reaching developments were under way. The gathering forces of feminism, deconstruction, and historicism would soon push new criticism aside, and profoundly change the nature of Dickens studies.                                         EW

**9. Post-structuralist** The terms 'post-structuralism' or 'deconstruction' designate a body of critical and philosophical writings that is difficult to summarize briefly. One way of approaching this topic is to distinguish between two broad strands of criticism with respect to Dickens. On the one hand there are readings that focus attention upon character, story, and setting. According to this approach, Dickens's novels are primarily of interest because of the portrait of Victorian life they provide us with; they are to be judged according to such concepts as 'realism', 'psychological acuity', and 'narrative plausibility'. Dickens's contemporaries tended to judge him in this manner, his works being praised for being 'true' (which is to say, conforming to a pre-existing notion of 'real life'), 'affecting' (emotionally engaging, in the same way real people are emotionally engaging), and so on.

A second broad approach to Dickens, on the other hand, has tended to stress the artificiality, the fictionality of Dickens's technique. In a 'structuralist' analysis, the novels are read as structures of symbolic meaning, often in terms of the binary oppositions they articulate, the patterning of theme and symbol that makes up the texture of the text. Such approaches can run the risk of being too obvious (Dickens's works are so patently structured according to binary oppositions— good/evil, male/female, city/country, and so on—that listing them adds little to our understanding) and too mechanistic (to ignore Dickens's humour and humanity is largely to miss the point of Dickens). Perhaps for this reason there have been few large-scale structuralist readings of Dickens's corpus, and critics have been content to notice patterns in individual novels (in the way that, for instance, W. H. Auden's classic essay 'Dingley Dell and the Fleet', explores *Pickwick*), or else to explore different sets of patterning in different novels whilst trying to retain a sense of Dickens's overall diversity and richness (J. Hillis Miller's early *Charles Dickens: The World of His Novels*, 1958, is a good example of this).

Although much post-structuralist thought is implicitly hostile to the totalizing, pseudo-scientific cast of structuralism, there is no denying the fact that deconstruction grew in large part out of structuralism. One structuralist insight is that the relationship between the 'signifier' (for instance, a word) and the 'signified' (the concept alluded to) is not natural or direct; it is defined not in terms of connection, but difference. This insight is behind a key concept of the influential post-structuralist Jacques Derrida, 'differance', a word which puns on the two French words meaning 'difference' and 'deferral'. Derrida's 'differance' extends the process of signification indefinitely. So the word 'foot' signifies by being different from 'knee', 'ball', and so on; which is to say, its meaning depends upon its being different from other words. But at the same time, the actual meaning of 'foot' (if, for instance, you look it up in a dictionary) is articulated via other words, which in turn need to be defined, just as their definitions need to be defined. That ultimate meaning, in other words, is deferred. Derrida cannot see any reason for this process to come

to an end—there is no transcendental 'meaning' that can be located, no ultimate benchmark against which all meanings can be checked. The effect of this is to see signification as a whole as a radically unstable, shifting, and ambiguous process.

'Deconstruction' tends to be fascinated with teasing out these uncertainties, with untying the binary oppositions that structuralism often presented as rigidly defining, with pinpointing those places in the text where it contradicts itself, or advances subtexts that undermine the apparent purpose of the work. Dickens is particularly ripe for this sort of criticism, and much of it is powerfully suggestive and fascinating; although it should also be noted that many critics (and not only of the more traditional cast) feel hostility towards post-structuralism. Some see 'deconstruction' as synonymous with 'destruction', as irresponsibly demolishing great works of literature, as perversely concentrating on the margins of the text instead of its central concerns (although deconstructionists might with validity question the whole notion of 'centre' versus 'margins' in textual production). Others see deconstruction as a sort of critical sausage machine, as productive of a huge amount of verbiage. This latter anxiety is in a sense significant, not only for criticism as a whole (critics are, after all, in the business of producing verbiage), but particularly with reference to Dickens, one of the most voluminous of canonized writers. Steven Connor's excellent deconstructionist reading of *Bleak House* (in his *Charles Dickens*, 1985) explores precisely the great length of Dickens's text, and the paradoxical mistrust of great length of written language evinced by the novel— embodied chiefly in the endless production of text by CHANCERY, all the legal documentation that is productive, ultimately, of nothing. Connor also explores the way the novel sets up the binary opposition between written and spoken language, only to problematize it. Derrida's *Of Grammatology* (trans. Gayatri Spivak, 1978) explores precisely this supposed opposition between speech and writing, and identifies what it calls 'logocentrism', the abiding sense that the spoken is somehow superior to the written (more immediate, more authentic, and so on). This hierarchical binary structure is then subjected to analysis that destabilizes it. The relationship is particularly important for Dickens, whose works occupy a middle ground between the written (as texts to be read) and the spoken (as texts to be read aloud, not least by Dickens himself in his famous PUBLIC READINGS).

It is not that deconstructionists set out to show that Dickens is somehow muddled or self-contradictory; *all* texts, to one degree or another, function in this manner, presenting a vision that purports unity whilst elaborating subtexts at odds with the surface meanings. Dickens's texts are so appealing to this school of thought partly because they are so multifarious, the proliferation of signification is so proudly displayed, the writing plays so joyously with the slipperiness of meanings. The novels are also peculiarly aware of their own textuality; they all in various ways express the potency of storytelling in making sense, albeit contingent sense, of the world. See also John Schad, *The Reader in the Dickensian Mirrors: Some New Language* (1992), a deconstructivist reading of Dickensian language; Audrey Jaffe, *Vanishing Points: Dickens, Narrative, and the Subject of Omniscience* (1991), a deconstruction of the Dickensian omniscient narrator. D. A. Miller's *The Novel and the Police* (1988) provides a deconstruction (via Foucault) of the representation of structures of power in Dickens's books. AR

**10. Textual scholarship on Dickens** Dickens poses many interesting challenges for the editor and textual scholar, partially because of the very richness of the surviving materials: notes Dickens used in planning serial structure, manuscripts, proofs, SERIAL publications, and a variety of book EDITIONS.

Dickens's manuscripts are the most important of these surviving documents, primarily because they are so rich in revisions—increasingly so over time, as Dickens took ever-greater care with his work (see COMPOSITION, DICKENS'S METHODS OF). The manuscript Dickens gave to the printer was an extensively revised draft, never a fair copy; as early as the 1840s, a single page of Dickens's manuscript might include dozens or even scores of alterations and revisions, many of them of great interest. Unfortunately, comparatively few of the deletions, and almost none of the substitutions and interlineations, are recorded in scholarly editions.

At least some holograph manuscript survives for each of Dickens's novels; though most of *Pickwick Papers* and *Nicholas Nickleby* and substantial portions of *Oliver Twist* are lost, the manuscripts of *The Old Curiosity Shop* and all the following novels survive in complete or nearly complete form. (Most are now in the VICTORIA AND ALBERT MUSEUM; see COLLECTIONS OF DICKENS MATERIALS.)

A significant amount of proof also survives, generally showing signs of far less revision than Dickens's manuscript, though in some cases there is evidence of as many as three different proof stages. Unfortunately, proofs of Dickens's novels were not kept systematically; the proof record is invariably incomplete, leaving textual scholars to puzzle over whether changes set in print in proofs or in the published text are the result of a compositor's efforts (or errors), or of Dickens's manuscript revisions to a lost set of proofs. Leslie Staples inaugurated serious consideration of the rare materials in the Forster Collection with his series of articles in the DICKENSIAN, entitled 'Shavings from Dickens's Workshop'; in these articles, he reprinted passages Dickens cut from the novels in the proof stage.

The earliest printed editions of Dickens's novels were published serially, whether in weekly or monthly 'numbers' or in such magazines as BENTLEY'S MISCELLANY, *Household Words*, or *All the Year Round*. These early serial instalments provide valuable evidence about Dickens's preferences regarding spelling and punctuation: for example, Dickens took pains with the idiosyncratic spellings in Mrs Gamp's speeches in the serial instalments of *Martin Chuzzlewit*, whereas these speeches are prone, in later editions, to be regularized. Nearly simultaneous with the concluding instalments of the serial publication, a first book edition in from one to three volumes was usually published.

After initial publication, most of Dickens's books went through several later editions in Dickens's lifetime, including but not limited to the Cheap Editions (1847–64), the Library Edition (1858–9), the illustrated Library Edition (1861–74), the People's Edition (1865–7), and the Charles Dickens Edition (begun in 1867 and completed five years after his death). Though Dickens never revised his text as extensively as, say, Henry James did, each lifetime edition bears at least some minimal signs of revision—and of textual corruption as well.

Modern textual scholarship on Dickens takes three principal forms. The most basic is the preparation and publication of facsimiles of important texts, whether of Dickens's manuscripts or of printed versions of his works. Micro Methods Ltd. produced commercial microfilm copies of most of Dickens's manuscripts in the Forster Collection in 1969. Facsimiles of Dickens's manuscript of *A Christmas Carol*, his working plans for his novels, and the book of memoranda he began keeping in January of 1855 have been published in book form, the latter two with transcriptions. Facsimile reproductions of original parts of *Pickwick Papers*, *Nicholas Nickleby*, MASTER HUMPHREY'S CLOCK (including *The Old Curiosity Shop* and *Barnaby Rudge*), and *The Mystery of Edwin Drood* have been published, but are not now widely available. Surprisingly, no publisher has produced a facsimile edition of Dickens's journals *Household Words* or *All the Year Round*, nor of any of the collected editions of Dickens's works published in his lifetime; facsimiles of the 'Cheap Edition' or the 'Charles Dickens Edition' would be of significant value to scholars without access to the originals.

A second and less successful set of projects (partly, perhaps, because the challenges are so much greater) involves the preparation of scholarly editions of Dickens's works, often attempting to establish an authoritative text. The Clarendon and Norton Critical editions, and the ongoing Pilgrim Edition of the LETTERS, are the most notable entries in this field thus far.

The most ambitious textual edition yet undertaken is the Clarendon Edition (Oxford UP: 1966– ). So far, volumes devoted to *The Pickwick Papers* (1986), *Oliver Twist* (1966), *Martin Chuzzlewit* (1982), *Dombey and Son* (1974), *David Copperfield* (1981), *Little Dorrit* (1979), *Great Expectations* (1993), *The Mystery of Edwin Drood* (1972), and *The Old Curiosity Shop* (1997) have been published. The editors of this series establish critical texts, attempting to purge the novels of disfiguring textual corruptions; demonstrate Dickens's process of revision by recording selected variants in an apparatus, and typically provide extensive and detailed introductions, useful in tracing the history of the text. The editions have, however, serious limitations. The editors typically (but not invariably) choose the first bound edition as copy-text; no Clarendon editor has based a text on Dickens's manuscript. Thus, the spelling, punctuation, and capitalization of the novels are invariably filtered through the regularizations and misreadings of compositors and printers, even where the editors restore the wording of Dickens's manuscript. Furthermore, the Clarendon Editions typically provide incomplete emendations lists: the editors make certain types of emendations and regularizations silently (that is, without recording the changes), so one cannot confidently reconstruct the readings of the copy-text. This is most striking in the case of pre-publication variants: most deletions from the manuscript are omitted, and almost all interlinear additions go unnoted. The Clarendon *Great Expectations*, based as it is on the 1861 three-volume edition, does not even record the spelling, capitalization, and punctuation of the original publication in *All the Year Round*, which reflected Dickens's manuscript preferences much more accurately. The Clarendon *Dombey* rejects some revisions from 1858 and 1867, specifically admitting them to be authorial, but not incorporating them into the text anyway. Some of the editors do not consult or record the readings of important documents (proofs, or early serial publications); in some cases the editorial construction rests on controversial assumptions, such as that a first edition 'obviously represents Dickens's final intentions'.

The other notable modern textual edition of the novels is the one undertaken by Norton; critical editions of *Oliver Twist* (1993), *David Copperfield* (1990), *Bleak House* (1977), *Hard Times* (1966; rev. 1990), and *Great Expectations* (1999) have now appeared. Of these, only *Bleak House*, *Hard Times*, and *Great Expectations* provide significant textual notes, and even these more ambitious efforts fail to provide that most basic piece of textual apparatus, an emendations list.

The Pilgrim Edition (1965– ) of Dickens's letters is more satisfactory; the editors make a serious attempt to transcribe Dickens's letters from the original sources, and, despite some errors and omissions, they generally do so extremely accurately. Though the edition has taken many years to prepare and is not yet complete, the project (especially when electronically searchable) will be of incomparable value.

A third and final category of textual scholarship includes interpretive scholarship and criticism based primarily on textual evidence. H. P. Sucksmith's *The Narrative Art of Charles Dickens* (1970) is the best study of Dickens's creative process as reflected in his manuscript and proof revisions, though the book is somewhat limited by an idiosyncratic transcription system and a diffuse critical focus. John Butt and Kathleen Tillotson's *Dickens at Work* (1957) and Sylvère Monod's *Dickens the Novelist* (1968) examine serial structure, Dickens's plans for his instalments, and the revisions between printed editions, but devote little or no sustained attention to revisions within the manuscripts. Surprisingly, no full study of Dickens's richly documented techniques of revision within the manuscripts has yet been published. JJB

**Cruikshank, George** (1792–1878), graphic artist, ILLUSTRATOR, and friend of Dickens from 1836 through the 1840s. Cruikshank first met Dickens at the artist's Islington studio on 17 November 1835. The publisher John MACRONE had hired Cruikshank to illustrate a volume reissue of the sketches and tales Dickens had been publishing in London periodicals. Artist and author met several times to discuss this project. Cruikshank eventually provided sixteen illustrations for the two-volume *Sketches by Boz*, First Series (February 1836), and ten more for the one-volume Second Series (December 1836). For the second edition of this Second Series (1837) the artist etched two more plates, and when both series were reissued in twenty monthly parts (November 1837–June 1839), he enlarged and re-etched his original images, added thirteen new plates, and designed the wood-engraved paper cover ('wrapper'). By the end of 1836 Dickens and his wife Catherine were friendly with Cruikshank and his wife Mary Ann; over the next few years they frequently socialized together.

When Richard BENTLEY hired Dickens to edit the publisher's new monthly magazine, BENTLEY'S MISCELLANY, he also hired Cruikshank to provide the illustrations and design

a wrapper. In the first number (January 1837), Cruikshank illustrated 'Public Life of Mr Tulrumble', and from February of that year he provided one steel etching per month illustrating Dickens's instalments of *Oliver Twist*. During the summer of 1838 Dickens wrote all of the remainder of the novel, as it was to be published in three volumes in November; Cruikshank also completed plates for those instalments not yet published in the *Miscellany*. When Dickens saw the last etchings for the first time (he had approved some preliminary designs earlier), he disliked the final image, of Oliver and the Maylie family by the fireside, and asked Cruikshank to redesign it. After trying to improve the existing plate, Cruikshank complied, substituting in later issues of the 1838 edition a picture of Rose and Oliver in church looking at a stone memorial to Oliver's mother Agnes.

Over the next few years Dickens discussed with Cruikshank various projects, including a novel to be written by Harrison AINSWORTH and Dickens and illustrated by Cruikshank and John LEECH, but little came of these discussions. Cruikshank contributed two etchings to the PIC-NIC PAPERS, which Dickens edited to raise money for Macrone's widow and family. Dickens composed a parodic Preface and notes for Cruikshank's illustrated Cockney poem, 'The LOVING BALLAD OF LORD BATEMAN' (1839), but as Dickens was under contract to Bentley 'not to commence or write an other work' besides *Barnaby Rudge*, he was anxious to conceal his part in this book. Dickens had hoped to publish *Barnaby* in *Bentley's Miscellany*, where it would have been illustrated by Cruikshank, but angrily terminated his relationship with Bentley and began issuing his own periodical, MASTER HUMPHREY'S COCK (1840–1). As Hablot Knight BROWNE and George CATTERMOLE were hired to illustrate that serial, Cruikshank was precluded from illustrating the novel he and Dickens had often discussed. In 1846 Cruikshank was Dickens's choice to refurbish his plates and design a wood-engraved wrapper for a reissue of *Oliver Twist* in ten monthly parts. Four years later, in response to Edward Chapman's enquiry about who was to draw a new frontispiece for the Cheap Edition of *Oliver Twist*, Dickens unhesitatingly replied, 'George Cruikshank, by all means' (13 February 1850; see CHAPMAN AND HALL).

Although Cruikshank illustrated only two of Dickens's titles, his representations of London lower-middle-class life in *Sketches* ('daguerres of London forms and faces', Ralph Waldo EMERSON called them), and his depictions of 'Oliver asking for more' and 'Fagin in the condemned Cell' in *Oliver Twist*, are among the most memorable illustrations to Dickens's books. Cruikshank's experience as a political caricaturist in the 1810s, as an illustrator of books about London life in the 1820s, and as the foremost illustrator of classic novels in the 1830s, provided him with a range of styles and effects to apply to Dickens's subjects.

Cruikshank also had strong ideas about what he wanted to represent: he enjoyed popular AMUSEMENTS at least as much as Dickens did, and had on the whole, despite drawing many melodramatic images of death, an optimistic view of life. He was skilful at choosing the optimal moment in a story for his picture, and at adding elements to the design that, in the manner of HOGARTH, provided further commentary on the central action. While his depiction of women was often faulted by contemporaries and later critics, Cruikshank's wiry, pulsing line and keen sense of dramatic design yields plates that are highly energized and theatrical.

In December of 1845 Dickens invited Cruikshank to join his AMATEUR THEATRICAL company. Thereafter Cruikshank acted character roles in plays by JONSON and SHAKESPEARE and in afterpiece farces and burlesques. He also drew a sketch for Dickens's pamphlet (never published) narrating the departure of the troupe for an out-of-town engagement from the viewpoint of Dickens's famous midwife, Sairey Gamp. At this time Cruikshank's wife was dying and the artist, formerly a heavy drinker, was turning to temperance propaganda for commercial support and as an outlet for his teetotal zeal (see DRINK AND TEMPERANCE). Dickens reviewed Cruikshank's series of cautionary plates, *The Bottle* (1847), favourably, but

gradually he took stronger objection, both in private and in public, to Cruikshank's 'fanaticism' on the subject of temperance. Dickens advocated moderation; Cruikshank believed that total abstention from spirits was the only possible course for many, including those in the lower economic classes. Personal relations became strained by the early 1850s: when Dickens published critiques of Cruikshank's temperance FAIRY TALES ('Frauds on the Fairies', *HW* 1 October 1853) and parliamentary testimony on behalf of prohibition ('The Great Baby', *HW* 4 August 1855), his declared opposition to Cruikshank's passionate teetotal rhetoric meant that their relationship was permanently severed.

At Dickens's death in 1870 Cruikshank is reported to have said, 'One of our greatest enemies gone'. On 30 December 1871, responding reluctantly to aspersions cast by FORSTER in the first volume of his biography of Dickens, Cruikshank in a letter to *The TIMES* stated his claim to have suggested the idea, plot, and characters of *Oliver Twist*. These claims he elaborated in an 1872 pamphlet, *The Artist and the Author*; Forster reiterated his position in the second volume of his biography published that December. Although at the time of its first publication THACKERAY among others had given Cruikshank equal credit with Dickens for originating *Oliver Twist*, by the 1870s Dickens was thought to be the embodiment of the powerful, controlling author, while Cruikshank was dismissed as 'deluded' in supposing that he had any hand in creating Dickens's works, or Ainsworth's, as he also (and justly) asserted. The disparity in the 1870s between Dickens's reputation and Cruikshank's created and perpetuated the image of the embattled and deluded artist and fostered a neglect of his contributions to Dickens's works that was only redressed in the 1970s. RLP

Cohen (1980).
Harvey (1971).
Patten (1992, 1996).

# D

**Daily News,** a morning paper started in 1846, with Dickens as its first editor. As early as 1840, Joseph Paxton (1801–55), superintendent of gardens at Chatsworth for the Duke of Devonshire and later knighted for designing the Crystal Palace, had expressed interest to BRADBURY AND EVANS (Dickens's publishers at the time) about starting up a paper. Coincidentally, Dickens's most recent contract with them, in 1844, had included a clause about the possibility of his editing a magazine or journal at some future date. By the autumn of 1845 a number of railway proprietors had been brought together by Paxton to set up the new paper, which was to be of 'Liberal Politics and thorough Independence' (advertisement, 1 December 1845), and Dickens was secured as the editor on 3 November 1845. No expense was spared to hire the best reporters away from other established papers: Eyre Evans Crowe, Albany FONBLANQUE, John FORSTER, and W. J. Fox as leader-writers; John Hill Powell and Thomas Hodgskin (both had been on the MORNING CHRONICLE with Dickens), and Frederick Knight Hunt (later to be editor 1851–4) as sub-editors; W. H. WILLS (later Dickens's sub-editor on *Household Words*) as secretary and sub-editor; Dudley Costello as foreign editor, with correspondents in more than ten cities in Europe, the Middle East, and India (Dickens tried to hire W. H. Russell, who went to the *Morning Chronicle* instead); John Towne Danson, a political economist; George HOGARTH as music and dramatic critic; and reporters such as Samuel Laman BLANCHARD, William Hazlitt (son), George Hodder, Thomas Holcroft, Douglas JERROLD, Blanchard Jerrold, and Mark LEMON. John DICKENS was put in charge of the reporters, a post he held until his death. Dickens himself was paid £2,000, double the annual salary of any other editor except Delane of *The* TIMES. The Times refused to carry any advertisements for the new paper and excluded it from arrangements with the *Morning Post* and *Morning Chronicle* for sharing the cost of foreign messengers. There was great trepidation about the new paper, which appeared for the first time on 21 January 1846 and sold 10,000 copies; it consisted of eight pages, three of them advertising (one page of railway ads alone). Most of the articles were on free trade and railways, and Dickens contributed a 'PICTURE FROM ITALY': this combining of literature and politics was considered new. W. H. Russell writes of Fleet Street's pleasure when the first issue turned out to be ineptly printed and laid out. The next day Dickens inserted a letter reassuring readers about the numerous errors. The circulation fell during February and March, but then so did those of other papers (the *Morning Chronicle* and *Morning Herald* were running at a loss at the time), and the reporters' salaries had to be reduced. More proprietors were brought in, and discussions about the future of the paper continued through the spring.

Meanwhile, it turned out to be a time of crisis for Dickens as well, as he proved to be unsuited to the constant grind of daily editorial attendance—he resigned on 9 February 1846. His editorship was criticized for not keeping up with the politics of the day. Forster stepped in as editor (until October 1846), and Charles Wentworth Dilke, who had made a success of the *Athenaeum*, became manager and set the paper on a firmer course. He lowered the price from fivepence to twopence-halfpenny, and circulation went from 4,000 copies in June to 19,500 in July. However, its losses (which James Grant says were £200,000 in the first ten years) forced a return to the original price. Dilke stayed on till 1849; the paper continued into the 20th century, merging with other papers to become the *News Chronicle*.

Before and after his resignation Dickens wrote various articles for the paper in 1846: 'Crime and Education' (4 February), 'Hymn for the Wiltshire Labourers' (14 February), 'Travelling Letters' (21, 24, 31 January; 9, 16, 26 February; 2, 11 March) and 'Letters on Social Questions: Capital Punishment' (23, 28 February; 9, 13, 16 March)—these are collected in his MISCELLANEOUS PAPERS.                KC

Britton, Thomas, in Justin McCarthy and Sir John H. Robinson, *The 'Daily News' Jubilee* (1896).

Roberts, David, 'Charles Dickens and the *Daily News*: Editorials and Editorial Writers', *Victorian Periodicals Review*, 22 (1989).

Tillotson, Kathleen, 'New Light on Dickens and the *Daily News*', *Dickensian*, 78 (1982).

**Davenport, Jean** (1829–1903). See INFANT PHENOMENA.

***David Copperfield*** Dickens's eighth novel, his first with a first-person narrator, published by BRADBURY AND EVANS in twenty monthly parts (as nineteen) 1849–50. Considered by many, starting with FORSTER, to be his masterpiece, it was Dickens's own 'favourite child' among his novels (1867 Preface) and draws more directly than any other on events in his life.

### Inception and Composition

Some time between 1845 and 1848—the exact date is uncertain—Dickens began to write his autobiography (see DIARIES AND AUTOBIOGRAPHICAL FRAGMENT). He showed parts of it to Forster and to Catherine, but upon reaching the period of his love for Maria BEADNELL he found the memories too painful and burned the manuscript (to Mrs Winter, 22 February 1855). The preoccupation during these years with his past found outlet in the Christmas books, and a child's view of experience was integral to his presentation of Paul Dombey. Forster, who says that his relationship with Dickens was then at its most intimate, proposed that, 'by way of change', Dickens might attempt to write a novel in the first person, a suggestion 'which he took at once very gravely' (6.6).

On 7 January 1849 Dickens travelled to Norwich and Yarmouth with John LEECH and Mark LEMON. He reported to Forster that Yarmouth was 'the strangest place in the world . . . I shall certainly try my hand at it' (12 January 1849), and on a walk saw a signpost for Blundeston, which he adapted to 'Blunderstone' for David's birthplace (to Mrs Watson, 27 August 1853). 'As a kind of homage to the novel he was about to write', he named his sixth son, born on 15 January, Henry FIELDING, instead of his original intention, Oliver GOLDSMITH (Forster 6.6). By early February he was 'revolving a new work', which put him in 'deepest despondency'—even

deeper than the customary birth-pangs of other novels (Forster 6.6).

He had great difficulty settling on a title; seventeen variants are recorded in his notes, including the name 'Charles Copperfield' for his hero. On 23 February he proposed 'Mag's Diversions', to Forster; dissatisfied, on the 26th he sent six more options, from which he chose 'The Copperfield Survey of the World as It Rolled'. This remained the working title for another month (but not as late as 19 April, as Forster claims; see Patten 1978, pp. 205–6), and he was 'much startled' when Forster pointed out that his hero's initials were his own reversed, declaring 'that it was in keeping with the fates and chances which were always befalling him' (Forster 6.6). At this stage he could still complain that 'My hand is out in the matter of *Copperfield*. Today and yesterday I have done nothing. Though I know what I want to do, I am lumbering like a stage waggon' (19 April 1949).

No. 1 did not fill 32 pages, and he added the account of Mrs Gummidge as a 'lone lorn creetur' and a passage foreshadowing Emily's seduction. Unlike *Dombey*, for *Copperfield* Dickens drew up no master plan in advance, often writing a chapter summary after the chapter itself. He made four late name changes (Traddles, Barkis, Creakle, and Steerforth —see Clarendon Introduction, p. xxix), debated about David's profession as late as November, when he had reached No. 8, and by 7 May 1850 had still not decided Dora's fate. Some things, however, were clear from an early stage: David's reunion with Aunt Betsey, Emily's fall, and Agnes's role as the 'real' heroine.

Once under way he was 'quite confident' and planning ahead (to Forster, 6 June 1849). He went for a long walk while meditating how to introduce 'what I know so well'—based on his experience in WARREN'S BLACKING warehouse—and once he had completed 'a very complicated interweaving of truth and fiction' he was delighted. 'I think I have done it ingeniously', he told Forster (10 July 1849). 'Once fairly in it, the story bore him irresistibly along', Forster observed (6.6); 'certainly with less trouble to himself in the composition, beyond that ardent sympathy with the creatures of the fancy which always made so absolutely real to him their sufferings or sorrows; and he was probably never less harassed by interruptions or breaks in his invention'.

He spent the summer in the Isle of Wight, where he fell ill briefly in August. He took Forster's advice and changed Mr Dick's obsession from a bull in a china shop to King Charles's head, topical in the bicentenary of Charles's execution (22 August 1849). Although sales were substantially lower than for *Dombey*, he was philosophical, and set about planning *Household Words*, the first number of which was published 31 March 1850 (to Forster, 22 September 1849). Although the journal took up increasing amounts of his time, it did not interfere with the writing of his novel, as the Christmas books had with *Dombey*. 'Between Copperfield and Household Words, I am busy as a bee', he cheerfully reported to Macready (11 June 1850). In December he had an unexpected setback when Mrs Seymour Hill threatened him with legal action because Miss Mowcher bore too close a resemblance to her. Embarrassed, Dickens placated her by changing his plans for the character, but not without loss to consistency of characterization (18 December 1849; see CHARACTERS—ORIGINALS). Stone (1987), praising Dickens's 'consummate fulfillment' of his design for *Copperfield*, calls the transformation of Miss Mowcher 'the only major departure from his original plans'.

On 16 August 1850 his third and last daughter, Dora Annie, named for David's child-wife, was born. Catherine was unwell for months afterwards and Dora, always frail, died on 14 April 1851. As Dickens finished writing the book on 21 October 1850, he felt 'strangely divided, as usual in such cases, between sorrow and joy. Oh, my dear Forster', he confided, 'if I were to say half of what *Copperfield* makes me feel to-night, how strangely, even to you, I should be turned inside-out! I seem to be sending some part of myself into the Shadowy World'. (See also COMPOSITION, DICKENS'S METHODS.)

## Contracts, Text, and Publication History

As with *Dombey*, there was no separate contract for *Copperfield*, only the general agreement of 1 June 1844 with Bradbury and Evans, which assigned them one-quarter share in whatever he might write for eight years. In response to a letter from the Secretary of the NEWSVENDORS' BENEVOLENT ASSOCIATION,

Dickens complained about his publishers' discount policy (to Evans, 5 May 1849). He warned Evans not to ask for copy (1 May 1849), and on several occasions asked for an incomplete number to be set up in type, so that he would know 'exactly where I am' and so that BROWNE would have material on which to base his illustrations (10 July 1849).

*The Personal History, Adventures, Experience, and Observation of David Copperfield the Younger, of Blunderstone Rookery (Which He Never Meant to be Published on Any Account)* appeared monthly from 1 May 1849 to 1 November 1850, with the cover title shortened to *The Personal History of David Copperfield* on the title-page. It was dedicated to the Honourable Mr and Mrs Richard WATSON. Holograph copies of trial titles, number plans, complete manuscript, corrected proofs, a list of chapter headings, and an errata list are all held in the FORSTER COLLECTION. A brief Preface, dated October 1850, stated publicly what Dickens had said to Forster, that he would leave unspoken the 'personal confidences, and private emotions' which the book aroused in him, and promised that another serial novel would follow. He used the same Preface for the Cheap Edition (1859) and altered it slightly for the Charles Dickens Edition (1867), adding that 'Of all my books, I like this the best'. He made little revision for these later EDITIONS.

Tauchnitz published the novel in three volumes in 1849–50 from corrected proofs (see COPYRIGHT), and the first American edition was published in monthly parts and two volumes by John Wiley and G. P. Putnam. It was reprinted widely after Dickens's death. The definitive Clarendon Edition (1981), based on the 1850 text, is edited by Nina Burgis.

## Illustrations

Dickens' principal ILLUSTRATOR, Hablot Browne, once again had sole responsibility. He prepared the wrapper design (with a baby in the centre, surveying a globe of the world —a remnant of the original working title), two engravings per number, a frontispiece, and vignette title-page. His illustrations contain details not in the text, which throw light on characters and events, thus forming 'part of the evidence of what the novel *is*' (Steig 1978). Dickens kept a sharp eye on minutiae, asking Browne, for example, to change

David's coat in the illustration of the friendly waiter to a 'little jacket' (9 May 1849). Browne offered several preliminary sketches for David's meeting with Aunt Betsey, reproduced in the Clarendon Edition, letting Dickens choose his favourite. Browne was one of the guests at a dinner party at Devonshire Terrace on 12 May, and visited Dickens at Bonchurch in August (Forster 6.3, 6). Dickens found Browne's work for *Copperfield* 'capital' and the illustration of Micawber for chapter 17 'uncommonly characteristic' (21 September 1849).

### Sources and Context

*David Copperfield* appeared the same year as the two other supreme English works of memory, WORDSWORTH's *The Prelude* and TENNYSON's *In Memoriam*. The Romantic concern with the moral and imaginative growth of the individual and the Victorian confrontation with change and doubt coalesced to make Dickens's novel 'a key text of mid-Victorian civilization, a text in which the self-fashioned hero is redefined for a post-Romantic generation' (Andrew Sanders, Introduction to World's Classics Edition, 1997).

Dickens's memories are intensely personal but marvellously transformed into fiction. His experience as the son of a debtor is comically celebrated in the resilience of Wilkins Micawber; his unrequited passion for Maria Beadnell is tenderly evoked in the doomed marriage of David and Dora. The decision to make David a novelist emphasizes the extent to which *Copperfield* is Dickens's stocktaking as an artist. 'The world would not take another Pickwick from me, now', he observed when the novel was barely under way, 'but we can be cheerful and merry I hope, notwithstanding, and with a little more purpose in us' (to Dudley Costello, 25 April 1949). The focus on an individual hero's adventures, on CHILDHOOD, and on a parade of comic and grotesque characters all look back to earlier work, even as the concern with individual development, the strain of pessimism, and the complex structural patterning foreshadow key characteristics of the later novels.

Charlotte BRONTË's intense first-person narrative, *Jane Eyre*, had appeared to acclaim in 1847 (although Dickens claimed years later never to have read it; see Jerome Meckier, 'Some Household Words', *Dickensian*, 71,

1975). Dickens did, however, read Elizabeth GASKELL's *Mary Barton*, with its concern to promote sympathy and understanding in a class-ridden society (to Rogers, 18 February 1849). *Pendennis* was appearing serially at the same time as *Copperfield*, but the rivalry mattered less to Dickens than to THACKERAY. The contemporary whose influence figures 'far more prominently' is CARLYLE, who laughingly quoted Mrs Gummidge that 'everything went contrary with him' at Dickens's dinner-party on 12 May 1849 (Forster 6.6). In his lectures *On Heroes, Hero-Worship, and the Heroic in History*, delivered in 1840, the year he and Dickens met, Carlyle had defined history as the biographies of Great Men. David, having made his own way by dint of hard personal experience, earnestness, and application, is precisely that 'most important modern person', the Hero as Man of Letters (see Sanders, World's Classics Introduction).

*Copperfield* also deals with specific social concerns. Martha and Emily reflect Dickens's efforts at URANIA COTTAGE to reclaim fallen women (see also PROSTITUTES). Their EMIGRATION, along with the Micawbers and Mr Mell, dramatizes Dickens's belief in the possibility of starting a new life abroad (see 'A Bundle of Emigrants' Letters', *HW* 30 March 1850). The depiction of Littimer and Heep in PRISON is generally seen as a journalistic excrescence, based on his article 'Pet Prisoners' (*HW* 27 April 1850) and on Carlyle's 'Model Prisons' (*Latter Day Pamphlets*, 1 March 1850). His views on EDUCATION and treatment of the insane feed into the depiction of Salem House and of Mr Dick, respectively (see MADNESS).

### Plot, Character, and Theme

David's childhood idyll with his young widowed mother and her kindly servant Peggotty is rudely interrupted when, on return from a holiday visit to Peggotty's family in Yarmouth, he discovers that his mother has remarried. His cruel stepfather, Mr Murdstone, abetted by his sister Miss Jane Murdstone, bullies Clara Copperfield into submission and terrorizes David by trying to 'form' his character. When Murdstone beats him for not knowing his lesson, David bites his hand and is sent to Salem House, a school conducted by the ignorant and brutal Mr Creakle. Among his fellow-pupils are the cheerful Tommy Traddles, who draws skeletons whenever he is caned, and Steerforth, a BYRONIC figure who patronizes David and is worshipped in return.

David's mother dies, whereupon Peggotty marries Barkis, the carrier, and David, taken from school, is sent to work in Murdstone and Grinby's warehouse. He boards with Mr Micawber, grandiloquent and improvident, who is arrested for debt. David runs away to Betsey Trotwood, his angular but kindly aunt, who, taking advice from her simple-minded ward Mr Dick, defies the Murdstones and offers protection to David, whom she renames Trotwood. David goes to Dr Strong's school in Canterbury, where he boards with Mr Wickfield, his daughter Agnes, and his 'umble clerk Uriah Heep.

David visits Yarmouth, accompanied by Steerforth, who carries off Mr Peggotty's niece, David's childhood sweetheart, Emily. Miss Mowcher, a dwarf, whom Dickens had introduced to assist in the elopement, is changed to an honest friend. David is articled to Mr Spenlow and falls in love with his daughter, Dora. Uriah, taking advantage of Mr Wickfield's drinking, gradually insinuates himself into power, sets his eye on Agnes, and assures Dr Strong his young wife is unfaithful. David knocks him down.

After Aunt Betsey is mysteriously bankrupted, David becomes a parliamentary reporter and then a novelist. He marries Dora, whose charming childishness results in chaotic housekeeping. The fallen woman Martha helps David and Mr Peggotty find Emily, who is berated by Rosa Dartle, companion to Steerforth's mother and herself passionately in love with Steerforth. Mr Dick reconciles Dr Strong and his wife. Mr Micawber exposes the villainy of Heep. Traddles recovers Aunt Betsey's property. Dora dies. In a great storm at Yarmouth, Ham Peggotty drowns trying unsuccessfully to rescue a sailor, whose corpse is found to be Steerforth's. The Micawbers, Mr Peggotty, Emily, and Martha emigrate to Australia. Some years later David marries Agnes.

Characters and themes in *Copperfield* are organized with intricate structural parallelism. The BILDUNGSROMAN teaches David to eschew the sternness of Murdstone on the one hand and the carelessness of Micawber on the other. David learns the pitfalls of an 'undisciplined heart', but the lesson of prudence is set against the lost joys of childhood, resulting in a prevailing tone of sadness.

## Reception

Reviews of *Copperfield* were mixed, and monthly sales hovered around 20,000, in comparison with 32,000 for *Dombey* and 34,000 for *Bleak House*. Nevertheless, as Forster proclaimed, 'Dickens never stood so high in reputation as at the completion of *Copperfield*' (6.7). 'Everyone is cheering David on', Dickens told Mrs Watson (3 July 1850). 'There seems a bright unanimity about "Copperfield" ' (13 July 1850). Thackeray found it 'charmingly fresh and simple', with 'admirable touches of tender humour' (*Punch*, 16, 1849). Ruskin thought the storm scene surpassed Turner's evocations of the sea (*Modern Painters*, 1843–60). Matthew Arnold described it as a work 'rich in merits' (Collins 1971, pp. 267–9), and Henry James recalled it as 'a treasure so hoarded in the dusty chamber of youth' (*A Small Boy and Others*, 1913). Thus, even though as late as 1861 'only Numbers I–V had been issued in more than 25,000 copies', its back numbers sold better than any other Dickens work; the Household Edition (1872) sold 83,000 copies, and in 1935 it led the Everyman and Collins lists (Collins 1971, p. 619; Patten 1978, pp. 209, 331).

It retained a special place in Dickens's affections. When he grew increasingly restless and dissatisfied in the 1850s, he asked, 'Why is it, that as with poor David, a sense comes always crushing on me now, when I fall into low spirits, as of one happiness I have missed in life, and one friend and companion I have never made?' (to Forster, 3 and ?4 February 1855). And as he began *Great Expectations*, he reread *Copperfield* 'to be quite sure I had fallen into no unconscious repetitions . . . and was affected by it to a degree you would hardly believe' (to Forster, early October 1860).

The number of DRAMATIZATIONS of Dickens's work, diminishing throughout the 1840s, increased markedly with *Copperfield*. Philip Bolton counts six productions before serialization was complete, and twenty in 'the first burst' of interest (Bolton 1987, p. 321). Dickens's PUBLIC READING version, prepared in 1861, was, like the novel itself, Dickens's own favourite, and the storm scene, the finale of the reading, was 'for most people who heard it . . . the most sublime moment in all the readings' (Collins 1975, pp. 216–17). One of the most distinguished FILM adaptations of Dickens is the 1935 MGM version, with Freddie Bartholomew as David, Edna May Oliver as Aunt Betsey, W. C. Fields as Micawber, Basil Rathbone as Murdstone, Lionel Barrymore as Dan Peggotty, and Maureen O'Sullivan as Dora.

For many critics *Copperfield* has been the foremost work in Dickens's career. Margaret Oliphant saw it as the culmination of Dickens's early comic fiction (*Blackwood's Magazine*, 109, 1871). K. J. Fielding (1965), and Geoffrey Thurley (1976), stressed its centrality, and Sylvère Monod (1968), celebrated it as the triumph of Dickens's art. Q. D. Leavis (1970) carefully explored its images of marriage, of women, and of moral simplicity. Richard Dunn (1981) lists issues which have figured most prominently in criticism of *Copperfield*: fictional autobiography, the characterization of the narrating hero, the question of heroism, the treatment of minor characters, the theme of memory, and the relation of *Copperfield* to Dickens's other works.                                    PVWS

Gilmour, Robin, 'Memory in *David Copperfield*', *Dickensian*, 71 (1975).

Needham, Gwendolyn, 'The Undisciplined Heart of David Copperfield', *Nineteenth-Century Fiction*, 9 (1954).

Patten, Robert L., 'Autobiography into Autobiography: The Evolution of *David Copperfield*', in George P. Landow (ed.), *Approaches to Victorian Autobiography* (1979).

Priestley, J. B., *The English Comic Characters* (1925).

**De Quincey, Thomas** (1785–1859), ESSAYIST, novelist, celebrated drug addict, much admired by Dickens. The story of De Quincey's early life, specifically his homelessness after running away from Manchester Grammar School and his descent into opium addiction, are documented in his *Confessions of an English Opium Eater* (1821), first published in the *London Magazine*. Most important for Dickens was De Quincey's metaphorical exploration of the city which anticipates Dickens's own urban GOTHIC. The confusing 'labyrinth of streets' (*BH* 57) Esther faces in her search for Lady Dedlock in *Bleak House* and the monotony of 'streets, streets, streets' and 'miles of close wells and pits of houses' Arthur Clennam observes in *Little*

*Dorrit* (1.3) owe a debt to De Quincey's vision of London. According to J. T. FIELDS, Dickens enjoyed discussing De Quincey's works (amongst others) while walking. De Quincey's autobiographical meditation is also fascinating for its exploration of the ways CHILDHOOD trauma manifests itself later in life as symbolic dreams. The influence of opium (not uncommon in his circle, which included WORDSWORTH and COLERIDGE) was one way to bring to the surface suppressed childhood experience (all of this long before Freud). Apart from his humour, De Quincey's focus on the darker side of human nature also appealed to Dickens.                        MWT

**death and funerals.** Dickens wrote naturally, movingly, and metaphorically about death as a fact of life, and of urban life in particular, but, as his novels suggest, he was much offended by the panoply of Victorian funeral customs. John RUSKIN, for one, noted that the death-rate in *Bleak House* functioned merely as 'a representative average of the statistics of civilian mortality in the centre of London'. In the novel Dickens varied the manner and the natural and unnatural causes of his characters' passing (suicide, disease, neglect, murder, spontaneous combustion, etc.) perhaps more than in any other of his fictions. As the last exits of both major and minor characters in the whole range of his novels, from the first to the last, indicate, Dickens was determined to incorporate death-scenes as both a contrast and a complement to his generally comic fictional drift. These contrasts and complements are as much emotional as they are dramatic. In *Pickwick Papers* deaths and hauntings are largely confined to the interpolated tales, but from *Oliver Twist* and *Nicholas Nickleby* onwards murder, suicide, and the Christianly resolved deathbed take on a new narrative, thematic, and structural significance. This may well be a consequence of Dickens's highly emotional reaction to the sudden death, in his arms, of Mary HOGARTH in May 1837. *The Old Curiosity Shop* in particular shows the impact of Mary's untimely death—referring publicly to the novel in 1841 Dickens stressed that he was not 'untried in the school of affliction, in the death of those we love' (*Speeches*, p. 10). If in *The Old Curiosity Shop* Dickens had avoided including an account of Nell's actual passing, his subsequent indulgence in extended and emotionally charged deathbed scenes (notably those of Little Paul Dombey, of Barkis and Dora in *David Copperfield*, and of Jo in *Bleak House*) suggests the extent to which he sought to vary and exploit their impact on his readers. Although some of these death-scenes have provoked charges of self-indulgence and SENTIMENTALITY from unsympathetic critics, they ought to be seen as integral to Dickens's exploration of a whole range of emotions and experiences. Their Christian base, and their implicit promise of an afterlife, was to be amplified in the scaffold meditations of Sydney Carton in *A Tale of Two Cities*. When called upon to comfort friends and correspondents on the death of their children, as he frequently was, Dickens was inclined to cite Matthew 18: 1–6.

Dickens's particular fascination with the Morgue in Paris is evident in two of the UN-COMMERCIAL TRAVELLER essays ('Travelling Abroad' and 'Some Recollections of Mortality'). The 'invisible force' which he claims 'dragged' him into the Morgue, even on one Christmas Day, may be linked less to an obsessive interest in exposed corpses than to an habitual concern with houselessness and lack of community (the corpses found drowned in the Seine, often of suicides, were exposed for purposes of identification). The Morgue was generally acknowledged to be one of the 'sights' of central PARIS, a city which, because of its revolutionary past, Dickens seems to have associated with mayhem and violent death.

Dickens's dislike of Victorian funeral customs is evident in the attack on undertakers as 'the Medicine Men of Civilisation' in the essay of that name (*UT*). He insisted to his sister that he had a deep-seated objection to attending funerals where his 'affections are not strongly and immediately concerned', for he could not 'endure being dressed up by an undertaker as part of his trade show' (to Mrs Henry Austin, 21 July 1868). His fictional undertakers—Sowerberry (*OT*), Mould (*MC*), Omer (*DC*), Trabb & Co. (*GE*)—are uniformly offensive and intrusive. As the pompous ministrations of Trabb in *Great Expectations* suggest, they can also be negative and absurd. Dickens particularly objected to the grand state funeral accorded to the Duke of Wellington, claiming in his *Household*

*Words* essay 'Trading in Death' that it had been perverted into a 'Public Fair and Great Undertaker's Jubilee' and a 'substitution of the form for the substance' (*HW* 27 November 1852). He was, however, favourably impressed by the desire for a modest funeral expressed by the Dowager Queen Adelaide in her will, trusting that the ceremony had been conducted 'with proper absence of conventional absurdity' ('Court Ceremonies', *Examiner* 15 December 1849). In his own will he 'emphatically' directed that he be 'buried in an inexpensive, unostentatious, and strictly private manner . . . and that those attending my funeral wear no scarf, cloak, black bow, long hat-band, or other such revolting absurdity'.                                                    ALS

Richardson, Ruth, *Death, Dissection and the Destitute* (1988).

Sanders (1982).

Wheeler, Michael, *Death and the Future Life in Victorian Literature and Theology* (1990).

**dedications.** Nearly all the novels, and a few other works, carried dedications, always to friends. Sometimes the reason for Dickens's choice is obvious, sometimes his selecting *this* friend is surprising when others seemingly closer never were honoured. All save Townshend (*GE*) were well-known personages, Dickens sometimes avowedly taking pride in thus linking his name with theirs. *Pickwick* had a long dedicatory letter to Serjeant [later Sir Thomas Noon] TALFOURD, MP, lawyer and author, a recent but soon close friend, whom he had met through Talfourd's activity over his COPYRIGHT Bill. *Nickleby*, much concerned with the theatre, went to the actor W. C. MACREADY; *MASTER HUMPHREY'S CLOCK* to the old poet Samuel ROGERS, with a dedicatory letter praising his generous sympathies, and *Chuzzlewit* 'with true and earnest regard' to the heiress Miss Burdett COUTTS with whose charities he had become involved (and 'Mrs Gamp' had worked in her household: see CHARACTERS—ORIGINALS). *Dombey* was dedicated 'with great esteem' to the Marchioness of Normanby; he had lately been seeing her at the British Embassy in Paris, where her husband was Ambassador. *Copperfield* was 'affectionately inscribed to the Hon. Mr and Mrs Richard WATSON of Rockingham [Castle]', close friends since 1846.

*Bleak House* was dedicated to his 'Companions in the GUILD OF LITERATURE AND ART', which he had helped found in 1850; he had since been active in 'friendly union' with them in fund-raising efforts. *Hard Times* was simply 'Inscribed to Thomas CARLYLE'. Seeking Carlyle's permission, he wrote: 'I know it contains nothing in which you do not think with me' (13 July 1854). *Little Dorrit* went to Clarkson STANFIELD, RA, from 'his attached friend', and *A Tale of Two Cities* to the politician Lord John RUSSELL, 'in remembrance of many public services and private kindnesses'. Russell had written a book on the French Revolution. The manuscript of *Great Expectations* was given to the eccentric cleric and author Chauncy Hare Townsend and the book 'affectionately inscribed' to him: 'I truly loved him' (12 March 1868). *Our Mutual Friend* was dedicated 'as a memorial of friendship' to Sir James Emerson Tennent, reformist politician, author, and traveller, an old friend whose death in 1869 much distressed Dickens.

AMERICAN NOTES had been dedicated to those American friends who had generously welcomed him, left him free to judge their country, and would not now resent his verdict, given 'good-humouredly, and in a kind spirit'. Two of the Christmas books contained dedications: The CRICKET ON THE HEARTH, 'with affection and attachment' to the veteran critic Lord JEFFREY, and The BATTLE OF LIFE 'to my English friends in SWITZERLAND' (where he had spent much of the previous year). A CHILD'S HISTORY OF ENGLAND was 'Dedicated to my Own Dear Children'. Finally, John FORSTER got his reward in 1858, when the Library Edition was dedicated 'to my dear friend . . . in grateful remembrance . . . and in affectionate acknowledgement' of much advice, care and sympathy 'during my whole literary life' (see EDITIONS OVER WHICH DICKENS HAD CONTROL).

Another form of 'dedication' may be mentioned, the names he gave his CHILDREN. Having paid his family dues with his first two, he named all the others after friends (except for Henry FIELDING)—the actor Macready, the authors LANDOR, Jeffrey, TENNYSON, Sydney SMITH, and BULWER-LYTTON, the dandy and painter Alfred D'Orsay, and—perhaps most surprisingly—William Haldimand, a philanthropic English banker who had retired to Switzerland, where they met.                    PC

**Defoe, Daniel** (1660–1731), novelist. Although Dickens observed that Defoe personally must have been 'a precious dry and disagreeable article' and found 'an utter want of tenderness and sentiment' in the death of Friday (to Forster, ?5 and 6 July 1856), from childhood *Robinson Crusoe* (1719) was one of his favourite books, and it powerfully influenced the world of his imagination. He quotes or refers to it frequently, and names it as one of the books which 'kept alive' young David Copperfield's fancy when the Murdstones imposed their regime (*DC* 4).     RCS

**detective fiction.** Shadowy pursuers, teasing suspense, ingenious plotting, and exposure of past injustices by amateur sleuths playing detective characterize several of the eight novels Dickens wrote before Inspector Bucket made his 'ghostly' appearance in *Bleak House* in September 1852. Materializing mysteriously, the 'stoutly-built, steady-looking, sharp-eyed man in black' who stepped forth noiselessly in the novel's twenty-second chapter left footprints discernible among Dickens's fellow novelists for decades to come. Bucket was called forth by the lawyer Tulkinghorn who, despite his own formidable sagacity, remained puzzled by Lady Dedlock's interest in the burial ground at Tom-All-Alone's. Solving this mystery, penetrating other equally dense secrets, and bringing a murderer to justice number among the Inspector's additional triumphs, executed with such flair and originality as to earn him recognition among literary historians as the progenitor of the detective in British fiction.

Despite the originality of Dickens's portrait, the standard of deductive ratiocination Bucket set in fiction was not without antecedents. Faintly foreshadowed in an earlier creation by Dickens himself—Nadgett, the secretive private-enquiry agent employed by Montague Tigg in *Martin Chuzzlewit* to dig out information on clients of his own fraudulent insurance company—Bucket's activities as a sleuth bear some slight resemblance to gifted amateurs like Godwin's Caleb Williams (1794) and the heroes and heroines of GOTHIC NOVELS who set out to trace distant crimes to their origins, expose their perpetrators, and force them to confess. Other antecedents include memoirs of Parisian police officers like E. F. Vidocq (1828) and the factual accounts of the pursuit of criminals published in *The Newgate Calendar* from 1773 onwards. In the 1830s Dickens, along with AINSWORTH and BULWER-LYTTON, was associated with in the so-called NEWGATE NOVEL; attacked at the time for romanticizing criminal heroes, Newgate fiction was also fascinated by the exposure of their crimes. Police forces in Paris and London were professionally organized during these years, and public interest in CRIME and its detection was tapped in Eugène Sue's *Mysteries of Paris* (1842), translated almost at once into English, and G. M. W. Reynolds's *The Mysteries of the Court of London* (1849–56: see READERSHIP). Several of Edgar Allan Poe's tales deal with the exposure of mysterious crimes, and his skilled and discerning Auguste Dupin, in *The Murders in the Rue Morgue* (1843), is generally recognized as the prototype of the amateur crime-solver in English.

Blathers and Duff, the incompetent and blundering pair of Bow Street Runners who investigate the attempted burglary in Chertsey (*OT* 30) pre-date Poe's hero, but they are objects of satire, not veneration. Plain-clothes thief-takers receive further criticism in *Great Expectations*, for their inability to find the culprit who attacked Mrs Gargery. Those 'worthies', about whom Dickens believed much humbug had been written, remained objects of scorn in his eyes, men destitute of ability, credibility, and integrity. Pip sarcastically reports how they took up obviously the wrong people, 'ran their heads very hard against wrong ideas, and persisted in trying to fit circumstances to the ideas, instead of trying to extract ideas from circumstances' (*GE* 16).

Rather it was the professional, notably Inspector Charles Frederick FIELD, who won Dickens's confidence, and whose exploits he admiringly depicted in several *Household Words* articles ('A Detective Police Party', and 'On Duty with Inspector Field', *HW* 27 July and 10 August 1850; 14 June 1851; repr. *Journalism* 2.265–82, 356–69; 'Three "Detective" Anecdotes', *HW* 14 September 1850). A later incarnation of Bucket appears in Mr Inspector in *Our Mutual Friend*, the efficient and imperturbable figure in charge of the waterside police station to which the corpse thought to be John Harmon's is taken, a man as studiously calm and as devoted to his

books as a monk 'in a monastery on top of a mountain' (*OMF* 1.3). The mysterious Dick Datchery in *The Mystery of Edwin Drood* belongs in the same category, an agent of some kind clearly intent on detection and revelation.

These descriptions, both factual and fictional, proved a dominant influence on Dickens's successors. Wilkie COLLINS's *The Moonstone* (1868), first published serially in *All the Year Round*, is generally considered the first detective novel in English. Detective themes and subplots dominate the SENSATION NOVELS of the 1860s and the popular fiction of Anthony TROLLOPE (*He Knew He Was Right*, 1869), Braddon, READE, and Le Fanu.

Explanations for Dickens's fascination with detectives vary. For Humphry HOUSE (1941), an answer must be sought in what he calls Dickens's authoritarian streak; for Philip Collins (1962), the source lies in the tension John FORSTER saw in Dickens's nature, which corresponds with his admiration of the police as keepers of public order and an imaginative understanding of criminals. Psychology aside, Dickens's introduction of Inspector Bucket remains a significant literary landmark equal to his unique employment of the detective story as a social fable rather than as a merely exciting expedient to introduce and manipulate narrative suspense.

It is worth reminding ourselves that Dickens did not write 'detective fiction' in either of the varieties the genre most commonly takes today. Monsignor Ronald Knox (1888–1957) and his famous Detection Club of detective fiction believed that the point of the detective novel was less the crime itself, and more the element of puzzle involved in unravelling the crime, and particularly uncovering the identity of the murderer. The common 'whodunnit' format, most associated with Agatha Christie (where the least-likely suspect turns out to be the murderer) is alien to Dickens's more literary conception of the form. Nor was he particularly interested in writing the second type of 'detective fiction' prevalent today, the *policier* with its stress on factually derived minutiae of police procedure. The belief that Dickens was writing the former of these sorts of detective novel in *Edwin Drood* has led to a variety of inappropriate readings of the novel, and has focused attention unduly on the identity of Drood's murderer, rather than (as Dickens would have conceived the point of a detective novel) on the psychological processes of the mind of the criminal (see MYSTERY OF EDWIN DROOD, SOLUTIONS TO). Dickens went to great lengths in his postscript to *Our Mutual Friend* to disavow any attempt to trick the reader, or to play 'whodunnit'-style games with the true identity of John Rokesmith.

The increasing body of contemporary criticism is interested in detective fiction from narratological and theoretical points of view (see CRITICISM AND SCHOLARSHIP: POSTSTRUCTURALIST). According to this school of criticism, detective fiction can best be understood in terms of its narrative strategies; specifically, a detective novel contains two narrative lines, the surface narrative concerned with detection and the buried narrative that the detection is seeking to bring to light. This is a more fruitful approach to Dickens's own novels of crime and detection. The late novels (*Bleak House, A Tale of Two Cities, Our Mutual Friend,* and *Edwin Drood* in particular) derive much of their power from the tension between surface and buried narratives, and the attempts by characters to draw these out. DHP

Glover, Dorothy, *Victorian Detective Fiction* (1966).

Most, Glen W. and Stow, William W. (eds.), *The Poetics of Murder: Detective Fiction and Literary Theory* (1993).

Ousby, Ian, *Bloodhounds of Heaven: The Detective in English Fiction from Godwin to Doyle* (1976).

**Dexter Collection,** a major COLLECTION OF DICKENS MATERIALS assembled by J. F. Dexter, held in the British Library.

**Dexter, Walter** (1877–1944), editor of the DICKENSIAN, 1925–44. Author of several still-useful works of Dickensian topography, e.g. *The Kent of Dickens* (1924) and *The England of Dickens* (1925), Dexter's chief importance in the history of Dickens scholarship is as collector and editor of Dickens's LETTERS and pioneer chronicler of his PUBLIC READINGS. He published new letters in almost every issue of the *Dickensian* and (in the case of Dickens's correspondence with his wife, and with Maria BEADNELL, Mark LEMON, and Thomas Beard) published them in volume form also. His edition of the letters for the Nonesuch Edition

(3 vols., 1938) is not yet wholly superseded by the Pilgrim Edition. MS

## diaries and autobiography of Dickens.

Diaries survive from 1838–41, published in editions of the LETTERS. Very fragmentary, they rarely record anything beyond social engagements, occasional notes on domestic life, and particulars of journeys, though 1838 begins in a more narrative form. Later diaries are mentioned in letters but none survives except for 1867; lost in New York and never recovered, it eventually came to the New York Public Library. It is most interesting for entries relating to Ellen TERNAN.

Letters of 1842 and 1845 show Dickens intending to write an autobiography, and he began one in 1845–9 (dating evidence is confusing). He later told Maria BEADNELL (Mrs Winter) that when the narrative approached the period of his frustrated romance with her 'I lost courage and burned the rest' (22 February 1855). But not everything was burned. Probably more than one manuscript existed, maybe written at more than one time. Certainly he had one before him when writing *David Copperfield*, chapter 11 (July 1849), because he there incorporated, often verbatim, its account of the WARREN'S BLACKING period, with 'my father' changed to 'Mr Micawber', etc. FORSTER too possessed a fragmentary version: substantial excerpts were published in the *Life* about the Blacking episode (1.2), and a paragraph about Wellington House Academy (1.3), the next stage of Dickens's childhood—nothing more about the years until he met Maria in 1830. Forster clearly had more material than he published, but no manuscript survives. In later years Dickens several times expressed his intention of leaving his children an autobiographical account—he 'always *intended* to do it', Georgina HOGARTH affirms. PC

**Dickens, Catherine Hogarth** (1816–79), Dickens's wife. Dickens was a regular guest at the home of George HOGARTH, his senior colleague on the MORNING CHRONICLE, and in the spring of 1835 he became engaged to Hogarth's eldest daughter Catherine. She was 'a pretty little woman' with 'heavy-lidded, large blue eyes', a retroussé nose, and a small rosebud mouth with a 'pleasant smiling expression' (Slater 1983, p. 109). Gentle and amiable, she was proficient in music and French and an excellent needlewoman.

During the period of their engagement Dickens's letters to his 'dearest Kate' show none of the passionate intensity of his feelings for Maria BEADNELL, but instead reveal a relationship based on common interests and enthusiasms and mutual affection. The letters are playful and tender, humorous and gossipy and full of childish endearments: she was his 'dearest Mouse', 'dearest darling Pig', 'Darling Tatie'. But he also had occasion to write to her more formally, reprimanding her for her tendency to sulks and 'cossness'. Although he had taken lodgings in Brompton so that he could be nearer to her, he was also working extremely long hours and evidently Catherine sometimes complained that he put his work before her: 'If the representations I have so often made to you about my working as a duty, and not as a pleasure, be not sufficient to keep you in the good humour, which you, of all people in the World should preserve—why, then my dear, you must be out of temper, and there is no help for it' (21 February 1836). They were married at St Luke's Church, Chelsea, on 2 April 1836 and spent a week's honeymoon in KENT returning to London to live in Dickens's bachelor chambers at Furnival's Inn (see INNS OF COURT). Nine months later Catherine gave birth to the first of her ten children, a boy, christened Charles Culliford Boz (see CHILDREN OF DICKENS).

Her younger sister Mary had become a regular visitor and continued to be a companion to the Dickenses until her sudden death soon after they moved into Doughty Street in April 1837 (see HOGARTH, MARY; HOMES OF DICKENS). In a letter to a cousin, shortly after Mary's death, Catherine expressed her grief:

'Since my marriage she had been almost constantly with us and my dear Husband loved her as much as I did. She died in his arms. We have both lost a dear and most affectionate sister and we have often said we had too much happiness to last, for she was included in all our little schemes and pleasures, and now every thing about us, brings her before our eyes' (Slater 1983, p. 111).

The letter also conveys, however, her happiness and pride as a young wife and mother: '. . . how proud I shall be to make you acquainted with Charles. The fame of his talents are now known all over the world but his kind affectionate heart is dearer to me than all . . . My darling boy grows sweeter and lovelier every day. Although he is my own I must say I never saw a dearer child' (Slater 1983, p. 111).

Catherine had a miscarriage just after Mary's death but her first daughter was born a year later and christened Mary (Mamie). As with her first child, Catherine suffered from a post-natal illness, but was well enough to spend the summer in the country entertaining visitors and guests. This set the basic pattern for the next fifteen years of her married life: childbirth, a slow recovery, managing the household, partnering her husband in public, and entertaining his guests at home.

In October 1839 daughter Katey was born and in February 1841 a second son, Walter. One of the Dickenses' many guests at Broadstairs in the summer of 1841 remembered Catherine's sense of fun and good humour, and her ability for making absurd puns. She also had a good line in Scottish jokes and anecdotes which was remembered affectionately many years later by her elder children (Slater 1983, p. 109).

Although very unhappy at leaving her children, Catherine dutifully accompanied Dickens on his tour of AMERICA in 1842. FORSTER saw the Dickenses off at Liverpool and commented to MACLISE on her 'cheerfulness about the whole thing. Never saw anything better. She deserves to be what you know she is so emphatically called—the Beloved' (Slater, p. 113). Throughout the exhausting tour Catherine fulfilled her role as celebrity's wife with grace and charm. Numerous descriptions of her, ranging from the New York press to private diaries and journals, attest to her resilience and amiability, her quiet dignity and sweetness of manner. Dickens himself wrote approvingly that she 'made a *most admirable* traveller in every respect . . . and proved herself perfectly game' (24/6 April 1842). In CANADA, indeed, she was 'game' enough to make her debut as an amateur actress playing, so Dickens wrote, 'devilish well' (26 May 1842).

On their return to England Catherine's younger sister Georgina HOGARTH became a regular member of the household, helping Catherine with the children. In the summer of 1844 the entire family, including the new baby Francis (born in January) moved to ITALY for a twelve-month stay in Genoa, during which time difficulties arose between Dickens and Catherine as a result of his preoccupation with his mesmeric treatment of Mme de la Rue (see MESMERISM). Back in England the following year, the demands on Catherine's skills as a hostess continued apace, especially when Dickens embarked on his AMATEUR THEATRICALS. In October 1845 Alfred was born. Two years later Catherine had a particularly difficult birth with Sydney, followed in December of that same year by another miscarriage. For the birth of her eighth child, Henry (January 1849), Dickens insisted on the use of chloroform which 'thank God . . . spared her all pain' (2 February 1849).

In 1851, soon after the birth of her ninth child, Dora, Catherine suffered a nervous illness, the cause of which is unknown and may have been due to emotional or psychological strain. Dickens arranged for her to go to Malvern for the water cure and spent as much time as possible with her there. When little Dora suddenly died, Catherine returned home at once. Dickens took her to Broadstairs for the summer, and at the end of the year they moved into Tavistock House. The same year also saw the publication of Catherine's only venture into authorship: *What Shall We Have For Dinner? Satisfactorily answered by numerous bills of fare for from two to eighteen persons*. It was published under the pseudonym of 'Lady Maria Clutterbuck', a character she had played in the farce *Used Up* at Rockingham Castle earlier in the year. This collection of rich and elaborate menus (which went into a second edition in the following year) gives evidence of the kind of table kept at the numerous Dickens dinner parties.

Catherine's tenth and last child, Edward, was born in 1852. By this time Dickens himself had begun to feel unsettled and dissatisfied. He wrote long, affectionate letters home to Catherine from Italy during his two-month tour there with COLLINS and Egg in Autumn 1853, but over the next four years his restlessness and volatility grew increasingly desperate and his marriage inevitably came under great strain (see DICKENS CIRCLE). He raged against everything, from the state of the nation to the untidiness and 'imbecility' of his in-laws. Meanwhile Catherine herself was becoming stout and matronly, ungallantly described by William Moy Thomas in 1853 as 'a

great fat lady—florid with arms thick as the leg of a Life Guard's man and as red as a beef sausage. Such an Agnes!' (Sophie Dupre [bookseller], Catalogue 17, item 381, 1990). In 1856 Dickens wrote to Forster 'The old days— the old days! Shall I ever, I wonder, get the frame of mind back as it used to be then . . . I find that the skeleton in my domestic closet is becoming a pretty big one' (13 April 1856). He bought Gad's Hill Place (1856), and the family spent the summer of 1857 there. Witnesses later testified to noticing frictions and unhappiness apparent between Catherine and her husband at this time.

In August 1857 Dickens's amateur production of *The FROZEN DEEP* (which had first been performed at Tavistock House in January) was performed at the Free Trade Hall in Manchester. The female roles were played by professional actresses including Mrs Frances Ternan and her two daughters Maria and Ellen (see TERNAN, ELLEN; TERNAN FAMILY). Dickens's strong attraction to Ellen brought his domestic misery into sharp and painful focus. He wrote to Forster:

'Poor Catherine and I are not made for each other, and there is no help for it. It is not only that she makes me uneasy and unhappy, but that I make her so too and much more so. She is exactly what you know, in the way of being amiable and complying; but we are strangely ill-assorted for the bond there is between us' (?3 September 1857).

Finding his domestic association with Catherine increasingly intolerable, in October of that year he gave instructions that his dressing-room be converted to a bedroom for himself, the doorway between his dressing-room and Catherine's room to be closed up and filled with shelves. There is no record of Catherine's response to this arrangement.

In late April or early May 1858 something happened which brought matters to a head. What it was exactly is not known, though some gossip about a present of jewellery from Dickens to Ellen somehow coming to Catherine's notice has been widely credited as the cause of the final rupture. There is also a story that Dickens, trying to prove that his relationship with Ellen was merely platonic, insisted that Catherine call on her (or possibly Mrs Ternan), which the weeping Catherine agreed to do despite her daughter Katey's outrage. After much negotiation involving Forster (acting for Dickens) and LEMON (acting for Catherine), on 14 May Lemon wrote to Forster that 'Mrs Dickens thankfully accepts the proposal—as made by you on May 7' (Slater 1983, p. 147). At this stage in the proceedings, Catherine's mother and sister Helen seem to have started spreading rumours about Dickens and his relationship with Ellen Ternan. Indignantly Dickens suspended all negotiations for a settlement on Catherine until the Hogarths had signed a statement saying that they disbelieved all rumours of his liaisons with other women. At first they refused, and Dickens became frantic with rage. Catherine evidently asked Miss COUTTS to act as an intermediary, but her attempt to heal the breach met with absolute failure. What Catherine felt, we do not know. On 19 May she wrote to Miss Coutts: | 'Many many thanks for your true kindness in doing what I asked. | I have now—God help me—only one course to pursue. | One day, though not now I may be able to tell you how hardly I have been used' (Pilgrim 8.565 n.).

On 26 May Dickens told his lawyer that Mrs Hogarth was still repeating 'smashing slanders . . . *since our negotiations have been pending*'. But, he continued, 'Pray do me the kindness to detach Mrs Dickens from these wrongdoings, *now*. I do not in the least suspect her of them and I should wish her to know it.'

Three days later he obtained the signatures of Mrs Hogarth and Helen to a statement he had drawn up, which included the assertion that the rumours 'are not believed by Mrs Dickens'. Negotiations for the settlement were resumed. Catherine was to have a house of her own and to receive an allowance of £600 a year. Her eldest son Charley was to live with her, and she was to have access to the other children and they to her at any time. He drew up the announcement which would make their separation public and sent it to Catherine with a covering note, asking her if she had any objections to its publication. Presumably she had none since the announcement appeared in *The* TIMES and other papers on 7 June and in *Household Words* on 12 June. It stated, after some preamble about Dickens's relations with his public:

'Some domestic trouble of mine of long-standing, on which I will make no further remark than that it claims to be respected, as

being of a sacredly private nature, has lately been brought to an arrangement, which involves no anger or ill-will of any kind, and the whole origin, progress and surrounding circumstances of which have been, throughout, within the knowledge of my children. It is amicably composed, and its details have now but to be forgotten by those concerned in it.'

With the separation 'amicably composed', it seems that Dickens had originally hoped that he and Catherine could remain on friendly terms. That is certainly the impression Catherine conveyed in a letter to her aunt written shortly after the separation, following a short visit from her youngest boys:

'I need hardly tell you, dearest Aunt, how very happy I have been with my dear boys, although they were not allowed to remain with me so long as I wished, yet I think we all thoroughly enjoyed being together. Of course, it has not been all pleasure, as their presence at times brought bitter recollections and feelings to my mind; for indeed, dear friend, you will understand and feel for me when I tell you that I still love and think of their father too much for my peace of mind. I have been told that he has expressed a wish that we should meet in society, and be at least on friendly terms. Surely he cannot mean it, as I feel that if I were ever to see him by chance it would almost kill me; but to return to my boys. I cannot tell you how good and affectionate they were to me. One of them, little Sydney, was full of solicitude and anxiety about me, always asking what I should do when they were gone, and if I would not be very dull and lonely without them: he should so like to stay. Upon the whole their visit has done me much good, and dear Charley is so kind and gentle, and tried to cheer me. I trust by God's assistance to be able to resign myself to His will, and to lead a contented if not a happy life, but my position is a sad one, and time only may be able to blunt the keen pain that will throb at my heart, but I will indeed try to struggle hard against it' (Pilgrim 8.749).

It was during that summer, however, that Catherine did or said something that Dickens found literally unforgivable. In August he wrote to Angela Burdett Coutts, who still sought to reconcile him with her, that Catherine had caused him 'unspeakable agony of mind' and adding 'I want to communicate with her no more' (23 August 1858). Two years later their younger daughter Katey married and Miss Coutts, who continued to befriend Catherine, suggested that she should be invited to the wedding. Dickens's response was unequivocal: 'It is simply impossible that such a thing can be. That figure is out of my life for evermore (except to darken it) and my desire is, never to see it again' (5 April 1860). His sentiments were still the same four years later when he responded to another of Miss Coutts's letters: 'a page in my life which once had writing on it, has become absolutely blank, and ... it is not in my power to pretend that it has a solitary word upon it' (12 February 1864).

Catherine moved into a house in Gloucester Crescent near Regent's Park. She continued to go into society, and maintained many of her old friendships with such eminent people as Millais and THACKERAY, who had pitied her for her separation from her children in 1858. She read her husband's works as they appeared and continued going to the theatre (on one occasion finding herself in the same theatre as Dickens, much to her distress).

Dickens wrote to Catherine only three times during the course of the twelve years from the separation to his death, all brief responses to letters from her. After the death of her mother he wrote about documents concerning the Hogarth grave at Kensal Green; he sent a brief acknowledgement of her letter of concern following his involvement in the Staplehurst railway accident (see KENT); and he acknowledged her good wishes for his American reading tour: 'Severely hard work lies before me; but that is not a new thing in my life, and I am content to go my way and do it' (5 November 1867). He seems not to have written to her after the death of their son Walter in 1863.

It was her daughter Katey who informed Catherine of Dickens's death. Catherine was not invited to the small family funeral, but she did receive a telegram of condolence from the Queen. After Dickens's death she was able to visit Gad's Hill and spent several Christmases there with Charley and his family enjoying her grandchildren. She was also visited by her sister Georgina. She died of cancer at her home on 21 November 1879. During the final stages of her long and painful illness she was nursed by her daughter Katey, who later told

George Bernard Shaw: 'During every day almost of that time she spoke to me, whenever I was alone with her, of my father. All her grievances against him came out ... Of course I did what any daughter would do. I tried to soften her remembrance of him. In a way I succeeded ...' (Slater 1983, p. 158).

As she lay dying Catherine gave Katey her collection of letters from Dickens, saying 'with great earnestness', 'Give these to the British Museum—that the world may know he loved me once' (G. Storey 1939, p. 164).

For many years Catherine received a bad press from Dickens BIOGRAPHIES, most notably and influentially from Johnson. She was portrayed as clumsy, torpid, and domestically incompetent. This was mostly based on Dickens's feverish comment during the collapse of the marriage in 1857/8. A very different picture of Catherine, both as wife and mother and as a member of the Dickens circle, has now emerged, mainly as a result of the evidence accumulating in the Pilgrim Edition of Dickens's LETTERS.          MS

Storey (1939).

**Dickens, Charles.** See AMATEUR THEATRICALS OF DICKENS; 'BOZ'; BROTHERS AND SISTERS OF DICKENS; CHILDREN OF DICKENS; COMPOSITION, DICKENS'S METHODS; DICKENS: PRIVATE LIFE; DICKENS: PUBLIC LIFE; ENGLISHNESS OF DICKENS; HISTORY, DICKENS'S ATTITUDES; HOMES OF DICKENS; JOURNALIST, DICKENS AS; NOVELIST AND MAN OF LETTERS, DICKENS AS; PETS BELONGING TO DICKENS; PLAYWRIGHT, DICKENS AS; POPULARITY OF DICKENS; PORTRAITS, BUSTS, AND PHOTOGRAPHS OF DICKENS; PUBLIC READINGS; RELATIVES AND DESCENDANTS OF DICKENS; REPUTATION OF DICKENS; STORY AND SKETCH-WRITER, DICKENS AS.

*1. private life; 2. public life.*

**1. Private life** Charles (after his maternal grandfather) John (after his father) Huffam (after his godfather, a naval rigger) Dickens was born on Friday, 7 February 1812, at 13 Mile End Terrace, Landport, Portsea (now 396 Commercial Road, Portsmouth, and the DICKENS BIRTHPLACE MUSEUM). The second child and first son of John DICKENS, a naval pay clerk, and Elizabeth Barrow DICKENS, he was baptised at St Mary's Church, Kingston, Portsea, on 4 March.

Following his father's postings, the family moved to London in January 1815, to Sheerness (KENT) in January 1817, and to Chatham in April 1817. His mother taught him the rudiments of reading, and he attended a day school with his sister Fanny, to whom he was particularly close (as later recorded in 'A Child's Dream of a Star', *HW* 6 April 1850; repr. *Journalism* 2.185–8). He next went to a school kept by William Giles, a Baptist minister's son, but this was broken off a year later when the family moved (with a reduction in John Dickens's income) to 16 Bayham Street, Camden Town. In 1823, although his father was in increasing financial difficulty, Fanny became a pupil at the Royal Academy of Music. His mother tried unsuccessfully to start a school, and later in 1823 he was sent to work in WARREN'S BLACKING factory. On 20 February his father was arrested for debt, and while his mother and younger siblings joined John Dickens in the Marshalsea prison, 12-year-old Charles was put into lodgings, first in Camden Town and then in Lant Street, Borough, near the prison. His father was released from the Marshalsea under the Insolvent Debtors' Act on 28 May, but Charles remained at the blacking factory until his father quarrelled with the proprietor and would not allow Charles to return, even after Elizabeth had patched up the quarrel. His employment there had lasted just over a year, but had a searing effect on his character. His loneliness and bruised sensitivity aroused despair over blighted hopes, an emotional trauma from which he never entirely recovered. As an adult he concealed this episode in his life from everyone but his wife and his most intimate friend John FORSTER, and in his autobiographical fragment he noted bitterly, 'I never afterwards forgot, I never shall forget, I never can forget, that my mother was warm for my being sent back' (Forster 1.2; see DIARIES).

In 1825, after his father retired from the Naval Pay Office on a pension, Charles was sent for about two years to Wellington House Academy, Hampstead Road, where he won the Latin prize. This was the end of his formal schooling, for in 1827 he was engaged as a law clerk and, having taught himself shorthand, he got work on his uncle's paper the *MIRROR OF PARLIAMENT* and as a staff reporter on the *MORNING CHRONICLE*, where he served

alongside his lifelong friend Thomas Beard (see DICKENS CIRCLE).

On his eighteenth birthday he acquired a reader's ticket to the British Museum, where volumes of SHAKESPEARE were among the first books he looked at. Around this time he began going to the THEATRE nearly every night, as well as organizing AMATEUR THEATRICALS at home, and in 1832 he was granted an audition at Covent Garden, but being ill on the day he missed the appointment, and by the next season was no longer interested in the stage as a possible career. As Kathryn Chittick has observed, by temperament the young Dickens was intensely ambitious, but the direction that ambition might take was undecided until his creative writing catapulted him to fame (1990, p. 13).

In 1830 he fell passionately in love with Maria BEADNELL, a romance which ended in frustration and, Dickens confessed to her years later, a habitual reserve, even with his own children (to Mrs Winter, 22 February 1855). Her middle-class parents discouraged the match, not considering Dickens's prospects good enough for their daughter—an attitude which, combined with his experience of his father's perpetual financial insecurity, fuelled his determination to succeed in life. Not long after finally giving up his hopes of Maria, Dickens met Catherine Hogarth, eldest daughter of George HOGARTH, formerly legal adviser to Sir Walter SCOTT and at that time a senior colleague of Dickens's on the *Morning Chronicle*. It was Hogarth who encouraged Dickens to develop his 'Street Sketches' for the *EVENING CHRONICLE*. Dickens and Catherine were engaged in the spring of 1835, and married on 2 April 1836, on the strength of his employment to write *Pickwick* (see DICKENS, CATHERINE). Although his affection for Catherine was never as passionately abandoned as his love for Maria had been, and although the marriage ended in separation after twenty years and ten children, there is abundant evidence to confirm that for many years they were very happy together (see Slater 1983).

The first of their ten CHILDREN, Charley, was born on 6 January 1837, and in April the young family moved to 48 Doughty Street, now the DICKENS HOUSE MUSEUM (see HOMES OF DICKENS). In later years it became a custom to celebrate Charley's birthday with a children's Twelfth Night party, with Dickens organizing and providing the entertainment. He was 'the best conjuror I ever saw', Jane Welsh Carlyle recalled (Collins 1981, 1.61). Tragedy struck that spring, when Catherine's young sister Mary HOGARTH, their frequent and beloved companion, fell ill one night when they returned from the theatre, and died some hours later in Dickens's arms. Dickens was devastated, and cherished her memory for the rest of his life.

By this time Dickens had formed some of his closest friendships, notably with John Forster, whom he met in December 1836, William Charles MACREADY, to whom Forster introduced him in June 1837, and Daniel MACLISE, who later painted the *Nickleby* POR-TRAIT of Dickens. In 1839 Dickens moved his growing family to 1 Devonshire Terrace, and in 1842, leaving the children behind, Dickens and Catherine travelled to AMERICA, an experience which severely dented his idealization of that nation as a great democratic republic. In subsequent years the family was to live abroad on a number of occasions—in Genoa (1844), Lausanne (1846), PARIS (1846, 1855–6) —and they spent long summer holidays out of London, principally at Broadstairs and at Boulogne (see ITALY; SWITZERLAND; FRANCE). If anything, living abroad made him more conscious of his ENGLISHNESS.

After the personal stocktaking of the mid-1840s, when he began then abandoned an autobiography and created his 'favourite child', David Copperfield, a number of sorrows contributed to the darkening social vision evident in his later novels. His sister Fanny died in 1848, followed a few months later by her crippled son Henry (the original of Tiny Tim). In March 1851 his father died, his infant daughter Dora died two weeks later, and then in quick succession in 1852 came the deaths of his friends Richard WATSON, Alfred D'Orsay, and Catherine Macready. Despite fame, fortune, and an adoring public, he was increasingly restless and unhappy. 'Why is it, that as with poor David, a sense comes always crushing on me now, when I fall into low spirits, as of one happiness I have missed in life, and one friend and companion I have never made?' (to Forster, 3 and 4 February 1853). In 1855 his unsettled state was increased by the comically disappointing reappearance of Maria Beadnell, now Mrs Winter, and in 1858,

nearly a year after meeting the young actress Ellen TERNAN, who became the great love of his twelve remaining years, he separated from Catherine, with her sister Georgina HOGARTH remaining as joint châtelaine of Gad's Hill with his eldest daughter Mamie. In the autumn of 1860 he built a bonfire, in which he burned twenty years' accumulation of letters and other papers.

In 1855 he happened to see that Gad's Hill Place, the 'dream of my childhood' which his father had told him long before could be his one day if he worked hard, was up for sale (to Wills, 9 February 1855; 'Travelling Abroad', *UT*). He purchased it the next year, and settled there permanently for the last decade of his life, in between his strenuous PUBLIC READ-ING tours.

On 9 June 1865, travelling back from France with Ellen Ternan and her mother, he was involved in a serious railway accident at Staplehurst in which ten people were killed. Although uninjured himself, Dickens was severely shaken and found railway travel upsetting for the rest of his life. He was in increasingly poor health, and aged dramatically thereafter. He visited America a second time, on an exhausting reading tour, in 1867–8. In April 1869, suffering from giddiness and paralysis, he was categorically ordered by his doctors to abandon his current reading tour, but the next winter, January–March 1870, he gave a final series of twelve readings in London. On 8 June he suffered a stroke, and died the following day at Gad's Hill Place.

His character and celebrity gave him a dominant position among his RELATIVES, as son, brother, and father, and he was frequently exasperated by their demands upon him. 'I seem to stop sometimes like a steamer in a storm,' he wrote to Wills on one such occasion (11 March 1861), 'and deliberate whether I shall go on whirling, or go down'. When John Dickens ran up bills against his son's supposed fortune, Dickens took out newspaper advertisements warning creditors that he would not pay, and in 1839 he tried moving his parents out of London, an experiment which worked only briefly. He harboured resentment against his mother ever after the blacking warehouse episode, but was close enough to his father to hire him in 1845 as a reporter on the *DAILY NEWS*, a position John Dickens retained until his death six years later. Dickens was deeply affected when his father died, and wept 'bitterly' afterwards, with his mother in his arms (Pilgrim 6.343n.). 'The longer I live, the better man I think him', Dickens wrote to Forster in 1865 (6.7).

Dickens remained close to Fanny until her death in 1848. He gave financial support to his brother Alfred's wife and children after his death in 1860, and to his sister Letitia after her husband's death in 1861. But he refused loans to his scapegrace brothers Frederick and Augustus, although he supported Augustus's abandoned, blind wife and the mistress with whom he eloped to America, after Augustus's death (see BROTHERS AND SISTERS OF DICKENS).

Dickens was a doting father with his children when they were young, giving them fanciful nicknames and organizing parties for them, but found them disappointing as they grew up. He sent several of them abroad at early ages, and all save Henry had undistinguished lives. Mary, who adored her father, never married but remained with him at Gad's Hill, whereas Katey, his favourite, married young, in order (as Dickens thought) to get away from home.

His friend and biographer Forster, who identified humour—'habitual, unbounded, and resistless'—as Dickens's leading characteristic, observed that no other author 'carried so little of authorship into ordinary social intercourse' (11.3). The depth and selflessness of his friendships were legendary. 'He was the best man I ever knew', recalled Marcus STONE; 'He was such a good man that you put his greatness in the second place when you knew him' (Collins 1981, 2.182). CARLYLE praised 'his rare and great worth as a brother man; a most cordial, sincere, clear-sighted, decisive, just and loving man', and THACKERAY's daughter Lady Ritchie spoke of his 'curious life-giving power' (Collins 1981, 1.63, 78). His energy was boundless. He dominated all activities in which he participated, looking after the minutest detail, and almost always found time each day for long walks as well as for simple domestic pleasures and much social entertaining.

Perhaps the clearest statement of the guiding principles of his private life is to be found in a letter that he wrote to his youngest son, 'Plorn', on the eve of his departure for AUSTRALIA. Impressing upon him 'the truth and beauty of the Christian Religion', he enjoined his son 'to persevere in a thorough determination to do whatever you have to do as well as you can do it' (Forster 11.3). See also DICKENS, CHARLES: PUBLIC LIFE.     PVWS
   Collins (1981).

**2. Public life** In a fragment of autobiography first published in FORSTER's *Life*, and written in 1847, Dickens speaks of how he accustomed himself at the age of 12 to working in WARREN'S BLACKING warehouse, and felt 'crushed in [his] breast' all his 'early hopes of growing up to be a learned and distinguished man' (see DIARIES AND AUTOBIOGRAPHY). By 1847, however, he was distinguished and widely read (if not classically learned), and considered himself 'famous and caressed and happy'.

The change was wrought in the 1830s. His appearance in the reporter's gallery of the House of Commons in 1832 was not stardom in itself, but it led to his achieving a high reputation within the profession and, equally importantly, to his future eschewal of POLITICS as a means of achieving distinction (see JOURNALIST, DICKENS AS). In 1833 his first imaginative work, 'A Dinner at Poplar Walk', appeared anonymously in print and was followed by five other unsigned pieces, 29 signed with the pseudonym 'BOZ', and 12 signed 'Tibbs' before 'Boz' was finally settled on. It was as 'Boz' that Dickens enjoyed his first taste of public notice, when REVIEWS of the first volume edition of *Sketches by Boz* in 1836 coincided with the widespread excerpting of *Pickwick Papers* in the national press. Although by no means uniformly favourable, the frequency of these notices gave an impression of ubiquitousness. Whether a new comic genius or merely a publishing breakthrough, 'Boz' seemed to be everywhere, and although Dickens gave up using the pseudonym on publication of the first edition of *Oliver Twist* (3rd issue), he continued to be known by it for many years afterwards.

So swift was his rise to fame that observers anticipated a parabolic trajectory. 'He has risen like a rocket, and he will come down like the stick', predicted Abraham Hayward in the *Quarterly Review* in October 1837, '. . . if he persists much longer' in the habit of writing 'too often and too fast'. Although conscious of numerous commitments, Dickens nevertheless accepted further writing engagements (the editorship of BENTLEY'S MISCELLANY, writing of material for the second series of *Sketches*, and two projected novels, plays, and so forth), all of which kept the name of 'Boz' in the public eye. His marriage to Catherine Hogarth in April 1836 and the birth of the first of their ten CHILDREN in January 1837 doubtless influenced these decisions (see DICKENS, CATHERINE).

Having cut short his promising career as a reporter, Dickens threw himself into the even less secure one of professional man-of-letters, in the execution of which his social and 'networking' skills were a valuable asset (see NOVELIST AND MAN OF LETTERS, DICKENS AS). 'What a face is his to meet in a drawing room!' exclaimed Leigh HUNT after dining with Dickens at Doughty Street in February 1839, 'It has the life and soul in it of fifty human beings' (Johnson 1.255). Between 1837 and 1839, during his editorship of *Bentley's Miscellany* and the writing and publication of *Oliver Twist* and *Nicholas Nickleby*, Dickens became acquainted, either through correspondence or in person, with many of the most prominent journalists and periodical contributors of the day (see ESSAYISTS, SKETCH-WRITERS AND HUMORISTS DURING DICKENS'S LIFETIME). Harrison AINSWORTH, Edward BULWER-LYTTON, Albany FONBLANQUE, Douglas JERROLD, Walter Savage LANDOR, J. G. LOCKHART, and T. N. TALFOURD also became friends and correspondents at this time. Following the immense popular success of *The Old Curiosity Shop*, no less a figure than Lord JEFFREY invited Dickens to Edinburgh, where he was honoured by a public dinner and the freedom of the city in June 1841. Dickens himself noted after the dinner that it was 'remarkable to see such a number of grey-headed men gathered about my brown-flowing locks', but, as he confided to Forster, the experience hardly overwhelmed him. When he rose to propose a toast to chairman John WILSON and to Scottish Literature, he remained 'quite self possessed . . . and, notwithstanding the enthoosemoosey, which was very startling, as cool as a cucumber'. On entering an Edinburgh theatre by chance later in his visit, he received a spontaneous ovation while the orchestra gave an impromptu rendering of 'Charley is My Darling' (Forster 2.10). It was not just portraits from *Pickwick* or *Nickleby* on clothes, chinaware, linen, billboards, and

posters that were bringing fame to their author: Dickens's own face was becoming well known to the nation through the widespread reproduction of PORTRAITS by Laurence, MACLISE, Alexander and others, quite apart from public appearances of this kind.

'Enthoosemoosey' was therefore to greet Dickens through much of his subsequent life, manifesting itself in its most extreme form in the continuous, and sometimes intrusive, attention which he received on his first trip to AMERICA in 1842. His plan had been to rest from the strain of popular authorship in England, and to travel and subsequently write a book for volume rather than periodical publication. Although the latter was for once achieved, Dickens enjoyed little rest in America, as his desire to tour and speak freely became more and more compromised by his celebrity status. The experience, it has been argued, stimulated deep-seated anxieties about his own character and social status, while the writing of AMERICAN NOTES itself was compromised in turn, becoming something of a 'containing' exercise in public relations (see Welsh 1987).

Quite apart from the unsettled feelings voiced in the autobiographical fragment, Dickens's life in the 1840s is characterized by a restlessness evident in changes of residence (from London to Genoa to Lausanne to PARIS to London), employment (from magazine editor to newspaper editor to author), and even publisher, with CHAPMAN AND HALL jettisoned in favour of BRADBURY AND EVANS (see also ITALY; SWITZERLAND). In his writing, however, he assumes the role of one constant in his affectionate relations to and dedicated service of the reading public. This is evident in prefaces such as that to the first edition of *Nicholas Nickleby* (1839) and particularly so in those written from 1847 onwards for the Cheap Edition of his works, a series which he hoped would show 'that Cheap Literature is not behind-hand with the Age [of reform], but holds its place, and strives to do its duty' (Preface to *Pickwick Papers*, September 1847; see EDITIONS OVER WHICH DICKENS HAD CONTROL). With the publication of *A Christmas Carol* in the hard winter of 1843, and four further CHRISTMAS BOOKS aimed at cheering the poor and stimulating good-will between all orders of society for their mutual benefit and security, Dickens succeeded in establishing a connection between himself and the popular celebration of a religious festival that is unique in cultural history (see READERSHIP; CHRISTMAS; CHRISTMAS STORIES).

There is little doubt that, at this time, Dickens was the most popular and widely read living author in both Europe and North America, and as such, was continually petitioned for public-speaking appearances, contributions to CHARITY and autographs (see POPULARITY OF DICKENS; SPEECHES OF DICKENS). On his return from America, he was increasingly in demand as a celebrity chairman and giver of toasts at fund-raising events, particularly those in support of working-class groups and initiatives (printers, governesses, newsvendors, mechanics, institutes, warehousemen and clerks' schools, etc.). The texts of over a hundred public addresses given by Dickens in the service of charitable and cultural causes are collected in K. J. Fielding's definitive edition of the *Speeches of Charles Dickens*, while his regular responses and spontaneous gifts to a range of charities and philanthropic initiatives are enumerated by biographers (e.g. Ackroyd 1990, pp. 533–5). Dickens himself describes how his home became 'a Receiving House' for begging letters from writers who had heard that he often gave money ('The Begging Letter Writer', *HW* 18 May 1850). Even letters declining assistance had their street value, as recipients in the know could 'always get one shilling for Charles Dickens's signature from Mr Waller', the Fleet Street autograph dealer (Ackroyd 1990, p. 534). This was fame indeed.

At the same period, Dickens actively courted the limelight in his organization of a number of AMATEUR THEATRICAL productions that attracted considerable media attention. This too was something that had started on his journey to North America, with the stage-managing of a charity programme at the Queen's Theatre, Montreal, by the Coldstream Guards stationed there (see CANADA). Between 1842 and 1850 Dickens became the driving force behind no fewer than ten productions of comedies and farces, in each of which he also played, while in the 1850s he appeared in the romantic dramas *The Lighthouse* and *The* FROZEN DEEP, and five further comedies. Fellow actors, audiences, and critics alike paid tribute to Dickens's acting

talent and organizational abilities, while Queen Victoria herself made it known in the spring of 1857 that she wished to attend one of the benefit performances of *The Frozen Deep* organized by Dickens in aid of the family of the late Douglas JERROLD: a Royal Command performance.

Under the spotlight of public scrutiny, it is perhaps natural that Dickens should have sought, like the medieval monarch, to identify himself with his office, and seek a kind of immunity by asserting the dignity of his calling. If the author was one who strove to do the public good, then the man behind the pen should be entitled to reciprocal good-will. In a speech made towards the end of his life, he announced that 'when I first took Literature as my profession in England, I calmly resolved within myself that whether I succeeded or whether I failed, Literature should be my sole profession . . . I made a compact with myself that in my person Literature should stand, and by itself, and for itself, and of itself' (*Speeches*, p. 389). This is a keynote speech as far as Dickens's conception of his role in public life is concerned, and his championing of the GUILD OF LITERATURE AND ART in the 1850s is eloquent of his belief that the services of the man of letters to society deserved broader public recognition than the aristocratic patronage bestowed by the ROYAL LITERARY FUND. The image of 'calm resolution' in the service of literature and his readers is one which he wished at all times to project: usually with admirable success, but unconvincingly on certain occasions. The announcements made in the last number of *Household Words* about his successful dissolution of that journal and the founding of *All the Year Round*, when read in conjunction with Bradbury and Evans's version of events, say more about the hastiness of Dickens's temper and the wilful nature of his professional dealings than they do about his calm resolution to serve Literature (*HW* 28 May 1859; Pilgrim 9.565–6).

Still more telling is the statement headed 'Personal' which he caused to be made public in *Household Words* on 12 June 1858, and which was the occasion of his quarrel with Bradbury and Evans. The first three paragraphs sum up Dickens's construction of the position he sought to hold in public life, and from which he was ill-advisedly about to depart, by dwelling on details of his private life:

'Three-and-twenty years have passed since I entered on my present relations with the Public. They began when I was so young, that I find them to have existed for nearly a quarter of a century.

'Through all that time I have tried to be as faithful to the Public, as they have been to me. It was my duty never to trifle with them, or deceive them, or presume upon their favour, or do anything with it but work hard to justify it. I have always endeavoured to discharge that duty.

'My conspicuous position has often made me the subject of fabulous stories and unaccountable statements. Occasionally, such things have chafed me, or even wounded me; but, I have always accepted them as the shadows inseparable from the light of my notoriety and success. I have never obtruded any such personal uneasiness of mine, upon the generous aggregate of my audience.'

In his allusion to the title of John Wilson's *Lights and Shadows of Scottish Life*, Dickens half implies that the light of *his* was his public success. As Butt and Tillotson justly observe, Dickens's love affair with his public was the most interesting of his life (1957, p. 75), and in later years it was manifestly dearer to him than his relationship with his wife. Although at the time Dickens was widely felt to be guilty of bad taste in deliberately subjecting Catherine to this kind of media attention, modern commentators are likely to find something both familiar and prophetic in the story of an unhappy superstar whose need for public affection destroyed personal relationships.

Dickens's decision in April of 1858, against the advice of Forster and other friends, to commence a series of paid PUBLIC READING tours is a further illustration of this desire for emotional bonding with strangers, a condition which at times seems to border on obsession, but which brought Dickens undisguised pleasure. 'I never beheld anything like the personal affection which they poured out upon me at the end', he wrote to Georgina HOGARTH of crowds at Exeter. 'I shall always look back upon it with pleasure' (5 August 1858). Over the next decade, the four series of reading tours which Dickens undertook in six countries were, judged as popular entertainment, a triumphant and unprecedented

success. They exacted a heavy price, however, again in personal terms, as Dickens's health deteriorated under what he described in one of his last essays as the 'constant strain on the attention, memory, observation, and physical powers'. The paper is an ironic protest over the 'remarkable' public misconception that the reading tours had made him seriously ill, but with hindsight, Dickens's usually surefooted satire can be seen to fail him here, and instead a picture is left of a man ill at ease with his celebrity ('A Fly-Leaf in a Life', *AYR* 22 May 1869; collected in *UT*).

Dickens's retrospective assurance that since an early age he had fixed his mind on serving Literature is also something which can be questioned. The evidence of his correspondence suggests that, until his journals gave him a steady income in 1850, he was frequently casting round for other kinds of role in public life. The first of these abortive public lives was that of a professional actor. A heavy cold prevented his attending an audition with the stage manager of Covent Garden in the spring of 1832, just at the time when his writing career was beginning to bring in the kind of money he had thought of turning to the stage to earn. 'See how near I may have been to another sort of life', he later remarked to Forster (1.4). 'Nature intended me for the lessee of a national theatre', he enthused during the Montreal amateur theatricals, '. . . pen, ink and paper have spoilt a manager' (to Cornelius Felton, 21 May 1842).

Then, for a number of years the notion of entering the LAW as a profession was one which Dickens seriously entertained. In December 1839 his name was entered among the students of the Inn of the Middle Temple, with his publisher Edward Chapman standing as 'surety' for his good behaviour while eating dinners there, 'and honourable intentions to pay for all wine-glasses, tumblers, or other dinner-furniture that I may break or damage' (to Chapman, 27 December 1839; see INNS OF COURT). Ten years later, during the writing of *David Copperfield*, he was still dining there when the throes of composition allowed: being called to the bar was still (and would remain) an unfulfilled ambition, sidelined by a different train of events (Forster 6.6). Other letters written during the 1840s show Dickens asking for advice about becoming a police magistrate or applying for 'some

Commissionership, or Inspectorship'. These details suggest that while he proclaimed Literature and Art as his mistresses, there was perhaps a lingering desire for the security of a more conventional kind of service.

Even his vigorous dislike of parliamentary procedure did not make the prospect of entering politics something impossible to consider. On being offered the candidature of MP for Reading in Berkshire in 1841, he declined it on the grounds that he 'could not afford a contested election', even though his 'principles and inclinations would lead me to aspire to the distinction' (31 May 1841). On at least two other occasions Dickens was offered the opportunity to stand for Parliament, declining it in 1852 on the grounds that, with *Household Words* and *Bleak House* to attend to, 'I should be worried to death if I did it now' (to Wills, 28 February 1852), and in 1869 for reasons that are finally consonant with his credo, announced in the same year, to stand or fall by Literature: 'if anything would induce me to forgo a determination I had formed in such wise long ago, the being offered the representation of Birmingham in conjunction with Mr Bright would do so. But . . . my mind was made up never to enter the House of Commons, and . . . I ha[ve] satisfied myself to rest content with the present sphere of my usefulness and occupation' (unpublished letter of 19 April 1869, quoted in G. Mott, 'I Wallow in Words: Dickens, Journalism and Public Affairs, 1831–38', unpublished Ph.D. Thesis, University of Leicester, 1984). Nevertheless, in his disgust at the kind of government neglect of duty and maladministration that came to light during the CRIMEAN WAR, Dickens became an active member of the Administrative Reform Association in 1855. The Association was a lobby group formed by the famous archaeologist and MP Austin Henry Layard (1817–94), whom Dickens admired and befriended. Not only did Dickens's journal *Household Words* come out strongly in favour of the Association's reforming ideals, but correspondence reveals that Dickens aimed to use his influence in media circles to swing PUNCH, the *Illustrated London News*, the *Weekly Chronicle*, and the EXAMINER behind the project (Letter to Layard, 3 April 1855). With his name on the masthead of every page, *Household Words* itself, and its even more widely read successor *All the Year Round*, were

just two of the means by which Dickens converted himself, in the words of Baldwin Brown, into one of the 'great social agencies' of the era.

The public life of an author, however reclusive, is closely bound up in and with his or her published works, and in Dickens's case the intense awareness which he possessed of his presence in the public eye, as transmitted by the medium of his writings and performances, was in many ways a defining influence. His remarks about the dignity of literature as a calling, and his emphasis as narrator on the establishment of intimate relations with his readers suggest a man whose ideal of public life was uniquely realized by his position as a popular periodical author, whose works were in circulation, month after month, for over thirty years. Nevertheless, the evidence which emerges from private letters and biographical research, of numerous plans, projects, and ambitions for achieving other kinds of social and professional recognition, suggests uncertainties and unfulfilled ambitions. Both kinds of 'history' need to be balanced to understand the 'public' side of Dickens's life and the complex way he responded to it. It is perhaps a fitting irony that Dickens's last effort to exert mastery over his progress through the world was overturned by the supreme act of public recognition awarded to him on his journey out of it. His wish to be buried 'in the small graveyard under Rochester Castle wall' (Forster 12.2) and 'in an inexpensive, unostentatious, and strictly private manner' went unheeded as, by general consent, a tomb in Poets' Corner of Westminster Abbey was prepared, and the nation mourned.     JMLD

> Collins, Philip, 'How Many Men Was Dickens the Novelist?', in Jean-Claude Amalric (ed.), *Studies in the Later Dickens* (1973).
> —— (1981).

**Dickens, Charles: works.** See under individual titles. See also ABRIDGEMENTS OF DICKENS'S WORKS; ADAPTATIONS OF DICKENS'S WORKS; ADVERTISING IN AND OF DICKENS'S WORKS; CHILDREN'S VERSIONS OF DICKENS'S WORKS; COLLECTIONS OF DICKENS MATERIALS; DRAMATIZATIONS AND DRAMATIZERS OF DICKENS'S WORKS; EDITIONS; LEGAL DOCUMENTS OF DICKENS; LETTERS OF DICKENS; LIBRARY OF DICKENS; MELODRAMA IN DICKENS'S WRITING; PUBLIC READINGS;

PUBLIC READING TEXTS; SEQUELS AND CONTINUATIONS OF DICKENS'S WORKS; SPEECHES OF DICKENS.

## Dickens, Elizabeth Barrow (1789–1863),

mother of Dickens. One of ten children, Elizabeth was the daughter of Mary Culliford and Charles Barrow, a music teacher who in 1801 obtained a position as a clerk in the Navy Pay Office. Within a year he had risen to the responsible position of Chief Conductor of Monies in Towns. In 1805 one of his younger sons, Thomas Culliford, also obtained a position in the Navy Pay Office, starting work the same day as another young clerk, John DICKENS. Over the next four years the friendship between John Dickens and Thomas Barrow developed and John fell in love with Thomas's pretty sister Elizabeth. He married her in June 1809 at St Mary-le-Strand in London. Their first child, Frances, was born the following year—the same year that Charles Barrow fled the country when his embezzlement of several thousand pounds from the Navy Pay Office came to light (see BROTHERS AND SISTERS OF DICKENS). Elizabeth and John enjoyed a modest prosperity for the first ten or eleven years of their married life, first in Portsea (where Charles was born in 1812 and a second son, Alfred Allen, was born and died in 1813), in London, and then Chatham (where Letitia was born in 1816) (see HOMES OF DICKENS). Elizabeth was, at this time, a pretty woman with dark ringlets and a narrow waist. Humorous and vivacious (she had been dancing at a ball just before Charles was born), she retained her ebullience and her love of dancing for the rest of her life. Her marriage to her beloved 'D', as she called him, was evidently a very happy one, and she remained devoted to him throughout all the fluctuations of fortune that befell them.

In Chatham she employed a nursemaid, Mary Weller, to help her with her growing family (Harriet, who lived only four years, was born in 1819, Frederick in 1820, and Alfred Lamert in 1822). Many years later Mary Weller described Elizabeth as 'a dear good mother and a fine woman'. It was Elizabeth who taught Charles to read, taking him even as far as the rudiments of Latin, and generally instilling in him a love of reading and a desire for knowledge (see DICKENS: PRIVATE LIFE).

Meanwhile John Dickens's extravagance and financial mismanagement was gradually leading to a decline in their living standards, and towards the end of 1822 the family moved to Camden Town, London. The following year, with her husband's financial state growing increasingly desperate, Elizabeth rented premises in Gower Street North and set up a school. She drew up a prospectus, copies of which Charles was sent out to distribute, and a brass plaque inscribed 'Mrs Dickens's Establishment' was displayed on the front door. 'Nobody ever came to the school,' Dickens remembered, 'nor do I recollect that anybody ever proposed to come, or that the least preparation was made to receive anybody' (Forster 1.13).

Some help for their plight came from James Lamert, stepson of Elizabeth's sister. The manager of the newly launched WARREN'S BLACKING factory, he suggested that Charles go and work there, pasting labels on bottles, for six shillings a week, an offer that was willingly accepted: 'My father and mother were quite satisfied. They could hardly have been more so, if I had been twenty years of age, distinguished at a grammar school, and going to Cambridge' (Forster 1.2). Deeply wretched, Charles began work in February 1824. A fortnight later his father was arrested for debt and imprisoned in the Marshalsea (see PRISONS). Elizabeth stayed on in Gower Street for a little while longer, selling almost all their possessions, including most of the furniture, and finally, with her younger children, went to live with John in his room in the prison. Charles, boarded out, remembered visiting his parents there and recalled that 'I was always delighted to hear from my mother what she knew about the histories of the different debtors in the prisons' (Forster 1.2). After going through the Insolvent Debtors' Court, John was released in April and returned to work in the Navy Pay Office (see LAW AND LEGAL INSTITUTIONS). Despite this turn of events, Charles continued, to his grief, to work at the factory until a few weeks later when John Dickens quarrelled with Lamert and Charles was dismissed. To his outrage and horror: 'My mother set herself to accommodate the quarrel, and did so next day. She brought home a request for me to return next morning . . . My father said I should go back no more, and should go to school. I do not write resentfully or angrily: for I know how all these things have worked together to make me what I am: but I never afterwards forgot, I never shall forget, I never can forget, that my mother was warm for my being sent back' (Forster 1.2). This sense of having been betrayed by his own mother was a resentment Dickens was to harbour all his life.

He did return to school, albeit briefly, and then in 1827 Elizabeth's seventh and last child, Augustus, was born. John could no longer pay the school fees, and it was again Elizabeth who helped Charles to a job. Her aunt kept a boarding house in Berners Street where lodged Edward Blackmore, a partner in the legal firm of ELLIS AND BLACKMORE. Elizabeth was a frequent visitor at Berners Street and she persuaded Blackmore to take Charles on as a clerk in his office. Later in 1832 it was on *The* MIRROR OF PARLIAMENT, a paper run by John Henry Barrow, one of Elizabeth's brothers, that Charles began his highly successful career as a JOURNALIST.

After Dickens became engaged to Catherine Hogarth, Elizabeth helped to prepare his bachelor chambers in Furnival's Inn for occupation by him and his bride, providing the linen and re-covering the sofa (see DICKENS, CATHERINE; INNS OF COURT). Elizabeth (along with Mrs Hogarth) attended Catherine when she gave birth to her first child, and Charles entrusted to her the task of inspecting possible new homes for himself and his new family. He was aware of her good sense and her canny eye for a bargain, and he used her skills again when he rented a cottage in Exeter for his parents in 1839: 'There are so many things she can make comfortable at a much less expense than I could' (6 March 1839). The move to Devon had been necessitated by his father's fresh financial embarrassments. John and Elizabeth were clearly not happy with this banishment to the country and Charles reported to FORSTER that he had received 'an unsatisfactory epistle from Mother' (? March 1839). 'I do swear,' shortly afterwards he wrote, 'I am sick at heart with both her and father too' (11 July 1839). He soon forgave them, however, and in the summer of 1841 they were staying with him and his family in Broadstairs. Another visitor there at the time recalled 'old Mrs Dickens' as a 'very agreeable woman'; who 'entered into youthful amusements with much enjoyment', and who loved

dancing, although 'Charles always looked as sulky as a bear' whenever she indulged in this pleasure (Slater 1983, 13).

By 1850 John was seriously ill. He and Elizabeth moved into Keppel Street; the home of a doctor called Mr Davey, and there John died in March 1851. Twenty-three years later Mrs Davey wrote a detailed description of Elizabeth:

'She had very bright hazel eyes, and was as thoroughly good-natured, easy-going, companionable a body as one would wish to meet with. The likeness between her and Mrs Nickleby is simply the exaggeration of some slight peculiarities. She possessed an extraordinary sense of the ludicrous, and her power of imitation was something quite astonishing. On entering a room she almost unconsciously took an inventory of its contents, and if anything happened to strike her as out of place or ridiculous, she would afterward describe it in the quaintest possible manner. In like manner she noted the personal peculiarities of her friends and acquaintants. She had also a fine vein of pathos, and could bring tears to the eyes of her listeners when narrating some sad event ... I am of the opinion that a great deal of Dickens's genius was inherited from his mother. He possessed her keen appreciation of the droll and of the pathetic, as also considerable dramatic talent. Mrs Dickens has often sent my sisters and myself into uncontrollable fits of laughter by her funny sayings and inimitable mimicry' (Collins 1981, p. 130).

After John's death Charles treated his mother kindly: 'he took her in his arms, and they both wept bitterly together. He told her that she must rely on him for the future. He immediately paid whatever his father owed; and relieved his mother's mind on that score' (ibid.).

In her widowhood Elizabeth continued to show her buoyant spirits: 'My mother has a strong objection to being considered in the least old, and usually appears here on CHRISTMAS Day in a juvenile cap . . .' (10 February 1855). Within four years, however, she had begun her decline into senility. In March 1860 the woman who had been living with Elizabeth to take care of her became 'terrified by the responsibility of her charge . . . Consequently', Dickens wrote 'I must at once devote myself to the difficult task of finding good hands for my mother, and getting her into them without alarming her' (28 March 1860). In August he wrote to a friend that she was 'in the strangest state of mind from senile decay; and the impossibility of getting her to understand what is the matter, combined with her desire to be got up in sables like a female Hamlet, illumines the dreary scene with a ghastly absurdity that is the chief relief I can find in it' (to Mrs Frances Dickinson, 19 August 1860). By then Elizabeth was living with a widowed daughter-in-law in a house that Dickens had found for them on Haverstock Hill. He visited her and found her 'much better than I had supposed ... the instant she saw me, she plucked up a spirit and asked me for "a pound"!' (27 November 1860). She finally died in September 1863.

In the fragment of his autobiography, published by Forster, it is clear that Dickens felt much more resentment towards Elizabeth than towards his father for his childhood misery (see DIARIES AND AUTOBIOGRAPHY). This resentment doubtless influenced the creation of so many unsatisfactory mothers throughout Dickens's fiction. Most directly Elizabeth has been credited with being the model for both Mrs Nickleby and Mrs Micawber. The former's ebullience and vanity, and her often ill-founded optimism, certainly suggest Elizabeth, though she herself failed to perceive the likeness, even asking Charles whether he 'really believed there ever was such a woman' (to Richard Lane, 2 January 1844). More obvious is the contribution made by John and Elizabeth and their precarious situation in the early 1820s to the portrayal of Mr and Mrs Micawber. The unsympathetic attitude of Mrs Micawber's family towards her husband's difficulties clearly echoes the irritation of Elizabeth's brothers whose names John used to raise money, Thomas Barrow eventually refusing to have him in the house; and the brass plate for Elizabeth's ill-fated school is recalled in *David Copperfield*, ch. 11: 'The centre of the streetdoor was perfectly covered with a great brass plate on which was engraved "Mrs Micawber's Boarding Establishment for Young Ladies".' Above all, Mrs Micawber's famous refrain, 'I will never desert Mr Micawber', seems to reflect Elizabeth's devoted loyalty through more than forty years of marriage to her charming but feckless husband.                                    MS

**Dickens, John** (1785–1851), father of Charles Dickens. John Dickens was a man of energy and humour, determined to live life at a level of comfort just beyond his means. It was a philosophy that led himself and his family through a tearful, demeaning, and infuriating existence, yet still, in the round, endeared him to his wife and to his famous son. 'My poor father,' Charles wrote in 1865, 'whom I regard as a better man the longer I live' (Forster 6.6).

John Dickens was born in London in August 1785, the second son of William and Elizabeth, elevated servants of John Crewe, a rich Cheshire landowner. William Dickens died two months later, and John was brought up by his mother, who remained an important part of the Crewe household. The Crewe family's lifestyle, spent as much in London as Cheshire, was sumptuous and high-profile, with the greatest politicians, writers, artists, and actors of the day, even the Prince of Wales, passing over their threshold. An upbringing in such surroundings gave John Dickens confidence, education, and an awareness of manners and style, all of which enabled him later to establish a position where he could behave, and be regarded as, a gentleman (see CLASS). At the age of 19, when he needed to make his own way in the world, the Crewes turned to one of their friends, George Canning, for assistance, who employed him as an 'extra clerk' in the Navy Pay Office, earning £78 a year, first at Somerset House in London and from 1807 at Portsmouth.

In 1809 he married Elizabeth Barrow, sister of a colleague, and set up home in Portsmouth, where they lived for six years and had three children, Frances, Charles, and Alfred—the latter of whom died at 6 months (see DICKENS, ELIZABETH; BROTHERS AND SISTERS OF DICKENS). They welcomed into the family a recently widowed sister-in-law, Mary Allen, whose small pension added to the family income. Through all the vicissitudes John and Elizabeth were a well-matched couple. 'Certainly there never was a Man more unselfish', Elizabeth wrote after the death of her beloved 'D', as she called him, 'and ever a Friend to those whom he could serve and a most affectionate kind Husband and Father' (quoted by Slater 1983, p. 4).

There was an excitement about John Dickens's job in Portsmouth—he was part of a major naval establishment fighting against Napoleon and later against America. The port town was rough and dangerous, filled with men hardened by their experiences at war, bustling with those involved in the provisioning and maintenance of ships. John Dickens's work included the paying of sailors and artificers, involving large sums, with hand-outs often made by candlelight and on board ship. Overpayment was deducted from pay clerks' salaries, and in bad weather the work could be hazardous, not only to the pocket. John Dickens was a reliable employee, and was promoted from fifteenth to eleventh Assistant Clerk, with an annual salary of £231.

The year 1814 saw Napoleon defeated and the war with America ended, resulting in reductions in personnel at Portsmouth dockyard, and John Dickens was moved to London in January 1815. It was during his two-year stay that he may have first experienced financial problems. His income dropped, and it seems likely he borrowed money from his mother. Nevertheless, he described himself as 'gentleman' on the register of baptisms for his second daughter, Letitia.

In 1817 he was moved again, first to Sheerness for a few months, and then to Chatham. Over the following five-and-a-half years his annual income rose from £200 to £441, but his expenditure rose even more. He was considered a good employee, eventually rising to the level of third clerk, with promotion to the Inspectors' Branch. It can only be surmised what he spent his money on. He certainly enjoyed parties and social gatherings. He took his family to the local theatre, and occasionally to theatres in London. For four years he lived in a new, if somewhat cramped, house, and employed two servants. No doubt clothing, feeding, and entertaining his growing family made heavy demands on his income. He borrowed £200 in August 1819, to be paid back at £26 per annum. However, the annual payments were not made, and the debt was paid by his brother-in-law Thomas Barrow in 1821, causing a family rift which lasted many years, with the amount still outstanding when Barrow died in 1857. John Dickens also borrowed from one of his neighbours in Ordnance Terrace.

It is difficult to identify any specific reason for John Dickens's financial difficulties—there is no hint of speculation on his part, or of gambling; he owned no horse or carriage; his house was modest, and his income satisfactory. It can only be assumed that daily living expenses were more extravagant than they should have been—too much spent on eating, drinking, and entertaining, on clothes and furnishings, on cutlery, crockery, and glassware.

Whatever the financial situation, John Dickens created a pleasant environment in which his children grew up. He was described as a fellow of infinite humour, chatty, lively, and agreeable. He sent Charles to school, introduced him to books, to the theatre, and to Gad's Hill Place, with the encouragement that he might live there one day if he worked hard. He helped create in his son an affection for a part of the country that was to stay with him for the rest of his life (see KENT).

Recalled to London in 1822 he carried with him not only a baggage of debts, but also a drop in salary, and the strains of his position told heavily. His decision to send Fanny to study music, with annual fees of 38 guineas, seems foolish, though under better conditions it could have been a sensible long-term strategy, leading to good teaching income. Charles's schooling, though, was discontinued and he felt neglected by his father. Twice in 1823 summonses were issued for non-payment of rates—perhaps rents received the same treatment, and debts built up with tradesmen. His wife set up a school in a suitably impressive house in Gower Street, but no pupils came. The scheme quickly failed, and Charles was sent to work at WARREN'S BLACKING warehouse. Eventually the whole façade collapsed and John Dickens was arrested for debt on 20 February 1824.

The long-term effect on his son of this period was profound. Charles went to see his father at the Sponging House—a holding-place, where the prisoner had a last-minute opportunity to resolve his difficulties. He was sent running errands and delivering messages for his father. It was heart-rending for the 12-year-old to see his father humiliated; and for the father, also, to be humiliated in front of his son. John Dickens's last words to his boy, before being carried off, were something to the effect that the sun was set upon him for ever.

Later, in prison, he broke down in front of Charles, and they both cried. 'And he told me, I remember, to take warning by the

Marshalsea, and to observe that if a man had twenty pounds a-year, and spent nineteen pounds nineteen shillings and sixpence, he would be happy; but that a shilling spent the other way would make him wretched' (Forster 1.1). The memory was bitter, but the now-famous homily from the autobiographical fragment was transformed in *David Copperfield* by the catalyst of humour; Micawber immediately borrows a shilling from David (see DIARIES AND AUTOBIOGRAPHICAL FRAGMENT). Dickens returned to his father's experience of debt again when drawing the portrait of the Father of the Marshalsea, William Dorrit, 'a very amiable and very helpless middle-aged gentleman', than whom 'nobody on the face of the earth could be more incapable of explaining any single item in the heap of confusion' that led to his imprisonment (*LD* 1.6).

John Dickens anxiously sought to secure his salary for that quarter, and excused himself from work for reasons of bad health, at the same time requesting retirement with superannuation. Two doctors visited him in prison, and produced a certificate stating that he was, 'from infirmity of body, arising from chronic infection of the Urinary Organs incapacitated from attending to any possible duty' (Allen 1988, p. 89). His infection was a genuine complaint, referred to in later Admiralty correspondence, and 27 years later his death certificate recorded that he died from 'rupture of the Urethra from old Standing Stricture and consequent mortification of the Scrotum from infiltration of urine'.

To obtain release from prison John Dickens had to declare himself an insolvent debtor—to detail all debts, hold goods valued at no more than £20, and agree, if able, to settle his debts at a later date. He was released from the Marshalsea on 28 May 1824, and the following week he came into possession of £450 from the will of his mother, who had died on 26 April. Even with this legacy his debts, in excess of £700, were not finally cleared until November 1826.

The Admiralty, meanwhile, granted his retirement and an annual pension of £146; and he found a new career, in journalism. He was able to take his son out of Warren's Blacking and send him back to school. This change of career direction for John Dickens indicates one more fundamental influence that he had

on Charles. He had first demonstrated an aptitude for journalism in 1820, when his account of a great fire at Chatham appeared not only locally but also in *The Times*. Now in 1825 he established himself as a correspondent for the *British Press*, and encouraged Charles to bring in reports of accidents, fires, police reports, and suchlike that escaped the regular reporters, for which Charles was paid a penny for each printed line.

Journalism, though, was no easy path to follow. In 1827 the *British Press* failed, and with insufficient income the family were evicted from their home in Johnson Street, Charles was taken away from school to begin work, and Fanny was withdrawn from the Royal Academy of Music. Many years of financial instability followed. Their income comprised the Admiralty pension, small payments for John Dickens's occasional journalism, fees paid to Fanny for teaching music (though this probably went, initially, to pay off debts accrued during training), and the gradually growing income of Charles. John Dickens consistently refused, or was unable, to live within this income, and was sued in 1831, 1834, and 1835. There were frequent changes of address.

Precarious and unsettled though this way of life was, difficulties were always overcome, and money found from somewhere. He must have looked to the future, then, with some confidence as Charles turned his pen to good use. His son moved out of the family home in 1834, but the two saw each other frequently, often in the company of Dickens's new friends and acquaintances—BENTLEY, CRUIKSHANK, FORSTER, AINSWORTH, MACREADY, TALFOURD, and CHAPMAN AND HALL.

For a time father and son seemed to get on well together—John Dickens helped with making fair copies of Dickens's plays and *MEMOIRS OF GRIMALDI*, and was invited to the theatre, to dinners, and parties. He treated Charles's good fortune as his own, and continued in his old way of spending money that he did not have. For Charles things came to a head, or were uncovered, in March 1839, when his solution to the problem was to send his parents to Devon, as far away from temptation as possible. On this occasion the cost to him was £300–£400.

John and Elizabeth Dickens's stay in Devon lasted from April 1839 to October 1842, but

John could spend money just as easily there as in London, and he drove Charles to new heights of exasperation. He started to sell samples of his son's writing and signature, and to write to Charles's publishers and bankers and friends begging loans. Charles described his father as a source of constant anxiety, uneasiness, and expense; 'How long he is, growing to be a man', he wrote (to Mitton, 4 April 1842). In his anger he suggested sending him abroad to live, and placed an entry in the main London newspapers repudiating debts made against his name by anybody other than himself or Catherine. Eventually the family were returned to London from Devon, though the problems continued. Charles wrote that his father had gone 'ravin'' mad with conscious willany. The thought of him besets me, night and day; and I really do not know what is to be done with him. It is quite clear that the more we do, the more outrageous and audacious he becomes' (20 February 1843). 'I am amazed and confounded by the audacity of his ingratitude ... Nothing makes me so wretched, or so unfit for what I have to do, as these things. They ... utterly dispirit me, and weigh me down' (28 September 1843).

It is a remarkable reflection of Dickens's relationship with his father that when, in 1845, he became editor of the DAILY NEWS, despite all the difficulties he had had with him, he appointed John Dickens to a responsible position organizing the reporters. He kept the post until his death six years later, even though Dickens's editorship lasted only a few weeks. This employment gave John Dickens, at the age of 60, a new lease of life—he relished being at the centre of things, being recognized for the abilities he had to offer, and he enjoyed a good, regular income. He was described as a short, portly, obese gentleman of enviable stamina, on whom time seemed to have made no impression, fond of a glass of grog and full of fun. Acrimony disappears from Dickens's letters and a more affectionate tone appears. He wrote that there was not attached to the paper a more 'zealous, disinterested or useful gentleman' than his father (26 February 1848). As financial difficulties eased, so did a softer nature surface; John Dickens spent time with Fanny during the illness leading to her death in 1848, and he was the only member of the family to attend the wedding of his son Fred, a wedding strongly disapproved of by Charles.

John Dickens's death was as dramatic as much of his life had been. Dickens wrote to Catherine: 'He was in that state from active disease [of the bladder] which he had mentioned to nobody, that mortification and delirium, terminating in speedy death, seemed unavoidable. Mr Wade was called in, who instantly performed (without chloroform) the most terrible operation known in surgery, as the only chance of saving him. He bore it with astonishing fortitude, and I saw him directly afterwards—his room, a slaughter house of blood. He was wonderfully cheerful and strong-hearted' (25 March 1851). He died six days later.

The obituary in the *Gentleman's Magazine* described him as one of the most efficient and most respected members of the press, possessed of great energy of character and thorough business habits, with a naturally generous disposition and kind heart. He would have appreciated these generous words, but they are reinforced by a passage in Dickens's autobiographical fragment, written many years before: 'I know my father to be as kindhearted and generous a man as ever lived in the world. Everything I can remember of his conduct to his wife, or children, or friends, in sickness or affliction, is beyond all praise. By me, as a sick child, he has watched night and day, unweariedly and patiently, many nights and days. He never undertook any business, charge or trust, that he did not zealously, conscientiously, punctually, honourably discharge. His industry has always been untiring' (Forster 1.1).                    MA

Allen, Michael, *Charles Dickens' Childhood* (1988).

**Dickens Birthplace Museum.** Dickens was born in a small Regency terraced house, not more than a few years old, in Mile End Terrace, Landport, Portsea. Unnumbered at the time, it later became known as 1 Mile End Terrace, later still as 393 Old Commercial Road, Portsmouth. Though a separate borough in 1812, economically Portsea was dependent on Portsmouth's naval dockyard.

At the time Dickens's father was a clerk in the Navy Pay Office in Portsmouth (see DICKENS, JOHN). He had rented the house in April 1809, two months before his marriage. The family vacated it in June 1812. George DOLBY reports that, in 1866, Dickens recognized the street in which he was born (Dolby 1885, pp. 37–8). It is more likely that he identified Wish Street (later Kings Road), where the family lived from 1813 to 1815 (Allen 1988, pp. 26–7).

Portsmouth Corporation bought the birthplace in 1903, and opened it as a museum of Dickens memorabilia in 1904. In 1967, however, the decision was taken to re-create the milieu of a Navy Pay Clerk and his family in 1812. From 1968 to 1970 the house was closed for investigation, major structural repair, and refurbishment. Original paint colours and wallpapers were identified. The parlour, the dining-room, and the bedroom in which Dickens was born, have all been decorated in the light of those discoveries, and furnished in the fashionable middle-class style of the era. The Museum also displays a collection of pictures and memorabilia, including the couch on which Dickens died, presented to the Museum by Georgina HOGARTH. DP

**Dickens circle, the.** Dickens's friends and acquaintances were numerous and various. Nationally famous in his mid-twenties, soon world-famous, he inevitably attracted attention and, though some friendships survived from his pre-fame years, his circle thenceforth consisted mostly of people more or less prominent in the arts, journalism, and public or social life. He lived mostly in London and participated in its vigorous routine of visiting and dining-out, and artistic and journalistic people institutionalized such opportunities. Though not an avid clubman like the quasi-bachelor THACKERAY, he belonged to the ATHENAEUM, GARRICK, and other more ephemeral and occasional clubs such as the SHAKESPEARE, whose weekly meetings were socially important to him in his early years.

In 1860 he sold Tavistock House and made Gad's Hill his family residence, though always retaining a London *pied-à-tèrre* and sometimes renting a town house to permit his unmarried daughter Mamie to enjoy the 'season' (see HOMES OF DICKENS). The break-up of his marriage (1858) had interrupted some friendships and diminished his social life: a very grand reception, attended by 'everybody', which he gave in 1870, was said by one guest to be his first return to general society since the

separation. But even in this final decade, when his PUBLIC READINGS restricted socializing, and his health and spirits were poorer, he was by no means reclusive, and he vigorously maintained his friendships by letter as well as reunions. Gad's Hill was in easy reach of London and he entertained there frequently, always filling the house at CHRISTMAS, with an overflow into the Falstaff Inn. Family holidays similarly had generally included friends. His sojourns over the years in AMERICA, FRANCE, ITALY, and SWITZERLAND established many friendships too, continued mainly by correspondence, and these included some of his warmest relationships.

Even at the age of 9 he was 'capital company', as his schoolmaster's sister recalled. By temperament he was genial and sociable, generally regarded as pleasant, socially delightful, an excellent host, with 'a great capacity for friendship' (Frederick Locker-Lampson): 'he warmed the social atmosphere wherever he appeared with [a] summer glow' (T. A. Trollope). He did not play the Great Man in society, was unegotistical in conversation and averse to discussing his work (did not, indeed, often talk on literary topics), but had plenty of agreeable light chat to put undistinguished or unintellectual companions at their ease. Thus, a guest at Gad's Hill was impressed by his kind attentiveness to 'a dull little woman', the shy wife of a naval officer (for he fraternized with his neighbours in Kent, including the local garrison). A minority report should be quoted: the Irish author and politician Justin McCarthy knew that other young men found him very 'kind and friendly and encouraging', but his acquaintance remained 'very slight and superficial . . . Dickens rather frightened me; I felt uneasy when he spoke to me . . . there was something physically oppressive about [his manner] . . . the very vehemence of his cheery good-humour rather bore one down.' Most people, however, found him accessible. 'Dickens most pleasant. No wonder people like him', noted W. P. FRITH, arriving to paint his portrait. His brother-in-law Henry Burnett recalled him, in the 1830s, as 'brimful of geniality and sociability . . . Nothing seemed more pleasurable to him than to be amongst his friends . . . It was natural to Dickens . . . to aim at making people happy.' For Lady Pollock, 'Charles Dickens was and is . . . the ideal of friendship', 'no work and no trouble of his own impeded him, if he believed that his friend wanted him'. (All quotations in this and following paragraphs are from Collins 1981.) Most of his friendships were durable; people were necessary to him and he had warm affection for many.

His first circle was, of course, his family, but here his record was patchy. He was a dutiful, sometimes fond, but often exasperated son, but his parents were not alone in preying upon him financially: brothers did so too (see BROTHERS AND SISTERS OF DICKENS). He was closer to his brother-in-law Henry Austin (husband of Letitia Dickens), a civil engineer who kept him usefully informed on PUBLIC-HEALTH matters. Unsurprisingly, he kept up with no companions from WARREN'S BLACK-ING, and unlike his fictional *alter ego* he carried no Traddles or Steerforth into his adult life, though he was affable when old schoolfellows contacted him; as one of them recalled, 'Mr D. *never* omitted anything in his power to do for old friends'. His oldest surviving friendships were with Thomas Mitton, his fellow-clerk in a solicitor's office, and Thomas Beard, a fellow-journalist. Mitton became a solicitor, and acted for Dickens for many years. (Frederic Ouvry, his later solicitor, was another close associate.) Beard stayed in journalism, was best man at Dickens's wedding, and always remained a fond friend, while his brother Francis became Dickens's physician. Another close early friend was Henry Kolle, who married MARIA BEADNELL'S sister.

The success of his first books launched Dickens into a wider world, at first literary and artistic but soon more generally social. His first well-known friend was the novelist and dandy William Harrison AINSWORTH, a frequent companion for a few years; Ainsworth's brilliant flare soon subsided and he sank into obscurity, a cautionary tale for Dickens, long insecure about his ongoing prosperity. He began to make friends in the artistic fraternity, initially with his ILLUS-TRATORS: CRUIKSHANK, a boon companion though increasingly cantankerous, BROWNE, CATTERMOLE, STANFIELD, and MACLISE (his 'Dear Mac', and he rarely abandoned surname formality, 'Kittenmoles'—or 'George'—and 'Stanny' being others so honoured). Soon he was familiar with most mainstream artists of the day—more artists indeed, probably, than authors—Wilkie, Leslie, Frith, LEECH, Frank

and Marcus STONE, the LANDSEERS, and Augustus Egg (1816–63). John FORSTER met him in the winter of 1836–7, and his centrality as closest friend and adviser and early-designated biographer needs no elaboration. Forster in 1837 introduced him to the leading actor MACREADY, 'a friend than whom he had none dearer' (Georgina HOGARTH attested): 'I love him dearly', meeting him almost daily and corresponding very frequently whenever out of London (1 September 1843). Macready's politics chimed with his, so his letters are expansive about this.

Macready had, however, to forgive Dickens's ungentlemanly boisterousness: 'Rather a noisy and vigorous day—not so *comme il faut* as I could have wished', 'a very merry—I suppose I must say *jolly* day—rather more tumultuous than I quite like' (diaries, 25 August 1840, 1 April 1846). Thackeray ran into the Dickens family on holiday, 'all looking abominably coarse vulgar and happy' (24 July 1849). Similarly, in Boston in 1842 'a considerable touch of rowdyism' in his manner was noted, a personality not 'altogether pleasing to [its] very refined and cultivated men and women'. Nevertheless, 'People *eat* him here!' reported W. W. Story: 'never was there such a revolution; LaFayette was nothing to it', and R. H. Dana, Sr., initially unattracted, soon remarked 'how dead the faces near him seemed'. Though ungenteel in origins and incompletely gentlemanly, he was attractive and sufficiently presentable to enter the 'highest' society. The well-connected Sir Mountstewart Grant Duff found him 'singularly unprepossessing' and unattractive at first sight 'but, when you became friendly with him, delightfully attractive . . . He talked . . . about Gore House and Count D'Orsay . . . and of Holland House.' As a young man he had thought it 'the thing to do' to attend Lady Blessington's Gore House receptions, he later recalled, and indeed he liked her and her dashing consort D'Orsay and the grander hostess Lady Holland (who had ascertained that he was 'presentable' before inviting him). These incursions into the fashionable houses soon ended, for 'what is called society . . . did not suit him, and he set no store by it', and he hated being lionized (Forster).

Nathaniel HAWTHORNE in 1856 heard murmurings that, 'though plebeian, [he] aspires to aristocratic society', but more often he was praised for his independence. CARLYLE disapproved of the admirers who surrounded him and 'did him no good' (Forster, JERROLD, Maclise), but at least he was 'seldom seen in fashionable drawing-rooms', and the authoress Eliza Lynn Linton contrasted him with Thackeray, who loved 'good society' whereas Dickens had few aristocratic friends. He had some, however; no inverse snobbery inhibited him from that, and in a speech (10 April 1869) he replied sharply to a suggestion that he was anti-aristocratic. He rather enjoyed proclaiming such friendships, indeed. (Why else dedicate *Dombey*, 'with great esteem', to the Marchioness of Normanby, a new-found and never very special friend?) The preceding novel was dedicated to the heiress Angela Burdett COUTTS (a baroness after his death), and its successor to the WATSONS of Rockingham Castle; he was very fond of them and their kinswoman the honourable Mary Boyle ('My dearest Meery'). Guest-lists of Dickens's dinners and receptions regularly contain a fair sprinkling of aristocratic names—indeed, a good spread of the Establishment in general—and to the end he was popular with great hostesses such as Lady Molesworth, to whom he was 'Ever affectionately Yours'. To the Duke of Devonshire, admittedly, he was rather obsequious: a Victorian quarter-million-pound income bought some deference.

Mostly, however, he mingled with his own kind: writers, publishers, and journalists, including the editor of *The* TIMES, Delane, and its illustrious correspondent W. H. Russell, and the *PUNCH* group (notably LEMON, Leech, and Jerrold), and theatre people (he knew most of the leading dramatists and performers). Few can be specified here. J. W. T. LEY in the 77 chapters of his useful survey *The Dickens Circle* (1918) examines 300 friendships, overlooking some significant ones, knowledgeable though he was. Another useful gazetteer is Anne Lohrli's list of the contents of *Household Words* (1973), identifying some 300 contributors, with many of whom he was acquainted or friendly. He was specially close to his assistant editor W. H. WILLS, as later to his readings managers Arthur SMITH and George DOLBY. Early in his career he was cordially welcomed by many leaders of the previous literary generation: Carlyle (always an important friend), ROGERS, JEFFREY,

HOOD, PROCTER, Leigh HUNT, MARRYAT, Sydney SMITH, and LANDOR (affectionately remembered in an obituary). To several he dedicated books or sons (see DEDICATIONS). One son was named after TENNYSON, whose poems and whose company he enjoyed, though Tennyson declined his invitation to join the family in Switzerland, fearing that his impatience with Dickens's SENTIMENTALITY would ruin their friendship. Later he saw BROWNING often, but seems not to have known Arnold and he only once met WORDSWORTH. Thackeray he knew before *Vanity Fair* made them rivals, but their relationship was always edgy. Other novelists he knew and liked included BULWER-LYTTON (a close friend from their GUILD OF LITERATURE AND ART days onwards), Mrs GASKELL, LEVER, READE, and Wilkie COLLINS, a boon companion and close colleague in later years. For George ELIOT's consort G. H. LEWES he had 'an old and fond regard' (Forster), and she derived 'great pleasure' from his visits: 'he is a man one can thoroughly enjoy talking to—there is a strain of real seriousness along with his keenness and humour' (letter, 11 November 1859).

'He knew us all', wrote the French novelist Paul Féval in an obituary, leaving it unclear whether he meant reading or personal acquaintance. Certainly in the 1840s he met Dumas, Hugo, Sue, Gautier, Lamartine, and others, and he was friendly too with Régnier, FECHTER, and other French actors. In America in 1842 he had much warmed to the Boston literati, and then and later formed many American friendships—with Longfellow, EMERSON, IRVING, Holmes, Lowell, Norton, and above all with Cornelius Felton, Professor of Greek and later President of Harvard, and the publisher J. T. FIELDS and his wife Annie (among his fondest friends). His sojourn on the Continent in the 1840s led to some enduring friendships, not literary or artistic, notably with the Watsons already mentioned, the de la Rues of Genoa, and the de Cerjats of Lausanne (both wives being English). His letters to de Cerjat are particularly informative.

Though scathing about lawyers, he had many legal friends. Closest was Thomas Noon TALFOURD, to whom *Pickwick* was dedicated, dramatist as well as MP, barrister, and judge, whom he affectionately obituarized in 1854.

Others included Lord Chief Justice Denman ('Denman delights me') and various advocates and Metropolitan magistrates. At one of his theatrical performances the audience included 'three fourths of the judges I know'—another Lord Chief Justice, the Lord Chief Baron, two others, with the Chief Justice of the Common Pleas attending another night (to Angela Burdett Coutts, 9 December 1856). His interest in PRISONS led to close friendships with leading prison governors Chesterton and Tracey and contact with reformists such as M. D. Hill, Recorder of Birmingham. Similarly, his philanthropic concerns led to his socializing with Lord Shaftesbury, the great EVANGELICAL akin to him in concerns but alien in temperament and convictions. His medical friends included the enterprising but eccentric Dr John Elliotson, to whom he turned for information on spontaneous combustion in connection with the death of Krook in *Bleak House* (an unwise choice).

In his final months, he breakfasted with Gladstone and dined agreeably with DISRAELI (besides calling upon the Queen), but the only prominent politician he knew well was Lord John RUSSELL, twice Prime Minister: 'there is no man in England whom I more respect in his public capacity, whom I love more in his private capacity' (speech, 10 April 1869). Several other friends were or had been MPs or were active in the Lords, but politicians were not his familiars. Nor were bishops, scholars, or scientists. Felton was 'heartiest of Greek professors', but the heartiness weighed heavier than the scholarship; professors were more to Tennyson's and Eliot's taste. His friend Babbage, inventor of the calculator, was a professor of mathematics who never lectured. The only notable scientist he knew was Sir Richard Owen, the opponent of Darwin. His circle included the great engineer Brunel. J. S. MILL met him in 1837 and was reminded of Carlyle's depiction of Camille Desmoulins, with 'his face of dingy blackguardism irradiated with genius'. Dickens thereafter had little or no contact with philosophers.

Despite this shortage of politicians, scientists, and philosophers, Dickens's wide circle makes an impressive list, containing many talented, prominent, and excellent people. But there was justice in Forster's judgement about his aversion to 'society', the pains he took to keep out of the houses of the great,

'not always wisely, it may be admitted', well-fitted though he was 'to adorn any circle', for he was certainly a gentleman (Forster's criterion here was less exacting than some others'), but 'if any one should assert his occasional preference for what was even beneath his level over that which was above it, this would be difficult of disproof'. That ponderously worded animadversion applied less socially, perhaps, than in terms of the weight and worth of his companions. In later years, when some older friends were dead or estranged or less accessible, Forster (who was himself now married, less available, and pricklier) was manifestly vexed by his resorting to such lightweights as Percy FITZGERALD and the dubious Edmund YATES, maybe because they would not be recalcitrant to what Yates called his *sic volo sic jubeo* principle ('my will is my command'), less apparent in his more equal friendships. And Wilkie Collins was arguably a declension from Forster as chosen companion. More endearingly, Dickens maintained friendships with older friends who seem worthy but dull, such as the music critic H. F. CHORLEY, a constant guest at Gad's Hill, and the eccentric cleric C. H. Townshend to whom he dedicated *Great Expectations*, even giving him the manuscript. Maybe their being so chosen should be explained by Forster's comment: 'No swifter or surer perception than Dickens's for what was solid and beautiful in character; he rated it higher than intellectual effort'—which may be counted as a sound and commendable instinct (Forster 6.6). His special liking for the journalist Charles KENT, who worshipped him, is more understandable. Sundry friends who were important to Dickens but fall outside most categories have gone unmentioned here, nor is this the place to explore Ellen TERNAN's place in his circle, or that of, say, 'our prononcée friend', 'My dear F.' (Mrs Frances Elliot, unhappy wife of the Dean of Bristol). Lucky, anyway, the man who was so amply friended. (See also DICKENS: PRIVATE LIFE; DICKENS: PUBLIC LIFE.)                    PC

Ley, J. W. T., *The Dickens Circle: A Narrative of the Novelist's Friends* (1918).
Collins (1981).

**Dickens Fellowship, the.** Organization of Dickens enthusiasts founded in London in 1902, with B. W. MATZ as the prime moving force. Its stated objects were to 'knit together in a common bond of friendship lovers of the great master of humour and pathos, Charles Dickens', to spread the love of humanity ('the keynote of all his work'), to campaign against those 'social evils' that most concerned Dickens, and 'to assist in the preservation and purchase of buildings and objects associated with his name or mentioned in his works'. Autonomous branches were established in many British towns as well as in North America and Australasia (today, 1997, there are 46 such branches as well as others in Boulogne, Tokyo, and Haarlem). Council, on which all branches are represented, was established as the Fellowship's governing body, its decisions being subject to confirmation by Conference, which meets annually. In 1905 the Fellowship began publishing its own journal, the DICK-ENSIAN, and in 1925 purchased Dickens's former home, 48 Doughty Street, and established the Dickens House Trust to run it as a museum and library (see HOMES OF DICK-ENS). The DICKENS HOUSE MUSEUM functions also as the Fellowship's headquarters. Although changing social circumstances have meant that the Fellowship's social and charitable work is less high-profile than it was during the first decades of its existence, many branches are still active in local charities and Council regularly makes donations to good causes. The preservation-society aspect of the Fellowship is still very strong; it has, for example, been much involved in recent conservation and renovation work at Dickens's last home, Gad's Hill Place. Fellowship Headquarters in London runs a full annual programme of lectures, conducted walks, and other events such as the Birthday Dinner on 7 February and the wreath-laying ceremony in Westminster Abbey on 9 June.          MS

**Dickens House Museum** (now the **Charles Dickens Museum**). Built in 1801, 48 Doughty Street is a terraced house, in the former London parish of Holborn, to the south of Mecklenburgh Square. In the 1830s it was a private road, with porters in mulberry-coloured uniforms and gold-laced hats on duty at gates at each end, desirable in view of its proximity to busy Gray's Inn Lane (now Gray's Inn Road). It was a good, but not grand address. Many houses in the street were occupied by members of the professional classes, some by successful tradesmen. Comic novel-

ist R. S. SURTEES quarters his sporting Cockney grocer, Jorrocks, in Doughty Street (*Jorrocks's Jaunts and Jollities*, 1838). Dickens was pleased with the house, however, and probably had it in mind when, in 1863, he spoke of 'a house which then appeared to me to be a frightfully first-class Family Mansion' ('Some Recollections of Mortality', *UT*). He rented it from the end of March or beginning of April 1837 to December 1839 (see HOMES OF DICK-ENS). He moved to Doughty Street with his wife Catherine, his brother Frederick, and his first-born child, Charles. His daughters, Mary and Kate, were born in the house. Catherine's sister, Mary HOGARTH, was a frequent guest, and it was at Doughty Street that she died.

Here Dickens completed *Pickwick Papers* and *Oliver Twist*. Here he wrote SKETCHES OF YOUNG GENTLEMEN, *Nicholas Nickleby*, the dramatic version of The LAMPLIGHTER, and various pieces for BENTLEY'S MISCELLANY, including The MUDFOG PAPERS. He also edited The MEMOIRS OF JOSEPH GRIMALDI here, and began *Barnaby Rudge*.

In 1923, 48 Doughty Street was threatened with demolition. It was saved by the DICKENS FELLOWSHIP, and in 1925 opened as the Dickens House Museum, under the direction of an independent trust established by the Fellowship. The Museum now houses major COLLECTIONS of books, manuscripts, letters, pictures, furniture, photographs, and personal possessions of Dickens. It is open to the public, and provides facilities for researchers.
                                                      DP

**Dickensian, The.** Journal of the DICKENS FELLOWSHIP, founded in 1902, and published monthly from 1905 until 1919 when it became a quarterly; since 1955 published three times a year. The magazine's projector, F. G. KITTON, died before preparations for the first number were complete and the first editor was B. W. MATZ. The journal would, he announced, be 'devoted to the vast subject of Dickens generally . . . original articles on the multifarious phases of Dickens's illustrations, reprints . . . of contemporary reviews of his works . . . indeed, anything and everything likely to interest the student and lover of England's great novelist'. Under him and his successors the *Dickensian* has become a great storehouse of (often very fully illustrated) biographical, critical, topographical, and bibliographical studies of Dickens; it also features reviews of all new books about him and new DRAMATIZATIONS and FILMS of his works, and it serves as a record of the activities of the worldwide Dickens Fellowship. (A continuing minor preoccupation of *Dickensian* contributors, attempts to solve the *Drood* mystery, manifested itself early in the magazine's history—see *MYSTERY OF EDWIN DROOD*, SOLUTIONS TO.) During the 1930s and 1940s, under Matz's successors Walter DEXTER and Leslie Staples, scores of Dickens LETTERS appeared for the first time in the *Dickensian*'s pages, as did T. W. Hill's excellent pioneering annotations to the novels. From the late 1940s onwards distinguished academic Dickens scholars began regularly to contribute articles and reviews, their work appearing alongside all the traditional amateur appreciations and investigations and reports of Fellowship activities. The *Dickensian* truly became, in K. J. Fielding's phrase, 'a meeting-place for all admirers' of Dickens, and very much remains so today as it approaches its centenary.          MS

**Dickens Quarterly** (1984–  ), formerly *Dickens Studies Newsletter* (1970–83). The journal began as a quarterly newsletter, ancillary to DICKENS STUDIES ANNUAL and designed to keep members of the Dickens Society of America (founded 1970) current with projects, exhibitions, and publications related to Dickens. In 1971 the Society assumed responsibility for the publication. Under successive editors, emphasis shifted to the publication of articles and notes, reducing 'news' to a perfunctory status. An extensive quarterly bibliography of Dickens studies ('The Dickens Checklist') and full-length reviews (both original features), together with articles and notes, continue to define the journal.          DHP

**Dickens Studies** (1965–9), an American 'scholarly periodical dedicated to serving a growing international community of Dickens students'. Following the death of its founder, Noel C. Peyrouton, the journal moved to Southern Illinois and resumed publication under a different format and title, as DICKENS STUDIES ANNUAL.          DHP

**Dickens Studies Annual** (1970–  ), a hardbound publication and successor, in expanded format, to DICKENS STUDIES. The first

seven volumes were edited by Robert B. Partlow, Jr. New editors broadened the volume's scope to include other Victorian novelists, hence the current title, *Dickens Studies Annual: Essays on Victorian Fiction.*          DHP

**diet, food, and nutrition.** See HEALTH; DOMESTICITY.

**Disraeli, Benjamin** (1804–81), statesman and novelist. Disraeli and Dickens shared a profound dislike of scientific rationalism as a means of social reform. But whereas Dickens's writings impelled his readers to consider radical social solutions, Disraeli hoped to strengthen society's institutions by effecting their political and ethical reform. Dickens professed to trust the People, and lauded their virtues. Disraeli's social philosophy reflected more what Dickens detested: narrow UTILITARIANISM stifling imaginative, creative social thinking.

Disraeli stated in 1857: 'I have never read anything of Dickens, except an extract in a newspaper' (Bradford 1982, p. 246). This is probably true: despite Disraeli's own considerable literary gifts he read little contemporary fiction. His novels were essentially political, working out his 'Young England' Toryism in *Coningsby* (1844), *Sybil* (1845), and *Tancred* (1847). Perhaps he found Dickens's exuberant style over-effusive, for in his novel *Endymion* (1880), Dickens is described by 'St. Barbe' [Thackeray] as 'that fellow Gushy', who would write descriptions 'like a penny-a-liner drunk with ginger beer' (*Endymion* 24).

Disraeli's first love was politics, where his greatest talents lay. He was Conservative Prime Minister in 1868 and 1874–80. In 1876 he was created Earl of Beaconsfield.          NR

Blake, R., *Disraeli* (1966).
Bradford, S., *Disraeli* (1982).

**dissent, religious.** 'Dissent' in the Victorian context refers to Christians who do not accept the doctrines of the CHURCH OF ENGLAND as embodied in the Thirty-Nine 'Articles of Religion' of the BOOK OF COMMON PRAYER—thus Dickens was himself, at least briefly and technically, a dissenter when he took regular sittings in UNITARIAN chapels in the 1840s; but dissenters in his writings typically appear as objects of satire, some of it quite fierce.

The terms 'dissenter' and 'nonconformist' are effectively synonymous (the former refers to dissent from doctrine while the latter refers to refusal to conform in matters of ritual) and were first used in the 17th century, around the time of the Civil Wars and Restoration.

The chief dissenting sects in Dickens's day were, in addition to the Unitarians, the Baptists, Congregationalists, Presbyterians, and largest of all, the Methodists, though there were numerous other smaller sects, and many still being invented during his lifetime. The consequences of being a dissenter, like those of being a ROMAN CATHOLIC or a JEW, could be considerably damaging. Until just after the mid-century, students at Cambridge were required formally to subscribe to the Thirty-Nine Articles in order to take degrees, and at Oxford subscription was required upon entering. The restrictions against dissenters' serving in Parliament had only recently been lifted when Dickens began his career, and dissenters were, along with everyone else, obliged to pay church rates—taxes that in part supported the Established Church—until just two years before Dickens's death.

The kind of RELIGION practised by most dissenters tended to be EVANGELICAL, and there was a tremendous overlap between these two large groups—so influential in imparting to the age its tone of moral earnestness—and especially among those whose beliefs derived from John Wesley's Methodist revival in the 18th century. But whereas many evangelicals were able to accommodate their beliefs to those of the Church of England, dissenters by definition were not, and most often the break was occasioned by differences about church government. Congregationalists and Presbyterians, of course, were distinguished precisely by their rejection of the episcopal structure, derived from that of Roman Catholicism and the medieval English Church, in which there is a clear hierarchy of bishops and priests over the laity. Congregationalists asserted the right of the church membership to govern itself, while Presbyterians even more fundamentally erased the distinction between laity and clergy and asserted the fundamental equality of rights among all members. They recognized but a single church office, that of presbyter, or elected ruling elder. Methodists had varying views of church polity—hence the fact that many remained in the Established Church after Wesley's death, though many others left.

The relatively democratic structure of most dissenting churches, the civil disabilities under which dissenters long suffered, and the great success of Methodist preaching among the working classes are among the reasons why dissent was particularly associated with the humbler orders (see CLASS). The term 'dissenter', indeed, most often intimated a person of the lower-middle or working class, even though plenty of technical dissenters could be found among the higher classes; the Unitarians, for example, drew heavily upon the professions for their membership. However good-humoured, there is certainly a trace of class condescension (as well as gender condescension) in Dickens's treatment of such dissenters as the second Mrs Tony Weller in *The Pickwick Papers*, Kit Nubbles's mother in *The Old Curiosity Shop*, or Jerry Cruncher's wife in *A Tale of Two Cities*, whose ignorance and superstitiousness render them easy prey to dissenting enthusiasms.

Sincere dissent of this order Dickens found vulgar; the dissenting minister, however, he typically found a great hypocrite. Although brought up chiefly in the Church of England, as a child in Chatham he was occasionally subjected to sermons in a Baptist chapel where he was 'steamed like a potato in the unventilated breath of Boanerges Boiler . . . until I have regarded that reverend person in the light of a most dismal and oppressive Charade' ('City of London Churches', *The UNCOMMERCIAL TRAVELLER*). Similar types can be found in Mrs Weller's mentor the Revd Stiggins, who preached abstinence while drunk, or the Revd Melchisedech Howler in *Dombey and Son* (another drinker), or—Dickens's greatest creation in this line—the Revd Mr Chadband in *Bleak House*, who positively gorges himself while blandly noting that it is our sinful material nature that requires us to take 'refreshment' (*BH* 19: see DRINK AND TEMPERANCE). It is surely significant that, while Dickens can easily imagine sincere if misguided religious enthusiasm on the part of females, a sincere religious enthusiasm on the part of males apparently was to him unimaginable (see SEXUALITY AND GENDER). At least, no such type appears prominently in his fiction.

That Dickens could himself embrace Unitarianism, even if briefly, shows that dissent as such held no dread for him. He was of such liberal, Broad Church views as to be entirely uninterested in doctrinal questions, and he was moreover suspicious of all doctrinal dispute as diverting attention away from the central active and practical lessons of Scripture (all having to do with love, toleration, and bringing comfort to others) and into fruitless speculation. For similar reasons, he heartily disliked church politics and any public display of piety. Since most forms of dissent were intensely interested in doctrine, in church politics, and in announcing their doctrines and politics to the world, it is safe to say that even though Dickens had no dislike for dissent in theory, he was certainly intensely hostile to it in its more evangelical manifestations. No doubt he would have found this *Companion*'s interest in such headings as 'dissent, religious' or 'evangelical religion' or the 'Church of England' quite beside the real point, which was to distinguish, as he says in the Preface to the Cheap Edition of *The Pickwick Papers* (1847), 'between religion and the cant of religion, piety and the pretence of piety, a humble reverence for the great truths of scripture and an audacious and offensive obtrusion of its letter and not its spirit in the commonest dissensions and meanest affairs of life'. RN

Pope (1978).
Walder (1981).

**Dolby, George** (d. 1900), Dickens's readings manager, 1866–70. In 1866, his PUBLIC READINGS career having faltered because he could find no suitable manager, Dickens invited the impresario firm CHAPPELL to become his agents. They appointed Dolby as manager. 'He had known me, and my reputation as a manager, for some years', Dolby recalled. Probably they met through Dickens's friendship with Dolby's sister, a famous singer; certainly Dickens had sought his advice about touring when a previous manager was ill. Dolby rapidly established himself as a wholly reliable, efficient, and devoted assistant, and a close friendship followed, Dolby receiving 'many tokens of his love and affection'. Between tours, and even after Dickens's retirement from the platform, Dolby lunched with him weekly. He and his wife visited Gad's Hill

and Dickens visited them at Ross on Wye, and Dolby was among the intimates who immediately went to Gad's Hill when Dickens's death was announced. In 1885 he published *Charles Dickens as I Knew Him: the Story of the Readings Tours in Great Britain and America (1866–1870)*, described by Mamie Dickens as 'the best and truest picture of my father that has yet been written. They were on the most intimate and affectionate terms.' They were indeed thrown together twenty-four hours a day in exacting conditions for long periods, and Dolby offers a uniquely unbuttoned account of 'my great hero—my "chief" ', lively with anecdote, with Dickens's moods varying from the ebullient, playful, and high-spirited to the sick, dejected, and exhausted. In these years Dickens's health was precarious, and he found Dolby 'as tender as a woman and as watchful as a doctor' (7 April 1868). Dolby praised Dickens's 'patience and good temper' even in discomfort and adversity, 'always more cheerful and good humoured than any public man with whom I have been associated', 'the best and dearest friend man ever had'. His determination to cheer and amuse Dickens could even take such extravagant forms as his twelve-mile pedestrian contest against a local 'champion', 'the Boston Bantam'; Dickens, duly diverted, elaborately documented this 'Great International Walking Match'.

Having managed readings tours in 1866 and 1867, Dolby was appointed to manage the American tour (November 1867–April 1868), Dickens having decided not to use an American agent. Dolby spied out the land, reported favourably, and preceded Dickens to AMERICA to finalize arrangements. Dickens's health gave great anxiety during this tour, and Dolby was solicitous in succouring and cheering him and easing his way. Dickens then undertook a farewell tour, winter 1868–9, further undermining his health by the violent and exhausting *Sikes and Nancy* reading, his addiction to which caused their only quarrel, when Dolby experienced 'the only time I ever heard him address angry words to any one' after his attempt to reduce the frequency of this item.

Dickens's death 'closed the brightest chapter of my life.' Dolby, notoriously extravagant, fell on evil days and died utterly destitute in Fulham Infirmary. He had owed Dickens money in 1870, and one of Dickens's friends, the actor Charles FECHTER, called him 'a traitor' who had overcharged Dickens for his services (but Mamie's praise suggests that the family rejected this accusation). Another friend, Percy FITZGERALD, described Dolby as 'wonderfully thick-skinned', 'not over-refined, but loud and a little noisy. He had the art, however, of now and then making his chief laugh'—an unkind underestimate of his services. He was a big man, rough, tough, forceful, somewhat vulgar ('a gladsome gorilla', said Mark Twain), but evidently his personality did not grate on Dickens's sensibility.

PC

**Dombey and Son** Dickens's seventh novel, begun while he was living in SWITZERLAND and PARIS. Published in 1846–8 by BRADBURY AND EVANS in twenty monthly parts, it is generally considered the first novel of his artistic maturity.

### Inception and Composition
The first definite word of *Dombey and Son* appears in a letter to FORSTER, nine days after the launch of the DAILY NEWS: 'I have been revolving plans in my mind this morning for quitting the paper and going abroad again to write a new book in shilling numbers' (30 January 1846). On 9 February he resigned his editorship and the next month wrote to the Countess of Blessington of 'vague thoughts of a new book' which had him 'wandering about at night in the strangest places, according to my usual propensity at such a time—seeking rest, and finding none' (2 March 1846).

On 31 May he left London with his family for Lausanne and almost at once announced, 'BEGAN DOMBEY!' (to Forster, 28 June 1846). Writing went slowly, and he confessed to missing the inspiration of streets to walk in, but he was certain he had a 'great surprise' in store, 'a new and peculiar sort of interest, involving the necessity of a little bit of delicate treatment' (to Forster, 5 July 1846). Confident that the 'leading idea' of the story was 'very strong' (?12 July 1846), he insisted that the title remain secret (18 July 1846), and on 25–6 July he sent the first number to Forster along with a detailed outline of the 'stock of the soup' which shows that the death of Paul, rejection of Florence, bankruptcy of Dombey, and loving constancy of Florence were planned from the start.

This is the first of Dickens's novels for which a complete set of working notes survives, planning every number in detail. Dickens was two full months ahead of the publisher at the outset (No. 1 was finished 23 July and published 30 September) but his lead was gradually eroded until he was barely a week ahead by the end. The notes show that Paul was 'born, to die'; that his illness was to be 'only expressed in the child's own feelings'; and that the 'thunderbolt' chapter was moved from the end of No. 15 'to leave a pleasanter impression on the reader'. They also indicate that Dickens changed his mind about three key ingredients: he postponed Paul's death from No. 4 to No. 5; he saved Walter, who had been intended to go to the bad; and he spared Edith from adultery and death, in response to a letter from Lord JEFFREY, who 'won't believe (positively refuses) that Edith is Carker's mistress' (to Forster, 21 December 1847).

Dickens overwrote each of the first four numbers and had to make cuts at proof stage. The amount of cutting in the first number, which eliminated much foreshadowing and emphasis on the leading idea is, in Alan Horsman's view, 'unfortunate' (Introduction to Clarendon Edition, p. xvi). He then underwrote No. 6 and had to race back to London in order to rectify matters (17 February 1847). Otherwise, letters indicate that Dickens wrote carefully, sometimes with difficulty, but always with confidence in the quality of his work. From the outset he had his mind on 'some rollicking facetiousness, to say nothing of pathos' (?12 July 1846), and after 'slaughtering a young and innocent victim'—as he described the death of Paul—he 'had no hope of getting sleep afterwards' and walked the streets of Paris all night long (to Charles Sheridan, 7 January 1847; to Miss Coutts, 18 January 1847).

Dickens read the first two numbers to friends before the work was published, and it was on the occasion of the second reading that he first broached with Forster the idea which was to consume his energies for the last twelve years of his life. 'I was thinking the other day that in these days of lecturings and readings, a great deal of money might possibly be made (if it were not infra dig) by one's having Readings of one's own books. It would be an *odd* thing. I think it would take immensely. What do you say?' (11 October 1846).

This was the germ of the PUBLIC READINGS, and it can be no coincidence that the first novel from which he extracted a story for performance was *Dombey.*

Several factors impinged on the writing. First, he was writing a version of the New Testament for his children at the time, which may account for the new religious tone in his work which critics have scented in *Dombey* (see LIFE OF OUR LORD). Second, in contrast to earlier practice, he found it nearly impossible to concentrate on two books at once. He nearly abandoned the Christmas book for 1846, *The* BATTLE OF LIFE (by general consent his least successful piece of fiction), and in 1847 did postpone writing *The* HAUNTED MAN until *Dombey* was finished. These difficulties indicate the new level of concentration he was expending on *Dombey.* Third, he was involved in trying to set up a model Ragged School, visiting several schools in spring of 1846 and reporting his findings to Angela Burdett COUTTS, James Kay-Shuttleworth, and Lord John RUSSELL (see CHARITY). EDUCATION is a recurring subject throughout Dickens's career, and Doctor Blimber's Academy in *Dombey* is one of his most incisive portrayals of a school. Fourth, he was working with Miss Coutts to establish a home for fallen women, from May 1846 until 1858; URANIA COTTAGE opened in November 1847. The portrait of Alice Marwood and the parallels between her and Edith, draw on this concern.

Above all, *Dombey* is inextricably tied to his own life, as no previous novel had been. 'I hope you will like Mrs Pipchin's establishment', he told Forster. 'It is from the life, and I was there' (4 November 1846). Forster identifies the original of Mrs Pipchin as Mrs Elizabeth Roylance, with whom Dickens lodged when his parents were incarcerated in the Marshalsea prison, and 'Mrs Roylance' is named in Dickens's notes for *Dombey.* As Forster explains, this recollection relates to Dickens's childhood sufferings which he committed to the autobiographical fragment written around this time (6.2; see DIARIES). What Valerie Purton describes as Dickens's 'intense identification' with the book's central characters, owes much to this autobiographical matrix, most particularly the presentation of scenes from a child's perspective (Introduction to Everyman Edition, 1997, p. xxvi). *Dombey* leads straight to Dickens's

next novel, the more overtly autobiographical *Copperfield.*

Dickens finished writing the novel in Brighton on 24 March 1848, and the next day remembered, at the last moment, to add the dog Diogenes to the final rounding up of characters. He held a celebratory dinner on 11 April. 'I have a strong belief', he later told Forster, 'that, if any of my books are read years hence, *Dombey* will be remembered as among the best of them' (?22 September 1849). (See also COMPOSITION, DICKENS'S METHODS.)

**Contracts, Text, and Publication History**

Dickens signed several agreements with Bradbury and Evans on 1 June 1844 regarding future publications. Forster states that 'no obligations were imposed as to what works should be written, if any, or the form of them' (4.2; see Pilgrim 4.691). There was no separate contract for *Dombey.* The publishers first advertised the novel on 18 April 1846. Although Dickens was dissatisfied and considered moving back to CHAPMAN AND HALL (to Forster, 25 June 1846), he remained with Bradbury and Evans until the breach of 1858. The novel was published as *Dealings with the Firm of Dombey and Son: Wholesale, Retail and for Exportation,* in twenty monthly parts (as nineteen) from 1 October 1846 to 1 April 1848 and as one volume on 12 April 1848. It was dedicated to the Marchioness of Normanby, with a brief Preface dated 24 March 1848.

The complete working notes, manuscript, and corrected proofs were all given to Forster and are now held in the VICTORIA AND ALBERT MUSEUM. A detailed account of the textual history and the 'unusual care' Dickens took is given in the Clarendon Introduction. Kathleen Tillotson (1954) describes *Dombey* as the earliest example in Dickens of 'responsible and successful planning'. He undertook no systematic revision for the Cheap (1858), Library (1859), and Charles Dickens (1867) EDITIONS. He added a new Preface in 1858, revised slightly for later editions, in which he responded to criticism of Mr Dombey's character by insisting on its consistency. The definitive Clarendon Edition, edited by Alan Horsman (1974), is based on the 1848 edition.

**Illustrations**

*Dombey* was illustrated by Dickens's principal ILLUSTRATOR, Hablot BROWNE, under his own name. Browne supplied 38 plates, the wrapper design, frontispiece, and vignette title-page. The cover allegorically depicts the course of Dombey's fortunes, and Dickens feared 'perhaps with a little too much in it'—as if it might give away some of the plot (to Forster, ?6 September 1846). Although Forster insisted that Mr Dombey had no particular original, Dickens did have an individual in mind for his protagonist's appearance, and urged Browne to look out 'Sir A—— E—— of D—— 's', which Browne was unable to do, sending various suggestions instead (Forster 5.3 and 6.2). In the vignette and one of the plates, Captain Cuttle's hook appears on the wrong arm. Dickens routinely suggested subjects, but gave Browne some freedom, and was more than once disappointed with the results. After No. 3 the gap between Dickens's completion of copy and publication was too narrow for Browne to base his sketches on text and he had to rely instead on letters sent by Dickens. Browne also drew fourteen etchings of characters, which were published separately from the novel. See Clarendon Edition, pp. 865–71, for details.

**Sources and Context**

Dickens's leading idea, according to Forster, was 'to do with Pride what its predecessor had done with Selfishness' (6.2). It is no coincidence that the play which Dickens chose for AMATEUR THEATRICALS in between the writing of the two novels was Ben JONSON's *Every Man In His Humour*. *Martin Chuzzlewit*, like *Dombey*, depicted central characters dominated by a single trait, or humour. As Horsman notes, both novels had the overthrow of a central character and a final reconciliation between characters as the 'primary structure' from the outset (Clarendon Introduction, p. xv). Both novels have (as earlier novels did not) elaborately recurring patterns of imagery, and Dickens's preliminary but abandoned thought for *Chuzzlewit* had been to introduce the sea as leitmotif (to Forster, 16 September 1842), as he in fact does with 'what the waves were saying' in *Dombey*. Despite the undoubted advance of placing a character divided against himself, and a relationship, at the centre, the single work which most evidently stands behind *Dombey* is *Chuzzlewit*.

A second literary source, which Alexander Welsh has examined, is *King Lear*. 'Most of the important configurations of characters in the novel bear some relation to the play, beginning with the perturbed estrangement of the hero from his own immediate family, which has its source in the failure of male inheritance' (Welsh 1987, p. 88). Where SHAKESPEARE's daughter figure 'redeems nature' (Act IV, scene vi), Welsh argues that in *Dombey* 'only this unchanging female principle makes death and history acceptable' (p. 101). Ever since Julian Moynahan's influential essay (1962), Freudian and feminist critics have seen subversive elements in Dickens's portrayal of Florence, and the parallel with Cordelia offers a stimulating perspective on the mythic female power which triumphs in the novel's conclusion, even as the comparison with Cordelia's father helps define the tragic stature of Dickens's protagonist.

*Dombey* is also a novel acutely attuned to contemporary issues. Hippolyte Taine declared that Dickens's 'princely merchant in his counting house' was a character which 'could only be produced in a country whose commerce embraces the globe, whose merchants are potentates' (*History of English Literature*, 1863–4; translated into English, 1871). Dickens was later to place institutions at the centre of novels (*Bleak House* and *Little Dorrit*) and, as the full title indicates, his original intention was to give the firm a more prominent place but, as Butt and Tillotson (1957) observe, despite its shrinkage in the novel as written, 'the pervasive suggestion remains that a family cannot be run on business lines'.

Early reviewers noted the topicality of the book's educational satire and its treatment of the railway mania of the 1840s, but what 20th-century commentators have stressed most is its response to an era of profound change, with the railroad presented as 'the great symbol of social transformation' (Marcus 1965, p. 306). The building of 4,538 miles of line was authorized by Parliament in 1846, the peak year of the railway boom, and 'it would be difficult to exaggerate the effect of those years on English social life' (House 1941, p. 138; see TRANSPORT). 'Stag' was a slang term of the day for someone speculating for a quick profit in shares, and Dickens's description of Stagg's Gardens emphasizes the cataclysmic impact of the railway: 'The first shock of the railway had, just at that period, rent the whole neighbourhood to its centre' (*DS* 6). Moreover, *Dombey* is the first of Dickens's novels 'in which a pervasive uneasiness about contemporary society takes the place of an intermittent concern with specific social wrongs' (Tillotson 1954, p. 157).

It is important, however, not to overstate the case. Philip Collins (1967) has argued that in *Dombey* 'Dickens is making a traditional moral point about pride and riches, not a specifically nineteenth-century one about an economic system'. The elopement of Edith with Carker, their confrontation in Dijon, and Carker's death in the maw of 'the fiery devil' of a train functions less as social realism than as a classic instance of Dickens's achievement in a MELODRAMATIC idiom. Florence too, is less a portrait of a young woman than a heroine from the 18th-century SENTIMENTAL tradition or FAIRY TALE, displaced from realism so that Dickens may explore taboos and fantasies. In nothing is *Dombey* more characteristically Dickensian than in its complex orchestration of a variety of literary modes.

### Plot, Character, and Theme

The novel begins with the birth of Paul and the death of his mother. Mr Dombey, who views his son exclusively as a new business partner, is forced to hire a wet-nurse, Polly Toodle. He neglects his daughter Florence, to whom Paul lovingly turns. Paul goes to Mrs Pipchin's school, then to Dr Blimber's Academy but, always fragile, dies.

Florence is kidnapped by Good Mrs Brown and rescued by young Walter Gay, nephew of the nautical instrument-maker Sol Gills. Mr Dombey appoints Walter to a post in the West Indies, and the ship on which he sails is lost. Mrs Brown's daughter, Alice Marwood, has been seduced and abandoned by Dombey's manager, Carker.

Dombey travels by train with the blustering Major Joey Bagstock to Leamington, where he meets the proud widow Edith Granger. She is humiliated at being sold in marriage by her mother, Mrs Skewton. Edith grows fond of Florence and quarrels with Dombey, who uses Carker to 'humble' her. When she elopes, apparently with Carker, Dombey strikes Florence, who flees to the nautical shop, now occupied solely by the retired seaman Captain Cuttle.

Edith meets Carker in Dijon and defies him. Pursued by Dombey, Carker is killed by a train. The Dombey firm collapses. Florence marries Walter and rescues her father from suicide. Her maid Susan Nipper marries Paul's old schoolmate, the good-hearted but simple Mr Toots.

In *Dombey* Dickens explores relations between business and private life, parent and child, male and female, wealth and poverty, old and new, and critics have found rich complexity in his treatment of these contrasts.

### Reception

After the disappointing reception of *Chuzzlewit*, *Dombey* was a triumph. Where the earlier novel had sold only 20,000 copies per month, the first number of *Dombey* quickly sold out its initial print run of 25,000 and was selling 34,000 copies by June 1848—in contrast to sales of 5,000 per month for THACKERAY's *Vanity Fair*, published serially at the same time by Bradbury and Evans (Patten 1970; Patten 1978, pp. 182–9). Moreover, after living in debt to his publishers ever since Chapman and Hall extricated him from his contracts to Richard BENTLEY, Dickens's profits from the first four numbers gave him financial security and, in Forster's words, 'all embarrassments connected with money were brought to a close' (Patten 1978, p. 186; Forster 6.1). Reviews were overwhelmingly favourable, and the response of contemporaries is legendary. Lord Jeffrey read the death of Paul and wrote, 'Oh, my dear, dear Dickens! What a No. 5 you have given us! I have so cried and sobbed over it last night, and again this morning; and felt my heart purified by those tears, and blessed and loved you for making me shed them . . .' (Collins 1971, p. 217). Thackeray burst into the *Punch* office with the same number in his pocket, exclaiming, 'There's no writing against such power as this—one has no chance! Read that chapter describing young Paul's death: it is unsurpassed—it is stupendous' (ibid., p. 219).

Only a single DRAMATIZATION appeared while *Dombey* was still being serialized, and only one other stage version, by John Brougham, enjoyed wide circulation (Bolton 1987, p. 306). Dickens's reading version, *The Story of Little Dombey*, had a mixed reception but remained in his repertoire throughout his professional reading career (Collins 1975, pp. 125–8). The readings 'probably' led Dickens to delete the final sentence of No. 5 ('To think . . .

that Dombey and Son should be a Daughter after all!') in later editions of the novel (Clarendon introduction, p. xxix).

Late-19th-century readers were more resistant to the novel's sentiment and melodramatic elements, but since CHESTERTON, critics have seen new seriousness, power, and structural coherence in Dickens's later art, starting with *Dombey*. Tillotson (1954) focuses on *Dombey* as one of four representative works of the 1840s, and Raymond Williams celebrates it as a great work of popular art, written in an age of uncertainty and distinctively different from more poised later works such as those of George ELIOT or Henry James (Introduction to Penguin Edition, 1970). It is the earliest of Dickens's novels which F. R. LEAVIS was prepared to discuss after he came to acknowledge Dickens's artistic seriousness (Leavis 1970). More recently, critics including Nina Auerbach and Helene Moglen have focused on the book's sexual politics, analysing the polarities between male and female spheres (see CRITICISM: FEMINIST; WOMEN AND WOMEN'S ISSUES). PVWS

Auerbach, Nina, 'Dickens and Dombey: A Daughter After All', *Dickens Studies Annual*, 5 (1976).

Collins, Philip, '*Dombey and Son*—Then and Now', *Dickensian*, 63 (1967).

Moglen, Helene, 'Theorizing Fiction/Fictionalizing Theory: The Case of *Dombey and Son*', *Victorian Studies*, 35 (1992).

Moynahan, Julian, '*Dealings with the Firm of Dombey and Son*: Firmness *versus* Wetness', in Gross and Pearson (1962).

Patten, Robert L., 'The Fight at the Top of the Tree: *Vanity Fair* Versus *Dombey and Son*', *Studies in English Literature*, 10 (1970).

Tillotson, Kathleen, *Novels of the 1840s* (1954).

**domestic fiction** (see also DOMESTICITY; NOVELISTS DURING DICKENS'S LIFETIME; SEXUALITY AND GENDER; WOMEN AND WOMEN'S ISSUES). The rise of domestic fiction was concurrent with the rise of both the novel and the middle CLASSES in England. Reaching its high-water mark in the middle of the 19th century, domestic fiction differed from 18th-century fiction through its articulation of human desires and actions in individualized MORAL terms, firmly establishing the novel as a moral form. Whereas in the 18th century novels tended to represent individual identity in terms of region, sect, or political faction,

19th-century domestic fiction 'unfolded the operations of human desire as if they were independent of political history' (Armstrong 1987, p. 9). In domestic fiction, the title and status of individuals is not so important as their own particular qualities of mind, their own personal characteristics, nuances of behaviour and, crucially, moral attributes. Such a change of emphasis can be related to the rise of individualism which accompanied the middle-class ascendancy in 19th-century Britain. Dickens's novelistic output both contributed to, and was formed by, the developing focus on individual morality as opposed to class or sect-based values in fiction. The reader is invited to judge characters as socially disparate as Mr Jarndyce, Betsy Trotwood, Wemmick, Joe Gargery, and Sissy Jupe for their essential individual 'goodness', as shown in private relationships, rather than for their social affiliations. In his early and middle fiction, it is individual goodness and morality which is prescribed as a remedy for social ills (*Oliver Twist, Nicholas Nickleby, Dombey and Son, A Christmas Carol*). In the later fiction there is a distinct movement away from the moral structure of domestic fiction inasmuch as that individual goodness no longer has the power to overcome social and political malaise (*Bleak House, Little Dorrit*).

In domestic fiction, modern domesticity is established as the only haven from the harsh vicissitudes of an unmerciful economic world. Modern domesticity is based on the so-called 'separate spheres' ideology, which itself derived from Puritan treatises on marriage and household government in the 17th century. John RUSKIN's 'Of Queen's Gardens' (in *Sesame and Lilies*, 1865) is the classic statement of the 'separate spheres' ideology which reached its apogee in the middle of the 19th century. Coventry Patmore, in his popular long sequence of poems, *The Angel in the House* (1854–63), also contributed significantly to the idealization of woman as the focal point of home life. According to Ruskin, the husband's duty was to get goods and money, to deal with many men, to travel and seek a living, and to take a full part in the 'public' world of economic and political life; the wife's duty, by contrast, was to save and garner the money and goods provided by her husband, to keep house, to talk with few, and to oversee and give order to the 'private', domestic sphere. Such a domestic arrangement is frequently idealized—if not always successfully realized—in Dickens's fiction. The Cratchits' domestic oasis (*CC*), the Toodles' similarly reassuring domestic haven (*DS*), and the projected marital life of David and Agnes (*DC*) and of John Harmon and Bella Wilfer (*OMF*), all approximate to the domestic ideal as promoted by domestic fiction.

Another significant characteristic of domestic fiction is its containment and domestication of sexual desire in general and of female desire in particular. Dickens's fiction is celebrated for its domestic set-pieces rather than for its account of sexual love. Sexualized females are either textually contained or erased in his novels. The body of the PROSTITUTE meets a brutal end in *Oliver Twist*; less brutal but no less final is the death of Lady Dedlock, mother to an illegitimate child (*BH*). Female sexual desire is expressed in a distorted way through the figure of Rosa Dartle (*DC*) and suffers a withering disappointment, Rosa playing only a marginal (if memorable) role in the narrative of David's life. Edith Dombey's sexuality has a terribly destructive effect, and she is banished from the re-established domesticity of the novel's close (*DS*). Louisa Gradgrind's sexual desire, repressed by the failure of her private life (*HT*), is sublimated through her obsessive fascination with the domestic fireside, the symbol, in Dickens's fiction, of modern domesticity.

Despite Dickens's undoubted contribution to the rise of domestic fiction in the 19th century, the frequent failure of the domestic ideal in his novels means that his work can by no means be understood in a wholesale way through its generic conventions. The many other novelists who were both influenced by and contributed to the rise of domestic fiction in the 19th century include George ELIOT, Charlotte BRONTË, Elizabeth GASKELL, and Charlotte Yonge. SL

Armstrong, Nancy, *Desire and Domestic Fiction: A Political History of the Novel* (1987).

**domesticity** (see also DOMESTIC FICTION; CHILDHOOD; CLASS; DIET; WOMEN AND WOMEN'S ISSUES). One of the hallmarks of Dickens's fiction is the centrality of the domestic ideal. Cosy, contented, cheerful, and sheltering homes are presented as a social and moral panacea from his early writings onwards. A writer for the MORNING CHRONICLE, reviewing *The* BATTLE OF LIFE on CHRISTMAS Eve 1846, identified Dickens's strengths as 'a writer of home life, a delineator of household gods, a painter of domestic scenes'. The domestic fantasy is epitomized in the Christmas books, where the essential ingredients of the domestic idyll are fully realized. Cleanliness, domestic order, and efficiency; a 'little woman' at the centre of the domestic space as a wifely and maternal paragon; a troop of happy, well-behaved children; a focus on the domestic hearth itself, and on warm, amiable family mealtimes—all these component parts of the domestic dream are to be found, for example, in *A Christmas Carol*. In this, the first of the Christmas books, the Ghost of Christmas Present reveals to the misanthropic and curmudgeonly UTILITARIAN, Ebenezer Scrooge, a vision of the poor-but-honest Cratchit family, whose house the spirit blesses. In the course of settling down to Christmas dinner, the reader, along with Scrooge, is introduced to Mrs Cratchit and her daughters. They are humbly but carefully dressed for the festivities—'brave in ribbons' (Stave 3). The daughters assist with the table-laying whilst a son (touchingly attired in his father's smart-but-too-large shirt) plunges his fork into a saucepan of potatoes in an attempt to help with the cooking. The children are happy, excited, and well-behaved as they dance around the dinner table awaiting their father and Tiny Tim, who, we learn, bravely bears with his invalidity. The weak and ailing younger son of the family reflects that 'he hoped the people saw him in church, because he was a cripple, and it might be pleasant to them to remember upon Christmas Day, who made lame beggars walk, and blind men see' (Stave 3) (see HEALTH, ILLNESS, AND DISABILITY). In Dickens, a well-ordered, loving domestic sphere produces morally upright, emotionally well-balanced individuals; the Cratchits are fine examples.

Food is recurrently used by Dickens, as with the Cratchits, as a gauge of the domestic ideal, the author invariably associating a good, hot cooked meal around a cosy table in amiable company with domestic well-being and security. When the domestic ideal fails to materialize, then mealtimes become a torture, as when Pip is subjected to Christmas Dinner with Mrs Gargery, his unfeeling older sister, and the reproving Uncle Pumblechook (*GE*). The absence of hot food at Paul's christening (*DS*) is likewise an indication of that family's frigid domestic arrangements.

The domestic idyll features throughout Dickens's fiction. The wedding scene in *Pickwick*, where the reader is shown a stable, happy home in the midst of festivities, is another example. Mr and Mrs Toodles (*DS*) have 'a clean parlour full of children', their particular domestic hearth functioning as an oasis of domestic contentment in a novel in which the eponymous family is dysfunctional and ultimately destroyed. Tom Pinch and his sister Ruth (*MC*), have their tiny lodgings transformed by Ruth's cheerful housewifely skills into a warm domestic sanctuary, despite its dampness and the obvious poverty of their surroundings. And the housewifely virtues of Agnes Wickfield, which transform her into a veritable Victorian 'angel in the house', suggest that David Copperfield will finally find the domestic bliss lacking in his marriage to Dora Spenlow.

The Victorian domestic ideal, although strongly associated with Dickens's fiction, was by no means his own invention, even though he undoubtedly contributed significantly to its dissemination in English culture. Victoria and Albert famously 'domesticated' the British monarchy (see ROYALTY); Coventry Patmore's immensely popular long poem sequence, *The Angel in the House* (1854–63), clearly articulated the domestic paradigm; the popularity of domestic DRAMA in the Victorian THEATRE—these and other manifestations of the mid-19th-century valorization of domesticity all suggest that Dickens, in his own obsession with domesticity, was thoroughly in tune with his time.

The rise of domestic ideology coincided with the Industrial Revolution and its aftermath. INDUSTRIALIZATION, gathering pace in the 19th century after its advent in the 18th, had as one of its effects the gradual separation of family life from working life. Prior to the Industrial Revolution most industry was home based, so that women, working from home, would not have experienced the conflict between the working world and the domestic sphere that so affected subsequent generations of women. Following the Indus-

trial Revolution, 'WORK' and 'home' slowly but surely became distinct, and this heralded the birth of that famous Victorian formulation of the 'public' and 'private' spheres. At precisely the moment that more and more women were necessarily moving *outside* the home in order to gain access to paid employment, Victorian domestic ideology promoted the idea that women should remain in the private, domestic sphere, leaving the public working world to men. Arguably this contradictory formulation was born of a fear that untethered women wandering around the urban and industrial landscapes of Britain would disrupt the public/private gendered division of labour on which the new bourgeois domesticity of the 19th century was predicated.

That the bourgeois domestic ideal was something of a chimera is borne out by many of Dickens's novels, despite his apparent fictional commitment to domesticity. A desire to contain those women who breach the boundaries of home and family is suggested by Dickens's response to such figures. The PROSTITUTE Nancy, although morally 're-claimed' through her attachment and loyalty to Oliver, is brutally murdered (*OT*); Martha (*DC*) is conveniently sent overseas by Dickens, where she is permitted to marry (one doesn't imagine he would have allowed the same outcome on home soil); Little Em'ly, a 'fallen' woman rather than a prostitute, also emigrates but cannot marry. Women who do not fulfil their domestic responsibilities in an appropriately supportive and virtuous way are often (although not always) severely punished in Dickens's fiction: Mrs Joe Gargery (*GE*) meets a grisly end; Mrs Jellyby (*BH*) is treated to Dickens's harshest satire, and Lady Dedlock in the same novel, whilst forgiven by her husband, is nonetheless subjected by Dickens to a cold and lonely death. The garrulous and maternally incompetent figure of Mrs Nickleby is treated in a lighter satirical vein, but there can be little doubt that the more domesticated, wifely, and maternal Dickens's fictional women were, the more he liked them.

Despite Dickens's ostensible promotion of the domestic ideal, there are more dysfunctional families and miserable marriages in his fiction than there are idyllic ones. Dombey denies his motherless children the emotional warmth they need, and the young Paul's death is strongly associated with parental neglect. The grotesque distortions of Miss Havisham's domestic arrangements (*GE*) pervert the course of the young Estella's emotional development, ruining her own prospects of domestic fulfilment. Amy (*LD*) makes a moving but pathetic attempt to sustain for her broken and bankrupt family a respectable domestic veneer in their Marshalsea prison 'home'. Arthur Clennam's cheerless domestic welcome when he returns home to the woman he thinks is his mother acts as an index to the sombre tone of this novel. The domestic idyll rarely triumphs in Dickens's later fiction. The very title of *Bleak House* serves as an implicit acknowledgement that domesticity is not an adequate response to the larger 'bleak house' of society with which the novel is concerned. John Jarndyce's heroic attempt to reconstitute the ideal family unit for the orphaned victims of CHANCERY, Richard Carstone and Ada Clare, is not enough to protect them from the slings and arrows of a maladjusted society. In *Hard Times* we have a novel in which the domestic dream is not even projected, let alone realized, making it one of Dickens's most austere works of fiction.

Whilst projected marriages—such as those between David and Agnes (*DC*), Florence Dombey and Walter Gay (*DS*), Esther Summerson and Woodcourt (*BH*)—are positively represented, actual marriages rarely match the ideal. Ill-tempered, recalcitrant, or simply irresponsible wives as disparate as Mrs Gargery (*GE*), Louisa Gradgrind (*HT*), Edith Granger (*DS*), and Mrs Jellyby (*BH*), thoroughly undermine the ideal of the 'angel in the house' on which bourgeois domesticity was predicated in the Victorian years.

Domestic happiness rarely thrives in the middle- and upper-class homes figured in Dickens's fiction. As Lady Dedlock stares gloomily out of her window near the start of *Bleak House*, she sees a small child run out of the lodge-keeper's cottage in the rain, to be caught up in the arms of her father. The lodge-keeper's house is illuminated brightly from within; domestic warmth is available in such humble abodes as this rather than in upper-class homes.

The broken and dysfunctional families which litter the pages of Dickens's fiction are offset not only by the domestic happiness of his more humble protagonists but also by a series of alternative domestic units. Oliver Twist finds a 'home' of sorts with Fagin's gang, which after all saves him from starvation; David Copperfield finds a domestic warmth denied him by the Murdstones and by Creakle's educational establishment first with the Micawbers and then with his eccentric aunt and the amiable lunatic Mr Dick in Dover; and Sleary's circus (*HT*) offers a limited but probably preferable alternative to the cold utilitarianism of the Gradgrind household. Wemmick (*GE*), eccentrically creates for himself a domestic 'castle' in which he nurtures his old father. The 'drawbridge' which physically separates the little house from its immediate environment is symbolic in its attempt to protect Wemmick's domestic haven from the social alienation of the city.

Dickens's simultaneous idealization of domesticity and acknowledgement of marital and familial misery had its correlate in his own life. His reputation, built as it was on his image as a champion of domesticity, suffered a severe blow when his marriage publicly broke down in 1858 (see DICKENS, CATHERINE). Dickens had met the young actress, Ellen TERNAN, and quickly developed strong feelings for her; he and his wife separated the following year. Long before this, though, Dickens's uneasy personal accommodation to the domesticity he so championed in his fiction had made for a troubled private life. On one level, he desperately wanted the solidly bourgeois domesticity which was denied to him in his childhood. His father had served time, like the fictional William Dorrit, in the Marshalsea prison for debtors; Dickens had had to work as a 12-year old in WARREN'S BLACKING warehouse; and all his life he felt that his mother had neglected to provide him with the emotional nurturing and support he needed (see DICKENS, ELIZABETH). His desire for domestic stability was, though, attenuated by his restlessness, his egotism, and by a desire for adventure and romance.

Dickens's marriage to Catherine Hogarth in 1836 had confirmed him as a bourgeois head of household, and many years after his death one of his daughters, Mamie, confirmed him as a patriarchal figure of domestic authority. She reflected that to his children he had been a 'strict master in the way of insisting upon everything being done perfectly and exactly as he desired . . . But, on the other hand, [he] was most kind, just and considerate' (Mamie Dickens, *My Father As I Recall Him*, 1900, p. 47). His desire beneficently to rule over a well-ordered domestic sphere, though, was marred by the failure of his marriage to match the ideal. Writing to his friend, Angela Burdett COUTTS, in the year of his marital breakdown, Dickens had claimed that his sister-in-law, Mary HOGARTH, had 'understood . . . in the first months of our marriage', that it was 'as miserable a one as ever was' (9 May 1858). Whether or not the early years of the marriage were as unhappy as Dickens suggests is a matter of some debate (Slater 1983 argues that they were not). Nonetheless, Dickens appears to have reacted with a bemused disgust to his wife's constant pregnancies, as if baffled by the fecundity of their imperfect union. He was also frequently worried by his large domestic expenditure, his substantial wealth an insufficient bulwark against the economic anxiety born of his financially insecure childhood. As, in middle life, Catherine became increasingly obese and frequently unwell, Dickens's feelings towards her became at best ambiguous. Earlier on in the marriage he seems to have escaped from the routine cares of domesticity, first by travelling, making a number of trips both to America and to the Continent, and secondly by romantically idealizing other, younger women as perfect spiritual sisters. These included Mary Hogarth and, after her death, her sister Georgina, who in her role as sister-in-law acted as Dickens's housekeeper for many years (see HOGARTH, GEORGINA). These sister figures he transformed fictionally into the idealized figure of Ruth, the sister of Tom Pinch (*MC*). He also took a great interest in other young women, such as Christiana Weller, a pianist, and Augusta de la Rue, whose neurological illness he had attempted to treat using the techniques of MESMERISM. Both these women he had met in 1844. Only four years later, after a theatrical performance in Glasgow, Dickens is reported to have railed against domesticity: 'Blow Domestic Hearth! I should like to be going on all over the kingdom, with Mark LEMON and Mrs Cowden CLARKE . . . and acting everywhere. There's nothing in the world equal to seeing the house rise at you, one sea of delighted faces, one hurrah of applause!' (Mary Cowden

Clarke, *Recollections of Writers*, 1878, pp. 305–25). Writing in the same month, he described his dissatisfactions thus: 'I have no energy whatever—I am very miserable. I loathe domestic hearths. I yearn to be a Vagabond . . . Why have I seven children . . . taken on for an indefinite time at a vast expense . . .?' (to Mary Cowden Clarke, 22 July 1848). The man who had, in his writings, elevated domesticity into a national totem, negotiated the demands it made upon him in his personal life with the greatest unease.  SL

Lane, Margaret, 'Dickens on the Hearth', in Michael Slater (ed.), *Dickens 1970* (1970).
Zaretsky, Eli, *Capitalism, the Family and Personal Life* (1976).

**Dostoevsky.** The then utopian socialist Fyodor Mikhailovich Dostoevsky (1821–81) first read Dickens in the 1840s, along with other 'progressive' writers like Soulié and George Sand. It was *Dombey and Son*, translated by Vvedensky, that first captured his attention (as it did Turgenev's). The critic Druzhinin compared the heroine's relationship with Larya in *Netotchka Nezhvanova*—published in 1849 at the time of Dostoevsky's arrest and condemnation to death—with Florence's to Paul Dombey.

During his imprisonment in Siberia in the 1850s Dostoevsky was at first allowed only the Bible, but later he was permitted other books. Two titles only are preserved: *Pickwick Papers* and *David Copperfield*. Dostoevsky's first post-Siberian novel, *The Insulted and the Injured* (1860–1), is also his most Dickensian, its heroine Nellie Valkovsky and her grandfather Jeremy Smith clearly modelled on *The Old Curiosity Shop*.

But no Dostoevsky novel lacks a Dickensian presence. The hero of *The Idiot*, for example, reflects Dostoevsky's admiration for Mr Pickwick and Don Quixote as types of the 'absolute beauty' embodied in Christ (and as with Tolstoy, the appeal of Dickens for Dostoevsky was in part as a disseminator of the Christian Gospel). That of the BILDUNGS-ROMAN *A Raw Youth* passes through a school that resembles Salem House in *David Copperfield*, and reads *The Old Curiosity Shop*.

Still, such particular borrowings are less important than the two-way general stylistic relationship between writers who shared a similar aesthetic. 'I have my own special view of reality (in art), and what the majority call almost fantastic and exceptional is for me sometimes the very essence of the real', wrote Dostoevsky. Dickens's own scattered remarks about art as well as his novelistic practice—his preoccupation with crime and evil, the suffering of children in dysfunctional families, and even more, the disconcerting shifts from tragedy to comedy and back—make it clear that his position was not dissimilar.     MH

Fanger, Donald, *Dostoyevsky and Romantic Realism* (1965).

Lary, N. M., *Dosteyevsky and Dickens* (1973).

Wilson, Angus, 'Dickens and Dostoyevsky', *Diversity and Depth in Fiction* (1983).

**Doyle, Richard** (1824–83), ILLUSTRATOR and painter. Doyle was the second son of the Irish artist John Doyle (1797–1868), a political caricaturist and portraitist who, because he signed his plates 'HB' (actually two 'JD's on top of one another) was therefore sometimes confused with Hablot BROWNE. Doyle was only 19 when he joined the PUNCH staff, bringing to the new humour magazine his exceptional facility in drawing fairy subjects. A year later BRADBURY AND EVANS asked him to help illustrate Dickens's second Christmas book, *The* CHIMES. Doyle supplied designs for the wood-engraved openings of each 'quarter'; he worked carefully to ensure that his imagery and portraits harmonized with those of Daniel MACLISE, John LEECH, and Clarkson STANFIELD, who shared with Doyle depictions of the neo-Gothic tower of the newly built St Dunstan's-in-the-West, Fleet Street. Combining delicately drawn, acrobatic 'elfin creatures' in the top half of each design with serious and substantial depictions of human suffering in the bottom half, Doyle provided a visual equivalent to Dickens's medley of FAIRY TALE and biting social criticism. One cut was, Dickens complained, 'so unlike my idea' that Doyle had to start 'afresh' (to Mrs Charles Dickens, 2 December 1844), but in the end Dickens was apparently satisfied both with Doyle's art and with his co-operation.

Accordingly, Dickens told Bradbury and Evans to engage the artist for the next book, *The* CRICKET ON THE HEARTH. Once again Doyle mixed cheerful elves with scenes of realistic humble life: varying the formula imaginatively, he supplemented the elves in the second scene with Caleb Plummer's toys, and

in the third he emphasized John Peerybingle's despair at his wife's supposed infidelity by surrounding him with protective spirits emblematic of the marital love the carrier cannot at that moment sense. In 1846 Doyle supplied three more designs introducing the sections of *The* BATTLE OF LIFE. Initially there was some confusion about whether Maclise would produce a frontispiece; when he decided to do so, he wanted the subject of the Jeddler daughters dancing under the apple trees, which Doyle had already worked up for his illustration. Doyle gave way without complaint. Once again he structured bifurcated designs; this time the top portion contains images of battle and death that transform into autumnal life in the third heading.

Dickens was often on the Continent when these books were being readied for the press, so Doyle usually communicated through John FORSTER. Doyle was never intimate with either man; nor did he, with his sweet and inexhaustible humour, get on comfortably with the rowdier *Punch* set. A devout ROMAN CATHOLIC like his friend Stanfield, Doyle resigned from *Punch* on 27 November 1850 over its attacks on the restoration of a Roman Catholic hierarchy in Great Britain. Thereafter he produced very popular series of gentle social satires, illustrated fairy tales by John RUSKIN and William Allingham, and painted large canvases of fairies and of landscapes. His younger brother Charles was the father of Arthur Conan Doyle.     RLP

## drama and dramatists before Dickens.

Dickens's reading and theatre-going, from an early age, exposed him to many of the dramas and dramatic genres of previous ages. On the early 19th-century stage SHAKESPEARE was still a favourite, especially through those plays which furnished strong roles for major actors: John Philip Kemble was renowned for his Hamlet, Macbeth, and Coriolanus; Edmund Kean won acclaim as Richard III, Iago, Othello, and Shylock. Some of the comedies of Ben JONSON, the romantic dramas of Beaumont and Fletcher, and Massinger's *A New Way to Pay Old Debts*, enhanced by Kean's terrifying performance as Sir Giles Overreach, were also popular. Performances of Shakespeare are often rendered absurd in Dickens's accounts. He recalls youthful visits to *Richard III* and *Macbeth*, 'where the witches bore an awful resemblance to the thanes, and other proper inhabitants of Scotland; and . . . the good King Duncan couldn't rest in his grave, but was constantly coming out of it and calling himself something else' (Forster 1.1). *Othello* and *Hamlet* are both made ridiculous by Mrs Joseph Porter's amateur theatricals ('Mrs Joseph Porter', *SB*) and Mr Wopsle (*GE* 31) respectively, whilst the Crummles version of *Romeo and Juliet* is made ludicrous not least through the casting of the apprehensive Smike in the role of the apothecary (*NN* 35). On a more serious level, David Copperfield witnesses *Julius Caesar* at Covent Garden (*DC* 19), whilst Dickens himself presented an AMATEUR THEATRICAL performance in 1848 of *The Merry Wives of Windsor* in which he played Shallow. He was also instrumental, through his support of MACREADY, in reinstating the Fool into stage versions of *King Lear*. His novels contain hundreds of references to nearly all of Shakespeare's plays. Dickens also revived Jonson's *Every Man in his Humour*, contemplated a production of Jonson's *The Alchemist*, and was strongly influenced as a novelist by the Jonsonian comedy of humours, especially as transmitted through the novels of such authors as FIELDING and SMOLLETT. For the benefit of Frances Kelly in 1846 he staged Massinger's and Fletcher's *The Elder Brother*.

Although Dickens jokingly described himself as 'the Congreve of the nineteenth century' in reference to a play competition organized by Benjamin Webster at the Haymarket Theatre (13 June 1843), Restoration comedy was rarely performed in the 19th-century (with the exception of Congreve's *Love for Love* and Farquhar's *The Beaux' Stratagem*). The development of SENTIMENTAL comedy in the 18th century had introduced a gentler and less salacious form of play, which in turn was satirized by GOLDSMITH in *She Stoops to Conquer* and *The Good-Natured Man* and SHERIDAN in *The Rivals* and *The School for Scandal*. Sheridan virtually reintroduced the comedy of manners in the late 18th century, but without the licentiousness of his Restoration forbears. Dickens often refers to Sheridan's plays, even parodying *The Rivals* in one of his letters (16 January 1854). The plays of Molière were also known to Dickens, who recounts a visit to Molière's *Don Juan* in Paris in 1847.

Tragedy moved from the Shakespearian to the more heroic mode of Dryden during the Restoration period, in turn to be replaced by domesticated, middle-class tragedies, of which *The London Merchant* by George LILLO, about the murderous George Barnwell, was a harbinger. Pip in *Great Expectations*, who listens to Mr Wopsle's lugubrious recital of the play, feels forced to identify with the play's moral lesson, 'as if it were a well-known fact that I contemplated murdering a near relation, provided I could only induce one to have the weakness to become my benefactor' (*GE* 15). Plays such as this, together with Moore's *The Gamester*, Rowe's *Jane Shore*, and Home's *Douglas*, introduced a new type of tragedy which, in turn, impacted upon the emergence of MELODRAMA in the late 18th century. Plays such as *The Stranger* and Sheridan's *Pizarro* (both adapted from the German playwright Kotzebue) are indicative of the transition towards a more romantic type of drama, which in turn helped to pave the way for the coming of melodrama. The first melodrama in English was Thomas Holcroft's *A Tale of Mystery* (1802), adapted from Pixérécourt's *Coelina*, one of many plays of this genre performed in France in the aftermath of the French Revolution. Prior to this many of the essential ingredients of GOTHIC melodrama had emerged in M. G. LEWIS's *The Castle Spectre* (1797), which Dickens was later to parody in a speech to the ROYAL GENERAL THEATRICAL FUND (*Speeches*, p. 125). Domestic melodrama, particularly in its nautical embodiment, was also much enjoyed by Dickens; whilst burlesquing the form with evident delight in *Great Expectations* (*GE* 47), he generously described Douglas JERROLD's seminal *Black-Ey'd Susan* as 'a remarkable illustration of what a man of genius may do with a common enough thing, and how what he does will remain a thing apart from all limitation' (*MP*, p. 163).

Farce and comedy were very popular throughout the 18th and 19th centuries. In the late 18th century some of the outstanding farces of the period were collected together in a series of volumes by Elizabeth Inchbald, including her own very popular *Animal Magnetism* and Foote's *The Mayor of Garrett*, both later revived by Dickens in amateur performances. Dickens recalls reading the collection, which would have introduced him to farces and afterpieces by James Kenney, David Garrick, Charles Macklin, Henry FIELDING, John O'Keeffe, Isaac Bickerstaffe, Arthur Murphy, Kane O'Hara, Charles and Thomas Dibdin, and the older and younger George Colman. Dickens was also well acquainted with the comedies of Colman the younger and Thomas Morton, together with Holcroft's *The Road to Ruin*, all popular around the turn of the century and beyond.

Music theatre had also developed in the 18th century, especially through such ballad operas as John GAY's *The Beggar's Opera*, which Dickens criticizes in his Preface to *Oliver Twist* for its attractive portrayal of Captain Macheath and of crime in general. Another legacy was burlesque, most famously, perhaps, in the Duke of Buckingham's *The Rehearsal* and Fielding's *Tom Thumb*, which was presented at the Devonshire House Christmas family theatricals in 1854. English politics are reduced to a similar level of burlesque in *Bleak House*, through the absurd confrontation of Lord Coodle and Sir Thomas Doodle (*BH* 40). The diminution of classical forms and heroic themes to serve the satirical intentions of their authors continued into the 19th century, but with the satirical edge much muted, as in *Bombastes Furioso* by W. B. Rhodes (1811). Another popular form which developed in the 18th century and continued into the 19th was the Harlequinade, the forerunner of the modern PANTOMIME. Performed at Christmas and Easter, these entertainments were based on characters and plots derived from the Italian *commedia del l'arte*, but very much adapted to the English theatrical context. Dickens attests to his fascination with this form in his Preface to Grimaldi's MEMOIRS.

Dickens's knowledge of English drama written in the 250 years prior to his birth was extensive. The influence of Shakespeare and Jonson, of sentimental comedy and domestic tragedy, of farce and melodrama, not to mention pantomime and burlesque, are all apparent in his work, sometimes through direct reference and sometimes by implication. Most significantly, the pleasures of live theatrical performance, imbibed from early childhood, lay at the heart of Dickens's love for the drama. 'And now, I see a wonderful row of little lights rise smoothly out of the ground, before a vast green curtain', mused Dickens, contemplating 'A Christmas Tree' and recalling youthful memories. 'Now, a bell rings—a magic bell, which still sounds in my ears unlike all other bells—and music plays, amidst a buzz of voices, and a fragrant smell of orange-peel and oil. Anon, the magic bell commands the music to cease, and the great green curtain rolls itself up majestically, and The Play begins!' (*CS*). JD

**drama and dramatists during Dickens's lifetime.** Dickens was born into an age of transition, in the THEATRE as in so much else. The rapidly growing urban population demanded entertainment, and throughout the century many old THEATRES were enlarged and new ones built, in both London and the provinces, to serve them. The drama shared the vital spirit of the age, and from early boyhood Dickens was entranced by it. By the time he was 7 or 8 his friend James Lamert was taking him to the Theatre Royal on Star Hill in Rochester. Here he observed the uninhibited acting styles and rough gusto of the provincial touring companies, where Richard III slept on a miniscule sofa on a tiny stage before battle, while in *Macbeth*, the murdered Duncan returned in different disguises to pad out the cast. Dickens was amused, but he was also captivated. In *Nicholas Nickleby* (1838–9), if he created a comic 'stage' world for the Crummles troupe, the 'serious' trials of the Nickleby family were also shaped by his MELODRAMATIC imagination.

Coming to London in 1822, the young Dickens found a theatre world of teeming diversity. By the licensing laws, repealed only in 1843, Drury Lane and Covent Garden, with the Haymarket in the summer, had exclusive rights to present serious plays, and it was partly to evade prosecution that the 'minor' theatres presented drama in many mixed forms, including dumbshow, burlesques, extravaganzas (entertainments, usually on mythical themes, with spectacle and music), melodrama (plays with acting to music), and burletta (plays with songs). The long mixed programme often featured music, dancing, and acrobatics. At Sadler's Wells, naval wars were re-enacted on a large water tank. Astley's Amphitheatre, rebuilt and enlarged in 1806, presented equestrian shows, CIRCUS displays, and military dramas such as J. H. Amherst's

*The Battle of Waterloo* (1824), where a cast of hundreds, with horses, enacted the battle complete. To compete with such attractions, the 'patent' theatres also mounted GOTHIC spectacles, such as Isaac Pocock's *The Miller and His Men* (1813), which ended with a full-scale windmill and its banditti crew blowing up on the stage. PANTOMIME, with its mime, acrobatics, and links with the *commedia dell'arte*, evolved at Covent Garden under the genius of Joseph Grimaldi (1778–1847). (Dickens, who had seen Grimaldi at Rochester as a child, later edited his MEMOIRS, 1838.) Annually from 1808 to 1835, Charles MATHEWS the elder performed his one-man 'At Homes' to packed houses, impersonating a dazzling succession of characters linked by commentary into a dramatic narrative, creating a form that Dickens carefully studied, and developed when, in 1854, he began his own PUBLIC READINGS.

At Drury Lane, the brilliant scenic innovations of Philippe Jacques de Loutherbourg (1740–1812) at Drury Lane had strengthened theatre's association with the visual arts. Scene painters were seen as artists in their own right, and were featured on playbills as more important than the playwright. These included Clarkson STANFIELD, who exhibited at the Royal Academy, and became a close friend of Dickens, painting the backdrop for Dickens's production of *The FROZEN DEEP* in 1857.

In this ambience, action, spectacle and music were more important than a spoken text, and in general it was an era of great acting but minor playwrights. WORDSWORTH, COLERIDGE, Keats, BYRON, and later BROWNING and TENNYSON all wrote plays for the theatre, but only Byron had significant success on the stage. The most effective playwrights were prolific journeymen whose work had little merit outside stage production, men like J. R. Planché (1796–1880), W. T. MONCRIEFF, and Edward STIRLING. Plots and characters were taken from any source to hand. Current fiction, including novels by Sir Walter SCOTT and, later, Dickens, was avidly plundered (see DRAMATIZATIONS).

Many plays were in translation. From 1802 the work of the German Augustus Kotzebue (1761–1819), whose *Lover's Vows* caused so much consternation in Jane Austen's *Mansfield Park* (1814), was superseded by plays from France. In that year *Coelina* by Guilbert Giles de Pixérécourt (1773–1844), adapted by Thomas Holcroft as *The Tale of Mystery*, made a sensational success at Covent Garden, and was rapidly followed by other Pixérécourt importations. Melodrama grew out of the idealism and turmoil of the Revolutionary period, and Pixérécourt claimed to write drama for a new proletariat who could not read. To realize their simple moral plots and intensified emotions, melodrama used stylized acting, partly in dumbshow, with the key passages accentuated by music. Its style was similar to that of the English circuit companies, trained in the rough life of the provincial playhouse circuits and fairground theatres. Their popular form of acting was introduced to London from the country by actors like Edmund Kean (1787–1833), who presented a sensational Shylock at Drury Lane in 1814, and T. P. Cooke (1786–1864), an ex-sailor who specialized in both nautical characters and stage monsters. In 1829 Cooke was acting William in JERROLD's *Black-Ey'd Susan* at the working-class Surrey Theatre on the South Bank, then hustling across Waterloo Bridge, costumed, in a hackney coach, to repeat the performance at Covent Garden. The play portrayed an honest sailor from Rye who saved his wife from assault by his captain, was condemned to death for striking an officer, and only saved by a stroke of fate. Featuring a wicked landlord, smugglers, a long-suffering heroine, and a last-minute reprieve, it became one of the most continuously popular plays of the century. Like J. B. BUCKSTONE's powerful play of the rural poor, *Luke the Labourer* (1827), Jerrold's drama showed a move from the Gothic towards domestic and social problem melodrama. This was taken further by Jerrold's *Fifty Years of a Drunkard's Life* (1828), and *The Rent Day* (1832), which 'realized' on stage two etchings by David Wilkie attacking oppressive landlords.

In the theatre world, Dickens was never a passive observer. Drama was in his blood. He dressed, spoke, and acted with thespian panache, and, in his imagination, shaped his reading into drama. At school at Wellington House, the 13-year-old Dickens staged melodramas, including Pixérécourt's *The Dog of Montargis*, with a white mouse acting the canine hero, on a toy stage. With characteristic thoroughness, he studied acting techniques, and considered becoming an actor. Only a heavy cold kept him from attending an audition at Covent Garden and perhaps changing his career. In 1838 his farce *The* STRANGE GENTLEMAN was enjoying a moderate success. *Pickwick Papers*, however, taking off like a delayed rocket, then confirmed his novelistic vocation.

But he never abandoned the theatre, contributing to the flourishing, often unnoticed, amateur stage activities of the Victorian middle class. Until the mid-century, the long performances and rowdy audiences of theatres like Drury Lane discouraged middle-class playgoing, but aspiring actors could pay to act in private theatricals, and many families created their own theatre, either on toy stages or, fleshed out and costumed, in informal productions. Even Queen Victoria, an avid playgoer, had a private theatre built at Windsor Castle. In 1833 Dickens and his family acted plays such as *Clari, the Maid of Milan* in his father's London home, and after he moved to Tavistock House in 1852 he annually turned the schoolroom into a theatre. When under pressure, Dickens turned for emotional release to the stage, acting and producing plays in London, the provinces, and even when visiting America (see AMATEUR THEATRICALS). He also moved in a circle of friends whose common interest was to revive serious drama in England.

Central to this was John FORSTER, who as chief dramatic editor of the EXAMINER, an enthusiastic amateur actor, and a discriminating critic, was well placed to put Dickens in touch with the London theatre scene. Another friend was the playwright and critic Sir Thomas Noon TALFOURD (1795–1854), whose tragedy *Ion* (1836), successfully produced at Covent Garden, reintroduced the classical unities and poetic verse on the stage: Dickens dedicated *The Pickwick Papers* to him. Still more important was BULWER-LYTTON (1803–73), a writer of many talents, whose verse dramas *The Lady of Lyons* (1838) and *Richelieu* (1839) remained popular throughout the century, and whose comedy *Money* (1840) brought a note of social realism onto a convention-bound stage. In 1850, after an amateur production at his country seat Knebworth Hall, Bulwer-Lytton and Dickens formed the GUILD OF LITERATURE AND ART to further the welfare of artists and writers.

Both Talfourd and Bulwer-Lytton were indebted for the successful staging of their plays to another member of Dickens's circle, William Charles MACREADY (1793–1873). Macready, with Edmund Kean, was the finest tragedian of the century. A passionate and often irascible perfectionist, he also worked as an actor-manager to free theatre from dependence on spectacle, and improve the quality of acting and production. Like Samuel Phelps (1804–76) and Charles KEAN (1811–68), he recovered accurate SHAKESPEARE texts, and produced them with carefully researched costume and scenery.

All this prepared the way for major changes in the theatre. At one end of the spectrum, the 1840s saw the opening of the Britannia Saloon in the London East End, which as a theatre (1850–1927) was to become the largest in England, and was described by Dickens in the second of his essays, 'The Amusements of the People' (*HW* 30 April 1850). Theatres like the Britannia created a distinctive style of popular melodrama, exemplified by G. Dibdin Pitt's *Sweeney Todd* (1842).

In the West End, a new generation of playhouses were being built which were respectable, comfortable, and planned for middle-class taste. The style of acting and timing of performance also changed. Performances started after dinner, at eight, and presented a shorter, more unified bill. In Charles Kean's Princess's Theatre, opened in 1850, great attention was paid to creating realistic effects with the aid of elaborate stage machinery and lighting. Lights were dimmed during the performances, and audiences sat silently through what was now a 'gentlemanly' style of acting. In 1861 the French actor Charles FECHTER (1824–79), another close friend of Dickens, broke with stage conventions and acted Hamlet at the Princess's in a reflective, naturalistic manner.

Dion Boucicault (1820–90) dominated the mid-Victorian stage. His adaptation of a French play, *The Corsican Brothers*, produced at the Princess's in 1852, showed his skill at sensational effect with the ghostly appearance of the dead Corsican twin, apparently through the solid stage. For such scenes, and startling twists of plot, which turned the old moral certainties of melodrama into mysteries of personal identity, his plays were called 'sensation dramas'. Their style was linked with contemporary fiction, and Dickens shifted from the melodrama of *Oliver Twist* (1827–8) to the revelations of *Great Expectations* (1860–1), which was classed as a 'SENSATION NOVEL' at the time. It also shaped the fiction and drama written by Dickens's friend and stage collaborator, Wilkie COLLINS.

Boucicault campaigned for the enforcement of dramatic COPYRIGHT, which Bulwer-Lytton had effected in 1833, and established the financial status of the professional playwright. The acting profession, too, was becoming respectable, and 'genteel' actors edged out the Crummles-style barnstormer. The old melodrama was modified into social-issue plays, such as Tom Taylor's *The Ticket of Leave Man* (1863), and took a psychological slant in Henry Irving's production of *The Bells* (1871). But the most significant move was towards the 'well made play', following the French example of Victorien Sardou (1831–1908). In 1865 Sir Squire (1841–1926) and Marie (1839–1921) Bancroft opened the Prince of Wales's Theatre, a small, genteel playhouse which staged T. W. Robertson's meticulous small-scale comedies *Society* (1865), *Ours* (1866), and *Caste* (1867). Although derided as 'cup-and-saucer' plays, they opened the way for the drama of Arthur Wing Pinero (1855–1934), Galsworthy (1867–1933), and Oscar Wilde (1856–1900).

For all these changes, however, there was nothing restrained about Dickens's readings of *A Christmas Carol*, or the murder of Nancy, in the last decade of his life. Although he had played his part in reforming English drama, it was his early theatre visits in Chatham that had baptized his imagination with stage fire. At a period when the literary traditions of Scott and the writers of the Romantic Movement were fading, the stage had given Dickens an entry into an alternative popular tradition—vital, physical, and in touch with the living voice. It offered him conventions of character and plot that he could transform into fiction. Today the early Victorian stage survives nowhere more vitally than in the 'theatre' of his novels.

LJ

Booth, Michael R., *Theatre in the Victorian Age* (1991).
Johnson, Edgar and Johnson, Eleanor (eds.), *The Dickens Theatrical Reader* (1964).

**dramatizations and dramatizers of Dickens's works.** Partly because staged PANTOMIME of children's stories had helped establish the 18th-century custom, what a multitude of 19th-century playwrights did with the plenitude of BOZ was only what the stage had been doing to the novel for decades. Behn, DEFOE, FIELDING, Godwin, GOLDSMITH, Richardson, SCOTT, and SMOLLETT were often dramatized. Pierce EGAN's *Life in London*, with its illustrations by Isaac Robert and George CRUIKSHANK, its fascination with the metropolis, and its presentation of ordinary people, formed a precedent to *The Pickwick Papers*—both as a book and as a derivative play.

Records of plays, FILMS, and radio and TELEVISION productions from his novels are probably the best single measure of Dickens's POPULARITY, which has extended far beyond audiences of readers. Moreover, the diaspora of his characters illustrates an almost universal appeal: they have been impersonated by actors from Moscow to California, broadcast from Melbourne to Manchester, and filmed from Spain to Scandinavia, Hollywood to London.

The history of these, mostly piratical, dramatizations of Dickens begins with the staging of an early story, 'A Bloomsbury Christening', at London's Adelphi Theatre in October 1834. Dickens himself reviewed the performance, whose characters he recognized as 'old and particular friends of ours'. The pirate BUCKSTONE's Preface to his play explains consequences of the recent Dramatic Authors Act: paltry remuneration for playwrights, who were effectively denied COPYRIGHT, caused Dickens seldom to write for the stage.

The first era in the wholesale dramatization of Dickens was that of *Pickwick Papers*, *Oliver Twist*, and *Nicholas Nickleby*—the late 1830s and early 1840s. Capitalizing on the enthusiasm for Boz, playwrights like J. B. Buckstone, W. T. MONCRIEFF, and Edward STIRLING earned small amounts; however, for a few years, actors and actresses could and did make handsome incomes playing characters from Dickens. W. J. Hammond profitably played Sam Weller for several seasons; and the wife of a famous manager and herself a famous actress, Mrs KEELEY played in succession Oliver, Smike, Little Nell, and Barnaby Rudge. To the novelist's delight and irritation, such plays often appeared long before the novels were complete, thereby promoting his popularity but also anticipating his plots and vulgarizing his characters. Even before 1840, *Pickwick Papers, Oliver Twist,* and *Nicholas Nickleby* had been staged at least 60 times.

After about 1845 a second period of Dickens dramatizing began, when the novelist had basically established his REPUTATION, and while the plays generated in the first period still remained in the popular commercial repertoire. Now the slope of the growth curve of the Dickens-dramatizing industry was declining even as his fame increased, albeit more slowly. Yet the industry was very substantial, so that by 1850 Dickens had been dramatized in at least 240 productions. Nearly 25 per cent of these were plays from *Nicholas Nickleby*. Another 10 or 15 per cent were stage versions of *Oliver Twist*. The CRICKET ON THE HEARTH supplied another 15 per cent, so that versions of only three narratives, among the thirteen major works that existed by 1850 accounted for about half the production. The first generation of playwrights, actors, and actresses to profit from Dickens began, after fifteen years, to turn their attention elsewhere. The Honners, who had staged *Oliver Twist* and other Dickens dramas as staples, continued with their old diet, including Dickens, well into the 1850s; but their more famous competitors, Mr and Mrs Keeley, were no longer dramatizing Dickens very often. Toward the end of the decade of the 1840s Dickens's most recent stories and novels were not so widely staged as the earliest: after great theatrical enthusiasm for *The Cricket on the Hearth*, subsequently *The* BATTLE OF LIFE, *The* HAUNTED MAN, and *Dombey and Son* were each less frequently staged than their immediate predecessors. Several important Dickens dramatizers—Edward Stirling and the Keeleys—ceased their efforts with *The Haunted Man*. The market for 'Dickens-dramas' was saturated. Almost exponential growth could not continue indefinitely; the large number of British theatres, provincial and metropolitan, did not continue to expand. Though Dickens continued to write prolifically—producing *David Copperfield, Bleak House, Hard Times, Little Dorrit,* and several Christmas stories between 1850 and 1860—during that decade only about 180 stagings of his stories have left their traces. This constituted a decline to

levels about 25 per cent less than in the decade previous. *Oliver Twist* and *Nicholas Nickleby* continued to be relatively strong attractions, between them producing about a third of the derivative dramas. *David Copperfield* made its contribution, too, inspiring about 15 per cent of the total output of dramatizations. But *Bleak House* and *Hard Times* were very little noted by playwrights of the 1850s.

A third epoch in the evolution of Dickens's popular, theatrical reputation occurred in the 1860s, after the novelist began to inhibit dramatization of his novels and stories by legal means, and as his narrative techniques became less obviously theatrical and harder to stage. The old favourites did not disappear, with *Oliver Twist* and *Nicholas Nickleby* continuing—though now Oliver and Fagin had become at least twice as popular as Smike and Squeers. Another generation of Dickens-dramatizers began to take over, led by Dion Boucicault whose new version of *The Cricket on the Hearth, Dot,* began in 1859 in New York, and came to the Princess Theatre, London, in January 1860. *David Copperfield* and versions of *Dombey and Son* that featured Captain Cuttle were also important in the 1860s. Captain Cuttle was especially prominent in America. These five novels bred about two-thirds of the dramas from Dickens's fictions during the decade. By contrast, the recent works, *A Tale of Two Cities,* 'A Message from the Sea' (*CS*), *Great Expectations, Our Mutual Friend,* and 'No Thoroughfare' (*CS*) played little part. The decline apparent from 1850 to 1860 thus continued, with still fewer British and American dramas, especially from Dickens's latest works, between 1860 and 1870. Therefore playgoers who were not also habitual readers of recently published novels knew mainly the Dickens of fifteen to twenty-five years before.

The industry of Dickens dramatizing had contracted now by about a third. Dickens, with Wilkie COLLINS's help, published a dramatic version of his most recent story, so that he could legally object to plays based upon 'A Message from the Sea' (*CS*). By similar means, he inhibited stagings of *Great Expectations,* publishing a legal device—a synopsis of a play from the novel—so as to be able to claim dramatic copyright. He instructed his solicitors to inform theatrical managers that he objected to without-your-leave productions from his last few works. He joined forces with Wilkie Collins and Charles READE to attempt to change the playmaking practice of his day, which assumed that all published narratives were, for theatrical purposes, in the public domain. Finally, Dickens embarked upon his own course of PUBLIC READINGS, which substantially though by no means entirely sated demand for dramatic versions of his works.

But Dickens's death altered everything. A fourth epoch arose during the early 1870s, when almost nothing restrained the dramatic adaptors, and the greatest burst of theatrical enthusiasm for Dickens occurred—greater even than in the first affection between the novelist and his adoring public during the late 1830s and early 1840s. England and America publicly mourned the passing of the prose bard, and theatrically celebrated his imagination for about fifteen years until, during the middle 1880s, enthusiasm began to wane. But during these years remarkable theatrical high-water marks were reached. A new generation of actors, soon to be led by Henry Irving, together with J. L. Toole and John Sleeper Clarke, established their places in the limelight partly by impersonating characters from Dickens. There was something nostalgic about this for certain older segments of the audience, doubtless, who remembered back over the turmoil and triumph of mid-century to the times when Dickens had first warmed their novel-reading and playgoing hearts. But during the 1870s, a whole new generation of playgoers learned their Dickens partly from the live drama. They therefore (as usual) knew vintage better than recent Dickens: *Oliver Twist* still predominated, leaving published and archival records of at least 40 more productions during the decade. *Nicholas Nickleby* continued to have some interest, though less than half as much as *Oliver Twist.* Now in New York *The Old Curiosity Shop* developed a minor vogue that involved 'living pictures' of Mrs Jarley's waxworks which, together with more truly dramatic versions of larger parts of the novel, generated at least forty-five stagings in the 1870s. *David Copperfield,* too, perhaps as an *alter ego* for its recently deceased author, was staged at least 40 times. Jo the crossing-sweeper of *Bleak House,* impersonated by Jennie Lee and a small host of her imitators, took the stages of two lands by storm; this novel has left records of at least 47 productions in the decade 1870–80. Because Albery's *The Two Roses* featured Digby Grant, as originally played by Henry Irving, and as derived from old Mr Dorrit, *Little Dorrit* too figures somewhat indirectly in this new churning out of Dickens dramas. All-in-all, more than 350 stagings of Dickens occurred in this prolific era.

A decline from this peak was inevitable, of course. Theatrical and social conditions had both changed. By 1890 some of the gravest ills of schoolroom and market-place had been a little ameliorated, so that stage mimicry of the suffering child was no longer so poignant and lucrative. *Little Nell and the Marchioness* and *Jo v. Jo* were burlesques that, during the 1880s, vented some affectionate exasperation with what playmakers had turned into Dickensian clichés. Passionate causes became sentimental memories. Thus, during the late 1880s and 1890s a fifth period in Dickens's theatrical posterity is apparent: the era when Ibsenism was transforming the British stage from an almost purely entertainment medium into something like a forum for social philosophizing. Interest in the melodramatic versions of Dickens continued to decline— though it certainly survived. *Oliver Twist* continued to ask for more, in at least forty-four productions over two decades. But Smike and Nicholas, though they continued in their struggles with Squeers and Ralph during the 1880s, virtually vanished in the 1890s. Little Nell, too, faded rapidly from sight. *The Cricket on the Hearth* continued to chirp, but more weakly now—at a minimal average rate of only about once in a year for the last two decades of the century. Versions of *Bleak House,* especially those featuring Jo, survived into the 1880s, with over thirty productions, but dwindled down to a dozen in the century's last decade. During the 1880s at least 200 plays from Dickens were performed; but during the 1890s only half as many saw the stage. Such simple arithmetic chronicles the closing of an era. Only *A Tale of Two Cities,* just as the century closed, demonstrated any potential for theatrical growth. *The Only Way,* MARTIN-HARVEY's enormous hit from Dickens's tale of the French Revolution, began life at the Lyceum Theatre, London, in October 1899.

After 1900 came a sixth period, when professional stagings of plays from Dickens did continue, though in diminished volume. *The Only Way* continued its long life of thirty years and more than ten London productions, providing a kind of climax in the history of Dickens-dramatizing, and eventually resulting in a 1925 silent film as well as a 1948 BBC television production. Already famous as an impersonator of Dickens himself in his avatar as a public reader, Bransby WILLIAMS now played Fagin in a 1909 New Cross Theatre *Fagin's Den*, making his first appearance in a dramatic version of Dickens. In the early 20th century, too, plays from *A Christmas Carol*, with Scrooge played, for example, by Sir Seymour Hicks, began to establish their modern significance—so much greater than any Victorian vogue. In the first decades of our century the professionals mixed freely with amateurs. J. L. Toole, who had been a famous Artful Dodger as well as a Caleb Plummer, together with Herbert Beerbohm Tree, who was even then a leading professional Fagin, very actively assisted at the gala charitable productions of the DICKENS FELLOW-SHIPS and their associated Theatre Societies. Enormous energies went into these productions after 1905; they raised thousands of pounds for various causes, especially those involving hospitals and children; the philanthropic spirit of Dickens was thus revitalized. In some ways the disinterested activity of devoted and gifted amateurs like Arthur Waugh, Walter DEXTER, Frederick T. Harry, and A. E. Brookes Cross paid even greater tribute to Dickens than the efforts of professional actors who, after all, had been earning their livings as characters from Dickens. The amateurs did it for love, and gave all the proceeds away. Many a Dickensian amateur ended life in the trenches of World War I, which closed this chapter in the annals of Dickens dramatizing. After the war, the records clearly indicate that personnel and enthusiasm for charitable Dickens dramatizing had been deeply wounded, though they lingered.

Yet this sixth era was also the time of the first silent films, a time of germinating technological possibility for the drama; and no novelist was more frequently filmed than Dickens, who flickered on the silver screen much to the consternation of those who wished to nurture his purely literary reputation, which was not in all circles by any means yet fully and firmly established. Nevertheless Bentley, Edison, Thanhouser, and others developed the silent film, whose very first example of a Dickensian drama came in 1903 from a few schoolroom scenes out of *Nicholas Nickleby*. All the while, Bransby Williams continued giving live stage versions of Dickens, even while he also crossed into the film medium as Gradgrind in *Hard Times* (1915) and Buzfuz in *Pickwick Papers* (1921).

A seventh era was the time between the two great wars, when interest in staging Dickens had all but died away among professional managers and actors, and even productions by the worldwide Dickens Fellowships were dwindling into mere scenes and songs from earlier plays, now nostalgically revived. Simultaneously, however, the first sounds of radio interest in Dickens emanated from the British Broadcasting Corporation. The earliest BBC radio reading from Dickens was probably 'Barkis is Willin'', broadcast on 29 July 1924. Dickens himself had been widely successful in public readings of his own works, and now radio revived that tradition in its new medium. Thus, Emlyn WILLIAMS, impersonating Charles Dickens in turn impersonating his own characters, led his career on the platform and the radio. Radio plays also naturally arose, though much less frequently than the simpler and more traditional readings. Now 'talking pictures' also sprang to life, so that Dickens lived again in this new medium. This seventh era was the time of a technological diaspora, when Dickens's characters emigrated from the novels and the stage to the several new mimetic media of radio, the talking picture, and even early television. In 1935 Sir Seymour Hicks, who had established himself as a stage Scrooge of an earlier era, played the part in a 'talking picture'. And as early as 1938 BBC television broadcast a version of *Pickwick Papers*.

After World War II came a time when radio dramatizations continued even while television and the colour film developed. Now the live stage had basically turned its attention elsewhere; however, during these late 1940s and early 1950s a wide variety of radio plays and readings from Dickens were given by the BBC—nearly two-dozen from *David Copperfield* alone in the ten years after World War II. Bransby Williams—now 80 years old!—even played Scrooge in a 1950 BBC television *Christmas Carol*. Television, especially in serial broadcasts, has been a very successful medium of Dickens-dramatizing. Both the new electromagnetic media have certain advantages over the live stage in the dramatization of long novels. Although technical problems of transforming the narrator's voice into other mimetic means than words will always remain, the possibility of multiple episodes and frequent changes of imaginary scene on radio and television make possible highly faithful renditions of even the most diffuse novels, like *Pickwick Papers*.

Our own era has been a time when Dickens's live theatrical posterity has been to some considerable degree reborn: *A Christmas Carol* has become much more an international theatrical institution during the holidays than it ever was in Dickens's time; and stagings of *Nicholas Nickleby* and *Oliver Twist* have had great vogue. Lionel Bart's musical *Oliver!* has been—and still is—enormously successful on stage, running for 774 performances in one New York production. It is as if Dickens's immortality survived, from 1920 to 1960, mainly in ghostlike electromagnetic form, to be reborn upon the stage in the gesturing, speaking bodies of actors. Our own era has of course tended to reduce Dickens on stage to Bart's *Oliver!* and those madly proliferating *Carols*. Such reductionism lies in the very nature of the process of popularizing. The modern mass audience seems ignorant of *The Cricket on the Hearth* and *The Old Curiosity Shop*, which the 19th-century stage had also greatly favoured. But Boz undoubtedly lives again in live performances—even in our own era of broadcast technology.

Measured by mere numbers of performances of the novel, *Oliver Twist* has proved the most popular of Dickens's full-length works —both in his day and (thanks to Bart's *Oliver!*) today. *A Christmas Carol* is the most enduringly popular of his stories—due to its 20th-century vogue on stage and screen, and even in Disney cartoon form. *The Only Way*, adapted from *A Tale of Two Cities*, may well have been the most popular Dickens-drama at the turn of the century; dramas from *Nicholas Nickleby, Bleak House, The Old Curiosity Shop*, and *The Cricket on the Hearth* have also inspired great enthusiasm. The greatest 19th-century roles were often suffering children as interpreted by actresses

—Oliver, Smike, Jo, Nell; the greatest 20th-century roles have been morally ambiguous adult males—Fagin, Scrooge, and Sydney Carton.                                        HPB

Bolton (1987).

**drink and temperance.** Dickens enjoyed alcoholic beverages all his life, portrayed in his fictions the vast range of Victorian drinking sites, brews, and customs, and argued in his prose against the zealotry of prohibition. During the 19th century the manufacture and sale of beers, ciders, spirits, and whisky were significant economic factors both in the home counties (growing hops and apples in Kent, for instance) and in Scotland. The government depended on the revenues from customs tariffs and excise taxes for imported spirits as well as from licensing domestic brews and their consumption. Long after mid-century places where alcohol was served provided their communities with heat, light, cheer, meals, lavatories, fellowship, mail, news and gossip, employment, games, entertainment, and sex. The government recruited for the armed services and held coroner's inquests there; politicians centred their campaigns on the 'local'. Factories distributed wages in taverns on Saturday night; since workers had to clear their slate of charges with the publican before taking home the remainder, many wives brought the whole family down to the pub in order to capture whatever was left of the week's pay, or at least to share in the drinking of it. Moreover, most public water supplies were unsanitary.

Drinking practices varied according to CLASS, and to some extent to region as well. The importation of gin ('blue ruin') from the Netherlands, and later the distillation, from virtually any vegetable refuse, of neutral spirits flavoured with angelica or juniper, sulphuric acid, and cayenne pepper, led to the construction of enormously profitable, garishly lit 'gin palaces' that catered to low clientele and lower morals. In the 1830s arguments that high excise taxes and restrictive government licensing encouraged smuggling, adulteration, high prices, poverty, and drunkenness prompted passage of the Beer Act, making beer much cheaper. Since it was manufactured out of boiled water and grains, there may have been some limited beneficial effect on the diet of the poor. Beer, ale, stout, and porter are consumed everywhere in Dickens—outdoors at rowing matches and on picnics, indoors at ordinaries (taverns with fixed-price meals), 'slap-bangs' (cheap restaurants), and below stairs. In the 'tap rooms' of public houses humbler customers sit on settles around a large fire (as in George CRUIKSHANK's illustration for 'Scotland Yard' in *Sketches by Boz*), and in the parlours a more select class of patrons, and on occasion the ladies, may be served by the barmaid.

Higher up in the drinking scale, various types of spirits were prescribed for different occasions: porter for nursing mothers, champagne for celebrations, home-made cordials to stimulate circulation, whisky to ward off cold, caudle or brandy-and-soda as a nightcap, ale for all the tenants when the squire came of age, and a drop of sherry to strengthen the enfeebled. Mixed drinks often included sugar, frequently paired with citrus juice for zest.

At the top end, the service of wines was extensive and elaborate. A full-scale banquet might require sherry with the soup, hock with the fish, claret with the roast, burgundy with venison and game, Madeira with the sweets, and port with the cheese. The cellars of some old families contained legendary vintages.

The representation of drink in all its variety and attraction was also an important element in Dickens's culture. While the gin mill is, for the most part, portrayed as a centre of factitious and dangerously delusive glamour, taverns, public houses, and the bars of coaching INNS are the scenes of countless encounters in the fiction, drama, and visual art of the 18th and 19th centuries. Some of these encounters turn violent—SCOTT's novels depict a number of frays in taverns. But many more are simply settings where all the business, from love-making to intrigue, take place. Dickens particularly enjoyed, and parodied, the convivialities attendant on brewing punch by the fire: compounding the steaming hot ingredients, delivering the orotund, formulaic toasts, and singing comic songs and risqué ballads.

There are hundreds of such scenes in Dickens's works. With George Cruikshank, he depicted the haunts of rivermen, coal-heavers, prostitutes, and thieves in *Sketches by Boz* and *Oliver Twist*. With Hablot Knight BROWNE ('Phiz') he images Bob Sawyer compounding

'a reeking jorum of rum punch', Sam and Tony Weller with their coaching friends 'Drinking to Mr Pell' (there are 250 references to drink in *Pickwick*; only the last is to abstinence), and David Copperfield giving his 'magnificent order at the public-house' for 'a glass of the Genuine Stunning'. With John LEECH, he shows Scrooge and Bob Cratchit sharing a Christmas bowl of smoking bishop. John Willet's Maypole Inn at Chigwell (*BR*), with its gables and huge zigzag chimneys and diamond-pane lattices, its ruddy fires and oak panelling and gleaming tankards, is the most elaborately described of Dickens's travellers' inns. The destruction of its bar—'the sanctuary, the mystery, the hallowed ground'—by the rioters, led by the former ostler Hugh and the hangman Ned Dennis, is, as Dickens's later running head names it, nothing less than a 'sacrilege in the sanctuary'. The snuggest of all Dickensian snuggeries may be the bar of the Six Jolly Fellowship Porters in *Our Mutual Friend*, presided over by the redoubtable Miss Abbey Potterson, a haven by the entrance, girt with casks and festooned with radiant grapes and winking lemons, divided from the rough world by a glass partition through which the proprietress can keep track of all the comings and goings of her customers. Despite the neighbourhood, it is a much better-run place than the Three Cripples, in the filthiest part of Little Saffron Hill, where Fagin spies on Noah Claypole through a peephole (*OT* 42).

It is hard to generalize about Dickens's own opinions concerning drink, or about changes in his personal or fictional attitudes over the course of his lifetime. Certainly drunkards come in for sound scolding, from the Revd Mr Stiggins in *Pickwick* to Melchisidech Howler (drunk on Jamaican rum) in *Dombey and Son* to Mr Dolls in *Our Mutual Friend*. Whereas the early novels seem to lampoon the hypocrisy of Squeers or Chadband as much as the drinking, later ones do seem to register the social cost of alcoholism more sensitively. Sairey Gamp, the inebriated midwife in *Martin Chuzzlewit*, has a drop whenever she is so 'dispoged', but although in the end old Martin rebukes her, she never, despite her patent incompetence, receives severe retribution. On the other hand, Krook, reeking with alcoholic fumes, spontaneously combusts in *Bleak House*. The heavy and almost indiscriminate drinking of the Regency era when Dickens was born, which is still present in the early novels, slowly gives way to more genteel beverages (the toothache-inducing iced champagne served at Paul Dombey's christening, for instance) and service, exemplified by the gloomy knowingness of the Veneerings' wine steward, the 'Analytical Chemist', in *Our Mutual Friend*. The CHRISTMAS holidays, notably in the Christmas books of the 1840s but also in Dickens's own holiday festivities when the children were young, were a time for quaffing wassail, lamb's wool, and smoking bishop. But though Dickens, both in his fiction and in his personal life, may have progressed from bon-vivant toping in his youth to more restrained consumption in the middle years, the novels are not, for the most part, the places where he registers his most intense feelings about alcoholism and teetotalers.

Despite the bouts of boozing when he was with Harrison AINSWORTH or the unreformed George Cruikshank or Wilkie COLLINS, Dickens was on the whole probably a moderate imbiber—more moderate as his health deteriorated in the 1860s. During the last PUBLIC READINGS drink became medicinal: he took a glass of 'flip'—sherry into which the yolk of a new-laid egg, powdered sugar, and nutmeg had been beaten—five minutes before going on stage. He also believed in the virtues of moderation, as personal and as public policy. Repudiating any interference with his own power to regulate his life, Dickens found himself in growing conflict with mid-Victorian social reformers who promoted abstinence from or prohibition of all spirits.

At first Dickens's disagreement with temperance was mild and humorous. Scrooge, the last paragraph of the *Carol* tells us, 'had no further intercourse with Spirits, but lived upon the Total Abstinence Principle, ever afterwards'; but nevertheless, 'he knew how to keep Christmas well, if any man alive possessed the knowledge'. With the campaign in the 1830s and 1840s to wean drinkers away from alcohol to tea and coffee (also adulterated, in some cases, but at least prepared with boiled water), Dickens seems to have had no quarrel; indeed, in *Copperfield* the consumption of tea is quite extensive. When George Cruikshank published his eight-plate temperance morality, *The Bottle*, Dickens hailed the

good it might do in pointing out to decent working men and women the dangers of indulgence. About Cruikshank's rendering of the violent effects of drinking on the family, Dickens said to John FORSTER: 'I question . . . whether anybody else living could have done it so well' (2 September 1847). Dickens himself wrote a review, in the 8 July 1848 *EXAMINER*, of Cruikshank's sequel, *The Drunkard's Children*, praising both its execution and its human sympathy. The power of the closing scene, when the daughter jumps from Waterloo Bridge, Dickens thought 'quite extraordinary'. 'It haunts the remembrance, like an awful reality.'

But Dickens disagreed with Cruikshank's moral. 'Drunkenness does not begin [in the gin shop]', he maintained in his review. 'It has a teeming and reproachful history anterior to that stage.' For Dickens, excessive drinking begins in sorrow, or poverty, or ignorance, and the government was as much at fault as individuals, especially for its failure to provide the working classes with education that would lift them out of poverty. So powerfully self-created by his own will, Dickens could not imagine that drinking might be addictive. For him, and for many moderationists, the use of liquor should not be prohibited by reformers simply because some weak persons abused it. Cruikshank, the son and brother of alcoholics, pointed out that education was no panacea, that learned persons were as likely to drink to excess as the ignorant. Moreover, while drunkenness might have a more immediate and visible effect on the poor, its long-term destructive consequences were not less, but simply better concealed, within the homes of the rich.

Their disagreements about temperance did not drive Dickens and Cruikshank apart until mid-century. In the late 1840s Cruikshank participated in Dickens's AMATEUR THEATRICALS, and Dickens wrote a very comical description of George's meeting with Sairey Gamp for an unpublished account of their Manchester tour. Dickens regaled his friends with stories about Cruikshank's inebriated antics, while becoming furious when the artist snatched a glass from the hand of one of Dickens's guests. But after the temperance party succeeded in banning alcoholic beverages from the refreshment stands at the Crystal Palace and Cruikshank became a more and more prominent spokesman for total abstinence, Dickens took umbrage.

In a *Household Words* leader, 'Whole Hogs' (23 August 1851), Dickens attacked the temperance, peace, and vegetarian societies, all of which had held huge gatherings during the Great EXHIBITION, and 'all of whom', Dickens wrote to his sub-editor W. H. WILLS, 'have lately been making stupendous fools of themselves' (10 August 1851). Dickens objected to the absolutism of these movements, their insistence on the 'Whole Hog' Responding to regenerators of all sorts who insisted that their programme be adopted without any exceptions, Dickens advocated 'the higher and greater work, called Education'. Temperance propagandists answered Dickens in publications sponsored by organizations of which Cruikshank was an officer; in such ways, the wedge between them was driven deeper.

Finally, in 1853, having only read Forster's enthusiastic review of Cruikshank's teetotal version of *Hop o' my Thumb*, Dickens told Wills that he wanted to write an article called 'Frauds upon the Fairies' (*HW* 10 Oct. 1853), protesting 'half playfully and half seriously' against any alterations 'of the beautiful little stories which are so tenderly and humanly useful to us in these times' (27 July 1853). The resultant essay attacked not only temperance but also reformist oratory, American prohibitionists, Mrs Bloomer, the women's suffrage movement, and literature that preached didactically. Infuriated by the censure and downcast by family troubles, Cruikshank replied in his own magazine in February 1854. He pointed out that fairy tales are constantly being altered in the retelling and wondered how the unexplained parental irresponsibility and ogre cruelty of *Hop* constituted beautiful, tender, humanly useful truths, whereas explaining these acts as the result of drinking did account for the 'unnatural brutality'. Dickens's whole hogs, Cruikshank concludes, should not be applied to the peace party or to teetotalers, but to drunkards, and 'I have therefore to beg, that in future you will not drive your "whole hogs" against us, but take them to some other market'.

Although there were favourable reviews of Cruikshank's Fairy Library, Dickens's notice and the general feebleness of the narratives killed its sales. That rankled. And for some reason Dickens persisted in his personal criticism of Cruikshank, caricaturing him as 'Mr Monomaniacal Patriarch' in an 1855 parody of Cruikshank's testimony about the benefits of abstinence before a Select Committee of the House of Commons looking into Sunday licensing hours. Cruikshank and Dickens never again spoke to one another; and having personalized his objections to temperance through Cruikshank, Dickens ceased after their break to comment further publicly about the movement.

Dickens's favourite potations included mulled wine with nutmeg ('negus'), milk punch (often served with his wife's ubiquitous toasted cheese), brandy, and gin slings. He loved compounding a bowl of hot or cold punch. Assembling the ingredients and utensils, holding forth while pouring, mixing, and tasting, passing round samples and discussing whether a little more of something might be added, and then serving up, exemplified the rather histrionic nature of Dickens's hospitality. While he continued to serve mixed drinks in his later years, the heavy, sweet punches, home-distilled liqueurs, and fortified wines of his youth declined in popularity. Gladstone's 1860 budget lowered tariffs on French wine. Dickens stocked up. His cellar at Gad's Hill Place, auctioned off on 13 August 1870, comprised dozens of cases of Iberian sherry and vintage port, French claret and champagne, 40 bottles of red burgundy, a selection of German hocks and Moselles, 11 dozen bottles of Highland whisky, 28 dozen bottles of French brandy, 17 bottles of the Regency favourite, curaçao, and a sampling of liqueurs and cordials. This was a well-chosen collection, appropriate for a middle-class host with wide-ranging tastes and knowledge of Victorian drinks.                                    RLP

Dickens, Cedric, *Drinking with Dickens* (1980).

Harrison, Brian, *Drink and the Victorians: The Temperance Question in England 1815–1872* (1971).

Hewett, Edward and Axton, W. F., *Convivial Dickens: The Drinks of Dickens and His Times* (1983).

Matz, B. W., *Dickensian Inns and Taverns* (1922).

**Ducrow, Andrew** (1793–1842), equestrian CIRCUS performer and proprietor of Astley's, 'scarcely to be classed', in Dickens's view, among the other 'mysterious beings' who enthralled him in the ring ('Astley's', *SB*). Ducrow's skill, daring, and grace made his name synonymous with excellence in horsemanship: apprehensive before a journey, Boz dreams of 'exhibiting *à la* Ducrow' ('Early Coaches', *SB*); reassuring his young fiancée of his safety, Dickens promises to avoid 'doing anything in the Ducrow way' (18 December 1853); a black coach-driver in America dances at the reins like 'the late lamented Ducrow on two of his fiery coursers' (*AN* 9).    PVWS

Saxon, A. H., *The Life and Art of Andrew Ducrow and the Romantic Age of the English Circus* (1978)

# E

**Easthope, Sir John** (1784–1865), Liberal MP (1826–47), knighted for political services in 1841. Shortly after Easthope bought the MORNING CHRONICLE in 1834, Dickens joined the staff, quickly earning attention as the paper's leading reporter (see JOURNALIST, DICKENS AS). He also contributed sixteen signed sketches under the name of 'BOZ', but left Easthope in November 1836 to edit BENTLEY'S MISCELLANY. Easthope's charge that Dickens received pay for three sketches he never delivered set the two apart. Social relations were later restored, but were strained again by Dickens's brief editorship of the DAILY NEWS in 1846. Easthope sold his interest in the *Chronicle* in 1847. DHP

**editions:** *1. collected editions over which Dickens had control; 2. collected editions published after Dickens's lifetime; 3. foreign English-language editions.*

**1. Collected editions over which Dickens had control.** Commenced in 1847, the Cheap Edition was a project involving the republication of all of Dickens's novels up to that date. FORSTER notes that Dickens, living in PARIS at that time, had travelled to London from 15 December to 23 December of 1846 to make the arrangements (5.7). In the first series everything appeared in three formats: weekly numbers of sixteen double-columned pages, monthly parts, and volumes. Margaret Dalziel in *Popular Fiction 100 Years Ago* (1957) called this the first successful attempt to provide cheap reprinted volumes of novels (p. 2). Dickens thus tapped every conceivable market, supplying his works both to those who wanted to read his writings as serial instalments and to those who wanted truly affordable volumes. 'In a sense he was merely keeping up with his time, since the ever-cheaper methods of printing and the ever-widening audience of literate readers meant that novels of his kind could be diffused far more widely than had been the case even ten years before' (Ackroyd 1990, p. 529). In the prospectus for this edition, published in the March number of *Dombey and Son*, Dickens

wrote that it had not been intended such an edition would be issued 'until the books were much older, or the Author was dead,' but the 'favour with which they had been received' justified republication. So as not to interfere with sales of his current works, he assured readers that 'Neither will any of the more recent writings of the Author; those now in progress of publication, or yet to come; appear in the CHEAP EDITION, until after a lapse of A VERY CONSIDERABLE PERIOD'. Dickens kept his word about letting time go by before allowing works to be included in this edition. Responding to a query about *Dombey*, Dickens wrote, 'Dombey & Son will *not* be included in the cheap edition, which is announced to close with Martin Chuzzlewit' (to Chaplin, ? January–21 March 1849). *Dombey*, in fact, did not appear in the Cheap Edition until 1858, ten years after its original publication. The prospectus gave the price of the weekly parts as 1½d each, the monthly parts as 7d. The original illustrations would not be reproduced; instead there was to be a new frontispiece 'engraved on Wood from a Design by some eminent Artist'. Dickens announced that he would revise and correct the text and provide a new preface to each work. The weekly numbers appeared each Saturday beginning 27 March 1847 and concluding 23 November 1850. The monthly parts were published at the end of each month. The volumes were published upon the completion of number publication. Prices for the volumes, bound in cloth, varied between 2s 6d and 5s. The nine titles in what turned out to be the first series of the Cheap Edition, published by CHAPMAN AND HALL, are *Pickwick* 1847, *Nickleby* 1848, *Old Curiosity Shop* 1848, *Barnaby Rudge* 1849, *Oliver Twist* 1850, *Chuzzlewit* 1850, AMERICAN NOTES 1850, *Sketches by Boz* 1850, and *Christmas Books* 1850.

BRADBURY AND EVANS, the publishers to whom Dickens had switched in 1844 because of his unhappiness with Chapman and Hall over *Chuzzlewit*, brought the Cheap Edition up to date by issuing a second series, all in volumes selling at 5s, comprised of *Dombey* 1858,

*Copperfield* 1858, *Bleak House* 1858, and *Little Dorrit* 1861. The Cheap Edition was completed by Chapman and Hall, to whom he returned in 1859, with the publication of the third series: *Great Expectations* 1863, *Tale of Two Cities* 1864, *The UNCOMMERCIAL TRAVELLER* 1865, *Hard Times* 1866, and *Our Mutual Friend* 1867. Of this edition Forster writes that 'Its success was very good, but did not come even near to the mark of the later issues of his writings'. Rather than being disappointed at sales, Dickens had a 'quiet confidence', which Forster thought well expressed in a dedication written for, but ultimately not included in, the edition: 'This cheap edition of my books is dedicated to the English people, in whose approval, if the books be true in spirit, they will live, and out of whose memory, if they be false, they will soon die' (5.7). Perhaps Dickens thought it best not to talk of an author's works dying.

Using the stereo-plates of the three series of the Cheap Edition, Chapman and Hall produced the People's Edition in 1865–7 in 27 volumes, issued at monthly intervals, at 2s per volume. This edition, aimed at the railway bookstall trade, dropped the prefaces, dedications, tables of contents, and frontispieces, but did include the engravings of the original editions. The longer novels were divided into two volumes. It was an exceptionally successful commercial venture, selling 382,317 volumes during the author's lifetime.

The Library Edition came about largely because of the suggestion of Forster that while Dickens's works were available in volumes in the Cheap Edition and in reprints of the serial parts, there was no high-quality edition that would appeal to the wealthy. Dickens eventually came round to the idea that an elegant edition could raise the stature of his writings. He faced a complication, in that the rights to the works were divided between Chapman and Hall and Bradbury and Evans. Consequently, the volumes contained the imprints of both publishers. With a dedication to Forster, the Library Edition appeared in 22 volumes in 1858–9 at 7s 6d per volume. Titles included *Pickwick*, *Nickleby*, *Chuzzlewit*, *Old Curiosity Shop*, *REPRINTED PIECES*, *Barnaby Rudge*, *Hard Times*, *Sketches by Boz*, *Oliver Twist*, *Dombey*, *Copperfield*, *PICTURES FROM ITALY*, *Bleak House*, *Little Dorrit*, and *Christmas Books*. The only illustrations were the

frontispieces. Between 1861 and 1874 this edition was reissued in 30 volumes with the addition of *Tale of Two Cities*, *Great Expectations*, *Our Mutual Friend*, *The Uncommercial Traveller*, *A CHILD'S HISTORY OF ENGLAND*, *CHRISTMAS STORIES*, and *Drood*. The reissue contained illustrations—the frontispieces plus additional illustrations by artists such as Marcus STONE, John LEECH, and Clarkson STANFIELD—and came to be known as the Illustrated Library Edition.

In 1866 Dickens began work on the Charles Dickens Edition, a 21-volume set in red cloth with his intertwined initials on the cover and his signature stamped in gold. The writer of the 1867 prospectus for this edition wrote that 'this title [The Charles Dickens Edition], appended to every volume, may suggest to the author's countrymen his present watchfulness over his own edition and his hope that it may remain a favourite with them when he shall have left them for ever'. The prospectus went on to state that each novel would be complete in one volume and that 'The page will be a flowing, open page, free from the objection of having double columns'. There was to be a descriptive headline by the author at the top of each right-hand page. Dickens wrote new prefaces, made minor corrections, and selected eight of the original illustrations for each volume, except for *Child's History of England* and *Uncommercial Traveller* with only four each. The longer books were priced at 3s 6d each, the shorter ones at 3s. The publishers undertook an extensive and expensive ADVERTISING campaign, as described by Patten (1978): 'One million three hundred and fifty thousand prospectuses were printed. Smith and Son placarded their English and Irish stations for six months; Willing and Co. posted the London, Chatham, and Dover railway; Robertson covered Australia. In newspapers and magazines £764 worth of advertising was placed in the first six months, more than half the nearly £1,400 spent by the end of 1867' (p. 312). The effort paid off because, as Patten notes, by June 1870 distributors had taken more than 500,000 volumes, and Dickens and his publishers split a profit of more that £12,500. Through the first half of the 20th century the text of the Charles Dickens Edition was generally regarded as the most authentic because it contained the author's last corrections for all his works except *Drood* and *Christmas Stories*, which were added after his death.                    JDV

Nowell-Smith, Simon, 'The "Cheap Edition" of Dickens's Works (First series) 1847–1852', *Library*, 22 (Sept. 1967), 245–51.

**2. Collected editions published after Dickens's lifetime.** In 1871, the year after Dickens's death, the publishers CHAPMAN AND HALL published *Oliver Twist*, the first volume in the Household Edition, playing on the public's fond memories of Dickens's magazine *Household Words*. Over the next eight years the edition grew to 22 volumes. Arthur Waugh calls the Household Edition one of Chapman and Hall's 'most ambitious ventures . . . a new complete edition of Dickens reset in large type on a quarto page, and furnished with entirely new illustrations by a fresh set of artists' (Waugh 1930). In particular, Waugh applauds the work of Fred Barnard who 'took the "Phiz" types and humanized them; they lost nothing of "Phiz's" creative interpretation, but they were stripped of the eccentricity which tended to emphasize the author's own trick of symbolic hyperbole' (see BROWNE, H. K.; ILLUSTRATORS). These illustrations were in addition to reproductions of previously published illustrations by Phiz and others. The 866 illustrations were published in 1908 by Chapman and Hall as a separate volume entitled *Scenes and Characters from the Works of Charles Dickens*. The Household Edition included Dickens's latest prefaces. Robert Patten says that Chapman and Hall may have been inspired to begin this edition by a comment in an OBITUARY in the *Graphic* complaining about the absence of a cheap edition of the novelist's works: 'For this reason the fame of Dickens is still chiefly confined to the middle and upper classes' in England, in contrast to the United States, where 'owing to the price at which his novels have been issued there, they have been read by a far greater number in proportion to population' (Patten 1978, p. 327). The Household Edition was available in monthly parts for one shilling, in penny parts, and in volumes. This was the first edition to include FORSTER'S *Life of Charles Dickens*.

Recognizing the continuing potential for sales of Dickens's works, Chapman and Hall in 1873 published a prospectus for the Second Illustrated Library Edition, containing, they contended, all the works the novelist wished to preserve. Calling it the first well-printed issue, with specially cast type and better paper than that used in previous editions, this set was published in 30 volumes between 1873 and 1876 and sold at £15 for the set, a high price for the time.

In 1897–8 Chapman and Hall issued the Gadshill Edition in 34 volumes. Arthur Waugh credits Oswald Crawfurd with originating the edition. Although it was announced as edited by Andrew Lang, who wrote the introductions, it was, in fact, edited by B. W. MATZ. This was the first complete edition and the first that can be called actually edited. One additional first was that it contained all the original illustrations. Matz says: 'The Original illustrations, by [Robert] SEYMOUR, Hablot K. Browne, [George] CRUIKSHANK, [Frederick] Walker, [Edwin] LANDSEER, [Daniel] MACLISE, [John] LEECH, Marcus STONE, [George] CATTERMOLE, Luke FILDES, are all printed from an unused Set of Duplicate Plates in the possession of the Publishers, or from Plates re-engraved for this Edition' (Matz 1905, p. 17). In 1903 the set was reissued as Edition de Luxe of the Gadshill Edition, and Forster's *Life of Dickens* was added. In 1908 the edition was extended to 38 volumes with the addition of MISCELLANEOUS PAPERS in which Matz reprinted many periodical writings, as well as speeches and poems. The Edition de Luxe was in turn reissued in 1910–11 in 36 volumes as the Centenary Edition. It contained the original illustrations but replaced Lang's introductions with all of Dickens's prefaces and dedications which had appeared in the various editions during his lifetime.

Waugh marvels at the sales of Dickens's works during the first decade of the 20th century: the Waverley Book Club purchased thousands of sets to resell on the instalment plan; a complete set of Dickens was given away with each purchase of the *Encyclopaedia Britannica*. He concludes that 'the volumes could hardly be printed fast enough to keep pace with the demand' (p. 251). The sales were so important to Chapman and Hall, said a company official, that 'If it weren't for Dickens . . . we might as well put up the shutters tomorrow' (p. 201). Thus the firm continued to turn out editions. The 22-volume Authentic Edition appeared in 1901–6, and the seventeen-volume Oxford India Paper Edition in 1901–2, with Forster's *Life* added as an eighteenth volume in 1907. The latter was reissued as the Fireside Edition in 23 volumes in 1903–7 and as the Eighteen Penny Illustrated Edition in 20 volumes in 1908. The plates of the Authentic Edition were used to print the Universal Edition, also 22 volumes, in 1912.

In 1902–3 Chapman and Hall published a nineteen-volume set at 3s 6d per volume and hoped to emphasize Dickens's connection with the firm by giving the collection the title of Biographical Edition. It reproduced the original illustrations and contained introductions by Arthur Waugh. An advertisement stated: 'These introductions are not technical or bibliographical; they aim at brevity and the narrative note; telling a story rather than arraying documents. No attempt is made at superfluous criticism; the biographical element is paramount; and the series of introductions present a clear and interesting story of the literary life of Dickens' (Matz, p. 21). A notable feature was the volume entitled *Collected Papers*, containing many minor writings not previously included in any collection.

The National Edition was published in 1906–8. Waugh credits the early Dickensian B. W. Matz, who was then a member of the firm of Chapman and Hall, with the idea for what at the time was the finest edition of Dickens. As well as conceiving the idea, Matz was also the editor. The Constable Company of Edinburgh was selected for its reputation for producing the best possible type work and press work. From the original steel plates, owned by Chapman and Hall, the illustrations were printed on Japanese paper. The publishers were able to procure from J. F. Dexter, a great collector of Dickensiana, many extra plates, vignettes, and title-pages which had been prepared by a variety of artists for other editions. As a final touch, the editor decided to include facsimiles of the wrappers of the novels issued in parts. The 40 volumes were to be priced at 10s 6d each with the edition to be limited to 750 sets. The publishers felt that this magnificent product was fit for a king. What, they asked themselves, could be more fitting than to call it 'The King's Edition' and dedicate it to King Edward VII? Unfortunately, royal permission was required and,

when applied for, brought the answer that the monarch could not lend his name to a commercial venture and that he could accept a dedication only from a close personal friend. Hence, the publishers settled for the title 'National Edition', which, Waugh writes, 'has no particular meaning' (p. 260).

Chapman and Hall were not alone in publishing editions of Dickens's works. The Macmillan Edition in 21 volumes, published between 1893 and 1925, is of interest for several reasons: it reprinted the text of the first editions, contained 'introductions, biographical and bibliographical', by Charles Dickens the Younger, and featured a collection of Dickens's LETTERS edited by his sister-in-law, Georgina HOGARTH, and his daughter Kate (see CHILDREN OF DICKENS). The J. M. Dent Company published the Temple Edition in 35 volumes in 1898–1903, edited by Walter Jerrold, and, from 1906 to 1921, the Everyman's Library Edition in 22 volumes with important introductions by G. K. CHESTERTON (except for *Barnaby Rudge* and *A Tale of Two Cities*, by Walter Jerrold). Methuen and Co.'s Rochester Edition of 1899–1901, comprised of only eleven volumes (containing *Pickwick Papers*, *Barnaby Rudge*, *Old Curiosity Shop*, *Oliver Twist*, *Nicholas Nickleby*, *Bleak House*), is of interest because of its introductions by George GISSING and notes by F. G. KITTON. Gissing's Introduction to *David Copperfield*, thought to have been lost, was later discovered and published in the *Dickensian* in 1977. In 1901–3 the Gresham Publishing Company also produced an incomplete edition, the Imperial Edition in sixteen volumes, including Gissing's *Charles Dickens, A Critical Study* and 'topographical illustrations' by Kitton. Yet another sadly incomplete edition is the Autograph Edition with fifteen volumes (containing *Pickwick Papers*, *David Copperfield*, *Old Curiosity Shop*, REPRINTED PIECES, *Barnaby Rudge*, *Dombey and Son*) appearing between 1903 and 1908. Published by George G. Harrap and edited by Kitton, it featured introductions by Percy FITZGERALD, George Gissing, George Edward Bateman Saintsbury, William Ernest Henley, Austin Dobson, and Edward Dowden. In 1903–4 Adam and Charles Black produced the twelve-volume Soho Edition. This was reissued in eighteen volumes in 1910 by the Educational Book Company, under the editorship of J. A. Hammerton, as the Charles

Dickens Library, of particular interest because it contained 1,200 illustrations, including 500 for this edition by Harry Furniss. Volume 17 was *The Dickens Picture Book: A Record of Dickens Illustratory*; volume 18 was *The Dickens Companion: A Book of Anecdote and Reference*. The 30-volume Waverley Edition, 1913–15, was illustrated with 'character studies' by Charles Pears and coloured reproductions of Fred Barnard's drawings. Introductions were written by various notables, including George Bernard Shaw and John Galsworthy. A handsome and affordable edition is the Heritage, with sixteen volumes issued at irregular intervals by the Heritage Press for members of the Heritage Club, beginning with *David Copperfield* in 1935. Each volume was illustrated by a different prominent artist of the day; most of the volumes are prefaced with an essay by John T. Winterich, 'How This Volume Came to Be', which places the writing of the book in the context of Dickens's life. These attractive volumes are printed in readable large Baskerville type on high-quality paper.

Great fanfare preceded the 1937–8 Nonesuch Edition. The 128-page Nonesuch *Retrospectus and Prospectus* (1937) contained 'Charles Dickens and His Illustrators' by Arthur Waugh; 'A Bibliographical List of the Original Illustrations to the Works of Charles Dickens' by Thomas Hatton; the 'Retrospectus', a brief summary of the four major previous editions—the Charles Dickens, the Second Illustrated Library, the Gadshill, and the National—with reproductions of specimen pages; and the 'Prospectus', describing the wonders and beauty of the forthcoming edition. (The terms 'Retrospectus' and 'Prospectus' were taken, one assumes, from Dickens's working notes for *Little Dorrit*.) The 23-volume Nonesuch Edition, edited by Arthur Waugh, Thomas Hatton, Walter DEXTER, and Hugh Walpole and published 1937–8 at 48 guineas, is indeed a handsome set. The Nonesuch Press had purchased from Chapman and Hall 877 plates, from which the original illustrations had been printed, and limited the edition to that number of sets, giving one plate to each purchaser. Hatton was in charge of collating and authenticating the illustrations. Dexter, then editor of the *Dickensian*, prepared the text, following the Charles Dickens Edition, and compiled a three-volume set of Dickens's letters which was the most complete until the publication of the Pilgrim Edition of the letters.

Perhaps the most inexpensive and readily available hardback edition is the 21-volume Oxford Illustrated Edition, known before 1966 as the New Oxford Illustrated Edition. Published between 1947 and 1985, the set reproduces the original illustrations or illustrations from early editions (AMERICAN NOTES from the Cheap Edition, *Christmas Stories* from the Charles Dickens Edition and the Illustrated Library Edition, *Great Expectations* from the F. W. Pailthorpe 'extra' illustrations of 1885). Unfortunately, these reproductions are sometimes pale. The introductions are of uneven quality, but those by Humphry HOUSE (*Oliver Twist*), Kathleen Tillotson (*Barnaby Rudge*), Lionel Trilling (*Little Dorrit*), and Leslie Staples (*The UNCOMMERCIAL TRAVELLER/Reprinted Pieces*) are noteworthy. Most of Dickens's works are available in inexpensive paperbacks in the Penguin English Library. These volumes generally have good introductions and useful notes. Similar in price, the Signet Library reprints often have excellent introductions but no notes. A new Everyman paperback edition, under the general editorship of Michael Slater began to appear in 1994. When complete, the Everyman Dickens will extend to 25 volumes and will include all the shorter fiction, plays, poems, writings for children, and travel writings as well as four volumes of the journalism, much of it never before collected. In most cases the editors have based their texts on the Charles Dickens Edition; special features are the inclusion of all the original illustrations, a section on 'Dickens and His Critics', and, where appropriate, historical appendices supplementary to the explanatory annotation, as well as text summaries.

There is no collected edition of Dickens's works in facsimile, although the Scolar Press announced one and in 1973 published a facsimile of *Nicholas Nickleby* in parts, edited by Michael Slater. One other notable example is the 1996 Easton Publishing Company facsimile of *Pickwick Papers*.

The writer of the Nonesuch *Retrospectus and Prospectus* quoted Waugh's statement about that edition: 'It will never be possible for a more complete and perfect edition to be put on the market' (p. 125). The Nonesuch editors, like others before them, used the text of the Charles Dickens Edition, secure in their knowledge that it was the last edition the novelist personally oversaw and was, to their minds, definitive. But scholars such as John Butt in 'Editing a Nineteenth-Century Novelist', *English Studies Today* (1961), pointed out that the manuscript and printed text sometimes disagreed because Dickens regularly wrote too much text for the serial parts and had to cut or condense (see CRITICISM: TEXTUAL SCHOLARSHIP). When he was 'revising' for the collected editions, he apparently rarely consulted his manuscript, almost never restored passages omitted from it, and sometimes left in errors introduced by the compositor. A careful, comprehensive examination of the variant texts had never been undertaken. In 1957 Butt and Tillotson declared that 'Dickens studies have hardly passed beyond the early nineteenth-century phase of Shakespeare studies; while the study of his text seems arrested in the early eighteenth-century' (Butt and Tillotson 1957, p. 8). In an effort to correct the foregoing deficiencies, the two scholars inaugurated the Clarendon Edition with the appearance of *Oliver Twist* in 1966. For most of Dickens's works, particularly the later ones, the Clarendon editors have manuscripts, as well as many working notes and proofs. The editors of these volumes restore deleted text and identify variant readings among the manuscript, the corrected proofs, and editions appearing during Dickens's lifetime. They also supply Dickens's number plans and reprint his prefaces for the various editions and the descriptive headlines he added for the 1867 Charles Dickens Edition.          JDV

Matz, B. W., *Two Great Victorians* (1905).
Patten (1978).
Waugh, Arthur, *One Hundred Years of Publishing* (1930).

**3. Foreign English-language editions.** Even in the absence of any strict rules on international publication, few authors in the 19th century could pride themselves as Dickens did on having their works published at home and abroad almost simultaneously in their original language. But it was also an ambiguous privilege, a combination of recognition and deprivation. For, in those days when the battle for a COPYRIGHT Law—to which the

novelist unremittingly contributed—was far from being won, publication was often synonymous with pirating (see PLAGIARISMS).

Pirating firms, 'Robbers' as Dickens called them (to Henry Austin, 1 May 1842), flourished in the United States, competing among themselves (see AMERICA). The first American firm to net money from the coming young writer was Carey, Lea, and Blanchard, of Philadelphia. Carey published the First Series of *Sketches by Boz* as *Watkins Tottle, and other sketches, illustrative of every-day life and every-day people* (1,250 copies of two volumes published in May 1836), followed by *Sketches by Boz, The Tuggses at Ramsgate, The Pantomime of Life, Public Life of Mr Tulrumble*, and *Oliver Twist* (1837). Dickens was not offered a single penny until it was perceived that his goodwill might be valuable (Patten 1978, p. 95). The publishers then offered him financial proof of their admiration, begging him to accept it, 'not as a compensation, but as a memento of the fact that unsolicited a bookseller has sent an author, if not money, at least a fair representative of it' (Pilgrim 1.652). Dickens indignantly refused the offer, but eventually stooped to conquer on realizing that the 'robbers' might bring money into his own pocket by helping his rise to fame. Carey purchased from Richard BENTLEY for £60 the manuscript of the last ten chapters of *Oliver Twist*, hoping to forestall the pirates; he also paid Dickens an additional £50, and the novelist received £75 for *Pickwick*. Carey proposed to purchase advance sheets of *Nicholas Nickleby*, but Dickens was 'rather behindhand than in advance' (18 July 1838) and so could not supply proofs prior to publication of the monthly numbers. It is true that bookselling was becoming a competitive enterprise and that there were rumours about an international copyright agreement on the verge of being signed, which accounts for Carey's trying to secure a profitable contributor by stealing a march on potential competitors (see PUBLISHING).

Competitors there certainly were. Perhaps chief among the American weeklies were the *New World* and *Brother Jonathan*, which on 7 November 1842 distributed copies of CHAPMAN AND HALL's sheets of AMERICAN NOTES —advertised as 'First American Edition'—as soon as the *Great Western* reached the docks of New York. Harper and Brothers (New

York) published an American version of the book a day later, followed by the *New York Herald* (Patten 1978, p. 131).

The competition between printers, publishers, and distributors would be a long and intricate story to tell. In 1851 T. B. Peterson and Brothers (Philadelphia) bought stereos and woodcuts from Carey, Lea, and Blanchard, Stringer and Townsend, Jesper Harding, G. P. Putnam and Harper's (Patten 1978, p. 297), but it was not until April 1867 that Dickens appointed TICKNOR AND FIELDS, publishers of the ambitious Diamond Edition, as his 'only authorized representatives in America', though FIELDS and his wife had long been very close friends of his. In the meantime, many American publishers succeeded in getting the books printed. *Bleak House* was serialized in *Harper's Weekly* (1852) and Dickens sent them advance sheets of *Little Dorrit*; Harper's and Brothers published *Nickleby* and *Bleak House*, had instalments of *A Tale of Two Cities* and *Great Expectations* delivered in advance, and published *Our Mutual Friend* and *The Mystery of Edwin Drood*. 'GEORGE SILVERMAN'S EXPLANATION' appeared in the *Atlantic Monthly*.

From the 1860s onwards the novels were also distributed in anglophone countries, Dickens's English publishers, Frederic Chapman in particular, having no qualms in exploiting foreign markets. 'The Library edition', Patten writes, 'was sold in quantity throughout the sixties to Ticknor and Fields, Scribner's, Appleton, Little and Brown, and Lippincott' and Australia became 'a steady customer' (p. 297).

A publisher who had Dickens's whole and constant trust was Baron Tauchnitz of Leipzig, whose house was founded in 1837. His 'Collection of British Authors' started in 1841, but he was licensed to publish for continental circulation only. Importation to England or British colonies was prohibited. He first approached Dickens in 1843 (Pilgrim 3.579n.) though he had already published *Pickwick*, *Oliver Twist*, *American Notes*, and *Nickleby* before that date. Their intercourse was friendly to the last. Tauchnitz always dealt very fairly with the novelist, and always paid liberally; Dickens's letters to him are the unfailing expression of his 'entire confidence in [Tauchnitz's] honour and integrity' (11 April 1847).

Tauchnitz published Dickens's complete works first in English between 1841 and 1870. During the years following the death of the novelist many American editions were also completed, but the publishers by then were not so much Dickens's publishers as the publishers of Dickens.

In anglophone countries other than Great Britain and the United States, there are few local editions to speak of. *A South African Bibliography* to the year 1925 lists only *A Tale of Two Cities*, published by T. Maskew Miller (Cape Town and Pretoria) some time in the 1920s. The first known AUSTRALIAN edition of a Dickens work is a pirated edition of *Pickwick* published in 1838 by Samuel Dowling (Launceston, Tasmania). The taste for Dickens in the colony was fed by serialization in local periodicals, the Sydney *Commercial Journal and Advertiser* (*Sketches by Boz* and *Oliver Twist* 1838, *Chuzzlewit*, 1845) the Sydney *Gazette* (*Pickwick*, 1838), the *Australasian Chronicle* (*Master Humphrey's Clock*, 1840–1), *Heads of the People* (*Dombey*, 1847). Dickens's attitude to such publications is clear in a letter he wrote to his lawyer, Frederic Ouvry, in 1865, complaining of 'a New Zealand vagabond playing the old nefarious game with Our Mutual Friend' and asking Ouvry to 'Terrify him, terrify him, terrify him!' (20 July 1865). Apparently, there was no real publishing trade in Australia till the 1940s. Only a few editions can be spotted at the turn of the century: *Our Mutual Friend* and *Bleak House* (E. A. Petherick, Melbourne, 1892 and 1898), *Oliver Twist* and *Barnaby Rudge* (E. W. Cole, Melbourne, 1900 and 1911), *Sketches by Boz* (Rigby, Adelaide, 1900).

Although Parliament during the 1840s tried to prevent inexpensive editions of British authors printed in the United States or elsewhere from entering CANADA, those restrictions were evaded and then relaxed in the hope that imposing a duty of up to 15 per cent would suffice to regulate the trade. Those hopes were delusory; free imports flooded the Canadian markets throughout Dickens's lifetime and thereafter. Various attempts were made from the 1840s on to print in Britain editions of popular authors for sale in the colonies; but though 'cheap books' were always in demand abroad, there were many difficulties to be solved before the books could be manufactured, shipped, and sold in

INDIA and elsewhere for a profit. Nonetheless, Dickens circulated the globe, brought in travellers' baggage if not bought in shops, and read to shreds not only by émigrés but also by Anglophone natives.                                        AS

Nowell-Smith, Simon, *International Copyright Law and the Publisher in the Reign of Queen Victoria* (1968).
Patten (1978).

**editor, Dickens as.** See WILLS, W. H.

**education.** Evidence of Dickens's interest in the important subject of education appears in his fiction, journalism, and public SPEECHES. While he was sensitive to the various educational developments which occurred in his lifetime, he stopped short of offering practical solutions to problems, and his work reflects only a selected range of issues and institutions. He saw education as the way to avoid social catastrophe; the Ghost of Christmas Present shows Scrooge the allegorical children Ignorance and Want, exclaiming, 'most of all beware this boy [Ignorance], for on his brow I see that written which is Doom, unless the writing be erased' (*CC* 3).

He was a strong believer in universal, non-sectarian education, though not necessarily under a state system. He never joined any of the reforming societies, and seemed more comfortable dealing with particular cases and large principles, rather than legislation and administration. His general outlook on the subject is encapsulated in a speech he gave in Birmingham in 1844; he said, 'If you would reward honesty, if you would give encouragement to good, if you would stimulate the idle, eradicate evil, or correct what is bad, education—comprehensive liberal education—is the one thing needful, and the one effective end' (*Speeches*, p. 63).

Dickens's early years coincided with the state's growing sense of responsibility for the instruction of its citizens. Access to education varied tremendously, according to location, gender, and class. Those who could pay for their schooling had access to several types of institution—though quality was by no means guaranteed. Dickens's own experience is a case in point: his education, which he acknowledged to have been 'irregular' (to J. H. Kuenzel, ?July 1838), and relatively slight, began in Chatham, where he was a pupil at a dame-school—a deficient private establish-

ment with an unqualified woman at its head, similar to the one run by Mr Wopsle's great-aunt (*GE* 7). Then in 1821 he moved on to the Revd William Giles's School, where his experiences were very positive, inspiring him with hopes of 'growing up to be a learned and distinguished man' (Forster 1.2). He parted with Giles in 1822 when the Dickens family transferred to London, and in 1824 his schooling was broken off when his father was imprisoned for debt. It resumed in 1825, when he was sent to Wellington House Classical and Commercial Academy, run by the sadistic William Jones, who was the original for Mr Creakle, and whose school was the inspiration for Salem House (*DC* 5–7). Dickens's experiences prompted two other recollections of Wellington House: in his essay 'Our School' he noted that Jones ('the Chief') had a penchant for ruling ciphering-books, and then 'smiting the palms of offenders with the same diabolical instrument' (*HW* 11 October 1851); in a speech of 1857 he remarked that it was Jones's business 'to make as much out of us and put as little into us as possible' (*Speeches*, p. 240). There were, however, positive aspects to Dickens's time at the school: he spoke well of the English teacher, Mr Taylor, who has features in common with Mr Mell (*DC* 5–7, 63), and the Latin master, who 'took great pains when he saw intelligence and a desire to learn' (*HW* 11 October 1851). By the time Dickens left in 1827 he had won the Latin prize.

While Dickens, as the son of a clerk, acquired some formal education, provision for the poor was far less readily assured. Wider access was facilitated by the non-sectarian British and Foreign School Society (founded 1808), and the strongly religious National Society for Promoting the Education of the Poor in the Principles of the Established Church (founded 1811); both used the large-scale monitorial system, and between them they administered over 18,000 schools by 1851. Dickens objected to the National Society's insistence on church intervention in education, declaring that the 'Catechism is wholly inapplicable to the state of ignorance that now prevails' (to Macvey Napier, 16 September 1843). This comment is characteristic of a larger controversy: for much of the 19th century the issue of religious education proved to be the key obstacle in developing a pervasive national school system. Dickens developed this idea imaginatively in 'A December Vision', which contains a portrait of priests and teachers arguing over—but never agreeing on—what to teach (*HW* 14 December 1850).

Dickens found an ally in his promotion of non-sectarian education and concern for the poor and deprived in James Kay-Shuttleworth (1804–77), a former assistant poor-law commissioner, statistician, and critic of the monitorial system, who in 1839 became the first secretary of the Committee of the Privy Council on Education, and laid the foundation for a national system of popular education. He opened the first teacher-training college (in Battersea, 1840); reported on the training of pauper children (1841); instituted the pupil-teacher apprentice system to counter the shortage and poor quality of elementary teachers (1846); and developed an inspectorate for those schools which received government grants. Dickens made his acquaintance in 1846, and found that they shared an interest in Ragged Schools—those institutions which, as their name suggests, accepted the raggedest of children (see CHARITY). In 1843 Dickens began his frequent visits to these schools, and became one of their most prominent supporters, though he was also aware of their limitations—particularly the lack of qualified teaching staff. Ragged Schools found their way into his journalism (*HW* 13 March 1852) and his fiction, where Charley Hexam's first school is described as a 'temple of good intentions' (*OMF* 2.1). Dickens even wrote to Kay-Shuttleworth proposing that they establish a model Ragged School; he enthusiastically declared, 'surely you and I could set one going' (28 March 1846).

While Kay-Shuttleworth's influence and expertise were recognized by both Dickens and Angela Burdett COUTTS (who enlisted the reformer's aid in developing the mark system for URANIA COTTAGE), there were other issues on which he and Dickens diverged—particularly educational methods, school inspections, and teacher training. One strategy singled out by Dickens for criticism in *Hard Times* was the object lesson, originally conceived by the Swiss educationalist Johann Pestalozzi (1746–1827) as a method of instruction deriving from children's own experiences, and suited to their particular stage of development, but distorted in its translation

to England by Charles and Elizabeth Mayo, particularly through the latter's *Lessons on Objects* (1831). Form acquired ascendancy over subject-matter, producing lessons whose vocabulary and content (including Latinate phrases and scientific jargon) were not suited to children's experience. Kay-Shuttleworth helped to popularize the object lesson by including it in the curriculum for his Battersea teacher-training college, which then became the model for many others. Dickens's critique is embodied in the exchange between Gradgrind, Bitzer, and Sissy Jupe over the proper definition of a horse. Bitzer, who has learned a definition by rote, classifies it as a 'Quadruped' and 'Gramnivorous', whereas Sissy, the horse-breaker's daughter dubbed 'Girl number twenty', is reprimanded for possessing 'no facts, in reference to one of the commonest of animals' (*HT* 1.2). The object lesson is also recalled in *Nicholas Nickleby*, where Squeers describes a horse 'as a quadruped, and quadruped's Latin for beast, as everybody that's gone through the grammar knows' (*NN* 8).

The educational critique in *Hard Times* confirms Dickens's familiarity with pedagogical developments. He had read Kay-Shuttleworth's *Public Education* (1853), and lamented the 'supernatural dreariness' of its supporting tables and statistics (to Coutts, 1 April 1853); also, Dickens asked W. H. WILLS to obtain for him a copy of the Education Committee's examination for teachers, for use in the opening chapters (25 January 1854). The novel's depiction of the government inspector, identified as the 'third gentleman' (*HT* 1.2), owes its inspiration to the art critic and designer Henry Cole (1808–82), one of the prime movers behind the Great EXHIBITION OF 1851, who had recently been appointed Superintendent of the Department of Practical Art. Dickens reflected the recent introduction of elementary drawing into the curriculum, and satirized Coles's direction of industrial design for consumer goods, by having this 'professed pugilist' test the children's judgement about whether or not to 'paper a room with representations of horses' (*HT* 1.2). The decidedly negative response, and the equation of taste with fact—which Cole seems to have received with good humour (to Cole, 17 June 1854)— confirms Dickens's disapproval of such unimaginative exponents of rational aesthetics.

The presentation of Mr M'Choakumchild is further evidence of Dickens's interest in contemporary developments. The schoolmaster is the product of Kay-Shuttleworth's pupil-teacher system, which apprenticed proficient boys and girls to school managers for five years, before allowing them to enter the training colleges for a maximum of three years, and then to graduate as certified teachers; the scheme produced its first 'Queen's Scholars' in 1853. While Dickens had argued against the employment of unqualified individuals as teachers (*HW* 13 March and 11 September 1852), he also deprecated what he considered 'Kayshuttleworthian nonsense' (to Coutts, 9 December 1856). Thus he presented M'Choakumchild as one of those who had 'been lately turned at the same time, in the same factory, on the same principles, like so many pianoforte legs' (*HT* 1.2). The list of subjects mastered, ranging from 'Orthography, etymology, syntax, and prosody' to 'all the productions, manners, and customs of all the countries', left little time to develop teaching skills. As Dickens noted, 'If he had only learnt a little less, how infinitely better he might have taught much more' (*HT* 1.2).

While M'Choakumchild features only briefly in *Hard Times*, in *Our Mutual Friend* a teacher occupies a far more prominent position in the narrative. Bradley Headstone, described as a 'highly certificated stipendiary schoolmaster' (*OMF* 2.1) is also a product of the training college system, and his conception follows the 1861 report of the Newcastle Commission, appointed to examine the possibility of extending sound elementary education to all classes. Its investigations revealed that the basics of education were being neglected, as Kay-Shuttleworth's colleges emphasized academic endeavour to the extent that graduates became out of touch with their pupils, and thus could not do their job properly. *Our Mutual Friend* considers the sociological development of the new generation of teachers: Headstone, and his pupil-teacher Charley Hexam, are products of the best education available to individuals from poor backgrounds, who are encouraged to rise above their social origins in their quest for respectability (see CLASS). The training college experience is again presented unsympathetically by Dickens: Headstone 'had acquired mechanically a great store of teacher's knowledge', to the point where his mental 'wholesale warehouse' was 'always ready to meet the demands of retail dealers' (*OMF* 2.1); though relatively well paid, and thus reflecting the enhanced status of qualified teachers, he has a passionate temperament which proves to be his undoing.

Headstone's respectability is precarious. He falls for Lizzie Hexam, but because of his obnoxious behaviour is rejected. Dickens exacerbates this feeling of injustice by positing as his rival Eugene Wrayburn—the indolent, briefless barrister, who has the benefit of a public-school education. Their confrontation serves as an indictment of the whole teaching profession. Dickens stresses Headstone's 'boyish weakness', 'great selfishness', short temper, and 'consciously bad grace' in the face of Wrayburn's 'dandy insolence' (*OMF* 2.6). By making the character of Headstone a significant element in the plot, Dickens highlights several considerations for the new generation of teachers: the struggle to achieve the essential certificate and become a 'Queen's Scholar'; the conceit prompted by the achievement of this status; the temptation to disregard their roots as a safeguard of respectability; and their jealousy of social groups who enjoy privilege without having to work for it.

Because the middle-class fee-paying institutions of Dickens's day did not depend on either charitable subscriptions or state funding, there was greater variation in standards and conditions, and thus more opportunity for imaginative expression. Many of the establishments for girls—about which Dickens knew relatively little—are presented comically, including Minerva House, in which the pupils 'acquired a smattering of everything and a knowledge of nothing' (*SB* 47); Westgate House, to which Mr Pickwick is lured by the threat of Jingle's elopement (*PP* 16); Mrs Wackles's day school, where 'writing, arithmetic, dancing, music, and general fascination' are taught (*OCS* 8); Miss Monflathers's Boarding and Day Establishment, into which 'nothing in the shape of a man—no, not even a milkman—was suffered, without special license, to pass' (*OCS* 31); the Seminary for Young Ladies of Miss Twinkleton, who 'didn't read fairly. She cut the love scenes, interpolated passages in praise of female celibacy, and was guilty of other glaring pious frauds' (*MED* 21); and the 'Lilliputian College' in

'Tom Tiddler's Ground' run by Miss Pupford, who gives a lecture on the mythology of the heathens, 'always carefully excluding Cupid from recognition' (*CS*). The perspective adopted in these portraits is that of a casual adult observer, who visits an establishment generally kept by a mature, narrow-minded spinster. The humorous character of these vignettes is evidence of a typically patriarchal perspective: Dickens shared with most men of his time an ideal of femininity which emphasized the teaching of domestic crafts and responsibilities, rather than imaginative or intellectual pursuits—although in real life he encouraged his daughter's career as a painter.

When Dickens turns his attention to fee-paying establishments for boys, they are treated far more seriously, and the perspective is generally that of the anguished pupil. Such is the character of Dotheboys Hall in *Nicholas Nickleby*, run by the sadistic Wackford Squeers (*NN* 8, 9, 12, 13). The novel served as a vehicle for exposing the dreadful conditions in the Yorkshire schools—those private venture boarding schools which catered for un-wanted—often illegitimate—children, who were kept throughout the year at cheap rates. Dickens denounced these establishments as examples of 'the monstrous neglect of education in England' and his attack helped to speed their demise.

While Squeers's designs are undeniably malevolent, in *Dombey and Son* Dickens focuses on a well-intentioned schoolmaster whose shortcoming is a deficient methodology. Little Paul progresses from Mrs Pipchin's, where the system was 'not to encourage a child's mind to develop and expand itself like a young flower, but to open it by force like an oyster' (*DS* 8), to Dr Blimber's academy, where he is sent by a father impatient for his son's advancement. The pompous Blimber runs 'a great hothouse, in which there was a forcing apparatus incessantly at work', assisted by his daughter Cornelia, 'dry and sandy with working in the graves of deceased languages', and Mr Feeder, BA, the 'human barrel-organ' (*DS* 8, 11, 12). Dickens seized the opportunity to offer a critique on the premature acquisition of mathematical skill, but more importantly of classical languages, which were not only essential for university entrance but were seen as valued culture-tokens for increasing

self-respect. The boys' plight is communicated through Mr Feeder's method of instruction: 'They knew no rest from the pursuit of strong-hearted verbs, savage noun-substantives, inflexible syntactic passages, and ghosts of exercises that appeared to them in their dreams' (*DS* 11). They reach the conclusion that 'all the fancies of the poets, and lessons of the sages, were a mere collection of words and grammar, and had no other meaning in the world' (*DS* 12). It is interesting to note that although Paul Dombey's death is accelerated by the Blimber regime, he—and other pupils like Toots—regard the school with affection.

While most of his fictional portraits are of children's schools, Dickens was also a strong, vocal supporter of adult education, particularly mechanics' institutes—those establishments offering instruction to subscribing artisans and skilled workers; by 1850 there were about 700 such foundations, claiming a membership of 100,000 (see SELF-HELP). Dickens was elected president of mechanics' institutes in Chatham, Birmingham, and Reading, and gave PUBLIC READINGS to raise funds for them; despite this seriousness of purpose, he was not averse to offering a comical account in 'Dullborough Town' (*UT* 12). He was also present at various foundings, soirées, and prize-givings from 1843 onward, giving speeches which reviewed resources and achievements, fees levied, number of volumes in the libraries, and courses offered. In 1844 he proclaimed of the Liverpool Mechanics' Institution: 'Every man who has felt the advantages of, or has received improvement in, this place, carries its benefits into the society in which he moves, and puts them out at compound interest, and what the blessed sum may be at last, no man can tell' (*Speeches*, p. 54).

Dickens believed in the extension of education on sound principles to all citizens; yet he did not offer specific strategies for achieving this aim. He exposed what he considered abuses and deficiencies, and praised what he believed were positive developments. He was a pioneer in introducing the theme of education into prose fiction, and proved, in his correspondence, journalism, and speeches, that he had greater familiarity with the subject than most of his rivals. In the year of his death Parliament passed the Elementary Education Act, which further raised the standard of teacher training and effectively inaugurated compulsory schooling. If Dickens made any practical contribution to achieving this end, it was by reinforcing the public's sense of moral feeling, and providing additional momentum for change. LL

Altick, Richard, 'Education, Print and Paper in *Our Mutual Friend*', in C. de L. Ryals (ed.), *Nineteenth-Century Literary Perspectives: Essays in Honor of Lionel Stevenson* (1974).

Collins, Philip, 'Dickens and the Ragged Schools', *Dickensian*, 55 (1959).

Collins (1963).

Gilmour, Robin, 'The Gradgrind School: Political Economy in the Classroom', *Victorian Studies*, 11 (1967).

Kay-Shuttleworth, James, *Four Periods of Public Education* (1862).

Shatto, Susan, ' "A complete course, according to question and answer" ', *Dickensian*, 70 (1974).

**Egan, Pierce** (1774?–1849), writer. When an anonymous critic saw 'a dash of a grammatical Egan' in *The Pickwick Papers*, he was referring to the rhetorical flourishes characteristic of Pierce Egan, Sr. Egan was the most popular SPORTING and CRIME journalist of the Regency era, and his ornate yet intimate writing set a model for 'real life' reporting which rubbed off on the young Dickens. But Dickens was not only indebted to Egan for elements in his style. Egan's *Life in London* (1820–1) was the literary sensation of the 1820s and foreshadowed Dickens's success with *Pickwick*. Accompanied by ILLUSTRATIONS by Isaac Robert and George CRUIKSHANK, it came out in shilling monthly parts. Anticipating Pickwick and Weller, Egan showed an innocent guided through London scenes by a streetwise initiate, thereby revealing its changing scenes and situations, although Egan's Jerry and Tom were Regency bucks very different to Dickens's pair. Most important, Egan's work pioneered romantic interest in the crowded life of London, with its contrasts of poverty and wealth, a vein Dickens was to develop and make his own. Egan later flattered Dickens by imitation in his picaresque novel *Pilgrims of the Thames* (1838). LJ

Reid, J. C., *Bucks and Bruisers* (1971).

**Egg, Augustus.** See DICKENS CIRCLE, THE.

**elections and the franchise.** During Dickens's lifetime franchise qualifications in the United Kingdom were radically altered on two occasions, in 1832 and in 1867/8. Latest estimates suggest that these changes increased the total electorate by about 55 per cent in the counties and 41 per cent in the towns, with an overall increase of approximately 49 per cent. The general effect of the so-called Great REFORM Act of 1832 was to enfranchise the lower middle classes of England and Wales. It was certainly not to make Britain more democratic. Both Dickens's journalism and his novels reflect the irritation and dismay felt by most radicals that post-1832 elections were not the sober, enlightened affairs they wished to see. The Reform Act did, however, increase the number of large parliamentary boroughs, not only in the industrial and commercial towns of the north and midlands, but also in Dickens's home city of London which gained ten additional seats, two each for Finsbury, Greenwich, Lambeth, Marylebone, and Tower Hamlets.

Dickens had been a close-hand observer of the debates of 1831–2 which preceded the 1832 Reform Act in his capacity as shorthand writer for the MIRROR OF PARLIAMENT, at that time an effective rival to *Hansard*. One of Dickens's first jobs was as polling clerk in December 1832 for the reformist MP Charles Tennyson, uncle of the poet, during the first elections held under the new system (Ackroyd 1990, p. 147). He became a keen observer of elections, not least in his capacity as parliamentary reporter on the Whig-supporting and reformist MORNING CHRONICLE from 1833. He was paid a salary of five guineas a week in this capacity. In 1834, for example, he reported on a dinner given in Edinburgh on 15 September for Lord Grey (*Journalism* 2.3–8). He wrote a bilious account of the Kettering by-election on 19 December 1835. 'No artifice has been left untried, no influence has been withheld, no chicanery neglected by the Tory party and the glorious result is that Mr Mansell is placed at the head of the poll, by the most ignorant, and brutal electors in these kingdoms, who have been treated, and fed, and driven up to the poll the whole day, like herds of swine' (Pilgrim 1.108n.).

Not surprisingly, therefore, Dickens's imaginative writings on elections evince both healthy scepticism and satirical comment. In *Sketches by Boz* he paints a jaundiced picture of the contest for parish beadle between the 'official' candidate, Spruggins, and the outsider, Bung. The comedy is sharpened by the fact that the beadle was not normally an elective office anyway. Bung was supported by a retired half-pay officer, Captain Purday, who engaged hackney coaches to transport electors to the poll—one for 'the drunken voters' and two for 'the old ladies, the greater proportion of whom, owing to the captain's impetuosity, were driven up to the poll and home again, before they had recovered from their flurry sufficiently to know, with any degree of clearness, what they had been doing'. Since elections after 1832 were not concluded in a single day, and since bribery and treating with liquor remained common in many constituencies, Dickens was satirizing the frequent electoral abuses to which radicals continued to draw attention after 1832.

*Pickwick* contains a famous account of the election for the borough of Eatanswill between 'the Blues and the Buffs'. This vividly captures both the venality and local excitement generated by a parliamentary election. The narrator confesses 'that we have in vain searched for proof of the actual existence of such a place at the present day'—an allusion to some of the smaller boroughs, like Calne, Rye, and St Ives, which survived the axe in 1832. Its electors 'considered themselves of the utmost and mighty importance' and divided their loyalties between 'Blue shops and Buff shops, Blue Inns and Buff Inns ... there was a Blue aisle and a Buff aisle in the very church itself'. Pickwick stands as the innocent who is amazed at the 'strange practices' involved in intoxicating and drugging the electors, while one of the candidates, Samuel Slumkey, has to be persuaded by his adviser to do his electoral duty in respect of one of the six 'children in arms' during the electoral procession: 'if you could manage to kiss one of 'em, it would produce a very great impression on the crowd'. Carried away by the occasion, Slumkey kisses them all and is elected (*PP* 13).

The effect of the *Pickwick* account is heightened by the fact that elections were still held without a secret ballot. Since electors had to declare their preference in a 'poll book', elections, particularly in the boroughs, retained something of the 18th-century atmosphere of carnival or even street theatre into the second half of the 19th century. Political processions, public hustings, and traditions

such as parading an elected MP around the constituency—'Chairing the Member'—continued. Popular participation in some elections was pronounced. Non-voters were encouraged to participate in the wider political culture at election times by attending meetings and demonstrations or by reading placards and party literature. Informal participation in the electoral process was thus more extensive than a calculation of the number of formally registered voters might imply.

Parliamentary elections were normally held only once every seven years. Members of Parliament were, therefore, not regularly held to account by their electors. In *Nickleby* the pompous MP Gregsbury who, while asserting that 'my time is yours—and my country's', has refused to honour pledges given to his constituents when he sought election, including 'that in event of your being returned, you would immediately put down the practice of coughing and groaning in the House of Commons' (*NN* 16).

*Our Mutual Friend* refers to the fact that some parliamentary seats remained effectively for purchase well after 1832. The wealthy Mr Veneering wishes to find a parliamentary seat, though 'not previously aware of having any' political opinions. Financial inducements having been provided, he is presented for the small borough of 'Pocket Breaches'. Lady Tippins remarks that 'she is pretending to be an electioneering agent' on Veneering's behalf, 'carrying on this little farce' of pretending that he is 'the dearest friend I have in the world' (*OMF* 2.3). The reference here is to the increased prominence of election agents after 1832 when a formal constituency register of electors was required. Robert Peel, as leader of the opposition in 1838, called this registration of voters 'a perfectly new element of political power ... a more powerful one than either the Sovereign or the House of Commons'. In many boroughs, particularly, the outcome of elections in the mid-19th century did indeed turn on the ability of party registration agents—often solicitors supporting one party or the other—to persuade known supporters to register. In the 1830s and early 1840s the Tories organized in London by F. R. Bonham co-ordinated electoral strategies much more effectively than the Whigs and reaped the electoral rewards. After the second

Reform Act of 1867, registration and party organization had an even higher premium.

'Doctor Marigold' (*CS*) contains an account of an electoral contest between Cheap Jack and 'Dear Jack', who vie with one another to persuade the so-called 'free and independent woters': 'I am going to give you such a chance as you never had in all your born days, and that's the chance of sending Myself to Parliament.' Dickens well knew that electors, especially in county constituencies where tenants occupying property worth £50 or more a year could vote, were frequently anything but 'free', since landowners were not above indicating that support for their preferred election candidate was a necessary requirement for the renewal of a lease. Norman Gash has estimated that up to 70 seats after 1832 remained under landlord control on terms not dissimilar to the situation before the first Reform Act (*Politics in the Age of Peel*, 1953). Gladstone, indeed, first became an MP in the elections held immediately after the Reform Act of 1832 and under the patronage of the Duke of Newcastle, who selected him because of his known strong Tory views.

Dickens's satires concentrate on what he saw as electoral malpractice and on the continuation of excessive landowner 'influence'. He did not draw attention to the frequent absence of any contest at all. After 1832, England and Wales had 254 constituencies. At no single election held between the two Reform Acts were more than 188 of these contested at any single election. In the general election of 1847 the number of contests was as low as 120 (47 per cent of the total). The increased electorate after 1832 did not necessarily have an increased opportunity actually to exercise a choice, especially in the smaller electoral boroughs.

Dickens himself was invited by the bookseller George Lovejoy to stand as Liberal candidate for Reading at the general election of 1841. Though probably tempted, not least because he had strong feelings against the new POOR LAW which he wished to air in Parliament, he declined the offer. Electoral opinion having moved decisively against Melbourne's government, he had little chance of success. Going with the national swing, Reading comfortably returned two Tories in 1841. He replied to Lovejoy's invitation courteously: 'I have no hesitation in saying plainly, that I cannot afford the expense of a contested election' (31 May 1841).                    EJE

**Eliot, George** (Mary Ann, later Marian, Evans) (1819–80), novelist, author of eight volumes of fiction written between 1857 and 1876: *Scenes of Clerical Life, Adam Bede, The Mill on the Floss, Silas Marner, Romola, Felix Holt, the Radical, Middlemarch*, and *Daniel Deronda*. She also translated Strauss's freethinking *Life of Jesus* in 1846, and Feuerbach's heterodox *Essence of Christianity* in 1854. In 1850 she met the publisher John Chapman and became a contributor to, and later assistant editor of, his *Westminster Review*. She first encountered Dickens at Chapman's house in 1852 where, at a meeting of writers, Dickens took the chair. Whilst admiring his chairmanly 'courteous neutrality of eyebrow', Eliot found Dickens's appearance 'disappointing—no benevolence in the face and I think little in the heart . . . he is not distinguished looking in any way—neither handsome nor ugly, neither fat nor thin, neither tall nor short' (Karl 1995, p. 141). She met George Henry LEWES, a friend of Dickens who was heavily involved in the latter's AMATEUR THEATRICALS, in about 1854. They lived together outside of marriage (his wife was still alive), and the relationship was generally accepted by their friends. Through Lewes, Dickens pursued Eliot as a contributor to *All the Year Round*, but without success. Dickens assured Lewes that were Eliot to write for the journal an immense new public would have been opened to her. Eliot's refusal frustrated him, and he put her reluctance down to a fear of the demands of SERIAL publication (to G. H. Lewes, 13 February 1860, and to Charles Lever, 15 October 1860).

Dickens admired Eliot's work, writing to his friend FORSTER of her *Scenes of Clerical Life*: 'Do read them . . . They are the best things I have seen since I began my course' (Forster 4.1). He also intuited that the pseudonymous author of *Scenes* was a woman (to George Eliot, 18 January 1858). For her part, Eliot had grave reservations about the merits of Dickens's fiction, lamenting in her 'Natural History of German Life' (1856) that whilst Dickens could render 'the external traits of our town people' he failed to 'give us their psychological character'. She objected too to 'his preternaturally virtuous poor children and artisans, his melodramatic boatmen and courtesans' (Eliot 1992, p. 264). Eliot seems to have felt competitive towards Dickens, even after his death. She was apparently nettled by the fact that Forster's *Life* sold more copies than *Middlemarch* in the early years of publication (Karl 1995, p. 490). Eliot's scientific and philosophical intellectualism, allied with her emphatically realist fictional style, made her a different kind of novelist than Dickens.   SL

Eliot, George, 'The Natural History of German Life', in Rosemary Ashton (ed.), *George Eliot: Selected Critical Writings* (1992).

Haight, Gordon, *George Eliot: A Biography* (1968).

Karl, Frederick, *George Eliot: A Biography* (1995).

**Ellis and Blackmore** were the Gray's Inn solicitors who employed Dickens as a clerk from March 1827 to November 1828. Edward Blackmore (1799–1879), the junior partner in the firm, was a boarder at the house of Elizabeth DICKENS's aunt (16 Berners Street, Oxford Street) in 1827, and he was asked by the family to find employment in his office for the young Dickens. On his first day, the 15-year-old Dickens turned up in a military-looking outfit and got a black eye from a heckler in the street.

F. G. Kitton, in *Charles Dickens by Pen and Pencil* (1890–2), reproduces a page from the firm's petty-cash book (now in Harvard's Widener Library) showing Dickens's handwriting for the entries from 5 January to 16 March 1828. Kitton also includes reminiscences by Blackmore and George Lear, an articled clerk, of the young Dickens at work. He used to be sent to government offices such as the Alienation Office, the Affidavit Office, and the Sixpenny Receivers' Office (there were 150 of them), on errands for Ellis and Blackmore, who acted as an agency office for solicitors in provincial centres like Bath and Chichester. Adept at these tasks, the young Dickens saw his weekly salary rise from the initial 10s 6d to a final 15s and also found endless material for satire of pre-Victorian officialdom. During this period, Dickens spent much of his time off going to the theatre with another clerk, Charles Potter, who was the model for 'the salaried clerk' earning a grand 30s per week in *Pickwick* (*PP* 30) and for the character of Thomas Potter in 'Making a Night of It' (*SB*). Lear said Dickens knew his London 'from

Bow to Brentford' and could imitate not only all the ancient office clerks but also all the varieties of street vendors in London. Blackmore published a letter about Dickens's experiences at Ellis and Blackmore (*Hampshire Chronicle*, 18 June 1870), just after Dickens's death.   KC

Carlton, W. J., 'Mr Blackmore Engages an Office Boy', *Dickensian*, 48 (1952).

**Emerson, Ralph Waldo** (1803–82). American Transcendentalist essayist, lecturer, and poet. Dickens satirized moonshiny Transcendental idealism in *Martin Chuzzlewit* but was not so hard on the Boston-based 'school' in AMERICAN NOTES: noting Emerson's debt to their common friend Thomas CARLYLE, Dickens found in Emerson's Essays 'much that is dreamy and fanciful' but 'much more that is true and manly, honest and bold'. Emerson granted *American Notes* was 'a readable book, nothing more'. Incapable of appreciating fiction, the New England moralist dismissed the little 'poor Pickwick stuff' he had seen and grumbled that Dickens could not write dialogue, that in *Oliver Twist* his 'eye rests always on surfaces[;] he has no insight into Character'. But when on 25 April 1848 Emerson dined with Dickens, he 'liked him very well' and came to respect him as a social critic. He mentions Dickens several times in *English Traits* (1856), but affords him the faint praise of having 'a preternatural apprehension' of 'municipal' detail. The Emerson children were caught up in the Dickens craze, attending costumed Dickens parties and hearing his PUBLIC READING of *A Christmas Carol* in December 1867. Finally hearing Dickens read for himself, Emerson reportedly 'laughed as if he must crumble into pieces' but could not overcome the old prejudice that 'Dickens is too consummate an artist to have a thread of nature left. He daunts me! I have not the key.'   WTM

**emigration and colonization.** Dickens had practical, fictional, and personal interests in emigration and colonization. The years of his life saw the development of AUSTRALIA, the settling of New Zealand, the Durham Report, Canadian Confederation, the expansion of South Africa, the exploration of tropical Africa, the establishment of coastal colonies, the extension of British rule in INDIA, and an uprising against colonial rule in Jamaica (see EYRE, EDWARD JOHN). By the later 1840s circumstances such as the increased pressures of industrial labour, coupled with bourgeois apprehension over the poor, the unemployed, and dissident workers, combined to inspire—among novelists as well as reformers—a popular advocacy of emigration as an acceptable panacea for social ills. From May 1846 onwards Dickens was involved in the URANIA COTTAGE project—the practical aim of which was to prepare its occupants for emigration, as well as to arrange their passage to the colonies, and their reception. As he proclaimed in the *Household Words* lead article which explained the scheme, 'there could be little or no hope in this country' for those who entered Urania Cottage; therefore the home only received 'those who distinctly accepted this condition: That they came there to be ultimately sent abroad' ('Home for Homeless Women', *HW* 23 April 1853). To demonstrate the effectiveness of the plan, Dickens reported on the progress of the women—many of whom ended up in Australia (see PROSTITUTES AND FALLEN WOMEN).

Concurrent with his interest in the reclamation and conveyance of fallen women was a growing concern with assisted emigration on a large scale. He acquired information from a variety of printed sources, including the Colonization Circulars issued annually by the Emigration Board, which included full details of the length and cost of voyages, as well as wages, prices, and the demand for labour in each of the British colonies. He was also attracted to the animated and widely circulated work of Samuel Sidney (1813–83), a polemical journalist who, assisted by his bushman brother John, published *Sidney's Australian Hand-Book* (1848) and *Sidney's Emigrant's Journal and Traveller's Magazine* (1848–50). Dickens wished to capitalize on this writer's popularity and avowed expertise by having him contribute to *Household Words* on the subject; Sidney agreed, and a series of historical accounts, adventure stories, and pieces offering practical advice appeared from 1850 onwards (see, for example, *HW* 16 November 1850 and 31 January 1852).

At about the same time Dickens came into contact with another potential contributor on Australia: Caroline Chisholm (1808–77), founder of the Family Colonization Loan Society. She developed a scheme whereby English families could be lent money for their passage, and would repay it when they had established themselves in the colony. She collaborated with both Dickens and R. H. HORNE to produce articles for *Household Words*, including 'A Bundle of Emigrants' Letters' (*HW* 30 March 1850), and 'Pictures of Life in Australia' (*HW* 22 June 1850). Chisholm's ethos influenced the tone of many Australian contributions to Dickens's journal.

Both Sidney and Chisholm promoted a vision of Australia as the solution to the perceived social distress plaguing England; their nostalgia for the Arcadian past of rural England influenced their language, as well as the lifestyle they advocated. The physical details they presented, and the sentiments they promoted provided a vantage point for Dickens in his depiction of Australia in *David Copperfield*—a novel in which emigration plays an important regenerative role. The colony is the final depository for the Micawbers, Martha Endell, the Peggottys, Mrs Gummidge, and Mr Mell. Micawber is unable to function in English society, but in Australia he enjoys a joyful if incompletely credible metamorphosis: after an interval spent in the bush, 'perspiring in the sun' (*DC* 63), he becomes a highly respected magistrate in Port Middlebay (Dickens's fictional appellation for Brisbane), and a leading contributor to the town's newspaper. Martha Endell also emigrates, thus allowing her to eradicate the stigma of the prostitute; she marries a farm labourer, and leads a productive life in the bush. She clearly conforms to the mould fashioned in the conception of Urania Cottage, and serves as a fictional testament to the success of the project. Daniel Peggotty becomes the epitome of the proletarian colonist lauded by Sidney and Chisholm; despite his seafaring background he takes to the bush and acquires consummate skill in agricultural pursuits, proudly proclaiming to David, 'What with sheep-farming, and what with stock-farming, . . . we've done nowt but prosper' (*DC* 63).

Dickens had further contact with Australia in the 1850s and 1860s through, among others, Horne, who emigrated in 1852, having been commissioned by the novelist to write a series of articles for *Household Words* on gold-mining (an activity of which Dickens disapproved). He also contemplated travelling to the colony for a PUBLIC READING tour, inspired by reports of 'the kind of reception that would await me', and enticed by the chance of gaining 'a great deal of curious experience for after use' (22 October 1862). While he did not go himself, two of his sons did: Alfred D'Orsay Tennyson Dickens sailed in 1865, and Edward Bulwer Lytton Dickens ('Plorn') emigrated in 1868 (see CHILDREN OF DICKENS). Alfred became moderately prosperous as a stock and station agent—a position he held until 1894. Plorn, whom Dickens thought 'may take better to the Bush than to Books' (24 August 1868), fell into debt, but was not allowed by his father to return to England. He eventually prospered, and served in the New South Wales Legislative Assembly from 1889 to 1894.

Other of Dickens's children also went abroad. Walter Savage Landor Dickens went to India at the age of 16, but as a soldier rather than an emigrant. After fighting in the Indian Mutiny he died there in 1863. In the same year Francis Jeffrey Dickens sailed to the subcontinent to join his brother, but arrived after his death; he joined the Bengal Police, and by 1874 had emigrated to CANADA, where, as an inspector in the North West Mounted Police, he helped in quelling the second Riel Rebellion in 1885, and in the defence of Fort Pitt.

In *Martin Chuzzlewit* Dickens showed a less positive side of the emigrant's experience. Not only Martin, but the typical emigrant family he and Mark Tapley meet on the *Screw* find themselves easy prey to the fraudsters and speculators waiting for the idealistic new settlers. Dickens's only other extended fictional treatment of emigration was in the UN-COMMERCIAL TRAVELLER, where, in 'Bound for the Great Salt Lake', he described the orderly behaviour of a group of 800 English and Welsh Mormons who were emigrating to Utah. The Traveller observes the behaviour of several families including the Dibbles and the Jobsons, commenting that there was 'no scrambling or jostling for the hot water, no ill humour, no quarrelling' on board the *Amazon*. The emphasis is on factual reporting, though he concludes on a note of doubt as to their future: 'What is in store for the poor people . . . what happy delusions they are labouring under now, on what miserable blindness their eyes may be opened then, I do not pretend to say' (*UT* 20).

Emigration was a popular way of tying up loose ends at the end of Victorian novels, but apart from *David Copperfield* Dickens avoids this particular tactic. On the other hand his novels are full of characters returning to England from the colonies—Magwitch returns from Australia (*GE*), Clennam comes back from China (*LD*), Rokesmith returns from the West Indies (*OMF*), and the Landlesses have lived in the east prior to the beginning of *The Mystery of Edwin Drood*. Taken as a whole, Dickens's novels are powerfully suggestive of a larger interest in British colonies, as well as more general political and commercial interests overseas.                                   LL

Hollington, Michael, 'Dickens and Australia', *Cahiers victoriens et edouardiens*, 33 (1991).
Lazarus, Mary, *A Tale of Two Brothers: Charles Dickens' Sons in Australia* (1973).
Litvack, Leon, 'Dickens, Australia, and Magwitch Part I: The Colonial Context', *Dickensian*, 95 (1999).
Simpson, D. H., 'Charles Dickens and the Empire', *Library Notes* (Royal Commonwealth Society), NS 162–3 (1970).

**Englishness, Dickens's.** 'Boz is a truly national author—English to the backbone', wrote the *Quarterly Review* (June 1839) in one early attempt to explain his POPULARITY. The next year Thomas HOOD was praising the 'Englishness' of *Pickwick*, 'to my taste a first-rate merit' (Pilgrim 2.221n.). His being 'so thoroughly English' and displaying an 'exquisite comprehension of the national character and manners' (*Fraser's*, 1850) was noted and welcomed throughout his career; he was 'national' in his fame and sympathies (*The Times*, 24 December 1857), 'his tastes and modes of thought were', wrote *Fraser's* (1870), narrowing this description, 'essentially middle-class English'. To discriminate further: he was a southerner, and by adoption, though not by birth, a Londoner. He never lived north of London.

Born in Portsea, Hampshire, and passing his happiest childhood years in Chatham on the Thames estuary, he was moved when 10 to London, where he resided until he bought a country-house in 1857, though he always retained a London *pied-à-terre*. His early journalistic duties took him sometimes into the provinces and to SCOTLAND, as later did public functions and family holidays (in south-coast resorts) and the PUBLIC READING tours. Researches for his writings occasionally made him visit unfamiliar areas: Yorkshire for its notorious schools (*Nicholas Nickleby*), or Preston, Lancashire, to observe a strike (which also suggested elements in *Hard Times*), or the Lake District for 'The LAZY TOUR OF TWO IDLE APPRENTICES' (though he shows little interest in the scenery). A brief jaunt to East Anglia suggested the Blunderstone and Yarmouth scenes of *David Copperfield*, but he mugged up the local dialect from a book. He was a stranger to the industrial north and midlands, and was ignorant of agricultural areas; the villages in his novels are very thinly presented (contrast David's Blunderstone and Pip's unnamed birthplace with George ELIOT's or Hardy's villages). He makes little attempt to depict regional types and characteristics, and the only dialect he is at ease with is Cockney, though he makes conscientious efforts with John Browdie's Yorkshirisms (*Nickleby*) and with Stephen Blackpool in *Hard Times*, his only novel set wholly outside London, which is overwhelmingly his main fictional locale.

'He was a master in London; abroad he was only a workman', judged his colleague John Hollingshead. 'There are scarcely anywhere such pictures of London as he draws', wrote Walter BAGEHOT (*National Review*, October 1858); '. . . He describes London like a special correspondent for posterity.' Most of the action of his novels occurs there, though the characters may originate in or make forays into the provinces, always to towns or areas Dickens knew. The novels also use countries he had visited (AMERICA, ITALY, FRANCE) but never Scotland, Wales, or IRELAND, and surprisingly he never resorts to the traditional English jokes about Scottish stinginess, Irish blarney and stupidity, and Welsh wiliness and verbosity. Mrs Woodcourt (*Bleak House*) is a feeble attempt at Welshness; otherwise he showed no interest in the Welsh, but seems to have held the common English view that Scotsmen were rational if idiosyncratic adults (he had a special fondness for Edinburgh) while the Irish were comic, crude, or violent. He was remarkably indifferent to the Irish potato famine of 1845–6, and never visited Ireland until his 1858 readings tour took him there.

For a well-to-do man in the steam age, he was not well-travelled overseas. Apart from a week in France and Belgium in 1837, his first encounter with foreigners was in the 1842 visit to America. In the next few years he moved his family to Italy, SWITZERLAND, and France, to economize, and from 1852 onwards was quite often in France for holidays and relaxation. He told his son Henry, 'laughingly, that his sympathies were so much with the French that he ought to have been born a Frenchman' (Henry Dickens 1928), and he sometimes favourably contrasted French civic arrangements and social customs with English (though on other occasions France was 'that detestable nation'). His more cosmopolitan colleague G. A. SALA, who spent time with him in PARIS, saw no evidence of his liking the French or appreciating their culture: he was a 'plain, downright Englishman', with 'a good-humoured contempt of foreigners' which in *PICTURES FROM ITALY* became 'aggravated into something like savage and ignorant ridicule' fed by 'an ample stock of the soundest of John Bull prejudices' (*Things I Have Seen*, 1894). In nothing, remarks Humphry HOUSE, 'was Dickens so much of an elementary John Bull as in his hatred of Catholicism' (see ROMAN CATHOLIC CHURCH; House 1941).

He was not, however, rabidly chauvinistic. George ORWELL indeed found it 'very striking . . . especially considering the time in which he lived', that, unlike THACKERAY, he was free of 'vulgar nationalism' (Orwell 1940). In a lively article, 'Insularities' (*HW* 19 January 1856), he attacks the tendency 'to be firmly persuaded that what is not English is unnatural', and in a letter (6 December 1846) he remarks: 'It is extraordinary what nonsense English people talk, write and believe, about foreign countries'—though he then proceeds with some confidently dismissive generalizations about the French, quoted below, while praising the Swiss as to be 'relied upon as steadily as the English'.

His career coincided with the peak of British international power, prestige, and commercial eminence. 'The modern world is theirs,' wrote R. W. EMERSON (*English Traits*, 1856). 'They have made and make it day by day . . . England is the best of actual nations . . . London is the epitome of our times, and the Rome of today'. Dickens, though indignant over his country's many shortcomings and often recording 'shameful testimony for future ages, how civilisation and barbarism walked this boastful island together' (*BH* 11), was not immune to the inevitable national afflatus. He mocks Mr Podsnap's conviction that other countries were 'a mistake' and that 'this island was Blest, Sir, to the Direct Exclusion of such other countries as—as there may happen to be' (*OMF* 1.11) but, as G. K. CHESTERTON observes, he was himself 'as English as any Podsnap or any Plornish' (Chesterton 1906).

The 'English-Saxon character', he tells children in his CHILD'S HISTORY OF ENGLAND, 'has been the greatest character among the nations of the earth . . . patient, persevering, never to be broken in spirit', etc. 'Wherever that race goes, there, law, and industry, and safety for life and property, and all the great results of steady perseverance, are certain to arise' (*CHE* 3). Addressing the grown-ups in *Household Words*, he praises 'the intelligence, steadfastness, foresight and wonderful power of resource, which in private [as against governmental] undertakings distinguish England from all other countries' ('That Other Public'), and their non-commercial virtues are equally conspicuous: '. . . remarkable for their domestic habits, and their household virtues and affections. They are, now, beginning to be universally respected by intelligent foreigners . . . for their unobtrusive politeness, their good-humour . . . [etc., and they] deserve this testimony . . . most honourably . . . The national vices are surprisingly few . . .' ('The Sunday Screw', *HW* 22 June 1850).

He was correspondingly aware of foreigners' deficiencies, such as their aversion to cleanliness and fresh air: here Emerson happily corroborates him ('A Frenchman may be clean: an Englishman is conscientiously clean'; *English Traits*, 1856). 'All the undrained, unscavengered qualities of a foreign town', Dickens grandly generalizes in *Pictures from Italy*, and he was worried when his cook, 'full of English notions of comfort and cleanliness and decency' (9 May 1845), married an Italian. Of the lower orders in Paris he writes: 'To the American indifference and carelessness, they add a procrastination and want of the least heed about keeping a promise or being exact, which is not surpassed in Naples. They have the American semi-sentimental independence too, and none of the American vigour or purpose . . . [Free trade would be fatal to them, in competition with English workmen.] Their inferior manual dexterity, their lazy habits, perfect unreliability and habitual

insubordination, would ruin them . . . instantly' (6 December 1846).

In America, 1842, he 'discovered his essential Englishness; indeed his need for English life . . . his sojourn on alien shores made him realise just how English in fact he was' (Ackroyd 1990). He had gone there with high expectations and the pious conviction 'that in going to a New World one must for the time utterly forget, and put out of sight the Old one' (12 October 1841), but he found this impossible. Though welcomed with acclamation and making many friends, he soon felt 'a yearning after our English customs and English manners such as you cannot conceive . . . I shall be truly glad to leave [America]' (12–21 March 1842), and when he reached Niagara he 'yearned to come over to the English [Canadian] side . . . You cannot conceive with what transports of joy, I beheld an English sentinel' (1 May 1842). AMERICAN NOTES ends with his joy 'which no tongue can tell' in returning to an English landscape—'pretty cottages . . . old church-yards, the antique houses, and every well-known object.' (Even on the voyage out, he had played 'Home, Sweet Home' on his accordion every night, with plaintive feelings.) Like many another national, even malcontents such as D. H. Lawrence, he pined when faced by other cultures for 'my own, my native land', and could echo Cowper's 'England, with all thy faults, I love thee still—| My country!' 'He had a very strong love of his country,' wrote his son Henry, 'was absolutely loyal', and Henry endorsed FORSTER's contention that 'his wish to better what was bad in English institutions carried with it no desire to replace them by new ones' (Henry Dickens 1928).

He struck visitors as very English in manner: 'anglais superlativement' in donning full evening dress when dining at home, noted a Frenchman (Paul Féval, 'Charles Dickens', *Le Gaulios*, 13 June 1870), 'essentially an Englishman in appearance', remarked an American: 'Among his minor characteristics was that essentially English one, his exceedingly poor taste in matter of dress' (G. D. Carrow, *University* [Princeton], winter 1965–6). In his life as well as his writings he fully shared the strong domestic feeling which all foreign commentators found specially English (see DOMESTICITY). *Fraser's* (December 1850) was not alone in holding that his 'wide-spread popularity' resulted 'above all' from 'his deep reverence for the household sanctities, his enthusiastic worship of the household gods'. Another English speciality which he happily celebrated was the comely but modest English rose: 'that fresh, pure, bright beauty which belongs exclusively to England', to quote one 1850s novelist, while another introduces her heroine as the quintessence of 'all things good and pure—a gentle, playful, kind English girl'. Dickens created many such 'pure', sexually unprovocative heroines, and though he derides Mr Podsnap's favourite question, 'would it bring a blush into the cheek of the young person', he never wrote, nor as editor published, anything that would, and had even anticipated Podsnap by assuring readers that *Pickwick* contained nothing that 'could bring a blush into the most delicate cheek' (1837 Preface, *PP*). He was much praised for this 'purity'.

'In England nowadays, novels are written for families; in France they are written for men' (*Spectator*, 11 July 1857). Such comparisons were frequent, with the 'lubricity' of French fiction and the laxity of French morality often being stigmatized. Dickens, who pointedly named his magazine 'Household Words', accepted these stereotypes about the French. Paris for him was always fascinating but wicked and wanton, and of a play he saw there he wrote, 'of course the interest of it turns upon a flawed piece of living China (*that* seems to be positively essential)' (25 November 1855). But a few days earlier, visiting an international ART exhibition, he found the English paintings 'niggling' compared with the boldness and passion of the French; in English art, as in English government and social arrangements, 'mere form and conventionalities usurp . . . the place of living force and truth' (to Forster, October 1855). He did not apply this judgement to areas of his own work, but others did.

Thus, the French critic Hippolyte Taine in 1856, having described Dickens's artistic personality, continues: 'Plant this talent on English soil; the literary opinion of the country will direct its growth . . . for this public opinion is its private opinion; it does not submit to it as an external constraint, but feels it inwardly as an inner persuasion.' (Dickens did indeed sit at ease with his readers' expectations.) So Dickens happily accepts its

injunctions to 'be moral' and be evasive enough to be 'read by young girls', to limit himself to blameless and uninteresting lovers, to shy away from any impropriety, to engineer anodyne happy endings, and so on. Balzac depicts the passions more daringly and with less moralizing; George Sand makes us desire to be in love, Dickens makes us desire to be married ('Charles Dickens: son Talent et ses Oeuvres', *Revue des deux Mondes*, 1 February 1856). Forster, much riled by Taine, summarizes his argument sarcastically: a great artist 'should be too much of a philosopher to remember that he is a respectable citizen. But this is what Dickens never forgets', and he cites a more congenial French professor's recognition that 'the great praise of English novelists' was that one 'closed their books the better for reading them' and that, true-to-type, Dickens stimulates 'noble sentiments, devotion to duty, and a passion for what was good'—quite unlike Balzac (Forster 9.1).

These are indeed valuable impulses, and being 'a respectable citizen', however Podsnappian this may sound (compare TENNYSON, 'The British Goddess, sleek Respectability'), can be advantageous to a novelist, but for any Victorian author some limitations were entailed. There are swathes of SEXUAL experience Dickens can hardly indicate, let alone explore. His heroes are singularly untempted by the flesh, and such seductions as are attempted (always by secondary characters) are unsuccessful or off-stage. The American critic E. P. Whipple remarked that 'as an English novelist' Dickens is prevented by his 'English sense of decorum'—which only a French critic would deplore—from describing those sensuous elements in Louisa Bounderby which Harthouse arouses, so the reader may be puzzled by her 'frenzy of soul'—but luckily there were many non-sexual passions for Dickens to be explicit about (*Atlantic Monthly*, March 1877).

Introducing his *The Englishness of English Art*, the German-born art-critic Nikolaus Pevsner lists characteristic impulses apparent in Dickens too: the very English HOGARTH's preference for 'modern moral subjects', English painters' tendency to preach and reform, and to depict the everyday world, the characteristic English philosophical inclination towards personal experience and observed fact, and the English medieval speciality of *baboonery* (grinning cathedral gargoyles and other such sculptural monstrosities). Following Pevsner and developing his last point, Andrew Graham-Dixon remarks on the 'uncontainability, irrepressible vigorous eccentricity at the heart of the national imagination' (cf. Emerson on England: 'I know not where any personal eccentricity is so fully allowed'; *English Traits* 1856), and he instances SHAKESPEARE's plays, 'so lively, so filled with the vitality and the freedom of the unfettered imagination, that they overflow their own structures, unmaking . . . the conventional dramaturgy of tragedy and comedy' (*History of British Art*, 1996). These terms fit Dickens, who inherits Shakespeare's multitudinousness and defends the 'streaky bacon' juxtaposition of the comic and tragic (*OT* 17).

Pevsner's remark on English empiricism reminds one of Dickens's anti-ideological stance, which can shade into anti-intellectualism, even Philistinism. '*Isms!*' he exclaims (27 April 1844). 'Oh Heaven for a world without an ism.' Characters who have a theory are generally wrong-headed and insensitive. For him, wrote G. B. Shaw, 'a philosopher, an intellectual, was a figure of fun . . . As to finding a character like Karl Marx among his characters, one would as soon look for a nautilus in a nursery' (Introduction to *GE*, 1947). He found worldly wisdom, simple man-to-man sympathy, and common sense (on which Englishmen pride themselves) sufficient: 'His common-sense had all the force of genius' (Matthew Browne, *Contemporary Review*, January 1880). His contemporary Tennyson, also very English, was similarly praised ('an immense sanity . . . the perfection of common-sense'), qualities for which few of their great continental contemporaries were prized. Dickens shared with Tennyson many national characteristics—that worship of hearth and home, 'a hatred of extremes', contempt for the 'blind hysterics of the Celt'—and he probably enjoyed Tennyson's favourite joke that Hell-gates now proclaimed 'Ici on parle Français'. These authors' styles gave impulse to the creation of a new term, 'word-painting', often involving comparisons with modern English painters. Taine does this, and also notes another Dickensian and English speciality, children ('We have none in French literature').

Dickens generally conformed to respectable English middle-class norms, even winning praise from the *Tailor and Cutter* (16 July 1870) for his sartorial correctness. When transgressing the mores, as in the Ellen TERNAN affair, he behaved discreetly, not with Bohemian defiance. His attitude to the CLASS-system was conventional enough to satisfy Queen Victoria: 'He felt sure that a better feeling, and much greater union of classes, would take place in time. And I pray earnestly it may' (diary, 11 June 1870; *Letters 1862–78*, ed. G. E. Buckle, 1906, 2.21). But American commentators remark that 'Americans find strange Dickens's [and David Copperfield's] shame over the warehouse' (G. H. Ford); 'It is hard for Americans, nurtured in the idealisation of the log-cabin and the rough suspender, to sympathise with the acute misery of Dickens [and Pip] in a class-conscious society' (Ada Nisbet, 'The Autobiographical Matrix of *Great Expectations*', *Victorian Newsletter*, 1959). Ford remarks elsewhere on his racism, typical of his age and nation, that he 'was not so much the friend of the common man as the friend of the common Englishman' ('The Governor EYRE Case in England', *University of Toronto Quarterly*, 1948). Dickens's journalistic colleague Hollingshead recalled him thus: 'With all his great commanding genius, he had many prejudices, and was somewhat "parochial" in his sympathies, except on abstract questions of personal liberty. He was an inspired Cockney. I use the term in no disparaging spirit, but as a brand of character' (*My Lifetime*, 1895). His genius was so commanding, however, that from early in his career onwards readers in many other countries have found his 'parochial' elements no great obstacle to their enjoyment of his work. His characters, said Tolstoy, 'are the friends of all mankind; they are a bond of union between man in America and man in Petersburg' (Aylmer Maude, *Life of Tolstoy*, 1929). For his Anglo-Saxon readers, Dickens was endowed, by his birth, upbringing, temperament and course of life, with the optimum set of characteristics and inclinations to embrace and express their typical interests and outlook. He belonged to the aspirant middle class and to the dominant southerner/metropolitan/urban culture, was a bourgeois reformer when that was the main ideology, but was neither an ideologue nor an extremist. Sensible, practical and intelligent, he was not, and made no show of being, a superior person— except of course in imaginative, narrative, and verbal skills. PC

**essayists, sketch-writers, and humorists during Dickens's lifetime.** The full catalogue of such writers during Dickens's lifetime is such as to defy classification. It would embrace every class of author, from the great quarterly reviewers and self-elected arbiters of public taste and opinion, to satirical columnists in metropolitan newspapers, and the penny-a-line contributors of puns, quips, and captions for cartoons. Every shade of political colour would be represented, and as many theories of wit and humour. However, a parameter is provided by the fact that, during Dickens's lifetime, in formal terms, the essay, the sketch, and the humorist's column gradually ceased to be the publishing media through which the most successful and admired writers of the day expressed themselves. By 1870 the novel was triumphant. Furthermore, Dickens himself, in his gradual self-education in such writings, seems to have been more concerned with individual authors, their works and personae, rather than with classifying trends and ideologies, and his selective approach may be imitated, where schematic categorization breaks down.

Edinburgh and London during the Regency of George IV (1811–20) witnessed an increasingly bitter rivalry between the reviews and periodicals of the two capitals, of which the northern was to retain its Augustan, preindustrial features, and sense of literary community long into the Victorian era, while the southern was propelled into the modern age, not so much by revolution of its traditional industries, as by the nature of its population problem (see NEWSPAPERS, PERIODICALS, AND THE BRITISH PRESS). Moral philosophy and campaigns for strict social, not to mention religious, reform also emanated from the northern capital. Francis JEFFREY and Sydney SMITH, two of the three founders of the prestigious Whig and liberal organ, the *Edinburgh Review*, were still publishing influential essays at this time, and were joined by William HAZLITT, publishing essays in literary criticism rather than political journalism. From 1809 Tory opposition to the opinions of the *Edinburgh* was provided by the *Quarterly*

*Review*, for which the poet laureate Robert Southey (1774–1843), Thomas Wilson Croker (1780–1857), and Walter SCOTT contributed regularly. From 1817 its somewhat ponderous offensives were complemented by the sharper attacks of *Blackwood's Edinburgh Magazine*, in which the pens of J. G. LOCKHART and John WILSON proved their proverbial superiority over the sword, in the wounds they inflicted on the 'Cockney School' of Romantic poets and essayists in England. The establishment of the *London Magazine* in the final year of the Regency provided an opportunity for essayists such as Hazlitt, Leigh HUNT, Charles LAMB, and Thomas HOOD to retaliate, but they did so by celebrating their city's folklore and eccentricities in a studiedly whimsical manner, in the face of the venomous criticisms issuing from 'secondary towns of the Kingdom' such as Edinburgh.

At the same time, London, its characters, and scenes were also being celebrated in Pierce EGAN's popular *Life in London* (1820–1). Although formally presented as a novel in the 18th-century mould, its essentially episodic and essayical nature was obvious during its publication in monthly parts, and its success catalysed the evolutionary development of the periodical essay into the urban sketch, which many saw as a degeneration. Washington IRVING's *Sketchbook*, with its discovery of the quaint and 'olde worlde' in the capital and environs, also achieved international renown in 1820, and the success of both works was such that Dickens came to know of both shortly after his arrival in London from Chatham. Up until then the bias of Dickens's childhood reading had been decidedly 18th-century, but after 1820 the ubiquity of humorous sketches and essays in London and about London, together with an intelligent child's desire to interpret city life and render it manageable, means that he is likely to have come across many of the successful urban humorists. His father's association with the *Morning Herald* in 1827, for example, is likely to have brought to his attention the comic sketches of John Wight, whose *More Mornings at Bow Street* was published in that year, with illustrations by George CRUIKSHANK. Wight's talent lay in exploiting the comic possibilities of describing the drunken, disorderly behaviour of would-be 'gentlemen' brought before the magistrate, in the grave and pompous manner of a national newspaper. The sketches of John Poole (1786?–1872) in the *New Monthly Magazine* (1826–34) and those of Robert SURTEES in the *New Sporting Magazine* (1831–8) described the comic mishaps of similar 'gentlemen' in their suburban lives and pastimes, and the influence of all three on Dickens's early writing has rightly been stressed. Apart from reporting on everyday life and people with an amusing archness, such writers tended to describe for comic effect the exploits of so-called 'Corinthian' gentlemen: young swells and amateur sportsmen, men about town who wanted to experience life among the highest as well as the lowest of society. It is easy to see the variation on such themes in *Sketches by Boz* and the *Pickwick Papers*, but the narratorial process they invited, of crossing perceived gulfs between different worlds within London, was to have a profound effect on Dickens's later and more serious works of social criticism.

Aside from London sketches in which the element of comic narrative was obviously attractive to a young male reader, essays by more 'respectable' authors who projected an essayical persona or club of characters in the *Spectator* tradition seem to have appealed particularly to Dickens in the 1820s (see ESSAYS AND ESSAYISTS BEFORE DICKENS; ADDISON). Neither the contributions of CARLYLE to the *Edinburgh Review* (1827–9) nor the 'Rural Rides' of COBBETT in the *Political Register* (serialized 1822–9) interested him then, though both were works he later read and owned. Instead, his correspondence and speeches suggest an early liking for Hood's whimsical comic annuals, verse, and puns, for Lamb's eccentric London clerk, 'Elia' (*London Magazine*, 1820–5), and for the whimsical Scottish characters depicted by Wilson, Lockhart, James Hogg (1770–1835), and William MAGINN in the *Noctes Ambrosianae* dialogues (*Blackwood's*, 1822–35). Wilson's *Lights and Shadows of Scottish Life* was the first book Dickens is known to have requested after gaining admittance to the British Museum reading room in 1830. At the same time, however, Dickens was embarking on a journalistic career that would shortly bring him into contact with every reviewer, essayist, and - humorist mentioned so far, with the exception of Southey and Croker. In particular, as

editor of BENTLEY'S MISCELLANY from 1837 to 1839, Dickens became actively involved with the writing of a high-spirited group of essayists, quondam and active contributors to the Tory-biased *Fraser's Magazine*, whose old-fashioned party antics were largely suppressed in the new publication. This heterogeneous group included a trio of Irish humorists—William Maginn, Francis Mahony ('Father Prout', 1804–66), and Samuel Lover (1797–1868)—Charles Ollier (1788–1859), William Jerdan (1782–1869), and the celebrated comic novelist, Theodore HOOK.

By the time of the grand Edinburgh dinner in Dickens's honour in 1841 (see Forster 2.10), the phenomenal success of 'BOZ'S' writing in *Bentley's*, and elsewhere, had gained for Dickens the admiration and acquaintance of a whole generation of elder literary statesmen: Sydney Smith, Lord Jeffrey, Lockhart, Hunt, Hood, and many others. Even Thomas Macaulay (1800–59), perhaps the most prestigious essayist of the day, desired to see Dickens 'inrolled [*sic*] in our blue and yellow corps' (i.e. writing for the *Edinburgh Review*), 'where he may do excellent service as a skirmisher and sharpshooter' (Macaulay's *Letters*, ed. Thomas Pinney, 1974–80; 19 October 1843). At the same time, Dickens's correspondence, works, speeches, and contemporaries now begin to document his reading and response to these authors, who may reasonably be regarded as his literary mentors. But Dickens was himself now a luminary of sufficient gravity to attract his own satellites, and the essayists, sketch-writers and humorists writing in the post-Pickwickian world were unlikely to escape his powerful influence. The sheer number of books of London sketches published in the late 1830s and early 1840s is indicative of the richness of the vein that Dickens had opened up. Of these, *The Great Metropolis* (1836), *Sketches in London* (1838; illustrated by 'Phiz') and *Travels in Town* (1839) by the journalist James Grant (1802–79) enjoyed perhaps the greatest currency. They confirm the impression given by both Dickens's and THACKERAY'S works of the same period, however, that facetious description of high- and low-life in the modern Babylon is gradually giving way to serious social observation. While Grant clearly owes a debt to Egan's unaffected enjoyment of London's contrasts, he could legitimately claim to have anticipated the earnest concern and meticulous reporting of Henry Mayhew (1812–87) in his acclaimed series of 81 *Morning Chronicle* 'letters', collected in *London Labour and the London Poor* (1851).

During the 'hungry forties', earnest concern for society's ills and meticulous observation of them did not necessarily result in 'serious' writing, although it did force Pickwickian humour into a SENTIMENTAL mode, where individual benevolence, however appealing in the individual, could quickly be perceived as ineffectual. Satire and the *reductio ad absurdum* were also weapons in the reformer's armoury, and Dickens became skilled in using them, following on many occasions the rhetorical models of Carlyle and of 'that great master of wit and terror of noodles', Sydney Smith (*OT*, Preface to Cheap Edition, 1850). Mayhew deserves mention again, as one of the founders of the radical magazine PUNCH in 1841, whose regular team of contributors and cartoonists—Douglas JERROLD, Mark LEMON, Thackeray, John LEECH, and John TENNIEL—were arguably Dickens's main rivals as satirists during the decade.

Although the accelerating expansion of the periodical press in the 1850s and 1860s brought new essayists, sketch-writers, and humorists to the fore, great numbers of budding authors turned their talents and attention to serial fiction. George ELIOT's progression from essayist to novelist was characteristic of a trend. Furthermore, literary critics of high standing were lamenting a widespread degeneration in the quality and creativity of non-fiction. The literary reviewer of the *Examiner* in 1860 voiced a general feeling in complaining that the 'taste of the day' had 'gone astray in the direction of affected smartness' and that 'our leading reviews . . . find few or none able to take the place of the brilliant essayists to whom they owed the credit of their youth' (20 October). The young writers encouraged by Dickens to write for *Household Words* and *All the Year Round* were frequently criticised for their 'smartness'; G. H. A. SALA, Edmund YATES, and Percy FITZGERALD in particular came under heavy fire. Fitzgerald himself prefaced a lecture in Dublin on 'Two English Essayists: Charles Lamb and Charles Dickens' by describing how the essay had descended from

being 'with Addison, STEELE and GOLDSMITH a miracle of pathos, humour and polish' to being 'in our time, a happy vehicle for interminable personal experiences and mild egotism' (May 1864).

By the time of Dickens's death the surviving exponents of the periodical essay and sketch no longer found themselves the object of such public admiration and critical acclaim as had attended their counterparts forty years before. 'Recreative literature' in 1870 principally meant SERIAL NOVELS. The essay *per se* still commanded respect as an analytic and philosophical tool, used with originality by the so-called 'Victorian thinkers' (Carlyle, John RUSKIN, J. S. MILL, Matthew Arnold, Walter Pater, *et al.*) and for general critical purposes in publications such as the *Saturday Review*, the *Fortnightly Review*, and the *Pall Mall Gazette*, representatives of what was later the 'Higher Journalism'. By 1870, however, the genre no longer afforded the scope it had offered Dickens and his contemporaries in their early careers, when 'descriptive sketches and personal traits, speculative suggestions and logical deductions, the force of direct appeal, the various powers of illustration, allusion and comment, [were] equally available to the essayist [whose] essay may be a lay-sermon or a satire, a criticism or a reverie' (Henry Tuckerman, 'Characteristics of Lamb', *Rambles and Reveries*, 1841; book in Dickens's library in 1844). JMLD

Gross, John, *The Rise and Fall of the Man of Letters; English Literary Life since 1800* (1969), chs. 1–3.

Jaeger, Muriel, *Before Victoria* (1956).

Martin, R. B., *The Triumph of Wit: A Study of Victorian Comic Theory* (1974).

**essays and essayists before Dickens.** In its many guises—familiar, critical, polemical, or philosophical—and as a publishing mode, the essay held a place in Dickens's idea of literature that was second to none. The 18th-century authors who made their names as essayists, and who found in the periodically published paper an ideal form for establishing a relationship with the reading public, were among those whom Dickens came to admire earliest and most enduringly. With admiration came desire for emulation, and the idea of writing series of periodical essays such as STEELE, ADDISON, FIELDING, GOLDSMITH, and JOHNSON had maintained in the 18th century, and as Leigh HUNT, Charles LAMB, and others had been publishing in the early 19th century, was a project foremost in Dickens's mind throughout the 1830s and 1840s. Indeed, the founding of *Household Words* in 1850—despite inevitable alterations made in style, presentation, and social agenda—was in many ways a tribute to his affection for the essay, and for essayists writing long before his birth. That Dickens came to be considered in his own lifetime, and posthumously, as a novelist rather than as an essayist *par excellence* is eloquent of a much broader shift in literary and critical perspectives, and the basis of an interesting paragraph in the history of English literature.

To summarize Dickens's reading of the essay is to name most of its canonized exponents, from the emergence of the form onwards. The works of Michel de Montaigne (*Essais*, 3 vols. 1588) and Francis Bacon (*Essays*, 3 edns. 1597–1625), traditionally regarded as the 'fathers' of the genre, were books Dickens owned and referred to. The former, in translations by Charles Cotton and HAZLITT, Dickens recommended to Wilkie COLLINS in 1854 (24 February 1854), while the Preface to the latter is quoted several times in Dickens's works (*BR* 37; *DS* 5, 17; to Lady Holland, 11 July 1842). The two authors are often held to represent two opposing schools as much of philosophy as of essay-writing: Gallic scepticism versus English empiricism, and the familiar, discursive essay versus the objective, inductive, and argumentative. Dickens's own essays display both tendencies. However, it seems likely that the influence of Bacon and Montaigne's speculative, almost treatise-like works (like Locke's *Essay concerning Human Understanding*, Dryden's *Essay of Dramatick Poesie*, and Hume's *Essays*, which were also in Dickens's library) was slight in comparison with the influence of the lighter periodical essays of the 18th-century, which Dickens not only quoted far more often, but encountered at a much earlier age.

Richard Steele and Joseph Addison made their names as pseudonymous authors of periodicals published in the reign of Queen Anne, and their essays, like the writings of SWIFT and the Scriblerus Club, partook of the spirit of satire and raillery which characterized the emerging factional politics of the Whigs and the Tories. In Dickens's boyhood anthologies of their works were still available in collections such as the 'Cooke's Pocket Library' owned by John DICKENS, but were admired not for their Whiggish satire but for their stylistic elegance, moral sentiments, and humorous depiction of fictional prototypes, such as the Tory baronet Sir Roger de Coverley, and the various personae who purport to narrate the journals ('Isaac Bickerstaffe', 'Mr Spectator', and 'Nestor Ironside'). FORSTER asserts that *The Tatler* (1709–11) and *The Spectator* (1711–12, 1714), along with Goldsmith's *Citizen of the World* (1760), were books of essays that Dickens read 'over and over' at Chatham, before he was 10 (Forster 1.1). In later life Dickens acquired complete editions of Addison and Steele, and his own essays, novels, speeches, and letters are dotted with quotations and references. Writing to Forster on 14 April 1855, Dickens confesses, however, to finding 'the serious papers in the Spectator . . . (whether they be Steele's or Addison's) . . . as indifferent as the humour of the Spectator is delightful', and it is perhaps the eccentric characterization of the personae and the 'clubs' of amusing gentlemen presented by Steele in particular, that influenced Dickens most. The original newspaper versions of the 'BOZ' sketches (1834–6), with their chatty introductions and asides (though these were mostly edited out for volume publication), were strikingly essayistic in manner, but the influence can be most clearly seen in the original presentation of the Pickwick Club (*PP* 1–5), and the group of cronies who meet to exchange stories in the ten numbers of MASTER HUMPHREY'S CLOCK which were not instalments of serial fiction. Dickens's Proposal for the latter, indeed, makes the debt clear: '[t]he best general idea . . . of the work might be given perhaps by reference to *The Tatler, The Spectator* and Goldsmith's *Bee* . . . I should propose to start, as *The Spectator* does . . . [and] to introduce a little club or knot of characters and to carry their personal histories and proceedings through the work' (14 July 1839).

This plan was sent to CHAPMAN AND HALL, via Forster, while Dickens holidayed in Petersham in the summer of 1839. From the same address he forwarded a 'carpet-bag-full' of holiday reading to a friend, which contained series of essays by Leigh Hunt and Thomas

HOOD, while for his own use he retained works by Swift, Fielding, Goldsmith, SMOLLETT, and a 45-volume collection of 18th-century essays called *The British Essayists* (ed. Chalmers, 1802, 3; to Cattermole, 21 August 1839). As well as Addison and Steele's essays, this last republished Samuel Johnson's *Rambler, Adventurer*, and *Idler* essay series (1750–2, 1752–4, 1758–60), George Colman and Bonnel Thornton's *Connoisseur* (1754–6), *The World* (Walpole, Chesterfield, *et al.*; 1753–6), and Henry MACKENZIE's *Mirror* and *Lounger* (1779–80, 1785–7). Johnson's essays, with their moral sententiousness and gravity, were prescribed reading for the young in the growing spirit of puritanism and REFORM which followed Waterloo. Dickens doubtless knew them, and parodies the Johnsonian manner with obvious delight in *Little Dorrit* (2.32), the essay 'Plate Glass' (with W. H. WILLS; *HW* 1 February 1851), and in his letter to Wilkie Collins of 24 May 1861. The elegant cynicism and worldly wit of Walpole and Chesterfield, on the other hand, seems to have repelled Dickens, and the openings of *Barnaby Rudge* chapters 23 and 29 show him imitating their fulsome style, in order to expose the affected virtues of Sir John Chester.

In the same period, Dickens gives an interesting description of himself in the Preface to the first volume edition of *Nicholas Nickleby* (1839). After quoting at length from the final number of Henry Mackenzie's popular periodical *The Lounger*, Dickens endorses Mackenzie's words, adding that it is '[w]ith such feelings and such hopes the periodical essayist, the author of these pages, now lays them before his readers in a completed form'. Clearly, at this stage in his life Dickens did not think of himself as a NOVELIST at all, but as a periodical essayist in the 18th-century mode. Similarly, in a letter to his former Chatham schoolteacher William Giles (31 October 1848), Dickens recalled how Giles had given him a copy of Goldsmith's short-lived periodical *The Bee* (1759) as a parting gift in 1822, adding that he has been 'fledging ... little Bees myself whose buzzing has been heard abroad'. Again, it is the periodical essay that is the yardstick against which Dickens measures his own work, rather than the novel.

It is not surprising, therefore, to find the narrative strategies and eidola typical of 18th-century periodicals repeatedly invoked in

Dickens's later plans for founding a journal. 'The Cricket, A Cheerful creature that chirrups on the Hearth' (the by-line is from Goldsmith's *History of the Earth*, 1774) was suggested to Forster as the basis for a magazine in 1845 (?early July 1845). Dickens felt that under this name he would be able to approach his public in a winning and immediate way, which would instantly distinguish his voice from that of any other contemporary magazine. In 1846, only months after devolving responsibility on to Forster for the editorship of the DAILY NEWS, Dickens was innocently confiding to him that it would be 'a great thing to found something'. Again, the basic model was to be the 18th-century *Spectator*, with something new and distinctive in its design (22 and 23 November 1846). After the writing of *Dombey and Son* (1846–8) Dickens's thoughts reverted to the 'old notion of the Periodical' which he had been nurturing for so long. Two weeks later he dreamed up a narrative persona into which he could pour his spirit and philosophy, to be called 'The Shadow': an intangible, omnipresent, critical but philanthropic creature that would establish itself as a power in the land. It was to be 'a creature which isn't the Spectator and isn't Isaac Bickerstaff' but which would charm people with its quaintness while arousing their curiosity to know its opinion on all subjects (24 September and [7 October] 1848). Forster rightly notes that hardly anything more characteristic of Dickens's imagination has survived him than the elaborate outline which he gives for 'The Shadow' in this letter (Forster 6.4). The powerful and continuing influence of 18th-century essays and essayists may also be noted, however.

Apart from the canonized work of *The British Essayists*, it is likely that Dickens also had knowledge of the more political and polemical essays of Daniel DEFOE and Henry Fielding, whose complete works he likewise owned and referred to. He also possessed 'Ned' Ward's *London Spy* (1698–1709) complete in eighteen parts, which comprised a series of sketch-essays narrating the adventures of a country yokel escorted over the sights of London by a knowing Cockney friend. The polemical review and the London sketch were to become characteristic of the new directions which the essay genre was to accommodate in the first decade of the 19th century, and while no strict dividing line can be drawn, the essay's most famous exponents of this period, and those whom Dickens seems to have read and learnt most from, were all instrumental in effecting these changes. Almost all, however, remained active and writing well into Dickens's lifetime.

The considerable influence which the essay and essayists exerted on Dickens's idea of literature can help explain aspects of his performance as a novelist which seem anomalous only from a somewhat anachronistic, novel-centred critical viewpoint. G. K. CHESTERTON's challenging assertion that 'Dickens's work is not to be reckoned in novels at all' (1906, p. 80) begins to make sense when it is remembered in what high esteem the essay was held by the literary arbiters and practitioners of Dickens's day. It was, traditionally, the form in which the finest and politest authors had appeared before the public in their *robes de chambre*, revealing something of themselves in a private and confidential manner. This interpretation may indeed have been the 'humanist fallacy', whereby readers erroneously sought to read texts as limpid transcripts of their authors' voices (T. Eagleton, *Literary Theory: An Introduction*, 1983, p. 120), but it was widespread. Thomas Macaulay's magnificent and popular eulogy on Addison in the *Edinburgh Review* (July 1843), reprinted in the numerous editions of his *Essays Critical and Historical* (1846, etc.), emphasizes the connection, and also the essay's potency as a valuable agent of social reform. Within Dickens's own circle, Forster published a major essay on Steele (*Quarterly Review*, 1855) and a *Life of Goldsmith* (1854); Henry MORLEY published editions of Bacon, Montaigne, and *The Spectator* (1868–91); Peter Cunningham edited Goldsmith's *Works* (1854); Percy FITZGERALD wrote on Lamb (1860, 1866); and W. H. Wills edited an anthology entitled *Sir Roger de Coverley, by The Spectator* (1850). Clearly, in an age when a leading London perfume manufacturer—Piesse & Lubin—could confidently market an aftershave under the legend 'Sir Roger de Coverley: hys Savour' (cf. *Illustrated London News*, 12 January 1861), the influence of the 'Spectator' tradition of essays and essayists died hard. Dickens was not alone in his admiration, though perhaps unique in the extent to which he transformed cherished

imaginative elements from the tradition into fiction for the industrial age.                JMLD

Andrews, Malcolm A., 'The Idea of a Miscellany: *Master Humphrey's Clock*', *Dickensian*, 78 (1982).
Smith (1996), ch. 4, 'Periodicals, Journalism and the Literary Essay'.

**evangelical religion,** whether Anglican or nonconformist, usually entails fervent and public professions of faith, which Dickens found almost as repellent as the ritualism of the High Church (of England) or ROMAN CATHOLICISM; and evangelicals generally returned his ill will, decrying the lack of piety in his novels (see CHURCH OF ENGLAND; DISSENT). As one evangelical newspaper put it, 'His writings are of the most questionable tendency in point of MORALS, and when he touches on RELIGION, he is often profane' (quoted in Pope 1978, p. 15). Nevertheless, Dickens often found himself in more comfortable practical alliance with evangelicals in several of his philanthropic enterprises (see CHARITY).

Evangelical beliefs are usually considered as deriving more from Martin Luther than from Calvin and the Puritans, and they stress the teachings of the Gospels and an intensely personal relationship with Christ and the Scriptures that is believed uniquely to provide the ground of faith. In England, evangelicals were particularly associated with John Wesley's Methodist revival in the 18th century. While many evangelicals left the Church of England following Wesley's death, many others remained. Thus the term 'evangelical' may refer to Anglicans, especially those belonging to the Low Church wing, as well as any number of nonconforming churches, including Methodism. Wesley's experience of conversion and energetic pursuit of evangelizing through missionary work have left indelible stamps on English evangelicals.

As an intensely personal religion, Victorian evangelicalism emphasized the importance of private judgement and conscience and the authority of the individual's reading of Scripture over the authority of the church hierarchy, and it was this family of beliefs—ones Dickens could himself very readily accept—that produced the tensions between evangelicals and the Church of England that led many to leave the latter. Those who remained within the Anglican communion generally stressed philanthropy and missionary work, and insofar as Dickens thought their philanthropy effectual in fact (it was, for example, evangelicals who were the main force behind Britain's withdrawal from the slave trade), he was happy to be their energetic collaborator.

In spite of the early opposition between evangelicals and Calvinists, evangelicals both within Anglicanism and without shared a deep sense of the sinfulness of human nature and stressed the need for personal conversion and salvation as well as Christ's crucial role in atoning for mankind's sins. Anglican evangelicals further were the chief power behind SAB-BATARIANISM—the strict observance of the Sabbath—in which Dickens saw a cruel discrimination against the working classes, since Sunday was the only day on which they were free to enjoy recreations—see his attacks in *SUNDAY UNDER THREE HEADS* (1836) and 'The Sunday Screw' (*HW* 22 June 1850) (collected in *Journalism* 1 and 2 respectively). It was these puritanical aspects of evangelicalism along with the often very public nature of evangelical professions of faith that Dickens could not bear. He was extremely quick—undoubtedly too quick—to suspect hypocrisy in anyone making a show of piety, and though very moderate in his own appetites, he was deeply suspicious of all ascetic impulses and the will to impose them on others.

There is a very long list of characters in his novels who are identifiably evangelical (sincere or otherwise), and Dickens's treatment of them is invariably harsh. The list begins with the Revd Mr Stiggins in *The Pickwick Papers*, who preys on the second Mrs Tony Weller and is to some degree implicated in her death (she has caught a fatal cold from 'imprudently settin too long on the damp grass in the rain a hearin of a shepherd who warnt able to leave off till late at night owen to his havin wound his-self up with brandy and water' (*PP* 52), and whose beating and near drowning by Tony in a horse-trough is the subject of the vignette on the novel's title-page. Kit Nubbles's mother in *The Old Curiosity Shop* is likewise in thrall to an evangelical minister who turns her naturally sweet disposition sour, and Mrs Jerry Cruncher in *A Tale of Two Cities* is given to enthusiastic praying that her husband dubs 'flopping' (*TTC* 2.1). Mr Chadband in *Bleak House* is perhaps Dickens's most successfully comic portrait of a hypocritical evangelical minister who literally fattens himself while preaching about the sinfulness of the human condition (*BH* 19). *Bleak House* supplies further examples of satire against evangelicals in the philanthropist Mrs Jellyby—she has no explicit religious position, but her scheme to cultivate coffee and the natives on the banks of the Niger would nevertheless have been readily associated with Exeter Hall, the bastion of Victorian evangelical philanthropy that promoted the ill-fated Niger expedition of 1846.

There is another important family of characters in the novels taken to task for their intense religiosity, though they might more accurately be characterized as Calvinist or Puritan. (Given Dickens's aversion to doctrinal questions, it is likely he would see no useful distinction between such terms as 'evangelical' and 'Puritan', nor would he be interested in fine differences between Lutherans and Calvinists.) In any case, its members significantly share the evangelicals' gloomy assessment of human nature, though they tend to be reclusive and thus less flamboyant in their display of faith, and they seem not particularly concerned about conversion, philanthropy, or missionary work. Dickens's portrayal of them is largely without humour, and he is generally far more bitter about their baleful influence than about the evangelicals he treats comically. The group includes Mr and Mrs Murdstone (*DC*), Miss Barbary (*BH*), and Mrs Clennam (*LD*). Inasmuch as Dickens strongly identifies with the young people subjected to their gloomy religious teaching, and certainly in the cases of Esther Summerson and Arthur Clennam sees lifelong difficulties traceable to their harsh upbringing, one may wonder where in his own life he found the model for such harmful and stern figures; but there is, however, no obvious prototype.                                    RN

Pope (1978), ch. 1, 'Dickens and Evangelicalism'.

***Evening Chronicle*** (31 January 1835–23 July 1847). The evening paper where Dickens published a series of twenty sketches, 'Sketches of London', from the paper's first issue until 20 August 1835. Set up by MORNING CHRONICLE proprietor John EASTHOPE, the paper appeared three times a week and was edited by

George HOGARTH and John Hill Powell, two of Dickens's colleagues on the *Morning Chronicle*. When planning for the paper was going forward, Dickens proposed a series of sketches like the ones that he had been doing for the *Morning Chronicle*. They describe various London landmarks with an ever-stronger emphasis on the sufferings of the lower classes. In this vein, the most outstanding feature is probably the loosely recurring set of sketches 'Our Parish', which invokes the same themes found at the beginning of *Oliver Twist*, though more comically. There is evidence that Dickens had been collecting this material for some time and from the beginning saw the parish stories as a series.    KC

Maxwell, Richard, 'Dickens and the Two *Chronicles*, and the Publication of *Sketches by Boz*', *Dickens Studies Annual*, 9 (1981).

**Examiner** (1808–86). The weekly paper where John FORSTER's first notice of Dickens's work—a drama review (not favourable) of *The VILLAGE COQUETTES* (11 December 1836)—appeared. Its fame was partly literary—in 1816 the article 'Young Poets' had helped introduce Keats and Shelley—but primarily it had been founded as a radical political journal in 1808 by brothers John and Leigh HUNT. HAZLITT wrote two series of familiar essays for the paper, 'Table Talk' (1813) and the 'Round Table' (1815), and was the regular drama critic from March 1815. Leigh Hunt was editor till 1821.

The property passed from the Hunts to Albany FONBLANQUE (1793–1872), who had been the *Examiner*'s main political commentator since 1826. As editor for the years 1830–47, Fonblanque brought in such contributors as John Stuart MILL, John Forster, and William Makepeace THACKERAY (who was briefly also a sub-editor). Fonblanque, who especially enjoyed Dickens's humour, wrote the *Examiner*'s first notice of Dickens's work (*Sketches by Boz*), which appeared on 28 February 1836; the paper's first notice of *Pickwick* appeared on 4 September 1836. Alex Brice (1972) calculates that over 70 reviews or mentions of Dickens appear in the *Examiner* during the years 1836–65 (many merely extracts) and are written by four reviewers: Fonblanque, Forster, Leigh Hunt, and Henry MORLEY. Kathryn Chittick (1989) lists 41 notices of Dickens (including minor works and plays)

appearing in the paper during the six years from 1836 to 1841 alone.

John Forster first reviewed Dickens's works as the *Examiner*'s dramatic critic from 1833, becoming its literary editor, sub-editor (from 1836), and editor (1847–55). As a reviewer he championed BROWNING especially, as well as TENNYSON ('The Charge of the Light Brigade' appeared first in the *Examiner*). Forster's reviews of Dickens (he did nine of *Nicholas Nickleby* alone) were generous but not uncritical; he particularly encouraged Dickens's development of FIELDINGESQUE realism (see review of *Pickwick*, 2 July 1837), and as Philip Collins (1970) points out, his notices provide the best clue to Dickens's own thoughts at the time. With Forster, the political aspect of literary criticism became less important than it had been during the Regency period of Hunt and Hazlitt, although Dickens clearly thought he was doing something 'radical' when he published his satirical ballad 'The Fine Old English Gentleman' on the Tories' accession to power (1841) in its pages (see POETRY BY DICKENS). Dickens published a number of articles there mainly during the years 1837–43 and 1848–9: some of these are found in *Miscellaneous Papers* (1908), which lists 21 pieces (plus three poems), and the Dent edition of Dickens *Journalism* (vol. 2), where Michael Slater estimates that there are probably over 40 contributions (including reviews of books and pictures) by Dickens. The early ones are mainly to do with literary controversies, especially concerning SCOTT and his publishers; the later articles deal primarily with miscarriages of justice.

Henry Morley (1822–94), who began writing for the paper in 1849 (and wrote over 250 articles for *Household Words*), later became editor (1861–7) and may have been the most frequent writer of the *Examiner* reviews of Dickens after 1855—these stressed the unity and plot control of his novels. After 1855 the reviews were less thorough, and its liberal non-partisan commentary, so unusual in the 1820s and 1830s, had become the rule in literary reviewing.    KC

Brice, Alex W., 'Reviewers of Dickens in the Examiner: Fonblanque, Forster, Hunt, and Morley', *Dickens Studies Newsletter*, 3 (September 1972).

Collins, Philip, 'Dickens' Self-Estimate: Some New Evidence', in Partlow (1970).

**Exhibition of 1851.** At the instigation of Prince Albert, the Great Exhibition was held in Hyde Park during the summer of 1851 to display goods and manufactures from all over the world. It was housed in the Crystal Palace, a massive glass greenhouse designed by Joseph Paxton (1803–65), chief financial backer of the DAILY NEWS. In a speech on 8 June 1851 Dickens marvelled at 'that wonderful building', and praised Paxton as a man of 'genius and good sense' (*Speeches*, pp. 133–5). Queen Victoria formally opened the exhibition on 1 May, and when it closed on 15 October it had attracted well over 6 million visitors.

Dickens visited the Palace with Paxton in February, before the building was complete, and he published several articles extolling it in *Household Words*. His letters indicate, however, that he was offended by the self-congratulatory spirit in which it celebrated British pre-eminence. In 'The Last Words of the Old Year' (*HW* 4 January 1851) Dickens enquired when the country would hold 'a great display of England's sins and negligences', and the gloomy opening of *Bleak House* contrasts starkly with the sense of beatitude on earth with which *The Times* (2 May 1851) celebrated the Exhibition. PVWS

Hill, T. W., 'Dickens and the 1851 Exhibition', *Dickensian*, 47 (1951).

**Eyre, Edward John** (1815–1901), explorer, colonial administrator, and Governor of Jamaica from 1862, where he became notorious for his brutal suppression of an uprising in 1865. Hundreds of Negro workers, seeking improved conditions, were flogged and hanged, with or without a cursory trial. Prosecuted unsuccessfully three times in Britain for contravention of the Colonial Governors Act of 1700, Eyre was viewed as tyrannical by liberal thinkers like T. H. Huxley and John Stuart MILL. Dickens, alongside TENNYSON, RUSKIN, and CARLYLE, defended Eyre and expressed contempt for those who displayed sympathy with 'the native, or the devil—afar off' (to de Cerjat, 30 November 1865). Dickens's endorsement of Eyre's conduct lends support to the view that an espousal of imperialist and racist sentiments accompanied the desire for national social reform that is to be inferred from his novels. SS

**Eytinge, Solomon, Jr.** (1833–1905), American ILLUSTRATOR. Eytinge became associated with Fields, Osgood & Co., Boston publishers, and through them came to render many Dickensian subjects, including a large work in which Sam Weller introduces Mr Pickwick to the characters in Dickens's other fictions. For volumes of the Diamond Edition which TICKNOR AND FIELDS prepared in anticipation of Dickens's second American tour, Eytinge supplied 96 designs for wood-engravings (see EDITIONS: FOREIGN ENGLISH-LANGUAGE EDITIONS). He also made two frontispieces for their edition of the PUBLIC READINGS and 25 illustrations for their edition of *A Christmas Carol*, and designed etchings for Houghton, Mifflin's *Dickens Dictionary*. Eytinge painted a portrait of Dickens, subsequently lithographed, in 1867–8, and visited Dickens at Gad's Hill in the summer of 1869. Dickens expressed a high regard for Eytinge's illustrations. RLP

# F

**Factory Acts.** Perhaps the fiercest campaign that Dickens waged in the pages of *Household Words* concerned factory accidents. While factory legislation dates from 1802, early reformers did not regard safety as a priority issue. Peel's Act of 1802, restricting the work of apprentices to twelve hours a day, was ignored, as was an Act of 1819 which banned the employment of children under 9 years old from cotton mills, and limited daily hours for all under 16 to twelve hours a day. Both Acts lacked proper means of enforcement and inspection. In 1831 Michael Sadler introduced a Bill for a ten-hour day, and had it referred to a Select Committee which he chaired. The evidence they amassed highlighted the harsh treatment of child labour in factories. When Sadler lost his seat in the elections of 1832, Lord Ashley (the Earl of Shaftesbury) took over the leadership of the Ten Hour Movement, introducing a Bill along the lines of Sadler's in 1833. This Bill to regulate the labour of children and young persons in mills and factories included the first attempt to compel industrial safety. However, the employers succeeded in stopping the Bill through the appointment of a Royal Commission to disprove the 'utterly unjustifiable' imputations against them. Its recommendations were a compromise, and were expeditiously enacted into law, thereby thwarting Ashley. It is probable that Dickens witnessed the defeat of Sadler's Bill and the rejection of Lord Ashley's Bill when he was a parliamentary reporter. He certainly heard the parliamentary debates concerning the conditions of factory operatives.

The 1833 Act banned the employment of children under 9 in textile factories, and limited the hours of children under 14 to nine hours per day plus two hours schooling. However, safety and compensation issues were ignored and adult male workers were not protected. The factory inspectorate created by the 1833 Act became increasingly concerned by the frequency and seriousness of accidents. Reform was not easily obtained in the face of opposition from the manufac-

turers. An Act of 1844 restricted female labour in textile industries to twelve hours a day and children to six-and-a-half hours, but allowed them to be employed from 8 years old. It also included the first legislative requirements concerning the fencing of machinery and compensation, albeit limited to those under 18. At the same time, Ashley sought to extend the range of trades covered by the legislation, notably, mining, but opposition from the colliery owners thwarted all but token provisions. An Act of 1847 imposed a ten-hour limit on women and young persons; but this was thwarted by the introduction of shift-working. The inspectors brought a test case, challenging the legality of this practice, but the courts sided with the employers.

Dickens himself promised an article for the *Edinburgh Review* on mining children (to Forster, 30 June 1841; to Macvey Napier, 26 July 1842), and was 'so perfectly stricken' by the 1843 Report of the Children's Employment Commission that he considered bringing out a pamphlet—'with my name attached, of course'—'on behalf of the Poor Man's Child' (to Southwood Smith, 6 March 1843), but wrote neither. He did, however, send an impassioned letter to the MORNING CHRONICLE (25 July 1842; repr. Pilgrim 3.278–85), commending Ashley's efforts to prohibit child and female labour in mines, and wrote a scathing review of an attack on Ashley by the Marquess of Londonderry, a colliery-owning peer who opposed the Bill (*Morning Chronicle* 20 October 1842; repr. *Journalism* 2.44–51).

Between March 1854 and January 1856 Dickens published eight articles in *Household Words* on industrial accidents, blaming mill owners and 'kind hearted interpreters of the law' for breaching the 1844 Factory Act and for failing to prevent accidents through the fencing of dangerous machinery. Seven articles were written by Henry MORLEY and one by Morley and Dickens. Long before, Dickens's visits to Lancashire to examine the conditions of the factory operatives caused him to resolve that he would 'strike the heaviest blow in my power for these unfortunate creatures' (to E. M. Fitzgerald, 29 December 1838), and his manuscripts show that a factory accident was to have played a significant role in *Hard Times*. As *Oliver Twist* assailed the New POOR LAW, and *Nicholas Nickleby* the Yorkshire schools, so *Hard Times* and the articles in *Household Words* ridiculed the economic rationalizations of Bounderby-like employers who pursued profit at the expense of physical safety and the life of the imagination. The National Association of Factory Occupiers (lampooned in *Household Words* as the 'Association for the Protection of the Right to Mangle Operatives') was one of several employers' groups critical of Dickens's stance. Harriet MARTINEAU attacked the articles on industrial accidents for containing many 'unscrupulous statements and objectionable representations'. In their riposte, Morley and Dickens refused to retract their accident statistics, mocking Martineau's arguments. The controversy brought to an end Martineau's contributions to *Household Words* and her friendship with Dickens. (See INDUSTRY.)                                    DS

> Bartrip, Peter, '*Household Words* and the Factory Accident Controversy', *Dickensian*, 75 (1979).
> Fielding, K. J., and Smith, Anne, '*Hard Times* and the Factory Controversy: Dickens *vs* Harriet Martineau', in A. Nesbit and Blake Nevius (eds.), *Dickens Centennial Essays* (1971).

**fairs and itinerant entertainers.** Dickens was enthralled by popular forms of entertainment, publishing articles on a variety of its aspects in his journals and writing about them from first-hand knowledge in his fiction and journalism.

Fairs flourished throughout Europe during the Middle Ages with trade as their primary purpose, but entertainment was an integral feature from the very outset. At least by the time Ben JONSON wrote his play *Bartholomew Fair* (1614) the commercial function of most fairs had declined, often to non-existence, and fairs became notorious as scenes of debauchery and vulgar AMUSEMENT, although patronized by visitors of every social CLASS. Changing patterns of entertainment, away from participatory amusements and one-man shows toward more commercialized, large-scale, organized forms such as the CIRCUS, MUSIC HALL, and profes-

sional SPORT, gradually diminished the importance of most fairs, even as their very existence was under attack by EVANGELICAL and UTILITARIAN forces. By Dickens's day fairs had taken on a symbolic function as a guarantee of the right of ordinary English men and women to traditional pleasures, and the suppression of the most famous of them, Bartholomew Fair, in 1840 by the Corporation of the City of London was widely seen as an attack on the rights of the common people (see LONDON: ENTERTAINMENT). Always as interested in the spectators as in the spectacle, Dickens was convinced that 'the many are at least as capable of decent enjoyment as the few' ('The Queen's Coronation', *Examiner*, 1 July 1838) and throughout his career he defended people's right to 'harmless recreations and healthful amusements' (*SUTH*), as relief from drudgery, opportunity for enjoyment, and stimulus to fancy.

The entertainment at fairs varied enormously in size, type, and quality, from the spontaneous patter of the cheapjack like Doctor Marigold (*CS*) selling his wares, to highly professional performances in RICHARDSON's booth theatre and the exhibition of exotic wild beasts in Wombwell's menagerie. What they had in common was that all were itinerant. Dickens describes the large fairground of Greenwich Fair in *Sketches by Boz*, and a little country fair in *Our Mutual Friend* (*OMF* 4.1). Entertainers would also perform at race meetings, where in Dickens's day the track was open to the public free of charge, the proprietors making their money from ground rents for gambling booths (*NN* 50) and for pitches of individual showfolk (*OCS* 19). Smaller shows and exhibits, such as 'the Fat Pig, the Wild Indian, and the Little Lady' seen in the streets by Dickens during his unhappy childhood days at WARREN'S BLACKING warehouse and described in his autobiographical fragment, would offer their delights wherever there was an audience to be found (see DIARIES). In *Nickleby* a delivery boy is delayed by the fascinations of a Punch show and stilt-dancers performing in the streets of Clerkenwell (*NN* 37), and in *Dombey* Paul's schoolmate Tozer is 'thrown in a state of mortal apprehension' at the thought that he will be examined on the classical implications of 'a Giant, or a Dwarf, or a Conjurer' (*DS* 14). The 1858 Christmas story 'Going Into Society' recounts the adventures of Chops, the fairground dwarf whose winning lottery ticket allows him to experience high society, but Dickens's most extended description of itinerant entertainers is to be found in *The Old Curiosity Shop*, in which Nell and her grandfather meet a Punch and Judy team, dancing dogs, stilt-walkers, a conjurer, and the proprietress of a travelling WAXWORKS exhibition.

PVWS

Schlicke (1985).

**fairy tales.** Dickens's favourite reading as a child had been fairy tales and he frequently invoked them in his novels and his occasional writing. In 'A Christmas Tree' (*HW* 21 December 1850) he ecstatically recalled some of his best-loved stories—Jack and the Beanstalk, Valentine and Orson, the Yellow Dwarf, Red Riding-Hood ('I felt that if I could have married [her] I would have known perfect bliss'), and above all the ARABIAN NIGHTS. He was often to allude to Sheherazade, Ali Baba, Aladdin, Sinbad, and lesser-known tales, and *Edwin Drood* opens with the opium smoker's blurred dream of ten thousand scimitars flashing in the sunlight, and dancing-girls strewing flowers to the sound of clashing cymbals. He satirized contemporary politics in 'Ten Thousand and One Humbugs' (*HW* 21 and 28 April, 5 May 1855). He probably read the tales in Jonathan Scott's six-volume edition of 1811—at that time there were few children's versions. *Tales of the Genii*, first published in 1764, was another favourite book, modelled on the *Arabian Nights* but unlike the tales there, moral and purposeful. Supposedly by 'Sir Charles Morell' it was in fact the work of the Revd James Ridley (1736–65), chaplain to the East India Company. The apparition in the opening story of a 'diminutive old hag' who night after night hops out of a box to haunt the merchant Abudah was one that gripped Dickens's imagination; there is something of her, for instance, in 'good Mrs Brown' who strips Florence Dombey of her clothes (*DS* 6).

It was the French fairy tales of Perrault that he knew (Red Riding-Hood, Cinderella, Diamonds and Toads, Bluebeard, Hop o' my Thumb, Sleeping Beauty), Madame D'Aulnoy's Yellow Dwarf, and English stories like Jack and the Beanstalk, Jack the Giant-killer, and Dick Whittington. Though careful parents did not usually then choose to give their children fairy tales (it was the Grimms' *German Popular Stories* of 1823, illustrated by George CRUIKSHANK, that began the acceptance of the genre among the educated), all these were available in chapbook form when he was a child, as were the medieval romances that he also referred to, such as the fantastic adventures of the twin brothers Valentine and Orson, Fortunatus with his magic purse and travelling hat, and Guy of Warwick the slayer of dragons and giants. Dickens execrated attempts to tamper with what he considered sacred text. In 'Frauds on the Fairies' (HW 1 October 1853) he lampooned George Cruikshank's *Fairy Library*, with its propagation of 'the doctrines of Total Abstinence, Prohibition of the sale of spirituous liquors, Free Trade and Popular Education' within the frame of the traditional tales (see DRINK AND TEMPERANCE). He himself wrote one fairy story for children, 'The Magic Fishbone', which formed part of 'HOLIDAY ROMANCE', but most of the Christmas books, with their accounts of miraculous transformations, take on fairy-tale shape; *The CHIMES* is directly described as 'a goblin story' and *The CRICKET ON THE HEARTH* 'a fairy tale of home'. Dickens was an admirer of Hans Christian ANDERSEN, whose fairy stories, translated by Mary Howitt, were immensely popular with the mid-Victorians.

GA

**Fechter, Charles** (1824–79) made his debut in 1840 in Paris, where he became a leading melodramatic actor, impressing Dickens as the original Armand Duval in *La Dame aux camelias*. Encouraged by Dickens to appear in London, he opened at the Princess's Theatre in *Ruy Blas* (1860), followed by *Don Caesar de Bazan*. His original, non-declamatory Hamlet (1861) was a revelation, as was his 'restrained, credible' Iago. His Othello was a disappointment, but *Ruy Blas* and his production of *The Duke's Motto* (1863) were also highly esteemed by Dickens, who subsequently assisted him in adapting Bellew's *The King's Butterfly* (1864). Dickens also assisted Fechter in staging *The Master of Ravenswood* (a dramatization of SCOTT's *The Bride of Lammermoor*), BULWER-LYTTON's *The Lady of Lyons*, and Wilkie COLLINS's *No Thoroughfare*. In the latter, which was based on the Collins/Dickens Christmas story, Fechter played the main role of the villainous Obenreizer. After he became manager of the Lyceum Theatre (1863–7) Fechter gave Dickens a small chalet which was erected in the garden at End's Hill and used by Dickens as a study. In 1870 Fechter toured in America, where he remained, apart from a short season in London in 1872. Prior to his departure Dickens wrote in *The Atlantic Magazine* (1869) about Fechter's qualities as a romantic and spontaneous actor, particularly in the role of stage lover, whilst also praising his 'passionate vehemence' and his sense of the picturesque. JD

**Field, Inspector.** Detective Inspector Charles Frederick Field (1805–74) of Scotland Yard contributed much to the character of Inspector Bucket in *Bleak House*, although Dickens denied drawing directly on Field's experiences (see DETECTIVE FICTION). Dickens first wrote of Field in *Household Words* articles ('A Detective Police Party', 27 July and 10 August 1850; 'Three "Detective" Anecdotes', 14 September 1850) that reveal a fascination for the work of the police detectives, and an uncritical attitude rare in his accounts of public functionaries. Dickens's patronage must have represented a public-relations coup for a small, recently formed Detective Department, then viewed with some distrust by the public. Field later conducted Dickens and others through London underworld scenes that have fictional counterparts in Tom-All-Alone's and the opium dens of *Edwin Drood*. Dickens referred to these expeditions as 'field-days', and Bucket, ready to expose Hortense, also prepares for a 'field-day' (*BH* 54). Field joined the New Police on their formation in 1829 and initially worked in the St Giles district, from where he and Dickens set off 'on duty' in another *Household Words* article ('On Duty with Inspector Field', 14 June 1851). Field became chief of the Detective Department in 1846 and, retiring in 1852, opened a private detective agency. Dickens felt that his admiration was reciprocated: '[Field]', he wrote to BULWER-LYTTON, 'is quite devoted to me' (9 May 1851). WFL

Long, W. F., 'The "Singler Stories" of Inspector Field', *Dickensian*, 83 (1987).

**Fielding, Henry** (1707–54), dramatist, journalist, novelist, and important influence on Dickens. Fielding was one of the great pioneers of the English novel in the 18th

century. His writings include political satires for the stage, such as *Pasquin* (1736) and *The Historical Register* (1737), and non-fiction for the anti-Jacobite periodical *The Champion*. However, he is now best known for his novels, including *An Apology for the Life of Mrs Shamela Andrews* (1741) and *The Adventures of Joseph Andrews* (1742), both of which parody Richardson's popular novel *Pamela*, and for *The History of Tom Jones, A Foundling* (1749). *Tom Jones* tells the story of a young man of humble origins who falls in love with a woman of more social prominence and who triumphs over circumstances and society, finally to marry his beloved. This foundling plot is one familiar to readers of Dickens; consider Pip in *Great Expectations*. Proclaiming in Book 2 of *Tom Jones* that he was 'the founder of a new province of writing', Fielding blurred the boundaries between fact and fiction, between historical and imaginative writing. For example, the Jacobite Rebellion of 1745 is fascinatingly interwoven into the structure of *Tom Jones*'s personal history and adventures. Tom Jones is one of the characters on whom young David Copperfield relies to escape the misery of the Murdstones (*DC* 4). Throughout his career Dickens's reviewers compared him with Fielding. FORSTER, reviewing *Nicholas Nickleby* for the EXAMINER, suggested that 'we see [Dickens], at no distant day, if he does entire justice to his powers, the not unworthy successor of our GOLDSMITHS and FIELDINGS' (27 Oct. 1839)—an apt appraisal of a writer who, like Fielding, was to become one of the most important innovators in the history of the novel. Dickens so admired Fielding that he named one of his sons after him. MWT

**Fields, James T.** (1817–81) and his enchanting young second wife **Annie** (1834–1915) were Dickens's closest American friends. He met James (partner in TICKNOR AND FIELDS, his Boston publishers) on his arrival in Boston in 1842; Fields gives a vivid account in his *Yesterdays with Authors* (1872)—Dickens 'seemed like the Emperor of cheerfulness on a cruise of pleasure'. James and Annie visited Dickens in 1859–60 and began urging him to give PUBLIC READINGS in AMERICA. They were much associated with the eventual American readings tour, 1867–8, during which their mutual affection increased. No two people 'could be more affectionately attached to a third', Dickens wrote (23 January 1868); she was 'one of the dearest little women in the world' (22 December 1867), and he told them: 'you will never know how I loved you both, or what you have been to me in America' (26 April 1868). They were, wrote Annie, 'truly penetrated with grateful love' for Dickens; 'we cannot help loving him as all must do who have the privilege of coming near him.' In 1869 they visited him, and Annie's diary—heavily drawn upon by James, and best available in George Curry's *Dickens and Annie Fields* (1988)—is uniquely full of detail about their encounters and of sympathetic insight. James was more aware of Dickens's energy and his being 'the *cheerfullest* man of his age'; Annie, a more penetrating observer, saw the pain and sadness underlying the ebullience, and noted the 'dear suffering face' and how his 'sad eyes' would suddenly flash into merriment: 'it is wonderful the fun and flow of spirits C.D. has for he is a sad man.' After his death she often thanked God 'that he is no longer in a world which held so much pain for him'.

PC

**Fildes, Samuel Luke** (1844–1927), ILLUSTRATOR and painter. John Everett Millais, knowing that Dickens sought an illustrator for his new serial, *The Mystery of Edwin Drood*, saw a picture in the first number (4 December 1869) of the *Graphic* that he thought might suit his needs. Dickens enquired about the young Liverpool-born artist, Luke Fildes, who had studied at the Royal Academy. After seeing specimen drawings, including a sketch of Little Em'ly and Peggotty, and then interviewing him, Dickens hired him. Fildes had to follow the figures and settings Charles COLLINS had already designed for the wrapper, but he also read proofs carefully and listened attentively to Dickens describing characters and situations. His pictures incorporated landmarks of the London and Rochester areas. As he gained Dickens's friendship and confidence, he was even able once to talk Dickens *out* of illustrating a scene. Fildes worked up his sketches very carefully, then transferred them photographically to woodblocks that his friend Charles Roberts engraved. When Dickens died Fildes had completed only six plates. On his own initiative he designed and executed

six more. He also painted a watercolour of Dickens's study, 'The Empty Chair', which appeared in the *Graphic*, and he remained friendly with the family, especially Kate. Fildes gave up book illustration by the end of the 1870s, and was elected RA in 1887; to the end of his long life he was pursued by Droodians convinced he knew more about the ending of the novel than he disclosed (see MYSTERY OF EDWIN DROOD, SOLUTIONS TO).

RLP

**films and film-makers of Dickens.** The films are many, the significant film-makers only two, D. W. Griffith and David Lean. At least 80 films have appeared since 1898 when an episode from *Oliver Twist*, 'Mr Bumble the Beadle', became the first screen adaptation of Dickens. And the Portuguese version of *Hard Times* (1988) ensured that all of the novels have been filmed at least once.

The connection between theatrical and filmed adaptation is clear (see DRAMATIZATIONS). By the time cinema began, theatrical adaptation had established itself as a form which began before *Pickwick Papers* had finished appearing serially, and it seemed natural that the reputations forged in one medium should be transferred to the other. The new form was desperate for material and for those—actors, writers, and producers—who could help to transfer it to the screen. Dickens was, then, an obvious source for a number of reasons. Theatrical reputations had been built on these foundations, especially by actors making a career out of specializing in a particular character role.

Dickens's immense popularity could be exploited for the benefit of film-makers, but as a popular genius whose work was beginning to achieve classic status he could also fulfil a purpose exploited by screen-adaptations of SHAKESPEARE, that of conferring a degree of respectability on a form that was dismissed in its earlier years as a vulgar, mechanical entertainment fit only for the humblest of audiences.

The seminal text in understanding the significance of Dickens's relationship to cinema is Sergei Eisenstein's essay, 'Dickens, Griffith and the Film Today' (1944), which contains masterly literary criticism in addition to its grasp of the historical and aesthetic forces crucial to the development of film.

Griffith made only one Dickens adaptation, The CRICKET ON THE HEARTH (1909), although his *Orphans of the Storm* (1922) a powerful melodrama of familial separation and reconciliation, set in revolutionary France, was influenced directly by Vitagraph's *A Tale of Two Cities* (1911). But Griffith's work as a whole—with its theme of the unprotected young women, for example—is pervaded by Dickens's moral vision, for reasons that have to do with his nurturing in an American theatre which inhabited the universe of MELODRAMA from which Dickens had drawn and to which he contributed so much.

Griffith's popularity and the critical esteem he engendered ensured that this system of values became part of the currency of the developing medium. For example, in the adaptation of *Bleak House* (1920) directed by Maurice Elvey, the cross-cutting between the interrogation of Hortense and Lady Dedlock's flight through the empty city is both Dickensian and Griffith-like in style, as is the strong visual emphasis on the latter's isolation.

But Griffith also acknowledged, and Eisenstein analyses brilliantly, Dickens's crucial influence on the medium's form. He demonstrates that the sensuous richness of detail found in chapter 21 of *Oliver Twist*, 'The Expedition', depicting the change from darkness to light and from stillness to uproarious activity, represents a plasticity vital to the development of the new form. Dickens's use of Oliver's journey with Sikes as a vehicle to evoke the gradually awakening city is, Eisenstein claims, essentially cinematic in its noise and movement.

Eisenstein identifies as Griffith's key—acknowledged—inheritance from Dickens, 'the method of a *montage progression of parallel scenes, intercut into each other*' (p. 217), through the structural breakdown of chapter 14 of *Oliver Twist* which shows how Dickens keeps a number of separate narrative strands running throughout the account of Oliver's errand for Mr Brownlow which results in his being dragged back to Fagin. Eisenstein's argument is rounded off by an examination of the 'streaky bacon' passage at the beginning of chapter 17 of the same book, which he sees as Dickens's own 'treatise' on the principles of montage as they operate within melodrama

'as if Dickens had placed himself in the position of the connecting link between the future, unforeseen art of the cinema, and ... the traditions of "good murderous melodramas" ' (p. 224).

In the light of this analysis, the history of the actual film adaptations is varied and interesting but, on the whole, fails to live up to the promise of these origins. What Eisenstein suggests is a work which captures some essential spirit of the novel, but in a new form which is interesting in its own right. These are exacting standards, and it is not clear that they have often been met although a great deal of fun and enjoyment has been generated along the way.

Many adaptations of the novels have started life as vehicles for established theatrical stars, for example, Paramount's 1935 version of *A Christmas Carol* starring Sir Seymour Hicks, Noel Langley's 1951 adaptation with Alastair Sim, and the Leslie Bricusse musical *Scrooge* (1970), which boasted Albert Finney in the title role and Alec Guinness as Marley's ghost. In 1984 a full-scale Americanization of the *Carol* saw George C. Scott in the lead, while Disney's *A Muppet Christmas Carol* (1992), with Michael Caine as Scrooge and Kermit the Frog as Bob Cratchit, represents an even more radical Americanization.

The concept of star as matinee idol offered sumptuous opportunities for a series of Sydney Cartons, including Ronald Colman (1935), produced by the redoubtable David Selznick, and Dirk Bogarde (1957) in an adaptation by T. E. B. Clarke who first achieved fame as a key writer of Ealing comedies. This version of the star vehicle again evokes an earlier theatrical tradition, of the domination of a single role, sometimes continuously for years, by a romantic leading man.

Turning to the Dark Novels, we can note only two films of *Bleak House* (1918 and 1920). The two adaptations of *Our Mutual Friend* also belong to the silent period, while it is perhaps surprising to note the six films of *Little Dorrit* to the four of *Great Expectations* (all such figures are approximate; exact records are not available for the early period of cinema), but this number is dwarfed by the some fourteen film versions of *Oliver Twist*. The dominance of America in film-making may account for the existence of only two, early, *Martin Chuzzlewits*. On the other hand, it might be possible to adumbrate a British tradition in the work of Thomas Bentley whose career encapsulated some of the key features of Dickens adaptation. Not a great deal is known of Bentley (*c.*1880–1950) and his early work is not easily accessible. Trained as an engineer, he then worked in music hall and on the stage in the mode of Bransby WIL-LIAMS by impersonating Dickens characters. He moved into the new medium in 1910 and directed a number of silent films, including *Oliver Twist* (1912), *David Copperfield* (1913), *The* CHIMES (1914), *The Old Curiosity Shop* (1914), *Barnaby Rudge* (1915), and *The Adventures of Mr Pickwick* (1921); he also remade *The Old Curiosity Shop* (1935) as a talkie.

The history of film adaptation of Dickens is crammed with incidental delights and amusing oddities, among the more striking being the pairing of Jackie Coogan and Lon Chaney as Oliver and Fagin in 1922, and the Mr Micawber of W. C. Fields in MGM's film (1935) directed by George Cukor. But it is noteworthy how few works stand out in this history. Both the Hollywood and the British films of *A Tale of Two Cities* gain sweep and power in crowd scenes by drawing on expensive production values, but they hardly begin to suggest the depths and complexity of the novel, while inhibitions generated by their consciousness of bringing a 'classic' before a large public prevent a full expression of the text's wilder aspects. And even a director of real distinction, Carol Reed, was unable to liberate the energies of Lionel Bart's musical *Oliver!* (1968) into a different form. (One oddity does stand out as being truly striking, the Portuguese *Hard Times* (*Tempos difíceis, este tempo,* 1988) written and directed by João Botelho. Set in contemporary Portugal and filmed in black and white, the novel's Coketown becomes World's End, an emblematically rendered vision of industrial decay rather than a harshly vibrant picture of a manufacturing town.)

With David Lean we turn to a director of international renown, although one constrained to some extent by studio demands, whose films are generally regarded as the high watermark of adaptations of Dickens although this view has been challenged by Graham Petrie in an important article, 'Dickens, Godard, and the Film Today.' Petrie's argument centres on what he sees as the inextricable mingling of mundane reality and grotesque fantasy in Dickens's work, and his belief that Lean and his collaborators separate out these elements in a way that is fundamentally false to the spirit of the novels. For example, his adaptation of *Great Expectations* (1946) contrasts the 'real' world of Pip and Herbert with the 'dream' world of Miss Havisham. What this distinction ignores, in Petrie's view, is the way in which Pip's world, in the country as well as in London, is pervaded by prison imagery and the taint of criminality. And the excision of Orlick removes one of the novel's most powerful suggestions of the darker side of Pip's inner life.

These strictures, which many would dispute, seem not to apply to Lean's *Oliver Twist* (1948). Unlike the absence of Orlick, the removal of the Maylies streamlines the narrative effectively while eliminating one of the novel's less successful features, and Oliver's entrance into London, brilliantly managed from the child's viewpoint, has all the ingredients of noise, animals, and lowering glimpses of St Paul's omitted from the earlier adaptation. The film abounds in cinematic equivalents of the spirit of Dickens's novel: as Oliver's mother lies dying the sounds of footsteps and coughing are heard outside as the inmates head for a breakfast which begins with a grace shouted rather than spoken. The baby is then carried on a breathtakingly effective tour of the workhouse which begins with the screen divided between the tiny Oliver and his nurse on the right and a panorama of the dining-room on the left, the wall above the eaters defaced with the huge and ironic sign, 'God is Good'. The wordless sequence towards Oliver's asking for more is rendered with a power almost greater than that of the novel in the deep-focus shot of a tiny Oliver making his way with agonizing slowness towards his fate. The merging of reality and fantasy demanded by Petrie is embodied in the magnificently studio-bound 'exterior' of the precarious bridge leading from a relatively normal London to Fagin's hideout, with St Paul's again lowering in the background. The acceptance of this version as a masterpiece of Dickens adaptation has been hindered, perhaps, by the unease generated by Alec Guinness's portrait of Fagin, with make-up modelled on CRUIKSHANK's illustrations. Understandably, in the aftermath of the

Holocaust, this caused a furore, particularly in the United States where the film was withdrawn from circulation on its first appearance.

The major attempt at adaptation in recent years was written and directed by Christine Edzard, the six-hour *Little Dorrit* (1987) which is divided into two parts, 'Nobody's Fault' and 'Little Dorrit's Story'. One major feature of the film was the attention it devoted to costumes which were handsewn by studio staff, presumably in an effort to escape from the colourful uniforms characteristic of many film and, especially, television ventures into period drama, costumes that have never endured the rough-and-tumble that was clearly inseparable from Victorian living conditions. The film generated controversy, with some finding feminist strengths in its strategy of repeating material from Part I in Part II, this time from Little Dorrit's perspective. For others it was a Thatcherite celebration of heritage which failed to bring the novel's satirical criticism of money-grubbing and the City into a focused relationship with contemporary life. This large-scale attempt suggests perhaps that Eisenstein's lessons have still not been fully absorbed.                                    GFS

Eisenstein, Sergei, 'Dickens, Griffith, and the Film Today', *Film Form: Essays in Film Theory* (1949).

Paroissien, David, 'Dickens and the Cinema', *Dickens Studies Annual*, 7 (1980).

Petrie, Graham, 'Dickens, Godard, and the Film Today', *Yale Review*, 44 (1974).

Smith, Grahame, 'Dickens and Adaptation Imagery in Words and Pictures', in *Novel Images*, ed. Peter Reynolds (1993).

—— 'Novel into Film: The Case of *Little Dorrit*', *Yearbook of English Studies*, 20 (1990).

**Fitzgerald, Percy** (1834–1925), Irish lawyer turned journalist and author, contributed to *Household Words* from 1856, first met Dickens in Dublin in 1858, and became a close and devoted (maybe sycophantic) friend. His extensive contributions to the weeklies include five novels, and he wrote more about Dickens than any other contemporary—a two-volume *Life, Memoirs of Dickens* with particular reference to his periodicals, six books on *Pickwick*, and much else. These writings are repetitive and unreliable, but he had enjoyed ample opportunity to observe Dickens professionally and domestically, and

zealously frequented the novels, so he offers unique information. A rapid, non-stop writer —his *An Output* (1912) lists 120 works—he was careless and inaccurate, and Dickens protested when Fitzgerald was simultaneously writing serials for *All the Year Round* and two other journals: our art 'cannot be reasonably pursued in this way', he told him (9 March 1870). Similarly, over an article: 'For my sake—if not for Heaven's—do, I *entreat* you, look over your manuscript before sending it to the printer. Its condition involves us all in hopeless confusion' (18 November 1869).

A biographer of Boswell, Fitzgerald resembled him in his fond attachment to an illustrious elder, and Dickens, like JOHNSON, forgave shortcomings and felt affection for his admirer, even wishing his daughter Mamie to marry him—a signal compliment, since Fitzgerald was a ROMAN CATHOLIC. Fitzgerald's services included giving him an Irish bloodhound, which delighted Dickens but no one else (see PETS). In old age something of a figure of fun for his garrulous celebration of Dickens—which could seem a soft-headed spun-out exploitation of his acquaintance with the great man—he founded the Boz Club in 1900, and was First President of the DICKENS FELLOWSHIP, 1902.              PC

**Fonblanque, Albany** (1793–1872), radical journalist, editor 1830–47 of the *EXAMINER*, to which Dickens then contributed, leader-writer on the MORNING CHRONICLE, *The TIMES*, the DAILY NEWS, etc., widely recognized as England's wittiest journalist, 'a scourge of humbug' and 'moral-force' reformer. Dickens felt for him a 'warm regard and admiration' and thought him 'another Swift' (14 November 1839; 11 July 1842), and coincided with him (or was perhaps influenced by him) on many public issues, such as unpaid magistrates. In frequent contact in earlier years, they rarely met later; quitting journalism, Fonblanque dropped out of circulation.                                            PC

**Forster, John** (1812–76), Dickens's oldest friend and first significant biographer. Forster came from UNITARIAN stock in Newcastle, the second child of a butcher, a fact about which he remained touchy all his life; and was educated at Newcastle Grammar School. A fascination with literature and, in particular, with the theatre, drew him to London, and in 1828 he enrolled as a law student at the Inner Temple. Much of his energy went into theatre-going and cultivating the company of the surviving Romantics, Charles LAMB (whom he revered as a model of the artistic temperament), Leigh HUNT, and Walter Savage LANDOR, as well as the leading actor of the day W. C. MACREADY and the up-and-coming novelist BULWER-LYTTON. These friendships helped to establish Forster as, in effect, a potential literary agent and on the basis of this promise he abandoned the law for literature in 1832, becoming drama critic for the TRUE SUN newspaper—at the same time as Dickens was that paper's parliamentary reporter—and then in 1833 the literary and dramatic critic of the EXAMINER. It was a bold but timely move for a man like Forster, when an expanding mass market for literature required the particular combination of skills he was able to provide. He had a widening circle of writers to advise and he was able to bring something of a critic's sensibility, a lawyer's awareness of technicalities, and a businessman's hard-headedness to this task. Dickens owed a great deal to these and other qualities in Forster, and recognized as much.

The two men met at the end of 1836 and took to each other at once. They came from a similar lower-middle-class background and shared a love of the theatre and a passionate belief in the dignity of literature. They were also high-spirited, interspersing the business of literature with impromptu decisions to ride out of London to see the surrounding countryside and visit country inns, including a jaunt to Cornwall in 1842—something one cannot imagine Forster's later incarnation, Mr Podsnap, doing. Forster early recognized Dickens's genius and before they met had reviewed Sketches by Boz and Pickwick Papers favourably in the Examiner. His first important service to Dickens was to help him disentangle himself from the simultaneous commitments to different publishers which he had entered into at the start of his career. The success of Pickwick Papers had inspired MACRONE, who owned the copyright of Sketches by Boz, to bring it too out in green-wrapped monthly parts to capitalize on the later work: Forster helped persuade CHAPMAN AND HALL, whose literary adviser he became in 1837, to give Dickens the money to pay off Macrone and to make him a loan

enabling him to buy back the copyright of Oliver Twist and release himself from his other commitments to the publisher Richard BENTLEY. Now settled with a single publisher, Dickens was able to produce his novels in the form with which they are chiefly associated, the monthly SERIAL part. Almost from the start Forster saw the parts at proof stage: 'There was nothing written by him after this date [part 14 of Pickwick] which I did not see before the world did, either in manuscript or proofs; and in connection with the latter I shortly began to give him the help which he publicly mentioned twenty years later in dedicating his collected writings to me.' Proofs were sent to both Forster and Dickens, and Forster would enter Dickens's corrections and make his own, which were usually minor and to do with punctuation. Forster's influence could be more substantial, the most famous example being his claim that Dickens had not thought of the death of Little Nell in The Old Curiosity Shop until he suggested it. 'He had not thought of killing her', Forster wrote, until he mentioned to Dickens that her death might 'necessarily belong even to his own conception' of the character. Again, in Dombey and Son Forster advised against Dickens's original, and wiser, instinct to make Walter Gay 'gradually and naturally' fall away 'into negligence, idleness, dissipation, dishonesty, and ruin'. He also dissuaded Dickens from giving unnecessary offence, as in the subsequently discarded opening chapter of AMERICAN NOTES or the rejected 'Young England' gentleman in The CHIMES.

It is easy to forget that Forster was pursuing a public career of his own at this time. As the editor of the Examiner from 1847 to 1855 he was at the hub of London literary life, with a wide circle of friends who were actors, writers, and journalists. He was the friend of BROWNING, TENNYSON, and CARLYLE, among others, all of whose careers he helped to promote; but he was also quick to raise money for the less fortunate through the AMATEUR THEATRICALS which he and Dickens helped to organize. He was active in setting up the GUILD OF LITERATURE AND ART as a professional alternative to what was seen as the genteel amateurism of the ROYAL LITERARY FUND, and it was under the aegis of the Guild that in 1850 he and Dickens started the theatricals, the 'splendid strolling', to raise an endowment for indigent men and women of letters—which, however, came to very little. (Forster was by all accounts a mannered actor but an excellent reader of dramatic poetry.) His concern to improve the condition of his profession shows in a number of ways, from his campaign for a COPYRIGHT Act and his part in founding the London Library to his quarrel with THACKERAY, whose attitude of gentlemanly disdain (as he saw it) he deplored.

Forster had ambitions as a historian, his chief field of interest being the 17th century. From his Newcastle days, when he wrote a play (produced only once) called *Charles at Tunbridge*, he had been interested in the conflict between Parliament and King, his sympathies lying predictably with the former. Five volumes of his *Lives of Eminent British Statesmen* appeared in *Lardner's Cabinet Cyclopaedia* between 1836 and 1839, the last two devoted to Oliver Cromwell, followed by the volumes of *The Statesmen of the Commonwealth of England* in 1840. The same themes were taken up in his later *Historical and Biographical Essays* (2 vols., 1858), and then Forster moved into the 18th century with his biographies of GOLDSMITH (1848; second edn. 1854) and SWIFT (1875; unfinished). But none of these works has survived in the way that the *Life of Dickens* has, for obvious reasons. Forster had nothing new to say about the 17th or 18th centuries, but his closeness to Dickens made him a unique witness to genius.

Forster and Dickens were especially close in the 1840s. When Dickens visited AMERICA in 1842 he wrote a series of long letters to Forster which became the basis of his *American Notes* (1842). Similarly Forster was the chief recipient of the letters Dickens wrote home when he and his family spent a year in ITALY from July 1844 to July 1845, and Dickens drew on them when writing his *PICTURES FROM ITALY* (1846). Forster invited Dickens to contribute to the *Examiner* when he became editor in 1847, resulting in a number of reviews and articles over the next two years, including four trenchant pieces denouncing the neglect and mismanagement of a juvenile Pauper Asylum at Tooting which had led to the death of 180 children.

If Forster provided Dickens with a platform for social reform, he also offered him an ear for the most intimate of confessions. By chance he had heard about Dickens's experience in WARREN'S BLACKING warehouse. In 'March or April of 1847', he told Dickens, he had met Charles Dilke, a friend of Dickens's father, who recalled having once seen Dickens working in a warehouse near the Strand, 'at which place Mr. Dilke, being with the elder Dickens one day, had noticed him, and received, in return for the gift of a half-crown, a very low bow. He was silent for several minutes; I felt that I had unintentionally touched a painful place in his memory; and to Mr. Dilke I never spoke of the subject again.' Shortly thereafter Forster received the autobiographical fragment which is reproduced in chapter 2 of the *Life* and was to be its most startling revelation (see DIARIES). Forster claimed to be the only recipient of Dickens's confession, but this is contested by Charles Dickens the younger who said, 'on my mother's authority', that Catherine also read the Autobiographical Fragment and had remonstrated with Dickens about his harshness towards his mother (Introduction to the Macmillan edition of *David Copperfield*, 1892). Be that as it may, however, the two impulses worked together at this time—concern for the suffering children in Victorian society awakened awareness of his own suffering as a child—and Forster was intimately involved with both.

Forster was also close to Catherine, and the three of them for years made a practice of celebrating birthdays together. On the brink of his own marriage, years later, Forster wrote to her on her birthday, 19 May 1856: 'Many, many most happy returns to you, and to us all on this day which for so many years we have passed together. I do not know how it is that I associate you so much with the change that is about to befall me—and that I have never felt so strongly as within the last few months how much of the happiness of past years I owe to you . . .' (Pilgrim 1, p. xvii). With such closeness, inevitably there were disagreements, and occasionally serious rows. On one occasion, according to Macready, who was present (*Diaries*, ed. Toynbee, 1912, 16 August 1840) Forster 'waxed warm', Dickens lost his temper, and Kate fled from the room in tears. On another occasion the discord was so severe that Macready feared the friendship might end, but again intimacy was restored (*Diaries*, 4 November 1847).

Subtle changes began to take place after 1850, however. Forster started to move to the right and found the liberal policies of the *Examiner* increasingly hard to sustain. Combining the editing of a weekly journal with his other commitments was putting a strain on his health, never good and getting worse. And he was becoming lonely as old friends died and younger friends married and started to accumulate large families. Desperate to escape the strains of journalism, he eventually obtained the post of Secretary to the Lunacy Commission in 1855, through the influence of Lord John RUSSELL; his new salary of £800 enabled him at last to resign from the *Examiner*. This new position imposed its own strains in the travelling he had to do to inspect lunatic asylums throughout the country, and he continued to act as an unpaid adviser and agent to contemporary writers. It was Forster, for example, who encouraged Dickens to look on copyright as a form of capital which could provide future earnings. Forster's own financial anxieties were eased dramatically when, to the surprise of all who knew him, he married a wealthy widow, Eliza Colburn, in 1856; his situation improved further when he became a Commissioner of Lunacy in February 1861, at a salary of £1,500 per annum. He was now well-to-do, if not wealthy.

Forster and Dickens retained the closeness of old friendship, cemented by Dickens's confession about the blacking-factory and the knowledge that Forster was to be his biographer. But something of the old intimacy and mutual sympathy was starting to fade. Like many, Forster disliked 'the underlying tone of bitterness that runs through the books which followed *Copperfield*', and in 1856 he withdrew from *Household Words*, feeling that he had not been consulted sufficiently and disliking the editor, W. H. WILLS. The following year saw his last participation in amateur theatricals, and it may be significant that the play in question, *The* FROZEN DEEP, figured Ellen TERNAN, the young actress with whom Dickens fell desperately in love at this time. We know he disapproved of the profitable PUBLIC READINGS which Dickens began in 1858, considering them 'a substitution of lower for higher aims' which 'had so much of the character of a public exhibition for money as to raise, in the question of respect for his calling as a writer, a question also of respect

for himself as a gentleman'. But Dickens needed the money which the readings provided; and he needed youth, to help bridge the gap between his age and Ellen's. His chosen companions were now younger and more bohemian individuals, like Wilkie COLLINS and Edmund YATES, with whom Dickens could experience a much more daring life than with Forster. And so as Dickens moved away from respectability Forster moved towards it, eventually becoming a part of that 'Society' which is one of the chief satirical targets of *Our Mutual Friend* (1864–5). The development can be seen in the move from his relatively modest chambers in Lincoln's Inn Fields (the original for Tulkinghorn's rooms in *Bleak House*) to the grandiose mansion he had built for himself to his own plans, Palace Gate House, on ground which alone cost £4,000.

In the last decade of his life Forster suffered from ill health, and work for the Lunacy Commission took him away from literature until Dickens's death in 1870 made the biographical task urgent. Prosperity and respectability brought out the grain which had always been there in the wood, and there is undoubtedly much of Forster in Podsnap. He could be rude, loud, pompous, touchy about his origins, snobbish, and overbearing. But he was also capable of quick sympathy, personal loyalty, and great kindness, and these are not Podsnappian qualities. His wife was small and nervous, unlike the large, hard-featured Mrs Podsnap, and there was no 'young person' in their lives: the Forsters were childless. The similarities seem to have been in voice, manner, gesture, possibly insularity of attitude, and prudery. Philistinism does not seem to be a sustainable charge, given Forster's huge collection of books and scholarly interests in 17th- and 18th-century politics. It is interesting to note that Forster himself considered the portrayal of the 'vulgar canting Podsnap' to be one of the few aspects of *Our Mutual Friend* where 'all the old cunning of the master hand' was at work.

Despite their differences, Forster and Dickens remained good friends in later years. Forster took Dickens's side at the time of the separation from his wife and Dickens appointed him ('my dear and trusty friend') as co-executor, with his sister-in-law Georgina HOGARTH, of his will. The will is printed as an

Appendix to the *Life* (3 vols., 1872–4), which Forster completed against a background of increasing illness. Not only by far the most important book Forster wrote, this is also a document of the greatest significance for anyone seeking to understand Dickens. Forster was unique in having known Dickens from the start to the end of his career and in having had access to his friend's recollections of his childhood and youth. But Forster was as important, if not more so, as a sounding-board for ideas about the novels: he was virtually the only person with whom Dickens felt able to discuss the conception and progress of his work, and apart from the monthly number-plans, it is only in the letters to Forster that we can see evidence of planning and self-conscious artistry.

The *Life* is full of details about Dickens but its structure—just under two-thirds is devoted to his career up to and including *Copperfield*—reflects Forster's belief that that novel is Dickens's masterpiece from which the others are a decline; it also unwittingly reveals the nature of his relationship with Dickens, which was more intimate in the earlier period. As one would expect at this time, Forster is silent about Ellen Ternan (although in printing the will he leaves in the tantalizing £1,000 legacy he bequeathed her). His account of the separation from Catherine is necessarily too wary for fullness or clarity. More generally, the biography suffers from the Victorian vice of shapelessness and is open to the charge of giving undue prominence to the role played by Forster in Dickens's life: 'The Autobiography of John Forster with Recollections of Charles Dickens', as it was called at the time. But the *Life* should not be judged entirely by modern standards of revelation. If it does not attempt to tell the whole truth about Dickens this is partly because of the idealizing tendency in Victorian biography, and partly because so many of the individuals involved were still alive when he wrote it.

Today Forster would be a largely forgotten figure were it not for his relationship with Dickens. His solid qualities of honesty, integrity, and trustworthiness, allied to literary taste, were necessary for the stabilizing of Dickens's more mercurial temperament, until they hardened into Podsnappery. As for Forster, the death of Dickens removed most of his pleasure in life: 'nothing in future can, to me, ever again be as it was', he wrote on hearing of Dickens's death. 'The duties of life remain while life remains, but for me the joy of it is gone for ever more.' RG

Davies, James A., *John Forster: A Literary Life* (1983).
*Dickensian*, 70 (1974)—a special Forster issue, with important articles by Anthony Burton on Forster on the stage and David Woolley on Forster's *Swift*.

**Forster Collection.** The largest COLLECTION of Dickens manuscripts and proofs, given by Dickens to his friend and adviser John FORSTER, now held in the VICTORIA AND ALBERT MUSEUM.

**France.** Dickens's interest in France can be said, roughly speaking, to fall into three phases. The early phase culminates in his first journey abroad—across the Channel to France and Belgium in 1837, above all to Calais. Two letters from there survive, one to FORSTER dated 'le 2nd. July 1837', the other to BENTLEY dated 'le 2me. Juillet 1837'. This is not yet the 'CITOYEN CHARLES DICKENS' who wrote jubilantly in French to Forster in February 1848 on the fall of Louis-Philippe, but we can see the novelist already constructing a humorous French-speaking *alter ego*. His son Henry Fielding Dickens (1928) wrote later of such lifelong *jeux d'esprit* that he 'used to say, laughingly, that his sympathies were so much with the French that he ought to have been born a Frenchman'.

The reasons for the earliest phase of Dickens's interest in France may have something to do with his KENTISH background. 'There's milestones on the Dover Road', Mr F's Aunt exclaims (*LD* 1.23), and of course Dover is the setting-off point for Calais. 'When I retire from a literary life I think of setting up as a Channel pilot', he wrote jestingly to de Cerjat (25 October 1864), having lived since 1856 in a famous literary location on the Dover Road—Gad's Hill, with both Chaucerian and SHAKESPEARIAN associations—in the house of his childhood dreams (see HOMES OF DICKENS). Its proximity to France may have been part of the significance of those dreams, for Dickens rejoiced over the opening in June 1856 of a railway 'which connects Gadshill with the whole sea coast', and which he would use for numerous subsequent visits to France (Forster 8.3). See map p. 615.

Even more to the point, perhaps, Calais itself held a symbolic psychological significance, derived from childhood, as a bolt-hole for those quick-witted and well-connected enough to avoid imprisonment—for debt, in the Marshalsea, above all. His grandfather and namesake Charles Barrow had absconded to the Isle of Man when found guilty of - embezzling money from Somerset House, but Calais and Boulogne were more fashionable retreats for debtors and thieves. The most famous English inhabitant of Calais in the period of his youth was someone whom Dickens the dandy strove to imitate: Beau Brummell, on the run from gambling debts.

Following his example, those characters in Dickens's novels with something to hide regularly scurry across the Channel. Mr Sparsit dies at the age of 24, 'the scene of his decease, Calais, and the cause brandy'; 'he did not leave his widow . . . in affluent circumstances' (*HT* 1.7). 'English outlaws are half the population' of Calais when Clennam goes to look for Miss Wade (herself with Tattycoram a sexual outlaw, perhaps); the manuscript had 'three fourths' (*LD* 2.20). And there is sarcastic biblical prophecy at the end of *Our Mutual Friend*: 'having over-jobbed his jobberies as legislator . . . it shall come to pass next week that Veneering will accept the Chiltern Hundreds . . . and that the Veneerings will retire to Calais.'

The motif of theatrical self-reinvention that accompanies this nexus of associations also surfaces at an early stage. Jingle is one example: his fraudulent boast of having written in France an 'Epic poem—ten thousand lines —revolution of July—composed it on the spot—Mars by day, Apollo by night,—bang the field-piece, twang the lyre', attracts a humorous footnote: 'A remarkable instance of the prophetic force of Mr Jingle's imagination; the dialogue occurring in the year 1827, and the Revolution in 1830' (*PP* 2). Though the chronological mistake may initially have been Dickens's own, his continuing interest at the time of the 1832 REFORM Bill in prospects in post-Revolutionary France can be detected in the remarks of the 'Genius of Despair and Suicide': 'they're doing a pretty brisk business in my way over in England and France just

now, and my time is a good deal taken up' (*NN* 6).

So his first landing in Calais in 1837 carried much significance. Now at last the 'shadow of the Marshalsea' in Dickens's past was beginning to dissipate with the sensational success of his novelistic career. He travelled with his wife and Hablot K. BROWNE ('Phiz'), whose French Christian name, given him following the death of his sister's fiancé at the Battle of Waterloo, serves as a reminder that English sympathies with French republicanism had not completely vanished during the Napoleonic years. Looking about him, Dickens seems, as later in AMERICA, to be assessing social and political conditions—with the important difference that his first impressions of Calais under the July Monarchy are strikingly positive: 'We went this afternoon in a barouche to some gardens where the people dance, and where they were footing it most heartily—especially the women who in their short petticoats and light caps look uncommonly agreeable. A gentleman in a blue surtout and silken Berlins accompanied us from the Hotel, and acted as Curator. He even waltzed with a very smart lady (just to show us, condescendingly, how it ought to be done) and waltzed elegantly too. We rang for slippers after we came back, and it turned out that this gentleman was the "Boots". Isn't this French?' (to Forster, 2 July 1837).

Noting and characterizing here as distinctively French, first, a popular gaiety, with no dismal Sundays (see SABBATARIANISM), and secondly, a republican egalitarianism which indicates less overt and rigid CLASS divisions, he implicitly begins a long series of comparative meditations on England and France or London and PARIS—often to the advantage of 'the other side'—that culminates of course in *A Tale of Two Cities*. One of the finest of these is 'A Monument of French Folly' (*HW* 8 March 1851), where efficient French abattoirs are contrasted with their complacent, lax English counterparts, where 'you shall see the little children, inured to sights of brutality from their birth . . . up to their ankles in blood'. Savage and convincing mimicry of endemic British jingoism ensues: 'the French are a frog-eating people who wear wooden shoes, and it's O the roast beef of England, my boy, the jolly old English roast beef!'

But despite this evidence of the first phase of a strong interest, it would be misleading to suggest that France was as yet *implanted* in Dickens's sensibility. A second period of exposure, which began in 1844 with the journey through France described in PICTURES FROM ITALY, is decisive in this respect. He explores in that book, in descriptions such as those of Lyons or Avignon, the persona of a touristic *flâneur* casually observing or reading the physiognomical human signs around him that will become the basis of a method. It will develop above all in connection with Paris, which he also first visited and described at that time, referring to 'the enormous book that stands wide open there'. By November of that year, *en route* to London via Paris, he had formed the desire to spend a longer period there *en famille*, a plan not in fact realized until the winter of 1846–7, during the declining years of Louis-Philippe's reign.

Soon after his arrival in Paris Dickens witnessed the epiphany of the king's convoy passing through the city streets, physiognomizing in the gestures of his entourage an obsessive preoccupation with security: 'it was strange to an Englishman to see the prefect of Police riding on horseback some hundreds of yards in advance of the cortège, turning his head incessantly from side to side, like a figure in a Dutch clock, and scrutinizing everybody and everything, as if he suspected all the trees in the long avenue' (to Watson, 27 November 1846). On the basis of such observations he began to develop a theory of gestural behaviour in France, and how to represent this in art: as he put it to Forster, 'the French . . . are a demonstrative and gesticulating people . . . and what thus is rendered by their artists is the truth through an immense part of the world' (11–12 November 1855). Thus, in rendering Rigaud (*LD*) and Hortense (*BH*) we find close attention paid to speech accompanied by extravagant physical self-expression— Hortense's 'two sovereign' [*sic*] thrown on Tulkinghorn's floor 'with such violence . . . that they jerk up again into the light before they roll away into corners', or her pronunciation of 'enraged'; 'it appears impossible for Mademoiselle to roll the letter r sufficiently in this word, notwithstanding that she assists her energetic delivery, by clenching both her hands, and setting all her teeth' (*BH* 42).

But it is a later street scene observed on one of his walks—one of those great public Parisian literary funerals, at which thousands turn out on the streets to pay their respects to a dead writer—that forms the essential turning-point in Dickens's relation to France. He later told Féval what this event meant to him, how he had 'started to feel fond of France in 1847, being moved by the funeral of the author Frederic Soulié, at which a widespread popular respect for literature was manifest' (Collins 1981, 2.292). From that point onwards France stands above all for 'Citoyen Dickens', and in thoroughly practical ways, as a haven for writers and writing.

A letter of 27 March 1847 to de la Rue in Genoa conveys this new mood: 'the general appreciation of, and respect for, Art, in its broadest and most universal sense, in Paris, is one of the finest national signs I know. They are especially intelligent people: and though there still lingers among them an odd mixture of refinement and coarseness, I believe them to be, in many high and great respects, the first people in the universe'—an estimate shared by Wilkie COLLINS in his reaction to Forgues's appreciation of him in the *Revue des deux mondes* of November 1855: 'the start of a new man in literature or Art is a matter of intense moment to every educated individual in this city.' The developing friendship between the two men was indeed partly based on a mutual love of Paris and France and the respect paid to art there, which set Collins apart from the jingoistic Forster caricatured in Podsnap.

Thus it is that the third phase of Dickens's relationship with France centres on living and writing there. This began with a visit to Boulogne in October 1852, during which a number of *Bleak House* was written. The place seemed a good working environment, and Dickens wrote: 'please God I shall be writing on those said ramparts next July' (to Forster, ?October 1852). That wish was realized, and *Bleak House* was indeed completed in Boulogne in the summer of 1853. *Hard Times* was also completed there the following summer, and more of *Little Dorrit* than of any other novel was written overseas—first in Paris in the winter of 1855–6, and then again in Boulogne the following summer.

But Dickens's Boulogne also carries forward the Calais associations of the novelist's youth. During this third phase of his relation to France, the three summers and later visits found Dickens frequently rubbing shoulders with English families escaping debt and/or living in reduced circumstances. He may have enjoyed the *frisson* of knowing that by contrast he now could more than pay his own way. One such family was that of Richard Cattermole, the brother of the artist George CATTERMOLE who did specialist illustrations of old buildings for Dickens (especially for *The Old Curiosity Shop*). They were close neighbours of Dickens, and tenants like him of Fernand Beaucourt-Mutuel, whom Dickens immortalizes in 'Our French Watering-Place' (*RP*), and whose tombstone is inscribed: 'The landlord of whom Charles Dickens wrote "never did see such a gentle kind heart" ' (Pilgrim 7.118 n.).

Beaucourt-Mutuel's 'angelic' treatment of the Cattermoles is described in the letters and elsewhere. Richard Cattermole never paid the rent: his landlord would simply shrug his shoulders to Dickens and say: he 'promises always, but that's all'. Not only that, he took the Cattermoles' retarded son Vincent under his wing: 'I have him to work in the garden with me, good infant (for it keeps his brain sounder).' Transliterating Beaucourt-Mutuel's French for comic effect—'I am desolated for them all' is his attitude to the Cattermoles—Dickens describes this Guardian Angel to debtors 'backing up the Avenue, with such a generous, simple, amiable face, that I half expected to see him back himself straight into the Evening-Star . . . without going through the ceremony of dying first' (to Beard, 21 June 1856).

Furthermore, his estate on the heights of Boulogne is described by Dickens as a Garden of Eden. Besides the capacity to work fruitfully on his novels, it enabled him to enjoy 'a state of Elysian laziness' for the first time since ITALY. He writes of 'a paradise of roses and geraniums' over which Beaucourt-Mutuel rules: 'I am inclined to doubt whether anybody else since Adam, has been so fond and proud of a garden' (to Beard, 21 June 1856). An admirer of Napoleon I attempting to live out the glorious ideals of Revolutionary France, Beaucourt clearly stands in sharp contrast to 'the cold-blooded scoundrel at the head of France' (Dickens's phrase for Louis Napoleon) at that time. Though Boulogne was then the centre for Anglo-French troop collaboration during the CRIMEAN WAR, it was Beaucourt-Mutuel's microcosmic haven of peaceful integration between Britain and France that captured Dickens's moral imagination during the writing of *Little Dorrit* and epitomized 'the dear old France of my affections' ('Travelling Abroad', *UT*).

Another way in which Boulogne inspired Dickens, though, was as a reminder of the previous paradise in Italy. The code-word 'picturesque' resurfaces as he marvels at how English touristic sensation-seekers have overlooked a kind of Genoa on their doorstep: 'If this were but 300 miles farther off how the English would rave about it! I do assure you that there are picturesque people, and town, and country, about this place, that quite fill up the eye and fancy. As to the fishing people . . . and their quarter of the town cobweb-hung with great brown nets across the narrow uphill streets, they are as good as Naples, every bit' (to Forster, 13 June 1853).

But as Proust remarks, all paradises are lost paradises, and this one is no exception. Falling in love with Ellen TERNAN in 1857, Dickens stopped going to Boulogne for several years, though he left four of his sons at boarding school there for varying periods up until 1860, the year in which Beaucourt's divine generosity or imprudence forced him to sell Les Moulineaux and move to a more modest house at Condette by the sand-dunes to the south of Boulogne. This in turn became a refuge for Dickens; the 'Chalet Dickens' was constructed, and in the 1860s became a secret haven to which he might escape with Ellen. An authoritative account of these visits must await the publication of the final volumes of the Pilgrim letters, but it seems safe to say that, until his death, not only Boulogne and Paris but the entire world of France, just across the Channel, continued to resonate as the 'significant other' it had always been: the place of the benign and tolerant father in which Dickens, as an artist and as a man, experienced the freedom of becoming someone else.                                                              MH

Carlton, W. J., 'Dickens's Forgotten Retreat in France', *Dickensian*, 62 (1966).

Collins, Philip, 'Dickens and French Wickedness', *Charles Dickens et la France* (1978).

Delattre, Floris, *Dickens et la France* (1927).

Watrin, Janine, *De Boulogne à Condette* (1992).

**Frith, William Powell** (1819–1909), painter and friend of Dickens from the 1840s. Frith started his career as a painter of historical and literary genre works and later became famous for his scenes of Victorian life. Attracted by the idea of painting subjects from Dickens's novels, but deterred by the problems of modern dress, the young Frith found inspiration in *Barnaby Rudge* for a group of works showing Dolly Varden of which the best-known is in the VICTORIA AND ALBERT MUSEUM. Dickens ordered one of these paintings in 1842, also commissioning a portrait of Kate Nickleby (both private collection). He paid £40 for the pair. Dickens praised Frith's work at the Paris International Exhibition of 1855, particularly admiring a scene from Oliver GOLDSMITH's *The Good Natured Man: Mr Honeywood and the Bailiffs* (Victoria and Albert). In the 1856 Royal Academy Exhibition Dickens praised *Many Happy Returns of the Day* (Harrogate Art Gallery). Frith's 1859 PORTRAIT of Dickens shows him seated at his desk in Tavistock House working on *A Tale of Two Cities* (Victoria and Albert).      LO

Frith, W. P., *My Autobiography and Reminiscences*, 2 vols. (1887).

Noakes, A., *William Frith* (1978).

Ormond, L., 'Dickens and Painting: Contemporary Art', *Dickensian*, 80 (1984).

***Frozen Deep, The.*** A play written by Wilkie COLLINS with substantial assistance from Dickens, who suggested ideas and made extensive revisions to the script, as well as producing, managing, and starring in its original AMATEUR THEATRICAL production (see COLLABORATIONS). First performed on 6 January 1857 for invited guests in the schoolroom of Dickens's home, converted specially for the purpose, the play was revived that summer in a series of benefit performances in London and Manchester to raise money for the widow and daughter of Douglas JERROLD, plus a private performance before Queen Victoria.

Although it received great acclaim at the time, subsequent revivals without Dickens's participation were failures, and as a work of dramatic art *The Frozen Deep* holds little interest today. Its significance for Dickens was, however, immense. The energy with which he threw himself into every detail of the production is symptomatic of his profound restlessness at the time, which eventuated in the break-up of his marriage eighteen months later. The conception of the play's flawed but ultimately noble hero, Richard Wardour, marked a new departure in characterization for Dickens, who made the role his own, and it fed directly into characters in his subsequent fiction, most notably Sidney Carton. And the decision to replace amateur actresses with professionals for public performances in the large theatre in Manchester introduced Dickens to Ellen TERNAN, the young actress with whom he fell passionately in love.

The story, which dramatizes the self-sacrifice of Wardour in rescuing Aldersley, his rival in love, was inspired by the ill-fated Franklin expedition to Arctic regions in search of the Northwest Passage in 1845. The entire party perished, and first reports alleged cannabalism—not finally proved until 1997—among those who survived longest. Dickens published several articles about the expedition in *Household Words*, defending Franklin, and public interest was revived in 1857 when Lady Franklin launched an appeal for public support to discover her late husband's fate. Dickens, always enthralled by TRAVEL LITERATURE, saw Franklin as a type of noble hero. Wardour, tempted to murder, demonstrates innate goodness in giving up his own life to save that of Aldersley.

The primary impact of the play centred on Dickens's portrayal of Wardour. As Robert Louis Brannan (1966) observes: 'The performance, not the script, excited Dickens and his audiences.' Pathos was the emotion evoked. Dickens wrote long letters to Angela Burdett COUTTS (5 September 1857) and to Mrs Richard WATSON (7 December 1857) recounting in detail how the play left the entire audience and cast in tears. With sets by STANFIELD and actors hand-picked by Dickens, the play was praised by observers for its realism and naturalness.

Dickens reflected that producing *The Frozen Deep* was 'like writing a book in company' (to Tennant, 9 January 1857). A reconstructed script, with an extensive introduction, appears in Brannan (1966).

PVWS

Brannan, Robert Louis (ed.), *Under the Management of Mr Charles Dickens: His Production of 'The Frozen Deep'* (1966).

# G

**gambling.** Dickens never disguised his distaste for and disapproval of gambling. It was in a gambling club that Sir Mulberry Hawk and Lord Frederick Verisopht had the quarrel which led to the duel in which Verisopht died (*NN* 50); and an addiction to gambling (even if for a good cause, the future of Little Nell) delivered the grandfather in *The Old Curiosity Shop* into the hands of Quilp who had lent him the money, turned him into 'a monstrous distortion of his image', and ultimately tempted him to steal from Nell herself (*OCS* 9, 30, 31).

Gambling was an issue frequently in the public eye, and was closely associated with most SPORTS. From the 1830s onwards public concern began to focus on the links between horse-racing and gambling. As Dickens described it, race meetings offered innumerable opportunities for gambling, whether the pea-and-thimble tables for the unwary and poor or the gambling booths specializing in *rouge et noir* for a richer clientele (*NN* 50; *OCS* 19). In 1844 Select Committees of both Houses of Parliament on Gaming condemned 'common Gaming-houses' in towns and 'gambling-booths' at races, while determined to uphold horse-racing in the national interest. An Act of 1845 'to Amend the Law Concerning Games and Wagers' deprived those who lost in wagers from any protection in law, but did little to control the spread of betting. The problem for the legislature in controlling gambling was that it wanted to leave unaffected wagers between the well-off (regarded, amongst other things, as crucial to the survival of a good breed of horses), while suppressing opportunities for gambling for the bulk of the population. The issue came to a head in the early 1850s and, riding the tide (there was a similar article in *Chambers' Edinburgh Journal* in July 1852), Dickens described to readers of *Household Words* (26 June 1852) the world of the betting shop and of the sporting journals which were full of advertisements from touts. At the same time he put forward his preferred remedy. Consistent with his general view that the legislature should not intervene in a repressive way in matters to do with 'the amusements of the people', he opposed proposals for a new Act, but agreed with those who had raised the issue that the 'evil' of betting shops had 'risen to a great height'. The remedy, he believed, lay with parents, employers, and the police who should enforce existing legislation and apprenticeship indentures (which forbade gaming). But in suggesting this remedy, Dickens was a lone voice. When the Attorney-General in 1853 brought forward a Bill to suppress betting houses it went through all its stages without debate and became law—though the consensus of opinion is that it did little if anything to stop betting.                              HC

Clapson, M., *A Bit of a Flutter: Popular Gambling in England, c.1820–1961* (1992).

**Garrick Club.** A gentlemen's club, founded in 1831, named in honour of David Garrick, the foremost English actor of the eighteenth century. Predominantly for men active in the theatre, it has a superb collection of theatrical paintings. Dickens was elected a member in January 1837, soon after being appointed editor of BENTLEY'S MISCELLANY. His election was a clear indication that he was accepted into the literary and dramatic world, but his membership had its ups and downs. As early as November 1838 he resigned, having taken the side of MACREADY in his acrimonious dispute with Alfred Bunn, manager of Drury Lane Theatre.

After resuming his membership, he retired again on 27 December 1849 for a reason not entirely clear, but which might have been his annoyance at the election of Albert SMITH, whose penny paper *The Man in the Moon* had contained articles lampooning him.

Five years later Dickens rejoined, paid his subscription of 21 guineas, and immediately afterwards was invited to chair the committee. On 22 April 1854 he presided at the SHAKESPEARE Birthday Dinner held at the club when, according to one of those present (J. C. O'Dowd), his speech was 'one of the most brilliant efforts and the best after-dinner speech I ever heard' (Pilgrim 7.322 n.).

He frequently made appointments to meet friends or dine at the club, sending notes such as this: 'Place of meeting. Garrick. Time of dinner (I will order something) a quarter past five' (to Lemon, 22 January 1855). One day in the Strangers' Dining Room Dickens was sitting back to back with Douglas JERROLD, with whom he had not been on speaking terms for some years, when Jerrold suddenly turned round and, holding out his hand, cried: 'For God's sake, let's be friends again!' (20 November 1858).

In 1858 he found himself involved in a bitter dispute between two club members, Edmund YATES and William Makepeace THACKERAY. Dickens, having tried to mediate in vain, sent a letter on 12 July 1858 resigning from the Committee but not from the Club itself. His final resignation came later as a result of the blackballing of his sub-editor of *All the Year Round*, W. H. WILLS, whom he had proposed for membership (25 February 1865).

ASW

**Gaskell, Elizabeth Cleghorn** (1810–65), novelist, married to William Gaskell, minister at the Cross Street UNITARIAN Chapel in Manchester. She wrote *Mary Barton* (1848) partly to distract herself from grief at the death of her infant son. Her other full-length novels were *Cranford* (1853), *Ruth* (1853), *North and South* (1855), *Sylvia's Lovers* (1863), and *Wives and Daughters* (1866), which was left unfinished at her death. She also wrote the first and most celebrated biography of Charlotte BRONTË.

It was Gaskell's first novel, *Mary Barton*, which won the attention of Dickens. On 31 January 1850 he wrote to ask if she would contribute to his new weekly journal, *Household Words*, declaring that 'there is no living English writer whose aid I would desire to enlist, in preference to the authoress of *Mary Barton* (a book that most profoundly affected and impressed me)'. Dickens habitually courted and flattered his contributors to *Household Words*, and was especially successful with Gaskell, whom he called 'Scheherazade' and whose work he admired as a feminine and domesticated version of his own (see ARABIAN NIGHTS; DOMESTIC FICTION). Attractive to his middle-class readership, she became one of Dickens's most regular contributors. Dickens, in turn, became the chief publisher of Gaskell's shorter works: of 40 stories and articles written by Gaskell between 1850 and her death in 1865, two-thirds were published by Dickens. For a while theirs was a cordial and productive literary relationship, although the friendship eventually soured.

Initially Gaskell had been somewhat timid about committing herself to write for *Household Words*, fearful lest her writing should disrupt her domestic duties. Dickens promptly urged her to write only shorter fiction, and she responded with 'Lizzie Leigh', a tale of PROSTITUTION which appeared as the lead story for the first issue of the journal on 30 March 1850. Although Dickens published 'The Heart of John Middleton' in the 28 December 1850 issue, he told her that he found the death of the protagonist's wife 'an unnecessary infliction of pain upon the reader' (17 December 1850), and privately fulminated, 'I wish to Heaven, her people would keep a little firmer on their legs' (to W. H. Wills, 12 December 1850). He asked her to 'put a pleasanter end to the next one' (20 December 1850).

Gradually Dickens and Gaskell began to disagree about her work, gently differing over the first episode of *Cranford* and more fiercely over 'The Old Nurse's Story' (1852). The real dispute, though, was over *North and South* (1855). Gaskell feared that Dickens might borrow the themes of *North and South*—industrial strife, poverty, and a strike—for his own work. Hearing that *Hard Times* would be serialized in *Household Words* from April 1854, Gaskell wrote anxiously to John FORSTER, who was a mutual friend. Forster was unable to reassure her: 'As to the content which Dickens' story is likely to take I have regretted to see that the manufacturing discontents are likely to clash with part of your plan, but I know nothing yet from him as to how far he means to use that sort of material, nor do I think he knows himself . . . I am your witness, if necessary, that your notion in this matter existed before and quite independently of his' (John Forster to Elizabeth Gaskell, 18 March 1854). Dickens promised her that he had no intention, in *Hard Times*, of representing a strike: 'I am not going to strike, so don't be afraid of me' (21 April 1854). He approved of the first tranche of *North and South*, finding it 'full of character and power', but he was insistent that the second section, in which John Hale leaves the Church, should be compressed, since the episode dealt with 'a difficult and dangerous subject' (15 and 17 June 1854). Gaskell ignored his request, refusing to alter anything. Author and editor subsequently wrangled over the length of the novel (it was longer than agreed), over the advertising, over its title, and various other details. Their once affable relationship was by now at best difficult, with Dickens once exclaiming in frustration, 'If I were Mr Gaskell, O heaven how I should beat her!' (to Wills, 11 September 1855). After the break-up of Dickens's marriage in 1858 (see DICKENS, CATHERINE), Gaskell expressed some coolness towards him, reporting to a friend that 'Mr Dickens happens to be extremely unpopular just now,—owing to the well-grounded feeling of dislike to the publicity he has given to his domestic affairs . . .' (Gaskell to Charles Eliot Norton, 9 March 1858).                    SL

> Schor, Hilary, *Scheherezade in the Marketplace* (1994).
> Uglow, Jenny, *Elizabeth Gaskell: A Habit of Stories* (1993).

**Gay, John** (1685–1732), friend of Pope and SWIFT, was best known to Dickens for his ballad-opera *The Beggar's Opera*, produced by John Rich at Lincoln's Inn Fields Theatre in 1728. This was a new theatrical form, using ballads to create musical drama, set in a criminal milieu, and satirizing the SENTIMENTAL tendencies of contemporary drama (see DRAMA AND DRAMATISTS BEFORE DICKENS). His sequel *Polly* (1729) was banned and not performed until 1777. Dickens criticized *The Beggar's Opera* in his Preface to *Oliver Twist*, on the grounds that it glorified rather than deterred criminality. References to it also occur in *Little Dorrit* (2.12) and *Our Mutual Friend* (3.14).                    JD

**George IV.** See ROYALTY.

**'George Silverman's Explanation'** A SHORT story by Dickens, commissioned for £1,000 by the American newspaperman Benjamin Wood but not used by him. It was published in *Atlantic Monthly* (January–February–March 1868) and in *All the Year Round* (1, 15, 29 February 1868). 'The main idea', Dickens told W. H. WILLS, was 'the narrator's position towards other people . . .

Upon myself, it has made the strangest impression of reality and originality!! And I feel as if I had read something (by somebody else) which I should never get out of my head!!' (28 June 1867). Presented as the autobiography of an elderly man who writes in an attempt to exorcize feelings of self-repugnance, the story is focused on Silverman's psychology. Raised by sanctimonious DISSENTERS who took advantage of his docility even as they accused him of worldly self-interest, he sacrificed his love for his pupil Adelina Fareway by contriving her marriage to another pupil. Outraged, her mother forced him to resign his position and pursued him vengefully. At last he comes to rest in a sequestered parsonage.          PVWS

**Germany.** The primary childhood associations of Germany for Dickens are with GOTHIC terror and 'German castles where we sit up alone to wait for the Spectre' ('A Christmas Tree', *CS*). Illustrated images from the books he read remained vivid in his memory, and are referred to throughout his life. Holbein's *Dance of Death* is a continual reference-point; Mephistopheles, 'the snarling critter in the picters with the tight legs' ('A Message from the Sea', *CS*), also of importance in *Dombey and Son* and elsewhere (Dickens's favourite opera was Gounod's *Faust*); while the colourful Baron von Trenck (1726–94), whose autobiography recounts his imprisonment under Frederick II, crops up here and there as the archetypical prisoner 'dressed almost entirely in padlocks . . . in Jemmy's book' ('Mrs Lirriper's Legacy', *CS*).

In adulthood, these images informed Dickens's sympathy and practical help for numerous post-1848 German victims of 'tyrants and oppressors', such as Kinkel and Solger and von Corvin-Wiersbitzki, a *Household Words* contributor who learnt English in solitary confinement by reading Tauchnitz's reprints of that journal ('Whole Hogs', *HW* 23 August 1851; to Wills, 12 August 1856). Dickens was a hero to Germans of liberal inclinations, and Tauchnitz a model publisher, the first foreigner scrupulously to respect Dickens's COPYRIGHT, and to pay him handsomely. Dickens's sons Charles and Francis went to Berlin and Hamburg to learn German for business purposes—to follow this model perhaps; and in 1870 Dickens intended to do likewise. He did not live to savour the irony of the year: Von Moltke reading *Little Dorrit* during the siege of Paris.

MH

Gummer, Ellis, *Dickens's Work in Germany 1837–1937* (1940).

**ghost stories** occupied a significant place in Dickens's life and work. 'Among his good things', according to FORSTER, 'should not be omitted his telling of a ghost story' (11.3). However, despite Dickens's liking for such stories, he remained largely sceptical about their claims. In a 26 February 1848 EXAMINER review of *The Night Side of Nature; or, Ghosts and Ghost Seers* by Catherine Crowe, he demonstrated not only an extensive knowledge of the subject of ghosts but also a strong disposition to disbelieve in them. Eleven years later he was involved in a controversy with William Howitt, an ardent believer in spiritualism. 'The Haunted House', the Christmas number that Dickens produced for *All the Year Round* in 1859, derived from this controversy and debunked the idea of hauntings by anything other than one's own recollections (*CS*).

While suggestions of ghost stories appear in Dickens's novels throughout his career, as in Pip's encounter with Magwitch in the graveyard (*GE* 1), the number of individual ghost stories that Dickens wrote is small. Of these, perhaps only the first of the two such tales in 'To Be Read at Dusk' (1852), the story of the murdered bride in chapter 4 of 'The LAZY TOUR OF TWO IDLE APPRENTICES' (1857), and the especially skilful tale called 'The Signalman' ('Mugby Junction', 1866; *CS*) genuinely arouse a chill along a reader's spine, evoking the sense of ambiguity between the possible and the impossible often seen as a distinguishing characteristic of ghostly literature. Another ghost story, 'To Be Taken with a Grain of Salt' ('Doctor Marigold's Prescriptions', 1865; *CS*) is also eerily powerful. (Ruth Glancy, 1985, has resolved earlier uncertainty regarding the authorship of this story and has attributed it to Dickens.) Likewise noteworthy in the designedly unnerving vein are the series of ghostly vignettes encapsulated in Dickens's 'A Christmas Tree' (1850; *CS*), and his imaginative re-creation of the terrifying tales (although not literally ghost stories, for the most part) apparently told to him in childhood in 'Nurse's Stories' (*UT*). By the

1850s Dickens was intrigued by the psychological ramifications of ghost stories. As he remarked in a 25 November 1851 letter to Elizabeth GASKELL, he considered such stories to be illustrative of 'particular states of mind and processes of the imagination'.

Nevertheless, Dickens's most famous ghost story, *A Christmas Carol* (1843), is less concerned with psychology than with conveying a message about the importance of fellow feeling. Subtitled 'A Ghost Story of Christmas', this Christmas book provides a more sophisticated version of Gabriel Grub's transformation in 'The Story of the Goblins who stole a Sexton', part of the Christmas celebration at Dingley Dell (*PP* 29). Both the *Carol* and the earlier goblin story display Dickens's distinctive ability to mingle humour with horror, a combination also seen in the brief ghost story about Mr Testator included in 'Chambers' (*UT*). In addition, both works reflect and reinforce the link between ghost stories and Christmas, a link that Dickens borrowed from folk tradition (and Washington IRVING) and then riveted even more firmly with his later work. Three of the four Christmas books that Dickens published after *A Christmas Carol* in the 1840s also use supernatural machinery (*The* CHIMES, 1844, being described in its subtitle as 'A Goblin Story'). However, only the last of these books, *The* HAUNTED MAN (1848), whose subtitle calls attention to 'The Ghost's Bargain', resembles the *Carol* in emphasizing this supernatural element. This final Christmas book, which uses the technique of the double, also looks forward to Dickens's interest in the 1850s and 1860s in the psychological dimensions of ghost stories.

With the inauguration of *Household Words* in 1850 Dickens had an opportunity to express his interest in ghostly fiction as editor as well as author. Until 1867 a particular feature of this journal, and its successor *All the Year Round*, was the special Christmas number, including at various times ghost stories by Gaskell, Wilkie COLLINS, Charles COLLINS, and Amelia B. Edwards. In the last year of Dickens's life, ghostly tales by J. S. Le Fanu appeared in a few of the regular issues of *All the Year Round* (notably Le Fanu's powerful tale of hallucination or supernatural possession, 'Green Tea', 23 October–13 November 1869). Dickens thus not only wrote ghost stories and creatively used ghost-story elements in his own work but he also stimulated a popular taste for ghostly literature and encouraged other writers to satisfy that taste.        DAT

Collins, Philip, 'Dickens on Ghosts: An Uncollected Article', *Dickensian*, 59 (1963).

Stone, Harry, *The Night Side of Dickens: Cannibalism, Passion, Necessity* (1994).

Thomas, Deborah A., *Dickens and the Short Story* (1982).

**Gissing, George** (1857–1903), novelist and one of the foremost early critics of Dickens. As a realist Gissing found much to admire in Dickens, but also found a great deal which was deplorable or needed to be explained away. He praised Dickens's 'narrative involvement', his 'interest in the commonplace', his sympathetic understanding of human beings, and his pathos, and found humour the 'soul' of his work, but considered that a predilection for MELODRAMA and the ARABIAN NIGHTS 'sadly led him astray'. Gissing's principal statements come in *Charles Dickens: A Critical Study* (1898), and in his introductions to the aborted Rochester Edition of Dickens's works, which were collected as *Critical Studies of the Works of Charles Dickens* (1924) and again as *The Immortal Dickens* (1925). His introduction to *Copperfield* was unknown until Richard Dunn published it in the *Dickensian*, 77 (1981).        PVWS

Coustillas, Pierre, 'Gissing's Writings on Dickens: A Bio-bibliographical Survey', *Dickensian*, 61 (1965).

**Goldsmith, Oliver** (1730?–74), Anglo-Irish writer of poems, plays, essays, and other works, beloved by Dickens from boyhood on, and known for what Goethe identified as his 'benevolent irony' (John Forster, *The Life and Times of Oliver Goldsmith*, 1848; 6th edn. 1878, p. 2). In 1831 Dickens wrote a parody of Goldsmith's 'Retaliation' called 'The Bill of Fare' that Maria BEADNELL preserved along with Dickens's love letters. Goldsmith's one novel, *The Vicar of Wakefield*, had a deep influence on Dickens's earlier novels, especially *The Pickwick Papers*, and was also the work that indirectly provided him with his pseudonym 'BOZ' (a comical family corruption of the first name of Moses Primrose, the vicar's son). Although little read today, *The Vicar* was perhaps the Victorians' favourite 18th-century novel. FORSTER characterizes it in his biography of Goldsmith—dedicated to Dickens—

as 'our first pure example of the simple DOMESTIC novel' (p. 234).        RN

**Gothic fiction.** The great vogue for Gothic novels ran from the publication of Walpole's *The Castle of Otranto* in 1764 through to the 1820s. Whilst the vogue lasted, tremendous success was enjoyed by authors such as Ann Radcliffe, Matthew LEWIS, and Charles Maturin. On the other hand, as Jane Austen's satire on Gothic conventions, *Northanger Abbey* (1818), demonstrates, the MELODRAMATIC extremes of Gothic were easily ridiculed. Conventional criticism sees mainstream Victorian fiction, Dickens included, as moving sharply away from the artificiality and irrationalism of Gothic, towards a domestic realism and broad social concern (see DOMESTIC FICTION). Gothic itself does not reemerge until the later years of the century, with works of horror such as Stoker's *Dracula* and the science fiction of H. G. Wells.

That said, Gothic elements are certainly present in a wide range of Victorian fiction. Heathcliff, in Emily Brontë's *Wuthering Heights*, brings the chaos of Gothic into the otherwise conventionally conceived domestic realism of Thrushcross Grange. A large market for 'penny dreadfuls', and gory NEWGATE and SENSATION novels also existed throughout the period. In a broader sense, several critics have argued that Gothic was not so much bypassed by conventional Victorian fiction as repressed; that the irrationalism associated with Gothic, its fascination with SEXUALITY, violence, and DEATH, becomes pushed into the underground of a novelistic aesthetic that prided itself on its rationality, respectability, and bourgeois decency—in other words, that Gothic functions in a way as the subconscious for a literary mind whose conscious self or ego did not like to acknowledge those aspects of life. This is certainly a fruitful way for regarding Dickens's own relationship to the Gothic. There are Gothic interludes interpolated into the otherwise sunny, light-hearted picaresque of *Pickwick*, for instance: nine tales written not as Pickwickian comedy, but as tragic, melodramatic Gothic (e.g. 'A Madman's Manuscript'). These episodes stand out from the surrounding text stylistically as well as in terms of content, and give the impression of being rather out of place. Gothic elements in other early Dickens novels are similarly obtrusive: the vampiric Quilp, 'buried with a stake through his heart in the centre of four lonely roads' (*OCS* 73); the Gothic villainy of Monks in *Oliver Twist*; the themes of MADNESS and blood in *Barnaby Rudge*; the GHOST STORY of *A Christmas Carol*. But as his career developed Dickens found thematic and symbolic ways of registering the presence of this Gothic subconscious without resorting to the importation of Gothic archetypes wholesale into the text. The most notable of these is his relatively belated discovery of the mystery novel, where part of the text becomes necessarily hidden, the unknown or buried fact of a crime, murderous or sexual. The contrast can be illustrated with reference to a relatively early and a later novel. In *Martin Chuzzlewit* Jonas's murder is told entirely from the point of view of the criminal; it is the detective Nadgett who is the unseen presence, invisibly shadowing Jonas along the length of his journey. By the time we get to *Bleak House*, however, the pattern has been reversed; Bucket struggles to bring to light the buried text, the one that contains all those elements of sexual transgression, violence, and death that were the province of the Gothic. Something similar happens in *Our Mutual Friend*, while *Edwin Drood* likewise portrays a society domestic and TROLLOPIAN on the surface, but containing the orientalist and Gothic excesses of Jasper buried within it.                    AR

> Milbank, Alison, *Daughters of the House: Modes of the Gothic in Victorian Fiction* (1992).
> Wilt, Judith, *Ghosts of the Gothic* (1980).

**government.** Dickens's most famous public statement of his 'political creed' came in a speech at the Birmingham and Midland Institute on 27 September 1869: 'My faith in the people governing is, on the whole, infinitesimal; my faith in The People governed, is, on the whole, illimitable' (*Speeches*, p. 407). This was not a specific criticism of Gladstone's Liberal government, which had taken office nine months earlier, although many press comments of the time took it as such. Dickens was certainly no Tory. Rather, it reflects the author's wider, and long-standing, scepticism about both POLITICIANS and the political process. Six months before his death, implicitly acknowledging that he had no better system to propose, he quoted with approval H. T.

Buckle's assessment that 'the lawgivers are nearly always the obstructors of society, instead of its helpers' (*History of Civilisation in England*, 1857; *Speeches*, pp. 411–12). He privately noted to FIELDS his 'pride' that his speech had made 'the regular political traders, of all sorts, perfectly mad' (14 January 1870).

Dickens's journalism is littered with disparaging references to politicians, but he had no aspirations to emulate Walter BAGEHOT as a political theorist. In essence, he was a CARLYLEAN romantic, who wanted the people to advance by self-improvement and by help from above. Part of the frustration which so frequently surfaces in his writings derives from the failure of political REFORM in 1832 and even in 1867 to make much immediate impact on the social origins of the governors. As E. J. Evans (1996) observes, 'Aristocratic control over most of the levers of power remained extremely tight, at least until the 1870s'. Dickens was annoyed that such control remained in the hands of those whose primary qualification was birth rather than merit or the choice of the electorate (see ELECTIONS AND FRANCHISE).

Responding to 'the most singular charge' made by Lord Houghton 'that I have been somewhat unconscious of the merits of the House of Lords', he referred to his friendship with, and respect for, two peers. Lord Brougham, the founder of the SOCIETY FOR THE DIFFUSION OF USEFUL KNOWLEDGE, who had died the previous year, had been close to Dickens in 1840–3. They shared an interest in EDUCATIONAL advance. His closest friend in high politics was Lord John RUSSELL, of whom he said, 'there is no man in England whom I love more in his private capacity, or from whom I have received more remarkable proofs of his honour and love'. These were exceptions; Dickens made no attempt to disguise his distaste for the Lords as a political institution (*Speeches*, pp. 388–9). His most sustained bout of anti-aristocratic invective came during his campaign on behalf of the Administrative Reform Association during the CRIMEAN WAR, when he referred to conflict between the people and the governing classes. He chided Angela Burdett COUTTS in a letter of 15 May 1855 for criticizing Austin Layard, the Association's main sponsor: 'I differ from you altogether, as to his setting CLASS against class. He finds them already set in opposition . . . you assume that the popular class take the initiative. Now as I read the story, the aristocratic class did that, years and years ago, and it is they who have put their class in opposition to the country' (15 May 1855).

Dickens satirizes aristocratic control of government in *Bleak House*, when Lord Boodle tells Sir Leicester Dedlock 'that he really does not see to what the present age is tending . . . supposing the present government to be overthrown, the limited choice of the Crown, in the formation of a new ministry, would lie between Lord Coodle and Sir Thomas Doodle, supposing it to be impossible for the Duke of Foodle to act with Goodle' (*BH* 12). In *Our Mutual Friend* Lord Snigsworth does not directly appear, but his political influence is all-pervasive; his cousin Twemlow is used by the socially aspirant 'bran-new' Veneerings in their search for political influence (*OMF* 1.2).

Dickens's most sustained attack on aristocratic government is found in the Circumlocution Office (*LD* 1.10), 'the most important Department under Government', controlled by the Tite Barnacle branch of the Barnacle family and an object lesson 'in the art of perceiving—HOW NOT TO DO IT'. 'Dispersed all over the public offices', the Barnacles are found 'all over the world, in every direction—dispatch-boxing the compass' (*LD* 1.34). It is no accident that *Little Dorrit* was begun while Dickens's campaign on behalf of Administrative Reform was at its height and when the Aberdeen government was collapsing under the weight of criticism of its administration of the Crimean War—only to be replaced by a Liberal government headed by Lord Palmerston containing most of the same aristocratic names: Palmerston, Cranworth, Granville, Argyll, Russell, and the rest.     EJE

Evans, E. J., *Forging of the Modern State: Early Industrial Britain, 1783–1870* (2nd edn. 1996).

## Gray, Thomas (1716–71), English poet.

Dickens was fond of his *Elegy Written in a Country Church-Yard* (1751); 'I am ashamed to say of Gray's Church', he wrote to the Countess Blessington, 26 May 1846, 'that I know the Elegy better than the place.' Chapter 52 of *The Old Curiosity Shop* closely follows the cadences of the *Elegy*, although Dickens's sense of the sometimes ponderous sentiments

of that poem render it an appropriate text to be found in the mouth of Micawber (*DC* 49).     AR

**Great Expectations** Dickens's thirteenth novel, published in 1860–1, and (after *David Copperfield*) his second depicting the adventures of a boy's growth to manhood, narrated by the protagonist. Set partly in rural KENT, where much of Dickens's own childhood had been spent, it is one of his his best-loved stories, combining a thrilling plot with complexly varied tones of retrospection.

### Inception and Composition

Dickens's *Book of Memoranda*, begun in 1855, includes among possible names for characters Magwitch, Provis, Clarriker, Compey, Pumblechook, Horlick, Doolge, Gargery, Wopsle, Hubble, and Skiffins (see COMPOSITION, DICKENS'S METHODS OF). There is also a note about a 'knowing man' who may be an early conception of Bentley Drummle, and another about a 'House-full of Toadies and Humbugs', prefiguring Miss Havisham's visitors in chapter 11 (Kaplan 1981). Margaret Cardwell speculates that the first premonition of *Great Expectations* may occur in a letter to W. H. WILLS on 25 November 1858, in which Dickens contemplated recasting 'an odd idea' intended for that year's Christmas number ('A House to Let') into 'the Pivot around which my next book shall revolve'; the 'odd idea' involving 'some disappointed person . . . prematurely disgusted with the world', who 'retires to an old lonely house . . . resolved to shut out the world and hold no communion with it' (to Wilkie Collins, 6 September 1858; Clarendon Introduction, p. xiv).

*A Tale of Two Cities* and the first series of UNCOMMERCIAL TRAVELLER sketches intervened, however, before Dickens began writing *Great Expectations*. On 8 August 1860 he reported the restlessness usual with his initial planning of a novel. 'I am prowling about, meditating a new book', he wrote to the Earl of Carlisle. A month later he told FORSTER that 'a very fine, new, and GROTESQUE idea has opened upon me . . . I can see the whole of a serial revolving on it, in a most singular and comic manner' (?mid-September 1860). 'This', Forster explained, 'was the germ of Pip and Magwitch, which at first he intended to make the groundwork of a tale in the old twenty-number form' (9.3).

No sooner had Dickens begun writing the novel as a monthly SERIAL, in late September, than circumstances changed that plan irrevocably. The circulation of *All the Year Round* began to decline ominously when readers failed to respond favourably to Charles LEVER's novel *A Day's Ride*, which was then appearing in the journal. 'I called a council of war', Dickens declared. 'It was perfectly clear that the one thing to be done, was for me to strike in.' Accordingly, he changed the format of his new story into a weekly serial 'of the length of *A Tale of Two Cities*' (in fact, slightly longer: 36 instalments as opposed to 31 for the earlier novel), to begin publication on 1 December (to Forster, 4 October 1860). As Robert Patten observes, both the timing and form of *Great Expectations* were based not on artistic but on economic factors (1978, p. 287). Two days later Dickens wrote to Forster again, explaining that 'The property of *All the Year Round* is far too valuable, in every way, to be endangered'.

But despite this last-minute alteration of structure, despite the fact that (as with each of his previous novels published in weekly format) he found the short instalments frustrating, and despite the fact that he was in poor health for much of the time the story was in progress, Dickens appears to have proceeded with his new work with untroubled confidence. In the same letter in which he explained its change in length and shape he announced the book's title. 'The name is GREAT EXPECTATIONS. I think a good name?' A few days later he told Forster that it was to be written 'in the first person throughout' with the 'grotesque tragi-comic conception' as the story's 'pivot'; the opening, he added, seemed to him 'in its general effect exceedingly droll. I have put a child and a good-natured foolish man, in relations that seem to me very funny' (early October 1860).

During that month four weekly numbers were 'ground off the wheel' (to Wilkie Collins, 24 October 1860) and, with the Christmas number of *All the Year Round* to prepare as well, he firmly declined outside claims on his time. 'A certain allotment of my time when I have that story-demand on me', he wrote to A. H. Layard on 4 December, 'has, all through my Author life, been an essential condition of my health and success.' And although a single letter refers to the writing as 'bondage' (to Edmund Yates, 24 February 1861), the months during which *Great Expectations* was in progress are singularly free of the cries of anguish which punctuated his composition of other novels. The fortunes of the periodical immediately revived when the new serial began (*A Day's Ride* limped on alongside until its conclusion on 23 March), and Dickens was able to report *Great Expectations* 'a very great success and universally liked—I suppose because it opens funnily and with an interest too' (to Mary Boyle, 28 December 1860).

He gave six PUBLIC READINGS between 14 March and 18 April 1861, and in May spent a few days in Dover to convalesce from the strain of writing and performing readings. Characteristically, even then he was not idle: on 22 May, the day before he retired to Dover, he took a party of some 'eight or nine friends and three or four members of his family' for an apparently carefree steamer excursion from Blackwall to Southend, during which he kept a sharp eye out for details along the riverside in preparation for writing of Magwitch's attempted escape (Forster 9.3).

Cardwell notes only a single substantial revision, in which Dickens altered the presentation of Herbert Pocket and his family, perhaps in order to draw on his son Charley in the portrait of Pip's companion (Clarendon Introduction, pp. xxvii–xxx; see CHARACTERS—ORIGINALS; CHILDREN OF DICKENS). On 11 June Dickens wrote to MACREADY to say that the novel was finished, and on 15 June he asked the publisher to make arrangements for its volume publication. And then, just over a week later, Dickens made what has come to be the most-discussed revision of his entire career, dropping the originally written ending of the novel and, on BULWER-LYTTON's advice, substituting a revised conclusion. In the original ending Pip and Estella were to meet briefly and finally in London, with Estella, widowed and remarried, mistaking Joe and Biddy's son for Pip's. As revised and published in the serial version and first edition, Pip and Estella meet in the ruined grounds of Satis House, where they pledge friendship and Pip foresees 'the shadow of no parting from her' (in the Library Edition of 1862 this is changed to 'no shadow of another parting from her'; see Rosenberg 1981; EDITIONS OVER WHICH DICKENS HAD CONTROL).

Dickens's explanation of the change, to Wilkie COLLINS in a letter of 23 June 1861, rather lamely concludes, 'Upon the whole I think it is for the better'. Ever since Forster printed the original ending in his *Life of Dickens*, the relative merits of the two versions have aroused extensive controversy. On the whole, however, most readers have agreed with Forster that the first ending is both 'more consistent' and 'more natural' (9.3). George Bernard Shaw was the first to publish the novel with the original ending, in a Limited Club edition (1937).

### Contract, Text, and Publication History

Because Dickens and Wills were co-proprietors of *All the Year Round*, with Dickens having 75 per cent control, he was effectively his own publisher and therefore required no contract for work by him appearing in its pages (see Patten 1978, p. 271). *Great Expectations* shows meticulous care in its construction, and Dickens lamented to Forster that it was 'a pity the third portion cannot be read all at once, because its purpose would be much more apparent' (?mid-April 1861). No number plans have survived (if they ever existed), but Dickens did make detailed working notes on three subjects for the last stage of Pip's expectations: the book's chronology, setting out the ages of the main characters at the time of the story's climactic action; short notes on the events to be narrated from the time Pip arranges with Miss Havisham to give money to Herbert (ch. 44); and notes on Thames tides, in preparation for the attempted escape (ch. 54). These notes are preserved along with the manuscript, and are transcribed by Stone (1987) and by Cardwell in Appendix B of the Clarendon Edition.

Although designed for weekly publication, Dickens divided the heavily corrected manuscript into nine monthly parts, starting page numbering afresh for each part. He inscribed the manuscript to Chauncy Hare Townshend (to whom the novel was dedicated), and Townshend in turn bequeathed it to the Wisbech and Fenland Museum, Cambridgeshire (see DEDICATIONS; COLLECTIONS OF DICKENS MATERIALS). Corrected first proofs for chapters 1–4, 51–7, and most of 58 are held in the FORSTER COLLECTION. Proofs for the entire novel are owned by the Pierpont Morgan Library. The manuscript and proofs are described in detail in the Clarendon Edition.

*Great Expectations* appeared serially in *Harper's Weekly* from 24 November 1860 to 3 August 1861, and in *All the Year Round* from 1 December 1860 to 3 August 1861. Harper's is said to have paid Dickens £1,000 for American rights. In addition, Dickens signed a 'perfectly satisfactory' agreement with Tauchnitz to publish the novel in English for Continental readers (4 January 1861; see COPYRIGHT). Patten remarks on the 'extraordinary testimony' to the novel's popularity shown by the proliferation of editions in Europe and America, listing four American editions in 1861, beyond the serial publication there (1978, pp. 288–93). In quick succession CHAPMAN AND HALL published the first edition in three volumes (1861), which went through five impressions, called 'editions', between 6 July and 30 October 1861; a one-volume edition in 1862; the Cheap Edition of 1863; the Library Edition of 1864; and the Charles Dickens Edition of 1868.

There are two meticulous scholarly editions, the Clarendon Edition, edited by Margaret Cardwell (1993), and the Norton Critical Edition, edited by Edgar Rosenberg (1999).

### Illustrations

Although instalments of the *Harper's Weekly* serialization of *Great Expectations* were accompanied by illustrations by John McLenan, neither the serialization in *All the Year Round* nor the first edition was illustrated, making it the first (and only) novel of Dickens for which he did not collaborate from the outset with an artist. Not until a year later did an edition over which Dickens had control include illustrations, when Marcus STONE, the son of his old friend Frank STONE, was invited to supply eight woodcuts for the Library Edition. Although these were wholly undistinguished, Stone was hired to illustrate Dickens's next novel, *Our Mutual Friend*, and the woodcuts for *Great Expectations* were reprinted in the Charles Dickens Edition.

### Sources and Context

The single most obvious literary predecessor to *Great Expectations* is Dickens's own previous BILDUNGSROMAN, *David Copperfield*. Both novels trace the growth of a boy to manhood, moving between rural countryside and the metropolis, tracing vicissitudes of love, and scrutinizing youthful hopes and dreams in a richly complex first-person retrospective narrative. Dickens himself was well aware of the similarity. 'To be quite sure I had fallen into no unconscious repetitions', he wrote to Forster (early October 1860), 'I read *David Copperfield* again the other day, and was affected by it to a degree you would hardly imagine.' But where *Copperfield* touches more closely on actual events of Dickens's life, *Great Expectations* (depicting the first of his heroes who is not middle-CLASS in origin) is the more intimate spiritual autobiography.

During the years immediately preceding its composition, a number of factors converged which suggest personal restlessness and dissatisfaction, combined with a return to his earliest imaginings (see DICKENS, CHARLES: PRIVATE LIFE). He purchased Gad's Hill Place, the 'dream of my childhood', in 1856 and settled there permanently, out of London in rural Kent, in 1860. His marriage of twenty-one years broke up painfully in 1858, and he became deeply attached to the young actress Ellen TERNAN (see DICKENS, CATHERINE). He severed close friendships, notably with Mark LEMON, and broke with his publishers of the previous decade and a half, BRADBURY AND EVANS. He built a bonfire at the back of his house, in which he burned the accumulated letters of twenty years. 'Would to God every letter I had ever written was on that pile', he declared (to Wills, 4 September 1860; Storey 1939, pp. 106–7). He embarked on the public reading tours which consumed the greater part of his energies during the last twelve years of his life, and in which he drew primarily for subject-matter on the popular writings of his early career. He wound up his highly successful periodical, *Household Words*, and launched *All the Year Round* as its successor. In the 'Uncommercial Traveller' sketches which he began publishing in *All the Year Round* in 1859, he included semi-autobiographical reflections, some of which —notably 'Dullborough Town' and 'Nurse's Stories'—meditated on scenes of his CHILD-HOOD. In these circumstances, it is hardly surprising that the novel Dickens wrote at this time was a return to roots, set in the part of England in which he grew up, and in which he had recently resettled.

Cardwell notes that 'Going into Society', Dickens's Christmas story for 1858, features a character (Chops the dwarf) who is under the delusion that he is entitled to property and who is disappointed when he achieves his social ambitions (Clarendon Introduction, p. xiv). Harry Stone has traced sources for *Great Expectations* in GOTHIC FICTION and FAIRY TALES, in one of Charles MATHEWS the elder's 'At Home' entertainments, in details found in *Household Words* and HOUSEHOLD NARRATIVE articles, and in 'The LAZY TOUR OF TWO IDLE APPRENTICES' (Stone 1979, pp. 279–97). More generally, in the exciting events which propel its action, the novel has clear affinities with the SENSATION NOVEL which preceded it in the pages of *All the Year Round*, Wilkie Collins's *Woman in White*.

In addition to its biographical and literary context, *Great Expectations* can also be seen, in Robin Gilmour's words, as 'a representative fable of the age'. Pointing to Samuel SMILES's influential book of 1859, *Self Help*, Gilmour proposes that Dickens's novel 'spoke to a generation which was itself acutely conscious of having made advances in the civilisation of everyday life' (1981, p. 123; see SELF-HELP). Pip's aspirations to better himself, in other words, are not so much snobbery (as has often been claimed) as a quintessentially Victorian recognition that education, social refinement, and material advancement are desirable goals for which to strive. By showing that Pip's expectations are founded in self-deception, CRIME, and PENAL TRANSPORTA-TION to the colonies, and that they involve rejection of the less sophisticated goodness of a previous generation (as represented by Joe), Dickens presents a searching analysis of the underpinnings of Victorian achievement.

### Plot, Character, and Theme

Philip Pirrip, known as Pip, while visiting the desolate graveyard in which his parents and siblings are buried, is terrified to be confronted by an escaped convict, who demands that he fetch food and a file. On Christmas day a party of soldiers call on the blacksmith, Joe Gargery (married to Pip's shrewish sister) to repair manacles and, accompanied by Joe and Pip, they proceed in search of Magwitch, who allows himself to be captured in order to ensure the arrest also of another escapee, his hated enemy Compeyson.

Pip is invited by the reclusive Miss Havisham to visit her and 'play'. Jilted in love years previously, she has had her clocks stopped and shut herself up, attired in her wedding dress, in rooms in Satis House. She is raising her beautiful young ward Estella to break men's hearts. Estella scorns Pip, who falls in love with her. He meets toadies who have come fortune-hunting, and is invited to participate in fisticuffs with a 'pale young gentleman'.

Miss Havisham's lawyer, Jaggers, comes to the village and announces that Pip has 'great expectations' of wealth and social advancement from an unknown benefactor, whom Pip naturally supposes to be Miss Havisham. Joe releases Pip from his apprenticeship, and Pip goes to London, where he is befriended by Jaggers's clerk, Wemmick, and finds that Herbert Pocket, his new companion, is the pale young gentleman. Mrs Joe is bludgeoned to death by an unknown assailant using the convict's broken manacle.

Pip lives beyond his allowance, is ashamed of Joe, and is frustrated in love when Estella favours the boorish Bentley Drummle. Pip is horrified when Magwitch reappears one stormy night and reveals himself to be Pip's benefactor. As a returned transportation convict Magwitch is liable to execution if recaptured, and Pip, loathing him, plans to get him abroad. Pip returns to Satis House, where he asks Miss Havisham for money to set Herbert up in business. Her dress catches fire and Pip is burned putting out the flames. Imploring Pip's forgiveness, Miss Havisham dies. Pip deduces that Estella is the daughter of Magwitch and the murderess Molly, whom Jaggers, having defended from the charge, maintains as his housekeeper.

Shortly before the escape attempt, Pip receives a mysterious demand that he return to the marshes. There Joe's shadowy journeyman, Orlick, confesses to killing Mrs Joe and threatens to kill Pip, who is rescued by Herbert at the last moment. Returning to London, Pip is given a message, 'Don't go home', and realizes that he is being watched. The river escape is foiled when Compeyson appears in a boat with officers; he and Magwitch fight and Compeyson drowns. Magwitch is apprehended and condemned to be hanged but dies first, with Pip (whose feelings towards him have undergone a complete change) at his side.

Pip returns to the forge, intending to propose to his childhood confidante Biddy, only to find that she has married Joe. He joins Herbert in his shipping firm in Egypt and, years later, returns to England and meets Estella, now the widow of Drummle.

Besides the high excitement of the mystery plot, *Great Expectations* contains some of Dickens's most delightful comedy, particularly in the pomposity of Pip's Uncle Pumblechook, the theatrical aspirations of Mr Wopsle, the antics of Trabb's boy, and the courtship of Wemmick and Miss Skiffins, chaperoned by Wemmick's Aged Parent in a mock-Gothic castle.

**Reception**

Patten estimates that *All the Year Round* sold perhaps 100,000 copies weekly while *Great Expectations* was being serialized, and notes that Mudie, the 'Leviathan' of lending librarians, who purchased around 1,400 copies of *Great Expectations*, claimed 30 readers for each copy of books he loaned out (1978, p. 292; see LIBRARIES; READERSHIP).

When he began writing Dickens told Forster, 'You will not have to complain of want of humour as in *The Tale of Two Cities*' (early October 1860). Forster concurred entirely: 'Dickens's humour, not less than his creative power', he wrote, 'was at its best in this book' (9.3). This is a verdict which most readers have endorsed; indeed, part of the book's appeal is that it has virtues both of his early and of his later achievements. Although reviews were not all favourable (Margaret Oliphant was notably dismissive in her *Blackwood's* review, May 1862), before long *Great Expectations* came to be widely regarded as one of Dickens's crowning achievements.

It attracted few DRAMATIZATIONS, partly because Dickens attempted to prevent adaptation by publishing a stage version to establish dramatic copyright, but more importantly because, as Philip Bolton observes, by this point in his career Dickens's art is less theatrical (1987, p. 416). One of the most successful cinematic versions of Dickens to date, however, is David Lean's 1946 FILM based on the novel.

Many critics have written well about *Great Expectations*, from a variety of perspectives. G. K. CHESTERTON praised its optimism, whereas Edmund WILSON admired its pessimism. Humphry House (1941) discussed its social context; J. H. Buckley (1974) considered it as *Bildungsroman*; J. Hillis Miller (1958) wrote of Pip as 'the archetypal Dickens hero'; Q. D. LEAVIS (1970) offered a trenchant chapter entitled 'How We Must Read *Great Expectations*'; and more recently, Peter Brooks (1984) has offered a deconstructionist reading. Undoubtedly the most influential single discussion of the novel is Julian Moynahan's 1960 essay in which he proposed that Orlick exists as 'double, *alter ego* and dark mirror image' of Pip, an analysis which looks beyond the book's narrative voice for an explanation of Pip's expressions of guilt. Of several book-length studies of *Great Expectations*, Anny Sadrin's (1988) is the most distinguished.

PVWS

Brooks, Peter, *Reading for the Plot* (1984).

Buckley, Jerome Hamilton, *Season of Youth: the Bildungsroman from Dickens to Golding* (1974).

Gilmour, Robin, *The Idea of the Gentleman in the Victorian Novel* (1981).

Moynahan, Julian, 'The Hero's Guilt: The Case of *Great Expectations*', *Essays in Criticism* 10 (1960).

Rosenberg, Edgar, 'A Preface to *Great Expectations*: The Pale Usher Dusts His Lexicon', *Dickens Studies Annual*, 2 (1972).

—— 'Last Words on *Great Expectations*: A Textual Brief on the Six Endings', *Dickens Studies Annual*, 9 (1981).

Sadrin, Anny, *Great Expectations* (1988).

**Grimaldi, Joseph.** See MEMOIRS OF GRIMALDI.

**grotesque.** Dickens's contemporaries used the term 'grotesque' to describe central features of his writing, and he seems to have embraced it with enthusiasm. Thomas HOOD, reviewing *The Old Curiosity Shop* in the *Athenaeum* of November 1840, praises Dickens's 'striking and picturesque combination of images', and twice uses the word 'grotesque' to characterize this. Early in 1841 Dickens thanked him for what he said, and later, in his Preface to the 1848 edition, wrote: 'I had it always in my fancy to surround the lonely figure of the child with grotesque and wild, but not impossible, companions.' He seems, likewise, to acknowledge the praise of George Henry LEWES (and others) of his 'exquisite sensibility to the grotesque' when he describes

the germ of *Great Expectations* (the idea of Magwitch's sponsorship of Pip) as 'a fine, new and grotesque idea', and later as 'the grotesque tragicomic conception that first encouraged me'.

But Dickens's love of the grotesque was by no means acceptable to all Victorians. Thomas Mann saw how it belongs in a popular tradition, and carries elements of a subversion of Victorian bourgeois values, when he wrote in 1926, with reference to Conrad and Dickens: 'it will be conceded that the grotesque is an essentially anti-bourgeois style; and however bourgeois in other respects Anglo-Saxon culture may appear to be, it should be remembered that the comic grotesque has been its artistic strong point since way back.' Amongst those who reacted quite severely against it, despite their great admiration for Dickens, were RUSKIN—'it is Dickens's delight in grotesque and rich exaggeration which has made him, I think, nearly useless in the present day' (letter to Norton, 8 July 1870)—and FORSTER himself, commenting on how Dickens's humour tended to 'magnify out of proper bounds its sense of what is droll . . . to put the merely grotesque in its place' (Forster 9.1).

Following Bakhtin and Kayser, we may define grotesque art as a mixed hybrid form, in which heterogeneous elements (human and animal forms, the natural and the supernatural, comedy and tragedy, the sublime and the monstrous) are held together in an unstable, conflicting, paradoxical relationship. In this light, we may see the Dickensian grotesque as fed by three principal sources: popular elements in the 18th-century and romantic NOVEL, including the GOTHIC novel; popular DRAMA, the *commedia dell'arte* and PANTOMIME in particular; and the tradition of popular visual satire, which also influences the ILLUSTRATIONS to his novels, most notably those of CRUIKSHANK and 'Phiz' (see BROWNE, HABLOT K.).

Dickens himself often uses the word 'grotesque' in his work, most frequently in PICTURES FROM ITALY. But it is the thing itself everyone recognizes (CHESTERTON not least amongst the major Dickens critics)—initially, perhaps, in the inimitable, unsettling, humorous linkages of incongruous things: 'I think it is my infirmity to fancy or perceive relations in things which are not apparent generally', he wrote to BULWER-LYTTON (Forster 9.1). Verbal grotesquerie might be said to begin with the Wellerisms of *Pickwick Papers* ('Business first, pleasure afterwards, as King Richard the Third said ven he stabbed the t'other king in the tower, afore he smothered the babbies'), and to climax in the astonishing Venus/Wegg duo in *Our Mutual Friend*, whose scenes have been described by Hillis Miller in a recent essay in *Dickens Refigured* as 'at the highest level of Dickens's admirable pantomimic notations and wild verbal imagination'. Grotesque characters are legion; they might be subdivided, following Ruskin, into 'terrible grotesques' like Quilp, Heep, or Fagin ('fit for nothing but keeping as a curiosity of ugliness in a glass bottle, and I suppose they don't blow glass bottles large enough', says Sikes), and 'playful grotesques' like Mr Dick, 'a florid pleasant-looking gentleman, with a gray head, who shut up one eye in a grotesque manner, nodded his head at me several times, shook it at me as often, laughed and went away'.

But the Dickensian grotesque, which is ubiquitous, and not, as some have suggested, simply a feature of the early comic novels that tends to die out in the later serious ones, is more than a set of local effects. It is a vision of a world in which Freud's 'return of the repressed' finds powerful expression: in Dickens, the life of fancy and the imagination, apparently buried beneath modern capitalism and industrialization, ceaselessly resurfaces in the strange and unforgettable forms of the grotesque.                          MH

Bakhtin, M. M., *Rabelais and his World* (1968).
Hollington, Michael, *Dickens and the Grotesque* (1984).
Kayser, Wolfgang, *The Grotesque in Art and Literature* (1963).

Schad, John (ed.), *Dickens Refigured: Bodies, Desires and Other Histories* (1996).

**Guild of Literature and Art.** In 1850, when Dickens's AMATEUR THEATRICALS troupe was presenting *Every Man In His Humour* at Knebworth, BULWER-LYTTON suggested setting up a fund: 'To encourage life assurance, and other provident habits among authors and artists, to render such assistance to both as shall never compromise their independence, and to form a new institution where honourable rest from arduous labour shall still be associated with the discharge of congenial duties.'

To begin raising funds for an endowment, and build retirement homes at Stevenage, Bulwer-Lytton wrote a new comedy, *Not So Bad As We Seem*, and the Duke of Devonshire allowed the use of his Piccadilly home for the opening night. On 16 May 1851 the play was presented before the Queen and Prince Consort, with a second performance a few nights later. Tickets were £5 each, and the Queen donated £150. The play then went on tour. By June 1851 the fund had reached £2,500.

Dickens devoted a great deal of time and energy to the Guild, attending 31 of its management meetings, but in 1857 he was dismayed to find that several clauses in its bill of incorporation seriously restricted its activities; it could not, for example, award pensions until seven years had elapsed. Dickens at once reorganized the administration; he ordered the Guild's chambers to be given up, its clerk discharged, and the *Household Words* office and staff placed at its disposal. Although the Stevenage houses were completed in 1865, the legal restrictions and lack of enthusiasm in the intended beneficiaries proved fatal to the Guild's success. It was disbanded in 1897.

ASW

# H

**Hall, William** (1801–47). See CHAPMAN AND
HALL.

***Hard Times*** Dickens's tenth and shortest
novel, his only one set entirely outside London, in a provincial INDUSTRIAL town. Juxtaposing schoolroom with CIRCUS in a satirical
attack on UTILITARIAN attitudes, *Hard Times*
was not popular with 19th-century readers,
but has become one of his most-read titles
over the past fifty years.

### Inception and Composition
Ironically, the initial factor which led Dickens
to write his foremost celebration of fancy, in
opposition to calculating rationality, was a
hard-headed business decision. He had
finished writing *Bleak House* in August 1853
and 'intended to do nothing in that way for a
year' (to Mrs Richard Watson, 1 November
1854), only to be faced with a precipitous fall
in profits from his journal *Household Words*
during the six months up to 30 September
1853—from £900 to £1,300 per half-year they
dropped to £527 15s 10d (Patten 1978, p. 244).
To meet this crisis, his publishers, BRADBURY
AND EVANS, proposed that he write a new
novel, to run serially in its pages. 'It was considered, when I came home [from FRANCE,
SWITZERLAND, and ITALY, where he had
toured during October with Wilkie COLLINS
and Augustus Egg, after living with his family
in Boulogne since June] such a great thing
that I should write a story for Household
Words, that I am at present up to my eyes in
one', he wrote (to Emile de la Rue, 9 March
1854). The strategy was successful; whereas
the March 1854 profits sank even lower, to
£393 7s 2d, the September 1854 net receipts
rose by 237 per cent (Patten 1978, p. 246).

On 20 January Dickens sent a list of fourteen possible titles, including *Hard Times*, for
the story to FORSTER, and three days later he
was under way. On 25 January he asked his
assistant editor at *Household Words*, W. H.
WILLS, to provide him with the Education
Board's questions used in examining teachers, and three days later he travelled with Wills
to the northern industrial town of Preston, to

see for himself the effects of the strike and
lock-out which had been dragging on there
for 23 weeks. 'I am afraid I shall not be able to
get much here', he wrote to Forster (29 January 1854), and a few weeks later he vigorously
refuted a claim in the *Illustrated London News*
for 4 March 1854 that his story 'originated' in
the industrial troubles in Preston. 'The mischief of such a statement is twofold', he wrote;
'First, it encourages the public to believe in
the impossibility that books are produced in
that very sudden and cavalier manner ... and
Secondly it has this pernicious bearing: it localizes (so far as your readers are concerned)
a story which has a direct purpose in reference to the working people all over England'
(to Peter Cunningham, 11 March 1854). On
25 February Dickens wrote to Mark LEMON,
requesting that he 'note down and send me
any slang terms among tumblers and Circus-
people', and on 24 March he sent instructions
to Wills, asking him to commission Henry
MORLEY to write an article on factory accidents 'for our immediate publication' in
*Household Words*. 'Ground in the Mill', on
preventable factory accidents, duly appeared
on 22 April. He finished composing the novel
on 15 July.

*Hard Times* was the first novel Dickens had
written for weekly SERIALIZATION since *The
Old Curiosity Shop* and *Barnaby Rudge* appeared in MASTER HUMPHREY'S CLOCK in
1840–1; over the next twelve years *Chuzzlewit,
Dombey, Copperfield*, and *Bleak House* had all
followed a monthly format. The more rapid
deadlines did not trouble him but, he reported to Forster, 'The difficulty of space is
CRUSHING. Nobody can have an idea of it who
has not had an experience of patient fiction-
writing with some elbow-room always, and
open places in perspective. In this form, with
any kind of regard to the current number,
there is absolutely no such thing' (? February
1854). A few weeks later he wrote to Wills, 'I
am in a dreary state, planning and planning
the story of Hard Times (out of materials for
I don't know how long a story), and consequently writing little' (18 April 1854). He felt

'wooden-headed', and although he went with his family to Boulogne, where he was to be seen 'bobbing up, corkwise, from a sea of Hard Times', he remained 'addled' and 'stunned with work'; after he had finished the story he described his condition as 'dreadfully lazy' and 'used up' (20 April; 9, 12, 14, 31 July; 1 November 1854).

An additional worry while he was writing was the need to reassure Elizabeth GASKELL that Hard Times would not steal the thunder of the INDUSTRIAL NOVEL which she was writing at the same time. 'I have no intention of striking,' he told her, 'So don't be afraid of me' (21 April 1854). North and South began its serial run in Household Words on 2 September, three weeks after the final chapter of Dickens's novel was published. (See also COMPOSITION, DICKENS'S METHODS.)

### Contract, Text, and Publishing History

Dickens signed a contract for Hard Times with his partners on Household Words, Bradbury, Evans, Forster, and Wills, on 28 December 1853, in which he agreed to write a novel 'equal in length to five single monthly numbers of Bleak House', to be published in weekly portions within that periodical. In return, he was to be paid £1,000, not to be charged against the profits of Household Words, and copyright for separate publication was assigned 'solely and absolutely' to him (Pilgrim 7.911).

Besides the titles Dickens suggested to Forster, Dickens compiled a list more than three times longer in his working notes, including 'Prove It', 'A Mere Question of Figures', 'Hard Heads and Soft Hearts', 'Black and White', and 'Stubborn Things'. His opening note to himself calculated that he needed to fill about seven and a half pages of manuscript to achieve the quantity he wished to publish weekly. Gradgrind and Bounderby, Louisa, Sissy and Bitzer, Coketown, the school, and the circus are all there in the plans for the opening chapters, as is 'the man who by being utterly sensual and careless, comes to very much the same thing in the end as the Gradgrind school'. As early as chapter 15 he had thought of republishing the story in three books, 'Sowing', 'Reaping', and 'Garnering'. He considered and rejected the idea of a lover for Sissy. He made notes of his intention that Louisa's danger be 'slowly drawn about her',

and to show 'almost imperceptibly' 'how alike in their creeds' Gradgrind and Harthouse are (Stone, 1987, pp. 245–61).

Hard Times first appeared in twenty weekly instalments of Household Words, from 1 April to 12 August 1854 (vol. 9, no. 210, to vol. 9, no. 229), without chapter titles. The first volume publication, by Bradbury and Evans, was on 7 August 1854, with an expanded title, Hard Times. For These Times, division into three books, chapter titles, and a dedication to Thomas CARLYLE, to whom Dickens wrote on 13 July 1854, asking permission to inscribe the book to him and expressing hope that it 'will shake some people in a terrible mistake of these days'. There was no preface in this or in subsequent editions. The manuscript, number plans, and corrected proofs are in the FORSTER COLLECTION.

A significant omission, still present at proof stage but for unknown reasons never printed as part of the novel itself, is a passage which Dickens wrote for 1.13, in which Stephen explains that Rachael's little sister, now dead, had her arm torn off in a factory accident. The omitted passage supplies the motivation, otherwise unexplained, for Stephen's refusal (2.4) to join the strike.

Tauchnitz published editions of Hard Times authorized by Dickens in 1854, first as part of Household Words in volumes 303 and 305 of the Collection of British Authors, and later as an independent volume (no. 307), COPYRIGHT in Europe outside Britain. Two unauthorized editions were published in New York in 1854, but it was not until the Diamond Edition of 1867, with illustrations by S. EYTINGE Jr., that an authorized edition of the novel appeared in the United States, bound with Barnaby Rudge. CHAPMAN AND HALL published it, bound in a single volume of the Library Edition along with the concluding chapters of Barnaby Rudge, in 1858, reissued in 1862 with four illustrations by Frederick Walker (1840–75). Chapman and Hall published Hard Times twice more during Dickens's lifetime, as part of the Cheap Edition in 1865, with a frontispiece by Arthur Boyd Houghton (1836–75), and revised and corrected by Dickens, with the addition of running headlines, in the Charles Dickens Edition of 1868, bound with PICTURES FROM ITALY. The most notable edition after Dickens's death, based on a comparative study of manuscript, proofs, serial version, and 1854 and 1868 editions, is the Norton Critical Edition, edited by George Ford and Sylvère Monod, which lists textual variants (1966; 2nd edn. 1990). (See also EDITIONS.)

**Illustrations**

*Hard Times* and *Great Expectations* were the only novels by Dickens which appeared without illustrations in their first volume publication. As noted above, Frederick Walker supplied four illustrations for the 1862 reissue of the Library Edition: 'Stephen and Rachael in the Sick-room', 'Mr Harthouse Dining at the Bounderbys', 'Mr Harthouse and Tom Gradgrind in the Garden', and 'Stephen Blackpool Recovered from the Old Hell Shaft'. A. B. Houghton drew a frontispiece for the 1865 Cheap Edition, depicting Tom Gradgrind in his circus disguise and Mr Gradgrind with his head in his hands, with Sissy and Louisa standing by. F. O. C. Darley provided two illustrations for an 1863 American edition; S. Eytinge, Jr., drew six for the Diamond Edition of 1867; W. H. C. Groome drew seven for the Collins Illustrated Edition of 1907; and 'Kyd' (Joseph Clarke Clayton) made eighteen pen-and-ink and watercolour illustrations of characters from *Hard Times* (n.d.; in the Gimbel Collection at Yale University). (See also IL-LUSTRATORS AND BOOK ILLUSTRATION.)

**Sources and Context**

*Hard Times* deals with issues which were matters of concern for Dickens throughout his career: industrial relations, EDUCATION, CLASS, the right of common people to AMUSEMENT, and attitudes antithetical to that right. It also draws on contemporary concern with reforming divorce laws, coloured by his personal discontent at the time with his marriage, which broke down irretrievably four years later (see DICKENS: PRIVATE LIFE).

As early as 1838 he declared his outrage over advocates of the factory system—'the enemy's camp'—and the oppressive conditions under which cotton-mill workers suffered. 'I mean to strike the heaviest blow in my power for these unfortunate creatures', he declared (to E. M. Fitzgerald, 29 December 1838). Although *Nickleby*, the novel he was writing at that time, located the Cheerybles' business in Lancashire, and although LEECH's illustration of Ignorance and Want in *A Christmas Carol* included factories in the background, it was not until *Hard Times* that the blow was struck. By then a number of industrial novels had addressed what Carlyle defined as the 'Condition of England', most notably DISRAELI's *Sybil* (1845), Gaskell's *Mary Barton* (1848), and Kingsley's *Alton Locke* (1850).

But like his contemporaries, Dickens was no advocate of working-class revolution (see CHARTISM). In the article 'On Strike', which he wrote for *Household Words* (11 February 1854), he expressed sympathy for the workers' plight but also stated the 'profound conviction' that their strike was a 'mistake'. And although the article indicates that he was impressed by their calm refusal to be bullied by the outside agitator ('Gruffshaw'), in the novel Stephen Blackpool is ostracized from his fellows by the TRADE UNION demagogue Slackbridge, before being fired by the bullying factory owner, Bounderby. As ever, Dickens maintains the Carlylean view that an enlightened moral outlook is necessary to heal social divisions.

Dickens blames these divisions on Mr Gradgrind's philosophy of 'Fact', which conflates two prominent social theories of the age, utilitarianism and political economy. BENTHAM's utilitarian doctrines proposed bringing about the greatest happiness for the greatest number through government intervention, whereas Adam Smith's followers held that national prosperity, being governed by immutable economic laws, required a *laissez-faire* approach from the state. Dickens brushed aside the differences, finding in both views a fallacious conception of humanity: 'into the relations between employers and employed, as into all the relations of this life, there must enter something of feeling and sentiment; something of mutual explanation, forbearance, and consideration; something which is not to be found in Mr McCulloch's dictionary, and is not exactly stateable in figures; otherwise those relations are wrong and rotten at the core and will never bear sound fruit' ('On Strike').

Because he is concerned with the underlying attitudes which cause industrial strife, it is appropriate that the book includes a schoolroom where children are being indoctrinated. Eight years previously James Kay-Shuttleworth (1804–71) had established the most ambitious teacher-training scheme England had ever seen, but its approach was condemned at the time as overly mechanical and arid; Bitzer is Dickens's comment on what a prize pupil from such a regime would be likely to be.

In opposition to what he considered wrong-headed attitudes and stultifying systems, Dickens offered Sleary's circus as a contrary image. *Hard Times* was Dickens's first novel since *The Old Curiosity Shop* to include entertainers as key figures in the cast of characters, and here they exist not merely as colourful personages but as representatives of Dickens's belief that, in Sleary's words, 'People mutht be amuthed'. Many of the circus acts mentioned in *Hard Times* correspond to performances Dickens might have seen at Astley's in the previous year or two, but most had been staples of the English circus for decades. By the 1850s the circus had become the prime example of the commercialization of leisure, but although Dickens made clear that his performers worked hard at their profession, he depicted Sleary's Horse-Riding primarily as a repository for the values of fancy and fellow-feeling, an opportunity for momentary escape from everyday drudgery into a carefree world of colourful spectacle.

Divorce was expensive, legally difficult, and socially unacceptable in the 19th century. A Divorce and Matrimonial Causes Bill failed in Parliament in June 1854. In this context, and at a time when he was becoming increasingly discontented with his own marriage, Dickens published three essays (two by Eliza Lynn, the other by W. H. Wills) on the issue of divorce in *Household Words*, the first of which appeared in the same issue as chapters 9 and 10, in which Stephen's wife first makes her appearance ('One of Our Legal Fictions', 29 April 1854).

### Plot, Character, and Theme

*Hard Times* opens in a schoolroom, in which the imaginative attitudes of Sissy, the circus girl, are rejected in favour of the rote statistical knowledge of Bitzer. Mr Gradgrind, patron of this model school, which exists to promulgate his philosophy of Fact, is shocked to discover his own children peeping under a circus tent. Sullen and repressed, his daughter Louisa agrees to marry the braggart industrialist Bounderby, in hope of being of use to her brother Tom. Tom repays the favour by robbing Bounderby's bank and fleeing to America with the help of Sleary and the circus people.

Stephen Blackpool, one of the 'hands' in Bounderby's factory, suffers a series of calamities. Humiliated by the reappearance of his drunken wife, Stephen is unable to divorce her and marry Rachael, the woman he loves. Refusing to join his fellow workers in strike action, he is spurned by them, fired by Bounderby, and then accused of the robbery. Returning to clear his name, he falls into an abandoned mine shaft and dies just as rescuers find him.

Louisa, frustrated by a loveless marriage, is easy prey for the cynical idler James Harthouse and agrees to elope with him. She flees instead to her father, who sees in her collapse and his son's ruin the emptiness of his pet theories. Sissy, who has quietly provided moral support to Louisa and Rachael, convinces Harthouse to depart, and Bounderby's claim to be a self-made man is exposed as a sham.

The novel is constructed on a series of thematic contrasts, between fact and fancy, factory and circus, schoolroom and experience. It portrays the dreariness of life for industrial workers, the hopelessness of decent people trapped in a failed marriage, and the fallacy of mechanical theories of human nature.

### Reception

Although RUSKIN and Shaw admired *Hard Times*, Macaulay condemned it as 'sullen socialism', and it was not until F. R. LEAVIS celebrated it as a 'moral fable' in *The Great Tradition* (1948) that the novel gained widespread admiration. Despite the fact that Leavis excluded Dickens from the canon and relegated *Hard Times* to an appendix, his criticism transformed the book's reputation. Since then it has been one of Dickens's bestselling titles, widely taught (partly, no doubt, because it is the shortest of all Dickens's completed novels), and extensively discussed from a wide variety of perspectives. A notable exception to the chorus of praise is John Holloway, whose 1962 essay '*Hard Times*: A History and a Criticism' (Gross and Pearson 1962), describes the book as middle-class philistinism, based on the premiss that 'All work and no play makes Jack a dull boy'.

Reviewers were virtually unanimous in condemning *Hard Times* as dull and disappointing. The novel had only a single major DRAMATIZATION, by Frederick Fox Cooper, as *Hard Times: A Domestic Drama*, first produced at the Strand Theatre 14 August 1854, in which Stephen is allowed to marry Rachael and Louisa is reconciled with Bounderby.                                                      PVWS

> Baird, John D., ' "Divorce and Matrimonial Causes": An Aspect of *Hard Times*', *Victorian Studies*, 20 (1977).
>
> Carnall, Geoffrey, 'Dickens, Mrs Gaskell, and the Preston Strike', *Victorian Studies*, 8 (1964).
>
> Gilmour, Robin, 'The Gradgrind School: Political Economy in the Classroom', *Victorian Studies*, 11 (1967).
>
> Leavis (1970).

**Harley, John Pritt** (1786–1858), popular comic ACTOR and long-standing friend of Dickens. Harley took over many of Charles MATHEWS the elder's roles at Drury Lane Theatre, after Mathews had been incapacitated by lameness. Possessing a similarly volatile and eccentric manner of performing, Harley was a bustling, vigorous actor, whose special style was often described by the word 'buoyancy'. Drury Lane roles included Flexible (Mathews's role in *Love, Law and Physic*) and Captain Bobadil in JONSON's *Every Man In His Humour*. From September 1836 he became stage manager and leading low comedian at the St James's Theatre under BRAHAM. Harley played Martin Tapkins in The VILLAGE COQUETTES (1836), the published version of which was dedicated to him by Dickens. Dickens also wrote the farce The STRANGE GENTLEMAN, based on 'The Great Winglebury Duel' (*SB*), at Harley's request. Although Harley's performance ensured it a long run, *IS SHE HIS WIFE?* (1837), also written for Harley by Dickens, proved less successful.

Westland MARSTON claimed that Harley 'had too little depth, too little discrimination of character, to merit the name of a fine comedian, but he was, beyond doubt, a very amusing one. In his airy, chattering, mercurial way, he overflowed with fun and self-enjoyment' (*Our Recent Actors*, 1888, 1.293–4). Harley played a number of Shakespearean roles for Charles KEAN at the Princess's Theatre in the 1850s, including Bottom, Autolycus, Touchstone, Feste, and Caliban. Dickens later wrote: 'Harley was an excellent artist in his way; but was always full of his own humour and showed it, as much as to say, "See

how funny I am!" ' In some characters, added Dickens, 'Harley's face and style, expressing mirthfulness in activity, gave him an advantage', although he felt Harley lacked the range and pathos of Robert KEELEY (Walter Goodman, *The Keeleys on the Stage and at Home*, 1889, p. 158). Harley, who had a wide and respectable circle of acquaintances, was considered an honour to the profession.      JD

***Haunted Man, The*** Dickens's fifth and last CHRISTMAS BOOK, written after a year's delay in 1848. It had a mixed reception, but has come to be seen as a precursor to *David Copperfield* and as a document of biographical interest, especially with reference to Dickens's relationship with his sister Fanny, who died while it was being written (see BROTHERS AND SISTERS OF DICKENS).

Dickens first mentioned 'a very ghostly and wild idea' for the next Christmas book before he had written The BATTLE OF LIFE (to Forster, 30 August 1846). A year later, with *Dombey* taking up 'so much time', he consulted with FORSTER. 'I am very loath to lose the money', he wrote, after completing a few pages; 'And still more so to leave any gap at CHRISTMAS firesides that I ought to fill' (19 September 1847). Forster 'had no doubt of the wisdom of delay', and a year's postponement was announced on 1 December in No. 15 of *Dombey*.

He resumed writing in autumn 1848, 'sitting frowning horribly at a quire of paper' (to the Hon. Mrs Watson, 5 October 1848). 'In the act of grinding at my Christmas book' a month later, he told Miss COUTTS, 'I have hit upon a little notion . . . which I hope is a pretty one, with a good Christmas tendency' (7 November 1848). He finished it on 30 November in Brighton, and reported himself 'crying my eyes out over it—not painfully but pleasantly, as I hope the readers will' (to Bradbury, 1 December 1848). He read it to friends on 11 December, and *The Haunted Man and the Ghost's Bargain. A Fancy for Christmas-Time* was published by BRADBURY AND EVANS on 19 December, with ILLUSTRATIONS by John TENNIEL, Frank STONE, Clarkson STANFIELD, and John LEECH. That day he wrote to Thomas Beard, announcing that 18,000 copies were sold, but in fact sales were down 6,000 on *The Battle of Life*, and there were still copies unsold at the time of Dickens's death more than two decades later (Patten 1978, pp. 202–3).

Dickens inscribed the manuscript to Miss Coutts and gave it to her; it is now in the Pforzheimer Library (see COLLECTIONS OF DICKENS MATERIALS).

Dickens assisted Mark LEMON with a DRAMATIZATION at the Adelphi. Opening night, scheduled for 18 December, was postponed at Dickens's instance until the 20th; the play ran for 42 performances. It was revived in 1863 by Benjamin WEBSTER at the Adelphi, with Professor Pepper's ghost (an optical illusion) as the chief attraction (see Malcolm Morley, 'Pepper and *The Haunted Man*', *Dickensian*, 48, 1952).

The story concerns a scholar, Redlaw, embittered by past griefs, whose ghostly double offers him forgetfulness. Without his memories he is unable to sympathize with others, and he has a baleful influence on everyone he meets. Learning the necessity of cherishing sorrows as well as joys, Redlaw is restored to human feeling. Dickens insisted that 'a little dreaminess and vagueness' were 'essential' for the story to have effect (2 January 1849).

                                  PVWS

**Hawthorne, Nathaniel** (1804–64). American novelist. Dickens returned from his first AMERICAN tour enthusiastic about Hawthorne's early tales, and Hawthorne glowingly reviewed *Travelling Letters, Written on the Road* (an abridged version of PICTURES FROM ITALY; Salem *Advertiser*, 29 April 1846). But Dickens found Hawthorne's masterpiece *The Scarlet Letter* (1850) unconvincing. The 'psychological part of the story', he wrote Forster (summer 1851), 'is very much overdone'. Ironically, reviewers in America often compared Hawthorne's descriptions and character delineation favourably with Dickens's. Hawthorne delighted his wife Sophia by reading aloud *David Copperfield* in 1850–1. Yet he knew his own genius to be different from that of his English counterpart. Asked to write a SERIAL romance for the *Boston Museum*, he declined, explaining that serial publication suited Dickens and THACKERAY, whose works 'are distinguished by a great variety of scenes and multiplicity of character', whereas his own stories have 'one idea running through them like an iron rod'. US consul at Liverpool (1853–7), Hawthorne occasionally mentions Dickens in *English Notebooks*. 'I must see him before I finally leave England', he deter-

mined. Owing to his own reticence, he never did.                    WTM

**Hazlitt, William** (1778–1830), London journalist, best known as a familiar ESSAYIST who assessed the impact of the important Romantic figures in *The Spirit of the Age* (1825). He was the drama critic on the MORNING CHRONICLE and the EXAMINER, and wrote for the *Edinburgh Review* and the *London Magazine* (1820–3). He is also known for his lectures on SHAKESPEARE, *The Characters of Shakespeare's Plays*, published 1817.

With a shared passion for drama, social justice, and the familiar essay, Dickens and Hazlitt would seem a perfect match, but Dickens quotes from Hazlitt on only two recorded occasions: the first from Hazlitt's *Round Table* essay (1817) on 'Actors and Acting' (*Speeches*, p. 75); the second (*Speeches*, p. 89), on the beloved familiarity of the *Spectator* characters, from the *Lectures on the English Comic Writers*, 'On the Periodical Essayists' (1819).

Dickens worked with Hazlitt's son, William (1811–93), a reporter on the *Morning Chronicle*, who later wrote for the DAILY NEWS and *Household Words* and edited his father's works and *Literary Remains* (1836). At Dickens's death his Gad's Hill library contained over a dozen volumes of Hazlitt's works, most of them in the edition published by his son between 1836 and 1846.           KC

**health, illness, and disability.** Health, individual and social, was a fundamental concern both in Dickens's writings and in many of his personal crusades. It is hardly an original theme: afflictions of the body are ancient metaphors for man's spiritual condition. Dickens assumed an audience familiar with the BIBLE's account of redemption through suffering, slaughter of the innocent, and divine retribution through pestilence, but he also responded with the distinctive voice of the 19th-century progressive—that disease was not always divinely ordained, but sprang from individual or collective negligence. Vulnerable characters, such as David Copperfield's mother or the first Mrs Dombey, seem to die as much from marital oppression as from the complications of childbirth; in *Bleak House* (47), the fatal fever of Jo the crossing-sweeper results from social neglect.

In the DEATHS of his beloved sister-in-law aged 17, and of an infant daughter, and in the alarming illnesses amongst his circle, Dickens shared the common experience of his day (see HOGARTH, MARY; CHILDREN OF DICKENS). Sickbeds and premature deaths were a normal expectation, and the deaths of children feature from the earliest novels (*OT* 2) to the last (*OMF* 2.9), while *Great Expectations* begins with Pip amid the gravestones of his parents and five little brothers (see CHILDHOOD). The death of Paul Dombey in Dickens's PUBLIC READINGS reduced to unrestrained weeping audiences familiar with bereavement. The statistics for England and Wales were brutal, even though underestimated: during Dickens's creative lifetime, of every 1,000 babies born, over 150 would die before the end of their first year. For every 10,000 births, about five mothers died, around nine maternal deaths every day. Although the adult death rate was beginning to decline, infant and maternal mortality remained constant. Dickens, a supporter of the Health of Towns movement (1844), knew that the statistics also concealed great variations between town and country, rich and poor. In certain districts the infant death rate was over 200 per 1,000 births.

William Farr, the Registrar-General, tried to impose a standard classification of the causes of death, but medical certificates in mid-century still attributed infant death to meaningless conditions such as 'inanition' or 'convulsions'. Historians propose a range of causes, such as malnourished mothers, insanitary housing, poor midwifery, neglect, or improper feeding (see PUBLIC HEALTH). Dickens made a straightforward connection between infant death and the harshness of life, as in the bricklayer's 'five dirty and onwholesome children, as is all dead infants' (*BH* 8). Medical opinion also stressed the importance of breast-feeding, and Paul Dombey's decline begins when his wet-nurse is dismissed (*DS* 8). By contrast, Pip's surviving his savage sister's efforts to rear him 'by hand' causes surprise (*GE* 2).

If a child lived through its first year, its chances of survival were greatly increased, though the common childhood infections of measles, whooping cough, diphtheria, and scarlet fever were all potentially fatal. Adults were threatened by both epidemic and endemic infections. Dickens experienced the most dramatic of these—the great cholera

epidemics of 1831–2 and 1848–9, followed by two lesser outbreaks. His daughter Mary contracted and survived the disease. Typhus, spread by lice, and typhoid from contaminated food and water were rarely absent, and would flare up repeatedly, although medical knowledge could not distinguish one from the other until 1869, the year before Dickens's death. Although epidemics could produce sudden increases in the local death rate, the single most common reason for adult deaths, especially amongst younger adults, was bronchial infection, and especially tuberculosis.

The constant presence of death gave 19th-century novelists arbitrary powers over the survival of their characters, but, like contemporary medical men, Dickens is rarely specific on the causes of non-accidental death in his fiction. The Chancery prisoner in the Fleet with Mr Pickwick contracts 'consumption' (*PP* 44), but the illnesses of more important characters, like Dora Copperfield (*DC* 53) or Arthur Clennam (*LD* 2.29) are undiagnosed. The illness passed from the boy Jo to Esther Summerson, in spite of its crucial place in the plot, is simply 'a very bad sort of fever' (*BH* 31). Readers have tried to identify it either as typhus, spreading from the slums to the wealthy, or as smallpox, because it scars Esther. To Dickens it is not a specific disease, but an essential metaphor for deeper social ills. Bailin has shown how the sickroom of Victorian fiction had its own logic, where many characters experience personal crisis and, usually, redemption. Injury and illness lead Arthur Clennam, Eugene Wrayburn, and Dick Swiveller to their true loves; Pip and Martin Chuzzlewit come to understand their own failings. Women, including Agnes Wickham, Little Dorrit, and Clara Peggotty, show their essential characters in acting as devoted nurses. Fever is moral as well as physical, as in the great 'epidemic' of speculation in *Little Dorrit* (2.13).

Ironically, Dickens's most specific diagnosis was also his most controversial: Krook in *Bleak House* dies of spontaneous combustion. Dickens had read some of the current sceptical literature in forensic medicine textbooks, but preferred to use older testimonies since no other end fitted Krook so well, being 'engendered in the corrupted humours of the vicious body itself' (*BH* 32).

Dickens, who numbered many doctors amongst his friends, knew the limitations of their profession. Doctors appear in most of his books. They begin badly with the venal Wosky ('The Boarding House', *SB*) and the riotous medical students in *Pickwick* (30), but in later work Alan Woodcourt (*BH*) is worthy even of the heroine's hand, and Physician in *Little Dorrit* (2.25) is endowed with an 'equality of compassion' following the example of the 'Divine Master of all healing'. From the 1830s to the 1850s the profession underwent a massive struggle for self-regulation, culminating in the 1858 Medical Act which set up the General Medical Council to control the standards of medical education. Dickens admired reforming doctors such as the sanitarian Southwood Smith, or Thomas Wakley, the battling coroner (*UT* 19), but did not attribute more to them than they could deliver. Woodcourt is praised for his sanitarian's preventive eye in his midnight walks through London, but even he soothes and alleviates rather than cures (*BH* 67).

Various forms of deformity or disability occur amongst Dickens's characters. In some cases he simply follows the tradition of making physical appearance a guide to character, as with the vile (but sexually charismatic) dwarf Quilp (*OCS*). His other notable dwarf, Mowcher (*DC*), featured in one of his notorious plot adjustments, when he changed her from a malicious to a sympathetic character in the course of serial publication, as she had been hurtfully identified with a real, and well-known, person (see CHARACTERS—ORIGINALS). Other disabilities, like personal illness, have a wider meaning, and are dealt with compassionately. The reader never knows why Jenny Wren (*OMF* 2.1) or Tiny Tim is crippled, but it plainly arises from the poverty of their surroundings. Even these permanent afflictions may be alleviated by personal devotion: Scrooge is given the choice whether to save Tiny Tim; Jenny Wren is wooed from her self-imprisonment by an unlikely suitor, the boy Sloppy. Dickens also unwittingly contributed a name, 'the Pickwickian syndrome', to a real disability, caused by hypoventilation, which the medical professional later discerned in the Fat Boy's over-eating and somnolence. Dickens, however, did not regard this as disability, but comedy.

The disabilities of notable amputees such as Captain Cuttle (*DS*) and Silas Wegg (*OMF* 1.7) do not impede these energetic characters, and are realistic assessments of what surgery had achieved. More complex operations could not be attempted before the use of anaesthetics, which Dickens was quick to endorse. In 1849 he forced his practitioner to use chloroform in Mrs Dickens's latest delivery, having heard of it directly from the 'Edinburgh doctors' (see DICKENS, CATHERINE). Dying just as the medical revolution of Pasteur, Lister, and Koch was beginning, Dickens had seen illness as a personal and social, rather than a medical challenge.     MAC

Bailin, Miriam, *The Sickroom in Victorian Fiction* (1994).

Brain, Russell, 'Dickensian Diagnoses', *Some Reflections on Genius* (1960).

Smithers, David, *Dickens's Doctors* (1979).

Wohl, Anthony S., *Endangered Lives: Public Health in Victorian Britain* (1983).

**historical novel.** Dickens wrote two works that are commonly thought of as 'historical novels', *Barnaby Rudge* and *A Tale of Two Cities*, although very few of his other books were actually set contemporaneously: events in *Great Expectations*, for instance, take place during the period 1807–26. Most Victorian novels are set in some nebulously conceived recent past, twenty or thirty years previously. It is important to distinguish between this sort of loosely historicized tale and the genre that the Victorians thought of as 'historical fiction': which is to say, a romance in the manner of SCOTT set at some distinctive and eventful period in history, in which ordinary people are caught up in extraordinary events.

With the example of Scott's huge success before them, virtually every Victorian novelist made one or more attempts at historical writing: BULWER-LYTTON's *Last Days of Pompeii* (1834) and *Harold* (1848), THACKERAY's *Henry Esmond* (1852), Elizabeth GASKELL's *Sylvia's Lovers* (1863), George ELIOT's *Romola* (1863), and TROLLOPE's *La Vendée* (1850) all enjoyed considerable success. Some authors (G. P. R. James, for instance, or Harrison AINSWORTH) built whole careers on historical writing. What nearly all these books share is the so-called Whig conception of history as progress; a positive, linear development from barbarity to civilization, the view of history most famously advanced by Macaulay's *History of*

*England from the Accession of James II* (1849–61). By way of contrast, CARLYLE's *French Revolution* (1837) transformed history from a catalogue of facts into an epic narrative, self-consciously modelled on Homer; his history is not so much linear as cyclic, not the expression of a divine plan but the recurring struggle of mankind under various traumas.

Scott's novels are Whiggish in their sense of history; but although Dickens began with the desire to emulate Scott, his historical fiction is very different. *Barnaby Rudge* is often spoken of—to that novel's denigration—as the most Scott-like of Dickens's output; but the comparison rather misrepresents the text. Scott's novels work through historical oppositions (England versus Jacobites, Christian versus Saracen) towards a compromise in which the two elements can become synthesized, and so end happily; Dickens's own binarisms are more Manichaean (see HISTORY: DICKENS'S ATTITUDES). The riot scenes in *Barnaby Rudge* are filled with a destructive and demonic power unlike anything in the more genteel romances of Scott, or many of Dickens's own contemporaries. Far from embodying a Whig conception of history as progress, Dickens sees the irrationalism of mob behaviour equally present in the Gordon Riots, the French Revolution, or the CHARTIST tumults of the 1840s. Dickens resolutely refused to view the past through rose-tinted glasses. Any movement which idealized the past (such as the Young Englanders) earned his scorn. His own CHILD'S HISTORY OF ENGLAND is more Carlylean than Macaulayan; in it history is not progress but a panorama of brutality and violence. Far from seeing Henry VIII, for instance, as a hero of the progress from Catholicism to Protestantism, Dickens presents him as a particularly grotesque Dickensian villain: 'a big, burly, noisy, small-eyed, large-faced, double-chinned, swinish-looking fellow' (*CHE* 27). Henry's execution of the Countess of Salisbury is related with a mixture of slapstick and bloodiness quite startling in a book designed for children: 'When she was told to lay her grey head upon the block, she answered the executioner, "No! My head never committed treason, and if you want it you shall seize it." So, she ran round and round the scaffold with the executioner striking at her, and her grey hair bedabbled with blood' (*CHE* 28).

This mixture of comedy and bloodiness also largely informs Dickens's historical novels; and the personal, individually judgemental tone of the *Child's History of England* alerts us to the fact that Dickens conceived history in this personal, individual manner—that, in other words, history for him was primarily psychological. *A Tale of Two Cities* is similarly less historical (although Dickens undertook extensive historical research before writing it) and more psychological. In an essay published in *Household Words* in 1853 he recalled his childhood fascination with 'the wicked old Bastille' where 'was shut up, in black silence through so many years, that old man of the affecting anecdote, who was at last set free' despite 'pray[ing] to be shut up in his old dungeon until he died'. The fascination with PRISONS (evident throughout his life, but surfacing particularly with *Little Dorrit*) as symbols of psychological depression is linked with another lifelong Dickensian fascination with mob violence—the polar opposite, as it were; the untrammelled expression of energy and destructive passion. It is as symbolic narratives, in which Dickens uses historical events in order to articulate certain psychological and artistic concerns, that Dickens's historical novels really succeed.

AR

Fleishman, Avrom, *The English Historical Novel* (1971).
Sanders, Andrew, *The Victorian Historical Novel 1840–1880* (1978).

**history: Dickens's attitudes.** Despite the widespread prejudice that Dickens was intolerant of and insensitive to history, his response to the past is probably best described as ambiguous. This ambiguity is most emphatically signalled in the paradoxical opening paragraph of *A Tale of Two Cities*, where ultimately the past is seen as 'so far like the present period, that some of its noisiest authorities insisted on its being received . . . in the superlative degree of comparison only'. The 'voice of Time', cited in the third quarter of *The* CHIMES, may insist that 'ages of darkness, wickedness, and violence, have come and gone' and that Time arrested or turned back is like 'a mighty engine which will strike the meddler dead', but, as Dickens's two HISTORICAL NOVELS serve to suggest, history cannot be ignored when it stands as both a warning and as an example to the present. The ages of 'darkness, wickedness, and violence' certainly reappear in the wryly comic titles of the series of false book-backs first introduced into the study at his HOME in Tavistock Place and reused at Gad's Hill Place in the 1850s ('The Wisdom of our Ancestors', for example, consists of volumes purporting to be studies of 'Ignorance', 'Superstition', 'The Block', 'The Stake', 'The Rack', 'Dirt', and 'Disease'). This 'darkness' is not simply a feature of the medieval, Tudor, or Stuart past. Dickens's prejudices against torture, judicially imposed pain, and the excessive use of CAPITAL PUNISHMENT in the immediate past are also echoed in his two novels set in the late 18th century. Dennis the hangman's grotesque taste for his trade is parodied in the course of *Barnaby Rudge*, but the judicial retribution exacted by the authorities after the riots at the end of the novel appears equally grotesque in its excess. As Jerry Cruncher reminds readers of *A Tale of Two Cities*, Darnay's trial for treason at the Old Bailey could have resulted in his being executed by hanging, drawing, and quartering, a sentence paralleled in the judicial dismemberments of the *ancien régime* in France (notably that of François Damiens) which are glanced at in the novel's opening pages. This systematic violence is seen as the root from which revolutionary mayhem stems. Dickens the historical novelist expresses amusement at redundant fashions in manners and clothes, much as the writer of *A CHILD'S HISTORY OF ENGLAND* emerges as an out-and-out progressive, one determined that the clock should not be turned back, and much as the third-person narrator of *Bleak House* splutters against those 'dandies' in Church and State who seek to return to outdated modes of belief, thought, and action. In all of these issues, Dickens shows himself to be a disciple of CARLYLE, whose *The French Revolution* he once rashly claimed to have read 500 times. Carlyle also provided a list of titles as appropriate background reading when Dickens hit what he described as a 'knot in his planning' in the early stages of writing *A Tale of Two Cities*.

If both of his historical novels take a monitory view of the late 18th century, most of his other novels also make play with aspects of then-and-now. With the notable exceptions of *Oliver Twist*, *Dombey and Son*, *Hard Times*, and *Our Mutual Friend*, Dickens seems to have been inclined to set his fictions back in the stagecoach era of his childhood, and, in the instance of *Bleak House*, in the immediately pre-railway, pre-Reform period of 1830. This is not a result of nostalgia for lost security. As *Little Dorrit*, set at a time when the Marshalsea (closed 1842) was still functioning, serves to suggest, Dickens tellingly mixes details of life in the 1820s with contemporary satire (centred on the Circumlocution Office). He questioned and prodded the present as much as he did the past.          ALS

Goldberg, Michael, *Carlyle and Dickens* (1972).
Sanders, Andrew, *The Victorian Historical Novel 1840–1880* (1978).
—— *The Companion to A Tale of Two Cities* (1988).

**Hogarth, Catherine.** See DICKENS, CATHERINE.

**Hogarth, George** (1783–1870) and **Georgina** (1793–1863), Dickens's parents-in-law. George trained as a lawyer in Edinburgh. An amateur violoncellist and composer, he also gained a reputation as a music critic. In 1814 he married Georgina Thomson, daughter of George Thomson, musician, publisher, and friend of Robert Burns. Two years later his sister married James Ballantyne of Sir Walter SCOTT's publishing firm and Hogarth became Scott's intimate friend and legal adviser. At the age of 47 he abandoned his legal career and, in the hope of earning more money to support his increasing family, he became a full-time journalist. The family moved from Edinburgh, first to Halifax where Hogarth started the *Halifax Guardian* and then to London where, early in 1834, he became music critic of the MORNING CHRONICLE and met the young Dickens. He admired Dickens's 'Street Sketches' and when, in the following year, he was appointed editor of the newly established EVENING CHRONICLE he invited Dickens to contribute further sketches to that paper. During the next seven months Hogarth published twenty such pieces, and when the complete *Sketches by Boz* appeared he gave the volume a highly favourable review in the *Morning Chronicle*.

By now Dickens was well established in the Hogarth circle. At this time the family consisted of five sons and four daughters, the eldest being Catherine whom Dickens married in 1836 (see DICKENS, CATHERINE). Relations between Dickens and the Hogarths were very cordial at first and Dickens was proud of his in-laws' connections with the highest cultural circles in Edinburgh (see SCOTLAND). Mrs Hogarth attended Catherine's first confinement, and there was a warm and sympathetic correspondence between her and Dickens following Mary HOGARTH's death. George Hogarth contributed to BENTLEY'S MISCELLANY under Dickens's editorship, and later Dickens made him MUSIC critic for the DAILY NEWS. When Household Words began in 1850, Hogarth was employed to compile a monthly supplement, the HOUSEHOLD NARRATIVE.

Some time before the Dickens' separation relations between Dickens and the Hogarths (with the exception of Georgina) became distinctly strained (see HOGARTH, GEORGINA). In various letters Dickens expressed his impatience and disgust with them. While staying at Tavistock House Mrs Hogarth allowed the dust to gather 'an inch thick'. For months he had been 'dead sick of the Scottish tongue in all its moods and tenses' (24 March 1855), he could no longer 'bear the contemplation of their imbecility', and the sight of George Hogarth at breakfast had 'undermined' his 'constitution' (27 April 1856).

While Dickens was negotiating his separation from Catherine, he discovered that Mrs Hogarth and her youngest daughter Helen were continuing to circulate slanders about him. In the 'Violated Letter' Dickens referred to them as 'Two wicked persons who should have spoken very differently of me, in consideration of earned respect and gratitude . . .' (25 May 1858). George Hogarth prepared a statement saying that his family had never suggested 'any improper motive' for Georgina's remaining with Dickens. This failed to satisfy Dickens, however, who insisted that Mrs Hogarth and Helen themselves sign a statement denying belief in all rumours about Dickens. He also forbade his children 'ever to utter one word to their grandmother or to Helen Hogarth' and never to remain in the presence of either of them (?10–12 July 1858).

Mrs Hogarth died in August 1863 and Catherine wrote to Dickens for permission to bury her beside Mary. Dickens gave his consent in a brief note which did not include one word of sympathy. Despite his age George Hogarth continued as a working journalist until his death, five months before Dickens's.

MS

Adrian, A., Georgina Hogarth and the Dickens Circle (1957).

**Hogarth, Georgina** (1827–1917), sister-in-law, companion, and confidante, described by Dickens in his will as 'the best and truest friend man ever had'. She became an essential member of the Dickens household, and remained there, despite the breakdown of the Dickens marriage, until Dickens's death in 1870.

Georgina first went to live with the Dickens family when she was 15 years old. She helped Catherine in the house and became a companion to both her and Dickens (see DICKENS, CATHERINE). Above all, she helped with the ever-increasing number of Dickens children, teaching the younger boys to read before they went to school. Known affectionately as 'Aunt Georgy', she deputized on social occasions when Catherine was unwell and looked after the family during Catherine's confinements. She often accompanied Dickens on his long daily walks, and took part in his AMATEUR THEATRICALS. She went with the Dickens family when they lived abroad, and acted as Dickens's amanuensis when he was writing A CHILD'S HISTORY OF ENGLAND. Dickens promoted possible matches for her, all of which she resolutely refused. When she was 33 Dickens wrote to a friend: 'I doubt if she will ever marry' (3 May 1860). She never did.

Georgina worked hard to prevent the break-up of the Dickens marriage but when the separation became inevitable, she outraged her family and outfaced scandal by staying in the Dickens household to look after the children. The separation had given rise to numerous unsavoury rumours about Dickens's relationship with her, all of which he furiously denied. His most vehement defence of her came in the so-called 'Violated Letter': 'Nothing has, on many occasions, stood between us and a separation but Mrs Dickens's sister, Georgina Hogarth. From the age of fifteen, she has devoted herself to our home and our children. She has been their playmate, nurse, instructress, friend, protectress, adviser and companion . . . I do not know—I cannot by any stretch of fancy imagine—

what would have become of them but for this aunt, who has grown up with them, to whom they are devoted, and who has sacrificed the best part of her youth and life to them . . . [She] has a higher claim . . . upon my affection, respect and gratitude than anybody in this world' (25 May 1858).

Certainly he had grown increasingly to rely on Georgina for the management of his domestic affairs. Long before the separation he was corresponding with her instead of Catherine on such matters and afterwards she naturally played an even greater role in managing the household. She helped to organize and supervise the move from Tavistock House to Gad's Hill in 1860 and ran the household there (nominally in conjunction with Dickens's elder daughter Mamie) till Dickens's death (see HOMES OF DICKENS). She acted as chaperone and with Mamie entertained the numerous guests and visitors who came to Gad's Hill. In 1861 Dickens observed admiringly that 'Georgina is, as usual, the general friend and confidante and factotum of the whole party' (8 July 1861). During his frequent absences on business and pleasure, she took charge of the household accounts and dealt with his correspondence. She concerned herself with all the details of Dickens's family and friends, their health and welfare, and the frequent financial embarrassments and failures of her nephews. From 1865 onwards she became increasingly concerned about Dickens's health and tried hard to dissuade him from undertaking the American reading tour. She attended his final PUBLIC READING in London, and was relieved that he would read no more. She was alone with him at Gad's Hill on the evening of 8 June when he collapsed. His last conscious words were to her. When she wanted him to lie down, he said 'Yes—on the ground'. She helped him to the floor and then summoned the doctors, together with Mamie, Katey, and Charley. She may also have sent for Ellen TERNAN.

In his will Dickens left her £8,000 together with most of his personal jewellery and all of his private papers. Years later, with increasing age and penury, she sold many of these papers and mementoes.

For the remaining 47 years of her life she acted as 'the Guardian of the Beloved Memory', stoutly defending his life and work against all critics and detractors. She and Mamie returned to London and for many years shared a home. Together they worked on an edition of Dickens's LETTERS for publication. Georgina's scrupulous concern for his reputation meant that many of the letters were ruthlessly cut. Any comment which might reflect badly on Dickens and all references to private family matters were excised; all references to Ellen Ternan were of course inked out or even cut from the letters with scissors. Not all omissions were acknowledged.

Georgina continued to maintain contact with all Dickens's family and friends, including Ellen Ternan, and was venerated by the DICKENS FELLOWSHIP. She was reconciled with Catherine. Of the nine Dickens children she had watched grow up, she outlived all except Katey and Harry and outlived also her own nine brothers and sisters. She died in April 1917 and is buried in Mortlake Cemetery.

She has often been considered the 'original' for Agnes Wickfield in *David Copperfield*, though she herself strenuously denied this, conceding, however, that she might have been the model for Esther Summerson in *Bleak House* (Slater 1983, p. 177). She is most clearly the model for a character in a story Dickens never wrote though he jotted down the idea in his Memoranda Book: 'She—sacrificed to children, and sufficiently rewarded. From a child herself, always "the children" (of somebody else) to engross her. And so it comes to pass that she is never married; never herself has a child; is always devoted "to the children" (of somebody else): and they love her and she has always youth dependent on her till her death—and dies quite happily' (Kaplan 1981, p. 10).                                                     MS

Adrian, A., *Georgina Hogarth and the Dickens Circle* (1957).

**Hogarth, Mary Scott** (1820–37), Dickens's sister-in-law and companion, whose early death affected Dickens profoundly.

Aged 14 when Dickens first visited the Hogarth household, Mary was Catherine's constant companion and chaperone during the period of Dickens's courtship and soon after their marriage she made a month-long visit to the young couple in their three-roomed flat in Furnival's Inn (see DICKENS, CATHERINE). She was subsequently a frequent visitor and kept house there for Dickens when

Catherine was confined with her first child. Described by contemporaries as 'sweet', 'beautiful and lighthearted', Mary's surviving letters show her to have been lively and amusing. They also convey a loving concern for her sister Catherine and a warm admiration for her increasingly famous brother-in-law. Mary died at the Dickens's new home in Doughty Street only a few weeks after they moved in. On 6 May Mary had accompanied the Dickenses to the St James's Theatre. Soon after they got home Mary, Dickens wrote, 'went up stairs to bed at about one o'clock in perfect health and her usual delightful spirits' (31 May 1837). Hearing a cry from her room, Dickens rushed in and found that she had been taken severely ill. The doctor was sent for, but nothing could be done and Mary died at three o'-clock on the following afternoon: 'in such a calm and gentle sleep,' wrote Dickens, 'that although I had held her in my arms for some time before, when she was certainly living (for she swallowed a little brandy from my hand) I continued to support her lifeless form, long after her soul had fled to Heaven' ([8] June 1837). 'Everything that could possibly be done *was* done but nothing could save her. The medical men imagine it was a disease of the heart' (31 May 1837).

Dickens was shattered. He took a ring from her finger and wore it for the rest of his life. He kept a locket he had himself given her and had a mourning-locket made containing a lock of her hair. He kept her clothes. He was quite unable to write the next month's instalments of *Pickwick Papers* and *Oliver Twist* and a public announcement explained that he had lost 'a very dear young relative to whom he was most affectionately attached, and whose society has been, for a long time, the chief solace of his labours'.

In letter after letter he expressed his grief-stricken agony at the loss of the 'dear girl whom I loved, after my wife, more deeply and fervently than anyone on earth' (17 May 1837). He also constructed her as an icon of angelic sweetness and purity: 'I have lost the dearest friend I ever had. Words cannot describe the pride I felt in her, and the devoted attachment I bore her'; 'Thank God she died in my arms, and the very last words she whispered were of me . . . I solemnly believe that so perfect a creature never breathed. I knew her inmost heart, and her real worth and value. She had

not a fault' (17 and 31 May 1837). He composed the epitaph for her headstone in Kensal Green Cemetery: 'Young, beautiful, and good, God in His Mercy Numbered her with his Angels At the early age of Seventeen', and fervently hoped to be buried next to her. He suffered later when one of her brothers was interred there instead: 'The desire to be buried next her is as strong upon me now, as it was five years ago; and I *know* (for I don't think there ever was love like that I bear her) that it will never diminish . . . I cannot bear the thought of being excluded from her dust . . . It seems like losing her a second time' (25 October 1841). Later, he consciously reactivated his grief for Mary to help himself into the frame of mind for describing the death of Little Nell (*OCS*): 'Dear Mary died yesterday, when I think of this sad story' (8 January 1841).

For months after her death he dreamt of her every night, 'sometimes as a spirit, sometimes as a living creature, never with any of the bitterness of my real sorrow, but always with a kind of quiet happiness' (8 May 1843). These dreams, however, stopped as soon as he told Catherine about them and he did not dream of Mary again until 1844 in Genoa when she appeared to him as a figure draped in blue like a Madonna: 'I knew it was poor Mary's spirit. I was not at all afraid, but in a great delight, so that I wept very much, and stretching out my arms called it "Dear"' (?30 September 1844). He asked this vision which was 'the True religion' and it replied that for *him* the ROMAN CATHOLIC was the best, whereupon he awoke with tears running down his face.

He also felt her presence in times of exaltation in his waking life. In AMERICA in 1842, in the sublime surroundings of Niagara Falls, he sensed her and was convinced that she had been there 'many times, I doubt not, since her sweet face faded from my earthly sight' (26 April 1842). During his rapturous reception in the United States he 'felt something of the presence and influence of that spirit which directs my life, and through a heavy sorrow has pointed upward with unchanging finger for more than four years past' (29 January 1842).

Mary is clearly the model for Rose Maylie who appeared in *Oliver Twist* about a year after Mary's death ('She was not past seventeen. Cast in so slight and exquisite a mould;

so mild and gentle; so pure and beautiful; that earth seemed not her element, nor its rough creatures her fit companions'). Like Mary, Rose is taken suddenly ill and Dickens later relives in fiction that terrible May night of 1837 but with the power to make it end happily.

Many critics, notably Albert J. Guerard, have discussed this and other ways in which the '*conscious* fantasy and enduring daydream' (Guerard 1976, p. 73) of reunion with Mary infiltrated Dickens's fiction. One of the most elaborate examples is the story of David Copperfield and his beloved 'sister' Agnes, whom he is eventually free to marry. Just as he had once described how Mary's spirit directed his life, pointing 'upwards with unchanging finger', so he concludes his most overtly autobiographical novel with an invocation to Agnes: 'O Agnes, O my soul, so may thy face be by me when I close my life indeed; so may I, when realities are melting from me like the shadows which I now dismiss, still find thee near me, pointing upward!' (*DC* 64).
MS

Guerard, Albert J., *The Triumph of the Novel: Dickens, Dostoevsky, Faulkner* (1976), ch. 3.
Tillotson, K., 'A Letter from Mary Hogarth', *TLS*, 23 December 1960.

**Hogarth, William** (1697–1764), painter and engraver, satirist of 18th-century life. Dickens greatly admired Hogarth's work and knew well his series of engravings, including *The Harlot's Progress*, *The Rake's Progress* and *Marriage à la Mode*; 48 Hogarth prints hung at Gad's Hill. In reviewing George CRUIK-SHANK's *The Drunkard's Children* in 1848, Dickens praised Hogarth for his compassion, believing him to have been too aware of 'the causes of drunkenness among the poor' to draw a 'Drunkard's Progress'. In letters Dickens refers to Hogarth as a point of comparison for his own view of society, castigating his contemporaries for their outrage at Hogarth's 'indecent' and 'immoral' art (to the Editor of the *Morning Chronicle*, 25 July 1842) and accusing them of failing to recognize the serious import of the artist's work. *Oliver Twist* is subtitled *The Parish Boy's Progress* and, since the 1830s, Dickens's early work has been compared to Hogarth, notably by R. H. HORNE (*A New Spirit of the Age*, 1844). More recently it has been argued that the influence remains

apparent in later novels, including *Great Expectations*. In *The* LAZY TOUR OF TWO IDLE APPRENTICES of 1857 Dickens gave Wilkie COLLINS and himself names taken from Hogarth's *Industry and Idleness*.
LO

Davis, P., 'Dickens, Hogarth and the Illustrated *Great Expectations*', *Dickensian*, 80 (1984).
—— 'Imaging *Oliver Twist*: Hogarth, Illustration, and the Part of Darkness', *Dickensian*, 82 (1986).
Hunt, J. D., 'Dickens and the Traditions of Graphic Satire', in J. Dixon Hunt (ed.), *Encounters* (1971).

**'Holiday Romance'** Four interlinked stories for children which first appeared simultaneously in *All the Year Round* and the Boston periodical *Our Young Folk* in January, March, April, and May 1868. Four children each narrate a story. The 'Introductory Romance' is told by 'William Tinkling, Esq.', aged 8, who is 'married' to Nettie Ashford. His friend, 9-year-old 'Lieutenant-Colonel Robin Redforth', is married to Alice Rainbird. Tinkling describes how he and Redforth try to rescue their brides from their boarding-school. Alice Rainbird's story is 'The Magic Fishbone', the only story at all well known. Redforth contributes a saga about pirates where the Latin master is hanged at the yardarm, and Nettie Ashford 'aged half-past six', tells about a country where 'the grown-up people are obliged to obey the children and are never allowed to sit up to supper'. The stories are interestingly different from the CHILDREN'S LITERATURE of their day. With their affected hostility to adults and descriptions of the romantic attachments of childhood they foreshadow Kenneth Grahame's *The Golden Age* (1895). The work did not attract enough attention to be reprinted until this century, when the first three stories appeared individually in 1912. It has only once, in 1920, appeared as a complete entity.
GA

**homes of Dickens.** It is a supposed truth that a person's home reflects his or her position and fortune in life, and so it was with Dickens. Clearly he had no influence over the choice of his birthplace, nor of other childhood homes—the fortune of the young being inevitably determined by the fortune of the parents; and in Dickens's case his early lot in life, like that of his parents, was one of both happiness and misery. His childhood reflected an unsettled home life, involving fourteen addresses in as many years. Such childhood instability helped create an adult restlessness, taking him abroad to Switzerland, France, Italy, and America, and at home to such places as Richmond, Broadstairs, Cornwall, and the Isle of Wight. Yet still he needed the security of a home base that he never had as a child, which he achieved through the ownership of only three homes from the age of 27 through to the end of his life.

Dickens's birthplace was Mile End Terrace, Landport, Portsea, the first house in a brand-new terrace of four. It comprised: in the cellar, a kitchen, coal-store, and pantry; on the ground floor, a narrow entrance hall leading to the centre of the house, a parlour overlooking the small front garden, and a dining-room at the rear; on the first floor, reached by a narrow winding stair which stretched from the cellar to the attic, two bedrooms, the front one of which was Dickens's birthroom; and, at the top of the house, two cramped garrets off a small square landing. The privy was at the bottom of the garden. Oil and candles were used to light the house. Quite remarkably, the rent book covering the time of Dickens's birth has survived, as has the house itself, which was bought by Portsmouth Corporation in 1903 (at twice the cost of the house next door, sold at the same time), and is now open to the public as the DICKENS BIRTHPLACE MUSEUM.

The family left the birthplace when Dickens was only four months old, moving to lodgings at 16 Hawke Street for eighteen months, and then to 39 Wish Street, Southsea, for a year. The family next stayed in lodgings in London for two years, probably at 10 Norfolk Street, close to Tottenham Court Road, before John DICKENS's work took them to KENT. Following a short stay in Sheerness they moved to Chatham by Rochester, known as the birthplace of Dickens's fancy, living from 1817 to 1821 at 2 Ordnance Terrace. It was described at the time as 'commanding beautiful views of the surrounding country and fit for the residence of a genteel family' (Allen 1988, p. 40). The house was small, and a growing family, together with two servants, made it, for young Charles, a crowded, busy, happy home. The house still stands today, privately

owned. From Ordnance Terrace the family moved to The Brook, next door to the Providence Chapel, where Charles's schoolmaster William Giles was Minister (see EDUCATION). They stayed for one year only, before John Dickens was once again recalled to London.

The family's next residence, in 1822, was at 16 Bayham Street, Camden Town, about three miles north of Central London. It comprised a basement, two rooms at ground level, two on the first floor, a small garret, and a wash-house at the rear. Into this limited space were crammed the Dickens parents, their five children, their cousin James Lamert, and an orphaned servant. At Bayham Street Dickens learned much about London, but was unhappy: while here his father's financial difficulties started to bite. The move to a larger, more expensive house in Gower Street North, at Christmas 1823, with pretensions to establishing a school, was an attempted escape from those difficulties, resulting only in more problems, leading to Charles's employment at WARREN'S BLACKING and then his father's imprisonment at the Marshalsea. The family moved from their most expensive accommodation to their cheapest!

With the family in prison, Charles was found accommodation first with a friend of the family, Mrs Roylance, in Camden Town, and then in an attic in Lant Street, Southwark. This lasted for two months, until John Dickens's release, when the family stayed again with Mrs Roylance, and then at Hampstead. At Christmas 1824 a new home was found at 29 Johnson Street, Somers Town. Not long after moving in John Dickens was retired from the Navy Pay Office and took up journalism, while Charles was able to leave Warren's Blacking and start school at the Wellington House Academy. The family stayed at Johnson Street until 1827, leaving, with rates unpaid, for the nearby Polygon. A hundred years later the Johnson Street house was presented to the local authority and became 'David Copperfield's Library'.

In May 1827 Dickens left school to work in a solicitor's office. Over the following nine years family fortunes were unstable, and John Dickens moved house regularly, usually, though not always, with his family, as he sought to elude creditors. Dickens took up journalism, and as late nights necessitated his own lodgings he spent some time with his family and some time in rooms. Most addresses during this time were located around the Strand area and off the north side of Oxford Street, although twice there were escapes to the seclusion of Hampstead. Other addresses were in Selwood Terrace, Chelsea, where he stayed to be near his future wife Catherine Hogarth, and in Furnival's Inn, their first marital home (see INNS OF COURT).

As Dickens's writing career took off so did he seek to establish more secure living arrangements than he had enjoyed either as a child or as a young man. The Furnival's Inn rooms were taken on a three-year lease, and when these became insufficient for his rising status and income he took a three-year lease at 48 Doughty Street. The leases indicated stability, a demonstration that he would not be living, as his father had, from one Quarter Day to the next. Doughty Street was the largest, most attractive house that he had ever lived in, which he described as 'a frightfully first-class Family Mansion, involving awful responsibilities' (John Greaves, *Dickens at Doughty Street*, 1975, p. 19). Costing him £80 a year, the home was spread over five floors, including the garrett and the basement. There was ample room to accommodate himself, his wife, their young son Charles, and also Mary HOGARTH and his brother Fred (see BROTHERS AND SISTERS OF DICKENS; CHILDREN OF DICKENS). Doughty Street was a private road, gated at each end, with a porter dressed in mulberry-coloured uniform and gold-laced hat to ensure privacy and security. Dickens lived there for nearly three years, during which time he completed *Pickwick Papers* and *Oliver Twist*, wrote *Nicholas Nickleby*, and worked on *Barnaby Rudge*. The house also saw the untimely death of Mary Hogarth. It was purchased by the DICKENS FELLOWSHIP and opened to the public as the DICKENS HOUSE MUSEUM in 1925.

In December 1839 Dickens moved to 1 Devonshire Terrace, paying £800 for an eleven-year lease, plus £160 a year for rent. He described it as 'a house of great promise (and great premium) "undeniable" situation, and excessive splendour' (7 November 1839). Located opposite the York Gate entrance to Regents Park, it boasted a substantial garden, a rest and play area for himself and his family. Dickens made major improvements throughout the thirteen rooms, including the installa-

tion of mahogany doors, Italian marble mantlepieces, and a sound-proofed study door to keep out noise. An inventory of the house exists (Pilgrim 4.704–26). His study overlooked the lawn with its plane trees, and there is a description of him in summer, lying on the grass with a handkerchief over his face, every so often dashing into the study to make notes before resuming his relaxation. At Devonshire Terrace he wrote *The Old Curiosity Shop*, *Barnaby Rudge*, *Martin Chuzzlewit*, *A Christmas Carol*, *Dombey and Son*, and *David Copperfield*. Five children were born there, one of whom, Dora, died. Dickens held the tenancy of this house longer than any other, and though it gave him stability, his restlessness shone through, as he travelled to AMERICA for six months, lived in ITALY for twelve months, SWITZERLAND for six months, and PARIS for three months. The building stood until 1960, when, astonishingly for a house with such strong associations, it was razed to the ground.

After Devonshire Terrace Dickens looked at houses at Highgate and Hampstead, but finally moved, in November 1851, to Tavistock House, Tavistock Square, where he paid £1,542 for a 45-year lease. This was a grand house, with a stone portico, and boasted eighteen rooms, including space for the AMATEUR THEATRICALS he staged there. It was shut off from the road by iron gates and railings, and fronted by an attractive carriage-drive. Whilst here Dickens worked on *Household Words*, *Bleak House*, *Little Dorrit*, *A Tale of Two Cities*, and *Great Expectations*. It was while living here that Dickens separated from his wife. In 1856 he purchased Gad's Hill Place, and for more than four years he had two homes. He sold the lease in 1860, and the building survived until its demolition in 1901.

It had been a childhood dream of Dickens to one day live at Gad's Hill Place, near Rochester. He saw it for sale during a walk in the area on his forty-third birthday, and when he purchased it in March 1856, at a cost of £1,700, Gad's Hill became the first and only home that he was to own. Built in 1780, it was well appointed with bedrooms for his family and guests, and had enough space not only for a study, dining-room, and drawing-room, but also a billiard room and eventually a conservatory. There were servants' quarters, coach-houses, and stables as well as 26 acres of land. Part of his land was separated from the house by the public highway, and he had erected here a miniature Swiss chalet given to him by his friend Charles FECHTER. During his time at Gad's Hill he wrote *Great Expectations*, *Our Mutual Friend*, and *Edwin Drood*. He died at Gad's Hill, and though the house was sold after his death, it still stands today, used as a school, and the Swiss chalet forms part of the Charles Dickens Centre in nearby Rochester. A copy of the 1870 sale catalogue is held at Dickens House Museum, and a full description and account of life at Gad's Hill is given by Watts (1989).                                    MA

> Allen, Michael, *Charles Dickens's Childhood* (1988).
> Greaves, John, *Dickens at Doughty Street* (1975).
> Langstaff, J. B., *David Copperfield's Library* (1924).
> Watts, Alan, *Dickens at Gad's Hill* (1989).

**Hone, William** (1780–1842), radical author and publisher. From 1810 to 1823 Hone published inexpensive political satires and parodies, often illustrated by George CRUIKSHANK, lampooning repressive government practices. Tried for blasphemy and libel in December 1817, he successfully defended himself against three different charges on successive days, thereby establishing a substantial measure of freedom of the press. Hone, though impecunious himself, was Cruikshank's financial backer and caretaker during the artist's riotous Regency days, but they fell out over money matters in the 1820s. On his deathbed Hone and Cruikshank became reconciled. Hone then asked Cruikshank to introduce him to Dickens, as he had been reading nothing but Dickens's works. The meeting took place on 5 October 1842; Hone died a month later. Accompanying Cruikshank to the funeral, Dickens was so amused by the artist's whiskers and deportment that he wrote a very comic, though exaggerated, report of the affair to his American friend C. C. Felton (2 March 1843). He also worked with Cruikshank to obtain a grant of £50 from the Literary Fund for Hone's widow and her nine surviving children. When John FORSTER published Dickens's letter to Felton in the second volume of his *Life*, Cruikshank, the officiating minister the Revd Thomas Binney, and members of the family contradicted the account.

Dickens's description of the funeral was deleted from subsequent editions.        RLP

> Hackwood, Frederick W., *William Hone: His Life and Times* (1912).
> Hone, J. Anne, *For the Cause of Truth: Radicalism in London, 1796–1821* (1982).

**Hood, Thomas,** English writer and journalist (1799–1845). Hood wrote humorous prose and verse throughout the 1820s and 1830s. From 1841 to 1843 he was editor of the *New Monthly Magazine*, and in 1844 he edited the short-lived *Hood's Magazine*. Hood's review of MASTER HUMPHREY'S CLOCK in the *Athenaeum* (7 November 1840), by which date *The Old Curiosity Shop* serialization had only reached chapter 37, was one of the first major appreciations of Dickens's work, as Dickens himself acknowledged in his Preface to the 1848 edition of the novel. By March 1844 the financial support for *Hood's Magazine* had fallen through, and Hood himself was very ill (he was never to recover). Dickens agreed to help by writing something for his magazine. 'Threatening Letter to Thomas Hood from an Ancient Gentleman', a satirical dig at conservative prejudice, appeared in the May issue (repr. *Journalism* 2.67–73). Following Hood's death in May 1845 Dickens added his name to the 'Hood Fund' to raise money for his widow.

Elizabeth GASKELL's *Cranford* was first serialized in *Household Words* (13 December 1851); the first episode contains a debate between two characters as to whether old or new literature is the best, the disagreement centring on the respective merits of Dr JOHNSON and Dickens. Feeling it inappropriate to carry a story in which he himself was praised so highly, Dickens altered all these references to 'Mr Hood'; presumably reflecting his sense that Hood was a contemporary writer of comparable ability and esteem working within a comic tradition. Dickens also greatly admired Hood's more sentimental poetry, for instance 'Bridge of Sighs' (of which he said 'My God! How sorrowful and pitiful it is'), which was a significant influence on *The CHIMES*.                                    AR

**Hook, Theodore** (1788–1841), Regency wit and highly popular novelist of the 'SILVER FORK' school, with whom Dickens came into contact while editing BENTLEY'S MISCELLANY (1837–9), and whose acquaintance he sought (to Thomas Hill, ?18 February 1838). Although

Hook was a former crony of the Prince of Wales, and an editor of pro-Tory publications such as *John Bull* (1820) and the *New Monthly Magazine* (1836–41), his fame as a sketcher and chronicler of mock gentility among the middle classes, in such publications as *Sayings and Doings* (9 vols., 1826–9), meant that Dickens's early work was frequently compared to his.					JMLD

**Horne, Richard Henry** (later restyled Hengist) (1805–84), after an adventurous youth, became a prolific poet, journalist, author, and familiar figure in literary circles. For the Children's Employment Commission in 1841 he wrote a notable report, which Dickens admired. In 1843 he published his epic *Orion* priced at one-farthing, in contempt of the public's neglect of poetry; but it sold well and was critically acclaimed. He was nicknamed 'the Farthing Poet', '*Orion* Horne', and was an accordingly eccentric, flamboyant, and unreliable figure. His *New Spirit of the Age* (1844) featured Dickens in its first and longest chapter, seeing him as 'manifestly the product of his age . . . a genuine emanation of its aggregate and entire spirit', and offering an intelligent account of his writings, personality, and stature; but Dickens is said to have disapproved.

He contributed to BENTLEY'S MISCELLANY and the DAILY NEWS when Dickens was editor, and they became friendly. Horne played in his AMATEUR THEATRICALS (reminiscences of which he published) and visited Dickens on holiday and in London. He joined the *Household Words* staff in 1850, and though he was careless and W. H. WILLS thought him lazy, Dickens later testified (supporting his application for a ROYAL LITERARY FUND grant) to his 'perseverance, zeal, good faith, steadiness and integrity' (1 February 1862). In 1851 Horne joined the Australian gold-rush: Dickens assisted his emigration and organized a farewell dinner. Not striking gold, he existed precariously on government jobs and meagre literary and journalistic earnings, including *Household Words* contributions on Australian and other topics. His marriage had broken up and he was allegedly neglectful of financing his wife, and devoted his considerable sexual energies to mistresses. He returned to England in 1869. Dickens thought this unwise, and when Horne sought to resume their friendship he refused, disgusted by his behaviour, and publicly cut him. His subsequent writings on Dickens and his circle moved Georgina HOGARTH to vituperation: 'what a *bad* man . . . a little old conceited, selfish miserable specimen.'					PC

Blainey, Ann, *The Farthing Poet* (1968).
Fielding, K. J., 'Dickens and Horne', *English* (1952).

**House, Humphry** (1908–55), the pioneer of modern literary-historical scholarship of Dickens, a popular teacher at both Oxford and Cambridge, and frequent presenter of talks on the BBC (see CRITICISM: HISTORICAL). His *The Dickens World* (1941), in spite of some limitations associated with being completed when House was on active wartime service, remains the indispensable introduction to an understanding of Dickens in his age and provided a model for the subsequent work of Philip Collins, K. J. Fielding, and Kathleen Tillotson, among others. Believing that 'Dickens history is inseparable from Dickens reformism', House portrayed Dickens as a much more thoughtful, tough-minded, and informed writer than the sentimental, anti-utilitarian promoter of a vague benevolence that he had frequently and condescendingly been presumed to be. House's sudden and untimely death at 46 came when he was well into work on the complete edition of Dickens's LETTERS that has since been carried on (as the Pilgrim Edition) by his late widow, Madeline House, and Graham Storey, with the help of many others. His work on the letters is engagingly described in an essay in his *All in Due Time* (1955), alongside several other important pieces on Dickens as well as other Romantic and Victorian writers.					RN

***Household Narrative of Current Events***
A monthly supplement to *Household Words* published from April 1850 to December 1855. Each densely printed issue, price twopence, contained a heavily factual digest of the month's main news, organized under regular headings: 'Parliament and Politics', 'Law and Crime', 'Accident and Disaster', 'Social, Sanitary and Municipal Progress', 'Obituaries, Colonies and Dependencies', 'Foreign Events', 'Commercial Record', 'Stocks and Shares', and 'Emigration Figures'. It was compiled by George HOGARTH, with occasional leaders by

FORSTER, who, until 1854, ostensibly supervised its production. Telling correspondences between individual items and details in Dickens's fiction—*Bleak House*, particularly—have been identified. JMLD

**Household Words** A weekly magazine (1850–9) of topical journalism, essays, short fiction, and poetry which commenced publication under Dickens's editorship on 27 March 1850. From this date until his death in 1870 (albeit with a change of title and publisher in 1859) a journal bearing the legend 'Conducted by Charles Dickens' was published, week in week out. The founding of *Household Words* thus represents the beginning of an era in Dickens's career. No longer was he simply an author of monthly and weekly parts, reliant on publishers' contracts, advances, or royalties for his principal income: as editor and joint owner of *Household Words* Dickens received a salary and shared in the profits. In addition to the roles of author and editor, Dickens was now himself a publisher.

The journal was the realization of an aim that had been present in Dickens's mind since the late 1830s. The story of his involvement with BENTLEY'S MISCELLANY, the conception, publication, and winding-up of MASTER HUMPHREY'S CLOCK, his connection with the DAILY NEWS, and his association with the EXAMINER through the 1840s all mark the course of this ambition, as well as representing important stages in Dickens's career as JOURNALIST and essayist. His letters to FORSTER of the 1840s also plot the genesis of the project. Proposals such as 'The Cricket' and 'The Shadow' were suggested, but did not seem commercially or logistically viable to Forster, who, in his unofficial role as Dickens's business adviser, successfully argued against them (Forster 6.4). The eventual result was a working compromise between Dickensian idealism and Forsterian prudence, with an overall purpose succinctly formulated in Dickens's letter to Mrs GASKELL of 30 January 1850: 'the raising up of those that are down, and the general improvement of our social condition.'

The choice of a name for the periodical was not easy. After discarding a dozen possibilities, Dickens at last found a title in SHAKESPEARE, in Henry V's declaration that, to each survivor of Agincourt (1415), the names of his King and leaders would ever after be 'familiar in his mouth as household words' (*Henry V*, IV. iii). Announcements of the journal's launch appeared in the national press from January 1850, and premises were leased at No 16 Wellington Street North, in the Covent Garden area of London for the establishment of a *Household Words* office. Although the rooms where the staff worked were spartan enough, Dickens also had at his disposal three upper-storey bedrooms, two bow-windowed sitting-rooms, and a kitchen, scullery, and wine cellar, which were fitted up for his occasional residence. Contributors, guests, and friends could be entertained here. According to the partnership agreement of March 1850, while the publishers BRADBURY AND EVANS held only a 25 per cent interest in the magazine, Dickens held 50 per cent, which increased to 56.25 per cent in 1856, on Forster's relinquishing a one-eighth share that was divided between Dickens and sub-editor W. H. WILLS, who already held an eighth. He was also to receive an annual salary of £500 and payment for his own contributions to the magazine, though the amounts involved were not recorded in the otherwise scrupulously kept *Household Words* Office Book. (The disappearance of the Office Book for *All the Year Round* makes documentation of that journal far more problematic.)

The journal appeared every Wednesday, bearing as its date of publication that of the following Saturday. It cost twopence, and offered readers six to ten items of original material—improving in this respect on the largely reprinted contents of the penny weeklies—and covered twenty-four pages, staidly printed in double columns without illustrations: a total of over 22,000 words in each issue. The first number was indicative of the range and solid quality of writing which was to characterize the journal for the next nine years, and raise it above the so-called 'Saturday trash' purveyed in cheaper magazines (Report of the Committee on Public Libraries, 1849, p. 1310). After an opening editorial by Dickens came the first episode of a three-part tale by Mrs Gaskell ('Lizzie Leigh'), then a joint piece by Wills and Dickens about mail-sorting technology ('Valentine's Day at the Post-Office'), a Leigh HUNT poem ('Abraham and the Fire Worshipper'), a critique by

Dickens of the bill of fare at popular theatres ('The Amusements of the People'), a biographical 'Incident in the Life of Mademoiselle Clairon', another poem, a joint article by Dickens and Caroline Chisholm, founder of the Family Colonisation Loan Society ('A Bundle of Emigrants' Letters'), and finally a couple of half-column 'fillers'. From the outset the magazine was a considerable success, with a reported sale of over 100,000 for the first number, settling down to a steady 38,500 per issue, which was augmented not only by the sale of monthly parts at ninepence and bound six-monthly volumes at 5s 6d, but by the publication of the monthly HOUSEHOLD WORDS NARRATIVE, and the hugely popular Extra Christmas Numbers (1850–8), with sales of over 80,000 (see CHRISTMAS STORIES). Although these figures were not of the order achieved by a popular penny weekly such as the *Family Herald* (300,000 per week, according to Charles KNIGHT's 1854 estimate), the magazine was aimed at a more discerning and affluent class of reader, and capitalized to return a healthy profit at these circulation levels. After fifteen issues Dickens was reporting that, although an expensive venture, *Household Words* was taking 'a great and steady stand' and 'no doubt already yield[ing] a good round profit' (to the Revd James White, 13 July 1850). After one year of trading Dickens's optimism was justified by profits of £1,715, rising to a high of £2,270 in the third year.

All items were unattributed, but in the case of the opening and closing editorials ('A Preliminary Word', 30 March 1850; 'A Last Household Word', 28 May 1859) and a handful of other items, Dickens made it clear that he himself was the author. The first of these offers a valuable statement of the Dickens aesthetic, simultaneously cultivating the intimacy of tone between periodical and public that Dickens so admired in the 18th-century ESSAYISTS, while promising to show all classes of reader that real progress, 'Romance', and social harmony were not incompatible with the harshness of the industrial world. 'One main object of our Household Words', Dickens elaborates, is 'to teach the hardest workers at this whirling wheel of toil, that their lot is not necessarily a moody, brutal fact, excluded from the sympathies and graces of imagination' (p. 1).

Initially, Dickens's policy was to exclude SERIAL novels from the journal, and his efforts were focused on securing the services of a staff of regular writers, capable of treating non-fictional subjects in a lively manner, or of established authors of poetry and short fiction, as occasional contributors. Altogether, over 380 writers contributed to *Household Words*, including such well-known names as Elizabeth Barrett Browning (1806–61), Edward BULWER-LYTTON, Wilkie COLLINS, Mrs Gaskell, Sheridan Le Fanu (1814–73), Harriet MARTINEAU, George Meredith (1828–1909), Coventry Patmore (1823–96), Adelaide Anne PROCTER, Charles READE, and T. A. Trollope (1810–92). Almost 200 of these writers contributed only once, however, while over a quarter of the articles were penned by the editorial staff, which consisted of Dickens, Wills, R. H. HORNE, Henry MORLEY, and Wilkie Collins, who were contracted, for different periods, at five guineas a week. Over the years, a further thirty or so writers became *Household Words* 'regulars', contributing anything between twenty and 140 items. Many of the established older writers, like Mrs Gaskell, Harriet Martineau, Charles Knight, the Revd James White, and Samuel Sidney, were personally invited to contribute by Dickens. Douglas JERROLD declined to do so, however, humorously observing that although theoretically anonymous, all good items in the journal would in practice be 'mononymous', and attributed to Dickens, whose name appeared on every page. Nevertheless, at two guineas per double-column page, Dickens paid amply and promptly, and with his reputation was soon able to attract submissions from promising younger writers who soon became regulars. Often referred to disparagingly as 'Mr Dickens's young men', this loose group included G. H. A. SALA, James Payn (1830–98), Edmund YATES, Percy FITZGERALD, William Blanchard Jerrold, Walter Thornbury (1828–76), and John Hollingshead (1827–1904). Dickens deftly exploited their particular talents, sending Sala to St Petersburg and Thornbury to Spain, from where they dispatched colourful reports in the capacity of 'special correspondents'—then an innovation in magazine journalism—while others were used for their capacity for urban sketches or whimsical description. Most were content, at least initially, with the opportunity and the payment *Household Words* offered for their work. Sala later recalled that Dickens's acceptance of his first submission was the turning-point in his career. Nevertheless, other staff writers tended to agree in retrospect with Douglas Jerrold that the anonymity of articles in the journal worked in Dickens's favour. 'It was a common complaint, not without foundation,' Hollingshead concluded, 'that all good things in *Household Words*' were attributed to Dickens, 'who was always credited with [the] best productions' of the other staff writers (*My Lifetime*, 1895, 166, 96). Percy Fitzgerald remembered the constant pressure placed upon them to strain after the fanciful effects which Dickens desired, and to inflate ordinary descriptions (*Memories of Charles Dickens*, 1913, ch. 16). Certainly, criticism that a Dickensy flavour predominated in the journal, and complaints of its exaggerated manner, were not lacking in contemporary reviews. On the other hand, the prevalence of genuine Dickensian touches cannot be considered a fault in the journal, whatever the difficulties experienced by other contributors in living up to the exacting standards of the writer they acknowledged as 'Master'.

Aside from questions of style and taste, there can be no doubt that in its variety of topics *Household Words* was second to none of its rivals. While roughly a third of its pages were set aside for literary entertainment, a third was devoted to informative articles on an encyclopaedic range of subjects: science for the layman (medicine, physics, chemistry, astronomy, geology), natural resources, agriculture, art, natural history, national biography, trade, inventions, life in the colonies, ancient history, fashion, domestic economy, and so forth. Another third of the journal dealt with urgent social issues, which were aired, publicized, and debated from the platform of the leading articles, which were widely excerpted and sometimes reprinted in the national press. *Household Words* thus actively participated—at times as a valuable catalyst—in campaigns to improve urban sanitation and housing, establish free elementary and industrial schools for the poor, reduce preventable factory accidents, establish a feasible system of urban burial, and bring about changes in penological practice. Reform of abuses and corruption in the armed and civil services, the Church, and colonial government was stridently called for. Not surprisingly, the journal came in for criticism from vested interests in all these areas, as well as from better-informed and less opinionated commentators than Dickens and his editorial staff. Nevertheless, it is likely that James Baldwin Brown (1820–84) had *Household Words* prominently in mind when making his famous dictum in 1853 that the three great social agencies were cholera, the London City Mission, and Dickens's works.

Apart from his editorial function (perfectly illustrated in his business relations with W. H. Wills), Dickens was also a prolific contributor to *Household Words*. The canon of his writings there, posthumously identified by means of the Office Book, has allowed 20th-century readers to see how he brought to his role of Conductor not just an orchestrating talent but the ability to lead from first violin. Among his fictional and serialized contributions—which include A CHILD'S HISTORY OF ENGLAND (1851), The LAZY TOUR OF TWO IDLE APPRENTICES, and the numerous Christmas stories (1850–8)—*Hard Times* (1854) deserves special mention as the first piece of long fiction to be serialized in the journal. Its appearance, in response to a disturbing drop in profits to a mere £528 for the half-year to 30 September 1853, signalled an important change in editorial policy, bringing the magazine into line with other cheap weeklies of the period. Aside from serializations, however, Dickens contributed 108 full-length essays and articles, and co-wrote a further 45. While the range of subjects is enormous, the essayistic approach can be usefully classified into perhaps a dozen basic formats or sub-genres. Building on his early journalistic experience, Dickens offers comic, anatomizing sketches in the manner of a mature 'Boz', as well as reports of tours of inspection to different public institutions, such as those which made up AMERICAN NOTES. Such tours were often actually undertaken in company with other staff writers, and the resulting articles would be COLLABORATIONS, with Dickens supplying a fanciful narrative or dramatic framework for the more factual and explanatory material of his co-writer.

Dickens referred to many of these as 'process' articles because they revealed the secret workings of some modern enterprise or industry. In the same vein were his ground-breaking accounts of Metropolitan Police operations, which helped pioneer a permanent vogue for DETECTIVE FICTION in English and a short-term craze for guided tours of London's underworld. Frequently, however, the purpose of Dickens's investigations was to expose rather than explain, and his reports take on a tone of sober indignation—as in his accounts of the state of Metropolitan workhouses ('A Walk in a Workhouse', 25 May 1850, 'A Nightly Scene in London', 26 January 1856)—or of biting irony, reminiscent of the early instalments of *Oliver Twist* and the 'MUDFOG PAPERS'. Upwards of 40 leading articles show Dickens in command of an impressive satirical arsenal, using a kind of mixed shot to attack a range of different targets, or bombarding a single target from various angles. Papers such as 'A Few Conventionalities' (28 June 1851), 'Proposals for Amusing Posterity' (12 February 1853), 'Proposals for a National Jest Book' (3 May 1856), and 'Stores for the First of April' (7 March 1857) typify the miscellaneous approach, while a more concerted mode of attack is adopted in papers like 'The Sunday Screw' (22 June 1850), 'The Finishing Schoolmaster' (17 May 1851), 'The Worthy Magistrate' (25 August 1855), and 'From The Raven in the Happy Family [II]' (8 June 1850). Here, Dickens has old enemies in sight: the SABBATARIAN movement, public executions, the LAW, and the expensive sham of English funeral rites, respectively (see CAPITAL PUNISHMENT; DEATH AND FUNERALS). In some of the most striking pieces Dickens adapts the narrative patterns of allegory, fable, FAIRY TALE, and dream literature as satirical strategies for interpreting Victorian life and politics to his audience. The three instalments of 'The Thousand and One Humbugs' (21, 28 April and 5 May 1855) and 'A December Vision' (14 December 1850) are outstanding in this respect. On some subjects, however, Dickens preferred to speak plainly and without irony, in the manner of his serious reviews for the *EXAMINER*. His address 'To Working Men' (7 October 1854), and remarks on 'Pet Prisoners' (27 April 1850), 'Railway Strikes' (11 January 1851), or 'The Lost Arctic Voyagers' (2 and 9 December 1854) are illustrative.

When the artistic balance of the journal permitted, Dickens would contribute comic pieces, spoken through the mouths of wittily observed caricatures ('Lively Turtle', 26 October 1850; 'An Unsettled Neighbourhood', 11 November 1854; 'Cheap Patriotism', 9 June 1855), or familiar essays in which he offered pseudo-autobiographical narratives and seemed to reveal details of his own life. Papers like 'Where We Stopped Growing' (1 January 1853), 'Gone Astray' (13 August 1853), 'Lying Awake' (30 October 1852), 'Please to Leave Your Umbrella' (1 May 1858), and 'New Year's Day' (1 January 1859), with their unrestrained and confessional tone, have provided modern critics with tempting texts on which to base biographical and psychoanalytic interpretations.

Dickens's collected contributions to *Household Words* make difficult work for the reader. On the one hand, the lack, during most of the 20th century, of a complete, annotated edition has hindered discussion and debate over their literary value and relative importance in the Dickens canon, while on the other hand, their removal from the date-stamped columns of the periodical for which they were written deprives each piece of its natural context. Dickens's overriding concern in making up each issue was the stylistic balance and variety of the whole, so the experience of reading just one of the items can understandably leave an impression of tonal imbalance that needs the rest of the issue as a corrective. The essay 'A Child's Dream of a Star' (6 April 1850), for example, may strike modern readers as overly maudlin or personal (Dickens is recalling details of his childhood relationship with his sister Fanny, who had recently died—see BROTHERS AND SISTERS OF DICKENS), but it was composed and inserted with the calculated artistic aim of supplying the 'want of something tender' in the issue overall (to Forster, 14 March 1850). It was widely praised by contemporary readers.

The dissolution of *Household Words* in 1859 was the result of a crisis in Dickens's private life which became public in a manner worthy of Shakespearean tragedy. After separating from his wife in May 1858, Dickens had become aware of rumours and accusations of adultery apparently being circulated by members of the Hogarth family, and determined to end them by publishing a signed statement of his innocence in *Household Words* (see HOGARTH, GEORGE). The front page of the

12 June issue was given over to this purpose. In addition, Dickens quite unreasonably expected BRADBURY AND EVANS to reprint this statement in the magazine PUNCH, which they also owned. Their refusal precipitated Dickens's decision to terminate their partnership in *Household Words*, which he hoped to do by buying up their quarter share and finding another publisher. Bradbury and Evans's response was to declare that the manufacture of the title was their exclusive right, leaving Dickens with no option, to have his way, but to announce at a meeting in November the dissolution of the magazine and the founding of a new one. From February of 1859 work began on *Household Words*'s successor, *All the Year Round*, which commenced publication on a new proprietorial basis on 30 April. After a favourable court hearing in CHANCERY on 26 March, Dickens was permitted to discontinue *Household Words*, which appeared for the last time on 28 May 1859.          JMLD

> Lorhli (1973).
> Slater (1996).
> Stone (1968).

**Hullah, John Pyke** (1812–84), musician. In 1835 Dickens became acquainted with Hullah (probably through Dickens's sister, Fanny, who studied singing and piano at the Royal Academy of Music), and agreed to collaborate with him on a play with music. Dickens wanted to write 'a simple rural story' in the tradition of 'the old English operas'. This became The VILLAGE COQUETTES, an operetta set in an English village in 1729. The St James's Theatre presented it as an 'operatic burletta' in December 1836, with John BRAHAM as Squire Norton and Elizabeth Rainforth as Lucy Benson. Hullah recalled it as a 'very decided' success. The *Athenaeum*, however, suggested that Dickens would be better advised to stick to his comic prose (*Pickwick Papers* had begun appearing in serial form since 31 March) than to cultivate the musical stage.

From about 1838 Hullah turned his attention increasingly from composition to music education, at which he was successful and influential. He was professor of vocal music at King's College, London (1844–82), and, beginning in 1872, government music inspector.
                                                    RTB

> Hullah, Frances, *Life of John Hullah* (1886).
> Rainbow, Bernarr, 'Hullah', in *Grove Dictionary of Music and Musicians* (6th edn., 1980).

**Hunt, James Henry Leigh** (1784–1859), radical journalist, famous as co-founder of the *EXAMINER* (1808) and libeller of the Prince of Wales (1813), but also as a talented Romantic essayist, poet, and prolific founder of literary journals, in which capacities he became well known to Dickens. By the late 1820s Hunt had moderated his radical zeal, and his Romantic enthusiasm was carefully tailored for the middle classes. His ESSAYS contributed to the *TRUE SUN* during Dickens's employment there, published under the signature of 'The Townsman' (1833–4), show him posing as a connoisseur of the London streets, and expounding what he called his 'Townosophy' of aesthetic responses to the city. In his 'Streets of London' sketches (*Leigh Hunt's London Journal*, 1834–5), Hunt returned to the theme, proposing 'to go through London, quarter by quarter', noting as many associations of the city's past as possible. These sketches were collected as *The Town* (1848), a copy of which was in Dickens's library at his death. Even in the 1830s Dickens was an enthusiastic reader of Hunt, praising his 'faith in all beautiful and excellent things', and humanitarian sentiments (to Hunt, ?13 July 1838), and taking editions of Hunt's *Indicator* (1819–21) and *Companion* (1828) journals with him to Petersham in 1839 as holiday reading. In 1847 Hunt's perennial financial difficulties were partly solved by a Civil List pension of £200, but not before Dickens had decided to organize two theatrical benefits in his behalf. In Dickens's fertile imagination, however, Hunt's charming naivety of disposition and avowed eschewal of money matters later became transformed into something more sinister in the character of Skimpole in *Bleak House* (see CHARACTERS—ORIGINALS). The parody caused Hunt much distress, which Dickens's later retractions and apologies, culminating in the article 'Leigh Hunt: A Remonstrance' (*AYR* 24 December 1859), never successfully assuaged (Forster 6.7).     JMLD

**'Hunted Down'** A sensational short story of murder, detection, and suicide, based on the career of Thomas Griffiths Wainewright (1794–1847), a notorious poisoner whom Dickens had seen in June 1837 in Newgate (Pilgrim 1.277n.). In the story, narrated by Mr Sampson, manager of an insurance company, Julius Slinkton murders his niece for her insurance money and is exposed by Meltham, a young actuary who loved her. Dickens knew Henry Porter Smith (1797–1880), the insurance agent who investigated the suspicious death of Helen Abercromby (with whom he was rumoured to have been in love), whose life had been insured by Wainewright (Pilgrim 2.251–2n.). Commissioned by Robert Bonner, proprietor of the *New York Ledger*, who paid Dickens £1,000 for its serial rights, the story was published with seven woodcuts on 20 and 27 August and 3 September 1859. Advertised as having been 'written expressly and solely for an American periodical', it later appeared in two parts in *All the Year Round* (4 and 11 August 1860) and (without authority) as a separate volume, which included an account of Wainewright, published by J. C. Hotten (?1871). (See MONEY AND FINANCE.)                                                 PVWS

# I

**illustrators and book illustration.** (See also individual artists and works by name.) Although most of the editions of classic fiction Dickens read as a child were unillustrated, Georgian culture was strongly visual as well as verbal. Indeed, for many centuries popular EDUCATION reached the uneducated through appeals to eye and ear: church decoration performed in other media the function of sermons. At the time of the French Revolution much of the propaganda for presumably literate royalists as well as sometimes illiterate republicans was conducted through visual means; and the subsequent wars engaged graphic artists in a Europe-wide competition of popular imagery deployed to nerve nationals to fight battles and pay taxes. As literacy increased from the late 1700s onward, reading was taught through pictures, especially those in alphabet books and crudely illustrated chapbooks providing moral and religious instruction. Science depended on diagrams, schematic drawings, maps, and highly detailed engravings for communicating its discoveries. Political propaganda used caricatures that engaged a wide range of visual signs —emblems, rebuses, puzzles, and sophisticated allusions to other works of art. Regency political and personal satires spared no one, from king to commoner, and they employed a ribald and impious graphic vocabulary unrestrained by notions of taste, Aristotelian balance, or Augustan sobriety. Sheet music of the sort Silas Wegg hawks in *Our Mutual Friend* was often headed by vivid plain or coloured images. Theatrical posters and toy theatres assembled from brilliantly coloured stiff paper cut-outs replicated the scenes and costumes of the latest hit and transmitted the visual impact of drama and spectacle to the public. And beginning in the late 1820s publishers devised more and more elaborately illustrated collected editions of favourite authors, particularly Sir Walter SCOTT. Dickens grew up surrounded by vivid pictorial images.

His first story, 'A Dinner at Poplar Walk', was submitted to an unillustrated magazine. It, and eight further submissions to the MONTHLY MAGAZINE which Dickens later grouped under the title 'Tales', were reminiscent of minor THEATRE comedies. But the sketches and street scenes that Dickens submitted under the pseudonym 'BOZ' to the MORNING CHRONICLE and EVENING CHRONICLE, and in a few cases to other periodicals, grew in part out of a combined verbal and visual tradition, the street sketch (see SHORT-STORY AND SKETCH WRITER, DICKENS AS). This genre, used so effectively by Washington IRVING and influential in Britain and later on the Continent (especially in France), employed a detached observer who watched the life passing by in the streets or through the adjacent windows. This observer is able to identify the anonymities and analyse the confusions of undifferentiated urban life—to detect the impecunious clerk behind his gorgeous clothing, the respectable widow in a pawnshop, the underworld in all its guises and disguises. The sketch captures the momentary, the fleeting; its medium—line or letters—reflects the evanescent in its quick graphic gestures and improvisatory prose. 'Sketches' deal with time, its passing, memories of the past, the decay of traditions or buildings or people; they may be melancholy in tone or celebrate the renewal of seasonal observances. They are a good medium for recording impressions of travel. And they lend themselves readily to combining letterpress with pictures.

Therefore, when John MACRONE, an enterprising young publisher richer in ideas than capital, wanted to reprint Dickens's journalism, he teamed 'Boz' with the leading urban 'sketcher' and book illustrator of the day, George CRUIKSHANK. From that point almost all of Dickens's major and minor works illustrated at the time of their original publication; only *Hard Times* and *Great Expectations*, among the novels, were issued without plates.

The plates record the first response to Dickens's imagination. Dickens would have to inform his artist about a scene, often before he wrote it, and the most responsive illustrators, Cruikshank, Hablot Knight BROWNE, and Luke FILDES, realized in visual terms not only the characters and settings but also the mood, point of view, themes, symbolism, relationships among subplots and characters, and future trajectories of the story. Dickens often approved preliminary designs before completing his manuscript, so even before John FORSTER, W. H. WILLS, Wilkie COLLINS, or another of Dickens's trusted friends read the draft, the artist had completed his picture.

For SERIALS, written in the course of publication, it is crucial to devise a title so that an ADVERTISING campaign may begin even before the first chapter is finished. About these titles Dickens often consulted friends, especially Forster. Once that title was determined, Dickens turned to his illustrator. If the novel appeared in separately issued parts, the text would be encased around the front, back, and spine by a coloured paper wrapper. On the front of this wrapper would be imprinted the work's title, author, instalment number and date, price, name of publisher/printer/booksellers, and some fairly elaborate pictorial rendering or 'shadowing forth' of the book's entire content, for the wrapper would remain unchanged, except for date and part number, throughout the serialization. Robert SEYMOUR had already designed a wrapper for Dickens's first serial, *Pickwick Papers* (1837–8); but for the succeeding novels Dickens provided his illustrator with the earliest indication of his ideas for the new story.

Browne, who did most of Dickens's wrappers, structured them according to graphic conventions he inherited from Cruikshank and Seymour in particular. He usually surrounded the verbal information with a design that tracked a rise up the left-hand margin and a fall that descended along the right-hand margin. The result is a kind of Wheel-of-Fortune structure, perhaps most explicit in the wrapper for *Dombey and Son* (1846–8): a young man on the lower left, standing on a chequebook and a banker's book, adjacent to a hopeful traveller, rising sun, and merchant fleet sailing calm waters, easily balances on his head and forefinger a huge ledger, a court guide, cash-boxes, and other records of wealth. These precariously stacked accounts rise to a throne-like chair resting on a fat cash-box and day-book. In it sits a commercial Croesus (representative of Mr Dombey), but to his right a pack of cards, featuring the unfortunate combination of diamonds and hearts, tumbles down from a wedding scene to press heavily on the overburdened shoulders of an elderly, lame man standing on scrip (worthless paper IOUs) adjacent to a quarter moon signifying inconstancy, a rolling ocean on which a ship founders, and an old man being comforted by a woman (see illustration no. 44 on p. 517) Dickens thought there was 'a little too much in it', though he confessed to Forster that this was 'an ungrateful objection', and in the following month he recommended Browne's design as a model for the illustrations to CRICKET ON THE HEARTH (to Forster, ?6 September and 26–9 October 1846). Through such visual indirection Browne is able to hint at the principal pattern of action and something of the character of a leading figure without giving away specifics of a plot not yet devised.

Not all the wrapper designs were composed before the novel. *Sketches by Boz* and *Oliver Twist* were reissued in parts *after* they had been published in periodicals. These reprints, like the originals, were illustrated by Cruikshank. For *Sketches*, he designed large letters B, O, and Z, with figures weaving in and out of them. This wrapper appropriately images that meld of words and pictures characterizing late Georgian popular entertainments and reading. It was printed on pink paper to distinguish the publication from Dickens's original serials, his 'green leaves'. For *Oliver*, which did, misleadingly, appear within green wrappers, Cruikshank adapted the clockwise design of fortune, Oliver starting out on the lower left with Mr Bumble and ending with Mrs Maylie (or Rose) at the top, while the thieves tumble down the right, ending with Bill Sikes hanging himself and Fagin waiting in the condemned cell of Newgate. These are all small, self-contained rectangular vignettes depicting familiar scenes and characters; some of them are versions of the full-page plates Cruikshank designed for the first issue of the novel. There was no need to hint at future events, for the story, published eight years earlier, was widely known even by those who had not read the original.

The front wrapper to MASTER HUMPHREY'S CLOCK is an exception too. Dickens did not know what tales, by himself and others, the clock-case would contain when he projected this serial, to appear in weekly and monthly parts and in half-yearly volumes with special frontispieces. So all Browne could do was draw a curly twisting vine around which benevolent fairies, nymphs, sylphs, and other mythological creatures sport. An aged Father Time, hourglasses, a noon-time sun, and intimations of budding, leafing, blossoming, and harvesting running clockwise around the letterpress reinforce the theme of time proclaimed by the central image of a large clock decorated with allegorical devices.

The most intensely studied of all the wrapper designs is that by Charles COLLINS, Dickens's son-in-law, for *Edwin Drood*. Dickens gave Collins other wrappers to study in preparation for his own design. In his drawing and cover Collins alludes to the Wheel-of-Fortune design by surrounding the central letterpress with entwined roses (on the left) and thorns (on the right). But in other ways he inventively works both with and against that circular paradigm. Edwin and Rosa walk down from Cloisterham Cathedral on the left, ascending, side; pursuers rush up a circular staircase on the right, descending, side. In each case the emotional (Edwin and Rosa) or moral (pursuers) valence may contradict the direction of the stairs or the circle. Most examined are the picture at the bottom, of someone with a lantern confronting someone else in a close, dark space, and the figures (uniformed officers in the drawing, plain-clothesmen in the printed wrapper) chasing after someone up the stairs in the cathedral tower or possibly the postern stairs of Jasper's gatehouse. What Dickens told Collins, what Collins understood, and what hints or concealments these images contain are subjects of continued debate (see MYSTERY OF EDWIN DROOD, SOLUTIONS TO).

The monthly serials had two plates per part; these were printed together on heavy paper stock, then cut apart and bound into the front of each part, behind the front advertising supplement but before the text. Sometimes booksellers displayed the illustrations in the window as an inducement to buy the instalment. Thus Dickens's illustrators came to think of their images as paired, and readers sometimes studied the pictures closely as clues to the contents of the instalment. These graphic designs translate the verbal text into

visual terms. Like all translations, they approximate the source, critique it, supplement it, and employ a different vocabulary to enact in another language and tradition what the source text expresses.

An example is Browne's illustrations for *Bleak House*, Part 8, where two characters never paralleled by the text are juxtaposed: Mr Turveydrop in 'A model of parental deportment' (ch. 23) and 'Mr Chadband "improving" a tough subject' (ch. 24). These two embodiments of hypocrisy and selfishness are depicted in similar poses, and their surroundings, subtly mirroring each other, iterate their monomanias. But Browne goes even further in deepening his visual analogues. Mr Turveydrop models himself on the Prince Regent, later George IV; Phiz models his depiction of Turveydrop on famous depictions of the Regent by James Gillray and George Cruikshank. Their satiric portraits, ruthless in exposing the Prince's self-indulgences, are echoed by pose, expression, and details of setting in the first of Browne's illustrations. In the second, Browne alludes to his own previous design in order to extend and complicate the conflation of Regent, Turveydrop, Chadband, artistic precedents, and textual representation (Dickens describes Turveydrop in the same terms the Regent's contemporaries described him, as 'a fat old gentleman with a false complexion, false teeth, false whiskers, and a wig').

Inheriting Seymour's wrapper design and first portraits of the Pickwickians, Browne could not fully free himself throughout that novel from his predecessor's comedy, so dependent on somatic confrontations (fat versus lean, men fighting, clumsy bodies colliding). In the early 1840s, however, Browne developed a highly emblematic component to his style. William HOGARTH had provided for a century the pre-eminent example of graphic designs that illustrated modern moral subjects. He devised pictorial systems that employed structures of parallel and contrast, scenery and accessories juxtaposed with the central action, and elaborately developed thematic analogues. As Henry FIELDING's tribute to Hogarth in *Tom Jones* exemplifies, the British novel matured as a genre by incorporating the thematic, structural, and allusive complexities characteristic of Hogarth's engravings. The later Georgian illustrators and

George Cruikshank extended this tradition, and with *Martin Chuzzlewit* Browne demonstrates his familiarity with Hogarthian practices. Details that Browne sometimes added after Dickens approved the preliminary design and that underscore some aspect of the theme of 'self' that structures the novel include a pair of scales to indicate miserliness, allusions to Daumier's caricatures of the complacent, pear-shaped visage of Louis Philippe, spider-webs and mousetraps to capture innocent gulls in Eden, finger-posts that point in true and false directions, and designs that echo Hogarth's own plates and thereby suggest the pictorial tradition out of which stories about youthful progress and social hypocrisy grow.

Beginning with *Dombey and Son* and climaxing with *Bleak House* and *Little Dorrit*, Browne gradually shifts from emblematic details to more pictorial means for expressing the novel's tone and themes. Light and dark, the essentials of etching, take on huge symbolic significance, not only in the dark plates, but also in the more 'realistic' ones. Sources of light—candles, lamps, sun and moon—may indicate genuine material and immaterial illumination, but such lights may also, like will-o'-the-wisps, be deceiving. Things concealed in darkness are customarily bad; but in *Little Dorrit* the shadows cast by society are if anything more contaminating than the taint of the prison. By the end of his collaboration with Dickens, Browne was more inclined to rely on design elements than on accessories within the picture to express his interpretation of Dickens's story.

The last, double, part of a monthly serial included four plates—the customary two, plus a frontispiece and a title-page with an etched vignette. Browne's frontispiece for *Pickwick* puts Mr Pickwick and Sam on a stage, surrounded by emblems of comedy, tragedy, and the prototype of tragicomic master and servant, *Don Quixote*. This was as far as author and artist could go in trying to rewrite Seymour's initial tales of cockney sporting mishaps, to shift minor episodic humour toward the more spacious and serious comic tradition initiated by Cervantes. The next frontispiece to a novel that Browne illustrated, *Nicholas Nickleby*, does something even more important to the status of the novel. It is an engraved portrait of the author,

signed 'Faithfully yours, Charles Dickens'. This is the first novel to be issued in Dickens's own name, rather than under his pseudonym 'Boz', and in supplying his own picture opposite the title-page Dickens offers a portrait not of the titular character, as might be expected, but of himself, in his own name, as the guarantor of the quality of the book. In a sense, that picture and that signature come to stand in for all the embellishments of other illustrations; a replica of Dickens's autograph stamped in gold on the covers of the Charles Dickens Edition was the ultimate imprimatur.

Thereafter, Browne devised etched frontispieces and vignette titles that, facing one another in any bound edition of the parts, clearly relate to one another. Tom Pinch's selflessness and harmony, imaged in his playing the organ in the frontispiece to *Chuzzlewit*, contrast with Pecksniff's greed in receiving a new pupil for pay. A fanciful amalgam of Paul and Florence Dombey, the sea, and angels in the frontispiece of *Dombey* contrasts to the realistic vignette of Captain Cuttle inside the Wooden Midshipman listening to a cowed Rob the Grinder reading. Underneath apparent contrasts, however, subtle convergences can be discovered; sometimes Browne's pictures bring out aspects of Dickens's story unemphasized by the text. And though the plates for *Dorrit* show signs of Browne's slackening, the initial plates are striking. The frontispiece, of Amy and Fanny being welcomed—if such stiff and supercilious impassivity may be termed 'welcomed' —by the servants at the Merdle mansion, is paired by the vignette title, of Amy leaving the Marshalsea under the watchful eye of John Chivery. Text and illustrations together convey that society is at least as much a gathering of sinners as the Marshalsea. In addition, Phiz mocks the costumed figure of the Merdle butler by juxtaposing a nude neoclassical statue in the same pose—an addition to Dickens's satire denoting the inappropriate and conspicuous acquisitions of rapacious parvenus and the unnaturalness of their retinues.

Titles of plates were supplied after etching, when they were calligraphed by a copperplate engraver. These engraved titles sometimes differ from the titles in the List of Illustrations printed in the final double number, and though the differences are slight, they may in cases indicate an evolving understanding of the relation between plate and letterpress. Instructions were also provided to binders about where to insert the plates, facing that page most applicable to the image.

The Christmas books proceeded according to a different formula. Dickens determined that the first of these, A Christmas Carol, was to be a beautiful little book, scarlet-and-gilt cased, with four uncoloured wood-engraved vignettes and four hand-coloured etchings. To do these he hired his friend John LEECH, a shy young man who had unsuccessfully applied for the Pickwick commission at the behest of Cruikshank seven years earlier. Leech's preliminary drawings were quite sketchy, but Dickens trusted his friend, and despite Leech's fears the results were splendid: the Fezziwig ball and the Ghost of Christmas Present are two of the most enduring of Dickens's illustrations. The remaining four Christmas books were illustrated by several artists besides Leech, and all the plates, whether full-page etchings, wood engravings dropped into the text, or vignette title-pages, were uncoloured. Multiple artists might enhance sales, but coloured pictures were too expensive for these holiday commodities. For the most part, the illustrations, like the texts, combine fancy, allegory, and realism: Daniel MACLISE drew elves, goblins, and fairies, Leech depicted squalor and humour, Clarkson STANFIELD modelled picturesque buildings and seascapes, and Richard DOYLE displayed modest domesticity.

Master Humphrey's Clock and A Tale of Two Cities also deviated from the monthly part norm. For the former, Dickens hired two principal illustrators, Browne and the antiquarian painter George CATTERMOLE. Each artist provided designs for wood engravings which were printed with the letterpress so that text and picture intermingle. In addition, Maclise drew the picture of Nell looking down into a well, incorporating so many downward-pointing verticals that the plate is virtually a graphic analogue of the line of print directly above it: 'The child complied, and gazed down into the pit.' And Samuel WILLIAMS, primarily known for his wood engravings, provided one of the most indelible of the Clock images: Nell asleep in her bed in the Curiosity Shop in the first chapter of that novel.

Browne was still Dickens's principal illustrator for Tale of Two Cities, but the story appeared in the columns of Dickens's unillustrated periodical All the Year Round. Browne therefore prepared etchings for the eight monthly parts, whose letterpress was reset from the weekly numbers. The wrapper design was, as usual, created before the novel began, so as to be ready for the monthly instalments; but otherwise Browne had the luxury of preparing plates after publication, instead of before. For whatever reasons, that exceptional opportunity did not inspire him.

Great Expectations was unillustrated, and when Dickens planned his next twenty-part serial he asked Marcus STONE, the son of an old neighbour and friend, to do the illustrations. At first Dickens was tactful and meticulous in his supervision; Stone took instruction well. His wood engravings, except for the somewhat symbolic and allegorical wrapper design, depart from the Hogarth–Cruikshank–Browne vocabulary of internally commenting accessories; instead, Stone works within the sentimental-realist tradition of the black-and-white graphic artists of the 1860s. Fatigued from illness and labour and further depleted by his exertions in rescuing other passengers from a railway accident at Staplehurst (see KENT), Dickens retreated to Gad's Hill to write the last parts of the novel and never even saw Stone's preliminary drawings. The results were in keeping with the story and with modern illustration, but unmemorable.

Edwin Drood was to be illustrated by Wilkie Collins's brother, Charles, but the artist, married to Dickens's daughter Kate, broke down after designing the wrapper. His place was taken by Luke Fildes, a young social realist, who for his Dickens illustrations put live models in landmark settings and rendered them with vivid poses, gestures, expressions, and lines. Dickens was extremely gratified with Fildes's 'veritable photographs' of his characters. He invited the artist down to Gad's Hill in early June to view other settings for later instalments, including the interior of Rochester Cathedral and one of the Maidstone jails wherein John Jasper was allegedly to confess to the murder. But before Fildes could make his visit, Dickens died.

Illustrations also embellished other of Dickens's writing. Dickens hired Samuel

PALMER to design vignette wood engravings of Italian subjects for the republication of Dickens's travel letters from Italy. After much labour Palmer supplied four designs; he also chivvied the engravers to reproduce his delicate lines delicately. PICTURES FROM ITALY was not well received, and neither were the pictures—'paltry', one reviewer complained. Francis W. Topham tried an ambitious scheme for the frontispieces of the three-volume CHILD'S HISTORY OF ENGLAND: four circular vignettes in the corners of the plate stay the same throughout the three volumes, though each frontispiece is printed in differently tinted inks; the large central vignette, however, varies from volume to volume.

When Dickens's works were reprinted in collected EDITIONS, most of the illustrations were excluded. For the Cheap Edition (1847 ff.) the original illustrators provided new frontispieces. The Library Edition (1858) had 21 vignette title-pages by Browne; the Illustrated Library Edition issued three years later included plates by Charles Green, G. J. Pinwell, and Fred Walker. The Charles Dickens Edition (1867–8) published a selection of the original illustrations. And the Household Edition (1871–9) converted hundreds of Browne's loose drawings into wood engravings, accompanied with new pictorial embellishments by Fred Barnard, Charles Green, and others. The original illustrators also cashed in on their success: with Dickens's at least tacit approval Browne in the 1840s sold sep-arate suites of portraits of principal characters; both Cruikshank and Browne in old age painted watercolours of their illustrations for eager collectors; John TENNIEL and other artists plundered the illustrations for instances that could be modified and adapted to political cartoons; and a new generation of artists imitated or deliberately deviated from the originals in their plates for subsequent editions of the novels. There were also countless supplementary paintings, illustrations, and pictorialized editions; contemporary artists who rendered Dickens's work included 'Alfred Crowquill' (Alfred Henry Forrester), Sir John Gilbert, Arthur Boyd Houghton, 'Kyd' (J. Clayton Clarke), Charles Robert Leslie, Thomas Onwhyn, and F. W. Pailthorpe, and in America, Felix Octavius Carr Darley and Thomas Nast. In the 20th century, however, mass-market paperback editions reproduced few, if any, of the original illustrations, and those that were printed were, despite modern technology, for the most part very badly done.

Not only did Dickens's illustrators reach their public through their own virtuosity, they also communicated by utilizing images and styles of well-known predecessors and contemporaries to deepen and expand their appeal. Among the other artists (besides themselves) quoted by Dickens's illustrators are Thomas Bewick, Honoré Daumier, John Doyle ('HB'), James Gillray, William Hogarth, Charles Robert Leslie, John Martin, John Everett Millais, Francis Quarles, Moritz Retzsch, Thomas Rowlandson, Thomas Stothard, William Makepeace THACKERAY, Bertel Thorwaldsen, J. M. W. Turner, and David Wilkie. When the architects and designers of London's streets and buildings, and the artists and typographers who created the pictorial advertisements whose imagery also migrates into the texts and illustrations, are added, the extent of the novels' visual intertextuality expands even further.

Another way Dickens's illustrations became known was through DRAMATIZATIONS of the stories. Often the plates translated to the stage even better than the texts; Browne's and Cruikshank's settings and costumes were faithfully copied by stage designers, and productions led up to a climactic moment when the actors would 'freeze' into a living replica of the illustration. Some characters were so well known outside their textual embodiment that they would be recognized in incongruous settings: quick-change equestrian artists, for instance, would ride around the ring bareback costumed as one character, then disappear for an instant behind a screen and emerge as another character, usually of a contrasting age and class and sometimes of a different gender (see CIRCUS). Such performances tell us a great deal about how widely disseminated the images of Dickens's characters were.

In the best working relationships, Dickens collaborated with his artists to produce 'multi-media' books dramatizing stories through words and pictures. The wrapper designs, frontispieces, vignette titles, wood engravings dropped into the text, and full-page etchings or wood engravings speak through alternative means, reiterating, amplifying, anticipating, and independently interpreting

Dickens's prose. For the most part, Dickens counted on those illustrations, even when he tried through the powers of his description, impersonation, and imagination to usurp and absorb the visual into his verbal performance. And his first audiences responded enthusiastically to these pictorial 'embellishments'; visually as well as verbally literate, many could read the pictorial sketches with as much attention and enjoyment as they read the texts.                                    RLP

Cohen (1980).
Harvey (1971).
Kitton (1899).
Steig (1978).

**India.** Dickens's popularity in India offers a noteworthy contrast to the lack of reference in his novels to India and the rest of the Empire, except as a backdrop to his central concern with ENGLISH experience. India, along with Africa and the Caribbean, is only a convenient space to which characters are shipped off or where they can make their future (see EMIGRATION). In the novels, India is a land distant and exotic. It lends bogus respectability to Montague Tigg's Anglo-Bengalee Disinterested Loan and Life Assurance Company (*MC* 27 *et seq.*); it is responsible for the torments of Paul Dombey's schoolmate Master Bitherstone, 'born beneath some Bengal star of ill-omen' (*DS* 41) and for the blue face of Major Bagstock, served 'spirited unknown liquids' by his servant, the Native (*DS* 26). Imperialist sentiments evident in 'The Perils of Certain English Prisoners', co-authored with Wilkie COLLINS (*HW* 1857 Christmas number), and in a letter stating his wish to 'raze it ["the Oriental Race"] off the face of the earth' (to Miss Coutts, 4 October 1857) are coloured by the fact that his son Walter, then 16, was a cadet in the East India Company and arrived in India just as the Mutiny broke out (see CHILDREN OF DICKENS). He fought in ensuing battles and died there in 1863.            NN

Oddie, William, 'Dickens and the Indian Mutiny', *Dickensian*, 68 (1972).

**industrial novels.** The first industrial novels tended to concentrate on heart-rending stories of individual misery rather than attempting to describe or encompass the experience of increasing Victorian industrialization (see INDUSTRY). Harriet MARTINEAU'S story 'A Manchester Strike' (1835), often cited as the first example of the genre, deals in impassioned and sometimes sentimental style with the miseries of the factory-worker's life. Mrs TROLLOPE's *Michael Armstrong: The Factory Boy* (1839) and C. E. Tonna's *Helen Fleetwood* (1839) exposed the abuse of child workers in northern factories (see FACTORY ACTS). Greater political sophistication was introduced into the genre with DISRAELI's *Sybil*, 1845, with its theme of the widening gulf between the 'two nations' of rich and poor. Charles Kingsley's *Alton Locke* (1848) focuses its wide-ranging critique of contemporary industrial society on the figure of its CHARTIST hero, giving a powerful individual focus to the novel's portrayals of the grimness of industrial life. Elizabeth GASKELL's *Mary Barton* (1848) paints a powerful portrait of Manchester factory-workers and their suffering; Dickens himself, greatly impressed, commissioned another industrial novel from Gaskell (*North and South*) to appear in *Household Words*; although by the time it appeared (September 1854–January 1855) the tenor of the genre had shifted somewhat. Bourgeois authors such as Gaskell and Dickens had been alarmed by the working-class political agitation of the 1840s and had watched revolution sweep through Europe in 1848 with dismay. Post-1848 industrial novels tend to be self-consciously less inflammatory. Gaskell's *North and South* is actually more concerned with the difficulties endured by the mill-owners than the workers, and Dickens's own *Hard Times* (1854) ridicules the TRADE UNION leader Slackbridge as representing a wrongheaded approach to the problems of CLASS conflict. According to Raymond Williams (*Culture and Society 1780–1850*, 1958, p. 97), such backsliding epitomizes the inadequacy of the industrial novel as a force for positive good: in his opinion the genre represents 'more a symptom of the confusion of industrial society than an understanding of it'.

The 'Industrial Novel' as a genre has various aliases: critics sometimes talk of the 'Social Problem Novel', the 'Condition of England Novel', the *Tendenzroman*. But these names, sometimes treated as synonymous, in fact point to a series of quite different concerns. Dickens, for instance, had little against industrialization as such. Figures such as *Bleak House*'s Rouncewell, with his model iron factory in the north, represent a vigorous and progressive response to social problems that depends upon the wealth industry creates. There are plenty of fictional examples of his enthusiasm for entrepreneurial activity as the modern equivalent of the 'Parable of the Talents' (the biblical story which underlay much of his MORAL thinking). Dickens objects to industrialization, as to EDUCATION, employment, POOR RELIEF (all satirized in Dickens despite being, patently, good things) when, for whatever reason, they tend towards the dehumanization of the individuals concerned. This is a point forcefully made by Nell's encounter with the man who watches the foundry fire (*OCS* 44), an early instance of 'industrial novel' concerns in his fiction.

In fact, industrial life makes but few appearances in Dickens's fiction. *Oliver Twist*, sometimes cited as an industrial novel, contains no factories at all; in *A Christmas Carol*, which was partly Dickens's response to the Children's Employment Commission Report on the miseries suffered by many of the capital's children, they appear only liminally (for instance, in the background of LEECH's illustration of the two children 'Want' and 'Ignorance'). Dickens is, throughout his career, more comfortable portraying an old-fashioned mercantile or trading company (as with the Cheerybles, or Dombey and Son) than contemporary manufacturing industry. Even *Hard Times* is not concerned with the sorts of workers' sufferings detailed by Mrs Trollope or Tonna. Dickens actually cut out a passage from the manuscript of the novel that mentioned a child having its arm ripped off in a poorly maintained machine as being too gruesome, and as it appears in the novel factory work (whilst certainly hard) is never shown to be actively dangerous to life or limb. The novel's satirical focus is less industrial, more UTILITARIAN, and more particularly involved with those forces that would oppress individual and imaginative life. Stephen Blackpool's problems result not from industrialization as such, but from (in the first instance) the incapacity of the System, embodied by Parliament and the Establishment, to respond to the difficulties of his marriage; and (in the second instance) by his refusal to submerge his individuality in another dehumanizing and conformist System, Slackbridge's trade union.

AR

Gallagher, Catherine, *The Industrial Reformation of English Fiction 1832–1867* (1985).

Smith, Sheila, *The Two Nations: The Poor in English Novels of the 1840s and 1850s* (1960).

**industry.** During the years immediately before and after Dickens's birth, parts of Britain underwent a massive transformation which most economic historians are still prepared to call an 'industrial revolution'. It did not produce overnight a country of 'dark satanic mills': Britain's economy owed at least as much to commerce and the provision of financial services as it did to textile factories. Even in industrial Lancashire and Yorkshire the transformation had not proceeded as far by the 1840s and 1850s as historians once used to believe. A return of Lancashire cotton firms in 1841, for example, revealed that 70 per cent of factories employed fewer than 200 workers (Evans 1996, p. 424). Most towns outside Lancashire, West Yorkshire, and Lanarkshire remained workshop- rather than factory-based. Nevertheless, the speed and decisiveness of industrial transformation where it did occur alarmed contemporaries as much as it impressed them. On the one hand, the Victorians gloried in industrial advances which were making Britain the workshop of the world; on the other, they feared the implications. Manchester, the epicentre of the world's first industrial revolution, was also 'the shock city' where old social ties did not hold and where CLASS conflict threatened not only order but civilization itself. Tocqueville memorably called Manchester the 'filthy sewer' from which flowed 'pure gold' (quoted in Asa Briggs, *Victorian Cities*, 1963).

Dickens shared the ambivalence of his middle-class contemporaries, who tended to see the national interest polarized into the 'agricultural' and the 'manufacturing'. He was, in RUSKIN's phrase, 'of the steam-whistle party', but there is a strain of romantic melancholy over the old ways being superseded, as in his two-edged portrait of an 'engine driver', representative of the new industrial interest, 'besmeared with coal-dust and begrimed with soot; his oily hands, his knowledge of machinery; all point him out as one devoted to the manufacturing interest. Fire and smoke, and red-hot cinders follow in his wake. He has no attachment to the soil, but travels on a road of iron, furnace wrought.

His warning is not conveyed in the fine old Saxon dialect of our glorious forefathers, but in a fiendish yell' ('The Agricultural Interest', *Morning Chronicle*, 9 March 1844; repr. *Journalism* 2.64 ff.).

Dickens was neither anti-industrialist nor anti-worker. As editor of the DAILY NEWS, he published articles in favour both of free trade and of industry as routes to prosperity (Coles 1989). He was lavish in his praise of both employers and workers who strived for mutual harmony, praising 'large iron masters . . . who have proceeded on the SELF-HELP principle and have done wonders with their workpeople . . . Also other manufacturers in isolated places who have awakened to find themselves in the midst of a mass of workpeople going headlong to destruction and have stopped the current and quite turned it by establishing decent houses, paying schools, savings banks, little libraries etc.' (to Angela Burdett Coutts, 18 April 1852). He contrasted 'obnoxious manufacturers of Preston' with self-improving workers of Birmingham, evidently better treated by their masters who employed fewer hands: 'I have never seen . . . those working people collected in any numbers . . . without extraordinary pleasure —even when they have been agitated by political events' (27 November 1853).

We should not be surprised, therefore, to see Dickens use his fictional Coketown in *Hard Times* (1854) as an allegory, rather than a documentary depiction, of industrialism and to draw attention also to the dangers of social disharmony which exercised so many of his contemporaries and which he himself shared. Though *Hard Times* is Dickens's 'INDUSTRIAL NOVEL', his primary concern is not with industry as such but with the dehumanizing attitudes which both industry and the use of capital can give rise. He protested to Peter Cunningham, who had suggested in the *Illustrated London News* that *Hard Times* was based on the Preston strike, regretting that Cunningham's misapprehension 'localizes (as far as your readers are concerned) a story which has a direct purpose in reference to the working people all over England' (11 March 1854). When Charles KNIGHT, the author of *Knowledge is Power*, expressed the view that *Hard Times* 'bore too hardly upon those who held that the great truths of political economy were not an insufficient foundation for the improvement of society', Dickens replied that his satire was 'against those who see figures and averages, and nothing else—the representatives of the wickedest and most enormous vice of this time' (30 December 1854).

Although Dickens's first-hand knowledge of industrial Lancashire was not so extensive as that of Elizabeth GASKELL (whose *North and South*, which followed *Hard Times* in *Household Words*, also took inspiration from the weavers' strike), he did visit Liverpool and Manchester and other industrial towns. To gather material for *Hard Times* he spent 48 hours in Preston, during which he attended a meeting of weavers' delegates at Temperance Hall and, briefly, a mass meeting of strikers. He thought, as he had previously thought about the railwaymen's dispute in 1851, that strikes were 'a deplorable calamity' ('Railway Strikes', *HW* 11 January 1851). He urged moderation and, specifically, mediation: 'Gentlemen are found in great manufacturing towns, ready enough to extol imbecile mediation with dangerous madmen abroad. Can none of them be brought to think of authorized mediation and explanation at home?' ('On Strike', *HW* 11 February 1854). (John Bright, a native Lancastrian, intimately acquainted with the politics of industrial conflict, condemned the arbitration solution as 'absurd': Dutton and King 1981.)

Dickens informed Elizabeth Gaskell that *Hard Times* would deal with 'The monstrous claims at domination made by a certain class of manufacturers, and the extent to which the way is made easy for working men to slide down into discontent under such hands' (21 April 1854) and would not focus on the strike. Significantly, it is dedicated to Thomas CARLYLE, who had so powerfully attacked the 'Gospel of Mammonism' in his own *Past and Present* (1843), a work Dickens much admired. *Hard Times* is a sustained plea for that moderation and social harmony which he believed eminently attainable in a properly organized industrial society. The hero, Stephen Blackpool, is a victim of a society run on principles of greed and unheeding self-interest, whose leaders are activated, Carlyle judged, by 'Money . . . and nothing more' (*Past and Present*, 3.2). Dickens caricatures economic self-advancement unyoked to moral self-improvement in Josiah Bounderby, and points to the theories of Thomas Gradgrind, who understands political economy entirely as a matter of 'Fact' rather than understanding, as the root problem of industrial society.

His fiction portrays good employers sympathetically, as with the 'kindly' brothers Charles and Edwin Cheeryble (*NN* 37), modelled on the commercial magnates of Ramsbottom, Bury, and Manchester, William and Daniel Grant. The smith and engineer Daniel Doyce, is presented as an honest, steady, patient self-improver whose invention has been ensnared in the Circumlocution Office: 'No man of sense who has been generally improved, and has improved himself, can be called quite uneducated as to anything', he told his partner before going on to explain his invention 'with the direct force and distinctness with which it struck his own mind' (*LD* 2.8). The characterization of the self-improving, and self-possessed industrialist is brought to its peak in Rouncewell the iron-master in *Bleak House*, who represents enlightened progress and is the industrial counterpart to the aristocratic, landowning Dedlocks. The Dedlocks have inherited their position; Rouncewell has worked for his. 'I have been ... an apprentice and a workman. I have lived on workman's wages, years and years, and beyond a certain point have had to educate myself.' He has brought his children up 'to make them worthy of any station' (*BH* 28). Dickens presents him as 'a responsible-looking gentleman' with a 'shrewd though open face ... strong and active', but ambiguity remains: Trooper George, one of Dickens's most sympathetically portrayed characters, chooses in the end not to join his brother's firm but to serve the crippled Sir Leicester.

Dickens's views about industrial society are in part romanticized, probably impractical, and—considered as documentary evidence—under-researched. They are, however, both positive and heartfelt. Industry is not something to be feared for itself, but only for what narrow-minded, profit-dominated folk make it. In a speech at the Birmingham and Midland Institute on 30 December 1853 he urged his large audience to heed the principles of the Mechanics' Institution: 'the fusion of different classes, without confusion' and 'the creating of a better common understanding among those whose interests are identical, who depend upon each other ... In this world a great deal of the bitterness among us arises from an imperfect understanding of one another' (*Speeches*, p. 167).                EJE

Coles, Robert, 'Charles Dickens and the *Daily News*: Editorials and Editorial Writers', *Victorian Periodicals Review*, 22 (1989).

Dutton, H. I. and King, J. E., *Ten Per Cent and No Surrender* (1981).

Evans, E. J., *The Forging of the Modern State*, 2nd edn. (1996).

Rubinstein, W. D., *Capitalism, Culture and Decline in Britain* (1993).

**infant phenomena,** a term widely employed for child actors and actresses, facetiously adopted by Dickens to describe his first-born son (to Lover, 6 December 1837), and most memorably applied to Ninetta Crummles, the daughter of Dickens's strolling actor-manager in *Nicholas Nickleby*.

Children's acting companies date back to the 12th century, and they were prominent in the performance of drama during the reign of Elizabeth (see E. K. Chambers, *The Elizabethan Stage*, 1923). SHAKESPEARE refers to them in *Hamlet* as 'an aery of children, little eyases, that cry out on the top of question and are most tyrannically clapped for't' (II. ii. 354–7). But the vogue for individual child prodigies dates from 1804, when the 13-year-old William Henry West Betty (1791–1874), the 'Infant Roscius', took London by storm, appearing at Covent Garden and subsequently at Drury Lane as Hamlet, Romeo, young Norval, and other starring roles. According to Leigh HUNT, who virtually single-handedly drove Master Betty from the stage, at least a further nine prodigies had appeared before the 1804–5 season finished (*The News*, 19 May 1805).

Betty's popularity quickly passed and, hissed from the stage, he spent the rest of his long life in obscurity. But other prodigies soon followed: in 1817 Miss Clara Fisher, the 'Lilliputian Actress', age 6, made her debut at Covent Garden; Robert William Elliston's protégé, Master Burke, made his first appearance at the Theatre Royal, Dublin, in 1824, the same year that Master William Robert Grossmith, age 5, appeared at the Coburg Theatre in London, and was later featured by Elliston at the Surrey (1827–8). In 1832 Gilbert Abbott À BECKETT wrote a scathing attack on child actors performing that season at the City of London Theatre (*Figaro in London*, 1, 25 August 1832, 152).

Dickens's Infant Phenomenon, 'a little girl in a dirty white frock with tucks up to her knees . . . who turned a pirouette, cut twice in the air, turned another pirouette, then, looking off at the opposite wing, shrieked, bounded forward to within six inches of the footlights, and fell into an attitude of beautiful terror' (*NN* 23), is widely thought to have been modelled on Jean Margaret Davenport (?1829–1903), whom Dickens may have seen make her debut at the Richmond Theatre, Surrey, in 1836, and who was performing in Portsmouth (site of the theatre scenes in *Nickleby*) shortly before Dickens wrote the chapters introducing the Crummleses into the novel. Managed by her pompous father, Thomas Donald Davenport (1792–1851), the likely prototype for Vincent Crummles, Jean Davenport performed all over Britain, Ireland, Europe, and North America, and as Mrs Lander later enjoyed considerable fame in the United States as a tragedienne. PVWS

McLean, R. S., 'How "The Infant Phenomenon" Began the World: The Managing of Jean Margaret Davenport (1829(?)–1903)', *Dickensian*, 88 (1992).

Playfair, Giles, *The Prodigy: A Study of the Strange Life of Master Betty* (1967).

Schlicke, Paul, 'Crummles Once More', *Dickensian*, 86 (1990).

Waters, Hazel, ' "That astonishing clever child": Performers and Prodigies in the Early and Mid-Victorian Theatre', *Theatre Notebook*, 50 (1996).

**inns and taverns.** Dickens's early novels abound in inns and taverns. In *Pickwick*, which follows the 18th-century picaresque tradition, the action moves swiftly from one inn to another. It opens with Mr Pickwick and his friends leaving the Golden Cross in London bound for the Bull in Rochester. As the story proceeds they travel to various towns, staying at the large coaching inns of that day, such as the Hop Pole in Tewkesbury and the Angel in Bury St Edmunds. At the Great White Horse in Ipswich Mr Pickwick has the embarrassing adventure with the lady in yellow curl-papers. At the White Hart in Bath Mr Winkle finds himself locked out, scantily clad, on a windy night. Dickens had travelled these roads himself when a reporter, and utilized his knowledge of inns to introduce new characters and scenes. His early novels, therefore, provide a picture of travel before the

coming of the railways, and of the coachmen, hostlers, bagmen, and others who were engaged in this work.

Then there were places which could hardly be called inns but were rather more than mere public-houses. Such was the Valiant Soldier, by James Groves: 'Good beds. Cheap entertainment for man and beast' (*OCS* 31). The Crozier (*MED* 18) was a rather better establishment, and although not exactly cosy was able to offer a visitor a meal of 'fried sole, veal cutlets, and a pint of sherry'.

Dickens had an abiding love of taverns, and throughout his works revealed a wide knowledge of them. He never forgot the time when he was working in WARREN'S BLACKING warehouse and came out of a little public house close to the river to sit on a bench and watch some coal-heavers dancing, nor the hot evening when he went into a strange public-house and asked the landlord: 'What is your best—your *very best*—ale a glass?' He used both of these incidents in *David Copperfield*, chapter 11.

In *Pickwick* he mentioned the George and Vulture where Mr Pickwick lodged, the Blue Boar where Sam Weller composed his valentine, and the Spaniards where Mrs Bardell was arrested. Dickens's taverns vary considerably, and he had an eye for what was quaint. He saw in the Three Cripples at Saffron Hill the sort of place where Sikes and Fagin would plot their crimes (*OT* 15 *et seq.*). He knew that some London taverns had rooms such as the first floor of the Sol's Arms where inquests might be held, followed not long after by Harmonic Meetings like that chaired by Little Swills (*BH* 11 *et seq.*). Many early scenes in *Great Expectations* take place in the Three Jolly Bargemen, where Joe Gargery liked to smoke his pipe, and where Pip noticed 'some alarmingly long chalk scores on the wall by the side of the door, which seemed to me to be never paid off' (10).

But the best description of an old tavern is that of the Six Jolly Fellowship Porters, 'a narrow lop-sided wooden jumble of corpulent windows heaped upon one another as you might heap as many toppling oranges, with a crazy wooden verandah impending over the water', 'a bar to soften the human breast', and 'red curtains matching the noses of the regular customers' (*OMF* 1.6).

ASW

Matz, B. W., *The Inns and Taverns of Pickwick* (1921).

—— *Dickensian Inns and Taverns* (1922).

**Inns of Court,** the principal institutional home of the English common lawyers since medieval times. They are the oldest professional societies in England, pre-dating the creation of the Anglican clergy and the establishment of the Royal College of Physicians. Four inns, Gray's Inn, Inner Temple, Middle Temple, and Lincoln's Inn came to predominate as the home of the common law elite, the judges and the advocates specializing in court work. From the late 17th century, as admissions fell finances dwindled and chambers were let to increasing numbers of non-lawyers, who used them as workplaces or homes. The Inns ceased to perform significant educational functions and exercised little formal control over the entry and conduct of barristers.

Several other 'inferior' Inns existed and became associated with attorneys and clerks, 'the lower branch' of the profession. By 1500 these 'Inns of Chancery' were Barnard's Inn, which Pip describes as 'the dingiest collection of shabby buildings ever squeezed together in a rank corner as a club for tom-cats' (*GE* 30, 31); Clements Inn; Clifford's Inn, where Tip Dorrit 'languishes' for six months in a lawyer's office (*LD* 1.17), a 'mouldy little plantation . . . Sparrows were there, cats were there, dry-rot and wet-rot were there, but it was not otherwise a suggestive spot' (*OMF* 1.8); Davies' (subsequently Thavies') Inn; Furnival's Inn (John Westlock has rooms in this 'shady quiet place': *MC* 36); Lyon's Inn; New Inn; Staple Inn, where Mr Snagsby walks in summer (*BH* 10) and where Mr Grewgious has chambers (*MED* 11, 20); and Strand Inn. By the 1890s the Inns of Chancery had been dissolved.

Several of Dickens's characters lived in the Temple, the area of London occupied by Inner and Middle Temple, which 'had something of a clerkly monkish atmosphere, which . . . even legal firms have failed to scare away' (*BR* 15). The evil Slinkton lives in Middle Temple (*HD*), Pip and Herbert Pocket live in Garden Court (*GE* 39), and John Chester has rooms in Paper Buildings, 'a row of goodly tenements' (*BR* 15). In *Pickwick* Mr Perker and Mr Phunky have offices in Gray's Inn, and

Serjeant Snubbin has chambers in Old Square, Lincoln's Inn. Jack Bamber entertains Mr Pickwick and his friends with 'tale[s] of horror' about the Inns (*PP* 20–1). Mr Tulkinghorn lives in a large house in Lincoln's Inn Fields (based on the home of John FORSTER, who lived in 58 Lincoln's Inn Fields during 1834–56), 'let off in sets of chambers now; and in those shrunken fragments of its greatness, lawyers lie like maggots in nuts' (*BH* 10).

The Inns were also an integral part of Dickens's early working life. In May 1827 he enrolled as a 'writing clerk' in the office of ELLIS AND BLACKMORE, 'a poor old set of chambers of three rooms in Holborn Court'. Subsequently, during 1834–7, he lived in chambers in the newly rebuilt Furnival's Inn, a former Inn of Chancery.                    DS

Lemmings, D., *Gentlemen and Barristers: The Inns of Court and the English Bar 1680–1730* (1990).

**Ireland and the Irish.** The attitude Dickens adopted toward Ireland and the Irish was a fusion of objectified pronouncements and informed observation. His interest in the THEATRE ensured that he was familiar with the tradition of the stage Irishman (to Lewes, 16 April 1848; to Georgina Hogarth, 25 August 1858), and he acted in a play written by the Irish dramatist Dion Boucicault (to Lemon, 30 June 1848). He knew the work of prominent Irish balladeers and poets, particularly Thomas Moore (1779–1852), whom he first met in 1838, and to whose *Irish Melodies* and *National Airs* he alludes in his fiction (see *OCS* 23, 27, 58; *DC* 29).

Dickens's intimate knowledge of London ensured that the Irish—who formed nearly 5 per cent of the capital's population in 1851—frequently found their way into his work. They are often stereotyped in the fiction as part of the general atmosphere Dickens wishes to create—appearing as unnamed 'labourers' who have been 'alternately shak[ing] hands with, and threatening the life of each other' in the gin shop (*SB* 29); prisoners in Newgate, 'indifferent' to the presence of visitors (*SB* 32); occupants of Saffron Hill public houses, 'wrangling with might and main' (*OT* 8); servants to the likes of Harold Skimpole (*BH* 43); and as the mass of urban poor, whose 'miserable affairs' are observed by the UNCOMMERCIAL TRAVELLER (*UT* 30).

Dickens also focuses on the London Irish in his 'On Duty with Inspector FIELD'—an account in *Household Words* of a nocturnal visit to the St Giles rookery, the East End, and the Mint lodging-houses in the Borough. The 'tramps' lodging-house' features various Irish occupants who, when asked 'Does any body lie there?' reply with 'Me Sir, Irish me'; others are described as 'coiling' themselves about the visitors' feet (*HW* 14 June 1851; see LONDON: SLUMS).

A more particular focus on Irish politics appears in *Martin Chuzzlewit*. Martin and Mark attend the meeting of the Watertoast Association of United Sympathisers, where they learn of the group's support of a 'certain Public Man in Ireland', who 'held a contest upon certain points with England'—and this despite the fact that the members are 'horribly jealous and distrustful' of the Irish people (*MC* 21). The man in question was the Irish nationalist Daniel O'Connell (1775–1847), who campaigned for Catholic civil rights and the repeal of the 1800 Act of Union. The episode was inspired by a series of articles in *The* TIMES in June and July 1843 which satirized the anti-English meetings held by Americans in favour of Home Rule. Dickens, writing the Watertoast episode shortly after the appearance of these articles, takes a similar stance; however, in tracing the Association's dissolution to Choke's discovery of O'Connell's opposition to slavery, Dickens was able to evoke his own emancipatory sentiments.

Dickens visited Ireland three times on PUBLIC READING tours, in August–September 1858, March 1867, and January 1869. During his first sojourn he read in Dublin, Cork, Limerick, and Belfast, and was 'greatly surprised' that imagined stereotypes were not confirmed: Dublin, he noted, had 'far fewer spirit shops' than other 'great cities' (to Miss Coutts, 23 August 1858). He also noted the 'quickness' of the Irish humour, and the 'universal' crying at a reading of 'Little Dombey' (to Georgina Hogarth, 25 August 1858). He pronounced the readings 'great successes' (to F. D. Finlay, 2 September 1857), as did the local newspapers, which spoke of 'enraptured audiences', 'full to overflowing' (*Belfast News-Letter*, 28 August 1858). He received a similar reception in 1867, when he was accompanied by his Irish friend Percy FITZGERALD, but was

distressed by the Fenian disturbances of that year. Indeed, his apprehension about an insurrection marred the effect of the visit: from the outset he saw himself as a 'disconsolate Voyager with the Fenians before him', and spoke of 'considerable alarm', 'apprehensions' of 'disturbance', and of the whole of Dublin being 'secretly girt in with a military force' (to Wilkie Collins, 13 March; to Georgina Hogarth, 16 and 17 March 1867). His overall impression was 'Tremendous success in Ireland . . . notwithstanding the Fenian alarms' (to Frances Elliot, 20 March 1867). The third visit, when he read 'Sikes and Nancy' in Dublin and Belfast, passed off without incident, though he was aware of a growing nationalist sentiment, and observed, shortly before his departure, that 'these are not times in which other powers would back our holding Ireland by force, unless we could make our claim good in proving fair and equal government' (to W. F. de Cerjat, 4 January 1869).

Despite this anxiety about the country's political aspirations, Dickens was clearly well received in Ireland—both personally and through his publications. The Irish stereotypes he created were part of the imaginative currency of the period, and his concern over political developments was shared by many of his English contemporaries. Nevertheless, papers like the Dublin *Freeman's Journal* could appreciate the 'peculiarities of character' in Dickens's work, and could recommend that it 'must be read' by 'everybody' (5 June 1851). LL

Blaisdell, L. J., 'The Origins of the Satire in the Watertoast Episode of *Martin Chuzzlewit*', *Dickensian*, 77 (1981).

Fitzpatrick, D., ' "A Peculiar Tramping People": The Irish in Britain, 1801–70', in W. E. Vaughan (ed.), *A New History of Ireland*, vol. 5 (1989).

Lees, L., *Exiles of Erin: Irish Migrants in Victorian London* (1979).

**Irving, Washington** (1783–1859), American essayist, travel-writer, and author of folk tales, celebrated as the first US author to achieve worldwide recognition. Dickens claimed to be one of Irving's earliest admirers, writing to him on 21 April 1841 that he had 'worn to death in [his] pocket' a copy of Irving's successful burlesque *History of New York from the Beginning of the World &c.* (1809), by 'Diedrich Knickerbocker', while walking about London 'when a small and not over-particularly-taken-care-of boy'. Irving had visited Europe, including London, in 1804–6 and 1815–32, and many of his successful works after the *History* conjured up quaint Old World scenes for his American readers, in a style that blended the elegance of the 18th-century British ESSAYISTS, with fresh Romantic enthusiasm and droll urbanity. His friendship with Walter SCOTT brought about the successful publication in Britain of *The Sketchbook of Geoffrey Crayon, Gent.* (1820) and its successor, *Bracebridge Hall* (1822); both books contained old-fashioned distillations of English life and character which gratified readers on both sides of the Atlantic. An important early review of *Pickwick Papers* was quick to note suspicious similarities between Dickens's descriptions of Tony Weller and CHRISTMAS at Dingley Dell, and passages from 'The Stagecoach' in Irving's *Sketchbook*, where he introduced Bracebridge for the first time ([Abraham Hayward], *Quarterly Review*, 59). Nevertheless, a mutual admiration was established between the two authors in the late 1830s, and plans were discussed for publishing *Oliver Twist* in the American *Knickerbocker Magazine* in exchange for the appearance of papers by Irving in BENTLEY'S MISCELLANY (Pilgrim 1. 588 n.). Dickens enjoyed active encouragement from Irving when planning his first visit to AMERICA in 1842 but the friendly relations between the two cooled considerably after the publication of AMERICAN NOTES (Ackroyd 1990, p. 351; to Irving, 21 April 1841). JMLD

**Is She His Wife? or Something Singular** A comic burletta in one act, written 'long before I was BOZ' and revised by Dickens in February 1837 (to Harley, ?21 January and 6 February 1837). It was first performed at St James's Theatre on 6 March 1837. The plot consists of flirtations, jealousies, and intrigues of two married couples, resolved in mutual affection. The role of the vain bachelor Felix Tapkins was designed for John Pritt HARLEY, who selected it for his benefit night on 13 March. Surviving playbills attribute the play to Boz. The first known publication was not until 1877, by James R. OSGOOD in Boston. PVWS

**Italy.** Dickens's Italy was modern, not classical. The grand tour was now in decline: Joseph Tuggs, the grocer who is left £20,000,

goes to Ramsgate, not Rome, on the strength of it, and 'did not precisely understand what the grand tour was, or how such an article was manufactured'. ('The Tuggses at Ramsgate', *SB*; a foreshadowing of the difficulties of the Dorrits?) As for many Victorians, Dickens's main experience of the country was a period of residence there, from July 1844 to June 1845, rather than a grand tour of its ruins. The base he chose was Genoa, the birthplace of Mazzini (who himself reviled classicism) in Cavour's Piedmont, then the most progressive and nationalistic region of a country whose most pressing concern was liberation from tyranny. There he became friendly with Emile de la Rue, one of Cavour's closest associates. In the remark of one of the *Household Words* 'young men', Dudley Costello, in *Piedmont and Italy* (1859–61), that Garibaldi 'deserved to be ranked with the noblest heroes of antiquity', we may locate Dickens's own position on the question of ancient and modern Italy.

Although, as with all Dickens's fascinations with foreign countries, book illustrations seen in childhood play a major role—PICTURES FROM ITALY recalls how as a child the author had responded to 'pictures in school-books' depicting, amongst 'The Wonders of the World', the leaning Tower of Pisa—that with Italy was fed from more various sources. For example, Dickens was familiar from an early age with refugee Italian street boys—and English boys pretending to be Italians—earning their living playing barrel-organs and displaying white mice, or selling plaster statuettes of saints and politicians (see LONDON: STREETS). It is conceivable that during the period at WARREN'S BLACKING warehouse he would compare his own plight to theirs. Street organists and 'Italian image boys' figure, not only in WORDSWORTH, George ELIOT, and Mayhew, but in several Dickens novels, including *Nicholas Nickleby* and *The Old Curiosity Shop*. It is thought Dickens may have reported the Old Bailey trial on 2 December 1831 of men accused of 'the wilful murder of the Italian boy . . . Carlo Ferrari, otherwise Charles Ferrier'; if so, we have a possible source for the many fake Italians in early Dickens, such as Muntle or Mantalini in *Nicholas Nickleby*, Bill Smith or Billsmethi in 'The Dancing Academy' (*SB*), and 'the splendid tenor . . .

Lobskini' in 'Sentiment' (*SB*). Later, Mazzini was to become the benefactor of these boys, and FORSTER recalls 'one Sunday evening . . . [he] made memorable by taking us to see the school he had established in Clerkenwell for the Italian organ-boys. This was after dining with Dickens, who had been brought into personal intercourse with the great Italian by having given money to a begging impostor who made unauthorized use of his name' (Forster 6.6). That Dickens might be prone to such duping is indicated in a letter of 17 April 1846, when he was dying to return to Genoa: 'I talk to all the Italian Boys who go about the streets with organs and white mice, and give them mints of money *per l'amore della bell'Italia*.

Yet another, perhaps greater driving force behind Dickens's *amore della bell'Italia* was the theatre, and its 'impostures'. His archetypal clown was Grimaldi, whose MEMOIRS he edited in 1838, and through whom he gained access as a child to Italian *commedia dell'arte* as this form was transposed into English PANTOMIME. But Italy in opera and ballet were also important at a slightly later stage of Dickens's youth, in particular through the various versions of the story of Masaniello (Auber's *La Muette de Portici* as well as others), the Neapolitan fisherman who led a revolt against the Spanish in the 17th century.

Everyone in the 19th century seems to have known *Masaniello*. 'We shall make a decided hit in Masaniello', says the stage manager in 'Mrs Joseph Porter' (*SB*), adding knowingly: 'Harleigh sings that music admirably.' Dickens jokes from Genoa to three separate correspondents—Forster, Mitton, STANFIELD—that the standard bathing costume he and everyone else wears looks like Masaniello's black-and-yellow. The point is that in the 19th century *Masaniello* was a kind of symbol of the *Risorgimento*—when Garibaldi came to Britain on a state visit in the 1860s he attended a performance at Covent Garden, where 'people noticed his close attention to that portion . . . dealing with liberty and love of country' (Harry Rudman, *Italian Nationalism and English Letters*, 1940). In Italy Dickens made a particular effort to mingle with Neapolitan fisherfolk—'I have got to understand the life of Naples (among the Fishermen and Idlers)'—and renders his tribute in *David Copperfield*, where they are still lovers

of liberty and subverters of orthodoxy. It is thanks to a modern Masaniella of personal morality that Little Em'ly survives her flight from Steerforth and gets back to England.

Dickens's book about his Italian travels of 1844–5, *Pictures from Italy*, implies the key word 'picturesque' on which his impressions of Italy were centred. He disliked artists and writers who went to Italy with 'grand tour' preconceptions of the aesthetic beauties they would find, or of the 'picturesque' charm of people whose daily reality was crippling poverty and oppressive government. A letter to Forster from Naples in February 1845 proposes an alternative approach to the 'picturesque': 'I am afraid that the conventional idea of the picturesque is associated with such misery and degradation that a new picturesque will have to be established as the world goes on.' This 'new picturesque', *Pictures from Italy* asserts, must criticize and work obliquely in the direction of progress: 'Painting and poetising for ever, if you will, the beauties of this most beautiful and lovely spot of earth, let us, as our duty, try to associate a new picturesque with some faint recognition of man's destiny.'

Likewise, the 'new picturesque' in *Pictures from Italy* was indirect in its treatment of Italy's political and social problems. The narrator immediately declares his 'strong conviction' on the subject of misgovernment in Italy, 'but as I chose when residing there, a Foreigner, to abstain from the discussion of any such questions with any order of Italians, so I would rather not enter on the inquiry now'. Dickens adopts the persona of the *flâneur*, here posing as a tourist casually strolling about the streets of Italian cities and observing passers-by. But through this persona an indirect, *physiognomical* critique of Italian society is mounted. Eschewing the overtly political, the narrator looks into the outward appearance of Italians for 'marks of weakness, marks of woe' (Blake, 'London')— or for the villainy of their oppressors, in the appearance of the priesthood of Genoa, for instance: 'if Nature's handwriting be at all legible, greater varieties of sloth, deceit, and intellectual torpor, could hardly be observed among any class of men in the world.' The authorities were not fooled, however, and the book was not published in Italy until 1879.

In this critique a clear separation is made between the Italian people and their governments. The 1869 statement often quoted as an expression of the quintessence of Dickens's politics—'my faith in the people governed is on the whole limitless, my faith in the people governing strictly limited' (*Speeches*, p. 407) —may owe much to his experience of Italy. 'So many jewels set in dirt' is the phrase in *Pictures from Italy*, where he praises 'the smiling face of the attendant, man or woman; the courteous manner; the amiable desire to please and be pleased'. Visiting the Carrara quarries, he finds in the formidable difficulty of making sculpture out of marble an allegory of the 'virtue that springs in miserable ground' in Italy. On 3 February 1860 he argues against CHORLEY's negative representation of Italy in his novel *Roccabella*: 'I believe they have the faults you ascribe to them (nationally, not individually), but I could not find it in my heart, remembering their miseries, to exhibit those faults without referring them back to their causes.' And the writer of 'The Country of Masaniello' (*AYR* 23 August 1862), on Naples, undoubtedly quotes the dying words of Cavour with Dickens's approval: 'there is much corruption in their country; but it is not their fault, poor people, they have been so badly governed!'

Even so, Dickens was not really active on behalf of Italy until after 1848. The famous war-correspondent W. H. Russell (himself a contributor on Italy to Dickens's periodicals) said that, at the time of his brief editorship of the *DAILY NEWS* in 1846 Dickens 'was ignorant and indifferent to what are called "Foreign Affairs"; indeed, he told me himself that he never thought about them till the Revolution of 1848' (Collins 1981, 1.76). It was first-hand experience of Italy and friendship with distinguished refugees that altered and developed his attitudes. 'I have known Mazzini and Gallenga', he said in 1860; 'Manin was tutor to my daughters in Paris' (3 February 1860). In August and September 1849, after the fall of Rome, he wrote and published from Tavistock House 'An Appeal to the English People on Behalf of the Italian Refugees'. He was so publicly identified with the Italian cause at that time that 'Morna' (Thomas O'Keefe) in an 1849 DETECTIVE NOVEL entitled *The Battle of London Life; or, Boz and his Secretary*, takes as its central figure a government spy engaged

unwittingly by Dickens who is investigating the novelist's involvement with Mazzini.

Italian critics of Dickens have always been more conscious of such issues than their English counterparts. For a writer like Ugo Piscopo, *Pictures from Italy* 'constitutes one of the most living and passionate of documents on the tragic social situation in Italy ... without any rhetoric or mystification' (*Europe*, December 1969); for most English readers it is a book which primarily records Dickens's reactions to Italian ART. That these were indeed deeply felt, especially in Venice, can be attested, not only from the book itself but also from Dickens's return pilgrimage to Italy in 1853 in the company of the painter Augustus Egg and Wilkie COLLINS, the son of a painter. The three travellers conducted animated critical discussions of the works seen during that journey. Dickens's own 'modern', realist preferences can be seen in a letter to Forster of 28 November 1853; he praises Tintoretto, whose work is 'more delightful and masterly than it is possible sufficiently to express. His Assembly of the Blest I do believe to be, take it all in all, the most wonderful and charming picture ever painted', and condemns conservative guidebook recommendations of what to see: 'You immediately obey, and tell your son to obey. He tells his son, and he tells his, and so the world gets three-fourths of its frauds and mysteries.'

Nevertheless, the most important artistic consequences of the attachment to Italy are to be found in creative writing, where political commitment is never far beneath the surface. Italy forms a sinister backdrop to Dickens's story 'TO BE READ AT DUSK' (*MP*), and 'The Italian Prisoner' (*UT*) depicts in the year of Garibaldi's revolt 'one of the vile old prisons of Italy ... below the waters of the harbour': 'its condition was insufferably foul.' It is in such surroundings in *Little Dorrit* that we meet Dickens's major Italian character, Giambattista ('John Baptist') Cavalletto, who bears the Christian name of the patron saint of Genoa. He stands as a symbol of the Italian common people in his combination of patience and speed and agility of gesture, 'a sunburnt quick, lithe, little man' pacing out his cell 'at a grotesque kind of jog-trot pace'.

Here too Dickens's Molly Bloom, Flora Finching, in a passage that might come from the last chapter of *Ulysses*, celebrates Italy's natural and verbal fecundity: 'In Italy is she really? With the grapes and figs growing everywhere and lava necklaces and bracelets too that land of poetry with burning mountains picturesque beyond belief though if the organ-boys come away from the neighbourhood not to be scorched nobody can wonder being so young and bringing their white mice with them most humane, and is she really in that favoured land with nothing but blue about her and dying gladiators and belvederas though Mr F. himself did not believe for his objection when in spirits was the images could not be true there being no medium between expensive quantities of linen . . . all in creases and none whatever.' Her fittingly rambling, poetic discourse offers tragicomic tribute to a land of disasters and inequalities in which, nonetheless, human warmth has not been so catastrophically lost as elsewhere. See map p. 615. MH

Clark, Mia J., 'Il giro di boa: Charles Dickens a Genova', *Critica Letteraria* (1983).

Hollington, Michael, 'Dickens and Italy', *Journal of Anglo-Italian Studies* (1991).

# J

**Japan.** Lafcadio Hearn, who taught English Literature at Tokyo University (1896–1903), discouraged his students from reading Dickens. Dickens was so English in Hearn's view that Japanese students could hardly be expected to understand his novels until they had gone to England and experienced London life. But Shoyo Tsubouchi (1859–1935), a major figure in the modernization of Japanese literature, is remembered as the first Japanese Dickensian without experience of London life. His poor showing in an examination on *Hamlet* at Tokyo University stimulated Shoyo to read all the English novels available then in the university library. *Pickwick Papers* and *Oliver Twist* were of crucial importance to him in the formation of his theory of the novel—*Shosetsu Shinzui* (The Essence of the Novel, 1885–6), which was most influential in the making of modern Japanese literature.

There were at least two more great literary contemporaries with Shoyo who were very much concerned with Dickens. One was Roka Tokutomi (1868–1927), whose autobiographical novel *Omoide no Ki* (Memoirs, 1902) was inspired by *David Copperfield*. The other was Soseki Natsume (1867–1916), an outstanding figure in modern Japanese literature, who was endowed with a Dickensian vein of humour and social criticism. He had two years' experience of London life studying English Literature at the University of London (1900–2). Soseki's *Botchan* (Young Master, 1906) has aspects interestingly comparable with *Nicholas Nickleby*. Botchan is a loveable young hero, but he is 'too simple minded and inexperienced', as Soseki comments, 'to be reconciled to complex society'. At the denouement of the novel, Botchan plays the part of a Nicholas Nickleby against the senior master of the school where he was employed as a novice teacher.

No complete TRANSLATION of any of Dickens's major works appeared until January 1914, when a translation of *Oliver Twist* began to be serialized in a daily paper under the title *Kozakura Shinkichi. A Christmas Carol, Oliver Twist, A Tale of Two Cities* and *David Copperfield* were the four novels best known to a Japanese audience through translations or as textbooks in English classes. The new bearings of Dickensian interest in Japan were marked by two events: publication of Tadao Yamamoto's *Growth and System of the Language of Dickens* (1950; rev. edn. 1952) and the establishment of the Japan Branch of the DICKENS FELLOWSHIP in 1970. Many entirely new or improved Japanese translations of Dickens's novels have been published during the past few decades. *Nicholas Nickleby* and *Dombey and Son* are the only two major novels yet to be translated. Critical studies are also numerous.

Such a wide range of interest in Dickens's world and increasing reassessment of it have made an impact on some Japanese writers. For example, Kunio Tsuji, one of the representative contemporary writers, showed a lively response to Dickens, suggestively analysing Dickens's creative vision and comparing it with Proust's. And Kenzaburo Oe, the Nobel prizewinner in 1994, has written a novel *Kirupu no Gundan* (A Legion of Quilps, 1988), based, as the title suggests, upon *The Old Curiosity Shop*.  MM

**Jeffrey, Francis Lord** (1773–1850), a founder of the *Edinburgh Review* and its most influential editor (1803–29), was a warm admirer of Dickens, calling himself Dickens's 'Critic Laureate'. The first review of a Dickens work in the *Edinburgh Review* had been of *Oliver Twist* in October 1838, which Dickens assumed Jeffrey had written (in fact, it was by Thomas Lister). Jeffrey and Dickens met for the first time in 1839. The 67-year-old judge, Whig MP (1831–4), and literary critic was much taken with the 27-year-old novelist: 'I have struck up what I mean to be an eternal and intimate friendship', Jeffrey wrote (Cockburn 1852, 4 May 1841). Jeffrey was instrumental in setting up the Edinburgh dinner honouring Dickens in June 1841 (see SCOTLAND). Dickens asked Jeffrey to be godfather to his third son, Francis Jeffrey Dickens

(1844). When in London, Jeffrey used to drop in informally on Dickens, who for his part was charmed by 'the way in which he has lived through all that Blue and Yellow, and remained so tender, true, and earnest' (to William Empson, 28 November 1845).

Jeffrey's weeping over Little Nell is famous, and he was warmly appreciative of Dickens's advocacy for the poor in The CHIMES: 'Blessings on your kind heart . . . your great talisman' (Cockburn 2.308; 12 December 1844). The CRICKET ON THE HEARTH was dedicated to Jeffrey in December 1845. Jeffrey was loyal enough to praise even The BATTLE OF LIFE for its 'generous sentiments', though recognizing its artistic weaknesses (see Pilgrim 5.24 n.). The last work for which there is a record of Jeffrey's reaction was Dombey and Son, where he admired the death of Paul: he preferred Dickens's SENTIMENTAL characters to his GROTESQUE ones. Dickens sent him a proof of the tenth number of David Copperfield, found unopened beside his bed after his death in January 1850.                                    KC

Cockburn, H. T., The Life of Lord Jeffrey, with a Selection of his Correspondence, 2 vols. (1852).

**Jerrold, Douglas William** (1803–57), dramatist and journalist, first met Dickens in 1836 when, disillusioned by the meagre rewards of playwriting (despite the enormous success of his best-known play, the nautical MELODRAMA Black-Ey'd Susan, or All in the Downs, of 1829), he was switching to a primarily journalistic career (see DRAMA AND DRAMATISTS DURING DICKENS'S LIFETIME). Although Dickens failed to recruit him as a contributor to BENTLEY'S MISCELLANY, Jerrold and he became good friends, sharing as they did almost identical views on most political and social matters. (This ideological closeness made their famous later quarrel over the question of ending public executions —Jerrold feared, rightly, that this would simply delay the total abolition of CAPITAL PUNISHMENT—all the more noteworthy.) Dickens's most radical story, The CHIMES (1844), was strongly influenced by Jerrold and he was present when Dickens gave a private reading of it. Jerrold's fame and influence had increased considerably as a result of his writings for PUNCH from 1841; in the pages of this widely circulated comic weekly he waged bitter satiric warfare against well-fed, moralizing magistrates dealing out harsh justice to the desperately poor, pontificating high-earning prelates, game-reserving landowners, and all who exploited or were indifferent to the plight of the poor. Dickens applauded his work, so full of 'gallant truths' (16 November 1844), and praised his 'Story of a Feather' (about a lovely young orphan struggling to earn an honest living in the slums) as 'a wise and beautiful book'. He fully shared Jerrold's unease in 1846 when Punch appeared to be becoming less earnest in its concern with social matters and going in for an 'eternal gaffaw' about everything (Pilgrim 4.643 n.). Jerrold was professionally associated with Dickens only once, when he wrote leaders for the DAILY NEWS during Dickens's brief editorship (1846), but, like other members of the Punch circle, he acted in Dickens's AMATEUR THEATRICALS, his Master Stephen in Every Man In His Humour being much admired (by Queen Victoria among others). Dickens began a description, written as if by Mrs Gamp, of the Amateur Players' journey to Manchester and had the delightful idea of making Mrs Gamp an indignant defender of Jerrold's most famous creation in Punch, Mrs Caudle, deliverer of nightly 'curtain lectures' to her hapless spouse; Mrs Gamp sees Jerrold charming the ladies, 'pretty delooded creeturs which never know'd that sweet saint, Mrs C., as I did, and being treated with as much confidence as if he'd never wiolated none of the domestic ties, and never showed up nothing! Oh the aggrawation of that Dougladge!' (Forster 6.1). Jerrold never wrote for Household Words but his eldest son Blanchard contributed frequently. Following Jerrold's sudden death Dickens threw himself into organizing a series of readings, lectures, and dramatic performances to raise a fund for his widow and unmarried daughter (it was these activities that brought the TERNAN FAMILY into Dickens's life). Blanchard Jerrold's unavailing public protests that his family did not need financial help annoyed Dickens, but there was no permanent breach and Dickens responded to Blanchard's request to contribute some reminiscences to a biography Blanchard was writing of his father by supplying a most tender and moving account of his first and last meetings with Jerrold.                    MS

Jerrold, Blanchard, Life and Remains of Douglas Jerrold (1859).

Jerrold, Walter, *Douglas Jerrold, Dramatist and Wit* (1914).

Kelly, R. M., *Douglas Jerrold* (1972).

Slater, Michael, 'Carlyle and Jerrold into Dickens: A Study of *The Chimes*', *Dickens Centennial Essays*, ed. A. Nisbet and B. Nevius (1971).

**Jews.** Dickens was relatively free of the conventional anti-Semitism prevalent among the early Victorians especially. As a Christian of extremely Broad Church, even at times UNITARIAN views, who was disgusted by sectarianism and debates about doctrine, he had no strong theological reason to be hostile to Judaism (see CHURCH OF ENGLAND). He disliked what he understood to be the letter and spirit of the Old Testament, but his recognized enemies in this regard were Christians —Puritans, Calvinists, EVANGELICALS. There is little evidence that he thought about Judaism in connection with the Old Testament or religious ideas very much at all. In *A CHILD'S HISTORY OF ENGLAND* he sadly records in some detail the inexcusable and cruel persecutions and expulsion of the Jews by Edward I in 1290 (*CHE* 16), and in 1861 he reports with great distaste Thomas CARLYLE's intensifying 'aversion to Jews' (Johnson 2.969).

But if Dickens was relatively free of anti-Semitism, he was certainly not entirely free of it. The depiction of Fagin in *Oliver Twist*, of course, drew upon many Jewish stereotypes. In a letter to FORSTER, Dickens refers to Richard BENTLEY, with whom he was quarrelling about money among other things, by quoting Bill Sikes' characterization of Fagin as an 'infernal, rich, plundering, thundering old Jew' (?5 August 1837). The reference underscores Dickens's prejudice, but also complicates it, for, as well he knew, Bentley was not Jewish. The expression, that is, both embodies a stereotype and self-consciously deploys it *as* a stereotype. There are other repugnant instances of such expressions scattered casually among the early works especially and in a few letters.

Dickens experienced a change of heart thanks to Eliza Davis, the wife of the Jewish banker to whom Dickens had sold the lease on his residence Tavistock House, and with whom he had had very congenial dealings. She pointed out to him that the portrait of Fagin did 'a great wrong' to Jews, and though Dickens tried to defend his representation, he was also evidently sufficiently troubled to take positive steps to correct it (Johnson 2:1010). Thus, in *Our Mutual Friend* Dickens introduces the character Riah, a noble old man whose unhappy employment is to play the stereotypical Jewish moneylender as a front for a Christian. Riah both belies the stereotype and speaks eloquently about prejudice: as he says, 'it is not, in Christian countries, with the Jews as with other peoples. Men say, "this is a bad Greek, but there are good Greeks. This is a bad Turk, but there are good Turks." Not so with the Jews . . . they take the worst of us as samples of the best; they take the lowest of us as presentations of the highest; and they say, "All Jews are alike" ' (*OMF* 4.9). In fleeing her two would-be lovers, Lizzie Hexam in the same novel hides in the country among a small Jewish community that befriends her. And in revising *Oliver Twist* for the Charles Dickens Edition of 1867, finally, Dickens eliminated or altered most of the many references to Fagin as 'the Jew'.     RN

**Johnson, Samuel** (1709–84), lexicographer, biographer, critic, essayist, and colossus of 18th-century letters, whose works remained prescribed reading throughout the 19th century, as Mrs GASKELL's *Cranford* (1853, ch. 1) suggests. Dickens was familiar with Johnson's *Lives of the Poets*, with *Rasselas*, the *Rambler*, and above all with his opinions and conversation as revealed in Boswell's famous *Life* of 1791. Dickens's efforts to provide for Johnson's penniless god-daughter in 1855–6 testify to his long-standing admiration for Johnson's contribution to the dignity of literature (see Pilgrim 7 and 8, Appendices).     JMLD

**Jonson, Ben** (1572–1637), poet and playwright. Jonson was best known for such comedies as *Every Man In His Humour* (1598), *Volpone* (1605), *Epicoene; or The Silent Woman* (1609), *The Alchemist* (1610), and *Bartholomew Fair* (1610). Many of his plays, intricately plotted and highly moralistic, have a feel for London low life; he depicts con-men and their dupes and creates a gallery of low comedy characters, developing a tradition which was to influence subsequent generations of comic dramatists and novelists, including FIELDING and Dickens. His comedies are usually set in contemporary London, refer to local topography, use the vernacular language of the time, and have a topicality which, again, is reflected in Dickens's work. Like Dickens he is at his weakest in portraying female characters, unless they are grotesques or eccentrics.

Northrop Frye has argued that Dickens uses the New Comedy structure, transmitted from Terence and Plautus via Jonson and Molière, in his novels. The far-fetched plots, a society divisible into the congenial and obstructive, and obsessive characters identified by specific humours, are common to both authors. Jonson had developed the notion of the comedy of humours not only to ridicule characters dominated by a single obsession, but also to create the need for action through their obsessions. In characters such as Bounderby in *Hard Times*, Pecksniff in *Martin Chuzzlewit*, or Ralph Nickleby, Dickens also draws on this technique, which is pervasive throughout his novels. In 1845 Dickens organized an AMATEUR THEATRICAL performance of *Every Man In His Humour*, the play through which Jonson introduced the 'comedy of humours' to the English stage, playing the boastful and cowardly Captain Bobadil, 'with an air of supreme conceit and frothy pomp', to great acclaim. He repeated this performance on subsequent occasions and also commenced rehearsals of *The Alchemist*, in which he was to play Sir Epicure Mammon, in 1847. Although the latter production was abandoned after a couple of rehearsals, FORSTER says the latter role was 'as good as anything he had done' (6.1). Dickens's admiration for Jonson was tempered by a sense that, whilst he may be rare, he could be heavy too (to Macready, 2 September 1845).

JD

Northrop Frye, 'Dickens and the Comedy of Humors', in Roy Harvey Pearce (ed.), *Experience in the Novel* (1968).

**journalism.** See JOURNALIST, DICKENS AS; NEWSPAPERS.

**journalist, Dickens as.** For so much of the 20th century Dickens studies have revolved around assessing and reassessing Dickens the novelist that perhaps inevitably assessments of Dickens as a journalist, if they have been made at all, have tended to place the two roles in a kind of binary opposition that would have puzzled his contemporaries. Almost everything that Dickens published, by virtue of appearing in NEWSPAPERS, magazines, or 'numbers', could be technically classified as journalism—and frequently was by early reviewers—while its internal structure, narrative strategies, its very topicality gave it an intrinsically journalistic flavour. According to the influential mid-Victorian critic Walter BAGEHOT, the grid-like structure of the modern city and its buildings had made London 'like a newspaper', and Dickens had succeeded in describing it 'like a special correspondent for posterity' ('Charles Dickens', *National Review*, 7, 1858). For Dickens's contemporaries, it may be surmised, Dickens's unique talent lay neither in novel-writing nor in journalism *per se*, but rather in brilliantly combining the two, and in so doing, changing the generic definitions of literature. Nevertheless, through a process Dickens himself introduced, it quickly came to be his works of fiction—periodical novels, the Christmas books and stories—that were rescued into volume form, acknowledged by the author, and republished cheaply, while the non-fiction—reports, sketches, articles, reviews, essays, and so forth—tended to remain in perishable form, untouched and often unascribed. *Sketches by Boz*, REPRINTED PIECES, and *The UNCOMMERCIAL TRAVELLER* were in fact the only collections of journalism republished by Dickens during his lifetime, but they together represent less than half of the canon. In round figures, Dickens published some 350 self-contained papers in magazines and newspapers (not including collaborations), which, for want of more comprehensive definition, may be constructively considered as journalism. At a conservative estimate, this is well over a million words, and substantial enough as an oeuvre to be assessed in its own right. Three main, overlapping phases can be distinguished in Dickens's journalistic career, in which he functions principally as a newspaper reporter and sketch-writer (1831–6), as a reviewer and commentator (1834–49), and as an editor and essayist (1846, 1850–70).

### Newspaper Reporter and Sketch-Writer (1831–6)

The story of Dickens's introduction to the craft of reporting has often been told, but usually as a preliminary to profiles of Dickens the novelist. At the age of 16, shortly before leaving employment as a lawyer's clerk in the firm of ELLIS AND BLACKMORE, Dickens acquired a half-guinea copy of Thomas Gurney's popular shorthand treatise, *Brachyography* (1750), probably in the fifteenth edition (1824), edited by the author's grandson. Until the advent of Pitman's superior system in 1837 Gurney's was the method commonly used by parliamentary reporters, at a time when the speed and accuracy of their transcripts of debates could make or break a newspaper. Dickens patiently set about teaching himself the system, but early in 1829, while his knowledge was still imperfect, found work as a freelance shorthand writer at Doctors' Commons, a series of law courts near St Paul's Cathedral dealing in naval and ecclesiastical affairs. This general career move seems to have been prompted by his father, John DICKENS'S, successful re-employment as a journalist, variously, for the *British Press* (*c*.1826), the *Morning Herald* (1827–8), and subsequently as a shorthand reporter for the MIRROR OF PARLIAMENT, which had been set up in 1828 by Dickens's maternal uncle, John Henry Barrow (see RELATIVES AND DESCENDANTS OF DICKENS). Having eventually tamed 'the savage stenographic mystery' (of which he was to leave a memorable description in chapter 38 of *David Copperfield*), Dickens joined the staff of the *Mirror* in 1831, and in 1832, in a supernumerary capacity, that of the TRUE SUN, a radical evening newspaper which boasted John FORSTER, Douglas JERROLD, and Leigh HUNT as contributors. For at least three sessions of Parliament (1832–4) Dickens recorded debates from the galleries of the old Houses of Parliament: exhausting and high-pressure work, in which he came to excel. According to fellow-reporter and friend Thomas Beard (1807–91), Dickens's command of Gurney's system was nothing short of 'perfect' and 'there never was such a reporter', while the journalist Charles Mackay (1814–89), sub-editor of the MORNING CHRONICLE during Dickens's time there, concluded that his young colleague was 'universally considered the rapidest and most accurate shorthand reporter in the gallery'. While Dickens was making what he called this 'great splash in the gallery' (Forster 1.4), the most eminent and grandiloquent politicians of the day were debating such key issues as Parliamentary REFORM, Catholic emancipa-

tion, the abolition of slave labour in the colonies, the future of the East India Company, amendments to the Poor Law, reductions in the taxes on newspapers, Sunday observance, and dozens of other legislative proposals which were to affect British society at the start of the Victorian era (see ROMAN CATHOLIC CHURCH; MONEY AND FINANCE; POOR RELIEF). In the process of transcribing such debates, first in shorthand, and then in longhand for the compositors, Dickens was clearly absorbing a great deal of information, and forming opinions about politicians and the parliamentary process, that were to stay with him for the duration of his life (see POLITICS). He was paid an average of 15 guineas a week for the privilege, but the work was sessional, which helps explain why, in December 1833, he found time to contribute papers to the MONTHLY MAGAZINE, and why in the autumn of 1834, he accepted a post as a staff reporter on the *Morning Chronicle* for the smaller, but regular, salary of 5 guineas a week (see MONEY VALUES).

Over the next two years, the Whig-owned *Morning Chronicle* provided Dickens with an intense and varied experience of newspaper reporting. 'There never was anybody connected with newspapers, who, in the same space of time, had so much express and post-chaise experience as I', he recalled in 1845 (Forster 1.4), and he announced in 1865 that he had 'never forgotten the fascination of that old pursuit' (*Speeches*, p. 347). The *Chronicle*'s veteran editor, John BLACK, seems to have known how to exploit Dickens's talents. In addition to being sent to cover public events and ceremonies throughout the country, from October 1834 his pen was also requisitioned for numerous theatrical reviews and 'Street Sketches' in the *Chronicle*, and, from January 1835, for 'Sketches of London' in its tri-weekly offshoot, the EVENING CHRONICLE. In recognition of this extra work, 2 guineas a week was added to his salary. In all that has been identified of Dickens's early work for the paper, a distinctive journalistic voice may be detected, sprightly and genial in tone, precise in its recording of detail and dialogue, but merciless in its ridicule of sham and imposture. Nevertheless, Dickens's brief as a reporter and sketch-writer did not require him to produce in-depth analyses of public affairs, and when permitted to trespass into politics, in such papers as 'The Story Without a Beginning' (18 December 1834), he always did so in a humorous and satirical vein. It was in just such a guise—comic, critical, political, but relatively non-party—that Dickens began to make an impact independently in literary circles, with his collected volumes of sketches and papers published under the pseudonym 'BOZ' (*SB* First and Second Series, *PP*, *OT*, *SYG*, *SYC*). As a literary figure, however, he was still unavoidably 'connected with the newspapers'. Boz was, above all, a journalistic personality, and it was the name Boz that publisher Richard BENTLEY wanted to acquire, when he employed Dickens as the editor of his monthly *Miscellany* in November 1836, following the latter's resignation from the staff of the *Chronicle* (see BENTLEY'S MISCELLANY). This newspaper connection in part accounted for the bafflement of early reviewers with the success of Dickens's writing as 'literature', and their bafflement is as eloquent of changing trends in the definition and status of literature and journalism at the start of the Victorian period, as it is of the essentially journalistic nature of Dickens's comic fiction.

### Reviewer and Commentator (1834–49)
Due to the nature of Bentley's venture, Dickens's opportunities for shaping and directing the *Miscellany* as its nominal editor were limited, and in his farewell 'Epistle', resigning from the post, he lamented that it had 'always been literally Bentley's . . . and never mine' (vol. 5, no. 26 (February 1839), p. 220). His 'Stray Chapters by Boz' and the two 'MUDFOG PAPERS' constitute some attempt to inject something satirical and topical into the journal, but for the most part it lacked direction. Thereafter, Dickens proceeded on the one hand to enhance, as he saw it, the literary value of his serial fiction, by imitating in *Nicholas Nickleby* and MASTER HUMPHREY'S CLOCK the manner of the well-known 18th-century periodical ESSAYISTS, and on the other, to progress to a more serious kind of journalistic work, through his connection with the weekly EXAMINER newspaper. With John Forster as sub-editor from 1836 and then editor of the *Examiner* from 1847 to 1855, Dickens was able and invited to commentate on or review a wide range of topics and publications. The result was a total of over 40 art-

icles, many lengthy, which not only display a serious commitment to liberal reform, in line with the well-known ethos of the paper, but also reveal surprising areas of personal interest and expertise on the part of the author. Sir Walter SCOTT's relationship with his publishers is analysed, and the dignity of literature asserted in a series of three carefully researched articles (2 September 1838, 31 March and 29 September 1839). Opinions on art and drama are given an aesthetic and ethical framework, when Dickens discusses the virtues of MACREADY's acting, the engravings of CRUIKSHANK in aid of the temperance movement (see DRINK AND TEMPERANCE), and the dainty caricatures of John LEECH (4 March 1843, 8 July and 30 December 1848). The existence of ghosts and the status of GHOST STORIES is considered in a sceptical review of Catherine Crowe's *Night Side of Nature* (26 February 1848). The wisdom of the foreign, as opposed to the home MISSION, and colonial attitudes to Africa are questioned at length in an article on the disastrous Niger Expedition of 1841 (19 August 1848) (see TRAVEL AND EXPLORATION). Opinions on challenging discoveries in the fields of biology, geology, astronomy, and chemistry, and their presentation to the world, are delivered in a review of a recent scientific publication (9 December 1848). The case of the notorious Mr Drouet, accused of criminally neglecting the children living in his 'Infant Pauper Asylum', is analysed and followed through the courts, in a series of four cogently argued articles (20 and 27 January, 3 March, 21 April 1849). Numerous articles, based as much on factual material (government statistics, commissioner's reports, recent court cases, etc.) as on fanciful personal observation, deal with the spirit and application of the LAW, CRIME, punishment, and the influence of EDUCATION and environment on all three (see PRISONS). In writing these papers, as the 20th-century experts who have brought many of them to light conclude, Dickens 'learned to be a journalist rather than a reporter' (A.W. Brice and K. J. Fielding, 'A New Article by Dickens' etc., *Dickens Studies Annual*, 9, 1981).

### Newspaper and Magazine Editor (1846, 1850–70)
Dickens was never more than an occasional contributor to the *Examiner*, however, and

throughout the 1840s seems to have aspired to a more central role in the mediation of public affairs to the people, and the addressing of urgent social issues. The letters written and journal kept during his American trip in 1842, for example, later worked up into AMERICAN NOTES, show a remarkable seriousness of purpose, and a strict, journalistic preoccupation with attempting to capture all impressions of a scene, whether flattering to his hosts or no. Shortly after his return he expressed an interest in reviving the recently defunct *Courier* newspaper, writing to Lady Holland that '[t]he notion of this newspaper was bred in me by my old training—I was as well acquainted with the management of one, some years ago, as an Engineer is with the Steam Engine'. Dickens also felt that it was the subjects which most newspaper writers left unhandled which were 'exactly the questions which interest the people . . . most' (11 July 1842). His correspondence also shows him seriously considering becoming a police magistrate, or applying for 'some Commissionership, or Inspectorship', in order to turn his 'social knowledge to practical account' (? June 1842; 20 June 1846), and it was during this period that he first began to act as a consultant and agent for Angela Burdett COUTTS and assist her in her philanthropic projects (see CHARITY). It is in this context of frustrated idealism searching for a practical outlet that his questionable decision to take on the editorship of the DAILY NEWS must perhaps be viewed. At first sight, the episode appears to gainsay Dickens's presumption of familiarity with the management of a newspaper. Recriminations and accusations of incompetence abounded, none acuter than the recollections of J. T. Danson, the man engaged by Dickens to write on financial and commercial topics, and who wrote two of the three leaders in the first edition of the paper. Dickens, Danson recorded in 1895, understood nothing of political economy or finance, which was a considerable failing in one whose post made him responsible for taking an intelligent and well-considered stance upon every public question. Dickens was in favour of good government and against corruption, like the rest of the liberal-minded public, 'but of how he was to serve them, except by giving way to their chief popular tendencies, as touching such matters he was really ignorant,

and felt himself so' (see K. J. Fielding, 'Dickens as J. T. Danson Knew Him', *Dickensian*, 1972). For his part, the great TIMES correspondent William Howard Russell (1820–1907) concluded that while Dickens 'was the best reporter in London . . . as a journalist he was nothing more', lacking political understanding and knowledge of or interest in foreign affairs (J. B. Atkins, *Life of Sir William Howard Russell*, 1911, vol. 1, p. 58).

Russell's conclusion from the affair that 'Dickens was not a good Editor' should perhaps be emended by the insertion of the word 'newspaper' as a qualifier, as the history of Dickens's triumphant founding, management, and editing of *Household Words* (1850–9) and *All the Year Round* (1859–70) suggest. The early-20th-century press baron Lord Northcliffe (1865–1922) redressed the balance appropriately, when praising Dickens as 'the greatest magazine editor either of his own or any other age', and it was doubtless these highly successful and durable examples of popular journalism that he had in mind (Johnson 2.717). Their history should be read as the natural continuation of Dickens's early training as a reporter and sketcher of metropolitan life, and his later experience as a reviewer and commentator.

While it is true that in simple terms of output Dickens contributed far less to *All the Year Round* than he had to *Household Words* (49 articles in *AYR* as opposed to 108 in *HW*, aside from COLLABORATIONS), numerous critics and admirers over the years have been in accord with Grahame Smith's recent conclusion that the later publication represents 'the summit of [Dickens's] journalistic career' and 'the climax' of his work as a periodical essayist (1996, pp. 80, 82). This is mainly on account of the papers collected under the title *The Uncommercial Traveller* (1860; first complete edn. 1898), which, as well as testifying, in design, research, and execution, to Dickens's consummate skill as an investigative journalist, arguably contain some of Dickens's finest writing in any genre.

Apart from *The Uncommercial Traveller*, Dickens republished only two other collections of his own journalism: *Reprinted Pieces* (1858), containing 28 items from *Household Words*, somewhat randomly selected, and *Sketches by Boz* (complete edn. 1839), to which he added a Preface in 1850, apologizing for the many 'imperfections' of the sketches, and their 'marks of haste and inexperience'. The first major posthumous collection, by no means complete, was made by B. W. MATZ in volumes 35 and 36 of Chapman and Hall's 'National Edition', which appeared in 1908 as MISCELLANEOUS PAPERS. This was supplemented 60 years later by Harry Stone's two-volume edition of composite articles by Dickens and one or more collaborators, taken from *Household Words* (*Uncollected Writings*, etc.). *The Dent Uniform Edition of Dickens's Journalism* in four volumes (1994–   ), edited and annotated by Michael Slater, promises to be the first scholarly collection and listing to be published. Readers of such collections of Dickens's journalism may occasionally feel disposed to question its literary merit, and may perhaps agree with B. W. Matz that 'some of the material . . . is of quite ephemeral interest and value' ('Dickens as a Journalist', *Fortnightly Review*, NS 498 (1 May 1908). On the other hand, G. K. CHESTERTON puts aesthetic considerations into perspective when he concludes that Dickens was 'a great novelist; but . . . also, among other things, a good journalist . . . it is often necessary for a good journalist to write bad literature' (1911, p. 242). A case in point might be Dickens's impassioned address 'To Working Men' on the subject of a recent cholera epidemic, which replaced a more frivolous piece as the *Household Words* leader for 7 October 1854. 'It behoves every journal-

ist', Dickens wrote (including himself under that denomination) 'at this time when the memory of an awful pestilence is fresh among us . . . to warn his readers . . . that unless they set themselves in earnest to improve the towns in which they live, and to amend the dwellings of the poor, they are guilty . . . of wholesale murder' (p. 1). In such cases, questions of literary value become immediately obscured by, if not secondary to, those of social message, dissemination, and propaganda, which beg for historical contextualization or other imported forms of information in order to be judged. While readers of Dickens's fiction might find it hard to overturn G. M. Young's famous verdict that in 'all Dickens's work' he seems 'equally ready to denounce on the grounds of humanity all who left things alone, and on the grounds of liberty all who tried to make them better' (*Early Victorian England*, 1934, vol. 2, p. 456), informed readers of Dickens's non-fiction are likely to agree with Humphry HOUSE that this 'is hardly true at all of the occasional journalism' (1941, p. 201 n.). Furthermore, few readers will fail to discover in much of Dickens's periodical and newspaper journalism, the same capacity to move to anger, laughter, or sorrow, and the same linguistic artistry that characterizes his periodical novels.

JMLD

*Dickens' Journalism*, ed. Michael Slater, 4 vols. (1994–2000).

# K

**Kafka, Franz** (1883–1924), Expressionist prose writer. Dickens was important for Modernist writers like Eliot and Joyce, and widely read in liberal Jewish circles of the period (Freud, Adorno, Zweig). It is not altogether surprising, then, that Kafka should have found both technical and thematic inspiration in his work.

An entry in Kafka's *Diaries* for 1917 ('Dickens's *Copperfield*. "The Stoker" a sheer imitation of Dickens, the projected novel even more so'), indicates why his novel *Der Verschollene* (*The Man Who Was Lost*, published 1927 with the title *Amerika*) is frequently studied as a rewriting of *David Copperfield*. Its itinerant 16-year-old hero Karl Rossmann has been rejected by his parents because of his sexual indiscretions with a servant-girl and sent to America, where he encounters various more and less satisfactory foster-parents. Like David, he is an innocent who is exploited and subjected to various forms of cruelty by the predators he encounters, rather than a conventional street-wise *picaro*. In particular, his attempts to defend a box containing his most precious possessions echo incidents in David's life, particularly during the flight to Dover.

But Kafka's later novels also bear considerable traces of Dickens's influence. The same diary entry comments on Dickens's 'use of vague, abstract metaphors', also manifestly to be found in *Der Prozeß* (*The Trial*), which has been persuasively compared to *Bleak House* and *Das Schloß* (*The Castle*), which has been linked, with somewhat less success, to *Great Expectations*. In this perspective, *Der Verschollene*, with its combination of social and psychoanalytic motifs, could be seen as a key transitional work connecting Dickens's 'Romantic Realism' to full-blown Modernist abstraction. The comparison between Dickens and Kafka thus offers two-way illumination —of Dickens as proto-Modernist as well as of Kafka as Expressionist Realist—and militates against the simplistic Modernist–Realist binary opposition too frequently encountered in contemporary criticism.  MH

Spilka, Mark, *Dickens and Kafka* (1963).

**Kean, Charles** (1811–68), son of the actor Edmund Kean and a leading member of the theatrical profession during the lifetime of Dickens. As one of MACREADY's chief rivals he was never part of Dickens's immediate circle; and although Dickens's public references to Kean were always respectful, in private letters to FORSTER, his wife, and Edmund YATES he was largely disparaging: 'Kean be blowed', he wrote of the acclaim for Kean's Drury Lane Hamlet in 1838 (see DICKENS, CATHERINE). In 1854, after an approach from Samuel Phelps concerning relief for the actress Mrs Warner, Dickens refused to allow his name to be used to justify a representation to Kean. In 1848 Kean was appointed Queen Victoria's director of private theatricals at Windsor, and he achieved considerable renown after he and his wife became co-managers of the Princess's Theatre from 1850 to 1859. During these years he employed members of the TERNAN FAMILY at various times. He was very concerned to foster the social respectability of the profession and, like Dickens, was involved in the ROYAL GENERAL THEATRICAL FUND and the founding of the Royal Dramatic College. Of Kean's involvement with the latter charity Dickens declared that 'the large spirit of an artist, the feeling of a man, and the grace of a gentleman have been most admirably blended' (*Speeches*, p. 276).  JD

**Keeley, Robert** (1793–1869) and **Mary** (1806–99). Robert Keeley, a popular comic actor who gave acting lessons to Dickens in his youth (Johnson 1.60), specialized in passive, cowardly roles, requiring bewilderment and resignation. Dickens admired his restraint and pathos, praising his ability to range from SHAKESPEAREAN clowns to broad farce. In 1829 he married Mary Ann Goward, whose strength was in soubrette parts and waifs. She was famed for breeches roles such as Jack Sheppard and Smike (in STIRLING's 1838 Adelphi *Nicholas Nickleby*), as whom Dickens felt she was 'excellent, bating sundry choice sentiments and rubbish regarding the little robins in the fields' (to Forster, 23

November 1838). Concerning these interpolations, Dickens reputedly turned to the prompter, saying, 'Damn the robins; cut them out' (*Westminster Gazette*, 13 March 1899). In subsequent Dickens adaptations at the Adelphi Mrs Keeley played Oliver Twist (1839) and Little Nell (1840) and, at the Strand, Barnaby Rudge (1841). In 1844 the Keeleys became the managers of the Lyceum Theatre, where they staged Stirling's *Martin Chuzzlewit*, with Mrs Keeley as Master Bailey and Keeley as Sairey Gamp. Dickens advised them during rehearsals and subsequently assisted them with staging The CRICKET ON THE HEARTH (1845), and The BATTLE OF LIFE (1846), which opened two days after the story's publication. The Keeleys had also presented The CHIMES in 1845, with Keeley as Trotty Veck. Dickens had much admired their performances in MACREADY's Drury Lane *The Merchant of Venice* (1841) and felt that Keeley's Verges (Drury Lane, 1843) was so striking that it put Dogberry in the shade. The Keeleys were also associated with Benjamin WEBSTER at the Haymarket and, briefly, with Charles KEAN at the Princess's Theatre. Mrs Keeley was often present at Dickens's private theatricals and readings. JD

**Kent.** London excepted, no part of the British Isles features more prominently in Dickens's life and art than Kent. FORSTER declared Rochester 'the birthplace of his fancy' (1.1). Kent might be deemed its native soil.

Dickens's first experience of Kent was probably at the beginning of 1817, when his father, a clerk in the Navy Pay Office, was attached to Sheerness dockyard (see DICKENS, JOHN). He found lodgings for himself and his family, it is believed, next door to the Sheerness Theatre.

In April John Dickens was transferred to the dockyard in Chatham. He rented a house overlooking Rochester and the dockyard basin, at 2 Ordnance Terrace, Chatham (see HOMES OF DICKENS). The next five years were probably the happiest of Dickens's childhood. Rochester, contiguous with Chatham, remained dear to him throughout his life. In Chatham the foundations of his EDUCATION were laid, first by his mother, next at a dame-school in Rome Lane, and finally, from 1821, at a school in Best Street conducted by William Giles. Giles was a son of a minister of the Baptist chapel next door to 18 St Mary's Place, The Brook, to which the Dickens family moved that summer. Though some of his financial problems date from this period, John Dickens evidently cut something of a figure in Chatham. Allowances and increments increased his income substantially. He was gregarious and took an active part in local affairs. He encouraged ambition in his son, Charles. A favourite country walk took them past Gad's Hill Place, in the village of Higham. His father promised Dickens that 'he might himself live in it, or in some such house when he came to be a man, if he would only work hard enough' (Forster 1.1).

In June 1822 John Dickens was transferred to the headquarters of the Navy Pay Office in London. Dickens remained in Chatham at school, under Giles's care, possibly for another three months, before joining the rest of the family in Camden Town.

There is evidence to suggest the family kept in touch with friends in Kent during the intervening years, but the next well-documented visit to the county by Dickens was in 1836. In April of that year he spent his honeymoon in the village of Chalk, near Gravesend. In February the following year he returned to the village with Catherine DICKENS for a month's holiday.

Later in 1837 they took a summer holiday in Broadstairs. In 1839 they returned with their growing family and, except in 1844 and 1846, did so annually until 1851, sometimes more than once, for protracted periods. Dickens found accommodation for his family in Broadstairs, at 12 (now 31) the High Street (1837), at 40 Albion Street (1839 and probably 1843), at the Albion Hotel into which it was later incorporated (1845 and 1849), at 37 Albion Street (1840), at Lawn House on the Kingsgate Road (1840, probably 1841 and 1842), at 1 or 6 Chandos Place (1847 and 1848), and at Fort House (1850 and 1851). He stayed alone at the Albion Hotel, during a short holiday he took in September 1859.

In Broadstairs, Dickens worked on *Pickwick Papers, Nicholas Nickleby, The Old Curiosity Shop, Barnaby Rudge*, AMERICAN NOTES, *Martin Chuzzlewit, Dombey and Son, The HAUNTED MAN*, and *David Copperfield*. From Broadstairs, he explored north-east Kent: Canterbury, Whistable, Margate, Ramsgate.

The development of railways during the 1840s enabled Dickens, often with friends, to make day trips into Kent, particularly to Chatham and Rochester, and to nearby towns such as Gravesend and Maidstone (see TRANSPORT). Not all of his railway experiences in Kent were happy, however. In 1865 a train on which he was travelling from Dover was involved in an accident at Staplehurst. Many passengers were killed or injured. Unhurt, Dickens comforted the injured and dying, but evidently suffered for some time from what today is called post-traumatic stress disorder.

He was travelling from Dover after visiting France. From 1844, when he began frequently to travel to the Continent, Dickens became familiar with the ports of Dover and Folkestone. He settled his family in Dover for the summer of 1852, and stayed there briefly without them in 1856, 1861, 1862, and 1864. In 1855 the family holiday was spent in Folkestone. Deal was one of the places he visited from Dover and Folkestone.

Dickens intensified his exploration of Kent when, once again, he acquired a home there. Walking from Gravesend to Rochester on his birthday in 1855, Dickens saw that Gad's Hill Place was offered for sale. He bought the house in March 1856, and used it as a country retreat until September 1860 when, having sold the lease of Tavistock House, he made it his principal home. Though he spent much of his time in London and travelling, Rochester again became central to Dickens's life. He continued to live and work at Gad's Hill until his death in 1870.

The growth of interest in Dickens's works after his death coincided with the growth of the rambling movement. Early ramblers liked to combine exercise in the country with pursuit of intellectual and literary interests. Kent and Dickens offered them clear opportunities to do so. A number of the earliest studies of Dickens are written in the form of ramblers' guides, particularly, though not exclusively, to parts of Kent with Dickensian connections. John R. G. Hassard's *Pickwickian Pilgrimage* (1879) is one such, Thomas Frost's *In Kent with Charles Dickens* (1880) another. Alfred Rimmer's *About England with Dickens* (1883) is clearly written with the rambler's needs in mind, and the title of Robert Allbut's *Rambles in Dickens-Land* (1903) speaks for itself. The

classic of the genre, however, is William R. Hughes's *Week's Tramp in Dickens Land* (1891). Hughes tracked down informants who had known Dickens, and provides scholars with invaluable primary source material. While this is no longer possible, books and pamphlets on Dickens and Kent still often take the form of rambling (or motoring) guides. *The Kent of Dickens* by Walter DEXTER (1924) is the most valuable work on the subject.

Many of today's readers are likely to be dissatisfied by the way the relationship between topographical fact and fiction is conceived in such works, which tend to speak of topographical 'originals' rather than 'models', and often forget Thomas Frost's warning that 'All the localities mentioned by Dickens in his narrative of the Pickwickians' journey and their sojourns at Manor Farm must be regarded . . . as being equally with Mr Wardle and the fat-boy the creations of his fancy' (p. 114). Even so, guides of this kind record valuable data about Dickens and Kent, and offer hypotheses, many as yet unfalsified, about topographical models (see CHARACTERS—ORIGINALS).

Often, of course, no hypothesis is needed. Chatham and Rochester feature under their own names, without disguise, in *Pickwick Papers* (2–5), *David Copperfield* (13, 19), and 'The Seven Poor Travellers' (*CS*). The subject of 'Chatham Dockyard' (*UT*) is declared in its title. Few would dispute that Rochester is also the model for 'Mudfog' in the MUDFOG PAPERS, 'Dullborough Town' (*UT* 12), the 'Market Town' (*GE* 8), and 'Cloisterham' (*MED*). It has been argued that Rochester is the model for the eponymous town of 'The Great Winglebury Duel' (*SB*).

David Copperfield lives with Mr Wickfield and Agnes in Canterbury, and attends Dr Strong's school there (*DC* 15–18 *et seq.*). There is evidence to suggest Dickens intended that the closing scenes of *Drood* should take place in Maidstone Gaol, and Maidstone is commonly held to be the model for Muggleton (*PP* 7), although arguments are also put forward in favour of West Malling (formerly known as Town Malling). Paddock Wood Station is believed by some commentators to have been the model for the setting in which Mr Carker is run down (*DS* 55).

Dickens strives for the essayist's generic inclusiveness in 'Our English Watering Place'

(*RP*), but there are sufficient corresponding contingencies to leave little doubt that his model was Broadstairs. The same may be said of 'Pavilionstone' in 'Out of Town' (*RP*), evidently modelled on Folkestone. Dickens alludes to Folkestone directly in 'A Flight' (*RP*). Dover was the model for the watering-place described in 'Out of the Season' (*RP*).

Ramsgate, unsurprisingly, is the setting of 'The Tuggses at Ramsgate' (*SB*). Betsey Trotwood's home is in Dover (*DC* 12, 13, 39), but the donkey business was inspired by a Broadstairs resident. It is in the 'Royal George Hotel', Dover, probably modelled on the Ship, that Mr Lorry tells Lucie Manette her father is not dead as she had supposed (*TTC* 1.4). As a soldier, Richard Carstone is posted to Deal, and is visited there by Esther Summerson (*BH* 45). Deal was probably the model for the town to which the narrator walks from the watering-place described in 'Out of the Season' (*RP*).

Nor did Dickens lack a sense of Kent as a whole. 'A Flight' (*RP*) describes a late-summer railway journey from London to Paris, affording glimpses on the way through Kent not only of hop-gardens but also of 'pools and rushes, haystacks, sheep, clover in full bloom delicious to the sight and smell, cornsheaves, cherry-orchards, apple-orchards, reapers, gleaners, hedges, gates, fields that taper off into little angular corners, cottages, gardens, now and then a church'. Kent was a principal market garden for London. On his long walk from London to Dover, David Copperfield encounters migrant labourers attracted by the fruit and hop harvests (*DC* 13). We are introduced to more in 'Tramps' (*UT* 11).

'God made the country, and man made the town', said the poet Cowper. Like many in the generations that constructed the Romantic movement, Dickens too was tempted to see the country as a paradise, out of which it is a misfortune to be cast. And since experience had made Kent for him the rural antithesis of London, in his earlier works Kent is sometimes the place where innocence, security, and social harmony are chiefly to be found. Serpents, to be sure, are found there too. Mr Jingle undermines the harmony of Dingley Dell (*PP* 9). Uriah Heep blights the innocence of Canterbury (*DC* 19 *et seq*.). But Manor Farm, Dingley Dell, is a memorable seat of innocence and good fellowship (*PP* 5–8 *et seq*.),

and it is in Dover that David Copperfield finds love and security (*DC* 13, 14).

Dickens's vision, however, rarely descends to the formulaic. Ultimately he recognized that innocence was no more secure in Kent than it was in London. His purchase of Gad's Hill Place signalled no retreat from London to a childhood paradise. Dickens became a commuter, travelling by train back and forth between London and Gad's Hill, sometimes daily, often at longer intervals. In his personal life and in his imaginative life he balanced London and Kent. His sensibility had changed. He abandoned his reflexive interest in little victims denied a country paradise, and began to look for the roots of evil and suffering in personal choice. In *Great Expectations* Pip is sinned against, but it is not this that makes him acquire ambitions that have to be unlearned, more like those of his sister and Mr Pumblechook than of Joe whom he loves.

Unsurprisingly, then, it is in *Great Expectations* that we find Dickens's most challenging representation of Kent. No longer is the county depicted as a seat of happiness and innocence. The Kent countryside and the 'nearest town' are no paradise from which Pip is snatched. Good is to be found there, in Joe Gargery, but Mrs Joe is cruel, Uncle Pumblechook self-important, Orlick brutal, Miss Havisham morally blighted. Both London settings and Kent settings, in this novel, are permeated with a mournful sense of lost innocence.

Perhaps the most fascinating feature of the novel, in this respect, is the way Dickens models his settings, for the most part, on places important in his life (see W. Laurence Gadd, *The Great Expectations Country*, 1929). He suffuses almost all of them with a sense of trouble and loss.

The countryside near Gad's Hill is the model for Pip's childhood milieu, and Rochester the model for the 'nearest town'. Despite his having spent the happiest part of his childhood nearby, the Rochester of *Great Expectations* is troubled and blemished. The garden of Satis House is no Garden of Eden, but a 'wilderness' (8). Quite apart from what transpires there, it is 'a rank ruin of cabbage stalks', 'overgrown with tangled weeds'. It does not compare, in fact, to Wemmick's suburban garden in Walworth.

The model for Joe Gargery's forge, where Pip is brought up, was evidently a forge in the village of Chalk, two or three kilometres from Gad's Hill Place. The Chalk blacksmith in the 1850s and 1860s was a prizewinner at one of the SPORTS days organized by Dickens at Gad's Hill. He is said to have employed a journeyman blacksmith, declared by some local sources to have resembled Orlick physically, by others to have resembled him in character too. The forge, the house adjoining it, and the garden all at one time corresponded closely to what is found in the novel. To this day, there is a roof coming down to within four feet of the ground, lending substance to Mr Pumblechook's theory that the convict acquired the file and 'wittles' by climbing onto the roof and letting himself down the chimney. Alas for Mr Pumblechook, the theory is demolished by the dimensions of the chimney. The forge is only a few hundred yards from the site of the cottage in which Dickens spent his honeymoon. He had separated from his wife in 1858, two years before he began *Great Expectations*. There can have been few places for Dickens more likely to call up a sense of lost innocence, than Chalk.

The churchyard in which the opening of *Great Expectations* is set had at least two models. Gad's Hill Place is in the parish of Higham. The parish church is St Mary's. Like the churchyard in chapter 1 of the novel, St Mary's churchyard abuts directly on to what used to be marshland, fringing the Thames. Looking north from the churchyard wall, it was possible to see, as Pip did, a beacon by which sailors steered, an old gibbet that once held the body of a pirate, and an old battery built in 1539, demolished in 1869. It was at St Mary's that Dickens's daughter Kate had been married, three months before he began the novel. Thanks to the separation, Kate's mother had not been present, and Dickens had been convinced his daughter was marrying to get away from him (see CHILDREN OF DICKENS). Once again, it must have been a place imbued with anxiety for Dickens.

The churchyard of Cooling Church was less stressful for him, but perhaps sad for all that. Three miles away from St Mary's, it contains models for the gravestones of Pip's little brothers, still to be seen—thirteen in fact (eight more than Dickens describes in the novel), all of children of the Comport family

of nearby Cooling Castle, though not all of one branch or generation. Dickens took friends to see these graves, and acknowledged them as his inspiration.

If the fictional topography of the novel is compared with the actual topography of the Hoo Peninsula, it is possible to deduce that the hulk Dickens was thinking of when he imagined the one in which Magwitch and Compeyson were imprisoned (5), was one in Egypt Bay, nine miles downriver from Higham. It was in fact a coastguard hulk, not a prison hulk. The actual prison hulks he had known as a child were moored off Upnor Castle, in the basin of Chatham dockyard. Needless to say, PRISONS were a source of anxiety for Dickens. Memories of prison hulks in the basin of the dockyard where his father had worked would scarcely have been untroubled.

Quaint old houses in 'the birthplace of his fancy' are given worrying or sinister qualities in *Great Expectations*. Mr Pumblechook's home, and corn and seed shop (8), is modelled on an establishment in an ancient three-gabled building in Rochester High Street. When Dickens was writing the novel it was occupied by a corn and seed merchant, John Bye Fairbain, in whose shop there were indeed 'many little drawers', like those Pip peeps into, wondering 'whether the flower seeds and bulbs ever wanted of a fine day to break out of those jails and bloom'. Examination of the gables of the building confirms that a bed in the attic might well induce an occupant to calculate 'the tiles as being within a foot of my eyebrows'.

The model for Miss Havisham's home, Satis House, is Restoration House, situated in Crow Lane just off Rochester High Street. Forster confirms this (8.3). The house is entered through an iron gate like the one Estella opens for Pip, and across a paved yard such as the novel describes. There was a disused brewery next to the house, and there is a detached dwelling nearby, Vines Cottage, corresponding to the one Estella takes Pip to on his second visit to Satis House (11). Built between 1580 and 1600, it is called Restoration House because Charles II slept there on his journey from Dover to London at his Restoration in 1660. Dickens was not immune to the romance of these connections, but he writes against the grain of it. Evidently he knew the interior. He made the room in which King Charles slept Miss Havisham's room. The drawing-room, across the landing, is where he places her rotting wedding feast.

The name, Satis House, Dickens took from another dwelling in Rochester, on Boley Hill. During the reign of Elizabeth I it belonged to a mayor of the city, Richard Watts. The queen was once his guest, and it is said he apologized to her for the modesty of his home. Her reply, in Latin, was 'Satis': 'It is enough.' Hence the name. Needless to say, the novel confers powerful irony upon it.

In *Great Expectations*, then, folly and knavery, pain and suffering, abound in Kent. The novel effectively repudiates the myth of the country paradise, and speaks to us instead of lost innocence. The same may be said of the treatment of Kent in *Edwin Drood*. Closely modelled on Rochester, Cloisterham is, for the most part, dismal and sinister. Yet among the last words Dickens wrote is a description in the novel of the city and its cathedral in the summer sunlight (23). 'Its antiquities and ruins are surpassingly beautiful', the reader is told. 'Changes of glorious light from moving boughs, songs of birds, scents from gardens, woods, and fields—or, rather, from the one great garden of the whole cultivated island in its yielding time—penetrate into the Cathedral, subdue its earthy odour, and preach the Resurrection and the life.' Dickens's final words on Kent are religious in mood, and optimistic. DP

**Kent, Charles** (1823–1902), journalist, poet, and miscellaneous author. Dickens (wrote Percy FITZGERALD) 'never had a more faithful follower' than this 'exuberant, affectionate, romantic' admirer: and Dickens doubted 'if I have a more genial reader in the world' (24 December 1856) than 'my faithful Kent', as he called him, in King Lear's phrase. They met through Dickens's gratitude for his review of *Dombey* in the *Sun*, which he edited, and became close friends. Kent contributed to the weeklies, organized the remarkable farewell dinner before the American PUBLIC READING tour, 1867 ('Nothing like it has ever occurred in London before', reported the *New York Tribune*), and became, with Dickens's blessing, the readings' official chronicler. His *Dickens as a Reader* (1872) and other reminiscences of Dickens are invaluable, and he compiled collections of his *Humour and Pathos* (1884) and *Wellerisms* (1886), also editing selections from other popular authors. PC

**Kitton, Frederic George** (1856–1904), Dickens scholar. Born near Norwich, he was apprenticed at 17 as a wood-engraver on the staff of the *Graphic* in London and contributed regularly to the magazine (1874–85). He also worked for the *Illustrated London News* and for *The English Illustrated Magazine*. He became a noted etcher and a prolific drawer of landscapes and of scenes and sites associated with Dickens. He contributed illustrations to W. R. Hughes's *A Week's Tramp in Dickens-Land* (1891) and was the author of *Dickensiana: A Bibliography of the Literature Relating to Charles Dickens and His Writings* (1886), *Charles Dickens by Pen and Pencil* (1890), *The Novels of Charles Dickens: A Bibliography and Sketch* (1897), *Dickens and His Illustrators* (1899), and the posthumously published *The Dickens Country* (1905). He was a founder and a vice-president of the DICKENS FELLOWSHIP (1902), and his appointment as the first editor of the DICKENSIAN was only prevented by his death. He was particularly active in the campaign for the purchase of Dickens's birthplace by Portsmouth Corporation (see DICKENS BIRTHPLACE MUSEUM). Following his death his library was purchased as the basis of the proposed national Dickens Library to be formed within the Guildhall Library (transferred to DICKENS HOUSE in 1926). ALS

*DNB: Supplement 1901–1911* (1912).

**Knight, Charles** (1791–1873), author and publisher, who issued numerous SERIALS and miscellanies designed to make entertaining and informative reading material cheaply available to a mass audience (see READERSHIP). His most notable publications include the *Penny Magazine* (1832–46, on behalf of the SOCIETY FOR THE DIFFUSION OF USEFUL KNOWLEDGE), *Half-Hours with the Best Authors* (1847–8, 1866), *The English Cyclopedia* (1854–70), *The Popular History of England* (1856–62), and several editions of SHAKESPEARE'S works.

Knight and Dickens met in the late 1830s, through the short-lived SHAKESPEARE CLUB. They corresponded through the 1840s, displaying a common interest in cheap publication, extended EDUCATION, and international

COPYRIGHT. Knight publicly praised Dickens's talents in the Introduction to his *Mind Among the Spindles* (1844), calling him 'a writer whose original and brilliant genius is always under the direction of kindly feeling towards his fellow-creatures'; he also included an extract from *Nicholas Nickleby* in the various editions of *Half-Hours with the Best Authors*. Dickens reciprocated by inviting Knight to serve as 'Director of General Arrangements' for his touring production of *The Merry Wives of Windsor* in 1848, and by purchasing Knight's Cabinet Edition of Shakespeare for the company.

The two writers enjoyed a closer relationship from the early 1850s: Knight participated in Dickens's AMATEUR THEATRICALS, and accepted an invitation to write for *Household Words*. He contributed nineteen articles to the journal, including a practical series of 'Illustrations of Cheapness' (1850), and a biographical collection of 'Shadows' (1851–2), described by Dickens as 'most excellent' (27 July 1851).

Dickens possessed several copies of Knight's publications, including the *Pictorial History of England* (1838) which, as Stonehouse notes, 'bears in the margins the marks of Mr. Dickens's study for his CHILD'S HISTORY OF ENGLAND' (*Catalogue of the Library of Charles Dickens*, 1935, p. 69). LL

Clowes, Alice A., *Charles Knight: A Sketch* (1892).

Knight, Charles, *Passages of a Working Life during half a Century*, 3 vols. (1864–5).

**Knowles, James Sheridan** (1784–1862), playwright and actor, of Anglo-Irish descent, cousin of Richard Brinsley SHERIDAN. His plays, which were thought to herald the dawn of a new legitimate drama, contained strong situations, often of a DOMESTIC nature, but were rather old-fashioned. As an actor he was, in MARSTON's opinion, overly emotional and tedious. Among his 23 plays, *Virginius* (1820) and *William Tell* (1825) provided star turns which MACREADY made his own. Dickens, learning of Knowles's bankruptcy in 1848, organized an AMATEUR THEATRICAL benefit on his behalf at the Theatre Royal, Haymarket. The pieces chosen were *The Merry Wives of Windsor*, in which Dickens played Justice Shallow, and Mrs Inchbald's farce, *Animal Magnetism*, followed by performances two nights later of JONSON's *Every Man In His Humour* and the farce *Love, Law and Physic*. A series of performances in the provinces followed. Plans to use some of the proceeds for funding the curatorship of SHAKESPEARE's house at Stratford, of which Knowles was to be the first incumbent, proved unnecessary as Knowles was also granted a government pension. Dickens may have used Knowles's *The Daughter* as an inspiration when he was working on *Our Mutual Friend*. JD

# L

**Lamb, Charles** (1775–1834), Romantic ESSAYIST, critic, and miscellaneous writer revered by early Victorian men of letters, members of the DICKENS CIRCLE, and latterly Dickens himself. Lamb's eccentric wit—what he called a 'self-pleasing quaintness'—was revealed through the persona of 'Elia' in *The London Magazine* (1820–5), and his unfashionable commitment to London life as subject-matter earned him a place in the new Cockney School of metropolitan poets and essayists. By 1838 Dickens was writing to acquaintances recommending the work of 'the original kind-hearted, veritable Elia' (8 February 1838), and Lamb's influence on several of Dickens's own essays is discernible.

JMLD

*Lamplighter, The* A farce written by Dickens in 1838 for production by MACREADY, who found it 'a manifest disappointment', claiming that FORSTER had 'goaded' Dickens to write it. Its slight plot concerns a jolly lamplighter, Tom Grig, who avoids matrimonial entanglement promoted by a foolish old astrologer. Dickens withdrew the play from rehearsal on 13 December, without ill feeling, and subsequently revised it slightly for publication as 'The Lamplighter's Story', his contribution to *The* PIC-NIC PAPERS (1841), which he edited for the benefit of John MACRONE's widow. It was not collected in either version during his lifetime.

PVWS

**Landon, Letitia Elizabeth** ('L.E.L.'), English poet (1802–38). Landon began publishing poetry at the age of 16, and by the time of her father's death in 1825 she was able to support her mother and brother on the strength of her earnings, particularly from the hugely popular sentimental verse-tale *The Improvisatrice* (1824). As a self-supporting and independent woman she attracted a certain amount of notoriety, and her name was linked scandalously with various men, including BULWER-LYTTON, who was by that time married. She herself became engaged to John FORSTER, but the rumours of her infidelity were too much for him. She denied them, but felt bound to

free him from the engagement, which was broken off in 1834. In 1837 she met and married Captain George McLean, Governor of Cape Coast Castle in West Africa, and sailed with him for the Gold Coast. She died there on 15 October 1838 of an overdose of prussic acid, possibly deliberate although her friends insisted it was accidental. Dickens consoled Forster on the news—'The comfort is, that all the "strange and terrible" things come uppermost, and that the good and pleasant things are mixed up with every moment of our existence so plentifully that we scarcely heed them' (Forster 2.2)—and contributed £10 to a fund on behalf of Landon's widowed mother.

AR

**Landor, Walter Savage** (1775–1864), English poet and man of letters, author of the epic poem *Gebir* (1798) and a series of prose recreations of famous people from history, *Imaginary Conversations* (1824–9). A friend of FORSTER's since 1836, he first met Dickens in 1840 and the two became firm friends. It was whilst visiting Landor in Bath that Dickens first thought of Little Nell—Landor later claimed to have deeply regretted not buying this house in order to destroy it and ensure 'no meaner association should ever desecrate the birthplace of Nell' (Forster 2.7); in his conception of the beautiful, doomed young heroine, Dickens may have been influenced by Landor's 1806 lyric 'Rose Aylmer 1779–1800'.

Dickens's fourth child was born on 8 February 1841 and christened Walter Landor Dickens; Landor was godfather to the boy (see CHILDREN OF DICKENS). Landor's fierceness ('Landor is like forty lions concentrated into one Poet'; to Charles Sumner, 31 July 1842) and his scrupulous sense of personal honour are recorded in Dickens's genial caricature of him in the figure of Boythorn from *Bleak House*. Dickens's opinions of Landor, published after the latter's death in *All The Year Round* ('Landor's Life', 24 July 1869) cast light upon his conception of that character: 'Like Hamlet, Landor would speak daggers but use none . . . his animosities were chiefly referable to the singular inability of his to dissociate other people's ways of thinking from his own.' Landor's biography was written by Forster (1869).                                    AR

**Landseer, Sir Edwin** (1802–73), painter of animal subjects, friend of Dickens from the 1830s. Dickens also knew Landseer's brother and his father John, and John Landseer's memories of the Gordon Riots provided background material for *Barnaby Rudge*. Prints of two Edwin Landseer works were in Dickens's collection, and the stags' heads which hung at Gad's Hill were his gift. Landseer's one illustration for Dickens, showing the Peerybingles' dog, Boxer, was for *The* CRICKET ON THE HEARTH. Dickens's essay 'The Friend of the Lions' (*HW* 2 February 1856) recounts Landseer's complaints about the poor treatment of lions in London Zoo. In the later part of his life Landseer became increasingly unstable, and his friendship with Dickens declined as a result.                   LO

Lennie, C., *Landseer: The Victorian Paragon* (1976).
Ormond, R., *Sir Edwin Landseer* (1981).

**law and legal institutions.** The law has long been the butt of writers, artists, and popular culture, quick to seize upon the disjunction between its lofty claims and its debased reality. Dickens drew freely upon these traditions, centring much of his writing on wills, legacies, villains, and crime. His concern with the law was constant, sustained, and serious. He created a gallery of characters and narratives which offered an unforgettable depiction of law and society in Georgian and Victorian England. His celebrated denunciations of the complexity, mystification, hypocrisy, and self-serving inefficiency of the legal system reflected the events of his time, often following the charges already levelled in parliamentary reports and debates, newspapers and magazines. These reproofs underpinned his reputation as a reformer. He probably did more than anyone to dramatize the plight of imprisoned debtors and of paupers; he actively championed substantive law reforms, as in the field of industrial accidents, and he is often credited with hastening the abolition of imprisonment for debt and of public executions (see CAPITAL PUNISHMENT).

But there is also another Dickens, the one who contemplated practising at the Bar, who wanted to become a stipendiary magistrate, who was a friend of judges, lawyers, stipendiary magistrates, detectives, and prison governors, who witnessed murder trials and public executions, who idealized the New Police, who supported the authorities' 'firm' treatment of mobs, who frequented criminal districts, PRISONS, and madhouses, who became a warm supporter of flogging, and whose son Henry became a successful lawyer and later a judge. Dickens's appeal to a wide audience, and his larger importance in shaping ideas and values, derives in part from his richly paradoxical treatment of law and modernity. He articulated the powerful and contradictory feelings about law, lawyers, CRIME, criminals, criminal justice, policing, and punishment that lay beneath the surface of Victorian society.

For many looking back on the legal system of the late 18th and early 19th centuries, it was an irrational and brutal *ancien regime*. Dickens experienced this *ancien regime* at first hand, living through the most prodigious period of legal and penal reform in British history. His writings illuminate this transitional period, the medieval juxtaposed alongside the modern. His intense interest in occupational groups and how people earned a living, and the impact of WORK on how people flourish, encouraged him to probe the culture of the legal community, how lawyers justified their work, and the lawyers' 'ideology of advocacy', namely, the obligation to be blind to the MORAL implications of their work, with its chill, mechanical view of law and life, one that absolved opportunism and selfishness. In these ways, Dickens made a valuable contribution to the history, sociology, and anthropology of law.

The law loomed large over Dickens's early life. In 1824, when he was 12, his father was arrested for debt and imprisoned in the Marshalsea prison (see DICKENS, JOHN). Dickens visited his parents there weekly. Like a criminal, he experienced being an outsider, suffering shame and various humiliations at the hands of the law. He developed a 'profound attraction of repulsion' to the criminal districts of London, which he frequently visited throughout his life. After six months in prison John Dickens was released. For his son the lessons of this experience were clear, and were recorded in the novels, in which children were frequently born prisoners, and feel injustice intensely; he showed that we live in an arbitrary, brutish world and that the law, as Mr Bumble famously discovered, 'is a ass—a idiot' (*OT* 51).

Dickens's most immediate involvement with the legal world came when, at 15, he began the first of two periods of clerkship, first in the offices of ELLIS AND BLACKMORE, attorneys of 1 Holborn Court (later 1 Raymond's Buildings, Gray's Inn), from May 1827 to November 1828, and for a few months subsequently in the offices of Charles Molloy, an attorney of 6 Symond's Inn. He was a keen observer, and with an ear for legal jargon, able to mimic clients. Edward Blackmore subsequently recalled that several of the incidents and clients Dickens encountered in his office became well known in *Pickwick* and *Nickleby*. Names such as Bardell, Corney, Rudge, and Weller came from the petty-cash book maintained by Dickens at Ellis and Blackmore. But Dickens was soon bored. 'I didn't much like it', he later wrote; it was 'a very little world, and a very dull one' (to J. H. Kuenzel, ?July 1838). So he became a law reporter, transcribing cases in Doctors' Commons, the Court of CHANCERY, and police courts, a parliamentary reporter, and a reporter for various papers and magazines. In 1839, despite his early success as a JOURNALIST, editor, and author, he registered as a student barrister at Middle Temple. It was a kind of safety net, should his writing career fail, and a means of acquiring gentlemanly respectability. There were long-standing connections between the law and letters, and Henry FIELDING, the reformer magistrate whose novels Dickens admired, may have been a role-model. Yet Dickens never ate sufficient dinners to be called to the Bar, and he resigned his membership of Middle Temple in 1855.

In 1846 he inquired about obtaining a paid magistracy in London. Although he took the matter no further (he lacked the qualifications) he was not infrequently involved in litigation and allied legal matters. He insisted upon the prosecution of a young woman charged with using bad language in the street, and brought a private prosecution against a fraudulent begging-letter writer, was a witness in an infanticide case, sat as a common juror and on a coroner's jury, and assisted the prosecution of several pickpockets. He also suffered from the shortcomings of Chancery in 1844 when he successfully obtained an injunction to prevent breach of COPYRIGHT with respect to pirated versions of *A Christmas Carol*. The defendants declared themselves bankrupt and Dickens had to pay his own considerable costs. He was friendly with several leading legal figures, including Chief Justice Cockburn, Baron Bramwell, Mr Justice Willes, Lord Denman, Lord Chief Baron Pollock, and Lord Campbell, although not all were charmed by his representations of legal matters. His long and close friendship with Serjeant TALFOURD (later Mr Justice Talfourd) provided Dickens with legal advice in both his personal affairs and also on the legal aspects of his writings. *Pickwick Papers* was dedicated to Talfourd, and Dickens is said to have modelled Tommy Traddles in *David Copperfield* on him.

Dickens was particularly prone to mine the years of his youth for material. Since much of his formative period was enclosed within the world of law and law talk it is hardly surprising that his novels abound with legal life. Nine of his novels, and many of his short stories, contain lawyers. There are 34 lawyers altogether, as well as judges, magistrates, law clerks, notaries, law writers, copying clerks, court clerks and ushers, jurymen, a law student, clients, a bailiff and bailiff's men, various police and prison officers, prisoners, and a hangman.

Dickens often spoke of his respect for the higher judiciary (there were 'no authorities in England so deserving of general respect and confidence, or so possessed of it': *Daily News*, 16 March 1846); and perhaps this explains why he was easy on them. *Bleak House* contains Dickens's only sketch of the Lord Chancellor, the head of the English judiciary and highest legal officer in the land, based on Lord Lyndhurst, whose court he had reported. While there is brief mention of other judges (Pip is offered a 'full view' of the Lord Chief Justice for half a crown: *GE* 20), the only portrait of a judge is Mr Justice Stareleigh, who presides over *Bardell* v. *Pickwick*. His irascibility, deafness, pomposity, and physical appearance ('a most particularly short man, and so fat, that he seemed all face and waistcoat': *PP* 34) were based upon Mr Justice Gazelee, of the Court of Common Pleas, whom Dickens had studied.

"AU REVOIR!"

'Au Revoir!': Dickens wishes John Bull farewell as he departs for America. Engraving by J. Proctor published in *Judy*, 30 October 1867. After the controversy and ill-feeling which surrounded his first visit to America in 1842, the second visit, on a public reading tour, was a huge financial success but irretrievably damaged his health.

## EXTRAORDINARY GAZETTE.

### SPEECH OF HIS MIGHTINESS
#### ON OPENING THE SECOND NUMBER OF
## BENTLEY'S MISCELLANY,
### EDITED BY "BOZ."

On Wednesday, the first of February, "the House" (of Bentley) met for the despatch of business, in pursuance of the Proclamation inserted by authority in all the Morning, Evening, and Weekly Papers, appointing that day for the publication of the Second Number of the Miscellany, edited by ".Boz."

Publishing day of *Bentley's Miscellany*; an 'Extraordinary Gazette.' Woodcut from a drawing by Hablot Knight Browne ('Phiz') published in March 1837. Dickens edited the *Miscellany* for the first two years of its existence, from 1837 to 1839. *Oliver Twist* made its first appearance at the time in serial format in its pages.

Dickens surrounded by his characters. Drawn by J. R. Brown for F. G. Kitton's *Dickens by Pen and Pencil* (1889-90). The front central figure, accompanied by Sam Weller, is Mr Pickwick, pointing to Pecksniff, Micawber, and Bumble. Little Nell and her Grandfather are seated before them, while the travelling showfolk from *The Old Curiosity Shop* draw up behind.

Manuscript page of *The Mystery of Edwin Drood*, chapter 22, written 8 June 1870. A few hours after writing these words Dickens collapsed from a stroke, and died the next day without regaining consciousness.

Newgate Prison. Engraving from *Picturesque Sketches of London* (1852). Dickens took great pains over 'A Visit To Newgate', written specially for his first book, the first series of *Sketches by Boz*, and years later Newgate is central to the powerful evocation of a criminal atmosphere in *Great Expectations*.

'Public Dinners', *Sketches by Boz*. Illustration by George Cruikshank. Dickens is the second adult figure from the left; Cruikshank, third from the right.

Miniature locket portrait of Catherine Dickens by an unknown artist, c.1830s. Dickens met the daughter of his colleague on the *Morning Chronicle*, George Hogarth, in the winter of 1834–5. They were married on 2 April 1836 and had ten children together. The marriage broke down in 1858.

Dickens in the blacking warehouse. Illustration by Fred Barnard for the 1892 edition of Forster's *Life of Charles Dickens*. 'No words can express the secret agony of my soul as I sunk into this companionship ... and felt my early hopes of growing up to be a learned and distinguished man crushed in my breast.'

Dickens photographed by John Watkins in 1861, the year of *Great Expectations*. Dickens also gave public readings in London this year, and began his third provincial reading tour, 46 readings between 28 October and 30 January 1862.

Elizabeth Dickens (1789–1826), the novelist's mother. Oil painting by John W. Gilbert. 'I never afterwards forgot, I never shall forget, I never can forget, that my mother was warm for my being sent back [to continue working at age 12 in the Blacking warehouse]', Dickens confided in his autobiographical fragment, written in the 1840s.

John Dickens (1785–1851), the novelist's father. Oil painting by John W. Gilbert. 'The longer I live, the better man I think him', Dickens wrote to Forster in 1865.

The opening of the Dickens House Museum (now the Charles Dickens Museum), 48 Doughty Street, by Lord Birkenhead on 9 June 1925. Dickens and Catherine lived here from spring 1837 to the end of 1839, during which time Mamie and Katey were born and Mary Hogarth died. While living at Doughty Street Dickens finished *Pickwick* and wrote both *Oliver Twist*

DOLBY.—" Well, Mr. Dickens, on the eve of our departure, I present you with $300,000, the result of your Lectures in America."
DICKENS.—" What! only $300,000? Is that all I have made out of these penurious Yankees, after all my abuse of them? Pshaw! Let us go, Dolby!"

Satirical cartoon of Dickens and his faithful readings manager George Dolby in America by an unknown artist, 1868. Dickens made a fortune from his reading tour of America, netting £19,000 even after changing dollars to sterling at a disastrous rate.

Dickens in 1859. Oil painting by W. P. Frith, RA (replica 1886). This year saw the replacement of *Household Words* by a new weekly periodical, *All the Year Round*, in which *A Tale of Two Cities* appeared as the first serialized novel. Dickens also undertook his second provincial reading tour that October.

Cooke's Circus at Astley's Amphitheatre, by an unknown artist, c.1852. 'Made up with curls, wreaths, wings, white bismuth, and carmine, this hopeful young person [Master Kidderminster] soared into so pleasing a Cupid as to constitute the chief delight of the maternal part of the spectators' (*HT* 1.6).

*A Girl at a Waterfall* (Georgina Hogarth) at St Nighton near Tintagel. Oil painting by Daniel Maclise, RA, 1842. 'The best and truest friend man ever had', Georgina Hogarth (1827–1917), youngest sister of Dickens's wife, lived with Dickens and Catherine and even after the breakdown of their marriage remained at Gad's Hill Place as Dickens's house-keeper until his death.

Mary Hogarth (1820–37), Dickens's beloved sister-in-law. Watercolour by F. G. Kitton (1856–1904) after an oil painting by Hablot Knight Browne ('Phiz'). Constant companion to Catherine during her courtship and the early days of her marriage to Dickens, Mary died suddenly after a night together at the theatre, and her death affected Dickens profoundly. 'Young beautiful and good, God in His Mercy Numbered her with his Angels At the early age of Seventeen.'

The little garret at 16 Bayham Street, Camden Town. In December 1822 the Dickens family moved from Chatham to this address, where they lived until October 1823. Dickens's schooling was broken off, and the next year, shortly before his father was arrested for debt, he was sent to work in the blacking warehouse.

Rear view of 1 Devonshire Terrace, Regent's Park. Dickens lived here from December 1839 with his growing family to May/June 1851. Six of his ten children were born during these years, and five novels, the two travel books, and the five Christmas books were written.

Rear view of Tavistock House. Dickens lived here from November 1851 to July 1860. The first productions of *The Lighthouse* and *The Frozen Deep* were staged in the schoolroom by Dickens's amateur players.

Dickens reading in the front garden of Gad's Hill Place, near Higham in Kent. Photographed by R. H. Mason, 1866. ' "Bless you, sir," said the very queer, small boy, "when I was not more than half as old as nine, it used to be a treat for me to be brought to look at it. And now, I am nine, I come by myself to look at it. And ever since I can recollect, my father, seeing me so fond of it, has often said to me, 'If you were to be very persevering and were to work hard, you might some day come to live in it' " …' ('Travelling Abroad', *UT*).

'The Nickleby Portrait.' Dickens by Daniel Maclise, RA, 1839. Engraved by Finden as the frontispiece to *Nicholas Nickleby*, the portrait, widely considered the best likeness of Dickens, was purchased by Chapman and Hall, who presented it to Dickens at the banquet celebrating the completion of the novel. It is now in the National Portrait Gallery.

K Cruikshank, Del                                  G. W. Bonner, Sc.

## Animal Magnetism.

**Doctor.**  This Lisette is so furious, she makes me tremble.

*Act II, Scene 1.*

---

'*Doctor*. This Lisette is so furious, she makes me tremble.' *Animal Magnetism*, Act II, Scene 1, illustration by Robert Cruikshank (1786–1856), engraved by G. W. Bonner. This farce by Elizabeth Inchbald (1753–1821) was performed by Dickens's amateur players in 1847. In addition to its comic potential, animal magnetism (mesmerism) seriously interested Dickens as a psychic phenomenon.

commanding tone.

"Sir," said the green-grocer.

"Have you got your gloves on?"

"Then take the kiver off."

"Yes Sir."

The green grocer did as he was told with great humility, and obsequiously handed Mr Tuckle the carving knife; in doing which, he accidentally ~~~~~ supfob.

"What do you mean by that, fellow?" said Mr Tuckle, with great asperity.

"I beg your pardon Sir," replied the crest-fallen green grocer, "I didn't mean to do it Sir; I was up very late last night—"

"I tell you what my opinion of you is, Harris," said Mr Tuckle with a most impressive air "you're a vulgar beast."

"I hope gentlemen," said Harris "that you won't be ~~too hard~~ severe with me, gentlemen. I'm very much obliged to you indeed gentlemen for your patronage, and also for your recommendations gentlemen whenever additional assistance in waiting is required. ~~and I hope~~ I hope gentlemen, I give satisfaction."

---

Manuscript page of *Pickwick Papers*, from chapter 37, recounting the tribulations of the greengrocer attending the soirée of select footmen of Bath, to which Sam Weller has been invited.

'A Court for King Cholera', wood-engraved cartoon by John Leech, *Punch*, 25 September 1852. There were four major epidemics of cholera in Britain during Dickens's lifetime. In a speech to the Metropolitan Sanitary Association in 1850 he was reported as saying, 'Of the sanitary condition of London at the present moment, he solemnly believed it would be almost impossible to speak too ill' (*Speeches*, p. 106).

Dickens reading in March 1870. Watercolour by an unknown artist. Dickens devoted the major part of his energy for the last twelve years of his life giving public readings from his works.

Dickens exhausted after reading Sikes and Nancy, March 1870. Illustration by Harry Furniss, undated. Dickens's lifelong friend, the actor-manager William Charles Macready, said of this reading, 'It comes to this ... TWO MACBETHS!' Dickens terrified audiences and ruined his health with his rendition of Nancy's murder, from *Oliver Twist*.

Dickens reading to his daughters Katey (standing) and Mamie in the garden at Gad's Hill Place. Photographed by R. H. Mason, 1866.

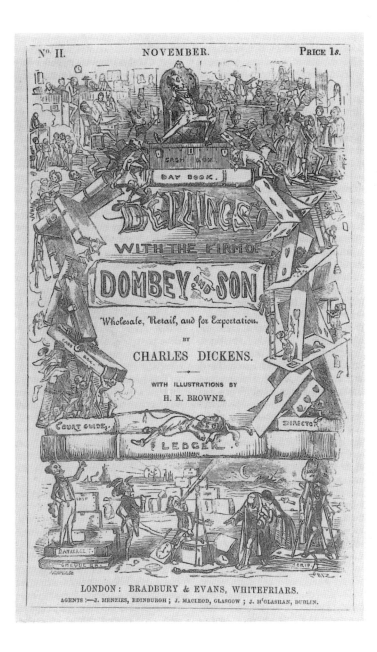

Cover to the second monthly part of *Dombey and Son*, illustrated by Hablot Knight Browne ('Phiz'). Elaborate cover designs such as this hint allegorically at the plot of Dickens's novels, and indicate how closely author and artist worked in collaboration.

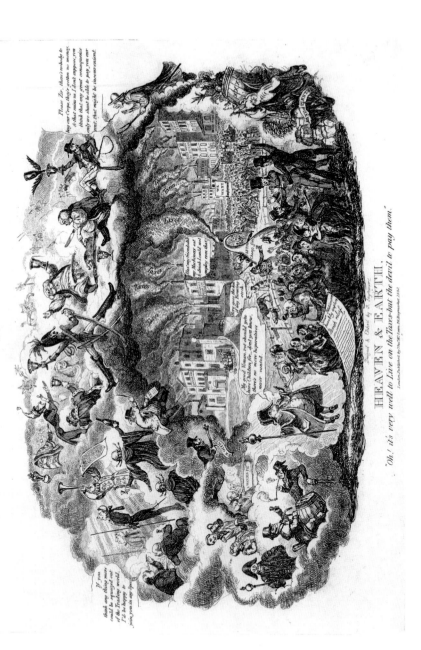

'Heaven & Earth. "Oh! it's very well to Live on the Taxes—but the devil to pay them."' The plight of the poor, drawn and etched by Robert Seymour, 1830. It was Seymour's idea for a series of comic sketches of Cockney sporting life which led to Dickens being invited to write *Pickwick*, and the pompous figure of authority who dominates this scene is evidence that the beadle was a stock figure well before Dickens created Bumble in *Oliver Twist*.

Dickens working in his study at Tavistock House. Oil painting by E.M. Ward, 1854. Dickens kept to a rigorously disciplined schedule when he was writing a novel, and needed familiar objects on his desk, as well as solitude and silence. Once he emerged from his study, however, he kept up a whirl of activities, and depended on the stimulus of London streets to fire his imagination.

Nelly Ternan in acting costume, late 1870s. Dickens met the young actress when she took on a role in his production of *The Frozen Deep* in 1857, and fell passionately in love with her. Dickens covered his tracks so well that their relationship did not become public knowledge until 1934, and to this day much about it remains unknown.

Warren's Blacking Warehouse (building to the right) at Hungerford Stairs, Westminster, *c.*1823. Drawing by G. Harvey, with figures added by D. Dighton. 'I know I do not exaggerate, unconsciously and unintentionally, the scantiness of my resources and the difficulties of my life … I know that, but for the mercy of God, I might easily have been, for any care that was taken of me, a little robber or a little vagabond.'

Dickens in 1870. Caricature from memory, by Leslie Ward ('Spy'). Dickens's extraordinarily energetic life took its toll, ending in his premature death at the age of 58.

While Dickens generally respected the metropolitan stipendiaries (who were paid and came to be drawn from the Bar), he was deeply hostile to the lay magistracy, whom he (and popular culture) depicted as arbitrary, harsh towards the poor, bumbling, pompous, and largely unaccountable, since the general public were frequently barred from observing their proceedings. He satirized many lay magistrates, including Alderman Cute of *The* CHIMES (based on Sir Peter Laurie, the Middlesex magistrate), Mr Sapsea of *Edwin Drood*, the Lord Mayor in *Barnaby Rudge*, and Mr Nupkins in *Pickwick*. When Pickwick insists on knowing the charge levelled against him, Nupkins furtively asks his clerk, 'Must I tell him?' The notoriously bad-tempered Mr Laing, the stipendiary magistrate who presided over the Hatton Garden Police Court, became the target of a sustained campaign in the press. Dickens joined this hue and cry. He was smuggled into Laing's court so that he could observe the magistrate at work. Subsequently, Laing appeared thinly disguised as 'the renowned Mr Fang' in *Oliver Twist* and was shortly after removed from office. Forster and others claimed that the authorities were at least partly influenced by Dickens. Whereas in his earlier work it was the magistrate as bully that loomed large, increasingly he castigated their leniency. In these ways, the magistracy were damned both for being too tough and for not being tough enough.

The barrister or 'upper branch' of the profession, which during Dickens's lifetime increasingly specialized in litigation and, therefore, advocacy, did not receive his detailed attention. 'The Bar', the phrase used to denote the profession of practising barristers as a whole, is the name given to one of the 'magnates'—'Bar, with his little insinuating Jury droop, and . . . his persuasive double eyeglass' (*LD* 1.21)—who seeks to influence Mr Merdle in *Little Dorrit*. Mr Tangle, who addresses the court in the first chapter of *Bleak House*, is the only king's counsel of whom there is any description. Tangle's presentation is tedious, uninvolved, and obscure. He 'knows more of Jarndyce and Jarndyce than anybody. He is famous for it—supposed never to have read anything else since he left school' (*BH* 1).

Throughout the period when Dickens wrote his novels, the Bar grew in size and competition for work within the Bar intensified. In *A Tale of Two Cities* we have portraits of Mr Stryver, the common law pleader and rising lion, and his jackal-like 'devil', Sydney Carton, 'fully half-solvent' like so many other impecunious barristers of the period, preparing briefs for Mr Stryver at half the fee. It has been suggested that Stryver's cross-examination in the trial episode in *A Tale of Two Cities* was inspired by Wetherall's cross-examination of Castel in the treason trials associated with the Spa Fields riots of 1816. Dickens satirized the forensic skills of the serjeants-at-law, who kept until 1846 a monopoly of appearing in the Court of Common Pleas, in his depictions of Serjeant Buzfuz (Mrs Bardell's counsel, modelled on Mr Serjeant Bompas) and Serjeant Snubbin (counsel for Mr Pickwick).

Dickens also conveyed the coercive structures of dread, awe, uncertainty, frustration, and absurdity experienced by lay people in the presence of the law, typified by the rituals of the courtroom. Here, for example, is his description of barristers, just before the business of the court began:

'Mr Pickwick stood up in a state of great agitation, and took a glance at the court. There were already . . . a numerous muster of gentlemen in wigs, in the barristers' seats, who presented, as a body, all that pleasing and extensive variety of nose and whisker for which the bar of England is so justly celebrated. Such of the gentlemen as had a brief to carry, carried it in as conspicuous a manner as possible . . . to impress . . . the spectators. Other gentlemen, who had no briefs to show, carried under their arms goodly octavos . . . which is technically known as 'law calf'. Others, who had neither briefs nor books . . . looked as wise as they conveniently could . . . content to awaken the admiration and astonishment of the uninitiated strangers. The whole, to the great wonderment of Mr Pickwick, were . . . chatting and discussing the news of the day in the most unfeeling manner possible,—just as if no trial at all were coming on' (*PP* 34).

The 'lower branch' of the legal profession was constituted by attorneys, who practised in the common law courts, and solicitors who practised in the Court of Chancery. By the time Dickens wrote they had in effect amalgamated so that all attorneys were solicitors and vice-versa. The lower branch was not only larger in size than the Bar but also more variegated, embracing respectable 'eminent attorneys' and so-called 'pettyfoggers' or 'hedge attorneys', which implied a low and rascally trickster. Dickens evoked the gradations within the 'lower branch', illuminating how the profession exercised power through its specialist knowledge, its expertise in the interpretation of the law, and the existence of law in written form. He also explored the tensions between the practice of the law and the moral life, and how professional success and 'professional neutrality' often produced individuals who were lonely, driven, impersonal, and passionless. The sinister Mr Tulkinghorn is a case in point. He was a pre-eminently successful 'eminent attorney', who undertook high-class work for titled personages. Tulkinghorn was 'passionless . . . mechanically faithful without attachment, and very jealous of the profit, privilege and reputation of being master of the mysteries of great houses . . . He is indifferent to everything but his calling. His calling is the acquisition of secrets, and the holding possession of such power as they give him' (BH 2).

'The one great principle of the English law', asserts Dickens, 'is to make business for itself' (BH 39). ' "Think," says Mr Snitchey [of Messrs Snitchey and Craggs] with such great emotion that he actually smacked his lips, "of the complicated laws relating to title and proof of title, with all the contradictory precedents and numerous acts of parliament connected with them; think of the infinite number of ingenious and interminable chancery suits, to which this pleasant prospect may give rise" ' (BL 1). One attorney in Bleak House is called Vholes: a 'vole' is a type of rat or, in a card game, a situation in which the dealer has all the winning cards. Mr Vholes is perhaps the archetypal modern lawyer. He 'is a very respectable man . . . He never misses a chance in his practice, which is a mark of his respectability; he is reserved and serious, which is also a mark of his respectability; his digestion is impaired, which is *highly* respectable' (BH 39).

Mr Jaggers, who specializes in the criminal law, is a tough lawyer in a tough world, regarded with awe by his clients, whom he bullies (GE 20). Beneath his grim exterior, however, Jaggers is a humane man made cynical and tough by his professional experience. He has the habit of washing his hands with scented soap whenever he comes from court, perhaps in recognition of the tainted nature of his work. Wemmick, his assistant, is a kindly, generous man at home, and an agent of violence and avarice at work. Fascinated by the interpenetration of home and the workplace, Dickens highlights the divisions within people, and the ways that the demarcation between 'home' or 'the private' and 'work', the 'legal', or the 'public', are easily overwhelmed.

Dickens modelled Perker, Mr Pickwick's solicitor, on his former employer, Mr Ellis. Decent, able, and reliable, he is nonetheless no match for Dodson and Fogg, the unscrupulous lawyers who persuade Mrs Bardell to sue Pickwick for breach of promise as a result of a misunderstanding. Pickwick's refusal to pay the damages and costs awarded against him results in Mrs Bardell's being unable to pay Dodson and Fogg's fees; they therefore have her committed to prison as a debtor. The appearance and names of the characters reveals much about them. Fogg 'was an elderly, pimply faced . . . man; a kind of being who seemed to be an essential part of the desk at which he was writing, and to have as much thought or sentiment'. Despite their improprieties, Dodson and Fogg survived in business 'from which they realize a large income, and in which they are universally considered the sharpest of the sharp' (PP 20). At the lower end of the profession were Solomon Pell, the attorney of the Insolvent Court, who had no fixed office, his 'legal business being transacted in the parlours of public houses, or the yards of prisons' (PP 43), and the City of London attorney, Sampson Brass, who was a criminal (OCS). By the end of his life, the reputation of the 'lower branch' had improved, and although they were by no means exempt from popular criticism or accusations of fraud, Dickens's last, unfinished novel portrays the solicitor, Mr Grewgious, in the form that was to become common by the Edwardian period, namely, as the trusted, respectable, family adviser (MED).

As one might expect, Dickens's novels contain many lawyers' clerks. These include the conscientious and ambitious cockney, William Guppy (BH 3), the aged and eccentric Jack Bamber (PP 20), the 'umble Uriah Heep (DC 15), and the mannish Sally Brass (OCS

33). Here, as in his depiction of law stationers, such as Snagsby and Tony Jobling, and copyists, such as Nemo (*BH* 5, 7, 10), he communicates their sordid employment conditions, their drudgery, and threadbare clothes.

Dickens's descriptions of courts, their offices, and lawyers' dwellings are rich in detail and humour. They uniquely convey the topography of legal London prior to the unification of the higher courts (epitomized by the opening of the Royal Courts of Justice at the Strand in 1884), when the courts were dispersed all over London and its maze of buildings, squares, gardens, and alleys (see INNS OF COURT). He depicted the atmosphere of the unreformed legal system with its complex and fragmented court structure, where courts competed with one another for business, and where judges and court officials were frequently dependent upon court fees and bribes for their incomes. Dickens portrays the self-importance, the dust and disorder, the bear garden, the noise and smell, the accumulation of paper and parchment, the theatre and the farce, that characterized the operation of the law. Here, for example, is Dickens's sketch of the offices of the higher bureaucracy of the courts, the Masters':

'Scattered about in various holes and corners of the Temple, are certain dark and dirty chambers, in and out of which, all the morning in Vacation, and half the evening too in term time, there may be seen constantly hurrying with bundles of papers under their arms, and protruding from their pockets, an almost uninterrupted succession of lawyers' clerks . . . These sequestered nooks are the public offices of the legal profession, where writs are issued, judgements signed, declarations filed, and numerous other ingenious machines put in motion for the torture and torment of His Majesty's liege subjects, and for the comfort and emolument of the practitioners of the law. They are for the most part low roofed, mouldy rooms, where innumerable rolls of parchment, which have been perspiring in secret for the last century, send forth an agreeable odour, which is mingled by day with the scent of dry rot, and by night with the various exhalations which arise from damp cloaks, festering umbrellas, and the coarsest tallow candles' (*PP* 31).

Dickens's many and varied portraits of the courts, their offices and their practitioners

include depictions of Doctors' Commons, the Prerogative Office ('Doctors' Commons', *SB*), the Insolvent Debtors Court (*PP* 41), the High Court of Chancery sitting at Lincoln's Inn (*BH* 1), the Old Bailey ('Criminal Courts', *SB*; *OT, TTC, GE*), police courts (*OT* 11, 43), the Court of Common Pleas sitting at the Guildhall and its offices (*PP* 40), and there are three inquests in Coroner's Courts. Usually they are portrayed as farcically incompetent and corrupt. Sheriff's officers appear in several of Dickens's novels, being responsible for apprehending, arresting, and taking into custody those so required by the law (*BH* 6, 15; *PP* 40). Neckett, for example, 'was never tired of watching' for his prey, sitting 'upon a post at a street corner, eight or ten hours at a stretch' (*BH* 6).

Jeremy BENTHAM's assault against the 'lying' fictions and self-interest of the lawyer generated much controversy during the 1830s, 1840s, and 1850s, as law reformers agitated for the elimination of the absurd fictions obstructing justice, and was reflected and sustained in the popular novels of the day, including those of Dickens. Dickens's novels include several fictionalized legal proceedings, some loosely based on real cases, that have since become notorious. *Bardell* v. *Pickwick* (*PP* 34) highlighted the absurd rules of evidence and legal fictions that were central to litigation, notably the rule that excluded the evidence of all interested parties, including the parties to the action; and, most famously, the presumption that if a wife commits a crime in the presence of her husband she is presumed to have done it under his coercion. *Jarndyce* v. *Jarndyce*, the seemingly interminable case heard in the Court of Chancery (a metaphor for the pervasiveness of law) concerns a disputed will that is the scourge of numerous innocent persons (*BH* 1). In these cases he bitterly satirizes the antiquated jargon, inefficiency, procrastination, and absurdity of the courts, demonstrating how lawyers exploit their weaknesses for their own ends.

Dickens described the interiors of lawyers' offices with some particularity, notably Serjeant Snubbin's chambers (*PP* 31), Mr Tulkinghorn's office (*BH* 10), Mr Jaggers's office (whose walls contained the busts of two clients who died on the gallows (*GE* 20, 24), Snitchey and Craggs, the country solicitors

(*BL* 1), Kenge and Carboy of Lincoln's Inn (*BH* 3), and Spenlow and Jorkins's of Doctors' Commons (*DC* 23). Most of these offices are portrayed as drab, dusty, dirty, dark, and daunting, cluttered with old and rickety furniture, papers, parchments, books, and boxes, padlocked and fireproof, with people's names painted outside containing all manner of secrets.

Debt, bankruptcy, and business failure were major themes for many 19th-century novels (see MONEY AND FINANCE). In this chancy world, people can rise or fall without warning, depending upon the state of their finances and the whims of their creditors. Debtors accounted for nearly 60 per cent of the institutional population of prisons in Howard's census of 1777. In *Pickwick Papers*, *Little Dorrit*, *David Copperfield*, and *Dombey and Son* Dickens portrayed the ease with which it was possible to be arrested and imprisoned for debt, and the mixed feelings that the prison evoked in some prisoners. His plots reflect a Victorian ambivalence about and fear of debt as a dangerous and antisocial activity. Within two years of the publication of *Pickwick Papers* (1836), arrest on mesne (i.e. middle) process was abolished; and many authorities report that arrest on final process (i.e. imprisonment for debt) was abolished in 1869. In fact imprisonment for debt was retained after 1869 for small (largely working-class) consumer debtors whose grinding poverty disabled them from paying for basic household items. Only in 1970, 134 years after the first appearance of Mr Pickwick, was imprisonment for debt finally buried by the Administration of Justice Act.

Dickens also took issue with wide-ranging matters of substantive law and procedure, such as the anomalies of divorce law (*HT*), the law of distress (*DC*, *BH*), safety and compensation issues arising from factory accidents, the defects of grand juries, the high cost of litigation, and the excessive formalism of the courts (see FACTORY ACTS).

For many contemporaries the worst aspect of England's *ancien regime* was its criminal justice system. Under the Bloody Code, over 200 small as well as grave crimes were capital offences. The sanction of the gallows and the rhetoric of the death sentence were central to all relations of authority in Georgian England. Executions were watched by crowds of

thousands. However, very few of those found guilty were actually executed. Most were reprieved and sent to prison hulks or transported. A mixture of humane and coercive motivations underpinned a new scientific rationalism that argued that this *ancien regime* was inefficient in terms of the detection, prosecution, punishment, deterrence, and the refashioning of criminals. This critique was underpinned by the belief that crime, principally crime against property, and public disorder, were significantly increasing. The movement for reform was rapidly successful. Most capital offences were repealed in 1837, and hanging was thereafter largely confined to murderers, though public executions continued until 1868. Nonetheless, the ambit of the ordinary individual's potential criminal liability was significantly enlarged as the scope of larceny was extended and a host of new crimes were created. These changes were inextricably linked to the emergence of imprisonment as the pre-eminent penalty for serious offences, the creation of a new, professionalized police, and new expert knowledge on the circumstances and bases of crime, punishment, and policing.

Imprisonment had been used on a small scale prior to 1770. These local prisons varied considerably. Prisoners were often free to mingle with family and friends, gamble, and drink beer sold by the jailers. At worst, prisons were unsanitary, noisy, poorly administered institutions run by corrupt gaolers. A prison reform movement emerged in the 1770s. The influence of penal experiments in the United States led to sustained efforts in England to transform the prison. Pentonville, opened in 1842, epitomized the new model prison, with its regime of hard labour, solitude, religious indoctrination, and its starker separation of the prisoner from the outside world.

Policing was in the hands of parish constables and watchmen, who were neither a preventative nor a detective police force. The establishment of the metropolitan police in 1829 (prefigured by Sir John Fielding's Bow Street Runners, established in the 1750s) marked a gradual but radical change in policing as increasing numbers of professionals were employed to combat crime. As the general public became less directly involved in the detection and prosecution of crime, and less familiar with the inside of prisons, so policing, prosecution, and prisons loomed larger in the public's imaginations, influenced by the increasing factual and fictional accounts of crimes, criminals, detectives, and prisons. This, in turn, induced more rather than less anxiety about crime, criminals, and disorder.

Dickens's writings played an important role in this process whereby images and stereotypes were constructed and transmitted. Crime, criminals, punishment, and policing were pivotal to his analysis of social problems and his understanding of the human condition. In the wake of the Gordon Riots, the French Revolution, and the increase in crime and popular disorder, the fragility of civilization and the unleashing of aggressive impulses (within and without oneself) haunted English society from the 1780s to the 1850s. It was also in this period that a particular construction of human nature and its dangers began to take shape in contemporary debates about the meaning of crime and the purposes of law, punishment, and the legal system. The educative role of law and punishment, fostering public or bourgeois character-building, was increasingly recognized. Dickens's moralistic and titillating treatment of crime and criminals, his images and stereotypes, pointed up these discussions and processes and seemed to corroborate and endorse them. His work seemed to echo and sustain a contemporary fascination with and horror of violence (typified by Sikes's murder of Nancy, *OT* 47), the attempt to separate out criminals from the rest of society as an underclass identified by its perverted psychology and poor, working-class rookeries. For Dickens, as for many of his contemporaries, the fear of irresistible impulse, lawlessness, and the breakdown of society were particularly associated with riots, mobs, gangs of unemployed labourers, TRADES UNIONS, and populist demagogues. Thus, without any seeming irony, Dickens portrays the burning of the cruel and harsh Newgate prison during the Gordon Riots as symbolic of the threat that the 'dangerous classes' (a term first coined in the 1840s) posed to civilized society (*BR* 44), portraying the rioters as 'wild animals' and bloodthirsty savages. Similarly, Dickens watched the levity of the crowd at public executions with deepening hostility.

Although he reversed his earlier opposition to capital punishment, the fears that he projected on to the scaffold crowd underpinned his campaign against public executions (to the editor of *The Times*, 13 and 17 November 1849).

Dickens constantly returned to the prison, both as a frequent visitor and in his writings. He explored the attitudes and conditions of many prisoners, being particularly drawn to the condemned man, as in his celebrated portrait of Fagin's last night alive (*OT* 52). There are detailed accounts of executions in *Barnaby Rudge* and *A Tale of Two Cities*, and in his journalism. The Marshalsea, the debtors' prison, whose customs and characters he came to know well as a young boy, figures prominently in *Little Dorrit* and *Pickwick Papers*. Other debtors' prisons are also described in detail: notably, the Fleet in *Pickwick Papers* and the King's Bench in *David Copperfield*. Dickens's first book, *Sketches by Boz*, contains extended descriptions of Newgate, as do *Oliver Twist*, *Great Expectations*, and *Barnaby Rudge*. *A Tale of Two Cities* includes depictions of the Bastille and La Force as well as Newgate, while the prison is the central symbol of *Little Dorrit*. AMERICAN NOTES includes his visit to the most famous prison of its day, the Philadelphia penitentiary, and several other American prisons. Moreover, his journalistic writings are replete with references to prisons and the contemporary literature thereon (see especially 'Pet Prisoners', *HW* 27 April 1850; repr. *Journalism* 2.212–27). Dickens's position on prison reform was ambiguous. The conditions of the old, unreformed gaols, which in Dickens's mind was forever associated with Newgate, were scandalous. Yet his account of Newgate was probably the least critical of contemporary accounts, and over time he became even less critical of its conditions.

Dickens generated a penological controversy when, following his visit to the Philadelphia prison in 1842, he subsequently condemned its punishment by solitary confinement as 'cruel and wrong', claiming that the silent system adopted at the Coldbath Fields and Tothill Fields prisons, where prisoners were forbidden to speak, was superior (*AN* 7). He also censured the French version of solitary confinement, as depicted in *A Tale of Two Cities*, and its English variant, as administered at Pentonville. Through these critiques, Dickens acquired a liberal reputation on prison discipline. Ironically, his attacks on Pentonville, both in the press and in his satire on the Pentonville experiment in *David Copperfield*, admonished the Pentonville regime and the prison reform movement for being too soft on offenders, views that he expressed more vehemently as he grew older. He consistently argued that penal hard labour (epitomized by the treadmill) was essential to prison discipline; that some prisoners were irredeemable, like 'savage beasts'; and that it was wrong to teach prisoners trades. While his views probably reflected public opinion, Dickens's satires and polemics helped to sustain the view that prison reform had gone too far, making it more difficult to liberalize a cruel and severe regime.

Dickens also wrote a good deal about the police, and is generally credited with introducing the detective into English fiction (see DETECTIVE FICTION). He helped to construct the modern image of the police in opposition to 'the criminal classes'. He was one of the earliest authors to explore the criminal districts of London, guided by the new Metropolitan Police (see LONDON: SLUMS AND ROOKERIES). His influential accounts of these explorations, such as 'On Duty with Inspector FIELD' (*HW* 14 June 1851; repr. *Journalism* 2.356–69), and his portrayal of Inspector Bucket (*BH*)—who was modelled on Field—celebrated the detective's knowledge of the underworld, his dogged professionalism, his efficiency, and the 'wholesome dread' that he engendered among the dangerous classes. Dickens relished the detective's power: like a novelist, the detective could observe and investigate the whole of society, resolving mysteries. Henceforth, Dickens's enthusiasm for the new police was almost unbounded. He fabricated those qualities traditionally associated with the British bobby that accounted for his popular appeal and mystique—imperturbability, character, and impersonal professionalism—in the same way that he idealized the English people. Writers had long ridiculed the unreformed police, as did Dickens in his treatment of Dubbley and Grummer in *Pickwick Papers*. Prior to encountering the new police, Dickens had portrayed the Bow Street Runners not unsympathetically (Blathers and Duff, *OT* 31); subsequently, however, he controversially attacked their honesty and

efficiency (*GE* 16), exaggerating the differences between the old and the new police. Overall, Dickens the celebrated critic of the law helped to sustain wider support for the legal order. As Humphry HOUSE observed, there was 'a strong authoritarian strain' in Dickens which 'helps to explain his fanatical devotion to the Metropolitan Police ... [His] obvious delight in disorder has tended to obscure an underlying cause of it—the natural preoccupation with order. He loved to describe the muddle he hated' (House 1941).

Dickens's depiction of legal issues is often characterized by a thinness of detail, an excessive reliance on the material of his youth, and by anachronism. He was not a lawyer and he made mistakes about the law. Yet the noted legal historian, Sir William Holdsworth, praised his writings for providing 'a very valuable addition to our authorities ... of unique value to the legal historian ... They give us information which we can get nowhere else ... [They are] a source of information which, in its range and lifelike character, is superior to that possessed by the historians of any other period' (Holdsworth 1928). Moreover, the fog of *Bleak House* has not yet lifted: the law still offers many of those caught in its web any number of frustrations, delays, confusions, and miscarriages of justice. The continuing power of Dickens's critique of law and legal ethics lies in the fact that we can all too readily comprehend its existence.          DS

Collins (1962).

Holdsworth, William S., *Charles Dickens as a Legal Historian* (1928).

Sugarman, David, *In the Spirit of Weber: Law, Modernity and 'the Peculiarities of the English'* (1987).

Wiener, Martin J., *Reconstructing the Criminal: Culture, Law and Policy in England, 1830–1914* (1990).

**'Lazy Tour of Two Idle Apprentices, The'** A five-part autobiographical account, written in collaboration by Dickens and Wilkie COLLINS, of a tour taken by the two of them in the north of Britain (*HW* 3–31 October 1857). FORSTER attributes specific portions to Dickens and to Collins respectively, in the appendix, 'The Writings of Charles Dickens', in his *Life of Dickens* (1872–4 edn. only), but the Pilgrim editors suggest that the potentially revealing episode in Doncaster in Part 5, all of which Forster attributes to Collins, is actually by Dickens (8.448n.). The central conceit, taken from HOGARTH's series of engravings *Industry and Idleness*, portrays Dickens and Collins as idle apprentices, Francis Goodchild and Thomas Idle respectively, and characterizes them as embodiments of contrasting types of idleness. Whereas Thomas Idle is passive and indolent, Francis Goodchild is the very picture of uncontrollable nervous energy (a reflection of Dickens's own wild restlessness at the time his marriage was breaking down), whisking them from London to Carlisle, up Carrock Fell in pouring rain, on to Wigan, Allonby, Lancaster, Leeds, and finally Doncaster (see DICKENS: PRIVATE LIFE).

The journalistic account of a holiday in unfamiliar locations is infused with a whiff of surrealism, which prepares the ground for two uncanny tales of passionate, unfulfilled love. The first, by Collins, concerns the horror of discovering a corpse in a double-bedded room, the greater horror of finding it alive after all, and the pathos of the protagonist's subsequently empty life of negation and forgetfulness. The second, by Dickens, concerns a man who orders his wife to die. Apprehended and hanged, the murderer is thereafter fated, like COLERIDGE's Ancient Mariner, to live forever telling his tale.

'The Lazy Tour' makes the pretence that the destination of the journey was immaterial, but in fact the primary motive was Dickens's desire to see Ellen TERNAN again, whom he had first encountered that summer. The article is filled with references to Francis Goodchild's lovelorn condition, especially the 'dreadful state concerning a pair of little lilac gloves and a little bonnet that he saw there'.      PVWS

Stone, Harry, *The Night Side of Dickens* (1994).

## Le Sage, Alain-René (1668–1747), French novelist and dramatist. In SMOLLETT's translations, the child Dickens grew to love *The Devil Upon Two Sticks* (1707) and *Gil Blas* (1715–35), which counts among the precious books that David Copperfield reads 'as if for life'. The former, about the lame devil Asmodeus imprisoned in a bottle, who rewards his saviour with a revelatory flight over Madrid, inspired Dickens's panoptic city vision, in (for instance) the 'good spirit who would take the house-tops off' in *Dombey*

*and Son*. The latter fuelled a feeling for picaresque forms and themes—the road, roguery, and role-playing.      MH

## Leavis, F. R. (1895–1978), polemical and influential critic. In *The Great Tradition: George Eliot, Henry James, Joseph Conrad* (1948), Leavis dismissed Dickens as 'a great entertainer', a valuation which impeded serious academic consideration of Dickens for a generation, even as an appendix celebrating *Hard Times* as a 'moral fable' directed attention to that previously much-neglected novel (see REPUTATION OF DICKENS). In 1970 Leavis made an unacknowledged recantation in *Dickens the Novelist*, co-authored with his wife Q. D. Leavis, analysing selected novels from *Dombey* to *Great Expectations*, and silently revising negative judgements in the reprinted *Hard Times* essay.      PVWS

Ford, George H., 'Leavises, Levi's, and Some Dickensian Priorities', *Nineteenth-Century Fiction*, 26 (1971).

## Leech, John (1817–64), caricaturist and ILLUSTRATOR. Educated at Charterhouse, where he first met his lifelong friend William Makepeace THACKERAY, Leech tried hard, albeit unsuccessfully, to become Robert SEYMOUR's replacement as illustrator for *Pickwick Papers*. In the later 1830s Dickens and Harrison AINSWORTH, along with Leech and his etching teacher George CRUIKSHANK, thought of issuing an illustrated serial about old and new London. After Dickens returned from his AMERICAN tour in 1842, Leech again approached the author for a commission; the artist had by then established himself as a leading comic illustrator, especially for the novels of SURTEES and the new magazine *PUNCH*.

But though Dickens invited Leech to dinner in November 1842, the beginning of a warmly sympathetic friendship, he could not employ him as an artist until the following year, when Leech provided four black-and-white and four hand-coloured plates for *A Christmas Carol*. Having supplied the copyist with a master print indicating every shade for the tinted illustrations, Leech was dismayed at the coarse results. But they looked better bound up 'in a neat book', as Dickens assured him (14 December 1843). The reviewers agreed. Leech was commissioned for all the successive Christmas books, paired with various other artists from the *Punch* staff and the DICKENS CIRCLE. He supplied five designs for wood-engravings for *The* CHIMES; the lower figure in one of these, of Richard the blacksmith slouching home from a night's dissipation, had to be redrawn and re-engraved on wood because the first version bothered the author (1 December 1844). These, and all the subsequent illustrations, were uncoloured.

The next year's book, *The* CRICKET ON THE HEARTH, eschewed overt social criticism in favour of cozy and parodic DOMESTICITY. Leech infused what RUSKIN called his 'loving wit' into a cover design and seven wood engravings. He brightened the close by picturing the dance—Dickens thought Leech's portrait of the carrier '*hardly* handsome enough' (?29 November 1845)—instead of the melancholy final sentence, where 'a broken child's-toy lies upon the ground; and nothing else remains'.

*The* BATTLE OF LIFE, produced in the same format, contained thirteen plates, of which Leech contributed only three. These were not very successful, and the last, depicting Marion's departure, mistakenly included Michael Warden, holding her as if they were eloping. This was the story believed by Marion's family and friends for six years; evidently Leech didn't read the conclusion, where it is revealed that Marion only ran away to her aunt's. Dickens didn't cancel the block, however, because he feared giving Leech pain a second time.

Dickens took especial care to make Leech's assignments for the last Christmas book, *The* HAUNTED MAN, pleasant. Leech designed five of the seventeen illustrations. His is the brooding, eerie illustration of Redlaw and the Phantom, and his too are two versions of the 'baby savage, a young monster', who visits Redlaw. But Leech, who wanted 'some comedy' (to Leech, 1 December 1848), also got twice to draw the contrasting 'baby savage' Sally Tetterby, the young 'Moloch' to whose care Johnny is martyred. On the whole, Leech's images balance each other and are consistent in their evocation of homely humour and terror.

Leech's friendship with Dickens grew, as did his fame as principal *Punch* artist. He adapted many of Dickens's illustrations to political cartoons. He also participated skilfully, though with increasing impatience, in Dickens's AMATEUR THEATRICALS. In September 1849, at Bonchurch on the Isle of Wight, Dickens used MESMERISM to cure Leech of sleeplessness after he had been knocked down by a huge wave. While the intensity of their friendship lessened in the 1850s, Leech could still be counted on for an excursion or a dinner; he was especially solicitous of Dickens's son Sydney, a sailor. In the 1860s the nervous artist retreated more from society; his overly acute hearing was assaulted by London noise. A few months after Thackeray's funeral, Leech died in November 1864 and was buried near his old friend in Kensal Green Cemetery.                RLP

**legal documents of Dickens.** Dickens entered into many agreements, deeds, bonds, and other arrangements during his lifetime. He married, leased and purchased domiciles, took out loans, assigned power of attorney, insured his life, sued PLAGIARISTS, produced plays and PUBLIC READINGS in Britain and America, sold and bought COPYRIGHTS, and made many other personal and professional commitments that involved legal proceedings. Of most interest, perhaps, are Dickens's publishing agreements and his will. The full text of these is printed in the relevant volumes of the Pilgrim Edition of the *Letters of Charles Dickens*. Here summaries must suffice.

Dickens's agreements with publishers for his writings go through three phases: none, or simple letters at first; then increasingly complex, detailed documents that attempt, unsuccessfully, to anticipate the skyrocketing worth of his literary properties; and later on, when Dickens reliably commanded the market-place, agreements with clear-cut terms that reserved most of the value of his properties, and their release in any form or place, to his discretion.

There was, of course, no contract for his first published stories, and nothing beyond additions to his pay-packets for stories he contributed when employed by the MORNING CHRONICLE and EVENING CHRONICLE. For his first book titles, letters setting forth terms were all that was needed. But with the runaway success of *Pickwick*, Dickens's price outstripped his agreements. Whereas John MACRONE paid Dickens £100 in January 1837 for the copyright of Dickens's previously published tales and sketches, CHAPMAN AND HALL paid Macrone £2,250 for the copyright and stock of those same pieces republished as *Sketches by Boz*, six months later. In the single year 1837, with *Pickwick* and *Oliver Twist* both serializing in monthly instalments, Dickens was involved in nine agreements concerning copyright. Over four years, 1836–40, he negotiated nine formal agreements with Richard BENTLEY. These dealt with the editing of *BENTLEY'S MISCELLANY* and the *MEMOIRS OF GRIMALDI* and with two novels, *Oliver Twist* and *Barnaby Rudge*. The most complex, signed 22 September 1838, contained 25 articles.

The September 1841 agreement with Chapman and Hall for *Martin Chuzzlewit* exemplifies the provisions governing the production of Dickens's monthly-part novels. It specified the format and timing of the next SERIAL. It dictated in minute particularity how the new serial was to be produced and costed, and how and when written accounts were to be submitted for Dickens's inspection. The £200 paid Dickens for each instalment was stipulated as an expense not to be deducted from his share of profits. He also retained three-quarters of the profit from the serial throughout its run and for six months thereafter, when the publishers could buy from him one-quarter of the back stock and share thenceforth as equal partners in any net revenue.

These provisions illustrate the power to dictate to publishers that Dickens had gained during the preceding five years. But there was more: the agreement also specified that Dickens was *not* to write for a year, but to receive £1,800 in equal instalments of £150 each over twelve months beginning 1 November 1841. This sum was to be repaid with 5 per cent interest from his three-quarters profit on the as-yet-unwritten twenty-part serial to commence publication in November 1842.

The agreement indicates how commercially viable both parties were: Chapman and Hall had money enough to finance their leading author's extended vacation, and Dickens had enough clout to secure a loan on the strength of his reputation. But the agreement also exposes Dickens's weakness: without a current publication he had no income. When the sales of *Chuzzlewit* proved insufficient to retire his debt and William Hall suggested withholding a quarter of Dickens's £200

monthly payment, Dickens was so enraged he determined to leave his publishers as soon as the contract was fulfilled.

The switch to BRADBURY AND EVANS was complicated and took place over a long time, but the basic provision of their agreement was simple: Dickens owned three-quarters of his copyright, Bradbury and Evans one-quarter, for anything he might write from 1844. When in the late 1850s Dickens returned to Chapman and Hall, he managed to buy back Bradbury and Evans's share in old titles and to sell it to Chapman and Hall, so that for previously published books he and his publishers were equal partners. But Dickens reserved to himself the option to make any arrangement he wanted on future books. And he gave his publishers no share in his new journal, *All the Year Round*.

In addition to these contracts, and to others that regulated the purchase and sale of back stock, of reprints, and of minor works, Dickens also made arrangements, at first informally and later formally, with American, German, and French publishers for other editions and translations of his works. He also negotiated with many of the artists who illustrated his books, though he did not enter into agreements himself with them. In all these negotiations, from 1837 on, Dickens was advised by John FORSTER and by a succession of legal friends, chief among whom, in the early years, was Thomas Mitton of Smithson and Mitton, and in the later years Frederic Ouvry, who represented him in the separation from Catherine DICKENS, drew up the papers for the Gad's Hill sale, and advised Dickens about his last will and testament.

That will, composed by Dickens and signed 12 May 1869, was, for the most part, unexceptionable. After specific bequests, Dickens left his estate, including copyrights, to his children, naming Georgina HOGARTH and John Forster as trustees. Georgina received outright £8,000, Dickens's jewellery, and his personal papers; Catherine Dickens got the income on £8,000 during her lifetime. Dickens left all his manuscripts (and, as it turned out, some proof sheets as well), to Forster, who in turn bequeathed them to the VICTORIA AND ALBERT MUSEUM. By a codicil appended only a few weeks before his death, Dickens gave his eldest son Charles Culliford Boz Dickens his share in *All the Year Round* (see CHILDREN OF DICKENS). Two provisions were noteworthy. Dickens 'emphatically' directed that his burial be 'inexpensive, unostentatious, and strictly private' and conjured his friends to make no 'monument, memorial, or testimonial'. Insofar as this was possible for an interment in Westminster Abbey, this request was honoured (see DEATH AND FUNERALS). And as the first clause in the will, Dickens left £1,000 to Ellen Lawless TERNAN, whose financial well-being he presumably secured by means of previous gifts. RLP

**Lemon, Mark** (1809–70), co-founder and editor of PUNCH from 1841 until his death, and one of Dickens's closest friends. Although Lemon contributed to BENTLEY'S MISCELLANY during Dickens's tenure as editor, they seem not to have met until 1843, when they began dining regularly with one another. Lemon served on Dickens's sub-editorial staff on the DAILY NEWS and contributed to Household Words, sometimes collaborating on articles with Dickens. Dickens, however, never contributed to Punch (his one submission, in 1849, about the abysmal quality of London's drinking water, was never printed), though allusions to him and his works in the magazine were numerous, and often ILLUSTRATIONS from Dickens's novels were mimicked in Punch with well-known political figures substituted for Dickens's characters. On one occasion at least Dickens provided Lemon with material for an article spoofing literary begging letters. After Dickens comforted Lemon following the death of his 2-year-old daughter in January 1851, and after Lemon remained all night with Dickens as he sat beside the body of his infant daughter Dora in April 1851, their friendship moved to a first-name basis and they shortly became so close that Dickens's children referred to Lemon as 'Uncle Porpoise' or 'Uncle Mark'. Lemon was the author of an extraordinary number of plays, many of them burlesques, farces, and 'burlettas'. He collaborated with Dickens on an 1851 farce, MR NIGHTINGALE'S DIARY, in which Dickens appeared in six different roles and Lemon in three. Lemon also DRAMATIZED several of Dickens's works. He and Gilbert à BECKETT adapted The CHIMES for the stage and he alone dramatized The HAUNTED MAN in 1848. Lemon was also an avid participant in many of the AMATEUR THEATRICALS staged by

Dickens. He became especially well known for his Falstaff in SHAKESPEARE'S Merry Wives of Windsor, to which Dickens played Shallow, and which Lemon later developed as a one-man show. Among other roles, Lemon also triumphed as Lafleur to Dickens's deluded doctor in Inchbald's Animal Magnetism and as Lieutenant Crayford to Dickens's Richard Wardour in the adaptation of Wilkie COLLINS'S The FROZEN DEEP (later productions of which would give Dickens his introduction to the TERNAN FAMILY). Dickens repeatedly praised Lemon's acting, for instance, writing to BULWER-LYTTON that 'Lemon is so surpassingly sensible and trustworthy on the stage that I don't think any actor could touch his part as he will' (5 January 1851) and 'we have a sort of reputation for farce-acting (Lemon and I) which induces people to make up their minds beforehand, to be made to roar' (23 March 1851). From 1858 until 1867 Dickens refused to have any contact with Lemon, objecting to his conduct as one of Catherine DICKENS'S representatives in the negotiation of their legal separation and because Lemon almost certainly supported the decision of the publishers BRADBURY AND EVANS not to publish in Punch the mysteriously worded public statement which The TIMES and other newspapers did print and which Dickens did insert in Household Words (12 June 1858) regarding his separation and the rumours that a certain innocent young woman was the cause. Lemon seems to have attributed Dickens's anger to FORSTER'S influence. They did not speak again until they were reconciled at Clarkson STANFIELD'S graveside. Lemon poured the majority of his energies into the improvement of Punch, and has often been quoted as saying that he was made for the magazine, and the magazine for him. Nevertheless, in his later years he also produced a number of novels which, like his dramatic writings, have not secured an enduring reputation. LDB

Adrian, Arthur A., Mark Lemon: First Editor of 'Punch' (1966).

Altick, Richard, 'Punch': The Lively Youth of a British Institution, 1841–1851 (1997).

Fisher, Leona Weaver, Lemon, Dickens, and 'Mr. Nightingale's Diary': A Victorian Farce (1988).

**letters of Dickens.** Dickens's letters (the standard edition is the Pilgrim Edition, hereafter Pilgrim) bear witness to the physical and mental intensity of his life, even while constituting a significant body of work, important not only as biographical materials or a commentary upon his age, but as part of the Dickens canon. Few other literary figures can match the extent and intrinsic interest of Dickens's correspondence. While Walter SCOTT and George ELIOT approach Dickens's volume of production, neither's letters can claim such liveliness or so wide a range over an individual's life and times. Amongst notable Victorian letter-writers, only Elizabeth GASKELL, Edward Fitzgerald, and Jane Carlyle can compare in interest and vividness.

Dickens wrote letters throughout most of his life: the first known dates from about 1821 and the last were written on 8 June 1870, the day of his fatal collapse. Their concerns span the vast range of his activities and interests: on business, they involve PUBLISHERS, ILLUS-TRATORS, contributors, tradesmen, lawyers, begging-letter writers, the rehabilitation of PROSTITUTES, EDUCATION, sanitary reform, working-class political power; on personal matters, they include family, friendships, outings on foot and by train, money, AMA-TEUR THEATRICALS, charitable activities for orphans and indigent artists, holidays, life abroad. Early active as a reporter and writer, Dickens wrote large numbers of letters and the fame of *Pickwick Papers* ensured that people kept them. Most suggest little hesitation or pause in composition, apart from occasional stumbles and slips and the common kinds of misdating. Dickens only occasionally drafted letters, though drafts dealing with legal and sensitive personal matters survive (some, on advice or further thought, never sent).

Letters were a natural form of communication, especially in London, where besides frequent postal deliveries (reformed but not instituted by Rowland Hill in 1840), servants or porters carried messages. Increasingly from the 1850s, as Dickens spent summers abroad in FRANCE or lived out of London at Gad's Hill, he kept in touch by post with the *Household Words* office and with business affairs. Dickens never employed a secretary to handle his correspondence, though at *Household Words* and later *All the Year Round* W. H. WILLS and others carried on much routine business; for the PUBLIC READING tours,

Arthur SMITH and later George DOLBY were responsible. How many letters Dickens wrote it may not even be helpful to conjecture: allowing for occasional exaggeration, and that some replies were short, even curt, he frequently claims in later life to answer a dozen or twenty letters at a sitting and as a matter of course. It is reasonable to assume that a high proportion of his correspondence survives: in 1995 the Pilgrim editors, on publication of Volume 8, knew of 14,089 letters, an increase from 11,956 since the first volume was published in 1965.

Dickens's letters survive in a great variety of forms. The first to survive chronologically was retrieved from the memory of its recipient in the late 19th century. The majority exist in manuscript, including fragments taken as autographs or mutilated by censors. Others survive in printed form, the most extensive series being in John FORSTER's *Life of Dickens*. Some are preserved as paraphrases or reports in the minutes of Societies and Associations, while many are known only through sales catalogues. A significant class included in the Pilgrim Edition is 'Mentions', letters clearly referred to by Dickens as written or by others as received, yet not otherwise traced. Letters known only from catalogue entries or as 'Mentions' surface from time to time: others previously unrecorded come to light, by sale or donation from private ownership or by the publicity associated with publication of a Pilgrim volume or by archival research.

The distribution of Dickens's letters is widespread, the consequence of fame during his lifetime and since. Holdings are sometimes large, sometimes only a few or a single example, in both public collections and private hands. The largest single collection is that of the DICKENS HOUSE in London, constantly enlarged by purchase and donation. Amongst British libraries with holdings are the VICTORIA AND ALBERT MUSEUM (chiefly in the FORSTER COLLECTION) and the British Library. There are extensive American holdings, including the Berg Collection (New York Public Library), the Henry E. Huntington Library, the Pierpont Morgan Library, and the Free Library of Philadelphia. Through the original recipients or subsequent dispersal, letters of Dickens can be found in most countries, including France, Germany, Denmark, Hungary, Russia, South Africa, Japan, and

Australia. Private holders include descendants of the original recipients as well as collectors of literary manuscripts (see COLLECTIONS OF DICKENS MATERIALS).

The Dickens correspondence is largely a one-sided survival. Early in life Dickens began the destruction of letters, often expressing a horror of the publication of private correspondence; one notable bonfire was that of 3 September 1860 at Gad's Hill, 'the accumulated letters and papers of twenty years', and another that of 1869. His papers, left by Dickens in his will to Georgina HOGARTH, were further weeded after his death. Nearly 150 letters to him survived by being deposited with his lawyer, Thomas Mitton, in 1841, and more than 100 others survive, like those from Frederick Maynard and his sister Caroline Thompson, which Dickens sent interleaved with comments to Angela Burdett COUTTS in 1854. While Dickens's own letters have survived in large numbers, many have necessarily perished. Besides chance destructions, many people habitually do not keep letters or else discard them once their purpose has been served. Other correspondents deliberately destroy letters sent to them, because letters are personal and therefore private or sensitive or potentially scandalous. Sydney SMITH, the clergyman and wit, whom Dickens met in the 1830s and to whom he wrote frequently, was a destroyer of correspondence: not a single letter from Dickens to Smith is known to survive. While references in letters to Wills make it clear that Dickens wrote to Ellen TERNAN, again not one is known to survive. Other people, equally deliberately, kept Dickens's letters. Catherine DICKENS, as the rejected wife, believed that his letters to her would show he had indeed loved her. Before her death in 1879 she passed them to her elder daughter Kate, who in turn (1898) gave them to the British Museum (now the British Library). Dickens's friendship with John Forster is preserved in The Life of Dickens, while the friendships with Thomas Beard, Thomas Mitton, and William Harrison AINSWORTH, all figures elided by Forster's biography, flourish in the letters to them. Later friendships that survive in letters are those with Angela Burdett Coutts (marked by a break after Dickens's marital separation) and with Wilkie COLLINS. It must always be recognized, though, that as a record of Dickens's whole life his letters have gaps and absences: some, significant but irretrievable in detail, as with the missing letters to Ellen Ternan; others, too often unnoticed, as with those to Sydney Smith. Dickens has not generally attracted the attention of forgers and their work is usually easily detected. In his lifetime Dickens suffered forgery of a different kind: letters produced to defame him, as with a fake insulting the Americans published by the New York Evening Tattler (11 August 1842; Pilgrim 3, Appendix). Good facsimiles also exist, and their possessors sometimes believe them to be originals.

Comparatively few of Dickens's letters were meant to be or were actually published in his lifetime. He was not a habitual correspondent to newspapers; besides occasional letters, largely about deserving individuals and causes, important (and very different) exceptions include the two letters to The TIMES on the public execution of the Mannings (13, 17 November 1849) and the so-called 'Violated' letter, a justification of his separation circulated by Dickens amongst his friends in May 1858 and printed in the New York Tribune (16 August 1858; Pilgrim 8, Appendix) and thence reproduced in London newspapers. Different in kind were the letters to Forster from AMERICA (1842–3), intended to be the basis of AMERICAN NOTES, and the 'travelling letters' from ITALY (1846) to the DAILY NEWS, revised and enlarged as PICTURES FROM ITALY.

The first great publication of the letters was in 1872–4, in John Forster's Life of Dickens, much of it based upon the letters written to him. Nearly 1,000 are quoted in the Life: of these, some 55 survive in manuscript, the rest having been destroyed by Forster and his executors, or (in the later stages of composition) having been stuck directly into the biography's manuscript. The survivors indicate that Forster altered and added to the letters in various ways, misdated and ran together letters, and 'improved' the style, besides allowing it to appear that letters to others (Georgina Hogarth, for instance) were addressed to himself (see Pilgrim 1, pp. xi–xiii). For the bulk of Dickens's letters to Forster, the Life is the only text, however much it must be approached with caution.

There have been three large-scale general collections of Dickens's letters. The first, by

Georgina Hogarth and Mamie Dickens, was intended as a 'Supplement' to Forster's *Life*, in the conviction that since no man 'ever expressed *himself* more in his letters' than Dickens, this would be 'a portrait of himself by himself'. Two volumes were published in 1880, followed by a third in 1882, giving nearly 1,000 letters to 200 correspondents. The completeness as a portrait claimed by the editors was more apparent than real. Many letters about sensitive matters—his family's sponging on him, for example, or Dickens's separation from his wife—were, regrettably if understandably, omitted. Besides, the texts were handled extremely cavalierly (even by the standards of the time), not only by cutting but also by reorganization, inserting of paragraphs into quite other letters, and carelessness over dating (see Pilgrim 1, pp. ix–xi, and Arthur Adrian, *Georgina Hogarth and the Dickens Circle*, 1957, pp. 206–25). Georgina Hogarth's work in bringing letters into print was part of a family desire both to promote and to control. Not only did the edition present, effectively, a new book by Dickens, but Georgina also suppressed what seemed undesirable representations. In 1908 she asserted the family's copyright to prevent publication in Britain (though not in the United States) of Dickens's early love letters to Maria BEADNELL.

As people in Dickens's circle died, so their holdings of letters were published, collections focused on a single correspondent, sometimes with a thematic emphasis as in *Dickens as Editor* (1912), letters to his sub-editor Wills. These caches included the letters to Wilkie Collins (1892), to Mark LEMON (1927), and to Angela Burdett Coutts (1931), especially important as revealing Dickens's practical involvement in social work. With the deaths of Kate and Henry Fielding, Dickens's last two surviving children, Mrs Dickens's letters, held under wraps by the British Library, became available (1934).

The second significant general collection was three volumes edited by Walter DEXTER (1938) as part of the Nonesuch Edition of Dickens's works (see EDITIONS PUBLISHED AFTER DICKENS'S LIFETIME). While this gave 5,811 letters to just under 1,000 correspondents, it was only available as part of the complete edition, itself expensive, limited to 877 sets, and very much aimed at the private collector. The editing was careless and the notes virtually non-existent. In 1951 Humphry HOUSE proposed, in a broadcast, 'A New Edition of Dickens's Letters' (repr. *All in Due Time*, 1955). The plan was to publish all of Dickens's letters, however seemingly trivial a mere refusal or an appointment time might be deemed, to offer the fullest detail of the pattern and significance of Dickens's life and a sense of his engagement with his age. The fullness and accuracy of the texts was to be matched by thorough annotation: a history of Dickens's letters and the editorial principles are set out in the Introduction to the Pilgrim Edition's first volume. The first stage of the enterprise was to collect the texts and much time was initially and necessarily spent on this. The project was unshaken by the death of Humphry House (1955), whose work was taken up by his widow Madeline, Graham Storey, and Kathleen Tillotson as general editors, assisted by numerous Dickens scholars. An initial grant by the Pilgrim Trust ensured the project's financial viability and provided the name of the edition. The British Academy became an important continuing source of funding, adopting the edition as an official research project, a fact recognized by the Academy's name being added to the title description of Volume 8. The first volume, covering the years 1820–39, was published by the Clarendon Press in 1965; Volumes 2 and 3 each covered two years, and currently each volume covers three years. The edition was completed in 12 volumes in 2002. Supplements are published annually in the *Dickensian*. The edition includes surviving letters to Dickens within the richly detailed annotation and gives an important range of related materials in appendices, amongst them Dickens's DIARIES; agreements with publishers; prospectuses for the periodicals; a house inventory, including books, of 1844; programmes for theatricals; and lists of engagements for the public readings. Volume 7 has an important Addendum of new and improved texts keyed chronologically to earlier volumes, and the final volume will offer another. Throughout, the Dickens family has lent its help and enthusiastic support, not least by permission to publish copyright material.

At one level, Dickens's letters help to build up a record of his life. This is true even of the briefest, whether standard circular letters, signed by him, urging, for example, attendance at crucial meetings of the ROYAL LITERARY FUND in June 1855, or a note appointing 'Halfpast three accordingly' for an expedition to Greenwich (to Lemon, 12 May 1855). The vast bulk of his correspondence confirms the energy of Dickens, as it does his ability to discipline and direct himself. What is more remarkable still is the length of many of the letters, whether personal or business, when it is realized just how many, among his other avocations, he was writing. In the 1850s he not only read through proofs of *Household Words*, but commented in detail about individual articles, the make-up and tone of whole numbers, while urging on the magazine's social and educational programme. During the CRIMEAN WAR, when positive support of the French alliance was needed, an article by Eliza Lynn ('this Balzac-imitation in poking with a little knife into the social peculiarities of France') proved unsatisfactory in both style and mood (to Wills, 14 October 1854). The letters, while they can be sober and forceful, in a plain style, as explanation or argument or instruction, make clear in their often exuberant description and imaginative play how far Dickens's fictional style was habitual to him. Forster wrote of the letters that were the basis of *American Notes* that they display 'the rare faculty of seizing out of a multitude of things the thing that is essential, the irresistible play of humour, such pathos as only humourists of this high order possess, and the unwearied unforced vivacity of ever fresh, bouyant, bounding animal spirits' (Forster 3.5). In the early letters Dickens shows his Regency upbringing, with a readiness for puns and jokes (never lost to him) along with a delight in the mildly improper: his supposed infatuation with the young Queen Victoria, for example, or a cod illustration to a NEWGATE NOVEL, with 'Jonathan Wild forcing Mrs. Sheppard down the grown-up seat of a gloomy privy, and Blueskin . . . cramming a child . . . down the little hole' (to Forster, 18 September 1839). Dickens is never more exuberant than in adversity, whether travelling to report parliamentary elections, threatened by storms on the Atlantic, or enduring bad inns and helpless companions in Italy. He is acute in observing his fellows, not least the British abroad, about whom he can be hilariously

scathing. But he is not given to lengthy introspection or brooding, though the comparisons thrown up by a second Italian tour (1853) and particularly by the second American visit (1867–8) are illuminating. Nor, though many incidental acute remarks are struck out, does he analyse his own art or that of others. Dickens is an observer, a commentator, and a man bent upon getting things done: his characteristic emotions are active ones. Despite the claims of Georgina Hogarth and Mamie Dickens, Dickens's rhetoric is a virtuoso construction that creates a visionary world rather than offering a revelation of the inner self: Elizabeth Gaskell or Jane Carlyle are known in their letters, where Dickens's verbal magic holds off even while it hints at a hidden (because absent) self. It is the more striking, therefore, in high emotional moments, when Dickens is angry or depressed or under stress, to feel that the man usually concealed now reveals himself. One such moment is identified by the Pilgrim editors during the first American visit, when Dickens's idealization of this new nation collapsed (Pilgrim 3, p. x). Again, in the struggle to establish the *Daily News* (1845), Dickens, overwhelmed, abandons anger or even feelings of physical grogginess for despair at the prospect of 'the maimed hands of this wounded Newspaper dragging . . . night and day' (to Bradbury and Evans, 6 November 1845). Or more crucially yet, the continued pressure of late 1854 and early 1855, when his mounting anger, the anger of a patriot, over the follies and wilful destructiveness of the Crimean War, the unchecked ravages of cholera, and political indifference at home, the strain of work, intertwined with increased dissatisfaction with his marital and emotional life, produces letters that show a man on the verge of breakdown, yet determined to go on, to explain his political ideas, to engage with administrative reform, to foster the first ideas of *Little Dorrit*, and to bring off amateur theatricals in *The Lighthouse* of the very highest quality.

Dickens's letters diffuse out into his times: through the vast range of correspondents (far more than Forster or even Georgina Hogarth and Mamie Dickens suggested), the range of interests, and the range of activities. It is not true, as has been rather hyperbolically claimed, that Dickens engaged with every aspect of his age: for all his intelligence, there is no sustained intellectual involvement, philosophical or SCIENTIFIC. But there is that unbounded activity, expressed most basically and also symptomatically in a physical vigour, even restlessness, fully engaged in social pleasure and social reform, in high and low culture, responsive to other societies and other people. Without his letters, Dickens would be the less as man and writer.     AE

The British Academy Pilgrim Edition of The Letters of Charles Dickens, ed. Madeline House, Graham Storey, Kathleen Tillotson, et al., vols. 1–12 (1965–2002).

**Lever, Charles** (1806–72), Irish novelist. Lever began his writing career with the success of his first outing into fiction, *The Confessions of Harry Lorrequer* (1839), published first in Dublin and afterwards issued in London in Dickens-style monthly parts, complete with illustrations by 'Phiz' (March 1839–January 1840; see SERIAL FICTION; BROWNE, H. K.). He went on to publish a great deal, specializing in broad Irish comedy. Dickens's friendship began in the 1840s; in 1846 he visited Lever in ITALY. In August 1860 Dickens began publishing serial instalments of Lever's latest novel, *A Day's Ride; A Life's Romance* in *All The Year Round*. The undertaking did not prosper. 'We drop,' Dickens mournfully reported the circulation figures to Lever in a letter 'we drop, rapidly and continuously, with The Day's Ride. Whether it is too detached and discursive in its interest for the audience and the form of publication, I can not say positively' (6 October 1860). To rescue his periodical Dickens began serializing *Great Expectations*—'a book I had intended for one of my long twenty number serials. I must abandon that design and forego its profit (a very serious consideration, you may believe), and shape the story for these pages.' This latter hint that Dickens had been put out of pocket by Lever's lack of popularity clearly stung the Irishman to a wounded reply, as Dickens's anxious next letter (15 October 1860) makes evident. A dozen subsequent letters from Dickens to Lever show him trying to smooth the novelist's ruffled feathers.     AR

**Lewes, George Henry** (1817–78), writer, best known in his secondary role as partner to George ELIOT, whom he was unable to marry because his estranged wife was still alive.

Lewes and Eliot lived openly together, and he wrote on aesthetics, philosophy, and science, as well as writing plays, a biography of Goethe (1855), and a novel, *Ranthorpe* (1847). He was also a semi-professional actor and played in Dickens's AMATEUR THEATRICAL company in 1850, in a production of JONSON's *Every Man In His Humour*. The play went on tour in order to raise funds for impoverished writers. Dickens had 'an old and great regard' for Lewes (Forster 6.6). Lewes had said of Dickens that he 'would not give you a farthing of money, but he would take no end of trouble for you. He would spend a whole day, for instance, in looking for the most suitable lodgings for you, and would spare himself neither time nor fatigue' (Kaplan 1988, p. 228). A year after Dickens's death, however, Lewes published a paper on 'Dickens in Relation to Criticism' (*Fortnightly Review*, February 1872) which greatly annoyed FORSTER because of an implied depreciation of the talent for 'fun' in Dickens's writing and a demeaning of his popularization of literature (Forster 9.1). Lewes's claim that Dickens's vivid imagination was merely 'hallucinative', and that Dickens had once told him that every word uttered by his characters was distinctly *heard* by him before it was written down, was also angrily refuted by Forster.     SL

**Lewis, Matthew Gregory** (1775–1818), novelist and playwright. Lewis's impact on Dickens was as the foremost exponent of GOTHIC literature in England through his novel *The Monk* (1795), with its fiend-like protagonist (possibly the source of the name of Dickens's villain, Monks, in *Oliver Twist*). The dungeon scene in his sensational drama *The Castle Spectre* (Drury Lane, 1797) may have influenced *A Tale of Two Cities*. Dickens makes a burlesque reference to this play in a speech to the ROYAL GENERAL THEATRICAL FUND in 1851 (*Speeches*, p. 125). His *Timour the Tartar*, in which Crummles's pony 'goes on' (*NN* 22), introduced horses onto the Covent Garden stage in 1811.     JD

**Ley, J. W. T.** (1878–1942), Dickens scholar, author of the first detailed study of the novelist's friendships, *The Dickens Circle* (1918), and a prolific contributor to the DICKENSIAN. His greatest achievement was a monumental annotated edition of FORSTER's *Life of Dickens* (1928). In this he drew on his own research for

The *Dickens Circle* as well as the pioneering biographical researches of Robert Langton, F. G. KITTON, and B. W. MATZ to supplement Forster, particularly as regards Dickens's love-affair with Maria BEADNELL, the breakdown of his marriage, and his relations with BRADBURY AND EVANS. Some of this new information had been unknown to Forster, much of it he could not (and would not have wished) to use when so many of those intimately involved were still alive. Ellen TERNAN does not figure anywhere in Ley's annotation, but so good is his work generally that A. J. Hoppé's 1969 Everyman edition of Forster, which does have extensive notes on the Ternan matter, has not superseded Ley, whose edition is still the one most regularly cited by Dickens scholars.                                             MS

**libraries.** We associate Dickens with cheaper forms of publication (SERIAL PUBLICATION and publication in NEWSPAPERS AND MAGAZINES in particular), but the general state of the mid-Victorian book market was one of very high book prices. In 1852 Gladstone addressed the House of Commons on the subject of what he called 'the enormously high price of books': 'You go into the houses of your friends, and, unless in the case of books for which they have a professional want that must be satisfied, or unless they happen to be persons of extraordinary wealth, you do not find copies of new publications upon their tables, purchased for themselves; but you find something from the circulating library, or something from the book club' (*Hansard*, 13 May 1852). Three-volume novels might retail at 31s 6d, more than the average middle-class reader could afford. Circulating libraries grew up to cater for this market; for a fee, usually a guinea, readers could borrow as many books as they could read in a year. The success of the libraries tended to entrench the practice of publishing three-volume novels (the advantage to the libraries of the triple-decker format was that each of the three volumes could be loaned out to different customers, tripling income). Some critics have even argued that libraries 'preferred nominally high prices as a kind of insurance that readers would be compelled to borrow' (Griest 1970, p. 11).

There were a number of circulating libraries in the 1840s and 1850s, the most significant being Mudie's. Established by Charles Edward Mudie in 1842, it began to grow after relocating to New Oxford Street in 1852, thereafter swiftly dominating the market. By the 1860s it had no competitors of any size except for the circulating library of W. H. Smith (established 1860), which, being based chiefly in railway stations, did not compete directly. Libraries were established in the major cities, but also in holiday resorts (particularly Bath and seaside resorts), and as the railway network spread so libraries appeared throughout the whole country. By 1861 Mudie claimed to be buying some 180,000 volumes a year, and his decision to stock a book could make or break a title (as with the 430 copies of THACKERAY's *Henry Esmond* ordered in 1852). This purchasing power gave Mudie's tremendous influence over the publishing market, and his strong views on the proper moral tone he considered fiction ought to strike had a direct effect on the literary scene. Meredith's 1859 novel *The Ordeal of Richard Feverel* was deemed unacceptable by the library, without whose sales the book flopped. Meredith himself believed it took his reputation ten years to recover (Horsman 1990, p. 3).

Dickens rarely published triple-decker novels (an exception is *Great Expectations*, which came out in three volumes in 1861, perhaps specifically to appeal to the circulating libraries: Mudie's purchased 1,400 copies of the first edition), and his success at other modes of publication gave him an independence from the perceived power of the big libraries.                                             RCS

Feltes, Norman N., *Modes of Production of Victorian Novels* (1986).
Griest, Guinevere, *Mudie's Circulating Library and the Victorian Novel* (1970).
Horsman, Alan, *The Victorian Novel* (1990).

**library of Dickens.** After Dickens's death his library was sold and duly listed in Sotheran's 'Price Current of Literature,' giving a record of the works he then possessed. This was edited by J. H. Stonehouse as *The Library of Charles Dickens from Gadshill* (1935). In 1844 when Dickens let his London home in Devonshire Terrace, his books had been inventoried, when there were at least 2,000 volumes (see Pilgrim 4.711–26). Making all allowances for incompleteness, lost works, and such questions as how far owners read all their books, the catalogue provides a guide to

Dickens's concerns. It may even help to show something of his intellectual world, its eccentricities and limitations, and point to interests and connections we might otherwise miss.

The books have been dispersed and few can now be located. Even so, as long as they are genuine, they can be identified by a label said to have been placed in each volume, and by a bookplate showing Dickens's crest of a couchant lion in most of them. It is surprising that the whereabouts of so many obviously valuable works, apart from the Dickens connection, have been lost track of. Many would certainly be helpful for Dickens studies insofar as they are catalogued as having his autograph notes. His edition of S. Hibbert, *Philosophy of Apparitions* (1824), had marginalia including 'a rather long note', p. 371, on 'the man who took every woman to be his wife'. It is suggested that he read R. Dale Owen, *Footfalls on the Boundary of Another World* (1860) with a view to supernatural events in *Edwin Drood*. There were notes on the flyleaf of Captain Charles Johnson, *General History of the Pyrates* (1724), and so there were on the five volumes of Lord Braybrooke's edition of Pepys's diary (1828) 'for quotation if need be' (see *Speeches*, pp. 201–2, 356–7). The catalogue does not record all such notes, as Dickens's set of FIELDING's *Works*, ed. A. Chalmers, 10 vols. (1806), now in Edinburgh University Library, has some highly uncomplimentary marked passages with comments added in Dickens's hand linking them with John FORSTER, Lady Morgan, and LANDOR.

*Bleak House* is typical of some of the novels which can lead us back to his reading, and then point in other directions. The reference to the megalosaurus may come from two of the *Bridgewater Treatises*, which Dickens acquired; we know from what Dickens says of spontaneous combustion that he resorted to his set of the *Annual Register*, and also to Dr Robert MacNish, *The Anatomy of Drunkenness* (1840), and possibly to his *The Philosophy of Sleep* (1840); the bound volume of pamphlets on 'sanitary subjects' leads straight to Jo's graveyard. The library held numerous works on dreams, which Dickens claimed to have read and observed 'with greatest attention and interest', either connected with *Bleak House* or reaching out to the whole dubious world of the supernatural, animal magnetism

(see MESMERISM), mental instability, and curious tales and wonders. For though Dickens was usually dedicated to resisting the irrational, his imagination was fascinated by the extraordinary.

His reading is such a vast and vague field that it remains largely unexplored, and it is hard to be specific about suggestions for further inquiry. Clearly there is an interest in his works of French literature or of foreign translation, including his German and Italian folk tales, which happen to be in duplicate. He had a set in thirty volumes of the works of Paul de Kock, said by Paul Feval to be one of Dickens's favourite authors. Yet there may be some doubt about whether he settled all his French works in his regular library. From boyhood he had, as he said of himself, 'a greedy relish' for TRAVEL LITERATURE, acquiring whole sets of such books, from Hakluyt to the latest exploration of Africa and the Arctic. Other subjects that caught his particular attention were London (either historical or topical), British history, medicine, and anything connected with the theatre, particularly SHAKESPEARE.

Underlying the collection may have lain the wish to have a balanced library, and perhaps to repossess the authors or works that we know him to have read and reread when no more than 9 or 10, such as DEFOE, Fielding, SMOLLETT, STERNE, GOLDSMITH, CERVANTES, and the 18th-century ESSAYISTS (Forster 1.1). He made a point of reacquiring *Ballantyne's Novelists' Library*, edited by SCOTT (1821–4). We can see Dickens's library-building in process at an auction sale (10–11 March 1841): sound sets and steady classics, probably far from showy.

The catalogue is indispensable for a thorough biography, if only because of its presentation copies. Some included material from Dickens's friends that can be found nowhere else, as in John Poole's or Leigh HUNT's annotations, or an original dedicatory poem by HOOD. Books came from figures who would otherwise be unknown to us. It is not a matter of there once having been attractive association copies, as with the signed works from FORSTER or Wilkie COLLINS, but what they have to tell that is otherwise unknown. Even the printed dedication of LANDOR's *Imaginary Conversations* in the 1853 edition and year of Boythorn shows us his judgement of Dickens, that 'in breaking up and cultivating the unredeemed wastes of Humanity, no labours have been so strenuous, so continuous, or half so successful as yours. While the world admired in you an unlimited knowledge of mankind, deep thought, vivid imagination, and bursts of eloquence from unclouded heights . . . I see you at the schoolroom you have liberated from cruelty, and at the cottage you have purified from disease.'

The Stonehouse catalogue is not complete. Its thin list of CARLYLE's works, for example, is made good by another catalogue in manuscript, recorded slightly earlier, which is in the Pierpont Morgan Library, New York. There are still discoveries to be made. (The contributor plans an updated catalogue.)     KJF

***Library of Fiction*** was a monthly magazine appearing from April 1836 until July 1837 (subtitled 'Family Story-Teller; consisting of Original Tales, Essays, and Sketches of Character'), where Dickens published two early sketches: 'The Tuggses at Ramsgate' (April 1836) and 'A Little Talk about Spring, and the Sweeps' (June 1836, reprinted as 'The First of May' in *Sketches by Boz*, Second Series). *Library of Fiction* was published by CHAPMAN AND HALL and edited by Charles Whitehead (1804–62). Its first number came out the same day as the first number of *Pickwick Papers*, and Hablot Knight BROWNE was the illustrator for both.     KC

***Life of Our Lord, The*** The published title of a simplified version of the life of Christ written by Dickens in 1846 for reading aloud to his children. His own title was 'The Children's New Testament'. FORSTER says that nothing would have shocked Dickens so much as the suggestion that it be published (Forster 5.2), and Dickens's express wish that it not be published was honoured by his last surviving child, Henry Fielding Dickens, who nevertheless in his will freed his heirs to do with it as they saw fit. According to A. J. Hoppé in his edition of Forster's *Life*, the manuscript and copyright were sold for £40,000 to the *Daily Mail*, and in 1934 the work appeared in many newspapers as well as a hardback edition.

Dickens's account is theologically mixed. Christ's miracles and resurrection are recounted, but there is no mention of virgin birth or atonement, and the angel announcing his birth says that he 'will grow up to be so good that God will love Him as His own

Son'—a UNITARIAN interpretation. It is Christ's roles as teacher and comforter that are stressed: 'He was always merciful and tender. And because He did such good, and taught people how to love God and how to hope to go to Heaven after death, he was called *Our Saviour*.'     RN

**Lillo, George** (1631–79), playwright. His *The London Merchant or the History of George Barnwell* (1731) and *Fatal Curiosity* (1736) initiated a new type of bourgeois tragedy, strong in pathos and MORAL instruction, which influenced both the development of 18th-century sentimental DRAMA and of MELODRAMA (see SENTIMENT). Dickens saw *The London Merchant* as a child in Rochester (Ackroyd 1990, p. 37), and refers to it familiarly in *Barnaby Rudge* (4) and in an EXAMINER review of LEECH's *Rising Generation* (*Examiner*, 30 December 1848; repr. *Journalism* 2.145). During Wopsle's lugubrious parlour representation of *George Barnwell* (*GE* 15), Pip is made to feel 'positively apologetic' when Wopsle and Pumblechook identify his 'unoffending self' with the apprentice who steals from his master and then murders him.     JD

***Little Dorrit*** Dickens's eleventh novel, published in twenty (as nineteen) monthly parts between December 1855 and June 1857. His most politically outspoken novel, and also the most overtly symbolic in structure, it initially attracted mixed critical reception but achieved initial sales higher than any of his previous monthly SERIALS, and has come to be admired as one of his greatest works.

### Inception and Composition

Dickens began his *Book of Memoranda*, in which he noted ideas for future works, in January 1855 (Forster 9.7; Kaplan 1981; see COMPOSITION, DICKENS'S METHODS OF). His jottings included 'a series of little closets squeezed up into the corner of a dark street [in] a fashionable neighbourhood', which became the Barnacle residence; a bedridden person 'brought out of doors by an unexpected exercise of . . . strength of character', who became Mrs Clennam; a man who sees 'much less difference than you would suppose between an honest man and a scoundrel', who became Henry Gowan; and an 'unwieldy ship, taken in tow by the snorting little steam Tug', which became Casby and Pancks.

On 6 February 1855 Dickens remarked to Angela Burdett COUTTS that he had 'motes of new stories floating before my eyes in the dirty air', and soon he was 'writing and planning and making notes over an immense number of little bits of paper' (to Wilkie Collins, 4 March 1855). By the beginning of May he reported to FORSTER that 'the story is breaking out all round me' (?2–3 May 1855), and later that month he instructed his publishers BRADBURY AND EVANS to advertise a new work for November publication (21 May 1855; Pilgrim 7.625–6n.).

But although Dickens was always restless when starting a novel, he had greater difficulty getting under way with *Little Dorrit* than with any other of his novels. His letters and working notes indicate considerable indecisiveness, and by 19 August, still no further than the second number, he told Forster he 'had half a mind to begin again, and work in what I have done, afterwards'. By 11 September, he told WILLS, he was 'in a hideous state of mind' over No. 3—a complaint he repeated five days later. His original idea, according to Forster, consisted 'of a leading man for a story who should bring about all the mischief in it, lay it all on Providence, and say at every fresh calamity, "well, it's a mercy, however, nobody was to blame, you know!"' (8.1). This idea appears in Dickens's notebook entry, 'The people who lay all their sins negligences and ignorances, on Providence', and is not finally rejected until his working notes for No. 4 (Kaplan 1981; Stone 1987).

In their study of the evolution of Dickens's conception of the novel, John Butt and Kathleen Tillotson point to the change of title as the key to understanding how the book took shape (1957, pp. 222–33). On 8 May he told Miss Coutts that he had a 'capital name' for the novel, and as late as 16 September he was able to report to Mrs WATSON that his title was 'Nobody's Fault'. On 13 October, however, the book was advertised as *Little Dorrit*, a change which indicates a shift in focus away from social criticism to 'optimism about humanity'. 'The original title', H. P. Sucksmith states, 'would no longer do for a novel that did in fact blame a system rather than individuals', whereas the new one points 'away from the negative and pessimistic theme of deception, imprisonment and irresponsibility in society towards a more positive, hopeful balance

through the counter-theme of enlightenment, freedom, duty and love' (Clarendon Introduction, p. xxi).

That autumn Dickens began at last to proceed with confidence. On the same day that he revealed the old working title to Mrs Watson, he told Forster, 'I have a great idea of overwhelming that family with wealth. Their condition would be very curious. I can make [Little] Dorrit very strong in the story, I hope.' He was soon reporting to friends his delight with chapter 10, 'Containing the whole Science of Government'—'a scarifier', he exclaimed to Wilkie COLLINS (30 September 1855), and on 29 October he announced to Bradbury and Evans that he intended to divide the story into two books, 'Poverty' and 'Riches'. In mid-October he moved to PARIS, where he remained (with occasional dashes back to London, and PUBLIC READINGS of *A Christmas Carol* in Peterborough and Sheffield) until the end of April, and from June to September he was in Boulogne, moving back to London only on account of an epidemic.

After autumn 1855 the one interruption to otherwise smooth progress on the book came in January, from frustration at being unable to write while sitting to Ary Scheffer for his PORTRAIT. 'Society, the Circumlocution Office, and Mr Gowan are of course three parts of one idea and design', he wrote confidently to Forster (?29–30 January 1856). That winter he closed an agreement to purchase Gad's Hill Place—'the dream of my childhood'—which he had seen for sale the previous winter; he moved in shortly after completing *Little Dorrit* in May 1857 (to Wills, 9 February 1855; see HOMES OF DICKENS). On 7 April 1856 he exclaimed to Forster that some things in his depiction of Flora seemed to him 'extraordinarily droll', and before writing No. 9 he told Forster, 'The story lies before me, I hope, strong and clear. Not easily to be told, but nothing of that sort is to be easily done that I know of' (?11 June 1856).

After writing Book II, chapter 1, in which the travellers meet at the Convent of the Great St Bernard in the Swiss Alps (an idea recorded in his working notes for No. 1, and mentioned again to Forster in a letter of 20 January 1856), he reminded Mrs Watson and M. Cerjat of visiting that place with them years previously (see SWITZERLAND). 'A new and serious piece', he called the chapter; 'how good it is!!!' (5 October 1856, 19 January 1857). From October 1856 he was embroiled in preparations to stage an AMATEUR THEATRICAL production of Wilkie Collins's play The FROZEN DEEP, but work on the novel continued to proceed smoothly. He allowed that he was having to work hard 'bringing a pretty large field of characters up to the winning post' (to G. F. Hudson, 11 April 1857), but he finished writing on 9 May, having three days previously paid a visit to the site of the Marshalsea, where his father had been imprisoned for debt many years previously (to Forster, 7 May 1857; to Collins, 11 May 1857; see DICKENS, JOHN).

### Contract, Text, and Publication History

The publishing agreement of 1844 between Dickens and Bradbury and Evans expired with Bleak House (1851–3), and Hard Times, first published serially in Household Words (1854), was subject to a separate contract. Accordingly, Little Dorrit was published under a new agreement, by which the publishers were to receive, as before, a fourth share of such books as he would write, but with their percentage no longer charged on partnership accounts, and with a clause permitting Dickens to withdraw 'when he pleased' (Forster 7.2). This reduction in Bradbury and Evans's commission, even when sales for the final numbers were lower than those for Bleak House, gave Dickens profits which were 'the best of his career' (Patten 1978, p. 251). Relations between author and publishers were amicable.

The number plans, heavily revised manuscript, dedication, and Preface (all complete), plus the corrected proofs (incomplete) are in the FORSTER COLLECTION. Additional proofs are in the DEXTER COLLECTION. Details are given in the Clarendon Edition, pp. xliv–xlix. Chapter 4 of Book I was interpolated into the text; chapters 2 and 3 of Book II were transposed from the order in which they were written; chapters 16 and 17 of Book II originally comprised a single chapter.

Two errors caused Dickens some consternation. In No. 13 he had left a description of Casby as having 'baptismal water on the brain' in the corrected proof, as a private joke for Forster, and it was not removed by the printer. Fearing to offend religious sensibilities, he wrote to the publishers, 'I never was so vexed in my life', but he had spotted the phrase in time for it to be deleted before the number appeared (to Bradbury and Evans, 29 November 1856; Pilgrim 8.227 n.). The second error occurred when Dickens wrote 'Blandois' instead of 'Rigaud' in No. 15 and did not notice it until after publication. An erratum slip was included with the next number (to Bradbury and Evans, 5 February 1857; Pilgrim 8.274 n.). A third 'serious blunder' was overlooked until the Clarendon Edition, in which three lines from No. 6 were dropped by the printer and not restored (Clarendon Introduction, p. xxix).

Little Dorrit was dedicated to Dickens's close friend and sometime illustrator, Clarkson STANFIELD, for whom a specially bound presentation copy was made (to Stanfield, 20 May 1857).

Dickens's Preface, dated May 1857, noted the unity of the work as a completed whole, pointed to the historical basis for his satire of the Circumlocution Office and Mr Merdle, and described the visit he made to the remains of the Marshalsea prison three days before finishing the book. He concluded with a personal message of appreciation to his readers and a hope to meet them again.

Simultaneously with the completion of its monthly serialization, Little Dorrit was published in one volume by Bradbury and Evans on 30 May 1857. There were three further major editions during his lifetime: the Library Edition (1859), the Cheap Edition (1861), and the Charles Dickens Edition (1868). Sucksmith observes that later editions are textually more corrupt than the first (Clarendon Introduction, pp. xxxviii–xli; see EDITIONS OVER WHICH DICKENS HAD CONTROL). Tauchnitz issued Little Dorrit on the continent initially in parts, starting in 1856, and then in four volumes (see COPYRIGHT). Harper's paid £250 for advance sheets of the novel for American publication (Patten 1978, p. 251; see EDITIONS: FOREIGN). The definitive Clarendon Edition (1979) is based on the 1857 text.

### Illustrations

Dickens's principal ILLUSTRATOR, Hablot BROWNE, supplied the cover, frontispiece, title-page vignette, and illustrations for Little Dorrit. His work has been seen as uneven at best, technically and conceptually 'diminished' at worst. F. G. KITTON notes that, uncharacteristically, none of the plates bear Browne's signature (1899, p. 112), a fact which Jane Rabb Cohen interprets as a sign of 'total exhaustion' (1980, p. 117). Dickens briefed Browne 'at full explanatory length' in early October 1855, and the cover wrapper design (analysed by Butt and Tillotson 1957, pp. 224–5, and by Steig 1978, pp. 159–61), depicting characters and foreshadowing themes of the novel, reveals Browne's familiarity with Dickens's intentions (to Wills, 19 October 1855).

But several of Dickens's surviving letters of instruction to Browne indicate that novelist and illustrator were not in full accord. On 8 November 1856 Dickens reminded Browne to 'please keep Clennam, always, as agreeable and well-looking as possible'. On 6 December he objected to a drawing of Lord Decimus with his hand out, 'because that looks condescending, and I want him to be upright, stiff, unmixable with mere mortality'. And on 10 February 1857 the sketch for Mr Dorrit before his collapse was decidedly at odds with Dickens's wishes. 'He is too comic now . . . and what he imperatively wants, is an expression doing less violence in the reader's mind to what is going to happen to him, and much more in accordance with that serious end which is so close before him.' In view of this dissatisfaction, it is unsurprising that Browne was hired only once more (for *A Tale of Two Cities*) to illustrate a novel by Dickens.

## Sources and Context

In the months prior to and during the composition of *Little Dorrit* there was widespread public concern, which Dickens shared, over the administration and GOVERNMENT of the country. The Northcote-Trevelyan report, published in February 1854, vigorously attacked the system of 'political and personal patronage' by which civil servants were recruited. The debacles of the CRIMEAN WAR during the autumn and winter of 1854 led Dickens to write a clutch of angry articles for *Household Words*, including 'Prince Bull' (17 February 1855), 'Nobody, Somebody, and Everybody' (30 August 1856), and 'The Murdered Person' (11 October 1856). In January 1855 a Select Committee chaired by J. A. Roebuck was formed to investigate the administration of the war. Roebuck's report, published in June, 'had a crucial effect' on

Dickens's conception of *Little Dorrit* (Clarendon Introduction, p. xvii). That winter his friend Arthur Layard was agitating unsuccessfully for administrative reform, and although Dickens turned down (not for the first time) an invitation to stand for election to Parliament (to unknown correspondent, 17 March 1857), he was more politically active than at any other time of his career, joining the Administrative Reform Association in May 1855 and making a speech to a crowded audience at Drury Lane Theatre at the Association's third meeting, in which he spoke of the government's 'theatricals'—'*The Comedy of Errors* played so dismally like a tragedy that we cannot bear it' (*Speeches*, pp. 197–208).

His letters of the time indicate despair of the country's political process. 'I am really serious in thinking', he told Forster on 30 September 1855, 'that representative government is become altogether a failure with us, that the English gentilities and subserviences render the people unfit for it, and that the whole thing has broken down since that great seventeenth-century time, and has no hope in it.' A few days later he wrote to MACREADY, saying 'I have lost hope even in the Ballot. We appear to me to have proved the failure of Representative Institutions' (4 October 1855). And he held Palmerston, who became Prime Minister when the Aberdeen government fell in consequence of maladministration of the Crimean War, 'the emptiest imposter and the most dangerous delusion, ever known' (to Angela Burdett Coutts, 13 August 1856).

On 16 February 1856 the suicide of the financier John Sadlier (1814–56) caused a sensation when a career of fraud and forgery was revealed. 'I had the general idea of the Society business before the Sadlier affair', Dickens wrote to Forster (?29–30 March 1856), but I shaped Mr Merdle himself out of that precious rascality' (see Smith, 1971; MONEY AND FINANCE).

A number of essays in *Household Words*, notably 'A Walk in a Workhouse' (25 May 1850), 'A Poor Man's Tale of a Patent' (19 October 1850), and 'Red Tape' (15 February 1851), prefigure themes and subjects in *Little Dorrit*. In summer of 1854 Dickens considered writing a series of papers for his journal under the title 'The Member from Nowhere'—foreshadowing 'Nobody's Fault'—to convey his 'contempt for the House of Commons' (to

Forster, ?30–1 July, ?6 August 1854). He thought of starting the series with a discussion of 'the Sunday question', which erupted the next year in the Hyde Park riots (24 June and 1, 8 July, over a bill to prevent Sunday trading), and which is reflected in chapter 3 of the novel as the 'gloomy, close, and stale' Sunday (see SABBATARIANISM).

Other subjects in *Little Dorrit* reach farther back in time. 'How Not To Do It' patently owes something to CARLYLE's 'Donothingism' (*Past and Present*, 1843). The Continental scenes draw explicitly on Dickens's travels in FRANCE, Switzerland, and ITALY in the 1840s, and the depiction of the Marshalsea prison derives from his personal experience of it in 1824. The portrait of Flora was directly based on Maria BEADNELL, whom he had loved passionately as a young man, and whose reappearance in his life as Mrs Winter in February 1855 had a profoundly unsettling effect (see CHARACTERS—ORIGINALS). 'We all have our Floras', he wrote to the Duke of Devonshire on 5 July 1856; '(mine is living, and extremely fat).'

As with *Bleak House*, *Little Dorrit* shows less influence by previous literary tradition than it was itself to have on later literature, although the idea of prison as a world unto itself—which had already appeared in *Pickwick* and in *Copperfield*—may owe something to SCOTT's *The Heart of Mid-Lothian* and to SHAKESPEARE's *Richard II* (see Clarendon Introduction, p. xxxiv).

Two topics in the novel which were *not* topical were Doyce's problems with getting his invention recognized and Mrs Clennam's house falling down. A Patent Law Amendment Law of 1852 simplified patent business and reduced costs (House 1941, p. 175), and Dickens had planted clues foreshadowing the collapse of the house well before 'recent and convenient' newspaper reports of houses in Tottenham Court Road falling down (see 'Curious Misprint in the *Edinburgh Review*', *HW* 1 August 1857, repudiating James Fitzjames Stephen's charge in 'The License of Modern Novelists', *Edinburgh Review*, 106, July 1857).

### Plot, Character, and Theme

The most sombre and oppressive of Dickens's novels, *Little Dorrit* is organized around a pervasive central symbol of imprisonment, manifest in a wide variety of instances. The novel begins in an actual cell in Marseilles, then moves to a group of travellers detained in quarantine, and on to a woman confined to a wheelchair. The most prominent prison is the Marshalsea debtors' prison in which the Dorrit family is incarcerated. As the book proceeds, examples of imprisonment—physical and psychological, institutional and individual, political, administrative, and economic—proliferate, establishing Dickens's vision of society at large as a kind of prison which entraps everyone save those (principally the story's heroine) who can find spiritual freedom through the power of love.

After being delayed by quarantine on his way home to England after twenty years in China, Arthur Clennam is coldly received on a dismal Sunday by his crippled mother and her servant, Jeremiah Flintwinch. Suspecting a wrong committed by his deceased father, Clennam resigns his share in the family business. He meets Amy, known as Little Dorrit, who does casual sewing jobs for Mrs Clennam, and follows her back to the Marshalsea, where she lives with and looks after her father, her ne'er-do-well brother, and sister (a dancer in a minor theatre). Clennam seeks information about Dorrit's creditors but learns nothing at the Circumlocution Office. He meets his acquaintance from Marseilles, Mr Meagles, and the engineer Daniel Doyce. Clennam becomes reacquainted with the love of his youth, Flora Finching, widowed daughter of Mr Casby, the landlord of Bleeding Heart Yard, and is dismayed to find her fat and silly, although good-hearted. As a legacy from her late husband Flora has a companion in Mr F's Aunt—one of Dickens's most extraordinary comic characters—a ferocious old lady given to gnomic utterances and vigorously hostile to Clennam.

Clennam and Doyce visit Meagles in Twickenham, where they meet the cynical dilettante Henry Gowan, who is courting Meagles's daughter Pet. Clennam suppresses his own attraction for Pet (who seems to love Gowan), and enters into partnership with Doyce. Little Dorrit is taken by her sister Fanny to meet the Society *grande dame* Mrs Merdle, whose fatuous son Edmund Sparkler admires Fanny, and who proceeds to buy her off. The sinister and haughty Rigaud (alias Blandois), first seen in the Marseilles prison, calls on Mrs Clennam. Gowan marries Pet.

Pancks, rent-collector for Casby, proves, after extensive researching, that Dorrit is heir to great wealth and secures his release from prison.

The Dorrit family, Gowan and Pet, and Rigaud/Blandois, unknown to one another, meet at the Convent of the Great St Bernard. At Martigny Mr Dorrit is outraged to find that his reserved room has been used by another, but is appeased by its occupant, Mrs Merdle. Despite coaching from Mrs General, hired by Dorrit to 'polish' his daughters, Amy cannot adjust to her new status as a 'fine lady'. Rigaud/Blandois accompanies the Gowans to Venice and kills Gowan's dog after it attacks him. Clennam unsuccessfully pursues Doyce's claim to an invention at the Circumlocution Office. At a grand dinner at Merdle's, a brief conversation between Merdle and Lord Decimus Tite Barnacle results in the appointment of Sparkler to the Circumlocution Office. Fanny and Sparkler are married. At another grand dinner, given by Mrs Merdle in Rome, Mr Dorrit's mind wanders; he imagines himself back in the Marshalsea, addresses his fellow-diners as fellow-prisoners, collapses, and soon dies. Miss Wade, a paranoid, self-tormenting woman, who has influenced Pet's maid Tattycoram to run away, is traced by Clennam to Calais. She has papers beneficial to Little Dorrit stolen by Rigaud from Mrs Clennam which she refuses to surrender. She gives Clennam a written account of her life.

Merdle's bank fails, and he commits suicide. Numerous investors, including Clennam, are ruined, and he is imprisoned in the Marshalsea, where his health and spirits fail. In a complex unravelling, it is revealed that Mrs Clennam is not Arthur's mother but his stepmother, and that she has suppressed a codicil of her husband's will by which Little Dorrit would have been made rich. Despite her paralysis, she rises from her wheelchair and runs to speak to Little Dorrit. When she leaves, her house falls down, killing Rigaud, who had been attempting to blackmail her. Tattycoram returns the stolen papers. Arthur, released from prison and restored to partnership with Doyce, at last recognizes the nature of Little Dorrit's love for him and marries her.

## Reception

Bradbury and Evans printed 32,000 copies of the first number of *Little Dorrit*, but two reprintings of 3,000 copies each were needed that month, and by 8 February Dickens reported to Georgina HOGARTH that 40,000 copies had been sold. 'A brilliant triumph', he declared to his publishers (2 December 1855). '*Little Dorrit* has beaten even *Bleak House* out of the field', he wrote to Forster; 'It is a most tremendous start, and I am overjoyed at it' (?1 and 2 December 1855). Despite a decline in the press run to 31,000 for the final numbers, Dickens could still claim in his Preface, 'I have never had so many readers'.

REVIEWS, however, were decidedly mixed. Politically motivated hostility—notably from James Fitzjames Stephen in the *Edinburgh Review*, who called the book 'false' and 'in the highest degree mischievous'—contrasted sharply with buoyant sales. Even Dickens's admirers were unconvinced. Forster detected a 'droop in his invention' and a 'want of ease', and judged that *Little Dorrit* 'made no material addition to his reputation' (8.1). GISSING, while allowing that *Little Dorrit* contained 'some of the best work Dickens ever did', found it a 'weary' book, and CHESTERTON called it Dickens's 'one collapse'. George Bernard Shaw, on the other hand, declared it 'the most complete picture of English society in the XIX century in existence', adding that it was 'a more seditious book than *Das Kapital*' (Laurence and Quinn 1985, pp. 51, 64).

Like other of Dickens's later books, *Little Dorrit* was adapted for the stage less frequently than his early works. On the other hand, a DRAMATIZATION by James Albery, *The Two Roses*, featuring Henry Irving as Digby Grant (a character based on William Dorrit), was performed frequently throughout the 1870s, and one of the most ambitious FILM adaptations of Dickens to date is Christine Edzard's two-part, six-hour version of 1987.

Undoubtedly the single critical assessment most influential in establishing the novel's present status as one of Dickens's masterpieces was Lionel Trilling's Introduction to the New Oxford Illustrated Edition of *Little Dorrit* (1953). Trilling argues that this novel, 'marked not so much by its powers of particularization as by its powers of generalisation and abstraction', is 'about society in its very essence'. The prison, he suggests, surpasses all other symbols used by Dickens because it 'is an actuality before it is ever a symbol', and the character of Little Dorrit herself is 'the Paraclete in female form'. *Little Dorrit* is the subject of a brief monograph by J. C. Reid and of a stimulating chapter by F. R. LEAVIS (1970).                                    PVWS

> Collins, Philip, 'The Prison and the Critics', *Times Literary Supplement*, 18 April 1980.
> Leavis (1970).
> Reid, J. C., *Charles Dickens: Little Dorrit* (1967).
> Smith, Grahame and Smith, Angela, 'Dickens as a Popular Artist', *Dickensian*, 67 (1971).
> Trilling, Lionel, '*Little Dorrit*', *Kenyon Review*, 15 (1953); repr. as 'Introduction' in New Oxford Illustrated Edition of *Little Dorrit* (1953); as '*Little Dorrit*' in *The Opposing Self* (1955); and elsewhere.

**Lockhart, John Gibson** (1794–1854), editor of the *Quarterly Review* (1825–53), commissioned an important early review of Dickens in October 1837. Lockhart had been notorious as 'the Scorpion' on *Blackwood's Magazine* in the early 1820s but is most famous as the son-in-law and first biographer (1837–8) of Sir Walter SCOTT, whom he met in 1818. George HOGARTH, Dickens's father-in-law, claimed to have introduced Lockhart to Scott.

Dickens did not hold Abraham Hayward's condescending tone in the *Quarterly Review*'s October 1837 article against Lockhart, for a year later he inscribed a copy of *Oliver Twist* to him. Dickens also sympathized with Lockhart's controversial pamphlet at this time that depicted Scott as an author exploited by publishers, an image Dickens identified with: he defended it (anonymously) in three EXAMINER reviews (2 September 1838, 31 March and 29 September 1839). Dickens and Lockhart met around this time, and Richard Ford was commissioned to write another, more favourable, review of Dickens in the *Quarterly* (June 1839). However, Lockhart was critical of Dickens's radical tendencies and thought the inflammation of discontent with the ruling classes in *The CHIMES* irresponsible (see Pilgrim 4.212 n.). Although their relationship was never intimate, Dickens visited Lockhart in Rome during his last illness in 1853.    KC

> Fielding, K. J., 'Scott and His Publishers', *Dickensian*, 46 (1950).

**London:** 1. bridges and the river; 2. buildings and building; 3. business London; 4. docklands; 5. entertainment London; 6. fashionable London; 7. growth; 8. markets; 9. residential segregation; 10. slums and rookeries; 11. streets and street traders; 12. topography. See map p. 614.

**1. Bridges and river.** Betsey Trotwood proves to be 'quite gracious on the subject of the River Thames' which looks 'very well with the sun upon it, though not like the sea before [her] cottage' (*DC* 35). The tidal Thames dominated much of London's early economic life and determined both the nature of its historic expansion and its development as Britain's largest port. The conservancy of the river, from the mouth of the Medway to Staines, was consigned to the Corporation of the City of London in the 12th century, and the disputatious Corporation retained control of an increasingly polluted and crowded waterway until 1857 (when a Thames Conservancy Act was finally passed by Parliament and a Board of Conservancy formed). A new Thames Conservancy Board, with control over the whole navigable river, emerged after a second Act of Parliament in 1866. The embanking of the Thames, linked to a new sewer system, had been proposed in the 1830s by Sir Frederick Trench. A second proposal was put forward in 1857 by the painter John Martin, but the present system of embankments which was constructed between 1868 and 1874 and which reclaimed some 32 acres of mud, was to the design of Sir Joseph Bazalgette, the chief engineer of the Metropolitan Board of Works. It was a scheme much admired by Dickens at the end of his life. The unbanked Thames, its commercial traffic and its pleasure craft, is described in 'The River' (*SB*) and the observation of the intense activity on the river provides a diversion for Tom and Ruth Pinch during their morning excursions (*MC* 40). 'Down with the Tide' (*RP*) describes a night out with the River Police (a force formed in 1798, preceding the Metropolitan Police by some 31 years). The river, which remained the source of much of London's 19th-century wealth, particularly from the long system of docks developed downstream of the Pool of London from the early 19th century, figures widely in Dickens's fiction, perhaps most memorably in *Our Mutual Friend*.

The first bridge over the River Thames was probably a wooden structure built during the period of the Roman occupation. The first stone bridge was constructed in the 12th century, its nineteen arches crowned by houses. Much of the structure of this bridge survived until 1831, though the houses were removed 1758–62 during a period of radical reconstruction which included replacing the two central arches with a single navigation span. The parapet of the bridge was decorated with a series of stone niches or alcoves at this period. This was the bridge familiar to Dickens as a boy, who would have crossed it regularly on his way to the Marshalsea. David Copperfield describes 'lounging . . . in one of the stone recesses, watching the people going by' on his early morning journey from the King's Bench prison to Murdstone and Grinby's (*DC* 11). It is this old bridge which also figures prominently in *Barnaby Rudge* and *Great Expectations* (Pip remarks on the 'race and fall of water' when the tide changed which gave the narrow arches a 'bad reputation' amongst rowers, *GE* 47). A new London Bridge, designed by John Rennie, was constructed upstream of the old between 1823 and 1831. It is on an angle of the steps on the Southwark side of this bridge that Noah Claypole hides when Nancy makes her fatal disclosures to Mr Brownlow and Rose Maylie (*OT* 46). This is also the London Bridge mentioned in the opening chapter of *Our Mutual Friend*. Rennie's bridge was replaced 1967–72 and re-erected in Lake Havasu City, Arizona.

London Bridge remained the only crossing of the Thames in London until the construction of Westminster Bridge, 1738–50 (replaced 1854–62) and of Blackfriars Bridge 1760–9 (replaced 1860–9). The subsequent realignment of streets south of the river enables many of Dickens's characters to take short cuts in crossing central London on foot and avoiding the wide bend of the river. To these bridges were added two further bridges designed by Rennie, both of them charging tolls, the handsome nine-arch, granite Waterloo Bridge of 1811–17 and the three-arch cast-iron Southwark Bridge of 1814–19 (the 'iron bridge' referred to in the first chapter of *Our Mutual Friend*). A daring and elegant suspension bridge at Charing Cross, linking Hungerford Market on the north bank to the south bank, was built 1841–5 and was replaced by the Hungerford railway bridge in 1864. Charles Fowler's Hungerford Market (1833) had been built on the site of WARREN'S BLACKING warehouse, which lay to the east of Hungerford Stairs. Westminster Bridge, linking up south of the river with the Dover Road, would have been used by the Pickwickians on their way to Rochester by coach from the Golden Cross at Charing Cross. With Blackfriars Bridge it figures prominently as a crossing point for the Gordon Rioters in *Barnaby Rudge* (the rioters break open the toll-houses). It is on a corner of the old Blackfriars Bridge that Jo pauses, 'munching and gnawing, and looking up to the great cross on the summit of St Paul's Cathedral' (*BH* 19). It is near the same bridge that Mr Peggotty and David catch sight of Martha, and subsequently follow her (*DC* 46). Waterloo Bridge, the arches of which once provided Sam Weller with overnight accommodation (*PP* 16), is crossed by the UNCOMMERCIAL TRAVELLER, who seeks 'to have a half-penny worth of excuse for saying "Goodnight" to the toll-keeper, and catching a glimpse of his fire' ('Night Walks'). It was in a house on the southern side of Southwark Bridge that the boy Dickens pretended to live as a ruse to be rid of Bob Fagin who had accompanied him home from Warren's Blacking warehouse ('home' was then the shameful Marshalsea). The old Southwark Bridge was where Little Dorrit loved to take her solitary walks, because 'if you go by the Iron Bridge . . . there is an escape from the noise of the street', and where John Chivery, after paying his toll, proposes to her 'towards the Middlesex side' (*LD* 18). The cast-iron Vauxhall Bridge, originally called the Regent's Bridge, was opened in 1816 (replaced 1895–1906). It is crossed by Bradley Headstone and Charley Hexam after a visit to Lizzie, he 'giving her his hand at parting and she thanking him for his care of her brother' (*OMF* 2.1).　　　　　　　　　　　ALS

Chancellor, E. Beresford, *The London of Charles Dickens* (1924).

Croad, Stephen, *London's Bridges* (1983).

de Mare, Eric, *London's Riverside* (1958).

Dexter (1923).

Weinreb and Hibbert (1983).

**2. Buildings and building.** Dickens takes most of the 'sights' of London for granted as part of his urban landscape. St Paul's, for example, is remarked on or simply encountered *en route* by a considerable number of his characters, yet the only ones who venture into it are the exploratory Master Humphrey and David Copperfield conducting Peggotty around the metropolis. Its 'great black dome' bulges behind Newgate in *Great Expectations*; it proves to be an object of ignorant curiosity for Jo who stares at the cross on its summit as he munches and gnaws on Blackfriars Bridge; John Browdie sets his watch by its clock in *Nicholas Nickleby*. The Tower of London, also visited by David Copperfield and Peggotty, otherwise functions merely as Lord George Gordon's prison in *Barnaby Rudge*. The Monument, under whose shadow Todgers's lies, proves to be a significant, if confusing, landmark in *Martin Chuzzlewit*, though it is perhaps most memorably described by Mr F.'s aunt in *Little Dorrit* as having been 'put up arter the great Fire of London . . . though not the fire in which your Uncle George's workshops was burned down!' Although Pip and Herbert attend a service at Westminster Abbey, the church, Dickens's final resting place, is perhaps most memorable in his works for being assumed by some muddled 'waterside heads' to be the origin of Abbey Potterson's Christian name in *Our Mutual Friend*. The London buildings Dickens uses most systematically in his novels were its PRISONS (Newgate, the Fleet, the King's Bench, the Marshalsea, and by implication, Millbank) or its almost random architectural collections (such as the INNS OF COURT and the Adelphi). Although Westminster Hall figures significantly in both *Barnaby Rudge* and *Bleak House*, the new Houses of Parliament (spectacularly reconstructed after the 1834 fire, and completed in 1860) merit scarcely a mention. Those of Dickens's characters who either are, or who encounter, MPs perhaps do so either in the old building or in the temporary structures which Dickens himself knew as a parliamentary reporter (1831–6).

The London of Dickens's fiction is physically Georgian London, but a Georgian London given a newly intense charge by the burgeoning of its Victorian population. Its vast suburban expansion is frequently noted and exploited, but much of its newly respectable westward development seems to be of little residential concern to Dickens's characters. The new suburbs of his fiction are generally those Regency developments (Is-lington, Somers Town, Camden Town, Kennington, Camberwell) which Dickens himself had known since his childhood. Nevertheless, the universal suburban sprawl and the grand schemes for metropolitan redevelopment, improvement, and reconstruction of the mid-century necessarily affected ways in which Dickens's contemporaries viewed changes in the capital. Sir John Summerson has estimated that in the 1860s alone some 73,000 new structures were built in the metropolitan area. The 1861 census returns reveal that London contained 3,845 builders, 1,459 architects, and 749 surveyors, some 24 per cent of all builders in England and Wales, 38 per cent of its architects, and 40 per cent of its surveyors. Two notable London builders, George Myers and Thomas Cubitt, employed respectively 2,000 and 3,000 men. ALS

Dexter (1923).
Olsen, Donald J., *The Growth of Victorian London* (1976).
Stamp, Gavin, *The Changing Metropolis: Earliest Photographs of London 1839–79* (1984).
Summerson, John, *The London Building World of the Eighteen-Sixties* (1973).

**3. Business London.** (See also MONEY AND FINANCE.) In chapter 16 of Book 3 of *Our Mutual Friend* Dickens describes the City of London in the evening when 'most of its money-mills were slackening sail, or had left off grinding for the night . . . there must be hours of night to temper down the day's distraction of so feverish a place'. In Dickens's lifetime the City of London had steadily asserted itself as the core of British finance and as the major centre of international banking, commerce, and trade. It had steadily transformed itself from what had long been established as the centre of small counting- and trading-houses (such as those of Scrooge and Marley, the Cheerybles, Dombey and Son, the Chuzzlewits, and the Clennams) into the vital and feverish hub of Britain's 19th-century capitalist enterprise. Indicative of this new enterprise was the emergence of the Bank of England as a central bank. The bank's headquarters in Threadneedle Street had been reconstructed after the assault on them by the Gordon rioters in 1780. From 1788, under the direction of Sir John Soane, the new building had been enclosed in a windowless, neoclassical wall, relieved by blank niches, pilasters, and columns. This is the wall circuited by the UNCOMMERCIAL TRAVELLER in 'Night Walks', thinking of 'the treasure within' and of 'the guard of soldiers passing the night there' (the soldiers had been stationed there nightly since the Gordon Riots). The mercenary Bella Wilfer, glancing at 'the mighty bank', also thinks 'how agreeable it would be to have an hour's gardening there, with a bright copper shovel'. Although the Bank of England had lost its old monopoly with the formation of joint-stock banks under Acts of Parliament passed in 1826 and 1833, it was enabled to open branches in prominent provincial cities. The Bank Act of 1833 had also made its notes legal tender. In 1844 the Bank Charter Act limited the issue of notes by other banks and separated the Bank of England's functions into a Banking and an Issuing Department. The Issuing Department was permitted to issue £14 million in notes backed by government securities, thus gradually leading to the situation where Bank of England notes replaced those issued by other banks and became the standard paper currency. By the mid-1860s the Bank of England employed upwards of 800 clerks and its deposits amounted to some £20 million.

A similar growth in financial influence is evident in the flourishing states of London's merchant banks, two of the most prominent among them being roughly coeval in foundation with the Bank of England. Child's & Co., established at no. 1 Fleet Street in 1673 (premises rebuilt in 1879), was supposedly London's oldest and is probably the bank to be identified with the 'old fashioned' Tellson's 'by Temple Bar' in *A Tale of Two Cities*. Coutts's Bank, originally established in St Martin's Lane by a goldsmith banker, John Campbell, in 1692, moved to the Strand in the 18th century. In 1755 James Coutts married into the Campbell family and was made a partner (later to be joined by his brother Thomas). Under Thomas Coutts's directorship the bank first began to hold the private account of the monarch. Thomas's fortune passed in 1837 to his granddaughter, Dickens's friend Angela Burdett COUTTS. Dickens himself banked with Coutts's. The London money market became internationally acknowledged as the most efficient during the opening decade of the 19th century. Nathan Meyer Rothschild from Frankfurt settled in

England in 1798 and opened a bullion-dealing firm and bank at New Court, St Swithin's Lane, in 1809, enjoying spectacular success during and after the Napoleonic Wars. By 1850 Peter Cunningham could confidently refer to the Rothschilds as 'the greatest people on 'Change', and recommend the corner of the Royal Exchange where they transacted business to the particular attention of visitors to London.

The Royal Exchange building, which was burnt to the ground in 1838, was replaced by an extended new building, designed by Sir William Tite and opened by Queen Victoria in 1844. This building, like its predecessors, provided not only a meeting place for prominent merchants and traders but also accommodation for Lloyd's (which had officially begun business in 1774). Lloyd's functioned both as a centre for insurance broking and as a rendezvous for merchants, shipowners, underwriters, and stock- and exchange brokers. Here news of the arrival and sailing of vessels, losses at sea, and other shipping intelligence was first obtained. The Royal Exchange figures unflatteringly and briefly in both *Sketches by Boz* ('Shabby Genteel People') and in *Great Expectations*, when Pip notices 'fluey men sitting there . . . whom I took to be great merchants though I couldn't understand why they should all be out of spirits'. In the same chapter (*GE* 21) Herbert Pocket, 'when he felt his case unusually serious . . . would go on 'Change at a busy time and walk in and out, in a kind of gloomy country dance figure, among the assembled magnates'. The Exchange is also frequented by Scrooge, Flintwich (*LD*), and Mr Dombey.

The Stock Exchange, described by N. M. Rothschild as 'the Bank for the whole world' and by Cunningham as 'the ready-money market of the world', moved to premises in Capel Court in 1802. Business in foreign funds moved here from the Royal Exchange in 1822. The building was centred on a rectangular trading room where brokers (some 550 in 1802) congregated. With the increase in the number of brokers (864 by 1853) a larger building was constructed on the same site (expanded 1882–8; replaced 1972). A fine new Coal Exchange in Lower Thames Street was constructed to the designs of J. B. Bunning and opened in 1849 by Prince Albert (demolished 1963). The Corn Exchange in Mark Lane was rebuilt 1827–8 and extended in 1850. The Baltic Exchange (which provides facilities for the fixing of cargoes for merchant vessels) moved into new premises in Threadneedle Street in 1810, but the increase in trade following the repeal of the Corn Laws in 1846 required a move to the old South Sea House in 1855–6 (demolished 1900).

The City was partly enabled to maintain its financial prominence thanks to the steady reform of its infrastructure, transport, and planning. Charles Pearson, the City Corporation's Solicitor, 1839–62, pioneered efforts to connect the area by railway to the new termini elsewhere in London, an effort which culminated in the construction of the Metropolitan Railway, London's first underground, in 1863. With the expansion of horse-drawn public transport after the formation of the London General Omnibus Company in 1855, commuting to and from the City was greatly facilitated. Despite the multiple changes evident in his lifetime, the City as it now looks and operates would be largely unrecognizable to Dickens. ALS

Cunningham (1850).

Gomme, G. Laurence, *London in the Reign of Victoria* (1898).

Timbs, John, *Curiosities of London* (new edn., 1868).

Weinreb and Hibbert (1983).

**4. Docklands.** London's river trade was historically concentrated in the Pool of London, the reach of the River Thames stretching from Limehouse Cut to Cherry Garden Pier, Rotherhithe (the 'Lower Pool'), and from Rotherhithe to London Bridge (the 'Upper Pool'), an area now roughly divided into two by Tower Bridge (opened in 1894). Docks had existed in the Upper Pool since Roman times and it was here that London's main docking facilities remained until the construction of enclosed wet docks in the early 19th century. In 1796 a Parliamentary Commission reported on the congestion of the existing port and recommended expansion. As a consequence a number of large-scale projects were proposed, but the main development proved to be piecemeal and the result of private rather than public enterprise. This development was to the east of the Tower of London along a ten-mile stretch of both banks of the river. In Dickens's day the most significant of these docks were the West India Docks on the Isle of Dogs (1802), the London Docks at Wapping and the East India at Blackwall (both 1805), the Surrey Docks (two miles east of London Bridge on the Surrey side, 1807), St Katherine's Dock (1828), the West India Dock South (1829), the Royal Victoria Docks (1855), and the Millwall Docks (1868). All of these docks were enclosed on the landward side by high brick walls pierced by monumental gateways. They were also of some considerable size—the West India Docks alone had some 54 acres of water and were connected to the river by a series of basins and locks. Many also had links to the canal system. The London Docks, designed by Daniel Alexander, were bordered with four-storey brick warehouses built above extensive brick-vaulted wine cellars. The designs of the great engineer, Thomas Telford, for St Katherine's Docks (just east of the Tower) necessitated the removal of a medieval hospital. The warehouses surrounding Telford's dock basins (some ranges of which still survive) were collaboratively designed by the classical architect Philip Hardwick. The 295 acres of the West India Docks were described by Peter Cunningham in his *Hand-book of London* (1850) as 'the most magnificent in the world'. Throughout the 19th century London's docks provided the city with its main industrial base. The Court of Directors of the London Docks controlled a capital of some £4 million and employed up to 2,900 labourers per day in the 1850s. The docks began to close in the 1960s and their sites were gradually redeveloped. The much reduced Port of London is now concentrated at Tilbury.

Brig Place, 'on the brink of a little canal' in the region of the West India Docks, is the residence of Captain Cuttle in *Dombey and Son*. It is eastward of the Tower that Mortimer Lightwood searches for news of John Harmon, and it is 'by the Docks; down by Ratcliff' that the Hexams live in *Our Mutual Friend*. Ratcliffe Highway and 'the houses where the sailors dance' is also visited by the intrepid Inspector FIELD in 'On Duty with Inspector Field' (*RP*), but Dickens's most memorable account of life 'Down by the Docks' is that in the UNCOMMERCIAL TRAVELLER essay 'Bound for the Great Salt Lake'. ALS

Cunningham (1850).

Ellmers, Chris, and Werner, Alex, *London's Lost Riverscape: A Photographic Panorama* (1988).

Weinreb and Hibbert (1983).

**5. Entertainment London.** For 'Boz', London was a place teeming with sources of recreation and AMUSEMENT. 'What inexhaustible food for speculations do the streets of London afford!' he exclaims ('Shops and the Tenants', *SB*). *Sketches by Boz* alone takes readers on visits to pleasure gardens ('Vauxhall Gardens by Day'), the CIRCUS ('Astley's'), a tavern saloon (precursor to the MUSIC HALL; 'Miss Evans and the Eagle'), the THEATRE ('Private Theatres', 'The Misplaced Attachment of Mr John Dounce', 'Making a Night of It'), private celebrations ('A Christmas Dinner'), holiday festivities ('The New Year'), formal gatherings ('Public Dinners'), and boat outings ('The River', 'The Steam Excursion').

As the population of London burgeoned, so too did the variety and extent of its provision of entertainment. Although no new THEATRES were built in the metropolis between 1843 and 1866, for most of Dickens's lifetime there were about 30 establishments licensed for theatrical entertainment—a figure which does not include private theatres, penny gaffs, song and supper clubs, and taverns in which entertainers performed. Dickens, who went to the theatre nearly every night as a young man, knew them all and wrote numerous drama reviews and essays, in addition to pursuing his own AMATEUR THEATRICAL activities.

PANORAMAS—vast paintings depicting scenes such as London as seen from the Dome of St Paul's or the Mississippi River—were hugely popular, and Dickens wrote about them on several occasions, notably in two articles on the Colosseum (*Morning Chronicle*, 10 and 13 July 1835; repr. *Journalism* 2.14–18); in 'The American Panorama' (at the Egyptian Hall, Piccadilly): *Examiner*, 16 December 1848; repr. *Journalism* 2.134–7; and in 'Some Account of an Extraordinary Traveller' (*HW* 20 April 1850; repr. *Journalism* 2.201–12).

The Zoological Gardens opened in 1828, replacing the dilapidated exhibition of lions in the Tower and greatly surpassing the menagerie at the Exeter Change, where the rampaging elephant Chunee had to be put down in 1826, an event still vivid to Dickens ten years later ('Scotland Yard', *Morning Chronicle*, 4 October 1836, in a passage deleted in the *SB* version; repr. Butt and Tillotson 1957, p. 55).

Madame Tussaud, after touring Britain with her WAXWORKS exhibition for 33 years, settled into permanent rooms in Baker Street, a short walk from Dickens's home at Devonshire Terrace. Dickens published an article on her show by Dudley Costello, 'Our Eye Witness in Great Company' (*AYR* 7 January 1860), and in *David Copperfield* David takes Peggotty to see a rival waxworks (*DC* 33).

The foremost 19th-century exhibition room for paintings, artefacts, and curiosities living and dead was the Egyptian Hall, built in 1811, where, among other wonders, the Siamese twins Chang and Eng appeared in 1829 (mentioned in *NN* 21 and *MC* 16), as did P. T. Barnum's famous dwarf, Charles Sherwood Stratton, known as General Tom Thumb, in 1844 and 1846 (mentioned in *PFI* 11).

In addition to entertainments in permanent venues, London was filled with itinerant shows. Ralph Nickleby's home in Golden Square is noisy with street bands and glee singers (*NN* 2), and in the same novel the errand boy dispatched to deliver a hat to Tim Linkinwater's sister is distracted by stilt-walkers and a travelling Punch and Judy show (*NN* 37). The Single Gentleman outrages Sampson Brass and delights Dick Swiveller by inviting Punch showmen to perform outside his lodgings (*OCS* 37). Although Dickens's tastes for amusement were nothing if not tolerant, some of these entertainers tried his patience, and he published a 'Chip' by J. D. Lewis, 'A Voice from a "Quiet" Street' (*HW* 2 November 1850) which deplored the cacophony of street musicians. In *The Old Curiosity Shop* Dickens portrays itinerant one- and two-man shows in decline, an assessment confirmed by a chorus of lament from the showfolk interviewed by Henry Mayhew, who was repeatedly told of the deteriorating quality of shows and of dwindling profits (*London Labour and the London Poor*, 4 vols., 1861–2, *passim*).

In even more serious decline were the ancient London FAIRS, most notably Bartholomew Fair, held in Smithfield at the end of each summer for centuries, but severely restricted in scope by civic decree in 1840, and defunct by 1855. It succumbed to vigorous opposition which faced all forms of entertainment, from EVANGELICAL and SABBATARIAN do-gooders, who incurred Dickens's wrath throughout his lifetime. Much of the energy in Dickens's celebration of entertainments and in his defence of people's right to amusement—his pleas for the opening of museums on Sundays, his subscription in support of Sunday band concerts—was predicated on the beleaguered state of entertainment, in London and elsewhere.  PVWS

Altick, Richard D., *The Shows of London* (1978).
Schlicke (1985).

**6. Fashionable London.** The success of *Pickwick Papers* and other early novels opened up fashionable London to Dickens. In 1836 he became a frequenter of the Countess of Blessington's salon at Gore House, mingling with such luminaries as Wellington, DISRAELI, LANDOR, and Sydney SMITH. In 1838 he began to attend Lady Holland's Whig salon at Holland House, and was elected a member of the ATHENAEUM CLUB, meeting-place of leading writers, artists, scientists, and politicians. His observation of the fashionable world was maintained through acquaintance with such figures as Lord John RUSSELL and the Duke of Devonshire; through friendship with such figures as Alfred Count D'Orsay, Angela Burdett COUTTS, and Edward BULWER-LYTTON, first Baron Lytton.

Close observation was necessary. The expansion of the middle classes during Dickens's lifetime, and the general growth in prosperity complicated distinctions between the fashionable and the unfashionable. There was a *beau monde*—'Society'—but its composition changed, and its fashions were imitated, particularly in London where they were most visible. At Mr and Mrs Waterbrook's dinner party members of the professional classes discuss 'Blood', and David Copperfield reflects that 'we should have got on better, if we had not been quite so genteel' (*DC* 25).

Specifically middle-class and working-class fashions evolved, moreover. Dickens took as much interest in these, and in fashion out of date or out of context, as in the latest and smartest styles of behaviour, expenditure, grooming, and costume. The middle-class Mr

Turveydrop's eccentric adherence to aristocratic styles made fashionable by the Prince Regent forty years earlier (*BH* 14) is as closely described as the behaviour of the mighty Barnacle family (*LD* 1.10 *et seq.*).

Perhaps Dickens's closest study of the world of high fashion is to be found in *Bleak House* (2 *et seq.*). 'It is not a large world', the narrator declares. '. . . There is much good in it; there are many good and true people in it; it has its appointed place. But the evil of it is, that it is a world wrapped up in too much jeweller's cotton and fine wool, and cannot hear the rushing of larger worlds, and cannot see them as they circle round the sun.' Sir Leicester and Lady Dedlock dominate this world. She, we are told, 'is perfectly well-bred. If she could be translated to Heaven tomorrow, she might be expected to ascend without any rapture.' Sir Leicester 'is an honourable, obstinate, truthful, high-spirited, intensely prejudiced, perfectly unreasonable man'. Other traditional leaders and followers of London fashion depicted by Dickens include James Harthouse (*HT* 2.2 *et seq.*), Mr Twemlow (*OMF* 1.2 *et seq.*), the predatory Sir Mulberry Hawk, together with his dupe Lord Frederick Verisopht (*NN* 19 *et seq.*), and Cousin Feenix, retired to Baden before the action of *Dombey and Son* begins, but cherishing memories of the *beau monde* he had inhabited (*DS* 21 *et seq.*). The portraits are hostile or disparaging for the most part, but Dickens often shows such characters behaving honourably, despite failings of understanding. Cousin Feenix, for instance, makes himself responsible for Edith Dombey in her disgrace (*DS* 61). It was the hostility, though, that doubtless helped to stimulate contemporary criticism of Dickens's ability to depict gentlemen.

During the course of Dickens's career, the fashionable world opened its doors wider, and became more sedate. Earlier novels depict members of the aristocracy and gentry behaving with Regency abandon. In *Nicholas Nickleby* we witness dissolute behaviour at a race-meeting, gambling, and a duel (*NN* 50). But, significantly, in *Dombey and Son* a society wedding is described, of an eminent merchant, Mr Dombey, with a lady of gentle birth, Edith Skewton (*DS* 31). In *Little Dorrit* we see the fashionable of London flocking to a reception at the home of Mr Merdle, a financier: 'Society was aware of Mr and Mrs Merdle. Society had said "Let us license them; let us know them" ' (*LD* 1.21). The marine insurance broker, Mr Podsnap, never doubts he is a member of 'Society'. Despite humble beginnings and eventual bankruptcy, his friend Mr Veneering gathers such figures as Lady Tippins and Boots and Brewer round his dining table, to provide a choral commentary of Society's views on the episodes and characters of *Our Mutual Friend* (1.2 *et seq.*).

Dickens carefully distinguishes the social tone of fashionable districts in London. He places his dissolute young aristocrats, and decayed older ones, among the clubs, apartment houses, and mews of St James's (*NN* 26, *OMF* 1.2), to distinguish them from more sedate beings who tread the 'aristocratic pavements of Belgrave Square' (*NN* 21). Mr and Mrs Wititterly are among the occupants of Cadogan Place, who do not claim to be 'on precisely the same footing as the high folks of Belgrave Square and Grosvenor Place', but who 'look down upon Sloane Street, and think Brompton low. They affect fashion too, and wonder where the New Road is' (*NN* 21). 'Stucconia', Dickens's term for the streets and squares north of Oxford Street, is where he lodges his successful businessmen, such as Mr Veneering (*OMF* 1.10) and Mr Dombey (*DS* 3).

Miss Tox and Major Bagstock, with their quarters in Princess's Place (*DS* 7), Mr Tite Barnacle, with his house in Mews Street, Grosvenor Square (*LD* 1.10) are among characters who tolerate cramped, airless, and inconvenient accommodation for the sake of the address.

Dickens also writes powerfully about fashion in London when he describes followers of relatively humble fashions, pretenders to styles that elude them, and candidates for entry into 'Society' from which they are in some way disqualified. Many of the *Sketches of Boz* are devoted to observation of such figures: pieces from the Characters group, such as 'Miss Evans and the Eagle', with its detailed descriptions of costume; pieces from the 'Tales' group, such as 'Horation Sparkins', the story of a mysterious fashionable young man who is revealed to be a draper's assistant. In a similar class are Dickens's accounts of Mrs Boffin's resolve to 'go in strong' for fashion (*OMF* 1.9 *et seq.*), and of efforts made to sustain gentility by the Kenwigs family (*NN*

14 *et seq.*) and by the Micawbers (*DC* 11 *et seq.*).

DP

**7. Growth.** By the end of the 18th century London contained just under 1 million inhabitants; it was already eleven times larger than any other British city and had almost double the population of PARIS, its chief European rival. In each decade of the 19th century its population rose steadily by a further 20 per cent. The 1841 census revealed that 1,870,727 people lived in the urban area, making up more than half of the population of the surrounding counties of KENT, Surrey, Middlesex, and Essex (3,052,630). By 1851 London's population had risen to 2,363,341 in the urban area and an estimated 2,651,939 if the immediately surrounding districts, later to be known as Greater London, are included. As the censuses taken in Dickens's lifetime suggest, an average of 300,000 newcomers arrived in the city in each decade, one-third of these immigrants being drawn from the home counties and nearly a half from the southern part of England. The remainder came from the rest of the United Kingdom, some 15 per cent arriving from Ireland in the years of the Famine, and from other European countries (including political refugees from Spain, Italy, France, and Germany). In the census taken the year after Dickens's death the population of the built-up area of London was revealed to be 3,261,396, while that of Greater London was 3,840,595.

In 1850 Peter Cunningham estimated that the limits of London, as defined by Act of Parliament as 'the circumference of a circle, the radius of which is the length of 3 miles from the General Post Office', to be twenty miles in circumference. He added that it was generally agreed that the circumference was in fact nearer to thirty miles. Cunningham also noted that the north side of the river, containing the cities of London and Westminster and their outlying parishes, occupied an area of some 43 square miles, while the southern or Southwark side covered around eight square miles. The shape of Victorian London continued to be determined by its river and by its twin focuses provided by the City and Westminster. The areas south of the River Thames had been opened up for development by the new bridges constructed in the 18th century (Westminster and Blackfriars) and in the opening decades of the 19th century (South-wark, Hungerford, and Waterloo). The concentration of administration and fashion in Westminster and of commerce in the City had also determined the nature and development of residential suburbs and the classic divide between 'West End' and 'East End', the process being accentuated by the construction of the new docks on the reaches of the Thames east of the Pool of London. Nevertheless, as Dickens's novels suggest, the early- and mid-Victorian City of London remained both commercial *and* residential with prosperous citizens and modest tradesmen—e.g. Scrooge, the Chuzzlewits, Sol Gills (*DS*), the Clennams (*LD*)—living above or close by their business premises. In 1841 125,008 people still lived in the City (with a further 265,043 in Finsbury to the north); in 1871 the population had fallen to 74,494 and 120,282 respectively. Other rich merchants or men with City connections in Dickens's novels—Ralph Nickleby, Mr Dombey, Mr Merdle (*LD*)—had, however, already transferred their residences to the more fashionable West End or in the case of Mr Carker (*DS*) to villa-land in the outer suburbs.

The West End of London still came to an abrupt, but nonetheless ceremonial, end at Hyde Park Corner in the early 19th century (hence the common description of the Duke of Wellington's mansion, Apsley House, as 'Number One, London'). The development of Kensington as a fashionable suburb, north, south, and west of Hyde Park, was very much a feature of the years after the Great EXHIBITION OF 1851. It is not an area that figures prominently in Dickens's novels. In Dickens's youth, however, the construction of largely middle-class residential suburbs north of the 'New Road' (opened 1757; now known as Marylebone and Euston Roads) was proceeding apace. This rapid, speculative development of uniform brick squares, terraces, and streets in the 1820s was part-celebrated, part-bemoaned, in George CRUIKSHANK's cartoon 'London going out of Town—or—The March of Bricks and Mortar!' (1829). Cruikshank, who lived in precisely the kind of terraced house in Islington that he had satirized in his cartoon, also perhaps used it as the model for his depictions of the interiors of Mr Brownlow's house in *Oliver Twist*. Dickens too chose to live in late-18th- or early-19th-century

houses in a relatively narrow segment of the respectable streets near the New Road (a decision perhaps determined by his parents' choice of lodgings in the cheaper streets of Bloomsbury, Camden Town, and Somer's Town during his boyhood). Somer's Town, north of the New Road, had, for example, been ambitiously begun with the Polygon in the mid-1780s, but had declined socially as more cramped terraced housing was constructed in the 1820s, thus wrecking the area's semi-rural pretensions. The Dickenses lived at 29 Johnson Street, Somers Town, 1824–5 after John DICKENS's release from the Marshalsea. The area was already popular with Spanish refugees, a feature which Dickens makes a point of when he gives Harold Skimpole lodgings in the Polygon (*BH* 43). Mr Snawley also lives modestly in Somer's Town in 'a little house one storey high, with green shutters' (*NN* 38). Further north, at 16 Bayham Street, Camden Town, the Dickenses lodged 1822–3 (see HOMES OF DICKENS). It shared a rapidly declining rural aspect with Somers Town and had once also aspired to rural prospects (the adult Dickens remembered once having looked over 'the dust-heaps and dock-leaves and fields . . . at the cupola of St Paul's looming through the smoke'). No. 16 Bayham Street was probably the model for the Cratchits' house in *A Christmas Carol*. In a 'little street near the Veterinary College at Camden Town' lives Traddles, the street being used by its inhabitants as a repository 'for any little trifles they were not in want of . . . which not only made it rank and sloppy, but untidy, too, on account of the cabbage leaves' (*DC* 28).

On the main arteries leading out of London, and notably on those leading south-wards, late-18th-century housing had been developed on the 'ribbon' principle with both terraces and detached and semi-detached villas. From the 1820s to the 1850s what had once been separate suburban parishes or settlements (Chelsea, Brompton, Kennington, Brixton, Camberwell, Walworth, Islington, Paddington) were gradually merged with the sprawl of London. If Camberwell retained its pretensions (the house where Ruth Pinch is a governess is 'so big and fierce, that its mere outside . . . struck terror into vulgar minds and made bold persons quail', *MC* 9), the Walworth which is the site of Wemmick's castle in *Great Expectations* is far less socially and architecturally daunting. Dickens's descriptions of the mixed and often ambiguous nature of London's inner suburbia are numerous. Perhaps most memorable is his account of the wholesale reconstruction around the fictional 'Staggs's Gardens' at 'Camberling Town', and the upheavals attendant upon the advent of the London and Birmingham Railway in the 1830s (*DS* 15). The process of redevelopment destroyed not only the fictional 'Staggs's Gardens' but also the schoolroom of Dickens's former school, the Wellington House Academy, Mornington Place.

As was the case with the London of the 18th century, most residential development was in the hands of large, speculative landowners offering property either on a long lease or for rent. Only the development of South Kensington, 'Tyburnia', and Bayswater was, however, to rival the substance and fashionable pretensions of the earlier aristocratic speculations in Mayfair, Bloomsbury, and Belgravia. Smaller estates, especially in areas given over to lower-middle-class, artisan, or working-class housing, were often developed on a more piecemeal basis. The very poor remained confined to inner-city slums, though much of the expansion of the East End, especially after the extension of railway lines into east London, was specifically intended for those surviving on modest incomes. This was, however, largely, a development of the years following Dickens's death. The indeterminate and uncontrolled sprawl of London's northern suburbs, the 'blighted country, not town', is well described in chapter 33 of *Dombey and Son*.

By an Act of Parliament passed in 1855 the Metropolitan Board of Works, London's first metropolitan-wide local authority (apart from the jealously preserved rights and privileges of the City), came into being. Also under this Metropolis Management Act the old parish vestries, which had formerly, somewhat creakily, administered much of the London area, were reconstituted as 38 elected bodies. The Board consisted of 46 persons elected by ratepayers and was charged with the management of existing streets, drains, and buildings. It was also empowered to construct a new main drainage system, to improve streets, to build and name new ones, and to provide parks. It was superseded

by the London County Council only in 1889. ALS

*Black's Guide to London and its Environs* (1873).
Cunningham (1850).
Olsen, Donald J., *The Growth of Victorian London* (1976).
*The Pictorial Handbook of London* (London, 1854, 1862).
*The Survey of London* (vols. 37, 38, 41) (1972–83).
Weinreb and Hibbert (1983).

**8. Markets.** Not long after he arrived in London in 1822, a description of Covent Garden in George Colman's *Broad Grins* prompted the boy Dickens to visit the market. 'He remembered', Forster records, 'snuffing up the flavour of the faded cabbage-leaves as if it were the very breath of comic fiction' (1.1). For Dickens, London's markets focused its vitality and complexity. Little wonder that, during the last decade of his life, his London home was over the offices of *All the Year Round* in Wellington Street, Covent Garden.

Founded in 1670, Covent Garden was a market for fruit, vegetables, and flowers, largely wholesale by Dickens's time. For Little Dorrit, aware of the neighbouring coffee-houses and theatre, the plenty on sale, and the homeless children who haunted the market, it is 'a place of past and present mystery, romance, abundance, want, beauty, ugliness, fair country gardens, and foul street gutters; all confused together' (*LD* 1.14). The market is also featured in 'The Streets—Morning' (*SB*), *The Old Curiosity Shop* (1), *Martin Chuzzlewit* (40), *The* UNCOMMERCIAL TRAVELLER (13), and *Our Mutual Friend* (4.9). Bill Sikes alludes to it as 'Common Garden' in *Oliver Twist* (19), and there are other brief references in *Pickwick Papers* (47), *David Copperfield* (12, 24), and *Great Expectations* (21).

Dickens refers occasionally to the fish market of Billingsgate, entirely wholesale by the 19th century. Tip Dorrit is declared to have worked briefly 'in the Billingsgate trade' (*LD* 1.7), Pip and Herbert Pocket contemplate it from the Thames (*GE* 54), and the Uncommercial Traveller visits it on a night walk (*UT* 13). 'A Popular Delusion,' by Dickens and W. H. WILLS (*HW* 1.217), is also about the market.

At Leadenhall Market, a medieval foundation like Billingsgate, meat, poultry, fish, fruit, and vegetables are sold, both wholesale and retail. Tim Linkinwater defends city life on the strength of the new-laid eggs obtainable there (*NN* 40).

But Dickens's most active involvement was with Smithfield, London's principal cattle market from about 1150 to 1855. By the mid-19th century the growth of London's population had overloaded the market's capacity, and calls were being made for it to be moved to the suburbs, but the City Corporation resisted. Dickens used *Household Words* to campaign for the move. 'The Heart of Mid-London' (1.121) is by Dickens and Wills, but Dickens was sole author of 'A Monument of French Folly' (*RP*), published in 1851. He had been impressed by the Paris cattle market at Poissy, and the Montmartre and Genelle abattoirs. A member of the Court of Common Council, however, had observed that, 'the French are a frog-eating people, who wear wooden shoes'. 'It may generally be summed up, of this inferior people,' Dickens comments, 'that they have no idea of anything.' Ironically, he contrasts the space, order, and cleanliness of the French institutions with the clutter, chaos, and squalor of Smithfield.

In 1852 the Smithfield Market Removal Act was passed, providing for the removal of the beast market to Islington. From 1855 no more live beasts were sold at Smithfield, and a covered market for carcasses was built (1866–8). Dickens, then, saw Smithfield reformed and reconstructed but, characteristically, it was the old Smithfield that held his imagination. Hustled through it by Bill Sikes, Oliver Twist found it 'a stunning and bewildering scene, which quite confounded the senses' (*OT* 21; see also 16). Pip complained that 'the shameful place, being all asmear with filth and fat and blood and foam, seemed to stick to me' (*GE* 20).

Passing allusions are made in Dickens's works to the Borough Market (*PP* 10, 32), Clare Market (*PP* 20), Fleet Market (*BR* 8, 69), and Newgate Market (*BH* 5). DP

**9. Residential segregation.** Contrary to a commonly held belief, CLASSES and economic groups were not rigorously segregated in Victorian London. The physical shape of the city and the nature of its development in the 18th and early 19th centuries had rendered such segregation virtually impossible. There were,

of course, quarters which were exclusively inhabited by the very rich. St James's and Mayfair retained their well-established claim to be the centre of fashionable life (a claim helped by proximity to the Court and to the Royal Parks), but were beginning to be rivalled by Belgrave Square (constructed 1825) and its adjacent squares and terraces. Nevertheless, the proximity of the less salubrious streets of Pimlico (where, for example, Lady Tippins 'dwells over a staymaker's in the Belgravian Borders' in *Our Mutual Friend*) suggests a lack of clear social and architectural segregation. Equally, when Dickens notes of Cadogan Place (the residence of Mrs Wititterly in *Nicholas Nickleby*) that it was 'the one slight bond that joins two great extremes . . . the aristocratic pavements of Belgrave Square and the barbarism of Chelsea', he was also indicating the extent to which even in relatively newly developed areas rich and middling Londoners lived cheek by jowl. On the Crown estate developed by John Nash north of the Marylebone Road in the second decade of the 19th century, grand terraces were designed to face Regent's Park, but the area was also to contain expensive detached villas set in the Park, less pretentious villas in the two 'Park Villages', and, to the east, a commercial and service development around a market. Other central parishes of the West End of London (notably St George's, Hanover Square, and Marylebone) retained pockets of real poverty, not all of it genteel, amidst general prosperity. The tone of the West End was still set as much by the grand, detached mansions of the aristocracy as by its residential squares and streets. Apsley House, since 1820 the London residence of the Duke of Wellington, Devonshire House, the home of Dickens's friend the sixth Duke of Devonshire, and Burlington House helped Piccadilly retain its singularly patrician air despite being surrounded by commercial property. Burlington House and its gardens were to be purchased by the government in 1854 and transformed into the home of six learned societies. Other aristocratic families preferred to live in often spectacularly grand houses hidden behind the uniform façades of West End squares. These families, like the Dedlocks in *Bleak House*, would be expected to divide their time between London and their country estates.

*Bleak House* also serves to demonstrate much of the intimate intermixture of classes in central London. The novel is centred on Lincoln's Inn, a site at the core of Victorian London and sandwiched between the great east–west arteries of Holborn and the Strand and Fleet Street. The Inn contained both the chambers of lawyers, such as Messrs Kenge and Carboy, and, like other INNS OF COURT, sets of rooms let out to gentlemen. Immediately beyond the bounds of the Inn the legal character of the area had enforced itself. Mr Tulkinghorn lives in a fine 17th-century house in Lincoln's Inn Fields (almost certainly based on John FORSTER's house at no. 58). Tulkinghorn's house has, however, seen better days (it is let off in chambers, 'and in those shrunken fragments of greatness lawyers lie like maggots in nuts'). To the east of the Inn, off Chancery Lane, lie Chichester Rents (the probable site of the Sol's Arms and Krook's Rag and Bottle Warehouse). Krook's tenants, Nemo and Miss Flite, have both fallen on hard times. On the other side of Chancery Lane, in Cursitor Street, is Coavinses' sponging house (based on the famous Sloman's) and in Cook's (properly Took's) Court is Mr Snagsby's law stationer's shop. To the south in Symond's Inn Mr Vholes has his chambers. To the north, off Holborn, lay Thavies' Inn, the residence of the Jellyby family. All of these sites are identifiable, but the fictional slum, Tom-All-Alone's, evidently is close at hand. It is probably based on the decaying streets of 17th-century wooden houses which once lay to the south-west of Lincoln's Inn Fields around Wych Street, the extension of Drury Lane (the burial ground has been identified as Russell Court). These streets disappeared during the construction of Kingsway and the Aldwych *c*.1900. Thus, as the novel demonstrates, prosperous lawyers, independent tradesmen, the barely housed, and the unhoused all live within easy walking distance of one another.

Early Victorian Londoners could have experienced a similar juxtaposition of respectability and festering slum in walking southward from Bloomsbury, a professional residential area protected by gates and liveried porters, or from the British Museum, into the notorious streets around the church of St-Giles-in-the-Fields. This area was described by Peter Cunningham in 1850 as 'long the abode of wretchedness, so that St Giles has become synonymous for squalor and dirt'. Much of the slum had in fact been swept away in 1847 with the construction of New Oxford Street, though Dickens describes it memorably in several of the *Sketches by Boz* (notably 'Seven Dials' and 'Meditations in Monmouth Street'). Multiple occupation of once-grand houses in an area like Soho, such as the one where Emily is discovered (*DC* 50), also suggests that it is often difficult to determine the precise social standing of any given area in mid-Victorian London.

As the coloured maps produced by Charles Booth at the end of the 19th century indicate, most of the main arteries leading out of central London contained a mixture of commercial property, inhabited by relatively prosperous tradesmen, and well-maintained residential property. Behind these roads, particularly from the 1850s onwards, were often-modest, newly built streets of terraced houses inhabited by clerks, artisans, and the 'respectable' poor. Certain suburbs already had a distinctly lower-middle-class flavour by the 1830s, notably Islington in the north and parts of Kennington in the south (the former is the residence of the Pinches; the latter of Mr Guppy). The Cratchits' house in Camden Town, probably based on the Dickens family's in Bayham St., may well be typical of the kind of property aspired to by a London clerk (see HOMES OF DICKENS). Richer business- and professional men and their families steadily seem to have preferred property in the outer suburbs of London, probably with the intention of persuading themselves of the prestige of a villa near 'the country'. Mr Carker lives in 'the green and wooded country near Norwood' in *Dombey and Son*; the same area is chosen by Mr Spenlow in *David Copperfield*, while the Steerforths live in a genteel 'old brick house . . . on the summit of the hill' at Highgate. In *Little Dorrit* Mr Meagles has his 'cottage-residence' at Twickenham.

ALS

Cunningham (1850).
Dexter (1923).
Olsen, Donald J., *The Growth of Victorian London* (1976).
Richardson, John, *Islington Past* (1988); *Highgate Past* (1989).
Saunders, Ann, *Regent's Park: A Study of the*

*Development of the Area from 1086 to the Present* (2nd edn. 1981).

Summerson, John, *Georgian London* (1962).

Stamp, Gavin, *The Changing Metropolis: Earliest Photographs of London 1839–1879* (1984).

Tallis, John, *London Street Views 1838–40* (repr. 1969).

**10. Slums and rookeries.** In Dickens's youth and early manhood London's most notorious slum was probably that of St Giles, situated in the southern part of the parish of St Giles-in-the-Fields off the dog-leg in London's main east–west axis formed by St Giles High Street. This was almost certainly the site of HO-GARTH's celebrated etching *Gin Lane* (1751; Hogarth shows the nearby spire of St George's, Bloomsbury in the background rather than that of Henry Flitcroft's St Giles's Church). The rookery at St Giles's provided an easy, and frequently exploited, contrast with the area of high fashion centred in the parish of St James's. The rookery largely disappeared with the construction of New Oxford Street in 1847, but the southern parts of it survived around its 'Gordian knot', Seven Dials. The slum was memorably described by Dickens in the sketch by 'BOZ' published in BELL'S LIFE IN LONDON in September 1835 as 'Seven Dials'. His childhood fascination with the area is also recalled in Dickens's fragment of autobiography reprinted by FORSTER: 'what wild prodigies of wickedness, want, and beggary, arose in my mind out of that place!' (1.2; see DIARIES AND AUTOBIOGRAPHY). The construction of Shaftesbury Avenue (completed 1886) involved the demolition of many of the surviving courts and narrow alleys off the former Monmouth Street (once the centre of the second-hand clothes trade and itself described in a further sketch by Boz of 1836). This 'labyrinth of streets which lies between Seven Dials and Soho' is also where Mantalini is discovered in a cellar, turning a mangle (*NN* 64).

For most of Dickens's career the worst rookeries and slums, and the worst human degradation of London were widely distributed throughout the metropolis. There were areas of dire poverty in and around Clerkenwell and the eastern part of Holborn throughout the first half of the 19th century, the worst part being concentrated near Saffron Hill. The 'maze of shabby streets' surrounding Bleeding Heart Yard in *Little Dorrit* were one thing, but the streets, courts, and alleys leading down to the valley of the open sewer of the old Fleet Ditch were quite another. Oliver Twist is conducted by the Artful Dodger through a labyrinthine descent from Islington towards Fagin's den in Field Lane: 'A dirtier or more wretched place he had never seen. The street was very narrow and muddy; and the air was impregnated with filthy odours' (*OT* 8). In 'the filthiest part of Little Saffron Hill' lay 'The Three Cripples', the insalubrious public house frequented by Sikes and Fagin, 'a dark gloomy den, where a flaring gas-light burnt all day' (*OT* 15). Much of this area disappeared when Farringdon Road was pushed through (by covering the Fleet Ditch) in 1845–6, further demolitions and rearrangements of street-plans being necessitated by the works involved in the construction of the Holborn Viaduct in 1868–9. Phil Squod describes working as a tinker in the area: 'poor neighbourhood, where they uses up the kettles till they're past mending' (*BH* 26). Equally depressing were the Westminster slums, lying to the west and south west of Westminster Abbey and largely destroyed by the gradual construction of Victoria Street in the late 1850s and early 1860s. As late as 1861 the Bishop of London felt obliged to remind the House of Lords that 'their Lordships were perhaps in the habit of thinking that the East-end of London was inhabited almost solely by the poor; but he believed that they would find that nearer to their own doors there was more squalid misery than in the East-end'. The run-down nature of the region extended into Millbank, a particularly 'dreary' neighbourhood, 'as oppressive, sad and solitary by night as any about London' (*OMF* 2.1). In one of the dilapidated Georgian houses around the 'blind' Smith Square lives the Dolls' Dressmaker and her drunken father (a place with 'a deadly kind of repose on it, more as though it had taken laudanum than fallen into a natural rest').

South of the River Thames lay some of the most noxious and disease-ridden rookeries, notably Jacob's Island in Bermondsey and the Mint in the Borough. Jacob's Island, 'the very capital of cholera', was joined to the Thames by the filthy inlet formed by the River Neckinger (a river said to have taken its name from 'the Devil's Neckerchief'). According to

Dickens, it was 'surrounded by a muddy ditch, six or eight feet deep and fifteen or twenty wide when the tide is in . . . known in these days as Folly Ditch' (*OT* 50). Here Sikes meets his death. Dickens felt obliged to insist on the veracity of his account of Jacob's Island in his Preface to the 1867 edition of *Oliver Twist*, when he complained about the declaration of an 'amazing alderman' (Sir Peter Laurie) who had claimed in 1850 that the place 'did not exist and never has existed'. The disease-ridden nature of Jacob's Island had also been harrowingly described in Charles Kingsley's *Alton Locke* (1850). The most notorious and longest-lasting of the transpontine slums was the Mint in Southwark, ironically described by John Hollingshead in 1861 as 'still the dear old collection of dens which it was in the days of our grandfathers, and, if it has no murky cellars like old St Giles's, this virtue is due more to its geological formation than to its local self-government. The foundations are nothing but rotten muck.' In 1842 Dickens, accompanied by Forster, MACLISE, and Longfellow, was guided through the 'worst haunts of the most dangerous classes' by two police officers. At the first of the Mint lodging-houses they visited, the squeamish Maclise was, according to Forster, 'struck with such a sickness . . . that he had to remain, for the time we were in them, under the guardianship of the police outside' (Forster 3.8). Dickens was vividly to describe a later nocturnal visit to the remains of the St Giles rookery, the East End, and the Mint lodging-houses in his essay 'On Duty with Inspector FIELD' (*RP*). Under Field's expert guidance Dickens observes an 'infinitely quieter and more subdued' place than he recalled from his earlier visits, but he still notes the survival of 'intolerable rooms, burrowed out like the holes of rats or the nests of insect-vermin, but fuller of intolerable smells', holding 'crowds of sleepers, each on his foul truckle-bed coiled up beneath a rug'.

Perhaps the most notorious of all London slums were, however, those concentrated in the inner East End of London, and particularly in the vicinity of the Ratcliff (or Ratcliffe) Highway and Whitechapel. These too are visited by night in 'On Duty with Inspector Field'. For Hollingshead in 1861 the Whitechapel Road opened up on either side to 'about twenty narrow avenues, leading to thousands of closely packed nests, full to overflowing with dirt, and misery, and rags'. In 'On an Amateur Beat' Dickens's UNCOMMERCIAL TRAVELLER describes how, in a single stride eastwards from Houndsditch Church, everything changed for the worse. Whitechapel, 'that pretty densely-populated quarter', is 'not a wery nice neighbourhood' according to Sam Weller, and occasions Sam's famous observation that 'poverty and oysters always seems to go together' (*PP* 22). In the area around Ratcliff Highway the often desperately poor population trebled in the first 60 years of the 19th century (reaching a peak of *c*.17,000 in 1861). Here probably was the site of the opium den in *Edwin Drood*, situated in 'a miserable court, specially miserable among many such' (*MED* 23). A marine-store dealer's 'in that reservoir of dirt, drunkenness, and drabs: thieves, oysters, baked potatoes, and pickled salmon—Ratcliff Highway', is described in 'Broker's and Marine-store Shops' (*SB*).

It is possible that this same marine-store dealer's contributed something to the far later account of Krook's warehouse in *Bleak House*, a shop situated close to Dickens's most significant fictional slum, Tom-All-Alone's. Tom-All-Alone's remains notably unlocated, though it must be close enough to Chancery Lane and Lincoln's Inn Fields to allow for the easy crossings from areas of prosperity to areas of dire deprivation in the novel. It would seem to have been linked in Dickens's mind to the decaying area of 16th- and 17th-century wooden housing which survived at the southern end of Drury Lane, around Wych Street, an area which disappeared in the construction of the Aldwych and Kingsway *c*.1900.      ALS

Dexter (1923).

Hollingshead, John, *Ragged London in 1861* (1861).

Mayhew, Henry, *London Labour and the London Poor*, 4 vols. (1861–2).

Stedman-Jones, Gareth, *Outcast London* (1971).

**11. Streets and street traders.** Dickens's career as a writer literally grew out of the London streets. In 1835 two of his earliest publications were the sketches 'The Streets—Morning' and 'The Streets—Night' published in the MORNING CHRONICLE and the genesis of his first book, *Sketches by Boz*. As he himself says, 'What inexhaustible food for speculation, do the streets of London afford!' ('Shops and Their Tenants', *SB*).

Dickens never lost this intense connection to the London streets, and as late as the 1860s he is still wandering them as the UNCOMMERCIAL TRAVELLER. He confessed to his friend John FORSTER that he found the streets 'a marvellous MAGIC LANTERN' and was unable to work for long without the stimulation they brought him. His novels are 'crammed'—as his biographer Edgar Johnson says—with lively evocations of the byways of London, 'from the narrow lanes darkened by the walls of Lincoln's Inn to the tall genteel houses between Portland Place and Bryanston Square'. Little escaped him. The narrator of the *Sketches* exuberantly describes the slum 'Seven Dials' and the racks of old clothes in 'Meditations in Monmouth Street'. Oliver Twist has a grimmer, even phantasmagoric, experience as he is dragged by Sikes on foot across all of London—from Bethnal Green in the far east to the far west suburb of Halliford (*OT* 21). The profusion of goods and faces which greet Nicholas Nickleby on his arrival in London both promise and overwhelm. But Florence Dombey's early life is forever marked by being lost on the London streets, 'stunned by the noise and confusion' (*DS* 6). This threatening mixture of crime and commerce is repeated in Pip's first encounter with the London streets as he disembarks from the coach on to Little Britain Street 'just out of Smithfields' (*GE* 20), the site of Jaggers's law office, a few steps from the criminal courts, and still there today. Little Dorrit and Arthur Clennam achieve a qualified happiness walking hand in hand in the anonymous 'roaring streets' at the end of their novel.

What was the 'attraction of repulsion' (as he put it to Forster) of the streets for Dickens? In a time without cinema or television or other kinds of access to the world beyond the home, the noisy, crowded, narrow London streets were a place of stimulation, excitement, adventure, challenge, and danger. People of all classes and occupations rubbed shoulders with each other. Rich and poor lived in the same quarters; the Houses of Parliament and Westminster Abbey backed on to some of the worst districts in the city. The sinister but fascinating slum Seven Dials (possibly a model for Tom-All-Alone's in *Bleak House*) was only a few blocks from Trafalgar Square and the National Gallery.

But the mass of people milling about the streets were not all just moving from place to place—either on foot or by omnibus, cab, or private carriage. (The large number of horses on the streets gave rise to a whole industry of crossing-sweepers like Jo in *Bleak House*, who, in return for a tip, swept the horse manure and other debris away from the well-dressed men and women who wanted to cross the street.) In addition, 40,000 men, women, and children made a living—and sometimes lived on—the streets of London (30,000 costermongers or traders in fresh food and 10,000 others). Though this mass of workers in the underground economy could seem alien, they were for the most part very hard-working and very law-abiding.

Early in the morning hundreds of petty traders filled baskets or barrows with fruits, vegetables, and flowers at the central markets like Covent Garden or Farringdon. Others got fish from Billingsgate or meat and dairy products from Smithfield and Leadenhall and then spread out through the streets of the metropolis to provide what was the only source of food and goods for many of the people living in London. Some rose early to prepare food—coffee and other drinks, baked potatoes, hot eels, pies, and sweet stuff which they hawked either from trays slung around their necks moving through regular rounds or from fixed wagons in busy thoroughfares where they and their parents had traded for years.

In addition there were people who sold all manner of goods on the streets—live animals and birds or manufactured goods like shoelaces, tinware, blacking, and glue—anything portable. Some, like Silas Wegg in *Our Mutual Friend*, sold ballads, books, and pamphlets. There were also many entertainers on the streets—sword swallowers, acrobats, hurdy-gurdy men and Punch and Judy shows. All these sellers hawked their wares at the top of their lungs; as Henry Mayhew, the great chronicler of the London street folk and an exact contemporary and sometime acquaintance of Dickens, put it, 'all are bawling together—salesmen and hucksters of provisions, hardware, and newspapers,—till the place is a perfect Babel of competition'.

There were also crowds of 'finders'—like the children who collected cigar butts discarded in the gutters to sell to those who would make new cigars from the leavings, or the 'pure finders' who collected dogs' dung to sell for use in tanneries. Of course there were plenty of pickpockets like Fagin's gang, and PROSTITUTES, estimated in 1855 to number 80,000. And there were beggars with an amazing range of appeals and cons, from little girls selling violets (and perhaps themselves), to the crippled nutmeg-grinder seller or Blind Sarah with her hurdy-gurdy whom Mayhew befriended.

At night this astonishing crush of humanity, vehicles, and animals was transformed by the hundreds of gas streetlights (well established by 1835) and by the recurrent dense fogs caused by damp air and smoke from the coal fires that heated all the London buildings (and which provided the memorable opening of *Bleak House*), one of the most enduring of London's images. Lit only by golden haloes of light from a gaslight, the narrow night streets were filled with indistinct and slightly threatening (or inviting) figures that flitted through narrow passageways or into sudden doors. In all this, Dickens found his creative energy: 'Put me down on Waterloo Bridge at eight o'clock in the evening,' he wrote to Forster, 'and I would come home, as you know, panting to go on.'                                    AH

Hibbert, Christopher, 'Dickens's London', in E. W. F. Tomlin (ed.), *Charles Dickens: A Centennial Volume* (1969).

Korg, Jacob, *London in Dickens' Day* (1960).

Mayhew, Henry, *London Labour and the London Poor*, 4 vols. (1861–2).

Porter, Roy, *London: A Social History* (1994).

Winter, James, *London's Teeming Streets 1830–1914* (1993).

**12. Topography.** London was founded, probably by the Romans, because its site flanks the lowest stretch of the Thames with a gravel bed. The river could thus be forded there, and eventually bridged. Gravel subsoil beneath the banks ensured firm landing-ground for boats. Thanks to its position on the Thames, the city grew to become a major junction for road, river, and maritime traffic. Roads converged on it because a bridge crossed the river there. Boats plied back and forth, from the mouth of the Thames, through the city, and through much of south-east England. Larger vessels sailed downriver and overseas. Inevitably, it attracted trade and population.

During the century preceding Dickens's birth, London had been growing at an unprecedented rate, and the population had more than doubled, to well over 1 million. During his lifetime the city grew even more rapidly. Between his arrival there as a boy and his death, the population increased from about 1,400,000 to about 3 million, and the city spread over much of the surrounding countryside, creating hybrid areas on the outskirts, like the neighbourhood of John and Harriet Carker's house: 'It is neither of the town or country. The former, like the giant in his travelling boots, has made a stride and passed it, and has set his brick-and-mortar heel a long way in advance; but the intermediate space between the giant's feet, as yet, is only blighted country, and not town ...' (*DS* 33).

The rapid growth of the city led to massive changes in infrastructure. From the middle of the 18th century turnpike trusts had begun to improve the network of roads converging on London, and in 1826 the Metropolis Roads Commission became responsible for road development in north London. Thanks to new techniques of road construction and surfacing, the number of passengers carried by coach in and out of the capital increased sixteenfold between 1790 and 1835, the year before railways began to take passengers from coaches (see TRANSPORT). Within London, too, the road system was being improved and extended. Built between 1756 and 1761, the New Road (today's Marylebone Road, Euston Road, and City Road) provided a northern bypass around the congested centre. A southern bypass was provided by Westminster Bridge, opened in 1750, and the roads running from it, through St George's Circus and south of the Borough.

The clearing of areas for new roads, though, pushed the poorest Londoners into even more crowded and dilapidated slums, such as those described in 'On Duty with Inspector FIELD': 'Ten, twenty, thirty—who can count them! Men, women, children, for the most part naked, heaped upon the floor like maggots in a cheese ... Thus we make our New Oxford-streets, and our other new streets, never heeding, never asking, where the wretches whom we clear out, crowd' (*RP*).

London indeed remained predominantly a labyrinthine city of convoluted streets and small alleys on ancient ground-plans, reflected by Dickens in descriptions such as that of the district near the Monument in which Mrs Todgers's boarding-house was to be found: 'You couldn't walk about in Todgers's neighbourhood, as you could in any other neighbourhood. You groped your way for an hour through lanes and bye-ways, and court-yards, and passages; and you never once emerged upon anything that might be reasonably called a street' (*MC* 9).

Westminster Bridge was the first to be built across the stretch of the Thames between the medieval London Bridge and Putney Bridge (1729). By the time of Dickens's birth there were six bridges between the Pool of London and Kew. Six more road bridges, and seven rail, were constructed before he died. Railways began to converge on London, and to carry passengers within it, from 1836. By 1870 the greater part of the network found today was complete.

During the years immediately before and after Dickens's birth, far-reaching changes were made to the port of London, not least in response to the challenge of west-coast ports such as Bristol and Liverpool. London's riverside wharves were becoming insufficient and inadequate. Secure deep-water docks were constructed, flanked by massive warehouses. New roads were constructed, such as Commercial Road and East India Dock Road, new canals, such as the Grand Surrey Canal, the Grand Junction Canal, the Kennet and Avon Canal, and the Oxford and Coventry Canal. These linked the docks to each other, to the heart of London, and to the manufacturing centres of the south and the midlands.

London, however, was largely untouched by the factory system, so much a part of the INDUSTRIAL revolution in the midlands and the north. In 1851 only seventeen industrial employers in the city had more than 250 workers; 86 per cent had fewer than ten. London remained a city of small counting-houses and workshops. The latter were sometimes called factories, but giant manufacturing establishments featured little in London's landscape.

Dickens was more attentive to man-made structures than he was to the geological structure of London. Like Sam Weller's, his knowledge of the city was 'extensive and peculiar' (*PP* 20), more piecemeal, that is, than fundamental. Geological continuity interested him less than historical change. He was fascinated by such notions as the supposition that 'a brook "as clear as crystal" once ran right down the middle of Holborn, when Turnstile really was a turnstile, leading slap away into the meadows' (*BH* 10). There is some evidence that he thought about the geological structure of the city, but he drew attention to it chiefly to generate comedy. Only Pickwick at his most absurd would act geographer, and trace 'to their source the mighty ponds of Hampstead' (*PP* 1).

One geological feature, however, did occupy a central place in Dickens's imagination. The identity of London is inseparable from its position on the Thames, and of this Dickens was acutely conscious. The river and its environs seized his imagination at an early date. On London Bridge, as a boy, he told the young servant who assisted his parents in the Marshalsea 'quite astonishing fictions about the wharves and the tower' (Forster 1.2). His unfailing interest in the river, his intimate and thorough knowledge of it, is revealed in Dickens's last completed novel by Rogue Riderhood's observation about the slow progress of a rower upstream, after he has 'lost the tide' (*OMF* 4.1). This is an allusion to the point at which, during a flood tide, the upstream current is lost, overwhelmed by the downstream current of landwater.

Dickens's consciousness of the proliferation of bridges across the Thames, and of their sequence, is marked by Wemmick's enumeration of the ones between the City and Chelsea Reach: London Bridge, Southwark, Blackfriars, Waterloo, Westminster, and Vauxhall (*GE* 36), none built later than 1819. The list helps us date the action of the novel.

His travels about the country as a young journalist, before railways became common, familiarized Dickens with turnpike roads. Their personnel and hardware are featured in *Pickwick Papers*. A bribed turnpike-keeper obstructs the pursuit of Mr Jingle and Rachael Wardle into London (*PP* 9). The coachman, Tony Weller, threatens to betray his calling by becoming a turnpike-keeper (*PP* 56). Dickens's fascination with stagecoach travel, and with travel on foot by those unable to afford it, is reflected in the way he repeatedly features the roads converging on London: from the north (*OT* 8; *NN* 5; *BH* 6), from the north-east (*PP* 22; *DC* 5, 54), from the south-east (*PP* 2, 28; *DC* 12), from the south-west (*NN* 22, 32), from the west (*PP* 35; *OT* 21; *MC* 8, 36; *OMF* 3.8), and from the north-west (*PP* 50; *OCS* 15, 69).

*Dombey and Son* registers Dickens's awareness of railways, and the way they were changing the appearance of London. 'Away, with a shriek, and a roar, and a rattle' is the refrain of his description of Mr Dombey's journey by train from London to Leamington (*DS* 20). The cutting of the London and Birmingham Railway through Camden Town is described as 'the first shock of a great earthquake' (*DS* 6). 'A Flight' (*RP*) describes a journey from London Bridge Station to Paris.

Dickens's awareness of the docks is most straightforwardly registered in 'Bound for the Great Salt Lake' (*UT* 20), which paints a vivid picture of the dockland milieu in the 1860s. Other powerful evocations of the quarter are to be found in *Great Expectations* (46) and *Our Mutual Friend* (1.3, 2.12). Captain Cuttle has lodgings in the region of the West India Docks (*DS* 9).

Dickens faithfully depicts the kind of workplace that continued to predominate in London during his lifetime. Evidently, neither Murdstone and Grinby's wine warehouse (*DC* 11), nor Doyce and Clennam's factory (*LD* 1.23), nor the Harmony dust-mounds (*OMF* 1.5) employs more than a handful of workers. The same seems to be true of the Cheeryble brothers' counting house (*NN* 35, 37), of Chicksey, Veneering and Stobbles's counting house (*OMF* 3.16), even of the grand establishment of Dombey and Son (*DS* 13).

Characteristically, Dickens encapsulates London in imaginative prose. To poor travellers approaching its outskirts, it is 'the monster, roaring in the distance' (*DS* 33). On a cold spring evening, with an east wind blowing, it becomes 'a black shrill city, combining the qualities of a smoky house and a scolding wife . . . a beleaguered city, invested by the great Marsh forces of Essex and Kent' (*OMF* 1.12). Such visions, however, are underpinned by a clear sense of the city's structure, man-made and natural. DP

### 'Loving Ballad of Lord Bateman, The'

A comic ballad that George CRUIKSHANK turned into a party performance. Cruikshank set down his version in Cockney dialect and illustrated it with charming line drawings and musical staves drawn by Dickens's brother-in-law Henry Burnett (1839). A facetious introduction and notes, purportedly by Cruikshank, were actually by Dickens, who because of his agreements with Richard BENTLEY not to publish elsewhere had to conceal his part in this collaboration. Having heard Dickens perform the same ballad, William Makepeace THACKERAY wrote and illustrated his own version, but it was never published during his lifetime. RLP

**Lytton, Edward Bulwer** See BULWER-LYTTON, EDWARD.

# M

**Mackenzie, Henry** (1745–1831), novelist, ESSAYIST, and successful Edinburgh lawyer whose farewell to the public as editor of *The Lounger* (1785–7) is quoted by Dickens in his Preface to *Nicholas Nickleby* (1839). Here Dickens describes himself as a 'periodical essayist' like Mackenzie, and endorses the intimate relationship between author and public of which Mackenzie speaks. Described by SCOTT as the 'Northern ADDISON', Mackenzie was also co-author of *The Mirror* (1779–80) and three novels of sentiment: *The Man of Feeling* (1771), *The Man of the World* (1773), and *Julia de Roubigné* (1777). His collected *Works* (1808) were in Dickens's library by 1844. JMLD

**Maclise, Daniel** (1806–70), historical painter and ILLUSTRATOR. Born in Cork, Maclise early gained a reputation as a skilled portraitist and draughtsman. Abandoning his plan to study medicine, he enrolled as a student at the Royal Academy in 1828, exhibited there from 1829, and was elected RA in 1840, an extraordinarily swift recognition by his peers. Good-looking and charming, Maclise soon moved easily among the political, social, and artistic circles around Harrison AINSWORTH, the Countess of Blessington, and the journalists who wrote for *Fraser's Magazine*. Quickly adopted by them, he provided line portraits of notable figures for the periodical from 1830 to 1838. As soon as he was introduced to Dickens they became close friends, often forming a 'trio' with John FORSTER for dinner, outings, and charitable projects.

Maclise's full-length PORTRAIT of Dickens at his writing desk was completed by June 1839 and engraved by Finden. This was published as the frontispiece to *Nicholas Nickleby*, and though George ELIOT deplored the 'keepsakey, impossible face', most thought it a good likeness. CHAPMAN AND HALL presented the oil (now at the National Portrait Gallery) to Dickens at the dinner celebrating the conclusion of *Nickleby*. In 1840 Maclise supplied the design for one wood engrav-ing illustrating the *Old Curiosity Shop*, chapter 55: the sexton showing Nell the church well.

A favourite around the Dickens household, Maclise was asked by Catherine DICKENS to paint a watercolour of the four children for her to take on the 1842 AMERICAN tour (circular group portrait, private collection). Perhaps at this time, and for the same purpose, Maclise drew for wood engravers a picture of the Devonshire Terrace house (in the FORSTER COLLECTION). A tour to Cornwall following Dickens's return from America, with Dickens, Forster, and Clarkson STANFIELD, resulted in Maclise's painting *Waterfall at St Nighton's Keive near Tintagel* (Forster Collection), for which Georgina HOGARTH posed as a peasant girl crossing the stream barefoot while balancing a ewer on her left shoulder. Knowing that the painter would try to give him the picture if he asked, Dickens used a ruse to buy it at auction. Maclise was at first upset, but soon afterwards friendly relations were resumed; he drew a triple portrait of Dickens, Kate, and Georgina (1843, Forster Collection) and painted Kate twice (DICKENS HOUSE MUSEUM).

For the second Christmas book, *The CHIMES* (1844), Dickens increased the number of illustrations from eight to thirteen and hired three artists to supplement the contributions of John LEECH. Maclise prepared the drawings for the steel-engraved frontispiece and title-page vignette. Used to full-scale canvases, he found it difficult to cram his pictures into the compass of a small page; the results were acceptable to Dickens, although the *Christian Remembrancer*, 9 (January 1845) castigated the 'monstrous mélange of kicking, sprawling nudities'. When Dickens returned from ITALY to London for a week in December, he read his new Christmas book to friends on two occasions. Maclise was present both times; he sketched the auditors and Dickens, light radiating from his head. This record of a 'triumphant hour' he presented to Catherine (drawing now in the Forster Collection).

Having been selected to execute frescos for the rebuilt Houses of Parliament, Maclise was not keen to contribute to another cramped fancy book. But he was persuaded by Dickens, and after fussing repeatedly about the woodblocks the publishers provided for him to draw on, he completed on time, for *The* CRICKET ON THE HEARTH, a very complex frontispiece of the Peerybingles and the cricket by the hearth, and a simpler design of holly and naked elves for the vignette title. The indecency of these figures was reprobated in the press, and Dickens failed to communicate his appreciation, so relations between artist and author cooled noticeably.

However, Forster, who had been superintending the production of the Christmas books while Dickens was abroad, managed to cajole Maclise into contributing to the next holiday offering, *The* BATTLE OF LIFE. Determined to prove his critics wrong, Maclise contributed four subjects—the frontispiece and title-page, and two further illustrations, of Clemency Newcome in despair at Michael Warden's interview with Marion, and of the two sisters reunited at the end. Though cut into the block by a master engraver, John Thompson, Maclise hated the result; 'mortified and humiliated by the effect of these damnable cuts' (Kitton 1899, p. 167), he withdrew from any further illustrating for Dickens.

The perfectionist artist laboured strenuously on his parliamentary murals, eventually completing two huge paintings for the Royal Gallery in the House of Lords. He had neither time nor inclination to participate much in Dickensian AMATEUR THEATRICALS or parties, though he helped design costumes for the 1845 production of *Every Man In His Humour* and attended many of the amateur players' performances. He grew more melancholy and reclusive, and although Dickens persuaded him to join in brief visits to PARIS in 1850 and 1855, thereafter Dickens was unable to breach the artist's solitude. When Maclise died in April 1870, Dickens at the annual Royal Academy dinner delivered a powerful eulogy upon 'the gentlest and most modest of men'. It was Dickens's last public speech.

RLP

**Macready, William Charles** (1793–1873), actor, manager, and one of Dickens's most intimate friends. They were introduced by FORSTER on 16 June 1837, and although Macready was a prickly and morose egotist of violent temper, he seems never to have quarrelled with Dickens, alone of his friends, from that date until Dickens's death 33 years later. Dickens was 'a friend who really loves me', Macready confided in his diary on 1 January 1842, and years later he meditated, 'If it were right to have a personal friend, Dickens is the person most fit' (Macready 1912, entry for 9 January 1851).

Within days of their meeting they were walking, dining, and consulting together frequently, a pattern broken only when they were physically separated. Dickens stood as godfather for Macready's son Henry (1839–57), a role which Macready reciprocated by standing as godfather for Dickens's first daughter, Kate Macready Dickens (see CHILDREN OF DICKENS). Catherine DICKENS and Georgina HOGARTH were frequent guests at Macready's home, and Dickens and Catherine regularly dined with Macready and his wife on their wedding anniversary. Macready greatly relieved Catherine's anxieties about accompanying Dickens to AMERICA in 1842, by making himself responsible for the safekeeping of her children during her absence. Recognizing that the hostile reception accorded to AMERICAN NOTES (which Macready did not admire) might extend to his friend, Dickens refrained from publicly seeing Macready off on the actor's visit to America in 1843. Macready attended the celebratory dinners which marked the completion of Dickens's novels, and was deeply moved by the 'high compliment' when Dickens dedicated *Nicholas Nickleby* to him—although the novel containing Vincent Crummles might be considered a doubtful compliment to a great actor. Perhaps his most important service to Dickens was his intervention, preventing an irreconcilable breach, on an evening when Dickens and Forster quarrelled violently, with Catherine rushing from the room in tears (Macready 1912, entry for 16 August 1840).

The son of a theatre manager, Macready was studying at Rugby, intending a career at the bar, when his father's arrest for debt led him to quit school and take up acting to rescue the family fortunes. A widely read and cultivated man, he loathed the stage and the low status of the actor, but made it his career.

He made his debut at the age of 16 in Birmingham as Romeo, and spent the next four years acting for his father's company. He made his London debut at Covent Garden Theatre in 1816, soon established himself as rival to the great romantic actor Edmund Kean, and on Kean's premature death in 1833 Macready stood at the forefront of his profession, 'the eminent tragedian', until he retired in 1851. 'The great representative English actor', he was a perfectionist who excelled in domestic roles, such as the father in KNOWLES'S *Virginius* (Lawrence Barrett, 'William Charles Macready', in Brander Matthews and Lawrence Hutton (eds.), *Actors and Actresses of Great Britain and the United States*, 1886).

Macready's accession to the management of Covent Garden Theatre in 1837–9, dedicated to a policy of mounting major revivals of SHAKESPEARE'S plays and to promoting new works by contemporary dramatists, raised hopes that he would halt what was widely seen at the time as a disastrous decline in dramatic art and restore the English stage to something approaching its Elizabethan glory (see DRAMA AND DRAMATISTS DURING DICKENS'S LIFETIME). Dickens shared these hopes, and although his own dramatic pieces were scarcely attempts to revive the drama, he offered them to Macready for production—all were declined, as was Forster's suggestion of a dramatization of *Oliver Twist*—and he worked tirelessly as an artistic adviser to Macready (see PLAYWRIGHT, DICKENS AS). The ambitious repertoire included thirteen titles by Shakespeare and plays by BULWER-LYTTON, Knowles, and TALFOURD.

Macready's most important single production, and the one which had the greatest impact on Dickens's writing, was a revival of *King Lear*, first performed on 25 January 1838, in which he overturned 150 years of stage tradition by discarding Nahum Tate's sentimental version of the play and returning to Shakespeare's text. Forster, who had planned to review it, was ill on opening night and quoted at length from 'a friend'—almost certainly Dickens—in the EXAMINER on 28 January (but Dickens did *not* write 'The Restoration of Shakespeare's Lear to the Stage', *Examiner*, 4 February (*RP*), misattributed to him by B. W. MATZ but shown by W. J. CARLTON (1965) to have been Forster's work).

Dickens, who wrote a thoughtful review, 'Macready as Benedick' (*Examiner*, 4 March 1843; repr. *Journalism* 2.55–9), in which he defended the actor's right to challenge an audience's preconceptions, also reviewed a later performance of *Lear* by Macready in the *Examiner* of 27 October 1849 (*Journalism* 2.170–2). Macready's conception of *Lear*, in terms which we would today consider more MELODRAMATIC than tragic, was shared by Dickens and fed directly into the portrayal of Nell and her Grandfather in *The Old Curiosity Shop* (see Schlicke 1980).

Macready's management met with mixed critical success and financial loss, and he resigned after less than two years. Dickens presided at a meeting of the SHAKESPEARE CLUB in Macready's honour on 30 March 1839, and on 20 July 1839 offered a public eulogy at a banquet in Macready's honour on his ceasing to manage Covent Garden (*Speeches*, pp. 2–3). He wrote a prologue, spoken by Macready, for MARSTON'S play *The Patrician's Daughter* (first performed 10 December 1842). He also spoke, proposing a toast to Bulwer as chairman, at the banquet on 1 March 1851 in honour of Macready's retiral from the stage (*Speeches*, pp. 113–18).

Macready not only valued the friendship of his 'dear' Dickens, but considered him a literary 'genius'. He sobbed openly over *The Old Curiosity Shop*, *Dombey and Son*, and *The* CHIMES (although it is a noteworthy comment on Dickens's alleged SENTIMENTALITY that he was impatient with Macready's grief over the DEATH of an actual child, when the actor's infant daughter Joan died only weeks before the fictional death of Little Nell: to Maclise, 27 November 1840). Macready, generally contemptuous of non-professional acting, considered Dickens one of only two amateurs 'with any pretension to theatrical talent' (a Miss MacTavish was the other; Macready 1875, 1.112), and he coached Dickens on his AMATEUR THEATRICAL performances. Of all the accolades Dickens ever received, perhaps the one he cherished most was Macready's verdict on the PUBLIC READING of *Sikes and Nancy*. 'In my—er—best times—er—', Dickens recorded Macready as saying (to James T. Fields, 15 February 1869), 'you remember them, my dear boy—er—gone, gone! . . . it comes to this—er—TWO MACBETHS!'

Macready's daughter Kate contributed three poems to *Household Words* in 1856.

PVWS

Carlton, William J., 'Dickens or Forster? Some *King Lear* Criticisms Re-examined', *Dickensian*, 61 (1965).

Collins, Philip, 'W. C. Macready and Dickens: Some Family Recollections', *Dickens Studies*, 2 (1966).

Downer, Alan S., *The Eminent Tragedian, William Charles Macready* (1966).

Macready, William Charles, *Macready's Reminiscences and Selections from His Diaries and Letters*, ed. Sir Frederick Pollock, 2 vols. (1875).

—— *The Diaries of William Charles Macready 1833–1851*, ed. William Toynbee, 2 vols. (1912).

Schlicke, Paul, ' "A Discipline of Feeling": Macready's *Lear* and *The Old Curiosity Shop*', *Dickensian*, 76 (1980).

**Macrone, John** (1809–37), Dickens's first publisher, described later by him as someone 'in the prime and vigour of his years' who had died 'at that moment his prospects were brightest' (*PIC-NIC PAPERS*, p. 2). The two probably met in 1835, introduced to each other by AINSWORTH (Forster 1.5), whose popular *Rookwood* (1834) Macrone had published through his own company founded in September 1834.

No agreement between Macrone and Dickens for collecting his *Sketches by Boz* has come to light. We know, however, that Ainsworth urged Dickens to seek a publisher and that Macrone asked CRUIKSHANK to illustrate the volume. This decision guaranteed public interest and engaged an artist whose knowledge of London life matched Dickens's. For his part, Dickens was equal to the challenge. If the whole collection fell short of the two projected volumes, he told Macrone, 'I will be ready with two or three new Sketches to make weight' (?27 October 1835).

Success with the *Sketches* drew Dickens and Macrone together. On 9 May 1836 Dickens wrote to express 'great pleasure' in accepting Macrone's offer of £200 for the COPYRIGHT of a three-volume novel 'entitled *Gabriel Vardon, the Locksmith of London*'. The letter also stated that Dickens would deliver the entire manuscript by 30 November 1836 or shortly afterwards. This was an impossible promise given Dickens's other commitments, as events soon revealed.

Complications began that summer when Dickens signed his first agreement with BENTLEY on 22 August 1836. The contract does not name 'Gabriel Vardon' as one of the two novels Dickens agreed to write. But when Bentley raised the copyright price of each to £500 he opened the door to a breach with Macrone. Dickens's relations with the latter were further strained when he agreed to edit the new monthly periodical Bentley proposed on 4 November 1836. Shortly afterwards, Dickens wrote to Macrone saying that he wished to withdraw from his agreement on 9 May to write 'Gabriel Vardon'.

This request left Macrone few options. Ainsworth advised him to bid for the novel; instead, he tried to hold Dickens to their May agreement. Under pressure, Dickens agreed to accept £250 for the copyright of the *Sketches* (both series) in return for regaining possession of the 9 May 1836 letter (?31 December 1836). Determined to make the best of events, Macrone announced the next year his intention to republish the *Sketches* in monthly parts, exploiting the format used so successfully by CHAPMAN AND HALL for *Pickwick*. Help from Chapman and Hall enabled Dickens to block this move when his publishers bought the copyrights of the *Sketches* from Macrone for £2,250. Macrone's victory was short-lived. His premature death on 9 September 1837 left his widow and three children with few resources. Dickens raised £450 on their behalf from the benefit publication of *The Pic-Nic Papers*, published in three volumes in 1841, to which he contributed an Introduction, 'The Lamplighter's Story', a revised version of his farce *The LAMPLIGHTER*, and his editorial labours.

DHP

**madness, lunacy, and insanity.** Into the very texture of Dickens's novels is woven an array of characters who lack sanity, common sense, or rationality. Many of these characters are memorable even for brief appearances in the novels—for key phrases which epitomize their mental disarray: 'Seventy-six hundred thousand million of parcels of bank-notes' (Grandmother Smallweed, *BH*), or 'she is come at last—at last—and all is gas and gaiters!' (Mrs Nickleby's mad neighbour, the 'gentleman in small clothes'). But Dickens did not limit himself to exploring insanity in characterization alone; madness is a recurrent theme in his novels, which he developed as he matured as a writer.

Born when a mad king was on the throne, whose insanity highlighted issues both medical and social, Dickens also inherited a strong imaginative tradition in representing madness. While conscious of changing social attitudes towards the insane, he drew on established conventions in his fiction. A reformer in his age, yet influenced by fictional tradition, Dickens did not always see the need to resolve contradictions between these strands.

There was widespread debate in the 19th century about the care of the insane (considered in recent years by Michel Foucault and others). Dickens's reading public would have been aware of the concern, even if not acquainted with the minutiae of such discussion. Several Acts during the century reflected public interest in this subject. That Dickens was aware of changing attitudes to madness is suggested by his long-standing friendship with John FORSTER, who was a Lunacy Commissioner, and by his scattered references to John Haslam (medical officer at Bethlem Hospital—Bedlam—from 1795–1816), and to abuses in the asylum system.

Dickens was acquainted with John Conolly (Professor of the Practice of Medicine in London University, 1827–31), an inspecting physician in lunatic houses, who helped plan Dickens's visit to Highgate's asylum. Dickens also sought out establishments for the insane in his travels, recording in AMERICAN NOTES disapproval of New York's asylum. In his view, this institution failed to promote either purposeful activity or even an orderly and clean environment for its inmates. By contrast, he applauded the approach adopted towards inmates at the State Hospital for the Insane in South Boston.

Besides asylums at Massachusetts and Glasgow, Dickens also visited St Luke's Hospital, London—the subject of 'A Curious Dance Round a Curious Tree' (HW 17 January 1852), an article describing the practice of inviting celebrities to asylum balls, and vividly contrasting contemporary treatments of the insane with descriptions of earlier, less humane methods.

As editor of Household Words, Dickens published several articles dealing with insanity, including a description of a lunatic asylum

at Palermo. He rejected, however, 'Gilbert Massenger', a tale written by Harriet Parr (under the pen name Holme Lee) describing hereditary madness. While he himself had explored this theme (in 'A Madman's Manuscript', PP 11), Dickens's postscript to this tale explains that the madman suffers because of his own immorality. Dickens as editor was aware both of the theme's potentially negative effect upon the sales of Household Words, and of its possible impact upon sufferers' families.

A personal experience of madness, of a very different kind, came through his friendship with Mme de la Rue. Dickens tried MESMERISM as a means of combating Mme de la Rue's emotional difficulties which had left her deeply distressed, although his wife, Catherine, was unhappy with this developing relationship.

Dickens's editorial stance, personal experience, and attempts to help Mme de la Rue, indicate a broadly sympathetic approach to the care of the insane. Yet his encounter with one individual in 1861 proved a notable exception. His observations of his visit to 'Mad Lucas' (later woven into 'Tom Tiddler's Ground', CS) were unsympathetic to the hermit, whom Dickens criticizes for laziness and irresponsibility.

If Dickens was conscious of changing attitudes towards the treatment of the insane, he was also familiar with a wide range of literature in which insanity was explored. In the biblical tradition, madness was portrayed as an outcome of moral failure—an attitude later emphasized in Massinger's drama A New Way to Pay Old Debts, and in writings of Dickens's contemporaries. He was familiar with works of 17th- and 18th-century playwrights who used insanity for sensational purposes (see DRAMA AND DRAMATISTS BEFORE DICKENS), and with writers from another literary tradition with a strong dramatic element— the GOTHIC NOVEL. Madness as a commentary on human frailty, observed in the writings of SHAKESPEARE, is a theme later employed in the fiction of SCOTT, among others, while the use of insanity to highlight both wisdom and folly has been explored in the writings of Erasmus and SWIFT, as well as those of Shakespeare and Scott. Although a range of contemporary literature described abuses of the asylum system, this theme was not taken up by Dickens in any detail. He did, however, explore the restorative potential of insanity—a New Testament theme, reflected later in the writings of Charlotte BRONTË and Elizabeth GASKELL.

In his treatment of madness, Dickens explored a range of themes, including madness and the environment ('Our Parish', *SB*); madness and morality ('The Drunkard's Death', *SB*; 'A Madman's Manuscript', *PP* 11; in the vegetable-throwing wooer, *NN* 41); madness and social collapse (in his representation of the crowd in *Barnaby Rudge* and *A Tale of Two Cities*); madness as thematic underlining (in *Barnaby Rudge* and Miss Flite, *BH*); madness as innocence (in Mr Dick, *DC*); madness and imprisonment (in Mr Dorrit); madness and recovery (in Dr Manette, *TTC*); and madness as monomania, cunning, and revenge (in Mme Defarge, *TTC* and Miss Havisham, *GE*).

In 'Our Parish' and 'The Drunkard's Death' (both *SB*), he interweaves themes of poverty and insanity, prefiguring later exploration of the malevolent aspects of city life and its blighting consequences. In his earliest fiction, indebted to those traditions in which insanity is an outcome of the Fall, Dickens explores madness as a means of illustrating mismanagement, drunkenness, selfishness, and criminal activity, portrayed comically (as in Mrs Nickleby's mad neighbour), or, as with the memorable tale 'A Madman's Manuscript' inset in *Pickwick*, to underline the tragic effects of moral degeneracy. He uses dramatic devices drawn from farce, comedy, MELODRAMA, and the Gothic tradition in a crudely dramatic representation of insanity to underscore his moral purpose.

In *Barnaby Rudge, Copperfield, A Tale of Two Cities*, and *Great Expectations*, he explores the potential of unfortunate victims of circumstance, using Mr Dick and Miss Havisham as catalysts in his plots. In *Barnaby Rudge* Dickens dropped his original idea of having three madmen as the riot's leaders, in favour of developing the contrasting roles of Lord George Gordon and Barnaby. Barnaby starkly illustrates for the reader the consequences of the riots upon an individual who lacks the capacity to reason, with Dickens underlining parallels between this figure and the dazed character of Gordon.

By contrast, in *Copperfield*'s Mr Dick Dickens demonstrates that even the most vulnerable member of society can effect beneficial change. From the outset Mr Dick is depicted as a grotesque, comic creation. For Forster, his rescue from a private asylum provides a remarkable example of alternatives to institutional care. However, Dickens's concentration on Mr Dick's madness, illustrated by his kite-flying and Memorial, declines as Dickens loads his character with moral purpose, with the attempt to rescue the Strongs' marriage in an uncomfortable denouement scene. The novel does, however, contain a contrasting cameo of insanity in the disquieting detail of the lunatic observed by Copperfield when revisiting his old home. The solitary madman staring out of David's old bedroom window not only underlines changes in Copperfield's life since childhood, but also challenges the rationality and purpose explored elsewhere in the novel.

Unlike some of Dickens's mad characters, Miss Flite was not mentally deranged from birth, her plight illustrating in *Bleak House* the effects of intense personal suffering. Members of her family are victims of legal injustice, Miss Flite's prophetic role in the novel providing a warning to other characters. The few trappings she possesses underline her association with the great CHANCERY case of Jarndyce and Jarndyce at the heart of the novel— her reticule stuffed with paper scraps and dry lavender, and her significantly named cage-birds.

In *A Tale of Two Cities* we encounter a very different victim of circumstance. In Dr Manette Dickens explores the interconnection between confinement and insanity and the effects on one individual of political unrest. Dr Manette is a portrait of human frailty, though Dickens prefers not to explore his inner thoughts and compulsions. Manette's incapacity to assist his family in escaping their impending doom provides a remarkable contrast with Carton's sacrificial action. Unreason is contrasted with reason and the restoration of Manette's sanity in Carton's prophetic vision illuminates the far-reaching effects of Carton's sacrifice, as Dickens interweaves themes of sacrifice and redemption. In contrast to Dr Manette's inner turmoil and actual restoration, Mme Defarge is a figure maddened by passion. Scarred by bereavement, she becomes locked in the desire for retribution and embodies the destructive effects of human vengeance.

As Dickens explores the impact of the French Revolution, descriptions of wild mob activities inject a terrific sense of energy into his narrative. Dickens draws upon impressions recorded in 'Mad Dancing' (*HW* 4 October 1856, by Louisa May Costello), of a festival in Dinant, the description in *A Tale of Two Cities* highlighting the warping effects of the French Revolution upon groups of people, much as his portrayal of Dr Manette illustrates its destructive impact upon one individual.

Later, *Great Expectations* contains a memorable study of monomania. Swindled and abandoned by her suitor, Miss Havisham becomes tragically warped. Like Mr Dick, she is obsessional. Unlike Mr Dick, though, Miss Havisham is an agent of revenge. While both Barnaby and Mr Dick are asexual in nature, Miss Havisham's monomania is linked with Dickens's exploration of SEXUALITY in *Great Expectations*. A possible source for Dickens's portrayal of this revenge-seeking, jilted bride is his article 'Where We Stopped Growing' (*HW* 1 January 1853), which describes a woman 'dressed entirely in white', 'a conceited old creature', becoming 'simpering mad on personal grounds alone'. This character's plight is not sympathetically portrayed, for although abandoned prior to her wedding, and still wearing her bridal dress, the account notes by her 'mincing step' and 'fishy eye' that she would have led her husband a 'sharp life'.

Elements from this account, amongst others, may have moulded Dickens's description of Miss Havisham—yet she is a distinctive creation, whose vulnerable figure is both haunting and grotesque. In Miss Havisham, confined amidst rotting emblems of her wedding, Dickens explores the malevolent effects of monomania in a remarkable female, and the part it plays in the maturing process of his hero, Pip.

Dickens's varied treatment of madness, which shifted in its focus as he matured as a novelist, reflected his changing vision and purpose as a writer, and his enduring interest in this subject. There is some disparity between Dickens's personal knowledge of the effects of insanity upon individuals and their families, and his fictional usage.

Although care of the insane became accepted as a public responsibility during the 19th century, in Dickens's novels the task is commonly undertaken by individuals, for he characteristically advises the reader that we should do a little in any good direction when assisting the mentally deranged, for it 'will be much, some day'. HAP

McKnight, N., *Idiots, Madmen and Other Prisoners in Dickens* (1993).

Scull, A., *The Most Solitary of Afflictions: Madness and Society in Britain 1700–1900* (1993).

**magic lanterns** were a widespread medium for instruction and entertainment in the Victorian period, part of a movement towards visualization which forms an important context for Dickens's work (see AMUSEMENTS AND RECREATION). Writing *Dombey and Son* in Lausanne, he complained of the 'absence of streets' provided by the 'magic lantern' of London (30 August 1846). By Dickens's day they had achieved a high level of sophistication. Multiple projection made possible dissolves from one image into another and the simulation of such effects of movement as the passing of clouds. These shows were an early form of mass entertainment, catering for audiences of a thousand. GFS

**Maginn, William** (1793–1842), a brilliant Regency journalist, was hired by BENTLEY to provide the Prologue to BENTLEY'S MISCELLANY, edited by Dickens from 1837 to 1839. Maginn, revered for his wit and scholarship, had written for *Blackwood's*, and in 1830, set up the high-spirited *Fraser's Magazine*, which quickly became the best-selling magazine of the day—both were models for *Bentley's Miscellany*.

In his only published reference to Dickens, Maginn observes, 'Boz the magnificent (what a pity it is that he deludes himself into the absurd idea that he can be a Whig!—Mr Pickwick was a Whig, and that was only right; but Boz is as much a Whig as he is a giraffe' (*Fraser's*, August 1836). KC

**Malthus, Thomas,** English political economist (1766–1834), who argued, in his immensely influential *Essay on the Principle of Population* (1798, rev. edn. 1803), that population growth necessarily tended to exceed the means of subsistence. This thesis helped to foster both the general principle of *laissez-faire* and the specific objective of 'less eligibility' which underlay the POOR LAW Amendment Act of 1834. Malthus was a *bête-noire* of Dickens, who considered him, correctly, as one of the intellectual progenitors of political economy and, with less justification, of UTILITARIANISM. Neither philosophy accorded with his own understanding of human nature. Scrooge sees off the charity collectors with Malthusian jargon, commenting that those who would 'rather die' than enter a workhouse 'had better do it, and decrease the surplus population' (*CC* 1). Thomas Gradgrind's younger children are named Adam Smith and Malthus, and the dummy book-backs in Dickens's study included *Malthus's Nursery Rhymes*.      EJE

**Marryat, Frederick** (1792–1848), distinguished naval commander, novelist, and friend of Dickens from 1841. 'Captain Marryat' established his popular reputation in the early 1830s with nautical adventure stories such as *Peter Simple* (1834), although he later turned to children's novels, such as *The Children of the New Forest* (1847). In preparation for his trip to AMERICA in 1842, Dickens read Marryat's TRAVEL BOOK, *A Diary in America* (1839); both writers petitioned for international COPYRIGHT when touring in America. There are interesting parallels in their fiction as well, for example, the prominence of foundlings. The two were warm friends, and according to FORSTER, Marryat 'was among the first in Dickens's liking' (Forster 6.6).      MWT

**Marston, Westland** (1819–90), playwright and theatre critic. His verse drama, *The Patrician's Daughter*, was performed by MACREADY at Drury Lane in 1842. Dickens, who admired the play, wrote a Prologue, 'Awake the present!', in support of its poetic handling of contemporary life, but audiences found the blending of verse and modernity incongruous, and it ran for only eleven performances. Marston said his intention was to 'write a Tragedy entirely indebted for its incidents, and passion, to the habits and spirits of the age' and to present the conflict between aristocracy and democracy. Marston also wrote *Anne Blake* (1852), another verse play with a contemporary setting, and a number of prose plays, including *A Hard Struggle*, by which Dickens was greatly moved when he saw it at the Lyceum in 1858. Marston, who was highly esteemed as a serious dramatist in his own lifetime, also wrote dramatic criticism for *The Athenaeum* in the 1860s and published *Our Recent Actors* in 1888.      JD

**Martin Chuzzlewit** Dickens's sixth novel, written after his first visit to AMERICA and CANADA. Containing controversial scenes in the United States, it is generally considered a transitional work between Dickens's early phase and the novels of his maturity.

### Inception and Composition

In August 1841, with *Barnaby Rudge* more than half written, Dickens determined he should take a break from novel writing. For the previous five years his serialized fiction had been appearing regularly—indeed, he produced instalments of two different novels each month for the duration of *Oliver Twist*'s serial run—with only the single break in June 1837, following the death of Mary HOGARTH. Citing the declining sales of MASTER HUMPHREY'S CLOCK and the precedent of SCOTT's last years, Dickens weighed options, decided to 'pause for a year', visit America, and then begin a new monthly serial, to commence in November 1842 (to Mitton, 23 and 30 August 1841).

On return from America, and before he had finished writing his TRAVEL BOOK AMERICAN NOTES, Dickens turned his mind to the next novel. 'I have some notion of opening the new book in the lantern of a lighthouse', he told FORSTER (early August 1842). A month later he still thought of the Cornwall coast as its setting—perhaps, as Michael Slater suggests, with a view to developing the sea 'as symbol or *leitmotif*, as he was to do in the novel which followed *Chuzzlewit*, *Dombey and Son*—and at the end of October he went with Forster, MACLISE, and STANFIELD on an expedition to Cornwall (Introduction to Everyman edition, 1994, p. xxvi). By now the publication date of the first number had been moved to 1 January 1843, and on 12 November, after trying out a variety of permutations for his protagonist's name (among them 'Chubblewig', 'Chuzzletoe', 'Sweezleden', and 'Sweezlewag') he announced the title to Forster: *The Life and Adventures of Martin Chuzzlewig, his family, friends, and enemies. Comprising all his wills and his ways. With an historical record of what he did and what he didn't. The whole thing forming a complete key to the house of Chuzzlewig*. The part issues boasted an even more elaborate version, but when the title-page did appear it was more sedate: *The Life and Adventures of Martin Chuzzlewit*.

Although that autumn he declared himself 'in the agonies of new harness' (to Hood, 12 November 1842), he found time to write a blank-verse prologue for MACREADY's forthcoming production of MARSTON's *The Patrician's Daughter*. It included the rejected line, 'Yourselves the Actors, and Your Homes the scene', which Dickens proposed using as a title-page motto for *Chuzzlewit* to drive home the nature of his satire, until Forster talked him out of it (Forster 4.2). By early December the first number was nearly written, and 'he was so eager to try out the effect of Pecksniff and Pinch that he came down with the ink hardly dry on the last slip to read the manuscript to me' (Forster 4.1). As Margaret Cardwell observes, Dickens's experience of writing *Chuzzlewit* was one of 'exhilaration'; 'I particularly commend . . . one Mr Pecksniff and his daughters, to your tender regard', he wrote to an American friend the day the first number was published (Introduction to Clarendon edition, p. xix; to Felton, 31 December 1842). Pinch was a special favourite with him, frequently mentioned in letters, and he marvelled to Forster at 'the way these characters have opened out' (?mid-February 1843). As the novel neared completion he allowed that Tom and his sister were 'two of the greatest favourites I ever had' (to Lady Holland, 10 June 1844).

Although Dickens indicated in advance publicity on 29 October that his subject was to be 'English life and manners', at the end of the May number young Martin announces his resolve to go to America (*MC* 12). Often condemned as an abrupt response to poor sales of the novel's first numbers, the change of scene allowed Dickens to 'distil' the 'sublimated essence of comicality' he had found there (to Forster, 26 April 1843) and, as Forster judged, to take up the 'challenge' presented by his 'American assailants', outraged by *American Notes* (Forster 4.2). He found that this episode took him 'at least twice as long, every line of it', to write as the rest (to Mitton, 7 June 1843), but 'everything that he hated' about America is, as the Pilgrim editors observe, 'concentrated' into Martin and Mark's first 24 hours there (Pilgrim 3, p. xvi). 'Martin has made them all stark raving mad across the water', Dickens gleefully reported to Forster (15 August 1843).

He was himself made furious when, in late June, his publisher William Hall suggested that his salary might have to be reduced on account of poor sales (see below, 'Contract'). Nevertheless Dickens remained supremely confident about his novel. Only days later he sent Forster the manuscript pages introducing Mrs Gamp, with a covering note declaring, 'I mean to make a mark with her' (6 or 7 July 1843). The next month he told Mitton, 'I have nearly killed myself with laughter at what I have done in the American no.' (13 August 1843). Despite financial worries which had him meditating on the possibility of taking his family to live abroad for an extended period (he moved to ITALY for a year soon after *Chuzzlewit* was finished), he maintained his self-belief: 'You know, as well as I, that I think *Chuzzlewit* in a hundred points immeasurably the best of my stories. That I feel my power now, more than I ever did. That I have greater confidence in myself than I ever had. That I *know*, if I have health, I could sustain my place in the minds of thinking men, though fifty writers started up to-morrow. But how many readers do *not* think! . . .' (to Forster, 2 November 1843). That such confidence was justified is manifest from the extraordinary fact that he managed, even as *Chuzzlewit* was in full flow, to find time to write his short masterpiece, *A Christmas Carol*, published in December 1843. He finished writing the novel in mid-June of 1844.

Dickens chafed against the constraints of SERIAL publication, explaining in a letter, 'It is the great misery of such a form of publication that conclusions are necessarily arrived at, in reference to the design of the story, before the design becomes apparent or complete' (10 June 1844). But in the Preface, dated 25 June 1844, he wrote, 'I have endeavoured in the progress of this Tale to resist the temptation of the current Monthly Number, and to keep a steadier eye on the general purpose and design'. Evidence of planning survives in scanty working notes, along with lists of possible names and alternative wordings of the title-page (reproduced in Stone 1987), and in a meticulously detailed letter to Hablot Knight BROWNE, giving instructions for the frontispiece, title-page, and final two illustrations

(?June 1844). (See also COMPOSITION: DICK-ENS'S METHODS.)

## Contract, Text, and Publication History

With the help of Forster and his lawyer, Thomas Mitton, Dickens negotiated a contract in the summer of 1842 with CHAPMAN AND HALL for the novel which was to become *Martin Chuzzlewit*. Patten describes it as 'a remarkable document': Dickens, already £3,000 in debt to his publishers, demanded and got a further advance of £2,000 for a year's holiday, in return for the promise of an unwritten book, for which he was to receive three-quarters of the profits, excluding losses (Pilgrim 2.478–81; Patten 1978, p. 126). Mitton was 'quite aghast at the brilliancy of the C. & H. arrangement', Dickens exulted to Forster (9 September 1842). Fatally, however, the contract included a clause which allowed the publishers to deduct £50 per month from his salary should profits not be sufficient to repay the debt. When Hall, faced with sales of 20,000 per month (*Nickleby* had topped 50,000, and weekly sales of *The Old Curiosity Shop* exceeded 100,000), suggested that the clause might have to be invoked, Dickens was outraged. 'I am bent on paying Chapman and Hall *down*', he told Forster, and vowed to write for them no more (28 June 1843). In the event their mutual interests were so intertwined that he never did sever relations completely. Both *Chuzzlewit* and *Christmas Carol* were published by Chapman and Hall, and in 1858, long after Hall's death, Dickens returned to 'the best of booksellers, past, present, or to come' (to Chapman, 14 November 1839).

The complete manuscript of *Martin Chuzzlewit* is preserved in the FORSTER COLLECTION, along with eight pages of notes, an errata slip, the Preface, and Dedication to Angela Burdett COUTTS. Incomplete proofs are held in the Forster Collection, the Free Library of Philadelphia, and the British Library. The manuscript shows many false starts, including one for chapter 6 which extends to seven folio leaves; second thoughts, and slips pasted on.

The novel was published in twenty numbers (as nineteen), which appeared monthly from January 1843 to July 1844. These were gathered for a one-volume first edition, published 16 July 1844, with 38 illustrations by Browne, plus frontispiece and vignette title-page.

In consequence of the hostile reception his remarks on international COPYRIGHT received during his American trip, Dickens publicly declared his intention of no longer supplying advance proofs to American publishers until the law was changed, and courteously rejected 'on principle' an approach from the Philadelphia publishers with whom he had previously made arrangements, Lea and Blanchard (7 July and 28 December 1842). Three unauthorized editions were published in New York in 1843 and a fourth in 1844; Lea and Blanchard issued an unauthorized edition in 1844. Dickens sanctioned a Continental edition in 1844 by the Leipzig publisher Bernhard Tauchnitz.

He did little revision for subsequent EDITIONS over which he had control. The Cheap Edition (1850) had a new Preface, dated November 1849, and a new frontispiece, designed by Frank STONE. The Library Edition (1858) and the Charles Dickens Edition (1867) were printed from the 1850 text with some corrections. The Clarendon Edition (1982), edited by Margaret Cardwell, is the definitive scholarly edition. (See also PUBLISHING; MONEY VALUES; COLLECTIONS OF DICKENS MATERIALS.)

## Illustrations

When *Martin Chuzzlewit* was advertised for publication in October 1842 it lacked not only a title but also any indication as to illustrator. Dickens was still negotiating on 5 November when he wrote to John LEECH: 'If it can possibly be arranged, consistently with that regard which I feel bound to pay to Mr Browne, I shall be truly happy to avail myself of your genius in my forthcoming Monthly Work.' Clearly the proposed arrangement proved impossible, for Dickens wrote to Leech two days later declaring it 'impracticable', and Browne supplied the customary two illustrations per monthly number. They were attributed to him as 'Phiz' and not under his own name, as in *The Old Curiosity Shop* and *Barnaby Rudge*.

## Sources and Context

The most immediately evident inspiration for *Martin Chuzzlewit* was Dickens's experience in America. Dickens drew directly upon characteristics (boasting, spitting), character types (journalists, literary ladies), institutions (slavery), and events (levees) which he had encountered there. But America provided him with more than ingredients for his satire. 'He returned from America with wider views than when he started, and with more maturity of mind', Forster judged; 'it was the turning point of his career' (4.2). Whereas his previous novels show him trying forms which he inherited from past masters, from this stage onward the influence of previous writers upon his art is less striking than the artistry which he pioneered. Young Martin's journey to America represents the last time that Dickens structures a story on picaresque travel, but even that is a less powerful unifying force than Dickens's new-found interest in character development and his focus on a single central theme. As Forster notes, 'The notion of taking Pecksniff for a type of character was really the origin of the book; the design being to show, more or less by every person introduced, the number and variety of humours and vices that have their root in selfishness' (4.1).

As ever, specific contemporary sources can be identified for particular aspects. Thus, Pecksniff is modelled upon the art critic Samuel Carter Hall (1800–89), and Mrs Gamp upon a nurse hired to care for the companion of Angela Burdett Coutts, but to identify originals reveals little about two of the great comic figures in English literature (see CHARACTERS—ORIGINALS). In Pecksniff Dickens has clearly assimilated the pith of Ben JONSON's humour characters, Molière's Tartuffe, and CERVANTES's Don Quixote ('There is nothing more powerfully humorous than what is called *keeping* in comic character', observed HAZLITT; 'this truth of absurdity to itself . . . is the surprising thing': *Works*, ed. P. P. Howe, 1931, 6.11). And Mrs Gamp is perhaps the most SHAKESPEAREAN of all Dickens's characters, in her kinship to Juliet's Nurse and to Falstaff.

Tigg's fraudulent Anglo-Bengalee Disinterested Loan and Life Assurance Company is a refraction of the West Middlesex General Annuity Company, whose self-made directors absconded with its funds in 1840. Todgers's and its neighbourhood are Dickens's quintessential development of the vision of urban life which he first depicted in the 'Boz' *Sketches*, and owing something to DE QUINCEY and to Pierce EGAN.

The opening sentence of *Chuzzlewit* traces the family back to Adam and Eve, and young Martin reaches his turning-point in a dystopia called Eden. These and numerous other references to gardens and family relationships show Dickens developing a mythic pattern, based on the first book of the BIBLE, in which the theme of self assumes wider significance than selfishness, but (as many critics have suggested) refers also to self-discovery, identity, human nature, and one's place in the world.

### Plot, Character, and Theme

*Martin Chuzzlewit* opens with a facetious genealogy, a keynote quite unlike anything Dickens had written before, which introduces a gathering of the Chuzzlewit clan in the house of Mr Pecksniff in a village near Salisbury. Old Martin Chuzzlewit, whose fortune the assembled family members are fighting over, takes the opportunity to decamp with his young companion Mary Graham.

Pecksniff, a platitudinous hypocrite, seconded by his daughters Charity and Mercy, is admired by his pupil Tom Pinch, who naively accepts his master's pronouncements of moral sentiment. Young Martin Chuzzlewit arrives to study architecture with Pecksniff, patronizes Pinch, and is dismissed at the instance of his grandfather, with whom he has quarrelled. Desperate, he sails with the resolutely jolly Mark Tapley to America, where nearly everyone he meets is vulgar, brash, and boastful. A land speculation takes him to a swamp out West, where he catches fever and undergoes moral revaluation.

Meanwhile back in England Martin's cousin, the brutish Jonas, pays his attentions to Charity Pecksniff and then proposes to her sister. In the ensuing farcical confusion, old Martin arrives at Pecksniff's as a houseguest. When Pinch discovers that Pecksniff has underhandedly paid court to Mary Graham, for whom Pinch has unrequited love, his eyes are opened and he goes to London, where he rescues his sister Ruth from servitude as a governess.

Jonas's father Anthony dies in suspicious circumstances, and the garrulous, drunken midwife Mrs Gamp is called to lay out the corpse; later to look after Anthony's senile servant Chuffey (Sydney SMITH's favourite character). Blackmailed by the chameleon rascal Tigg Montague (formerly Montague Tigg), Jonas persuades Pecksniff to invest ruinously in Tigg's fraudulent company and then murders Tigg. Apprehended by the shadowy detective Nadgett, Jonas commits suicide. Old Martin exposes Pecksniff and, reconciled with his grandson, gives blessing to his betrothal to Mary. Charity is jilted on her wedding day, and the book ends with Tom playing dreamily alone on the organ.

### Reception

Various explanations have been offered for the low initial sales of *Martin Chuzzlewit*, but the most likely cause is the trade depression of 1842, which seriously affected publishers generally (see Patten 1978, p. 133, and Pilgrim 3.516–17n.). Reviews were mixed. A number, especially in America, were exceedingly hostile. Forster considered the book's structure defective (4.2), but other of Dickens's contemporaries were delighted. Pecksniff and Gamp were immediately accorded a place in the inner circle of favourite Dickens characters, and in 1861 an anonymous reviewer in the *National Review* praised *Chuzzlewit* as 'the most brilliant and entertaining of all the works of Mr Dickens' (repr. in Collins 1971, pp. 192–7)—a judgement which prefigures the assessment of later critics such as Steven Marcus and Robert Polhemus, who find the quality of writing 'Joycean' and place it among the comic masterpieces in the language (Marcus 1965; Polhemus, *Comic Faith*, 1980).

Although adapters tended to cut the American scenes (as did David Lodge in his 1994 BBC TELEVISION dramatization), the novel had a 'considerable' stage history (Bolton 1987, p. 222). Robert KEELEY was 'immense' as Mrs Gamp in STIRLING's version at the Adelphi Theatre, and some later stage versions were devoted to that character alone. Dickens himself returned to Mrs Gamp on three separate occasions, in addition to forays into her speech mannerisms in letters. In 1847 he began (but soon abandoned) an account, as if by Mrs Gamp, of one of his AMATEUR THEATRICAL tours ('A New Piljians Projiss', Appendix G of the Clarendon Edition). Mrs Gamp was one of the character impersonations he interpolated into Mark LEMON's

farce, *Mr NIGHTINGALE'S DIARY* (1851), in which Dickens performed a quick-change routine in the roles of several of his best-loved characters. And his PUBLIC READING version, first performed on 17 June 1858, was unusual in being based not on a short work or a single episode from a longer one, but on selected passages from the entire novel; it was also the most revised of all his PUBLIC READING TEXTS.

Modern criticism has accorded high praise to *Chuzzlewit*, although its bibliographer, Robert Lougy, suggests that puzzlement has been the dominant response (Lougy 1990, p. xix). Dorothy Van Ghent's landmark essay on Dickens's STYLE uses Dickens's description of Todgers's as its starting-point (Van Ghent 1950). J. Hillis Miller, also focusing on Todgers's, discusses the novel as a search for 'an authentic self' (Miller 1958). Myron Magnet, picking up Dickens's references to Lord Monboddo and Blumenbach in the novel's opening chapter, suggests that, like those sources, Dickens's concern is the question of human nature (*Dickens and the Social Order*, 1985). Most challengingly, Alexander Welsh explores Dickens's 'creative use' of Shakespeare, Molière, and Milton, and suggests that Dickens's experience at WARREN'S BLACKING mattered less in itself than in his later revaluation of it in the work of his middle years, including, centrally, *Chuzzlewit* (Welsh 1987).

PVWS

Curran, Stuart, 'The Lost Paradises of *Martin Chuzzlewit*', *Nineteenth-Century Fiction* (1970).
Monod, Sylvère, *Martin Chuzzlewit* (1985).

**Martineau, Harriet** (1802–76), journalist, novelist, and economist, and a regular contributor to *Household Words*. She also contributed to the Christmas numbers (see CHRISTMAS STORIES), 'What Christmas is in the Country' (1851) and 'The Deaf Playmate's Story' (1852). She and Dickens differed sharply on matters of political economy and factory employment, with Martineau favouring the manufacturers' interests rather than the employees' (see FACTORY ACTS). Having attacked what she regarded as Dickens's 'mistake' in *Oliver Twist* (she charged that he 'confounds' the new POOR LAW with the old), their five-year journalistic connection was severed following the publication of *Hard Times*, which she angrily dismissed in her *Autobiography* (1855) for what she regarded as its 'vigorous erroneousness about matters of science' in connection with 'the controversies of employers' (2.378). She also wrote a pamphlet, *The Factory Controversy: A Warning Against Meddling Legislation* (1855), in which she upbraided Dickens for his publication in *Household Words* of a series of what she regarded as unduly alarmist articles about industrial accidents. Dickens and his co-author, MORLEY, defended themselves in a reply to Martineau ('Our Wicked Mis-statements', *HW* 19 January 1856), in which they reaffirmed their commitment to factory legislation to improve safety at work. Martineau also wrote in her *Autobiography* of her resentment of what she saw as Dickens's prejudice against ROMAN CATHOLICS, and she objected, too, to his attitude to the social role of WOMEN, claiming that in his own contributions to *Household Words* Dickens had ignored the fact that the vast majority of English women were wage-earners. After his marriage broke down in 1858, Martineau wrote contemptuously of Dickens's 'self-love' (Slater 1983, p. 160). For his part, Dickens humorously described Martineau's grim determination on 'the enlightenment of mankind' (to W. H. Wills, 14 October 1854). His humour deserted him when he later confided to the same friend that he deplored Martineau's 'vomit of conceit' and declared, 'there never was such a wrong-headed woman born—such a vain one—or such humbug' (to W. H. Wills, 6 January 1856). SL

> Fielding, K. J. and Smith, Anne, '*Hard Times* and the Factory Controversy: Dickens *vs* Harriet Martineau', in A. Nesbit and Blake Nevius (eds.), *Dickens Centennial Essays* (1971).

**Martin-Harvey, John** (1863–1944), actor. His most significant role was that of Sydney Carton in *The Only Way*, a DRAMATIZATION of *A Tale of Two Cities* by the Revd Freeman Wills and the Revd Canon Langbridge, first performed at the Lyceum Theatre in 1899. Martin-Harvey's pictorial production, which made his fortune, realized at its conclusion Fred Barnard's illustration of Carton mounting the scaffold, which also became the basis of John Hassell's poster for the production. With its heavy emphasis on self-sacrifice,

Harvey's romantic portrayal of Carton, pale-faced, dark-haired, and dissipated, maintained its popularity well beyond the 1914–18 War. JD

**Master Humphrey's Clock** A weekly journal, 4 April 1840–4 December 1841, conceived and written entirely by Dickens, in which *The Old Curiosity Shop* and *Barnaby Rudge* first appeared. It was also issued in monthly parts and in three volumes. Despite his unhappy experience of editing BENTLEY'S MISCELLANY, Dickens retained a keen interest in conducting a popular periodical (see JOURNALIST, DICKENS AS). On 14 July 1839, when *Nicholas Nickleby* was in its final stages (the seventeenth of twenty monthly parts was published two weeks later) he wrote a long letter to FORSTER outlining a proposal for a new miscellany. He planned to introduce a small group of solitary men, withdrawn from the world, who would gather by the fireside of a gentle old cripple, Master Humphrey, in the case of whose beloved old grandfather clock manuscripts of 'sketches, essays, tales, adventures, letters from imaginary correspondents and so forth' would be stored. Mr Pickwick and Sam and Tony Weller were to be reintroduced, along with topical satire and stories about 'London long ago'. Dickens anticipated that the journal would include writing by contributors other than himself, and he planned to visit Ireland or America, 'where he would travel specially for the purpose' of sending copy from abroad (to Forster, 14 July 1839).

The conception had its origins in 18th-century precedents which Dickens had admired from an early age: ADDISON and STEELE's *Tatler* and *Spectator*, GOLDSMITH's *Bee*, and MACKENZIE's *Lounger* (see ESSAYS AND ESSAYISTS BEFORE DICKENS). It gave him an opportunity to draw on his experience as a journalist, to develop a more distinctive editorial persona of an author-observer than that of 'BOZ', and to try his hand at the framed-tale device which so fascinated him in *The ARABIAN NIGHTS*. He was full of confidence for the project, but also concerned lest the public tire of his novels—he had been producing two SERIAL works of fiction simultaneously for most of the previous two and a half years—and lest, like SCOTT, whose biography by LOCKHART had been published the previous year, he burn himself out by overtaxing his imagination.

Dickens formally agreed with CHAPMAN AND HALL on 15 October 1839 to undertake the new journal, and a contract was signed on 31 March 1840 (Pilgrim 1.681, 2.464–71). The terms were designed to ensure that he could exercise editorial control over the work, such as he had never enjoyed with Bentley, and that the primary financial rewards would accrue to him instead of to the publisher.

Dickens began writing in January (to Forster, 10 January 1840) and on 4 April the first number appeared. In the event, the contents—autobiographical writing by Master Humphrey, 'Mr Weller's Watch' (a below-stairs parody of the 'Clock' device), 'chronicles' of Gog and Magog, the giants who stood outside the Guildhall—lacked the variety of the proposal, and after initial high interest, sales plummeted for subsequent numbers. In these circumstances Dickens decided to expand a story, 'The Old Curiosity Shop', which had appeared in the fourth number as the first of an intended series, 'Personal Adventures of Master Humphrey'. It was continued in the seventh number, after which it took over as the entire contents of the miscellany. Master Humphrey briefly reappeared at the conclusion of *The Old Curiosity Shop* to make the improbable announcement that he was himself Nell's great-uncle, the Single Gentleman, and to introduce *Barnaby Rudge*, at the conclusion of which *Master Humphrey's Clock* ceased publication.　　PVWS

Andrews, Malcolm, 'Introducing Master Humphrey', *Dickensian*, 67 (1971).

Chittick, Kathryn, 'The Idea of a Miscellany: *Master Humphrey's Clock*', *Dickensian*, 78 (1982).

Mundhenk, Rosemary, 'Creative Ambivalence in Dickens's *Master Humphrey's Clock*', *Studies in English Literature*, 32 (1992).

Patten, Robert L., ' "The Story-Weaver at His Loom": Dickens and the Beginning of *The Old Curiosity Shop*', in Partlow (1970).

**Mathews, Charles,** the elder (1776–1835), comic ACTOR greatly admired by Dickens. Frustrated with the limited roles offered by regular stage comedy and lamed by an accident, Mathews developed a series of solo entertainments, 'At Homes', for which he was famous. Appearing on stage not in a role but as himself, Mathews narrated a journey he had taken—his 'Trip to Paris', 'Mail Coach Adventures', or a balloon trip through 'Earth, Air, and Water'—interspersed with songs, recitations, and character impersonations. This was followed by a stage farce, or 'monopolylogue', in which, by means of quick changes of costume, ventriloquism, and sharp differentiation of character, he played all the roles. In an era of theatre reliant on stock character types, Mathews's performances were distinctive in his individuation of character.

As an avid theatregoer, Dickens claimed that he went 'always to see Mathews when he played'. Aspiring to become an actor himself, he worked up one of Mathews's routines, but on the day appointed in 1832 for an audition at Covent Garden he was laid up with 'a terrible bad cold and an inflammation of the face', and before he could try again next season, successful parliamentary reporting turned his energies in other directions (Forster 1.4 and 5.1; Pilgrim 1.3–4n.).

Dickens's later PUBLIC READINGS owed much to Mathews. Appearing like Mathews in his own person, he too used narration as the primary structure of solo performances, which were predominantly comic, developing mimicry of a variety of characters. Like Mathews again, he relied centrally on the rapport he established with his audience in a distinctive combination of sincerity and impersonation, to nurture 'sympathies and graces of imagination' (*HW* 30 March 1850).　　PVWS

Klepac, Richard L., *Mr Mathews at Home* (1979).

Schlicke (1985).

**Mathews, Charles James** (1803–78) and **Vestris, Madame Eliza** (1797–1856). Mathews, the most outstanding light comedian during Dickens's lifetime, was the son of Charles MATHEWS the elder. He made his debut at the fashionable Olympic Theatre in 1836 under Madame Vestris, whom he married in 1838. From 1830 to 1839 Vestris managed the Olympic, where she became renowned (with J. R. Planché) for her elegant staging of burlettas and extravaganzas and her innovative use of real furniture and authentic props. Dickens was a regular visitor and boasted that his AMATEUR THEATRICAL production in CANADA of *Past Two*

*O' Clock in the Morning*'was as well furnished as Vestris had it; with a "practicable" fire place blazing away like mad' (to Forster, 26 May 1842), although Douglas JERROLD joked about this tendency to present comedies only 'susceptible to upholstery' (Pilgrim 3.246n.). Mathews and Vestris became co-managers of Covent Garden, 1839–42, exasperating MACREADY, whose own negotiations for the theatre had fallen through. Dickens, who had a poor opinion of Covent Garden's offerings under their management, was later to refer to the 'offensive conduct' of Mathews and his 'estimable lady' when, as managers of the Lyceum Theatre, they would not allow HARLEY, the KEELEYS, Mrs Nisbett, and Mrs Stirling to appear in the benefit he had organized at the Haymarket for the family of the drowned actor, Elton. Mathews again irritated Dickens through suggesting changes to the programme for Fanny Kelly's benefit in 1853. In 1854 Mathews—whose co-management with Vestris of the Lyceum (1847–55) ended in bankruptcy—visited Dickens to seek advice on his financial problems, saying he 'only' wanted capital 'to set the Lyceum going. And he went away shaking hands with me with his right hand and respectfully poking me in the waistcoat with his left, exactly as he goes off the stage' (to William Brown, 3 May 1854). Mathews, who was particularly adept in light, effervescent roles in farce and extravaganza, was a skilled mimic and an effortless performer of patter songs. Among his best performances was Sir Charles Coldstream in *Used Up* (Haymarket, 1844), which Dickens himself played in private theatricals in 1851 in a performance some felt superior to Mathews's own. Yet FORSTER more than once wrote to Mathews to inform him that he and Dickens had enjoyed productions at the Lyceum. Mathews's memoirs were completed and edited by Dickens's son, Charles. JD

**Matz, B. W.** (1865–1925), Dickens scholar and first editor of the DICKENSIAN. Matz, with his editorial policy of including in the magazine 'anything and everything likely to interest the student and lover of England's great novelist', was primarily responsible for the initial success and subsequent flourishing of the *Dickensian*. This was his greatest contribution to Dickens scholarship, but there were others. His *Inns and Taverns of Pickwick* (1922)

is still the standard work on the topic and his Memorial Edition of FORSTER's *Life of Dickens* (2 vols., 1911) is a treasure-house of information on all aspects of Dickens's life and times. He was, moreover, the first to attempt, in his MISCELLANEOUS PAPERS (1908), a collected edition of Dickens's uncollected journalistic writings in the EXAMINER, *Household Words*, and elsewhere (also including Dickens's plays and various stray Prefaces), and it is only very recently that his work here has begun to be superseded. MS

**Meadows, Joseph Kenny** (1790–1874), illustrator. Meadows published portraits of characters from *Pickwick Papers* and *Oliver Twist* in 1838 numbers of BELL'S LIFE IN LONDON. In the following year he issued in six half-shilling instalments portraits of 24 characters from *Nicholas Nickleby*, allegedly derived 'from drawings by Miss La Creevy'. These were subsequently republished without the Dickensian identifications. Between 1839 and 1843 Meadows realized his life's ambition by illustrating an edition of SHAKESPEARE published by Charles KNIGHT. This was very successful and led to collaborations with members of the PUNCH circle. He depicted Dickens, John FORSTER, Douglas JERROLD, John LEECH, and Mark LEMON acting in *Every Man In His Humour* for a review in the *Illustrated London News* (22, 29 November 1845; see AMATEUR THEATRICALS), and he tried the Dickens market one more time with a picture of Barbara, the Garlands' maidservant, timed to coincide with the release of the Cheap Edition of *The Old Curiosity Shop* in 1848. RLP

**melodrama in Dickens's writing.** As a pejorative term, 'melodrama' has often been used as a stick to beat Dickens with. His stagey villains, too-good heroines, improbable plots, and heightened rhetoric bear close relation to the hackneyed stereotypes of popular 19th-century theatre, and detractors have been quick to point to the similarities as evidence of Dickens's artistic failings. But historical research by scholars such as Michael Booth, Martin Meisel, and Peter Brooks into the nature of dramatic art and theatrical production, and into the reconception of genre in the 19th century, has empowered critics in recent decades to invoke 'melodrama' as a more neutral, descriptive term, one which sees what Brooks calls 'the mode of excess' not as crude lack of control but as *method*, conscious, deliberate, and artistically legitimate.

Strictly speaking, melodrama is a stage play ('-drama') with musical accompaniment ('melo-') (see DRAMA AND DRAMATISTS). It first emerged in France in the late 18th century, and quickly crossed the channel, often in crude translations of French plays. Thomas Holcroft's *Tale of Mystery* (1802) is generally credited with being the first English melodrama, and the genre dominated the British stage for most of the ensuing century. A key factor in its rise was the licensing law, which forbade 'legitimate' (i.e. spoken) drama in any THEATRE save Covent Garden and Drury Lane, and later the Haymarket and various provincial Theatres Royal. This necessitated reliance on action, spectacle, and instantly recognizable characters—elements which Dickens found congenial to his own creative instincts and appropriate for his SERIALIZED narratives.

Peter Brooks has argued that melodrama and melodramatic fiction represent not 'degraded near-tragedy' but 'the principal mode for uncovering, demonstrating, and making operative the essential moral universe in a post-sacred era'. Simplification to achieve moral clarity, and an inherent tendency toward abstraction, are defining characteristics of such art. Thus Oliver Twist is described by Dickens as 'the Principle of Good surviving through every adverse circumstance, and triumphing at last' (1841 Preface), and Little Nell compares herself to Christian in BUNYAN's allegory, *The Pilgrim's Progress* (*OCS* 15). The division of characters into morally polarized groupings accounts for the purity of Dickens's heroines and the villainy of characters like Monks (*OT*), Ralph Nickleby, Rudge, Blandois (*LD*), and Orlick (*GE*). The guilty secrets and past crimes which set plots in motion are devised not for probability but to dramatize ideal values. Villainy is overturned, often by comic figures like Newman Noggs (*NN*) or Trabb's boy (*GE*), whose very lack of sophistication authenticates the desired 'natural' morality.

Melodrama is a means of ordering and making sense of a complex and frightening world. Dickens's art is concerned with the 'hidden and private world of dream and death, out of which all the energy of life comes' (Frye 1968). It offers a means of

expressing the powerless rage of victimized classes (Vicinus 1981). In so doing it explodes classical stability of genre: as Martin Meisel has shown, narrative art freezes action into tableau, with characters placed in a static picture—Vincent Crummles locked in an embrace with the departing Nicholas (*NN* 30), Sidney Carton standing beside the guillotine (*TTC* 3.15)—even as the ILLUSTRATIONS, by indicating action prior and subsequent to the moment depicted, take on a narrative function, complementing the text.

Melodrama is a key to an understanding of Dickens's essential vision. As narrator of *Pickwick* and as editor of BENTLEY'S MISCELLANY, he casts himself in the role of 'Stage Manager' (with 'scenery' supplied by CRUIKSHANK, 'machinery' by Samuel Bentley, and Richard BENTLEY 'presiding over the Treasury department' (*BM* June 1837); see RICHARDSON, JOHN). In addition to his PLAYWRITING and AMATEUR THEATRICALS, between 1834 and 1849 he contributed more than twenty theatrical reviews for the MORNING CHRONICLE and EXAMINER.

From very near the beginning of his career, he was himself both conscious of the reputation of melodrama as a somewhat subliterary genre and aware also that his own art was analogous to it. In *Oliver Twist* Dickens justified the abrupt transitions in his novel from the pathetic to the ridiculous on the grounds of realism, citing 'the custom on the stage, in all good murderous melodramas, to present the tragic and the comic scenes in a regular alternation, as the layers of red and white in a side of streaky bacon' (*OT* 17). And in his next novel, *Nicholas Nickleby*, he interrupted the serious melodramatic plot involving the hero, his wicked uncle, the besieged heroine, her threatening father, and the comic man, Newman Noggs, by enlisting Nicholas in a troupe of laughably inept provincial actors who specialize in the most excessive forms of melodrama, providing a parody of his own novelistic practices from within the novel itself. In *Great Expectations* the posturing of Mr Wopsle as Hamlet in a cheap London theatre reduces tragedy to ridiculous melodrama. Directly after the performance he divulges that Compeyson, the villain of the novel's own melodramatic plot, has been stalking or following Pip 'like a ghost'. The self-conscious artistry which this awareness

# Memoirs of Grimaldi

implies allowed Dickens to use the emotions aroused by melodrama, impotent rage and an imperative for revenge, in a controlled manner. Dickens's later fiction moves on from the relatively 'straight' melodrama of *Oliver Twist* and the interpolated tales of *Pickwick*, but for all its subtlety and complexity it remains melodramatic to the core.

In his works the world-view of melodrama exists, not as the entire vision, but one of several visions, to be balanced by or perhaps even contradicted by other, opposing world-views. William Axton has shown how Dickens employed differing prose rhythms, a device which Axton sees as itself derived from melodrama, to contrast the visions and emotions represented by the railroad and water passages in *Dombey and Son*. A similar contrast controls the interplay of the revenge and the Christian themes of *A Tale of Two Cities* and of the light versus the dark visions of many of the late novels, the 'sunshine' and the 'shade', as Dickens puts it in the last sentence of *Little Dorrit*.                                    EME

Axton, William F., *Circle of Fire: Dickens' Vision and Style and the Popular Victorian Theatre* (1966).
Booth, Michael, *English Melodrama* (1965).
Brooks, Peter, *The Melodramatic Imagination: Balzac, James, Melodrama, and the Mode of Excess* (rev. edn. 1995).
Meisel, Martin, *Realizations: Narrative, Pictorial and Theatrical Arts in Nineteenth-Century England* (1983).
Vicinus, Martha, 'Helpless and Unfriended: Nineteenth-Century Domestic Melodrama', *New Literary History*, 13 (1981), 127–43.
Worth, George J., *Dickensian Melodrama* (1978).

***Memoirs of Grimaldi*** A work edited by Dickens as 'BOZ' in 2 volumes, with illustrations by George CRUIKSHANK. BENTLEY, whose *Miscellany* Dickens was editing at the time (see BENTLEY'S MISCELLANY), purchased the manuscript autobiography from T. Egerton Wilks, who had made an unsuccessful attempt to edit it for publication, and commissioned Dickens to re-edit it. Mere hack work, the *Memoirs* were poorly received.

Joey Grimaldi (1778–1837), the greatest of PANTOMIME clowns, was almost single-handedly responsible for developing the satirical potential of pantomime in its heyday, 1800–30, at a time when it was 'the only effective

means of satire to hold the stage' (Mayer 1969). Dickens had fond childhood memories of seeing Grimaldi perform (to the sub-editor of *Bentley's Miscellany*, March 1838). He 'set great store' by the 'Introductory Chapter', containing reminiscences of his youthful love of clowns, and the concluding chapter, which described Grimaldi's death and assessed his character (to Bentley, 21 February 1838).
                                                        PVWS

Findlater, Richard (ed.), *Memoirs of Joseph Grimaldi* (1968).
Mayer, David, *Harlequin in His Element: The English Pantomime 1806–1836* (1969).

**Memorials to Dickens.** In his will, Dickens stipulated that on no account was he to be 'the subject of any monument, memorial or testimonial whatever' (Forster 3, Appendix 2). Consequently, he was laid to rest without ostentation in Poets' Corner at Westminster Abbey (see DEATH AND FUNERALS). The flat grave marker set into the floor reads 'Charles Dickens | Born 7th February 1812 | Died 9th June 1870', plainly inscribed in brass letters. Since then, he has been memorialized more than any other British author. Surprisingly, Dickens's eldest daughter Mamie was an early perpetrator, presenting St Thomas's Mission Church in Manchester with a memorial cross bearing the inscription 'To the Glory of God and in Memoriam | Charles Dickens June 9th, 1870'. It remained there until the church's demolition early this century. In Rochester Cathedral is a brass tablet, one of many memorials in KENT celebrating Dickens's close association with the county. His London residences and workplaces are indicated by blue ceramic plaques, the best example being 48 Doughty Street, the DICKENS HOUSE MUSEUM. Dickens's first HOME is commemorated with a bronze bust, one of a number by Percy FITZGERALD. It stands above a memorial plaque on the site of Furnival's Inn, High Holborn. A bas-relief frieze depicting Dickens and a number of his characters occupies part of the site of 1 Devonshire Terrace, his home from 1839 to 1844.

Certain memorials exist abroad. Embedded in the wall of a chalet at Condette, near Boulogne, is a plaque showing Dickens's head in profile. It commemorates the author's intermittent visits and is inscribed '1860–1864', although it is more probable that these began *c*.1862 and lasted to mid-1865 (Ackroyd 1990, p. 913).

Of the two statues of Dickens, one is in Clark Park, Philadelphia, USA. Cast in bronze in 1891 by Edwin Elwell (1858–1922), it was originally intended to be set up in Britain, although this idea was abandoned due to the requirements of the author's will. Dickens is seated upon a raised plinth with a figure of Little Nell at his feet. Vandalized during the 1980s, it has since been restored.

Another statue stood in Centennial Park, Sydney, Australia. Finely executed in Carrara marble, it was vandalized in 1988 and subsequently placed in storage.                        AX

Matz, B. W., 'Memorials and Tablets to Dickens', *Dickensian*, 11 (1915).

**mesmerism,** an early type of hypnotism, named after its formulator Franz Anton Mesmer, who, discredited in Vienna in 1778, continued his operations in Paris until a commission appointed by Louis XVI in 1784 ruled Mesmer's claims insupportable. Though the practice was always controversial (Mozart mocked it in *Cosi fan tutte* in 1790), pockets of supporters continued to appear in Europe and America until late in the 19th century. Mesmerism, also known as animal magnetism, apparently to distinguish it from the variations, gravitational and mineral magnetism, was presented as a cure for the world's troubles. If the basic element of human energy, an invisible fluid, could be harnessed and directed by a strong will, then anything would be possible. Dickens became convinced of the reality of mesmerism after attending demonstrations performed by Dr John Elliotson in 1838. Elliotson, who became Dickens's family doctor and one of his longest-standing friends, was a strong advocate of both PHRENOLOGY and mesmerism, and pressed for the alliance of the two movements. When Elliotson felt compelled to submit his resignation to University College London in late 1838, Dickens stoutly defended him and continued to do so until Elliotson's death in 1868. Another long-standing Dickens friend instrumental in his developing interest in mesmerism was the Revd Chauncey Hare Townshend, a scholar-poet who undertook a number of mesmeric experiments and recorded them in *Facts in Mesmerism* (1840). Dickens himself learned to mesmerize, but

seems never himself to have undergone the procedure, preferring always to be the operator. He reported that he mesmerized Catherine into a hysteric fit in Pittsburgh during his 1842 American trip (see DICKENS, CATHERINE). He later mesmerized Catherine and her sister Georgiana HOGARTH, and in September 1849 he operated on John LEECH after a bathing accident while at Bonchurch. Dickens was convinced that he had substantially aided Leech's recovery. His most extensive experience as a mesmeric operator began during his Italian stay in Genoa in 1844, with his English-born Swiss friend Madame Emile de la Rue (née Augusta Granet), who suffered from a number of neurasthenic symptoms, including a nervous tic, convulsions, headaches, and insomnia. He treated her over a period of years, believing that he was struggling for control of her psyche with a sinister evil phantom. His fascination with her case and the extraordinary measures he undertook to treat her produced a severe early strain on Dickens's marriage. His recognition of the potentially negative effects of mesmerism emerged in his fiction, where many of his most terrifying evil characters, such as Quilp and Carker, are portrayed as having a form of mesmeric power over others. However, during Dickens's participation in AMATEUR THEATRICALS in the 1840s and 1850s, he often appeared in Elizabeth Inchbald's *Animal Magnetism* (a farce he apparently knew from his childhood reading), performing in the role of a doctor who is tricked into believing he can mesmerize his patients. He wrote that he had 'seen people laugh at the piece, until they hung over the front of the boxes, like ripe fruit' (to Mary Boyle, 16 September 1850).

                                                                    LDB

Kaplan, Fred, *Dickens and Mesmerism: The Hidden Springs of Fiction* (1975).

**Mill, J. S.** (1806–73), philosopher and political economist, the leading Victorian proponent of UTILITARIANISM, and perhaps as much misunderstood by Dickens as Dickens was by him. The two had numerous mutual friends and might have joined forces in many causes, but Mill seems to have disliked Dickens (he described Dickens's face as one of 'dingy blackguardism irradiated with genius'), and the two had little contact. Possibly Dickens modelled Gradgrindean education in *Hard Times*, with its 'infinite grinding at the mill of knowledge' (1.9), on J. S. Mill's extraordinarily demanding education by his father James Mill (he was set to work learning Greek at the age of 3), which Dickens may have learnt about from CARLYLE or through literary gossip. Mill was especially critical of Dickens's treatment of the rights-of-WOMEN question in *Bleak House*, and they found themselves on opposite sides in the Governor EYRE controversy. When Mill writes in *Utilitarianism* (1863) that 'In the golden rule of Jesus of Nazareth, we read the complete spirit of the ethics of utility', he appears to be answering Dickens's satire in *Hard Times*, where Sissy Jupe is ridiculed by M'Choakumchild for believing that the first principle of political economy is 'To do unto others as I would that they should do unto me' (1.9). RN

***Mirror of Parliament*** (January 1828–October 1841), a weekly record of debates in both Houses of Parliament, founded and edited by John Henry Barrow (1796–1858), Dickens's maternal uncle, who taught him the Gurney system of shorthand. Dickens worked here, as did his father, perhaps as early as the first debates on the REFORM Bill (1–9 March 1831; see JOURNALIST, DICKENS AS).

*The Mirror of Parliament*, relying on its own shorthand reporters, is considered a more authentic record of Parliament during the 1830s than *Hansard*, which relied on copy from the daily papers and did not hire reporters until 1878. Gladstone paid tribute to the *Mirror* in the House of Commons 50 years after its inception: 'I do not hesitate to say that Barrow's *Mirror of Parliament* is the primary record, and not *Hansard's Debates*, because of the great fullness which Barrow aimed at and obtained' (*Hansard*, 233: 1577; 20 April 1877). KC

Carlton, W. J., *Charles Dickens, Shorthand Writer* (1926).

Grubb, Gerald G., 'Dickens's First Experience as a Parliamentary Reporter', *Dickensian*, 36 (1940).

***Miscellaneous Papers*** A collection of Dickens's articles, plays, and poems uncollected during his lifetime and first gathered together in two volumes by B. W. MATZ for the National Edition of 1908 (see EDITIONS PUBLISHED AFTER DICKENS'S LIFETIME). Included

are 21 pieces from the EXAMINER, 83 from *Household Words*, and 12 from *All the Year Round*. These were reprinted by Walter DEXTER, with additional previously uncollected pieces, as *Collected Papers* in the Nonesuch Edition of 1937. A reprint edition of *Miscellaneous Papers*, with an introduction by P. J. M. Scott, was issued in two volumes in 1983. A detailed listing is provided in an appendix to *Dickens's Journalism*, ed. Michael Slater (4 vols., 1994– ), which reprints a larger selection of Dickens's periodical writing. PVWS

***Misnar, the Sultan of India***. Dickens's earliest known work, a tragedy written when he was 9, based on 'The Enchantress', a tale from James Ridley's pseudo-Oriental *Tales of the Genii* (1764; see ARABIAN NIGHTS). The manuscript has not survived. PVWS

Stedman, Jane W., 'Good Spirits: Dickens's Childhood Reading', *Dickensian*, 61 (1965).

**missions and missionaries.** British missionary enterprises—particularly overseas—reached the height of their popularity and influence in Dickens's day. Organizations which benefited from the Victorian concatenation of philanthropic sentiments and an EVANGELICAL ethos included the Society for the Promotion of Christian Knowledge, the Society for the Propagation of the Gospel, the London Missionary Society, and the Church Missionary Society. Dickens's somewhat overstated disapproval of the activities of such bodies surfaced in his published work, speeches, and correspondence.

Though a vocal and material supporter of such domestic charitable endeavours as the Ragged School movement, Dickens objected strongly to what he called 'the cant of philanthropy' (*Speeches*, p. 132), that is, the misuse of CHARITY for arbitrary relief and self-seeking ends. He believed that the privileging of foreign missionary work over more pressing domestic concerns was evidence of snobbery and hypocrisy, and it called forth such satirical portraits as Mrs Jellyby and Mrs Pardiggle in *Bleak House*, as well as a poignant indictment of the Society for the Propagation of the Gospel in Foreign Parts, whose doorstep Jo sweeps, though he has 'no idea, poor wretch, of the spiritual destitution of a coral reef in the Pacific' (*BH* 16).

Such portrayals of excessive—and misdirected—religious enthusiasm may be found throughout Dickens's oeuvre, from the 'distributionist' Mrs Johnson Parker in 'The Ladies' Societies' (*SB*) to the 'gunpowderous' Mr Honeythunder (*MED* 6). Though he referred to missionaries generally—with the exception of David Livingstone—as 'perfect nuisances' (30 November 1865), he did approve of some projects sponsored by the non-denominational London City Mission, including the educational and reformatory initiative in the 'Devil's Acre', Westminster; the founding of the Field Lane Ragged School in Saffron Hill; and the promotion of sanitary reform (see PUBLIC HEALTH).                          LL

**Moncreiff, William (George) Thomas** (1794–1857), one of a generation of theatre craftsmen whose prolific output was the stock fare of early-19th-century theatre. His dramatized version of Pierce EGAN's *Life in London* (1820–1), *Tom and Jerry; or Life in London* (1821), showed the skills of an innovative craftsman, using Isaac Robert and George CRUIKSHANK's illustrations to pioneer an influential stage iconography of London scenes. *The Cataract of the Ganges* (Drury Lane, 1823) and a succession of spectacular MELODRAMAS extended his reputation. Complaining of PLAGIARISTS himself, he was an indefatigable adapter of other writers' material. His *Sam Weller; or the Pickwickians* was produced in July 1837 before Dickens had completed the serialized novel. It compacted the available episodes of the novel into five scenes, and not knowing Dickens's ending, he wrote his own, in which Pickwick and Weller celebrate the accession of Queen Victoria. Dickens furiously lampooned Moncreiff in *Nickleby* (48) as 'the literary pickpocket' who 'dramatized two hundred and forty-seven novels as fast as they had come out—some of them faster than they had come out.' Although writing nearly 200 plays, he died blind, unrecognized, and a pauper.       LJ

Moncreiff, W. T., *A Selection from the Dramatic Works* (1851), vol. 1.

Reid, J. C., *Bucks and Bruisers* (1971).

**money and finance.** When little Paul Dombey asked his celebrated question: 'Papa! what's money?' (*DS* 8) he was told that it was 'gold and silver, and copper, Guineas, shillings, half-pence'. And so it was: Mr Dombey summarized quite neatly the metal coinage found in purse and pocket. Perhaps

he liked the sound of 'Guinea', the gold coin worth 21 shillings, last struck in 1813. It was replaced by the new gold sovereign of twenty shillings value, with its accompanying gold half-sovereign, after Britain returned to the gold standard in 1816.

There were, too, copper pence and farthings. Crowns and half-crowns were of silver, as were the sixpenny and threepenny pieces. From 1836 to 1856 there was a silver fourpenny piece. In 1849, the year following the appearance of *Dombey and Son* in book form, the silver florin, worth two shillings, was first minted.

Bank notes started at five pounds, the one-pound notes having been withdrawn after 1816. The Bank of England's notes were always safe, and reigned supreme in London. The paper notes of the many country banks were often unsafe, as Charles READE demonstrated very dramatically in *Hard Cash* (1863).

Mr Dombey's reply had been framed in simple terms for a child to understand. To his adult mind the question conjured up different words: 'circulating-medium, currency . . . paper, bullion, rates of exchange, value of precious metals in the market.' For Paul's father, as for other merchants and City folk, the word 'money' connoted a wider world of finance and investment, where commercial credit and the means of obtaining it were of infinitely greater power than the gold, silver, and copper coinage in circulation.

When Mr Dombey thought of 'paper', he was recalling a term that embraced not only the share and stock certificates of commercial ventures but also the negotiable inland and foreign bills of exchange, which could be endorsed and used to pay debts to third parties. Specialist firms, called bill-brokers, had developed to deal exclusively with such transactions. (Dickens introduces the wording of a foreign bill of exchange in *A Christmas Carol*, 1843, as a means of suggesting that Ebenezer Scrooge was an exporting merchant of some sort.) Throughout Dickens's life the City was awash with paper, including cheques—personal bills of exchange—the use of which grew rapidly with the establishment of joint-stock banks after 1826.

Central to the world of business were the Bank of England and the Stock Exchange. The Bank was officially a joint-stock company trading on its own account. In practice it was the country's Central Bank, and although it experienced some nail-biting episodes during times of financial crisis, it was rightly regarded as a pillar of stability and probity, holding as it did a monopoly of the banking business of the state. Scattered throughout London were 62 private banks, and there were nearly 800 privately run country banks eager for deposits.

The Bank's near neighbour, the Stock Exchange, had attracted an antagonistic literary tradition since the 17th century, when stock-jobbing (amassing the paper of government funds and private stocks in order to sell them at a profit) came into being. Stock-jobbers had fomented frenzied and shady speculation in the South Sea Company, resulting in the disastrous bursting of the Bubble in 1720.

Dickens makes little use of this anti-jobber tradition, which is best illustrated in BULWER-LYTTON's *The Disowned* (1829). However, in *The Pickwick Papers* (1837) he reveals a sound understanding of Stock Exchange practice. When old Mr Weller decides to invest £200 for Sam in the four and a half per cent reduced Consols, Wilkins Flasher, Esquire, a broker, takes him to the Bank of England Consols Office to sign the transfer register. Afterwards they go to the Stock Exchange, then as now a private institution, where Mr Flasher leaves Mr Weller at the gate while he enters the building and sells the remainder of his client's holding. He returns with a cheque for £530 drawn on Smith, Payne, and Smith, a real bank of high repute. Mr Weller cashes his cheque at Smith's, and is paid in five-pound notes.

The early decades of the 19th century saw an intense public interest in the growing institutions of capitalism, with their potential for both investment and speculation. Most poor people, of course, had nothing to invest, but those with even modest property very easily yielded to the fever of speculation, and adjusted themselves to the seemingly inevitable ten-year cycles of boom, crisis, and depression.

Perhaps the most severe commercial crisis occurred in 1825, following a mania for foreign investment, notably in the national loans of the newly independent South American states. Numerous companies were floated in London to exploit the silver-mines of Mexico, Peru, Chile, and Brazil. The banks were eager to advance money cheaply, and during 1824 and 1825 no fewer than 624 company schemes of all sorts were floated.

By November 1825 the Bank of England, its bullion reserve down to just over £3 million, suddenly took fright and turned off the tap. With money no longer plentiful some 80 country banks failed, followed by the vast majority of the new company schemes. Of the 624 companies floated only 127 survived into 1827. The investments in South American loans and silver-mines yielded no interest, and many of the mining projects were simply abandoned. Their stock was thrown on to a depressed market, where it became so much waste paper.

Dickens was only a teenage boy when these traumatic events took place, but in common with other Victorian novelists he saw the creative possibilities of this year of financial panic. The opening chapters of *Nicholas Nickleby* (1838) echo the hectic atmosphere of 1825. The feckless Mrs Nickleby urges her husband to 'speculate' with their joint assets of £2,000 and a farm. The outcome is virtually inevitable: 'a mania prevailed, a bubble burst . . . four hundred nobodies were ruined.' One of them was Mr Nickleby, who very soon afterwards died of a broken heart. (So, incidentally, did Mrs Pipchin's husband (*DS* 8), having broken his heart in 'the Peruvian mines'.)

These speculative manias and their resultant crises were a reminder to novelists of the precariousness of the commercial system. There was a frantic scramble for railway shares in 1836, echoed in the second and third of Dickens's MUDFOG PAPERS (*BM* October 1837 and August 1838). Here Dickens creates Mr Jobba, who invents a 'forcing machine' designed to bring the new railway shares prematurely to a premium. 'Mr Jobba said that the whole machine was undoubtedly liable to be blown up, but that was the only objection to it.' In real life the objection was overruled, and thirty-five railway Bills passed into law at a cost to the proposers of £17,500,000.

The possibility of taking part in these colossal schemes helped to establish popular capitalism during the century, and the urge to invest was brought to fever-pitch during the great Railway Mania of the mid-1840s, when 270 further railway Bills were sanctioned, with powers to raise £131,713,206 from the investing public. The inevitable crash came after the repeal of the Corn Laws in June 1846. By 1847 a depressed market saw £78 million knocked off the value of railway shares.

Company law formulated during the early decades of the century was imperfect and unwieldy. Thousands of technically illegal partnerships traded as though they were legal entities, because they could not afford the archaic means of legal recognition available either through the granting of charters of incorporation or the passing of an Act of Parliament.

This state of affairs made it very easy for rogues to establish undertakings designed to defraud the public. There was no legal redress, as such 'companies' had no legal corporate existence. An Act of 1825 made joint-stock enterprises amenable to common law, and a further Act in 1837 provided the choice of voluntary registration. Neither of these Acts achieved much by way of regulation. Order was finally brought to the chaos of Company Law by the Limited Liability legislation of 1856 and 1862. The Companies Act of 1862 laid down the main lines of constitution and government for every limited liability company, including banks.

Insurance companies offered dazzling prospects to the swindler. All that was required to reap a fortune was seductive advertising and sumptuously furnished offices. One such undertaking was the Independent and West Middlesex Fire and Life Assurance Company, one of the most gigantic and impudent insurance frauds ever perpetrated. It was established in 1836 by Thomas Knowles, an ill-educated former smuggler and shoemaker, assisted by William Hole, another ex-smuggler turned footman, a bell-hanger, and a domestic servant.

After a period of impressive advertising the company opened grand offices in London, Edinburgh, Glasgow, and Dublin. They claimed to have a working capital of £1 million, and to have been 'established and empowered under the several Acts of Parliament'. Those words in their advertisements should have alerted the prudent investor. In terms of the Companies Act of 1825 the firm was merely a common law joint-stock partnership, and none of 'the several Acts of Parliament' empowered it to do anything.

The unregistered West Middlesex flourished, even though its porter was also its auditor, and the sweeping-boy was often called in to sign annuity deeds for thousands of pounds. The company was exposed as a gigantic swindle during the course of 1839, and the directors absconded. The capital of £1 million had never existed. The loss to the public in stolen premium money was in the region of £250,000.

In *Martin Chuzzlewit* (1843) Dickens created a powerful echo of the West Middlesex fraud in 'The Anglo-Bengalee Disinterested Loan and Life Assurance Company'. This fictional company, like the West Middlesex, carried on its business during the time when the largely ineffective Company Act of 1837 was in force. The real-life ex-smuggler Thomas Knowles is paralleled by Montague Tigg, a smooth-tongued mendicant who is tellingly transformed into a fashionable beringed dandy. Only the gullible can fail to see through the glitter to the tarnished, tawdry reality.

Other details of the Anglo-Bengalee, its methods of business and its personnel, strongly suggest that Dickens had remembered many facts about the West Middlesex affair of four years earlier, and one may assume that many of his readers very soon realized what was going to happen to Tigg Montague's company.

As *Martin Chuzzlewit* progresses, Dickens remoulds Tigg in a new, more spectacular image, that of the blackmailer murdered by his victim. By now, the sponging mendicant is 'the great speculator and capitalist'. Tigg becomes involved with the vicious Jonas Chuzzlewit in a drama of his own, and Dickens begins to lose interest in his fictional insurance company. In chapter 54 of the novel he leaves old Martin Chuzzlewit to give a confused and financially dubious account of the fate of the Anglo-Bengalee.

In January 1838, when the West Middlesex was in mid-career, Dickens took out a life policy with the Sun Life Assurance Society, and in November 1841 he effected another policy with Eagle Life Assurance. The secretary and actuary of this company, H. P. Smith, was largely instrumental in the arrest of Thomas Griffiths Wainewright, the poisoner and insurance defrauder. Dickens was impressed with Smith, and presented him as Meltham, the young actuary of the 'Inestimable', who unmasks the villainous Julius Slinkton in 'HUNTED DOWN' (1859).

The 1850s witnessed an alarming moral decline in commercial life. Following the frantic gambling of the 1840s railway mania, very old established firms of high repute secretly embarked on reckless speculation, inevitably resorting to fraud. Particularly disturbing were the 'high art crimes', as they were called, a series of criminal bank failures in 1855 and 1856, when Dickens was occupied in writing and issuing the monthly parts of *Little Dorrit*.

Dickens was engaged on the first chapters of *Little Dorrit* in June 1855, a month which saw the spectacular criminal failure of the ancient banking-house of Strahan, Paul, and Bates, and the commencement of proceedings against its principals. The case remained before the public throughout the summer and autumn. The bank's owner, Sir John Dean Paul, Bart., was sentenced to fourteen years' transportation.

Meanwhile, John Sadleir, MP, a Junior Lord of the Treasury who was revered as a financial wizard, was quietly and effectively plundering the Tipperary Bank, which he owned. His particular genius was forgery, and when his issue of false shares to the value of £150,000 was discovered, his hollow shell of a bank collapsed with debts of £400,000.

Sadleir's Tipperary Bank was the 'certain Irish bank' mentioned by Dickens in his Preface to the one-volume edition of *Little Dorrit* (1857). John Sadleir, unable to face the shame of trial and sentence, committed suicide on 17 February 1856.

Dickens began writing the sixth number of *Little Dorrit*, in which Mr Merdle made his debut, two days later. The 'precious rascality' of Sadleir gave him the idea for the character whose 'complaint' is fraud and forgery, involving so many others in the novel in his own suicidal ruin (?29–30 March 1856).

This spate of criminal bank failures would still have been in Dickens's memory when he created Tellson's Bank in *A Tale of Two Cities* (1859). It was important that the 18th-century Tellson's, a bastion of stability in a revolutionary world, should be distanced from the marble and mahogany palaces that housed the brash new banks of the 1850s, which is one reason for its rather endearing mustiness. It

carries on its business in 'a miserable little shop, with two little counters' (*TTC* 2.1). The partners, we learn, are proud of its reassuring dinginess (*TTC* 2.1).

Tellson's is in Fleet Street, 'in the heavy shadow of Temple Bar' (*TTC* 2.1), and according to Jarvis Lorry, its devoted clerk, it has been established for nearly 150 years. Many Victorian readers would have seen in Tellson's an echo of the distinguished private bank of Child & Co., established at 1 Fleet Street since the early 17th century. Child's produced the first printed banknotes, which had a picture of Temple Bar in the corner. With Tellson's it shared a penchant for 'extemporised strongrooms made of kitchens and sculleries' (*TTC* 2.1). Child's old premises, with their gloomy front kitchen, were demolished in 1879, but the bank flourished independently until an amalgamation in 1924.

Tellson's had a branch in Paris, which enjoyed that rare banking phenomenon, 'a run of confidence' (2.21), when aristocratic customers hurriedly consigned their valuables to it, but the function of both branches of Tellson's is to link the Two Cities by a common bond, a 'great gathering-place' (*TTC* 2.24), for those characters who are to provide the novel with some of its most moving and memorable episodes.

Dickens creates four mercantile firms in his major works. They are all initially depicted with some fidelity to reality, and then shaped into an imaginative mould to conform with Dickens's preoccupation with theme or character.

Cheeryble Brothers (*NN* 35) are German-merchants, a point which Dickens emphasizes by telling the reader about Frank Cheeryble's four-year stint looking after the business in Germany. (German-merchants imported fine wool from Saxony and exported finished textiles, notably worsted, to Germany). However, once Dickens moves away from young Frank, he develops the Cheeryble brothers as good fairies to balance the evil Ralph Nickleby. Their goodness stretches their credibility as businessmen to the limit, as do the terms of Nicholas's engagement (*NN* 37) and the repetitive, non-progressive nature of Tim Linkinwater's daily round as depicted in the same chapter.

Anthony Chuzzlewit and Son are Manchester-warehousemen, distributive merchants and export factors for Lancashire cotton goods and Yorkshire linens. This was a thriving trade, but their dingy, rotting premises are created to symbolize their moral degradation. They are not seen exercising their trade. Instead, they are depicted as usurious and grasping money-getters.

The same suggestion of decay and usury surrounds the firm of Scrooge and Marley. Scrooge is presented as an exporting merchant of some sort, with a name 'good upon 'Change for anything he chose to put his hand to' (*CC* 1). ('''Change' means the Royal Exchange, Cornhill, where merchants met to transact business. It should not be confused with the Stock Exchange, which was in Capel Court.) However, it is not long before the shades of the moneylender's den begin to gather stylistically. Scrooge the merchant yields to Scrooge the miser and, by implication, usurer.

Mr Dombey is a West India merchant. In real life he would have belonged to the powerful West India Interest, giving him power and prestige far greater than that enjoyed by any other class of trader. It may seem that this power fed his complacency, letting him idle away three years while his business is plundered by Carker. In fact, even while the first four chapters were still in manuscript Dickens had tired of the idea of Dombey as a merchant. He wanted to concentrate on the dramas of Florence and Edith, and so reshaped the realities of business life to serve his literary purposes. Dombey wilfully neglects his business only because his creator leaves him no option!

Dickens was a shrewd, careful man of business, investing throughout his career in steady government, Russian, and Indian stock, railway paper, and property. His bank accounts in later years showed huge deposits, and some American newspapers waxed satirical over his apparent financial acquisitiveness. When he died in 1870 Dickens left £93,000. The sum, in present-day values, would exceed £1 million (see MONEY VALUES).

Dickens, in common with other Victorian novelists, showed an ambivalent attitude to wealth-creation, an activity seen both as a vital element in the progress of the nation and as a potential corrupter of public and private morality. When little Paul Dombey presses his question by asking 'what's money after all', his Papa furnishes him with some ingeniously evasive answers.　　NR

Brown, J. M., *Dickens: Novelist in the Market-Place* (1982).
Russell, Norman, *The Novelist and Mammon* (1986).
Smith (1968).

**money values** in Dickens's time manifestly differed greatly from today's, but no precise overall multiplier can be given, because the relative costs of various services, commodities, and property varied enormously. To cite a famous if trivial example: 'poverty and oysters always seems to go together', Sam Weller remarks about the oyster-stalls lining a 'crowded and filthy' Whitechapel street (*PP* 22): oysters, now a luxury item, then cost a penny each. Costs also varied regionally: Yorkshire schools were so located because living was relatively cheap there—but only metropolitan prices matter much for Dickens. Some references to wages, etc., in the novels and in actuality will, however, suggest what scale of multiplication is appropriate. Happily, inflation on a modern scale was then unknown, so, despite fluctuations in the cost of living (rising in the first half of Dickens's career but falling in the second), money-values during this period remained fairly stable, as did the dollar exchange-rate (£1 = $5).

Farm-labourers got as little as 7 or 8 shillings a week, sometimes but not always with perquisites; Midlands weavers could drop in times of depression to 4s 6d (see WORK). The working-class aristocracy—craftsmen and skilled industrial operatives—got around 40 shillings. Domestic SERVANTS (numerous and, because 'living-in', they were 'all found') ranged from the annual 50 shillings and a few clothes that the ex-workhouse skivvy Guster got from the Snagsbys (*BH* 10) to the £60 for the housekeeper, and more for the butler, in a prosperous family ('per annum' should be understood throughout this item). Sam Weller jumps at Pickwick's offer of £12 and two suits of clothes. No wonder teenage Kit Nubbles thinks himself lucky on £6 (though David Copperfield pays his pageboy £6 10s). After his first quarterly payment, Kit can treat his and Barbara's families to an outing to Astley's Circus followed by 'three dozen of your largest oysters' and beer (*OCS* 39). Another treat, Guppy's ample

'Slap-bang' dinner for three, including second-helpings, cheese, beer, rum, and a tip costs 8s 6d (42.5p) (*BH* 20). But it is evident how kindly restrained was David Copperfield's protest that it was 'more than we can afford' (*DC* 44) when Dora, hearing that he 'would like a little bit of fish', bought a whole salmon costing £1 6s (around £100 in 1990s currency).

A lower-middle-class clerk, Bob Cratchit, threadbare but respectable in attire though unable to afford an overcoat—having a wife and six children, only two of them working—'had but fifteen "Bob" [shillings] a week' (under £40 p.a.) and is obviously underpaid, as the converted Scrooge recognizes. 'In such matters as this Dickens was normally a good observer,' remarks G. Kitson Clark (*The Making of Victorian England*, 1962), citing this and reckoning that lower-middle-class incomes ranged from £60 to £200. Another historian, John Burnett (*A History of the Cost of Living*, 1969, here drawn upon) compares Bob with the senior clerks at a Burnley mill, enjoying 'near Utopian conditions', their employers claimed, on 21 shillings a week for an eleven-hour day; in the winter they had to bring daily 4 pounds of coal. Burnett cites Thomas and Jane CARLYLE (no children), living in a twelve-room house in Chelsea on £300: their major expenses were £75 on food, £35 for rent, £25 for Jane's clothes, £12–16 for a live-in maid, and £25 for rates and taxes (then a relatively low proportion of income).

A useful indication is what income a young professional man needed before marrying. *The Times*, 1858, debated whether £300 was enough for a 'gentleman' to marry on, but Tommy Traddles (*DC*), a young lawyer, marries on £250, having to economize (no silver, only Britannia metal) but able—a little implausibly?—to accommodate five sisters-in-law. Entrants to the Civil Service got £80 (John DICKENS) or £90 (Anthony TROLLOPE); John Dickens, on £350 in the 1820s, should have been living comfortably, not going bankrupt. Teachers, joining a humbler but advancing profession, earned much less but had to live 'respectably'. Mr Marton is rightly happy to move to another parish as clerk and schoolmaster to earn 'a fortune . . . Five and thirty pounds!' (*OCS* 46). By the 1860s certificated teachers averaged £94 and uncertificated ones £62, some teachers enjoying

rent-free accommodation. Living-in governesses earned anything from £10 to a rare £100; Jane Eyre's £30 was normal. In the 1870s a university Principal, on £700, could save £200, employ two maids, and take two-month holidays. Mrs Beeton (*Domestic Management*, 1861) reckoned that families on £150–200 could afford one maid, adding a nursemaid at £300, a cook at £500, and on £1,000 luxuriating on a cook, nursemaid, two maids, and a manservant. In the Church, curates might earn as little as £30, bishops as much as £10,000; parish clergy's stipends varied enormously.

Literary earnings could be substantial—much higher, as were other professional incomes, than in France, as Hippolyte Taine observed around 1860. Trollope in his better years averaged £4,500, TENNYSON in 1869 negotiated an annual £5,000 from his new publishers. Both George ELIOT and DISRAELI were offered £10,000 for a novel. Dickens received £11,000–12,000 for his final full-length novels, and in his later years his writings (including back-sales) were producing £10,000–13,000 a year (the income of many peers, and of leading bankers and industrialists, though seriously rich grandees such as his friend the Duke of Devonshire had around £200,000; see Patten 1978). For his farewell PUBLIC READINGS Dickens received £80 a night, all expenses paid, but had earned three times that in AMERICA. He bequeathed £93,000. In 1856 he had bought Gad's Hill for £1,700 and then spent £1,000 on improvements; last time it was on the market, it fetched £500,000.

These figures are a reminder that the one shilling for a monthly part of a Dickens SERIAL novel was not a throwaway amount, though spreading the cost of a novel over a year and a half made novel-buying possible for many who could never have afforded a new novel in three volumes at 31s 6d. Serial purchasers would expend 20 shillings plus the cost of binding—more than Bob Cratchit's weekly wage. Novel-buying was a quite expensive middle-class luxury. Dickens's weeklies, *Household Words* and *All the Year Round*, sold for twopence. Tickets for his public readings cost 1 to 4 shillings or 5 shillings, rising to 7 shillings for his Farewells; in America, all seats cost $2.00.

As was stated earlier, the wholly different pattern of life then and today and the wide range of variants in the relative costs of various commodities, etc., make it impossible to offer any single figure which will reliably convert Dickens's money-values into ours. Readers who want a quick fix which will most often give them some guidance will, however, get a *very approximate* notion of present-day values if they multiply Dickens's figures by 70. But how imperfect even this 70 is as an indicator appears if one applies it to Bob Cratchit's weekly wage. 15s × 70 = £52 50p, and no family with children could survive, let alone maintain a precarious lower-middle-class gentility, on that income. The multiplier works better, however, for Traddles's longed-for £250 p.a., which is probably the best and easiest figure to bear in mind. £250 × 70 = £17,500, on which a newly wed childless couple could indeed manage to start life together in a frugal and marginal but recognizably middle-class fashion.                        PC

***Monthly Magazine*** (1796–1843), the magazine where Dickens published his first sketch, 'A Dinner at Poplar Walk' (December 1833). It was not at the time a prominent monthly though still respected for its venerable history, having been founded as a progressive magazine in 1796 by Richard Phillips, a radical bookseller who published Mary Wollstonecraft and endured imprisonment for selling Paine's *Common Sense*. Its original description of itself—as 'an enterprise on behalf of intellectual liberty against the forces of panic conservatism'—should be seen in the context of the repressive atmosphere after war with France was declared in 1793. The magazine's ethos was DISSENTING and UNITARIAN. Recurrent topics were scientific discoveries, travels abroad, especially the United States, the reform of injustice, and foreign literature. Among the contributors from its most famous period as a repository of liberal dissent, up to 1824, were COLERIDGE, LAMB, Southey, and HAZLITT.

At its peak, the *Monthly* circulation reached 5,000; by Dickens's time, when it was colloquially called the 'Old Monthly', this was more like 600. Sold in 1824, the *Monthly* became Tory; under new ownership again, from 1833, it became radical—a typical history in magazines during the period. The owner and editor in 1833 was a Captain Holland, who had been in the Napoleonic wars and then, like other disbanded veterans at this time, had joined Bolivar's South American campaign in 1817. He edited the *Monthly* from 1833 to 1835, hoping 'to make it a popular mouthpiece for his ardent liberalism' (Forster 1.4), and reminding his readers that the magazine had been 'founded upon the principle of political freedom and reform' in an editorial of February 1834. After Holland gave up the magazine in 1836 because of failing health, Dickens continued to see him socially—Forster mentions seeing him at Doughty Street in 1837—and at last mention, in 1838, Dickens sent him twelve guineas in Paris.

After December 1833 the *Monthly* published eight more of Dickens's tales: 'Mrs Joseph Porter "Over the Way" ' (January 1834), 'Horatio Sparkins' (February 1834), 'The Bloomsbury Christening' (April 1834), 'The Boarding-House' (May 1834), 'The Boarding-House, No. II' (August 1834; the first to be signed 'BOZ'), 'The Steam Excursion' (October 1834), 'Passage in the Life of Mr Watkins Tottle, Chapter the First' (January 1835), and 'Watkins Tottle, Chapter the Second' (February 1835).                        KC

Carlton, W. J., ' "Captain Holland" Identified', *Dickensian*, 57 (1961).

**Moore, Thomas,** Irish poet (1779–1852), the author of a great many popular lyrics and songs, as well as comic verse and the orientalist *Lallah Rookh* (1817). Dickens met Moore on a few occasions, although the two men were never friends. There are over 30 allusions to Moore's songs in Dickens's novels, the majority appearing in *The Old Curiosity Shop* and involving quotation and parodic variation by Dick Swiveller. His version of Moore's ' "Twas Ever Thus' (from *Lallah Rookh*) is correct up to the final four words: ' "Twas ever thus, from childhood's hour I've seen my fondest hopes decay, I never loved a tree or flower but 'twas the first to fade away; I never nursed a dear Gazelle, to glad me with its soft black eye, but when it came to know me well, and love me, it was sure to marry a market-gardener' (*OCS* 56; the original has '. . . to die'). Moore's popular and SENTIMENTAL verse represents in many senses a verse forerunner of Dickens's own early success in prose.                        AR

**morality and moral issues.** Dickens's writings, whether fiction or journalism, are imbued with a sense of morality, and frequently engage with the moral issues of his time. In the words of the *Wesleyan-Methodist Magazine* in 1853, 'He has morality shining upon his page' (quoted in Pope 1978, p. 16). Yet, as the writer noted, it appeared to be a morality without Christianity, or at least a morality which did not prevent Dickens from satirizing Christians. For Dickens the apparent conundrum was easily resolved: he based his morality on the New Testament, the book which, 'putting aside the interpretations and inventions of Man . . . teaches you the best lessons by which any human creature who tries to be truthful and faithful to duty can possibly be guided' (to Plorn [Edward Dickens], 26 September 1868). These lessons were succinctly conveyed in Betsey Trotwood's advice to the young David: 'Never be mean in anything, never be false, never be cruel' (*DC* 15). If Christians departed from these simple rules, as all too often they seemed to, then they became targets of Dickens's wrath. Scrooge, and the solitary selfishness which he embodied, was the epitome of immorality, as was the Old Testament morality of Mrs Clennam (*LD*) and of Esther's aunt Miss Barbary (*BH*).

Like his contemporary Thomas CARLYLE, for whom he felt something close to reverence, Dickens trained the searchlight of morality on the problems of his day. This brought him into opposition to two of the great forces shaping the Victorian age, EVANGELICALISM and UTILITARIANISM. Evangelicalism, which can be dated back to the 1780s, was the force which Dickens had most firmly and consistently in his sights. He identified it with a meanness of spirit and hypocrisy which sought to control and repress people's sense of enjoyment, and opposed it in all its manifestations, taking the general line that 'whatever Exeter Hall [the meeting place of evangelical societies] champions, is the thing by no means to be done' (*Examiner*, 19 August 1848). This was particularly the case with two moral and political issues which greatly exercised Dickens and his contemporaries: SABBATARIANISM and temperance (see DRINK AND TEMPERANCE).

The sabbatarian issue came to the fore when Dickens was a young man with the formation in 1831 of the Lord's Day Observance Society, and the attempt, under the leadership of Sir Andrew Agnew (1793–1849), to push sabbatarian legislation through Parliament. Dickens opposed this with vigour. He knew that for many people Sunday was in effect the only day of leisure in the week. In SUNDAY UNDER THREE HEADS (1836) he painted a picture of 'Sunday As it is', 'As Sabbath Bills would make it', and 'As it might be made', the proposed Bills being directed 'exclusively . . . against the AMUSEMENTS AND RECREATIONS of the poor'. The evangelicals were unsuccessful in the 1830s, but the issue did not die away, and Dickens was always ready to defend Sunday against restrictions, as well as, in *Little Dorrit* (1.3), painting the classical picture of the repressed English Sunday. His line of argument was entirely consistent: where there was entertainment on offer on a Sunday, the people were 'decent, orderly, quiet, sociable among their families and neighbours. There is a general feeling of respect for religion, and for religious observances' ('The Sunday Screw', *HW* 22 June 1850). If some behaved badly, that was no reason to repress the pleasures of the majority.

A similar argument underlay his attitude to temperance. The temperance movement, like the sabbatarian, was a product of the 1830s, and it met with Dickens's unqualified scorn in the exposure in *Pickwick Papers* (33) of the Brick Lane Branch of the United Grand Junction Ebenezer Association, and in a fear of its consequences in his remark that popular discontent 'could be expected when Temperance Societies interfere with the amusements of the people' (Butt and Tillotson 1957, p. 44). Temperance advocates, he believed, mistook effects for causes and misused the language, calling for temperance but meaning the total abstinence of teetotalism. The causes were environmental and EDUCATIONAL, and the cure lay there rather than in restrictions of the kind temperance advocates wanted (*Examiner*, 8 July 1848).

The utilitarians were a harder target, for it was difficult to take exception to many of the reforms they wanted to introduce, such as mechanics' institutes, public LIBRARIES, or public parks. What angered him about utilitarianism was not so much what it advocated as its negative reasons for doing so: these things, said the utilitarians, were a cheaper route to a stable society than prisons; they were to be valued not for themselves but for the ulterior purpose they served. For Dickens they should be advocated and justified for the positive function they served, to bring pleasure into people's lives. In *Hard Times* he brought the full force of his dislike of utilitarianism to the fore in the portrait of Mr Gradgrind, a man who had dedicated his life to facts and closed it to the play of the emotions.

Dickens, then, set himself up in opposition to the powerful forces of evangelicalism and utilitarianism. And yet in many respects his attitude to morality was what we might think of as quintessentially that of a middle-class Victorian: a belief in SELF-HELP, combined with a commitment to CHARITABLE activity on behalf of deserving groups, and a willingness to treat the undeserving as beyond the pale. The crucial differences from the stereotype are these: first, in an age of individualism he clung to a morality of sociability, believing that social life brought out the best in people, a message most powerfully conveyed in *A Christmas Carol*. Secondly, though an embodiment himself of the WORK ethic, he fought to introduce more pleasure and leisure into the lives of the people. Thirdly, he preached a tolerance of other people's behaviour. And finally, linked to this, he delighted in exposing the cant and hypocrisy which, he believed, underlay the words and actions of those most anxious to inject moral behaviour into the people—most memorably in his portrait of 'the moral Pecksniff', serenely selfish in accordance with his own maxim, 'There is nothing personal in morality, my love' (*MC* 2).

Believing, as he did, that attitudes to morality were displayed in the physique and bearing of a person, he did much to create for his own generation and his successors the image of moral reformers whose own lives were not all they should be. In place of their moral absolutes, which even they could not live up to, he based his own morality around the twin ideas of a 'Let well alone' tolerance of others' behaviour ('The Sunday Screw', *HW* 22 June 1850) and an endorsement of sociability as the key to the creation of the moral person.                                                    HC

Pope (1978).

**Morley, Henry** (1822–94) had been a schoolmaster and occasional journalist when in 1851 Dickens appointed him to the *House-hold Words* staff; he stayed with the weeklies until 1865 when he became a Professor of English, thenceforth publishing extensively on literary and other scholarly topics. He was *Household Words's* most prolific contributor, mainly on sanitary, educational, and other social matters, though sometimes uncomfortable with its chirpy style. He felt great affection for Dickens and warmly appreciated his genius but, as the only in-house graduate, was conscious that Dickens's was not a cultured or critically refined mind. Never an intimate friend, though a much-esteemed and dependable colleague, he wrote intelligently about him, in the office and at home, in letters.                                                    PC

Solly, Henry Shaen, *The Life of Henry Morley* (1898).

*Morning Chronicle.* The most influential liberal newspaper of Dickens's day, at its height second in circulation only to *The TIMES*, and which provided Dickens with his first position as a regular reporter from 1834 (shortly after its ownership changed hands and the new owners infused a good deal of money into it) to 1836, when he resigned to assume the first editorship of BENTLEY'S MISCELLANY. The rivalry between the *Chronicle* and *The Times* was intense and may have provided Dickens with the model for the battles between Pott and Slurk in *The Pickwick Papers*.

The *Chronicle* was one of the first papers to print parliamentary debates verbatim (for which it was unsuccessfully prosecuted), was often in legal difficulties (frequently for alleged libels), and, especially under the editorship of John BLACK in the 1820s and 1830s, pioneered sharply critical investigations into such previously sacrosanct institutions as the law and police courts and battled for freedom of the press, notably in the area of religion. Here Dickens worked with his good friend Thomas Beard (who had recommended his appointment as a reporter) and met his future father-in-law, the music critic George HOGARTH. And here too he very probably received his most concentrated education in the essentials of reformism amidst editors and reporters closely connected to BENTHAMITE and other radical circles and causes (Black was close to James Mill and Lords Brougham and Melbourne; he was a staunch supporter of the New POOR LAW of 1834, which Dickens hated to the end of his life and was the occasion of countless arguments between him and Black; and among the reporters with whom Dickens was friendly was a former private secretary to Bentham). While Dickens certainly never identified himself with utilitarianism as a school, he nonetheless throughout his life had in his sights exactly the sort of institutional inefficiency and absurdity that aroused the Benthamites' wrath.

Nine of the pieces that became *Sketches by Boz* were first published in the *Chronicle*, and several others were first published in the companion EVENING CHRONICLE, which was launched in 1835 under Hogarth's editorship.
RN

**Mr Nightingale's Diary,** a farce by Mark LEMON, extensively revised by Dickens. It was used as an afterpiece for their AMATEUR THEATRICAL production of BULWER-LYTTON'S *Not So Bad As We Seem*, in aid of the GUILD OF LITERATURE AND ART, founded by Dickens and Bulwer-Lytton. Dickens's role, Gabblewig, involved the kind of quick-change routine he admired greatly in Charles MATHEWS the elder's 'At Home' performances—a series of five impersonations while wooing the heroine in the face of opposition from her hypochondriac uncle—'fourteen costume changes in the course of the night', he reported to George Beadnell (4 May 1852). The first performance was in the Duke of Devonshire's house on 27 May 1851, and toured to Birmingham, Liverpool—where the audience 'cannot have heard half of it, they laughed to that amazing extent', Dickens wrote to Catherine (12 February 1852)—Manchester, and Nottingham. The script was privately printed in 1851 and published by James OSGOOD in 1877, but there was so much improvisation from night to night that the text was never stable (Pilgrim 6.398–9 n.).
PVWS

**Mudfog Papers, The** The title of Dickens's contributions, other than *Oliver Twist*, to BENTLEY'S MISCELLANY, written when he was editor of that journal and illustrated by George CRUIKSHANK, but not published as a collection until 1880. 'The Public Life of Mr Tulrumble, Once Mayor of Mudfog' (*BM* 1 January 1837) describes the farcical results of Nicholas Tulrumble's procession celebratin his investiture as Mayor of Mudfog. 'Full Re port of the First Meeting of the Mudfog Assc ciation for the Advancement of Everythin; appeared in October 1837, when Dickens's di: pute with Richard BENTLEY determined hii to write no number of *Oliver Twist* for th; issue. It satirizes the British Association fc the Advancement of SCIENCE (founded 1831 as does the next, 'Full Report of the Secon Meeting . . . ', published in September 183; again in place of a serial instalment of *Oliv Twist*. Three further items were included i the collection: 'The Pantomime of Lifk (March 1837), which draws parallels betwee life and the stage; 'Some Particulars Concerr ing a Lion' (May 1837), about the lionizing c writers; and 'Mr Robert Bolton' (Augu: 1838), an anecdote by 'a gentleman connecte with the press', which was not in fact writte by Dickens. Dickens located Oliver's birth place in Mudfog in the original serialize version of *Oliver Twist*, but removed th specificity in all later editions. PVW

Chaudhry, G. A., 'The Mudfog Papers', *Dick ensian*, 70 (1974).

**music and musicians evoking Dick ens's works.** In Dickens's lifetime numei ous composers from England and the Unite States based comic and sentimental parlou pieces on characters and incidents from hi novels. Examples of instrumental music ai Brinley Richards's 'The Dolly Varden Polk; W. M. Parker's 'Little Dorrit's Schottische and Charles Coote's 'Mugby Junction Galoj Among the parlour songs and ballads in spired by Dickens's works are Henry Russell 'The Ivy Green' (*PP*), Stephen Glover's 'Wh; the Wild Waves Are Saying' (*DS*), and Georg Linley's 'Little Nell' (*OCS*).

Claude Debussy evoked Dickens in th quirky piano piece from his second book c Preludes, 'Hommage à S. Pickwick'. In 196 John Dankworth created a jazz suite of Dick ens pieces collectively titled 'What the Dick ens!'

Several 20th-century composers have writ ten effective 'background' scores for Dicken sian FILMS, notably Herbert Stothart fo George Cukor's version of *David Copperfiel* (1934), Walter Goehr for David Lean's *Grea Expectations* (1946), and Arnold Bax fo Lean's *Oliver Twist* (1948).

There have been several film musicals based on *A Christmas Carol,* among them *Scrooge* with songs by Leslie Bricusse (1970), the Walt Disney animated version, *Mickey's Christmas Carol* (1983), with songs by Buddy Baker and Irwin Kostal, and *The Muppet Christmas Carol* with songs by Paul Williams (1992).

The most popular 20th-century musical comedy adaptation has been Lionel Bart's long-running *Oliver!* (1960; screen version 1968). Other musical versions include Cyril Ornadel's *Pickwick* (1963), with Harry Secombe in the title role; Roger Holman's *Smike* (1973); *Copperfield* (1981), with book, lyrics, and music by the team of Al Kasha and Joel Hirschhorn; Rupert Holmes's *The Mystery of Edwin Drood: The Solve-it-yourself Broadway Musical* (1985); and *A Christmas Carol,* performed seasonally at New York's Madison Square Garden since 1994 (music by Alan Menken and Lynn Ahrens).

The Royal Shakespeare Company's nine-hour *Nicholas Nickleby* (1980) made effective use of songs and instrumental interludes composed by Stephen Oliver. Several operas have been based on Dickens's works. Albert Coates composed *Pickwick* (1936), and Arthur Benjamin set *A Tale of Two Cities* (radio broadcast 1953; first staged performance 1957).

The Christmas books have attracted the most sustained attention as inspirations for music dramas. Alexander Mackenzie set music to *The CRICKET ON THE HEARTH* (1914, revised version 1923). There had been two earlier full-scale operatic versions: Riccardo Zandonai composed the romantically lush *Il grillo del focolare* (Turin, 1908). Most notable is Karl Goldmark's version, the intensely dramatic and exceedingly beautiful *Das Heimchen am Herd,* first performed in Vienna in 1896.

Ralph Vaughan Williams used *A Christmas Carol* as the basis for a masque with singing, dancing, and mime (*On Christmas Night,* 1926). More recently, Thea Musgrave's opera *A Christmas Carol* was given its first performances in Norfolk by the Virginia Opera Company (1979). RTB

**music hall** developed during Dickens's lifetime into one of the most important and characteristic forms of 19th-century popular entertainment. The music hall implies a specific venue, a characteristic programme, and a particular cultural product—the music-hall song with its inevitable chorus.

The origins of music hall lie in diverse forms of later Georgian commercial entertainment, including 'pleasure gardens' such as Vauxhall and those attached to taverns such as the Eagle in the City Road, tavern rooms with informal singing, and song and supper rooms of 1820s London. Dickens vividly describes a 'harmonic meeting' in 'The Streets—Night' (*SB*); a number of characters in *Pickwick*—the dying clown, Tom Smart, Dodson and Fogg's clerks, Lowten—frequent song and supper clubs. Fagin visits the Three Cripples, a crowded tavern which boasts a chairman and blue-nosed piano-player (*OT* 16); Swiveller is 'Perpetual Grand' of the 'select convivial circle called the Glorious Apollers' (*OCS* 13). Nemo's inquest is held in the Sol's Arms, otherwise the home of entertainment twice a week, with a gentleman 'of professional celebrity' faced by Little Swills, the comic vocalist (*BH* 11). From these precursors emerged a group of comedian-singers who became early music-hall stars. Generally, the whole range of diverse popular entertainments, so significant a part of the texture of Dickens's work, contributed something to the music hall.

If the music hall started as a cellar or tavern room where beer and chop suppers were consumed during performances, it ended as a variety theatre where audiences sat in rows of seats and drinks were not allowed in the auditorium. If it started as a participatory form where all present were expected to contribute, it ended as professional entertainment, although an element of participation remained in the form of chorus singing. The music hall drew heavily on the popular traditions of English song, but by the mid-century a genre of specially created songs was emerging.

Dickens pays surprisingly little attention to the music hall. In 'The Amusements of the People' (*HW* 30 March and 13 April 1850) he follows 'Joe Whelks, of New Cut Lambeth', to the Britannia Saloon, and years later in *All the Year Round* Andrew Halliday took the same fictitious character to a variety of working-class amusements, including a well-ordered north-west London hall, complete with chairman and 'beadle', featuring singing, dancing, acrobats, 'a negro melodist', and a comical sketch with a sound moral. 'If the entertainment were somewhat vulgar, and wanting in taste,' Halliday observed, 'it was on the whole, well meaning.' Halliday thought that music halls could help improve taste and refine morals, but in the end safety regulations, licensing laws, and the pursuit of profits dictated their development (*AYR* 16, 23, 30 June, 7 and 10 July 1866).                          VG

Schlicke, Paul, 'Glorious Apollers and Ancient Buffaloes', *Dickensian*, 90 (1994).

**music, musicians, and song.** At the beginning of his career Dickens wrote the words to an operetta set to music by John HULLAH, *The* VILLAGE COQUETTES. Performed at the St James Theatre (6 December 1836), it was a modest success with the public. Hullah and Dickens's sister Fanny, a talented singer and pianist, were both students at the Royal Academy of Music, and she introduced the two men.

Dickens's most obvious interest in music was his love of ballads and popular vocal music, both comic and sentimental. These play an important role in several of Dickens's novels and are often integral parts of his comic characterizations. James T. Lightwood and J. W. T. LEY have shown how frequently Dickens alludes to songs from GAY's *Beggar's Opera*, MOORE's *Irish Melodies*, songs and lyrics by Charles Dibdin, T. H. Bayly, Sir Henry Bishop, George Linley, and many others.

The use of songs and singing—quoting, distorting, remaking songs into something new—is one way Dickens creates characters who are themselves creators, characters for whom creative imagination is at life's centre. Dick Swiveller (*OCS*) constructs a life-affirming version of himself partly by his imaginative singing. A central aspect of Captain Cuttle's vivid personality (*DS*) is his ability to quote from his extensive repertory of popular songs. Ominously, Rosa Dartle, accompanying herself on a harp while singing for David and Steerforth, transforms an Irish song into something 'unearthly' and 'fearful', expressing the 'passion within her' (*DC* 29). And Silas Wegg (*OMF*) demonstrates the moral ambivalence of song; in Wegg's re-creation of lyrics Dickens analyses an imagination where distinctions between a generous

potential to create and a selfish compulsion to destroy are blurred.

Allusions to songs and ballads are important parts of Dickens's artistic engagement with music as part of the texture of his novels, but he also alludes more generally to the emotional power of music to create powerful (or comical) associations with memory. Dickens's writing often suggest that, as the 20th-century composer Paul Hindemith maintained, music evokes not feelings but 'memories of feelings' (*A Composer's World*, 1952), and indeed in Dickens's novels musical reactions are often closely tied to dreams and memories.

Sometimes the association between music and memory is as straightforward as Mr Pickwick's tipsy attempt to remember the songs of his youth (*PP* 19). This power can reside literally in musical sounds, or figuratively in a creative listener's ability to transform other sounds into a 'fireside song of comfort', such as the non-verbal 'song' sung by the kettle and the cricket at the beginning of *The* CRICKET ON THE HEARTH ('Chirp the First'). In *Oliver Twist*, the narrator remarks that music can create 'sudden dim remembrances of scenes that never were, in this life' (30). In *The Old Curiosity Shop* a fire is both music and memory to the factory labourer (*OCS* 44). David heard 'sorrowful distant music' when Agnes touched the chords of his memory 'so softly and harmoniously' (*DC* 60). In *Little Dorrit's* voice, Arthur Clennam heard all the 'soothing songs' which Nature sings and which bring healing memories of 'every merciful and loving whisper' he had ever heard (*LD* 2.34). And in *Our Mutual Friend*, Nature's voice in the falling water of Plashwater Weir Mill Lock constituted an 'outer memory' for a 'contemplative listener' (4.1).

When Dickens's musical characters do not sing, or make allusions to songs, they sometimes produce lugubrious instrumental sounds. The jilted Swiveller relieves his burden of self-pity by picking up a flute to play 'Away with Melancholy' before going to sleep (*OCS* 58). Mr Mell, the poor schoolteacher so abused by Steerforth, also produced a 'dismal sound' with his flute (*DC* 5). Mr Morfin the bachelor consoled himself with a cello and every Wednesday joined with other players in executing 'quartettes of the most tormenting and excruciating nature' (*DS* 13). By contrast,

*Martin Chuzzlewit* ends with an extended image of good Tom Pinch creating a kind of musical analogue for poetic justice with the 'noble music' of his organ (54). Little Dorrit's shabby uncle Frederick reverts to the unhappy norm, played 'a clarionet as dirty as himself' in a theatre orchestra (*LD* 1.7). In both the opening and closing chapters of *Drood*, there are portentous sounds from the organ of Rochester Cathedral. In the same novel, by contrast, Mr Crisparkle is described as both musical and kind, holding alternate musical Wednesdays and keeping a portrait of Handel above his dining room closet (*MED* 2, 10). Handel, composer of 'The Harmonious Blacksmith', is the name Herbert Pocket gives to his friend Pip because 'we are so harmonious and you have been a blacksmith' (*GE* 22). Handel's 'Dead March' (*Saul*) is mentioned in *Dombey and Son* (5), *Bleak House* (21), and *Our Mutual Friend* (2.8).

Dickens knew the composer Francesco Berger, who was studying music in Leipzig at the same time that Dickens's son Charley was there, and Berger wrote incidental music for *The* FROZEN DEEP. Berger stated in his autobiography that Dickens's taste in music, as in all art, 'was for the unsophisticated, the obvious. Art for art's sake, the Art that we spell with a capital A, did not appeal to him' (*97*, 1931). An early example of Dickens's love of private theatricals is his directing for family and friends a version of Henry Bishop's opera *Clari: or, the Maid of Milan*, on 27 April 1833. From time to time Dickens toyed with the accordion, and on his first visit to AMERICA, among the pieces he played to entertain his fellow passengers on the crossing, one, 'Home Sweet Home', was from this same opera (to Forster, 22–3 March 1842).

His daughter Mamie and his son Henry both reported that later in life he loved to hear Mamie sing ballads. He also attended many operas. He wrote to Forster excitedly of the 'prodigious' acting of Grisi, Mario, and Fornasari in Bellini's *Il Pirata* at Her Majesty's Theatre in the Haymarket (?13 December 1844).

During the 1860s a newly composed opera appealed to him strongly, Gounod's setting of Goethe's *Faust*. He saw it first in Paris and wrote to Forster that it was a 'very sad and noble rendering of that sad and noble story'.

As the opera approached the part of Marguerite's seduction, 'I couldn't bear it, and gave in completely' (19 February 1863). Next to *Faust* he was most moved by the revival in Paris of Gluck's *Orphée* which Berlioz prepared. He was impressed by the power of Pauline Viardot-Garcia's acting in the title role. He had already come to admire her in London as Fides in Meyerbeer's opera *Le Prophète*. He wrote to MACREADY that in *Orphée* hers was 'a most extraordinary performance—pathetic in the highest degree, and full of quite sublime acting'. After the performance Viardot's husband took Dickens backstage 'to her dressing-room. Nothing could have happened better as a genuine homage to the performance, for I was disfigured with crying' (to Forster, November 1862).

Dickens heard Arthur Sullivan's incidental music to *The Tempest* performed at the Crystal Palace concerts in Sydenham. He praised the young composer, just back from his musical studies at Leipzig, his enthusiasm increased and possibly aroused by the encomia heaped on Sullivan in the *Athenaeum* by his friend, the influential reviewer Henry Fothergill CHORLEY. In the summer of 1865 Dickens joined Chorley and Sullivan in Paris to hear Viardot again perform *Orphée*. Sullivan found Dickens at that time 'a delightful companion . . . the best of good company' (Henry Saxe Wyndham, *Arthur Seymour Sullivan (1842–1900)*, 1926, p. 78). In 1862 Dickens met and became friends with the violinist Joseph Joachim.

In *Household Words* and *All the Year Round* Dickens published several articles about music by authors such as Percy FITZGERALD, George HOGARTH, G. A. H. SALA, Richard Albert Smith, and John Hollingshead. Chorley's articles argued vehemently that instrumental music by Schumann and operas by Wagner were indications of cultural degeneracy ('Old, New, and No Music', *AYR* 22 October and 5 November 1864; 'Music About Music', *AYR* 9 and 16 March 1867; and 'Depths and Heights of Modern Opera', *AYR* 9 October 1869). About one of Chorley's blasts, Dickens wrote to his sub-editor WILLS that he had 'been down on it' because it was 'a little bit too personal', but that in general 'them's my sentiments too of The Music of the Future' (8 Oct. 1864).

One of Dickens's own articles, 'A Christmas Tree' (*HW* 21 December 1850), joins music and memory most characteristically, memorializing 'the images once associated with the sweet old Waits, the softened music in the night, ever unalterable! Encircled by the social thoughts of Christmas time, still let the benignant figure of my childhood stand unchanged!'                                    RTB

Bledsoe, Robert, 'Dickens and Opera', *Dickens Studies Annual*, 18 (1989).

Cupers, Jean-Louis, 'Approches musicales de Charles Dickens', in Raphaël Celis (ed.), *Littérature et Musique* (1982).

Ley, J. W. T., a series of articles on Dickens and popular songs, *Dickensian*, 26–7 (1930–1).

Lightwood, James T., *Dickens and Music* (1912).

Ruff, Lillian M., 'How Musical Was Charles Dickens?' *Dickensian*, 68 (1972).

**Mystery of Edwin Drood, The** Dickens's last novel, left tantalizingly incomplete at the time of his death. It has inspired a vast amount of speculation in search of an appropriate ending, and although some readers have considered the completed portion the tired work of a dying author, it is more often regarded as containing some of Dickens's very best writing (see MYSTERY OF EDWIN DROOD, SOLUTIONS TO).

### Inception and Composition

Dickens finished writing *Our Mutual Friend* in September 1865, and the next autumn he wrote to his friend James T. FIELDS to say that after his upcoming series of 42 PUBLIC READINGS he hoped in early summer 1867 to 'get to work upon a new story that I have in my mind' (16 October 1866). Other activities—notably his reading tour in AMERICA—intervened, however, and it was only after his health broke down in April 1869 and his doctors ordered him to abandon further reading tours that he started thinking seriously about writing a new novel. According to his readings manager George DOLBY, it was after his collapse that Dickens 'began to cast about for a subject for a new book' and except for his ill health might have travelled to AUSTRALIA in search of material (1885, pp. 417–18). FORSTER claims that it was mid-July 1869 that Dickens disclosed the 'first fancy for the tale', which was to trace the separate lives of a boy and girl 'going apart from one another, pledged to be

married' (11.2), but, as Margaret Cardwell points out, this same idea is recorded, 'perhaps several years earlier', in Dickens's *Book of Memoranda* (Clarendon Introduction, p. xiii; Kaplan 1981).

Dolby and Forster are agreed that Dickens was thinking hard about the novel later in the summer, and he compiled a list of trial titles on 20 August (Dolby 1885, p. 434; to Forster, 6 August 1869; Clarendon Edition, Appendix A). He was, according to Dolby, 'sorely puzzled' over the title, but by 27 September *The Mystery of Edwin Drood* had been determined upon, and a little 'christening party' held in celebration (Dolby 1885, p. 436).

On 18 October Dickens reported to MACREADY that he was in the 'preliminary agonies' which invariably attended the commencement of a new novel. The first number was complete a week later, and he read it 'with great spirit' to Forster on the 26th (12.1). Despite the setback of having to find a new ILLUSTRATOR to replace his son-in-law Charles COLLINS, who had to withdraw on account of ill health, he finished the second number by the end of the next month, only to learn 'to my horror' that the two numbers were twelve printed pages too short. To deal with this unaccustomed shortfall, just as he was preparing his farewell readings, he added a passage about Rosa's birthday party in chapter 3, moved chapter 5, 'Mr Durdles and a Friend', from the second number into the first, and wrote a new chapter, 'Birds in the Bush', for No. 2 (to Forster, 22 December 1869; Clarendon Introduction, pp. xxii–xxiii).

On 31 December he declined an engagement with J. H. Chamberlain, citing his concentration on writing as his 'virtuous cause'. He was pleased with his progress, reporting to Fields that Forster considered No. 2 'a *Clincher*' and that the next numbers were developing intriguingly. 'There is a curious interest steadily working up to No. 5, which requires a great deal of art and self-denial. I think also, apart from character and picturesqueness, that the young people are placed in a very novel situation. So I hope—at Nos. 5 and 6 the story will turn upon an interest suspended until the end' (14 January 1870).

But he was using up material faster than anticipated. Forster observes that he had misgivings lest he had introduced Datchery too soon (11.2), and Harry Stone notes that the number plans are 'atypical' in the number of times they indicate that an incident has been 'done already' (1987, p. 379). There is also the puzzle about the 'Sapsea Fragment', five manuscript sheets numbered 6 to 10, involving Mr Sapsea with characters who make no appearance in *Drood*. Forster, who discovered it among Dickens's papers and printed it in the *Life*, speculated that it was an attempt to pad out the book's materials 'to suspend the final development' (11.2). Other critics have suggested that it is more likely to be an early, rejected draft, or even a false start 'having no connection' with *Drood* (see Charles Forsyte, 'The Sapsea Fragment: Fragment of What?', *Dickensian*, 82, 1986). Nevertheless, Cardwell argues, the manuscript shows that Dickens structured the book 'deliberately', and the fact that he left it unfinished at the time of his death makes it 'perhaps not surprising that rumours as to his difficulties spread' (Clarendon Introduction, pp. xxv–xxvii).

As the writing progressed, however, he was overtaxing his strength. Against medical advice, he gave a farewell series of twelve readings (11 January–15 March), and he had an audience with Queen Victoria on 9 March. 'Between my readings, my book, my weekly journal', he confided to LEWES, 'I really am hard put to it occasionally' (26 February). Although working 'most perseveringly and ding-dong-doggedly', he told Charles KENT, he was 'making headway but slowly' (25 April 1970). A recurrence of symptoms which had afflicted him intermittently from the winter of 1865 left him crippled; what he called a 'neuralgic' condition left his foot 'a mere bag of pain' (to William Ralston, 16 May 1870). He worried that his youngest son, 'Plorn', was not 'taking to' Australia (to Alfred Tennyson Dickens, 20 May 1870; see CHILDREN OF DICKENS), and he was shocked by the deaths of two of his closest friends, Daniel MACLISE (25 April) and Mark LEMON (23 May). On 8 June he worked on the manuscript of *Drood*, completing the 6th number (although it turned out to be two pages short), which includes the passage about beauties of nature which 'penetrate into the Cathedral, subdue its earthy odour, and preach the Resurrection and the Life' (*MED* 23). That evening he suffered a stroke, and he died the next day without regaining consciousness.

**Contract, Text, and Publication History**

On 20 August 1869 Dickens wrote to Frederic Chapman of CHAPMAN AND HALL proposing that his new novel be published either in twelve monthly numbers or in weekly instalments in *All the Year Round*. Robert Patten suggests that the shorter length (all of Dickens's previous novels published in monthly parts had extended to twenty numbers) is not necessarily an indication of Dickens's ill health but a 'realistic' response to the changing nature of the PUBLISHING market (1978, p. 316; see SERIAL LITERATURE). Although the original contract no longer exists, it is known that Chapman agreed to pay Dickens £7,500 for 25,000 copies, with profits shared equally thereafter. As in the contract for *Our Mutual Friend*, there was a clause to compensate Chapman in the event of Dickens dying before the work was complete.

The manuscript (complete except for one folio containing the first five paragraphs of chapter 11) is in the FORSTER COLLECTION, along with a list of projected titles, chapter headings, the Sapsea fragment, the number plans, and the proofs for No. 5. A complete set of proofs, sent by Dickens to his illustrator, Luke FILDES, is in the Gimbel Collection of the Beinecke Library at Yale University (see COLLECTIONS OF DICKENS MATERIALS).

American rights became greatly confused when Dickens, forgetting that he had signed an agreement on 15 April 1867 naming TICKNOR AND FIELDS his 'only authorized representatives in America', accepted an offer of £2,000 from Harper's for advance sheets (quoted by Patten 1978, p. 317). When Fields reminded Dickens of the prior contract, Dickens had to back out of his agreement with Harper's (to Harper and Brothers, 13 November 1869). Matters did not rest there; in February Harold Ticknor proposed publishing instalments of *Drood* in America *before* its publication in Britain, and Dickens protested that he would thereby lose his English COPYRIGHT. Thereupon Harper's renewed their offer to publish the work. On 5 March Dickens assured them that were he free he would 'place myself in your hands', and on 14 May he wrote to Fields, Osgood, and Co. warning them that he had referred matters to his solicitor, to prevent prior publication in America (Clarendon Introduction, pp. xxx–xxxii; Patten 1978, pp. 317–19).

*The Mystery of Edwin Drood* was published in six monthly parts from April to September 1870, and in one volume on 31 August 1870. The Library Edition was published in 1873, and the Charles Dickens Edition in 1875 (see EDITIONS OVER WHICH DICKENS HAD CONTROL). Dickens saw only Nos. 1–3 through publication and had corrected the proofs for No. 4. Nos. 5 and 6 were altered after his death, restoring cuts made for reasons of space and dividing the final chapter of No. 5 in two, with the second half published as the first chapter of No. 6 (see Stone 1987, p. 379). Tauchnitz as usual published an English-language edition in Leipzig, and Dickens accepted £50 by giving permission for a translation into German (to Mrs F. Lehmann, 14 April 1870). The authoritative modern edition is the Clarendon Edition, edited by Margaret Cardwell (1972).

### Illustrations

For the illustrations to accompany *The Mystery of Edwin Drood* Dickens looked not to his long-time illustrator Hablot BROWNE nor to the artist who had executed the engravings for his previous work, Marcus STONE, but to his daughter Katey's husband Charles Collins. Dickens set him to work on the wrapper design first of all, and asked Frederick Chapman to send him copies of 'any of our old green covers that you may have by you'—that is, covers designed by Browne (24 September 1869). He insisted that Collins be paid the same rates as Stone (to Frederick Chapman, 29 October 1869), and considered the completed cover 'excellent' (to Forster, 22 December 1869), but the illness which was to lead to Collins's early death three years later prevented him from continuing, and on 28 November Dickens wrote to Chapman alerting him to the need of finding a replacement.

Cardwell copies a delightful letter from W. H. Chambers to Howard Duffield, dated 28 November 1927, describing what happened next: John Everett Millais, the PRE-RAPHAELITE painter, who was visiting Dickens at Gad's Hill at the time, was so impressed by an illustration which had appeared in the first issue of the *Graphic*, 'Houseless and Hungry' by Luke Fildes, that he 'rushed into Dickens' room waving the paper over his head exclaiming "I've got him"—"Got who" said Dickens. "A man to illustrate your Edwin Drood" ' (Clarendon Introduction, pp. xxi–xxii; Kitton 1899 gives a slightly varied version of the same anecdote, p. 206). Fildes offered Dickens trial drawings and warned the author that his skills lay more in grave than comic subjects. He was duly hired but, unhappy with the reproduction of his drawings (engraved by a new method, using photographic transfer), asked Dickens to employ an engraver with whom the artist had worked previously and Dickens graciously complied (to Frederic Chapman, 14 March 1870; Patten 1978, pp. 321–2; Cohen 1980, pp. 221–6). A month later Dickens, obviously pleased with Fildes's work, wrote to his long-time friend the artist W. P. FRITH to say that he had 'great hopes' of Fildes (16 April 1870).

Fildes quickly gained Dickens's admiration and friendship, and had been invited to visit him at Gad's Hill on the weekend of 11 June before death intervened (Cohen 1980, p. 225). Fildes had completed six illustrations before Dickens died, and drew six more to accompany what remained of the unpublished manuscript. The results are generally regarded as uneven.

### Sources and Context

A significant indication of factors which led Dickens to choose the title he did for *Drood* is contained in a letter he wrote around the time he was getting under way, to Robert Lytton, son of his old friend and fellow-novelist, Edward BULWER-LYTTON. Dickens had agreed to publish a work by young Lytton, *John Acland*, serially in *All the Year Round*, but urged him to alter his intended title (presumably 'The Murder of John Acland') to *The Disappearance of John Acland*, which was the title actually used. The latter, Dickens explained, 'will leave the reader in doubt whether he really *was* murdered, until the end' (2 September 1869). Although we have the testimony of Dickens's eldest son that Edwin Drood actually was murdered, the combination of title and unfinished state leave open the possibility, entertained by many readers, that he was only missing and presumed dead (Charles Dickens, Jr, introduction to the Macmillan edition of *Drood*, 1923).

The opening setting in an opium den derives in the first instance from visits Dickens paid to such places with James FIELDS, George Dolby, and a police escort, at around the time he was writing the first chapter and, in all probability, at earlier dates also. 'The opium smoking I have described', he wrote to Sir John Bowring (5 May 1870), 'I saw (exactly as I have described it, penny ink-bottle and all) down in Shadwell this last autumn. A couple of the Inspectors of Lodging-Houses knew the woman and took me to her as I was making a round with them . . .' (see Ray Dubberke, 'Dickens's Favourite Detective', *Dickensian*, 94, 1998). Somewhere behind the scene, with its clear implication of importance for later developments in the story, lurks also Thomas DE QUINCEY's *Confessions of an English Opium Eater* (1821), which Dickens knew well, and (more proximately) Wilkie COLLINS's *The Moonstone*, first published by Dickens in *All the Year Round* in 1868, in which the mystery revolves around opium-eating.

Jasper's powers over Edwin and Neville are evidently a form of MESMERISM, reflecting Dickens's keen interest in that subject, dating back to the 1840s when he closely followed the experiments of his friend Dr John Elliotson. In 1844 he himself attempted to cure the wife of Émile de la Rue of a nervous disorder by means of animal magnetism—an episode which still fascinated him 25 years later when he was writing *Drood*, as he explained at length in a letter to J. S. Le Fanu on 24 November 1869.

The Cloisterham setting plainly derives from Rochester, adjacent to Chatham, where Dickens spent the happiest days of his boyhood. The cathedral town atmosphere may owe something to the Barchester novels of Anthony TROLLOPE, but a more important influence is Victor Hugo's more sinister novel of 1831, *The Hunchback of Notre-Dame*. The character of Mr Crisparkle shows the influence of Charles Kingsley's (1819–75) championship of 'muscular Christianity', and that of Mr Honeythunder of John Bright's (1811–89) pugnacious politics.

More than any of Dickens's novels, *The Mystery of Edwin Drood* reflects England's role as the centre of a worldwide empire. The dark-skinned Landless twins come from the east, and Edwin's supercilious behaviour towards Neville betrays the worst sort of colonialist condescension. Edwin himself plans to go to Egypt, which was in English minds at the time as the gateway to the East, after the Suez Canal opened in 1869. Edgar Johnson suggests that the social themes of *Drood* deal specifically with 'a dark resentful conflict of East and West' (2.1124–5). Above all, in the most famous reading of the novel, Edmund WILSON proposes that the murder is carried out as a Thug ritual, as performed by members of a Hindu religious sect in India who worshipped Kali, the goddess of destruction. Jasper's black silk scarf, in this reading, is the murder weapon, and he is to be exposed because he was unaware of the gold ring in Edwin's pocket, which would not corrode in lime.

### Plot, Character, and Theme

John Jasper, the respectable choirmaster at Cloisterham Cathedral, wakes from a nightmare in an opium den in London. Back in Cloisterham, Edwin discusses his betrothal to Rosa, which was arranged when they were infants, with Jasper. The 'jackass' auctioneer Thomas Sapsea consults Jasper about his recently deceased wife's epitaph. The twins Neville and Helena Landless, introduced by the blustering philanthropist Luke Honeythunder, arrive from the East in Cloisterham, where Neville is placed under the tuition of Canon Crisparkle. Neville, having previously revealed his violent temper, quarrels with Edwin, and Jasper, pretending to break up the fight, gives them drugged wine. Jasper feigns to reveal fears for Edwin's safety to Crisparkle. Neville is attracted to Rosa but is advised by Crisparkle not to pursue his love. Edwin visits Rosa's guardian Hiram Grewgious in Staple Inn, where he is given Rosa's mother's ring. When Durdles guides Jasper round the Cathedral by night, Jasper drugs him and temporarily steals his keys.

Edwin and Rosa agree to break off their engagement. Neville prepares for a walking expedition. Edwin sees the opium woman, Princess Puffer, who warns him that the life of someone named Ned is in danger. After a violent storm Edwin disappears. Neville is apprehended, and Jasper collapses when told by Grewgious of the broken engagement. Crisparkle discovers Edwin's watch and shirt-pin in the weir. Jasper devotes himself to detecting Edwin's murderer. The mysterious Dick Datchery arrives in Cloisterham. Jasper declares his love to Rosa, who flees in terror to Grewgious and is given shelter by his neighbour, the naval officer Tartar. The schoolmistress Miss Twinkleton visits Rosa; together they lodge with Miss Billikin. Jasper visits the opium den again, and is followed back to Cloisterham by the opium woman. Collecting evidence, Datchery observes her spying on Jasper. Here the story breaks off, halfway through its intended length.

Forster, Charles Collins, Fildes, Charles Dickens Jr., and Kate Dickens Perugini all made statements about what they claimed to know of Dickens's intentions. According to Forster, the story 'was to be that of a murder of a nephew by an uncle; the originality of which was to consist in the review of the murderer's career by himself at the close, when its temptations were to be dwelt upon as if, not he the culprit, but some other man, were the tempted' (11.2). Collins observes that in the cover design Jasper, who leads the search for the missing Edwin, points to himself (letter of 4 May 1871, quoted by Steven Connor in Everyman edition of *Drood*, 1996, p. 283). Fildes reported that Dickens explained to him the importance of Jasper's scarf, which was to be the means of Edwin's death, and said that Dickens planned to take him to Maidstone gaol, in order that he might make a drawing 'better than CRUIKSHANK' of the felon in a condemned cell (reported by Thomas Hughes, *A Week's Tramp in Dickens-Land*, 1891, p. 140; also letter to *Times Literary Supplement*, 13 November 1905).

Dickens's eldest son, as mentioned above, affirmed that his father had been emphatic that Edwin was indeed dead. Of all the reported evidence the most significant is that of his daughter Katey, who insisted that Dickens aimed to present 'his strange insight into the tragic secrets of the human heart'. Quoting Forster's account, she declared that no reader 'will be able to detect any word or hint from my father that it was upon the Mystery alone that he relied for the interest and originality of his idea. The originality was to be shown, as he tells us, in what we may call the psychological description the murderer gives us of his temptations, temperament, and character, as if told by another' ('*Edwin Drood*, and the Last Days of Charles Dickens', *Pall Mall Magazine*, June 1906).

### Reception

When *Drood* commenced publication in April 1870, its initial sales of 50,000 copies quickly surpassed those for *Little Dorrit* at 38,000 and *Our Mutual Friend* at 40,000 (Patten 1979, p. 216). 'We have been doing wonders with No. 1 of Edwin Drood', Dickens wrote triumphantly to Fields; '*It has very, very far outstripped every one of its predecessors*' (18 April 1870). Initial reviews, responding to Dickens's first novel for the unprecedented gap of four and a half years, rose to the 'sense of occasion' and praised him as a writer 'who has had the privilege of delighting two generations' (*Athenaeum* 2 April 1870; quoted in Collins 1971, p. 542). Although some later reviews returned to the knee-jerk complaint of Dickens's 'declining powers', Forster voiced the majority opinion when he declared that *Drood* showed 'his imaginative power was at its best' and possessed 'something of the old lightness and buoyancy of animal spirits' (11.2; see Everyman edition, pp. 308–9).

Before long a veritable industry of mystery-solving arose, as readers attempted to guess how the story would have proceeded had Dickens lived. In the early 20th century there was a vogue for mock-trials of Jasper, most famously one in London in 1914 which lasted four and a half hours, ending only when George Bernard Shaw as jury foreman returned a verdict of 'Not Proven' without first consulting his fellow-jurors. For decades interest in the plot distracted attention from the book's themes, and it was left to Edmund Wilson to identify 'a new intensity' in Dickens's last book, in which, Wilson claims, 'every descriptive phrase is loaded with implication' (Wilson 1941, p. 82). As Steven Connor notes, for Wilson 'Dickens's manic-depressive instability is the key to his artistic greatness', with the result that *Drood* is 'the key to understanding Dickens's work as a whole' (Everyman edition, p. 310). Although critics such as Edgar Johnson have argued for social as well as psychological interest in *Drood*, Wilson's identification of a divided self as the centre of achievement in the novel has remained the dominant view. PVWS

Sanders (1982).
Wilson (1941).
Wright, James, 'Afterword to *The Mystery of Edwin Drood*' (1961); repr. in A. E. Dyson (ed.), *Dickens: Modern Judgements* (1968).

***Mystery of Edwin Drood, The*, solutions to.** Dickens's unfinished mystery has provided a Do-It-Yourself kit on which the imagination of would-be authors and solvers has been unleashed. Edwin could be alive, and hiding, ill, disguised, a sailor, or in Egypt. He may have been murdered by Jasper, or by others. Where did the murder take place, and was the victim drugged, strangled, thrown from a height? Durdles, Datchery, or Deputy could find the body in the Sapsea tomb, the crypt, a lime heap, or elsewhere. How and by whom is the murderer caught? He may then confess through drugs, hypnotism, repentance, or change of personality. It is probable that there are hidden relationships and motives. Jasper has been seen as Edwin's half-brother or an impostor, and his motive as pure evil, opium, lust, love, hatred, or greed. Princess Puffer may be his grandmother, mother, mother of a ruined girl, Rosa's relative, or a blackmailer. The Landless twins may also be relations, and Neville may die or be murdered, and Helena may impersonate Neville, his ghost, Datchery, Edwin, a Lascar, or a Chinese. Jasper's fits, the East, the ring, the Church, Crisparkle, Grewgious, Tartar, and the scene at the bottom of the cover that is not in Dickens's text, may each fit in many patterns. The permutations of these possibilities are endless, and this is their fascination.

Dickens had guarded his secret closely. He revealed only to FORSTER his 'very curious and new idea' for the murder of a nephew by an uncle, that a ring which survived the lime into which the body had been thrown would reveal the murderer, whose story would be elicited from him in the condemned cell 'as if told by another'; Rosa would marry Tartar, and Crisparkle would marry Helena Landless; less certainly, Neville Landless would be killed assisting Crisparkle and Tartar in unmasking and seizing Jasper. Forster's account (1874) was doubted, and it was the next century before the artist Luke FILDES disclosed that Dickens told him Jasper would strangle Drood with his scarf, and wanted an illustration of the condemned cell. So Victorian readers were free to use their imaginations. Speculation about the ending of *Drood* began immediately after Dickens's death, and has continued ever since. Solutions have taken two main forms: 'continuations', which are fictional completions, and argued cases, usually called 'solutions'.

Soon after his death three very different continuations were published in America, but all assumed that Edwin had survived. This was to be the main pattern of Victorian reaction: readers were reluctant to accept that the sympathetic eponymous hero could be murdered. In England 'Gillan Vase' [Elizabeth Newton] wrote a long, sentimental continuation as a love story in which Edwin finally marries Rosa, shrewdly using one of Jasper's fits to explain Edwin's escape (*A Great Mystery Solved*, 1878). Vase's Edwin was improbably disguised as Grewgious's new clerk. A solution by Richard Proctor then offered a more satisfying answer: Datchery is Edwin himself, trying to discover who had attacked him (*Watched by the Dead*, 1887). There was wide agreement that this solved the mystery. Jasper was usually considered a hypocritical villain, and some saw *Drood* as a religious and moral tale in which Jasper would ultimately repent.

Then in 1905, in *Clues to Dickens's Mystery of Edwin Drood*, John Cuming Walters published a solution maintaining that Edwin must have been murdered. It was not a new idea, but it seemed revolutionary, and aroused wide interest and support. It also changed the whole focus. With murder, *Drood* became a DETECTIVE story. To a generation fascinated by Sherlock Holmes, the detective was the main character, and the evidently disguised Datchery now became the centre of interest. Cuming Walters made a plausible case that he was Helena Landless, but there were other candidates: Bazzard, Grewgious, Neville Landless, Tartar, a new character, a private detective, even Dickens himself. This debate went on for years.

A fresh idea was that Jasper was a member of the sect of Thugs, who worshipped Kali, a Hindu goddess of destruction, and carried out ritual strangulations (Howard Duffield, 'John Jasper—Strangler', *American Bookman*, 70, 1930). This idea was taken up by Edmund WILSON in a seminal essay suggesting that in Jasper Dickens was fictionalizing his own divided self (1941). It marked the start of a trend to see *Drood* as a psychological study, as Dickens's daughter Kate Perugini believed, more a whydunit than a whodunit. So the focus now began to move onto Jasper. This was reinforced in the 1950s when critical interest in Dickens grew, and scholars increasingly saw

*Drood* as a Dickens *novel* with themes. The Eastern theme was used by Felix Aylmer for an original interpretation of Jasper as the *protector* of his half-brother Edwin from assassins in an Egyptian family feud (*The Drood Case*, 1965). Charles Forsyte's combined solution and continuation agreed with an Egyptian connection, while seeing the theme of duality permeating the novel, and in Jasper a dual personality whose fits mark his personality changes (1980). The religious theme has been taken up by John Thacker, for whom Jasper is a figure of evil, Antichrist in the cathedral (*Edwin Drood: Antichrist in the Cathedral*, 1990). The weight of modern opinion is that Jasper is in some sense a divided personality and that he murdered Edwin, a view reinforced by Dickens's working notes, which twice refer to 'murder'. However, the survival school has always retained support, and scholarly study of the theme of resurrection in Dickens's works has provided some critical justification.

Arguably the best pastiche of Dickens's style is a continuation by Leon Garfield (*The Mystery of Edwin Drood . . . Concluded*, 1980). There is also a trend to postmodernist fantasy, such as new scenarios in which well-known fictional detectives set out to solve the mystery—Carlo Fruttero and Lucentini France, *The Drood Case* (1981), who conclude that Wilkie COLLINS murdered Dickens, and Peter Rowland, *The Disappearance of Edwin Drood* (1991); or that Edwin is a rapist killed by Helena Landless (Benny Reece, *Edwin Drood Solved*, 1989).

Versions of *Drood* have appeared on the stage, in films, and television, but the requirements and limitations of these media inhibit adequate solutions of this literary mystery.

GP

Beer, J., '*Edwin Drood* and the Mystery of Apartness', *Dickens Studies Annual*, 13 (1984).
Connor, Stephen (ed.), Appendix C, *The Mystery of Edwin Drood*, Everyman edn. (1996).
Cox, Don Richard, *The Mystery of Edwin Drood: An Annotated Bibliography* (1998).

**myth.** See CLASSICAL MYTH AND LEGEND.

# N

**Newgate novels,** fiction published in the 1830s that dealt with criminals' lives. Many of the biographies were taken from *The Newgate Calendar*, sensationalistic accounts that often appeared at the time of the subject's execution. A four-volume compilation was published in 1824 and a six-volume *New Newgate Calendar* came out two years later. John GAY's *Beggar's Opera* (1728), Henry FIELDING's *Jonathan Wild* (1743), and William HOGARTH's series of didactic narrative prints, *Industry and Idleness* (1747), were often cited as precedents for their 19th-century successors. Edward BULWER-LYTTON published two novels portraying criminals in a sympathetic manner in the early 1830s; in 1834 Harrison AINSWORTH's *Rookwood*, which features a glamorous highwayman, took London by storm. John MACRONE published a fourth edition of the novel, illustrated by George CRUIKSHANK, at the same time that Richard BENTLEY was launching a new humour magazine, BENTLEY'S MISCELLANY, edited by Dickens and illustrated by Cruikshank. Into the columns of that magazine Dickens inserted *Oliver Twist*. The novel appeared complete in three volumes in November 1838, though it did not finish its magazine run until April 1839. However, in January 1839 it was displaced as the lead story by Harrison Ainsworth's pot-boiler about the young 18th-century thief and Newgate escape-artist, *Jack Sheppard*, also, of course, illustrated by Cruikshank.

That succession of wildly popular illustrated novels portraying criminals as victims of society, idealists, or captivating rogues provoked opposition from those who disliked their 'radicalish tendency'. William Makepeace THACKERAY offered in *Catherine* (1839–40) a 'cathartic' for the town's taste: 'it is not everybody who can take a scoundrel, and cause us to weep and whimper over him as though he were a very saint.' He and his fellow critics censured novels about 'dandy, poetical, rosewater thieves' on three grounds: the depictions of low life were shams, far from the sordid reality; the novels cultivated in their readers a debased taste in fiction; and by looking to a large public for support writers were turning literature into a trade. Further outcry greeted the many theatricalizations of *Jack Sheppard*; John FORSTER savaged 'the rank garbage stewed up' at the popular theatres (*Examiner*, 3 November 1839). The Lord Chamberlain banned one staging of Ainsworth's novel, and writers and publishers quit the field of rogue literature in favour of other stimulating topics, including INDUSTRIAL unrest and CHARTISM.

Critics did not always exclude Dickens from the company of 'gallows-school' novelists, a company from which Dickens emphatically and repeatedly tried to separate himself. 'I am by some jolter-headed enemies most unjustly and untruly charged with having written a book after Mr. Ainsworth's fashion', he told R. H. HORNE (?February 1840). But the publication of *Barnaby Rudge* in 1841, with its central episode of the rioters burning down the old Newgate prison during the anti-Popery riots of 1780, seemed to reinforce Dickens's long associations with the prison, going back to one of the papers he composed for the First Series of *Sketches by Boz*, 'A Visit to Newgate'. His ambivalent portrayal of the leaders, the Maypole ostler Hugh and the hangman Ned Dennis, distinguished this Newgate novel from those that had gone before. And in the Preface to the Third Edition of *Oliver Twist* (April 1841), Dickens further discriminated his fiction from Bulwer's and Ainsworth's. His 'few words of explanation' begin by declaring that 'a lesson of the purest good may . . . be drawn from the vilest evil'. He then defends Oliver as 'the principle of Good surviving through every adverse circumstance', and emphasizes how wretched and squalid are the lives and circumstances of the thieves. He instances the examples of Hogarth and many 18th-century novelists who also dimmed 'the false glitter' illuminating the 'unattractive and repulsive truth' of the debased lower classes, and he defends Nancy, whom Thackeray thought absurdly unreal, as 'TRUE': 'From the first introduction of that poor wretch, to her laying her bloody head upon the robber's breast, there is not one word exaggerated or overwrought.'  RLP

Hollingsworth, Keith, *The Newgate Novel, 1830–1847: Bulwer, Ainsworth, Dickens, and Thackeray* (1963).

**newspapers, periodicals, and the British press.** Dickens straddled the contemporary news-publishing world in the range of his periodical ventures, and yet it can also be said that he stood aloof amid the growth of the popular press that is the defining feature of the Victorian age. He was both a reporter and an editor; he wrote both for daily and weekly papers and monthly serials and magazines (see JOURNALIST, DICKENS AS). He wrote novels in the shape of periodicals, and most paradoxically, he was a popular writer but not a 'cheap' one in the Victorian sense. Yet at the end of his life he had brought the lower classes middle-class literature and made the middle classes readers of twopenny weeklies. He had given literature the journalistic immediacy of politics.

In 1812, the year of Dickens's birth, the country was in a state of crisis: Britain was at war with both France and the United States, and the Prime Minister was assassinated. Governmental censorship of news was severe, and yet there was an unprecedented demand for periodicals of all kinds. The 19th-century's enfranchisement of a new political CLASS is at the same time a history of how the literary market opened up to middle-class, and eventually after 1855 to lower-class, ownership of books and papers (see READERSHIP). The sales of SCOTT's and BYRON's poetry, and of the great quarterly reviews during this pre-REFORM time, showed that literature could be moved across publishers' transoms in record time. By the end of the Napoleonic wars in 1815, the decorous upper-class trade in literature had been joined by a new reading market. Francis JEFFREY, in 1812, noted that the number of readers in the middle classes was ten times the number of those in the upper classes, who had traditionally formed the most profitable market for literature. COBBETT's *Political Register*, begun in 1806, was taken notice of by the great *Edinburgh Review*, not so much for its literary merit as for the fact that Jeffrey deemed it the most influential of all journals—ten years later, its

circulation had risen to over 40,000 copies a week, the highest of any publication.

However, by conventional standards the most prominent papers at this time were the four upper-class dailies: the MORNING CHRONICLE (established 1769), the *Morning Post* (1772), the *Morning Herald* (1780), and *The* TIMES (1785). Their origins and ethos lay in party politics. The *Morning Chronicle*, famous for its parliamentary reporting, was Whig; the *Morning Post*, known for its coverage of the fashionable world, was court Tory. The *Morning Herald*, originally established in rivalry with the *Morning Post*, as a 'liberal' paper in support of the Prince of Wales, then became a Tory paper (still in support of the future George IV), until the early 1820s, when it became an admirer of Henry Brougham and supporter of the Whigs. *The Times* declared itself non-partisan, meaning that it usually supported the government of the day. By comparison to Cobbett, it is important to note, their sales ranged only from 2,000 to 5,000 copies nationally. The weeklies (BELL'S WEEKLY MAGAZINE, *John Bull*, and the *Observer*, for example), which were considered much more popular than the dailies, sold between 4,500 and 7,000 copies. At the grandest end of the political press, the quarterlies, the *Edinburgh Review* (1802) and the *Quarterly Review* (1809), at their height (1814–17) sold around 14,000 copies each and were considered best-sellers. Both had been established for political reasons. But while there is thus a general expansion of the press because of political excitement, Cobbett's sales of 40,000 —so unusual in the era of Dickens's childhood—suggest the existence of another market and another category alongside the traditional readers of news. This popular market and Cobbett's figures were not to be reached again until the 1850s. Dickens's popularity is not more extraordinary than Cobbett's, and until the Cheap Edition and *Household Words*, Dickens is the more expensive author. Nor did the government regularly attempt to prosecute Dickens for his radical views, as they did Cobbett.

The example of Cobbett brings to light the government's deliberate control of the press through taxation and the crucial question of price in determining who would read newspapers. In part, because of taxation designed to censor the press, the cost of a daily newspaper from Dickens's childhood (1815) until *Pickwick Papers* (1836), was sevenpence. The newspaper tax of a penny that was first instituted in 1712 had been repeatedly raised, until in 1815 it represented 60 per cent of the cost of a paper (fourpence out of sevenpence). It did not go back down again to a penny, the pre-1776 rate, until 1836. Duty on paper, also used to suppress mass circulation of the papers, was cut in half in 1837 (at the beginning of the century it had been threepence a pound); only in 1861 was the paper tax repealed altogether. Thus these 'taxes on knowledge' reached their zenith in the war years, fell somewhat in the 1830s, but were not abolished altogether until the 1860s. Dickens, like *The Times*, stood slightly aloof from the campaign in the 1850s to repeal the paper tax, arguing that the window tax was a hardship for a greater number of people.

All this meant that the daily newspaper was not something typically bought by an ordinary working person. There were coffeehouses and newspaper societies in which a few or more families shared the cost of a subscription. It was through the growth of reading rooms and coffee-houses during the Napoleonic wars that newspaper reading became an interest of people who were politically unenfranchised. News of national importance was only obtainable through the London papers circulated through the country—no daily papers were published outside London until 1855. Once a paper received a stamp its postage was paid indefinitely, and a paper might be mailed repeatedly to a series of readers throughout the country. The weekly Sunday papers were most commonly associated with the new involvement of lower-class readers in reading and thinking about politics. The growth of these liberal Sunday weeklies and high reading-room circulations caused the government to redouble its efforts at censorship. In fact, Raymond Williams says 'the most significant error' made in understanding the meaning of the 'popular' press in the 19th century is to identify it with the reading of *daily* papers (more applicable after the 1890s), whereas 'the real history' lies in the reading of the *Sunday* paper (*Communications*, 1962).

The definition of 'periodical' is complicated somewhat by the amount of publishing in 'numbers' that was done in the 19th century. Before *Pickwick Papers* started the possibility that *new* fiction could be obtained cheaply in monthly numbers, COPYRIGHT laws made most newly published books expensive to own (see SERIAL LITERATURE). Hence the appeal of circulating LIBRARIES. The books that middle-class readers might *own* would likely be classics issued in reprinted number series. The BIBLE, histories of the French Revolution, *Robinson Crusoe*, BUNYAN, the ARABIAN NIGHTS, Hume's *History of England*, and Richardson's *Pamela* were popular titles for republication in numbers, and Dickens has said that some of these were favourite titles of his childhood (see DEFOE; CARLYLE). This new mass market was cultivated by the publishers in monthly and quarterly magazines that had started up in the times of political excitement and partisanship. There was a growing appetite for *series*, and the publication of Byron's *Childe Harold* and Scott's Waverley novels at recurrent intervals was a feature in their being purchased and talked about. Contemporary observers noted that the number of readers in the lower classes had quadrupled.

During the 1820s an interest in news for political reasons among the working classes gave way to the appetite for SELF-HELP and improvement. There was a dip in optimism after the troops came home from war in 1815, and the post-war years, the years of Dickens's childhood near the navy dockyards of Chatham, were difficult economic times. The excitement of war and then, after 1815, the great domestic unrest caused by demobilized men continued right through to the passing of the REFORM Bill of 1832. Between 1800 and 1830 the number of newspaper stamps sold increased by 14 million, nearly doubling (to 30 million), while the population increased from 10 million to 16 million, even with the EMIGRATION of nearly 1 million. Virtually half the population was under 16 at this time, and after demobilization the crime rate rose. There was an attempt on the life of the Prince Regent in 1817, and not until 1818 was the act suspending Habeas Corpus repealed. Repression of the press perhaps reached its height with passage of the 'Six Acts' in 1819, after the 'Peterloo Massacre', when the army was called out to control a mass gathering near Manchester.

However, the press was cowed in the mid-1820s, not so much by governmental edicts as by the economic disasters of 1825–6. During the years Dickens was at school the publishing industry collapsed. The failure of Constable, Scott's publisher, in particular, meant that the initiative no longer rested with Edinburgh, and the centre shifted once more back to London: hence in the 1820s the fashionable novel craze that combined parliamentary politics and London drawing-room gossip. In the context of a renewed focus on Parliament, the plans of John Murray, Byron's publisher, to set up a new daily called *The Representative* were timely, but these were pre-empted by the crash of 1825–6. Publishers after that played it safe with reprints and encyclopaedic series of 'useful knowledge'. These series seem invariably to begin with a history of Napoleon or a life of Byron. Typically, the 1820s reprised the excitement of earlier years in the format of self-improvement textbooks.

In 1824 Constable put forward his ideas for *Constable's Miscellany*, a series of 3s 6d volumes of non-fiction to be published every three weeks. The crash of 1825–6 slowed down Constable's plans but the *Miscellany* eventually started to appear in 1827. Still, both the seriousness of the books offered and the price of 3s 6d remained too high for a mass market. Fiction reached its highest price, a rise in cost to the buyer that had been going on for 50 years (with the war lasting virtually half those years), since 1780. At the very same time, Brougham's SOCIETY FOR THE DIFFUSION OF USEFUL KNOWLEDGE began publication of the *Library of Useful Knowledge*, 32-page parts selling every two weeks at 6d, on topics of mechanical and scientific interest. These parts sold initially 22,000–28,000 copies: this is only just beginning to approach the volume of Cobbett's twopenny papers and is still not considered mass marketing. In 1829 the Society then began issuing the *Library of Entertaining Knowledge* in 2 shilling parts or 4s 6d a volume. Even in this case the emphasis seems to fall more on the knowledge than the entertainment. Also in 1829 appeared Murray's *Family Library* (history, biography, travel), Lardner's *Cabinet Library*, Oliver and Boyd's *Edinburgh Cabinet Library*, and Colburn and Bentley's *National Library*. The price per volume for each of these was 5 shillings, as yet more of a middle-class investment than a working-class possibility.

The first *cheap* periodical might be considered the twopenny weekly, the *Mirror of Literature, Amusement, and Instruction*, begun in 1822 by John Limbird, a sixteen-page miscellany consisting of reprints from other periodicals and books. Typically, it might contain biographical memoirs, descriptions of famous landmarks, chronologies of kings and queens, antiques, anecdotes, and extracts from new novels: for 24 years it ran in this format. Limbird also issued a series of reprinted English classics, including essays, poetry, and fiction, for only pennies per volume. Not until the 1850s did British publishers offer the public new fiction in serial form at the same price.

This was partly what made *Pickwick Papers* an innovation. Strictly speaking, its origins merely as copy-text to more valuable sporting illustrations did not place it in the category of fiction, and there was no notion of its adding up to a novel until some way through its publication as a periodical. At 1 shilling per month, it is priced neither like reprinted fiction (5 shillings per volume) nor Limbird's non-fiction compilations (twopence weekly). It is more useful to keep in mind the fact that, in the format of *Pickwick*'s original parts, the illustrations appear at the front with tissue paper covering them: thus they could be framed separately and represent most of the value of the shilling.

The economic crisis of 1826, combined with the sense of impending social revolution during the lead-up to the Reform Bill of 1832, meant that any investment in new literature was highly unlikely while politics occupied so many energies. However, newspaper reading rose again to wartime levels as people waited for some sort of apocalyptic reaction after the passage of Catholic Emancipation: the Duke of Wellington was forced to barricade his house, and the House of Lords threatened to defy a national uprising by their stand against Reform. Figures show that sales of the dailies came to a combined total of nearly 40,000 copies (7 morning papers = 28,000; 6 evening papers = 11,000). But the more telling statistic is the continued growth of the Sunday papers associated with radicalism, which sold 110,000 weekly. Finally, one could understand what was meant by 'public opinion':

Macaulay's remark, about the newspaper press sitting in the House public gallery being 'the fourth estate of the realm', was made in 1828. At the same time, Dickens himself was caught up in the parliamentary excitement that may be said to have dominated the national news at this time, when he became a shorthand reporter on the MIRROR OF PARLIAMENT, a rival to *Hansard*. When the Houses of Parliament were rebuilt after the fire of 1834 they contained, for the first time, a gallery exclusively for newspaper reporters. And when Dickens was hired by the *Morning Chronicle* (1834), it was because money was being poured into the paper as a vehicle for Whig propaganda; Dickens, as his letters indicate, spent much of his time on the road covering the speeches of Whig politicians such as Lord John RUSSELL.

Joel Wiener, in *Unstamped British Periodicals* (1970), has singled out the years 1830–6 as 'a watershed in the history of British journalism'. Because of the government's continuing prosecution of 800 publishers and newspaper vendors, the 'war of the unstamped press' arose: in the atmosphere of the July 1830 Revolution in France and pressure for reform in Britain, a campaign grew in which hundreds of periodicals were published without paying the stamp tax. Dickens again should be seen as standing aside from this. His reporting career for the *Morning Chronicle* may owe something to the widespread excitement of reform in the early 1830s, but the paper he wrote for was still part of the stamped press and cost sevenpence, far beyond the means of working-class people, and it was a Whig, not a radical, publication. He earned five guineas a week, with two more guineas for his sketches. On the other hand, Henry Hetherington, printer of the *Poor Man's Guardian*, a penny weekly, went to prison three times and was finally brought before the Exchequer, where the government decided not to define his paper as a newspaper rather than stir up public opinion with another court case. It was reported in *Hansard* that between 100,000 and 200,000 such papers were sold weekly (1834). The result was the reduction of the tax to one penny in 1836 and the renewed determination to eliminate it altogether.

This did not mean that 'cheap' literature had arrived. The lowering of the stamp tax to a penny per sheet was accompanied by conditions such as the posting of expensive bonds against libel. The reduction in the price of daily papers meant that their price was now fivepence instead of sixpence, still too dear to own. The trend of coffee-house reading continued: Arthur Aspinall (1949) says that London had 1,600–1,800 coffee-houses, each offering perhaps 43 daily papers, eleven weekly papers, 24 magazines, and four quarterlies. In fact, most coffee-houses carried only papers; a minority carried periodicals such as the magazines and quarterlies, and *Chambers's Journal* and the *Penny Magazine*.

The confluence of newspapers and literature in parts occurs in 1832, with the launching of these last two, *Chambers' Edinburgh Journal* and Charles KNIGHT's *Penny Magazine*, two 'family periodicals for the working classes'. Chambers included short stories, while Knight was publishing on behalf of the Society for the Diffusion of Useful Knowledge and was not allowed to include fiction in his weekly line-up of useful knowledge. The *Penny Magazine* had the advantage of being illustrated and is said to have reached a circulation of 200,000 at one point. Both differed from earlier cheap papers in being respectable: they were not GOTHIC, gossiping, coarsely comic, or SENSATIONALIST. For alongside the cheap diffusion of knowledge, the other feature that sold the new threepenny weekly papers of the late 1830s and early 1840s was an increase in 'criminal intelligence' items. If politics had been the *raison d'être* of the late-18th-century daily, crime and disaster were the selling features of the new cheap journalism. THACKERAY, in his article 'Half a Crown's Worth of Cheap Knowledge' (*Fraser's Magazine*, 1838), also noted with disgust the traffic in pornographic and low-life journalism, which had increased after 1836.

Weekly papers were the ones that families typically might buy. During the early 1840s, the *Weekly Dispatch* appears to have been the most popular (55,000). Other papers, such as the *Sunday Times* and BELL'S *LIFE IN LONDON* (both established in the early 1820s) sold around 20,000 copies each. This was also the area of greatest growth, especially as the use of illustrations became the most notable feature. By 1850 the best-selling papers were the *Illustrated London News* (established 1842), *News of the World* (1843), *Lloyd's Weekly Newspaper* (1842), and *Weekly Times* (1847).

The daily papers also achieved circulation in six figures, after the complete repeal of the stamp tax in 1855. The end of the newspaper tax and finally the repeal of the paper tax in 1861, plus introduction of the Hoe rotary press in the mid-1850s, set up a great increase in periodical publishing generally. After 1855 Manchester, Sheffield, and Liverpool got their first daily papers. *The Times* may have adopted steam-printing in 1814, but this innovation was not widely taken up till the 1840s, and it was the rotary press that in fact made the increase in numbers possible. Not until government duties were eliminated could such innovations actually improve profitability. It is important to distinguish between the growth of the press associated with the expansion of public opinion during the radical times of the early 19th century of Dickens's childhood ('the pauper press') and the full capitalization of the popular press achieved after the 1840s with the technological innovations of steam and steel in printing machinery and railways. The use of libel prosecution by the government to control the press declined notably during Dickens's lifetime even as the means of production and distribution grew.

Paradoxically, again, economic factors exerted more of a controlling influence on the movement of the press. Whereas in the period 1790–1820 it might have cost £2,000–5,000 to establish a paper, by the 1830s it would have cost ten times that. Where in the 1780s daily papers might have one to two parliamentary reporters and no foreign reporters (foreign news was often excerpted from the Dutch papers that came in), by 1850 a newspaper reader would expect twelve to sixteen parliamentary reporters, six law reporters, and a foreign correspondent in every European capital. W. H. Russell's reporting of the CRIMEAN WAR for *The Times* created an unprecedented interest in foreign and investigative reporting. Any paper established in the 1850s had to compete with *The Times*; it was estimated that £100,000 was needed in 1846 to fund the DAILY NEWS. *The Times* continued to consolidate its dominant status, so that by 1855 TROLLOPE could satirize its editorial offices in *The Warden* as 'Mount Olympus'.

The weekly papers begun in the radical atmosphere of the early 1820s defined a 'popular' press—this Romantic radicalism was transformed into Gladstonian liberalism later in the century. Popular weeklies included, in descending respectability, the *Observer*, the *Sunday Times*, *News of the World*, the *Weekly Times*, the *Weekly Dispatch*, *Lloyd's Weekly Newspaper*, and *Reynolds' Weekly Newspaper*. The price of a newspaper was widely reduced to as little as a penny, by the *Daily Telegraph*, the *Standard*, the *Daily News*, the *Pall Mall Gazette*, the *St James's Gazette*, and the *Morning Post*. *The Times*'s sales fluctuated around 50,000–60,000, but those of the *Daily News* and the *Daily Telegraph* went up to over 150,000 by 1870, the year of Dickens's death. However, Altick (1957) points out that these papers still largely catered to middle-class readers with an interest in politics. The mass daily actually bought by the working class, and inevitably featuring more crime and sporting news, does not really arrive until 1896 with the *Daily Mail*. With the arrival of illustrations, it was entertainment not politics that sold papers in quantity.

Dickens is often vaguely associated with some notion of cheap publishing, but in fact his readership should probably be considered middle class (even if his celebrity, especially after the PUBLIC READING tours, was broader). The trend of serially published fiction begun with *Pickwick Papers* in 1836 was not in the same category as the fiction published a few years later in cheap newspapers. Nor was BENTLEY'S MISCELLANY, his first editorial venture, aimed at the working classes—it was essentially a frivolous publication aimed at a leisured, educated readership. Dickens, in taking up the editorship of *Bentley's*, is still in the realm of expensive Regency literature: the magazine sold for 2s 6d a month, considered 'moderate' in a market where rivals charged 3s 6d. By comparison, an outstanding lower-class publication, *Chambers's Journal*, sold for a fraction of that cost and printed improving moral tales. Papers such as the *Family Herald*, *London Journal*, and *Reynolds' Miscellany* retained higher circulation figures with their melodramatic fiction. All these comprise the lower end of the market. During his stint as editor of *Bentley's Miscellany* (1837–9), Dickens published Gothic tales by authors who had made their

name in the 1820s. *Oliver Twist* itself had unexpectedly progressed from being a satire on
the new POOR LAW to a MELODRAMA of crime
in the LONDON SLUMS—this was accentuated
by the coincidence of AINSWORTH's *Jack
Sheppard* serial happening to follow *Oliver* in
the *Miscellany*. Thus, from the genial comic
humour of *Pickwick Papers*, Dickens was
launched on to another form of popular success, with the low-life criminal adventures of
Fagin's gang and Nancy. The success of both
*Oliver Twist* and *Jack Sheppard* retrospectively
made Dickens a sensationalist author, but still
a middle-class one.

After Dickens resigned from *Bentley's
Miscellany* in 1839 he still very much wanted
to be involved in the periodical market; however, he wanted *not* to write as much as he had
to for *Pickwick*, *Nickleby*, and *Oliver*, *and* he
wanted to have more control than *Bentley's*
had given him. MASTER HUMPHREY'S CLOCK
(1840–1), a threepenny weekly, was Dickens's
next venture as a periodical 'editor' rather
than 'author'. He had fond notions of recap-
turing the affectionate place in readers' hearts
that *Pickwick* and *Nickleby* (the CHAPMAN
AND HALL periodicals) had given him and of
freeing himself of the 'smart' market of *Bentley's* and the sensationalist one of *Oliver*. In
outlining his ideas for *Master Humphrey's
Clock* he makes reference to Isaac Bickerstaff
and the *Spectator* (see ESSAYS AND ESSAYISTS
BEFORE DICKENS). Contemporary readers
were quick to pick up on the resemblances
also to Washington IRVING's *Sketch-Book*
(published in Britain in 1820), and indeed Irving was initially invited to contribute. But it
turned out that readers did not want short
whimsical tales from Dickens. In his own
conscious plans for serials Dickens is oddly
out of touch with his public, as can be seen
again later, when he proposed to call the projected *All the Year Round* 'Household Harmony'—this after the public scandal of his
separation in 1858—and FORSTER actually
had to explain to him why such a title would
not work. It could be argued that the notion
of *Master's Humphrey's Clock* as a new *Spectator* was seriously out of date, however charmingly Dickens might reminisce about his
childhood reading of the last century's classics. In any case, he ended up writing *The Old
Curiosity Shop* (which sold about 100,000
monthly) to save the weekly *Clock*, which was

eventually abandoned after *Barnaby Rudge*.
Washington-Irving-like imitations may have
been a hit in the refined market of the early
1820s, but they did not work in the increasing
momentum of the 1840s market.

Dickens's brush with the serious capitalism
of this market came in 1845–6, when he was
co-opted by a consortium of railway speculators for the editorship of the *Daily News*—
there could have been nothing further from
Washington-Irving sentimentalism. Despite
his newspaper background, he proved surprisingly unequal to the pressures of producing a modern paper with its express foreign
news and heavy advertising. Nor could he
keep up with the political news.

Still, the notion of editing a periodical did
not leave Dickens (it is worth noting that he
never gave up the desire to be an editor), and
he next spoke of plans for a new periodical
apart from his serials to Forster in 1849.
Incredibly, even then, he still clung to a
*Spectator*-like plan of a 'Shadow' who would
perambulate the streets of London silently
observing. This time Forster was emphatic
that such whimsicality would not go and insisted on the journal's being a real miscellany
without an excess of SENTIMENTAL imagination (Forster 6.4). Fortunately, Forster appears to have prevailed, even while all that was
valuable about the Dickensian 'man of feeling' figure was still used to effect. It could be
argued that the figure of the 'UNCOMMERCIAL
TRAVELLER' in *All the Year Round* during the
1860s is ultimately Dickens's most successful
rendition of this sentimental ideal.

Dickens wrote that *Household Words*
would focus on 'all social evils, and all home
affections' (to Mrs Howitt, 22 February 1850).
Among the social evils treated early on was
sanitary reform, and Philip Collins points out
that the magazine's discussion of contemporary affairs brought it serious attention (see
PUBLIC HEALTH). At the same time, Dickens
continually urged *imagination* as a desirable
feature of all contributions and refused to
allow the magazine to succumb to the dour
blight of *useful* knowledge—in this way, he
distinguished *Household Words* from the
tediously moral stream of working-class literature. Equally important was his refusal to
fall into the other trap of appealing to the
lower classes through sensationalist stories,
and he also emphasized *wholesomeness*

('home affections') in its offerings. In this respect his periodical more resembled *Chambers's Journal*, which outlasted its useful knowledge competitor, Knight's *Penny Magazine*.

The next time Dickens published any fiction in a weekly magazine rather than in his characteristic green parts, it was *Hard Times* (1854), in *Household Words*, which began in 1850 at a circulation of 100,000 and sold a steady 50,000 copies weekly throughout the decade. Its Christmas numbers, which substituted for the best-selling Christmas books of the 1840s, annually pushed the magazine's sales up to 250,000. *Household Words* was the price of a cheap weekly (twopence), but the sophistication of its fiction and political outlook were middle class. The contributions of Dickens and writers such as Mrs GASKELL and Henry MORLEY compelled the attention of middle-class readers to a cheap paper, and its usual circulation figures indicate that, despite its price, it appealed to a more exclusive market from that of the sensationalist threepenny papers.

The market the middle-class *Household Words* readers aspired to was that of the monthly magazine, which cost two shillings or half-a-crown. For that price one could buy, not an array of 'cheap knowledge' but one issue of say, the *Fortnightly*, the *Contemporary*, or the *Nineteenth Century*. The market that emerged, between the twopenny or threepenny 'family' papers with their escapist romances of high life and melodrama and the serious intellectual monthly, turned out to be the new shilling monthly, a feature of the early 1860s. Particularly outstanding was the *Cornhill*, established by Smith, Elder in 1859 and edited by Thackeray until 1862; it first sold 120,000 copies. Thackeray's last novels were serialized there, and other contributors included Elizabeth Barrett Browning, Robert BROWNING, and Trollope (*Framley Parsonage*). *Macmillan's Magazine* also started at this time, and the shilling monthly becomes more of a publisher's vehicle for advertising a stable of authors rather than the early-19th-century magazine of a literary club recalled in *Pickwick Papers* and *Master Humphrey's Clock*. The Regency reader would have had to come from a higher rung of fashionability to afford a monthly costing 2s 6d or 3s 6d and would have been happy with a few short Gothic tales

as a minor attraction: for a shilling the middle-class Victorian reader expected a continuing serial from a reliable author of known family values at the front of the magazine and more fiction from minor authors besides.

Less weighty imitators also sprang up, such as *Tinsley's Magazine* (1867), *Temple Bar* (1860), *St James's* (1861), and *Belgravia* (1866). Circulation of the shilling magazines typically settled down to well below 100,000, whereas papers costing twopence or threepence, such as the *Family Herald*, *London Journal*, *Cassell's Family Paper*, and *Reynolds' Miscellany*, variously sold between 200,000 and 450,000 copies. *All the Year Round*, the successor that Dickens set up to *Household Words* after he fell out with BRADBURY AND EVANS, began in 1859 with a circulation of 120,000 and grew to 300,000. This time he made sure that the magazine always opened with a serial by a well-known writer—the first was *A Tale of Two Cities*, followed by Wilkie COLLINS's *The Woman in White*—and that the name of the writer always appeared in the advertising.

In fact, in all his periodical undertakings, whether by design or not, it should be emphasized that Dickens was in a class by himself. In speaking of Dickens's writing for a weekly market where *Great Expectations* was serialized in *All the Year Round*, E. S. Dallas points out that Dickens has once again been part of an innovation like the one that *Pickwick Papers* had represented in the context of the fiction market 25 years earlier. Formerly, the weekly selling at a penny or three-halfpennies had always been associated with 'low' writing, where 'the favourite subjects were stories from high life, in which the vices of an aristocracy were portrayed, now with withering sarcasm, and now with fascinating allurements' and where 'Lust was the *alpha* and murder the *omega*' (*The Times*, 17 October 1861). Previous attempts to introduce better writing in these periodicals had failed. From the outset, Dickens's periodical had addressed a higher class of reader, giving them the connected fiction otherwise associated with monthly publication. In *Household Words*, and later *All the Year Round*, he had serialized not only his own *Hard Times*, *A Tale of Two Cities*, and *Great Expectations*, but also such classics as Mrs Gaskell's *Cranford* and *North and South* and Wilkie Collins's *Woman in White* and *The Moonstone*. Thus he straddled both the middle-class (one shilling) and the lower-class (twopenny) markets, combining in all his serials, monthly and weekly, both editorial comment and entertainment, politics and literature. He sold a middle-class product at a 'cheap' price and proved that weekly publication did not have to appeal to a degraded taste in order to sell: in this way, at the end of his career, he had finally become a *popular* writer.                                    KC

Altick (1957).
Aspinall, Arthur, *Politics and the Press 1780– 1850* (1949).
Boyce, George, *et al., Newspaper History* (1978).
Fox Bourne, H. R., *English Newspapers* (1966).
Kellett, E. E., 'The Press', in G. M. Young (ed.), *Early Victorian England, 1830–1865* (1934).
Vann, J. Don, and Van Arsdel, Rosemary T., *Victorian Periodicals: A Guide to Research* (1978; 1989).

**Newsvendors Benevolent Association.** As a journalist himself, Dickens readily supported an organization founded to provide pensions and financial assistance to newsmen in need. In November 1849 he gave the first of a number of outspoken addresses at its annual dinners. In 1852 he referred in barely disguised terms to the tightly muzzled press of France under Louis Napoleon. He was elected President in 1855, when he spoke of parliamentary inefficiency and family influence. He presided again in May 1862, and one of the last speeches he ever made was to this Association on 5 April 1870.                                ASW

***Nicholas Nickleby*** Dickens's third novel, published 1838–9, best known for its attack on Yorkshire schools and for its comic depiction of a travelling theatre company. Its fame achieved a new lease of life in the 1980s when a two-part, nine-hour theatrical adaptation played to turn-away audiences in Britain and America.

**Inception and Composition**
In November 1837 *Pickwick* was completed, and although it was to be another year before Dickens finished writing *Oliver Twist*, in January 1838 he began work on a new novel. On the 30th he travelled with his illustrator, Hablot BROWNE, to Yorkshire, in order to gather information about the notorious boarding schools there, and on ?21 February he announced to FORSTER that 'the first chap-

ter of Nicholas is done'. The next day he wrote to his publishers assuring them that he intended to 'begin in earnest tomorrow night, so you can begin to print as soon as you like. The sooner you begin, the faster I shall get on.' SERIAL publication began on 31 March.

Characteristically, he was soon 'behind-hand', completing each number only 'a day or two before its publication' (to Carey, Lea and Blanchard, 18 July 1838). *Nickleby* 'has scarcely advanced a jot', he lamented (to Forster, ? March 1838). *Nickleby* 'does *not* go on well' (to Forster, ?8 March 1838). 'I couldn't write a line 'till three o'clock, and have 5 slips yet to finish, and don't know what to put in them for I have reached the point I meant to leave off with' (to Forster, ?15 April 1838). Nevertheless, no instalment missed its publication date.

In early September he went on holiday to the Isle of Wight, passing through Portsmouth on the way, and in No. 7, dated 1 October, Dickens sent Nicholas to Portsmouth, scene of his adventures with the theatre company of Vincent Crummles (Forster 1.1; James G. Ollé, 'Where Crummles Played', *Dickensian*, 47, 1951). The absence of any sign of actors on Phiz's cover design for *Nickleby* suggests that Dickens had not conceived of this episode when the novel began. From 29 October to 7 November Dickens toured the Midlands with Browne, stopping briefly in Manchester, where he met Daniel and William Grant, originals of the Cheeryble brothers (Pilgrim 1.471n.).

On 19 November the first DRAMATIZATION of *Nickleby*, adapted by Edward STIRLING and produced by Frederick YATES, opened at the Adelphi Theatre and ran for over a hundred performances. Dickens, who went to see it on the 21st, considered it 'admirably done in every respect' (to Yates, ?29 November 1838), but he was distinctly annoyed by an adaptation in May 1839 by William MONCRIEFF, in which Smike was revealed to be Ralph's son— a disclosure Dickens had not yet made in the novel's serial run. He gave vent to his indignation in chapter 48, in which Nicholas derides hack dramatists—an attack to which Moncrieff retorted at length (see S. J. Adair Fitz-Gerald, *Dickens and the Drama*, 1910, pp. 121–6).

In December Dickens received a letter from the 5-year-old William Hughes (1833– 1907, younger brother of the author of *Tom*

*Brown's Schooldays*), advising him to punish Squeers, and wrote one of his most charming letters in reply, praising Master Hughes's drawing of Fanny ('very like . . . it will make her very cross when she sees it, and what I say is I hope it may'), and reporting that he had given Squeers 'one cut on the neck and two on the head, at which he appeared much surprised and began to cry' (12 December 1838).

On 30 April 1839 Dickens rented a cottage in Petersham for four months, and in June went to the races at Hampton, scene of the quarrel between Mulberry Hawk and Lord Frederick in the July number of *Nickleby* (Pilgrim 1.640; to Forster, 7 June 1839). On 20 September he finished writing the novel (Pilgrim 1.642), and the following day wrote to MACREADY asking permission to dedicate it to him. On 5 October a dinner to celebrate the completion of *Nickleby* was held at the Albion in Aldersgate Street, at which CHAPMAN AND HALL presented MACLISE'S PORTRAIT of Dickens to him. (See also COMPOSITION, DICKENS'S METHODS.)

## Contracts, Text, and Publication History

In the summer of 1837 Chapman and Hall, publishers of *Pickwick*, were eager to secure Dickens's services to write a successor to that triumphant venture. Having signed an agreement with Richard BENTLEY the previous summer to undertake 'no other literary production' until he had delivered one novel to that publisher and had given him the option on a second, Dickens wrested a new agreement on 22 September 1838 from Bentley, exempting *Pickwick* and *Nickleby*, and on 18 November signed a contract with Chapman and Hall to write a work 'of similar character and of the same extent and contents in point of quantity' as *Pickwick* (Pilgrim 1.648–9, 658–62, 666–74). Dickens was to receive £150 per month, less than two years after he had found the offer of £14 per month to write *Pickwick* 'too tempting to resist' (to Catherine Hogarth, 10 February 1836). COPYRIGHT was to revert wholly to Dickens after five years.

*The Life and Adventures of Nicholas Nickleby, Containing a Faithful Account of the Fortunes, Misfortunes, Uprisings, Downfallings and Complete Career of the Nickleby Family, edited by 'Boz'* was published by Chapman and Hall in twenty monthly parts (as nineteen) between 31 March 1838 and 30 Septem-

ber 1839. The first volume publication, in October 1839, had the simpler title of *The Life and Adventures of Nicholas Nickleby*, and Dickens was named as author. It had a Preface and the dedication to Macready. Dickens made minor revisions and wrote a new Preface for the Cheap Edition of 1848. For the Charles Dickens Edition of 1867 he made slight alterations to the 1848 Preface, added running headlines, and systematically altered most references to the foolish young nobleman from 'Lord Verisopht' to 'Lord Frederick' (see EDITIONS).

Carey, Lea and Blanchard, Philadelphia publishers, enquired about making an agreement to receive advance proofs for American publication, but Dickens had to decline on the grounds that he generally completed each number only a day or two before its London publication (18 July 1838). It was published in 1839 in Paris by Galignani and in New York by Colyer, and in 1843 in Leipzig by Tauchnitz. After Dickens's death it has been published many times, but there has been no textually definitive edition.

*Nickleby* marks the first recorded instance of Dickens's attempt to preserve his manuscript (to Hicks, ?20 September 1838), but only fragments survive. The largest, over 100 pages (chapters 9, 16, 17, and 20), is in the Rosenbach Foundation in Philadelphia; smaller bits are scattered elsewhere. (See also COLLECTIONS OF DICKENS MATERIALS.)

## Illustrations

Hablot Browne collaborated with Dickens on *Nickleby*, supplying the cover wrapper and two illustrations per number. William Finden made an engraving for the frontispiece, of Daniel Maclise's oil painting of Dickens, known as the 'Nickleby portrait'. Under the pseudonym of 'Peter Palette' the artist Thomas Onwhyn produced 40 engravings (ten portraits and 30 scenes) issued separately as 'extra illustrations', starting with No. 4 of Dickens's novel. Another series of 24 engravings by Kenny MEADOWS was published by Robert Tyas in 1839 as *Heads from Nicholas Nickleby drawn by Miss La Creevy*. For the Cheap Edition a new frontispiece, depicting the Yorkshire school, was designed by Thomas Webster (to Webster, 26 November 1847), and for the same edition three portraits by Frank STONE, of 'Tilda, Kate, and

Madeline, were engraved by Edward Finden and inserted as extra plates (Pilgrim 5.222n.). (See also ILLUSTRATORS AND BOOK ILLUSTRATION.)

## Sources and Context

Of all Dickens's novels, *Nicholas Nickleby* most closely follows the 'life and adventures' pattern of FIELDING, SMOLLETT, and other 18th-century NOVELISTS whose works he had loved from childhood, in which a young hero encounters a variety of colourful characters and meets with diverse experiences in the course of his travels. Nicholas's education from his experiences, although not developed with the sophistication later seen in *David Copperfield* and *Great Expectations*, gives the novel affinities in particular with the BILDUNGSROMAN. Some critics have sought to identify more complex organization in *Nickleby*, but its most obvious source of unity is the centrality of Nicholas to the novel's random adventures.

Cheap boarding schools in Yorkshire dated from the 18th century, and their emphasis on 'no holidays' made them a convenient place to dispose of unwanted children, as Snawley discusses with Squeers (*NN* 4). Dickens claimed in the 1848 Preface to have known about them from childhood, and on his fact-finding trip with Browne in January 1838 he called on William Shaw, headmaster of Bowes Academy in Greta Bridge, who had been prosecuted in 1823 for negligence when two boys went blind. Squeers, whose blandishments for Dotheboys Hall closely parody actual advertisements, was modelled on Shaw, and Dickens said that a grave-marker he saw in the churchyard near the school 'put Smike into my head' (to Mrs S. C. Hall, 29 December 1838). A number of details about Nicholas's journey to Dotheboys Hall—the bitter weather, the praise for the inn at Grantham, the letter rebuking a boy for refusing to eat meat, the lady's maid watching for an oncoming coach—were developed from observations Dickens recorded of his own coach trip to Yorkshire (to Catherine Dickens, 1 February 1838). John Browdie was based on a Yorkshireman who warned Dickens to have nothing to do with Shaw (1848 Preface).

The episode depicting the theatrical company of Vincent Crummles draws on Dickens's lifelong fascination with the THEATRE and is widely thought to be modelled in particular on the pompous manager T. D. Davenport (1792–1851), whose chief claim to fame was his promotion of the juvenile career of his daughter Jean (1829–1903) as an INFANT PHENOMENON. The novel's MELODRAMATIC incidents, set-piece scenes, heightened rhetoric, and typecast characters have led a number of critics, most notably Michael Slater in his Introduction to the 1978 Penguin edition of the novel, to identify theatricality as the 'living heart' of *Nickleby* (p. 15).

The bankruptcy of Nicholas's father and the early episode concerning the United Metropolitan Improved Hot Muffin and Crumpet Baking and Punctual Delivery Company are Dickens's response to the commercial crisis of the 1820s, in which speculation in joint-stock companies led to the collapse of banks and the ruin of thousands of small investors (see MONEY AND FINANCE). The satirical portrait of the novel's aristocrats and of Mrs Wititterly's literary tastes in particular, parodies the SILVER FORK NOVEL, formulaic tales of fashionable life, a popular form of the 1820s and 1830s. More generally, CLASS figures as a central concern throughout the novel, reflecting and commenting on contemporary uncertainties of social position which resulted from the tension between the new wealth of the emerging middle classes and the continuing political and social power of the aristocracy. Noggs is a failed gentleman and Nicholas the son of a failed gentleman, whereas Ralph owes his status to wealth rather than gentility. The Kenwigses are obsessed with their precarious respectability; Hawk makes his living as a leech on a foolish aristocrat.

The earnest young hero, determined to make his way, sensitive to slights, and 'lion-hearted' (as Crummles calls him) in his chivalric readiness to defend moral justice, owes more than a little to the character of Dickens himself, a parallel reinforced by the frontispiece depicting the young author with eager look and piercing eyes. Dickens's mother, Elizabeth DICKENS, the original of the comically illogical Mrs Nickleby, apparently did not recognize the likeness, asking him 'if I really believed there ever was such a woman' (to Forster, 27 September 1842; see CHARACTERS—ORIGINALS).

# Nicholas Nickleby

## Plot, Character, and Theme

Upon the death of his father, the penniless young hero, Nicholas Nickleby, throws himself, his mother, and sister upon the mercies of his wealthy uncle. Resenting the imposition, the mercenary Ralph sends Nicholas far off to Yorkshire as an assistant to the rascally schoolmaster Squeers, and places Kate in arduous and socially degrading millinery work with Madame Mantalini. Nicholas, embarrassed to find Squeers's acerbic daughter flirting with him and appalled by the ignorance and cruelty at Dotheboys Hall, thrashes Squeers and runs off with Smike, a pupil pathetically retarded by Squeers's bullying (see SENTIMENT).

Returning to London, Nicholas goes to Ralph's clerk, Newman Noggs, who finds him employment as tutor to the Kenwigs children. Kate, tormented by the foolish attentions of the spendthrift dandy Mantalini and by the threatening behaviour of the gambler and roué Sir Mulberry Hawk, leaves the ladies' millinery to serve as companion to the pretentious Mrs Wititterly. Nicholas and Smike walk to Portsmouth, where they are hired by the grandiloquent theatrical manager Vincent Crummles. Nicholas immediately becomes a star of the stage, and much fancied by the leading lady, Miss Snevellicci. The Kenwigses' uncle, the dour water-rate collector Mr Lillyvick, follows the actress Miss Petowker to Portsmouth and marries her, to the Kenwigses' consternation.

Hawk continues to pursue Kate, while her uncle refuses protection and her mother is flattered by the attentions. Warned of Kate's danger by Noggs, Nicholas returns once more to London where he overhears Hawk jesting about Kate and assaults him. Nicholas finds employment with benevolent merchants, the Cheeryble brothers. Smike is abducted by Squeers, then released by the genial Yorkshireman John Browdie, visiting London on his honeymoon with Fanny's friend 'Tilda Price. Nicholas falls in love with Madeline Bray, whom the miser Arthur Gride is conspiring with Ralph to marry. A lunatic makes love to Mrs Nickleby by throwing vegetables over the wall and climbing down the chimney of her house.

Hawk quarrels with Lord Frederick, who is killed in the ensuing duel, forcing Hawk to flee. The plot against Madeline is frustrated by her father's death, and Nicholas carries he off. Ralph hires Squeers to recover incrimir ating papers from Gride's servant Peg Slide skew, but is intercepted by Noggs and th Cheerybles' nephew Frank. Smike dies, cor fessing that he loves Kate; it is revealed that h is Ralph's son. Ralph commits suicide; afte scruples are overcome, Kate marries Fran Nicholas marries Madeline, and Dotheboy Hall is broken up.

## Reception

In an attempt to thwart his PLAGIARIST Dickens issued a 'Proclamation' threatenin the pirates with a 'summary and terribl reprisal, but several were immediately in th field with serial imitations and theatric adaptations, and one, calling himself 'Bo (T. P. Prest, author of *Nickelas Nickelbery* impudently issued a counter-proclamatior Imitation did not detract from sales of th real thing, however; the first number of *Nick leby* sold nearly 50,000 copies, and the initi circulation held up, earning profits of £14,00 for the serial publication alone (Forster 2.2; t Mitton, 26 July 1839). *Nickleby* attracted mor notice than Dickens had received previousl but although reviewers praised his humou and observation, they were largely conten with quoting extracts rather than offerin serious criticism (Chittick 1990, p. 120).

By 1863 more than 100,000 copies of *Nick leby* had been sold in book form alone, but i did not sell particularly well in the Cheap Edi tion or the Library Edition, and it was DRA MATIZED far less than *Pickwick* or *Oliver Twis* (Patten 1978, p. 101; Bolton 1987, p. 154). Des pite its initial popularity, *Nickleby* did not es tablish itself as an especial favourite eithe with the general reader or with critics. Sur veying sales of Dickens's works in the Unite States for the year 1968, George Ford estim ated 3,300 copies of *Nickleby* sold, compare with 293,060 of *A Tale of Two Cities* an 238,670 of *Great Expectations* ('Dickens in th 1960s', *Dickensian*, 66, 1970), and writing i 1994 David Parker observed, '*Nicholas Nick leby* has received surprisingly little critical at tention' ('Dickens and His Critics', Everyma edition, p. 803). A few critical analyses d stand out, however. George GISSING and G. K CHESTERTON celebrated the power of Dick ens's comic characterization in the novel Steven Marcus praised its combination of th

vitality of *Pickwick* with the moral seriousness of *Oliver Twist* (Marcus 1965, pp. 92–128),
and more recently John Bowen has examined
'the peculiarly ambivalent transformational
energies' of *Nickleby*.

On the other hand, the PUBLIC READING
version which Dickens devised in 1861,
'Nicholas Nickleby at the Yorkshire School',
became one of his standard repertoire pieces.
'I think Nickleby tops all the readings', Dickens reported. 'Somehow it seems to have got
in it, by accident, exactly the qualities best
suited to the purpose, and it went last night
not only with roars, but with a general hilarity and pleasure I have never seen surpassed'
(to Georgina Hogarth, 30 October 1861). And
over a century later David Edgar's dramatization, written for the Royal Shakespeare
Company in 1980, was enormously successful,
playing in Stratford, London, and New York
in its initial production. The play was video-
taped for serialized television transmission in
1982 as the first major arts programme on
Britain's newly opened Channel 4, and was revived for the stage by the RSC with an entirely
new cast in 1985.                        PVWS

Bowen, John, 'Performing Business, Training
Ghosts: Transcoding *Nickleby*', *English Literary History*, 63 (1996).

Clinton-Baddeley, V. C., 'Benevolent Teachers
of Youth', *Cornhill Magazine*, 169 (1957).

Edgar, David, 'Adapting *Nickleby*', *Dickensian*,
79 (1983).

Gilmour, Robin, 'Between Two Worlds: Aristocracy and Gentility in *Nicholas Nickleby*',
*Dickens Quarterly*, 5 (1988).

Russell, Norman, '*Nicholas Nickleby* and the
Commercial Crisis of 1825', *Dickensian*, 77
(1981).

Slater, Michael, *The Composition and Monthly
Publication of Nicholas Nickleby* (1973).

**novelist and man of letters, Dickens
as.** One extraordinary consideration for the
modern commentator looking at Dickens's
posthumous reputation as the greatest English novelist is that, at the outset, neither he
nor his contemporaries considered the work
he was publishing to be novels. A novel, according to the conception of the time, was an
extended work of fiction published in three
volumes, as popularized by SCOTT. Imaginative sketches and stories published serially,
even when linked by plot and character, were
considered to be miscellaneous writing, and

were reviewed as such (see SERIAL FICTION;
PUBLISHING; REVIEWS). *Pickwick* began life as
little better than hack work, letterpress to
accompany a series of comic illustrations;
*Oliver Twist* started as Dickens's editorial contribution to BENTLEY'S MISCELLANY and was
the subject of acrimonious negotiation between author and publisher as to whether it
could fulfill Dickens's contractual obligation
to supply Richard BENTLEY with a novel;
*Nickleby* was contracted by CHAPMAN AND
HALL to follow the success of *Pickwick* by
imitating its format and content; *The Old
Curiosity Shop* was expanded from a short
sketch in MASTER HUMPHREY'S CLOCK when
that weekly miscellaneous publication proved
unpopular. It was only when Dickens chose to
publish his long-delayed historical novel
*Barnaby Rudge*—his fifth extended work of
fiction—within the pages of *Master Humphrey's Clock* that it finally became clear that
he was writing a new kind of novel and offering it to a new reading public in a new mode
of publication. By the end of his career the
day of serial publication of fiction was passing, as the lending LIBRARY came to dominate
modes of distribution, but his pre-eminence
and achievement as the foremost Victorian
novelist were integral with his success in
forging a new form.

Our present-day sense of Dickens as a novelist can distract us from the range of writing
he undertook throughout his life. A 'man of
letters' in the fullest sense, he contributed diverse materials to journals and newspapers,
wrote fiction of many different kinds and
lengths, published pamphlets, and accepted a
variety of different commissions. Early in his
career he edited two periodicals (*Bentley's
Miscellany* and *Master Humphrey's Clock*),
and two others (*Household Words* and *All the
Year Round*) occupied a major portion of his
time for two full decades, when he was simultaneously writing what is now seen as his
greatest fiction. He carried on active correspondence throughout his life, served briefly
as editor of a daily newspaper (the DAILY
NEWS), was a much-sought public speaker
and a gifted amateur actor-manager, and latterly devoted his primary energies to performing PUBLIC READINGS from his works.
For all his accomplishment and enduring
fame as a writer of long works of fiction,
he was far from being 'only' a novelist (see

Dickens was 24 years old, and already known in select circles as an outstanding reporter and writer of imaginative sketches, when Chapman and Hall approached him in 1836 to collaborate with Robert SEYMOUR on *The Pickwick Papers* (see SHORT-STORY AND SKETCH WRITER, DICKENS AS). Dickens's role was intended to be strictly subordinate: comic engravings were a formula of tested popularity, and not he, but Seymour, had the existing reputation which was to be the project's selling point. Dickens was to supply copy to accompany the ILLUSTRATIONS. What happened in the next few weeks changed the course of 19th-century publishing. Dickens, characteristically, took charge of the project; Seymour committed suicide; Chapman and Hall had sufficient confidence in Dickens not to abort publication but hired Hablot BROWNE ('Phiz') to replace Seymour, and soon the Pickwickians and Sam Weller were the talk of the town. Dickens gradually introduced elements of plot to give the work added coherence, but it remained to the end primarily an episodic series of adventures, with the comic scenes and dialogue and the relationship between Mr Pickwick and Sam the chief attractions. What was important, in terms of Dickens's subsequent career, was that the monthly serial part, selling for one shilling, was the format in which he rocketed to fame. He was still using it in his last works, *Our Mutual Friend* and *The Mystery of Edwin Drood*.

It is an indication of Dickens's own conception of the ephemeral nature of *Pickwick* that later in 1836, when it was less than halfway through its serialization, he agreed to edit a new miscellaneous periodical for Richard Bentley and to write two three-volume novels for the same publisher. *Oliver Twist*, his own contribution to the *Miscellany*, was a story in a different key from *Pickwick*, and it constituted only a portion of each month's contents of the periodical. It drew on materials of the sort Dickens had previously used in the 'Our Parish' pieces in *Sketches by Boz*, and it was organized as a moral allegory or Hogarthian 'progress' (its full title is *Oliver Twist, or the Parish Boy's Progress*). But like *Pickwick*, it was an extended work of fiction published in monthly instalments. Dickens, soon over-burdened with commitments, asked Bentley to treat *Oliver* as one of the two contracted novels, on the basis that it could be—indeed, was—published in three volumes when complete. Bentley understandably demurred, not wishing to pay twice under separate contracts for the same work, and controversy ensued. The question was not whether *Oliver Twist* was a novel, but whether it was *the* novel Dickens had agreed to write for Bentley. Nevertheless, the dispute highlights the problematic conception at the time of what constituted a novel. Dickens eventually won the argument, and Bentley lost his star writer.

While all this was going on, Chapman and Hall, eager to secure Dickens's services when *Pickwick* was complete, negotiated a new contract on 18 November 1837 for a successor, 'of similar character and of the same extent and contents in point of quantity' as *Pickwick*. Significantly, the contract did not specify that Dickens was to write a novel, but a 'new Book or work' (Pilgrim 1.659). But whereas *Pickwick* never fully abandoned its origins as comic sketches of Cockney sporting life, and *Oliver* owes at least as much to the example of the allegories of BUNYAN and HOGARTH as to the novels of FIELDING, SMOLLETT, and Scott, *Nicholas Nickleby* is, as its full title indicates, emphatically in the tradition of the 18th-century 'life and adventures' novel (see NOVELISTS AND THE NOVEL BEFORE DICKENS). Centred on the encounters of a young hero with a variety of people and places during his episodic wanderings, *The Life and Adventures of Nicholas Nickleby, Containing a Faithful Account of the Fortunes, Misfortunes, Uprisings, Downfallings and Complete Career of the Nickleby Family*, looks back to *Tom Jones* and *Roderick Random* far more than it looks forward to later developments in the novel, even as Dickens was to write it. Like *Pickwick*, *Nickleby* was published in twenty monthly numbers (as nineteen), and on its completion sold in a one-volume edition.

But as Kathryn Chittick (1990) has shown, it was reviewed primarily for its local felicities, and links between episodes were largely ignored. Moreover, it was while he was writing *Nickleby* that Dickens charted his future course, not as a novelist, but as the editor of his own weekly miscellany, modelled on 18th-century precedents. It was with the failure of *Master Humphrey's Clock* that Dickens emerged, not as the successor to Scott, but as a distinctive novelist in his own right.

First, Dickens almost extemporaneously transformed the short sketch of a child living in a curiosity-dealer's shop into an extended work of fiction. Like *Oliver*, *The Old Curiosity Shop* (1840–1) is overtly plotted as a 'progress', and its counterpointed contrasts provide its structure. Thematically *The Old Curiosity Shop* clarified Dickens's central preoccupation with the power and nature of imagination, but its journey through dreamlike countryside, extravagant characterization, and FAIRY-TALE motifs, which pushed harder against the limits of realism than he ventured in any other extended story, offered a precedent he would follow in many of his shorter Christmas writings, but never again in a full-length work of fiction.

Second, Dickens followed *The Old Curiosity Shop* with *Barnaby Rudge* (1841), a work which had been contracted as 'Gabriel Vardon' five years previously, first with MACRONE and later with Bentley. This was a HISTORICAL NOVEL, conceived in conscious imitation of Scott, and with a subtitle ('A Tale of the Riots of 'Eighty') deliberately echoing Scott's precedent (the subtitle of *Waverley* is 'Or, 'Tis Fifty Years Since'). Whereas each of his previous works of fiction emerged from the contingencies of publishing arrangements which were from the outset designed for serial publication, *Barnaby Rudge* was planned from its inception—and even begun, in 1839—as a novel in three volumes. That it first saw the light of day in serialized form, at a time when CHARTIST agitation gave it urgent contemporary significance, is evidence that Dickens was not, finally, a writer in Scott's mode, but something different—a Victorian novelist (see Chittick 1990, p. 166).

Dickens followed the completion of *Barnaby Rudge* by taking the first extended break in his career as a writer of fiction, travelling to AMERICA and publishing a travel book, *AMERICAN NOTES* (1842), as his next work. The novel which followed, *Martin Chuzzlewit* (1843–4), although in some ways following in the 'life and adventures' tradition, marks a decisive break from his earlier fiction. Here, as FORSTER observes, Dickens centred the book on a single theme, selfishness, and planned 'old Martin's plot to degrade and punish Pecksniff' as early as the third number (4.1).

Despite the scanty working notes which survive, the book's systematic patterns of imagery also suggest more careful planning than in any previous novel he had written.

*Dombey and Son* (1846–8), often seen as the first work of Dickens's full artistic maturity, followed *Chuzzlewit* by taking a single theme, pride, as its organizing principle (Forster, 6.2). It is the first of his novels for which a complete set of number plans survives, and its structural complexity and coherence surpass anything he had previously achieved. In Harry Stone's words, *Dombey* is 'the first novel to exhibit that profound and sustained integration of theme, fable, image, and mood that would characterize all his later works' (Stone 1987, p. 49). The orchestration of so many layers of artistry in a work of such scope was something entirely new in fiction, and exemplifies Dickens's supreme achievement as a novelist and his distinctive contribution to the history of the novel.

It is perhaps evidence of the magnitude of Dickens's advance that it was preceded by the longest fallow period up to that point in his career: *Chuzzlewit* was complete in July 1844, and *Dombey* did not begin appearing until the end of September 1846. Dickens was no less active than usual, and *The CHIMES*, *The CRICKET ON THE HEARTH*, and *PICTURES FROM ITALY* all intervened, but he wrote no novel between *Chuzzlewit* and *Dombey*. Another indication of the development can be seen in the retrospective nature of the novel which followed, *David Copperfield* (1849–50). The first of his overtly autobiographical novels, narrated in the first person by a character whose growth to maturity the novel charts and whose eventual choice of career is to become a novelist, *Copperfield* represents a taking of stock by Dickens (who had embarked on writing a straightforward autobiography some months previously but soon abandoned the attempt; see DIARIES). *Copperfield* has all the structural complexity of *Dombey* but, dealing primarily with the hero's maturation, is less socially oriented.

*Copperfield* was followed by what is widely considered the crowning achievement of Dickens's career, *Bleak House* (1852–3). A panoramic novel which is intricately plotted with a web of interconnections between the many characters, it is the first of Dickens's works to be organized around a central symbol, an institution which impinges on the life of every personage in the book. By focusing upon the Court of CHANCERY, notorious for its abuses and subject of outcry even as he was writing, Dickens was addressing an issue of topical moment, with an artistry which locates the source of wrong in the system itself. Whereas Dickens's earlier satire had been directed at specific, remediable (or eradicable) targets, in *Bleak House* the pervasiveness of the court's influence generates great pessimism as to the possibility of escaping its clutches. This pessimism is not merely the result of Dickens's darkening social vision as he grew older, but also of the increased sophistication of his artistry (see Smith 1968). His development of techniques for exposing root causes of social evils generates institutional satire of a power seldom seen in fiction.

Dickens's next work of fiction was his only INDUSTRIAL NOVEL, and also his shortest, *Hard Times* (1854), which juxtaposes the social philosophy of 'Fact' (Dickens's attack on UTILITARIANISM) with the values of fancy, as represented by Sleary's CIRCUS. Its brevity gives it atypical spareness and abstraction, and ever since F. R. LEAVIS praised it as a 'social fable' in *The Great Tradition* (1948), it has attracted much critical attention. First published in the pages of *Household Words* to revive flagging sales, it was, like *The Old Curiosity Shop* and *Barnaby Rudge*, serialized in weekly instalments.

He returned to twenty monthly parts in the second of his social panoramas, *Little Dorrit* (1855–7), which, like *Bleak House*, is organized around a central institutional symbol, in this case the prison. The book depicts a number of physical prisons, and also economic, social, and psychological 'prisons', in a way that makes it the most tightly organized of Dickens's long novels, and also the most oppressive, despite the countervailing force of the eponymous heroine's goodness.

In order to inaugurate his new weekly periodical *All the Year Round* in 1859, Dickens wrote the second of his historical novels, *A Tale of Two Cities*. Although criticized for lack of humour, it quickly established itself as one of his most popular works for its vivid presentation of the violence of the French Revolution, and its depiction of the ultimate self-sacrifice for love by Sidney Carton. Crit-

ical opinion has not, by and large, seen it as a major achievement nor as an advance in artistry.

The following year, once more to halt declining sales of a periodical he was editing, Dickens wrote the second of his BILDUNGSROMANE, *Great Expectations*. The delicacy with which he interweaves the immediacy of the hero's thrilling adventures with the sadder-but-wiser reflections of the mature Pip who tells the story is a triumph of narrative art, and the course of Pip's adventures has been seen as a 'fable of cultural emergence', reflecting the emergence of Victorian society out of Regency roughness (see Gilmour 1981).

In the last decade of his life Dickens devoted more of his energies to giving public readings than to writing fiction, and he completed only one further novel, *Our Mutual Friend* (1864–5), leaving another, *The Mystery of Edwin Drood*, unfinished at his death in 1870. *Our Mutual Friend*, the third of his social panorama novels, uses dust-heaps and the river as organizing symbols, and by means of the benevolent deception of Noddy Boffin, the Golden Dustman, finds more grounds for optimism than *Bleak House* or *Little Dorrit*. *Drood* gave promise of developing psychological themes more completely than ever, through the split personality of John Jasper, but Dickens guarded his mystery so well that his intentions remain a matter for speculation (see MYSTERY OF EDWIN DROOD, SOLUTIONS TO).

Throughout his career Dickens insisted upon the factual authenticity of his fiction, declaring 'IT IS TRUE' of Nancy in *Oliver Twist*, and making similar claims for Mrs Gamp (*MC*) and for the spontaneous combustion of Krook in *Bleak House*. He also proclaimed a desire to amuse as a primary aim, which he modulated into a statement of the kind of fiction he wrote, when he declared in the Preface to *Bleak House* that he had 'dwelt upon the romantic side of familiar things'. He was also emphatic that he wrote with thematic purpose, as indicated, for example, in a letter written at the height of his career: 'Pray do not suppose', he wrote, 'that I ever write merely to amuse, or without an object. I wish I were as clear of every offence before Heaven, as I am of that . . . Without it, my pursuit— and the steadiness, patience, seclusion, regularity, hard work and self-concentration, it demands—would be utterly worthless to me' (to Mrs Cropper, 20 December 1852).

It is perhaps fitting to note, in conclusion of this survey, that the final words of fiction which Dickens wrote, a few hours before suffering the stroke from which he died, describe a character (Mr Tope), who 'falls to with an appetite' (*MED* 23). The gusto and vitality of Dickens's fiction remain, along with his extraordinary organizational powers and his Inimitable STYLE, hallmarks of his achievement as a novelist. (See entries on individual novels under their titles.) PVWS

Chittick (1990).
Gilmour (1981).
Patten (1978).
Smith (1968).
Stone (1987).

**novelists and the novel before Dickens.** Early in *David Copperfield*, when David is at the Murdstones', whose 'gloomy theology . . . made all children out to be a swarm of little vipers', the young boy takes refuge in fiction and the power of his own imagination. Indeed, fiction is the 'one circumstance' which makes David's life bearable and it is a comforting and consoling indulgence:

'My father had left a small collection of books in a little room upstairs, to which I had access (for it adjoined my own) and which nobody else in our house ever troubled. From that blessed little room, Roderick Random, Peregrine Pickle, Humphrey Clinker, Tom Jones, the Vicar of Wakefield, Don Quixote, Gil Blas, and Robinson Crusoe, came out, a glorious host, to keep me company. They kept alive my fancy, and my hope of something beyond that place and time,—they, and the *ARABIAN NIGHTS*, and the *Tales of the Genii*,— and did me no harm; for whatever harm was in some of them was not there for me; *I* knew nothing of it. . . . I have been Tom Jones (a child's Tom Jones, a harmless creature) for a week together. I have sustained my own idea of Roderick Random for a month at a stretch, I verily believe . . . This was my only and my constant comfort. When I think of it, the picture always rises in my mind, of a summer evening, the boys at play in the churchyard, and I sitting on my bed, reading as if for life' (*DC* 4).

Young David's passion for reading is that of young Dickens; for Dickens, whose father was imprisoned in the Marshalsea, suffered similar humiliations and despair. As FORSTER recounts in his *Life*, a number of chapters in *David Copperfield* were really based on an autobiographical fragment which Dickens had written; the idea of an autobiography was abandoned but the germ of Dickens's life remains, particularly in chapter 4 (see DIARIES AND AUTOBIOGRAPHY OF DICKENS). And, of course, like Dickens, David Copperfield becomes a successful novelist.

In the catalogue of literary heroes who were so important to David's childhood, we see many of the novels which represent important developments in the early history of the novel: CERVANTES's picaresque, DEFOE's TRAVEL narrative, FIELDING's mock-heroic. The novel before Dickens, like the novel in Dickens's own time, offered a rich variety of subjects, styles, and forms. It is this diversity which we must recognize in order to understand the literary culture which so influenced Dickens, and which he reshaped and experimented with for the 19th century.

One of the primary ways we have to come to understand the novel is through the emphasis on individual lives which can be seen in fiction of the early 18th century, when the first novels in English were being written. This interpretation of the rise of the novel— why the form arrived when it did—links the genre to the emergence of the bourgeois middle CLASSES and a consequent burgeoning of literary culture. The emphasis on individualism is reflected in the full titles of the books David Copperfield reads: for example, Henry Fielding's *The History of Tom Jones, A Foundling* (1749), Tobias SMOLLETT's *The Adventures of Roderick Random* (1748), Daniel Defoe's *The Life and Strange Surprising Adventures of Robinson Crusoe* (1719), to which we might also add Laurence STERNE's *The Life and Opinions of Tristram Shandy* (1759–67). One of the primary subjects, then, of the 18th-century English novel is the individual; not the aristocratic or noble individual of romance and epic; rather, the middle-class man or woman, or even, in the case of Defoe's Moll Flanders, the low-born prostitute. That this focus on individualism in the novel continued into the 19th century can again be illustrated through the titles to some Victorian novels: Dickens's *David Copperfield*, Charlotte BRONTË's *Jane Eyre*, and Elizabeth GASKELL's *Ruth*, to name but three.

Another way we can discuss the novel in the early 18th century is to consider the range of literary forms out of which the novel grew: romance, epic, but particularly journalistic forms such as the ballad and the periodical. It is worth noting that the English novel derives from the French word *nouvelle*, meaning 'new' (in the temporal sense) and 'news' (in the journalistic sense). This is interesting in relation to Dickens if we consider his formal innovation in adapting the serial form of the 18th-century ESSAY to the writing and publishing of fiction. Dickens's early fiction particularly was REVIEWED as magazine miscellany material rather than as novels, let alone as serious literature, and one of Dickens's achievements in his career was in narrowing the gap between popular, essentially ephemeral literature and 'high' literature. In the first Preface to *Nicholas Nickleby* (1839), Dickens quotes the 18th-century sentimental novelist Henry MACKENZIE on writing for the SERIAL form:

'The author of a periodical performance has indeed a claim to the attention and regard of his readers, more interesting than that of any other writer. Other writers submit their sentiments to their readers, with the reserve and circumspection of him who has had time to prepare for a public appearance ... But the periodical essayist commits to his readers the feelings of the day, in the language which those feelings have prompted. As he has delivered himself with the freedom of intimacy and the cordiality of friendship, he will naturally look for the indulgence which those relations may claim; and when he bids his readers adieu, will hope, as well as feel, the regrets of an acquaintance, and the tenderness of a friend.'

Dickens is well known for the speed with which he produced his weekly parts especially, ensuring always a feeling of 'newness' and topicality. Along with the later *Nicholas Nickleby*, the *Pickwick Papers* is particularly noteworthy in relation to journalism and periodical literature. The roots of the word 'novel' (of 'new' and 'news') indicate an intersection between both fact and fiction, real and unreal. Therefore, we can trace the development of the novel to the dissemination of the discourse of journalism in ballads and later in periodicals, especially since so many novelists were also working journalists. One of the things which the early novel did was to blur the boundaries between what is true and what is false, and the diversity of the novel form in the 18th century points to the hybridity of its roots.

If we return to those novels which David Copperfield reads, we can illustrate this point. In the Preface to *Roderick Random*, Smollett writes that 'every intelligent reader will, at first sight, perceive I have not deviated from nature, in the facts, which are all true in the main, although the circumstances are altered and disguised to avoid personal satire'. This work of fiction, Smollett tells us, is really not a fiction at all; rather, it is a true story in which the names (particularly his own) have been changed for the sake of propriety. If we look at the first chapter in Book 2 of Fielding's *Tom Jones*, the author invites us to consider what constitutes the discourse of 'history':

'Tho' we have properly enough entitled this our work, a history, and not a life; nor an apology for a life, as is more in fashion; yet we intend in it rather to pursue the method of those writers, who profess to disclose the revolutions of countries, than to imitate the painful and voluminous historian, who, to preserve the regularity of his series, think himself obliged to fill up as much paper with the detail of months and years in which nothing remarkable happened, as he employs upon those notable areas when the greatest scenes have been transacted on the human stage.'

Like Smollett, Fielding complicates the notion of history or biography and fiction, and in so doing challenges the reader's understanding of literary genre. It is a radical move, and later in the same chapter Fielding claims to be 'the founder of a new province of writing', a province which we might now simply call the novel. Finally, we can look at the Preface to Defoe's *Robinson Crusoe*: 'The editor believes the thing to be a just history of fact; neither is there any appearance of fiction in it: and however thinks, because all such things are dispatched, that the improvement of it, as well to the diversion as to the instruction of the reader, will be the same; and as such, he thinks, without farther compliment to the world, he does them a great service in the publication.' Here, Defoe presents himself as an editor rather than an author, and the story is said to be a factual account rather than a fiction. As it happened, Defoe did base Robinson Crusoe on a real castaway; but the source of the story is not the same thing as that source transformed into fiction by Defoe's powerful imagination. The blurring of boundaries between history, biography, journalism, and other literary genres, it seems, is part of the project of early innovators of the novel. And it may still be part of the project of Victorian autobiographical novels, such as *David Copperfield* or Charlotte Brontë's *Villette* (1853).

It is important to consider what the early 18th-century novelists were doing, partly because Dickens was so influenced by them and partly because reviewers of Dickens's fiction continually linked his novels with his predecessors. Nowhere is this more obvious than in the early numbers of the *Pickwick Papers*. The weekly literary review, the *Athenaeum*, wrote that 'the *Pickwick Papers*, in fact, are made up of two pounds of Smollett, three ounces of Sterne, a handful of HOOK, a dash of a grammatical Pierce EGAN—incidents of pleasure, served with an original *sauce piquante*' (3 December 1836). Not a bad recipe for literary success. Such comparisons, while more numerous regarding his early fiction, continued throughout his life, and Dickens was particularly likened to Fielding who happened to be one of his favourites. Reviewing one of the parts to *Nicholas Nickleby*, the *Sun* boldly asserted that 'there is nothing in Fielding better than this' (4 July 1839). That Dickens, like Smollett, Fielding, Defoe, and many other 18th-century writers, was a JOURNALIST further linked him with the literary culture of a century before.

Much of the fiction being written in the 18th century might be contained under the broad category of realism, in the sense that it wishes to convey truth. What exactly 'truth' means may vary—is it verisimilitude? Historical fact? Moral truth?—but realism, with an attempt simultaneously to educate and to entertain, was an important way of thinking about the early novel. One need only note the ways writers attempted to offer their fictions as factual. However, despite the best efforts of writers to present 'truthful' accounts of the world around them, the novel was not a unanimously applauded form. The cultural value of the novel was continually debated, for example, in periodicals such as the *Monthly Review* and the *Rambler*. Some of the anxiety about the popularity of the novel stemmed from the subject-matter. Whereas the romance and epic traditions generally focused on aristocracy and noble heroes, the novel often depicted bawdy 'low life'. Furthermore, novel-writing was seen less as an art form and more as a commercial enterprise, with writers being forced to produce their fiction more quickly to meet deadlines. While the instructive and educative purpose of realist fiction was asserted, there was no unified belief in the value or purpose of the novel, or what form the novel ought to take.

Under the umbrella term 'realism' were many and varied manifestations of real life, of 'truth'. Defoe, for example, used the travel and adventure narrative as a framework for his fiction, but his version of the real differed radically, from, say, SWIFT's allegorical satire in *Gulliver's Travels* (1726). Even more different were the novels of Richardson—whom Dickens thought 'never seems to me to take his top-boots off' (28 January 1847)—such as *Pamela* (1741); the epistolary form suggests the real by using the most personal of documents, the letter, to structure the narrative, so that the intimacies of private life are made public. The use of letters provides a sense of immediacy and plausibility which lends a kind of realism to what is, after all, still fiction. Sterne, along with Richardson and Fielding, pioneered the novel of SENTIMENT, in which virtue and sympathetic feeling mark the truly developed individual. Sterne's *Sentimental Journey* (1768), a travel narrative in which the narrator is often reduced to tears in his wanderings through Europe, is one of the chief texts in the genre, and Dickens greatly admired both *Sentimental Journey* and *Tristram Shandy*. The sentimental novel reached something of an apogee in Henry Mackenzie's extremely popular *The Man of Feeling* (1771), a story depicting one young man's emotionalism, innocence, and benevolence. Dickens drew heavily from the sentimental tradition, most obviously in the depiction of Little Nell in *The Old Curiosity Shop*, but the pathos of sentimentalism is felt broadly throughout his fiction. The fashionable rage for sentimentality was ridiculed for its over-indulgence by some contemporaries and in *Sense and*

*Sensibility* (1811) by Jane Austen, a writer whom Dickens did not read, if at all, until late in life. The popularity of the sentimental novel was perhaps only exceeded by the vogue for GOTHIC FICTION, most prominent in the final decade of the 18th century. Although the Gothic novel had been around since Horace Walpole's *The Castle of Otranto* (1764), it is Ann Radcliffe's 1794 novel *The Mysteries of Udolpho* which remains the most popular of the early Gothic works. Dickens drew on the Gothic in a number of ways, including his use of the supernatural, the depiction of social decay, and the complicated relationship between past and present. However, more important as a precursor for Dickens was the NEWGATE NOVEL, itself a sub-genre related to the sensationalism of the Gothic.

The Newgate novel, which took as its central theme the life of the criminal, was popular from the 1820s to the 1840s. Drawing on the criminal biographies published in the 18th century in the *Newgate Calendar*, the Newgate novel was popularized by a range of writers including Edward BULWER-LYTTON and William Harrison AINSWORTH. Bulwer's *Paul Clifford* (1830) tried to use the focus on the criminal life to draw attention to social problems. In the Preface to *Paul Clifford* he states that one object in writing the novel is 'to draw attention to two errors in our penal institutions, viz., a vicious Prison-discipline and a sanguinary Criminal Code'. He was conscious of the need to suggest a moral value in a genre largely focused on the often-enjoyable escapades of highwaymen and murderers. Ainsworth's *Rookwood* (1834)—illustrated by CRUIKSHANK, who also illustrated Dickens's *Sketches by Boz*—contains a sub-plot built around the highwayman Dick Turpin. Dickens was associated with Bulwer and Ainsworth in the 1830s especially, and a novel such as *Oliver Twist* (1837–8), taking juvenile crime as its primary subject, certainly overlapped with the Newgate novel (it preceded Ainsworth's *Jack Sheppard*, a high-point of the Newgate genre, in BENTLEY'S MISCELLANY), although it also contains a strong element of social criticism. However, Dickens distanced himself from the Newgate fiction which romanticized its criminal heroes, as he plainly states in the third Preface to *Oliver Twist*:

'What manner of life is that which is described in these pages, as the everyday existence of a Thief? What charms has it for the young and ill-disposed, what allurements for the most jolter-headed of juveniles? Here are no canterings upon moonlit heaths, no merrymakings in the snuggest of all possible caverns, none of the attractions of dress, no embroidery, no lace, no jack-boots, no crimson coats and ruffles, none of the dash and freedom with which "the road" has been, time out of mind, invested.'

Indeed, although Dickens does draw on the conventions of the Newgate tradition—as he draws on the sentimental and the gothic novels—he transforms these sub-genres into a hybrid fiction all his own.

Another sub-genre worth mentioning in discussing the novel before Dickens is the fashionable or SILVER FORK NOVEL of the 1820s–1830s. Essentially, popular fictions describing the high life of London's *beau monde*, the silver fork novels gave readers a voyeuristic insight into the lives of the upper classes. The dandyism of Regency London was the particular backdrop for these novels, by writers as various as Benjamin DISRAELI, Bulwer-Lytton, Catherine Gore, T. H. Lister, and Caroline Norton. On the publication of Disraeli's *Vivien Grey* (1826–7), the *Star* recorded that 'a new class of novels has lately sprung up, which has attained a very great celebrity: we allude to those which relate to fashionable life . . . we do not pretend to know who is the author of "Vivien Grey", but that he is a lively and accomplished writer will be seen at once from his work, which details the adventures of a young man of ambition in varied circumstances and often in very critical situations . . .'. Dickens parodied the silver fork novel in the story of Lady Flabella, which Kate Nickleby reads to Mrs Wititterly (*NN* 28).

Yet more inspiration for Dickens came from comic novels of the early 19th century. Robert SURTEES's great comic figure John Jorrocks, a cockney greengrocer who emerged out of the author's magazine sketches, was an important predecessor to Mr Pickwick. Also significant was Theodore Hook, another silver fork and comic writer with whom Dickens was often compared in early reviews. Hook's *Gilbert Gurney* (1836), a series of essays and sketches focused on a single central character, and *Jack Brag* (1837), with its emphasis on farcical adventures rather than meticulous plotting, was typical of his output.

Although Dickens greatly enjoyed the popular fiction of the 1820s and 1830s, his most beloved novelist remained Oliver GOLDSMITH, whose *Vicar of Wakefield* (1766) Dickens believed had 'done more good in the world, and instructed more kinds of people in virtue, than any other fiction ever written' (to Miss Coutts, 29 March 1849). Goldsmith's novel was Dickens's favourite but his most revered novelist was Walter SCOTT, who wrote hugely popular HISTORICAL NOVELS in the first decades of the 19th century. No one, according to Dickens, came near to Scott's achievement in the novel form: 'Foremost and unapproachable in the bright world of fiction, gifted with a vivacity and range of invention scarcely ever equalled, and never (but in the case of Shakespeare) exceeded; endowed as never fabled enchanter was, with spells to conjure up the past, and to give to days and men of old the spirit and freshness of yesterday; to strip religion of her gloom, Virtue of her austerity, and present them both in such attractive forms that you could not choose but love them ...' (Collins, 1981, 2.228). High praise, indeed. For Dickens, as for so many Victorian novelists, Scott's fiction was the supreme example of the heights the novel could reach. Dickens's work was often very favourably compared with Scott's, as an obituary on the death of Dickens in 1870 suggests: 'To a degree unequalled by any other novelist except perhaps SCOTT, [Dickens] had the power of making the reader feel thoroughly at home in an imaginary world, and of being and living and moving in it naturally' (*Saturday Review*, June 1870). In addition to their literary merits, both Dickens and Scott were the most popular and famous novelists of their day.

From Defoe's island adventure to Scott's historical romance, the novel before Dickens offers a remarkable diversity in form, style, and subject-matter. The attempt to present a fully unified account of its history before Dickens is difficult at best, not least because what constituted the novel was regularly debated. In the century of novels before *Pickwick*, what is most impressive is the range of experiments in subject-matter and form. The travel narrative, the epistolary novel, the picaresque adventure, the novel of sentiment, the Gothic, the fashionable novel, the historical romance: all of these were crucial developments before Dickens, and all, in some way, shaped Dickens's own extraordinary imagination. The influence of Fielding's comic adventures, of Sterne's sentiment, of Smollett's grotesques, of Goldsmith's tenderness, of Radcliffe's melodramatic Gothic, of Scott's unique development of the theme of past and present can all be felt in the pages of his fiction.

Dickens's novels, however, are not merely a textual mosaic of all that came before him, and it may be useful to return to *David Copperfield* to see how Dickens's imagination works. In chapter 11, David tells us how he used his childhood reading to shape the people and events around him into stories: 'I fitted my old books to my altered life, and made stories for myself, out of the streets, and out of men and women...' Later in the chapter, he admits that fact and fiction, the real and unreal, history and the imagination have been blurred: 'When my thoughts go back, now, to that slow agony of my youth, I wonder how much of the histories I invented for such people hang like a mist of fancy over well-remembered facts! When I tread the old ground, I do not wonder that I seem to see and pity, going on before me, an innocent romantic boy, making his imaginative world out of such experiences and sordid things!' David here fictionalizes his own past. His extensive reading in novels of the 18th century, like Dickens's own reading, shapes the power of his imagination. Not merely a process of synthesizing the fiction of the past, story-telling for Dickens is far more active, creative, and transforming. One of his great achievements in the varied and disunified history of the novel is his ability to convert forms and literary modes from the past into meaningful fiction for the present. Steeped in the literature of his heroes, Dickens's fiction remains as much of a new province as his favourite Fielding. (See also NOVELISTS AND THE NOVEL DURING DICKENS'S LIFETIME; PUBLISHING, PRINTING, AND BOOKSELLING; READERSHIP AND THE READING PUBLIC.)    MWT

Adburgham, Alison, *Silver Fork Society: Fashionable Life and Literature from 1814–1840* (1983).

Davis, Lennard J., *Factual Fictions: The Origins of the English Novel* (1983).

McKeon, Michael, *The Origins of the English Novel, 1600–1740* (1987).

Mayo, Robert D., *The English Novel in the Magazines, 1740–1815* (1962).

Spencer, Jane, *The Rise of the Woman Novelist: From Aphra Behn to Jane Austen* (1986).

Watt, Ian, *The Rise of the Novel* (1957).

## novelists and the novel during Dickens's lifetime.

One sense of the huge importance of Dickens to the development of the 19th-century novel can be gauged from the adjective derived from his name. The *Oxford English Dictionary* has no entry for 'Eliotic' or 'Lyttonesque', but 'Dickensy' and 'Dickensian' were in use from 1856 (when the *Saturday Review* made reference to 'a Dickenesque description of an execution'). A commonplace of the OBITUARIES upon his death was that he was the characteristic Victorian novelist: 'He was', wrote the *Daily News* (10 June 1870) 'emphatically the novelist of his age. In his pictures of contemporary life posterity will read, more clearly than in contemporary records, the character of nineteenth-century life.' But for many of his contemporaries, astonished at his unparalleled popular success, Dickens was not exactly an artist—more the pre-eminent entertainer of the age (see POPULARITY); and many would have followed TROLLOPE when, in his posthumously published *Autobiography* (1870), he identified THACKERAY as the greatest novelist of the period. David Masson presciently wrote in 1859 (in his *British Novelists and their Styles*): 'there is a Dickens faction, and there is a Thackeray faction; and there is no debate more common, wherever literary talk goes on, than the debate as to the respective merits of Dickens and Thackeray.' For Walter BAGEHOT ('Charles Dickens', *National Review*, October 1858), Dickens may have been popular, but Thackeray was the artist; 'Mr Thackeray . . .', Bagehot opined, 'exercises a more potent and plastic fascination within his sphere'; whereas Dickens, for all that he amuses, 'wholly wants the two elements which we have spoken of as one or other requisite for a symmetrical genius'—which is to say, 'the faculty of reasoning' and the ability to 'give a unity' to his novels. This assumption, that Thackeray was more technically proficient, but Dickens was somehow spontaneous, populist, broadly conceived, was common even to defenders of Dickens. Edward Fitzgerald cannot keep the CLASS snobbery out of his praise: Dickens is 'a little SHAKESPEARE—a Cockney Shakespeare, if you will: but as distinct, if not so great, a piece of pure Genius as was born in Stratford . . . had I to choose but one of them, I would choose Dickens's hundred delightful Caricatures rather than Thackeray's half-dozen terrible Photographs' (letter to Fanny Kemble, 25 April 1879). There is little doubt that there is a large class-bias in this Victorian opposition between Thackerayan technical accomplishment and sophisticated realism on the one hand, and Dickensian crude populist entertainment value and roughly structured accretions of caricature on the other. Richard HORNE, for instance, mournfully concedes that Dickens has 'been accused of a predilection for the lower classes of society' (*A New Spirit of the Age*, 1844); a curious ground for accusation by contemporary standards. The point here is that present-day grounds for judgement differ in fundamental respects from those of contemporary Victorian criticism. The Victorians had a more stratified conception of their literature; Dickens was certainly raised above the level of the pulp fiction of the day (produced by writers such as G. W. M. Reynolds), but he lacked the serious combination of morality and realism that was regarded as the highest form of fiction.

Both Dickens and Thackeray started writing in the 1830s, at a time when the novel in English literature was a fragmented body of sub-genres. As Michael Wheeler puts it, at this time 'the variety of sub-genres of fiction in vogue—HISTORICAL, SILVER FORK, NEWGATE and social problem novels, marine, sporting and Irish rogue novels—puts one in mind of Polonius's generic division and sub-divisions in *Hamlet*: "tragedy, comedy, history, pastoral, pastoral-comical, historical-pastoral" and so on' (*English Fiction of the Victorian Period*, 1994, p. 16). Thackeray was largely content to use these various genres for his own purposes—to write a satire of the Newgate novel in *Catherine* (1840), to write comedy in *The Great Hoggarty Diamond* (1841), to rework satirically the Irish novel in *Barry Lyndon* (1844), and so on. Dickens, on the other hand, worked in a largely synthesizing manner. Even novels rooted very clearly in a certain generic context grow in the telling into something cross-generic, something larger. *Pickwick* was originally conceived as what we might call 'sporting-comical', as humorous text to accompany sporting illustrations, but evolved into an infinitely broader literary conception—effectively defining its own genre, a combination of 18th-century comic picaresque, of BILDUNGSROMAN, of social portrayal, and the inflection of individual character. Even *Oliver Twist*, an apparently straightforward Newgate novel (for all that Dickens denied this), changes as the story develops into something more broadly concerned with humanity.

Like Dickens, Thackeray began his career in the 1830s writing comic journalism; but even his early writings for PUNCH demonstrate an experimental fascination with different narrative modes and points-of-view. From the earliest Thackeray was the more cynical, worldly wise, and sharply satirical writer of the two. His first substantial novel, *Catherine*, contains a cast of 'scoundrel' characters; scenes are set in the grimy Bugle Inn, a dark version of the Merrie England hostelries of *Pickwick*. *Barry Lyndon* (1844) adopts the intriguing device of being narrated by a liar, the Irish adventurer of the title. Lyndon's career as a card-sharp and confidence trickster elaborates the attitude (which was to find its most famous expression in the character of Becky Sharp in *Vanity Fair*, 1848) that only a fool takes the world at face value. The contrast with Dickens, whose literary ingenuousness never slips into such world-weary cynicism, is striking; and the notion that Thackeray was embodying, somehow, a more 'adult' aesthetic (with Dickens the more 'childish') goes some way towards explaining the high esteem in which he was held by many contemporaries. But whilst Thackeray prided himself on portraying the shabby reality behind the shows of the world ('if Philip's boots had holes in them,' the narrator declares at the end of *Philip* (1862) 'then I have written that he has holes in his boots'), he also had no patience with Dickens's specific concerns with named and correctable social ills. Thackeray's youthful bitterness matures into a world-weary cynicism, a sense of the inevitability and changelessness of human suffering. 'Is not one story as stale as another?' says a character in *The Virginians* (1858). 'Are not they all alike? What is the use, I say, in telling them over and over?' At the beginning of *The Newcomes* (1855) the narrator asserts, 'all types of all characters march through all fables . . . there may be nothing new under and including the sun'. It is in this sense that G. K. CHESTERTON called four of Thackeray's masterpieces (*Vanity Fair*, *Pendennis*, *The Newcomes*, and *Philip*) 'in one sense all one novel'. Once again we are struck by the contrast with Dickens, whose entire aesthetic (we might say without exaggerating too greatly) is based upon an energetic, inventive, and even strenuous attempt to make things new. It is the energy of Dickens that marks him out, here as elsewhere in the Victorian novel; for all that such vigour was sometimes seen by his contemporaries as somehow vulgar, it opened up the novel to a wider audience than had ever been seen before, and continues as the basis of Dickens's appeal even today. This is perhaps the key fact of Dickens's place in the traditions of the 19th-century novel: his colossal popularity. Dickens was a literary superstar, an international figure, and not even SCOTT had enjoyed such fame.

One important factor in Dickens's rise to fame was the mode of SERIAL PUBLICATION that he established so successfully with *The Pickwick Papers*. As John Sutherland has pointed out (in *Victorian Fiction, Writers, Publishers, Readers*, 1996), part of Dickens's success in this respect was a matter of good timing (see PUBLISHING). The book-trade slump of the 1830s had left a relatively attenuated network for distributing published volumes (in terms of, for instance, booksellers and bookshops); the great advantage of the serial instalment was that it could be distributed nationwide via the same networks that distributed newspapers and journals. More than the overall structure of his novels was determined by what Dickens called (in his Preface to the first edition of *Pickwick Papers*) 'this detached and desultory form of publication'. His success set up something of a vogue for publishing in this fashion. This resulted in (one of the complaints of contemporary critics) a looser conception of overall plot, certainly; but it also focused attention more directly on the text in hand. Audiences had to be kept interested from month to month, and the novel responded with a tighter sense of narrative tension (predicated chiefly upon narrative postponement), finer localized comic effects, and descriptive passages often focused on the ILLUSTRATIONS provided for the issue. Having said this, however (to quote John Sutherland again), 'the novel in monthly numbers was a bow of Ulysses which only Dickens could draw with consistent success'. Fifty novels were being serialized in this manner in 1850, but this number subsequently fell away until in 1870 there was only one (*Edwin Drood*). Nonetheless, the basis of the serialized novel's appeal, its strong combination of immediate reader satisfaction and subtle postponement of conclusion, determines the form for almost all forms written until Dickens's death. Variations on the form included magazine publication (favoured by Elizabeth GASKELL, Anthony Trollope, Wilkie COLLINS, and others, and which Dickens also utilized) and publication of novels in 'books' (George ELIOT's *Middlemarch* was published as eight 'books' between 1871 and 1872). Dickens was again central to this mode of novelistic production; the huge success of his journal *Household Words* spawned copycat publications, but also provided significant boosts for the careers of Elizabeth Gaskell and Wilkie Collins, along with G. A. SALA, Percy FITZGERALD, and Harriet Parris. All these writers benefited from their association with Dickens; it would be misleading to talk of a Dickens 'school', and in certain respects (particularly STYLISTICALLY) these writers differ considerably from Dickens; but in terms of the broader aesthetic associated with the man, they belong to him.

If anything, publication in magazine format was even more exacting than monthly serialization; if a novel was not keeping the interest of the readership, as measured directly in sales (as was the case with LEVER's *A Day's Ride*, serialized in Dickens's *All The Year Round*) it would be unceremoniously supplanted by a more likely candidate. Following the Dickensian path, a novelist such as Charles READE could claim with a certain pride: 'I write for the public, and the public doesn't care about the dead. They are more interested in the living, and in the great tragicomedy of humanity that is around them and environs them in every street.' The sentiment, and the novelistic aesthetic it implies, is pure Dickens.

If Dickens's success with serializing *Pickwick* helped the democratization of the novel, it also laid the blueprint for the novel of character. Victorian fiction was written, and was received by its READERSHIP, as a means of presenting 'well-drawn' (which is to say, distinctive, interesting, and engaging) characters; and Dickens scaled new heights with this. 'Character' had always played a large part in the novel, of course, but with Dickens it reached a new pinnacle of success. People thought of Pickwick (say) in the same sort of ways they thought of their real-life acquaintances; they *cared* about him (a concept contemporary criticism, and particularly critical theory, finds it difficult to encompass). Dickens's genius was not 'caricature' (although he is often accused of precisely this) any more than it was the minute delineation of individual psychological complexity that we find in Jane Austen or Henry James. Instead, he produced Theophrastan 'types', shorthand embodiments of general human characteristics. As Anthony Trollope put it:

'No other writer of English language except Shakespeare has left so many types of character as Dickens has done, characters which are known by their names familiarly as household words, and which bring to our minds vividly and at once, a certain well-understood set of ideas, habits, phrases and costumes, making together a man, or woman, or child. . . Every hypocrite who knows his part, wears the Pecksniff shirt-collar. Every detective is to us a Bucket' ('Charles Dickens', *St Paul's Magazine*, July 1870).

In this manner Dickens engaged the reader, in a collective as well as an individual sense, directly in the construction of his literary architecture. Much of Dickensian humour depends upon recognition, and this recognition in turn depends upon the sheer range of characters represented. Oliver asking for more, Fagin and the Artful Dodger, the brutality of Bill Sikes and the loyalty of Nancy became for 19th-century, as for present-day, readers archetypes of human experience.

Dickens was archetypal in another sense as well: topographically. His version of LONDON dominates our imagination in similar ways to his characters. Topographically expressive novels were invented by Scott, of course, with his particularized Scottish historical romances; and in the Victorian period Dickens was preceded by the success of the derivatively Scott-like Harrison AINSWORTH, whose historical fictions were centred less on famous historical personages and more on places. Ainsworth's version of London was particularly popular, as seen in *The Tower of London* (1840), *Old Saint Paul's* (1841), and particularly in *Windsor Castle*, whose success was helped by lavish illustrations of sites of local colour and interest. But Ainsworth's 16th- and 17th-century London lacks the specificity, not to mention the outstanding literary skill, of Dickens's version of the city.

Through the 1850s and 1860s, partly under the influence of Dickens's huge success, the myriad sub-genres of previous fiction coalesced into broader categories. Religious problem novels (such as Newman's *Loss and Gain*, 1848), historical fiction, DETECTIVE FICTION (particularly the work of Wilkie Collins) and social problem novels were all popular. Dickens was never drawn to religious topics, and his historical novels (*Barnaby Rudge* and *A Tale of Two Cities*) are occasional forays into the field rather than concerted attempts to write in that genre. But detective fiction influenced several later novels (*Bleak House, Our Mutual Friend*, and *Edwin Drood*), and in a sense Dickens had always been a 'social problem' novelist, with later works such as *Hard Times* merely the development of his earlier concern at specific social ills. Something different is seen in works such as Elizabeth Gaskell's *Mary Barton* (1848) and *North and South* (1855) or Disraeli's *Sybil* (1845), which are more properly termed 'Condition of England novels', insofar as they attempt, however crudely, to view the problems of England systemically instead of as a matter of individual abuses. Dickens's late novels, and particularly *Bleak House* and *Little Dorrit*, pick up on this impulse, and attempt to conceive of social ills as a network of interrelations and issues, rather than the doings of a few evil individuals.

But having identified a few dominant genres during this period, it has to be said that placing Dickens aesthetically amongst his fellow novelists is a less than satisfying business. There seem to be very few vectors of influence from other writers to Dickens's work. Partly this is because Dickens was so unique, a fact recognized at the time (for instance, in his nickname the 'inimitable'). There are many places where Dickens drew in one form or another from the fiction of his contemporaries, but the itemization of these borrowings does little actually to contextualize Dickens's output. For one thing, the novelists he was most likely to be influenced by are not those from the 19th-century who have been canonized as classics. There are, for instance, very few female novelists whose fiction impinges on Dickens. Charlotte BRONTË and her sisters failed to impress him: a memoir of his conversation at Gad's Hill towards the end of his life records him as saying that he 'had not read *Jane Eyre* and said he never would as he disapproved of the whole school. He had not read *Wuthering Heights*' (quoted in Ackroyd 1990, p. 837). His notion of the more 'passionate' branches of Victorian fiction is brutal in its reductiveness ('They met she shrieked and married him'). The more balanced, and conventionally DOMESTIC, FICTION of Mrs Gaskell was more to his taste. He highly praised *Mary Barton*, offered his suggestions on *Ruth* (1853), and serialized *Cranford* (1851–3) and *North and South* in *Household Words*. But his attitude to female authors was dependent upon them remaining within their appropriate (i.e. domestic) sphere (see also DOMESTICITY; WOMEN'S ISSUES). Not for nothing does *Bleak House* contain a satire upon the movement for female enfranchisement (Mrs Jellyby's last and, it is implied, ridiculous cause). On 19 January 1856 he used *Household Words* as a platform from which to attack a prominent campaigner for women's rights, Harriet MARTINEAU ('Our Wicked Mis-statements'); even the placid Mrs Gaskell could provoke his fury (at one time he commented to a friend that, were he her husband, he would feel compelled to 'beat her' (to Wills, 11 September 1855).

It is worth wondering how he would have greeted the developing career of the period's most gifted woman novelist, George Eliot. The gentle, pastoral domesticity of *Scenes of Clerical Life* (1858) met with Dickens's highest approval; indeed, he refused to believe the author's pseudonym correctly reflected her gender. 'I think [*Scenes of Clerical Life*] so truly admirable,' he wrote to Joseph Langford on 18 January 1858, 'but if those two volumes, or a part of them, were not written by a woman, then I should begin to believe I am a woman myself.' He even wrote to 'George

Eliot' herself, voicing his suspicions ('I have observed what seems to me to be such womanly touches, in those moving fictions . . .', 18 January 1858). What this suspicion allows us to do is access what Dickens considered a proper 'womanly' fiction (see SEXUALITY). It was to be 'moving' (or as we would put it today, SENTIMENTAL), limited in scope to the domestic sphere, gentle, kindly, mildly humourous. The essentialism and restrictiveness of this model of the 'womanly' seems narrow today. *Adam Bede* (1859) also met with Dickensian approval; again it is a pastoral tale, in which the woman who conforms is rewarded with marriage and the woman who transgresses is punished severely. Dickens wrote to Eliot that 'Adam Bede has taken its place among the actual experiences and endurances of my life. Every high quality that was in [*Scenes of Clerical Life*] is in that, and with a World of Power added thereunto' (10 July 1859). But he seems to have been rather nonplussed by the strenuous intellectualism of Eliot's historical novel *Romola* (1863) and he died before the publication of her late masterpieces *Middlemarch* (1872) and *Daniel Deronda* (1876). The move away from the comfortable domesticity of *Scenes* was far from his own notion of the proper area of the woman novelist.

But there were several male Victorian novelists, now considered to be somewhat of the second rank, whose influence upon Dickens is more palpable. One is Edward BULWER-LYTTON, whose novels are now unread but who was popular enough in his own day. Critics have discerned the influence of Lytton's Newgate novel *Paul Clifford* (1830) upon *Oliver Twist*, of *Night and Morning* (1841) upon *Bleak House*, and of the Gothic-magical *Zanoni* (1842), set partly in the French Revolution, upon *A Tale of Two Cities*. Dickens thought highly enough of Bulwer-Lytton's judgement to follow his advice and change the ending he had originally planned for *Great Expectations*. On the other hand, it is difficult to establish any pattern of influence from Bulwer to Dickens more substantial than the occasional plot device or character-quirk. Temperamentally, Bulwer-Lytton as a novelist was urbane, aristocratic, often prolix, and almost wholly lacking in humour; it is difficult to imagine four terms less applicable to Dickens.

A similar problem presents itself when we deal with another accredited influence upon Dickens, Wilkie Collins. Collins's great contribution to 19th-century letters is, broadly speaking, twofold: plot, which Collins refigured as a dense, carefully worked through, and complicated network of references, usually predicated upon a mystery which has to be brought to light (what we now think of as 'the detective plot'); and narrative technique, or more specifically his dividing narrative viewpoint between several witnesses, after the manner of courtroom testimony (a technique used most famously in *The Woman in White*, 1860, and *The Moonstone*, 1868). Dickens thought very highly of Collins's technical abilities in these two spheres. He commissioned work from Collins for *All the Year Round* (the short stories collected as *After Dark*, 1856, and the novel *The Moonstone*, 1868), and Collins even wrote and acted in a play with Dickens, The FROZEN DEEP (1857). Yet when Dickens tried to adapt Collins's techniques for his own work the results were not happy. The over-complicated inheritance and hidden-identity plot of *Our Mutual Friend* collapses halfway through the novel, leaving Dickens to all but disclaim it in an afterword ('Postscript in Lieu of a Preface'). Once again we are left with the sense that, however much Dickens read, corresponded with, and interacted with his fellow novelists —however much he was a vital and active part of the Victorian literary scene—he was too much the distinctive original ever to really fit neatly into a particular historical period. Dickens's own genius, in a significant sense, set him apart from the novel of his own age.

AR

Gilmour, Robin, *The Novel in the Victorian Age: A Modern Introduction* (1986).
Hawthorn, Jeremy (ed.), *The Nineteenth-Century British Novel* (1986).
Sutherland (1976).
Wheeler, Michael, *English Fiction of the Victorian Period* (2nd edn. 1994).

**nursery rhymes.** To Dickens the traditional rhymes of childhood were part of the fabric of English life, and he alludes to them in many of his novels. There are several references to 'Cock Robin', 'Mother Hubbard', 'Little Jack Horner', and the 'House that Jack Built'. 'Old King Cole', 'Ride a Cock Horse',

'Peter Piper', 'Sing a Song of Sixpence', 'Tom, Tom, the Piper's Son' are also mentioned, and 'No little Gradgrind had ever learnt the silly jingle, Twinkle, twinkle, little star' (*HT* 1.3). This last, by Jane Taylor, which first appeared in 1806, is one of the very few nursery rhymes actually written for children and with a known author. Though many rhymes are of great antiquity, for centuries they were orally transmitted, and it was not until the 1740s that anyone thought to collect and print a selection for children (*Tommy Thumb's Pretty Song Book*, 1744, apparently preceded by *Tommy Thumb's Song Book* which has disappeared). *Mother Goose's Melody* was another important 18th-century compilation which probably made its first appearance in 1780; here again whole editions have disappeared without trace. Many rhymes are to be found in early 19th-century chapbooks—'Cock Robin' was a particular favourite—but more lavish illustrated collections did not begin to appear until James Orchard Halliwell's *The Nursery Rhymes of England* (1842) and *Popular Rhymes and Nursery Tales* (1849), and Dickens probably originally knew most of them from hearing them repeated. Indeed, his rendering of 'I'll tell you a story | About Jack a Nory' as a story about 'Jack a Manory' (*OMF* 2.16) suggests this.                                              GA

Opie, Iona and Peter, *The Oxford Dictionary of Nursery Rhymes* (1951).

# O

**obituaries.** 'It is an event world-wide', Carlyle wrote on Dickens's death (9 June 1870); 'a *unique* of talents suddenly extinct; and has eclipsed ... "the harmless gaiety of Nations".' It was lamented by the Queen ('a very great loss') and by an illiterate costermonger's girl ('Dickens dead? Then will Father Christmas die too?'—which would have charmed him). His death created 'a blank in our own existence', wrote the *New York Times* (11 June), which celebrated him with 150 column-inches that day and much more over the next fortnight. Obituaries, recognizing him as 'the most popular and most personally regarded novel-writer that ever handled pen' (*Fraser's*, July), sought again to explain this POPULARITY, assess its likely survival, and determine which phases and modes of his work were most effective, and they stressed his peculiar status as literary genius, great entertainer, and eminent public man. Obituaries did not then say much about their subjects' private lives, but friends of Dickens described his personality, habits, and demeanour; Sir Arthur Helps, for instance, writing about his outlook, appearance, and powers of observation (*Macmillan's*, July) and G. A. SALA expanding his *Daily Telegraph* obituary into an illuminating booklet (1870).

The TIMES (10 June) foresaw that Dickens would be 'regarded with more honour, as time passes and his greatness grows upon us'. It thought *Pickwick* his masterpiece; the *Athenaeum* (18 June) chose *Copperfield*; almost everyone preferred his earlier work, with the *Carol* and *Chuzzlewit* also attracting special praise. Of the later novels, only *Little Dorrit* was considered a total failure. All agreed that he was a great humourist, with an exceptionally wide range of characterization; his pathos was more controversial. He was seen as very much the man of his age, not only depicting it with such vigour, amplitude, and accuracy that posterity would see it through his eyes, but also, while criticizing its shortcomings, sharing its mainstream values—'his tastes and modes of thought were essentially middle-class English' (*Fraser's*), 'he was the man of his epoch, and had the time-spirit throbbing within him' (*Temple Bar*, July). This included his reformism; he was a radical, but a moderate, helpful, unthreatening one.

He appealed to the heart, was loved not just admired, and considered a friend: obituaries hailed the home, hearth, and family as his empire, his eminent 'purity' being helpful here ('he never wrote a line which his daughter would blush to read aloud in miscellaneous company': *Sunday Times*, 12 June). His extra-literary skills and public stature were noticed, such as his oratory: 'He spoke so well, that a public dinner became a blessing instead of a curse, if he was in the chair' (Anthony Trollope, *St Paul's*, July). Even irrespective of his literary genius, he was 'an able and strong-minded man, who would have succeeded in almost any profession to which he devoted himself' (*The Times*). Thus, he would have been 'a gain to physic' (*British Medical Journal*, 18 June); his medical observations were so accurate that they had entered the textbooks. There is a selection of obituaries in Collins (1971).    PC

## Old Curiosity Shop, The
Dickens's fourth novel (1840–1) which consolidated his fame and sold better during its SERIAL run than any of his previous novels (over 100,000 copies per week), but which later became a prime target for attacks on his alleged vulgar sentimentality.

### Inception and Composition
The idea for the child Nell, surrounded by old and grotesque objects, came to Dickens when he and John FORSTER were visiting Walter Savage LANDOR in Bath in February 1840. Landor later reported (with 'a thundering peal of laughter') that he wished he had bought the house and then burned it to the ground, to ensure that 'no meaner association should ever desecrate the birthplace of Nell' (Forster 2.7 n.). At that date Dickens was under way writing the initial numbers of his new weekly miscellany, MASTER HUMPHREY'S CLOCK. What was to become chapter 1 of *The Old Curiosity Shop*, written in March, initially

appeared as a single episode in no. 4 of the *Clock*, describing Humphrey's night-time meeting with Nell, their walk to the shop where they meet her grandfather and Kit Nubbles, the grandfather's departure, and Humphrey's meditations on the scene. Dickens's interest in the conception and an alarming decline in sales of the miscellany determined him to turn the single episode into an extended story, which engulfed *Master Humphrey's Clock* entirely after no. 11. Dickens discarded Master Humphrey as narrator at the end of chapter 3, reintroducing him only after the final chapter, where the improbable announcement that he is the Single Gentleman serves as transition to *Barnaby Rudge*, the story which followed *The Old Curiosity Shop* in the *Clock*.

Although Forster reported that *The Old Curiosity Shop* evolved 'with less consciousness of design' than any other of Dickens's works, and claimed that he was himself responsible for the 'valued suggestion' made halfway through the writing that Nell should die (Forster 2.7), Dickens stated that the design and purpose were 'distinctly in my mind, from its commencement' (13 March 1841). He found the space available for weekly instalments constricting, but composed the story quickly and easily, with few manuscript corrections—notably, the suppression at proof stage of a passage from chapter 66 which indicated that the Marchioness was the illegitimate child of Sally Brass and Quilp. Shortly after he began extending the story, he described himself as 'warmly interested' in it, and particularly in Dick Swiveller ('I *mean* to make much of him', he told Forster, ? May 1840). In a revealing glimpse at his use of observation to inspire his imagination, he reported in August that he had been to Bevis Marks 'to look at a house for Sampson Brass' (to Forster, ?19 August 1840). His letters of the time make it clear that Dickens was characteristically energetic and in good spirits while writing most of the novel, but his 'anguish unspeakable' for his beloved sister-in-law Mary HOGARTH reawakened as Nell's death approached (12 November 1840). After he had finished writing the novel he confessed that 'I think I shall always like it better than anything I have done or may do' (13 March 1841). (See also COMPOSITION, DICKENS'S METHODS.)

## Contracts, Text, and Publication History

*The Old Curiosity Shop* was not subject to an independent contract, first appearing as it did within the pages of *Master Humphrey's Clock*, for which Dickens had signed a contract with CHAPMAN AND HALL on 31 March 1840 (Pilgrim 2.464–71). The complete manuscript and corrected proofs, plus the first surviving number plans for a Dickens novel, are held in the FORSTER COLLECTION at the VICTORIA AND ALBERT MUSEUM; galley proofs for chapters 29, 30, 31, and 37, with corrections in Dickens's hand, are in the DEXTER COLLECTION at the British Library. Chapter 1 was published in No. 4 of the miscellany on 25 April; chapter 2 appeared in No. 7 on 16 May, and thereafter instalments of the story appeared weekly until the final chapter was published in No. 45 on 6 February 1841.

The weekly numbers were collected and issued in monthly parts as well, and *Master Humphrey's Clock*, including both *The Old Curiosity Shop* and *Barnaby Rudge*, was published in three volumes, with a dedication to Samuel ROGERS and prefaces dated September 1840, March 1841, and November 1841. The first edition of *The Old Curiosity Shop* to be published independently of the *Master Humphrey's Clock* framework was printed in 1841, largely from the original plates, retaining the original running headline, '*Master Humphrey's Clock*' and the original pagination. A second set of page numbers indicated junctions where *Clock* material had been excised, and at the end of chapter 1, where excision had created a gap, Dickens added three new paragraphs, transforming the opening episode from a self-contained short story into the beginning of a longer narrative, and including the observation that Nell seemed to exist in 'a kind of allegory' (an interpretation suggested by Thomas HOOD in a review written before the story was half completed—*Athenaeum* 7 November 1840). During Dickens's lifetime *The Old Curiosity Shop* was reissued as part of the Cheap Edition (1848), for which he wrote a new Preface, the People's Edition (1865–7), the Library Edition (1858), and, with new running titles, the Charles Dickens Edition (1868). Dickens also paid to have a raised-letter edition published by the Perkins Institute for the Blind in Massachusetts in 1869. He made no substantial emendations of the text for any of these editions.

Editions published after his death have generally been based on the first volume edition of 1841 or the Charles Dickens Edition, although some subsequent editions, notably the Macmillan Edition, with an introduction by his son, Charles Dickens the younger (1892), and the Everyman's Library Edition, with an introduction by G. K. CHESTERTON (1907), return to the text as it originally appeared in *Master Humphrey's Clock* (which is now usually published as a separate volume). The definitive Clarendon edition (1997), edited by Elizabeth Brennan, is based on the 1841 edition. (See EDITIONS.)

## Illustrations

As with the later Christmas books, for *Master Humphrey's Clock*, including *The Old Curiosity Shop* and *Barnaby Rudge*, Dickens had his ILLUSTRATORS supply woodblock engravings dropped into the text, as opposed to the steel etchings on separate pages used for his other full-length illustrated works. This had the advantage of linking illustration and text far more closely; MACLISE's engraving of 'Nell and the Sexton' (*OCS* 55) has been identified as a particularly fine example of such a marriage (John Harvey, *Victorian Novelists and their Illustrators*, 1971, pp. 103–29). But the preparation of the illustrations by this method was a slower and more painstaking process than steel engraving, at precisely a time when greater speed was necessary to meet a weekly rather than monthly publication schedule. In consequence, rather than the customary illustrator taking sole responsibility for supplying plates for a text, for *The Old Curiosity Shop* four artists were hired: Samuel WILLIAMS, Daniel Maclise, George CATTERMOLE, and Hablot BROWNE. In the event, Williams and Maclise supplied only a single illustration each—'The Child Asleep in her Bed' (*OCS* 1) and 'Nell and the Sexton' (*OCS* 55) respectively—with Cattermole and Browne sharing the remainder. Browne concentrated on the scenes involving figures, especially the grotesque comic characters, while Cattermole's drawings were more stately and architectural, a contrast which reinforced the diverse moods of the story itself. His letters reveal that Dickens took great care over the content and placing of the illustrations, and commentators have generally regarded the result with great admiration.

Browne in particular 'artistically came into his own' as a Dickens illustrator (Cohen 1980), making it fitting that *The Old Curiosity Shop* was the first illustrated book in which he was identified by his own name rather than by his soubriquet 'Phiz'. Dickens, however, apparently preferred Cattermole's work to Browne's, commissioning two watercolours in 1842 based on his illustrations, *Little Nell's Home* (*OCS*, frontispiece) and *The Grave of Little Nell* (*OCS* 72). Among illustrations for later editions, Fred Barnard's drawings of Dick Swiveller and Charles Green's of Quilp are particularly noteworthy. There is a statue of Nell by Ball Hughes, first exhibited at the Great EXHIBITION OF 1851 and now on display at the Athenaeum in Boston, and a bronze statue of Dickens with Nell by Edwin Elwell in Philadelphia. A grave-marker in Tong churchyard commemorates Dickens's heroine.

## Sources and Context

*The Old Curiosity Shop* is almost universally thought to have its origin in Dickens's grief over the death in his arms of his beloved young sister-in-law, Mary Hogarth, three years previously. Dickens himself wrote to Forster that 'old wounds bleed afresh' when he came to write of Nell's death (?8 January 1841), and the treatment of his heroine's fate has been at the centre of most controversy over Dickens's ability to deal—whether artistically or personally—with deep emotion. His letters show, however, that far from being obsessed with Mary's memory, he seems consciously to have reactivated his grief in order to write about Nell's last days, and in any case, Nell shares little of Mary's distinctive personality (see Kathleen Tillotson, 'A Letter from Mary Hogarth', *Dickensian*, 57, 1961).

The attention to this biographical source has distracted attention from the fact that Dickens was writing within a popular tradition at the time, of edifying accounts of mortality. A stream of EVANGELICAL tracts recount the death of pious young persons, and more generally, Dickens was drawing on Romantic celebrations of CHILDHOOD (WORDSWORTH's 'We Are Seven' was one of his favourite poems) and of the 'pleasures of melancholy' (the title of the most famous work of Samuel Rogers, to whom *The Old*

*Curiosity Shop* was dedicated). Nell herself compares her wanderings to those of Christian in *The Pilgrim's Progress* (*OCS* 15), and the absence of place names, the passing over water and through fire, the evocations of Vanity Fair and the Delectable Mountains, all reinforce the relation between the novel and BUNYAN's allegory of a soul's journey.

Quilp too has clear antecedents in traditional popular sources, most notably the puppet Punch, but also the Yellow Dwarf of FAIRY TALE, the Dandy Lover of PANTOMIME, and SHAKESPEARE's *Richard III*. It also seems evident that Dickens was consciously thinking of *King Lear* in creating his image of a wilful old man, partially out of his senses, supported in adversity by the love of a spiritually pure young woman. A number of critics have explored parallels between the works (see Jerome Meckier, 'A Myth for Victorian England', *South Atlantic Quarterly*, 71, 1972; Paul Schlicke, 'A Discipline of Feeling', *Dickensian*, 76, 1980; Alexander Welsh, 'King Lear, Père Goriot and Nell's Grandfather', in Joseph P. Strelka (ed.), *Literary Theory and Criticism*, 1984).

If *Lear*'s themes of disorder and alienation provide a literary context, *The Old Curiosity Shop* also shows Dickens participating in troubling social issues of the hour. Overtly, the torchlight parade of unemployed workers (*OCS* 45) is a nightmare vision of popular unrest occasioned by trade recession and bad harvests and finding its principal outlet in CHARTIST protest, which had erupted in alarming riots only months before Dickens began writing the novel. Nell's sense of loss and insecurity mirrors widespread contemporary anxiety in the face of CLASS tensions, population explosion, URBANIZATION, INDUSTRIALIZATION, disappointment in REFORM, and controversial social legislation, presided over by weak governments and an inexperienced young Queen. A decline of some traditional forms of AMUSEMENT AND RECREATION, is depicted in the financially hard-pressed entertainers Nell meets on her travels (see FAIRS AND ITINERANT ENTERTAINERS; Schlicke 1985). *The Old Curiosity Shop* is thus a highly topical work, even as its deliberate blurring of time and place and its affinities with pantomime, fairy tale and Punch and Judy lift it into a timeless world of imagination.

## Plot, Character, and Theme

*The Old Curiosity Shop* begins with Nell Trent, a 13-year-old girl, lost at night in the streets of London. Master Humphrey (unnamed in the novel) takes her home to her grandfather in the curiosity shop, where he is struck by the incongruous contrast of her childish innocence surrounded by ancient and GROTESQUE objects. In hope of winning riches for her, Nell's grandfather leaves the shop for nightly bouts of GAMBLING, and his losses put him in the power of the malicious usurer, Daniel Quilp. When Quilp takes possession of the shop and of Nell's bed, Nell flees with her grandfather, who is now debilitated by MADNESS. Wandering aimlessly in a landscape from which Dickens withholds place names, Nell meets a variety of people, including a schoolmaster whose favourite pupil is dying; the Punch and Judy exhibitors Codlin and Short; and Mrs Jarley, proprietress of a travelling WAXWORKS show. When her grandfather's gambling mania returns and he steals the last of Nell's money, they pass through a nightmarishly frightening industrial town; Nell collapses and is taken by the schoolmaster to a rural village where she dies peacefully.

The demonically energetic Quilp, meanwhile, has been pursuing her, tormenting his wife and mother-in-law, devising plots against Nell's reverently faithful servant Kit Nubbles, and toying with Dick Swiveller, a raffish 'gent' with careless matrimonial designs upon Nell. Quilp secures Swiveller a job as clerk to the toady lawyer Sampson Brass and his mannish sister Sally, where a small, ill-used servant-girl captures the engaging wastrel's imagination. Swiveller entertains her and names her the Marchioness; in return she runs away, nurses him through a near-fatal illness, and exposes the villainy of Quilp and the Brasses. Quilp drowns while trying to escape; Kit marries his fellow-servant Barbara, and Swiveller marries the Marchioness.

The plot—or rather, plots—of *The Old Curiosity Shop* are loosely improvisatory and episodic, arranged primarily in broad contrasts of comedy and pathos, darkness and light, city and country. On the other hand, each of the central characters can be seen to move, like Oliver Twist, through a 'progress' within a clear moral framework. Little Nell, beset by fears and threats, represents a 'Principle of Good surviving through every adverse circumstance' (as Dickens described his intention with Oliver in his 1841 Preface to *Oliver Twist*)—with the crucial distinction that Nell lacks the strength and support to survive in a wicked world. Daniel Quilp, systematically cutting himself off in frenzied violence from wife and accomplices, hurls himself to a dark and lonely death which the coroner's verdict fittingly declares to be suicide. Dick Swiveller, his moral sensibility awakened by his imaginative response to the Marchioness, undergoes a symbolic death and rebirth to emerge as the true hero of the story.

In her lonely wanderings, Nell is the quintessentially Dickensian representative of childhood—sensitive, frightened and prematurely responsible. In her innocence and selfless goodness she is also representative of Dickens's tendency to idealize young women, in this case saved from sexual maturity by an early death (see SEXUALITY AND GENDER; WOMEN'S ISSUES). Her antithesis is Quilp, grotesque and iconoclastic, whose manic hilarity gives him greater kinship to an ogre of folklore than to any merely human character. And Dick Swiveller, with his delight in observation, theatre, and song, and his name which echoes that of his creator, is Dickens's supreme embodiment of the beneficent power of a comic imagination.

Thematically *The Old Curiosity Shop* is concerned with the contrast between city and country, with youth and age, with innocence and wickedness, and above all with life and death, not so much as death affects the person facing it as in its meaning in the memory of those who survive. In the final summing up, Dickens points to Kit, who gathers his children round to 'tell again the story of good Miss Nell who died' (*OCS* 73). In its abstraction, idealization, and grotesquerie it is the least realistic of all Dickens's novels, and the one which has elicited the greatest extremes of response from readers over the years.

## Reception

There is a famous (unconfirmed) legend that crowds would gather at docks in America as the ship sailed in with the latest instalment of *The Old Curiosity Shop*, shouting 'Is Little Nell still alive?', and it was above all the pathos of the story which its first reviewers praised. By the time of Dickens's death, however,

bewilderment at such a response was commonplace, and the most famous witticisms at Dickens's expense are directed at Nell, 'a monster as inhuman as a baby with two heads' in Swinburne's words ('Charles Dickens', *Quarterly Review*, 196, 1902). According to Oscar Wilde, 'One must have a heart of stone to read the death of Nell without laughing' (Violet Wyndham, *The Sphinx and Her Circle: A Biographical Sketch of Ada Leverson, 1862–1933*, 1963), and many have agreed with Aldous Huxley's judgement that Nell is a classic instance of 'vulgarity' (*Vulgarity in Literature*, 1930).

Opinion about the book has never been unanimous, however; there were dissenting voices among its first reviewers, and defenders such as E. P. Whipple (*Charles Dickens: the Man and His Work*, 1912) and George GISSING, even when its critical fortunes were at their lowest. Nell and Quilp have caused controversy from the outset, but Swiveller has widely been considered 'the noblest of all the noble creations of Dickens' (Chesterton, 1906, p. 122). 19th-century readers praised the book's pathos, moral elevation, and comedy; Charlotte Young's song, 'They told him gently she was gone', was 'sung for a generation in nearly every British home' (Edwin Charles, *Some Dickens Women*, 1926), and Lotta Crabtree played both Nell and the Marchioness for 20 years (1867–87) in John Brougham's burlesque DRAMATIZATION.

In the 20th century, Freudian critics stood appraisal of the book on its head, deploring Nell but praising the depiction of sexual vitality in Quilp (see CRITICISM: FREUDIAN). Gabriel Pearson's analysis (1962), seeing the book's structure organized into three 'fields of force', was influential in directing attention away from isolated parts of the book, and there have been lengthy assessments by J. C. Reid (1962), who found a balance between realistic and fairy-tale elements, and by Mark M. Hennelly Jr. (1993), whose Bakhtinian approach defined Dickens's achievement as 'carnivalesque'. Perhaps the most perspicacious modern assessment has been made by Edwin Eigner (*The Metaphysical Novel*, 1978), who finds a clash of world views in which realism is negated by romance.                    PVWS

Hennelly, Mark M. Jr., 'Carnivalesque "Unlawful Games" in *The Old Curiosity Shop*', *Dickens Studies Annual* (1993).

Pearson, Gabriel, '*The Old Curiosity Shop*', in Gross and Pearson (1962).

Reid, J. C., *The Hidden World of Charles Dickens* (1962).

Schlicke, Paul, 'The True Pathos of *The Old Curiosity Shop*', *Dickens Quarterly*, 7 (1990).

**Oliver Twist** Dickens's second novel, first published SERIALLY 1837–9, distinguished by trenchant social satire and vivid evocation of criminal low-life, and, in the mythically evocative depiction of Oliver asking for more, containing perhaps the most widely known image Dickens ever created.

### Inception and Composition
Of all Dickens's novels, *Oliver Twist* had the most troubled birth pangs. It occasioned bitter controversy between author and publisher while it was being written and published serially, and to this day its origins are fraught with controversy.

On 2 November 1836 Dickens agreed to edit a new monthly miscellany for the publisher Richard BENTLEY. Dickens was to contribute 'an original article' of sixteen pages for each issue, but—the cause of much discord in months to come—there was no explicit indication that this was to be a serialized novel. He signed a contract on 4 November, and although he resigned the next day from the MORNING CHRONICLE, he remained heavily committed elsewhere: twelve numbers of *Pickwick* were still unwritten; *Sketches by Boz* (Second Series) was unfinished; *The* VILLAGE COQUETTES was being prepared for production in December; he was under contract to write a three-volume novel for John MACRONE and two more of equal length for Bentley.

Dickens's contribution to the first number of BENTLEY'S MISCELLANY, published on 1 January 1837, was a farcical tale, 'Public Life of Mr Tulrumble, Once Mayor of MUDFOG'. On 6 January his first child was born. On 18 January he announced to Bentley that he had 'hit upon a capital notion' and expected the next number to be 'an exceedingly good one'; two days later, in the first specific reference to *Oliver Twist*, he asked whether Bentley had met his hero. 'I have taken a great fancy to him—I hope he deserves it', Dickens wrote.

Thereafter Dickens generally devoted the first two weeks of each month to *Oliver Twist* and the *Miscellany*, and the latter two to *Pick-*

*wick*; from May 1838 he reversed this pattern, working first on *Nickleby*, which had succeeded *Pickwick* as his serialized novel for CHAPMAN AND HALL, then on *Twist*. At first Dickens consistently wrote fewer pages of *Oliver Twist* than his contract stipulated (the January 1838 number was the first to extend to sixteen pages), filling the remaining pages of the February number with 'The Pantomime of Life' and adding 'Some Particulars Concerning a Lion' in May. Relations with Bentley were generally cordial during the first months; it was only after Dickens discovered in May 1838 that Bentley was docking his pay for shortfalls that he made certain each subsequent instalment ran to its full extent.

The first interruption to monthly publication occurred in June 1837, when Dickens was recovering from the double shock of Mary HOGARTH's death on 7 May and his wife Catherine's subsequent miscarriage. Tension between Dickens and Bentley developed that summer, when Dickens proposed that *Oliver Twist* be considered the second novel ('Gabriel Vardon', eventually published by Chapman and Hall as *Barnaby Rudge*, was the first) (to Bentley, 14 July 1837). Bentley understandably objected that Dickens was demanding to be paid twice for the same work; Dickens equally understandably considered that his value had increased enormously since the initial agreements were reached. By August relations had reached the point that Dickens was applying Sikes's description of Fagin to Bentley: an 'infernal, rich, plundering, thundering old Jew' (to Forster, ?5 August 1837). By 30 August Dickens had decided to write no number of *Oliver Twist* for October; on 16 September he threatened to resign the editorship of *Bentley's Miscellany*. Bentley eventually backed down, and signed a revised agreement on 28 September (Pilgrim 1.654–5).

Resuming work on the novel, Dickens reread the opening chapters before writing chapter 17, in which the narrative returns to Oliver's birthplace, with a famous defence of scene changes contrasting like 'layers of streaky bacon'. He had some breathing space between November, when *Pickwick* concluded its serial run, and February, when he began writing *Nickleby*, but characteristically there were other projects: SKETCHES OF YOUNG GENTLEMEN, published 10 February by

Chapman and Hall, and MEMOIRS OF GRIMALDI, published by Bentley on 26 February. In March Dickens opened negotiations with Frederick YATES for a DRAMATIZATION of *Oliver Twist*—in the event Dickens did not turn it into a play himself, but two rival adaptations, one by Gilbert À BECKETT and another by C. Z. Barnett, were staged that spring, although Dickens was 'satisfied that nobody can have heard what I mean to do with the different characters, inasmuch as I don't quite know, myself' (to Yates, ?mid-March 1838).

The agreement of 28 September 1837 stipulated that *Oliver Twist* would continue in *Bentley's Miscellany* until 'Midsummer 1838'. By July 1838 that date had been moved to September, and in the event Dickens was unable to deliver the final chapters to the printer until 20 October. Even then there were last-minute changes to be made; publication of the three-volume edition, overseen by FORSTER, was postponed from 6 November; Dickens returned from Wales on the 8th for final corrections, and the book was published the following day. Serialization continued until April 1839, with AINSWORTH's *Jack Sheppard* replacing it as lead story, but Dickens took little interest in the final instalments, having 'burst the Bentleian bonds' and resigned from the *Miscellany* (to Talfourd, 31 January 1839).

In her introduction to the Clarendon edition Kathleen Tillotson proposes that Dickens had conceived of *Oliver Twist* as early as 1833, citing a letter of ?10 December to Henry Kolle which refers to 'my proposed Novel' (p. xv), and arguing further that extensive revisions made for the 1846 edition indicate that 'until then, Dickens was still writing his novel' (p. xl). Her case is disputed by Burton M. Wheeler, who argues that *Oliver Twist* 'was begun as a short serial', that it had advanced to four instalments before Dickens decided to convert it to a novel, and that 'its plot did not take shape even in general form' until seven instalments had appeared (Wheeler 1983, p. 41). Based on close scrutiny of Dickens's letters, on the three interruptions to the work's serial progress, and on textual changes Dickens made for the three-volume edition of 1838, Wheeler offers a persuasive hypothesis, but at the expense of evidence of planning by Dickens.

The novel's inception is complicated further by the claim of George CRUIKSHANK, the novel's illustrator, that he 'was the originator of *Oliver Twist*' ('The Origin of Oliver Twist', *The Times*, 30 December 1871). Cruikshank said that he proposed to Dickens a story which would 'raise a boy from a most humble position up to a high and respectable one'; the boy would fall among thieves, including a receiver of stolen goods who was a Jew, and who would be shown in a prison cell. Cruikshank's claim, which has aroused 'fierce controversy' (Forster branded it a 'monstrous absurdity': 2.3), is judiciously examined by Robert Patten, who demonstrates how close was the collaboration between author and illustrator (Patten 1996, 2.50–94). (See also COMPOSITION, DICKENS'S METHODS.)

### Contracts, Text, and Publication History

Dickens signed a contract to write two novels for Bentley on 22 August 1836, and on 4 November entered into an agreement to edit *Bentley's Miscellany* (Pilgrim 1.648–50). This agreement was modified on 17 March 1837, on 28 September 1837, and on 22 September 1838 (Pilgrim 1.650–1, 654–5, 666–74). *The Adventures of Oliver Twist, or the Parish Boy's Progress*, by 'BOZ', with illustrations by Cruikshank, was serialized in *Bentley's Miscellany* from February 1837 to April 1839, with three breaks, in June and October 1837 and September 1838. Chapters were numbered in three books of unequal length, a division which was eliminated in subsequent editions. Dickens revised the first eighteen instalments extensively in autumn 1838 for the three-volume edition, which was published by Bentley on 9 November 1838, and reissued a few days later with a new title-page naming Dickens as author. A 'second edition', published 17 December 1838 and dated 1839, was actually a reprinting with the words 'second edition' added to the title-page. It was reissued by Bentley as a 'new edition' in October 1839 and, with authorship reverting to 'Boz', again in March 1840. An incomplete manuscript, consisting of chapters 12–13 and 23–43 (according to the final chapter numbering), is in the FORSTER COLLECTION, and a few scraps of manuscript are in the Berg Collection, the Gimbel Collection, and the DICKENS HOUSE.

Dickens's long and acrimonious dispute with Bentley—'war to the knife . . . with the

Burlington Street Brigand'—continued after the formal agreement of 27 February 1839 terminating Dickens's editorship of *Bentley's Miscellany* (to Talfourd, 17 December 1839; Pilgrim 1.675–80). Settlement was ultimately agreed on 2 July 1840, whereby Dickens was released from his obligations to Bentley, and Chapman and Hall advanced £2,500 on Dickens's behalf for COPYRIGHT, plates, and unsold stock of *Oliver Twist* (Pilgrim 2.471–5). Chapman and Hall reissued the 1840 sheets as the 'third edition' with new title-page and a Preface, written in March 1841 and dated April 1841, described by Tillotson as 'Dickens's longest and most ambitious preface, an important critical manifesto containing a reasoned defence of the novel' (introduction to Clarendon Edition, p. xxvii).

Dickens continued to revise the novel, extensively repunctuating, curbing MELODRAMATIC style, and altering chapter divisions for the next edition, which was brought out in 1846 by BRADBURY AND EVANS in ten monthly parts from 1 January to 1 October, and in one volume on 26 September. This is the text controversially chosen for the Clarendon Edition of 1966. During his lifetime the novel was republished, without the subtitle but with little further revision other than a new Preface and a new frontispiece by Cruikshank, in the Cheap Edition (1850, reissued without Preface or contents in 1865 as the People's Edition); in the Library Edition (1858); and, with running headlines and a revised version of the 1841 Preface, in the Charles Dickens Edition (1867) (see EDITIONS). In this final edition over which Dickens retained control he replaced most references to 'the JEW' with 'Fagin' or 'he'.

*Oliver Twist* was published in Philadelphia in 1838 (dated 1839) by Lea and Blanchard, in Paris in 1838 (dated 1839) by Baudry, and in Leipzig in 1843 by Tauchnitz. No edition contained a dedication. (See also COLLECTIONS OF DICKENS MATERIALS.)

### Illustrations

Cruikshank, who had collaborated previously with Dickens on *Sketches by Boz*, was hired by Bentley to supply one plate a month for *Bentley's Miscellany*. Announcing his initial conception of Oliver to Bentley, Dickens confidently predicted that it 'will bring Cruikshank out', as indeed it did; the resulting illustration was the incomparable 'Oliver Asking For More' (18 January 1837). The plates of Sikes on the rooftop ('The Last Chance') and of 'Fagin in the Condemned Cell' are among the most admired of all Cruikshank's works.

Dickens undertook to have copy to Cruikshank by the fifth of each month, to give the artist time to execute his engravings, but he was chronically late, and some illustrations were drawn before Dickens had written the monthly number (to Cruikshank, ?26 November 1836). Others show Cruikshank picking up details from Dickens's text, or adding to it. As Patten observes, regardless of which of them originated specific ideas, the collaboration was particularly close: 'the illustrations reflect and comment not only on the text, but also on themselves, forming their own narrative of the progress of Oliver and his acquaintances' (Patten 1996, 2.73).

Cruikshank supplied 24 plates for *Oliver Twist*. During the dispute between Dickens and Bentley in autumn 1838 (in which Cruikshank sometimes acted as intermediary, apparently retaining the confidence of both parties) publication was erratic: there was no instalment of Oliver in the September number, no illustration to the novel in October, both novel and plate in November, but the plate in the December number illustrated a scene from the August number. The final design depicting Rose Maylie and Oliver (the 'fireside' plate) met with disapproval from Dickens, and was replaced in later copies of the first three-volume edition by another, of Rose and Oliver in Church. Cruikshank supplied a new wrapper design for the 1846 edition, and a new frontispiece for the Cheap Edition. (See also ILLUSTRATORS AND BOOK ILLUSTRATION.)

### Sources and Context

It is appropriate to think of *Oliver Twist* as the first Victorian novel—its serialization had reached chapter 8 when the young Queen acceded to the throne on 20 June 1837. Dickens's great original stroke in *Oliver Twist* was to place a child at the centre of the novel, thereby developing in a contemporary context WORDSWORTH's idea of CHILDHOOD as a special state. His portrait of Rose Maylie owes something to Dickens's memory of Mary Hogarth.

The art of both Dickens and Cruikshank has been widely seen as a new version of HO-GARTH—a similarity emphasized by the novel's original subtitle, *The Parish Boy's Progress*. Both had previously used London low life as subject-matter, notably in their collaboration on *Sketches by Boz*. Some *Sketches* directly anticipate *Oliver*: 'The Hospital Patient' (Nancy), 'Criminal Courts' (Dodger), 'A Visit to Newgate' (Fagin in the condemned cell). Cruikshank imagined the story as a re-enactment of Francis Goodchild's 'progress' in Hogarth's *Industry and Idleness* (Patten 2.53), and in its allegorizing tendency the tale bears resemblance to an earlier progress as well, that of BUNYAN's Pilgrim. In the initial serialized version Oliver's birthplace is named as Mudfog, linking it with other papers Dickens wrote for *Bentley's Miscellany* (the location is unspecified in later editions).

Dickens drew on his nightmare experience in WARREN'S BLACKING warehouse as background to Fagin's lair, and took the villain's name from one of his fellow-workers, Bob Fagin. He was familiar with criminal cases from his days as a reporter for the *Morning Chronicle*, and to gather material for the scene depicting Oliver's appearance before Mr Fang (*OT* 11) he arranged to be smuggled into the police magistrate's court of the 'notoriously severe' Allan Stewart Laing (1788–1862) (to Thomas Haines, 3 June 1837 and note; see LAW AND LEGAL INSTITUTIONS). He had also reported the parliamentary debates concerning the New POOR LAW of 1834, which aroused widespread protest during the harsh winter of 1836–7. The savage satire in the book's opening chapters on the treatment of paupers attacks the conception of human nature associated with Jeremy BENTHAM and Thomas MALTHUS which lay behind the law, and the depiction in chapter 1, and subsequently, of the power of clothing to characterize a person suggests the influence of CARLYLE's *Sartor Resartus* (1836).

In language, characterization, and action *Oliver Twist* is by far the most melodramatic of Dickens's novels, even after revisions to reduce its excess, and Dickens's deep familiarity with the THEATRE is everywhere in evidence: the rhetorical flourish of speeches, accompanied by violent gestures, the moral polarization of characters, and improbable plot by which the story's resolution is achieved.

Monks is a two-dimensional stage villain, Nancy the whore with a heart of gold, and the beadle was a stock comic figure which Dickens himself had drawn previously, in the 'Our Parish' section of *Sketches by Boz*. Theatricality is the source at once of the artistic limitations of *Oliver Twist* and of its supreme power. (See also CRIME; LONDON: SLUMS.)

## Plot, Character, and Theme

The story begins with Oliver's birth as an illegitimate child in a workhouse. Lacking individuating characteristics—his mother (with no wedding ring) dies in childbirth and Bumble, the pompous beadle, invents his name—Oliver serves less as a character than as a representative of oppressed childhood. Having outraged the Poor Law authorities by asking for more food, he is apprenticed to Mr Sowerberry the undertaker, and is soon in trouble again when he hits the charity boy Noah Claypole for insulting his mother's memory. With inexorable logic, his oppression leads him into the criminal underworld; the first person he meets after running away to London, Jack Dawkins (better known as the Artful Dodger), takes him to Fagin's den. Oliver's survival is miraculous; the more likely consequences of the environment Dickens portrays is seen in the death of the orphan Dick (*OT* 7) and the cowardly later career of Noah as an informer. Fagin's explanation to Noah how self-interest benefits all is a brilliant parody of the philosophy which underpinned the Poor Law (*OT* 43).

Oliver is apprehended when his companions pick the pocket of Mr Brownlow, who takes him home and looks after him after securing his release from the police magistrate's court of Mr Fang. On his first errand out of Brownlow's house Oliver is kidnapped by the prostitute Nancy and the house-breaker Sikes and returned to Fagin. Taken by Sikes to assist at a robbery, Oliver is shot and captured, but the occupants of the house, Rose Maylie and her aunt, believe Oliver's pleas, and their friend Dr Losborne persuades the Bow Street Runners that he is innocent.

Halfway through the novel Dickens introduces a shadowy villain named Monks, who turns out, in the complex plot which follows, to be Oliver's legitimate half-brother, conniving at Oliver's ruin for financial gain. The centre of interest shifts from Oliver to Nancy, whose revelation of the scheming to Rose and Mr Brownlow, on the steps leading down to the river at the side of Old London Bridge, is overheard by Noah. Fagin reveals Nancy's action to Sikes, who murders her then flees in guilty terror, eventually falling to his death from a rooftop. Fagin is apprehended and condemned to be hanged; Bumble and his wife are convicted for destroying evidence, and Oliver is revealed to be Rose's nephew and the nephew of the woman Brownlow had loved.

### Reception
Dickens's new-found fame from *Pickwick* and the monthly serialization of *Bentley's Miscellany* ensured that *Oliver Twist* was widely reviewed, overwhelmingly with admiration. The novel was read as much as a social document as a work of art; the young Queen Victoria found it 'excessively interesting' but was unable to convince her Prime Minister, Lord Melbourne, who declared, 'It's all among Workhouses, and Coffin Makers, and Pickpockets ... I don't *like* those things; I wish to avoid them; I don't like them in *reality*, and therefore I don't wish them represented' (Collins 1971, p. 44). THACKERAY attacked Dickens for romanticizing crime, linking *Oliver Twist* with Ainsworth's *Jack Sheppard* and BULWER-LYTTON's *Eugene Aram* as a NEWGATE NOVEL ('Horae Catnachianae', *Fraser's Magazine*, 1839; '*Catherine*', *Fraser's Magazine*, 1839–40; 'Going to See a Man Hanged', *Fraser's Magazine*, 1840).

PLAGIARISTS were active, and more dramatizations of *Oliver Twist* have been staged than of any other Dickens work, despite censorship for some twenty years by the Lord Chamberlain, who considered it dangerous to public peace (Bolton 1987, p. 105; Jame F. Stottlar, 'A Victorian Stage Censor: The Theory and Practice of William Bodham Donne', *Victorian Studies*, 13, 1970). Arguably the greatest FILM based on a Dickens novel is David Lean's *Oliver Twist* (1948), with Alec Guinness as Fagin, and Lionel Bart's musical, *Oliver!* (1960), has been enormously popular on stage and in a film version. But incomparably the most important adaptation of the novel was by Dickens himself, in the PUBLIC READING version, 'Sikes and Nancy', first performed on 14 November 1868. His rendition of the murder electrified audiences ('TWO MACBETHS!',

MACREADY declared it: to Fields, 15 February 1869), and radically undermined Dickens's health, contributing significantly to his death at the age of 58.

From the first appearance of the novel, critics have debated the relative merits of Dickens's comedy, as epitomized by *Pickwick*, and his depiction of low life, crime, and violence, as seen in *Oliver Twist*. In a famous essay, Graham Greene proposed that Dickens's vision in *Oliver Twist* is Manichaean, a war of spiritual forces; Arnold Kettle identified conflicting structures of 'pattern', based on a contrast between rich and poor, and 'plot', in which distinction is made between deserving and undeserving poor; and John Bayley located the book's power in its combination of 'social denunciation' and 'GOTHIC nightmare'.                                               PVWS

Bayley, John, '*Oliver Twist*: Things as They Really Are', in Gross and Pearson (1962).
Greene, Graham, 'The Young Dickens', *The Lost Childhood and Other Essays* (1951).
Kettle, Arnold, 'Dickens: *Oliver Twist*', *An Introduction to the English Novel* (1962).
Patten (1996).
Wheeler, Burton M., 'The Text and Plan of *Oliver Twist*', *Dickens Studies Annual*, 12 (1983).

**Orwell, George,** pseudonym of Eric Blair (1903–50), journalist, broadcaster, and novelist, whose essay 'Charles Dickens' (*Inside the Whale*, 1940) was a milestone in the history of Dickens's REPUTATION. Orwell's Dickens was 'generously angry', a revolutionary whose social and political outlook was 'almost exclusively moral'. 'His whole message', Orwell wrote, 'looks like an enormous platitude: if men would behave decently the world would be decent.' Calling Dickens the best writer on CHILDHOOD, Orwell claimed that his concern for the child and for EDUCATION arose because he abhorred violence and distrusted politics. Orwell found grave limitations in Dickens's novels: 'large areas of the human mind that he never touches ... no poetic feeling anywhere in his books and no genuine tragedy'. His 'good' characters are 'a collection of village idiots', and he was a writer 'whose parts are greater than his wholes. He is all fragments, all details.' But for Orwell this was, paradoxically, Dickens's greatest strength: 'The outstanding, unmistakable mark of Dickens's writing is the *unnecessary detail*.' By arguing a case for Dickens as a serious novelist and not merely a popular entertainer, Orwell, along with Edmund WILSON and Humphry HOUSE, led the way for much subsequent study of Dickens. PVWS

**Osgood, James Ripley** (1836–92), Boston publisher. As a junior partner of TICKNOR AND FIELDS, Osgood travelled to England in 1867 to solicit texts from Dickens and to negotiate for his firm to be named Dickens's sole authorized American publisher. Osgood also suggested, and later, with George DOLBY, planned and made arrangements for Dickens's American PUBLIC READING tour of November 1867 to April 1868, during which he acted as Dickens's escort. On 29 February 1868 (competing as 'the Boston Bantam') he defeated Dolby (as 'the Man of Ross') in 'The Great International Walking-Match', a burlesque competition organized for Dickens's amusement. MW

**O'Thello** A Shakespearean 'burlesque burletta', written by Dickens in 1833, for private performance by his family and friends. The 'juvenile indiscretion' survives only in his father's prompt copy of his role as 'The Great Unpaid', seven manuscript pages of doggerel verse and songs written to be sung to popular tunes, which were sold by John DICKENS in 1842 and are now scattered in several collections. The comic misadventures in Dickens's 1834 sketch, 'Mrs Joseph Porter, "Over the Way" ' (*SB*), suggest why a private theatrical production of *Othello* might best admit a ludicrous aspect. PVWS

Haywood, Charles, 'Charles Dickens and Shakespeare; or, The Irish Moor of Venice, O'Thello, with Music', *Dickensian*, 73 (1977).

**Our Mutual Friend** Dickens's fourteenth and last completed novel, published in twenty monthly parts (as nineteen) in 1864–5. The third of his great panoramic depictions of English society, it is dominated by the symbols of dust-heaps and the river.

### Inception and Composition

The gestation of *Our Mutual Friend* was unusually prolonged and frustrating. Between 1860 and 1861 Dickens chose his title and discussed with FORSTER ideas which he recorded in his *Book of Memoranda*. These included a number of names used in the book—Podsnap, Lightwood, Riderhood, Wegg, Boffin, Headstone, Lammle, Twemlow, and

Wilfer—and plot notions which he was to develop—a man 'feigned to be dead, and *being* dead to all intents and purposes external to himself'; 'a poor imposter of a man marrying a woman for her money; she marrying *him* for *his* money; after marriage both finding out their mistake, and entering into a covenant against folks in general', with both of them connected with 'bran new' people; and an 'uneducated father in fustian' with an 'educated boy in spectacles' (Forster 9.5; Kaplan 1981).

Dickens's letters of the next several years are a litany of woe: first, an inability to get under way, and then trouble in proceeding. Poor health added to his difficulties. In April 1862 he wrote to Forster: 'Alas! I have hit upon nothing for a story. Again and again I have tried, but this odious little house [in Kensington, where he was staying temporarily] seems to have stifled and darkened my invention.' Six months later he wrote again to Forster to say that he doubted whether he 'could force an original book out' (5 October 1862). The better part of a year passed, and on 9 August 1863 he lamented to Wilkie COLLINS, 'I am always thinking of writing a long book, and am never beginning to do it'. In October he told Forster that he was 'exceedingly anxious to begin my new book', and insisted that 'I see my opening perfectly', but wanting to have at least five numbers in hand before he began publishing feared lest he should 'drift off again, and have to go through all this uneasiness once more'.

Finally, on 15 January 1864 he was able to announce to Collins that 'I have done the first two numbers, and am now beginning a third. It is a combination of drollery with romance which requires a great deal of pains and throwing away of points that might be amplified; but I hope it is *very good*.' But even then, he confessed, he felt 'dazed' by the 'large canvas'. Moreover, he explained, 'I have grown hard to satisfy, and write very slowly' (to Forster, 29 March 1864). Serial publication commenced in May, and by summer his lead of completed numbers was being eroded. 'I have not been wanting in industry,' he told Forster (29 July 1864), but 'wanting in invention.' Although he was more cheerful about the book by the start of the new year, expressing amusement that Charles KENT could not see his way 'with a certain Mutual Friend of ours' (17 January 1865), by May he confided to Forster that he felt near to breaking down.

Then, on 9 June 1865 (five years to the day before his death), he was involved in a serious railway accident at Staplehurst, KENT, after which he 'clambered back' into a teetering carriage to retrieve a portion of manuscript (to Thomas Mitton, 13 June 1865; Postscript in lieu of a preface). The next month he fell further behind, and found that he had underwritten No. 16 by two and a half pages—'a thing I have not done since Pickwick!', he exclaimed to Forster (July 1865). That month he declared himself 'tied by the leg to my book' (to Edward Bulwer-Lytton, 20 July 1865), and to both MACREADY and WILLS he reported that he was 'working like a Dragon' (to Macready, 22 April; to Wills, 27 August 1865). He finally finished writing the novel on 2 September (to Thomas Beard, 21 September 1865; see COMPOSITION, DICKENS'S METHODS).

A number of Dickens's LETTERS relating to *Our Mutual Friend* await publication in volume 11 of the Pilgrim Edition (forthcoming). In an interview with F. G. KITTON, Dickens's illustrator Marcus STONE revealed that Dickens's original intention was to have Eugene die as a result of Bradley's attack (Kitton 1899, p. 197).

### Contract, Text, and Publication History

On 8 September 1863 Dickens wrote to CHAPMAN AND HALL offering them half of the COPYRIGHT during SERIAL PUBLICATION of *Our Mutual Friend* for £6,000, and the contract was signed on 21 November (Pilgrim 10.477–8). There was a clause which entitled the publisher to cancel the agreement if publication had not begun by the end of 1864, and to claim compensation should Dickens die before completing the work. Robert Patten notes that the contract gave Dickens 'unprecedented' control: 'Chapman risked the whole sum in advance without security, while Dickens guaranteed to himself £6,000 ... plus half of whatever the number sale netted, plus the whole of whatever the novel produced following the first volume issue' (1978, pp. 302–3).

The manuscript and number plans, which Dickens gave to E. S. Dallas in gratitude for his favourable review of the novel in *The TIMES* (29 November 1865), are held by the Pierpont Morgan Library. The corrected proofs, presented to Marcus Stone, are in the Berg Collection (see COLLECTIONS OF DICKENS MATERIALS).

The novel is dedicated to James Emerson Tennant (1804–69), an old friend of Dickens and Forster (see DEDICATIONS). It was published serially from May 1864 to November 1865, and in two volumes, divided into four books, in February and November 1865. It was brought out in four volumes in Leipzig by Tauchnitz, 1864–5, and serially in America in *Harper's New Monthly Magazine*, June 1864–December 1865. A German TRANSLATION by Marie Scott was published by J. J. Weber in five volumes, 1864–5. The Cheap Edition and the Library Edition both appeared in 1867, the Charles Dickens Edition in 1868 (see EDITIONS OVER WHICH DICKENS HAD CONTROL). There is no authoritative modern text.

### Illustrations

*Our Mutual Friend* was illustrated by Marcus Stone, the son of Dickens's close friend and neighbour Frank STONE, who had died in 1859. Dickens promptly took the young man under his wing, treating him like a member of the family and giving him work. Fresh and biddable, Marcus Stone drew the frontispiece for the Cheap Edition of *Little Dorrit* and eight engravings for the Library Edition of *Great Expectations*. His work marked a distinct break from the caricature tradition of HOGARTH and CRUIKSHANK which Hablot BROWNE had followed. Less adept at grotesque art, Stone's figures were larger and more realistic, and his work for Dickens was, as Jane Rabb Cohen observes, 'more ornamental than integral' (1980, p. 205).

Dickens discussed some of the illustrations in great detail with Stone. He considered the wrapper design 'excellent', but made several suggestions regarding detail. He wanted the word 'Our' in the title to be drawn as large as the other two words, and the dustman's face 'droll, and not horrible ... I want Boffin's oddity, without being at all blinked, to be an oddity of a very honest kind, that people will like'. He made a similar observation about Stone's drawing of the dolls' dressmaker. 'A weird sharpness not without beauty is the thing I want' (23 February 1864).

Dickens allowed Stone to select some of his subjects and let the artist decide which of

Wegg's legs should be wooden (Kitton 1899, p. 197), but he made specific suggestions for other illustrations. The frontispiece for the second volume, for example, 'should be the dustman with the three mounds, and Mr Boffin digging up the Dutch bottle, and Venus restraining Wegg's ardour to get at him. Or Mr Boffin might be coming down with the bottle, and Venus might be dragging Wegg out of the way as described' (13 September 1865).

Although some commentators have suggested that Dickens was largely uninterested in the illustrations for *Our Mutual Friend*, Cohen argues that he participated actively in the collaboration and was 'judicious' in his appraisal of Stone's work (1980, pp. 203–9).

Undoubtedly Stone's most valuable contribution to the novel was to take Dickens round to St Giles's to see the establishment of one Mr Willis, a taxidermist (Kitton 1899, pp. 199–200). As Dickens reported to Forster, this inspired the creation in the novel of Mr Venus, preserver of birds and animals and articulator of human bones (25 February 1864; see ILLUSTRATORS; CHARACTERS—ORIGINALS).

### Sources and Context

*Our Mutual Friend* opens on the River Thames, London's great commercial highway which Dickens had previously described as a 'deadly sewer' (*LD* 1.3; see LONDON: BRIDGES AND RIVER). After years of dispute between the City of London Corporation and the Crown over its ownership, the City had withdrawn its claim and in 1857 the first Thames Conservancy Act was passed. By Dickens's day watermen were less ubiquitous than historically, as new bridges were built, but boat traffic remained heavy. G. A. SALA describes a 'strong-boned' female waterman in a *Household Words* article ('Powder Dick and His Train', *HW* 7 May 1853). In the novel as in fact the river's complex function was a source both of livelihood and of death.

Refuse collection was a major source of wealth in the 19th century, and CARLYLE had written of dust-heaps in his *Latter-Day Pamphlets* (1850), making the connection between money and dirt. R. H. HORNE wrote an article on the business of collecting refuse ('Dust; or Ugliness Redeemed', *HW* 13 July 1850), describing the dust-heaps and recount-

ing an anecdote of a dust-contractor's daughter, who is offered a dowry of £20,000 or a dust-heap. She chooses the money, and the heap is 'subsequently sold for forty thousand pounds'. Other *Household Words* articles describe reclamation of waste: 'Penny Wisdom' (*HW* 16 October 1852), 'Important Rubbish' (*HW* 19 May 1855), 'A Way to Clean Rivers' (*HW* 10 July 1858), 'Dirty Cleanliness' (*HW* 24 July 1858).

Favourite Dickens themes—CLASS, EDUCATION, mercenary marriage—reappear in *Our Mutual Friend*. 'The Decline and Fall Off The Rooshan Empire', which Wegg reads to Boffin, alludes (with pointed relevance to the British empire of the 19th century) to Gibbon's great work, *The History of the Decline and Fall of the Roman Empire* (1776–88), in which a great commercial empire crumbles. Dickens introduced the character of Riah in a conscious attempt to 'atone for a great wrong', the slur against JEWS which Fagin was seen to be. Mrs Eliza Davis, whose husband (described by Dickens as a 'Jew money-lender', to Thomas Mitton, 16 August 1860) had purchased Tavistock House from him in 1860, wrote to him on 22 June 1863 to complain about the prejudice he encouraged, and he replied defending himself. 'I have no feeling towards the Jewish people but a friendly one', he declared (10 July 1863; see Cumberland Clarke, 'Fagin and Riah', *Dickensian*, 17, 1921).

Earle Davis (1963, pp. 266–9) has shown that central situations in *Our Mutual Friend* bear striking resemblance to two plays by Sheridan KNOWLES, one of the most popular 19th-century playwrights. *The Daughter* (1837) concerns salvagers of dead bodies on the Cornish coast and opens with a scene depicting these men at work pulling floating bodies out of the water. The heroine, who is ashamed of her father's mode of earning his living, is deceived into thinking that he has murdered one of the dead men. The villain turns out to be responsible both for the murder and the deception. The relations of Lizzie Hexam, Gaffer Hexam, and Rogue Riderhood are essentially similar.

In an earlier play by Knowles, *The Hunchback* (1832), the heroine is forced to choose between money and love. Her guardian (who is actually her father in disguise) pretends to demand that she marry for wealth and position, but she chooses instead the man she loves, who serves as a supposed rich man's secretary. Her father then reveals that the deception was carried out to test her character, and she is rewarded with a blessing on her marriage to the man she loves and the money as well. Boffin's deception to test Bella, who (as she thinks) rejects his wealth to marry Rokesmith the secretary, has basic affinity.

Another theatrical source, discussed by Edwin Eigner (1989) is the 'pious fraud' of PANTOMIME, in which a benevolent character deceives the hero or heroine for their own good, as Boffin does to Bella.

Famously, the character of Podsnap is said to be based on Dickens's closest friend, John Forster, who saw in the portrait only 'all the old cunning of the master hand' (9.5).

### Plot, Character, and Theme

*Our Mutual Friend* is the most complexly plotted of all Dickens's novels, with multiple strands skilfully interwoven. It opens with Gaffer Hexam, assisted by his daughter Lizzie, salvaging a corpse from the river. At a society dinner at the 'bran new' home of the Veneerings, it is disclosed that the heir to a fortune has been found drowned. Mortimer Lightwood and Eugene Wrayburn leave the dinner and go to view the body. With the dust-collector's heir, John Harmon, presumed dead, Noddy Boffin, servant to the late misanthrope, Harmon's father, stands to inherit the fortune. Boffin hires Silas Wegg, a one-legged ballad seller and a thorough rascal, to read to him, and hires John Rokesmith as his secretary. Mr and Mrs Boffin invite Bella Wilfer, betrothed from childhood to John Harmon, to live with them, and they adopt an orphan who dies.

Patronized by the Veneerings, Mr and Mrs Lammle are married on the presumption of each other's wealth, only to discover that neither has any. They vow vengeance on society and befriend 'the Young Person', Georgiana Podsnap, daughter of the pompous and opinionated John Podsnap, and encourage a match between her and the mean and hypocritical Fascination Fledgeby. Gaffer Hexam, falsely accused by another riverside scavenger, Rogue Riderhood, of murdering Harmon, drowns. Eugene is fascinated by Lizzie, as is her brother's schoolmaster, Bradley Headstone. When Charley Hexam and Bradley call on Eugene and reproach him for his atten-

tions to Lizzie, Eugene infuriates them with his supercilious coolness. Wegg and the comically lugubrious bone articulator Mr Venus begin a 'friendly move' to find a will in the dust-heaps which will deprive Boffin of the fortune. Rokesmith, who is Harmon in disguise, proposes to Bella, who rejects him from mercenary motives. Bradley proposes to Lizzie, who rejects him and runs away.

The genial Mr Boffin gradually becomes miserly, to Bella's dismay. When he denounces Rokesmith, Bella leaves his patronage and, on second asking, accepts Rokesmith's offer of marriage. Eugene bribes the drunken father of Jenny Wren (the crippled friend of Lizzie, who earns her living as a dolls' dressmaker) to find where Lizzie is hidden. Followed by Headstone, Eugene finds Lizzie in her country retreat. Headstone assaults Eugene and leaves him for dead; Lizzie uses her boating skills to rescue Eugene. While his life is still in danger they are married. Riderhood, recognizing that Headstone has modelled a disguise on his dress, blackmails the schoolmaster; they fight and both are drowned. The Lammles' conspiracies are foiled, as is Wegg's. Harmon's disguise is uncovered, and Mr Boffin reveals to Bella that his miserliness was pretence to educate her away from mercenary aspirations.

In Betty Higden, who runs away with funeral money sewn into her dress to avoid a pauper burial, Dickens works a reprise on his Poor Law satire in *Oliver Twist* (see POOR RELIEF). In Podsnap he ridicules John Bullish insularity and sanctimoniousness. Mrs Wilfer is one of the most comic of a long line of Dickensian termagants, and the 'innocent elopement' of Bella on an outing with her father displays Dickens's domestic humour at its most genial. Conversely, the violent Bradley Headstone's unrequited passion for Lizzie makes him perhaps the most terrifying psychological portrait Dickens ever drew. That the self-made man Bradley perishes, whereas the idle gentleman Eugene is redeemed, shows how complex Dickens's MORAL outlook had become. But despite its implacable attack on class prejudice and mercenary attitudes, *Our Mutual Friend* is less pessimistic than *Bleak House* or *Little Dorrit*, for Dickens grants John and Bella wealth, comfort, and respectability at the novel's conclusion.

## Reception

Sales for the opening number of the novel surpassed those for any previous work by Dickens, and he reported triumphantly to Forster, 'Nothing can be better than Our Friend, now in his thirtieth thousand, and orders flowing fast' (3 May 1864). Sales dwindled to 19,000 by the final number, however, and although Dickens made £12,000, Chapman and Hall lost £700 (Patten 1978, p. 308). Reviews were decidedly mixed: Henry CHORLEY declared it 'one of Mr Dickens's richest and most carefully-wrought books' (*Athenaeum* 28 October 1865), whereas young Henry James considered it 'the poorest of Mr Dickens's works' (*Nation* 21 December 1865). And although many critics have admired it greatly—Jack Lindsay (1950), for example, judging it 'one of the greatest works of prose ever written'—acclaim has never been universal. Stephen Gill, in his introduction to the Penguin edition (1971), is guarded in his praise, and Grahame Smith (1968) sees it as a work of 'failed genius'.

A. O. J. Cockshut (1961) has written insightfully on the book's symbolism, and Sylvère Monod (1968) looks carefully at Dickens's STYLE.

Undoubtedly the best-known evidence for the novel's impact, reflecting Angus Wilson's (1970) judgement that it was 'a novel before its time', is its direct influence on two great works of modernism. Ibsen's *The Doll's House* (1879) picks up Bella's declaration that she does not want to become 'a doll in a doll's house', and T. S. Eliot's *The Waste Land* (1922) originally began with a section inspired by Betty Higden's description of Sloppy's reading abilities: 'He do the police in different voices.'

PVWS

Cockshut, A. O. J., *The Imagination of Charles Dickens* (1961).

Davis (1963).

Eigner (1989).

Lindsay, Jack, *Charles Dickens: A Biographical and Critical Study* (1950).

Monod (1968).

Smith (1968).

# P

**Palmer, Samuel** (1805–81), artist, member of the Royal Society of Painters in Water Colours, and ILLUSTRATOR for *PICTURES FROM ITALY*. Known today primarily for his landscape paintings of Shoreham, Kent, and as a disciple of William Blake (1757–1827), Palmer was more highly regarded at that time for his Italian scenes. He was recommended to Dickens after Clarkson STANFIELD withdrew from illustrating *Pictures from Italy*. Author and artist met only once, and Palmer provided four woodcut vignettes, which he both designed and cut (a fifth design was prepared but not published). Palmer, a perfectionist, was disappointed with the results, but the illustrations pleased Dickens, who insisted that Palmer's name appear on the book's title-page. PVWS

**panoramas.** An entertainment of visual spectacle, invented in 1788, in which the audience was surrounded by a 360-degree painting of an urban scene, landscape, or battle. Increasingly sophisticated uses of lighting, sound effects, and music created an experience akin to the cinema in its verisimilitude. Commentary by a lecturer added instructional value. Some of the largest panoramas were set up in permanent rotundas, and spectacular effects were also possible outdoors, such as the eruption of Vesuvius at the Surrey Gardens. Dickens depicted his apartment on the Champs Elysees as having 'a moving panorama always outside, which is PARIS in itself' (21 October 1855), and he wrote an article about the adventurous Mr Booley, who travels the world while remaining in London ('Some Account of an Extraordinary Traveller', *HW* 20 April 1850). GFS

**pantomime** is popular theatre, derived from the Italian improvisatory street theatre, *commedia dell'arte*. In Britain it has flourished with radical and persistent changes since the 18th century, and then as now many British theatres depended on Christmas pantomime for financial stability. Dickens was a close friend of pantomime writers, scene designers, and reviewers, and an enthusiastic pantomime critic, contributing articles to the journals he edited in the course of his long career, most notably 'The Pantomime of Life' (*BM*, March 1837) and 'A Curious Dance Round a Curious Tree' (*HW* 17 January 1852). Pantomime influenced the structure, characters, and world-view of much of his fiction.

In 18th-century pantomime, Harlequinade interludes alternated without plot connection with scenes of serious drama, but when Dickens saw his first pantomime, the Harlequinade and attending story-line were more closely linked. Regency pantomime begins with a romantic scene based on a New Comedy formula: the young lovers are blocked by a greedy father who demands his daughter marry a wealthy but unattractive suitor. When the lovers despair, this plot is interrupted by the appearance of the Benevolent Spirit, often a popular fairy-tale figure, who transforms the characters into their *commedia dell'arte* equivalents and sets the Harlequinade in motion. The lovers are aided by Clown, who, as played by Joseph Grimaldi, had become the most important and the only speaking part in the Harlequinade (see *MEMOIRS OF GRIMALDI*). In the finale or transformation scene, the Benevolent Spirit waves her magic wand, transporting the entire cast to a magnificent, fairyland setting.

In later years the Harlequinade diminished in importance and eventually was dropped altogether. But it was the integrated pantomime of his childhood, with its lavish spectacle, genre transformations, and delight in the magical properties of ordinary objects, which fired the imagination of Dickens. In 'The Christmas Tree' (*HW*, Christmas Number, 1850) he wrote of this Regency pantomime as a 'stupendous Phenomenon!—when Clowns are shot from loaded mortars into the great chandelier, bright constellation that it is; when Harlequins, covered all over with scales of pure gold, twist and sparkle, like amazing fish . . . when Everything is capable, with the greatest ease, of being changed into Anything; and "Nothing is, but thinking makes it so".' EME

Eigner (1989).

Mayer, David, *Harlequin in His Element: The English Pantomime, 1806–1836* (1969).

**Paris.** Dickens first visited Paris in July 1844 *en route* to Italy. The impression the city made on him was, he later reported to Count D'Orsay, 'immense'. He found it 'the most extraordinary place in the World', and went on to describe its impact: 'I was not prepared for, and really could not have believed in, its perfectly distinct and separate character. My eyes ached and my head grew giddy, as novelty, novelty, novelty; nothing but strange and striking things; came swarming before me' (7 August 1844). Much of this pleasure in the distinctive novelty of Paris never wore off. Twenty years later he put into the mouth of Mrs Lirriper something of his continuing sensual delight. Paris, she found, was 'town and country both in one ... clean table-cloths spread everywhere for dinner and people sitting out of doors smoking and sipping all day long ... and every shop a complete and elegant room ... and the crowd of theatres and the crowd of people and the crowd of all sorts, it's pure enchantment' ('Mrs Lirriper's Legacy', *CS*). Relatively few of his other characters share Mrs Lirriper's enchantment, though their jadedness may well be indicative of a dulled sensibility. The newly married Mr and Mrs Dombey reportedly find Paris 'dull' during their honeymoon (*DS* 35). Lady Dedlock is typically 'bored to death' at the Hotel Bristol in the Place Vendôme (*BH* 12). The narrator of *Our Mutual Friend* notes that it is a city 'where nothing is wasted, costly and luxurious city though it be, but where wonderful human ants creep out of holes and pick up every scrap ... There, sharp eyes and sharp stomachs reap even the east wind, and get something out of it' (*OMF* 1.12).

The Paris Dickens saw in 1844 had approximately 900,000 inhabitants (though the number swelled to just over a million if the surrounding department of the Seine was taken into account). It thus held around half the inhabitants of contemporary London, already by far the most populous city in Europe. As Paris expanded in the 19th century (its overall population had risen to 1,825,274 in 1867) it remained much more physically contained than London. In 1844 its limits were still determined by the *octroi* or customs wall

constructed in 1785, but on 1 January 1860 the government of Napoleon III redefined its official boundaries with the new *enceinte continue*, a line of fortified wall of more than 21 miles in circuit pierced by some 67 gates. This new definition expanded the official size of the city from some twelve to 30 square miles. The city was divided into twenty arrondissements.

Napoleon III's Paris was also to be notable for the immense changes in its physical appearance and in its circulation wrought by the Prefect of the Seine, Baron Haussmann, in the 1850s and 1860s. Haussmann gave Paris an enforced coherence both in terms of its street plan and in its new urban architecture, extending the improvements begun in the reign of Louis Philippe. What had been a city of narrow, four-storey houses and pavementless streets in the 18th century was transformed in the 19th by conspicuously sited public buildings and by high apartment blocks lining grandiose boulevards and avenues. Dickens was well aware of the historic significance of these changes. He knew, for example, of the disappearance of buildings with prominent Revolutionary connections (notably clubs and prisons), and that Sydney Carton's winding route from the Conciergerie to the guillotine had largely been swept away by 1859. The Bastille, which plays so dramatic a role in *A Tale of Two Cities*, had been demolished by the triumphant people of Paris in 1789–90. At the end of the same novel Dickens also allows the visionary Carton to look forward to the improvements made to the Place de la Concorde under Louis Phillipe ('a place fair to look upon, with not a trace of this day's disfigurement'). Haussmann's radical alterations to the Île de la Cité are referred to at the opening of 'Some Recollections of Mortality': 'Notre-Dame was before me, but there was a large open space between us. A very little while gone, I had left that space covered with buildings densely crowded; and now it was cleared for some new wonder in the way of public Street, Place, Garden, Fountain, or all four' (*UT*). Dickens seems to have few regrets about the disappearance of the old Paris. He refers, for example, to the city as 'very full, extraordinarily gay, and wonderfully improving. Thousands of houses must have been pulled down for the construction of an immense street [the extension of the Rue de

Rivoli] . . . It will be the finest thing in Europe' (to Mrs Charles Dickens, 13 October 1853).

'Some Recollections of Mortality' and 'Travelling Abroad' (*UT*) deal primarily with Dickens's fascination with one particular building on the Île de la Cité, the Morgue. There was no real equivalent to this particular edifice in Victorian London and it was well known to contemporary British visitors to Paris (and recommended to them by guidebooks). 'Whenever I am at Paris', the UNCOMMERCIAL TRAVELLER remarks in 'Travelling Abroad', 'I am dragged by invisible force into the Morgue.' Here he saw the bodies of suicides and of others found drowned in the River Seine publicly exposed for purposes of identification. The two essays suggest a man both haunted by, and darkly speculative about what he had seen. On one occasion he claims to have been intrigued by the body of 'a large dark man whose disfigurement by water was in a frightful manner comic'; when he later swims at one of several bathing-establishments on the river he suddenly feels nauseous at having taken some water into his mouth, 'for I fancied that the contamination of the creature was in it'. The disturbing image continues to haunt him at a fencing display in the Rue St Honoré, as he gazes in shop-windows in the Palais Royal, and even amidst his commonest Parisian distractions, trips to the theatre.

It is possible that Dickens's fascination with the Morgue is rooted in his essentially ambiguous response to Paris. The city was, on the one hand, the revelatory *ville lumière* of his first visit. That it remained the centre of 'elegance, variety and beauty', a place typified by 'brilliant cafés' and by 'the light and glitter of houses turned as it were inside out' is suggested vividly by the essay 'A Flight' (*RP*). But it was also a city darkened and bloodied by its Revolutionary history. On a visit in 1847 Dickens described a typical tourist itinerary as consisting of trips to 'Versailles, the Prisons, the Opera, the Hospital, the Conservatoire and the Morgue' (27 January 1847). The prisons he visited would have probably included both the Conciergerie and the Abbaye, both replete with Revolutionary associations, the latter being particularly notable for its reminders of the horrors of the September Massacres. In January 1847 he also recorded a visit to a MELODRAMA at the Cirque

Olympique in the Boulevard du Temple. The melodrama re-enacted scenes from the Revolution and contained 'the most tremendous representation of a *people* that can be imagined . . . there is a power and massiveness in the Mob, which is positively awful'. That Revolutionary Paris, as the city of a blood-thirsty mob and of untimely death, worked powerfully on Dickens's imagination can be adduced not simply from *A Tale of Two Cities* but also from the fact that he exaggeratedly claimed in 1851 to have read 'that wonderful book', CARLYLE's *The French Revolution* (1836) some 500 times.

Dickens's Paris residences include the Hotel Meurice, 42 (later 228) Rue de Rivoli (July 1844; February 1855); the Hotel Bristol in the Place Vendôme ('the best I ever was in'; November 1844); the Hotel Brighton, 30 Rue de Rivoli (November 1846); 38 (formerly 48) Rue de Courcelles (1846–7); the Hotel Windsor, 38 Rue de Rivoli (June 1850); the Hotel Wagram, 28 Rue de Rivoli (February 1851); the Hotel de Londres in the Rue Castiglione ('a second rate affair and a poor dinner'; October 1853); 2 Rue St Florentin (October 1855); 49 Avenue des Champs Elysees (1856). He appears to have dined regularly at the Trois Frères Provençaux in the Galeries Beaujolais at the Palais Royal.                          ALS

Harrison, Wilmot, *Memorable Paris Houses* (1893).
*Galignani's New Paris Guide* (1842).
*Murray's Hand-Book for Visitors to Paris* (1882).
Sanders (1988).

**Peacock, Thomas Love** (1785–1866), self-educated satirical novelist, poet, essayist, and East India Company administrator, who apparently never met or corresponded with Dickens. However, some shorter work, especially two 'Paper Money Lyrics', appeared in 1837 and 1838 in BENTLEY'S MISCELLANY, then edited by Dickens. Dickens almost certainly drew on the corrupt election in Peacock's *Melincourt* (1817) in creating Eatanswill (*PP* 13–15), and may have recollected *Crotchet Castle*'s miserly financier Ebenezer McCrotchet when naming Scrooge and Bob Cratchit. In Peacock's final year, rereading much of Dickens as 'a rest from more serious study', he was 'continually in fits of laughter over *Pickwick*' and said he had quite 'fallen in love with Lizzie' Hexam of *Our Mutual Friend*.    LDB

Brett-Smith, H. F. B. and Jones, C. E. (eds.), *The Halliford Edition of the Works of Thomas Love Peacock*, 10 vols. (1924–34; repr. 1967).

**penal transportation.** See PRISONS; EMIGRATION AND COLONIZATION.

**penny dreadfuls.** While at Wellington School academy, the teenage Dickens pored over weekly numbers of *The Terrific Register* (1824–5?). Its contents, illustrated with lurid woodcuts, included accounts of torture, bizarre figures such as Sawney Beane, the 'Monster of Midlothian', who fed his family on human flesh, and the inevitable downfall of evil-doers. Such accounts provided a fertile ground for the imagination that was to create Squeers, Bill Sikes, Quilp, and the self-combusting Krook. The *Register* was a twopenny precursor of the 'penny dreadfuls' that became staple reading for the Victorian working classes, and illicit reading for many of the younger middle classes (see READERSHIP). These were launched in the 1830s by penny-issue PLAGIARISMS of *The Pickwick Papers* (1836–8), and flourished in the 1840s and the early 1850s, when crude SERIALS such as Thomas Rymer's *Varney the Vampire* (1846–7) were joined by better-written works such as G. W. M. Reynolds's *The Mysteries of London* (1846–8). By the 1860s, with improved literacy and literature for the masses, penny dreadfuls became lower-middle-class juvenile reading. By about the end of the century, the 'penny dreadful' may be said to have become the modern 'comic'.                    LJ

Stone (1994).
Turner, E. S., *Boys will be Boys* (rev. edn. 1957).

**pets belonging to Dickens.** Dickens's first pets seem to have been ravens. The first shared a stable with a Newfoundland dog, possibly the first of Dickens's dogs. Grip in *Barnaby Rudge* was based partly on this bird but mainly on its more gifted successor, whose death grieved Dickens although, as he recorded, 'The children seem rather glad of it. He bit their ankles' (to Maclise, 12 March 1841). A third raven with none of Grip's gifts was later kept at Gad's Hill.

In 1842 Dickens brought an eagle and a white spaniel back from America. The eagle so frightened the children that on the family's departure for Italy it was left with LANDSEER. When Dickens moved to Gad's Hill he acquired two large dogs to protect the property—Turk, a bloodhound, and Linda, a St Bernard. After Turk was killed by a train, Dickens obtained Don and Bumble, both Newfoundlands. He was then given an Irish bloodhound, Sultan, which proved so savage and uncontrollable that it had to be shot.

Dickens also possessed a canary, 'Dick, the best of birds', which died in 1866 aged 15, and a deaf kitten, known merely as 'The Master's Cat', which learned the trick of extinguishing a candle by a deft stroke from its paw.
                    ASW

**phrenology,** the scientific study of the mental faculties, meant for Dickens the theories of Franz-Joseph Gall adapted and popularized by Johann Kaspar Spurzheim, the Scots George and Andrew Combe, and by Dr John Elliotson, Dickens's longtime friend and family physician, who in 1824 founded and served as first President of the London Phrenological Society. Phrenology defined the brain as the organ of the mind, or, more accurately, as a number (usually 26, sometimes 33) of independent competing organs (e.g. of benevolence, amativeness, adhesiveness) that could be enhanced or controlled through the proper exercise of the will. Phrenologists studied the particular shape of individual skulls only to secure clues to the relative size of the particular mental organs, but were often derided as 'craniologists' who believed the shape of the skull itself to be a determinant of character. Like a number of 19th-century literary figures such as Charlotte BRONTË and George ELIOT, Dickens believed phrenology worthy of serious attention, and often used its jargon, from *Sketches by Boz* to *Edwin Drood*. When Pecksniff falls and hits his head, the Misses Pecksniff must attend 'to an entirely new organ, unknown to phrenologists' (*MC* 2). Dr Chillip notes the 'strong phrenological development of the organ of firmness, in Mr Murdstone and his sister' (*DC* 59). And Fezziwig's famous laugh from his 'shoes to his organ of benevolence' is well known (*CC* 2). Dickens shared Elliotson's conviction that phrenology enabled the discovery and treatment of criminal dispositions, attending the execution of the murderer Courvoisier with Elliotson, who produced a reading of the murderer Rush's skull. However, Dickens demonstrates his awareness of the uncertain status of phrenology on a number of occasions, often in relation to his AMERICAN experiences. He deftly satirizes the American appetite for phrenological instruction when he describes the lecturer Dr Crocus (*AN* 13). Dickens mocks the American frenzy to examine his own head (L. N. Fowler did so on 5 February 1842 in Worcester, Massachusetts) in *Martin Chuzzlewit*, where at the levee organized for Chuzzlewit by Captain Kedgick at the Watertoast National Hotel, 'Amateurs in the physiognomical and phrenological sciences roved about him with watchful eyes and itching fingers, and sometimes one, more daring than the rest, made a mad grasp at the back of his head, and vanished in the crowd' (*MC* 22). Nevertheless, Dickens was pleased by the theatrical performances given in Boston on 24 January 1842 in his honour, where the programme included Joseph M. Field's *Boz! A Masque Phrenological*, in which the actors represented, besides BOZ (Field himself) and many of his literary creations, phrenological 'faculties' such as 'Identity' and 'Wonder'.

LDB

Collins, Philip, ' "When Morals Lay in Lumps": The Victorians and Phrenology', *Listener* (August 1973).

**Pickwick Papers, The** Dickens's first novel, published in monthly parts from March 1836 to November 1837, which catapulted him to fame 'like a skyrocket', as one early review put it (Abraham Hayward, *Quarterly Review*, 59, 1837), and which remained his best-loved novel among general readers for decades after his death.

### Inception and Composition

In November 1835 the artist Robert SEYMOUR proposed to the young publishers CHAPMAN AND HALL a series of engravings depicting Cockney sporting life, to be issued SERIALLY with accompanying text. After approaching other writers unsuccessfully, Chapman and Hall contacted Dickens on 10 February 1836, just two days after *Sketches by Boz* (first series) had been published by John MACRONE. 'They (Chapman and Hall) have made me an offer of £14 *a month*', Dickens wrote that evening to his fiancée Catherine Hogarth (see DICKENS, CATHERINE), 'to write and edit a new publication they contemplate, entirely by myself; to be published monthly and each number to contain four wood cuts . . . The work will be no joke, but the emolument is too tempting to resist'.

The offer was little more than hack work, with his own role subordinate to illustrator and publisher, and Dickens later recalled that 'My friends [AINSWORTH and BULWER-LYTTON] told me it was low, cheap form of publication, by which I should ruin all my rising hopes' (1847 Preface). That he agreed with this verdict is clear from the number of other commitments he took on while *Pickwick* was under way: he continued his full-time job as parliamentary reporter for the MORNING CHRONICLE, wrote three theatrical pieces (*The VILLAGE COQUETTES*, *The STRANGE GENTLEMAN*, and *IS SHE HIS WIFE?*), composed a political pamphlet SUNDAY UNDER THREE HEADS, produced a second series of *Sketches by Boz*, agreed to write a novel for Macrone ('Gabriel Vardon', not completed until 1841 as *Barnaby Rudge*) and a children's book for Tegg ('SOLOMON BELL THE RAREE SHOWMAN', in the event never written), and signed a contract with Richard BENTLEY to write two novels and edit BENTLEY'S MISCELLANY. But far from 'ruining' his 'rising hopes', *Pickwick* became the publishing sensation of the century and in the process utterly transformed the very nature of book production.

From the outset, Dickens assumed control of the project. 'I objected, on consideration, that although born and partly bred in the country I was no great sportsman, except in regard of all kinds of locomotion; that the idea was not novel, and had been already much used; that it would be infinitely better for the plates to arise naturally out of the text; and that I should like to take my own way, with a freer range of English scenes and people, and I was afraid I should ultimately do so in any case.' A mere eight days after the project was first put to him, Dickens was under way. 'My views being deferred to, I thought of Mr Pickwick, and wrote the first number' (1847 Preface). He promised to have it to the publishers on 1 March, but on the 4th he wrote to Catherine, 'Pickwick is not yet completed. The sheets are a weary length—I had no idea there was so much in them.' The first number was published on 31 March. This was to be the pattern to the very end: a mad dash every month to finish copy, and text delivered late to the printer. But with a single exception, each number was published on schedule.

On 2 April Dickens and Catherine were married. On the 20th Seymour committed suicide. Despite poor sales, author and publishers agreed to proceed with the project. For an increased salary (20 guineas a month), Dickens was to write more copy (32 instead of 26 printed pages), and each number would contain two rather than four plates. A new illustrator, R. W. BUSS (1804–75), was hired—then summarily fired when his work proved unsatisfactory. He was replaced by the young Hablot BROWNE (1815–82), who was to be Dickens's chief collaborator for the next 23 years.

The first number which Browne illustrated, No. 4, which was published on 29 June, was momentous in other ways: in chapter 10 Dickens introduced Sam Weller, whose presence in the work was to transform Mr Pickwick from a comic butt to an incomparable comic character. Two chapters later, Mrs Bardell's misunderstanding of Pickwick's announcement that he intended to hire Sam introduced an element of plot, and without ceasing to be an episodic miscellany, from this point *The Pickwick Papers* became a novel.

From the August number onwards (No. 6), Dickens began to synchronize the story with the season in which each serial part appeared, most notably for the CHRISTMAS number (No. 10, published 1 January 1837), and the March number (No. 12), in which Sam writes a Valentine to Mary, and Mr Pickwick is put on trial for breach of promise of marriage.

On 4 November Dickens agreed to edit *Bentley's Miscellany*, and the next day he resigned from the *Morning Chronicle*. On 6 January his first child was born; two weeks later Dickens was elected a member of the GARRICK CLUB. The first instalment of *Oliver Twist* appeared in *Bentley's* on 31 January, and thereafter, until the final double number of *Pickwick* in November, Dickens was writing two novels simultaneously, a task which he accomplished by devoting the first two weeks of each month to the *Miscellany* and the latter half of the month to *Pickwick*. On 31 March Dickens and Catherine moved from chambers in Furnival's Inn to 48 Doughty Street (see HOMES OF DICKENS), and on 8 April Chapman and Hall hosted a celebratory dinner, at which they presented Dickens with a cheque for £500 and a set of SHAKESPEARE. This month the first of many DRAMATIZATIONS of *Pickwick* was produced (STIRLING'S adaptation at the City of London Theatre), as was the first sustained critical appraisal of the work (in the *Court Magazine*, 10, 1837).

For all the prodigious activity of these months, the sole interruption to the serial publication of *Pickwick* occurred when, on 7 May, Dickens's sister-in-law Mary HOGARTH, only 17 years old, died unexpectedly. Dickens and Catherine were devastated, and went into seclusion in Hampstead for a fortnight. No June number of *Pickwick* or *Oliver* appeared. In July Dickens, Catherine, and Browne travelled to FRANCE for a week, and in September Dickens took the first of many family holidays at Broadstairs. In early October he was 'obliged in violation of my established usage' to write in the evening in order to finish the final double number of *Pickwick*, which was published on 30 October (Pilgrim 1.315 hn). (See also COMPOSITION: DICKENS'S METHODS; ILLUSTRATORS AND BOOK ILLUSTRATION; PUBLISHING.)

### Contracts, Text, and Publication History

On 18 November 1837 a 'semi-business semipleasure kind of dinner in honour of the completion of Pickwick' was held at Degex's in Leicester Square, at which 'the pleasant and uncommon fact was stated . . . that there had never been a line of written agreement' for the serial (to Samuel Lover, 16 November 1837; William Jerdan, *Autobiography* 4.365, quoted Pilgrim 1.330 n.). Chapman and Hall had, however, formally outlined the proposal in a letter dated 12 February 1836 (Pilgrim 1.648); Dickens had responded with written acceptance on 16 February, and there were numerous letters regarding progress of the work between author, illustrators, and publishers. A deed, assigning one-third of copyright to Dickens after five years and contracting for another novel to follow (*Nicholas Nickleby*), was drawn up at FORSTER'S instance, approved on the date of the dinner, and signed on 24 November 1837 (Pilgrim 1.330–1n., 658–62).

Only fragments of the manuscript survive, primarily of chapters 36 and 37, scattered among several COLLECTIONS (see Engel, pp. 15–16). *The Posthumous Papers of the Pickwick Club*, by BOZ, was initially published by

Chapman and Hall in twenty (as nineteen) monthly parts from March 1836 to November 1837, with a break in June 1837 occasioned by the death of Mary Hogarth. Addresses to the reader announced the death of Seymour (No. 2, May 1836), the revised format (No. 3, June 1836), the intention to complete the work in 20 numbers (No. 10, January 1837), and 'severe domestic affliction' which interrupted publication (No. 15, June 1837). Chapter 29 was misnumbered 28, throwing off chapter numeration for the remainder of the work, an error not corrected until the Cheap Edition. The final double number included a frontispiece, vignette title-page, table of contents, Preface, and a dedication (written 27 September 1837) to Thomas Noon TALFOURD. *Pickwick* was issued in one volume, from existing plates, by Chapman and Hall on 17 November 1837 at 21 shillings. For the Cheap Edition of 1847 Dickens made haphazard corrections and wrote a new Preface. BRADBURY AND EVANS published *Pickwick* as volumes 1 and 2 of the Library Edition in 1858, from corrected copy of the 1847 edition, with a new dedication to Forster. In 1867 Chapman and Hall published the final version overseen by Dickens, with descriptive headlines, as volume 1 of the Charles Dickens Edition (see EDITIONS).

*Pickwick* was quickly published in Philadelphia by Carey, Lea and Blanchard in 1836–7; in Calcutta in 1837–8; in Tasmania in 1838; and in Leipzig by Frederick Fleischer in 1839. Within 100 years there were at least 96 separate English editions and 127 American ones (Patten, Introduction to Penguin edition, 1972, p. 19). The most carefully edited scholarly edition is the Clarendon, edited by James Kinsley and published in 1986.

### Illustrations

As explained above, *Pickwick* was originally conceived by Robert Seymour as a series of comic engravings of cockney sporting misadventures, with accompanying text. But Dickens immediately insisted on more extensive subject-matter and a reversal of priorities; he wanted the engravings not to dictate what he wrote, but to 'arise naturally out of the text', and he began issuing demands that Seymour alter the illustrator's designs to meet the writer's conception. The two met only once, 'to take a glass of grog' on 17 April

(to Seymour, 14 April 1836; 1867 Preface). Seymour made some alterations to the three plates he had finished for the second number, and then, leaving a note of apology to the 'best and dearest of wives', killed himself.

Buss, who was hired to succeed him, was inexperienced at etching and dismissed after supplying only two plates, which were suppressed shortly afterwards and replaced by new ones drawn by Browne. Hearing that a new artist was wanted, THACKERAY (1811–63) offered himself, but his services were declined. Browne, first as 'Nemo' and then as 'Phiz' (to complement 'Boz') quickly proved himself the ideal illustrator for Dickens: a skilled and rapid draughtsman, with a visual imagination that particularly lent itself to comic and grotesque designs, and a tractable nature which enabled him to give satisfaction according to Dickens's instructions—in the case of *Pickwick*, often given verbally before Dickens had written the scene to be illustrated. The history of the *Pickwick* illustrations is further complicated by the fact that increasing print runs necessitated the etching of two copies of each plate, from the tenth number onwards, with considerable variation of detail.

Many other artists, beyond the three with whom Dickens worked, tried their hand at illustrating *Pickwick*—Thomas Onwhyn, 'Alfred Crowquill', Thomas Sibson, John LEECH, and Fred Barnard, among others. In 1899 Joseph Grego collected 350 illustrations, including portraits based on stage adaptations, with notes and commentary (*Pictorial Pickwickiana*, 2 vols.).

### Sources and Context

Comic misadventures of cockney sportsmen were a popular subject in the 1830s, having been depicted by CRUIKSHANK in his *Comic Almanack*, by John Poole in the *New Monthly Magazine*, and by Seymour himself in illustrations to Richard Penn's *Maxims and Hints for an Angler, and Miseries of Fishing* (1833). Robert SURTEES's sporting adventures of a London grocer, *Jorrock's Jaunts and Jollities*, appeared serially in the *New Sporting Magazine* (1831–4) and were published in 1838 in volume form with illustrations by Leech. Dickens included Mr Winkle among Pickwick's companions in deference to Seymour's initial conception.

But the primary influence on *Pickwick*, as developed by Dickens, was the fiction, drama, and pictorial art of the 18th and early 19th centuries. The reviewer in the *Athenaeum* (3 December 1836) provided the recipe: 'two pounds of SMOLLETT, three ounces of STERNE, a handful of HOOK, and a dash of a grammatical Pierce EGAN', correctly identifying Dickens's ingredients as a combination of episodic adventure, SENTIMENT, lampooning wit, and graphic observation. In one of the earliest notices, BELL'S LIFE (12 June 1836) called Boz 'the literary HOGARTH of the day', a comparison which has been made repeatedly since. From FIELDING Dickens not only inherited many devices, including mock-heroic rhetoric and adventures on the open road, but gained 'a clearly defined view of "comic Romance" and the "true Ridiculous" ' (Kinsley, Introduction to Clarendon Edition, p. xxxix). From CERVANTES and the eighteenth-century stage he took the motif of an unworldly master with a worldly wise servant; the club device, the reluctant duellists, and the nocturnal adventures were other stock motifs. The satire on Nupkins is Shakespearean; on Stiggins JONSONIAN; Jingle's staccato patter derives from Charles MATHEWS the elder's comic character impersonations. The nostalgia for coaching days and the cheerful celebration of 'old-fashioned' CHRISTMAS festivities had precedent in the work of Washington IRVING. The ingredients were all well known, but the mixture was distinctively Dickens's.

For a number of episodes Dickens drew on personal experience. His father's imprisonment for debt in 1824 left him well aware of the inside of a prison (see DICKENS, JOHN). His reporting for the *Morning Chronicle* provided topical issues. The altercation between Mr Pickwick and Blotton draws on his familiarity with parliamentary debate. His coverage of corrupt elections, particularly that in Ipswich in May 1836, fed into the account of Eatanswill. His 26-column account on 23 June 1836 of the notorious Melbourne–Norton trial, in which the estranged husband of a society belle unsuccessfully sued the Prime Minister for adultery, provided material for the novel's trial scene. (See also NOVELISTS AND THE NOVEL BEFORE DICKENS; DRAMA AND DRAMATISTS BEFORE DICKENS.)

## Plot, Character, and Theme

Samuel Pickwick, a balding, bespectacled, good-natured man, descended from the 18th-century tradition of sentiment, first appears as a figure of ridicule, archly mocked by the narrator for the scrapes in which his naivety land him and his companions. But, in CHESTERTON's memorable words (adapted from GOLDSMITH), 'Dickens came to the Pickwick Club to scoff, and Dickens remained to pray' (Chesterton 1906, p. 96). In his relationship with Sam Weller, his cheerfully cynical manservant, Mr Pickwick develops into an 'angel in tights and gaiters', whose benevolence brings goodness and happiness to a naughty world.

With three of his Club companions (Winkle, Tupman, and Snodgrass) Mr Pickwick travels in search of sights and adventures. He promptly meets the strolling actor Alfred Jingle, who impudently leads the Pickwickians a merry chase as they righteously attempt to thwart his matrimonial designs on unwary spinsters. Eventually Mr Pickwick encounters a chastened Jingle in the Fleet prison and gives him and his servant Job Trotter money for passage to Demerara (see EMIGRATION).

Mr Pickwick's travels take him to Manor Farm, in KENT, where he is the guest of the hospitable Mr Wardle; to Eatanswill, where he witnesses an election and attends a fancy-dress party; to Bury St Edmunds, where he is discovered at night in the garden of a young ladies' boarding school while trying to thwart Jingle; to Ipswich, where he inadvertently finds himself in the bedchamber of a 'lady in yellow curl-papers'; back to Manor Farm for Christmas festivities; to a bachelor party in the London lodgings of two medical students, Ben Allen and Bob Sawyer; to Bath, where Sam attends a 'swarry'. Meanwhile, the machinations of the rascally lawyers Dodson and Fogg lead to Mr Pickwick being tried and convicted for breach of promise of marriage to Mrs Bardell, and when he refuses to pay damages, he is committed to prison. Only when he learns that Mrs Bardell has likewise been imprisoned does he relent, in order that she may be released and he may travel to Birmingham to seek reconciliation between the Winkles, father and son, after the latter has eloped with the lovely but penniless Arabella Allen.

Sam Weller faithfully serves Mr Pickwick all this while, instructing him in the ways of the world with anecdotes and 'Wellerisms'— cheerfully grotesque similes which defuse horror by absurdity ('Business first, pleasure arterwards, as King Richard the Third said when he stabbed t'other king in the Tower, afore he smothered the babbies'). Sam also finds time to pay visits to his father Tony, a rotund coachman with an aversion to 'widders', on account of finding himself married to one who spends her time with a drunken 'shepherd', the hypocritical EVANGELICAL Revd Mr Stiggins. Sam courts and marries the housemaid Mary, whom he has met in the course of his travels with Mr Pickwick.

These adventures are interspersed with nine inset tales, grotesque, macabre, or fabulous, which are unconnected with the main action and provide sharp contrast in tone. Generally seen either as mere filler, included because Dickens was hard-pressed to meet publishers' deadlines (seven appear in the first half of *Pickwick*), or as displays of virtuosity, they have precedent in narrative forms well known to Dickens, and some modern critics have claimed greater integration for them than is at first apparent (see Robert L. Patten, 'The Art of *Pickwick*'s Interpolated Tales', *English Literary History*, 34, 1967).

### Reception

Chapman and Hall envisaged a sale of around 500 copies a month. They printed 1,000 of the first number but sold fewer than half of them. Sales were still poor with number 3, but started to increase with number 4; by February 1837 they had reached 14,000, and by the end of 1837 part sales had reached 40,000. By then *Pickwick* was a sensation. At least five theatrical adaptations had appeared before the work completed its serial run; there were *Pickwick* hats, cigars, china figurines, songbooks, picture books, and jest books. There is even a disease named in honour of the Fat Boy (see HEALTH). Dickens himself contributed to the list of imitators, first reintroducing Sam, Tony, and Mr Pickwick in MASTER HUMPHREY'S CLOCK and then devising two PUBLIC READING versions, one of which, 'The Trial from Pickwick', was by far the most frequently performed of all his readings. And the novel itself continued to sell: 31,000 copies of the Cheap Edition (1847) in

the first year alone; by the end of 1878, 1,600,000 copies had been sold in England and America combined.

Serialization meant that it was being REVIEWED far more widely and frequently than any novel appearing in volume form would be. Reviewers quickly recognized that *Pickwick* was something special: comparisons were made with Fielding and Smollett, with Cervantes, with SCOTT, and with Shakespeare.

For generations after its first appearance, *Pickwick* remained evergreen. Percy FITZGERALD alone produced five volumes of *Pickwick* studies, notes, commentaries, riddles, and perplexities. G. K. Chesterton declared that *Pickwick* was 'something nobler than a novel' (1906, p. 79), and W. H. Auden, in a famous essay, proposed that it was a mythic retelling of the Fall of Man. Following Auden, critics have argued whether or not Mr Pickwick learns from his experiences. But its generic looseness—is it a novel, or isn't it?—has left some modern readers uncomfortable; A. E. Dyson's survey of Dickens's fiction, *The Inimitable Dickens* (1970), for example, silently refrains from discussing *Pickwick*. Nevertheless, Dickens's first novel continues to receive its meed of delight from readers, as well as scholarly and critical attention.     PVWS

Auden, W. H., 'Dingley Dell and the Fleet', *The Dyer's Hand and Other Essays* (1963).

Butt and Tillotson (1957).

Marcus, Steven (1965).

——'Language into Structure: Pickwick Revisited', *Daedalus* 101 (1972); rptd. *Representations* (1975).

Patten (1978).

**Pic-Nic Papers, The** (London: Henry Colburn, 1841), a three-volume anthology of miscellaneous pieces by various authors, edited by Dickens, to benefit the widow and infant children of 28-year-old publisher John MACRONE, who died suddenly in September of 1837. Dickens began assembling contributions for the book in February of 1838; eventually he contributed a brief Introduction and a short tale, 'The Lamplighter's Story', adapted from his unsuccessful farce *The LAMPLIGHTER*, as well as editing contributions by William Harrison AINSWORTH, Thomas MOORE, Leitch Ritchie, Agnes Strickland, and others. After many frustrating delays the anthology was finally published on

9 August 1841; it included six engravings by Hablot K. BROWNE and two by George CRUIK-SHANK. The frontispiece, an illustration for 'The Lamplighter's Story' titled 'The Philosopher's Stone', proved to be Cruikshank's last collaboration with Dickens. Mrs Macrone ultimately received £450 from this charitable publishing venture.                                    JJB

**Pictures From Italy** Records Dickens's residence in ITALY from July 1844 to June 1845 and was clearly intended to defray some of the costs of the expedition. The first third of the book began life as a series of eight 'Travelling Letters', published in the DAILY NEWS from 21 January to 11 March 1846. In order to write these 'Letters' (and the later *Pictures from Italy*), Dickens drew upon his own Italian correspondence, borrowed back from friends and family, and in particular from John FORSTER (see LETTERS). Following Dickens's departure from the editorship of the *Daily News*, the 'Travelling Letters' came to an early end. When *Pictures from Italy* was published by BRADBURY AND EVANS in May 1846, several additional passages had been added while others had been deleted from the 'Travelling Letters' texts. The manuscripts of a part of the seventh 'Travelling Letter' and of the whole of the eighth are in the FORSTER COLLECTION, but there is apparently no extant manuscript of *Pictures from Italy*.

The ILLUSTRATOR originally chosen for *Pictures from Italy* was Clarkson STANFIELD, but he resigned his commission to supply twelve plates because the book seemed to him to have an anti-Catholic bias (Stanfield later converted to ROMAN CATHOLICISM). Samuel PALMER was appointed in Stanfield's place, but was able to complete only four woodblocks, showing the Villa d'Este, the Colosseum, the Street of the Tombs at Pompeii, and a group of peasants harvesting in a vineyard. Marcus STONE contributed four illustrations to the Library Edition of 1862 (see EDITIONS OVER WHICH DICKENS HAD CONTROL).

*Pictures from Italy* belongs to a tradition of 19th-century TRAVEL LITERATURE written by established writers of fiction. It follows works on Italy by Mary Shelley and Frances TROLLOPE and looks forward to those by William Dean Howells and Henry James. These are all records of the writer's personal experiences and responses, rather than guidebooks.

Dickens either knew or owned the best-known guidebooks for the 1840s, those by Maria Starke and John Murray, but he is often scornful of more conventional travel writers, such as J. C. Eustace, whose opinions are mocked in *Little Dorrit* (2.5). The one work which he notes with pleasure is Louis Simond's *A Tour in Italy and Switzerland* of 1828.

Within Dickens's own oeuvre, *Pictures from Italy* follows fairly closely on his earlier travel book, AMERICAN NOTES of 1842. In both Dickens's approach to the scene is expressed in a strongly independent voice and with a degree of iconoclasm. In *Pictures from Italy* he is determined to question conventional ideas and to avoid giving yet another predictable account of the famous paintings and the tourist sights.

Characteristically, Dickens draws his readers' attention to those places and activities which particularly captured his own imagination, such as a puppet-show depicting the death of Napoleon ('the drollest exhibition I ever saw in my life'), and the prisons and cemeteries of the towns and cities. On several occasions Dickens's fascination with prisons leads him to refer to the poems of BYRON, whose influence on English perceptions of Italy he was well aware of. In two cemeteries he particularly noted the graves of English writers, that of Tobias SMOLLETT (whose *Travels through France and Italy* probably influenced Dickens) in Livorno, and, in the Protestant Cemetery of Rome, the tombs of Keats and of Shelley.

Dickens begins his book with his family's departure from PARIS, and then describes their journey through FRANCE, with particular attention to Avignon and its Palace of the Popes, scene of a massacre during the French Revolution. Early chapters tell of life in Genoa, where the Dickens family were based during their stay in Italy, and Dickens then turns to his journey back to London (to read *The CHIMES* to a group of friends) in November to December 1844, travelling through the north Italian cities of Modena, Bologna, Ferrara, Padua, Venice, Verona, Mantua, Cremona, and Milan. Venice particularly attracted Dickens and is the subject of a separate chapter, 'An Italian Dream'. In his accounts of these places Dickens mingles some attention to the famous landmarks with a more idiosyncratic account of his own reactions and of his meetings with local residents or other travellers.

In the second half of *Pictures from Italy* Dickens writes of his two visits to Rome, the first to participate in the Carnival and the second to see the ceremonies of Holy Week, which he reports rather mockingly. He then describes his travels in the Bay of Naples which took him to Pompeii and to the summit of Vesuvius on an icy night. Finally, he compresses his return journey to Genoa and his departure from Italy into the two closing chapters, giving a brief glance at Florence, and ending his book in SWITZERLAND on the homeward route. During Dickens's visit, Italy was in the early stages of the revolutionary ferment which led to the Risorgimento, but, perhaps because of hostile responses to *American Notes*, Dickens states that he will omit all references to the Italian political scene. This promise he largely keeps, and the reader is only occasionally aware of the author's movements between self-governing principalities and Papal States.

Dickens's openly hostile responses to Roman Catholicism, however, aroused strong reactions amongst some readers, provoking a seventeen-page denunciation in the *Dublin Review* of September 1846. Other critics felt that Dickens was not sufficiently well educated to write of Italy or that he was an amateur in Italian affairs. Those reviewers who praised the work, usually commented with pleasure on his prose STYLE and on the openness of the book to the general reader, ill served by many of the earlier works which concentrated entirely on art treasures or the historical background.         LO

> Ormond, Leonée, 'Dickens and Painting: The Old Masters', *Dickensian*, 79 (1983).
> —— and Schwarzbach, F. S. (eds.), *American Notes and Pictures from Italy* (1997).
> Paroissien, David, '*Pictures from Italy* and its Original Illustrators', *Dickensian*, 67 (1971).
> —— (ed.), *Pictures from Italy* (1973).
> Thurin, Susan Schoenbauer, '*Pictures from Italy*: Pickwick and Podsnap Abroad', *Dickensian*, 83 (1987).

**plagiarisms of Dickens.** Dickens's early writing suffered more plagiarism than any English literary work then or since—on the stage, in sheets of spurious illustrations, and, in particular, in cheap SERIALIZED novels

based on his plots and characters. Literary hacks plagiarized Dickens in the first place to avoid the law. By the 1814 COPYRIGHT Act an author's actual text was protected for 28 years, but as Dickens found to his cost, there was little redress against the most blatant imitation (see CHANCERY). Plagiarisms also adapted Dickens's writing to suit the tastes of a rapidly expanding lower-class readership. Although no exact statistics are available, these imitations enjoyed sales which rivalled and probably outnumbered that of Dickens's originals.

*Pickwick Papers* (1836–8) offered an easy target for the plagiarist. Dickens's contribution was first conceived as copy-text to accompany comic etchings of cockney life by Robert SEYMOUR. Like Seymour's preceding series, *Humorous Sketches* (1833–6), it was to be based on the genre of comic stereotypes, whose visual idiosyncrasies could be easily copied. Pickwick's plump figure, green spectacles, and gaiters, however crudely drawn, were immediately recognizable. The episodic plot also offered few restraints to the plagiarist, for 'Pickwickian' adventures could be adapted or invented for as long as the readers kept buying the serial. The first and most successful of these plagiarisms was *The Posthumourous Notes of the Pickwick Club* (1837–9), also called *The Penny Pickwick*. This was by 'Bos', probably the playwright and general literary hack Thomas Peckett Prest, and published by Edward Lloyd, who used it to pioneer 'penny issue' fiction. It first appeared in April or early May of 1837, at the height of *Pickwick*'s popularity, exploiting the fashion for things Pickwickian. Instead of Dickens's monthly shilling numbers, Lloyd sold his serial weekly at a penny, exploiting the market further with fourpenny monthly issues. These were sold on Sunday, when working-class people had their leisure, and through tobacconists and small shops, so reaching a market of semi-literate readers outside the range of middle-class booksellers.

In June 1837 CHAPMAN AND HALL tried legally to restrain Lloyd's publication of his penny *Pickwick*, but failed on the counter-claim that no one could confuse the two productions. Lloyd's 'Bos' declared 'that every author has a right to take a popular subject' and that he 'had used none other *but his own materials*'. The differences are, however, in

ADAPTATION rather than innovation. His 'Club' consists of Christopher Pickwick, Arthur Snodgreen, Matthew Winkletop, with the addition of a military type, Captain Julius Caesar Fitzflash. Sam is called Samivel Veller throughout the story, and is joined in Pickwick's service by an ancient black man called John White. Jingle becomes Shirk.

The Guzzleton (Eatanswill) episode is typical of the way 'Bos' turns Dickens's work into gross slapstick. Pickwick stands as candidate, and, under the able supervision of Samivel Veller, is beating the corrupt Tory incumbent, Sir Gregory Graspall. 'Bos' begins to give a political edge to Dickens's send-up of a Rotten Borough election. However, then Pickwick is discovered, costumed as Cupid in a fancy-dress masquerade, kissing the wife of Mr Squib, editor of the opposition paper. Pickwick's 'unwhisperables' are punctured by Squib in a duel, and it is Squib, not Mrs Bardell, who initiates the trial against Pickwick. Refusing to pay damages, Pickwick goes to the Fleet prison, an episode extended with much expert information about gaol life. Samivel is the real hero of the story, and although Pickwick gains some dignity as the narrative meanders on, he is largely drawn in the way that a costermonger in real life might have seen him, as an object of ridicule. Apparently when 'Bos' came to the end of the story as Dickens had written it, he found sales still buoyant, and the serial was padded out for a further ten months. For all its crudity, the serial's jaunty energy, supported by crude woodcuts by C. J. Grant, gave it wide popular appeal, and G. A. SALA in his biography *Charles Dickens* (1870) declared that 'this disgraceful fabrication had an enormous sale'.

Lloyd was also milking the market with *Pickwick in America!*, again by 'Bos' (1838–9), in which Pickwick, accompanied by the Pickwick Club, is called to America to correct the mismanagement of his large estate there. Perhaps emboldened by Dickens's failure successfully to prosecute *The Penny Pickwick*, the Pickwickians, and even Sam Weller, have the same names as in Dickens's original, although Jingle is replaced by an American, Jonathon Junket, who exploits the tall-story humour currently being popularized in the transatlantic tales of 'Sam Slick' (T. C. Haliburton). There is a visit to the Shakers, a comic duel,

and Mr Tupman—who, as an ageing Romantic, Dickens pointedly did *not* marry off—is wed. The material proved foreign to 'Bos' in more senses than one, and the plantation episode is particularly awkwardly handled. 'Bos' may have been confused by the fact that slavery still continued in the Southern States, while slaves in British possessions had been emancipated in 1836. Pickwick expresses sympathy with freeing the slaves, and they chair him round the grounds, then the subject is abruptly dropped. This weakest of the 'Bos' plagiarisms ended after 44 numbers.

'Bos' may also have been over-extended, for Lloyd was simultaneously publishing a third Dickens plagiarism, *Oliver Twiss*. This commenced in March 1838, while Dickens's *Twist* was still running in BENTLEY'S MISCELLANY, and before Dickens had revealed the story's conclusion in the three-volume edition. *Twiss* ran for 78 weeks, with some success. It was closer to the original than *The Penny Pickwick*, for *Twist* told the story of Oliver's progress, and offered less scope for deviation. 'Bos' exploited *Oliver Twist*'s links with the popular traditions of GOTHIC melodrama, crime reporting, and stage comedy. Banks (Monks) is a complete Gothic villain living in a ruined castle; a mysterious gypsy appears to tell Oliver's fortune. The melodramatic love of Polly (Nancy) for Jem Blount (Bill Sikes) is drawn out, and Poll goes to jail to save her lover. The comic element in Mumble (Bumble) courting Mrs Stint'em (Mrs Corney) is played up as slapstick farce, although 'Bos' also introduces more realistic elements, for Mumble marries because the Poorhouse Guardians want a married man for beadle (see POOR RELIEF).

Throughout, 'Bos' adds more background about the criminal world than does Dickens, and the JEWISH identity of Solomans (Fagin) is never disguised. 'Bos' evidently knew his criminal LAW. In Dickens's version Fagin hangs for being accessory to Nancy's murder, though as he was absent at her actual death this was legally unlikely at the time. Solomans is hanged for the actual murder of a gypsy, dying with the flourish of a repentant broadsheet villain, acknowledging 'the fate I have been condemned to undergo has been richly merited'. Twiss retires to live out a happy life in a country mansion, with Mr Beaumont (Brownlow).

In March 1838 Dickens, having failed to stop plagiarism of his work by legal means, preceded publication of *Nicholas Nickleby* with an attack on the 'dishonest dullards' who produced 'cheap and wretched imitations of our delectable works'. Lloyd responded with a fair imitation of Dickens's polemic, and at the end of the month, using advance advertisements of *Nickleby*, published *Nickelas Nickelbery* by 'Bos' concurrently with Dickens's original, with the claim that 'Boz' was a plagiarist. In spite of this flourish, however, even Lloyd's semi-literate readers must have found the muddled story disappointing. The Crummles plot gave 'Bos' a congenial theme, and the theatre episodes are expanded, but when Nicklebery leaves the troupe, 'Bos' brought the story to an abrupt end, with Snike (Smike) inheriting a fortune through a will that had been concealed by Roger (Ralph) Nicklebery.

Lloyd's vein of Dickens plagiarism was becoming worked out. *The Sketch Book by 'Bos'* (1837), *Barnaby Budge* (1841), and *Master Humfries' Clock* (1840) were short lived. His novelette *A Christmas Log* (1846) exploited the popularity of Dickens's Christmas books. In a hackneyed plot a benevolent uncle returns in disguise to witness how his grasping relatives mistreat his granddaughter. In a final tableau all is revealed, and everyone is forgiven, but the story totally lacks the Dickensian CHRISTMAS spirit. Meanwhile the success of *The Penny Pickwick* itself was creating imitators. These included *The Posthumous Papers of the Cadger's Club* (1838), based on the scene of a beggars' masquerade drawn by George CRUIKSHANK for Pierce EGAN's *Life in London* (1820). *The Posthumous Papers of the Wonderful Discovery Club, edited by 'Poz'* (1838) began by satirizing the contemporary popularity of Mechanics' Institutes, but lacking a story, itself fell back on snippets of pedantic 'popular knowledge' to fill the pages (see SELF-HELP). A radical *Oliver Twiss* (1838) by 'Poz' also appeared, attacking the Poor Law system, and the inadequate provision of EDUCATION for the working classes (see À BECKETT). Few apparently read it, for it only lasted four numbers.

If Lloyd's publications were directed towards the semi-literate audience unlikely to read Dickens's originals, plagiarisms for a more educated audience was written by G. W. M. Reynolds. The son of a post-captain in the navy, Reynolds had wasted his inheritance in France, and returned to pursue a journalistic career in Britain. As editor of the old MONTHLY MAGAZINE, he began *Pickwick Abroad; or the Tour in France* (1837–9) in its pages, concluding it in monthly parts, and the work remained in print throughout his life. Reynolds claimed that although he took Dickens's characters, the story was his own: 'if the talented "Boz" have [*sic*] not chosen to enact the part of Mr Pickwick's biography in his continental tour, it is not my fault.' In Pierce Egan's *Life in London* (1820–1), a work that also prepared the way for Dickens, Egan had used the innocent Jerry and the experienced man-about-town Tom as viewpoints on city life. Reynolds uses Pickwick and Sam Weller to introduce Paris, backing up the text with engravings of Parisian sites. The Pickwickian narrative itself is the least interesting element in this long work, for Reynolds's characters are shadows of Dickens's ebullient originals. Their mildly salacious adventures through Parisian society are little more than the pretext for Reynolds's account of racey life in France, and a framework for a succession of interpolated stories.

Reynolds enjoyed some success as a 'Dickensian' author. When editing *The Teetotaller*, he boosted its circulation with 'Noctes Pickwickianae' (27 June–8 August 1840), showing Pickwick and both the Wellers becoming converted to the temperance cause, signing the pledge book of 'the London United Temperance Association' at the Aldersgate Street Chapel (see DRINK AND TEMPERANCE). This was followed (23 January–19 June 1841) by *Pickwick Married*. Here Pickwick saves a Miss Sago from the undesired attentions of a policeman, and after a heavily comic courtship, he marries her in a double ceremony, together with Sam Weller who is marrying for a third time. The ceremony is attended by the rest of the Pickwickians, including Jingle, freshly arrived from America. The story was reissued, abbreviated, in early editions of *Mister Timothy's Bookcase, or the Magic Lanthorn of the World* (1841), itself loosely modelled on Dickens's MASTER HUMPHREY'S CLOCK.

Other middle-class plagiarisms may be mentioned. *Scenes from the Life of Nickleby Married* (1840), edited by 'Guess', with illustrations by 'Quiz', was ostensibly a continuation of Nicholas's story, although in part it rehearses Dickens's plot, with a replay of the Mantalini story. Mrs Squeers now runs a coffee-house, while Wackford makes a living writing begging letters. Sir Mulberry Hawk pursues criminal activities, and a rich heiress. Nicholas Nickleby and the Cheerybles are now partners, and the main plot concerns the theft and recovery of money from their firm. The main interest of the story, however, is a Mayhew-like account of London low life. A vivid urban realism also enlivens Renton Nicholson's *Dombey and Daughter* (1847), a work whose main debt to Dickens lies in the title. The story is of a waif, Clara George, whom Mr Dombey acknowledges as his natural child. However, at the end it is revealed that her legitimate father is in fact Mr Dombey's brother George, an army captain, who has left her an heiress. The plot is played out against a background of London low life that no doubt drew on Renton Nicholson's own racy experiences while he was presiding as 'Baron' of the disreputable Coal Hole Tavern just below the Strand.

By the time he wrote *Dombey* in 1847–8 Dickens's development as a writer had made plagiarism of his work difficult and unrewarding. The PUBLISHING market had also changed. The first flood of imitative works had been produced to fill a dearth of literature demanded by a rapidly increasing mass reading public. By the 1840s this was being supplied by a new generation of popular writers. Significantly, the leaders in this field included the publisher Edward Lloyd and the novelists G. W. M. Reynolds and Thomas Peckett Prest, all of whom had been launched to success by their plagiarisms of Dickens. Through them, if indirectly, Dickens played a part in developing genres of reading that were to be the basis of today's mass literature. (See also READERSHIP.)                                    LJ

The Lesley Staples Collection of Dickens plagiarisms, in Dickens House Museum, London.

James, Louis, *Fiction for the Working Man* (1963; rev. edn. 1974).

**playwright, Dickens as.** Although all of Dickens's writings reflect the glare of 'a circle of stage fire' (Ruskin, *Unto This Last*, 1860, 1862, repr. in Collins 1971, p. 314), his plays are far inferior to his fiction and journalism.

Fascinated by all aspects of the stage from an early age, Dickens was an inveterate theatre-goer all his life. He nearly became an ACTOR, before the success of *Pickwick* turned his ambition in a different direction. In mid-life he threw himself into AMATEUR THEATRICAL productions, and for the last seventeen years of his life spent much of his energy giving PUBLIC READINGS, his own type of one-man theatrical show.

From early childhood he wrote, produced, and acted in plays. The first was MISNAR, THE SULTAN OF INDIA, based on one of *The Tales of the Genii*, written when he was 9. No copy is known to exist. At the age of 16 he wrote *The Stratagems of Rozanza*, concerned with love adventures at a Venetian inn and evoking the atmosphere of Vauxhall Gardens. A 131-page holograph copy of this piece of juvenilia was discovered in Paris in 1926, but it subsequently disappeared. Besides a brief description by Van Amerongen (1926, pp. 115–16) no record of it exists. In 1833 Dickens wrote an operatic SHAKESPEAREAN travesty, *O'THELLO*, which was performed by members of his family. Fragments of his father's prompt copy survive.

The first of Dickens's plays to be produced on the public stage was *The STRANGE GENTLEMAN* (1836), a comic burletta based on 'The Great Winglebury Duel' (*SB*). It ran as an afterpiece at the St James's Theatre for an entire season and was published by CHAPMAN AND HALL. Even at the time Dickens dismissed this as a mere farce, but he set great store by his next play, *The VILLAGE COQUETTES* (1836), a pastoral operetta. He confided to John HULLAH, who wrote the music, that he hoped it would 'introduce me to the Public, as a dramatic Writer' (?May 1836). Offering it to Richard BENTLEY for publication, Dickens explained that it was 'the first time that a "drama" has been united to music, or poetry to songs; and a great many competent judges who have heard it, consider it to possess both, in a high degree' (?27 August 1836). Dickens's libretto was poorly received, and the play closed after sixteen performances.

He wrote two more farces, IS SHE HIS WIFE?, staged for a few nights at the St James's Theatre in January and February 1837, and *The LAMPLIGHTER*, which he hoped MACREADY would produce at Covent Garden. It went into rehearsal but was withdrawn before it could be performed. These were to be his final solo attempts at playwriting. He substantially rewrote Mark LEMON's farce MR NIGHTINGALE'S DIARY, as a vehicle for his own performance in 1851. In 1857 he worked closely with Wilkie COLLINS on The FROZEN DEEP, and collaborated with Collins again in 1867, turning their Christmas story, 'No Thoroughfare', into a play.

None of these plays holds much intrinsic interest. It is a paradox that the most theatrical of novelists could not write a good play, but it seems apparent that he needed the greater canvas of the printed page and above all the controlling authority of a narrative voice, to breathe life into stock MELODRAMATIC plots and type figures.          PVWS

**poetry and poets before Dickens.** Dickens had an appreciation of the work of SHAKESPEARE, Milton, Pope, SWIFT, Cowper, GRAY, and GOLDSMITH, as well as the more recent productions of WORDSWORTH, Southey, BYRON, HOOD, ROGERS, and MOORE. As a young man he wrote very good imitations of Goldsmith ('The Bill of Fare') and Southey ('The Devil's Walk') for Maria BEADNELL. In his artistic development there is a discernible pattern of growing poetic awareness: once confirmed as a successful author with the publication of Pickwick Papers, Dickens began to purchase canonical literature, to aid his transformation from popular entertainer to serious novelist attuned to literary tradition. This growing attention was complemented by his fondness for popular song—an affinity which he maintained throughout his career (see MUSIC). In 'The Bloomsbury Christening' the Kitterbell guests join in Thomas Bayly's 'We met—'twas in a crowd' and 'I saw her at the fancy fair' (SB), while in Pickwick Sam Weller sings 'Bold Turpin'—an adaptation of Horace Smith's 'Turpin and the Bishop' (PP 43). In The Old Curiosity Shop Dick Swiveller, Grand Master of the 'Glorious Apollers', quotes from or alludes to a wide range of songs, including Bayly's 'Oh give me but my Arab steed' and 'I saw her at the fancy fair', and Thomas Dibdin's 'All's Well' (OCS 2, 13, 56). These are augmented by an enlarged range of poetic reference, including Gray's 'Elegy', Moore's Irish Melodies, and Wordsworth's 'We are Seven' (OCS 17, 23, 53). On a more personal note, Dickens acknowledged

the encouragement and hospitality he had received from the banker-poet Samuel Rogers in 1839–40 by dedicating The Old Curiosity Shop to him, and by recalling his poem 'Ginevra' in the SENTIMENTAL description of Nell's grandfather's 'seeking something' but finding 'no comfort' after her death (OCS 72).

In later novels poetic allusion serves a more serious critical purpose. Whereas in his early sketch 'The Boarding House' Dickens comically depicts Septimus Hicks, the 'Byron-quoter', uttering observations from Don Juan (SB 45), by the time of David Copperfield and Bleak House he uses the model of the psychologically complex Byronic hero to explore the motivations of Steerforth and, to a lesser extent, Lady Dedlock (DC 7, 32; BH 18). In Great Expectations Dickens recalls Paradise Lost, presenting Pip as a type of Milton's Adam, gaining knowledge of good and evil, and enabled through his 'fall' to live a morally conscious and socially integrated life (GE 58).

An increasing intertextual engagement with poetry did not, however, mean that Dickens ever abandoned his love of more popular forms; this amalgamation is evoked in Our Mutual Friend through the ballad-monger Silas Wegg, who quotes from Bayly's 'The Soldier's Tear' and Elizabeth Hamilton's 'Nae falsehood to dread', as well as Burns's 'Auld Lang Syne' and Scott's Marmion (OMF 1.5, 3.6).          LL

Harvey, W. R., 'Charles Dickens and the Byronic Hero', Nineteenth-Century Fiction, 24 (1969–70).

Kitton, F. G., Dickensiana (1886).

Ley, J. W. T., a series of articles on songs Dickens knew, Dickensian, 26–9 (1930–3).

**poetry and poets during Dickens's lifetime.** Dickens admired the 'Genius' of TENNYSON, and ever after the publication of the two-volume Poems of 1842 read his lyrics assiduously. Otherwise, however, he had little time for what are today considered some of the most significant varieties of Victorian poetic expression. He had little sympathy with the more experimental or 'grotesque' verse of BROWNING or Meredith (although he admired Browning's plays); neither was he drawn to poetry exploring religious doubt, the more mournful lyrics of Arnold or Clough. But two important modes of Victorian poetic output were important to

Dickens: SENTIMENTAL poetry and comic verse.

Sentimental verse flourished exceedingly in the 1820s and 1830s, particularly with female poets such as Felicia Hemans and Letitia LANDON, and the mode of publishing lady's magazines or lavishly illustrated ANNUALS. On the one hand Dickens was perfectly capable of ridiculing the excesses of this genre, as with Mrs Leo Hunter in *Pickwick* and her 'Ode to an expiring Frog', which 'appeared originally in a Lady's Magazine':

> Can I unmoved see thee dying
> > On a log,
> > Expiring frog!
> > > (*PP* 15)

Nonetheless, when Dickens began editing *Household Words* it was precisely this sort of poetry, often written by women (for instance Adelaide PROCTOR, for whose collected poems Dickens wrote a preface) that he chose to include in the journal. This is poetry that is 'sentimental' in the sense that Dickens's novels are sometimes accused of being: verse that seeks to evoke an emotional response on the principle that it is emotive sympathy that makes us most human. To contemporary tastes the seemingly never-ending stream of poems with titles such as 'Friendship's Valentine' or 'Gentleness of Death' can overwhelm with their saccharine, as with the cloying 'A Child's Prayer' (it appeared in the 13 December 1851 number of *Household Words*):

> The bee is hushed within the hive
> > Shut is the daisy's eye;
> The stars alone are peeping forth
> > From out the darkened sky.
>
> No, not the stars alone; for God
> > Has heard what I have said;
> His eye looks on His little child
> > Kneeling beside its bed.

He admired poetry that could make him cry (of HOOD's 'Bridge of Sighs', for instance, he approvingly noted 'My God! How sorrowful and pitiful it is!'), and he sometimes quoted Tennyson's mournful refrain to 'Mariana' ('I am aweary, aweary | I would that I were dead') with reference to himself.

His taste for comic verse is easier to endorse today; but for Dickens laughter and sentiment were both indices of the ability to empathize with fellow men and women, and as such represented two aspects of his humanity, and of the MORAL basis of his art. He particularly admired the comic poetry of Thomas MOORE, Thomas Hood, Richard BARHAM, and THACKERAY. His own comic poetry was produced only occasionally, chiefly at the beginning of his career, and tended to make broad points at the expense of more localized effects, although it can often be very funny. 'The Fine Old English Gentleman: New Version', for instance (printed in the *Examiner*, 7 August 1841), is a fiercely comic satire on Tory nostalgia for 'the good old days':

> The good old laws were garnished well with gibbets, whips and chains,
>
> With fine old English penalties, and fine old English pains,
> With rebel heads, and seas of blood once hot in rebel veins;
> For all these things were requisite to guard the rich old gains
> > Of the fine old English Tory times;
> > Soon may they come again!

AR

**poetry by Dickens.** As a young man Dickens wrote doggerel verses for the amusement of the BEADNELL circle, such as 'The Bill of Fare' (1831), parodying GOLDSMITH's 'Retaliation', and four poems written in Maria Beadnell's album, including an eight-verse parody of Southey's 'The Devil's Walk'. He wrote three poems for inclusion in *Pickwick Papers* ('The Ivy Green', 'A Christmas Carol', and 'Gabriel Grub's Song') and the lyrics for the sixteen songs in *The VILLAGE COQUETTES*. In August 1841 he published three anti-Tory verse satires in the EXAMINER ('The Fine Old English Gentleman', 'The Quack Doctor's Proclamation', and 'Subjects for Painters'), and in 1842 wrote a blank-verse prologue for a play by Westland MARSTON, *The Patrician's Daughter*. In 1844 he contributed a poem on religious intolerance, 'A Word in Season', to an ANNUAL, *The Keepsake*, edited by Lady Blessington. Two more political verse satires appeared in the DAILY NEWS in 1846 ('The British Lion' and 'The Hymn of the Wiltshire Labourers'), and in 1855 he wrote a Prologue and 'The Song of the Wreck' for Wilkie COLLINS's *The Lighthouse*. His last published verse was the Prologue to Collins's *The*

FROZEN DEEP (1857). The early private verses were first collected in volume 2 of *Collected Papers* in the Nonesuch Dickens (1938); the published poems were first collected by F. G. KITTON (1903) and subsequently included by B. W. MATZ in *MISCELLANEOUS PAPERS* (1908); Kitton included some verses from *Household Words* and elsewhere, such as 'Hiram Power's Greek Slave', which have subsequently been shown not to be by Dickens.    MS

**politics and politicians.** With a few notable exceptions—Lord John RUSSELL and the humanitarian reformer the seventh Earl of Shaftesbury stand out—Dickens had little time either for politicians or for the forms of politics practised in 19th-century Britain. His own political position was broadly reformist, but it was neither consistent nor particularly coherent. His main concern was with what CARLYLE called 'The Condition of England' question, as expressed in a long letter to the *Morning Chronicle* on 25 July 1842, attacking members of the House of Lords—who included the Duke of Wellington—for seeking to 'pare, cut, and fritter . . . away' Shaftesbury's Bill to abolish child and female labour in the mines. He saw the excessive aristocratic control, venality, amateurism, and lack of clear focus of contemporary politics as impediments to making the country a more civilized place. These are richly satirized in his novels, particularly *Bleak House*, *Little Dorrit*, and *Our Mutual Friend*. What he saw of the behaviour of politicians in the Commons, as a parliamentary reporter on John BLACK's *MORNING CHRONICLE* in the 1830s, he did not care for, although he greatly enjoyed the excitement of the work and also the travel to political meetings which it entailed. He wanted change but he seems to have had little idea about how the changes he wanted might be brought about, or indeed—beyond improving people's standards of living and improving the efficiency of GOVERNMENT—what these changes were. He held no brief for Tories—'people whom, politically, I despise and abhor' (Ackroyd 1990, p. 327). In August 1841, as they came into office after a large general ELECTION victory, he published three anti-Tory verse satires in the *EXAMINER* (see POETRY OF DICKENS). When in the United States in 1842, he wrote enquiring of Albany FONBLANQUE, 'How long will the Tory Min-

istry [of Peel] last? Say six months, and receive my blessing' (12 and ?21 March 1842). He abhorred violence in the furtherance of political objectives (see CHARTISM). He favoured 'Progress', believed in the decisive contributions of 'Great Men', and was sceptical about theories of government, such as the then-dominant idea of *laissez-faire* which seemed, paradoxically, to Dickens to subordinate individuals to systems.

Dickens did, however, warm to Peel after he repealed the Corn Laws—thus, so the theory went, giving working people access to cheap bread. He wrote to Thomas Chapman on 3 July 1846: 'I little thought, once upon a time, that I should ever live to praise Peel. But D'ISRAELI and that Dunghill Lord [Bentinck] have so disgusted me [by their tactics in opposing repeal], that I feel disposed to champion him.' He also shared in the outbreak of national grief at Peel's sudden death in a riding accident on 2 July 1850. He wrote to Mrs Richard WATSON the next day: 'I am in a very despondent state of mind about Peel's death. He was a man of mark, who could be ill-spared from that Dung Heap down at Westminster.' He could even summon up valedictory sympathy for the Duke of Wellington, perceived as the quintessence of reactionary Toryism, when he died in 1852, writing to Angela Burdett COUTTS (whom at one time Wellington seemed likely to marry) that he was 'a great old man' (14 September 1852). He was, however, appalled by the pomp and expense of Wellington's funeral.

One issue which concentrated Dickens's mind constructively upon political issues was the CRIMEAN WAR, and especially the administrative shortcomings which made its winning such a problematic and protracted affair. His alliance with the archaeologist-turned-politician Austen Layard over the Administrative Reform Association evoked his most consistently 'political' speech. It began with a direct attack on the House of Commons as 'a set of men who "thought they should be heard for their much speaking"', and continued with a PANTOMIME reference to the Prime Minister, Viscount Palmerston, as 'the comic old gentleman'. Parliament gives 'little adequate expression of . . . or apparent understanding of the general mind', its debates representing a phoney war: 'a great deal of the reproof valiant and the counter check quarrelsome.' Dickens concluded: 'The great, broad, true case' was that 'our public progress is far behind our private progress, and that we are not more remarkable for our private wisdom and success in matters of business than we are for our public folly and failure' (*Speeches*, pp. 197–208).

Dickens used his literary contacts to aid Layard. His letter of 3 April 1855 mentioned a recent confidential meeting with Mark LEMON, the editor of PUNCH, which seems to have led directly to the publication on 7 April of a cartoon, 'The Member for Nineveh Digs Out the British Bull', which supported Layard, the excavator of Nineveh, against Palmerston, represented as the British bulldog. Dickens urged Layard to present him with 'any new loophole, cranny, needle's eye' for use in *Household Words*. He duly wrote four stinging attacks on the government: 'The Thousand and One Humbugs' (*HW* 28 April 1855), 'The Toady Tree' (*HW* 26 May 1855), 'Cheap Patriotism' (*HW* 9 June 1855), and 'Our Commission' (*HW* 11 August 1855). A further letter to Layard on 10 April bemoaned 'the alienation of the people from their own public affairs' which Dickens attributed to 'English Tufthunting, Toad Eating, and other manifestations of accursed Gentility'. Anti-aristocratic sentiment was a pronounced feature of Dickens's politics.

Dickens's literary references to Members of Parliament and their concerns are not extensive but they are almost all damning. The MP Gregsbury (*NN* 16) had 'a loud voice, a pompous manner, a tolerable command of sentences with no meaning in them, and, in short, every requisite for a very good member indeed', who employs empty patriotism—'this great and free and happy country'—as a means of deflecting his listeners' attention from pertinent, practical politics. The image of the garrulous, mendacious politician is also cleverly invoked in 'Doctor Dulcamara MP' (*HW* 18 December 1858), a piece written with Wilkie COLLINS. Like the quack doctor of Donizetti's popular opera *L'Elisir d'amore*, this Dulcamara travels the country to proclaim 'his discovery of a new soothing syrup to be taken in a great many table-spoonfuls, called, "Social Science" '. Dickens also felt that the atmosphere of the Commons militated against effective legislation. Twemlow tells

Veneering that the House of Commons 'is t| best club in London' (*OMF* 2.3).          E|

## poor relief and the New Poor Law (

1834 were highly topical subjects when Dic|| ens took them up in *Oliver Twist* (1838), a| his related sense of outrage at the misery | pauper children brought up in baby farn| and adults living in workhouses remain| strong right through to the end of his life. I| deed, he had already taken up the subject| early as 1835 in one of the sketches later i| cluded in the section of *Sketches by Boz* titl| 'Our Parish'. He returned to the theme | three articles for the EXAMINER (collected | MISCELLANEOUS PAPERS) in 1849 concerning| scandal at a baby farm at Tooting in whi| scores of neglected children died of choler| in an article in *Household Words* in 1850 (| Walk in a Workhouse', included in REPRINT|| PIECES); in *Bleak House* (1853), through t| orphan Guster, whose 'fits' are by implicatic| a result of her being brought up in a ba| farm (*BH* 10); in *Little Dorrit* (1857), throu| the workhouse inhabitant old Nandy (*L*| 1.31); and in *Our Mutual Friend* (1865| through Betty Higden, who literally choos| death rather than resort to the workhou| (*OMF* 1.16, 3.8–9). These later treatment| however, are relatively short and predictab| compared with the satire in *Twist*.

The evolution of English poor law in th| period is very complicated—but also impor| ant, involving as it does some of the fir| moves toward the modern centralized sta| and introducing problems of social enginee| ing in the area of welfare that remain ve| much with us. Under the system in effe| when the law was amended in 1834, parish| were responsible for poor relief, which w| funded by alms and the local rates; and reli| was administered both in workhouses an| through direct, so-called outdoor relief. In t| 18th century the control exercised central| by Parliament was not great and consiste| largely of such measures as vagrancy an| settlement laws that regulated the movemen| of people between parishes. The large di| placements of sizeable populations and dra| tic variations in prices and wages associate| with the rise of INDUSTRIALISM in the lat| 18th century necessitated stronger mea| ures. In 1782 an Act was passed that, amon| other things, allowed a parish to provide t|

able-bodied poor with work outside the workhouse, and in 1795 a relatively generous system was inaugurated whereby a worker whose wages fell below subsistence received supplementary wages on a scale tied to the price of bread and the size of the family. The combination of these two liberal measures, however, proved both expensive and degrading, for it encouraged farmers to hire workers at artificially low wages with the assurance that the parish would bring them up to subsistence level. The Poor Law Amendment Act of 1834 was one of the most dramatic legislative measures following the triumph of the Whigs and Radicals with the passage of the First Reform Bill in 1832 (see REFORM). It aimed to bring order to what had become a chaotic as well as much-abused system by creating both an efficient centralized authority—the Poor Law Commission (though local administration was put into the hands of a Board of Guardians elected from among propertyholders)—and a coherent set of policies and procedures informed by the latest theory, which in this case was supplied by the recently deceased Jeremy BENTHAM's disciple Edwin CHADWICK. Recognizing that an automatic supplement to workers' wages provided little incentive to workers or employers to break the vicious cycle of relief, Chadwick thought it would be most effective to restrict relief for the able-bodied to the workhouse; and in regulating the life of the workhouse he resorted to what he called the principle of 'less-eligibility', which quite intentionally made the workhouse the least pleasant possible place, second only to the prison in unattractiveness. Among the more prisonlike provisions were those separating husbands and wives, adults and children. Inmates, in fact, could not under ordinary circumstances leave the workhouse. Meals were to be taken in silence, and a diet that was in theory to be just barely adequate was in practice often far less than wholesome—hence Dickens's characterization of the Act's philosophy as providing the poor with a choice between 'being starved by a gradual process in the house, or by a quick one out of it' (*OT* 2). Many workhouses became in fact rather less attractive even than many prisons—a theme of much of Dickens's later writing about workhouses—and the amendment proved so widely unpopular that it is usually reckoned among the

causes of CHARTISM and a powerful new force unifying the working CLASSES, hence important as background to the development of the TRADE UNIONS and labour as a political force. In spite of the central authority of the Commissioners, practices varied enormously from county to county, and many features of the older system, including its abuses, persisted. (*Oliver Twist*'s rather confused chronology covers a period that appears to span the older system and the new, and of course the detestable beadle Bumble survives the transition, eventually to become Master of the workhouse.) There was great dissension even within the Commission and more or less continual tinkering with its policies for the next decade. The Commission was replaced by a more politically responsive and less powerful new Poor Law Board in 1847, but the law itself remained in effect, and life in the workhouse, at least in some places, continued to be sufficiently miserable as to justify Dickens's unhappy and lifelong attention to it.

Dickens quarrelled with the new and old systems on several grounds, the chief (and common) ground being that neither worked. Aimed at providing 'relief', both systems produced a great deal of misery for the people whom they were supposed to help while providing ample opportunities for corruption and exploitation on the part of providers and overseers. The beadle Bumble's bullying and venality make a mockery of his being an official of the church; the Board's complacency and incompetence make a mockery of their positions as responsible public servants. Officialdom, as always, provided Dickens with an easy and abundant target. The peculiar features of the New Poor Law that drew his bitterest scorn, however, were its reliance on fashionable 'philosophical' assumptions derived from Enlightenment thought about human nature that Dickens found intolerable—notably, that people are naturally selfish beings and that a successful social policy, therefore, will draw upon that selfishness as providing the great social machine's motive power. Dickens certainly had a much too simple understanding of the ideas of the 'philosophers', but he equally certainly understood very well that Chadwick's schemes were not working—though whether that was because of flaws in Chadwick's theory or problems with putting it into practice remains a

complicated question. In his own philan-
thropical ventures—notably URANIA COT-
TAGE, the Home for Homeless Women which
he managed for the Baroness Angela Burdett
COUTTS for several years beginning in 1847—
Dickens demonstrated tough-mindedness
about motivating and disciplining his charges
and a zest for efficiency that have a distinctly
UTILITARIAN flavour. The fact is, Dickens was
highly ambivalent about the question of relief, and it can easily be argued that his quarrel with the New Poor Law, a supposedly
Benthamite affair, was made on the perfectly
good Benthamite grounds that, instead of
producing the greatest happiness of the greatest number, it simply produced a lot of pain,
especially for many entirely innocent children
and adults.

The question of innocence is of course an
important one, which Dickens tends to fudge,
or at least gloss over, especially early on and
especially, perhaps, in *Twist*. His ideal workhouse inmates—the people he imagines as
the poor when he is satirizing the Poor Law—
are generally, like Oliver, assumed to be
blameless. This is in sharp contrast to the
shameless criminals of Fagin's circle on the
one hand, and the equally shameless representatives of officialdom on the other. Therefore the immensely difficult problem of how
one relieves the pains of poverty without creating circumstances that may themselves attract and be exploited by the unscrupulous is
one he need not explicitly face in the novel,
though he certainly encountered it in life. It is
a measure of the uncertainty of Dickens's
satire, however, that while he decries the
philosopher's supposed assumptions about
the selfishness of human nature, he in fact
presents in *Twist* a world populated chiefly by
immensely greedy and unscrupulous people
—whether the parish surgeon and his attendant crones, or Bumble, or the 'Board', or
Gamfield the chimney-sweep, or Noah Claypole and Charlotte, or the magistrate Mr
Fang, or Fagin and his gang. The only exceptions really are Oliver himself, the family and
family friends that Oliver miraculously encounters once he flees to London (the Brownlow and Maylie circles), and Nancy—perhaps
the novel's most interesting character—for
her conscience is powerful enough to lead her
to rescue Oliver, but not powerful enough to
lead her to leave the irredeemably bad Bill

Sikes. Nancy's divided loyalties belie the assumptions made about human nature both
by the 'philosophers' and by Dickens the
satirist of the Poor Law.                          RN

Collins (1962), ch. 4.
Finer, S. E., *The Life and Times of Sir Edwin Chadwick* (1952).
Hammond, J. L. and Hammond, Barbara, *The Bleak Age* (2nd edn., 1947).
Webb, Sidney and Webb, Beatrice, *English Local Government*, vols. 7–10 (1927–9).

**popular culture.** See AMUSEMENT; SELF-
HELP; SPORT.

**popularity of Dickens.** Dickens's popularity was almost instantaneous, relatively
classless, and soon worldwide; it has endured
and remains unique in literature. England, to
its great good fortune, has produced in him
and SHAKESPEARE the best-known and best-
loved novelist and dramatist internationally,
their currency having been aided by English
having become the dominant world language. Dickens has enjoyed several advantages over Shakespeare: he was born into and
wrote about an urban culture which has become almost universal, his debut coincided
with steam technology which quickly spread
his fame nationwide and soon worldwide
(Shakespeare was little known outside Britain
until the 18th century), and Dickens, being
born into an age of publicity and photography, became and has remained a personality—and predominantly a likeable and
estimable one—as Shakespeare could never
do, since we know so little about him. When
Dickens arrived in Boston in 1842, less that six
years after *Pickwick* had shot him to fame and
with four other novels to his credit already, he
could justly, if immodestly, record, 'There
never was, and never will be, such a triumph',
and a prominent Bostonian (William Whet-
more Story) agreed: 'People *eat* him here!
never was there such a revolution; Lafayette
was nothing to it' (see AMERICA). When he
returned to Boston in 1867, Longfellow reported: 'The enthusiasm for him and his
Readings is immense. One can hardly take in
the whole truth about it, and feel the univer-
sality of his fame.'

That PUBLIC READING tour resembled such
later British invasions of the American market as those by the Beatles and the Rolling
Stones, but those groups could never have

envisaged such a send-off as Dickens got, a Farewell Banquet attended by 450 notabilities, with speeches by the Lord Mayor of London, the Lord Chief Justice, and other such grandees and with the support of two Prime Ministers and most of the leading figures in literature, the arts, the theatre, and public life generally. 'Nothing like it has ever occurred in literature before', reported the *New York Tribune*, and the event's organizer was hardly exaggerating when he remarked that this readings tour was 'in no respect [to] be considered a private event but, from first to last, was regarded, and reasonably regarded, as a public and almost an international occurrence'. Dickens then travelled to Liverpool by the royal train. Such an apotheosis is inconceivable for any other English author. Dickens was not only the most admired entertainer of his age but he also commanded a peculiar homage and—in a phrase repeated in his letters—a 'particular relation (personally affectionate and like no other man's) which subsists between me and the public'. As the *Daily Telegraph* remarked after his death (18 June 1872), 'his current story was really a topic of the day; it seemed something almost akin to politics and news—as if it belonged not so much to literature but to events'.

Early REVIEWERS were commendably prompt and assured in recognizing this phenomenal popularity, in realizing that it was no nine-days wonder, and in trying to account for it. By the second half of 1837 all the leading critical journals had discussed this at length, noting Dickens's formidable literary skills—the range and accuracy of his observation, his wit and humour, his inventiveness in creating characters and incident, and (less often) his linguistic dexterity and originality —but also the special warmth and generosity of his personality, his benevolence, and his indignation over social injustice and institutional inefficiency and his sympathy for the poor and afflicted. In these earlier years his pathos—at its most intense over the sufferings and deaths of his younger characters— contributed as much to his popularity as his humour (see SENTIMENT). He had strikingly demonstrated his range and versatility when, halfway through *Pickwick*, he started serializing *Oliver Twist*, with its child-centred pathos, political protest, and depictions of low life, crime, and evil. It was an important factor in establishing his special status that, amusing though he was, he was manifestly not only a great entertainer but also a genial and heart-warming personality, a moral force, very English but justly and eloquently critical of his country's shortcomings (see ENGLISHNESS, DICKENS'S).

In 1844 he occupied the first and longest chapter of R. H. HORNE's *The New Spirit of the Age*: 'The secret of Dickens's success doubtless is, that he is a man with a heart in his bosom', besides 'a strong perception of all the commoner class of excitements' and other such literary gifts. Commentators noted another cause of his popularity: the publication of his works in SERIAL form made them available to many readers who could never have afforded them in hardback, and the novels' appearing over a long period maintained them as 'a topic of the day'. It was as if, today, the favourite current television serials were being written by an author seen as creatively in the Shakespeare class but who was, unlike Shakespeare, a highly visible narrator with a large and esteemed public presence and, unlike successful television authors, a household name.

In a much-quoted letter (30 June 1837) the novelist Mary Russell Mitford, comparing him to HOGARTH and Shakespeare, reports that 'All the boys and girls talk his fun—the boys in the streets', which is equally relished by the Lord Chief Justice and other such top professionals (see REPUTATION), while the *Quarterly Review* noted (October 1837) that before the end of 1836 Pickwick chintzes and Weller corduroys and other such spin-offs were on sale. The London telephone directory shows that Pickwick and Weller are still efficacious trade-names. Anthony TROLLOPE reported in 1879 that in a frenzy of free-gift-offers a tea-dealer had ordered 18,000 copies of Dickens, and when his supplier suggested other titles he memorably replied that 'the tea-drinking public preferred their Dickens'. This remained so in the 1930s, when four rival newspapers were offering his *Complete Works* to readers who would subscribe to their product.

*Fraser's* in 1850, renewing the enquiry into Dickens's popularity, attributed it to his charity, humour, tenderness, purity, his Englishness, but 'above all' to 'his deep reverence for the household sanctities, his enthusiastic

worship of the household gods' (see DOMES-
TICITY). He warmed his readers with his very
genuine attachment to such values, and with
his reformism (not so radical as to be alarming), so that Trollope could not unjustly call
him 'Mr Popular Sentiment' (*The Warden*,
1855). Also important is that, though he rat-
tled some conservative readers by his attacks
on the legal and parliamentary systems and
on aristocratic privilege, he never supported
the unpopular causes espoused by more radical contemporaries such as CHARTISM or, in
the 1850s, opposition to the CRIMEAN WAR or
disquiet about British suppression of native
uprisings in the Empire (see EYRE, E. J.), or
disbelief in God. (His religious convictions
were orthodox but unobtrusive on doctrine
or dogma. He was a Broad-Churchman, regarded as somewhat lax by some keenly partisan readers but enjoying the advantage of not
being so partisan himself, in High or Low
Church directions, as to offend or deter substantial groups of believers: see RELIGION.)
Another important negative quality in his
work is suggested by *Fraser's* praising—as
critics did throughout his career—his 'purity'.
'Three words—nay, three letters—would
have lost him his tens of thousands of readers
in nearly every class of society', remarked
R. H. Horne: but happily Dickens never used
any fatally rude three- (let alone four-) letter
words. *Pickwick* contained nothing 'unpleasant', Miss Mitford remarked; 'a lady might
read it all *aloud*', and indeed Dickens had assured readers in his Preface that it included
'no incident or expression ... which could call
a blush into the most delicate cheek'. A century later another very popular novelist,
Marie Corelli, when asked 'Why is Dickens so
abidingly and powerfully Popular?', replied:
'Because he never soiled the pen with degrading "sex problems" '—not the highest or most
positive estimation of his merits, but not an
insignificant one.

Dickens's instinctive avoidance of material
or sentiments which would offend substantial
numbers of the public removed one possible
obstacle to his popularity. Another obstacle
avoided was sneeringly noted by the *Spectator*
(31 March 1838): 'He calls upon his reader for
no exertion—requires from him no mental
elevation; he who runs can read Boz—"he is
plain to the meanest capacity".' Whatever further riches accrue to the more sensitive and

thoughtful reader, the least sophisticated and
instructed can indeed get much from the
novels—a strong narrative drive with a wide
variety of attractive incidents, vigorously distinctive characters, plenty of agreeable fun
and thrills, and acceptably uplifting sentiment. He is the most abundantly comic
English author, and his stories have happy
endings (if the happiness is less facile in later
novels). Posthumously some elements in his
work, such as his deathbed pathos and his
milk-and-water heroines, became less attractive, but his viewpoint has not seemed so
stuffily 'Victorian' as to dismay or bore.

His human centrality is well instanced by
his attachment to CHRISTMAS, the greatest demotic and international festival, with its emphasis on family, children, simple fun, and
shared feasting, all precious to him: and the
annual re-appearance of the *Christmas Carol*
—Western literature's supreme Christmas
text—in DRAMATIZATIONS, FILMS, and readings keeps alive his memory as the spirit of
warmth, generosity, humour, and good fellowship. 'It seems to me a national benefit,'
THACKERAY had presciently announced in a
review of the *Carol* (*Fraser's*, February 1844),
'and to every man and woman who reads it a
personal kindness.'

On the day of his death, while the Queen at
Windsor was lamenting this 'very great loss,' a
costermonger's girl in Drury Lane was overheard saying: 'Dickens dead? Then will Father
Christmas die too?' This juxtaposition
catches his wide appeal, his almost mythological status, and his special association with
Christmas. The girl probably knew of Dickens through staged versions rather than reading. The intrinsically theatrical nature of his
work (see THEATRE AND THEATRICALITY) and
its ready-made popularity, together with the
absence of COPYRIGHT protection, meant that
theatres were full of him; in late 1845 there
were seventeen versions of *The* CRICKET ON
THE HEARTH running in London theatres
alone. 'What will become of the English stage',
asked the *Saturday Review* after his death,
'when the public has grown weary, if it ever
does grow weary, of dramatic versions of
the stories of the late Mr Dickens?' Stage versions are now infrequent, though in recent
decades the musical *Oliver!* and the Royal
Shakespeare Company's *Nicholas Nickleby*
have been hugely popular: but he has become

stock-dramatist for film, radio, and television. When the English film industry got going at the turn of the century, Dickens was its 'most bankable commodity' (Joss Marsh), and since the BBC's first Dickens television dramatization in 1950 (inevitably, of the *Carol*), serializations of the novels, increasingly elaborate in form, have become an almost annual television event. Bookshop sales figures show Dickens still enjoying a steady high circulation, although interviews with candidates for English degree courses suggests that, of the classic English novelists, Austen and the Brontës and Hardy are more likely to be read by adolescents; the length of his novels is one of his few disadvantages. His popularity today is probably sustained as much by performed versions, which offer a strong if incomplete impression of his genius, as by the words on the printed page.

His celebrity, wrote the Harvard professor C. C. Felton in 1843, was 'without a parallel in the history of letters'. 'Probably,' wrote *Fraser's* in 1850, twenty years before his death, 'there is no single individual who, during the last fourteen years, has occupied so large a space in the thoughts of English folk as Charles Dickens.' Justin McCarthy, a young Irishman embarking on his career about that time, recalled in his *Reminiscences* (1899) that 'No one born in the younger generation can easily understand, from any illustration that later years can give them, the immensity of the homage which Dickens then enjoyed'. Such superlatives can be multiplied, and this fame was international too (see entries relating to various countries). 'You cannot think how pleasant it is to me to find myself generally known and liked here', Dickens wrote from PARIS on 24 October 1855. 'If I go into a shop to buy anything and give my card, the officiating priest or priestess brightens up, and says, "Ah! C'est l'écrivain célèbre! Monsieur porte une nomme très distingué ... Je lis un des livres de Monsieur tous les jours".' In London, he did not need to present his card. 'To walk with him in the streets of London was in itself a revelation', recalled his son Henry (1928); 'a royal progress; people of all degrees and classes taking off their hats and greeting him as they passed.' He was, wrote an OBITUARIST, 'the one writer everybody read and everybody liked ... People who never read any novels, read Mr Dickens's' (*Daily News*, 10 June 1870).

On the same day *The TIMES*, in a leading article, recognized that his death would be 'felt by millions as nothing less than a personal bereavement,' for he was 'the intimate of every household'. 'It needs an extraordinary combination of intellectual and moral qualities', *The Times* continued (as reviewers had been doing for over 30 years), 'to gain the hearts of the public as Dickens has gained them'. Not all of these have been fully explored above. His case remains unique.      PC

Collins (1971).
Collins, Philip, 'The Popularity of Dickens,' *Dickensian*, 70 (1974).
Smith (1996).

**portraits, busts, and photographs of Dickens.** The earliest Dickens portrait of confirmed authenticity is an 1830 miniature on ivory by his aunt, Janet Barrow (Ackroyd 1990, pl. IV). Drawn full-face, a slight smile plays across the lips and the hair is full but not yet the length that would characterize Dickens's appearance from the late 1830s to the late 1840s. An earlier unsigned miniature said to be Dickens shows a somewhat idealized view of him in childhood (Ackroyd 1990, pl. III), although its validity is unconfirmed. A drawing formerly in the collection of the late Percy FITZGERALD, by Thomas Uwins, RA (1782–1857), shows Dickens in 1831 (Ackroyd 1990, pl. V). The expression is softer than in the Barrow miniature, the eyes more stylized and the hair longer.

A number of other artists portrayed him in the 1830s. In July 1835 Dickens presented Catherine with a miniature by Rose Emma Drummond to mark their engagement (Ackroyd 1990, pl. VI; Pilgrim 1.69). It has been suggested that Miss Drummond was the prototype of Miss La Creevy, the good-natured miniature painter in *Nicholas Nickleby* (Kitton 1890, p. 15). In April 1837 George CRUIKSHANK made numerous sketches of Dickens sitting in an armchair by the window of the drawing-room at 48 Doughty Street. It seems Cruikshank took his work very seriously, so much so that Dickens was unable to receive his uncle Edward Barrow during the sitting (Pilgrim 1.248). Another of Dickens's illustrators, Hablot K. BROWNE tried his hand at representations of the author. One appeared in the April number of the *Court Magazine*. It is said that the artist later refused to acknowledge it; 'Phiz's forte was evidently not portraiture . . .' (Kitton 1890, p. 23). However, the previous month had seen Phiz's fine cartoon entitled *Publishing Day of* BENTLEY'S MISCELLANY which appeared in the third issue of that magazine. An energetic Dickens is seen leading a stout, breathless porter by the lapel. On his head, the weary man carries an enormous bale of the magazines and enthusiasts eagerly scramble for stray copies as they fall from the top.

The year 1837 also saw Dickens sitting to Samuel Laurence (1812–84), an artist accomplished in portraiture whose particular strength lay in the use of chalk and crayons. There is some confusion over the number of drawings made by Laurence, but it would seem that the earliest dates from late October (Pilgrim 1.324 n.). To this Dickens added his signature, and the artist would never part with it, keeping it above his mantelpiece until his death (Kitton 1890, p. 20). It is now in the DICKENS HOUSE MUSEUM, along with a companion portrait of the author's wife Catherine DICKENS. A second, dated 1838, came into Dickens's possession and he inscribed it with his pseudonym 'BOZ'. Lithographed shortly after by both Weld Taylor and Laurence himself, it was the first portrait to be sold to the public. However, it is said that Dickens did not care for it (Kitton 1890, p. 23) and shortly afterwards presented it to his sister Fanny. A watercolour by Laurence also exists and was formerly in the possession of the Comtesse de Suzannet, also a later depiction executed after Dickens grew his beard (listed in the Christie's Catalogue for 22 November 1912, but now of unknown whereabouts).

In 1839 Dickens sat to his great friend Daniel MACLISE for the famous 'Nickleby' portrait, now in the National Portrait Gallery (Ackroyd 1990, pl. XI). Dickens was unsatisfied with the face on Maclise's first effort, but considered the second to be 'astonishing'. Dickens's peers reacted to the finished version in different ways. George ELIOT thought it to suffer from 'odious beautification', whereas THACKERAY described it as 'perfectly amazing' (Pilgrim 1.558 n.). The portrait was painted for Dickens's publishers CHAPMAN AND HALL, who had it engraved by William Finden for the frontispiece of *Nicholas Nickleby*. Dickens tried to pay Maclise for his efforts but the painter returned the cheque and, despite

Dickens's remonstrations, continued t refuse payment (Pilgrim 1.577n.). In April c the same year Dickens sat to the sculptc Angus Fletcher (1799–1862). The bust, exe cuted in marble, shows Dickens somewhat a he appears in the Maclise painting. It was ex hibited at the Royal Academy later in the yea but did not come into Dickens's possessio until 1841 and is now in the Dickens Hous Museum.

Another oil painting dating from thi period is by Samuel Drummond ARA (1765 1844), father of Rose Emma Drummond. C all the portraits of Dickens, this one is re markable for the debate it has excited. Due t a number of errors made earlier this centur its authenticity has long been questionec principally because it offers an image un welcome to Dickens scholars. Painted in th majestic style of Sir Thomas Lawrence RA Drummond's near contemporary, it show Dickens with brilliant eyes, dark, irregula hair, flaring nostrils, and a curling upper lir similar indeed to Lawrence's portraits o BYRON. Nevertheless, there can be little doub that it is of Dickens and was painted aroun the time of the Nickleby portrait. There is n record of Dickens having sat to Drummond but the artist worked from the same addres as his daughter. It was bought by the heires and philanthropist Angela Burdett COUTTS who knew the author as a young man an never had any doubt that it was a genuin likeness.

Dickens's friend Count D'Orsay (1801–52 made two drawings of him, the first in De cember 1841, and another in December 184 which the artist believed to be more pleasin and subsequently inscribed it 'the best of th two'. The sitter was also satisfied but foun the chin in need of remodelling (Pilgrin 3.419 n.). Both versions are now in the Dick ens House Museum.

During 1842 Dickens fulfilled a promise t sit to Francis Alexander while he was i Boston on his first trip to AMERICA. The resul is comparable to the D'Orsay drawings and a later miniature by Margaret Gillies (1803–87) although it has been criticized for lackin character (Pilgrim 3.26 n.).

The American sculptor Henry Dexte (1806–76) married Alexander's niece, and i was no doubt through this connection that h managed to get Dickens to sit in late Januar

1842. Dexter's marble bust was much admired by the subject and he is said to have repeatedly alluded to it during his stay (Pilgrim 3.18 n.). Despite plans to send the original to England, it remained in America and has since disappeared. A cast formerly in the possession of the sculptor's granddaughter was presented to the Dickens House Museum in 1962 (frontispiece to Pilgrim 3).

Dickens sat to Margaret Gillies six or seven times in 1843 and her miniature on ivory was later displayed at the Royal Academy in May 1844. The whereabouts of the original is unknown, but it was engraved by J. C. Armytage for HORNE's *A New Spirit of the Age* (1844). The engraving was not to Dickens's taste and he commented that he had the look of the iron mask without the man in it (to Talfourd, 19 March 1844).

Two other drawings, showing Dickens with others, were done in 1843 and 1844 respectively by Maclise. The former shows Dickens, his wife, and sister-in-law Georgina HOGARTH in profile and was much admired by John FORSTER (Pilgrim 3.440 n.). In December 1844 Dickens read *The CHIMES* at Forster's house to a group of friends. Maclise drew the scene, showing Dickens seated in the centre of the composition surrounded by, amongst others, JERROLD, BLANCHARD, and CARLYLE. As a light touch, he added two phantom goblins and deified Dickens, surrounding his head with a halo of solar rays.

Over the next decade, and particularly after the advent of photography, the number of portraits begin to subside. In 1849 Augustus Egg, RA (1816–63) painted a fine portrait in oils of Dickens as Sir Charles Coldstream in an AMATEUR THEATRICAL performance of Charles MATHEWS's *Used Up*. It was the first major painting to come into the collections of the Dickens House Museum. In the following year Dickens sat to William Boxhall (1800–79). He later told his friend William Powell FRITH that the portrait worsened with each sitting, seeing him resemble an ugly boxer of the day and later a murderer. The picture was left unfinished.

The first daguerreotype Dickens ever sat for was taken by John Edwin Mayall (1810–1901) in 1852. Dickens applauded the outcome (to Coutts, 23 December 1852) and Mayall took further daguerreotypes around the same time, although there is no record of the sittings.

Edward Matthew Ward, RA (1816–79) began a painting of Dickens in his study at Tavistock House, one of a series of 'in character' portraits which included Thackeray and BULWER-LYTTON. Due to illness and travel, Dickens was unable to sit again until the following year, and the portrait was completed in late 1854. It is the first portrayal showing Dickens with the characteristic beard he so favoured in later life. Another daguerreotype by Mayall, tenuously dated 1855, in the Dickens House Museum is the first photographic image to show Dickens with a moustache.

Whilst working in Paris on *Little Dorrit* Dickens sat for the French painter Ary Scheffer (1795–1858) from 1855 to 1856, when Dickens wrote to Forster 'the nightmare portrait is nearly done . . .' (6 January 1856). The lengthy periods spent at the studio and Scheffer's unhappiness with his work had prevented Dickens from writing, but despite disappointing both artist and sitter, the portrait was displayed at the Royal Academy in May 1856.

The final great painting of Dickens during his lifetime was begun in 1859 by Frith (Ackroyd 1990, pl. XXI). The portrait, in oils, is almost full length, showing Dickens seated at a writing table, his head turned slightly to the left and his right arm resting on the back of the chair. The facial expression, although admirably portrayed, inspired Dickens to remark that 'it is a little too much (to my thinking) as if my next-door neighbour were my deadly foe, uninsured, and I had just received tidings of his house being afire . . .' (to the Hon. Mrs Watson, 31 May 1859). As with the Scheffer portrait the sittings were lengthy, and in an effort to combat this Dickens was photographed by one of the Watkins brothers (there were three; Herbert, John, and Charles of 34 Parliament Street, London). It was hoped that Frith might work from the photograph, but he found it of no assistance whatsoever (Kitton 1890, p. 75).

During the late 1850s and early 1860s photographs of Dickens became prevalent and he found himself widely recognized. He was not entirely pleased by his image being so extensively dispersed, particularly as he generally disliked the photographs. This did not deter him from occasionally requesting a sitting. In May 1858 he desired the 'best photograph' of himself to be produced by Herbert Watkins so that he might place it in an elegant case and have it sent to a friend in ITALY, the banker Émile de la Rue (to Herbert Watkins, 31 May 1858).

A fine selection of poses taken by John Watkins date to 1861. Although deemed mostly satisfactory by Dickens and his family, one in particular caused 'a general howl of horror' followed by an effort to throw it from the window (to Watkins, 28 September 1861). In 1861 a curious anonymous caricature became popular in shop windows showing Dickens with an oversized head and a miniature body. He sits at his desk, holding his left hand aloft, 'tapping his forehead to knock out an idea ... it made me laugh when I first came upon it, until I shook in open sun-lighted Piccadilly' (to the Hon. Mrs Watson, 8 July 1861). It is fittingly captioned 'From whom we have Great Expectations', and Dickens's friend Charles Kent (1823–1902) recounted that it was among the novelist's favourite portrayals (Wilkins 1924, p. 56).

In 1864–5 Dickens sat for Robert Hindry Mason, which culminated in the photographer visiting Gad's Hill Place in August 1866 (to Mason, 3 August 1866). The result was a splendid series of photographs of Dickens and members of his family and friends in various poses, as well as interiors of the house. The finest of these shows the author, his daughters Mamie and Katey, Henry CHORLEY, Charles COLLINS (Katey's husband), and Georgina Hogarth on the steps of the porch. Dickens holds a glass of claret in his hand and looks straight towards the viewer. Even he was satisfied with Mason's work, declaring the camera had let him off more easily than usual. Only one 'griffin' had to be cancelled (to Mason, 28 November 1866).

On his second trip to America (November 1867 to April 1868) Dickens must have realized that a sitting to a major photographic house would add to the receipts of the PUBLIC READINGS as well as publicize them. Consequently he chose Jeremiah Gurney (1812–86) & Son who were able, in December 1867, to advertise their success in procuring the only sitting. The photographs show a variety of poses (*Dickensian*, 54, 1958, pls. I–XII) published in both cabinet and *carte-de-visite* sizes, and although Dickens vowed never to sit to a photographer again, he thought them the best to have ever been done (Kitton 1890, p. 88). In 1983 a photograph of Dickens by

Gurney & Son's rival Mathew Brady (c.1823–96) came to light, showing Dickens seated and wearing a melancholy expression (*Dickensian*, 79, 1983). Whether it was taken before or after the Gurney series is a mystery, but it discounts their boast that they had secured an exclusive sitting.

Not all the American portrayals were done with Dickens's approval. Many of the comic periodicals criticized his reading tour as cashing in on a nation he had scorned. One, entitled 'Dickens' farewell to Hamerica', is a double cartoon, showing two images of Dickens, back to back. In the first he holds his hand to his nose in a derisive gesture, while in the second he strides away carrying a large bag of money (Wilkins, pl. XXVI).

Towards the end of his life, in February 1870, Dickens was sketched by Leslie Ward (the *Vanity Fair* cartoonist 'Spy', 1851–1922). He is seen out walking carrying a cane and wearing a short overcoat, a top hat balanced rakishly over his left ear. The face is that of a very old man, the weary expression sombre and the beard and hair protruding in tufts (*Dickensian*, 66, 1970). Another Ward drawing of the same year is the only known portrayal of Dickens wearing spectacles.

The day after Dickens's death, 10 June 1870, brought John Everett Millais RA (1829–96) to Gad's Hill Place, who made a fine pencil sketch of Dickens's profile (see PRE-RAPHAELITE BROTHERHOOD). The bandaged head is on a pillow with the sparse beard resting on a sheet drawn up to the chin (Johnson 2, pl. 85). The sculptor Thomas Woolner (1825–92) took a death mask from which he produced a marble bust. Dickens had promised to sit for the sculptor in December 1870 on the completion of *Edwin Drood*.

Dickens's death did not end the interest in producing his image, and copies and reworkings of original portraits continue to the present day. Perhaps the most famous and most reproduced of these is the unfinished 'Dickens's Dream' by Robert William BUSS, painted in 1875 and now in the Dickens House Museum. The novelist is represented seated in his library at Gad's Hill Place dreaming of his works and surrounded by a number of his characters. The setting is carefully modelled on Luke FILDES's drawing 'The Empty Chair' and the figure of Dickens copied from an 1859 photograph by (Herbert?) Watkins.

One of the most recent reworkings of Dickens's face appears on the current £10 note. Drawn by Roger Withington of the Bank of England in 1992, it is based on later photographs that show the effect of the many strains on Dickens. The artist has softened the lines around the eyes and rendered the face less gaunt (*Dickensian*, 88, 1992).    AX

Kitton (1890).

Peyrouton, N. C., 'The Gurney Photographs', *Dickensian*, 54 (1958).

Wilkins, W. G., *Dickens in Cartoon and Caricature* (1924).

Xavier, A., 'Charles and Catherine Dickens: Two Fine Portraits by Samuel Laurence', *Dickensian*, 92 (1996).

**Pre-Raphaelite Brotherhood.** The initials 'PRB', for Pre-Raphaelite Brotherhood, first appeared on a number of paintings exhibited at the Royal Academy in 1848. The title was adopted by a group of young British ARTISTS who wished to revive the freedom from academic rules and conventions which they associated with pre-Renaissance painters. They were not antagonistic to Raphael, but to 'Raphaelitism': that is, they objected to the hackneyed, mannered work of disciples and later followers of Raphael. The Brotherhood in its earliest years consisted of William Holman Hunt, Dante Gabriel Rossetti, John Everett Millais, William Michael Rossetti, Thomas Woolner, George Frederick Stephens, and James Collinson. Other painters became associated with the group in later years, notably Ford Madox Brown and Arthur Hughes. Their aim was to choose subjects from everyday life or from literature or the Bible, and to paint them with a luminous naturalism, often through painstaking location work in order to capture in precise detail a riverbank or old grange as the setting for the literary or religious subject. In their fidelity to natural detail and their radical challenge to post-Renaissance academic conventions they won the powerful support of John RUSKIN.

Dickens, who loathed most contemporary forms of romantic medievalism, wrote a fierce critique of Millais's painting *Christ in the House of His Parents* (*HW* 15 June 1850). He regarded it as an instance of vulgarizing naturalism in the representation of the Holy Family. He went on to attack what he called the 'great retrogressive principle' of the PRB and satirically invoked various imaginary forms of this 'principle', including a Pre-Galileo Brotherhood which would ensure that the earth no longer revolved around the sun.

The PRB was never as consolidated as their title suggested, and the painters drifted apart in later years, many abandoning the first principles that had brought them together. Dickens admired the later work of Millais, who became a friend. It was Millais who introduced Dickens to the work of Luke FILDES, and who drew a delicate pencil portrait of Dickens on his deathbed.    MYA

**prisons and penal transportation.** Dickens's sustained fascination with prisons was in many ways a reflection of a wider interest in penal reform. Building upon the early efforts of John Howard (1726–90), Jeremy BENTHAM (1748–1832), and Elizabeth Fry (1780–1845), enthusiastic legislators and publicists recommended changes of system, organization, and even architecture, in an effort to effect the systematic reclamation of prisoners.

The fictional portraits of prison life are varied, encompassing both foreign and domestic experience. Dickens was able to evoke the atmosphere of the Marseilles prison (*LD* 1.1), the Conciergerie (*TTC* 3.6), and the Abbaye (*TTC* 2.24) with as much insight as he devoted to depictions of the Fleet (*PP* 41–7) and the King's Bench (*DC* 11). He inspected prisons and met with penal reformers on his travels through England, SCOTLAND, SWITZERLAND, FRANCE, and AMERICA, and demonstrated acute sensitivity to both the physical and psychological effects of incarceration.

Dickens's penological reading was geared towards sharpening his imaginative rejoinder to the specific issues he championed. His chosen volumes included Wakefield's *Facts Relating to the Punishment of Death* (1831), a personal account of imprisonment in Newgate; Field's *Prison Discipline* (1848), which advocated a religious approach to inmates; Kingsmill's *Prisons and Prisoners* (1849), describing conditions at Pentonville; and Hill's *Crime: Its Amount, Causes, and Remedies* (1853), a prison inspector's plea for tolerance. He also read various pamphlets by the reformer Alexander Maconochie (whom he first met in 1836), and whose 'marks system' he adapted as the basis for discipline in URA-NIA COTTAGE. The combination of personal experience and penological reading produced a response which focused on the plight of the individual. Such is the thrust of 'A Visit to Newgate', where he concentrated on the condemned man in his cell, whose 'fears of death amount almost to madness' (SB 32). Dickens continued to visualize Newgate—one of the worst prisons in England—as a dark repository of suffering in 'Fagin's Last Night Alive' (OT 52), in Barnaby Rudge, where a break-in raises the threat of prisoners being burned alive (BR 63–4), and in Great Expectations, where Pip reflects on the 'ugly, disorderly, depressing scene' (GE 32).

By the late 1840s Dickens had acquired sufficient confidence in his ability to comment poignantly on the penal process to enter the debate concerning the relative merits of the 'Silent' and 'Separate' systems of incarceration. The Silent System—of which Dickens and the public at large generally approved—involved close surveillance by prison staff to prevent inmates from communicating with one another; it was in operation at Coldbath Fields, where Dickens was a frequent visitor. He supported the harsh regime, including purposeless walking of the treadwheel—a tedious, irksome task which supposedly acted as a deterrent. Most English legislators and penologists, on the other hand, preferred the Separate System, instituted at such 'Model Prisons' as Pentonville, Reading, and Preston, featuring a limited period of solitary confinement and a commitment to teaching prisoners a trade. Dickens spoke out against Pentonville in particular in 'Pet Prisoners', claiming that it was expensive, encouraged 'pattern penitence', and offered superior diet and conditions to those in the workhouse; crime, he noted, seemed to have gained a 'manifest advantage' over poverty (HW 27 April 1850). This critique found fictional expression in David Copperfield's encounter with the 'two interesting penitents', Littimer and Uriah Heep (DC 61).

While Dickens was keen to expose the English Separate System's laxity, he was far more troubled by the excessive severity of its American counterpart, which he observed at the Eastern Penitentiary in Philadelphia in 1842. He recorded his impressions in AMERI-CAN NOTES, emphasizing the 'morally un-

healthy and diseased' state of mind produced by extended isolation (AN 7). This sense of haunting mental anguish is effectively conveyed in the depiction of Dr Manette, who suffers permanent damage to his personality as a result of his confinement in the Bastille (TTC 1.6). Dickens also considered how characters imprisoned for debt—particularly George Heyling (PP 21) and William Dorrit (LD 2.19)—suffered adverse effects after being released. It is significant that both were confined in the Marshalsea, where Dickens's own father, John DICKENS, was held in 1824; this painful boyhood experience certainly helped to fuel his fictional expressions about prisons, his comments on penal reform, the painful recollections of the autobiographical fragment (Forster 1.2; see DIARIES), and such comments as those in 'Where We Stopped Growing', where he notes that 'We have never outgrown' the walls of any prisons; within there is still 'the same blank of remorse and misery' (HW 1 Jan-uary 1853).

On the subject of penal transportation to AUSTRALIA Dickens had far less factual information. Begun in 1787, with the sailing of the 'First Fleet' to New South Wales, transportation was initially deemed a fitting sentence for a range of crimes, from petty theft to murder; despite various reforms and attempts at abolition, the scheme persisted until 1868, by which time over 160,000 men and women had been forcibly dispatched to the Antipodes. Though he played no part in reforming the system, Dickens believed in the potential for deterrence embodied in the threat of transportation; he wrote to the Home Secretary, Lord Normanby, offering to produce a pamphlet to be placed 'on the pillow of every prisoner in England', containing a 'vivid description' of the terrors of convict life (3 July 1840). The plan was, however, never executed.

The incidents of transportation in Dickens's fiction owe their scanty details to his reading of parliamentary reports, journalism, travelogues, and novels; his scrutiny of contributions to Household Words and All the Year Round; and his involvement with emigration schemes such as those promoted by Samuel Sidney (1813–83) and Caroline Chisholm (1808–77). In his early work characters like John Edmunds, in 'The Convict's Return', are depicted as having suffered greatly in the 'distant land' of 'bondage and infamy' (PP 6). In

*Oliver Twist* Dickens introduces elements of irony and the picaresque in reporting how the Artful Dodger acquired the 'distinction' of being 'lagged' (transported for life) at his tender age (*OT* 43). In *Nicholas Nickleby* New South Wales is deemed an appropriate depository for the incorrigible Wackford Squeers, who cannot be accommodated in England (*NN* 64). A similar fate awaits Uriah Heep and Littimer (*DC* 61), though in *David Copperfield* Dickens widens the range of possibilities offered by Australia: as free settlers, Micawber, Mr Peggotty, and Mell succeed, while Martha finds a husband (*DC* 63).

Dickens only offers one extended treatment of a transported convict: his portrayal of Magwitch in *Great Expectations*. He first appears to Pip on the marshes, having escaped from the hulks—those decommissioned troop transports and men o'war used as floating prisons (*GE* 1). After being recaptured he leaves the narrative, during which time he works as an assignee in New South Wales and, after obtaining his ticket-of-leave (a form of parole), makes his fortune as 'a sheep-farmer, stock-breeder, and other trades besides' (*GE* 39), before returning to declare himself Pip's benefactor. Magwitch plays the key role in the scheme for Pip's elevation upon which the plot depends. The fact that he conceives the plan in a 'solitary hut', where he conjures up an image of Pip 'looking at me whiles I eats and drinks' (*GE* 39), confirms Dickens's continued interest in the individual psyche and its appeal to the imagination, and establishes a connection between prisoners and transported convicts as subjects of immense psychological interest for Dickens.
                                                                          LL

Collins (1962).
Easson, A., 'Marshalsea Prisoners', *Dickens Studies Annual*, 3 (1974).
Easson, A., 'Imprisonment for Debt in *Pickwick Papers*', *Dickensian*, 64 (1968).
Litvack, L., 'Dickens, Australia, and Magwitch Part I: The Colonial Context'; 'Part II: The Search for *le cas Magwitch*', *Dickensian*, 95 (1999).

**Proctor, Adelaide Anne.** English poet (1825–64). The daughter of Dickens's friend Bryan Waller Proctor ('Barry Cornwall'), Proctor wrote poetry from an early age. Fearing her father's friendship with Dickens would unfairly colour his judgement of her writing, she submitted a poem to *Household Words* in 1853 under the pseudonym of 'Miss Mary Berwick'. The poem was printed, and was followed by many others; it was not until Christmas 1854 that Dickens discovered the actual identity of the contributor. Proctor's poetry consists largely of morbid but pious lyrical meditations on death and Christianity, and her own early death seems many times prefigured (see POETRY AND POETS DURING DICKENS'S LIFETIME). Dickens wrote a Preface to her posthumously published collection *Legends and Lyrics* (1866) in which he dramatizes the scene at her deathbed in a manner familiar from his earlier novels: ' "Do you think I am dying, mamma?" "I think you are very, very ill to-night my dear." "Send for my sister. My feet are so cold. Lift me up! . . . It has come at last!" And with a bright and happy smile, she looked upward, and departed.'
                                                                          AR

**prostitutes and fallen women** haunt the pages of Dickens's fiction, as they haunted the public places of London and many other Victorian towns. The 'great social evil' generated intense MORAL concern, yet the facts about prostitution, known to social investigators of the time, bore little relation to the mythology circulating among the middle classes. Dickens can be accused of the same double vision. He was well acquainted through his reform work with prostitutes and the conditions of their profession. There is no actual proof that he ever used prostitutes, though a veiled reference to the 'conveniences' of Margate in a letter to Daniel MACLISE (16 August 1841) and his later social jaunts with Wilkie COLLINS suggest that he was far from criticizing his friends' behaviour in this respect. He may have kept a young actress, Ellen TERNAN, as his mistress for over a decade, thus putting her in the situation of the 'fallen woman' condemned by contemporary morality, and there are a couple of references in his surviving letters of 1859 that suggest he may have resorted to prostitutes, or at least to women of what was called 'easy virtue', around this time. Yet for all his personal knowledge, he presented fallen women in his fiction as the most blatant of cultural stereotypes.

Prostitutes in 19th-century art and literature were sensationally depicted as sexual and sinful whores, the dark opposites of 'angels in the house'. Once fallen, victims of their own sexuality or seduced by an unscrupulous suitor, they slid quickly down the social scale into a life of common prostitution and crime. Whether guilt-ridden or flagrantly lacking in remorse, these imaginary girls were merciless sirens to respectable men, pariahs among women. Many ended their wretched careers by drowning themselves in the Thames. However, the life of the real prostitute typically followed a different course. She was likely to have lapsed into prostitution in her late teens, primarily out of economic choice when faced with other gruelling low-paid employment. The majority of prostitutes worked from lodgings, enjoying at least a measure of independence and supportive female companionship from landladies and other prostitutes. Far from being trapped for ever on the streets, most women appear to have returned to mainstream society after a couple of years, married, and brought up families of their own.

Prostitutes awakened Dickens's sympathy, and intrigued him. He showed practical kindness in individual cases, as with the working prostitute whom he attempted to establish as a respectable London landlady in the mid-1850s (see Pilgrim *Letters* 7.467–9 and Appendix D). For over a decade from 1846 he was actively involved in URANIA COTTAGE, a home for the reclamation of London prostitutes and the support of other young women at risk, who were encouraged along the path of reform by the hope of EMIGRATION. This was the fate allotted to Martha Endell in *David Copperfield*, written at the inception of the Urania Cottage project, who was saved from suicide on the banks of the Thames to live out Dickens's dream of a remorseful prostitute rewarded by a decent husband in AUSTRALIA. But Dickens's understanding of prostitutes and the lives of lower-class women had remarkably little effect on his fiction. Fallen women lurk in the shadows in many places in his writing, a threat to middle-class decency and the DOMESTIC ideal. The sisters taken off to jail in Dickens's early sketch, 'The Prisoners' Van' (*SB*), are depicted in stereotypical terms, their influence on society likened to a 'wide-spreading infection'. The younger is still ashamed of her exposure to the public gaze; the elder girl's features are marked by 'two additional years of depravity . . . as legibly as if a red-hot iron had seared them'.

The sketch moralistically traces the harlot's progress from a 'hopeless' beginning, through a 'loathsome and repulsive' course, to a 'friendless, forlorn, and unpitied' conclusion.

Dickens's main thematic variation lies in his sympathy for fallen women. In *Dombey and Son* he repeatedly underscores the parallel between Alice Marwood on the streets and Edith Dombey in the upper-class marriage market in order to shock the reader into a better understanding of both situations. In *David Copperfield* fallen Martha Endell plays a noble part in saving Little Em'ly from a brothel. Even the prostitute who disappears 'with a strange, wild, cry' in *Little Dorrit* is described as 'not wicked-looking', and appeals pathetically to Little Dorrit: 'Kiss a poor lost creature' (*LD* 1.14). Dickens was not alone in this forgiving attitude. The religious thinking which inspired the Magdalenism movement for prostitute rescue reverberates in the phrase 'the ruined Temple of God', used of the whore on the staircase in *The* HAUNTED MAN (2); Lilian in the vision sequence of *The* CHIMES, having made her melodramatic entrances bearing the purse containing her wages of sin, explicitly compares herself to Mary Magdalene before dying of a broken heart. It was not unusual to locate some blame for women's fall elsewhere. The sisters in 'The Prisoners' Van' and Alice Marwood in *Dombey and Son* (whose surname suggests a fall from natural goodness) are sold onto the streets by their mothers; Little Em'ly, who is rescued from a brothel in the nick of time, has been betrayed by a cynical seducer. In *The Chimes* Dickens is reflecting the research of social investigators into the connection between prostitution and low pay: Lilian's decision to become a whore rather than face more 'long, long nights of hopeless, cheerless, never-ending work' (Third Quarter) is justified in terms of the text when Meg, her good counterpart, continues with her honest toil as a seamstress only to end in destitution and despair.

The vivid character of Nancy in *Oliver Twist* is in some ways an exception. Since she was situated in the East End underworld, she was perhaps not envisaged as a typical common prostitute and therefore invited different fictional treatment. Indeed, her profession is not distinctly identified in the novel, so the moral issue is submerged. She is a whore with a heart of gold, fulfilling in some semblance the roles of wife and sister in her relationships with Sikes and Oliver. Her terrible murder, a scene which engaged Dickens's intense imaginative commitment in PUBLIC READINGS in the last year of his life, can be construed as the punishment of a whore, whose good intentions and good works cannot save her. For the modern reader it invites another interpretation, as a rendering of the violence men do to women through direct acts of physical brutality and through the kind of sexual relationships and fantasies epitomized by prostitution where men hold the money and the power.

There is no doubt that many Victorians would have been unable to accept Dickens's forgiving approach to fallen women, however limited it may appear today. Indeed, mainstream Victorian morality labelled women who had committed adultery or fallen to a single seducer as no better than prostitutes, and artists and writers who aired the subject were greeted with dismay by reviewers and the reading public. Elizabeth GASKELL was appalled by the reception of her novel *Ruth* (1853), which attempted to show the situation from a woman's viewpoint. In *Past and Present*, a sequence of three paintings by Dickens's friend Augustus Egg (exhibited 1858), the discovery of a wife's infidelity ensures her banishment from the comfortable family drawing-room; in the third picture she is depicted in a wretched condition under the arches beside the River Thames, nursing an emaciated baby. The moral message was harsh, but many reviewers were unhappy that the subject had been dealt with at all.

Dickens played some part in awakening public sympathy on behalf of fallen women. He deliberately intended to arouse pity in the readers of *David Copperfield* through Mr Peggotty's search for Little Em'ly, a story which inspired Holman Hunt's controversial painting 'The Awakening Conscience' (exhibited 1854), in which a kept mistress realizes her wrongdoing. He serialized Elizabeth Gaskell's 'Lizzie Leigh' in the opening numbers of *Household Words*, a tale of a family reunited with a lost daughter who earned a living by prostitution after having a child. And he refused to present illegitimate children like Esther Summerson and Oliver Twist as tainted by their mothers' fault, though he showed

how they suffer from the circumstances of their birth. However, despite his compassion, Dickens still punished his fictional women for their fall. Little Em'ly is not permitted to marry; nor indeed is Louisa in *Hard Times*, who does not actually succumb to her seducer but falls instead at her father's feet. There is no evidence in his novels that fallen women could save themselves or that prostitutes could keep control of their own lives, and he was less successful than his contemporary Elizabeth Gaskell in departing from moral and literary conventions to give the woman's side of the story.                     EW

Armstrong, Nancy, *Desire and Domestic Fiction* (1987).
Mason, Michael, *The Making of Victorian Sexual Attitudes* (1994).
Nead, Linda, *Myths of Sexuality: Representations of Women in Victorian Britain* (1988).
Walkowitz, Judith R., *Prostitution and Victorian Society: Women, Class, and the State* (1980).

**public health, sanitation, and housing.** 'In all my writings', Dickens noted in November 1849 (in the Preface to the first Cheap Edition of *Martin Chuzzlewit*), 'I hope I have taken every available opportunity of showing the want of sanitary improvements in the neglected dwellings of the poor.' By 1851 Dickens was prepared to state his belief in sanitary reform even more strongly. All the information that he had been able to acquire, he told the Metropolitan Sanitary Association, 'has strengthened me in the conviction that Searching Sanitary Reform must precede all other social remedies' (*Speeches*, p. 129). Of 'the preventible wretchedness and misery in which the mass of the people dwell,' he wrote in 1854, 'the reform of their habitations must precede all other reforms . . . without it, all other reforms must fail' ('To Working Men', *HW* 7 October 1854; repr. in *MP*).

Dickens's outspoken, public commitment to the cause of sanitary reform and his active involvement in sanitary politics were in large measure a response to state inertia in the face of the 1848–9 cholera epidemic—culpable negligence (again at the national level) that was repeated during the 1853–4 epidemic, which Dickens likened to wholesale murder. Yet a concern with issues of public health, sanitation, and working-class housing should come as no surprise from an author long known for depictions of insalubrious environments. 'Gin Shops' and 'Seven Dials' in *Sketches by Boz* come quickly to mind. Jacob's Island in *Oliver Twist* is a still more celebrated example. Also notable is the powerful passage in *Dombey and Son* where Dickens invited readers to 'follow the good clergyman or doctor, who, with his life imperilled at every breath he draws', goes down into the dens of society's outcasts: 'Look round upon the world of odious sights . . . Breathe the polluted air, foul with every impurity that is poisonous to health and life; and have every sense, conferred upon our race for its delight and happiness, offended, sickened and disgusted, and made a channel by which misery and death alone can enter. Vainly attempt to think of any simple plant, or flower, or wholesome weed, that, set in this foetid bed, could have its natural growth, or put its little leaves off to the sun as God designed it' (*DS* 47).

This striking aside, written in October or November 1847, probably owed a good deal of its urgency to recent cholera rumours, the result of a series of letters published in *The TIMES* and elsewhere noting the alarming reappearance of cholera in Eastern Europe, and its likely return to England. But if a newly heightened consciousness of epidemic disease lay behind this passage—conscious propaganda for the public health and sanitary cause—the aside also owes much to Dickens's prior connections with sanitary and public-health reform. These connections were both intellectual and personal. The most important personal connection was Dickens's brother-in-law, Henry Austin, who had been one of the founders and honorary secretary of the Health of Towns Association (see BROTHERS AND SISTERS OF DICKENS). A civil engineer by training, Austin attributed his own interest in sanitation to his experiences in the construction of the Blackwall Railway, where he saw at first hand the appalling condition of the working-class suburbs through which the railway was built (a link between railways and the exposure of slum ills that has its own direct echo in *Dombey*). By 1841 Austin had contributed an important article on metropolitan improvements to the *Westminster Review*, and he was asked to prepare a paper for Edwin CHADWICK's celebrated 1842 sanitary report. Allegedly Chadwick's 'favourite engineer', Austin continued to work closely with

Chadwick in the years that followed—for example, on the 1847 Metropolitan Sanitary Commission (an appointment for which Dickens lobbied), on the first Metropolitan Commission of Sewers, and on the General Board of Health. As early as 1842 Chadwick asked Austin to present a copy of his sanitary report to Dickens, in the hope that Dickens might help win influence for the sanitary cause. Dickens acknowledged the importance of the sanitation, though he went on privately to express his strong disagreement with Chadwick on what he took to be Chadwick's chief subject, the new POOR LAW. In the end, Dickens concluded AMERICAN NOTES with a nod toward sanitary reform and a very brief commendation of Chadwick's report.

Dickens's other personal connection with the public-health cause was Dr Thomas Southwood Smith, an ardent BENTHAMITE reformer and by the 1840s a leading figure in the sanitary movement. Smith had been appointed medical advisor to the Poor Law Commission in 1832, and at the end of the decade he had helped to produce the series of extremely important studies on the physical geography of fever that provided key medical arguments for sanitary reform. Like Austin, Smith was one of the founders of the Health of Towns Association; and he was also appointed to the General Board of Health in 1848. Dickens was in contact with Smith by the end of 1840, in connection with a sanatorium that Smith had established in London, and in connection with the Children's Employment Commission. Smith was a member of the latter commission, established by Lord Ashley, whose report on women and children employed in the coal-mines proved to be one of the most sensational Blue Books of the century—a report that Dickens had planned (but failed) to write an article about for the *Edinburgh Review*.

Despite these ties, Dickens's name did not appear publicly in connection with organized sanitary reform until the start of 1848, when he was listed as a subscriber (and thus member) of the Health of Towns Association—at a time, however, when the passage of the Health of Towns Bill seemed very likely, and when the work of the Association, established as a pressure group to secure public-health legislation, was very nearly over. What accounts for this timing? As noted, the ominous reappearance of cholera altered the significance of sanitary reform. Although England's 1832 cholera epidemic had aroused considerable anxiety, the way in which the contagion spread was not understood. Moreover, sanitary ills were quickly overshadowed by such things as CHARTISM, opposition to the New Poor Law, FACTORY REFORM, extensive unemployment, and free-trade radicalism. (Early public-health reformers were criticized by both Chartists and members of the Anti-Corn Law League for diverting support from more fundamental change.) In addition, despite the increasing degradation of the urban environment, particularly in older, central-city areas, many urban reformers were preoccupied with issues of CRIME and MORAL decay, which progressives (including Dickens) associated primarily with ignorance and poverty. Finally, filth and disease were simply so ubiquitous in early Victorian slums that they could easily be taken as inevitable, rather than as remediable evils.

The cholera episode that aroused Dickens's greatest indignation was the Tooting disaster, in January 1849. In this needless tragedy, cholera claimed the lives of 150 helpless pauper children at a commercial baby farm run by Bartholomew Drouet. Drouet had not followed any of the precautionary measures recommended by the Board of Health (in a memorandum drawn up by Henry Austin) to lessen the likelihood and dangers of cholera. Moreover, when the news of fever at Tooting reached the Board of Health, a medical inspector was sent quickly to the scene, even though Tooting, about eight miles south-west of London, was excluded from the Board's jurisdiction. The inspector recommended the immediate removal of all uninfected children —advice that was flatly rejected. When the circumstances of the tragedy came to light, including the everyday treatment of the pauper children in Drouet's care, Dickens was outraged, and he wrote four scathing articles on the subject for the EXAMINER (three of which are reprinted in *MP*; one in *Journalism* 2). More than any other single incident, this example of callous neglect brought Dickens out as a powerful proponent of sanitary reform, allying him closely with Austin, Chadwick, and Southwood Smith in favour of a centralized public-health authority, capable of overriding petty local interests and red tape.

Dickens was soon able to argue this viewpoint from the platform of the Metropolitan Sanitary Association, an organization established to bring London within the provisions of the Public Health Act (an omission that Dickens likened to *Hamlet* with only the gravedigger). The Association's backers urged, among other things, that the failure of London's local authorities to take vigorous preventive measures before and during the cholera epidemic was directly responsible for up to half of the metropolis's 16,000 cholera deaths. Dickens was a speaker at the Association's inaugural meeting in February 1850, and he identified those responsible for obstructing sanitary reform: these were 'the small owners of small tenements, who pushed themselves forward on boards of guardians and parish vestries, and were clamorous about the ratings of their property', and also gentlemen of a higher class 'who had a weak leaning to the words "self-government" ' (*Speeches*, p. 107). Dickens was again a speaker at the Association's 1851 meeting, where he vigorously defended the Board of Health (on the basis of information supplied directly by Chadwick), argued strongly for centralization, and condemned the inactivity of metropolitan vestries during the cholera epidemic.

From March 1850 onward, Dickens was able to use his newly established journal *Household Words* as a powerful voice for sanitary reform. He was 'sincerely anxious to serve the cause', he wrote to Austin in May 1850—in this case, with reference to metropolitan interments—'and am doing it all the good I can, by side-blows in ... Household Words—[and] in the . . . "narrative" too' (12 May 1850). 'You will see that I have done something sanitary this week', he wrote to Austin the following November, noting that two numbers later he had also 'kept the subject alive' (28 November 1850). Indeed, up through 1854 barely a month passed without *Household Words* or its monthly supplement carrying some discussion of sanitation or housing. Moreover, Dickens remained in very close contact with Austin, soliciting his suggestions for articles, showing him proofs, and receiving information and documents.

One such document was the Board's *Report on a General Scheme for Extramural Sepulture*. 'I began to read it last night, in bed,' Dickens wrote to Austin, 'and dreamed of putrefaction generally' (27 February 1850). This report certainly supplied part of the basis for the noxious cemetery where 'Nemo' is buried in Bleak House. But it is also suggestive at a deeper level: putrefaction, decay, and their social consequences pervade the novel's literal and metaphorical landscape, from Krook's rag-and-bone shop to Tom-All-Alone's, the pestilential slum where, as Jo explains, the inhabitants 'dies more than they lives'.

By the time Bleak House was under way, in March 1852, the Board of Health was coming increasingly under criticism—though for doing too much, rather than too little. Yet despite effective campaigns by the numerous interest groups that had clashed with the Board (from Poor Law Guardians to water companies to undertakers), Dickens remained firmly committed to the idea of a strong central authority, armed with coercive powers. Although the cholera of 1853–4 was less lethal than the epidemic of 1848–9, it nevertheless had a harsh impact on the poor, particularly in the north of England. Newcastle was worst hit—where the city corporation had long resisted the Public Health Act.

Dickens's views on sanitary reform in the aftermath of the 1853–4 cholera epidemic were expressed most forcibly in a series of angry articles in Household Words in the autumn of 1854. The first, 'To Working Men' (7 October 1854; MP 1), was by Dickens himself; it called upon the working classes to unite with the middle classes to insist that the central government discharge its 'first obligation': to secure 'to the people Homes, instead of polluted dens'. 'A Board of Health can do much,' Dickens wrote, 'but not near enough. Funds are wanted, and great powers are wanted; powers to over-ride little interests for the general good; powers to coerce the ignorant, obstinate, and slothful, and to punish all who, by any infraction of necessary laws, imperil the public health.' A subsequent article by Henry MORLEY ('A Home Question', 11 November 1854) called for a new People's Charter, containing five points of sanitary reform, and it again stressed the need for a powerful central authority able to override local interests. Though the article praised the work of John Simon, Officer of Health for the City (of London) Sewers Commission, it condemned the generality of local authorities for

obstructing sanitary reform. Indeed, All the Year Round was still making this point a decade later. Though centralization was often viewed as 'an ugly bugbear . . . you and I and every Londoner who reads this page, are in daily and increasing peril of being sacrificed to the fine old conservatism of that obstinate blockhead the British vestryman'. The article went on to ask 'whether it be beneath the dignity of parliament to check the wholesale dissemination of poison, and the recklessly indiscriminate dealing out of death?' (11 November 1865). By this date no appeal could be made to the Board of Health, which had been dismantled in 1858 as a result of continuing opposition to its activities and approach. But its functions had been transferred elsewhere rather than abolished, and a series of Nuisances Removal Acts and Sewage Utilization Acts in the late 1850s and 1860s in fact enabled many local authorities to make significant sanitary improvements in their localities.

If moral indignation was a powerful catalyst for Dickens's public stand on sanitary reform, his knowledge of the realities of working-class housing drew him into an overlapping cause, that of housing reform (see LONDON: SLUMS). 'Thus, we make our New Oxford Streets, and our other new streets,' Dickens wrote in 1851, 'never heeding, never asking, where the wretches whom we clear out, crowd' ('On Duty with Inspector Field', HW 14 June 1851). Reformers concerned with slum ills were increasingly forced to ask this question, as the shortage of decent working-class accommodation in central urban areas became more and more apparent. For people too poor to move to outlying suburbs, the consequences were obvious: overcrowding emerged as a leading problem, both for health reformers charting the epidemiology of infectious disease, and for moral and religious reformers worried about (and eager to regulate) the indiscriminate aggregation of large numbers of people in common habitations, often with common sleeping arrangements.

The first explicit evidence of Dickens's interest in housing reform was a visit he paid in 1846 to the newly completed Model Houses in Pakenham Street, Bagnigge Wells, constructed by the Society for Improving the Condition of the Labouring Classes. Two years earlier Miss COUTTS had made a modest donation to this society, which was predominantly EVANGELICAL in its sponsorship and management. Over the next decade the society emerged as one of the leading influences in the model dwellings movement. Dickens and Miss Coutts visited its Model Houses for Families (in Streatham Street, Bloomsbury) in 1852, and the society went on to attempt to recruit Dickens—unsuccessfully—as a speaker for its next annual meeting.

The other important housing society in this period was the Metropolitan Association for Improving the Dwellings of the Industrious Classes, which had been formed in 1841. Unlike the SICLC, which was entirely charitable, this organization sought to provide a modest return for investors to attract capital to working-class housing, thereby inaugurating the 'philanthropy and five percent' movement. In November 1849, probably at Southwood Smith's urging, Dickens purchased a £25 share in the Association. The great advantage of the association, Dickens later explained to Miss Coutts, was that one became a shareholder rather than a subscriber—though Dickens's return seems to have been only 3 per cent per annum, far short of the returns that a speculative builder might expect, and far short of the 12–15 per cent that slum landlords often earned by simply neglecting repairs.

Dickens's most active involvement in housing reform, however, was through Miss Coutts. From January 1852 Dickens was involved in planning the large housing project that Miss Coutts eventually built at Nova Scotia Gardens in Bethnal Green, known as Columbia Square. While this project was delayed by legal difficulties (including a dispute with the site's main tenant, a large dust contractor), Dickens sought to help Miss Coutts improve the sanitary arrangements of a slum neighbourhood in Westminster. Finally, in late 1852 and early 1853 Dickens and Miss Coutts contemplated refurbishing a slum house as a showpiece of sanitary reform, to demonstrate to local landlords that improved sanitation was inexpensive and in their long-term interests.

This last project does not seem to have got off the ground. In an effort to find a suitable location for the project in early 1853, for example, Dickens visited an area near Jacob's Island known as Hickman's Folly—which he regarded as 'the last hopeless climax of everything poor and filthy'. His conclusion was that 'it would be of no use to touch a limb of Hickman—his whole body is infected, and would spoil the mended part' (7 January 1853). Dickens continued to examine potential sites at least through March 1853, before the idea was abandoned, perhaps because the more ambitious Westminster project had run into difficulties. This project was intended to facilitate the introduction of efficient drainage and water in a bad district of Westminster through a combination of modest philanthropic expenditure, SELF-HELP, and moral pressure. Miss Coutts paid for a survey, plans, and estimates (which she guaranteed); it was then hoped that the landlords could be persuaded to pay the cost of connecting their houses to the main street drains and water supply (partly out of humanitarian concern, partly to avoid the higher cost of compulsory hook-up later on, and partly to raise property values). Around 150 houses were involved, owned by eighteen separate proprietors. In the course of protracted negotiations, some of the landlords most hostile to the plan attempted to use their opposition to force Miss Coutts to pay part of their costs—a step that Dickens recommended against. The final outcome of the negotiations with the Westminster landlords has not been recorded. Suffering from overwork, Dickens left for a long stay on the Continent before any conclusion was reached.

The first portion of the Nova Scotia Gardens project was finally completed in 1859, and the entire square was finished in 1862. It consisted of four apartment blocks arranged around a courtyard, able to accommodate 1,000 people in 183 separate flats. Rents ranged from 2s. 2d. for single rooms, to 5s. 6d. for three-room flats, and all tenants had access to laundry rooms, club rooms, play areas, and storage areas. The project returned a very philanthropic 2½ per cent on Miss Coutts's outlay of £43,000. An article in *All the Year Round* warmly praised Columbia Square when it was completed, although there is no evidence that Dickens ever visited it. By this time his separation from his wife had ended his close association with Miss Coutts.

More generally, the appalling problems of filth and disease identified in the 1840s were gradually being addressed by the 1860s, making slums somewhat less lethal. But the problem of overcrowding, only dimly recognized in the 1840s and 1850s, worsened. By the mid-1860s *All the Year Round* admitted that benevolence had not solved the housing problem, and urged that the state make low-interest loans available for slum rebuilding. Moreover, the demands of sanitary reformers and housing reformers were no longer always compatible: the tenants of properties condemned for lack of sanitation had nowhere else to live. Dickens unquestionably deserves credit for helping to advance sanitary reform, particularly in the period from 1848 to the mid-1850s. In this he allied himself with an emerging group of public-health professionals whose own expertise, authority, and standing were closely bound up with the sanitary cause and with the expansion of state activity in this area. But like most other reformers of his generation, Dickens lacked a full understanding of the systematic pressure of urban demolition and displacement. Influential in the sanitary cause, he played a more limited role in the battle to end overcrowding and to increase the supply of decent working-class housing.                                          NP

Fielding, K. J. and Brice, A. W., '*Bleak House and the Graveyard*', in Partlow (1970).

Pope (1978), ch. 5.

Wohl, Anthony, *Endangered Lives: Public Health in Victorian Britain* (1983).

**public readings.** Dickens's public readings, described at the time as 'a novelty in literature and in the annals of "entertainment" ' and 'a wholly unexampled incident in the history of literature'—for no great author had thus performed his works in public—were enormously successful, artistically and financially. Audiences relished this opportunity to see so long-loved and illustrious an author and hear him brilliantly enacting his own creations: he was 'the greatest reader of the greatest writer of the age'. There were objectors: John FORSTER thought this activity was a substitution of lower for higher aims, a dereliction of Dickens's duty to literature, and a dubious occupation for a gentleman. Others thought that the touring, and especially his addiction to the last item he devised, the spectacular but exhausting 'Sikes and Nancy', had caused his premature death. Certainly, the time and energy he gave to the reading left less time for writing, while the substantial box-office income reduced the incentive to write. Dickens found that he could earn more, and more quickly, by reading than by writing, and in these 'restless' unhappy later years he could more easily force himself to repeat a performance than undertake the long, lonely task of creating a new novel. But also he enjoyed the footlights, the adoration of a visible audience, the exercise of his considerable histrionic skills, and the kudos of his success. Moreover, as the success of such later Dickens-readers as Bransby WILLIAMS and Emlyn WILLIAMS has shown, no classic English novelist's work lends itself so well to such purposes, for his prose is highly auditory and his stories offer strong narrative, emotional, and comic opportunities.

Before becoming an author Dickens had most wanted to be an ACTOR, and later he often maintained that he would have been as successful, and happier, on the stage. Giving readings from his works gratifyingly combined his two great talents and ambitions, being even more inspiriting than the AMATEUR THEATRICALS which he had organized and starred in during the 1840s and 1850s, for now he was scriptwriter, and took all the parts and collected all the applause. From early in his career he had read his latest compositions to family and friends, and these private readings sometimes became elaborated—notably the CHIMES readings to distinguished friends which he dashed home from ITALY to deliver.

After further such performances, to English expatriates in Italy and SWITZERLAND, he mooted the possibility of making a fortune by repeating them in England, 'in these days of lecturing and reading' (11 October 1846). Conditions were indeed propitious, and it is surprising that Dickens delayed so long, given his skills and delight in performance and the dramatic quality of his fiction. Mechanics' Institutes and such-like recent establishments provided suitable audiences and auditoria, respectable people for whom theatres were taboo yearned for more admissible stage performances, and steam transport facilitated such touring ventures. Literary men were more commonly giving lectures (COLERIDGE, HAZLITT, and CARLYLE are obvious instances), and actors and recitalists, professional, semi-professional, or amateur, were increasingly offering recitals of prose or verse. The most illustrious and sustained effort of this kind was the actress Fanny Kemble's: in 1848, like her father Charles Kemble before her, she abandoned play-acting in favour of giving solo readings of SHAKESPEARE's plays, touring AMERICA as well as Britain. Such events were more fully organized and better rewarded there, so British recitalists and lecturers were increasingly being attracted; notably, THACKERAY preceded Dickens on American platforms, lecturing there profitably in 1852–3 and 1855–6. One other precedent, or inspiration, for Dickens was the actor he most admired in his youth, Charles MATHEWS the elder, and his imitators. These 'monopolyloguists' devised entertainments in which the soloist performed a dazzling range of characters, with lightning changes of costume.

Appropriately, Dickens's first public readings were given in aid of an adult-EDUCATION establishment in Birmingham, late December 1853. (He strongly supported adult-education, and most of his subsequent 'CHARITY' readings were for similar institutions.) He read *A Christmas Carol* and *The* CRICKET ON THE HEARTH, with huge success, and was inundated with invitations to perform for cash, but although tempted towards this, 'if they *will* have him', he continued only with occasional 'charity' readings (always of the *Carol*). Late in 1857 his 'paid' idea quickened: he needed much ready cash to refurbish Gad's Hill, recently purchased, and was very 'restless', his marital unhappiness having been exacerbated by his infatuation with Ellen TERNAN. It was no coincidence that his marriage broke down within weeks of his starting paid readings, on 29 April 1858 (at the height of the London 'season'). He gave more-or-less weekly performances in St Martin's Hall, Long Acre, London, so successfully that he soon expanded his plans. His original repertoire consisted of Christmas books (*Cricket*, *The Chimes*, and the *Carol*). Soon only the *Carol* survived (always remaining the quintessential reading), joined by episodes from the novels ('The Story of Little Dombey' and 'Mrs Gamp') and abbreviations of *Household Words* Christmas stories ('The Poor Traveller' and 'Boots at the Holly Tree Inn'; see PUBLIC READINGS TEXTS). With this expanded repertoire he undertook a substantial tour,

including SCOTLAND and IRELAND, August–November 1858, adding a new item which became his most frequently given one, 'The Trial From Pickwick', and returning to London for a Christmas/ New Year series. He then concentrated on writing *A Tale of Two Cities*, never undertaking substantial reading engagements while composing a novel. Having completed it, he made a short readings tour in October 1859, followed by a short Christmas series—his last in St Martin's Hall, which burned down soon after, destroying much of his equipment.

Dickens had designed a transportable stage-rig, slightly modified over the years—desk, carpeting, screens framing gaslights—which helped audiences to see and hear him better. (Emlyn Williams used a replica of his desk, now in the DICKENS HOUSE MUSEUM, for his Dickens performances, and found it technically ingenious.) A small team of around half-a-dozen accompanied him, including his manager (the experienced and efficient Albert SMITH, until his premature death), a valet-dresser, a gasman, and sundry odd-job and clerical staff. It was a highly professional organization and Dickens gave it his full-time attention, meticulously supervising arrangements and never accepting hospitality while touring. During his first tour he sometimes managed seven performances a week, including matinées (though he disliked these, as CLASS-divisive, and always insisted on seats being available at working-class prices). Later, four became his maximum. It was exhausting work: having to project his voice into large auditoria under the heat of the gaslamps left him in need of a rubdown and change of clothes after performing. Nevertheless, having begun the readings under financial necessity and in the emotional turmoil of 1858, he kept returning to the platform between novels (which, partly though not wholly because the readings produced ample cash, now declined in frequency). In his amateur theatrical days, he had exclaimed, 'There's nothing in the world equal to seeing the house rise at you, one sea of delightful faces, one hurrah of applause!' This thrill never palled. 'It was not applause that followed' his performances, one admirer wrote, 'but a passionate outburst of love for the man'—and Dickens may be forgiven for relishing this, especially when his emotional life was unsatisfactory.

His rapport with audiences was remarkable, his eyes—'like two exclamation points' —commanding their attention and his skill in gesture being uncanny. By contemporary standards, his manner was restrained: he drew no attention to himself or his legendary fame, he eschewed claptraps and took no curtain calls, he narrated in a lively but 'natural' fashion as if telling a story in a 'gentlemanly drawingroom', not a barnstorming actor tearing every passion to tatters. He found an acceptable mode which, while using histrionic skills, was not 'acting thoroughly *out*': unlike an actor, he did not pretend that there was no audience but acknowledged their presence and joined in their amusement or grief. But, as another reviewer remarked, 'He does not only *read* his story; he *acts* it', taking on the visage, body-shape, and gestures, besides the voice of his characters—and, with up to a score of characters in an item, he had splendid opportunities to show the skills earlier apparent in his theatricals, where he usually starred as a 'character'-actor. Verbally, he enhanced audiences' apprehension of his texts 'a thousand-fold', as enthusiasts said, disclosing to them unnoticed nuances, felicities, implications, and jokes.

For his next readings, March–April 1861 weekly, he chose St James's Hall, off Piccadilly, a large auditorium holding 2,127 people which remained his usual London location. He was still writing *Great Expectations* and found the 'fatigue and excitement' of performing 'very difficult to manage in conjunction with a story'; he never attempted this again. Finishing the novel in June, he prepared an autumn tour, re-rehearsing the existing repertoire, but substantially enlarging it with six new items. Of these, two—long readings based on his two last novels—were never performed, and a third, 'Mr Chops the Dwarf' (from a Christmas story), remained unperformed until 1868, when it was unsuccessful. The tour began in October 1861 with two new items, 'David Copperfield' (initially a two-hour reading, but later reduced) and 'Nicholas Nickleby at the Yorkshire School' (usually paired with 'The Trial from Pickwick'). Another new item joined the repertoire in December: 'Mr Bob Sawyer's Party' (from *PP*). Introducing new items was hard work: never remiss, Dickens had become more exacting, and came to regard 200 rehearsals as necessary, sometimes culminating in private 'trial' performances before family and guests. The three new items proved triumphant successes. 'Copperfield' became his favourite item; its main plot concerned Steerforth's seduction of Em'ly and ended with his and Ham's death in the storm—an impressive moment—with the comic relief and light pathos of David and Dora's 'Courtship and Young Housekeeping', including a fine Micawber episode. The 'Nickleby' reading ended with cheers as Nicholas thrashed Squeers (enacted with 'startling reality', a reviewer noted), before the high-spirited encounter with John Browdie and the pathos of Smike. 'Bob Sawyer', with its tipsy medical students, offered Dickens new comic opportunities, gleefully taken.

Arthur Smith was dying when this tour began, and no satisfactory replacement emerged. Dickens gave short spring seasons in London, 1862 and 1863, and three triumphant 'charity' readings in PARIS, January 1863: henceforth the Parisians' quick, intelligent response became the standard by which other audiences were assessed. Edinburgh and Manchester audiences ranked high. Specially responsive audiences inspired Dickens to extra efforts and inventiveness: he was very sensitive to the 'feel' of a house. For over three years there were no more paid readings, partly because he lacked a reliable manager but also because he was writing *Our Mutual Friend* (serialized May 1864–November 1865). He gave occasional Christmas 'charity' readings, however, for the local (Chatham) Mechanics' Institute, of which he was a loyal supporter.

Early in 1866 he contracted with CHAPPELL, the impresarios, to give 30 readings in London and elsewhere, from April to June. The manager they appointed, George DOLBY, soon became a trusted associate and friend. For this season Dickens devised a new reading from his latest Christmas story, 'Doctor Marigold', the monologue of a market trader, which evoked a highly popular blend of laughter and tears. A similar but longer tour followed, January–May 1867, with Chappell raising his nightly expenses-paid fee from £50 to nearly £60, further raised to £80 for the 1868–9 farewells. Even at £50 Dickens was earning more than MACREADY had commanded as leader of the English stage. For the 1867 tour Dickens created three new items from his 1866 Christmas story: 'Barbox Brothers', 'The Boy at Mugby' and 'The Signalman'. The last of these was never performed (the fate also of another late Christmas story reading, 'Mrs Lirriper's Lodgings') and the other two were failures.

Still beset by 'enormous' expenses, Dickens now ominously began 'to feel myself drawn towards America, as Darnay in the Tale of Two Cities was attracted to the Loadstone Rock, Paris' (10 May 1867). He had been considering an American tour since 1858—AUSTRALIA was another possibility he contemplated—but the Civil War intervened, though he was also reluctant to endure a long separation from home and from his beloved Ellen. Moreover, railway travel was irksome to him after his involvement in the Staplehurst accident, June 1865 (see KENT), and for a while he refused to travel express (and he found American railroads 'truly alarming'). But the lure of America prevailed: the opportunity to revisit old friends, to astound his American admirers, and to amass a large dollar nest-egg. Like Thackeray, a predecessor on the American circuit, he was conscious of needing to bequeath substantial funds to dependent womenfolk. Dolby spied out the land and reported favourably, and in September, despite Forster's predictable opposition, Dickens agreed to go, with Dolby as manager. As the readings' official chronicler, Charles KENT, remarked, this tour was regarded 'as a public and almost international occurrence', and he organized a farewell banquet, on 9 November, attended by over 500 notabilities from public and artistic life. The banquet was unprecedented, 'a high historical event' (*New York Tribune*), and appropriately Dickens then travelled to Liverpool in a royal saloon carriage.

He rested in Boston, and there triumphantly began his tour on 2 December with the *Carol* and 'The Trial', the pairing with which he opened in every American city. His repertoire was unadventurous, consisting of his nine most popular items. These were published by the Boston firm of his great friend J. T. FIELDS—the basis of all collections of the readings until Philip Collins's 1975 edition. The tour was enormously successful: Dickens netted £19,000, though he had lost performances during a political crisis and changed dollars into sterling at a disastrous rate. But the work was gruelling (American auditoria were often huge, and the weather severe), and Dickens's health and spirits were often wretched. He was sustained by Dolby's devotion, the loving care of Fields and his adorable wife, and an old-trouper sense of duty which infallibly brought him up to scratch. He 'felt nearly used up', beset by sleeplessness, 'climate, distance, catarrh, travelling, and hard work' (30 March 1868), but the local press reported how much more 'genial' he appeared that night than his photographs suggested—'a hearty, companionable man, with a great deal of fun in him'.

The tour ended on 20 April 1868 and he soon recovered from its effects. He had agreed to undertake a long farewell tour of 100 performances, beginning on 6 October, for which he devised a new item to ensure that Chappell did not lose on their generous terms but also to display his power in 'very passionate and dramatic' narration, 'the murder from Oliver Twist'. Hesitant about the wisdom of performing it, he eventually gave a 'trial' performance before an illustrious audience (14 November 1868). Everyone was impressed, but family and friends argued that its effects on himself and his audiences would be damaging. 'Sikes and Nancy' went into repertoire, however, on 5 January 1869, and he became obsessed with giving it, despite its evident toll upon his emotional and physical wellbeing. His health so deteriorated that his doctors made him abandon the tour on 22 April. They rashly permitted him a short farewell series in London in 1870. After his final performance, 15 March (inevitably, the *Carol* and 'Trial'), he said, 'From these garish lights I vanish now for evermore'—words inscribed on his funeral card less than three months later.    PC

**public readings texts.** Dickens said little about why he chose particular items for performance or how he adapted them, but ample evidence survives, notably his own desk-copies, most of which are extant. Also there are many contemporary accounts of the PUBLIC READINGS, some by enthusiasts who with book on knee recorded textual revisions. At first his task was simple, since all the 'charity' readings (1853–8) were of Christmas books (the *Carol* and CRICKET ON THE HEARTH), joined in the opening 'paid' readings by *The CHIMES*. These were popular stories, needing little cutting to be suitable for performance, and had been printed in easily legible typography, so pages from a commercial edition were inset into a larger page, in the margins of which Dickens wrote rewordings and stage-directions ('Tender', 'Cheerful narrative', 'Very strong', etc.), while cutting the text to the requisite length. Early performances of the *Carol* took three hours, but progressively it was reduced—as later happened to all the readings—until in May 1858 it took two (henceforth his standard performance-length). Later in 1858 he moved to a two-item pattern, so another 30 or 40 minutes'-worth of material was cut from these longer items, to accommodate a shorter 'afterpiece'.

Meanwhile the repertoire was expanding beyond the Christmas books. Here printed editions tended to be less legible and the textual revision was usually more complex, so Dickens did a quick scissors-and-paste job and had this mock-up printed and well-bound before undertaking further revision. Occasionally this further revised version was printed. The short Christmas stories presented few problems—mainly abbreviation and some verbal heightening and sharpening. From the novels, he usually selected an episode ('The Trial from Pickwick') or short swathe of the action ('The Story of Little Dombey', 'Nicholas Nickleby at the Yorkshire School'), eliminating irrelevant characters and developments, coalescing characters, and sometimes raiding the novel for choice phrases and speeches. In 'Mrs Gamp' he centred the reading on one favourite character but experienced difficulty in devising a coherent and telling narrative to contain this character display. He needed self-contained narratives ending with effective curtain-lines and not requiring elaborate introductions—though he could reasonably assume that his audiences knew why, for instance, Pickwick was on trial, or who Micawber was.

The texts never achieved definitive form. He knew them by heart, varied and improved them from night to night, sometimes spontaneously inventing verbal felicities (not written into his copies but recorded by audiences). His last-devised item, 'Sikes and Nancy' (1868), contained more drastic rewriting than before; rarely elsewhere did he substantially alter the narrative or point of view. Various performance indications were

written into his copies, including underlining for special effects. There are facsimiles of *Mrs Gamp*, ed. John D. Gordon (1956), *A Christmas Carol* and *Sikes and Nancy*, ed. Philip Collins (1971, 1982), and *Nicholas Nickleby at the Yorkshire School*, ed. John Greaves (1973).

Some readings were prepared but never delivered, Dickens having decided that they were not up to scratch; others were dropped after a few performances. The basic repertoire consisted of eleven items. Humour predominated, though pathos marked 'Little Dombey' and featured in many others, while the terrific prevailed in 'Sikes and Nancy'. The storm which concluded the *Copperfield* reading was the readings' great sublime moment. No novels after *Copperfield* yielded a reading which entered the repertoire, though several of the later Christmas stories did (some were evidently written with performance in mind: as first-person narratives, they easily became character-monologues). One element in the fiction was barely represented in the readings —political satire and social protest—though such passages as the *Carol* vision of Ignorance and Want, originally included, had impressed audiences. Evidently Dickens decided that such notes were inappropriate in an evening of entertainment.

Most of Dickens's platform copies remained in his possession. He intended them to go to FORSTER's archive, but they were sold with other items of his LIBRARY and thus became dispersed. Later almost all of them were reassembled in two COLLECTIONS—the Berg (New York Public Library) and the Suzannet (DICKENS HOUSE MUSEUM). For particulars, see Collins 1975.                                        PC

**publishing, printing, bookselling: modes of production.** Dickens's career spanned the years during which publishing changed from family-run, petty-commodity businesses meeting local needs to large, sometimes vertically integrated firms servicing international markets. This transformation was effected by improvements in book technology and in TRANSPORT, by reforms in banking and credit, by revisions in national and multinational COPYRIGHT laws, by reductions in 'taxes on knowledge', by dramatic increases in the speed of production and stable or decreasing costs for materials and labour, by expansion of the reading and buying public, and by successful innovations at every stage in the production cycle, from writing to selling (see MONEY AND FINANCE; READERSHIP). In some of these developments Dickens, his agents, friends, lawyers, booksellers, publishers, writings, magazines, speeches, and readings played an influential role. Although the material transformation of publishing was not alone responsible for Dickens's unprecedented popularity, then or now, it did significantly influence his career. The contrary is equally true: Dickens showed the industry what could be done, and his example was widely imitated.

Dickens never earned anything from his first publication. Beginning in the autumn of 1833 and extending to 1835, he submitted tales anonymously, later pseudonymously as 'BOZ', to the MONTHLY MAGAZINE. This was owned and edited by Captain J. B. Holland, had a circulation of around 600, and from January to August 1834 was published by James Cochrane and John MACRONE. In February 1836 Dickens wrote to Captain Holland, saying that he wanted payment for future contributions. Holland, meanwhile, had sold the *Monthly*. The new editor, James Grant, replied, asking Dickens's terms for continuing his monthly sketches indefinitely. By that point Dickens had committed to writing a monthly SERIAL for CHAPMAN AND HALL, so the connection with the *Monthly* ceased.

Meanwhile, Dickens had established a connection to a newspaper, the MORNING CHRONICLE, which with its sister publication the EVENING CHRONICLE published a total of 28 pieces between 26 September 1834 and 26 October 1836. In January 1835 Dickens requested, and received from George HOGARTH, co-editor of the *Evening Chronicle*, an increase in his weekly wages from £5 to £7, in recognition of his extra articles. Other editors bought some of Dickens's sketches as well. Thus periodicals became Dickens's first source of income from writing fiction.

John Macrone, a Manxman, was Dickens's first book publisher. Having ceased publishing the *Monthly*, in September 1834 he set up in business for himself. Soon thereafter he met Harrison AINSWORTH, and through him Dickens. Macrone's slender capital was largely borrowed from a woman who was for a brief time in the autumn of 1834 his fiancée, before

he married Eliza Bordwine in January 1835. He therefore depended on his wits and ramifying connections within London literary life to keep his publishing enterprise going. It occurred to him that there might be value in republishing, in an illustrated edition, Dickens's magazine and newspaper sketches. To this end he secured the agreement of Dickens and the well-known book illustrator and caricaturist George CRUIKSHANK. *Sketches by Boz*, First Series, in two volumes, appeared on 8 February 1836, and a Second Series, in one volume, caught the Christmas trade in December of that year. Both series were reprinted. During this period Macrone and Dickens became great friends; Macrone was chosen to be Dickens's best man, and both families were busy establishing households and having children (Macrone's first son, born 20 October 1835, died 16 November; his second son was born 30 September 1836; Dickens's first son was born 6 January 1837). Dickens agreed on 9 May 1836, for £200, to write for Macrone a three-volume novel, provisionally entitled 'Gabriel Vardon, the Locksmith of London'. Throughout that summer and autumn Macrone also held discussions with Ainsworth about other projects, including a serial about old and new London to be illustrated by Cruikshank and John LEECH. Ainsworth encouraged Macrone, whose business was constantly outstripping his capital resources, to sign up all the 'gentlemanly' authors he could. Macrone found those contracts expensive and not always rewarding. When Ainsworth failed to produce a promised novel in time, and Dickens got caught up with other publishers and projects, Macrone in June 1837 ventured on the desperate expedient of republishing the *Sketches* yet again, bringing them out in the twenty monthly-part serial format popularized by *Pickwick Papers*. Dickens took offence at this exploitation of his format. His new publishers, Chapman and Hall, convinced that the venture could realize a profit, arranged with Dickens to purchase in equal shares for £2,250 the copyright and stock from Macrone and to issue the *Sketches* on their own in the *Pickwick* mode. Two months before this venture could be launched Macrone suddenly died on 9 September, leaving Eliza and two surviving children destitute. Dickens edited *The* PIC-NIC PAPERS, three volumes of illustrated stories, to benefit the widow, raising £450 by the end of 1841.

Macrone's is not an untypical story of the way entrepreneurs could enter into publishing at the beginning of the century, risking a little capital and essentially relying on friendships, contacts, and reviews to sustain the enterprise. Nothing of real value accumulated —this hand-to-mouth publishing garnered no valuable back stock, copyrights, or other assets. It was mostly a matter of brains and bravura.

Chapman and Hall, by contrast, were cautious men of business who started out owning a retail store selling stationery and books and offering inexpensive periodicals and serials, some of which they co-published. Two days after *Sketches by Boz*, First Series, appeared, on 10 February 1836, William Hall called on Dickens in Furnival's Inn to offer him the opportunity to write letterpress for comic sporting plates designed and etched by one of the illustrators Chapman and Hall had published, Robert SEYMOUR. From that date forward, Chapman and Hall were Dickens's principal publishers. They, with Dickens, were responsible for devising the shilling monthly-part format for issuing original novels as serial literature, and they worked with Dickens to expand his circulation and tap new markets at home and abroad.

At the start of their relationship Chapman and Hall concentrated on the retail side of the business. They hired out the printing, first to Charles Whiting in Beaufort House, Strand, then, beginning with *Pickwick*, to BRADBURY AND EVANS. As publishers, they devised the projects, hired the writers and ILLUSTRATORS, ran the promotions, managed the stock and inventory, and produced the accounts. There were a number of ways publishers could make money: they could publish on commission, being paid a percentage of the costs or profits but taking no risk themselves; they could buy the copyright outright or share profits with the author, taking all the risk; they could publish reprints, especially of popular books out of copyright and books that had hitherto appeared only in limited or expensive editions; they could, and did with *Pickwick* and subsequent serials, pay the author and publish in instalments, recycling their investment; they could publish magazines and newspapers, profiting from those sales and from sales of books made up out of the contents of the periodicals; and they could share with other publishers in producing works, usually expensive ones such as dictionaries and atlases. Publishers might also make money on the sales of items in their own shop, and take a commission on all sales to other retailers.

In the 18th century successful publishers reaped huge profits and entertained the best society. Though a few gentlemanly publishers traded in the 19th century (notably the John Murrays, son succeeding father in name and firm throughout the century), most were frankly, and sometimes frenetically, in business. Dickens socialized with Macrone, as we have seen, and carried on cordial relations for a time with other early publishers—Richard BENTLEY in particular. By the 1840s Dickens's relationship with his publishers was rather more professional than personal. Exceptions were made for the German publisher Bernhard Tauchnitz, and towards the end of Dickens's life for James T. FIELDS, partner in the American publishing firm of Ticknor and Fields.

At every point along the line from manuscript to sales the direct relationships between writer and publisher, publisher and printer, printer and retailer, were gradually mediated. Soon after Dickens met him, John FORSTER became an unofficial agent, entrusted by Dickens with responsibility for negotiating agreements for new works and escapes from previous commitments. In time Forster also became Chapman and Hall's principal adviser, the most important one in their more than 100-year history. Dickens's skyrocketing fame sent publishers flocking to him with proposals; he began making contracts, more and more complex ones as experience exposed disagreements about what constituted fair publishing practices. Thus lawyers began negotiating for Dickens, alongside Forster or in place of him. On the publishers' side, early negotiations were conducted by one or more of the principals; sometimes, especially in the case of Richard Bentley, a trusted employee might deputize.

Dickens's third book publisher, Richard Bentley, combined a number of the advantages separately represented in earlier firms. Though by 1837 Bentley was only in publishing, from 1819 to 1829 he had been in partnership with his elder brother, Samuel, who owned a substantial printing establishment in Dorset Street. Samuel continued to print many of Bentley's publications, including the magazine he initiated in January 1837, BENTLEY'S MISCELLANY, and portions of the three-volume edition of *Oliver Twist*. That Richard Bentley owned a periodical gave him access to writers he would pay to compose magazine articles or poems that he could then republish as books, and a monthly magazine kept his brother's presses going between other jobs. Thus the interconnections between publishing books, issuing periodicals, and running a printing firm enabled Bentley to attract some of the leading writers of the day, including 'Boz' and Ainsworth, and prominent artists such as Cruikshank and Leech. But those entanglements meant that if Bentley quarrelled with a contributor in any of that person's capacities—as editor, essayist, novelist, poet, or graphic artist—he might lose all the services. That is what happened with Dickens, Ainsworth, and Cruikshank, all of whom associated with, and then broke from, *Bentley's Miscellany* and Bentley as publisher.

Much of the accounting for magazines was similar to that for books: costs of production had to be subtracted from sales and advertising revenue. But magazines entailed other kinds of calculation as well. Contributors might be paid per column inch, as Dickens was; one or more might also, as Dickens was, be paid for editing. A successful editor—like Dickens—might be paid a bonus if the magazine's circulation exceeded a set figure. And while illustrators during this period customarily sold their plates and copyrights outright, authors might expect to receive additional sums when their columns were reissued as books. The connections between sales and payments made authors and editors more interested in bookkeeping than when they sold copyrights outright, without recourse to further emolument in the case of an unexpectedly large sale.

For those reasons, among others, Dickens's nine formal agreements with Richard Bentley between 22 August 1836 and 2 July 1840 record in ever-increasing particularity the ways shares and leases of copyright, length and due date of articles, rates and dates of pay, sales calculations, printing and distribution costs, commissions, profits, and republication rights and formats were to be determined.

Some of these agreements specify that Dickens and his solicitor or agent may examine the books and make copies of them. While these provisions manifest Dickens's growing distrust of Bentley, they evidence more widespread and long-standing frictions between authors and publishers. Authors seldom appreciate all the publishers' costs that are charged against income, and frequently believe that either too much advertising was spent in the wrong places, or too little in the right ones, to hike the sales as high as they should go. Publishers, on the other hand, argue that they risk their capital, often paying authors in advance, and are entitled to cover not only the tangible costs of producing and promoting this title but also an appropriate fraction of the intangible costs—editorial time, literary and legal counsel, space, utilities, maintenance, warehousing, insurance, taxes, and other overheads—of running the business. These charges begin to be broken out in 19th-century publishers' accounts, and as they ramify they display the increasing specialization of publishing.

Dickens's phenomenal POPULARITY enabled him to lever better and better terms from a reluctant and growingly irascible Bentley. *Oliver Twist* eventually satisfied *both* the obligation to furnish in each monthly number of the magazine 'one or more Original Article or Articles of his own writing' (Agreement, 22 September 1838, Pilgrim 1.667) *and* the first of two three-volume novels promised in an earlier agreement of 22 August 1836. And when Bentley's exasperation and meddling in the make-up of issues collided with Dickens's temper and determination to direct his energies into more lucrative projects, no agreement could keep the two parties collaborating. Dickens withdrew from editing and contributing to the *Miscellany* and in 1840 wrested both *Oliver Twist* and *Barnaby Rudge* from Bentley's contractual grip.

Meanwhile, Chapman and Hall perfected serial publication with *Nicholas Nickleby* and were happily anticipating a further serial, when Dickens proposed instead to start up and edit a weekly illustrated magazine containing stories by him and other writers. Dickens was still trying to devise a system whereby he did not have to write every minute in order to have an income; but so long as he had to sell his copyrights outright, or to receive income only during composition, the only alternative was to lessen the strain on his fancy by editing a publication to which his friends might contribute stories. Reluctant at first, Chapman and Hall conceded to their star turn's terms, and the resulting venture, MASTER HUMPHREY'S CLOCK, was a considerable success—not as great a moneymaker for the publishers as they first thought, however, because the costs of the wood-engravings and of all the inventorying of weekly parts ran much higher than estimated. And not as great an energy-saver for the editor, either, because he soon found that the public only wanted a continuing story by him, so he had to produce two in succession, *The Old Curiosity Shop* and *Barnaby Rudge*.

Dickens's fame provided his publishers with other opportunities to profit. From *Pickwick* onward, American publishers had sent small sums either directly to the publishers or to Dickens, in order to secure their good-will and early proofs. (As there were no reciprocal copyright agreements among nations, British publishers were free to issue foreign authors' writings, and vice versa.) By the time of *Master Humphrey's Clock*, American demand was so well established that Chapman and Hall arranged to ship, via steam packets, early proofs of every instalment, at £2 10s each, to the Philadelphia firm of Lea and Blanchard. Dickens himself contracted for early proofs to Germany.

The lack of control over his copyrights in other countries infuriated Dickens and many other authors: 'Is it not a horrible thing', Dickens railed during his AMERICAN tour in 1842, 'that scoundrel-booksellers should grow rich here [the United States] from publishing books, the authors of which do not reap one farthing from their issue?' (to Henry Austin, 1 May 1842). Although publishers could send out copies of books printed in England to America and the colonies, and did so to some extent during the 1830s and 1840s, it was often much cheaper to print so-called 'pirated' texts in the country where they would be distributed. Dickens's American tour increased his popularity and stimulated the market for his AMERICAN NOTES, but it did not achieve one effect for which he hoped: the passing of a binational copyright agreement. Consequently, on his return he and Chapman and Hall

profited to some extent from the publication of his travel account, but continued to have to expand in foreign markets by means of indirect rather than direct publication.

To finance a year's break from writing and his tour of the United States and Canada, Dickens had borrowed from Chapman and Hall, using as a principal security the expected profits from his next serial. However, *Martin Chuzzlewit* did not sell particularly well. The economies of Britain and the United States were in a slump, the hiatus may have interrupted the public's habit of buying Dickens's instalments, his reputation had suffered as a result of the tepid response to his previous novel and the furore over *American Notes* and International Copyright, and the new work started out unpromisingly. Whatever caused the slump, the poor sales meant that Dickens's serial was not earning enough to repay the loan. William Hall suggested invoking a clause in Dickens's agreement whereby £50 out of his contractual £200 monthly stipend for writing *Chuzzlewit* would be withheld and applied against the balance owing. Furious, and undoubtedly anxious about whether his profitability would be permanently impaired, Dickens determined to break with his publishers.

But first, in order to increase his income, Dickens devised a little tale that could be marketed as a holiday offering—*A Christmas Carol*. He forced Chapman and Hall to publish on commission: that is, they took his directions, paid themselves the costs of printing and distribution, took a commission on gross sales, and then turned all the profits over to Dickens. Theoretically, by this arrangement Dickens would have absolute control over costs. In a sense he did, but he was his own undoing. Caught up and mastered by the story, he insisted that it be produced beautifully, with hand-coloured etchings, coloured endpapers, and a cloth binding stamped in gold. The book was so expensive to manufacture, and at Dickens's insistence sold so cheaply (5 shillings), that though within a year 15,000 copies had been purchased his net profits were only £726, when he had been hoping for at least £1,000. Dickens wrested one-third of Chapman and Hall's sales commission back from them, and then persuaded his reluctant printers, Bradbury and Evans, to start publishing his future works.

There were, theoretically, some advantages in combining publisher and printer: one firm intervened between manuscript and print instead of two, and one rather than two entities took a share of the receipts. Moreover, Dickens started afresh with his new publishers: all arrangements would be for new works, of which Dickens retained three-quarters of the copyright. But he also brought with him various complex arrangements about previous titles in which Chapman and Hall still had an interest. Bradbury and Evans advanced money to buy out some of these shares and stock, but in the end Dickens had to propose, as part of paying off his new publishers' advances (he also wanted another paid holiday), that Chapman and Hall combine with Bradbury and Evans in issuing his previous work in a uniform edition. While this idea did not materialize right away, it did eventually lead to a succession of collected EDITIONS, beginning with the Cheap Edition (1847–52), which tapped markets largely untouched by serial publication.

At first Bradbury and Evans, whose only substantial publishing experience involved the still-marginal humour magazine PUNCH, depended on Chapman and Hall for help in issuing the Christmas books that succeeded the *Carol*. But they gained confidence, and when Dickens's first twenty-part novel for them, *Dombey and Son* (1846–8), succeeded beyond anyone's projections, they settled down for a long and profitable run. Dickens's mid-career fiction was published in monthly part issues by Bradbury and Evans: after *Dombey* came *David Copperfield* (1849–50), *Bleak House* (1852–3), and *Little Dorrit* (1855–7). They also reissued *Oliver Twist* in ten monthly numbers (1846), Dickens revising the text and Cruikshank etching a wrapper design. And they profited from a share in Dickens's new periodical, *Household Words*, and from the books republished from those pages, the three-volume CHILD'S HISTORY OF ENGLAND (1851–3) and *Hard Times* (1854).

Typically, for the long novels Bradbury and Evans would, once Dickens decided on a title, start up an ADVERTISING campaign, stimulating the public to buy copies when issued and advertisers to sign up for space in an inserted advertising supplement even before the first page was written. As publishers, they also alerted their distribution network, and assisted when needed in facilitating arrangements for overseas issue, either by sending printed sheets or stereotypes or by forwarding advanced proofs for resetting and printing abroad. When manufacture began they had to order four different kinds of paper (cheap for ads, better for text, flimsy coloured paper for wrappers, and substantial stock for imprinting the etched illustrations); set type, proof, correct, and finally stereotype it; supervise the collation and binding of the sheets; send out the copies, account for all sold, returned, or damaged stock, and keep track of inventory and reprint on demand; collect what was owing from wholesalers, retailers, advertisers, and agents; pay staff and suppliers and overheads and overtime; render accounts to copyright shareholders (Dickens scrutinized his carefully and often consulted Forster or another trusted friend about disputed figures); adjudicate disagreements, often surrendering skirmishes in order to avoid losing the war; and then gear up for another monthly cycle, all the while maintaining the complex machinery of the presses and keeping them running with other jobs.

And that was simply the normal routine. Bradbury and Evans also had to manage their banking, drawing sums against future profits, paying off their own advances, purchasing new machinery, and financing expansion; they had to keep a keen eye on promising new endeavours, flatter and cajole current customers, and tactfully disentangle themselves from unprofitable accounts; they had to socialize with authors, buyers, and politicians, at guildhalls, clubs, and taverns, and to participate in the heavy round of mid-Victorian entertainment and charitable enterprises to keep their name and their firm's credit in circulation; and they had to oversee the day-to-day operations of a complex, many-sided operation. Authors who knew little about the kinds of problems caused by a slipping gear or a defalcating wholesaler frequently accused publishers of inflating their charges and cheating the poor chaps who, by writing, made it all happen. That was never a fair telling of the whole story.

When Dickens examined his semi-annual author's statements, themselves assembled by the publishers from a range of books that separately recorded materials, inventory, sales, and costs of manufacturing a product, he usually learned about gross sales and net income from retail commissions, about the actual costs of production (not hidden ones such as overheads, warehousing, and office-staff wages), and about the commissions to publishers and net profits to partners in the copyright lease. Thus the second half-yearly account from Bradbury and Evans on *Bleak House*, which covered new parts from July to December 1852 (but indicated the expense of printing a month ahead of publication, so the July number's costs appeared in the preceding account and the January 1853 costs appear in the December 1852 accounts) and reprintings of earlier parts (March to June), arrived in the spring of 1853. It showed that the number of each part printed declined from 35,000 for no. 7 (September 1852) to 34,000 for no. 11 (January 1853), and that the quantity of each part sold declined over the same span from 34,000 to 32,500. (These figures were not alarming; there was usually some drop from the sale of the first part, though for *Pickwick* the sales hugely increased for the later parts as the novel caught fire.) Total sales for the period, including back sales of earlier parts, amounted to 202,724 parts, yielding, after all retail discounts, nearly £7,150. To this was added the revenue from advertisements printed in the parts, £654; and this sum total was reduced by about £3,650 of specified production expenses, including Dickens's £200 monthly stipend for writing. The net profit was split 75 : 25 per cent, Dickens receiving £3,100 and Bradbury and Evans £1,035, plus a commission on sales of £767 that was figured in the expenses and added to their income. Not a bad six-month's earnings for publishers who had already paid their bills, and not bad for an author who was getting £4,000 just to write the novel, as well as receiving the majority of the income from this title and a hefty sum from previous titles in their original or reprinted formats, and who retained a three-quarter share of the *Bleak House* copyright in any future republications.

What disturbed this profitable routine was another crisis in the accelerating shift of power away from the publishers to Dickens. Once he abandoned the pseudonym 'Boz', Dickens worked to make his name a trade mark. He was scrupulous about fashioning a public persona and an authorial self identified with certain broadly conceived political and social causes: humanitarianism, non-denominational Protestantism, EDUCATION reform, CHARITY as opposed to UTILITARIAN welfare, the professionalization of letters, the reclamation of worthy unfortunates (prisoners and PROSTITUTES), the wholesomeness of DOMESTIC values, and the sanctity of CHILDHOOD imagination. When he separated from his wife, Catherine DICKENS, in 1858 he expected his publishers to print in *Punch* his explanation of an event that might otherwise seem to contradict everything he stood for as man and writer. Their refusal infuriated him even more than William Hall's parsimonious banking had. With a good deal of subterfuge Dickens arranged matters so that he returned to Chapman and Hall, with whom he had continued to share some copyrights and receipts throughout the 1840s and 1850s, and ruined Bradbury and Evans's one continuing shared property, *Household Words*. By this point in mid-Victorian Britain it was not that *publishers* were 'gentlemen' but that *Dickens* was; not that *publishers* were patrons of learning but that *Dickens* was a writer whose life and lessons were, so far as the public was concerned, an integrated and seamless whole. Out of this claim of authorial exemplarity came a highly saleable product: books that delighted and instructed, by a man who practised what he preached. This became the nexus of Dickens's projection of himself over the last decade, when as author, editor, and reader he became to many of his contemporaries the greatest reader of the greatest writer in the world (see PUBLIC READINGS).

That reputation, and those audiences, expanded still more in the 1860s, as customs acts and bi-national copyright agreements protected publication in English and TRANSLATION of Dickens's titles throughout the British dominions and in parts of Europe. At home, growing populations and increasing working-class literacy, marginal improvements in wages and leisure time, ramifying and accelerating transportation systems on land and at sea, and lower prices for printed products all fuelled dramatic multiplications of the book trade. Publishers began buying and selling Dickens in bulk, bringing out new collected editions to capitalize on the American tour, for instance, or after his death to supply what the *Graphic*, in its obituary, called for: 'cheap popular editions which have secured to other writers so enormous a sale.'

Whereas in the 1840s Dickens wrote five novels, five Christmas books, and two TRAVEL BOOKS, all prompted in part by a strenuous effort to produce enough new work to steady and augment his income, in the 1860s he only completed two novels and some miscellaneous journalism (see JOURNALIST, DICKENS AS). He no longer needed a publisher to act as the promoter of his work; he did that himself. He needed a manufacturer and wholesaler who could churn out old texts in different formats for multiple markets. While the campaigns for *Our Mutual Friend* and *Edwin Drood* were planned meticulously, keeping in mind all the lessons learned over a lifetime, and while Dickens's interest in every part of issuing his periodical *All the Year Round* and his serial fictions, including the illustrations and the marketing, never flagged, his revenue derived more from republication and public readings than from new material, and thus his publishers became less his partners in venturesome entrepreneurial experiments and more the large distributors of a brand-name product. Over 100 years after his death, the evolution of Dickens has gone farther: his name has become a byword for literacy, for reading itself. Anyone who has not read Dickens and SHAKESPEARE, Anglophone newspapers around the world declare, is not literate. At this point, with copyright expired (except in unpublished material), Dickens belongs to anyone who can reproduce in any medium or obtain in any form a version of his work.

                                                              RLP

Altick (1957).
Feltes, N. N., *Modes of Production of Victorian Novels* (1986).
Patten (1978).
Sutherland (1976).

**Punch** began its long career as a threepenny comic weekly on 17 July 1841, not long after Dickens began his. Its original staff belonged to his generation; he already knew some of them and soon met others, and its publishers BRADBURY AND EVANS were soon his too. 'Punch is better than ever', he told them (13 August 1843), and a diarist recorded (October 1843) that he 'admired JERROLD [then its dominant contributor] and lauded Punch, which, he said, he "generally saw before it was

in print" ' (Pilgrim 3.577 n.). Most of the non-family guests at the *Chuzzlewit* dinner, June 1844, were *Punch* men, as were nearly half the actors in his 1845 AMATEUR THEATRICAL production of *Every Man In His Humour*: of its staff only THACKERAY and two others did not participate. Of the six who did, three were long among his closest friends—its editor Mark LEMON, its chief graphic artist John LEECH, and its leading wit and social commentator Douglas Jerrold. *Punch* men whom he engaged for the DAILY NEWS, 1846, included Jerrold and W. H. WILLS, later his coadjutor on his weeklies. But *Punch* men contributed little to *Household Words* and, though Dickens furnished material for a *Punch* item in 1843 (Pilgrim 3.469n.), his only other offering (on metropolitan water-supplies, 1849) was rejected.

*Punch* began as an irreverently raffish and radical publication, but soon was moving 'from the journal of Bohemia to the mouthpiece of Belgravia', 'keeping to the gentlemanly view of things'. Jerrold's mordant radicalism was sidelined by the 'gentlemanly' party led by Thackeray, Leech, and Shirley Brooks. Dickens warmly agreed with Jerrold's disquiet over *Punch*'s 'new spirit', its 'eternal guffaw' over issues inappropriate for such comicality (24 October 1846), and later expressed 'disgust' about its 'base flunkeyship' in supporting Palmerston, one of his *bêtes noires* (31 August 1861). By then Lemon's view of Reform was that 'we should stand by and see how the stream runs,' not give a lead. Reform, Evans and Leech agreed, had gone quite far enough and by then, comments on Dickens round the *Punch* table were decidedly snide.

The break-up of Dickens's marriage in 1858 had involved his rupture with Bradbury and Evans and quarrels with Lemon, Leech, and Thackeray. The friendships were later resumed, though less warmly. But in the 1840s and 1850s there had been a considerable overlap between Dickens's and *Punch*'s attitudes, joke-situations, and satirical butts. Philip Collins (1967) instances the closeness of *Bleak House* (1852–3) to *Punch* in concerns, stances, and even phraseology: thus, the 'Telescopic Philanthropy' theme had been anticipated by *Punch* (15 April 1848)—'Exeter Hall (the EVANGELICAL headquarters) is a little too apt to search for distant wretchedness, with a telescope; forgetting the misery that lies at its very feet'—and Mrs Jellyby's obsession with Borrioboola-Gha follows many *Punch* jokes about futile MISSIONS to comically named tribes. Not that Dickens raided *Punch* for jokes; he and it shared a common joke-pool and started from a common stock of early Victorian radical ideas (and middle-class masculine prejudices)—on EDUCATION, CRIME, the POOR LAW and the Corn Laws, the legal system, the sanitary question, CAPITAL PUNISHMENT, SABBATARIANISM, EMIGRA-TION, Puseyites and 'Papal Aggression', the WOMAN QUESTION, and much else (see also LAW; PUBLIC HEALTH). Dickens brought genius to projecting these issues, which *Punch* handled sometimes with satirical talent but often with dismal facetiousness and dire repetition. His humour proved more long-lasting, and though he later became reactionary (on penology, for instance; see PRISONS), he never became as complacently 'gentlemanly' as *Punch*.                    PC

Altick, Richard D., *Punch: The Lively Youth of a British Institution, 1841–51* (1997).

Collins, Philip, 'Dickens and *Punch*', *Dickens Studies* (1967).

Price, R. G. G., *A History of Punch* (1957).

**Putnam, George Washington** (1812–96), 'my faithful secretary . . . from Boston' (*AN* 9) who accompanied Dickens throughout his first tour of AMERICA in 1842. Dickens, who nicknamed him 'Q' and joked in *Martin Chuzzlewit* about an ardent young aspirant to literary fame named 'Putnam' Smif, was amused by his appearance 'in a cloak, like Hamlet' and 'a cap like Harlequin's', by his sentimentality, his singing and his painting, and above all by his 'marvellous lies concerning his past life' (to Frederick Dickens, 22 March 1842). Catherine DICKENS did not like him, but Dickens found him 'modest, obliging, silent and willing' (to Forster, 29 January 1842). Putnam, who admired 'the beauty and purity' of Dickens's nature and 'the singular lighting up of his face', published a memoir circumstantially recounting Dickens's American experience ('Four Months with Charles Dickens', *Atlantic Monthly*, 26, 1870).   PVWS

# R

**radicalism.** See POLITICS.

**Reade, Charles** (1814–80), dramatist, novelist, and friend of Dickens. Reade began his literary career in the late 1840s with adaptations for the stage, but in the 1850s he turned to novels, for which he became well known. Like Dickens, Reade was concerned to expose social injustice in his fiction, and in his first major success, *It Is Never Too Late To Mend* (1856), Reade used his research into PRISONS to reveal the inhumanity of incarceration. The novel established him as one of the finest and most popular writers of SENSATION fiction, a sub-genre particularly popular in the 1860s with which Dickens was also associated. Reade's sensational *Hard Cash*, with its provocative asylum scenes, was first serialized as *Very Hard Cash* in Dickens's magazine *All the Year Round* in 1863; however, the serial's frank madhouse depictions were not popular with readers (see MADNESS). In a letter to his publisher, Reade asserts that Dickens thought *Hard Cash* his best novel. Because of the sensational contents of his fiction, with its focus on the horrors of social injustice and often with sexually suggestive material, Reade was a controversial figure. The all-powerful Mudie's Circulating Library refused to take Reade's novel *Cream* in 1859 (see LIBRARIES). In the furore over another novel, *Griffith Gaunt, or Jealousy* (1866), which graphically describes the effects of sexual infidelity, Dickens was asked to support Reade; Dickens said he admired the novel but could not fully endorse it since some of the passages, in the wrong hands, could be interpreted as obscene. Dickens, unlike Reade, was more adept at gauging the mood of the mid-Victorian reading public (see READERSHIP). In addition to campaigning novels, Reade wrote HISTORICAL NOVELS (*The Cloister and the Hearth*, 1861) and he continued to produce plays, often borrowing his plots from the novels of his contemporaries.                                    MWT

**readership: literacy and the reading public.** The phrase 'reading public' is a 19th-century coinage, a fact which reflects not only the increasing levels of public literacy but also the new ways in which writers began to conceive of their audience. Authorship no longer addressed itself to a select or elite group. In 1816 COLERIDGE (in *The Statesman's Manual*) had trumpeted his own elitism, and echoed the more narrowly conceived literary philosophy of the previous century, saying that true writing was aimed at 'men of clerkly acquirements' and expressing a wish that 'the greater part of our publications could be thus directed'. But, he continued, this was no longer possible: 'for . . . we have now a Reading Public . . . a strange phrase . . . our readers have in good truth, multiplied exceedingly.' This exceeding multiplication of readers continued and increased its pace during the Victorian period, and Dickens was at the forefront of this explosion in audience.

The growth involved two chief factors; first, a great increase in levels of literacy, and secondly, a shift in taste towards reading fiction. The latter fact can be indicated with two statistics. The Victorian publisher Charles KNIGHT (in his *Passages of a Working Life*, 1853, 3.195) calculated the total number of different books published during the whole period 1816 to 1851 as 45,260 (of which the largest number —10,300—were 'works on divinity', and only 3,500 were fiction). With an average print run of less than a thousand, this means something like 40 million actual copies of books being bought over forty years. By way of comparison, Robert L. Patten (see Collins 1971, pp. 617–20) estimates that in the dozen years following Dickens's death alone, some 4 million copies of his novels were sold. The total sale of all his editions is incalculable, but evidently huge. Dickens's readership, then, was large.

When trying to determine just how large, it is necessary to gain some sense of the levels of literacy amongst the Victorian general public; but this is not easy. As Gertrude Himmelfarb puts it, literacy figures for the 19th century 'are notoriously difficult to come by, not only because the sources are inadequate but because the definition and measurement of literacy are debatable. Is schooling an appropriate index of literacy, or reading and writing, or reading alone, or signing the marriage register?' (Himmelfarb 1984, p. 413). With Dickens the situation is complicated by the fact that he was an author enjoyed by both the literate and the illiterate (who had access to the novels via readings-aloud that took place regularly in coffee-rooms, public houses, family environments, working men's clubs, and so on).

One of Dickens's contemporaries gives a sense of the numbers of readers amongst the upper CLASSES. In an essay on Crabbe in his *Contributions to the Edinburgh Review* (1844), Lord JEFFREY asserts that 'in this country there probably are not less than three hundred thousand persons who read for amusement and instruction among the middling classes of society. In the higher classes, there are not as many as thirty thousand.' There is clearly some element of guesswork in Jeffrey's figures (most scholars would suggest higher figures), but his general sense that 'the larger body' of middle-class readers 'are to the full as well educated and as high minded as the smaller' of upper-class ones is a crucial insight. Jeffrey here ignores the proletariat, but as E. P. Thompson (1968) points out, over the first half of the century 'as the effect of the Sunday schools and day schools increasingly became felt . . . so the number of the illiterate fell'. With CHARTISM and the increasing drive to promote working-class EDUCATION (for instance, through the Ragged Schools with which Dickens was involved; see CHARITY), literacy levels climbed as the century progressed. By the time of the Education Act of 1870, the year of Dickens's death, the reading public had grown by (estimates vary) between ten and twenty times. Gertrude Himmelfarb (1984, pp. 411–12) suggests that in the mid-Victorian period between two-thirds and three-quarters of the population had some reading ability (in 1851 the population was 18 million); although only a relatively small proportion of this would have had the necessary sophistication and predisposition to read fiction regularly. In other words, the 'reading public' in the 1840s can be thought of as a core of perhaps half a million sophisticated and relatively affluent readers, with a body of several million less-skilled readers; these figures growing steadily throughout the 1860s and 1870s (although the real explosion in literacy was not to come until after the

establishment of compulsory education in 1871). The sheer size of this constituency represents something quite new in literary history. In November 1844 Thomas HOOD wrote to the Prime Minister, Peel, to complain that literature did not have a high enough official profile. The occasion was a speech in which the Queen replied to a civic address, and Hood deplored the fact that Her Majesty had not mentioned what he considered to be the people's pastime: reading. 'Whatever differences may obtain in a society', he wrote, 'that will be an unlucky one which distinguishes a sovereign from a reading public, rapidly becoming a reading people.'

Dickens must, of course, be understood primarily as the first great unofficial laureate of this new reading people. Partly this has to do with his resolutely populist approach to writing and publication, and in particular the mode of SERIAL PUBLICATION that rendered his works cheaply available to a broad audience. A weekly instalment of *The Old Curiosity Shop* might sell as many as 100,000 copies, and each instalment could well be read by (or recited aloud to) a great many more people than the purchaser. Even assuming the relatively conservative figure of an average four readers per instalment it is clear that Dickens is reaching four-fifths of the core reading population of the country; with readings-aloud to often packed rooms, the number of less-literate fans was perhaps ten times this. As a statistical indication of the reach of a writer's contemporary popularity this is unprecedented, even compared to SCOTT. It is inconceivable that a writer could have such a wide following today.

The point here is that, to put it baldly, Dickens was read by just about everyone, from the bottom of society to the top. As Walter BAGEHOT noted, there was no other Victorian writer 'whose works are read so generally through the whole house, who can give pleasure to the servants as well as to the mistress, to the children as well as to the master' ('Charles Dickens' 1858, in *Literary Studies*, 1898, 12.128). Queen Victoria read *Oliver Twist* and found it 'excessively interesting' (*The Girlhood of Queen Victoria: A Selection from her Diaries 1832–1840*, 1912, 2.86). Dickens was read widely amongst the aristocracy (although for some of the upper-classes he was perceived as a little vulgar); his name crops up endlessly in the letters of virtually every figure on the 19th-century literary scene; and he is often seen as the pre-eminent middle-class author. At the other end of society, there is 'the [illiterate] old charwoman who never missed a subscription tea . . . at a snuff shop over which she lodged when the landlord read the newest number of *Dombey and Son* to his assembled guests' (Altick 1957, p. 2). Himmelfarb notes how widespread were reports of 'the poorest people reading Dickens, and those who could not read listening to the latest instalment read aloud in the servants' hall, lodging house, public house or tea shop' (1984, p. 455). Dickens's reputation amongst the illiterate was maintained by these sorts of impromptu readings, but also by widespread (and often illegal) ADAPTATIONS, PLAGIARISMS, and DRAMATIZATIONS. Thackeray might have possessed more cachet amongst the upper classes, and there may have been SENSATION NOVELS that sold more copies amongst the working classes, but no other writer commanded so widely defined and so large a general readership.

This last point needs stressing, because critics sometimes talk of other writers as having had a larger reading public than Dickens. George Reynolds (1814–79) is one such author sometimes presented as more 'popular' than Dickens, a fact based chiefly on the runaway success of his serial publication *Mysteries of London* (1845–55), a piece of gory sensation fiction that sold widely amongst the lower classes. This work clocked up perhaps as many as a million sales over its ten-year run, and Dickens could never boast that sort of instant success. But Reynold's career began completely in Dickens's shadow (his first success was a plagiaristic continuation of *Pickwick* called *Pickwick Abroad; or the Tour in France* (1837–9), and he never matched either the breadth of Dickens's appeal or the consistency of his success. Similarly, Harriet Beecher STOWE's *Uncle Tom's Cabin* (1852) is sometimes bruited as the first million-selling book, but this represents a highpoint in a career that, whilst certainly productive, never achieved Dickensian levels of general public saturation or renown.

As a writer whose readership spanned the literate and the illiterate, it is perhaps not surprising that literacy is a key theme in much of Dickens's work. In general the power over words represented by the ability to read functions in his novels as an index to the relative empowerment of characters as a whole. We might take as an example *Our Mutual Friend*, a novel particularly concerned with issues of literacy. As the narrator says early on in the book (Dickens's idiosyncratic punctuation emphasizing the weightiness of the point): 'No one who can read, ever looks at a book, even unopened on a shelf, like one who cannot' (1.3). In that novel literacy equals empowerment in a straightforward way: Gaffer Hexam's unconsidered hostility to the very idea of himself or his children being taught to read is a badge of his obstinacy, of the dead hand of a past that must die to release his daughter: similarly, Lizzie Hexam's decision to learn to read signals her passage away from the dead-end (literally) world of her father, and towards a marriage with a gentleman. In the same book Boffin's illiteracy puts him to one degree or another in the power of the scheming 'literary man' Wegg (Wegg's wickedness is signposted by the fact that he can't actually read very well); a thraldom that it requires Rokesmith as secretary to undo. But mere literacy, unleavened by any engagement of the heart, is not enough. Headstone's dry and fruitless reading has given him no moral core: he 'could have told to the letter' all about Wat Tyler's treacherous murder by Lord Mayor Walworth, but he cannot see the applicability of the lesson to his own circumstances as a would-be murderer (*OMF* 4.1). This is why Eugene's tutoring of Lizzie Hexam is so positive, whilst Headstone's tutoring of her brother is so barren.

The representations of literacy and illiteracy in the other novels tend towards the same point. Joe's halting steps towards reading and writing in *Great Expectations* are presented comically but affectionately, as a correlative to his growing independence, moving out of the tyrannical influence of Mrs Joe towards his happy marriage with Biddy; whereas the illiterate Krook in *Bleak House* is never able to capitalize upon the power represented by his documents (because he can never read them) and dies. A great many of Dickens's plots hinge upon the reading of documents. On the other hand, it is interesting to consider that Dickens rarely represents a reader in his fiction: his rendering of English culture seems to have no place for the self-reflexive tableaux of the Micawbers (as it might be) settling down to hear Mr Micawber read out the latest Dickens instalment. RCS

Altick (1957).
Flint, Kate, *The Woman Reader 1837–1914* (1993).
Ford (1965).
Himmelfarb, Gertrude, *The Idea of Poverty: England in the Early Industrial Age* (1984).
Sutherland (1976).
Thompson, E. P., *The Making of the English Working Class* (1968).
Webb, Richard, 'The Victorian Reading Public', in *From Dickens to Hardy: Pelican Guide to English Literature*, vol. 6 (1958).

**reform.** Dickens entered upon professional parliamentary reporting just as 44 years of Tory rule were coming to an end and the reform of Parliament was being undertaken. In 1831 he gained a position as a shorthand parliamentary reporter with the MIRROR OF PARLIAMENT. As a reporter, Dickens may have recorded the early debates about reform, which took place 1–9 March 1831. The Bill passed in the Commons by one vote. Only after three tries did it get through the Lords. During all this time there was real fear of revolutionary insurrection, and it seemed as though the Lords, in defying the will of the populace, would destroy the country. The Bill was passed in June 1832, and a general election held, in which Dickens worked in Lambeth recruiting poll clerks for TENNYSON's uncle.

It was a time of exceptional political excitement—Gladstone later remembered it as the last time when NEWSPAPERS were created just to record the events surrounding reform (one example being the *Mirror of Parliament* itself). Dickens's hiring on the MORNING CHRONICLE, which had been refurbished to support the Whigs, is thus part of the historical changes of the time. It can be seen that parliamentary reporting and Dickens's part in it come to prominence because of the issue of reform. His letters describing his adventures as a reporter of politicians' speeches on the hustings in 1833 convey some of this excitement.

The First Reform Bill increased the electorate by 217,000 but still excluded much of the working classes and lower middle classes by retaining a property qualification. The franchise was redistributed geographically, with old rotten boroughs in Cornwall and Wiltshire dating from the medieval period losing representatives (–28 and –15 seats, respectively), and the new industrial Midlands gaining representation for the first time (Lancashire +11; West Riding of Yorkshire +8).

The passage of the Reform Bill inaugurated a series of Whig measures reforming social legislation (the end of slavery, a new POOR LAW, municipal government reform) and eventually during the 1840s PUBLIC HEALTH, EDUCATION, and poor relief all were reorganized. In 1842 and 1847 two FACTORY ACTS were passed, stopping the employment of children and women in mines and limiting the number of hours children could work in textile factories. In 1848 the first national Public Health Act was passed, and 'sanitary reform' became a function of government. All these specific acts were evidence of a new attitude that saw government intervention as desirable.

Liberalism, which had been regarded early in the century as a dangerous atheistical doctrine among the masses, now became a prevailing ethos associated with the earnest improvement of material conditions for the poor. The most controversial was probably the new Poor Law, which antagonized radicals and Tories alike with its MALTHUSIAN justification for breaking up families. In a review of the Cheap Edition of Dickens's works (1857–8), Walter BAGEHOT draws attention to the harshness of the early 19th century ('we cannot comprehend its having existed'), and says that Dickens's 'sentimental radicalism' is perfectly explicable as a reaction against this aristocratically governed world that knew no sympathy with ordinary human suffering. Bagehot argues that it was utterly necessary for people such as Dickens to emphasize the pain endured by the lower classes in order to counter the 'harsh unfeelingness which is of all faults the most contrary to any with which we are chargeable now' (*National Review*, October 1858). This puts Dickens's invocation of SENTIMENTALISM in his writings in context, seeing it against the ethos of the pre-reform era in which he came to his first maturity. It also explains somewhat his distrust of governmental authority. Dickens, who consistently refused nomination as candidate for Parliament, looked upon the House of Commons as merely a chamber for empty speechifying. He played a more active role by publicizing issues of social reform in his writing, and in the mid-1840s intended to write an article on the Factory Acts in the *Edinburgh Review*. The mandate of *Household Words* in 1850 was to expose 'all social evils' and to offer at the same time the cultivation of DOMESTIC feeling as a partial solution. He also proselytized for reform of the PRISON system (see the *EXAMINER*, 1848–9) and worked tirelessly with Miss COUTTS to provide shelter and hope for the 'fallen' women who were the female criminals of this society (see PROSTITUTES).

The Second Reform Bill, introduced by DISRAELI and the Conservatives in 1867, doubled the electorate and added 938,000 new voters. There were 45 new seats, created by siphoning off one member from each borough of fewer than 10,000 people. This increased the weight of the urban population in electoral representation. There was still no enfranchisement of agricultural labourers until 1884 and no universal male suffrage until 1918. The secret ballot, agitated for since the turn of the century, did not win approval until 1872, two years after Dickens's death.                                            KC

> Carlton, W. N., 'Dickens and the Two Tennysons', *Dickensian*, 47 (1951).
> Evans, Eric, *Social Policy, 1830–1914* (1978).
> —— *The Great Reform Act of 1832* (2nd edn. 1994).

**relatives and descendants of Dickens.** In 1993 a great-great-grandson of Dickens, Mark Dickens, compiled a family tree showing 137 direct descendants of the author alive at that time, all deriving from just two of Dickens's CHILDREN, Charles and Henry. The Dickens surname survives only through Henry's branch of the family, and is shared by seventeen descendants, whilst fourteen people with other surnames use Dickens as one of their forenames. In a celebration to launch the family tree nearly 100 direct descendents gathered at DICKENS HOUSE in London, the largest family gathering there has ever been. The head of the family is Christopher Charles Dickens (1937–   ).

Ever since its foundation in 1902 the DICKENS FELLOWSHIP has been strongly supported by members of the family, with thirteen holding positions of President or Vice-President. As might be expected in such a large family,

a variety of careers have been followed, including the law, the church, the army and navy, publishing, and industry—acting and journalism are represented among the current generation. Two have been novelists, his granddaughter Mary, writing between 1891 and 1912, and his great-granddaughter Monica Dickens, who died in 1992. The latter wrote more than 50 books, not all novels, and for 20 years had a column in the magazine *Woman's Own*. Books have also been written by Captain Peter Dickens (1917–87) and Cedric Dickens (1916–   ). Since the time of his own children members of the Dickens family have given readings from the books, written articles, and given lectures, traditions that have continued into the 1990s.       MA

> Dickens, Monica, *An Open Book* (1978).

**religion** figures far more explicitly and insistently as an interest in Dickens's works and in the Victorian novel generally than it does in much fiction of the 20th century, even though Dickens—a Christian of the broadest kind—goes to great lengths to erase all traces of the merely sectarian from his work, and much of his MORAL thinking is consistent with a highly secular interpretation.

The language of the BIBLE and the BOOK OF COMMON PRAYER, as well as, of course, BUNYAN's *Pilgrim's Progress*, were so deeply impressed upon his culture—and upon the always-responsive ear of Dickens—that religious references come thick and fast even in contexts that seem hardly to put religion at issue. In giving a chapter of *Bleak House* the title 'Our Dear Brother' (11), for example, Dickens draws on a phrase out of the funeral service that all his readers would readily recognize, and thereby simply announces that a burial is going to take place without calling up any specifically religious issues—though he does make a moral point through a characteristically Dickensian irony: the 'dear brother' will hardly be treated as dear or a brother at all, for he is to be laid to rest in a filthy and overcrowded burying ground in a noisome slum, good for nothing but spreading disease. There is thus a large body of nominally religious allusion whose function may be best described as literary.

This is by no means to say that Dickens held no religious views, but rather that his frequent allusions to scripture and Anglican liturgy provide no very sure guide to them. In all his writings, Dickens is outspoken in his dislike of EVANGELICALISM and ROMAN CATHOLICISM, but, especially in his fiction, he is very reluctant to make professions of a specific faith beyond the most general sort of Christianity. Nothing more surely aroused his suspicions about a person's religious faith than a public profession of it, and this aversion formed a fundamental feature of his dislike of evangelicals and DISSENTERS. It is likely too that his awareness that his readers held widely differing religious views—that he numbered many Roman Catholics and JEWS among his audience as well as Anglo-Catholics and every conceivable variety of Protestant—provided additional motivation for avoiding circumstances that would touch off sectarian debate, which he characterized in a letter as 'unseemly squabbles about the letter which drive the spirit out of hundreds of thousands' (to the Revd R. H. Davies, 31 December 1856).

Dickens's parents were Anglican, but evidently entirely uninterested in the dogmas of the CHURCH OF ENGLAND and probably not very regular in their worship. As a small boy in Chatham Dickens seems to have attended services at a nearby Baptist chapel. There is little positive evidence about Dickens's religious thinking throughout the 1820s and 1830s, but it is in the latter decade, a period of significant REFORM in England, that he was at his most unrestrained in his religious satires —for example, upon SABBATARIANISM (in the pseudonymously published SUNDAY UNDER THREE HEADS, 1836) and upon hypocritical dissenting preachers (in the form of Mr Stiggins in The Pickwick Papers, 1837). It is evident at the time of his first AMERICAN trip in 1842 that he was hopeful of finding in the United States political and religious institutions more progressive and effective than Parliament and the Church of England. At the time he looked enthusiastically to the new nation's ideals of liberty and equality as promoting a future that might reward merit and free itself of ancient and hidebound class prejudices. He was, moreover, certainly attracted by the separation of church and state in the United States, and while he was soon to be profoundly disappointed in American politics, he was very taken at least by the UNITARIAN circle that he encountered in Boston. Indeed, his

interest in Unitarianism was virtually the only enthusiasm he managed to bring back with him undamaged at the end of the trip, and it survived for at least a year or two and possibly as many as five.

It was in these years too that Dickens first felt the need to impart some religious instruction to his CHILDREN and, significantly, undertook to do this himself by writing a simplified version of the Gospels designed for reading aloud (not published until 1934, when it was dubbed The LIFE OF OUR LORD). Given the intended audience, it is hardly fair to infer the specifics of Dickens's faith from this slight work, which is in any case theologically rather inconsistent. But it is often taken as expressing a Unitarian outlook, and certainly what Dickens stresses is Christ as model, teacher, and healer—the comforter of the distressed rather than the saviour of mankind through the crucifixion and atonement. A letter to his youngest son, 'Plorn', on the occasion of his emigration to AUSTRALIA, is extensively quoted by Forster (11.3) and also provides useful insight into Dickens's religious views.

According to Forster—himself a lifelong Unitarian—Dickens eventually was able 'to accommodate all minor differences' with Anglican doctrine, and his will contains a highly orthodox committing of his soul 'to the mercy of God through our Lord and Saviour Jesus Christ' (Forster 4.2). Among the very last words Dickens wrote is a description of a brilliant spring morning in Rochester in which 'Changes of glorious light from moving boughs, songs of birds, scents from gardens, woods, and fields . . . preach the Resurrection and the Life' (MED 23).

Immortality of the soul, a favourite rock upon which a Victorian's faith might founder, seems in fact to have constituted the one article of faith about which Dickens was troubled by no doubts. His notion of heaven, however, is notably worldly. It is 'where we hope to go, and all to meet each other after we are dead, and there be happy always together' (LOL 1). Heaven is where the good go to be reunited with their friends, and heavenly bliss is thus rather like a permanent stay at the ideal Pickwickian inn. Although Dickens mentions Christ's coming again 'to judge the world' (LOL 11), he seems never to have taken seriously the possibility of eternal damnation and is always bitterly critical of the harm done by those who hold out the threat of hellfire, especially over the young.

The extent to which Dickens's religious thought bears a secular reading is evident if one asks the fundamental ethical question: where does he locate the good? Not, very clearly, in religious or moral thought, but rather in immediately and self-evidently useful actions. In this he much resembles his mentor Thomas CARLYLE. As he says to another correspondent who had turned to him for guidance, 'Be earnest—earnest—in life's reality and do not let your life, which has a purpose in it—every life upon the earth has —fly by while you are brooding over mysteries . . . Our Saviour did not sit down in this world and muse, but labored and did good' (to Emmely Gotschalk, 1 February 1850). The goods that he associates with Christ are—appropriate to Dickens's rather DOMESTIC conception of heaven—the goods of a kindly companionship: healing, teaching, loving. They can be summed up in one word (one of Dickens's favourites): 'comfort.' They are conspicuously not such traditional religious goods as obedience, which figures prominently in Roman Catholicism, nor the traditional religious good of self-denial, which figures prominently in Roman Catholicism and in evangelical and dissenting versions of Protestantism.

Sometimes the contrast between traditional religion focused on the otherworldly and the religion of doing good—providing comfort and pleasure—in the here and now is sharply drawn, as in the early interpolated tale of the five sisters of York in *Nicholas Nickleby*, in which five lovely young sisters are urged by one of the 'black monks of St Benedict' to eschew their pastime of embroidery and to be mindful of eternity by taking up the veil. After many misfortunes and the death of the youngest and loveliest sister, the monk seeks out the four survivors and urges them again not to fritter away their lives on 'geegaws', but to take up the veil. Though initially tempted in their grief, instead they decide to celebrate precisely 'the harmless mirth' of their embroidery by commissioning 'artists of great celebrity' to copy in 'richly stained glass' for York Minster 'a faithful copy of their old embroidery work' (*NN* 6). Sometimes the contrast is more subtly drawn, as when the illegitimate child Esther Summerson in *Bleak House* turns the sternly Calvinistic precepts of her godmother Miss Barbary ('Submission, self-denial, diligent work, are the preparations for a life begun with such a shadow on it') into a rather different set of maxims; Esther vows instead 'to be industrious, contented, and kind-hearted, and to do some good to some one, and win some love to myself if I could' (*BH* 3).

In both these examples, there is a studied rejection of pure self-denial even as the needs of self are sensitively attuned to the larger claims of community. For Dickens resists a crude worldly doctrine of self-interest as powerfully as he resists crude otherworldly doctrines of selflessness. 'Duty' is certainly a powerful word in his vocabulary, but duty is located not in institutional authorities, which are very often corrupt and inefficient; rather the 'duty' that is compelling is one's obligation to the community—the more immediate the better. Esther Summerson, again, is exemplary. Rather than adopt the mechanical protocols of organized philanthropy, she thinks 'it best to be as useful as I could, and to render what kind services I could to those immediately about me; and to try to let that circle of duty gradually and naturally expand itself' (*BH* 8).

Is Esther's programme 'religious'? It is fully consistent with Christian principles of a broad and rather dilute sort, but also, arguably, is equally if surprisingly consistent with the famous UTILITARIAN good of promoting the greatest happiness of the greatest number. (Broad Christianity and utilitarianism had in fact already been similarly combined in the moral philosophy of William Paley, whose works were standard texts at Cambridge in the late 18th and early 19th centuries and thus had been widely disseminated via the liberal Victorian Anglican clergy; Paley is classed as an ethical utilitarian because he argues that we should imitate God's benevolent desire that we realize as much happiness as possible.)

Dickens would no doubt have argued that Esther's programme was *essentially* religious —that it preserved the spirit of the New Testament while dispensing with the mechanical letter. Believers less willing to dismiss the letter for the spirit—whether because they doubted the spirit could be known other than through the letter or just because they liked the letters for their own sake—might not be so sure. Dickens was no favourite with the evangelical and dissenting press, and he was the very embodiment of the kind of liberalism anathematized by the Oxford Movement and its most famous convert to Roman Catholicism, John Henry Newman. John RUSKIN, the great art critic, perhaps put the case for the secular interpretation of Dickens's ethics most sharply in a letter to their mutual friend Charles Eliot Norton shortly after Dickens's death—and in spite of the fact that Ruskin himself was generally a great admirer of Dickens and had had an experience of loss of faith that he referred to as an 'unconversion': 'He knew nothing of the nobler power of superstition—was essentially a stage manager, and used everything for effect on the pit. His CHRISTMAS meant mistletoe and pudding—neither resurrection from dead, nor rising of new stars, nor teaching of wise men, nor shepherds' (*Letters of John Ruskin to Charles Eliot Norton*, 1905, 2.5). The description may be undermined by language such as that from *Edwin Drood* quoted above, but if Ruskin is unfair to Dickens's religious feeling here, it is also in part because Dickens indeed goes to great lengths to purge his works of professions of faith that appear much more than ornamental. RN

Walder (1981).
Welsh (1971).

***Reprinted Pieces*** A collection of 31 essays, stories, and sketches written by Dickens between 1850 and 1856, first published in *Household Words*, and gathered by him under this title to bulk out volume 2 of *The Old Curiosity Shop* in the Library Edition of 1858 (see EDITIONS OVER WHICH DICKENS HAD CONTROL). They include several Christmas stories and one entry, 'A Plated Article', not by Dickens but by WILLS. PVWS

**reputation of Dickens.** Dickens's first success came with *Sketches by Boz*, and this established his earliest reputation as a writer of sketches, contemporary REVIEWERS comparing him with other sketch-writers like Pierce EGAN. T. H. Lister thought him 'like Washington IRVING in his detached tales', cannily introducing an American dimension to give some sense of how populist—how democratic, in a sense—Dickens's appeal was. But Lister went on, even more acutely, to add: 'but

his own manner is very distinct—and comparison with any other would not serve to illustrate and describe it. We would compare him rather with the painter HOGARTH. What Hogarth was in painting, such very nearly is Mr Dickens in Prose fiction' (*Edinburgh Review*, 86, 1838). In other words, Dickens's early reputation was that of a direct and affecting satirist, a writer of sketches on a par with the best. (See SHORT STORY AND SKETCH WRITER, DICKENS AS.)

But this reputation was very soon to be expanded by the immense POPULARITY of *Pickwick*, *Oliver Twist*, and *Nickleby*. Reviewers widened their comparisons—Dickens was now like SCOTT, like FIELDING, like SHAKESPEARE, like nobody before. An elderly, and crotchety, WORDSWORTH wrote to his publisher wondering why his books were not selling as well as they might: 'the young men in the Universities cannot be supposed to be straitened in their allowance, yet I find that scarcely any books are sold them. Dr Arnold told me that his lads care for nothing but Bozzy's next No., and the Classics suffered accordingly. Can that Man's public . . . materially affect the question? I am quite in the dark' (Wordsworth to Edward Moxon, 1 April 1842). The late 1830s and the early 1840s are the period of what contemporary reports called 'Bozmania' or 'Boz-i-ana'. A much-quoted letter by Mary Russell Mitford illustrates both the range and some of the attributes of Dickens's reputation in these early years. Mitford is amazed at the ignorance of her correspondent, who lives in Ireland: 'So you have never heard of the *Pickwick Papers*! Well, they publish a number once a month and print 25,000 . . . It's fun—London life—but without anything unpleasant; a lady might read it all *aloud*; and it is so graphic, so individual and so true, that you could courtsey to all the people as you met them in the streets. I did not think there had been a place where English is spoken to which "Boz" had not penetrated. All the boys and girls talk his fun—the boys in the streets; and yet those who are of the highest taste like it the most. Sir Benjamin Brodie [a famous surgeon] takes it to read in his carriage, between patient and patient, and Lord Denman [Lord Chief Justice] studies *Pickwick* on the bench while the jury are deliberating' (Collins 1971, p. 36).

The approval with which this educated and morally self-conscious woman talks ('a lady might read it all *aloud*') makes clear that what Dickens enjoyed is more than just fame, it is 'reputation' in the societal sense of that word—that Dickens's fame was of the sort that decent society might commend. Despite his often passionate engagement in his various social causes and his satirical attacks on much of society's establishment, Dickens clung hard to his reputation as a writer as concerned with propriety, in the broadest sense. This achievement was the greater when we consider, as Mitford suggests, the extent to which Dickens's popularity crossed CLASS barriers (see READERSHIP). For Mitford, Dickens's appeal was grounded in his skill as an entertainer ('it is fun'); but for many working-class readers his reputation as a man engaged in ameliorating social injustice was just as important. Dickens's son Henry reported an anecdote from the day of Dickens's death. A friend of Henry's was in a tobacconist's: 'Whilst there a working man came in for a screw of tobacco and, as he threw his twopence on the counter, he said: "Charles Dickens is dead. We have lost our best friend"' (1928, p. 29).

This reputation, that of the friend and helper of ordinary people, began with *Oliver Twist* and grew throughout Dickens's career. It was felt keenly on both sides; ordinary people loved Dickens, and Dickens was fiercely proud of his reputation amongst them. Kathleen Tillotson's famous remark sums up the depth of the relationship between Dickens and his readers: 'with *Pickwick*, Dickens embarked upon his lifelong love-affair with his reading public; which, when all is said, is the most interesting love-affair of his life' (Butt and Tillotson 1957, p. 75). Both in his writing and his public (and private) life Dickens vigorously cultivated this reputation. The list of societies (for instance) with which he was connected, and which were engaged in improving conditions for the poorest classes, is an index of his growing reputation as a tireless worker for social justice and benefactor of the disadvantaged: the Administrative Reform Society; the Birmingham Industrial and Literary Institution; the Governess's Benevolent Institution; Great Ormond Street Hospital; the Liverpool Mechanics' Institution; the Manchester Free Library; the News-vendors' Benevolent Association; the Playground and General Recreation Society; the Royal Hospital for Incurables. Dickens's reputation as public benefactor and his literary reputation went, of course, hand in hand (see CHARITY).

A key date in the development of Dickens's reputation was 25 June 1841, when the first of what was eventually to be a long series of great public dinners was held in Dickens's honour. This first, in Edinburgh, saw 450 people, including 200 women, attend ('the room was crammed,' a delighted Dickens wrote to Forster, 'and more than seventy applicants for tickets were of necessity refused yesterday') to hear a speech in which John WILSON (the famous 'Christopher North' of *Blackwood's Magazine*) described Dickens as 'perhaps the most popular writer now alive'. Wilson went on to argue that whilst Dickens's representation of female character was not fully successful, he nonetheless deserved his reputation for the MORAL basis, the propriety, of his art: 'he has represented his female characters as inspired with the love of domestic duty, of purity, innocence, charity, faith, and hope ... and always brings over their path on earth some glimpses of the light of heaven (Loud cheers)' (Pilgrim 2.310 n.). This dinner —a particular honour for a man not yet out of his twenties—represents the first acknowledgement of the literary establishment of Dickens's unique literary and popular reputation. Other dinners were to follow. The point to stress here is the extent to which Dickens's involvement in projects for ameliorating the lot of the poorer classes (from charitable donations to his patronage of Mechanics' and Literary Institutions), as well as the satirical effectiveness of his fiction, all contributed towards his reputation as a friend of the poor, a social reformer, and a man with a profound moral sense. It was in these terms that R. H. HORNE characterized him in his *A New Spirit of the Age* (1844); the fact that Dickens merited the first chapter in this survey of early-Victorian worthies is particularly significant. For Horne, Dickens was an artist whose works 'have a direct moral purpose in view, viz., a desire to ameliorate the condition of the poorer classes by showing what society has made of them, or allowed them to become'.

But it is with *AMERICAN NOTES* and *Martin Chuzzlewit* that another sort of Dickensian reputation begins to emerge. If in the early 1840s his reputation was of a hugely entertaining morally and socially engaged writer and do-gooder, there were many in AMERICA who felt his negative portrayal of their country was unjustified. Ralph Waldo EMERSON, for instance, confided his dissatisfaction with *American Notes* to his journal (25 November 1842): 'Truth is not his object for an instant, but merely to make good points in a lively sequence ... We can hear throughout every page the dialogue between the author and publisher—"Mr Dickens, the book must be entertaining—that is the essential point. Truth? Damn truth! I tell you, it must be entertaining" ... Monstrous exaggeration is an easy secret of romance.' Dickens's reputation as an exaggerator has stayed with him to this day, and it cropped up with increasing frequency as he consolidated his other reputation as the world's most successful author. In his Preface to *Bleak House* he could easily ridicule the CHANCERY judge who thought his satire of the Court of Chancery in that novel exaggerated beyond truthfulness; but John Stuart MILL had more reason to object to the novel's caricature of a feminist in Mrs Jellyby. 'That creature Dickens', Mill wrote, 'has had the impudence in this thing to ridicule rights of WOMEN. It is done too in the very vulgarest way, just the style in which vulgar men used to ridicule "learned ladies" as neglecting their children and household' (Mill, letter to his wife, March 1854)—though Mrs Chisholm, the 'original' for Mrs Jellyby, did neglect her children in just that way. Mill's charge of 'vulgarity' is evidence that a reputation for popularity and popularism can be a double-edged thing, particularly in the hands of those who consider themselves social superiors. Anthony TROLLOPE's novel *The Warden* (1855) is perhaps the fullest elaboration of this sense of Dickens as a man who exaggerates to be entertaining at the expense of the truth. In that novel, the complex moral ambiguities of the situation in Barchester become flattened and distorted when 'Mr Popular Sentiment' (a fictional version of Dickens) decides to take up the cause of Hiram's Hospital in his latest book. This sense of Dickens as vulgar, driven by Popular Sentiment rather than truth, liable to exaggeration and caricature, is in a sense the flip-side of his reputation as the greatest popular entertainer of his day.

In one instance a reviewer criticized Dickens in *Little Dorrit* for straying beyond the bounds of mere entertainer and for libelling the upper classes and establishment, which provoked a waspish reply in *Household Words*. The review, entitled 'The License of Modern Novelists' appeared anonymously in the *Edinburgh Review* in 1857. In it, the author (James Fitzjames Stephen) attacked Dickens for 'his injustice to the institutions of English society' and his 'animosity to particular classes [i.e. the upper classes] in that society.' Stephen, rather like Trollope, accuses Dickens of having an eye for the main chance, a fascination with topicality that distorts his art: 'If there was a popular cry against the management of a hospital, he would no doubt write a novel on a month's warning about the ignorance and temerity with which surgical operations are performed; and if his lot had been cast in the time when it was fashionable to call the English law the perfection of reason, he would probably have published monthly denunciations of Lord Mansfield's Judgement in *Perrin v. Blake*, in blue covers adorned with curious hieroglyphics . . . Even the catastrophe in *Little Dorrit* is evidently borrowed from the recent fall of houses in Tottenham Court Road, which happens to have appeared in the newspapers at a convenient moment' (*Edinburgh Review*, 106, July 1857). Dickens's reply, 'Curious Misprint in the Edinburgh Review', appeared in *Household Words* on 1 August 1857; in it he points out that the collapse of the house in *Dorrit* is prepared for at the very beginning of the book, and he argues wittily for the fundamental justice of his satire on government red tape. He concludes with a proud assertion of the 'just respect' due 'himself, and his calling; beyond the sound, healthy, legitimate uses and influences of which, he has no purpose to serve, and no ambition in life to gratify'. Apart from anything else, the incident suggests that by the mid-1850s Dickens was becoming fiercely protective of his reputation—his reputations, we might say, as a writer, entertainer, friend to the people, and man of honour.

Dickens's literary reputation began to change with the publication of *Bleak House* in 1852–3. Philip Collins calls *Bleak House* 'a crucial item in the history of Dickens's reputation. For many critics in the 1850s, '60s and '70s, it began the drear decline of the author of *Pickwick*, *Chuzzlewit* and *Copperfield* (1971, p. 272). This view of Dickens as changing his aesthetic from bright sunny comedy in the early novels to dark and serious social comment in the later has endured, although most critics today would dismiss it as a caricature of his career. But contemporary reviews increasingly accuse Dickens of being dreary; the *Spectator* called *Bleak House* 'a heavy book to read through at once . . . dull and wearisome as a serial'; Richard Simpson, in *The Rambler*, characterized *Hard Times* as 'this dreary framework'; *Fraser's Magazine* thought *Little Dorrit* 'decidedly the worst of his novels' (Collins 1971, pp. 284, 303, 356). A. W. Ward, recalling the mood amongst educated readers as the later novels emerged, pinpoints the sense that his literary reputation was wilting: 'I well remember, at the time of its publication in numbers, the general consciousness that *Little Dorrit* was proving unequal to the high-strung expectations which a new work by Dickens then excited . . . Nothing is more remarkable in the literary career of Dickens than this speedy decline in his power' (Collins 1971, p. 356). But Ward is astute enough to recognize that, despite increasing reservations amongst reviewers and the chattering classes, 'the public never deserted its favourite'. Dickens's reputation as the foremost novelist of the day might have suffered with the later novels (Trollope's *Autobiography* famously declared THACKERAY, not Dickens, to be the greatest novelist of the age); but Dickens's popular reputation was undented. Sales continued to rise, and *Household Words* and later *All the Year Round* were hugely successful.

With the commencement of his series of PUBLIC READINGS, his reputation as the greatest popular entertainer and communicator of the age soared. On one reading tour in Ireland Dickens was approached by a man in the streets of Belfast who shook his hand, saying: 'Do me the honour to shake hands, Misther Dickens and God bless you sir; not only for the light you've been to me this night, but for the light you've been in mee house sir (and God love your face!) this many a year!' (Forster 8.4). Several critics have noticed that Dickens's choice from his novels for readings tended to be passages of human interest, the entertaining, comic, and sometimes SENTIMENTAL parts of his work; that his conception of himself as a reader had no place for his

darker, more satirical attacks on social injustice. That, in other words, Dickens's sense of himself and his popular reputation was grounded first and foremost in what Grahame Smith has called 'celebratory entertainments' (1996, p. 117). There is little doubt that it was his popular reputation that mattered most to Dickens. He consistently refused the suggestion of honours or titles, always despised flunkeyism; but was also always profoundly moved, sometimes to tears, by the spontaneous and genuine love demonstrated by his ordinary readers.

The biggest threat to this popular reputation came with his separation from his wife, Catherine DICKENS, in 1858, and particularly with his relationship with Ellen TERNAN. The almost obsessive secrecy with which he veiled this latter relationship is testament to his fear that, were it to become widely known, his public and popular reputation would be irredeemably damaged. This touchiness explains actions such as his publication of the 'personal statement' concerning the separation, with its public announcement of the trouble between husband and wife, and the outraged insistence that 'this trouble has been made the occasion of misrepresentations, most grossly false, most monstrous, and most cruel—involving, not only me, but innocent persons dear to my heart' (*HW* 12 June 1858; repr. Pilgrim 8.744). It seems clear that Dickens misjudged the extent of his reputation in this matter; or at least misjudged the extent to which his popular audience were privy to the intimate goings-on of his life, and the gossip that attached to that. Percy FITZGERALD, a young man at the time of the publication of the 'personal statement', later said: 'I well remember the feeling of surprise and regret which the article created among us of the general public . . . So far as one could learn at the time, no great dissimilarity existed between the author and the man' (*Memories of Charles Dickens*, 1913).

There was some newspaper condemnation of Dickens in 1858 that suggests his reputation as the moral entertainer of the masses was damaged by the separation. Gossip (that Dickens was enamoured of his wife's sister, Georgina HOGARTH, for instance) circulated. Later in the year Dickens's reading tour took him to Aberdeen, where the local paper carried letters from local clergymen deploring his advocacy of amusements on the sabbath (see SABBATARIANISM), and urging people not to attend the readings because Dickens ridiculed Christianity and to support him would be to strengthen 'the enemy' (*Aberdeen Free Press*, 1 October 1858). But such extreme reactions were rare, more likely in bastions of nonconformist religion like Aberdeen than in Dickens's heartland. A week after the letter in the Aberdeen paper, Dickens gave FORSTER a very different sense of how deeply loved his reading audiences made him feel: 'As to the truth of the readings, I cannot tell you what the demonstrations of personal regard and respect are. How the densest and most uncomfortably packed crowd will be hushed in an instant when I show my face. How the youth of colleges, and the old men of business in the town, seem equally unable to get near enough to me when they cheer me away at night. How common people and gentlefolks will stop me in the street and say: "Mr Dickens, will you let me touch the hand that has filled my home with so many friends?" ' (to Forster, 10 October 1858).

Benjamin Jowett's sermon on Dickens's death (19 June 1870) captured this sense of the reach Dickens had into the lives of ordinary people: he 'occupied a greater space than any other writer in the minds of Englishmen during the last thirty-five years. We read him, talked about him, acted him; we laughed with him, we were roused by him to a consciousness of the misery of others, and to a pathetic interest in human life.' Dickens's contemporary reputation encompassed all these things.                                              AR

Collins (1971).
—— (1981).
Smith (1996).

**reviews and reviewing.** From the beginning, Dickens's REPUTATION was not esoterically derived; the weighty critical reviews came after his POPULARITY was already a recognized phenomenon.

From December 1833 Dickens published in the MONTHLY MAGAZINE nine sketches receiving about 40 notices. Most merely remarked that the tales were 'clever', only the *Sun* going so far as to say that BOZ was 'too ambitious of saying smart things' (1 April 1834). There was a convention by which most of the seven-penny daily papers printed a column at the

beginning of each month, in which they reviewed 'The Magazines', and so the chances of Boz's receiving some passing notice were regular.

After this, Dickens was not reviewed until February 1836, when the first collected volume of *Sketches by Boz* appeared. In between, the five MORNING CHRONICLE, twenty EVENING CHRONICLE, and twelve BELL'S LIFE IN LONDON sketches, despite showing some distinct improvement on the *Monthly* sketches, received no notices, since it was not customary to review newspaper sketches. It was the reception of *Pickwick Papers* that materially changed Dickens's direction as a writer, although there were some good notices of *Sketches by Boz*, First Series ('a perfect picture of the morals, manners, habits of a great portion of English society'—*Metropolitan Magazine*, 15, March 1836).

However, *Sketches by Boz* was quickly overtaken by *Pickwick*, which had started to run serially in April 1836. Alongside the discrete reviews of Dickens's *Sketches* appear, without any critical commentary, the ubiquitous *Pickwick* excerpts that were to make his fame. Because of these regular monthly notices, *Pickwick* appeared to be an ongoing series of sketches under one title that appeared, like the magazines, at the beginning of each month. It could be relied upon as filler, and the sayings of Sam Weller enjoyed an incremental value as the months passed by. Whereas Dickens's first book disappears into the maw of the *literary* market, Dickens's SERIAL, a magazine complete in one article, turns up month after month to create its own market. The popularity becomes noticeable after the introduction of Sam Weller in the September 1836 number (the fifth). His sayings were highly useful to editors who saw nothing wrong with lengthy extracting. The paradox is that *Pickwick* as a book would probably have received no more notices than *Sketches by Boz*. Published in increments, however, Sam Weller might be compared to a novelistic character, without having to meet the same demands for coherence. Dickens, as a recurrent 'magazine' (which is the category under which *Pickwick* appeared in many columns), thus found himself in the public eye every month—often in papers that normally carried no literary reviews—for the better part of two years. And this was reinforced by the appearance of *Oliver Twist* in BENTLEY'S MIS-CELLANY from February 1837, when *Pickwick* still had ten more numbers to run.

When the Second Series of *Sketches by Boz* came out late in 1836, it was not widely noticed, and indeed MACRONE and Dickens were no longer speaking, after Macrone's decision to reissue it in parts (pink) like those of *Pickwick*. Dickens did not like this trading on the *Pickwick* phenomenon and flooding the market with similarly produced Dickens works. But obviously Macrone, like everyone else, had seen the significance of the periodical format to Dickens's success. At this point, John FORSTER wrote one of the first significant reviews of Dickens's work, the EXAMINER review of *Pickwick*'s fifteenth number. The month of July 1837 marks an early turning point in Dickens's reputation: Forster and the *Sun* reviewer were comparing the narrative skills found in *Pickwick* to FIELDING'S novels, and in the same month Charles Buller gave him his first critical attention in a quarterly, the *London and Westminster Review*. The latter remarked how extraordinary it was that such a popular production should have attracted serious notice but that the fact of its extraordinary POPULARITY was precisely what made such attention necessary. Thus, Dickens's first review from a quarterly came, not because of literary merit, but because he was a publishing phenomenon who cut across the usual lines of literary decorum. The *London and Westminster Review* confirmed the opinion of *Sketches by Boz* as 'monotonous', yet also found that the same talent— appearing in two serials at once and excerpted in dailies and weeklies everywhere, month in and month out—had become essential reading.

Dickens's second major review, by Abraham Hayward in the *Quarterly Review* for October 1837, also spent time attempting to understand the anomalies of this phenomenon. Both quarterlies concluded that Dickens had yet to show any ability to sustain a narrative or depict a realistic character. Hayward famously predicted that 'he has risen like a rocket, and he will come down like the stick'. What they praised as original—though with misgivings about 'lowness'—was Dickens's rendering of lower-class speech: with this he had made a new source of language available to literature. This notion was developed in the next *Quarterly Review* article commissioned by the editor J. G. LOCKHART (seeking to make amends for the unexpected harshness of the first), where Richard Ford cheerfully called Dickens the 'regius professor of slang' (June 1839).

The reviews of *Nicholas Nickleby* the next year frequently commented on its literary self-consciousness—they complained of too much 'fine writing'. The case of *Nickleby* is a paradoxical one: there is copious extracting of 'bits'—Dickens's popularity is never more wholeheartedly displayed—but the critical comments become rarer. The *United Services Gazette* remarks that the Strand on the last day of the month is 'verdant' with green covers in everyone's hands (9 February 1839). However, the *Spectator* (March 1838) shrewdly notes that 'Had the *Pickwick* been first published in a volume, it is questionable whether its circulation would have reached one-fifth of its actual extent . . . the Sketches of this writer, collected into volumes, have a far less extensive demand.' When *Oliver Twist* ended its serialization in November 1838, this complaint was prominent. The *Spectator*, along with the *Edinburgh Review* (October 1838), again queried Dickens's ability to tell a story without being '*magazinishly* diffuse'. There was a general speculation about Dickens's ability to be anything more than a Cockney sketch-writer. In his letters, Dickens shows the same concerns.

He was also worried about working his popularity to death before he had even managed to write what he considered a first novel proper—that is to say, a HISTORICAL NOVEL in the SCOTT tradition. This was *Barnaby Rudge*, but both it and its predecessor, *The Old Curiosity Shop*, were sacrificed to Dickens's new periodical venture, MASTER HUMPHREY'S CLOCK. The latter had been started in order to give Dickens some relief from the pressure of a monthly serial but turned out to be commercially fragile. He responded by developing *The Old Curiosity Shop* in its pages and then continued with *Barnaby Rudge* as a serial, although the latter had been planned as his first three-volume novel. Nonetheless, the notices for *Barnaby Rudge* were 40 per cent fewer than *Nickleby* at its height in 1839. Edgar Allan Poe's review in *Graham's Magazine* of February 1842, where he praised Dickens for his genius but deplored his bungling of the mystery, is probably the best-known of the notices of *Barnaby Rudge*. The excerpting of bits continued routinely but without the same enthusiasm. Dickens's readers wanted a sustained narrative, not short stories, while his critics wanted to see if he could actually write a novel in the conventional three volumes. They regarded the writing of narrative by monthly instalments as a sleight-of-hand. In fact, Dickens was never to pass that particular test of the literary heavyweight.

Dickens thought he would write a serious novel after his sabbatical from serial-writing during the first half of 1842. His return to novel-writing, *Martin Chuzzlewit*, reaches for the 18th-century note, reminding us of Dickens's reverence for the classics he read as a child (see NOVELISTS AND NOVELS BEFORE DICKENS). But even though his critics shared this love, they thought his imitation of the Shandiean voice weak (see STERNE). The blame mostly has been put on the bad-tempered feeling invoked by AMERICAN NOTES, published two months before *Martin Chuzzlewit* began its serial run. Critics and readers, lovers of *Pickwick* and *The Old Curiosity Shop*, were not prepared for this misanthropy, and Dickens for the first time since his fame had begun had no surge of popularity to sustain him through any criticism.

It is hard to know when Dickens stopped reading serious criticism of his works (he said in 1843 that he had not done so for five years). However, the prefaces published for the publication of his works after their serial runs show a detailed knowledge of what his critics had said, and generally read like replies to them. Forster's reviews in the *Examiner*, always an indicator of what Dickens was thinking, also put forward arguments for the rightness of his artistic choices. Even if Dickens avoided the serious quarterlies' notices, it would have been impossible for him as a regular newspaper reader to have avoided everything, and often longer reviews were excerpted in the papers. We have a record, for example, of his response to *The* TIMES attack on *The* BATTLE OF LIFE (2 January 1847): 'Another touch of a blunt razor on B.'s nervous system . . . Dreamed of *Timeses* all night. Disposed to go to New Zealand and start a magazine' (to Forster, 7–8 January 1847). George Ford (1955) has an appendix showing specific cases for every work in which Dickens clearly

was familiar with at least one review. It may be, as Ford conjectures, that Dickens's resolve not to read criticism in fact specifically meant an avoidance, not of reviews but of *attacks*.

The 1840s were perhaps the period when Dickens was most unsettled by critical reaction. Subsequent to the AMERICAN trip, the travels in SWITZERLAND and ITALY were one way of licking his wounds after *Martin Chuzzlewit* and searching for inspiration. When *Martin Chuzzlewit* ended in June 1844, it was more than two years before *Dombey and Son* appeared, 'to general esteem' (Collins 1971, p. 212). In the meantime, instead of settling down to a career as a serious novelist, he became even more diversified in his writerly pursuits: the expensively produced *Christmas Carol* in Christmas 1843; the brief venture as editor of the DAILY NEWS in 1846; more Christmas books; another travel book (1846); and a series of public letters on social questions. The response to these was varied and uneven. A *Christmas Carol* was generously received, as Philip Collins says, something of a critical 'truce' being declared; it was recognized that as a phenomenon the story was beyond the usual criticism. THACKERAY probably expressed this most delicately in his review in *Fraser's Magazine* of February 1844, which hints at all the things wrong with Dickens's writing and then shows how none of that matters because of the way that *Christmas Carol* has touched so many hearts.

The sales of the Christmas books were at odds with the critical disapproval, and here we see the split that is confirmed after *David Copperfield*: whatever the vagaries of critical commentary, and with only a few dips, his sales continued to rise for the rest of his career —although those for *Copperfield*, widely proclaimed his masterpiece, were markedly down from *Dombey*. But the 1850s also represent the time when literary criticism began to eschew the crude political bias that was so important earlier in the century, and the rejection of Dickens became more commonplace. The *Saturday Review* was established, and the new generation of critics disliked the intrusion of public affairs into artistic works. Where the *Westminster Review* in 1843 had praised Dickens for his 'latent desire to improve and strengthen the charities of life', by 1864 it resented the perversion of the novel 'from a work of art to a platform for discussion and argument'.

Partly, the attitudes taken towards the full-blown satire found in Dickens's novels after *Copperfield* depend on who was being attacked. After the attack on the civil service in *Little Dorrit* (and also in *Household Words*), Fitzjames Stephen, whose father was thought to be the model for the elder Barnacle, wrote at least five of the articles in the *Saturday Review*'s pages that assailed Dickens in the two years between 1857 and 1859, culminating in 'The Licence of Modern Novelists' published in the *Edinburgh Review* (July 1857). Collins points out that the *Edinburgh Review* had not in fact seriously reviewed Dickens as a novelist since its first 'Dickens's Tales' in October 1838; Stephen's attack merely embodied the unspoken implication that the *Edinburgh* thought Dickens's work was too light to deserve thoughtful criticism. Dickens's response to these, 'Curious Misprint in the Edinburgh Review' (*HW* 1 August 1857), indicates that he must temporarily at least have broken his own vow never to read attacks. The Pilgrim editors quote one of Dickens's young men on *Household Words*, John Hollingshead (1827–1904), as remarking afterwards that 'This was his last answer to his critics or defamers. From that time till his death he read nothing and answered nothing' (Pilgrim 8.3893 n.).

In any case, *A Tale of Two Cities* and *Great Expectations* were well received, the latter being greeted (except by Mrs Oliphant, in a hostile review in *Blackwood's Magazine*, 91, May 1862) as a welcome return to the humour of the early works after the sourness of Dickens's tone since the mid-1840s, and so the attacks provoked by the 'Condition-of-England' novels, which had culminated in that on *Little Dorrit*, died down. In a general review of Dickens's career on the occasion of the Cheap Edition (1857–8), Walter BAGEHOT had outlined with some insight the origins of Dickens's 'sentimental radicalism' in an age of political repressiveness that now seemed foreign (*National Review*, October 1858). But in this last stage of Dickens's career the new literary criticism, which preferred to treat the novel as a serious art form and eschewed political topics, reverts to another version of the old criticism's complaint of 'lowness'. Dickens's portraiture was said to be too close to life and at the same time aesthetically lacking in realism. Specific instances of his drawing from recognizable public figures could be cited from *Oliver Twist* to *Little Dorrit*—Dickens even had to repair the damage done in *David Copperfield* and *Bleak House*, when a couple of the characters were too readily identified (see CHARACTERS—ORIGINALS). And yet, his depiction of the Victorian world did not meet the standards of the new realism found in ELIOT, GASKELL, and Thackeray. In the 1850s this criticism is best represented by David Masson's essay 'Dickens and Thackeray', first published in 1852 and reprinted well into the 20th century. Henry James's review of *Our Mutual Friend* (*Nation*, 21 December 1865) announced that Dickens's book had only 'figures not characters', and compared his late works unfavourably to his earlier ones in their 'humanity'. Both *Bleak House* and *Little Dorrit* had been 'forced', and *Our Mutual Friend* showed 'permanent exhaustion'.

Finally, in 1872 George Henry LEWES's essay on Dickens, 'Dickens in Relation to Criticism' (to which Forster felt compelled to reply in his biography), gives the argument that governed Dickens's posthumous reputation as it entered its late-19th-century decline: 'that there probably never was a writer of so vast a popularity whose genius was little *appreciated* by the critics . . . How are we to reconcile this immense popularity with this critical contempt?' Since then, it would appear that the worldwide popularity of Dickens for the last 150 years irresistibly suggests the irrelevance of professional criticism.   KC

Chittick (1990).

Rantavaara, Irma, *Dickens in the Light of English Criticism* (1944).

**Richardson, John** (1767?–1836), showman and fairground theatre manager. For several decades his show was, in Dickens's words, 'the very centre and heart of the FAIR'. Spectacle and action were the principal attractions of his brisk, formulaic melodramas, which offered a rapid sequence of sword fights, mad scenes, deaths, and invariably, a ghost. With lavish scenery and costuming, and high standards of production, his theatre booth packed in audiences of nearly a thousand for up to a dozen times a day during fair-time, and the showman, born in a workhouse, had amassed a fortune by the time of his death. Dickens mentions Richardson with delight in

'Greenwich Fair' (*SB*) and MEMOIRS OF GRIMALDI; the collection of dummy books in his library at Tavistock House included a twelve-volume set entitled *Richardson's Show of Dramatic Literature* (see HOMES OF DICKENS). He edited an obituary of Richardson by William Jerdan for BENTLEY'S MISCELLANY (1.178–86), and in the announcement appended to Part 10 of *The Pickwick Papers* he compared his role as 'Mr Pickwick's stage-manager' to that of 'the late eminent Mr John Richardson'.                                    PVWS

Schlicke, Paul, 'The Showman of *The Pickwick Papers*', *Dickens Studies Annual*, 20 (1991).

**Rogers, Samuel** (1763–1855), English poet, author of *The Pleasures of Memory* (1792) and the collection of verse tales, *Italy* (1822–8). He was friendly and supportive to a wide range of younger writers in the first half of the 19th century; Dickens first met him in 1839 and remained on good terms with him until his death. FORSTER records him leaving one of Dickens's dinner parties in (apparently) a state of some inebriation: 'I helped Rogers on with his over-shoes for his usual night-walk home. "Do you know how many waistcoats I wear?" asked the poet of me, as I was doing him this service. I professed my inability to guess. "Five," he said: "and here they are!" Upon which he opened them, in the manner of the grave-digger in *Hamlet*, and showed me every one' (Forster 6.6).

Dickens dedicated MASTER HUMPHREY'S CLOCK to Rogers; when *The Old Curiosity Shop* was published as a separate volume the dedication was printed with that book. Grandfather Smallweed, from *Bleak House*, is reputed to be a portrait of Rogers. In the Preface to *Barnaby Rudge* Dickens concedes that the image of the old man wandering in chapter 72 of *The Old Curiosity Shop* was taken from Rogers's verse ('Ginevra', in *Italy*): 'And long might'st thou have seen | An old man wandering *as in quest of something*, | Something he could not find—he knew not what' (Dickens's italics).                          AR

**Roman Catholic Church.** As much as Dickens disliked the enthusiasm of EVANGELICALS and DISSENTERS, his strongest religious antipathies were aroused by Roman Catholicism, and unfortunately he was by no means unusual among English Protestants in the strength of his prejudice. For whereas the age saw a gradual but steady decline in intolerant attitudes directed against dissenters and JEWS, there were notable Victorian outbreaks of anti-Roman Catholic feeling, especially occasioned by the Oxford Movement and the high drama of John Henry Newman's conversion in 1845, and the so-called 'Papal Aggression' scare of 1851, which was sparked by the decision of Rome to reinstate a Roman Catholic hierarchy in Great Britain. In these outbreaks Dickens was a spirited participant (see 'A Crisis in the Affairs of Mr John Bull', *HW* 23 November 1850; *Journalism* 2.297–305).

Although on good personal terms with many Catholics and sympathetic to individuals persecuted for their Catholicism (as, for example, in his treatment of the Gordon Riots of 1780 in *Barnaby Rudge*), Dickens was perfectly convinced that Roman Catholicism embodied the worst evils of the past, that it was the epitome of ignorance and superstition, slavish obedience to priestly authority, and unwholesome asceticism—as well, of course, as the whole gamut of cruelties represented by the Inquisition. Only a few months before his death, in a letter to John FORSTER, he referred to Roman Catholicism as 'that curse upon the world' (29 April 1870). The interpolated tale of 'The Five Sisters of York' in *Nicholas Nickleby* is an early and elaborate warning against the Catholic Church's gloomy, otherworldly call to take the veil (*NN* 6). The vanity, degradation, and cruelty of Catholicism are insistent themes in PICTURES FROM ITALY (1846), where Dickens's taste for the macabre is well satisfied by multitudes of relics and skeletons of saints dressed up in rich vestments and jewels. The Pope's celebration of High Mass strikes him as 'droll and tawdry' (*PI* 'Rome'). There are jibes at the Oxford Movement in *Bleak House*, and the evils of CHANCERY in that novel are often imagistically linked with Roman Catholicism. More outspoken is the account of the Reformation ('which set the people free from their slavery to the priests') in A CHILD'S HISTORY OF ENGLAND (1851–3). Without defending Henry VIII or the destruction of the monasteries as such (for 'the King's officers and men punished the good monks with the bad' and 'demolished many beautiful things and many valuable libraries' and otherwise 'did great injustice'), Dickens nonetheless believes 'that many of these religious establishments were religious in nothing but name, and were crammed with lazy, indolent, and sensual monks. There is no doubt that they imposed upon the people in every possible way; that they had images moved by wires, which they pretended were miraculously moved by Heaven; that they had among them a whole tun measure full of teeth, all purporting to have come out of the head of one saint, who must indeed have been a very extraordinary person with that enormous allowance of grinders . . . and that all these bits of rubbish were called Relics, and adored by the ignorant people' (*CHE* 27). This is strong language, and while one can find similarly strong views in the novels of Charles Kingsley and Charlotte BRONTË, for example—it exceeds Dickens's bigotry under other religious heads.

Passionate denunciations are often a sign of ambivalence, and Dickens's repulsions are frequently compounded with attractions. A strange dream experienced during his Italian journey in 1844 suggests this may have been the case here. In it, the spirit of his beloved Mary HOGARTH visits him, wearing 'a blue drapery, as the Madonna might in a picture by Raphael'. After begging for a sign that the visit is real, Dickens goes on to ask, 'What is the True religion? . . . You think, as I do, that the Form of religion does not so greatly matter, if we try to do good?—or . . . perhaps the Roman Catholic is the best?' To which Mary replies, 'for *you*, it is the best!' In recounting the dream to Forster, Dickens analyses the 'fragments of reality' that 'helped to make it up', but he later receives the sign he has asked for that the visitation was real (the extrication of his mother-in-law from distressing circumstances) and exclaims, 'I wonder whether I should regard it as a dream, or an actual Vision!' (Forster 4.5). Dickens certainly never after this wandered Romeward, nor wavered in his detestation of Roman Catholicism, but the dream surely hints at a much more complicated religious character than the explicit expressions of distaste denote.          RN

## Royal General Theatrical Fund.

Founded in 1839 to assist everyone connected with the stage by extending aid beyond that given to Covent Garden and Drury Lane performers, the General Theatrical Fund was warmly supported by Dickens. He was one of its original trustees and a regular speaker at its

dinners. It was after his speech in 1851 that FORSTER told him of the death of his infant daughter, Dora. In 1858, after a period when their relations had been notably cool, he proposed THACKERAY's health in such warm terms that his fellow novelist was almost too moved to reply. Dickens would have spoken at the 1870 dinner but was too ill to attend.

ASW

**Royal Literary Fund.** Founded in 1790 as the Literary Fund to give financial aid to distressed authors, their widows and orphans, it was incorporated in 1818 and accorded royal title in 1842 by Queen Victoria. Dickens became a member in 1837, made his first public speech at the Fund's 1837 dinner, and became a member of Council in 1838. Later he became highly critical, believing the Fund to be dominated by aristocrats and men of wealth who diverted its money to pay for lavish entertainments, administration, and upkeep of offices. He resigned from the Council in 1854, and in 1858, with the help of FORSTER and C. W. Dilke, wrote a pamphlet, *The Case of the Reformers in the Literary Fund*, in an unsuccessful attempt to rectify the situation and revise the Fund's charter.          ASW

**royalty.** As in so much else concerning POLITICS, Dickens's views on royalty were ambivalent, although he was certainly more comfortable with a constitutional monarch such as Victoria than with previous monarchs who had exercised real power. *A CHILD'S HISTORY OF ENGLAND* maintains a generally robust anti-royalist and 'popular' stance. The people of France in the 1780s were justifiably 'maddened' by the heartless government of Louis XVI. His behaviour, however, was no worse than the 'atrocities' of Judge Jeffreys in the Bloody Assize of 1685, undertaken with 'the express approval of the . . . detestable . . . King of England', James II (*CHE* 36). The atrocities 'form the blackest and most lamentable page in English history'. Similarly, he denies that Charles I was 'a martyr of the people', 'for the people had been martyrs to him, and to his ideas of a King's rights, long before' (*CHE* 33). He found the Stuarts a particularly loathsome dynasty: 'a public nuisance altogether' (*CHE* 37), who continued to make mischief down to the last Jacobite rising of 1745–6. Interestingly, his characterization of Henry VIII as 'one of the most detestable villains that ever drew breath' (*CHE* 27) is close to, if racily blunter than, recent reassessments of the King. He did not accept the predominantly Whiggish Victorian view that Henry was an agent of progress responsible for bringing Protestantism to England.

*Bleak House* satirizes the Prince Regent, later George IV, who had just assumed the regency on account of his father's mental instability at the time of Dickens's birth. Old Turveydrop christens his son 'Prince', in remembrance of the Prince Regent, whom he adores on account of his 'Deportment'. Old Turveydrop 'don't teach anything in particular . . . But his Deportment is beautiful'—a thinly veiled reference to the Regent and Dickens's dislike for an empty creature who maintained only an outward show of regality (*BH* 14).

Of William IV, who succeeded George IV in 1830, Dickens has little to say although he was close to the consequences of the last publicly independent exercise of royal power in November 1834 when William used the royal prerogative to dismiss Melbourne's government and install a Tory administration in its stead (see REFORM). Dickens extensively reported the general election campaign of late 1834 and early 1835 for the MORNING CHRONICLE and produced a lampoon of the dismissal for that paper on 18 December, 'The Story without a Beginning' (*Journalism* 2.10–13).

Dickens's general scepticism, shading in particular cases into virulent hostility of monarchs and monarchy, did not extend to Queen Victoria, who came to the throne in 1837. The last words of the *Child's History* provide an appropriate text: 'She is very good, and much beloved. So I end, like the crier, with GOD SAVE THE QUEEN!' The Queen, of course, exercised little direct power, and this was significant. She was not responsible for the enormities of GOVERNMENT. Dickens made frequent mention of the Queen's benefactions to good causes, most notably 'her usual annual donation of one hundred pounds' to the ROYAL GENERAL THEATRICAL FUND and donations to the Artists' Benevolent Fund. Acknowledging the Queen's donation to the latter in 1858, he stated that he wished to invoke 'a blessing' on her as one of her 'loyal and devoted subjects' (*Speeches*, pp. 119, 265).

Dickens's admiration for Victoria began early. He seems to have been genuinely beguiled by the glamour associated with the marriage of the 20-year-old Queen to Prince Albert in February 1840 and wrote a number of exuberant letters to friends at the time feigning undying devotion to her. 'Society is unhinged here, by her majesty's marriage, and I am sorry to add that I have fallen hopelessly in love with the Queen, and wander up and down with vague and dismal thoughts of running away to some uninhabited island with a maid of honor . . .' (to Walter Savage Landor, 11 February 1840). When the unhinged youth Edward Fox tried to kill the royal couple as they drove up Constitution Hill in June 1840, Dickens railed: 'It's a great pity they couldn't suffocate that boy . . . and say no more about it.' He was concerned that the publicity would encourage others, 'some of whom may perchance be better shots and use other than Brummagem firearms' (to Forster, ?12 June 1840).

In July 1857, with a group of amateur players, Dickens presented a private performance of Wilkie COLLINS's The FROZEN DEEP for the Queen at the Gallery of Illustration. The Queen noted in her *Journal* that 'The Play was admirably acted by Charles Dickens (whose representation of Richard Wardour was beyond all praise and not to be surpassed)'. She asked to see Dickens after the performance, but he felt himself obliged to decline the invitation because, as he told John FORSTER, he was still in 'Farce dress' and hoped that 'her Majesty would have the kindness to excuse my presenting myself in a costume and appearance that were not my own' (5 and 6 July 1857; Pilgrim 8.366 n.). In fact, Dickens and Victoria met only once, three months before his death, on 9 March 1870. The Queen found him 'very agreeable, with a pleasant voice and manner'. Their conversation encompassed the state of English society. The Queen noted that he 'talked of the division of CLASSES in England which he hoped would get better in time. He felt sure that it would come gradually' (*Letters of Queen Victoria*, 2nd ser., 1926, 2.9). When he died, she noted in her journal: 'He is a very great loss. He had a large, loving mind and the strongest sympathy with the poorer classes' (ibid. 2.26).

Dickens's admiration for Prince Albert was less. He acknowledged his interest in, and support for, the arts and sciences but his politics were suspect. In a letter to MACREADY on 4 October 1855 he made a veiled allusion to the Prince's alleged sympathy for the Prussians and even the Russians during the CRIMEAN WAR: 'making asses of ourselves for Prince Albert to saddle.' On his death in December 1861, Dickens wrote that the Prince was 'neither a phenomenon, nor the saviour of England; and England will do exactly the same without him as it did with him. He was a good example of the best sort of perfectly commonplace man' (to Cerjat, 16 March 1862).                                                    EJE

**Ruskin, John** (1819–1900), art and social critic, seems never to have met Dickens (who is recorded as having read his *Seven Lamps of Architecture* but nothing else), but he was a warm if incomplete admirer, finding in the novels one of his life's 'chief comforts and restoratives' and often praising their spirit and wisdom: 'No one has a deeper respect for the genius, and the practical goodness, and limitless good service of Mr Dickens' (letter, 30 October 1867). 'He is entirely right in the main drift and purpose in every book he has written; and all of them, but especially *Hard Times* ['in several respects the greatest he has written'], should be studied with close and earnest care by persons interested in social questions' (*Unto this Last*, 1860). The storm in *Copperfield* was 'incomparable'. But he could be exasperated. Little Nell 'was simply killed for the market', and the mortality rate in *Bleak House* was inexcusably sensational in a story not 'tragic, adventurous, or military' ('Fiction, Fair and Foul', 1880). Dickens was 'a thorough Cockney', who should stick to urban life. Nor had he any 'understanding of any power of antiquity'. He was 'a pure modernist—a leader of the steam-whistle party *par excellence* . . . his hero is essentially the ironmaster'.                                          PC

**Russell, Lord John** (1792–1878), British statesman and twice (1846–52 and 1865–6) Prime Minister. Russell was a leading member of the Whig/ Liberal hierarchy for almost 40 years. He was particularly associated with two policies, POLITICAL and EDUCATIONAL reform, which appealed to Dickens. He was one of the staunchest Whig supporters of parliamentary REFORM, having first introduced a Bill in unpropitious circumstances in 1822, and he led for the government in the Commons when the Reform Bill was first presented in March 1831. In 1836 he became a leading figure in the new Central Society of Education and, in 1839, Vice-Principal of the newly established Committee of the Privy Council on Education which introduced school inspections. Dickens encountered him first in the early 1830s as a reporter on the *MORNING CHRONICLE*, when he took notes of one of his speeches in pouring rain (Pilgrim 1.58 n.; *Speeches*, p. 347). He wrote papers for Russell on educational subjects, notably Ragged Schools (to Forster, ?28 June 1846; see CHARITY), and became a frequent dinner guest, freely speaking his mind about such subjects as the government's incompetent war policy in the CRIMEA (to Wilkie Collins, 7 July 1855). Russell was one of very few contemporary politicians whom Dickens admired. The relationship was enhanced by the considerable rivalry between Russell and Palmerston, whom Dickens detested. *A Tale of Two Cities* is dedicated to Russell.             EJE

**Russia.** The 'certain barbaric power' in *Little Dorrit*, begun during the CRIMEAN WAR, during which Dickens's sympathies were divided between anguish about bungling and red tape on the British side and anger against Russian aggression—'Russia *must* be stopped', he wrote on 3 January 1855, confessing to 'burning desires to cut the Emperor of Russia's throat' (1 November 1854). Yet, unlike 'civilized' Great Britain, Russia appreciated Doyce (*LD*), and certainly counts as one of the 'significant others' of Dickens's imagination, belonging with other geographical extremities like Swiss peaks, the Arctic, or AUSTRALIA. Childhood is again decisive. SWITZERLAND in 'Travelling Abroad' (*UT*) awakens 'associations long forgotten . . . I dreamed I was in Russia—the identical serf out of a picture-book I had . . . going to be knouted by a noble personage in a fur cap'. After Vvedensky (who TRANSLATED *Dombey and Son*) wrote in 1849 describing his great fame in Russia, where, from Gogol to Tolstoy and DOSTOEVSKY, he was widely revered, Dickens would periodically joke about fleeing British philistinism and emigrating to Siberia.             MH

# S

**sabbatarianism** in Christianity is the doctrine of the strict observance of Sunday as a holy day reserved for worship, vigorously attacked by Dickens throughout his career—most systematically in the pamphlet SUNDAY UNDER THREE HEADS: *As It Is; as Sabbath Bills Would Make It; As It Might Be Made* (1836; see also 'The Sunday Screw', *HW* 22 June 1850; rptd. *MP* and *Journalism* 2.249–57). Several Bills that would limit Sunday recreation beyond the harsh restrictions already in effect were proposed during Dickens's lifetime, and although none of these was successful, they served as a focal point for much controversy among Victorian Christian sects and reformers (see AMUSEMENTS).

Following Mosaic law, Judaism regards Saturday, the seventh day of the week, as a day of rest in remembrance of the Lord's resting on the seventh day of creation (see JEWS). Jesus, upbraided by the Pharisees for plucking corn on the Sabbath, replied 'The sabbath was made for Man, and not man for the sabbath' (Luke 2: 27, quoted both in *Sunday Under Three Heads* and 'The Sunday Screw'). Christians generally observe Sunday, the day of Christ's Resurrection, as the Sabbath. ROMAN CATHOLICS treat the Sabbath as a feast day, but the Protestant reaction (especially in its more EVANGELICAL varieties) often returned to a conception of the Sabbath that resembles Judaism's proscription of any activity that is not devotional.

Observance of the Sabbath became for many in the 19th century a crucial test of piety, a definitive demonstration of one's position on dogma, and a most public manifestation of religious identity. It seemed the lone defence against a tide of secularism eroding divine authority. But because Sunday was the only day free from work for most of the working class, policies regulating activities available to those at the bottom of the social pyramid also pointedly raised the question of CLASS. Restricting the behaviour of the working class on Sundays to worship was a powerful instrument of social control at a time when the upper and middle classes were extremely anxious about uprisings among the poor. It is difficult today to imagine how passionately people on all sides of the controversy felt, but the sabbatarian debate aroused as much public attention, occasioned the founding of as many organizations and leagues, and proved in general as troubling as such issues as abortion and gay rights have today.

Dickens was usually ambivalent about divisive social issues, and could appear, like his mentor Thomas CARLYLE, alternately profoundly radical and conservative; but his attitude towards sabbatarianism was one of unambiguous and profound detestation—so much so that he could quite uncharacteristically and wholeheartedly support the Hyde Park disturbances of 1855, during which an unruly crowd of many thousand working-class people menaced aristocrats displaying themselves in their carriages of a Sunday afternoon (to Miss Coutts, 27 June 1855). When during subsequent Sunday protests the crowds became much larger and more violent, the police responded brutally and Dickens again defended the protesters (to John Leech, 4 July 1855).

Sabbatarianism so strongly aroused Dickens's anger because it brought to a focus issues about which he was extremely sensitive. As a matter of RELIGION, it embodied for him the most harmful kind of resort to the letter of the law, and the law least attractive to him at that—Old Testament law. He hated doctrinal disputes of any kind as tending to absorb in idle speculation energies that would better be put into doing practical good, and this dispute in his eyes did nothing but harm—especially harm against those without the means to amuse themselves, unlike the rich who could join the Sunday parade of carriages in Hyde Park or be waited on in fashionable private clubs, while public inns and taverns were closed or their hours severely curtailed. Especially hypocritical in Dickens's eyes were the various provisions of the Sabbath Bills that exempted SERVANTS from enforced rest, thus assuring that the wealthy would continue to have their Sunday dinners cooked for them, while the poor who depended on bake shops for roasting their meat and fowl would have to make do with cold provisions.

Equally harmful among existing restrictions was the fact that even such manifestly improving institutions as the British Museum and the Crystal Palace were closed on the one day of the week when workers might visit them. But while Dickens was very active in his support of movements to open the museums and galleries on Sundays, it was concern for what he calls, in the dedication to *Sunday Under Three Heads*, 'the comforts and pleasures of the humbler classes of society' that most aroused him. The right of the poor to their pleasures on their one holiday is therefore the constant theme of this early work, and its satirical targets are those who would deny those pleasures out of a bullying inspired by either class or religious feeling. Nowhere is Dickens's ridicule of organized religion so pointed as in the twin portraits he offers here of worship in a fashionable church, on the one hand, rife with complacency and hypocrisy, and worship in a DISSENTING chapel on the other, rife with 'enthusiasm amounting almost to frenzy' (*Sunday Under Three Heads*). Perhaps regretting its outspokenness, Dickens never included *Sunday Under Three Heads* among his works reprinted or collected in any edition in his lifetime.

Although dissenters were strict observers of the Sabbath, in fact it was Anglican evangelicals who provided most of the political impetus behind Sabbath Bills (like Lord Ashley, Dickens's particular target in 'The Sunday Screw'; see CHURCH OF ENGLAND). Nevertheless, Dickens particularly associated the dreariness of Sundays with the kind of low-church Calvinism practiced by Arthur Clennam's mother in *Little Dorrit*, and his most eloquent writing about the misery of Sunday occurs in the chapter of that novel called 'Home', where sabbatarianism and the repressive religion of Mrs Clennam are thoroughly intertwined and representative of the emotional blight of the age. 'Heaven forgive me,' Arthur says to himself of Sunday, 'and those who trained me. How I have hated this day!' (1.3).                                                     RN

Pope (1978).

**Sala, George Augustus Henry** (1828–95), 'the most active and successful journalist of the Victorian era' (*Saturday Review*, 16 February 1895), was pre-eminent among 'Mr Dickens's young men' on *Household Words*, the one in whom Dickens felt the strongest personal interest, says FORSTER. Sala had seen Dickens when a boy (his mother performed in Dickens's stage-pieces, 1836–7) and in 1843 when, for her sake, Dickens tried to help Sala embark as a draughtsman, but their association began in 1851 when Sala, trading on this family connection, sent him 'The Key of the Street', an essay about a night spent locked out from his lodgings. Within four hours Sala received an acceptance and banknote, and Dickens, describing the essay to his sub-editor W. H. WILLS as 'a very remarkable piece of description ... exceedingly superior to the usual run of such writing', urged that 'There is nobody about us whom we can use, in his way, more advantageously than this young man' (13 August, 27 September 1851). This was 'the turning-point of my career', Sala recalled: he abandoned engraving for journalism, which he would never have done without Dickens's encouragement. He was also befriended, encouraged, and later employed by THACKERAY, who regarded 'The Key' as 'almost the best magazine paper that ever was written' and Sala as 'a man of curious talents certainly— perhaps a genius' (letter, 22 September 1855).

For six years Sala contributed almost weekly to *Household Words*, living on its £5 payments (generally needed in advance) and averaging four hours' work a week. Dickens found him in PARIS, 'living very queerly ... not doing himself much good ... [with] a strong flavour of the wineshop and the billiard table' (10 January 1856), but he remained uncommonly patient and generous until 1857 when Sala's laxity and financial demands caused a temporary exile from Dickens's columns and company. Sala later acknowledged that he was in the wrong and had been inexcusably idle and dissolute. He turned to the *Daily Telegraph*, with which he became prominently associated, though he wrote for many other periodicals (and returned to Dickens's) and produced over 40 books, many of several volumes.

'I am of the streets, and streety', wrote Sala who cultivated Dickens territory and aped his style—out-Dickensing Dickens in his 'affected, overstrained, laborious *badinage*', 'insufferably inflated and spasmodic' style of 'would-be jocular wordspinning' (*Saturday Review*, 11 September 1858). Matthew Arnold pilloried him as a 'rowdy Philistine'. Sala wrote about Dickens affectionately, shrewdly, and entertainingly in his *Charles Dickens* (1870) and memoirs (1894, 1895).       PC

**science.** It has been said that Dickens was 'indifferent or hostile to the scientific developments of his age' and that his novels show hardly a trace of the 'new theories that revolutionized man's view of himself and his universe in the nineteenth century' (G. S. Haight, 'Dickens and Lewes on Spontaneous Combustion', *Nineteenth-Century Fiction*, 11, 1955). It is a view that has come to be sharply challenged, and which now needs to be decided by the evidence.

In the MUDFOG PAPERS (1837–8), Dickens satirizes the absurdities of the influential British Association for the Advancement of Science. We have to wait until 9 December 1848 for his first and only direct piece of writing on the subject in 'The Poetry of Science', a review of Robert Hunt's book of the same title which appeared in the EXAMINER, and shows Dickens as a committed evolutionist. He strongly supported Robert Chambers's anonymous and Lamarckian *Vestiges of the Natural History of Creation* (1844), and showed himself an enthusiast for science in general. His imagination is stirred by geology; science, he wrote, has found in the rocks 'and read aloud the great stone book which is the history of the earth, even when darkness sat upon the face of the deep. Along their craggy sides she has traced the footprints of birds and beasts whose shapes were never seen by man.' Yet, in spite of the title, both Hunt and Dickens were practical; Hunt himself seems to have gone over to evolution soon after; and there is an excitement in their approach to nature which, with Dickens, led on to the preliminary address for *Household Words* and its promise to tell of the 'mightier inventions' of the time.

Dickens has been well known as being of 'the steam-whistle party' (in RUSKIN's phrase), and celebrating technology, its railways, factories, and INDUSTRIAL power, which helped bring him his new public. Yet he was also responding to the spirit of change himself. His library shows him acquiring the works of Cuvier and Buffon, books that tried to reconcile science and religion such as the *Bridgewater Treatises*, and apparently quick to buy Darwin's *Origin of Species* (1859), just as he was to have it noticed in *All the Year Round* three times within the first twelve months of its publication. As he emphasized in his review of 'The Poetry of Science', he admired liberty of thought and freedom of speculation. *Household Words* was receptive to the methods and discoveries of science; and so far as it reveals Dickens as an editor rather than a writer, he was right to claim that he made it imaginative, finding new metaphorical meanings in the natural world. *All the Year Round* remains to be investigated, and is less speculative; each periodical needs to be looked at as a whole rather than searched for special clues.

Even so, it is possible to go too far in claiming that some of the later novels 'reflect the leading scientific preoccupations of his time' (Ackroyd 1990, p. 663), including the second law of thermodynamics, the 'creation of entropy', and fields of force, as in Ann Y. Wilkinson's brilliant but unreliable 'Bleak House: From Faraday to Judgement Day', *English Literary History*, 34 (1967). For while Dickens had use made of Faraday's lecture-notes on 'The Chemistry of a Candle' in *Household Words* and, as she shows, was probably influenced by it in what he wrote about spontaneous combustion, there is no evidence to support the belief that Dickens knew about Faraday's other hard-won discoveries or the second law. Nor is it reasonable to see him as 'intuitively' anticipating what 'entropy' was in the sense of the term as introduced in the late 1860s. Apart from the lecture-notes on the candle, there is nothing to link him with such advanced discoveries, and even now— emphatically as such claims may be made— the 'evidence' lies only in seeing it somehow expressed in the 'form' of the novels. Even the 'death of the sun' allusions (*BH* 1 *et seq.*) do not involve the second law, as is sometimes suggested: and, to return to evolution, for all we know, Dickens's beliefs in the 1860s may have been closer to the anti-Darwinian Sir Richard Owen, whom he respected, than to Darwin.

Dickens was a man of his time, anxious to keep a place for the divine prescience in creation, whether shown in his sketch of *The HAUNTED MAN*, or in his telling his old friend William De Cerjat that 'it is contended that the science of geology is quite as much a revelation to man as books of immense age and of (at the best) doubtful origin and that your consideration of the latter must reasonably be influenced by the former' (21 May 1863). He repeated this in his speech at Birmingham in 1869 (*Speeches*, pp. 403–4), holding an equal balance between churchman and Huxleyan scientist. He argued through his JOURNALISM for the understanding of new discoveries, and the novels are informed by the same general view, yet there is nothing to show that they engage with science more closely than this: it is not their function: they are about humanity.                                                            KJF

Levine, George, *Darwin and the Novelists, Patterns of Science in Victorian Fiction* (1988).

Metz, Nancy A., 'Science in *Household Words*: "The Poetic . . . Passed Into Our Common Life" ', *Victorian Periodicals Newsletter*, 11 (1978).

**Scotland.** Dickens visited Edinburgh in September 1834 with Thomas Beard to report for the MORNING CHRONICLE on a banquet given to Lord Grey. That was his only direct experience of Scotland before he composed the only work he was to set there, chapter 49 of *Pickwick Papers*, 'Containing the Story of the Bagman's Uncle'. This amusing melodramatic tale of drunk-dreaming exhibits a considerable grasp of the topography and nocturnal atmosphere of the old part of Edinburgh, from the Canongate to Leith Walk. But on the whole Scotland was important to Dickens for the literary and popular receptions it offered him, rather than any literary inspiration. In all he visited Scotland twelve times, but by far the most important of these visits was in June and July 1841, when Dickens, still only 29, was received by Scotland's capital and its *literati* with unprecedented enthusiasm: FORSTER calls this 'his first practical experience of the honours his fame had won for him' (1.10).

On 25 June a public dinner was held in Dickens's honour, with Professor John WILSON ('Christopher North') in the chair, as Dickens's friend Lord JEFFREY was ill. Dickens described to Forster (26 June) 'the most brilliant affair you can conceive; the completest success possible, from first to last'. There were more than 250 gentlemen present, and nearly 200 ladies were admitted to the gallery to hear the speeches. He was fêted everywhere he went for ten days, dining and staying at the most exclusive houses, with foremost critics, academics, artists, and lawyers. On 30 June he writes that he has been 'voted . . . by acclamation the freedom of the city'. This was a rare honour, and his 'Burgess Ticket', the inscribed roll he was presented with, hung till his death in his Gad's Hill Place study (see HOMES OF DICKENS). This rapturous reception in 'the Athens of the North' was a source of intense pleasure for the young man, honoured so markedly by his distinguished seniors. When he went 'incognito' to the Adelphi Theatre on 3 July, the orchestra improvised 'Charley is my darling' on his entrance.

Dickens was proud of his wife's Scottish connections: she was born in Edinburgh and on this occasion visited the house where she was born (see DICKENS, CATHERINE). Her grandfather, George Thomson (1757–1851), was a prominent editor of Scottish songbooks, and her father, George HOGARTH, born in Edinburgh in 1783, was an intimate of SCOTT, LOCKHART, and other noted men of letters before he moved to London in 1831, after which he and Dickens were closely associated for many years in journalistic and literary work.

Immediately after the triumphant visit to Edinburgh, in July 1841 Dickens and his wife undertook their only relatively leisurely Scottish holiday in the Highlands, travelling to Lochearnhead, Killin and Ballachulish, and Inveraray, travelling through Glencoe, the scenery of which, combined with its dark history, had an unforgettable impact on Dickens. He found the place 'perfectly *terrible*' (9 July). The following day they had to retrace their steps through Glencoe because of appalling weather, and the writer was even more eloquent on the wilderness and dangers of the scene: 'perfectly horrific.' But typically he went on in his letter to Forster to make 'a good adventure' out of it, with a 'wild highlander in a great plaid . . . screeching Gaelic', and at the inn, 'fifty highlanders *all drunk*' (11 July 1841). The following year in AMERICA he found the dramatic journey from Harrisburgh to Pittsburgh 'immeasurably inferior to Glencoe, to whose terrors I have not seen the smallest *approach*' (28 March 1842).

The next journey north was in December 1847, when he was 'sorry to report the Scott Monument a failure'. This was a less happy visit, on the whole. Catherine had a miscarriage on the train between Edinburgh and Glasgow, and in Glasgow she was treated by Professor James Simpson, from whom Dickens learned about the use of chloroform, which would be used in her later pregnancies. Meanwhile, Dickens was shown Glasgow Royal Lunatic Asylum (see MADNESS) and a PRISON, 'a truly damnable gaol' (30 December).

The following summer Edinburgh and Glasgow were among the venues where Dickens's amateur players successfully performed *The Merry Wives of Windsor* (see AMATEUR THEATRICALS). But the first professional PUBLIC READING tour of 1858 was another outstanding triumph. He made record profits, and read to packed houses in Edinburgh, Dundee, Aberdeen, and Perth, and in Glasgow, where the audience got up 'and thundered and waved their hats with such astonishing heartiness and fondness that, for the first time in all my public career, they took me completely off my legs' (9 October 1858).

Dickens revisited Scotland for more readings in November and December 1861: in Glasgow, 'blazes of triumph' when an oversale of tickets precipitated a dangerously full house, with the platform crammed with people: 'I got them to lie down upon it, and it was like some impossible tableau or gigantic picture—one pretty girl in full dress, lying on her side all night, holding on to one of the legs of my table!' (3 December 1861). Apparently undeterred by the rigours of travel as well as the exertions of the readings, he was in Glasgow and Edinburgh on 16–21 April 1866, and in Aberdeen, Glasgow, and Edinburgh a month later, and Glasgow and Edinburgh in February 1867 and December 1868. Despite a brief postponement because of inflammation of the foot he was back again in three days, travelling back and forth from Edinburgh to Glasgow like a metronome.

The Post-Enlightenment Scottish intelligentsia markedly honoured the young Dickens, and the popular audiences for his later readings were gratifyingly large in all the cities. Glencoe for Dickens was sublime and unforgettable, and unforgettable too was the appalling poverty of city slums. One haunting memory was the subject of a passionate speech in February 1858 in support of the children's hospital in Great Ormond Street, London. In a desperate Edinburgh slum Dickens had found a quiet, dying child whose mother said he seldom complained: ' "he lay there, seeming to wonder what it was a' aboot". God knows, I thought . . . he had his reasons for wonder' (*Speeches*, pp. 250–1). This Scottish memory helped to raise £3,000 for the hospital on that night alone.                 IM

**Scott, Sir Walter** (1771–1832), poet and novelist, an important influence on Dickens's early career (1836–42). Scott represented the possibilities of novel-writing as a profession as well as the modern technical repertoire of novelistic discourse. An international celebrity at the time of his death (only four years before the first appearance of *Pickwick Papers*), Scott had raised the novel to the dignity of a national form, and in so doing acquired unprecedented wealth and status. Dickens was acutely aware of this achievement as a model for emulation and rivalry in the formation of his own career, as he turned from the journalistic sketch to extended fiction. Dickens thought it no small part of the prestige of George HOGARTH, his editor at the EVENING CHRONICLE, that he had been 'the most intimate friend and companion of Sir Walter Scott', as he would boast (with slight exaggeration, 31 March 1836) on his engagement to Hogarth's daughter.

Dickens read John Gibson LOCKHART'S *Memoirs of the Life of Sir Walter Scott, Bart.* (1837–8) in the flush of his own early triumph, and the story of the precarious financial arrangements behind the success of the Waverley novels, issuing in the ruin of Scott and his publishers, made a powerful impression. Dickens recurred frequently to the topic over the next few years, a period marked by his own struggles in the market-place. He intervened in the public controversy over Lockhart's account of Scott's ruin, writing a series of anonymous articles for the EXAMINER ('Scott and his Publishers': 2 September 1838; 31 March 1839; 29 September 1839) that vehemently affirmed the novelist's right to fame and fortune. On a visit to SCOTLAND in 1841 Dickens was fêted as Scott's successor. But by now admiration for Scott's achievement had given way to an obsession with his downfall, which culminated in Dickens's use of Scott to berate audiences in the international COPY-RIGHT dispute that vexed his AMERICAN tour in 1842. Scott's ruin encouraged Dickens to promote his own public visibility as a professional author in the market-place, striving to maximize legal and economic control over his work, in contrast to the genteel anonymity that had come to signify the Author of Waverley's failure to cope with the commercial realities of literary production.

Scott's name does not appear on the famous childhood reading list in *David Copperfield*. Dickens most likely read the Waverley novels in London in the early 1830s, the period of his self-education and literary apprenticeship. He learnt from Scott the narrative techniques of a mixed representation of a complex social universe, involving a polyphonic interplay of multiple styles, genres, and plots, a combination of the devices of realism with MELODRAMA and romance conventions, and vivid renditions of popular speech. Imitation of Scott's example framed the first stage of Dickens's career. At first he intended to write a HISTORICAL NOVEL ('Gabriel Vardon, the Locksmith of London', contracted in May 1836 but planned earlier) in the three-volume format made prestigious by Scott. Over the next four years, however, Dickens's own success transformed SERIAL PUBLICATION into a respectable medium for novels, and *Barnaby Rudge* appeared in weekly parts (1841). *Barnaby Rudge* emerges from the Scott-like antiquarian and tale-telling machinery of MASTER HUMPHREY'S CLOCK to reproduce many of the forms, topics, and character-types of Scott's historical romance. It draws variously on *Waverley* (the idiot Barnaby), *The Heart of Mid-Lothian* (the storming of the prison by rioters), *Kenilworth* (the opening scene in the inn, the weak lord manipulated by parasites), *Peveril of the Peak* (the Popish plot), and *The Fair Maid of Perth* (the triangle of strong master, fair daughter, and resentful apprentice). However, *Barnaby Rudge* rejects the Scott novel's ethical and political content of a resigned subjection to legality and historical process. The specificity of Dickens's imitation—in particular, of the analogy between civil disturbance and a conflict between fathers and sons—carries a defiance of the senior novelist's cultural authority. Later novels, from *Dombey and Son*

onwards, show Dickens's creative absorption of Scott's romance techniques rather than his historicism. In particular, despite the radical differences of culture and temperament between the two authors, Dickens's thematic focus on the redemptive or transformative energies of romance, often personified in a virtuous daughter, owes much to Scott novels like *Guy Mannering* and *The Heart of Mid-Lothian*.                                    IHD

Chittick (1990).

Duncan, Ian, *Modern Romance and Transformations of the Novel: The Gothic, Scott, Dickens* (1992).

Wilt, Judith, *Secret Leaves: The Novels of Walter Scott* (1985).

**self-help** was a crucial concept for Dickens. Widely associated in late-20th-century minds conditioned by a decade of Thatcherism and Reaganomics with greed, financial sharp practice, and selfishness, Dickens saw self-help differently. In this he was in line with his age. Samuel Smiles's famous tract *Self Help* (1859) preached hard work, thrift, and self-improvement as a way of life in which material advancement and moral enrichment went hand in hand. Although connotations of 'self-help' today are largely material, the Victorian perspective saw them much more in terms of character. Accordingly, it is never enough in Dickens's novels simply to help oneself, as do, for instance, Uriah Heep (*DC*) and Josiah Bounderby (*HT*); the approved road involves helping both oneself and others, out of a sense of social commitment allied to self-worth.

This theme runs strongly through novels, letters, and speeches alike. Though born into an apparently secure middle-class family, Dickens knew the need to raise himself by his own efforts after his loveable but feckless father, John DICKENS, squandered the family's domestic security and was imprisoned for debt in the Marshalsea prison when Dickens was 12 years old.

Dickens's belief in self-help as the route to progress and prosperity mirrored dominant Victorian perceptions. Smiles's *Self Help* was one of Victorian Britain's biggest best-sellers, having sold more than 250,000 copies by the time of its author's death in 1904. It owed its success not to the novelty of its ideas but to the prevailing temper of the times. Looked at in an unfavourable light, *Self-Help* is little more than a series of well-written rags-to-riches stories stitched together with crass homilies. An age of opportunity, expansion, and national pre-eminence found it comfortable to believe not only that hard work, honesty, and the right values were necessary for independence and self-fulfilment if not material success, but also that an absence of these attributes was evidence of that turpitude which rendered the subject an inappropriate beneficiary of CHARITY. As ever, Smiles had the moral ready to hand: 'National progress is the sum of individual industry, energy, and uprightness, as national decay is of individual idleness, selfishness and vice.'

Dickens was himself a spectacular exemplar of self-help. He used his acute powers of observation and literary skills to make his way as a political reporter in the early 1830s. He believed that material success was only a by-product of self-help, a message he conveyed regularly in his speeches to those quintessential agencies of self-improvement, the specialist libraries, clubs, and mechanics' institutes. When he addressed the first annual soirée of the Manchester Athenaeum in May 1843, he praised improvement through knowledge: 'The man who lives from day to day by the daily exercise in his sphere of hand or head, and seeks to improve himself in such a place as the Athenaeum, acquires for himself that property of soul which has in all times upheld struggling men in every degree, but self-made men especially and always . . . The more a man who improves his leisure in such a place learns, the better, gentler, kinder man he must become' (*Speeches*, pp. 48–9).

This improvement was related to another of his great themes: mutual harmony in society and respect between employers and employees. He had a special message for students in the 'industrial classes' at the Birmingham and Midland Institute when he addressed its inaugural meeting on 27 September 1869: 'Courage, Persevere . . . This is the motto of a friend and worker. Not because the eyes of Europe are upon them, for I don't in the least believe it . . . not because self-improvement is at all certain to lead to worldly success, but because it is good and right of itself; and because, being so, it does assuredly bring with it, its own resources and its own rewards' (*Speeches*, p. 405). TROLLOPE referred to self-

help as its own reward when, in an encomium published at Dickens's death, he noted that the novelist had refused all honours: 'He had a noble confidence in himself which made him feel that nothing Queen, Parliament or Minister could do for him would make him greater than he was' (*St Paul's Magazine*, July 1870).

Dickens believed that Mechanics' Institutes and other EDUCATIONAL organizations were ideal vehicles for self-improvement. He wrote a congratulatory letter to Lyon Playfair for advocating more SCIENCE-teaching there, but he also expressed worries. Too many institutes had 'fallen into the accursed habit of looking round for external patronage—of abandoning the self-reliance which should be a main part herein with his Employer, to the enduring advantage and improvement of both' (20 December 1853).

He supported EMIGRATION schemes, since those who emigrated had already given sufficient indication of their improving qualities: 'It is unquestionably melancholy that thousands upon thousands of people, ready and willing to labour, should be wearing away life hopelessly in this island, while within a few months' sail . . . there are vast tracts of country where no man who is willing to work hard (but that he must be, or he had best not go there) can ever know want . . . Nor is it to be contested—either that where it is possible for the poor, by great self-denial, to scrape together a portion of the means of going abroad, it is extremely important to encourage them to do so, in practical illustration of the wholesome precept that Heaven helps those who help themselves; or that they who do so help themselves, give a proof of their fitness for emigration . . . and establish a strong claim on legitimate sympathy and benevolence, to do the rest.' He urged charitable support to those who had given earnests of their intention to improve themselves by emigration, going 'from places where they are not wanted, and are miserable, to places where they are wanted, and can be happy and independent' ('A Bundle of Emigrants' Letters', *HW* 30 March 1850).

The theme of self-help through education runs through the novels. Pip, the eager blacksmith's boy, has a 'hunger for information' and a determination to make his way in the world. His alter ego is the morose, non-improving Orlick, who spends his precious Sunday leisure time lying 'all day on sluice-gates, or stood against ricks and barns. He always slouched, locomotively, with his eyes on the ground' (*GE* 15). As Robin Gilmour (1973) has pointed out, the improving heroes of the early novels 'get on', 'not so much to achieve status as to recover it ... to reassert a lost inheritance'. The reference to Dickens's own 'lost inheritance' is clear enough. The possible conflict is ironically presented by Newman Noggs: 'as to getting on in the world, if you take everybody's part that's ill-treated—Damn it, I am pleased to hear of it, and would have done it myself' (*NN* 15). The partly autobiographical David Copperfield looks back on 'the strong part of my character' which is 'the source of my success ... I could never have done what I have done, without the habits of punctuality, order, and diligence, without the determination to concentrate myself on one subject at a time ... My meaning simply is, that whatever I have tried to do in life, I have tried with all my heart to do well ... in great aims and in small, I have always been thoroughly in earnest' (*DC* 42). This attribute, along with self-reliance, he had learned from his 'brighteyed' and shrewd great-aunt, Betsey Trotwood: 'Earnestness is what Somebody must look for, to sustain him and improve him ... Deep, downright, faithful earnestness' (*DC* 35).

Dickens was, however, well aware of the greater character pitfalls presented by self-improvement shorn of the MORAL dimension. Some of his least attractive characters are self-improvers. Josiah Bounderby is a caricature of a self-made 'banker, merchant, manufacturer, and what not'. He boasts that 'I passed the day in a ditch, and the night in a pigsty ... I pulled through it, though nobody threw me a rope' (*HT* 1.4). Self-important and bellicose, Bounderby has money but the moral values only of the counting-house. Ironically, his start in life came not from his own efforts but from the self-sacrifice of his mother on his behalf. Charlie Hexam, offered the chance of self-improvement through education by his sister, and patronized as a star pupil by the precariously respectable schoolmaster Bradley Headstone, meanly rejects them when they seem to stand in his way. 'I have made up my mind that I will become respectable in the scale of society, and that I will not be dragged down by others' (*OMF* 4.7). Uriah Heep hides behind a pose of 'rightful umbleness' (*DC* 39) in his scheming to destroy Mr Wickfield, take over the business, and marry the heroine. His name has entered the language as the very type of oleaginous hypocrisy in the service of self-improvement.

The Victorian ruling classes as a whole believed in the improvement of working men. Friendly societies, co-operative societies, mutuality lodges, and savings banks were all advanced as 'proper' avenues to respectability and material comfort (see CLASS). Friendly Societies were enormously popular in mid-Victorian Britain. Their benefit funds protected by the Friendly Societies Act in 1855, they grew to sustain a bewildering variety of activities grounded in the principles of mutual support, self-help, thrift, and educational improvement. The Royal Commission on Friendly Societies in 1874 estimated that they had about 4 million members. They were particularly popular with skilled workers and especially in the industrial north. It has been estimated, for example, that about 80 per cent of Rochdale's population in 1887—including women and children—were in a friendly society (estimate in Rochdale *Observer*, 30 January 1891 and quoted in an unpublished paper by John Garrard, 'Friendly Societies, the Poor Law and Working-Class Politics in Rochdale'). Co-operative societies expanded both their numbers and activities in the second half of the 19th century. The Co-Operative Wholesale Society was established in 1863 and extended to Scotland in 1871, becoming one of the biggest food distributors in Britain. By the 1880s co-ops had their own parliamentary and education committees and a little later supported candidates for the infant Labour Party. In launching his Post Office Savings Bank scheme in 1861, for example, William Gladstone told the House of Commons: 'The establishment of savings banks has undoubtedly been of immense service to the humbler classes throughout the country' (*Hansard*, 8 February 1861). By 1878 its total deposits (mostly by small savers) totalled around £31 million (N. McCord, *British History, 1815–1906*, 1991). A state system of banking for the lower orders was necessary. Smaller banks could fail—and with disastrous consequences, as those small savers who entrusted their hard-earned cash to Merdle's bank discovered (*LD* 2.26).

Self-help strategies were diverse and widely practised, but two minatory points should be made. First, as Henry Mayhew's *London Labour and the London Poor* (1861) abundantly demonstrated, strategies dependent on regular savings, order, and thrift were of very limited applicability to that large proportion of working people who were casual labourers, or who suffered frequent unemployment. Secondly, such strategies were by no means *de haut en bas*. Skilled workers usually preferred to organize their own opportunities which, as with TRADE UNIONS or REFORM clubs, did not necessarily involve complaisant acquiescence with the governing classes. As we have seen, Dickens applauded this independence without necessarily understanding its consequence. Self-help was not always productive of that social harmony which Dickens strove so hard to promote. EJE

Evans, E. J. (ed.), *Social Policy, 1830–1914* (1978).

Gilmour, Robin, 'Dickens and the Self-Help Idea', in J. Butt and I. F. Clarke (eds.), *The Victorians and Social Protest* (1973).

Gosden, P. H. J. H., *Self-Help: Voluntary Associations in Nineteenth-Century Britain* (1973).

Morris, R. J., 'Samuel Smiles and the Genesis of Self-Help: The Retreat to a Petit Bourgeois Utopia', *Historical Journal*, 24 (1981).

Searle, G. R., *Entrepreneurial Politics in Mid-Victorian Britain* (1993).

**sensation novels** were a type of fiction, especially popular in the 1860s, which sought to arouse feelings such as excitement and fear in their readers by depicting extraordinary events in ordinary life. Stock situations include murder, MADNESS, mistaken identity, arson, or bigamy—situations that are presented in supposedly factual detail to evoke an impression of what Henry James called 'those most mysterious of mysteries, the mysteries which are at our own doors' ('Miss Braddon', in *Notes and Reviews*, 1921). An early study by Walter C. Phillips viewed the sensation novel as a distinctly Dickensian mode, whose principal practitioners—besides Dickens himself—were Wilkie COLLINS and Charles READE. More recent, feminist criticism (such as that of Elaine Showalter in *A Literature of Their Own: British Women Novelists from Brontë to Lessing*, 1977) has focused on the women writers of sensation fiction, notably M. E. Braddon and Mrs Henry Wood, and has seen their work as reflective of the frustrations of women in Victorian society. Reviewers often treated sensation novels with disdain, but readers of the 1860s were widely addicted to the fictional thrills that commercially astute writers—both men and women—were ready to provide.

As an influence on the sensation novel, Dickens's example was important. Long before the flood of sensation novels in the 1860s or even before his statement in the Preface to *Bleak House* about dwelling 'upon the romantic side of familiar things', what Donald Fanger has described as Dickens's 'romantic realism' (in *Dostoevsky and Romantic Realism: A Study of Dostoevsky in Relation to Balzac, Dickens, and Gogol*, 1965) is evident in the style of *Oliver Twist* and even some of the pieces in *Sketches by Boz*. Highly coloured or violent episodes occur freely in Dickens's early novels, such as the murder of Nancy in *Oliver Twist*. (Similarly violent or gruesome scenes can be found in William Harrison AINSWORTH's novels of the 1830s and early 1840s.) Not surprisingly, the sensation writers of the 1860s looked to the eminent Dickens as a prototype. He had an especially close relationship with Wilkie Collins, a literary protégé and later a frequent companion, who published what is sometimes considered the first and one of the most striking illustrations of the sensation novel, *The Woman in White* (serialized in *All the Year Round*, 1859–60).

Not only did Dickens influence the sensation novel but he was also influenced by it. There has been some discussion concerning the extent to which the increased tightness of his plots in the novels starting with *Bleak House* can be attributed to the example of Collins, noted for his handling of suspense. As Kathleen Tillotson has observed, however, 'the common view that Dickens's increased skill in plotting and construction is due to his admiring study of the younger novelist's work does not fit the facts—even, the dates' (Tillotson 1969, p. xxii). Nevertheless, while Dickens was by no means a slavish imitator of Collins, the evidence of Dickens's last novels suggests his awareness of and, to some extent, participation in the sensationist vogue. Both *Great Expectations* (which was reviewed by Margaret Oliphant in 1862 as a sensation novel) and *Our Mutual Friend*, as well as *The Mystery of Edwin Drood* (which Dickens began writing in 1869), resemble more typical sensation novels of the decade in a number of respects. For instance, all three of these novels of the 1860s give special prominence to lurid details (such as Magwitch terrifying Pip in the cemetery at the beginning of *Great Expectations*, Gaffer Hexam fishing for dead bodies at the opening of *Our Mutual Friend*, and the squalid opium den at the start of *Drood*). All three works also share a concern with criminality, mystery, and false identity—recurring ideas in sensation novels of the period. Even the resourcefulness of Lizzie Hexam's rescue of Eugene Wrayburn in *Our Mutual Friend* and the fearlessness of Helena Landless in *Drood* may owe something to the active women often found in sensation fiction. However, Dickens's novels go far beyond those of the pure sensation writers in symbolism, characterization, and social vision. Moreover, unlike the moral ambiguity that many Victorian critics perceived as a particularly troubling aspect of the sensation novel, the underlying MORAL order of Dickens's novels (as John R. Reed has discussed in *Dickens and Thackeray: Punishment and Forgiveness*, 1995) is clear-cut.          DAT

Hughes, Winifred, *The Maniac in the Cellar: Sensation Novels of the 1860s* (1980).

Phillips, Walter C., *Dickens, Reade, and Collins: Sensation Novelists* (1919).

Tillotson, Kathleen, 'The Lighter Reading of the Eighteen-Sixties', Introduction to the Riverside Edition of Wilkie Collins, *The Woman in White* (1969).

**sentiment.** An aspect of Dickens's writing often singled out adversely (and usually a-historically) by his detractors, sentiment as a purely descriptive term refers to a major literary and philosophical tradition which he inherited from some of his favourite authors.

In the 17th century, in reaction to Calvinist views on man's fallen nature and to Thomas Hobbes's (1588–1679) description of man as fundamentally selfish, Latitudinarian divines proposed the image of the man of feeling, predisposed instinctively to benevolence. Anthony Ashley Cooper, third Earl of Shaftesbury (1671–1713), developed these views into a secular humanism which linked ethics with aesthetics and located virtue in spontaneous human affections (*Characteristicks*, 1711).

Scottish Enlightenment philosophers Francis Hutcheson (1694–1746) and Adam Smith (1723–90) defined virtue in relation to beauty (Hutcheson, *An Inquiry into the Original of Our Ideas of Beauty and Virtue*, 1725) and posited that sympathy, by arousing interest in the feelings of others, provides the source of MORAL judgements (Smith, *The Theory of Moral Sentiments*, 1759). For all of these writers, man was a creature of natural goodness. Sensibility, the faculty of feeling, predominated over reason, and sentiment, the capacity for moral reflection, was innate.

Sentimentalism was popularized in the *Tatler* and *Spectator* essays of ADDISON and STEELE, and remained a dominant characteristic of the periodicals conducted by later ESSAYISTS such as GOLDSMITH's *Bee* and MACKENZIE's *Lounger*. Dickens knew all of these periodicals well and consciously looked to them as models when he first conceived MASTER HUMPHREY'S CLOCK (to Forster, 14 July 1839).

Early 18th-century DRAMA emerged in direct opposition to the urbanity, cynicism, and wit of Restoration plays, offering instead both comedy and tragedy rooted in feeling and moral outlook. Steele's *The Conscious Lovers* epitomized sentimental comedy, which sought 'a joy too exquisite for laughter' (Preface), by eschewing satire in favour of a depiction of moral characters emerging happy and successful from distressful situations. David Garrick, the foremost actor of the century, introduced a style which depended less on declamation than on the communication of emotion. Even the most celebrated later-18th-century plays, Goldsmith's *She Stoops to Conquer* (1773) and Sheridan's *The School for Scandal* (1777), written as 'laughing' rather than 'sentimental' comedies (the terms are Goldsmith's, 'A Comparison Between Laughing and Sentimental Comedy', *Westminster Magazine*, January 1773), for all their satire offered good-natured heroes and a morally wholesome tone. Such plays were part of the standard repertoire of the theatre of Dickens's day, and the heightened emotions and moral polarities of 19th-century MELODRAMA, so influential on his own work, descended directly from this tradition.

Dickens was also familiar with the sentimental outlook of 18th-century nature POETRY and of Pope's *Moral Essays*. The melancholy musings of GRAY's 'Elegy in a Country Churchyard' find direct echo in chapter 52 of *The Old Curiosity Shop*. WORDSWORTH, whose poetry 'loosed our heart in tears' (Matthew Arnold, 'Memorial Verses'), was one of Dickens's favourite poets, and he particularly admired the poem 'We Are Seven', in which the child's instinctive wisdom routs the more logical adult interlocutor. The very basis of Wordsworth's poetry was a poetics of sentiment; as he wrote of his artistic creed,

> And I have felt
> A presence that disturbs me with the joy
> Of elevated thoughts . . .
>                    . . . well pleased to recognize
> In nature and the language of the sense,
> The anchor of my purest thoughts, the
>     nurse,
> The guide, the guardian of my heart, and
>     soul
> Of all my moral being.
>
>                    ('Tintern Abbey')

But the dominant vehicle for sentimental attitudes, and the form in which Dickens knew and loved it best, was the 18th-century NOVEL. In FIELDING's *Tom Jones* (1749), the hero's carelessly exuberant good nature is juxtaposed to the calculating rationality of his chief antagonist, Blifil, and their patron, Squire Allworthy, is invariably benevolent when he follows his heart's impulse, and equally invariably misguided whenever he listens to apparently reasonable advice. In STERNE's *Tristram Shandy* (1759–67) the mutual affection of Uncle Toby and his man Trim causes tears to flow freely, and in one famous passage Toby's kindliness prevents him from killing a fly. Above all for Dickens, in Goldsmith's *The Vicar of Wakefield* (1766), 'that most delightful of all stories' (to Forster, ?6 October 1844), the unworldly Dr Primrose emerges uncorrupted from a series of misadventures which test his benign sentiments. Mr Pickwick, John Jarndyce, and Joe Gargery are among descendants of the 'good-natured man' to be found in Dickens's works.

Sentimentalism was always an adversarial posture, combating mechanical, rational, and deterministic forces, opposing realism with idealism. *Sense and Sensibility* (1811) by Jane Austen (1775–1817), a novelist whose works Dickens did *not* read with admiration (if he read them at all), is representative of anti-sentimental thought, contrasting in the sisters Marianne and Elinor the imprudence and vulnerability of excessive emotionalism with the wisdom and greater self-control of circumspect good sense. But the traditions of sentiment and sensibility were long-lived. Besides their offshoots into the extravagant emotions of GOTHIC FICTION and the celebration of imagination as the source of poetic creativity by the Romantic poets, the emphasis on moral uplift based on right feeling continued vigorously in tract literature, in the Victorian cult of DOMESTICITY, and in the poetry of TENNYSON and other Victorians. John Stuart MILL (1806–73), in his essay 'What is Poetry?' (1833), declared its object was 'confessedly to act upon the emotions', and later, in his *Autobiography* (1873), he described how Wordsworth's poetry, by promoting 'the cultivation of the feelings', rescued him from an emotional crisis when he was a young man.

'Sentiment' is the title of one of Dickens's earliest sketches, published in *Bell's Weekly Magazine* (7 June 1834) and collected as the third of the 'Tales' in *Sketches by Boz*. It comically recounts the elopement of a young lady from her finishing school, and Dickens was always ready to laugh at the excesses of sentiment—Julia Mills, at the age of 'almost twenty', 'having been unhappy in a misplaced affection, and being understood to have retired from the world on her awful stock of experience, but still to take a calm interest in the unblighted hopes and loves of youth' (*DC* 33); the love-lorn John Chivery, composing lugubrious epitaphs for himself (*LD* 1.18, 2.27); Mr Venus 'floating his powerful mind' in tea (*OMF* 1.7). But, especially early in his career, Dickens was famous—later notorious —for his willingness to play on readers' heartstrings. The death of Little Nell (*OCS*), the potentially fatal crippled condition of Tiny Tim (*CC*), and the death of Little Paul (*DS*) moved many early readers to tears and later attracted derision as the worst excesses of bathos—what Aldous Huxley condemned as *Vulgarity in Literature* (1930). What a historical view can clarify is that these evocations of sentiment are written to be *exemplary*: they are not mimetic, but idealized lessons for the feeling heart. FORSTER referred to the death of Nell as a 'discipline of feeling', an invigorating moral instruction, the very reverse of self-indulgent wallowing in grief. But it is equally true that such passages were also exercises in sensibility, intended to produce an intense outpouring of feeling, such as JEFFREY described on reading of the death of Paul Dombey: 'Oh, my dear, dear Dickens! what a No. 5 you have given us! I have so cried and sobbed over it last night, and again this morning; and felt my heart so purified by those tears, and blessed and loved you for making me shed them . . .' (Lord Cockburn, *Life of Lord Jeffrey*, 1852, 2.406). It is more difficult for narrative art than for a lyric outcry to convey the writer's sincerity, however, and there are certain always to be readers who react with embarrassment to Dickens's sentiment.

In addition to deathbed scenes, Dickens's fiction is concerned centrally with the depiction of emotion in a moral context. He routinely constructs scenes of heightened feeling to elicit an emotional response from the reader, and he confidently attributes innate moral sentiments to an otherwise degraded character such as Nancy, the lowly prostitute in *Oliver Twist*. His villains are notable for their lack of moral feeling; his heroines such as Agnes (*DC*), Esther (*BH*), and Little Dorrit are beacons of moral strength; and his heroes, most notably Pip, imbibe lessons in moral sensitivity in the course of their adventures.

Nevertheless, as Philip Collins has argued, it seems clear that a shift in taste occurred during Dickens's lifetime. Although some of his earliest readers refused to be moved by his rhetoric, and although some eyes were not dry when the sceptics waxed loudest, by the time of his death in 1870 OBITUARISTS routinely expressed bafflement over the enthusiasm which the previous generation had described as its response to Dickens's sentiment. And although Dickens continued to depict childhood mortality in his later works, the deaths of Poor Jo in *Bleak House* and of little Johnny in *Our Mutual Friend* are presented with a more complicated rhetoric than his treatment of Nell. Collins connects changing attitudes with 'the rise and decline of EVANGELICALISM, and to philanthropic and parliamentary concern with infant mortality' (Collins 1974, p. 18). Not coincidentally, it was in the early 20th century, when irony, indirection, and detachment were favoured narrative modes, that Dickens's sentiment came most

vigorously under attack (see CRITICISM: THE FIRST HUNDRED YEARS), whereas today, when melodrama and sentiment are being reconsidered and revalued, his pathos is once again finding defenders and admirers. It is probably best to accept that there can be no final verdict on Dickens's sentiment, for, as Kathleen Tillotson has observed, 'the response to such pathos must always be related to those changing things, manners and belief' (*Novels of the 1840s*, 1954, p. 49).     PVWS

Collins, Philip, *From Manly Tear to Stiff Upper Lip: The Victorians and Pathos* (1974).

Hardy, Barbara, *Forms of Feeling in Victorian Fiction* (1985).

Kaplan, Fred, *Sacred Tears: Sentimentalism in Victorian Literature* (1987).

Todd, Janet, *Sensibility: An Introduction* (1986).

**sequels and continuations.** Dickens himself reintroduced Mr Pickwick and the two Wellers into MASTER HUMPHREY'S CLOCK, but this was unsuccessful, and he never repeated such an experiment, although in 1847 he began (and then abandoned) 'A New Piljian's Projiss', an account of Mrs Gamp's travels with the Dickens AMATEUR THEATRICAL company (reprinted in Appendix G of the Clarendon *Martin Chuzzlewit*). His failure with *Master Humphrey's Clock* did not, however, discourage other writers, and many tried their hands at further adventures of his characters. T. P. Prest issued *The Post-Humourous Notes of the Pickwickian Club* in penny numbers between 1837 and 1839, and *Pickwick in America* in 44 weekly numbers which ran from 1838 to 1839. Another writer, often regarded as the most skilful of Dickens's imitators, George W. M. Reynolds, was responsible for two *Pickwick* sequels. The first, *Pickwick Abroad, or The Tour in France*, ran in the MONTHLY MAGAZINE from December 1837 to July 1839. The second, *The Marriage of Mr Pickwick*, appeared in Reynolds's journal *The Teetotaller* from 23 January to 19 June 1841. Other early Pickwick sequels were *The Pickwick Gazette*, a penny sheet recording Pickwick's further doings (it apparently lasted only two weeks in June and July 1837); *Pickwick in Boulogne* (September 1837), consisting mainly of pirated extracts but with a little invented dialogue; and *Winkle's Journal (Omitted in The Pickwick Papers)* appearing in the *Metropolitan Magazine* during October 1838.

From 1840 sequels began to tail off, but were followed by a miscellany of works, such as *Pickwick in India* (1839–40) published in the Madras journal *The Lighthouse*; *Mr Pickwick's Hat-Box* (January–November 1840) containing tales and poems attributed to Mr Snodgrass; and *An Omitted Pickwick Paper, Restored by Poz* (Boston, 1841). Then, half a century later, Sir Walter Besant and James Rice wrote a fictitious obituary, *The Death of Samuel Pickwick* (1895). In its 1902 Christmas number the *Shooting Times* included 'Mr Pickwick Goes Out Pike Fishing'. In 1903 John Gilbert Reid's *Pickwickians Abroad* was published in Shanghai. Reid also wrote a political article, 'Mr Pickwick Visits the Foreign Office', for the *Hamilton Literary Magazine*. In 1927 *Mr Pickwick's Second Time on Earth* by Charles G. Harper, published to coincide with the centenary of the Pickwickians' first departure from the Golden Cross Inn, records their amazement at the changes which had taken place. (A shorter version had appeared in *Autocar* in 1927.) 'An Unwritten Episode in the Life of Samuel Weller, Esq.', by Charles Robinson, appeared in *The Windsor Magazine* (1937).

A sequel to *Oliver Twist*, by 'Uncle Reg' (E. P. Woodcook), in his *Beautiful Bairns: Stories from Dickens* (1914) altered the setting, invented new dialogue, and radically changed the story (see CHILDREN'S VERSIONS). Another, 'Mr Bumble on Old Age Pensions', a political attack on government interference, appeared in the *Westminster Gazette* (9 January 1909).

Irene Howlett's *The Schoolmaster's Daughter* (1990) narrated the events following the transportation of Squeers. His daughter supported herself and her mother by opening a grocery shop, while young Wackford became a clergyman. Their father on his return home set up as keeper of an asylum for workhouse orphans. An earlier *Nickleby* sequel was *Scenes from the Life of Nickleby Married* (1840) by 'Guess'.

*A Christmas Carol* (1843) was followed by a whole host of continuations by various authors. 'The Final Stave of *A Christmas Carol*', in which Scrooge is dismayed to find that his descendants no longer observe Christmas, appeared in *Punch* (1905). 'Dickens Up to Date: A Christmas Carol in Two Staves' (*Funny Folks*, 1893) had a similar theme, Tiny Tim becoming a lecturer on 'the cant of Yuletide'. *Blackwood's Magazine* (1973) contained M. M. Markham's story, 'What Really Happened to Scrooge'.

In 1919 Sir Harry Johnston published *The Gay-Dombeys*, written during his explorations in Africa. Walter Gay having founded a successful business, adds his wife's family name to his own. The sequel opens with a dinner party in the Onslow Square home of Sir Walter and Lady Gay-Dombey. References to A. E. W. Mason, John Burns, and other contemporaries fix the date as the late 1800s. Johnston's characters are not confined to those in the parent novel. Doctor Sawyer (once late Nockemorf) attends the family as medical practitioner. Mr Weller presides over a livery stable, and mention is made of Harmon, Westlock, Hawk, and others.

Renton Nicholson, who published two sequels to Dickens in his weekly paper *The Town—Master Humphrey's Turnip, A Chimney Corner Crotchet*, 25 April–5 December 1840, and *Master Humphrey's Clock: Written by Himself*, 10 November 1841–26 January 1842 —turned in 1847 to *Dombey*, with *Dombey and Daughter*, which attended to the fortunes of Florence. Two other *Dombey* sequels appeared in *The Man in the Moon*, edited by A. Smith and A. B. Reach: 'An Inquest on the Late Master Paul Dombey' (March 1847), and 'Dombey and Son Finished: Part the Best and Last' (February 1848).

In 1854 Robert B. Brough produced a 're-vised ending' to *Hard Times*, 'Hard Times by Charles Dickens, Concluded as it Ought to Have Been', with an explanatory note 'that Dickens was not himself when he wrote the end of Chapter 34', which should therefore be disregarded. Brough produced another parody of *Hard Times* in 1856 (see ADAPTATIONS).

*Great Expectations*, with its ambiguous conclusion and lack of precise detail about Magwitch's time in Australia, has tempted more than one writer to expand the story; Sue Roe's *Estella, Her Expectations* (1982) and Michael Noonan's *Magwitch* (1982) are examples. There have been many attempts to write a conclusion to the unfinished *Mystery of Edwin Drood* (see MYSTERY OF EDWIN DROOD, SOLUTIONS TO). ASW

Davis, Paul, *The Lives and Times of Ebenezer Scrooge* (1990).

**serial literature.** All Dickens's major fiction was published serially. The mode he and his publishers CHAPMAN AND HALL devised in the course of issuing *Pickwick Papers*, monthly part issue, was used for nine original novels (*Pickwick, Nickleby, Chuzzlewit, Dombey, Copperfield, Bleak House, Dorrit, Our Mutual Friend*, and *Drood*), and in variations for most of the rest of his major work.

The standard format of a Dickens serial is 32 pages of letterpress and two ILLUSTRATIONS. These leaves, plus any ADVERTISING supplements, are gathered together, stitched, and bound in a coloured wrapper. Each instalment (also called a 'part' or a 'number') usually contains two or three chapters, the last of which ends on the last page of letterpress; Dickens is careful always to give full measure to his customers. The parts cost one shilling apiece. As winding up so many characters and plots at the end of a novel takes extra space, the last two parts are combined into a double number, 19 and 20, with 64 pages of letterpress and four plates—two illustrations, a frontispiece, and an etched title-page with a vignette picture on it. This last part costs two shillings. Among the pages of letterpress are the half-title, dedication, preface, table of contents, list of illustrations, and sometimes an errata sheet or directions to the binder about where to place the illustrations if the owner of the parts wants to reassemble them into a volume.

There were many variations on this format. *Pickwick* began with 26 pages and four illustrations, and did not reach 32 pages and two illustrations until the third instalment. *Our Mutual Friend* was designed to be rebound as two volumes. Therefore part 10 includes the half-title, printed (not illustrated) title-page for volume 1, dedication, list of contents, and list of illustrations; parts 19 and 20 include the half-title, printed title-page, contents, and illustrations for volume 2, plus a 'Postscript, in lieu of Preface' which makes explicit what earlier serials declared only implicitly, that the Preface is composed after the novel has been written, reviewed, and read by its initial audience. One of the four plates in this double number is the frontispiece for volume 2, but there is no plate here or in part 10 designated as the frontispiece for volume 1. By the mid-1860s, when *Our Mutual Friend*

appeared, shilling serials were being shoved aside by other, cheaper formats. Since the sales of that novel were disappointing, Dickens planned to issue *Edwin Drood* in only twelve monthly parts; he did not quite complete writing the sixth instalment before he died.

Dickens also republished as monthly serials works originally issued in other formats. *Sketches by Boz*, collections of tales and sketches Dickens had published in various periodicals between 1833 and 1836, appeared in two volumes (First Series) in February 1836, and in a further volume (Second Series) in December of that year. In this format they were illustrated by George CRUIKSHANK. When the publisher, John MACRONE, saw how successful *Pickwick* was in monthly parts, he proposed issuing the *Sketches* yet again, this time in shilling instalments. Dickens violently objected to having so much of his work offered for sale at the same time (*Pickwick* was concluding and *Oliver Twist* was in mid-story), and he was also angry that Macrone sought to capitalize on the successful *Pickwick* format. When it became clear that Macrone could make a lot of money nevertheless, Dickens talked Chapman and Hall into buying out Macrone and reissuing *Sketches* in the *Pickwick* format themselves. Cruikshank designed a wrapper; copied, enlarged, and etched his original illustrations; and produced thirteen new plates, for a total of 40, two per part. While the instalments look and cost the same as those for *Pickwick*, the letterpress runs to only 24 pages per part. Customers grumbled; in part 2 Chapman and Hall published an 'Address' explaining that the three volumes of *Sketches* cost 16 shillings more than the serial would cost, so buyers were getting a bargain for the text alone (not to mention the thirteen additional illustrations and the wrapper). What they were not getting was a serial conceived and executed in monthly parts; whenever 24 pages of type were filled, the text stopped, always in mid-story so that the next part had to be purchased to conclude it. In this case, dividing up a story between monthly parts was a strategy for inveigling customers to purchase the next part of a serial that contained no continuing narrative.

Dickens's second novel, *Oliver Twist*, also appeared in monthly parts, but a long time after initial publication. At first the text of *Oliver* fulfilled Dickens's contractual obligation to supply matter for each monthly number of the new periodical he began editing in January 1837, BENTLEY'S MISCELLANY. Midway through the novel Dickens compelled BENTLEY, the publisher, to accept *Oliver* also as the new novel Bentley had agreed to publish in three volumes. Nine years after *Oliver* appeared in the *Miscellany* (1837–9) and in three volumes (1838), Chapman and Hall reissued it in ten monthly shilling parts, January to October 1846, with Cruikshank's 24 original plates retouched and reprinted. The artist designed a new wrapper for this edition. Some of the instalments have two illustrations, some three; there is no frontispiece or vignette title accompanying the last part. All the parts finish with the end of a chapter except part 9, where chapter 50 runs over into the final part.

When Dickens published in weekly formats, he might also gather four or five of those instalments into a monthly issue. He did so with *The Old Curiosity Shop* and *Barnaby Rudge*, taken from the illustrated weekly MASTER HUMPHREY'S CLOCK (1840–1). As each weekly part cost threepence, the monthly issues cost 1 shilling or 1s. 3d. The wrapper for these parts was designed by George CATTERMOLE and engraved on wood by Ebenezer Landells. Dickens tried this expedient in part 'to baffle the imitators' (to Cattermole, 13 January 1840), who repeatedly anticipated his monthly episodes, staging or publishing variants even before Dickens could write the original. *Hard Times* ran in the pages of Dickens's unillustrated weekly *Household Words*, but was not issued in monthly instalments; it came out as one compact unillustrated 5 shillings volume at the end of its magazine run. When Dickens started off a new unillustrated weekly, *All the Year Round*, with *A Tale of Two Cities*, he tried reprinting the weekly instalments in the familiar 32-page shilling monthly parts, with two illustrations by Hablot Knight BROWNE, bound in a paper wrapper with a cover design that Browne also drew. This was issued in eight (as seven) parts, the last double number containing the usual front matter, two illustrations, a frontispiece, and a vignette title. The experiment failed, so it was not tried again when *Great Expectations* appeared in *All the Year Round*.

The other principal format in which Dickens issued his novels is weekly magazines. There were three of them, already mentioned, and in their pages Dickens published five novels: *Old Curiosity Shop, Rudge, Hard Times, Tale of Two Cities,* and *Great Expectations*. Dickens found the compression of weekly instalments ('thimblefuls'), usually running to twelve printed pages for the *Clock* novels, five or six double-column pages for the others, to be extremely taxing. Whereas with monthly parts he could complete all his work by the 25th of the month and have a few days for relaxation before tackling the next instalment (he hated the month of February because it was so short), with weekly numbers he began again every seven days. 'Mr Shandy's Clock [in Laurence STERNE's *Tristram Shandy*] was nothing to mine', he complained to Walter Savage LANDOR, '—wind, wind, wind, always winding am I; and day and night the alarum is in my ears, warning me that it must not run down' (to Landor, 26 July 1840). In the first instances, the novels that appeared in weeklies were not planned for that format: *Old Curiosity Shop* was a short story extended when no other expedient would keep buyers for the *Clock*, and *Rudge* had been promised as a three-volume novel to two different publishers before it succeeded the *Shop* in threepenny *Clock* parts. The other three novels were also thrust into Dickens's periodicals to pick up slack; and in the case of the last one, *Great Expectations*, Dickens continued to plan for it in monthly instalments although he published it weekly and republished it in three volumes.

Serialization was important to Dickens, his publishers, and his public. For Dickens, periodically issuing a text in progress gave him money while he wrote; he did not need to wait until a book was completed before selling it. Indeed, throughout his life he counted on the earnings from his current serial to support his increasingly expensive residences and family. It is frequently asserted that Dickens's novels are so prolix because he was paid by the word. That statement is not strictly true, and is not a cause of their length. In fact serial issue facilitated planning and structuring the fictions. Once Dickens determined the length of a serial, he could arrange his story over the whole. The first evidence of his planning instalments comes at the end of *The Old*

*Curiosity Shop*; having announced in the *Clock* when the next novel would begin, Dickens sorted out on a piece of paper what had to be said and done within the weekly parts remaining for that story. From *Chuzzlewit* forward, Dickens prepared 'number plans' in advance of writing. These consisted of sheets of paper folded in half. On the right side Dickens wrote the number of the part and the chapter numbers and titles, with some indication of the events therein; on the left, he tried out names and scribbled ideas. During the course of COMPOSITION he made further notes about what items he had or had not included, reminded himself of themes and phrases, and used these plans in other ways as aides-mémoires. Twenty-part novels have a clear turning-point midway through, and secondary points at numbers 5 and 15. Such structural hinges were helpful in deploying incidents; Dickens postponed the death of Paul Dombey from part 4 to part 5, so that the novel's first, fifth, tenth, fifteenth, and final parts all demarcate the loss or gain of a Dombey family member. In such ways the serial structure often inflects the novel's themes and action.

Two other aspects of serialization were advantageous to Dickens. He tended, in the longer novels, to invent two or three plots that intersect; in *Bleak House* he provided two narratives told by different narrators. By including something about each of the narratives in each instalment, he could parallel and contrast the events and characters, keep all the stories going forward, and provide climaxes to each part that, while they rarely indulge in the histrionics of early cinema serials, do sometimes end on notes of suspense or anticipation. The individual part may thus serve as a microcosm of the whole; and the challenge of composing a 500,000-word novel is broken down into much more manageable portions. The second helpful feature of serialization derives from the necessity of so much planning and commitment in advance of any publication. Before a novel was even begun, Dickens needed to decide on a title so that his publishers could start advertising for readers and, more important, for advertisers who would buy space in inserts to the monthly parts. Once Dickens settled on a title, he had to outline the whole story to his illustrator so that the design for the wrapper

of the first part would shadow forth something of the entire unwritten tale. Therefore serialization forced Dickens to do kinds of advance planning that committed him in print long before he finished writing; as a consequence, he tended to fix very early on principal elements of plot and character, to organize his narrative in terms of structural and thematic analogues, and to exfoliate images and patterns. Paradoxically, publishing as he wrote enabled Dickens to devise densely and complexly structured novels. By contrast, the fictional author Edwin Reardon, in GISSING's *New Grub Street*, never gets forward with his novels because after drafting a few chapters he gives up and starts anew. He is never committed to a story by publishing the beginning before he completes the ending. Moreover, Reardon, unlike Dickens, sells his entire COPYRIGHT to a publisher outright, thus earning nothing while writing and frequently running out of money before the next novel is ready. Also unlike Dickens, Reardon can expect nothing on the resale of his novels after initial issue. George Gissing was an ardent student of Dickens's work, but he knew from his own painful experiences as an author that in the 1880s it was impossible any longer to publish serials as Dickens had.

For a while, serialization had important advantages for publishers (see PUBLISHING). It took only a small outlay of capital, little more than one-twentieth of the amount for a whole book, to launch a title, and that capital was recycled many times in the course of the novel's production. Periodicity made serials good mediums for advertising; some firms took space for an entire run, and for the most popular of Dickens's titles the advertising inserts might number as many as 32 pages. In *Our Mutual Friend*, part 1, in addition to a 32-page 'Advertiser' ten firms printed and inserted their own flyers, adding a further 35 pages. This produced a substantial addition to the revenue of the book: for *Dombey* gross advertising revenues exceeded £2,000. Early in the Victorian period serials were popular with booksellers, because they ensured that customers would return to the shop at the end of each month to purchase the next instalment. Later on, however, the trade turned against serials, as it was hard to take stock of so many different parts coming and going month after month, and the individual transaction amounted to so little. In the early years serials were REVIEWED more than once in the course of a run; such multiple notices, often containing extracts of the month's instalment, repeatedly called attention to the work and thus contributed to its success. And because serial parts were hard to track and to care for over nineteen months, many customers bought the novel in parts as it came out, and also at its conclusion bought a second copy encased in hard covers to keep permanently. Alternatively, publishers offered various kinds of bindings for the parts, and did a lively business supplying missing parts before they were reassembled as volumes.

Serialization had many advantages for readers as well (see READERSHIP). Foremost was cheapness. Customers could spend a shilling a month for nineteen months and at the end own more text than if they bought outright a three-volume novel in hard covers costing 31s 6d. Serialization made owning original fiction possible for millions of newly literate customers with modest disposable incomes. That shilling might itself be reduced; weekly parts cost threepence. Twelve readers might each contribute a penny to buy the part; and we know of one charwoman whose landlord, on the first Monday of every month, provided tea (for a fee) and a reading of the latest instalment (for free) (Forster 5.7). Having the text in the home enabled families to experience the novel together as it was read aloud; it could also be taken to one's room to reread in privacy and to study the pictures. In such ways Dickens especially, and other serial novelists to a lesser degree, *belonged* to their readers. That belonging was enhanced by the gap between instalments and the long time it took for the novel to run its course; the characters and events were talked about, predictions were made, old parts were reread for clues, and in countless other ways the events in the novel became part of people's lives. While some serials were set in the past and suffused with nostalgia, others took place in the very present of their readers' world, further melding the fictional universe with the real one. 'Did Nelly die?' was as ubiquitous a question in 1841 as 'who shot J. R.?' nearly 150 years later. And serial publication, with its regularity and periodicity, fitted into the rhythms of life, measured by weekly and monthly observances that provided order in a rapidly changing environment.

Serial fiction lost out in the 1860s to other forms of publication that extended its benefits. If one novel at a shilling was a bargain, what about several for the same price? Shilling magazines, with two or more fictions running concurrently, were a better bargain than shilling parts. It was easier for low-wage earners to spend a few pennies a week than to save up twelve pennies a month; so weekly journals, inexorably cheapening as the century progressed, competed for the labourer's coppers. The middle classes often preferred to rent rather than to own. They joined circulating LIBRARIES, of which the largest was Mudie's. For a guinea (£1 1s) a year, they could take out one volume at a time; for two guineas, two volumes, and so forth. They could thus sample many books without committing to purchase any of them. And the guarantee of a sale to Mr Mudie of, say, 500 copies of a new novel secured profit to all concerned—author, publisher, bookseller, and Mudie. So novels issued in three volumes, costing a guinea and a half, remained a standard format for fiction from 1820 to 1894, even though for many writers (including Gissing's Reardon) and readers, that second volume, separating the initial complication in volume 1 from its resolution in volume 3, was a weary, wire-drawn affair.

By 1870 the circulating libraries were driving serial fiction from the field. And from 1870 onward, as state education and public libraries were mandated, there were more readers, more publications, and more competition for readers' money. Moreover, reading practices grew more cursory, abbreviated, discontinuous, and shallow. A generation of reviewers and cultural authorities decried literary 'snacking', but in the late 1880s entrepreneurs began catering to such 'debased' customers, providing snippets in inexpensive newspapers. George Newnes's *Tit-Bits* achieved an unprecedented circulation, and Alfred Harmsworth, imitating it, became the most powerful publisher in Fleet Street. The formula, as another character in *New Grub Street* explains with only slight exaggeration, was that 'No article in the paper is to measure more than two inches in length, and every inch must be broken into at least two paragraphs' (ch. 33).

Although the novels of Anthony TROLLOPE and Wilkie COLLINS were sold to republication syndicates for reprinting in newspaper columns as filler, such transactions did not shape or constitute original serial fiction. Dickens's monthly and weekly parts democratized literature, putting new work into the hands and homes of every economic and social class; subsequent stratification of markets and segmentation of reading and attention-spans combined with the cheapening of all categories of books to kill off original fiction in monthly parts. But the revolutions in authorship, publishing, distribution, and reading that part-issue instituted continued through new formats, technologies, and writing.                                                     RLP

Butt and Tillotson (1957).
Hughes, Linda K., and Lund, Michael, *The Victorian Serial* (1991).
Patten (1978).
Stone (1987).

**servants and domestic work** (see also CLASS; WORK). Dickens's paternal grandparents, William Dickens and Elizabeth Dickens, née Ball, had been respectively butler and housekeeper to the Crewe family (though this fact was not generally known until after Dickens's death: see DICKENS, JOHN). They were therefore part of the aristocracy of the below-stairs world and must have been a factor in Dickens's precise evocation of that world in his novels.

Butlers in Dickens's novels tend to be rather mysterious figures who exert inordinate power, like Mr Merdle's butler in *Little Dorrit*, or the Veneerings' in *Our Mutual Friend*. Servants can also be used metonymically to expose the social pretensions of their betters, like the butler hired by Mrs Skewton in *Dombey* to 'make a handsome appearance' for her daughter's wedding (*DS* 30). In contrast to the line of formidable butlers, housekeepers occur in Dickens as generally wholesome and well-ordered. There is a tribute to Dickens's grandmother, who did not die until he was 12, in Mrs Rouncewell in *Bleak House*—'a fine old lady, handsome, stately and wonderfully neat' (*BH* 7). The ability to create order is a cardinal virtue in the novels and its opposite is uniformly condemned. Dickens's values, it could be argued, are therefore very much those of his servant

grandparents rather than of his socially superior but feckless parents. His own servants remembered him writing out lists of instructions for them individually. He demanded from them an almost feudal loyalty, but in return seems to have been an understanding and sympathetic master.

Dickens's sympathy with servants is evident in the picture he gives of the cruel treatment meted out to household drudges like the Marchioness in *The Old Curiosity Shop* and to poor Guster in *Bleak House* (who 'goes cheap with [the] unaccountable drawback of fits'; *BH* 10) or, more farcically, to the black servant and to Withers, the wan page in *Dombey*. He can also set the warm, loving servant in opposition to the cold employer, as with Peggotty in *David Copperfield*. In *Dombey* this contrast becomes a central theme, with Polly Toodle embodying exactly the life-enhancing qualities Dombey so signally lacks. The power of Master over Servant is epitomized in the (historically accurate) episode in which Dombey assumes the right to change Polly's name while she is in his employment, to 'say, Richards—an ordinary name, and convenient' (*DS* 2). Dickens is similarly sensitive to the plight of the governess, which he presents vividly through Ruth Pinch in *Martin Chuzzlewit* and which he spoke feelingly about in a speech to the Governesses' Benevolent Association in 1843 (*Speeches*, p. 65).

There is a SENTIMENTAL side too to Dickens's treatment of servants. His most famous servant, Sam Weller in *Pickwick Papers*, owes a great deal to the sentimental image of the loyalty between Master and Man—evident in CERVANTES's Don Quixote and Sancho Panza and in several 18th-century NOVELS. Good servants are characterized primarily by absolute and unconditional devotion to their masters/mistresses. In this mould are Mark Tapley in *Martin Chuzzlewit*, Betsey Trotwood's devoted Janet in *David Copperfield*, and the redoubtable Miss Pross in *A Tale of Two Cities*. Clemency Newcome in The BATTLE OF LIFE, Tilly Slowboy in The CRICKET ON THE HEARTH, and Esther Summerson's hard-working maid Charley in *Bleak House* are all examples of what a servant ought to be.

However, in the patterning of the novels this idealized image is frequently subverted. The Pickwick/Sam relationship is parodied by that between Mr Jingle and Job Trotter; in *Barnaby Rudge* John Grueby, the good servant of Lord George Gordon, is balanced by the sharp and shrewish Miggs, Mrs Varden's servant and maid-of-all-work. Later novels have their share of discontented and even sinister servants. Jeremiah Flintwinch in *Little Dorrit*, a transgressive figure who 'might . . . be a clerk or a servant' (*LD* 1.3) exercises a tyrannical power over his wife, Affery, and over the Clennam household. Hortense, the lady's maid in *Bleak House*, acts out the hidden anger which her mistress, Lady Dedlock, cannot express, and becomes the murderess of their shared enemy, Tulkinghorn.

The Cinderella theme, centred on a servant, allows Dickens to deal gingerly with the issue of 'station': in *The Old Curiosity Shop* Dick Swiveller marries his Marchioness; in *Dombey* Toots raises Susan Nipper from lady's-maid to wife. Luckily, he 'had no relation to object or be offended on the score of station' (*DS* 60) (see FAIRY TALE). In each case the servant is presented as in some way superior to the master—but in each case too, Dickens, typically, tempers this radicalism by making the higher social figure unrepresentative of his class: Swiveller is penniless and Toots witless. In *Hard Times* there is a grotesque parody of the theme in the anti-love affair between the impoverished but well-bred Mrs Sparsit and her employer, the self-made man Mr Bounderby.

A particularly Victorian version of the Cinderella theme is the ideal of the 'Angel in the House' (the title of Coventry Patmore's popular book-length poem of 1854–62). Unstinting devotion, particularly in WOMEN, is responsible for all the 'unpaid housekeepers' in the novels—not servants, but women whose vocation is in fact apotheosized DOMESTIC work—notably Agnes Wickfield in *David Copperfield* and *Little Dorrit*, who can even make an idyll of home in the Marshalsea prison. The image of such devoted motherless daughters gladly carrying out what is effectively unpaid domestic work is a pervasive one. Poor Florence Dombey watches with envy the motherless family in the house opposite, in which the eldest child acts as a 'happy little housekeeper' to her father. Esther Summerson in *Bleak House*, though acting for a surrogate father in Mr Jarndyce, may stand as a paradigm. She receives her basket of housekeeping keys as a sacred trust and rejoices in her new role: 'I was full of business, examining tradesmen's books, adding up columns, paying money, filing receipts . . .' (9). She, like the others, is not to be seen as enslaved to domesticity, but rather exalted as homemaker and domestic angel.

Dickens's simplest use of servants is as a rich source of comedy, centred often on social pretension. Footmen in particular are almost always presented satirically, from the Bath footmen's 'swarry' in *Pickwick Papers* (36), to the Dedlocks' 'Mercuries in powder' (*Bleak House*), to the overdressed individual in *Martin Chuzzlewit* who was like 'a bluebottle in a world of cobwebs' (*MC* 9). In *Oliver Twist* the Maylies' comic band of servants bring some light to a dark novel. Perhaps most famous is the Fat Boy in *Pickwick*, noted for falling asleep and for informing on Mr Tupman to the deaf old lady: 'I wants to make your flesh creep' (*PP* 8).

Dickens could also convey comically the huge power of servants. He caricatures this in the innocent David and Dora's 'ordeal by servants' in *David Copperfield*. Pip in *Great Expectations* takes on a page ('the Avenger') whose demands keep his master, as Pip remarks ruefully, 'in bondage and slavery' (*GE* 26). On the other hand, Littimer, Steerforth's manservant in *David Copperfield*, attributes his own fall (he ends the novel in prison) to the follies of his master (*DC* 61). Dickens can deal seriously too with the darker side of servants' influence, particularly in the rearing of children. He writes feelingly of the power of nursemaids, notably in 'Nurse's Stories' (*UT*): 'I found I had been introduced to [frightening stories] by my nurse before I was six years old.' This suggests a tendency in 19th-century literature and society to see Upstairs as the world of light and reason and Downstairs as the world of dark imaginings. One of Dickens's nurses 'had a ghoulish pleasure in terrifying me to the utmost confines of my reason'. There are echoes of these figures in the lugubrious Nurse Wickham in *Dombey*. However, one of the two Portsmouth nursemaids, Mary Weller, lends her name in *Pickwick* to the upwardly mobile Mary, who begins as housemaid to Mr Nupkins, then becomes maid to Arabella Allen, then (after marriage to Sam Weller) reaches the heights of being housekeeper to Mr Pickwick.

Dickens's readers, whether above or below stairs, would understand the precision with which such social progress was charted.

Dickens's own servants left records of his benevolence, of his acts of individual charity, and of his tolerance (Ackroyd 1990, p. 534). He seems to have succeeded in that great Victorian test of keeping their loyalty, and guests commented on their efficiency and invisibility. In return he demanded punctuality, order, and absolute obedience (no servant, for example, was ever allowed into his study). Dickens died in the year of Forster's Education Act, but the revolutionary implications of such EDUCATIONAL reform for the serving classes are nowhere evident in his work or in his life. He never seems to have questioned the right of an employer to absolute power over his servants. (The Law of Master and Servant, making disobedience to the master a criminal offence, was not repealed until 1875, five years after his death.)

Dickens's edited journals reveal the continuing public interest in servants. 'Old and New Servants' (*AYR* 20 July 1867) explores, as the novels do, the ways in which servants can reveal the foibles of their masters. In Dickens, servants can thus appear metonymically to attack the pretensions of the well-to-do; they can be used metaphorically to represent the dark side of human nature; they can be woven into the Cinderella fairy-tale strand of the novels; and they can form a 19th-century chorus (notably in *Dombey*), before whom the major figures enact their more important stories. They can also be subjects in their own right, the texture of their lives captured unerringly by someone whose grandparents' lives did so much to form his own values. Even as minor characters, they can become almost mythical figures, like the bootboy in *Martin Chuzzlewit* (*MC* 8): 'What a life Young Bailey's was!'                                            VP

Horn, Pamela, *The Rise and Fall of the Victorian Servant* (2nd edn. 1990).

**sexuality and gender.** There is some historical basis to our popular image of Victorian prudery and polite literary discourse. Dickens mocked Mr Podsnap's pompous avoidance of any impropriety that might 'bring a blush into the cheek of the young person' (*OMF* 1.11), but he never forgot his own responsibility to the family circle. He policed his magazines carefully, revealing the sensitivity of his editorial antennae when a regular contributor to *Household Words* got 'so near the sexual side of things as to be a little dangerous to us at times' (to W. H. Wills, 6 October 1854). However, such an oversimplified view of Victorian sexual inhibition and self-censorship is a myth which performs its own cultural functions, as Michael Mason's research (1994*a*, *b*) has demonstrated, and bears a complicated relationship to behaviour and attitudes of the time. Societies that are repressive on the surface deal with sex on other levels in ways that can be picked up from a diversity of cultural signals: see, for example, the seamier side to male sexual behaviour documented by Steven Marcus in *The Other Victorians* (1969). Even among respectable Victorians it is possible to detect, or at any rate suspect, many variations in the extent to which individual men and women's sexual beliefs and practices mirrored the dominant ideology of their class. Some sexual matters were quite openly debated. The protection of PROSTITUTES' clients by the Contagious Diseases Acts, or the differing opinions of eminent doctors on sexual feelings in WOMEN, may not have been acceptable subject-matter for a family magazine like *Household Words*, but they did not pass without considerable published comment (see Mason 1994*a*, *b* and Vicinus 1973, 1977). So in Dickens's writing, as in Victorian society at large, it is not surprising to find more about sexuality than appears at first glance.

Sexuality is normally controlled through a MORAL scheme based on marriage. Dickens's novels strictly enforce a Victorian version of this morality. Where couples cannot consummate their love within marriage, like Stephen and Rachael in *Hard Times*, Dickens understands their suffering and deplores the inadequate divorce system that divides them, but unequivocally endorses Rachael's refusal to live with Stephen as man and wife. The responsibility for defending the moral high ground is placed mainly on the woman, especially where a working-class girl is pursued by an upper-class suitor who is unlikely to marry her (see CLASS). Lizzie Hexam resists the persistent attentions of Eugene Wrayburn until he has reformed on the threshold of death and made heroic efforts to speak the word 'wife'. Girls like Little Em'ly who allow themselves to be betrayed, however inexperienced they may be, have to suffer for their sin. The Victorian wife was expected to curb male sexual desire by regulating her own. However, this system relied on the Victorian husband finding her offer of DOMESTIC bliss irresistible, and a novel like *David Copperfield*, which presents Agnes Wickfield as the epitome of the self-disciplined homemaker, suggests that some men might be unwilling to see marital happiness in such terms. The text's official endorsement of Agnes and disapproval of David's 'undisciplined heart' fail to erase the sex appeal of pretty, undisciplined Clara, Em'ly, and Dora; on this evidence, men demanded incompatible qualities in desirable women and had difficulty in adapting their own taste to the recommended domestic ideal.

Elsewhere, Dickens takes evident delight in his bevy of attractive female characters, bestowing special approval on rosy, plump, and 'coquettish' young women. CHRISTMAS festivities at Dingley Dell are spiced with young ladies' screams, and repeated reference to such feminine attributes as black eyes and little furry boots (*PP* 28). Childlike Mrs Peerybingle in *The* CRICKET ON THE HEARTH seems to be merely playing at keeping house; she strikes a wifely pose of 'coquettish thoughtfulness' at the fireside, and charmingly fills her husband's pipe with her 'chubby little finger in the bowl'. Dickens's tone on such occasions can be described as thoughtlessly belittling to younger women. The flipside of this coin is sexual comedy at the expense of older women, who are, however, never so ugly that men can afford to ignore their marital designs. Mrs Bardell's breach-of-promise case may be only a passing threat to the genial bachelor culture of *Pickwick*, but Mrs Sparsit (*HT*) and Mrs General (*LD*) are more formidable forces to be reckoned with.

Dickens's male gaze is at its most suggestive where the narrator's eyes wander over the 'delicate bodice' and 'neglected dress' of Dolly Varden, while she bestows 'lavish caresses' on another woman (*BR* 59), but such sensual moments are few and far between. He is equally drawn to youthful innocence, a leaning that manifests itself in heroines with diminutives attached to their names—Little Nell, Little Em'ly, Little Dorrit—and in his understanding of the attraction felt by older men for young women, as with John Jarndyce's wish to make Esther his wife. The narrator in *A Christmas Carol* fantasizes about caressing a girl in the guise of a playmate, 'to have had the lightest licence of a child, and yet been man enough to know its value' (Stave 2). Some readers have found these sexual undercurrents disturbing, and while it has been argued that we are misreading Victorian sensibilities, it is worth noting that some of Dickens's contemporaries were also uneasy about the fondness for young girls expressed in his fiction (MACLISE confided to FORSTER, 'I'm never up to his young girls—he is so very fond of the age of "Nell" when they are most insipid'; Pilgrim 4.599 n.). There is, moreover, an odd blurring of relations between husband and wife, father and daughter, brother and sister. Victorian households often included sisters or daughters playing domestic roles—as Dickens's own sisters-in-law Mary HOGARTH and Georgina HOGARTH did—yet Ruth Pinch's coy behaviour to her brother, Bella Wilfer's flirtation with her father, Mr Dombey's response to his daughter, and Mr Peggotty's extravagant love for his niece sometimes play too close for comfort around the boundary with incest.

The lack of sexual attractiveness in Dickens's male characters is a matter that has caused little comment. The men provided as rewards for good women—Bella Wilfer's John Harmon and Ruth Pinch's John Westlock—are as unremarkable as their plain names. The honest sailors paired with Florence Dombey and Rosa Bud are utterly wholesome characters. By contrast, a BYRONIC figure like Steerforth wrecks lives: Rosa Dartle is literally and psychologically scarred, and Little Em'ly is ruined. David's adolescent infatuation with Steerforth is in part responsible for the catastrophe which comes to its climax in the tempest, the erotic element still latent in David's gaze as he looks at Steerforth's drowned body on the shore: 'lying with his head upon his arm, as [he] had often seen him lie at school' (*DC* 55). Dashing charm is clearly dangerous, displayed only by seducers and cads; acceptable suitors are expected to show restraint and chivalrous sensitivity. Even the 'feminine manner' of the little dancing teacher Prince Turveydrop meets with the approval of Caddy Jellyby and Esther Summerson (*BH* 14). The same novel draws the line at Harold Skimpole, though more for a fecklessness that undermines the work ethic than for a colourful extroversion that transgresses gender boundaries.

The sexual side of Dickens's characters is most interesting when denied direct expression. Self-denial and inhibition are striking features of several principal characters, both male and female, whose childhood experiences are responsible for their struggle to reach emotional maturity. Small wonder, as many critics have noted, that Dickens's work had a significant influence on Sigmund Freud (see Ned Lukacher, *Primal Scenes*, 1986; also CRITICISM AND SCHOLARSHIP: FREUDIAN). Pip (*GE*), brought up by an aggressive woman and a meek man, suffers for his adolescent desires at the hands of sexually manipulative Estella. She is cut off from her own emotions by the education she has received from her proxy mother Miss Havisham, herself deprived of a fulfilling marriage when she was jilted on her wedding day. Louisa Gradgrind attempts to explain herself to the aloof father who denied her any self-expression as a child by alluding to the fire that bursts out from Coketown's smoky chimneys at night, an image that evokes a yearning for fulfilment including sexual desire (*HT* 1.15). As a child, she finds her future husband Bounderby so repulsive that she threatens to cut out the place where he kisses her on her cheek with a penknife (*HT* 1.4). She later escapes from a union that disgusts her, though the reader has received no hints about her marital experiences in the meantime, but she is denied any opportunity to remarry. *Little Dorrit* is another novel centrally concerned with emotional deprivation. Miss Wade, locked up in a 'dead sort of house' with a dried-up fountain (*LD* 2.20), visits the kind of suffering she has experienced, as described in her autobiographical 'History of a Self-Tormentor', on the orphan servant-girl Tattycoram, drawing her into a mutually destructive relationship with unmistakable lesbian overtones. Disabled Mrs Clennam, imprisoned in one room of a decaying old house, with a damped-down fire that on rare occasions 'flashed up passionately, as she did' (*LD* 1.15), has inflicted her unhappiness on her adopted son, who is unable to assert his own desires until middle age. Yet Arthur Clennam and Little Dorrit show that it is possible to break free from the cycle of pain by seeking emotional satisfaction rather than responding with self-effacement to the needs of others. *Bleak House* renders an extreme case of self-denial with extraordinary insight through illegitimate Esther Summerson, deprived of her mother's love from birth. Esther is allowed her own slow flowering into marriage, but her surrogate father John Jarndyce must deprive himself of Esther's wifely companionship and give her up to a younger man. These novels say more about repression than sensuality or passion, but they give their endorsement to physical love and are not without moments of sexual resonance.

Sexuality is most powerful in Dickens's fiction where it is illicit or obsessive; indeed, the two aspects are linked, since any suggestion of undomesticated passion quickly shades into violence. Passionate women are immediately recognizable as wild and dangerous, yet their capacity to disturb the morality of the text is contained by a degree of stereotyping. Beautiful and imperious women like Edith (*DS*) and Estella (*GE*) predictably arouse and scorn sexual attention. Lady Dedlock still smoulders beneath her languidness. Rosa Dartle flies at Steerforth 'with the fury of a wild cat' (*DC* 29). The nature of Hortense (*BH*) is signalled by her foreignness, connoting strong un-English feelings, and specifically by her Frenchness, associating her with an ungovernable nation. Prostitutes and fallen women are conventionally depicted and appropriately punished.

Male characters driven by violence and lust, for whom there were few available stereotypes, exerted a more powerful hold on Dickens's imagination. There are certainly comic moments on this theme: sexually potent Quilp keeping his wife up all night while he blazes away with his phallic cigars (*OCS* 4–5) or avaricious Wegg displaying his excitement by the involuntary erection of his wooden leg (*OMF* 3.6). Though male pursuit can be presented as amusingly harmless in a ladies' man like Tracy Tupman (*PP*), flirtation is often close to harassment. The comic sexual patter of Mr Mantalini is juxtaposed with the predatory assault of Sir Mulberry Hawk (*NN* 19) and old Gride's lascivious designs on young Madeline Bray. Dickens's most memorable pursuers and tormentors of women are in deadly earnest. Bill Sikes bullies Nancy and—in a bloody passage that Dickens performed with relish in PUBLIC READINGS in the last year of his life—batters her to death. The overtly sexual Carker flashes his shark's teeth as he moves in for a kill. The lecherous dwarf Quilp coils suggestively into Little Nell's empty bed (*OCS* 11), one of the nastiest moments in a novel that plays on Nell's sexual vulnerability from the opening scene, where she walks the London pavements alone by night. In *Our Mutual Friend*, written at the time of his attraction to the young actress Ellen TERNAN, Dickens depicts Eugene Wrayburn's pursuit of Lizzie Hexam as voyeuristic and decadent, and in an extraordinary *tour de force* in the same book charts the parallel course of Bradley Headstone's murderous jealousy. Jasper is unusually close in his attachment to his young nephew Ned, and his sinister intensity makes schoolgirl Rosa Bud fear rape in the garden of the Nuns' House (*MED* 19). Sexuality is not one of the themes Dickens does best, but the darker side is done brilliantly. Yet Dickens passed himself off as a family writer always mindful of the young person. His contemporaries, and for a hundred years his critics, rarely focused on how he got 'so near the sexual side of things' as to be a little dangerous at times. (See also CRITICISM: FEMINIST.)                                   EW

Johnson, Pamela Hansford, 'The Sexual Life in Dickens's Novels', in Slater (1970).

Mason, Michael, *The Making of Victorian Sexuality* (1994*a*).

—— *The Making of Victorian Sexual Attitudes* (1994*b*).

Vicinus, Martha (ed.), *Suffer and Be Still* (1973).

—— (ed.), *A Widening Sphere* (1977).

**Seymour, Robert** (?1798–1836), graphic artist. The illegitimate son of a Somerset squire, Robert Seymour became in the early 1830s one of the more popular comic ILLUSTRATORS, adapting the unbridled political and social satire of James Gillray and Isaac, Robert, and George CRUIKSHANK to farcical lampoons about contemporary manners and customs, especially among urban dwellers playing at SPORTS in rural Islington where he lived. In the autumn of 1835 Seymour brought to CHAPMAN AND HALL, publishers of other of his works, drawings intended to illustrate the perils and mishaps befalling a 'Nimrod Club' of Cockneys who set themselves up as experts

in sports. After asking several writers to churn out letterpress to accompany the plates, and being turned down by all of them, Chapman and Hall approached Dickens, then known for his journalism and sketches. Dickens said 'yes', but from the start he intended to take his own way. The publishers had decided that Seymour's project would be issued in paper-covered monthly instalments, 24 pages of letterpress and four illustrations to retail at one shilling. Dickens wrote up to Seymour's designs for the first part, though Edward Chapman may have had a hand in changing the portrait of Mr Pickwick from a thin to a fat man, and consequently changing the conception of his character from splenetic to benevolent.

Seymour, despite his middling success as an artist, was depressed about finances and about the mediocrity of his career. His spirits were not enlivened when Dickens suggested that one of his drawings could be improved by altering the gesture of a figure; nor were they helped by the depressing story of a dying clown Dickens introduced into the plot, or by the friable metal on which he was trying to etch his designs. He had one face-to-face meeting with Dickens, on Sunday, 17 April 1836; issuing the invitation, Dickens asked the artist to change details in the design illustrating the dying clown. The evening in Furnival's Inn passed without incident. Seymour went home to Islington, finished biting in the third of four scheduled plates for Part 2, and then early in the morning of 20 April walked into his garden and shot himself.

Dickens, Chapman, and Hall scrambled to recover from this blow, and after a false start they succeeded. Mrs Seymour, however, had to struggle in dire poverty while the project her husband initiated catapulted the others to stardom. In the early 1840s she twice asked Dickens for assistance; he was unable to edit a volume on her behalf, but he did write a brief statement supporting an AMATEUR THEATRICAL performance to raise money for her. Nevertheless, his charity seemed to her grossly disproportionate to the fame and wealth he had won from her husband's idea. Rumours of her complaints reached Dickens, so in the Preface to the 1847 Cheap Edition of *Pickwick* he provided his own story of the novel's origin. Two years later, in considerable privation, Mrs Seymour once again demanded Dickens's help. This time he showed his response to her allegations to William Chapman and Mrs Samuel Carter Hall, a friend of Mrs Seymour as well as of Dickens. They substantiated his version of the story. Five years afterwards the unappeased widow printed her *Account*, overstating and even rewriting the record. The controversy flared up again in the 1860s, neither party being willing to let it rest. To the end of his life Dickens was adamant that Seymour's claims be contradicted and that all the evidence supporting his side be assembled and published.

Later research indicates that indeed Seymour may have prepared drawings to which Dickens wrote up for Parts 1 and 2, but the novel did not take off until after Part 4, by which stage Dickens had reconceived the original characters and plot, had added new ones, and with Hablot Knight BROWNE as his artist had substantially re-imaged the Pickwickians. Robert Seymour's contribution, therefore, was to bring to the fledgling publishing house another project turning the conventions and subjects of Georgian graphic humour on to city-bred men of modest independence who aspired to be taken as country squires. The notion in itself was not original. But Seymour's types became, under Dickens's hand, less stereotypical and far more influential figures of affectionate fun.          RLP

## Shakespeare, William (1564–1616), playwright and poet.

For Dickens Shakespeare was 'the great master who knew everything' ('Night Walks', *UT*), whose plays were 'an unspeakable source of delight' (to Forster, 22–3 March 1842). It has been well said that 'No one is better qualified to recognize literary genius than a literary genius' (Harbage 1976, p. 114), and no other author had so profound an influence upon Dickens. From the very outset of his career Dickens's achievement has been compared to that of Shakespeare, and it is a mark of his stature that to this day the comparison commands assent.

### Dickens's Engagement with Shakespeare

(See also DICKENS: PRIVATE LIFE; DICKENS: PUBLIC LIFE; DRAMA AND DRAMATISTS; NOVELIST AND MAN OF LETTERS, DICKENS AS.) Dickens's association with Shakespeare was lifelong. He knew 'all about' Falstaff as a 'very queer small boy' when his father took him for a walk at Gad's Hill ('Travelling Abroad', *UT*), and he included a characteristic paraphrase from *Macbeth* ('when it was really done, it seemed not worth the doing, it was done so soon') in the final chapter of the uncompleted *The Mystery of Edwin Drood*, written a few days before he died (*MED* 23; see *Macbeth* I.vii. 1–2).

Before he was 9 Dickens was taken by his cousin James Lamert to the Theatre Royal, Rochester, where he was terrified when Richard III 'backed up against the stage-box in which I was posted'. There he learned 'many wondrous secrets of Nature . . . of which not the least terrific were, that the witches in Macbeth bore an awful resemblance to the Thanes and other proper inhabitants of Scotland; and that the good King Duncan couldn't rest in his grave, but was constantly coming out of it and calling himself somebody else' ('Dullborough Town', *UT*). On the day after his eighteenth birthday, the earliest date he could gain admission to the library of the British Museum, among the books he checked out were two multi-volume editions of Shakespeare—one edited by a scholar suggestively named Samuel Weller Singer (Harbage 1976, p. 112; Pilgrim 1.9 n.). Dickens told FORSTER that as a young man he went to the theatre 'every night, with a very few exceptions, for at least three years' (Forster 5.1). In those days his chief ambition was the stage (Forster 1.4), and the description of 'Private Theatres' (*SB*), in which aspiring young actors paid money to assume roles such as that of Richard III, is likely to derive from personal experience. In 1833 he wrote and, with his family and friends, produced a Shakespearean travesty, *O'THELLO*.

He soon came to know leading Shakespeare scholars, critics, and actors, including John Payne Collier, Charles KNIGHT, and William Charles MACREADY. Macready, famous for his Shakespeare productions, was to become one of his most intimate friends for the rest of his life. Dickens was a trusted adviser during the actor's management of Covent Garden (1837–8), and dedicated *Nicholas Nickleby* to him. He was also a close friend of the artist Daniel MACLISE, whose fame was based in large part on his paintings of scenes from Shakespeare, which Dickens admired greatly. Later he became a financial backer and personal friend of the actor Charles FECHTER, whose performances as Hamlet and Othello impressed him greatly.

A regular member of the SHAKESPEARE CLUB during its brief existence (1838–9), Dickens was thereafter a member of Council (1843–4) for the Shakespeare Society, 49 of whose publications were in his library at the time of his death (Pilgrim 3.455n.). In 1838 he visited Shakespeare's birthplace in Stratford and left his autograph there (to Mrs Charles Dickens, 1 November 1838). Throughout 1848 he busied himself with the London Shakespeare Committee, which had purchased the birthplace, and Dickens was the driving force behind an AMATEUR THEATRICAL production of The Merry Wives of Windsor, which toured in order to raise money to endow a curatorship, to be offered to the playwright James Sheridan KNOWLES. (In the event, absence of government support prevented the creation of the post, but not for lack of effort on Dickens's part.) In 1855 Dickens was approached to propose to the Shakespeare Society the purchase of an alleged portrait of Shakespeare (to John Murray, 22 November 1855).

On the occasion of the first anniversary of the appearance of the first number of The Pickwick Papers his publishers CHAPMAN AND HALL presented him with a set of Shakespeare (Pilgrim 1.244n.), and when he sailed for AMERICA Forster gave him a one-volume Shakespeare, which, he reported, 'I constantly carry in my great-coat pocket' (22–3 March 1842). And when in 1856 he purchased Gad's Hill Place, his HOME for the remainder of his life, he commissioned and displayed an illuminated inscription (now in the DICKENS HOUSE MUSEUM), commemorating its associations with Falstaff.

## Shakespeare in Dickens's Writing

(See also under individual works.) Dickens's novels, JOURNALISM, and LETTERS are saturated with quotations, creative misquotations, and allusions to Shakespeare. The extent of Dickens's references to Shakespeare is suggested by the catalogue compiled by Valerie Gager, which, although admittedly incomplete, extends to some 120 pages (Gager 1996, pp. 245–369). In his early essay 'The Pantomime of Life', published in BENTLEY'S MIS-CELLANY (March 1837), Dickens refers to himself as a follower of Shakespeare, 'tracking out his footsteps at the scarcely-worth-mentioning little distance of a few millions of leagues behind', and in a speech honouring THACKERAY in 1858 he declared, 'Every writer of fiction, though he may not adopt the dramatic form, writes in effect for the stage' (Speeches, p. 262).

His fiction contains memorable comic descriptions of Shakespearean tragedies: Othello is the play chosen for amateur theatricals by the eponymous Mrs Joseph Porter (SB); Romeo is the character in which Nicholas Nickleby achieves his finest hour with Vincent Crummles's strolling players; and the most extended account of a Shakespearean performance appears in Great Expectations, when Pip and Herbert go to see Mr Wopsle undertake the role of Hamlet (GE 31).

Dickens wrote theatre reviews of Macready as Lear (Examiner, 28 January 1838 and 27 October 1849; Journalism 2) and as Benedick (Examiner, 4 March 1843; Journalism 2). In collaboration with R. H. HORNE, Dickens wrote a lead article for Household Words praising the Shakespeare productions of Samuel Phelps at Sadler's Wells Theatre (HW 4 October 1851; Uncollected Writings 1), and in August 1869 contributed an essay, 'On Mr Fechter's Acting', to Atlantic Monthly. In addition, he published essays on Shakespeare in his journals. Under his editorship, in Bentley's Miscellany alongside Oliver Twist he published a series of six studies of Shakespeare's characters by William MAGINN. Household Words included 'Something that Shakespeare Lost' (HW 17 January 1857), by Henry MORLEY, on contemporary reviewing of Hamlet; 'Touching the Lord Hamlet', a source study of Hamlet by John Oxenford (HW 17 October 1857); and 'Re-Touching the Lord Hamlet', by J. A. Heraud (HW 5 December 1857). In Nickleby Dickens ridicules both wrong-headed scholarship (Mr Curdle) and mindless gushing over the bard (Mrs Wititterly). Moreover, as Harbage has observed, Dickens was 'apt to quote Shakespeare whenever he stated his creed as a writer' (Harbage 1976, p. 118), perhaps most eloquently in the words of Nicholas Nickleby: 'He [Shakespeare] brought within the magic circle of his genius, traditions peculiarly adapted for his purpose, and turned familiar things into constellations which should enlighten the world for ages' (NN 48).

There are references by Dickens to the majority of Shakespeare's works, but the overwhelming preponderance come from two plays, *Hamlet* and *Macbeth*. These seem to indicate that Dickens uses Shakespeare's lines as vehicles for his own thought, both from the frequency of allusion and from the active way in which Dickens adapts quotations to suit his own purposes. But he also uses at least one play as a structural model for his novels; a number of critics, most notably Alexander Welsh, have explored parallels between *King Lear* and *The Old Curiosity Shop*, *Dombey and Son*, and *Hard Times* in particular. In Welsh's words, 'whenever Dickens required an exalted test of love and truth in his fiction, he tended to favour the Cordelia model of loyalty to a difficult father ... Dickens, in fact, cannot be said ever to have completed the study of *King Lear* inspired by Macready's production of 1838' (Welsh 1987, pp. 88, 104).

### The Nature of the Affinity

(See also STYLE OF DICKENS; COMPOSITION, DICKENS'S METHODS OF; MELODRAMA IN DICKENS'S WRITING; THEATRE AND THEATRICALITY.) Angus Wilson has well observed that literary influence is not the lifting of identifiable snippets, but a response which 'affects your whole outlook, the whole fictional world you live in, and that isn't a matter of taking little pieces and incorporating them, however transformed' (*Dickens Memorial Lectures*, 1970, p. 42). Dickens's art is like Shakespeare's in three major ways: it is entertaining, it is theatrical, and it is verbally inventive.

It is crucial to an understanding of Dickens's admiration for Shakespeare to recognize that he knew the plays both in theatrical production and as text. Theatre licensing laws up to 1843 dictated that 'legitimate' (i.e. wholly spoken) drama could be performed in London only in Covent Garden and Drury Lane (and at the Haymarket during the summer), and outside London in select Theatres Royal. Dickens knew such productions intimately. But Shakespeare was also performed in radically adapted form in the minor theatres, in FAIRGROUND booth theatres, in penny 'gaffs', and even on horseback in the CIRCUS. In such productions dialogue was largely eliminated in favour of action, spectacle, and music. 'The presence of Shakespearean adaptations outside the patent theatres offered Dickens a supreme example that popularity need not mean hackneyed frivolousness, and that achievement of lasting worth could exist within popular forms' (Schlicke 1991, p. 12). Like Shakespeare, Dickens was an entertainer who saw no conflict between popular appeal and artistic excellence.

Dickens's fiction is essentially histrionic: he visualizes the appearance of his characters; he depicts them dramatically interacting with one another; and when they talk, they invariably declaim. His daughter Mamie recounted how she watched one day as he wrote—grimacing in a mirror in order himself to enact the scene he would then retreat to his desk to transcribe (Mamie Dickens, *My Father As I Recall Him*, 1897, pp. 47–9). One of his richest and most typical comic veins is the pretence that people behave the same way in private as in public; that is, his characters are invariably seen performing their own distinctive roles. The law-clerk Mr Guppy proposes marriage to Esther by asking to be allowed to 'file a declaration' (*BH* 9); Mr Lillyvick talks in the argot of a water-rates collector in the Kenwigses drawing-room (*NN* 15). Often an audience gathers to witness set pieces: a crowd 'to the number of some five-and-twenty' follows Bounderby to his self-exposure as a fraud (*HT* 3.5); the village urchins watch Trabb's boy mimicking Pip (*GE* 30). Dickens has an eye for group scenes, in which characters are carefully placed in relation to one another, and action regularly ends in tableau, such as the finale of *Martin Chuzzlewit*, when Old Martin thrashes Pecksniff (*MC* 52). This is one reason why Dickens's fiction lends itself so well to ILLUSTRATION, and it is notable that some DRAMATIZATIONS of Dickens's works consisted of little more than tableaux in which actors arranged themselves in living representations of Phiz's drawings (see BROWNE, H. K.). Dickens was an inferior PLAYWRIGHT, but his novels are Shakespearean in their vital theatricality.

Finally, Dickens is like Shakespeare in his verbal inventiveness. Both writers extended and enriched the language; both delight in the novel turn of phrase, the vivid yoking of words not usually heard together. This produces the animism so characteristic of their language: inert things take on a life of their own, whereas living creatures are grotesquely reified. It produces the dynamic interrelation between the mundane and the imaginary, constantly testing the boundaries between the real and the fanciful. And it produces extraordinary richness of texture, in which the local life of a phrase encapsulates the wider themes of a work, functioning as an 'expanded metaphor'—Wilson Knight's description of Shakespearean language, which Steven Marcus tellingly applies to Dickens (1965, p. 40). In this sense Dickens, like Shakespeare, is a supreme poet of the English language. As F. R. LEAVIS observed about 'Dickens's command of word, phrase, rhythm and image: in ease and range there is surely no greater master of English except Shakespeare' (Leavis, 1970, p. 207). PVWS

> Gager, Valerie, *Dickens and Shakespeare: The Dynamics of Influence* (1996).
>
> Harbage, Alfred, *A Kind of Power: The Shakespeare–Dickens Analogy* (1975).
>
> —— 'Shakespeare and the Young Dickens', in G. B. Evans (ed.), *Shakespeare: Aspects of Influence* (1976).
>
> Schlicke, Paul, 'The Showman of *The Pickwick Papers*', *Dickens Studies Annual*, 19 (1991).

**Shakespeare Club,** an association of some 70 leading writers, actors, painters, and musicians, including Dickens, which was founded 'to combine intellectual with social enjoyment'. It met weekly on Saturday nights for readings, papers, and discussion, and monthly for supper. Dickens attended frequently during the two years of the club's existence, 1838–9. It broke up at the annual dinner, 7 December 1839, with Dickens in the chair, when FORSTER provoked an altercation. The following year former Club members founded the Shakespeare Society (1840–53), a subscription publishing venture in which Dickens served (1843–4) as a member of the Council. PVWS

> Stone, Marcus, 'The Shakespeare Club', *Dickensian*, 41 (1944).

**Sheridan, Richard Brinsley** (1751–1816), playwright. He wrote several plays well known to Dickens, including *The Rivals* (1775), a comedy mocking SENTIMENTALISM and introducing the comic characters of Bob Acres and Mrs Malaprop; *The School for Scandal* (1777); *The Critic* (1779), a satire on contemporary drama; and *Pizarro* (1799), a romantic drama adapted from the German

playwright Kotzebue. In 1776 he became manager of Drury Lane Theatre, maintaining his connection until its destruction by fire in 1809, and in 1780 he became a Member of Parliament. Dickens frequently refers to *The Rivals* and played Sir Peter Teazle (*The School for Scandal*) in AMATEUR THEATRICALS; he probably saw Charles MATHEWS play Puff in *The Critic* at Drury Lane in 1828. JD

**short-story and sketch writer, Dickens as.** Dickens's first imaginative writing, published in newspapers and periodicals and later collected as *Sketches by Boz*, consisted exclusively of tales and sketches, and these were forms to which he returned repeatedly throughout his career. There are short stories included within the main discourse of both *Pickwick* and *Nickleby*, and later Miss Wade's autobiography in *Little Dorrit* stands as an independent set-piece. The MUDFOG PAPERS (1837–8), MASTER HUMPHREY'S CLOCK (1840), The UNCOMMERCIAL TRAVELLER (1860–9), and the Christmas stories Dickens wrote between 1850 and 1867 are further examples of short narratives published in periodicals he edited. In addition he wrote the five novella-length Christmas books of the 1840s, two supernatural anecdotes for the *Keepsake* in 1851 ('TO BE READ AT DUSK'), and three stories for American periodicals late in his career: 'HUNTED DOWN' (1859), 'GEORGE SILVERMAN'S EXPLANATION' (1868), and 'HOLIDAY ROMANCE' (1868).

The early short stories are largely undistinguished, drawing without distinctive originality on conventions of theatrical farce, GOTHIC FICTION, and other forms which Dickens had enjoyed from childhood. The sketches, on the other hand, from the very earliest are fresh and original in their attention to everyday places and events, vibrant with sharply observed detail, and urgent in their sympathy with ordinary people. The late stories and sketches are remarkable for the sophistication of their narrative strategies, their complexities of tone, and their psychological subtlety.

The 'BOZ' sketches show Dickens forging an attractive narrative persona, genial, alert, ready to be amused, and impatient with cant. Master Humphrey, however, a lugubrious old cripple, lacked the versatility which Dickens needed, and was quickly jettisoned when

*Master Humphrey's Clock* evolved into *The Old Curiosity Shop*. Later stories deploy first-person narrators suitable to each, and several of the Christmas stories are conceived as dramatic monologues (the Boots at the Holly Tree Inn, Mrs Lirriper, Doctor Marigold, the Boy at Mugby). Most interesting of all is the persona of the Uncommercial Traveller, a figure whose sadder but wiser vision interfuses retrospection with stocktaking in the present, as Pip does with such delicacy in *Great Expectations*. For narrative technique alone, a story such as 'Dullborough Town' (*UT*) shows Dickens at the very height of his powers.

In contrast to the realism of *Sketches by Boz* and *The Uncommercial Traveller*, 'The Story of the Goblins Who Stole a Sexton' (*PP*), 'The Baron of Grogzwig' (*NN*), the Christmas books, and some of the Christmas stories are conceived as versions of FAIRY TALES. And although 'The Haunted House', the 1859 Christmas Number of *All the Year Round*, debunked supernaturalism, two of Dickens's most compelling stories, 'The Bride's Chamber' (in 'The LAZY TOUR OF TWO IDLE APPRENTICES', 1857) and 'The Signalman' (in 'Mugby Junction', the 1866 Christmas Number of *All the Year Round*) deal centrally with the uncanny (see GHOST STORIES).

In her study of Dickens's short stories, Deborah Thomas summarizes: 'In terms of such subjects as the supernatural, psychological abnormality, public entertainment, the idea of joint authorship, and the whole issue of "fancy" in a pervasively factual age, these stories occupied an important position in Dickens's thoughts' (Thomas 1982, p. 1).

                                                                    PVWS

**silver fork novels.** Novels of high society which dominated English and American fiction from the mid-1820s to the early 1840s. In Dickens's estimation they were 'mawkish tales of fashionable life'. American readers, he complained, fell down before them as if they were 'gilded calves'; in England, novels affecting an interest in gentility were 'snugly enshrined in circulating LIBRARIES' (to John Forster, 3 May 1842). The term was first used by William HAZLITT in 1827 before it took on a more specific application to describe novelists eager to chronicle the manners and morals of the aristocracy. Credit for the origin

of the genre usually goes to publisher Henry Colburn, who in the mid-1820s recognized and then exploited a Regency taste for details about high life. Theodore HOOK's *Sayings and Doings* (1824) and Benjamin DISRAELI's *Vivien Grey* were early successes, and the Countess of Blessington and Catherine Gore wrote prolifically in the genre. BULWER-LYTTON's silver fork novel *Pelham* (1828) was 'probably the biggest long-term best-seller of the century' (John Sutherland, *The Longman Companion to Victorian Fiction*, 1988).

Dickens offers an amusing burlesque of the genre in *The Lady Flabella*, a new novel in three volumes full of 'sweet descriptions', which Kate Nickleby reads aloud to Mrs Wititterly. In a single page he ridicules the use of French phrases, descriptions of 'half-playful half-angry' altercations between characters, and the delivery of amorous sentiments in scented *billets*. Taking one from 'a golden salver' held by a kneeling page, the Lady Flabella, 'with an agitation she could not repress, hastily tore off the *envelope* and broke the scented seal. It *was* from Befillaire—the young, the slim, the low-voiced—*her own* Befillaire' (*NN* 28).

Dickens's response to 'silver fork' society in real life was thoughtfully modulated. As early as 1836 he was introduced into the cosmopolitan set over which the Countess of Blessington presided at Gore House. For her, he complied with her request for a contribution to *The Keepsake* in 1843 despite his objection to ANNUALS; three years later he wrote appreciatively of contributions he solicited from her, a series of 'On Dits' published in the DAILY NEWS detailing 'that World' which she knew all about (16 January 1846). He also responded to an overture of friendship from Mrs Catherine Gore (1799–1861), the prolific author of numerous fictional accounts of upper-middle-class society in the 1830s. She sent him presentation copies of her books, dedicated *The Dean's Daughter* (1853) to him, and occasionally asked for help with literary projects. In return, Dickens maintained a discreet yet not unfriendly distance. Most remarkable is the frank account he sent her of his separation from Catherine DICKENS (31 May 1858).                                    DHP

Adburgham, Alison, *Silver Fork Society* (1983).

Rosa, M. W., *Silver Fork School* (1936).

**Sketches by Boz** Dickens's first book, which gathered, along with some new pieces, the sketches and tales which he had published between 1833 and 1836 in newspapers and journals. Inspired by his love of the writings of 18th- and 19th-century ESSAYISTS, with their distinctively crafted narrative personae (see 'BOZ'), the sketches attracted some attention and led CHAPMAN AND HALL to invite Dickens to collaborate with SEYMOUR on *The Pickwick Papers*. Although the huge success of that work quickly eclipsed the reputation of *Sketches by Boz* (FORSTER claimed (1.5) that Dickens 'decidedly underrated it'), Dickens retained an active interest in the sketch form, culminating in The UNCOMMERCIAL TRAVELLER pieces written in the last decade of his life (see SHORT-STORY AND SKETCH WRITER, DICKENS AS).

### Inception and Composition

Most of the stories and sketches collected in *Sketches by Boz* were first written as individual miscellaneous items for various periodical publications. Details can be found in Appendix F of volume 1 of the Pilgrim *Letters*; in Appendix A of De Vries 1976; and in *Journalism* 1, pp. xxiii–xxvi. Michael Slater's Introduction to that volume offers a succinct survey, and Maxwell (1981) examines the distinctly differing audiences at which the different newspapers and periodicals in which the pieces first appeared were aimed.

In the Preface to the Cheap Edition of *Pickwick* (1847) Dickens described the excitement he felt in seeing his first piece of creative writing ('A Dinner at Poplar Walk', later retitled 'Mr Minns and His Cousin') in print, and his surprise, when introduced several years later to the publisher William Hall, at recognizing him to be the man who sold him the December 1833 issue of the MONTHLY MAGAZINE in which the tale appeared—the kind of coincidence which always delighted him. He recalled purchasing 'my first copy of the magazine in which my first effusion— dropped stealthily one evening at twilight, with fear and trembling, into a dark letter-box, in a dark office, up a court in Fleet Street—appeared in all the glory of print; on which occasion by-the-bye,—how well I recollect it!—I walked down to Westminster Hall, and turned into it for half-an-hour, because my eyes were so dimmed with joy and

pride, that they could not bear the street, and were not fit to be seen there.'

Between January 1834 and January 1835 Dickens contributed one story, 'Sentiment', to BELL'S WEEKLY MAGAZINE (6 June 1834), and six more stories to the *Monthly Magazine*: 'Mrs Joseph Porter', 'Horatio Sparkins', 'The Bloomsbury Christening', 'The Boarding House' (in two parts), 'The Steam Excursion', and 'A Passage in the Life of Mr Watkins Tottle' (also in two parts). The *Monthly* requested more, but because they were ' "rather backward in coming forward" with the needful', he ceased sending contributions there once he could earn money by placing them elsewhere (to H. W. Kolle, ?10 December 1833). Except for 'The Boarding House', these farcical tales deal with a social sphere higher than the one he knew personally at the time, and as a result are largely unoriginal, lacking a distinctively Dickensian touch. In 'The Boarding House', however, Dickens focused instead on a lower-middle-class milieu and found 'his peculiar cast and territory' (Chittick 1990).

This territory served as the subject-matter for the quite different contributions Dickens published in the MORNING CHRONICLE in the autumn of 1834, after he was hired in August as a reporter for that newspaper. These were not tales but 'Street Sketches'—'Omnibuses', 'Shops and Their Tenants', 'The Old Bailey' (later entitled 'Criminal Courts'), 'Shabby-Genteel People', and 'Brokers and Marine-Store Shops'—which broke new ground by offering astonishingly vivid and accurate vignettes of London people and scenes. As Michael Slater notes, ' "Boz" is not simply an animated camera cum tape recorder. He has a heart and evokes our sympathy ... Already in these sketches Dickens is experimenting, very effectively, with that blending of the wildly comic and the intensely pathetic that was to win and keep him such thousands of devoted readers in after years' (*Journalism* 1, p. xiii).

In January 1835 Dickens was invited by George HOGARTH, editor of the newly founded EVENING CHRONICLE and father of the woman Dickens was to marry the next year, to contribute a sketch to the first number. Dickens responded by offering to write a series of sketches and deferentially asking if the proprietors (who also owned the *Morning Chronicle*) 'would think I had any claim to *some* additional remuneration (of course no great amount) for doing so' (20 January 1835). Both proposals were immediately agreed to: between 31 January and 20 August, 20 'Sketches of London' appeared in the *Evening Chronicle*, and during that period his salary was increased from five guineas per week to seven. As in the *Morning Chronicle* sketches, these pieces were notable for keen observation, humour, and pathos, intermingled with occasional bursts of sympathizing dismay at the sight of 'misery and distress' ('The Pawnbroker's Shop') and of outrage at what he considered misguided attitudes to DRINK ('Gin Shops').

In September 1835, on completion of the *Evening Chronicle* series, Dickens began a series of twelve 'Scenes and Characters' for BELL'S LIFE IN LONDON. Published under a different soubriquet, 'Tibbs' (the name of the 'melancholy specimen of the story-teller' in 'The Boarding House'), these pieces included five farcical tales—far more assured and individual than the *Monthly* stories—an extended character study ('Some Account of an Omnibus Cad'), four metropolitan sketches, and two seasonal pieces ('Christmas Festivities'—later retitled 'A Christmas Dinner'—and 'The New Year'). The last of Dickens's contributions to *Bell's Life*, 'The Streets—Night' (which was a counterpart to 'The Streets—Morning', published in the *Evening Chronicle* on 21 July 1835), appeared on 17 January 1836, just three weeks before the publication of *Sketches by Boz*, First Series.

Between the publication of the First and Second Series of *Sketches* Dickens wrote 'Our Next Door Neighbours', which appeared in both the *Morning* and *Evening Chronicle* on 18 March (see Graham Mott, 'The First Publication of "Our Next Door Neighbours" ', *Dickensian*, 80, 1984, correcting earlier claims that it was unpublished until the Second Series); 'The Tuggses at Ramsgate' and 'A Little Talk about Spring, and the Sweeps' (later retitled 'The First of May'), which first appeared in the LIBRARY OF FICTION in April and June 1836, respectively; and 'The Hospital Patient' and 'Hackney Cabs, and their Drivers' for the CARLTON CHRONICLE, 6 August and 17 September 1836, respectively; plus four further pieces—among the very best of the *Sketches* —for the *Morning Chronicle*: 'Meditations in Monmouth Street' (24 September), 'Scotland Yard' (4 October), 'Doctors' Commons' (11 October), and 'Vauxhall Gardens by Day' (26 October).

Finally, Dickens included two pieces specifically for *Sketches by Boz*, First Series— 'A Visit to Newgate' (a subject which he found 'a very difficult one to do justice to' because he had 'so much difficulty remembering the place, and arranging my materials': to Catherine Hogarth, 25 November 1835), and the macabre 'Black Veil'. A third item, 'The Great Winglebury Duel', was originally intended for the December 1835 number of the *Monthly Magazine* but did not appear there, perhaps (as the Pilgrim editors suggest: 1.83n.) because Dickens decided to rewrite it for theatrical production, as The STRANGE GENTLEMAN. One more tale was first published in the Second Series: 'The Drunkard's Death', written with 'great pains', to 'finish the Volume with *eclat*' (to T. C. Hansard, 7 December 1835).

### Contracts, Text, and Publication History

In October 1835 John MACRONE, having recently been introduced to Dickens by Harrison AINSWORTH, offered £100 for the COPYRIGHT of a collected edition of the pieces which Dickens had been writing over the previous two years—a very handsome sum for a first book (see MONEY VALUES; Forster (1.5) names the amount as £150; but Dickens later told his lawyer Thomas Mitton that he received £100 'three or four days after the publication': 13 May 1839). The Pilgrim editors speculate that there may have been a contract, but none has come to light (Pilgrim 1.647).

Dickens worked closely with Macrone (whom he asked to be best man at his wedding: Pilgrim 1.81 n.), and with George CRUIKSHANK, who illustrated the volumes. His surviving letters indicate his commitment to the project, his eagerness to see the book into print, and his frustration over delays. He revised all of the stories carefully, removing indelicacies and profanity, altering punctuation and style, and cutting back topical and political allusions. There has never been a reprinting of the stories in their original form, nor a systematic study of Dickens's revisions, but Kathleen Tillotson discusses, *inter alia*, types of changes between the initial and the collected versions (Butt and Tillotson 1957, ch. 2).

Planned to appear in time for the CHRISTMAS trade, *Sketches* was not published until

8 February 1836, the day after Dickens's twenty-fourth birthday. It sold so well that a new edition was published on 10 August, followed by a third on 11 March 1837. A Second Series in one volume (originally conceived as two volumes) appeared on 17 December 1836 and in a second edition on 21 March 1837. Meanwhile, Dickens took on far more commitments than even one so energetic as he could possibly fulfill: monthly numbers of *Pickwick* for Chapman and Hall; two plays, *The* VILLAGE COQUETTES and *The Strange Gentleman*; the editorship of BENTLEY'S MISCELLANY; 'Gabriel Vardon' for Macrone (eventually published by Chapman and Hall as *Barnaby Rudge*), another novel, to be written for Richard BENTLEY before any other literary work; and a children's book, 'SOLOMON BELL THE RAREE SHOWMAN', which was abandoned. In between times he married Catherine Hogarth on 2 April 1836 and continued reporting for the *Morning Chronicle* until November of that year.

As a result, when the Second Series did appear on 17 December 1836, it consisted of a single volume only, including one new piece, 'The Drunkard's Death', and all the rest of Dickens's previously published sketches and tales which had not appeared in the First Series (except 'The Tuggses at Ramsgate', omitted until the combined edition published by Chapman and Hall). Dickens revised the texts and amalgamated some existing sketches. By this time he and Macrone were in dispute over 'Gabriel Vardon' (see BARNABY RUDGE), and Dickens was further angered when the publisher proposed to cash in on the popularity of *Pickwick* by reissuing the *Sketches* in a monthly format similar to that of the novel (to Forster, ?9 June 1837). Matters were settled when Chapman and Hall bought the copyrights for both series for £2,250—for which Macrone had paid £100 only six months previously—and reissued the combined series (now arranged for the first time in the divisions which have been retained in all subsequent editions) in 20 monthly parts—with pink rather than Pickwickian green covers—between November 1837 and June 1839. Once again Dickens carefully revised the text, and added 'The Tuggses at Ramsgate'. When serialization was complete, Chapman and Hall brought out a one-volume edition of both series of *Sketches by Boz*.

Dickens, who received a total of £450 from Macrone, estimated that the publisher had cleared £4,000 from the venture (to Mitton, 13 May 1839)—a figure which Patten (1978) describes as 'wildly high'. Carey, Lea, and Blanchard of Philadelphia brought out an edition in 1836 as *Watkins Tottle and Other Sketches*; there were editions published in Calcutta (1837), Paris (1839), and Leipzig (1843), plus a German TRANSLATION by H. Roberts in 1838.

Dickens wrote two advertisements and four Prefaces to *Sketches by Boz*. Confiding to Macrone that 'I really can*not* do the tremendous in puffing myself' (2 February 1836), he sent a paragraph for insertion in the *Morning Chronicle* which described the first series as 'entertaining' and singled out 'A Visit to Newgate' as 'very powerful' (Pilgrim 1.123 n.). The first Preface, written the previous month but dated February 1836, described the work as 'a pilot balloon', and claimed as his purpose 'to present little pictures of life and manners as they really are'. The Preface to the second edition of the First Series, dated 1 August 1836, consisted entirely of an expression of 'deepest gratitude' for 'the kindness and indulgence with which these volumes have been universally received'. By the time of the advertisement to the first collected edition, dated 15 May 1839, Dickens was taking a more apologetic tone, noting that the pieces were 'the earliest productions of their Author, written from time to time to meet the exigencies of a Newspaper or a Magazine', and in the Preface to the Cheap Edition (1850), reprinted unaltered in the Charles Dickens Edition (1868), his tone was positively embarrassed, calling the *Sketches* 'often . . . extremely crude and ill-considered, and bearing obvious marks of haste and inexperience' (see EDITIONS OVER WHICH DICKENS HAD CONTROL).

**Illustrations**

From the inception of the project illustrations were conceived as an integral part of the book's appeal, and Macrone enlisted Cruikshank as artist. As Robert Patten notes (1978), the proposed titles all give Cruikshank equal billing with Dickens: 'Bubbles from the Brain of Boz and the Graver of Cruikshank', 'Sketches by Boz and Cuts by Cruikshank', 'Etchings by Boz and Wood Cuts by Cruikshank' (to Macrone ?27 October 1835; Pilgrim 1.82 n.), and the title chosen indicates the pictorial nature of Dickens's writing. Cruikshank was already a well-established artist, and his London street scenes were widely popular. Dickens and Cruikshank did not meet at once, but before they were introduced Dickens told Macrone that 'no one appreciates so highly as myself . . . the much appreciated talents' of the illustrator (7 November 1835). Initially Dickens blamed Cruikshank for causing delays in the book's publication, but soon author and illustrator were collaborating congenially, and the first Preface fulsomely praised Cruikshank's drawings.

Cruikshank supplied sixteen illustrations for the First Series and ten for the Second Series, plus two more for the second edition. When reissued by Chapman and Hall, page size was altered, forcing Cruikshank to re-etch the illustrations. One was omitted and thirteen new ones added. He also replaced the original cover design for the 1839 edition with a new cover featuring a balloon, reflecting his own interest in ballooning and Dickens's metaphor for the book in the first Preface.

### Sources and Context

The immediate literary context of the sketches was depiction of urban street scenes by the Regency writers of Dickens's youth, notably Charles LAMB, Thomas DE QUINCEY, Pierce EGAN, Thomas HOOD, Theodore HOOK, John Poole, and Leigh HUNT. Dickens was amused to note that one early reader identified Boz as Hunt (to Macrone, ?March 1836). Virgil Grillo (1974) has explored the relationship of *Sketches by Boz* with some of these writers, concluding that what makes Boz distinctive is the 'rhetorical relationship' he establishes with the reader, to draw the reader in and distil the essence of a scene.

More generally, Dickens is working within the tradition of essay-writing which dates back to ADDISON and STEELE and their 'Mr Spectator' essays, in which the genial narrative persona making observations is as essential as the subjects being observed. As readers have noted from the start, the vividly visual quality of the sketches, focusing on the bustle of London low-life, links them with the graphic art of William HOGARTH. 'The soul of Hogarth has migrated into the body of Mr Dickens', declared Sydney SMITH (Pilgrim 1.431 n.). A further tradition which fed into the sketches, as Edward Costigan has shown

(1976), is the melodramatic THEATRE of the day, with its emphasis on gesture, externalized detail, and eccentric speech patterns (see MELODRAMA).

### Plot, Character, and Theme

Michael Slater notes that the opening paragraph of the *Bell's Life in London* version of 'The Prisoner's Van', omitted from collected editions, 'might well serve as an introduction to Boz's sketches in general' (*Journalism* 1, p. xvi): 'We have a most extraordinary partiality for lounging about the streets. Whenever we have an hour or two to spare, there is nothing we enjoy more than a little amateur vagrancy —walking up one street and down another, and staring into shop windows, and gazing about as if, instead of being on intimate terms with every shop and house in Holborn, the Strand, Fleet Street and Cheapside, the whole were an unknown region to our wandering mind. . .'

Formally, the sketches and tales are organized in fundamentally different ways. The sketches generally lack plot and proceed wherever Boz's enquiring eye happens to alight. Their tone is genial, compassionate, and urbane. The tales, in contrast, are generally sardonic, moving boldly towards narrative climax, which often exposes vain or foolish characters to ridicule; a few other pieces, notably 'The Black Veil' and 'The Drunkard's Death', elicit GOTHIC horrors.

In both the sketches and the tales, Dickens's primary object is to entertain, through sensitive responsiveness to the variety of people and things in the mundane world about us. Social commentary is also an important element in many sketches. It was their fidelity to observed reality which impressed contemporary readers, whereas later readers have responded more to the interfusion of that reality with fanciful vision, perhaps most effectively in 'Meditations in Monmouth Street', in which clothes dancing on racks in the street set Boz speculating on the people who might have worn them.

### Reception

For a collection of miscellaneous imaginative writings, *Sketches by Boz* attracted a surprising amount of attention, which would seem more noteworthy had its fame not been rapidly eclipsed by the spectacular success of *Pickwick*. Even before they were collected, one of the stories, 'The Bloomsbury Christening', had been successfully adapted for the stage by J. B. BUCKSTONE—an accolade which Dickens wryly acknowledged in a letter to the editor of the *Morning Chronicle*, noting that 'Mr Buckstone has officiated as self-elected godfather, and carried off my child to the Adelphi' (October 1834). On the publication of the first series, George Hogarth wrote what Dickens described as a 'beautiful notice' for the *Morning Chronicle*, praising Dickens as 'a close and acute observer of character and manners, with a strong sense of the ridiculous', and singling out 'A Visit to Newgate' as 'the most remarkable paper' in the collection (to Macrone, 11 February 1836; Pilgrim 1.129 n.). The *Sunday Times* (21 February) declared that Boz surpassed Hood; the *Court Journal* (20 February) called him 'a kind of Boswell to society'; and John Forster (who had not at this stage met Dickens) praised him in the *Examiner* (28 February) for his perception of the ludicrous, his pathos, and his 'agreeable racy style'.

The 'great success', as Dickens called it at the time, of the *Sketches*, 'established [his name] among the Publishers' and enabled him to marry Catherine Hogarth at an earlier date than anticipated (to T. C. Barrow, 31 March 1836). The publication, Kathleen Tillotson concludes, was of 'signal importance as an event in literary history', and its contemporary fame crucially influenced Dickens's literary career (Butt and Tillotson 1957). There have been two book-length studies of *Sketches*, by Virgil Grillo (1974) and by Duane DeVries (1976), and an influential essay by J. Hillis Miller (1971) on metonymy as 'a structuring principle'. PVWS

Butt and Tillotson (1957).

Chittick (1990).

Costigan, Edward, 'Drama and Everyday Life in *Sketches by Boz*', *Review of English Studies*, N.S. 27 (1976).

DeVries (1976).

Dexter, Walter, 'The Reception of Dickens's First Book', *Dickensian*, 32 (1936).

Easson, Angus, 'Who is Boz? Dickens and His Sketches', *Dickensian*, 81 (1985).

Grillo, Virgil, *Charles Dickens's Sketches by Boz: End in the Beginning* (1974).

Maxwell, Richard, 'Dickens, the Two Chronicles, and the Publication of *Sketches by Boz*', *Dickens Studies Annual*, 9 (1981).

Miller, J. Hillis, 'The Fiction of Realism: *Sketches by Boz*, *Oliver Twist*, and Cruikshank's Illustrations', in *Charles Dickens and George Cruikshank* (1971).

**Sketches of Young Couples** *With an Urgent Remonstrance to the Gentlemen of England (Being Bachelors or Widowers) on the Present Alarming Crisis, by the Author of Sketches of Young Gentlemen, with Six Illustrations by Phiz.* A collection of eleven sketches plus an 'urgent remonstrance' and a conclusion, archly ridiculing contemporary types, in response to the announcement by Queen Victoria of her intention to marry Prince Albert (see ROYALTY). Written anonymously by Dickens, illustrated by Hablot BROWNE (as 'Phiz'), and published by CHAPMAN AND HALL in 1840, the sketches were not collected in any edition of Dickens's works during his lifetime. PVWS

**Sketches of Young Gentlemen** *Dedicated to the Young Ladies, with Six Illustrations by Phiz.* A companion piece to *Sketches of Young Ladies* (1837) by 'Quiz' (Edward Caswall), written anonymously by Dickens, illustrated by Hablot BROWNE (as 'Phiz'), and published in 1838 by CHAPMAN AND HALL. It consists of twelve facetious descriptions of contemporary types, a dedication, and conclusion. The sketches were not collected in any edition of Dickens's works during his lifetime, although they were reissued, attributed to 'Boz', along with SKETCHES OF YOUNG COUPLES in 1846, and, attributed to 'Quiz', along with *Sketches of Young Ladies* and *Sketches of Young Couples* in 1869. PVWS

**Smiles, Samuel** (1812–1904), popular advocate of SELF-HELP, whose belief in upward mobility and in a redefined notion of the gentleman resembles ideas Dickens explored (see CLASS). Familiarity with Smiles can be inferred from Dickens's comment to MORLEY that Smiles's biography of George Stephenson would make 'an interesting article' for *Household Words* (1 June 1857). Elsewhere Dickens anticipates in David Copperfield's 'golden rules' (*DC* 42) ideas Smiles formulated nine years later, a relationship which reverses when the reformed Pip speaks of the need for hard work and self-respect in language suggestive of Smiles's essay 'Character: The True Gentleman' (*Self-Help*, 1859). Assessments of harmful self-improvement appear in Mr Bounderby (*HT*) and in Charlie Hexam (*OMF*). DHP

Morley, Henry, 'Inch by Inch', *HW* 18 July 1857.

**Smith, Albert** (1816–60), comic writer and entertainer. A contributor to BENTLEY'S MIS-CELLANY and PUNCH, he moved in some of the same circles as Dickens. Dickens supplied Smith with advance proof-sheets of *The* CRICKET ON THE HEARTH and *The* BATTLE OF LIFE for authorized DRAMATIZATIONS, performed by the KEELEYS, but he was irritated by an ADVERTISEMENT for Smith's serial novel *The Struggles and Adventures of Christopher Tadpole* (1848) in the *Dombey* advertiser, which compared Smith's harmless amusement with the 'ponderous attempt' of other novelists to confront social issues (24 October 1846). Smith's one-man show, part travelogue, part comic entertainment, *The Ascent of Mont Blanc*, which ran at the Egyptian Hall from 15 March 1852 for some 2,000 performances, was an undoubted influence on Dickens's PUBLIC READINGS. Although Smith was widely scorned as a vulgar showman, and condemned in private by Dickens as 'the bothering Albert' (to Mark Lemon, 21 April 1855), Dickens publicly praised Smith's 'ability and good humour' (*Speeches*, p. 175) and hired his brother Arthur SMITH as manager for his own solo entertainments. PVWS

Cross, A. E. Brooks, 'Albert Smith, Charles Dickens and "Christopher Tadpole" ', *Dickensian*, 34 (1938).

Fitzsimons, Raymund, *The Baron of Piccadilly: The Travels and Entertainments of Albert Smith 1816–1860* (1967).

**Smith, Arthur** (1825–61), manager for his brother Albert SMITH's entertainments at the Egyptian Hall (1852–60), for the AMATEUR THEATRICAL tour Dickens arranged to raise money for Douglas JERROLD's family when Jerrold died, and for Dickens's PUBLIC READINGS from 1858 to 1861. Dickens admired him as 'the best man of business I know' (10 June 1857), 'all usefulness and service' (11 August 1858), and withheld all blame from him over the 'violated letter' entrusted to Smith, concerning rumours circulating after Dickens's marriage broke down (see HOGARTH, GEORGE). Dickens wrote an inscription for the gravestone when Smith died, 'zealous' about the readings to the last. 'I miss poor

Arthur dreadfully', Dickens lamented (1 November 1861). PVWS

**Smith, Revd Sydney** (1771–1845), Canon of St Paul's, essayist, pamphleteer, liberal-minded Whig, brilliant conversationalist, and, as Dickens called him, 'great master of wit, and terror of noodles' (1850 Preface, *OT*; alluding to his famous 'Noodle's oration' in a review of BENTHAM'S *Fallacies, Edinburgh Review* 1825), 'wisest and wittiest of the friends I have lost' (*Speeches*, p. 405). Smith had initially 'stood out against Mr Dickens as long as I could', suspecting vulgarity, 'but he has conquered me' (he wrote, after reading *Nickleby*). They met in 1839 ('Nobody more, and more justly, talked of than yourself', Smith's invitation said; Pilgrim 1.432 n.), became great friends and correspondents, and Dickens often quoted him, approvingly, both where Smith was reformist (on public schools) and reactionary (on penology), particularly admiring his popular *Lectures on Moral Philosophy* (1804–6). PC

**Smollett, Tobias** (1721–71), novelist and an important influence on Dickens. Smollett is best known for his novels *The Adventures of Roderick Random* (1748), *The Adventures of Peregrine Pickle* (1751; 1758), and *The Expedition of Humphry Clinker* (1771). His development of the picaresque novel in English was particularly significant, and in 1755 he published a translation of the classic picaresque tale *Don Quixote* by CERVANTES. Smollett is one of the novelists David Copperfield reads to console himself and indulge his imagination while at the Murdstones (*DC* 4), which reflects Smollett's importance in Dickens's own childhood reading. Dickens believed that 'Humphrey (*sic*) Clinker is certainly Smollett's best', and he was 'rather divided between Peregrine Pickle and Roderick Random, both extraordinarily good in their way, which is a way without tenderness . . .' (letter to Frank Stone, 2 November 1854). FORSTER suggests that in placing Sam Weller and Mr Pickwick together in prison, Dickens 'was perhaps thinking of his favourite Smollett, and how, when Peregrine Pickle was an inmate of the Fleet, Hatchway and Pipes refused to leave him' (Forster 2.1). Generally, Dickens's use of the GROTESQUE and his emphasis on exaggerated physical details in characterization further suggests Smollett's influence. REVIEWERS often linked Dickens's work directly to Smollett's, and generally 18th-century fiction was the yardstick by which Dickens's early work was measured (see NOVELISTS AND THE NOVEL BEFORE DICKENS). The *London and Westminster Review*, for example, suggested that 'the renown of FIELDING and Smollett is that to which [Dickens] should aspire, and labour to emulate, and, if possible, to surpass' (July 1837). The *Monthly Review* had already professed that 'BOZ is a perfect Smollett . . .' (February 1837). MWT

**Society for the Diffusion of Useful Knowledge.** This non-profit-making organization, founded in 1826, was dedicated to the cheap dissemination of entertaining and informative reading material. On its committee were such notable figures as Lord Brougham, Lord John RUSSELL, John Stuart MILL, and several members of the Royal Society. At a time when EDUCATION suffered from poor organization and misguided planning, the Society—acting on UTILITARIAN principles—issued cheap periodicals, and produced volumes and collections of pamphlets on a wide variety of subjects, including history, geography, architecture, biology, mathematics, mineralogy, and agriculture. Their most notable publications included the *Library of Useful Knowledge* (1828–46), the *Library of Entertaining Knowledge* (1829–38), the *British Almanac* (1829–86), and the illustrated *Penny Magazine* (1832–46). The Society officially suspended operations in 1846 owing to losses on its *Biographical Dictionary*.

Dickens became familiar with the Society in the 1830s, and possessed several of their publications (Pilgrim 4.712). He also knew the publisher Charles KNIGHT, who produced the mass-circulation *Penny Magazine*. While he was generally interested in the organization's aims, it seems that Dickens also hoped to derive some personal benefit from the association: after a period of difficulty with CHAPMAN AND HALL in 1840–1 he marked the restoration of cordial relations by recommending the firm as agents for some of the Society's monthly publications—an offer which was accepted in October 1841 (Patten 1978, pp. 115–17). He also recommended to Lord Brougham in January 1842 that the Society consider for publication the work of his father-in-law George HOGARTH

(3 January 1842); no such book was ever published. LL

Altick (1957).
Bennett, S., 'Revolutions in Thought: Serial Publication and the Mass Market for Reading', in J. Shattock and M. Wolff (eds.), *The Victorian Periodical Press: Samplings and Soundings* (1982).

**'Solomon Bell the Raree Showman'** The title of a projected children's book, for which Dickens accepted an offer of £100 from the publisher Thomas Tegg (1776–1845), but which he never wrote (11 August 1836). In 1839 Tegg published *Sergeant Bell and his Raree-show*, written not by Dickens but probably by George Mogridge. PVWS

*Dickensian*, 32 (1936).

**songs.** See MUSIC.

**speeches of Dickens.** Dickens, who was admired and even renowned as a public speaker, appeared on many CHARITABLE occasions, for schools, adult EDUCATION, SELF-HELP societies, hospitals, and at social celebrations. His speeches, given throughout Britain and on both visits to AMERICA, tell us much about himself, his times, his beliefs, and attitudes. They show his opinions on POLITICS and PUBLIC HEALTH, about fellow authors and artists, about writing as a profession, and even something about his approach to fiction, as in his toast to THACKERAY in March 1858. They let us see his importance as a public figure, and not only as an entertainer but as an intensely admired representative of his class and time.

No doubt it can be misleading to switch simply from speeches to novels, or from what he said to what he wrote. The occasions have to be seen in context. Yet they show Dickens's readiness to delight in an audience as much as through his acting, his JOURNALISM, or PUBLIC READING; and both in what they say and what they keep in reserve, they give us a great chance of coming to know him.

Some of the speeches are directly autobiographical in that, for example, he speaks of his first learning to read, his schooldays, his active life as a reporter, and his attitude to readers; this is especially true of some of the speeches given in America. He makes the casual remark of how the scenes of Yarmouth, in *David Copperfield*, really arose from boyhood memories of Chatham. The biographical aspect also comes out in the sense we have, from the first, that he knew he had Westminster Abbey always before him, the assurance he displays in his rather daunting reception in Edinburgh in 1841 (see SCOTLAND), and his verbal battles over slavery and COPYRIGHT in America in 1842, followed by his apology on his return in 1867–8. There is the speech to the Governesses' Institution from which we indirectly learn of his sister's having been a governess. He speaks for his newly founded GUILD OF LITERATURE AND ART. There is the occasion when he had to chair the annual dinner of the ROYAL GENERAL THEATRICAL FUND, when FORSTER'S tribute was greeted with a cry of 'Humbug,' after which he had to break the news to Dickens of the death of his youngest daughter (see CHILDREN OF DICKENS). In 1858 an outburst of oratory signalized a crisis in Dickens's relations with his public as he came to his separation from his wife.

In all this there is a Dickensian attitude to life, partly shown in his willingness to speak at all, uncommon with writers, and then in his choice of causes. They were largely for associations which combined self-help with help for others. No other writer has had the same ability or drawing power as Dickens; but no one else has ever been so willing to help in this way, even though it was probably never such a pleasure to him as acting. 'He spoke so well,' TROLLOPE wrote, 'that a public dinner became a blessing instead of a curse, if he was in the chair.' His last public speech, Gladstone noted, 'was one of the most finished performances of its kind that I ever knew' (quoted, *Speeches*, p. xix).

None of his speeches was written down in advance but many of them were carefully prepared. Dickens once told his readings manager, George DOLBY, that before giving a speech he usually took a long walk and decided on the 'heads to be dealt with. These being arranged in their proper order, he would in his "mind's eye", liken the whole subject to the tire of a cart wheel—he being the hub. From the hub to the tire he would run as many spokes as there were subjects to be treated; and during the progress of the speech he would deal with each spoke separately, elaborating them as he went round the wheel.' As the spokes dropped out, one by one, the speech came to an end; and Dolby

adds that, after this, he often noticed Dickens dismissing each spoke when he was speaking with a quick flick of his finger.

Forster mentions another aspect, that from his boyhood experiences had come the determination to assert himself against all authorities that seemed to stand in the way of progress. One of the most remarkable speeches of this kind was to the Administrative Reform Association in 1855, and a whole series in the same spirit was given to the ROYAL LITERARY FUND, not so much at its dinners as at Annual General Meetings when Dickens tried to upset, then wrest control from its administration. It combined with his campaigning for artists, actors, writers, and musicians demanding the same respect as their wealthy patrons. This runs through his career: the assertion of the right to be heard, not just for himself but for what he spoke of as the 'people governed' rather than 'the people governing'.

Forster linked this with his sympathy for suffering CHILDREN, and as a composition perhaps the finest is the speech given in aid of the Great Ormond Street Children's Hospital. It has something of the power of his writing, though this cannot be said of other speeches which were composed in his head, and not revised. His best speeches, given at times when he took an unequivocal public stand, include many expressive passages.

Nevertheless one is sometimes reminded of Thackeray's slightly sour response to a companion at a banquet to mark MACREADY'S final retirement. 'How delightful he looks,' said a young actor of Dickens, 'so frank.' 'Yes,' said Thackeray, 'Frank, frank as an oyster.' That is to say, allowing for Thackerayan cynicism, Dickens could also be unusually withdrawn in public and well in control of his feelings, as those who heard him often remarked. But there is something to be learned even from his calculated confidences.

He was not altogether free to choose his topics or his audience. Yet he made an almost independent platform for himself, free from affiliation with most social and political movements, by agreeing to speak at the 'Public Dinners' he had glanced at almost affectionately in *Sketches by Boz*. Elsewhere, in a letter to Douglas JERROLD (8 May 1843), he writes of one such dinner where the participants were like 'sleek, slobbering, bow-paunched, overfed, snorting cattle'. This kind of ambience was reflected even at his Farewell dinner in 1867, given Dickens by his friends on his leaving for America, which ended in drunken scuffles in the cloakroom. Even this aspect, however, throws light on the medium in which Dickens worked and the public he spoke for. As a reporter wrote in 1849, 'when such a man speaks, what he says is unlike all else you hear' (*Speeches*, p. 97).

KJF

*Speeches of Charles Dickens*, ed. K. J. Fielding (1960, rev. edn. 1988); earlier collections are incomplete and misleading.

**sport** does not feature to any great extent in Dickens's work. 'No great sportsman' (*PP*, 1867 Preface), as he admitted, he quickly shifted the emphasis of *Pickwick Papers* away from SEYMOUR's initial plan to focus on the well-established theme of Cockney sporting adventures. This lack of interest in sport is revealing, for Dickens's early writings draw on a tradition of writing about London, notably by Pierce EGAN, in which 'the sporting fraternity' was a prominent and positive feature; this was a world of prizefighting, pedestrianism, and horse-racing, all of which had GAMBLING as a central feature. Dickens dissociated himself from this world, and condemned it. In *Nicholas Nickleby* Sir Mulberry Hawk had been a patron of prizefighting, and it was in the gambling booth at a horse-race that his quarrel with Lord Frederick Verisopht took shape (*NN* 38, 50).

On a more positive note, Dickens used some sports, with deeper roots in the past, as symbols of innocent physical activity and harmonious and peaceful social relations. Contrary to his own self-assessment, his daughter claimed that he had a 'passion' for sports; but significantly the ones in which he participated—bar-leaping, bowling, and quoits—were all old-fashioned (Mamie Dickens, *My Father As I Recall Him*, 1897, pp. 41–2, 69–72). The same carefully nurtured sense of tradition surrounded the sport which he was most inclined to describe, cricket. *Pickwick Papers* (6) contains one of the most famous cricket matches in English literature, though the cricket itself is merely the setting for a particular kind of sociability. In *SUNDAY UNDER THREE HEADS* Dickens describes, under the ideal Sunday 'As it might be

made', an idyllic cricket match, encouraged by the vicar, which he had seen some 70 miles from London; he would like to see such scenes near London. In *The Old Curiosity Shop*, when Nell and her grandfather arrive at a village where 'The men and boys were playing at cricket on the green' (24), it is a shorthand way of indicating a safe place on their hazardous journey. And when Dickens returns to Rochester ('Dullborough'), one of the things he remembers from his childhood is cricket on the playing-field now taken over by the railway (*UT* 12). At Gad's Hill Dickens himself promoted cricket matches, and in 1866 he held a sports day there for the local people (see HOMES OF DICKENS). Nevertheless, what is striking is how rarely Dickens uses sport in this positive way. There were many contemporaries who celebrated traditional and old-fashioned pastimes which were likely to be on the wane; Dickens seems to have been relatively immune to this particular form of nostalgia.

Towards the end of Dickens's life there was occurring a transformation of sport: it was taking root as a central feature of the burgeoning public schools and it was beginning to be organized and codified and used by public-school missionaries as a means of civilizing the people. The Football Association was formed in 1863, rowing and athletics were set up as strictly 'amateur' activities, boxing began to lose its associations with prizefighting. These were changes which scarcely feature in Dickens's work (but see *MED* 6 for boxing), and of which he may well have been unaware. As late as the 1850s he was arguing that ' "Sporting" AMUSEMENTS' were not 'the sports of the PEOPLE . . . they are the amusements of a peculiar and limited class' (to W. H. Wills, 13 October 1852). It was a CLASS for whom Dickens had scant sympathy.  HC

Reid, J. C., *Bucks and Bruisers: Pierce Egan and Regency England* (1971).

**Stanfield, Clarkson** (1793–1867), painter, mainly of marine and landscape subjects. In 1812 he was pressed into the navy, for a number of years, during which, on one occasion, he painted scenery for theatricals organized by Douglas JERROLD. He became a professional designer and painter of stage scenery, in Edinburgh and London, once he had left the navy, but was also producing paintings for exhibitions. He was elected to the Royal Academy in 1835. Thereafter he returned to scene painting only at the request of personal friends, such as MACREADY and Dickens.

He first met Dickens in December 1837 and their friendship developed over many years. He painted the scenery for a number of Dickens's private and public AMATEUR THEATRICALS: *Every Man In His Humour* (1845); *Not so Bad as We Seem* (1851), with David Roberts and other painters; *The Lighthouse* (1855); *The FROZEN DEEP* (1857). Stanfield also contributed ILLUSTRATIONS to Dickens's Christmas books *The CHIMES*, *The CRICKET ON THE HEARTH*, *The BATTLE OF LIFE*, and *The HAUNTED MAN*. He was invited to illustrate PICTURES FROM ITALY but, as a Catholic, declined once he recognized Dickens's satirical treatment of ROMAN CATHOLICISM in that book. In 1847 he settled in Hampstead and enjoyed a circle of friends which included some of the most distinguished writers and ARTISTS of the age. He was highly esteemed by RUSKIN as one of the finest realists among the English painters, though Ruskin occasionally qualified this by remarks on Stanfield's superficial and rather formulaic picturesqueness. Perhaps Stanfield's most famous painting was *The Abandoned* (1854), the brooding portrait of a wrecked ship. It spawned many prints and was featured as a picture on the wall in the central painting of Augustus Egg's triptych *Past and Present*. *The Abandoned* was exhibited at the PARIS Exposition of 1855, where it won a gold medal. Dickens visited the exhibition and privately expressed his disappointment with what he felt to be the tame conventionality of the English paintings there: 'Stanny is too much like a set-scene.' But in his very affectionate obituary of Stanfield, in *All the Year Round* (1 June 1867), Dickens paid tribute to the painter's talents and his commitment to his art: 'No Artist can ever have stood by his art with a quieter dignity than he always did.' In the character of Henry Gowan in *Little Dorrit* Dickens attacked the cynical dilettante artists who represent the reverse of his friend's commitment to art. *Little Dorrit* was dedicated to Clarkson Stanfield.							MYA

**Steele, Richard** (1672–1729), Anglo-Irish ESSAYIST, dramatist, and politician greatly admired by Dickens for his humorous essays in *The Tatler* (1709–11) and *The Spectator* (1711–12, 1714), journals co-written principally with ADDISON. Steele's description of the informal 'clubs' of gentlemen meeting to exchange stories at 'The Trumpet' (*Tatler*, no. 132) and 'Mr Buckley's in Little Britain' (*Spectator*, no. 2 onwards), was an important influence on Dickens's conception of the Pickwick Club, MASTER HUMPHREY'S CLOCK, and his subsequent plans for founding a periodical. A spirited defence of Steele's life and work was published by Dickens in *All the Year Round* (5 December 1868).							JMLD

**Sterne, Laurence** (1713–68), novelist who influenced Dickens. He is best known for the bawdy and often satirical *Life and Adventures of Tristram Shandy* (published in separate volumes between 1759 and 1767) and for *A Sentimental Journey Through France and Italy* (1768). Along with works by Richardson and others, Sterne's *Sentimental Journey* was an important contribution to the 18th-century novel of SENTIMENT, with an emphasis on MORALITY and sympathy, which was important to Dickens. The pathos of the death of Little Nell in *The Old Curiosity Shop* places Dickens in a direct line to Sterne and the sentimental tradition. Sterne was also one of the early innovators of the novel form (see NOVELS AND NOVELISTS BEFORE DICKENS), and *Tristram Shandy* uses a range of narrative devices, particularly stream-of-consciousness. Dickens was fond of a line from *Sentimental Journey*, 'I can't get out—I can't get out', spoken by a caged starling whom the narrator Yorick is unable to liberate; Dickens often quoted this in his letters (see, for example, Dickens to Forster, ?10 October 1838) and he alludes to it in *Bleak House* (*BH* 37). In the Christmas number of *Household Words* for 1855, Dickens finds a copy of *A Sentimental Journey* at the Holly-Tree Inn and informs us that, 'I knew every word . . .' According to an *Athenaeum* review of the early numbers of *Pickwick*, in addition to 'two pounds of SMOLLETT', 'three ounces of Sterne' was also an important ingredient in the series (3 December 1836).							MWT

**Stirling, Edward** (1809–94), the most assiduous DRAMATIZER of Dickens's work, was born in Thame of middle-class parents. At 17, however, like Nicholas Nickleby, he joined a travelling acting company, RICHARDSON'S fairground tent theatre. In 1829 he appeared at the London Pavilion Theatre, beginning a career that was to take him to the Adelphi, Covent Garden, Surrey, Olympic, Lyceum, and Drury Lane. While at Birmingham he had written a successful extravaganza, *Sadak and Kalasrade*, and in November 1838 he adapted *Nicholas Nickleby* for the Adelphi, which ran throughout the season and into the next, and was often staged in the provinces. His first-hand experience of Crummles's world gave the play authenticity, and it gained a cautious approval from Dickens himself. Stirling's later adaptations included *The Fortunes of Smike* (Adelphi, 1836); *Pickwick* (City of London Theatre 1837); *Martin Chuzzlewit* (The Lyceum, 1844), and CRICKET ON THE HEARTH (Princess Theatre, 1846), in which Dot was played by Mary Anne Stirling (1815–95), his erstwhile wife. Stirling in his time was a respected actor, stage manager, and playwright, credited with writing over 200 plays. However, none have survived to posterity.

LJ

Edward Stirling, *Old Drury Lane* (London, 1881), vol. 1. *Actors by Daylight*, 1 (1838), p. 321.

**Stone, Frank** (1800–59), portraitist and ILLUSTRATOR. Dickens met Frank Stone at the SHAKESPEARE CLUB in the late 1830s. The self-made artist was both a tedious bore and a loyal, warm-hearted friend (to Maclise, 11 September 1845). Dickens invited Stone to join his AMATEUR THEATRICAL company; while Stone irritated him by criticizing, incorrectly, the authenticity of the period costumes, and was inconsistent as an actor, the friendship deepened. Stone was then invited to contribute to the last Christmas book, *The HAUNTED MAN*. He picked three scenes in which Milly Swidger figures, having been attracted to the pretty young woman who dispenses love and DOMESTICITY to all her extended family. These pictures escaped the general censure of the tale accorded by reviewers. Stone also did portraits of Kate Nickleby and Madeline Bray reproduced as steel-engraved extra illustrations for the Cheap Edition of *Nicholas Nickleby*, and designed the wood-engraved frontispiece to the Cheap Edition of *Martin Chuzzlewit* (see EDITIONS OVER WHICH DICKENS HAD CONTROL). Dickens commissioned from him a portrait of another of what THACKERAY called Stone's

'rococo rustics', Matilda Price, John Browdie's fiancée in *Nickleby*.

In 1851 the Stones moved out of Tavistock House and into the adjacent Russell House. Dickens took a lease on the vacated dwelling, and for the next eight years his family and Stone's were constantly in and out of each other's homes. Stone, nicknamed 'Pumpion', painted a number of pictures of Dickens's family and eagerly listened to the latest writing or reading, while 'Sparkler' in his turn did countless favours during Stone's life. At his death Dickens supervised the funeral and then helped the widow and her children, including Marcus STONE.                         RLP

**Stone, Marcus** (1840–1921), ILLUSTRATOR and painter. Frank STONE's son learned art informally from his father. When his father died, Dickens acted *in loco parentis* to all the children, who became sisters and brothers to the Dickens family. Dickens immediately recommended Marcus to CHAPMAN AND HALL, for whom the artist supplied the frontispiece to the Cheap Edition of *Little Dorrit* and supplementary illustrations for volumes in the Library Edition, which included the first illustrated *Great Expectations* (see EDITIONS OVER WHICH DICKENS HAD CONTROL). Stone was then picked to design the wood engravings for *Our Mutual Friend* (1864–5). At first Dickens supervised his protégé closely, but as trust and the press of other business built, Dickens often let Stone pick the subjects, though Dickens nearly always had some kind of discussion—in person or on paper—about the details. One day Stone took Dickens to St Giles's to visit a taxidermist's, which Dickens adapted for Mr Venus's shop in the novel. Shaken by a railway accident at Staplehurst in June 1865 (see KENT), Dickens recuperated at Gad's Hill where he completed his manuscript; for the last four illustrations he did not consult with Stone at all. Stone soon thereafter abandoned illustration for narrative painting, becoming a distinguished academician. In old age he dismissed his Dickens work as immature, but he always cherished the personal associations.                         RLP

**Stowe, Harriet Elizabeth Beecher** (1811–96), New England writer and philanthropist. She dedicated herself to the cause of anti-slavery, and her famous propagandist novel, *Uncle Tom's Cabin*, was published in 1852. Like

Dickens, she was hugely popular: *Uncle Tom's Cabin* sold more than 300,000 copies in its first year and became the most popular American novel of its time.

At the height of her fame Beecher Stowe made a trip to England (1853), where she was enthusiastically received. She met Dickens at a Mansion House Banquet. In her *Sunny Memories From Foreign Lands* (1854) she remembers that 'Directly opposite me was Mr Dickens, whom I now beheld for the first time, and was surprised to see him looking so young. Mr Justice TALFOURD made allusion to the author of *Uncle Tom's Cabin* and Mr Dickens, speaking of both as having employed fiction as a means of awakening the attention of the respective countries to the condition of the oppressed and suffering classes.' She also noted that it was because of Dickens that 'fashionable literature now arrays itself on the side of the working classes' (pp. 153–4). Whilst publicly Dickens praised Beecher Stowe (*Speeches*, p. 165), privately he expressed dislike, condemning her 'conceited affection of humility—moony . . . very silly . . . terrible humbug . . .' (4 August 1854).          SL

**Strange Gentleman, The** Dickens's first play, a comic burletta in two acts (see PLAYWRIGHT, DICKENS AS). Based on 'The Great Winglebury Duel' (*SB*), it consists of farcical confusion of cross-wooing and jealousy. It opened at the St James's Theatre on 9 September 1836 for a run of more than 50 performances, plus a revival in December of the next year. Dickens accepted £30 from John BRAHAM for the COPYRIGHT. He later offered it, along with The LAMPLIGHTER, to MACREADY, claiming that it ran for 'some seventy nights', with John Pitt HARLEY in the title role of Walker Trott ('the best thing he does'; ?19 November 1838), but Macready rejected both plays. Attributed to 'BOZ', it was published by CHAPMAN AND HALL in late 1836 or early 1837, with a frontispiece by 'Phiz' (Hablot Knight BROWNE) depicting Harley with the actress Julia Smith. Dickens had mixed feelings about a watercolour sketch of Harley as Trott drawn by John LEECH (to Harley, ?December 1836). The play was not collected during Dickens's lifetime. A heavily revised copy is in the Lord Chamberlain's collection; its five songs are printed in Appendix G of Pilgrim 1.695–7.          PVWS

**style of Dickens.** There are certainly novelists who may be said to possess *a* style (one thinks, for example, of Jane Austen, George ELIOT, Henry James, D. H. Lawrence, William Faulkner), and so distinctive is Dickens as a writer that one is tempted at first to believe that he must surely be one of these. But the style of Dickens turns out to be a medley of literally scores of styles—derived from every conceivable literary as well as real-world source: from the BIBLE and the BOOK OF COMMON PRAYER, from NEWSPAPERS, from FAIRY TALES, popular ballads, SHAKESPEARE, and MELODRAMA, even from ADVERTISEMENTS and business circulars, the jargons of particular trades and professions, and of course the slang of criminals and the streets—and their distinctiveness lies not so much in their sharing a surface family likeness—a cohesive body of stylistic features—as, rather, in their being to an extraordinary degree styl*ized* (see MUSIC, MUSICIANS, AND SONG). The styles of Dickens, that is, share the knack of drawing attention to themselves, often through their striking and carnivalesque juxtaposition. Self-consciousness or, to use David Parker's happy term, 'archness,' a certain knowing and mischievous theatricality, in short, is the most distinctive feature of Dickensian styles, and nowhere is this more apparent than in his various authorial voices, as Robert Garis has argued in *The Dickens Theatre* (1965). It may be testimony both to Dickens's lack of a single style and the peculiar self-consciousness of his language that he has never been very successfully parodied. Then again, his style is difficult to parody also because—being arch—it so often already has itself the flavour of burlesque.

Among the most fundamental features of Dickens's self-conscious use of language is his fondness for striking metaphors, especially the related tropes of metonymy (in which the name of some thing is replaced by an associated term—as in the substitution of 'crown' for 'country') and synecdoche (in which the name of a part substitutes for a whole—as in 'hands' for 'workers'). All metaphors yoke *somewhat* unlikely terms together; Dickens's, as we shall see, often happily border on the outrageous.

Another prominent aspect of linguistic self-consciousness in Dickens is evident in his sensitivity to the written language as a palpable object, whether it be in his description of the shapes of the letters of the alphabet as they appear to a child or an illiterate crossing-sweeper, or the reversed letters of a sign on a window seen from the wrong side, or the even more antic shapes of shorthand characters as they appeared to him (and to David Copperfield) as a young man attempting a career as a parliamentary reporter. In a letter to John FORSTER concerning the proofs to *The* BATTLE OF LIFE, Dickens urges his friend 'to knock out a word's brains here and there' should he find the text slipping into blank verse (13 November 1846).

Dickens was frequently criticized by his contemporaries not only for such mannerisms as SENTIMENTALITY, strained diction, and that tendency to fall into blank verse just referred to, but for the liberties he took with language, his defiance—or, less charitably, his ignorance—of the 'rules'. (The supposed solecism of 'our mutual friend', discussed by H. W. and F. G. Fowler in *The King's English*, 1931, 65–7, is perhaps the most famous example.) His freedom with language—the very trait we nowadays are apt to marvel at, the trait that more than any other prompts comparison with Shakespeare—was in the 19th century often felt to be debasing. Not only does Dickens delight in incorporating the linguistic oddities and novelties of every imaginable station and calling into the speech of his characters, but he adopts them himself, makes them his own. Knud Sørensen, in *Charles Dickens: Linguistic Innovator* (1985), has painstakingly compiled a list of more than 300 Dickensian neologisms—words and phrases that first appear in print in his works, and many of which are now common if not quite standard in English (such as 'butterfingers', 'the creeps', 'in the same boat', 'an acquired taste', 'round the corner', 'a good cry', 'clap eyes on', 'fork out', 'unapproachable' (of persons), 'take leave of one's senses', 'hardworked'). It is rarely easy to tell if a particular neologism registers an authentic Dickensian coinage or just Dickens's ever-alert ear, but in any case—and as in the case of Shakespeare—he exhibits a marvellous facility for being the first to publicize an abundance of striking words and phrases.

As early as the writing of *Pickwick Papers* Dickens was styled as 'the Inimitable' (Forster 1.1), and the phrase has stuck. But no less real

an aspect of his inimitability than his originality is also, perhaps somewhat unexpectedly, his own genius for apt imitation. He was by all accounts a great mimic from early boyhood on and a great student especially of the language of LONDON, its streets and shops, small counting-houses, newspaper offices, THEATRES, markets, inns, gin-shops, pawnbroker's shops and other lesser trades, the lawcourts, police stations, and PRISONS. It is the language of such locales that flows through a large class of great Dickens characters, from Sam Weller through Sairey Gamp and Jo the crossing sweeper to Silas Wegg. Dickens well knew how to record such speech with virtually stenographic fidelity, and he had of course been a shorthand reporter himself. (The language of Jo in fact was evidently based upon the verbatim report of a trial in which a young crossing sweeper had been called as a witness.)

But a great paradox of the language of such characters (and it is one that parallels larger critical paradoxes about what makes Dickens 'Dickensian') is that it seems at once to *typify* a certain class—the boots, the nurse, the ballad-monger—and to be utterly *individual*. What has often been said disparagingly of Dickens's characters is that they seem mere caricatures, greatly exaggerated in their features (see CHARACTERIZATION). But if one asks, 'caricatures of what, exactly?', the answer is not so ready. Mr Pecksniff may strike us as the very type of the hypocrite, but his manner of speaking is readily distinguishable from, say, Mr Chadband's (even though both parody scripture to hilarious effect), and Chadband is surely another excellent example of the very type of the hypocrite—as, for that matter, is Uriah Heep, whose speech is equally distinctive again. If Pecksniff, Chadband, and Heep are types, in other words, they must be said in the end to typify no one so much as themselves. Therefore while Dickens's works are an excellent place to go to learn about substandard speech, professional jargon, regional dialects, and the like among the Victorians (and fine work has been done by linguists on all these topics), it is the 'idiolects' of Dickens—the private speech habits peculiar to individuals—that are likely to be of most critical interest.

One widely recognized way in which Dickens individuates characters stylistically he borrowed from contemporary stage farce. This is the use of 'tags'—frequently repeated expressions (sometimes mere noises) tied to an individual, like Mr Snagsby's 'not to put too fine a point upon it' or his 'deferential cough' (*BH* 22 and 10) or Mr Micawber's constant expectation of something's turning up, or Mrs Micawber's 'I never will desert Mr Micawber' (*DC* 12). There is a, no-doubt primitive, but real pleasure in anticipating the repetition of such tags, and often Dickens will reintroduce us to a character after a long absence by letting us hear the tag before we have, as it were, seen the face.

There is, however, another whole class of characters we might think of as the tagless, and our pleasure in them is precisely that we never know just what they will say next nor how outrageously they will say it. Mrs Gamp may provide the foremost illustration. Here are several prime Gampisms: 'Some people may be Rooshans, and others may be Prooshans; they are so born and will please themselves. Them which is of other natures thinks different' (*MC* 19); 'Rich folks may ride on camels, but it an't so easy for 'em to see out of a camel's eye' (*MC* 25); 'we never knows wot's hidden in each other's hearts; and if we had glass winders there, we'd need keep the shetters up, some on us, I do assure you!' (*MC* 29); 'The torters of the Imposition shouldn't make me own I did it' (*MC* 29); of Young Bailey, presumed dead: 'He was born into a wale [vale] and he lived in a wale and he must take the consequences of sech a sitiwation' (*MC* 49); 'A pleasant evenin' though warm, which we must expect when cowcumbers is three for twopence' (*MC* 51). There are several characteristic 'substandard' features at work in Mrs Gamp's speech, but to list them in learned fashion is to miss the point and hardly explains the humour or captures its distinctiveness. Here the question of 'style' cannot usefully be separated from the question of content, or, most broadly, of imagination. (Perhaps the single best book on Dickens's style is Garrett Stewart's (1974), whose title in fact announces itself as a study of Dickens's 'imagination'.)

It is tempting to label not just Mrs Gamp's language as 'substandard', but her thought as well. There certainly are numerous ways in which she derails logic. Yet that logic is sometimes both weird and entirely apt. It may be a

perfectly good inference that if cucumbers are inexpensive, they must be in season, the season must be summer, and the weather must therefore be warm. What is striking here is not so much illogicality as rather an unexpected, incongruous logic. When Mrs Gamp confuses 'Inquisition' and 'Imposition', her malapropism makes a certain ironic sense: to be subjected to the tortures of the Inquisition is an imposition, to say the least. And while it is odd to think of the 'wale' of life as a 'sitiwation' (with its twin senses of 'predicament' and 'employment'), it may be perfectly good sense and even sound theology.

Because incongruity is the common denominator here, we might very broadly label Mrs Gamp's style as 'ironic'—putting aside the question of an intention to be ironic and thinking of irony most generally as always entailing some distance or disparity, whether between what is said and meant or between what is expected and what happens or is conveyed. As is so often the case with irony, moreover, the disparity or incongruity in this instance turns out to reveal some deeper similarity, a fit, a likeness, even a likelihood— although the affinity may still escape precise logical articulation.

Such an escape may indeed be the mark of a genius felt to be almost divine. When Mrs Gamp declares, 'Gamp is my name and Gamp my natur' (*MC* 26), we may laugh at her apparent innocence about language and, at the same time, long for a look into that transcendent dictionary—its pages evidently wide open to her—wherein 'Gamp' is defined.

Like other prolific and zany talkers in Dickens (e.g. Mrs Nickleby and Flora Finching), Mrs Gamp is so much herself that it is easy to forget that it is really Dickens who speaks through her. So forceful a presence is she that we may have the uncanny impression that it is really she who ventriloquizes him— an impression reinforced by G. H. LEWES's report that 'Dickens once declared to me that every word said by his characters was distinctly *heard* by him' (quoted in Collins 1971, p. 574). It is an impression that would no doubt have been further reinforced had we had the opportunity to attend the PUBLIC READINGS Dickens based upon Mrs Gamp. Utterly unlike one another in so many respects, Dickens and Mrs Gamp nevertheless do in fact speak the same language—not just on the literal-minded level where we recall that Dickens actually is her creator, but on some level deeper even than that of 'style'.

Indeed, flights of fancy and of logic that are broadly ironic, at once unlikely and apt, and that call attention to themselves as linguistic play or to their own manner of expression are as much the mark of the Dickensian narrative voice (and even Dickens's own private voice, as seen, for example, in the letters) as they are of any Dickensian characters. The chief difference is that writing in his own person (or his typical authorial personae), Dickens is sufficiently sensitive about his own social standing that he generally will not allow himself the luxury of slipping into the substandard without some knowing signal, even if it be only resorting to inverted commas.

A stylistic technique that further complicates the relationship between characters and narrative voice has been usefully and extensively analysed by Mark Lambert (1981). It is what he calls the 'suspended quotation', in which a character's words are interrupted by the narrator, who inserts a comment, a bit of mind-reading, or a stage direction (as in ' "It's not Madness, ma'am," replied Mr Bumble, after a few moments of deep meditation. "It's Meat" ': *OT* 7). Lambert provocatively argues that Dickens's extensive use of this technique in fact reflects a general 'hostility toward his own characters by an author who resents the special attractiveness those characters have for the audience. It is the resource of a jealous author' (p. 35).

A typical authorial flight of Dickens's fancy occurs at the beginning of *A Christmas Carol*, just after the narrator has announced that 'Old Marley was as dead as a door-nail'. The narrator continues by self-consciously animating the dead cliché (and such reanimations are typical, both in that Dickens frequently resorts to them and in that they produce, again, the strikingly Dickensian notes of verbal self-consciousness and the play of the novel against the conventional): 'Mind! I don't mean to say that I know, of my own knowledge, what there is particularly dead about a door-nail. I might have been inclined, myself, to regard a coffin-nail as the deadest piece of ironmongery in the trade. But the wisdom of our ancestors is in the simile; and my unhallowed hands shall

not disturb it, or the Country's done for' (*CC* 1).

*Bleak House* provides a more extended, sober, and softer example of Dickens's animating imagination, which is as fond of animating dead objects as dead phrases. (Indeed both animism and its opposite, reification—as when Dickens refers to Lord Stiltstalking as a 'noble Refrigerator [who] had iced several European courts in his time' (*LD* 1.26)—are favourite stylistic gestures.) Here, the omniscient narrator prefigures Lady Dedlock's downfall simply through a description of the play of light from the setting sun on the family portraits at Chesney Wold:

'Through some of the fiery windows, beautiful from without, and set, at this sunset hour, not in dull grey stone, but in a glorious house of gold, the light excluded at other windows pours in, rich, lavish, overflowing like the summer plenty in the land. Then do the frozen Dedlocks thaw. Strange movements come upon their features, as the shadows of leaves play there. A dense Justice in a corner is beguiled into a wink. A staring Baronet, with a truncheon, gets a dimple in his chin. Down into the bosom of a stony shepherdess there steals a fleck of light and warmth, that would have done it good, a hundred years ago ...

'But the fire of the sun is dying. Even now the floor is dusky, and shadow slowly mounts the walls, bringing the Dedlocks down like age and death. And now, upon my Lady's picture over the great chimney-piece, a weird shade falls from some old tree, that turns it pale, and flutters it, and looks as if a great arm held a veil or hood, watching an opportunity to draw it over her. Higher and darker rises shadow on the wall—now a red gloom on the ceiling—now the fire is out' (*BH* 40).

So emotionally laden do the merely natural phenomena of light appear here that this passage may seem to embody the RUSKINIAN pathetic fallacy in its most extreme form. And yet it may be viewed at the same time as wonderfully realistic, rendered with an extremely clear vision that knows (and lets us, moreover, see perfectly well) the difference between what is really out there and what is purely in the mind's eye. These alternate visions are reflected in the long history of debate about whether Dickens is essentially a realist, a virtually hallucinatory illusionist, or some combination of the two—as has been suggested by Dickens himself when he declares in the Preface to *Bleak House* that he has 'purposely dwelt upon the romantic side of familiar things', or refers to his observation as a 'fanciful photograph' (to Wills, 24 September 1858).

Critics have, from the earliest days of the cinema on, frequently noted how cinematic is the style of the omniscient Dickens narrator, and it is interesting to imagine this scene as it might be rendered on FILM. Apropos of the debate about realism versus illusion, two versions suggest themselves. In one, the visuals might be straightforwardly realistic and would be accompanied by a narrative 'voice-over' reading the passage quoted; in the second, the descriptive commentary would be dispensed with altogether, and the special-effects department would be called on to produce in the portraits unambiguous winks, dimples, and bosomy blushes as well as that great arm holding its veil or hood. Can we say with any assurance which treatment would be the more faithful to the Dickens style?    RN

Brook, G. L., *The Language of Dickens* (1970).
Golding, Robert, *Idiolects in Dickens* (1985).
Lambert, Mark, *Dickens and the Suspended Quotation* (1981).
Marcus, Steven, 'Language into Structure: *Pickwick Papers*', *Daedalus* 101 (1972); rptd. *Representations* (1975).
Page, Norman, *Speech in the English Novel* (2nd edn. 1988).
Parker, David, 'Dickens's Archness', *Dickensian*, 67 (1971).
Quirk, Randolph, 'Charles Dickens, Linguist' in *The Linguist and the English Language* (1974).
Stewart, Garrett, *Dickens and the Trials of Imagination* (1974).
Sucksmith, H. P., *The Narrative Art of Charles Dickens* (1970).
Van Ghent (1950).

**Sunday Under Three Heads** *As it is, As the Sabbath Bills Would Make It, and As It Might Be*, a political pamphlet written by Dickens under the pseudonym 'Timothy Sparks', with three full-page wood engravings and title-page vignettes by Hablot BROWNE, published by CHAPMAN AND HALL in June 1836, between the appearance of the first and second series of *Sketches by Boz* and concurrent with the fourth number of *The Pickwick Papers*. It was prompted by Dickens's opposition to a Sabbath Observances Bill, introduced to Parliament by Sir Andrew Agnew (1793–1849), MP for Wigtonshire, Scotland, on behalf of the Society for Promoting Due Observance of the Lord's Day, a SABBATARIAN pressure group founded in 1831. Two similar Bills of his had been rejected by Parliament in 1833 and 1834, and another was lost in 1837 when Parliament was prorogued on the death of William IV.

In common with radicals in the House, such as William COBBETT and Edward BULWER-LYTTON, whose arguments the pamphlet closely followed, Dickens saw the bill as a piece of CLASS legislation, cynically designed to forbid innocent AMUSEMENTS to the poor on their one day of rest, without interfering with the pleasures of the well-to-do (*Hansard*, 29 March 1833 and 30 April 1834). Dickens dedicated *Sunday Under Three Heads* to Charles Blomfield (1786–1857), Bishop of London, sarcastically remarking: 'That your Lordship would ever have contemplated Sunday recreations with so much horror, if you had been at all acquainted with the wants and necessities of the people who indulged them, I cannot imagine possible.' The pamphlet, which displays Dickens's characteristic sympathy for ordinary people, close observation of actual lives, and vigorous rhetoric, was still at press when Sir Andrew's Bill was rejected by the House on 18 May, but it received favourable notice in the press and articulates convictions which he held passionately throughout his life.    PVWS

D[exter], W[alter], 'Early Propaganda', *Dickensian*, 32 (1936).
Johnson, Edgar, 'Dickens and the Bluenose Legislator', *American Scholar*, 17 (1948).

**Surtees, Robert Smith** (1805–64), comic and sporting novelist. Perhaps the most popular of Victorian sporting novelists, Surtees is best known for *Jorrocks's Jaunts and Jollities* (1838), which features a masterful comic depiction of Jorrocks the cockney greengrocer, and *Mr Sponge's Sporting Tour* (1853), which recounts the fox-hunting adventures of one Soapey Sponge. The humorous escapades of Jorrocks partly inspired Dickens in *The Pickwick Papers*, and significantly, 'Phiz' (Hablot K. BROWNE) illustrated both *Pickwick* and some of Surtees's later books, linking the two authors in the public mind. Although trained in the legal profession, Surtees was more concerned with hunting than with the tedium of a career, and his passion for SPORT was the basis for much of his fiction. He began by writing comic sketches and sporting articles, published in periodicals, much in the way Dickens's early fiction evolved out of his journalism. Surtees was friendly with many prominent contemporary writers such as THACKERAY, and he was closely connected to several of Dickens's friends, including the PUNCH editor Mark LEMON and illustrator John LEECH (the main illustrator of Surtees's novels). Despite sharing a similar social circle and having literary interests in common, Surtees and Dickens never met. For the most part, Surtees remained outside the mainstream of popular Victorian writers (having only one major success), and was renowned mostly in sporting circles; Dickens, by contrast, wrote for the general public.      MWT

Gash, Norman, *Robert Surtees and Early Victorian Society* (1993).

**Swift, Jonathan** (1667–1745), satirist, pamphleteer, and poet. Undoubtedly his most popular work remains *Gulliver's Travels* (1726), a satire which begins with a ship's surgeon, Lemuel Gulliver, being shipwrecked on the island of Lilliput, inhabited by people only six inches high. Dickens was extremely fond of *Gulliver's Travels* and hoped that MASTER HUMPHREY'S CLOCK would be 'something between *Gulliver's Travels* and [GOLDSMITH'S] *Citizen of the World*' (to Forster, 14 July 1839). In another letter Dickens recounts spending an entire day cutting the pages of the complete works of Swift, 'looking into it with a delicious laziness in all manner of delightful places' (to Forster, 18 March 1841). Like Goldsmith, STERNE, FIELDING, and SMOLLETT, Swift was one of Dickens's cherished 18th-century writers.      MWT

**Switzerland.** In 'Lying Awake' (*RP*), the insomniac narrator wonders why he is obsessed with Switzerland: 'with the night-light before me, up I go, for no reason on earth that I can find out . . . up the Great Saint Bernard!' The answer might lie in the high-altitude morgue there that Dickens describes to FORSTER (?6 September 1846): 'in a little outhouse . . . are the bodies of people found in the snow who have never been claimed . . . some erect and horribly human, with distinct expressions on the faces . . . some tumbled down altogether, and presenting a heap of skulls and fibrous dust.' It recurs literally in *Little Dorrit*, and metaphorically in *Our Mutual Friend*, in Jenny Wren's London rooftop cry to Riah: 'Come up and be Dead!'

Certainly it was the experience of high mountains that fascinated Dickens during his residence in Lausanne between June and November 1846: '. . . whenever I live in Switzerland again, it shall be on the hill-top' (to Forster, 13 November 1846). The place itself, 'a mighty dull little town' (to Frederick Dickens, 16 June 1846), depressed him, as did the contemplation of people with grotesque deformities due to iodine deficiencies: 'Something of the *goître* and *crétin* influence seems to settle on my spirits sometimes, on the lower ground' (to Forster, 13 November 1846). He at first considered Neuchâtel as an alternative place of residence, but 'thought it best to come on here, in case I should find, when I begin to write, that I want streets sometimes' (to Forster, ?13, 14 June 1846). Its big attraction was its proximity to Geneva, where Dickens sought inspiration in his customary city *flânerie* during the writing of *Dombey and Son* and *The* BATTLE OF LIFE.

There too, for the only time in his life, he brushed shoulders with revolution. The Vaud had already experienced a civilized one in February 1845; in October 1846 it was Geneva's turn. 'My sympathy is all with the radicals', wrote Dickens, admiring 'the precision of the common men' with their 'smart guns': 'they picked out every officer and struck him down instantly . . . there were three or four of them; upon which the soldiers gravely turned round and walked off.' The experience appears to be connected with turning to CHILDHOOD injustice as a creative inspiration, for at this precise moment he wrote about lodging with Mrs Roylance [alias Pipchin] during his father's imprisonment: 'We should be devilish sharp in what we do to children. I thought of that passage in my small life, at Geneva' (to Forster, 4 November 1846).

Switzerland thus figures quite frequently in Dickens's imaginative work; before *Little Dorrit* there is *David Copperfield*, and after it, as a conclusion to the Swiss writings, 'No Thoroughfare' (*CS*), written in collaboration with Wilkie COLLINS (1867). In scenes that anticipate D. H. Lawrence's *Women in Love*, its hero Vendale is attacked in the snow by the villainous Obenreizer and left for dead—to be 'resurrected' by his fiancée Marguerite and the St Bernard dogs. There is, moreover, a major Swiss intellectual influence in his fiction—that of Lavater, the father of the 'science' of physiognomy, ubiquitous throughout his work (David can 'defy the science of physiognomy to have made out' the meaning of Aunt Betsey's facial expressions), but finally named in *Our Mutual Friend*, when Mrs Wilfer comically denounces Mrs Boffin, 'to whose countenance no disciple of Lavater could possibly for a single moment subscribe'. Dickens dedicated *The Battle of Life* to 'My English friends in Switzerland', and important friendships—with the WATSONS and W. W. F. de Cerjat—started there. See map p. 615. MH

# T

**Tale of Two Cities, A** Dickens's twelfth
novel and his second HISTORICAL NOVEL, set
in the time of the French Revolution. Although not generally held in high regard by
critics, it is one of his most popular works,
both as Dickens wrote it and in stage and
screen adaptations (see DRAMATIZATIONS;
FILMS).

## Inception and Composition
The first recorded evidence that Dickens was
thinking about the book which became A Tale
of Two Cities is found in a letter to Angela Burdett COUTTS on 5 September 1857. Referring to
the AMATEUR THEATRICAL production of
Wilkie COLLINS's The FROZEN DEEP, in which
he took the role of the hero, Richard Wardour,
who sacrificed his life in order to save that of
his rival for the woman they both loved, Dickens wrote: 'Sometimes of late, when I have
been very much excited by the crying of two
thousand people over the grave of Richard
Wardour, new ideas for a story have come into
my head as I lay on the ground, with surprising force and brilliancy. Last night, being
quiet here, I noted them down in a little book
I keep.' As the editors of the Pilgrim Edition of
Dickens's letters observe, 'There are in fact no
entries that connect Wardour specifically or
the themes of The Frozen Deep' (Pilgrim
8.432n.), but the Book of Memoranda does
record an entry which conceives of 'Representing London—or Paris, or any other great
city—in the new light of being utterly unknown to all the people in the story'. The
names Carton and Stryver are also recorded,
along with the idea of 'a story in two periods
—with a lapse of time in between, like a
French drama', and another concerning 'The
drunken?—dissipated?—What?—LION—
and his JACKAL and Primer, stealing down on
him at unwonted hours' (Kaplan 1981).

On 27 January 1858 Dickens wrote to
FORSTER of 'growing inclinations of a fitful
and undefined sort' which might lead to a
new book, and three days later of starting to
write, 'If I can discipline my thoughts into the
channel of a story'. On 15 March he sent

Forster three trial titles: 'Buried Alive', 'The
Thread of Gold', and 'The Doctor of Beau-
vais', but got no further. This was a time
of great personal restlessness for Dickens,
marked by his growing infatuation with Ellen
TERNAN and the first of his PUBLIC READING
tours, and culminating in his separation from
his wife in May (see DICKENS, CATHERINE). A
full year passed before he actually began writing, and even then he complained, 'I cannot
please myself with the opening of my new
story, and cannot in the least settle at it or take
to it' (to Forster, 21 February 1859).

Soon, however, he hit upon 'exactly the
name for the story that is wanted' (to Forster,
11 March 1859), and began consulting historical works sent to him from the London
Library by Thomas CARLYLE, to whom he had
turned for advice (to Carlyle, 24 March 1859).
'All the time I was at work on the Two Cities',
he told Forster afterwards (2 May 1860), 'I
read no books but such as had the air of the
time in them.' By 5 April he reported to
MACREADY that he was 'a *little* busy, and hard
at work on a new story', and on the 30th of
that month the first instalment appeared.

That summer he was in ill health and able
'to do no more than hold my ground, my old
month's advance' (to Forster, 9 July 1859), but
working 'doggedly' he continued to 'blaze
away with an eye to October', when another
reading tour was scheduled (to Collins, 16
August 1859). He explained to Forster that A
Tale of Two Cities was designed to be different
from his other novels. 'I set myself the little
task of making a *picturesque* story, rising in
every chapter with characters true to nature,
but whom the story itself should express,
more than they should express themselves, by
dialogue. I mean, in other words, that I fancied a story of incident might be written, in
place of the bestiality that *is* written under
that pretence, pounding the characters out in
its own mortar, and beating their interests out
of them' (25 August 1859). Forster (who gives
a slightly variant transcription of the letter)
calls this 'a deliberate and planned departure
from the method of treatment which had

been pre-eminently the source of his popularity as a novelist. To rely less upon character than upon incident, and to resolve that his actors should be expressed by the story more than they should express themselves by dialogue, was for him a hazardous, and can hardly be called an entirely successful, experiment' (9.2).

On 4 October he completed the novel, and two days later wrote to Wilkie Collins, explaining that he had not written in Collins's manner for fear the story would have been 'overdone' that way—'too elaborately trapped, baited and prepared'. Referring to his treatment of Dr Manette, he declared, 'I think the business of Art is to lay all that ground carefully, but with the care that conceals itself—to shew, by a backward light, what everything has been working to—but only to SUGGEST, until the fulfilment comes. These are the ways of Providence—of which ways, all Art is but a little imitation' (6 October 1859).

On finishing the book his confidence in it was high. 'I hope it is the best story I have written,' he declared to François Regnier (15 October 1859), and six months later he remained both pleased with the book and idealistic about the value of his fiction. 'As to my art,' he told Angela Burdett Coutts (8 April 1860), 'I have as great a delight in it as the most enthusiastic of my readers, and the sense of my trust and responsibility in that wise, is always upon me when I take pen in hand.'

Still later, in response to a letter from his friend and fellow-novelist Sir Edward BULWER-LYTTON, Dickens defended his novel on two counts, one historical and the other artistic. First, he declared, although 'feudal privileges' had been surrendered before the time of the Terror, he was confident that they were still in use 'to the frightful oppression of the peasants'. And he defended his design in making the death of Madame Defarge accidental rather than dignified, 'which she wouldn't have minded'. 'Where the accident is inseparable from the passion and emotion of the character, where it is strictly consistent with the whole design, and arises out of some culminating proceeding on the part of the character which the story has led up to, it seems to me to become', he wrote (5 June 1860), 'as it were, an act of divine justice'.

## Contract, Text, and Publication History

Dickens planned *A Tale of Two Cities* as a serial with which to launch his new periodical *All the Year Round*. Because he owned the journal, there was no contract and no additional payment for contributing a story (as BRADBURY AND EVANS had paid when *Hard Times* appeared serially in *Household Words*) but, as Robert Patten observes, Dickens 'worked his COPYRIGHT thoroughly' (1978, p. 273). Simultaneous with its weekly appearance in *All the Year Round* the novel was issued, with illustrations by Hablot BROWNE, in the familiar monthly numbers, and Dickens also sold advance copy to foreign publishers. On 17 March he signed a contract (agreed verbally a week earlier) with Thomas Coke Evans, who undertook to pay 'a thousand pounds for the first year, for the privilege of republishing [*All the Year Round*] in America one day after we publish here. Not bad?' (to Forster, 11 March 1859). Evans promptly found himself in financial difficulties, however, and sold the American rights to J. M. Emerson of New York without telling Dickens, who had meanwhile (despite an exclusive contract with Evans) sold American rights for *A Tale of Two Cities* to Harper's for £1,000 (to Wills, 23 July 1859; Pilgrim 9.98 n.; Patten 1978, pp. 274–6). In addition, a continental edition was published in Leipzig by Tauchnitz.

*A Tale of Two Cities* thus appeared in weekly instalments in *All the Year Round* from 30 April to 26 November 1859; in *Harper's Weekly* from 7 May to 3 December 1859; in monthly parts from June to December 1859, in one volume, published by CHAPMAN AND HALL in December 1859, and in two volumes, published by Tauchnitz in 1859, as volumes 479 and 480 in their Collection of British Authors series. The Cheap Edition, with a frontispiece by Marcus STONE, appeared in 1864, and the Charles Dickens Edition, with descriptive headlines added, was published in 1868 (see EDITIONS OVER WHICH DICKENS HAD CONTROL). Although it has been republished more than any other novel by Dickens, there is at present no authoritative scholarly text.

The heavily corrected manuscript, dedication, and Preface are in the FORSTER COLLECTION. No number plans or proofs survive. Dickens also expended much effort preparing a public reading extract from the novel, 'The

Bastille Prisoner', in late summer 1861, but he never performed it. The text of the reading version is included in *Readings* (see Michael Slater, '*The Bastille Prisoner*: A Reading Dickens Never Gave', *Études anglaises*, 33, 1970).

Dickens wrote a Preface, dated November 1859 from Tavistock House, in which he related that he 'first conceived the main idea of this story' while acting in *The Frozen Deep*. While writing it, he allowed, it 'had complete possession of me' and, paying tribute to 'Mr Carlyle's wonderful book' (*The French Revolution*, 1837), he declared that his intention was 'to add something to the popular and picturesque means of understanding that terrible time'. *A Tale of Two Cities* was dedicated to Lord John RUSSELL 'In remembrance of many services and private kindnesses' (see DEDICATIONS).

Dickens found the weekly format challenging and frustrating. 'The small portions', he told Forster (9 July 1859), 'drive me frantic.' The next month he remarked, 'Nothing but the interest of the subject, and the pleasure of striving with the difficulty of the forms of treatment, nothing in the mere way of money, I mean, could also repay the time and trouble of the incessant condensation ... If you could have read the story all at once', he added, 'I hope you wouldn't have stopped halfway' (to Forster, 25 August 1859). 'You can better perceive my design in seeing it all together', he wrote to Mrs William Howitt three days later, 'instead of reading it in what Carlyle (writing to me of it with great enthusiasm), calls "Teaspoons".' A few months later, however, in endeavouring (unsuccessfully, as it turned out) to tempt George ELIOT to contribute to *All the Year Round*, he took a more sanguine view. In response to her worry 'whether something was not sacrificed, through the necessities of such a plan, to terseness and closeness of construction', he replied that in *A Tale of Two Cities* 'this was its effect, but nothing more believe me' (to G. H. Lewes, 13 February 1860; see SERIAL LITERATURE).

### Illustrations

There were no illustrations in the story as published in *All the Year Round*, but Dickens's principal ILLUSTRATOR, Hablot Browne, supplied a wrapper design, frontispiece, title-page vignette, and two illustrations for each of the eight monthly numbers. These were reproduced in the first volume edition. But although the cover design has been admired, Browne's work as a whole for this novel has met with a chorus of disapproval. The plates appear hastily executed and poorly reproduced; the composition is undramatic; the costumes are historically inaccurate. 'Deficient in vitality' (Steig 1978, p. 171), the illustrations add nothing to the vivid prose in which Dickens tells his exciting story. As Jane Rabb Cohen concludes, 'the artist utterly failed to find a graphic correlative for the author's next stage of growth' (1980, p. 118). As if in acknowledgement of failure, Browne did not put his signature on a single plate. He never worked for Dickens again.

### Sources and Context

It is fitting that a novel constructed on contrasts, which has from the first evoked polarized response, should have had sources at once specific and general, public and private, historical and contemporary. As noted previously, Dickens pointed to the character of Richard Wardour in *The Frozen Deep* as the primary inspiration for his story. Another play, *The Dead Heart* by Watts Phillips, bears striking similarities in key elements of plot to Dickens's novel. Both are set in revolutionary FRANCE; in both, a character has been 'buried alive' for eighteen years, and in both the hero goes to the guillotine to save the life of another. *The Dead Heart* was not produced until three weeks before the novel was complete, and Phillips was accused of plagiarism at the time, but Carl Dolmetsch has argued that Dickens might easily have seen the play script much earlier and transformed the materials into superior art ('Dickens and *The Dead Heart*', *Dickensian*, 55, 1959; see MELODRAMA IN DICKENS'S WRITINGS).

Readers recognized at once that Carlyle's *French Revolution* was a major influence on Dickens's novel. Dickens himself claimed years previously, in 1851, that he was then reading 'that wonderful book ... for the 500th time' (Forster 6.3), and critics have argued the nature and extent of Dickens's debt (see Michael Goldberg, *Carlyle and Dickens*, 1972, and William Oddie, *Dickens and Carlyle: The Question of Influence*, 1972). In his long letter to Bulwer-Lytton of 5 June 1860, Dickens named works by Louis-Sébastien Mercier (1740–1814) and Jean-Jacques Rousseau

(1712–78) as other key sources. Andrew Sanders (1988), the scholar who has done more work on *A Tale of Two Cities* than any other, has explored these and other sources for *A Tale of Two Cities*, including the *Annual Register* for 1774, 1775, and 1776 and Arthur Young's *Travels Through France in the Years 1787, 1788, and 1789* (1792).

The French Revolution itself was overwhelmingly the single dominant historical influence on 19th-century Europe, and its aftermath still reverberated more than half a century later. As Dickens wrote in 'A Flight' (*HW* 30 August 1851), the French were 'always at it', and like Carlyle, Dickens stressed that events have their identifiable causes. Napoleon III declared himself emperor in 1852, and an assassination attempt on his life in 1858 was hatched in England, with grenades manufactured in Birmingham (Sanders 1988, pp. 10–11).

At least as important as these contexts was Dickens's personal unrest. At a time when he was rejecting his wife, his publisher, and some of his oldest friends, revolution must have seemed a singularly appropriate subject to use as a creative outlet. The character played by Ellen Ternan in *The Frozen Deep*, when Dickens first met her, was named Lucy, and Lucie Manette is said to have the physical appearance of Ellen. As Dickens wrote to Mary Boyle shortly after finishing the novel, 'I must say I like my Carton. And I have a faint idea sometimes, that if I acted him, I could have done something with his life and death' (8 December 1859)—words which echo the statement in his Preface: 'I have so far verified what is done and suffered in these pages, as that I have certainly done and suffered it all myself'.

### Plot, Character, and Theme
'It was the best of times, it was the worst of times': thus Dickens introduces the dual setting of London and Paris in 1775. Jarvis Lorry, a trusted employee of Tellson's Bank, takes Lucie Manette to Paris, where they find her father, long believed dead, in a room above Defarge's wine shop. His mind deranged by eighteen years' imprisonment in the Bastille, Manette occupies himself by shoemaking (see MADNESS).

Part 2 opens five years later in London. Charles Darnay is tried for treason and acquitted. In Paris a child is killed by the carriage of the Marquis St Evrémonde, driving furiously through narrow streets. Darnay, whose real name is Evrémonde, visits the Marquis and declares his opposition to the government. The Marquis is murdered that night in his bed.

A year later the self-important lawyer Stryver, whose success is founded on the cleverness of his 'jackal' Sydney Carton in preparing his cases, expresses indifference when Lorry dissuades him from proposing to Lucie. She urges Carton, who claims he would do anything for her, to abandon his dissolute ways. The wife-beater and grave-robber Jerry Cruncher exhumes the coffin of Darnay's servant Roger Cly. The government informer Barsad visits the shop of Defarge and his wife, who is always knitting. Lucie and Darnay are married. Dr Manette reverts to his derangement and resumes shoemaking.

The Revolution erupts in France, with M. and Mme Defarge among the leaders. During the storming of the Bastille, Defarge finds the cell where Manette was imprisoned. Darnay, responding to a plea for help from his agent Gabelle, who has been imprisoned by the revolutionaries, goes to Paris, as does Lorry, accompanied by Cruncher.

Part 3 opens with Darnay arrested and imprisoned. Dr Manette, Lucie and her child, and her servant Miss Pross, go to Paris. With a backdrop of executions, Darnay is tried, set free, then rearrested. Jerry Cruncher recognizes Miss Pross's brother Solomon as Barsad and reveals that Cly's funeral was bogus. Before the Revolutionary Tribunal Darnay is accused by M. and Mme Defarge, who produce a paper written by Manette in prison, denouncing Darnay. He is sentenced to death. Carton goes to Darnay's cell, drugs him, and having exchanged clothes, sends him back to England with Lucie and Lorry, while he remains in prison in Darnay's place. Mme Defarge, intending death to Lucie and her child, is killed in a scuffle with Miss Pross. Carton is executed in Darnay's place, exclaiming 'It is a far far better thing that I do, than I have ever done'.

### Reception
On 20 June 1859 Dickens wrote to Cornelius Felton that '*All the Year Round* is an amazing success. It has left the circulation of old

Household Words in remote distance, and flourishes amazingly. My story too, has taken a great hold, and strikes deeper every week.' A month earlier W. H. WILLS was able to report that 120,000 copies of the opening number had been sold, and although this settled down to 100,000, sales were far higher than the 40,000 copies per week which was the best that *Household Words* ever achieved (Pilgrim 9.81 n.). On 9 July Dickens repeated that *A Tale of Two Cities* had 'taken a strong hold', observing to Forster that 'The run upon our monthly parts is surprising, and last month we sold 35,000 back numbers'. Monthly part sales were held down by publication in *All the Year Round*, however, and on 13 March 1860 Dickens declared himself 'rather disappointed' by the profit achieved.

Contemporary response was starkly divided. Dickens was 'heartily delighted' with Carlyle's enthusiastic reaction (to Carlyle, 30 October 1859). Many REVIEWS were laudatory, but Mrs Oliphant commented that there was 'little of Dickens' in it (*Blackwood's*, 109, 1871) and James Fitzjames Stephen launched what has been described as 'the most infamous [review], perhaps in the whole record of English criticism' (William Robertson Nicoll, as quoted in Pilgrim 9.183 n.), calling the book a dish of 'puppy pie and stewed cat' which is 'not disguised by the cooking'; 'a disjointed framework for the display of the tawdry wares which form Mr Dickens's stock-in-trade' (*Saturday Review* 17 December 1859; reprinted in Ford and Lane 1961).

One of the most long-lived of all dramatizations of a Dickens novel was *The Only Way*, adapted by the two clergymen, the Revds Wills and Langbridge, and starring Sir John MARTIN-HARVEY as Carton. Even more famous were two films based on the novel, the first in 1935 with Ronald Colman as Carton, the second in 1958 with Dirk Bogarde in that role.

*A Tale of Two Cities* has not been a favourite with critics, but has remained hugely popular with the general reader. George Ford, surveying sales of Dickens titles in the United States in 1968, estimates that it sold 293,060 copies, some 54,390 more than the next-best seller, *Great Expectations* ('Dickens in the 1960s', *Dickensian*, 66, 1970). Taylor Stoehr (1965) has explored its STYLE in detail, and Chris Brook (1984) its Christian themes; Albert Hutter (1978) has written an influential psychoanalytical study.     PVWS

Brook, Chris, *Signs for the Times* (1984).
*Dickens Studies Annual*, 12 (1983), special *Tale of Two Cities* issue.
Hutter, Albert, 'Nation and Generation in *A Tale of Two Cities*', PMLA 93 (1978).
Stoehr, Taylor, *Dickens: The Dreamer's Stance* (1965).

**Tales of the Genii.** See ARABIAN NIGHTS.

**Talfourd, Thomas Noon** (1795–1854), barrister, MP, judge, and author. He was made a Serjeant in 1833 and a Judge in 1849. Dickens seems to have met him shortly after he had introduced his COPYRIGHT Bill into Parliament in May 1837 (when passed into law in 1842, it gave an author copyright protection during his life and for seven years after his death). Evidently, Dickens took very strongly to Talfourd and they became good friends. *Pickwick Papers* was dedicated to him (September 1837), Dickens writing in the dedicatory epistle, 'Many a fevered head and palsied hand will gather new vigour in the hour of sickness and distress from your excellent exertions', and referring to their friendship as 'the most gratifying . . . I have ever contracted'. Their common friendship with, and admiration of, MACREADY was a strong bond between Talfourd and Dickens (Macready did all he could to promote Talfourd's attempts to 'revive the drama' with *Ion* and other blank-verse melodramas straining at tragedy). Both as genial host and ever-welcome guest Talfourd played a prominent and much-valued role in Dickens's social life for twenty years, and FORSTER comments that Dickens 'had no friend he was more attached to'. He visited Dickens in SWITZERLAND in 1846 and in Bonchurch in 1849, immediately after his elevation to the bench ('I am really quite enraptured at his success', Dickens wrote to Forster). Dickens vividly recalls this latter visit in the fine tribute he paid to his friend in *Household Words* (25 March 1854). In it he writes of Talfourd: 'So amiable a man, so gentle, so sweet-tempered, of such noble simplicity, so perfectly unspoiled by his labours and their rewards, is very rare indeed upon this earth.' Talfourd is often cited as the 'original' for Traddles in *David Copperfield*, but there is no external evidence for this supposition.     MS

**Tauchnitz, Bernhard.** Leipzig publisher. See COPYRIGHT; PUBLISHING.

**television adaptations of Dickens** became an important feature of British life in the 1950s thanks to the work of the BBC's Children's Drama Department. A generation of children, and their parents, were introduced to Dickens through what rapidly became an institution, the Sunday tea-time serialization of a classic literary text. A remarkable range of Dickens's work was made available in this way, including *Our Mutual Friend* (1958), *Bleak House* (1959), *Oliver Twist* (1962), *David Copperfield* (1966), and *Great Expectations* (1967). The earliest of these black-and-white productions were made cheaply, and live, in the studio with occasional inserts of film to cover outdoor activities. They were, therefore, liable to the chances of live production and had on occasion to resort to desperate measures to effect transitions of scene and character. Many contained remarkable performances—for example, Ian McKellen as a charmingly distracted David Copperfield—and the murder of Nancy caused a public outcry because of its graphic depiction of violence in a melo-dramatically heightened manner. *David Copperfield* was remade, in colour and on videotape, in 1974, with an astonishing re-creation of Uriah Heep by Martin Jarvis.

The advent of competition to the BBC in the form of commercial television changed the context of production, leading to the landmark version of *Hard Times* made by Granada in 1977. The most expensive Dickens adaptation up to this point, Granada's version was overtly political in its stance and explicitly rejected what was seen as the 'safe' institutionalization of classics of English literature by the establishment. It aimed for a general effect of gritty realism and, in technical terms, attempted something of the breadth and detail of the cinema as opposed to conventional television (see FILMS). The rivalry thus engendered resulted in the BBC's attempt to emulate commercial television in its elaborate and expensive adaptation of *Bleak House* (1985), which was, again, seen as a response to the current political situation and, from a technical standpoint, was directed on film by an established film-maker, Ross Devenish. The cost of this production was felt to be prohibitive in a time of straitened resources, and nearly ten years passed before the re-appearance of the Dickens serial, partly made possible by the critical and commercial success of *Middlemarch*. Two very different productions appeared in 1994, *Martin Chuzzlewit*, adapted by the novelist David Lodge, and the version of *Hard Times* made for the BBC's Schools Programme. *Chuzzlewit* cost some £4 million and thus took its place in the tradition of sumptuous production values, lavish sets and costumes, and 'classic' English acting. *Hard Times*, on the other hand, cost only £800,000 to make and consciously rejected realism in its form and content for a heightened theatricality. This last production helps to focus the theoretical and practical issues involved in televised adaptations of Dickens. The classic serial has now become established as a television genre with all that this entails in terms of audience expectation and the conventions adopted, consciously or otherwise, by its makers. It has been argued that the heightening made possible by filmic devices can reinstate Dickens's 'dangerous' complexity.       GFS

**temperance and drink.** See DRINK AND TEMPERANCE.

**Tenniel, John** (1820–1914), graphic artist. BRADBURY AND EVANS hired Tenniel to design six wood engravings ('poor little contributions', he called them) for *The* HAUNTED MAN. Dickens found Tenniel 'very agreeable . . . and modest' (to John Leech, 30 October 1848). Tenniel acted with Dickens's AMATEUR THEATRICAL company and socialized often with the family in the 1850s. He succeeded LEECH as PUNCH's chief cartoonist in 1864 and illustrated Lewis Carroll's *Alice* books in 1865 and 1871. Many of his cartoons parodied illustrations to Dickens's novels. He was knighted in 1893.       RLP

**Tennyson, Alfred, Lord.** English poet (1809–92). Dickens wrote to Tennyson of 'the love I bear you, as a man whose writings enlist my whole heart and nature in admiration of their Truth and Beauty' (9 March 1843), and shortly afterwards the two men met. Echoes of Tennyson's 'Lady Clara Vere de Vere' appear in a speech he made in October that year (*Speeches*, p. 56) and an allusion to 'Mariana' occurs in stave II of *A Christmas*

*Carol.* There are many references to Tennyson in Dickens's journalism. The two continued to meet socially throughout Dickens's life, but were never intimate.                                    AR

**Ternan, Ellen Lawless** ('Nelly') (1839–1914), actress, intimate friend of Dickens from 1857 who may also have become his lover during the 1860s. Nelly was born at her uncle William Ternan's home in Rochester, Kent, on 3 March 1839, the third child (also third daughter) of Thomas and Frances Ternan, actors, and christened Ellen Lawless, the latter name deriving from the family name of her paternal grandmother's father, a Dublin brewer. During her early years her parents were going through difficult times (see TER-NAN FAMILY) and she was early enlisted in their struggle to keep afloat, being only 3 years old when she made her stage debut at Sheffield in Kotzebue's *The Stranger* (15 November 1842). Both before and after her father's death in 1846 she toured with the rest of the family, making what contributions she could as regards stage appearances (she shared a benefit night with her sister Maria at York in May 1845 and, together with both her sisters, supported Mrs Ternan at her benefit night at Newcastle in March 1849—playbills reproduced in Tomalin 1990, pp. 49 and 56), but not, apparently, showing any of the precocious theatrical talents manifested by her older sisters. By 1855 the family were settled in London with Mrs Ternan and the two older girls all in work.

Nelly did not get an engagement until April 1857 when she was cast as Hippomenes, a breeches part (i.e. girl-as-boy), in a burlesque of the classical legend of Atalanta at BUCKSTONE's Haymarket Theatre. *Atalanta*'s run ended in July and, Mrs Ternan and Maria being also then free, all three were recruited by Dickens who needed professional actresses to perform with his AMATEUR THEATRICAL company in The FROZEN DEEP in Manchester. Nelly had a minor role in the main piece and an ingénue part playing opposite Dickens in the Buckstone farce *Uncle John*, which concluded the evening.

That autumn Nelly and Maria went on to act at Doncaster during Race Week and Dickens, by now thoroughly infatuated with Nelly, followed them there, accompanied by Wilkie COLLINS. Ostensibly, the two writers were in Doncaster as part of their travels in connection with the writing of 'The LAZY TOUR OF TWO IDLE APPRENTICES', and it is only in cryptic references in Dickens's letters to WILLS as well as in certain passages in his section of the 'Lazy Tour' itself that we get glimpses of the real reason for his being in Doncaster.

Nelly returned to the Haymarket in the autumn and Dickens wrote to Buckstone expressing his keen interest in her career, adding, 'On the termination of the present engagement, I hope you will tell me, before you tell her, what you see for her, "coming in the future" ' (13 October 1857). Nelly continued acting at the Haymarket, with a summer season in Manchester, through 1858, the year of Dickens's separation from Catherine DICKENS, and into 1859. Her sister Fanny having left for Florence, chaperoned by her mother, to develop her musical career, Nelly lodged with her other sister, Maria, in Berners Street, near the theatres where they were working, and in October 1858 Dickens made, through Wills, a strong formal complaint to Scotland Yard about police harassment of the girls. In 1859 the two elder Ternan sisters took a long lease on a large house in Houghton Place near Mornington Crescent, 'selling' it a year later to Nelly when she reached her twenty-first birthday, and the presumption must be, in the absence of any evidence that she had suddenly come into some money independently, that this was all financed by Dickens. His accounts from 1859 show varying payments to 'H P Trust', 'HP', and 'HPN', convincingly conjectured by the Pilgrim Editors (9.11 n.) to relate to Houghton Place. Nelly made her last appearance as a professional actress at the Haymarket on 10 August 1859.

From then on nothing more is known (apart from Francesco Berger's memories of Dickens's presence at musical evenings in Houghton Place) about Nelly and her relations with Dickens until 1865 when, with her mother, she was travelling back from France with him and all three were involved in the Staplehurst railway accident (see KENT). As there is much evidence from accounts of her after Dickens's death, and from her own surviving papers, that she was a highly educated and cultured woman, it seems a fair assumption that during these years she was 'using her brains to educate herself' as Kate Perugini said she did (Storey 1939, p. 94). She seems to have sustained some injury in the Staplehurst accident and is often referred to in Dickens's subsequent correspondence as 'the Patient'. By 1866 she was living in Slough, in a cottage the rates for which were paid by a 'Mr Tringham' who sometimes became 'Mr Turnan', and in 1867 she moved to a substantial house in Peckham called Windsor Lodge, the rates being again paid by 'Mr Tringham' alias 'Turnham'. Dickens visited her frequently both at Slough and at Windsor Lodge. He hoped that she might come to America during his 1867–8 PUBLIC READINGS tour, but evidently decided soon after his arrival that this would be too indiscreet and Nelly went instead on a visit to her sister Fanny (Mrs Tom Trollope) in Florence. Wills acted as postman in the correspondence between them, such phrases as 'Another letter for my Darling, enclosed' (30 December 1867) occurring regularly in Dickens's business letters to him from America. On his return (end of April 1868) Dickens had a secret reunion with Nelly in Peckham before going home to Gad's Hill.

This, apart from some brief references to her (attending some of his public readings, for example) in his surviving correspondence is all that is positively known about their relations between 1868 and the time of his death. Kate Perugini is reported as stating that Nelly was summoned to Gad's Hill when Dickens was dying, but an alternative scenario has recently been proposed, on the basis of a curious story told in the family of the descendants of a Peckham neighbour of Nelly's. This has Dickens collapsing while on a visit to Windsor Lodge and having to be hastily transported, in an unconscious state, to Gad's Hill for the avoidance of scandal (see Tomalin 1991, pp. 271–83). The only public mention of Nelly in connection with Dickens before the 20th century occurs in his will, where her name stands first as being bequeathed the sum of £1,000; Dickens's motivation in this posthumous publication of her name after all the years of discretion has been the subject of much debate.

In 1876 Nelly married a young clergyman, George Wharton Robinson, and helped him to run a boys' school in Margate. They had two children, Geoffrey and Gladys. She kept in friendly touch with Georgina HOGARTH and on occasions gave public readings from Dickens for charity. In 1886 Robinson's ill health necessitated the giving up of the Margate school and for the rest of her life Nelly was to live in somewhat straitened circumstances (she sold the lease of the Houghton Place house in 1901, six years before her husband's death). Her last years were passed in Southsea, where she shared a house with her sisters, and she is buried in the cemetery there where, by a truly Dickensian coincidence, Dickens's first great love, Maria BEADNELL, also lies.

Dickens's long-standing intimate friendship with her, the subject of much private gossip since 1857, did not become public knowledge until the revelations of Thomas Wright and Gladys Storey in the 1930s (see BIOGRAPHIES AND BIOGRAPHERS OF DICKENS). Basing his comments on what he had been told by William Benham, a clergyman in whom an apparently remorseful Nelly had confided in Margate, Wright depicted her as having given herself reluctantly to Dickens, motivated by 'vanity combined with a desire for a competence', and as being very unhappy in the relationship, 'assailing herself with reproaches and drawing daily further and further from him' (*The Life of Charles Dickens*, 1935, p. 281). He began a reductively simplistic tradition in Dickens criticism of seeing Nelly as the model for the novelist's later heroines, especially Pip's tormenting Estella in *Great Expectations* and Bella Wilfer in *Our Mutual Friend* in her 'mercenary little woman' phase. This approach was developed by Edmund WILSON, most influentially in his seminal 'Two Scrooges' essay in *The Wound and the Bow* (1941) and appears also, in a somewhat more tentative form, in Edgar Johnson's monumental biography and elsewhere (for a different view see Slater 1983, pp. 213 ff.). Storey's book records Kate Perugini's fairly acerbic comments on Nelly and makes mention of Dickens and Nelly's having had a son who died in infancy.

Over the past half-century a number of scholars, notably Ada Nisbet, Felix Aylmer, Malcolm Morley and Katharine M. Longley, have made important additions to what we know about both Nelly herself and about her relationship with Dickens, but firm, unambiguous evidence that they actually were lovers is still lacking. Few will remain unconvinced that this was the case after reading

Claire Tomalin's carefully researched and deftly argued *The Invisible Woman* (1990, 1991) but students of the question should also note a persuasive alternative hypothesis put forward by Peter Ackroyd in his *Dickens* (1990), which argues for a non-sexual relationship on the grounds that it 'acted for Dickens as the realisation of one of his most enduring fictional fantasies . . . sexless marriage to a young, idealised virgin' (p. 916).

MS

Aylmer, Felix, *Dickens Incognito* (1959).
Longley, Katharine M., 'The Real Ellen Ternan', *Dickensian*, 81 (1985).
—— 'Ellen Ternan: Muse of the Readings?', *Dickensian*, 87 (1991).
Morley, Malcolm, 'The Theatrical Ternans, Parts 1–7', *Dickensian*, 54–7 (1958–61).
Nisbet, Ada, *Dickens and Ellen Ternan* (with foreword by Edmund Wilson) (1952).
Parker, David and Slater, Michael, 'The Gladys Storey Papers', *Dickensian*, 84 (1980).
Storey (1939).
Tomalin, Claire, *The Invisible Woman. The Story of Nelly Ternan and Charles Dickens* (1990; with a 'Postscript', 'The Death of Dickens', 1991).
Wright, Thomas, *The Life of Charles Dickens* (1935).
—— *Thomas Wright of Olney* (1936).

**Ternan family.** Frances Eleanor Ternan, mother of Ellen TERNAN, was born in Hull in 1802, her parents, John and Maria Jarman, both being members of Tate Wilkinson's company of strolling players which was based in York (John was the company prompter and Maria a leading actress). Frances appeared on the stage before she was 2 years old and continued to act with her mother (sometimes also with visiting stars like Mrs Siddons and Mrs Jordan) until the Wilkinson company broke up in 1813. Soon afterwards Mrs Jarman, having apparently lost her husband, joined the Bath theatre company and her daughter made her debut there in 1815. In 1822 mother and daughter went to Dublin, where Frances was an immediate success and over the next two years had no difficulty in obtaining touring engagements in both England and Ireland. Her London debut was at Covent Garden in 1827 but she did not succeed in establishing herself with metropolitan audiences in the way she had done with Irish ones, and in 1829 she was displaced by the sensa-

tional success of Fanny Kemble in Juliet, one of her chief roles.

After more years of working in the provinces and minor London theatres she married in 1834 an Irish actor, Thomas Ternan (born 1783), who had as yet made no great success in Britain and planned to try his luck on an American tour. The Ternans left for America immediately after their marriage and did well there, though Frances was certainly a greater draw than her husband. Their first child, Frances Eleanor (hereafter referred to as Fanny), was born in 1835 and a second daughter, Maria Susanna, soon after their return to England in 1837. Two years later Ellen was born in Rochester where Thomas's brother William was prospering as a barge-owner. Ternan subsequently became manager of theatres in Newcastle and Doncaster and for a while things seemed to go well. Frances appeared regularly and both Fanny and Maria made their stage debuts as 'INFANT PHENOMENA'. Fanny, in particular, made a great impression with her talent for singing as well as dancing and acting, and when the family's fortunes began to decline as Ternan's theatres became less profitable, her earnings in Newcastle and elsewhere became an important source of income. She had some good reviews for her London debut at the Strand in September 1843, *Oxberry's Weekly Budget*, for example, hailing her as 'without exception, the most clever child we ever remember seeing' (vol. 2, p. 83) but, as Claire Tomalin observes (1990, p. 45), 'she was a prodigy, a spectacle, but not yet an actress in London eyes'. Ternan had surrendered the Newcastle lease in 1842 and the next three years were difficult ones for the family as they moved from theatre to theatre in quest of work. The couple's only son (born 1842) died in infancy, and in 1845 Thomas was diagnosed as suffering from what was then termed General Paralysis of the Insane (i.e. syphilis) and confined in Bethnal Green Lunatic Asylum, where he died the following year.

By that time Mrs Ternan was consolidating her reputation as a fine Shakespearian actress through working with MACREADY in Dublin and in London, and over the next five years she and her daughters got what work they could both in London and the provinces. Fanny made her farewell appearance as an 'infant phenomenon' at Newcastle in 1849 and concentrated thereafter on her singing, giving her first London concert in 1853 but meeting with only moderate success. Mrs Ternan had by this time set up a permanent home in London, and found work first with Samuel Phelps at Sadler's Wells and later with Charles KEAN at the Princess's where both Maria and Fanny were also employed, the former specializing in comedy parts and the latter in singing ones.

In the summer of 1857, however, only Fanny was working and Mrs Ternan and Maria were happy to accept Dickens's offer (which also extended to Ellen, who had just made her London debut in a small part at the Haymarket) to join his AMATEUR THEATRICAL company, as paid professionals, in giving public performances of The FROZEN DEEP in Manchester. Dickens was enraptured by Maria's performance as the heroine Clara, especially in Wardour's death-scene ('she sobbed as if she were breaking her heart, and was quite convulsed with grief', he wrote to Miss COUTTS on 5 September 1857), and enraptured by Ellen in a different sense. His subsequent passionate involvement with her inevitably meant involvement with the rest of the family. He facilitated Fanny's going to Florence to study singing under a famous maestro, giving her letters of introduction to various acquaintances including Mrs Trollope who lived there with her elder son Tom, a good friend of Dickens's. Mrs Ternan accompanied her daughter, and Dickens was probably instrumental in settling Maria and Ellen, both now working at the Haymarket (Maria also at the Strand), in West End lodgings within walking distance of the theatres during their mother's absence. He may also have been responsible for establishing the family in a substantial residence in Ampthill Square after Mrs Ternan's return in 1859. In both 1861 and 1862 he wrote to theatre managers trying to push Maria's career but without any apparent effect, and then in 1863 Maria left the stage for marriage with William Taylor, the son of an Oxford brewer. The marriage seems not to have been a successful one and, although there was no formal separation and Maria remained in the Oxford home, she began to develop an independent career as a painter. Mrs Ternan remained with Ellen and was with her and Dickens in the Staplehurst railway disaster in 1865 (see KENT). She survived unscathed, however, and at the beginning of 1866 made her farewell to the stage in Dickens's friend Charles FECHTER's production of SCOTT's Master of Ravenswood, a production in which Dickens was closely involved. After Dickens's death Mrs Ternan, no longer needed to chaperone Ellen, spent her last years with Maria in Oxford, dying in 1873.

Meanwhile Fanny, having returned to England, was writing novels, the first of which, Aunt Margaret's Troubles, Dickens accepted for publication in All The Year Round. In 1865, Tom Trollope's wife having died and left him with a young daughter, Fanny agreed to return to his Florence household as a companion-governess and within a year had married him, in spite of his being her senior by twenty-five years. Trollope received a letter of warm congratulations from Dickens (1 November 1866) in which he alluded to Fanny's novel-writing: 'I have not the least doubt of her power to make herself famous.' He certainly did his best to increase her fame by publishing two more of her novels in All The Year Round. In 1872 the Trollopes moved to Rome, where Tom became Rome Correspondent for an English newspaper, the Standard, and a few years later Maria, having completed her studies at the Slade School of Fine Art, also came to Rome. Here, while continuing with her painting and achieving an Artistic-National Diploma, she developed a new career as a journalist and travel-writer, reporting on her adventurous tourism in Egypt and other North African countries. In 1886 she took over from Trollope as the Standard's Rome Correspondent. The Trollopes returned to England in 1888 and, after Tom's death in 1892, Fanny, still vigorously writing but now apparently in some financial difficulty (Gladstone granted her a Civil List pension in 1893) went to live with Ellen, now Mrs Robinson, at Calcot, near Reading. Here she was joined by Maria in 1898 and with her moved soon afterwards to Southsea where Maria died in 1904. After her husband's death in 1907 Ellen came to live with Fanny and tended her in her last illness in 1913. By her express wish Fanny was buried in the same grave as Maria in Southsea Cemetery.     MS

Morley, Malcolm, 'The Theatrical Ternans, Parts 1–7', Dickensian, 54–7 (1958–61).
Tomalin, Claire, The Invisible Woman. The Story of Nelly Ternan and Charles Dickens (1990, 1991).

**Thackeray, William Makepeace** (1811–63), the novelist then regarded as Dickens's main rival, was acquainted with him from 1836, when he applied to become illustrator for *Pickwick Papers* (he drew as well as wrote), and in 1837 Dickens published his first story in BENTLEY'S MISCELLANY. They met in literary circles, and a cordial though never intimate friendship developed. Much more of a 'gentleman' by birth and education (Charterhouse and Cambridge), Thackeray was conscious of their different social and cultural allegiances (see CLASS). Running into the Dickens family on holiday he described them as 'all looking abominably coarse vulgar and happy', and even in his very handsome review of *A Christmas Carol* ('It seems to me a national benefit, and to every man or woman who reads it a personal benefit') he had to point out that Dickens had 'little Latin and less Greek' and no higher education, though denying that this mattered. He consistently praised Dickens's genius and fecundity (which he envied) and generally reviewed him generously, though sometimes protesting against his unreality.

With *Vanity Fair* (1847–8) Thackeray belatedly emerged as a major novelist, and Dickens was seen to have at last a rival of comparable stature, maybe a superior (Thackeray being credited with a purer, more educated style and greater realism: see NOVELISTS AND THE NOVEL DURING DICKENS'S LIFETIME). When halfway through it Thackeray proclaimed that he was now 'having a great fight up [at the top of the tree] with Dickens', and he often thereafter measured himself for size against him, sometimes indeed suffering, as a friend said, from 'Dickens-on-the-brain'. But, while *Vanity Fair* was being serialized alongside *Dombey*, he famously acknowledged that the death of Paul Dombey was 'unsurpassed . . . stupendous!'—'There's no writing against this—one has no chance!'—and later, in a published lecture, he wryly and generously admitted that his little daughters, always specially delighting in *Nicholas Nickleby*, much preferred Mr Dickens's books to their father's, and often urged him to write 'a book like one of Mr Dickens's books. Who can?' For his part, Dickens often acknowledged the greatness of *Vanity Fair* but rarely spoke of the other novels (as a friend said, Thackeray appreciated Dickens's work much more than Dickens did his) and, unchallenged in popularity, Dickens could afford to be unaware of the 'great fight', though there were recurrent coolnesses and quarrels between the two novelists and their supporters over 'the Dignity of Literature' and other matters, most spectacularly in the 'GARRICK CLUB affair', which ended their friendship (see YATES, EDMUND). Dickens regarded Thackeray as lacking in professional solidarity and acknowledged, in the obituary he reluctantly provided for Thackeray's old monthly *The Cornhill*, that 'We had our differences of opinion. I thought he too much feigned a want of earnestness, and that he made a pretense of under-valuing his art, which was not good for the art that he held in trust. But . . .'—and he praised warmly, if in general terms, his literary brilliance and personal attractiveness. Privately, Thackeray often expressed major reservations about Dickens's art and asserted that Dickens hated him and that 'he knows that my books are a protest against his—that if the one set are true, the other must be false'. Evidence for these assertions is lacking. The Garrick Club affair most rankled with Thackeray but, on his initiative, they were reconciled shortly before Thackeray's death, which distressed Dickens. Kate Dickens Perugini wrote on 'Thackeray and my Father' (*Pall Mall Magazine*, 1911), and Victorian memoirs abound in anecdotes about them, and reviews in comparisons between their works. PC

**theatre and theatricality.** In chapter 39 of *The Old Curiosity Shop* Kit and Barbara celebrate their half holiday by taking their families to Astley's CIRCUS, where the highlight of the evening is a play on horseback. Their 'whirl of entertainments' epitomizes the diversity of theatrical entertainment in Dickens's day.

The root cause of this interfusion of forms was the legal position of dramatic performance in Britain. The Theatre Regulation Act of 1737 restricted performance of 'legitimate,' or spoken, drama to the two Patent houses, Covent Garden and Drury Lane, and although the privilege of staging drama was gradually extended to other theatres, the law, as interpreted and modified over the next century, effectively prevented most theatres in the land from putting on plays which relied on spoken dialogue. In practice this situation

forced the minor theatres to develop alternative forms of entertainment, and the inventiveness with which they combined music,
dance, scenic splendour, pageantry, costuming, and other sorts of spectacle made them
hugely popular. Indeed, the Patent houses
found that they had to mount comparable attractions in order to compete for audiences.
In 1823 Andrew DUCROW, the star of Astley's,
took his stud to Covent Garden, and in the
1838–9 season he shared top billing at Drury
Lane with the American lion-tamer Isaac Van
Amburgh—a show which proved a royal attraction, as young Queen Victoria attended
on six separate evenings between 10 January
and 12 February.

Even without circus acts, however, the
19th-century theatre offered a very considerable portion of entertainment which was
emphatically non-dramatic. Scene-painting
became increasingly elaborate and sophisticated, sometimes executed on a huge canvas
backdrop, or diorama, which allowed the
scenery to move on rollers behind the actors.
A new concern with historical accuracy in the
presentation of plays was manifest in the detailed attention lavished on sets and costumes, and the resulting visual effects often
gave productions more pictorial grandeur
than dramatic action. Actors grouped in
tableaux, reproducing on stage the image of
favourite paintings; some DRAMATIZATIONS
of Dickens's novels, indeed, consisted of little
more than a series of static groupings devised
to imitate the engravings of Hablot BROWNE,
and later in the century a particularly popular
entertainment was the staging of *Mrs Jarley's
Far-Famed Collection of Waxworks*, in which
amateur actors dressed and posed as the WAX-
WORK models Little Nell encountered in *The
Old Curiosity Shop*. Most spectacularly of
all, PANTOMIMES, at once the most expensive
and lucrative (or financially disastrous) of
all 19th-century theatrical entertainments,
depended on the mechanical ingenuity by
which a windmill would be magically transformed into a ship at the touch of Harlequin's
bat, a chair on which Clown is sitting would
suddenly fly into the air, or an entire set
would change from a dark cavern into a
sunny countryside.

Business on the stage routinely emphasized novelty and spectacle as well as plot.
Dog drama, with canine stars in leading roles,

was popular throughout the period. At
Sadler's Wells the stage was replaced by a massive water tank for the production of nautical
drama, including mock battles of warships.
There was invariably musical accompaniment—the 'melo-' of MELODRAMA—and
both within plays and during the intervals between plays actors would sing favourite
melodies, dance a polka (or a hornpipe in fet-
ters), juggle, tumble, or balance on a slack
rope. With the development of the type of entertainment known as 'burletta'—initially a
dramatic form which relied on recitative with
musical accompaniment and no spoken
dialogue, but by the 1830s so various as to
be quite indefinable—the legal distinction
between legitimate and illegitimate drama
broke down entirely, and the revoking of the
monopoly in 1843 merely confirmed what was
already established practice, namely, that
mixed forms of entertainment held sway in
theatres throughout Britain.

The acting style of the age was consonant
with the overall emphasis on colourful display. Boldly mannered, it relied on rhetorical
delivery of lines, sweeping gestures, and formal posturing, methods well suited both to
the cavernously large theatres and to the
polarities of melodrama. The toy theatre cut-
outs of actors frozen at steep angles, arms
aloft and faces defiant, accurately represent its
stylized manner. There was an implicitly recognized code, according to which inner
emotions were represented by externally expressed signs, and acting manuals of the day
spelled out in detail the gestures considered
appropriate means by which the actor could
convey particular feelings and attitudes. Acting was not so much *representation*, by which
an actor would attempt to lose his own personality in the character he was playing and
create the illusion of real life, as *presentation*,
by which he would rely on acknowledged
convention and artifice to evoke a character
(the terms are used by Joseph Donohue, *Theatre in the Age of Kean*, 1975, pp. 180–1).

As with the Hollywood star system in the
movies of our own century, an audience was
likely to be more interested in the actor who
was performing than in the role which he
was playing. This focus was intensified in the
early 19th century by the number of roles an
actor routinely undertook, not just during a
season but on a single night, and by the stock

character types of melodrama. An actor in Dickens's day had much in common with the skilled artiste of the circus; he was admired not only as an impersonator but also as a performer.

Reciprocally, the circus had close affinity to the theatre. The defining characteristic of the circus then and now was the mixed nature of the entertainment: whether the show was large or small, travelling or stationary, it always included performing animals, athletic artistes, and merrymen. But the circus in the 18th and early 19th centuries customarily had two further features which distinguish it from later circuses: it was housed in a large building which had a stage as well as an arena, and the chief attraction was the enactment of a melodrama on horseback, or hippodrama. Soon after his show settled in Lambeth Philip Astley had the amphitheatre covered, and in the 1780s a stage was built, with moveable ramps which allowed horses to move freely between ring and stage. Despite rebuilding on several occasions, the type of structure remained constant: seating, as in a theatre, was arranged in gallery, dress circle, boxes, and pit; a ring, thirteen metres in diameter, dominated the centre of the pit; and a stage, said to be 130 feet wide and described as the largest in London, had a proscenium arch which extended the full width of the auditorium. Contemporary illustrations reveal a highly decorated interior, with curtains, chandelier, gilding, and ornaments. Circuses elsewhere in England, in France, and in America were housed in similarly designed buildings, and even travelling shows, up to the middle of the 19th century, took place not in the huge tents of later years but in portable wooden structures, like the 'wooden pavilion' of Sleary's circus in *Hard Times*. The auditorium was fundamentally similar to that of a theatre; except for the ring, its interior arrangements were the same.

Furthermore, the nature of the entertainment had much in common with performances in the theatre of the day. The succession of variety acts, or scenes in the circle, which generally constitutes the whole of the show in a circus today, formed only a portion of an evening's attractions during the first half of the 19th century. Then top billing was given to a dramatized entertainment on horseback, in which riders and animals would enact a play.

The spectacle might be a mock battle, a melodrama, or a pantomime, but an essential element was its dramatic nature: a story was enacted by the company. Mr Sleary gives an indication of the nature of equestrian drama when he wheezes a description of one for Sissy: 'If you wath to thee our Children in the Wood, with their father and mother both a dyin' on a horthe—their uncle a rethieving of 'em ath hith wardth, upon a horthe—themthelvth both a goin' a black-berryin' on a horthe—and the Robinth a coming in to cover 'em with leavth, upon a horthe—you'd thay it wath the completetht thing ath ever you thet your eyeth upon!' (*HT* 3.7). Following the famous instruction of Ducrow, 'Cut the dialect and come to the 'osses!', dialogue was minimal, the emphasis falling firmly on feats of horsemanship, music, costumes, sets, and pageantry.

Individual horses were often billed by name as the leading actors, dancing, playing dead, rescuing heroines, and apprehending villains; sometimes elephants or lions were included in the cast. The foremost military spectacle, *The Battle of Waterloo*, first staged in 1824, was revived season after season, as was the dramatization of BYRON's *Mazeppa* (1831), in which a wild steed, with the hero tied naked to its back, galloped across the countryside, up precipices and over ravines. In 1853, immediately before Dickens started writing *Hard Times*, Astley's developed *Billy Button's Journey to Brentford* (one of Signor Jupe's routines) from a comic act of supposed bad riding into an elaborate Christmas pantomime, with more than thirty named roles. In these and countless other equestrian dramas, a thorough fusion of circus and theatre took place.

Recognition of these distinctive characteristics of the 19th-century theatre can clarify the theatricality in the writings of Dickens. A number of his characters—and not just actors—are closely related as theatrical entertainers. Sometimes they move between one kind of show and another, like Tom Codlin, the Punch and Judy operator in *The Old Curiosity Shop*, whose previous livelihood saw him cast as a ghost in fairground theatre booths; in the same novel, one of Jerry's performing dogs has graduated from the role of Toby in the puppet show. Chops the Dwarf (in the Christmas Story 'Going into Society') is exhibited alongside a giant, an albino lady, and wild Indian; Doctor Marigold, the cheap-jack, attracts customers by developing a patter as entertaining as that of any fairground barker. Matthew Bagnet plays the bassoon in a theatre orchestra (*BH*); Frederick Dorrit plays the clarionet; Little Swills (in *Bleak House*) is a stand-up comedian in a public house.

Among these and other such theatrical types, by far the most prominent are the actors in *Nicholas Nickleby* and the circus troupe in *Hard Times*. Crummles and Sleary are near cousins. Both managers offer shows which include dramatic pieces and variety acts: the actors in Portsmouth perform not only plays but the sword-exercise of the two Master Crummleses, the balletic duet of 'The Indian Savage and the Maiden', a variety of songs and dances, and they have the pony's talents on call; the equestrians in Coketown have riding routines in their repertoire and also full-length hippodramas of *The Children in the Wood*, *Jack the Giant Killer*, and the black-face play in which young Tom Gradgrind is cast. Moreover, all performers have several essential characteristics in common: they unashamedly present themselves as entertainers; they are hard-working, gregarious, cheerful, benevolent, and imaginative, but equally they betray pettiness and egotism sufficient to prevent their appearing wholly romanticized.

The diverse nature of their activities involves the artiste in appearing simultaneously as self and as other; he or she undertakes a role without disguising the actor who is performing that role. Performance thus becomes complex play with reality, at once asserting the actor's individual identity and reaching beyond that identity into an imagined one. Integrity, imagination, and desire to please are the essential ingredients of such theatricality, and they are represented as invaluable attributes of both Sleary's and Crummles's companies.

The diverse nature of 19th-century theatre, with its emphasis on spectacle as much as upon plot and character, was frankly committed to providing delight, just as we find Dickens insisting in his prefaces that the aim of his writing was to offer amusement. This entertainment, both in the theatre and in Dickens's fiction, reflected the realities of contemporary life without pretending to slavish imitation. Part of the fascination of such art lay precisely in the surprising ways in which the patent artifice could reflect the known reality. Dickens was explicit about the non-mimetic appeal of such art when he described the theatre as a 'delightful dream' in which one had the experience 'of having for an hour or two quite forgotten the real world, and of coming out into the street with a kind of wonder that it should be so wet, and dark, and cold, and full of jostling people and irreconcilable cabs' (*Speeches*, p. 316). Similarly, he spoke of the attraction of the 'jocund world' of pantomime:

'where there is no affliction or calamity that leaves the least impression; where a man may tumble into the broken ice, or dive into the kitchen fire, and only be the droller for the accident; where babies may be knocked about and sat upon, or choked with gravy spoons, in the process of feeding, and yet no Coroner be wanted, nor anybody made uncomfortable; where workmen may fall from the top of a house to the bottom, or even from the bottom of a house to the top, and sustain no injury to the brain, need no hospital, leave no young children; where every one, in short, is so superior to all the accidents of life, though encountering them at every turn, that I suspect this to be the secret (though many persons may not present it to themselves) of the general enjoyment which an audience of vulnerable spectators, liable to pain and sorrow, find in this class of entertainment . . . It always appears to me that the secret of enjoyment lies in the temporary superiority to the common hazards and mischances of life; in seeing casualties, attended when they really occur with bodily and mental suffering, tears, and poverty, happen through a very rough sort of poetry without the least harm being done to anyone—the pretence of distress in a pantomime being so broadly humorous as to be no pretence at all.'

'Much as in the comic fiction I can understand the mother with a very vulnerable baby at home, greatly relishing the invulnerable baby on the stage, so in the Cremorne reality I can understand the mason who is always liable to fall off a scaffold in his working jacket and to be carried to the hospital, having an infinite admiration of the radiant personage in spangles who goes into the clouds upon a bull, or upside down, and who, he takes it for granted—not reflecting upon the thing—has, by uncommon skill and dexterity, conquered such mischances as those to which he and his acquaintance are continually exposed' ('A Curious Dance Round a Curious Tree,' *HW* 17 January 1852; 'Lying Awake,' *HW* 30 October 1852).

The characteristics of the theatre of the age clarify the nature of this stimulus to the imagination. The theatre as Dickens knew it was not representational in the sense of creating an illusion of reality; its value was not the verification of a 'slice of life'. Rather, theatre was performance, pushing against the boundaries of known reality, revealing undreamt-of possibilities, shedding new light on ordinary existence, and thereby enlarging experience. So too Dickens in his novels, purposely dwelling on the romantic side of familiar things, created an art which expanded readers' perception through its appeal to their imagination. Mr Bounderby, the pompous blowhard of *Hard Times*, stands as the antithesis of such activity. Fabricating an utterly fallacious image of himself for his own personal aggrandizement, Bounderby rejects the 'exact truth' which must form the core of fanciful treatment. His invention is not fancy, but deceit; not role-playing for the delight of others, but misrepresentation at the expense of everyone around him. It is the very reverse of the theatrical values embodied by the artistes of Sleary's circus.

For Dickens, the relation between theatre and life was a fascinating mirror image. Such, at least, was the claim he made in his early essay 'The Pantomime of Life' (*BM* March 1837), in which he proposed that all men and women are actors in a great pantomime. It was a view he also articulated in *Oliver Twist*, in the course of his famous comparison of the alternation of comic and tragic scenes in melodrama to the 'layers of red and white in a side of streaky, well-cured bacon': 'Such changes appear absurd; but they are not so unnatural as they would seem at first sight. The transitions in real life from well-spread boards to death-beds, and from mourning weeds to holiday garments, are not a whit less startling; only, there, we are busy actors, instead of passive lookers-on; which makes a vast difference' (*OT* 17).

The wonderfully eccentric characters who populate his novels, with extravagant gesture

and idiosyncratic speech; the surprising coincidences of plot which foil the villain and bring hero and heroine together at last; the animate world in which vividly realized objects take on lives of their own—these are central characteristics of Dickens's art which his detractors call 'theatrical.' Theatrical they are, but in no derogatory sense: they highlight the absurdities which abound in everyday existence; they heighten realities which would otherwise pass unnoticed; they create new perspectives by juxtaposition, inversion, and surprising connection; they portray life with curiosity and wonder, finding novelty, amusement, and insight in everything.

Dickens believed that love of the theatre was an innate human characteristic, and for this reason he was confident that theatrical art had potency as a great educative force. By appealing directly to people, he felt, it could stimulate imagination as no other means, however pleasingly instructive, could do ('The Amusements of the People', *HW* 30 March and 13 April 1850). In a speech in honour of his fellow-novelist THACKERAY, Dickens said that 'Every good actor plays direct to every good author, and every writer of fiction, though he may not adopt the dramatic form, writes in effect for the stage' (*Speeches*, p. 262). While the applicability of the remark may not be as all-inclusive as Dickens claims, its relevance to his own artistry is patent. (See also AMUSEMENTS AND RECREATION; DRAMA AND DRAMATISTS.)                    PVWS

**theatres and other places of exhibition.** 'I tried to recollect . . . whether I had ever been in any theatre in my life from which I had not brought away some pleasant association, however poor the theatre,' said Dickens in 1846, 'and I protest . . . I could not remember even one' (*Speeches*, p. 76).

Throughout his lifetime Dickens was associated with and wrote about a large number of theatres. He recalls childhood visits to the Theatre Royal, Rochester ('the sweet, dingy, shabby little country theatre': Ackroyd 1990, p. 37), whilst the young David Copperfield, after watching *Julius Caesar* and the new pantomime at London's Covent Garden Theatre, finds that 'the mingled reality and mystery of the whole show, the influence upon me of the lights, the music, the company, the smooth stupendous changes of glittering and brilliant scenery, were so dazzling, and opened up such illimitable regions of delight, that when I came out into the rainy street at twelve o'clock at night, I felt as if I had come from the clouds ... to a bawling, splashing, link-lighted, umbrella-struggling, hackney-coach jostling, patten-clinking, muddy, miserable world' (*DC* 19). Dickens doubtless drew on his own youthful experience of Covent Garden, which he would have visited along with Drury Lane, the only two theatres officially licensed to open in London during the winter months up until 1843, although there were many minor theatres offering MELODRAMA and other fare throughout London at this time.

Dickens also describes the rather shabby private theatres, at some of which he may have performed as a young man: 'The theatre itself may be found in Catherine Street, Strand, the purlieus of the city, the neighbourhood of Gray's Inn Lane, or the vicinity of Sadler's Wells; or it may perhaps form the chief nuisance of some shabby street on the Surrey side of Waterloo Bridge' ('Private Theatricals', *SB*). He also describes Astley's Ampthitheatre, which was situated south of the river and consisted of a stage and CIRCUS ring, in which were presented equestrian and military spectacles ('Astley's', *SB*), as witnessed by Kit Nubbles in *The Old Curiosity Shop*. Dickens describes Astley's, 'with all the paint, gilding, and looking-glass; the vague smell of horses, suggestive of coming wonders; the curtain that hid such gorgeous mysteries; the clean white sawdust down in the circus; the company coming in and taking their places ... What a glow was that, which burst upon them all when that long, clear, brilliant row of lights came slowly up, and what the feverish excitement when the little bell rang and the music began in good earnest' (*OCS* 39).

Dickens's fascination with popular theatres such as Astley's resurfaces in 'The Amusements of the People', when he visited the Victoria Theatre, again south of the river, and the Britannia, Hoxton, in east London. At the Victoria he describes the gallery, full of 'attentive faces, rising one above the other, to the very door in the roof, and squeezed and forced in, regardless of discomfort' (*HW* 30 March 1850), whilst the Britannia is also crowded to excess with 'a large number of

boys and youths, and a great many young girls grown into bold women before they had well ceased to be children ... .'. The audience, he says, being 'able to see and hear, were very attentive' (*HW*, 13 April 1850). The Britannia, subsequently rebuilt, was revisited in 1860; Dickens saw a PANTOMIME and melodrama, comparing this with a Sunday service which took place there the following night. ('Two Views of a Cheap Theatre', *AYR* 25 February 1860). A slightly patronizing tone, combined with a concern for the moral efficacy of the theatre, characterizes Dickens's accounts, as can also be seen in a collaborative piece with R. H. Horne on Sadler's Wells, a popular neighbourhood theatre in north London, which under Samuel Phelps became a centre for SHAKESPEARE and the serious drama in the 1840s and 1850s (*HW* 4 October 1851). The backstage world of the minor theatres is evoked in *Little Dorrit*, when Amy and her sister enter 'a maze of dust, where a quantity of people were tumbling over one another, and where there was such a confusion of unaccountable shapes of beams, bulkheads, brick walls, ropes and rollers, and such a mixing of gaslight and daylight, that they seemed to have got on the wrong side of the pattern of the universe' (*LD* 1.20).

As a young man Dickens became associated with the St James's Theatre in London's West End. Opened by BRAHAM in 1836, it staged three of his plays during 1836–7 (see PLAYWRIGHT, DICKENS AS); he would also have visited the fashionable Olympic Theatre, under Madame Vestris's management, during the 1830s (see MATHEWS, CHARLES JAMES). Among other West End theatres with strong Dickensian associations were the Adelphi, where Charles MATHEWS the elder had performed his 'At Homes', which staged many Dickens DRAMATIZATIONS under Frederick YATES, and where J. L. Toole later made his debut on Dickens's recommendation; the Strand, also noted for its Dickens adaptations and later for Marie Wilton's male impersonations in burlesque; the Royalty, built in 1840 for Fanny Kelly and used by Dickens for AMATEUR THEATRICALS; the Lyceum, where the KEELEYS played several Dickens adaptations and which his friend Charles FECHTER later managed; and the Haymarket, frequently visited by Dickens for the comedies and farces presented under both WEBSTER'S and BUCKSTONE's management. Any theatre at which MACREADY was performing was attended by Dickens, especially Covent Garden in the late 1830s and Drury Lane in the early 1840s.

Dickens, a frequent visitor to provincial theatres, provides a strong impression of the Portsmouth Theatre in *Nicholas Nickleby* with 'its strong smell of orange-peel and lamp-oil, with an under-current of saw-dust' and its 'bare walls, dusty scenes, mildewed clouds, heavily daubed draperies, and dirty floors' (*NN* 23). Visiting a benefit at a theatre in a forlorn, out-of-season watering-place, he calculates the house to be 'four and ninepence to begin with', possibly warming up, in the course of the evening, to 'half a sovereign' ('Out of Season', *HW* 28 June 1856). On his travels abroad he also visited the French theatres in Paris, including the Odéon (where he saw Dumas's *Christine* with Macready), the Variétés, the Cirque, the Comédie-Français, the Porte-Martine, and the Ambigu. In Genoa, Italy, he describes the Theatre Diurno (a covered outdoor theatre), and was much taken with the puppet theatre, where marionettes from Milan performed. He remained an inveterate theatregoer throughout his life.                                   JD

**Ticknor and Fields** and successor firms, Boston publishers, issued American editions of many of the great literary works of the mid-19th century. James T. FIELDS and later James R. OSGOOD, both partners in the firm, became acquaintances of Dickens and were largely responsible for the organization of his second tour of AMERICA (1867–8) (see also PUBLIC READINGS). Upon becoming Dickens's sole authorized American publisher (1867), the firm issued his collected works in various styles (most notably the Diamond Edition, with illustrations by Sol EYTINGE Jr.; see EDITIONS: FOREIGN ENGLISH-LANGUAGE), his reading texts, several fugitive periodical pieces, and *Edwin Drood*. Dickens also contributed to the firm's periodicals: the *Atlantic Monthly*, *Our Young Folks*, and *Every Saturday*.                                   MW

**Times, The.** Dickens appears to have been a daily reader of the paper, whose editor, John Thadeus Delane (1817–79), he met by 1847 and continued to see on terms 'intimate and frequent', according to FORSTER (6.6). The paper

was founded in 1785 as the *Daily Universal Register* ('*The Times*' was added three years later) by John Walter (1739–1812), a coal merchant and Lloyd's underwriter. He handed over management of the paper to his son in 1809, and it was John Walter II (1776–1847) who brought it to prominence, making it the first paper to use a steam press (1814) and also to have a foreign correspondent in the Peninsular War. Walter acted as his own editor until 1813, but it was Thomas Barnes (b. 1785), editor from 1817 until his death in 1841, who gave the editing of *The Times* its legendary status. He was a journalist of liberal sympathies who had been associated with Leigh HUNT and the EXAMINER. Barnes is given credit for making the leading article a looked-for feature and for increasing the use of advertising and so gaining more independence from government patronage. The paper's nickname, 'The Thunderer', was gained in 1830 for a trivial society piece (by Edward Sterling), but the paper began to make use of the name's sterner connotations in 1831, urging the People to 'thunder for REFORM'.

Delane succeeded to the editorship in 1841 (when he was 23) and brought it to even greater influence upon political events. Barnes's articles had been a strong feature of the paper, whereas Delane wrote little but mingled tirelessly with the politicians of the day. The power of his leading articles has been ascribed to the fact that important government intelligence was given there and nowhere else in the paper. The paper's general air of authority was reinforced by the rigid anonymity imposed upon its writers.

Dickens was friendly with a number of *The Times*'s parliamentary reporters when he worked as a JOURNALIST for its main competitor, the MORNING CHRONICLE, in his early twenties, and they all competed on the road to file express reports of politicians' speeches during the elections of the early 1830s. Among these colleagues were Charles Ross (1800–84), the parliamentary reporter who gave Disraeli advice on public speaking and worked for *The Times* for 60 years, and his brothers, Francis Ross (b. 1804) and John Ross (1808–85). Dickens's maternal uncle, John Henry Barrow (1796–1858), who founded the MIRROR OF PARLIAMENT where Dickens did his first parliamentary reporting, was a Doctors' Commons reporter for *The Times* who gained a reputation for his shorthand reporting of Queen Caroline's trial in that paper in 1820.

Dickens fell out with *The Times* when the preparations for the DAILY NEWS began in 1845 (*The Times* refused to print the advertisements of its first appearance), and to this he attributed the hostile review of *The* CRICKET ON THE HEARTH and other derisory notices. However, even after the *Daily News* debacle, Dickens continued to read the paper and to write letters to the editor on public issues of the day such as CAPITAL PUNISHMENT (13 and 17 November 1849). He and *The Times* were in agreement that repeal of window tax was a more urgent social issue than that of the paper tax (31 January 1851), and the paper noted with approval Dickens's efforts to make the ROYAL LITERARY FUND more efficient (see *Pilgrim* 7.566, 640n). Dickens was full of praise for *The Times*'s dispatches from the CRIMEAN WAR and its resulting campaign for administrative reform (see *Speeches*, p. 201). He also customarily used its columns to make various announcements about himself and his publications: two letters disavowing an advertisement in *Household Words* which was anti-Catholic (9 and 19 July 1852; see ROMAN CATHOLIC CHURCH); another denying that he had used Inspector FIELD as a character in *Bleak House* or contracted to write his biography (18 September 1853); and two letters regarding the fund set up for Douglas JERROLD's family after his death (31? August–1 September 1857, 6 October 1857). The most famous of such announcements was the public letter on the separation from Catherine DICKENS. It was Delane who cast the deciding vote, against Forster, that Dickens should print the 'Personal Statement' (published 7 June 1858 in *The Times*). That Dickens should have relied upon Delane is hardly surprising—Delane's worldliness and independence of party have often been eulogized.

TROLLOPE satirized both *The Times* ('the *Jupiter*') and Dickens ('Mr Popular Sentiment') in his novel *The Warden*, where *The Times*'s premises are called 'Mount Olympus' and Delane 'Tom Towers': 'It is probable that Tom Towers considered himself the most powerful man in Europe; and so he walked on from day to day, studiously striving to look a man, but knowing within his breast that he was a god' (ch. 14).     KC

Cook, Sir Edward, *Delane of The Times* (1916).

Hudson, Derek, *Thomas Barnes of 'The Times'* (1943).

Times, *History of the Times: Volume 1, The Thunderer in the Making, 1785–1841* (1935); *Volume 2, The Tradition Established, 1841–1884* (1939).

Woods, Oliver and Bishop, James, *The Story of the Times: Bicentenary Edition 1785–1985* (1985).

**'To Be Read at Dusk'** Two brief tales of the supernatural, written by Dickens in 1851 for publication in *Heath's Keepsake*, an ANNUAL edited by Marguerite Power, niece of the late society hostess and writer, the Countess of Blessington. The tales are told as the sun glows red on the surrounding snow, by two of a group of five couriers gathered at the Great St Bernard hospice in the Swiss Alps. The first, which Elizabeth GASKELL accused him of stealing from her (Pilgrim 6.545 n.), draws upon Dickens's experience with Mme de la Rue (d. 1887), whom he tried to cure of a nervous disorder by means of MESMERISM in Genoa in 1844–5. It concerns an English lady who elopes, never to be seen again, from her home in Genoa with a man whose face has haunted her in a dream. The second tells of a man who hurries to his brother's bedside after seeing his phantom, arriving only in time to witness the brother's death.    PVWS

**trade unions.** The contradictions in Victorian responses, including those of Dickens, to trade unions must be set in their historical context to be fully understandable. English common law regarded combining with the aim of controlling conditions of work, wages, and hours as illegal in being a conspiracy to restrain trade. Theoretically, this prohibition applied equally to masters and workers, but in practice it was more severely applied in the case of the latter (see CLASS). The traditional legal position was reinforced by an Act of Parliament of 1800 partly stimulated by the agitation generated by the French Revolution and the fear of its spreading to the United Kingdom. Partial recognition of unions was implied in the Act of 1859, which accepted the validity of peaceful persuasion in the field of hours and wages, although the formation of unions still remained an unlawful, if not necessarily a criminal, activity. Agitation against these prohibitions led to a series of what were regarded as 'outrages' in Sheffield and Manchester in 1865–6. This in turn resulted in the setting up of a Royal Commission which sat from 1867 to 1869 to review the whole matter. These deliberations led to the Trade Union Acts of 1871 and 1876 which set the pattern for the legal development of union activity which remained dominant in the United Kingdom until recently.

The core texts for an understanding of Dickens's attitude towards unions are *Hard Times* and his *Household Words* article of February 1854, 'On Strike'. However, it is also useful to consider another *Household Words* article of December 1853, 'The Preston Lock-Out.' Although this was by James Lowe, it is well known that nothing appeared in his periodical without Dickens's approval and so its critical sentiments towards trade unions must be seen as part of the total picture of responses in this field. Although not the direct inspiration for *Hard Times*, the Preston difficulties were sufficiently well known to encourage Dickens to visit the town as part of the preparation for his novel. The fact of some 20,000 to 30,000 cotton spinners being unemployed, and so entirely dependent on support from fellow unionists and charitable contributions, for seven to eight months in 1853 was a cause of national concern and interest. The tone of Lowe's article can be felt in his reference to the 'mob-orators [who] appear in times of trouble and contention, to excite, with their highly spiced eloquence, the thoughtless crowd; over whom they exercise such pernicious sway'. The tone, as well as the content, of 'On Strike' is markedly more balanced, but it has to be assumed that Lowe's stereotypical view of glib outsiders holding sway over honest, but rather dim, workers was not unacceptable to large sections of the Victorian middle class. A representative of this class, 'Mr Snapper', is the object of Dickens's attack in the course of the train journey he takes to see the Preston situation for himself. Dickens is clear that the 'hands' have a 'perfect right to combine in any lawful manner' and that this is 'a protection to them'. And he accepts also that the 'blame of this business is not all on one side. I think the associated Lock-out was a grave error.' However, Dickens cannot bring himself to accept that the workers are in the right, as he fears that 'they are at present engaged in an unreasonable struggle', and this unwillingness to take sides is rooted in his belief that 'into the relations between employers and employed . . . there must enter something of feeling and sentiment; something of mutual explanation, forbearance, and consideration'.

This attempt to see both sides of the question motivates the treatment of trade unionism in *Hard Times*, and can seem pusillanimous to modern readers, especially those of a left-wing tendency; and to some extent it runs counter to the expressions of support for union, and other forms of working-class activity contained in, for example, Dickens's letters. However, in addition to being a deeply held conviction, Dickens's tone and attitude can be understood as the best means of combating, without alienating, the no-doubt vulgar prejudices that existed in much of his audience. The presentation of the union 'agitator' Slackbridge, very much in the terms of Lowe's article, as a manipulator might be seen as a sacrifice to this viewpoint. But a higher artistic purpose is also at work in the novel, one in which union pressures can be seen as threatening the individuality that it is part of the novel's essential purpose to defend against the forces that menace it.        GFS

**translations of Dickens.** Dickens's works of fiction have long been translated into all major European languages since Dickens's lifetime, with most of his works appearing in foreign-tongue versions almost as soon as they were published in English. Today, many novels and stories are also available in exotic and minor languages (including Esperanto), and it would take several volumes to provide an approximately exhaustive bibliography. This entry is bound to be drastically selective.

German translators were the pioneers, followed closely by the French. As early as 1837 there began to appear a five-volume translation of *Pickwick Papers* in Leipzig, *Die Pickwickier*. Dickens expressed his pleasure at his unforeseen popularity in GERMANY (to Kuenzel, 9 July 1838), and his London publishers soon came to an arrangement with J. J. Weber, the Leipzig publisher, by which the proofs of his new novels were to be sent directly for translation into German. H. Roberts, the translator, was very explicit about his intentions to do justice to the text, and his achievement is still held in high esteem by contemporary scholars, despite the subsequent appearance of many excellent alternative versions.

Not so the first French translation of the same novel, *Le Club des Pickwistes (sic)*, 'traduit librement de l'anglais' by Eugénie Niboyet in 1838. Many liberties indeed were taken by Mme Niboyet and by other early French translators, one of the often-quoted instances being Amédée Pichot's rendering of *David Copperfield* as *Le Neveu de ma tante* (1851). It was not until 1859 that a proper translation (by P. Grolier) was published by Hachette in a series edited by Paul Lorain 'avec l'autorisation de l'auteur' (an agreement had been signed in 1856 giving Hachette the exclusive rights of translation into French). Dickens certainly sanctioned the series somewhat hastily when he declared it 'perfectly faithful to the English text' while rendered 'in elegant and expressive French', but it was a real improvement on earlier attempts, 'fragmentary and unauthorized translations over which', as the novelist rightly complained, he had had 'no control' (Archives Hachette). Lorain was a scrupulous academic, a good coordinator and proof-reader, and misinterpretations are scarce. At a steady pace, between 1857 and 1874, the 28 volumes of the complete works came out in the 'Bibliothèque des meilleurs romans étrangers', some of which were reprinted by Jean Gattégno in the late 1980s in the paperback series '10/18'. But these translations had long been superseded by better ones, especially Sylvère Monod's published singly in the 'Classiques Garnier' or in the famous series 'La Pléiade', the last three volumes of which he edited, annotated, and prefaced (following the death of Pierre Leyris, the former editor). Of all his translations, *La Maison d'Âpre-vent (Bleak House)* is perhaps Monod's outstanding achievement.

In the Netherlands, the journal *De Gids* ran translations of *Pickwick* near-contemporaneously with the British publication (although the total amount translated amounted to only a few chapters); and Hendrik Frijlinck's abridged translation of *Nicholas Nickleby* appeared in another journal, *Het Leeskabinet*, in 1838–9. Other pieces by Dickens appeared in Holland (for instance, J. L. van der Vliet's 1845 translation of *The CHIMES*), but a complete Dutch translation of Dickens only appeared much later (see below).

Dickens's reputation soon reached far beyond the borders of neighbouring countries, often preceding translations of his works. His name was mentioned for the first time in Russia in 1837 when *Pickwick* was recommended in *Bibliotheka dlya Chteniya*. At the end of 1838 this novel was partly translated in the same journal and in *Syn Otechestva*. Some of the sketches were translated in 1839, *Nicholas Nickleby* in 1840. In 1841 translations of *Sketches by Boz* and *Oliver Twist* appeared in *Literatornaya Gazeta* and *Otechestvennye Zapiski*, where Dickens was described as 'the best English writer'. Most of the translations were anonymous until 1849, when a new version of *Pickwick* came out, signed Irinarkh Vvedensky. This excellent translator played an important part in strengthening the popularity of Dickens in Russia with further translations until his death in 1855. In the meantime he corresponded with the novelist, whom he met in London in 1853.

In Northern Europe the need for translations was not so urgently felt by educated readers who had a good mastery of English. The first Danish translation, *David Copperfield* by L. Moltke, appeared as late as 1849–50. From that date onwards Moltke translated all Dickens's major works simultaneously with their appearance in English. No fewer than ten out of the 23 collected editions distributed over 123 years bear Moltke's name, making him the pre-eminent Danish translator of Dickens. This translator's competence, however, was severely questioned in 1872 and many revisions were made henceforth, while new translations, particularly by Henrik Carl Bering Liisberg, Oluf Petersen, Else Brudenell-Bruce, Ejnar Reeslev, and Eva Hemmer Hansen, came out between 1905 and 1981. Written Danish and Norwegian were virtually the same language in the 19th century, which accounts for the small number of translations published in Norway in those early days. Similarly, few translations appeared in Flanders, Flemish being a variant of the Dutch language. In the Netherlands an edition of the complete works in 22 volumes, *Geïllustreerde complete werken van Charles Dickens voor het huisgezin*, finally appeared in 1889, most of the novels being translated by C. M. Mensing. In 'Dickens in English' (*Stockholm Papers in English Language and Literature*, April 1984), Ishrat Lindblad asserts that 'there is no complete edition of Dickens' collected works in Swedish'. He also informs us that, strangely enough, 'Dickens was introduced to Sweden via Germany', since the first translations (*Pickwick Papers* and *Sketches by Boz*), by Henrik Bernhard Palmaer, were based on H. Roberts's. This, at any rate, would seem to confirm the quality of those early German translations.

Few Spanish or Italian translations of Dickens's works were available during the lifetime of the novelist. Even PICTURES FROM ITALY did not inspire translators until 1911, when *L'Italia. Impressioni e descrizioni di Carlo Dickens* by Edoardo Bolchesi was published in Milan. Dickens's love of ITALY was not fairly reciprocated until the 20th century. But Italian academics are making up for lost time and new translations are currently in progress.

In *El inglés de Charles Dickens y su traduccion al espanol* (1993), Adolfo L. Soto Vazquez analyses the difficulties met by Spanish translators, most of them from the 20th century, in rendering the flavour of Dickens's style and finding equivalents for typically English concepts and institutions. Such puzzles must be far more difficult to overcome in non-European countries. How, we wonder, can Oriental or African countries cope with such problems? How can translators mediate between totally different languages and totally different cultures, landscapes, and climates? Indeed, significantly, an early and approximative JAPANESE translation of SKETCHES OF YOUNG COUPLES (1882) was rendered as something like 'Sketches of Man and Wife of the West'. The addition of 'of the West' is a clever trick to bridge the gap between mores that are poles apart, a sign that translators will not let themselves be deterred by difficulties.

The *British Museum General Catalogue* lists titles in a most astonishing range of languages and dialects besides those mentioned above: Afrikaans, Arabic, Armenian, Bengali, Bulgarian, Catalan, Chinese, Czech, Estonian, Finnish, Georgian, Greek, Hebrew, Hungarian, Icelandic, Irish, Kazak, Latvian, Lithuanian, Marathi, Panjabi, Persian, Polish, Portugese, Romanian, Serbo-Croat, Slovack, Slovene, Tamil, Ukrainian, Welsh, Yiddish. Chinese translations were among the earliest productions from the Far East, with *Ku chi*

*wai shih* (*Nicholas Nickleby*) in 1907, *Tsei shih* (*Oliver Twist*) in 1908, and *Hsiao nü nai êrh chuan* (*Old Curiosity Shop*) in 1915 by Lin Shu and Wei I. Lin Shu, in fact, went on to translate the whole of Dickens, and other Western authors, despite not actually speaking any English—by the expedient of getting friends to describe the novels to him and on that basis translating them into Classical Chinese.

Apart from the sketch mentioned above and a chapter from *David Copperfield* published in 1892 in a magazine, all Japanese translations have appeared in the 20th century: the first complete translation of *David Copperfield*, by Tokuboku Hirata, the leading scholar in English studies in pre-war Japan, appeared in four volumes from 1925 to 1928. Most of the major novels came out in Japanese after the war, though *Nicholas Nickleby* and *Dombey and Son* are still waiting to be translated.

Superficial though it is, this survey should convey an idea of Dickens's widespread and lasting POPULARITY. The dissemination of Dickens through all five continents reflects that his enduring appeal is based less on cultural specifics, and more on an underlying humanism. For example, *A Christmas Carol*, always the great favourite in Europe, where it underwent countless translations and adaptations, also finds favour in contemporary Africa: between 1983 and 1986 it was translated into various South African languages: Zulu, Tsonga, Tswana, Xhosa, Venda. It would seem that humane values and the CHRISTMAS spirit are universally transmittable and translatable. AS

Collins (1971).

Delattre, Floris, *Dickens et la France* (1927).

Fridlender, Iu. and Katarsky, I., *Charl'z Dikkens, bibliographfiia russikh perevodov i kriticheskoi literatury na russkom iazyke, 1838–1960* (1962).

Gummer, Ellis M., *Dickens's Works in Germany, 1837–1937* (1940).

Mikdadi, F. H., '*David Copperfield* in Arabic', *Dickensian*, 75 (1979).

Nisbet, Ada, 'Charles Dickens', in Lionel Stevenson (ed.), *Victorian Fiction: A Guide to Research* (1964).

Nolin, Joseph, 'The Appreciation of Dickens by his French Contemporaries', *Dickensian*, 13 (1927).

Waley, Arthur, 'Notes on Translation', *Atlantic Monthly* (1958).

Wellens, Oscar, 'The Earliest Dutch Translations of Dickens (1837–1870): An All-Inclusive List', Dickensian, 93 (1997).

Wilkins, W. Glyde, 'Early Foreign Translations of Dickens's Works', Dickensian, 7 (1911), 35–7.

## transport: roads, coaches, railways, omnibuses, cabs.

'It is very generally allowed that public conveyances afford an extensive field for amusement and observation', wrote Dickens in one of his earliest 'BOZ' sketches ('Omnibuses', SB). While the period of his lifetime coincides neatly with that of the celebrated 'Railway Age', readers of his works are as likely to connect him with the heyday of what may be termed the 'Coaching Era'. In fact, in his fictional and non-fictional writings Dickens has left a vivid, impressionistic account of almost every form of transportation available to him, and by extension to the characters who inhabit his literary representations of the world. For him, as for many contemporary writers and pictorial artists, it was easy to see transport and communications, by a characteristically metonymic imaginative displacement, as indexes to the age and embodiments of its *Zeitgeist*.

### Roads and Coaches

During the regency of George IV, long before the locomotive steam engine was seriously considered as a means of conveyance, important advances were still being made in the development of road networks in the United Kingdom. In the period 1730–70 England and Wales had already seen a huge increase in the provision of well-maintained high-roads. Steady expansion of inland consumption and trade encouraged the establishment of numerous private turnpike trusts, and the parishes adjacent to highways such as the Great North and Great West Roads were no longer burdened with their maintenance. Tolls were charged to rich and poor alike, affording foreigners a notable example of the relatively egalitarian principles obtaining in British society. A guide to the new national network was given in Daniel Paterson's indispensable *New and Accurate Description of all the Direct and Principal Cross Roads in Great Britain* (1771), familiarly known to those of Dickens's generation as 'the Book of Roads' (*Speeches*, p. 172). Radical further improvement came with the appointment of John Loudon McAdam (1756–1836) as Surveyor-General of the Bristol Roads in 1815, and the publication of his *Present State of Road-making* (1820). The 'macadamizing' of roads —the building up of graded courses of broken stone to withstand heavy traffic and improve drainage—soon became widespread in Britain and 'in all parts of the civilized world' (*DNB*). By 1830 the journey time by coach from Edinburgh to London had been cut to around 36 hours, from nearly a fortnight in 1745. McAdam's countryman Thomas Telford (1757–1834) also opened up swathes of the nation to road traffic, with the provision of 120 new bridges and 920 miles of roads in northern counties of Scotland, and similar feats in England (*DNB*).

Telford was equally prominent in canal construction, engineering the Ellesmere Canal in Wales and Cheshire (commenced 1793), the Caledonian Canal (1803), and the Göta canal connecting the Baltic and the North Sea (1808). As with the roads, commercially motivated co-operation between landowners and industrialists resulted in the creation of a privately funded communications infrastructure, until all the major navigable rivers in Britain were connected, and Birmingham could boast more miles of canal and waterway than Venice. The first two decades of the 19th century saw the completion of the Grand Junction Canal between London and Birmingham (1805), the Kennet and Avon between London and Bristol (1810), the Wey and Arun between London and Portsmouth (1816), and within London, the Surrey and the Regent's Canals (1803, 1820), linking the north-west to the south-east. All this before the railways arrived.

Despite being later viewed as overly leisurely and inefficient forms of transportation, by the time of Dickens's youth the British system of roads and of 'broad' and 'narrow' canals, accommodating boats of different beams and lengths, was without rival in Europe and technologically highly advanced. As in ancient times, the nation took pride in the construction of her chariots and the speed of her charioteers. In his essay on 'The English Mail-Coach' (1849) DE QUINCEY writes informatively about the way the royal mail coach, as established by the Bath MP John Palmer (1742–1818), became 'the national organ for publishing the ... mighty events' of the Napoleonic Wars, and of how it was in 'itself a spiritualised and glorified object'. Before 1829 the mails left between 8.00 and 8.20 p.m. from the old General Post Office on Lombard St., and after from outside Smirke's neoclassical façade to the new building on St Martin's-le-Grand (*NN* 39; *MC* 11). Each carriage (originally chocolate brown) underwent a rigorous daily inspection before being approved for use and polished up for its journey. The guards, rather than the coachmen, were royal appointees and, as such, were entitled to wear the royal livery. The mails plied between the metropolis and Aberdeen, Bristol, Edinburgh, Glasgow, Gloucester, Holyhead, Lincoln, Manchester, Newcastle, Oxford, Perth, Portsmouth, Stirling, Winchester, and York, and were often tied to a strict time allowance of eleven miles every 50 minutes—meaning an average speed of over 13 m.p.h.—and were thus considered the epitome of speed and purpose, gloriously harnessed to the national interest.

Fierce competition was provided by commercially operated stagecoach companies covering a wider selection of routes. Speed was the key, hence names such as 'Tallyho', 'Flyer', and the French 'diligence' (from *carosse de diligence*, 'speedy coach'). A would-be commercial proprietor (or 'coachmaster') first needed to get his 'plates' (licences), at a cost of £5 per vehicle. He would then choose his 'ground' (route), contract with a coachbuilder to 'mile' an appropriate number of coaches (construct individualized coaches, at so much per mile), 'horse' the coaches (contract with 'postmasters', usually innkeepers, to provide relays of horses between stages), and man them with coachmen and guards. Every coachmaster, finally, needed a headquarters to work from, with stabling for horses and accommodation for employees and passengers. These were the coaching INNS or yards, hives of social, commercial, and 'SPORTING' activity. London had dozens, many of which were represented frequently in the drama and fiction of the period as scenes of meeting, departure, and comic 'business'. Dickens's works alone feature at least thirteen, with no less than five occurring in *Pickwick*. One of the reasons for the success of Dickens's writing as 'Boz' and of Robert SURTEES with *Jorrocks* in the 1830s, was doubtless their perceptive and humorous rendering of the coaching yards and of 'sporting' activity generally.

As the well-known story of the origin of *The Pickwick Papers* suggests, sporting prints and sketches such as those in which Robert SEYMOUR specialized were popular predecessors of the literary sketch, as were paintings of coaching activity such as those of James Pollard (1792–1867), Charles Cooper Henderson (1803–77), and the prolific Henry Alken (1785–1851). The latter's painting *The Carlisle to London Coach in Snow, Trains Passing* transcends the genre of sporting art, however. Alken died in poverty following the decline of the coaching yards in the 1840s, and his undated canvas shows the London-bound mail coach foundering in a snow drift, with the passengers forced to alight and help the guard to push, while speeding northward to Carlisle on clearly separate lines, glide not one, but two sleek steam trains. Another reason for Boz's success with *Pickwick* was surely that by 1836 his readers recognized nostalgically that the coaches' glory had finally departed. This vein of sentiment is humorously touched on in Dickens's final contribution to *Bentley's Miscellany* ('Familiar Epistle', 5.219–20; repr. *Journalism* 1.552–4) and during Tony Weller's fleeting reappearance in MASTER HUMPHREY'S CLOCK (*MHC* 3), when he denounces the railways as 'unconstitutional'. Dickens later provides a more serious exploration of these issues in the meditative essay 'An Old Stage-Coaching House' (*UT* 24), while reflections on the attractions of travel in a private coach can be found throughout PICTURES FROM ITALY, and in 'Travelling Abroad' (*UT* 7).

## Railways

It was the commercial possibilities of the locomotive as a freight-handler that first attracted investment and engineering expertise. The planners of the Liverpool and Manchester line, on which George Stephenson's 'Rocket' made its fateful inaugural journey in 1830, claimed that its 'immediate and prominent advantages' lay in reducing transport time from an average 36 hours by canal to a mere '4 or 5' by rail, and transport costs by 'at least one-third' (*Prospectus for the Liverpool and Manchester Railway*, 1826). As well as being attractive to the cotton and coal producers in many areas of Britain, the actual construction of railways, with their associated demand for raw materials and human labour, was a massive stimulus to the national economy. In the 40 years to 1870, with periodical stockmarket booms and busts, a railway network thus sprang up in Britain with extraordinary speed. In 1830 there were under 100 miles of public railway open in Britain; in 1850 there were 6,000, and by 1870, 15,310 miles, much of it double track, costing well over £10,000, and using an estimated 156 tons of iron, per mile. By 1870 a comprehensive network was in place, consisting of giant companies such as the London and North Western, the Great Western, the Midland, the Great Eastern, Great Northern, and North Eastern, with numerous smaller local operations. SER and the London, Chatham and Dover, for example, were just two of the rival companies vying for ascendancy in Kent and the south-east in the 1860s, when Dickens was commuting regularly from Gad's Hill to central London (*UT* 8, 12). Dickens himself was involved in a disastrous railway accident at Staplehurst in June 1865 (see KENT), prompting him to write scathingly later in the year of 'a muddle of railways in all directions possible ... with no general public scheme, no general public supervision, enormous waste of money . . . [and] no accountability but under Lord Campbell's Act [of Railway Regulation, 1844]' (13 November 1865). The piecemeal structure of the network overall was the major obstacle to efficiency, despite the introduction of a Clearing House in 1842 to calculate through-rates for freight and passengers using a combination of companies. Not until the creation of British Railways in 1948 was a national 'British Rail' network finally forged —temporarily, as it turns out—from this agglomeration of private-sector initiatives.

The speed of locomotives was also a cause both for concern and admiration. Engineers on the Liverpool and Manchester in 1828 expected 8 or 10 m.p.h. but achieved 28 to 29 m.p.h. from their prototypes. In 1841 the five fastest train companies listed in George Bradshaw's first *Monthly Railway Guide* were advertising speeds of 29 to 36 m.p.h. By 1848 the *Great Britain* was running from Didcot to London at over 67 m.p.h., and Edinburgh could be reached by express from London in thirteen hours. This ferocious energy, coupled with unreliable braking, fire risks, and (doubtless) widespread public recollection of the death of William Huskisson, president of the Board of Trade (1770–1830), under

the wheels of a train at the opening of the Manchester–Liverpool railway in 1830 led to a justifiable suspicion of the engine. Dickens famously capitalized on this in making a railway engine the agent of Carker's destruction (*DS* 55), equivalent to the fire-breathing, all-devouring dragon of Teutonic fairy-tales. Apart from *Dombey and Son*, with its detailed description of a railway journey (*DS* 20) and of the effects of railway construction on the neighbourhood of 'Stagg's Gardens'—probably the Somers Town and Figs Mead areas of London, redesigned to accommodate the construction of Euston Station (*DS* 6 *et seq.*) —Dickens does not appear particularly anxious in the 1840s and 1850s to incorporate the railway into his novels and stories. At this time, indeed, it is steamboats rather than engines which seem to have appealed more consistently. His experience of travelling across the Atlantic on the Cunard steam packet *SS Britannia* in 1842 is fully recorded in AMERICAN NOTES (1, 2) and lively animadversions are offered in chapters 9 to 11 on canal-boat life, including the advisability of finding a berth 'as far aft as possible' due to the well-known propensity of steam-packets to 'blow up forward'. Mrs Gamp elaborates gloriously on the vices of steamboats during her quest to locate the 'Ankworks package' (Antwerp packet) from the steam-boat pier by London Bridge (*MC* 40; see also 'The Steam Excursion', *SB*). After 1850, however, with editorial command of his own journal, Dickens ensured that railway engines and railway culture were frequently handled topics. His own essay, 'A Narrative of Extraordinary Suffering' (*HW* 12 July 1851), highlights the problems of ordinary citizens in mentally adjusting to new, impersonal timetables and systems such as the notoriously baffling 'Bradshaw' guide. 'A Flight' (*HW* 30 August 1851) describes a high-speed journey on the South Eastern Railway's recently-introduced London-to-Paris express, and is strikingly modernistic in style, anticipating later 'stream of consciousness' approaches to narration in order to convey the traveller's displaced sensations of time and space; 'The Calais Night Mail' (*AYR* 2 May 1863; *UT* 18) does the same for cross-channel ferries. In the following year Dickens incorporated a witty compendium of early railway history—social, political, and financial—into the description of Jemmy Lirriper's model railway (*AYR* extra Christmas number, 'Mrs Lirriper's Legacy'; *CS* 17). Two years later the railway provided the literal and figurative network for an entire Christmas number of *All the Year Round*, 'Mugby Junction'. Further examples of the varied fictional and dramatic uses to which the railways and their social impact could be put by Dickens and his co-writers can be found in Ewald Mengel's anthology, *The Railway through Dickens's World* (1989), which republishes 24 essays on different aspects of railway culture published by Dickens in his journals between 1850 and 1866. Only the essay 'An Unsettled Neighbourhood' (*HW* 11 November 1854), which returns to the theme of the civil disturbance caused by railway works, is by Dickens himself.

## Omnibuses and Cabs

No reader of early Dickens can fail to notice his fondness for descriptions of public transport in London. 'Cab' was the abbreviation of 'cabriolet' (a hooded, one-horse, one-seater chaise), one of many French terms imported into English to describe different models of horse-drawn carriage and equipage. The 'fly' was a covered version, with its origin in the wheeled sedan chair, invented by John Butcher in 1809 and (according to E. C. Brewer in his *Dictionary of Phrase and Fable*, 1870) used by the Prince Regent to 'fly-by-night' from nocturnal escapades in Brighton. In the mid-1830s the rather unsafe 'outrigger' cab, with the driver perching level with the passenger—perfectly illustrated in CRUIK-SHANK's etching (see *Journalism* 1.143)—was replaced by J. A. Hansom's 'Patent Safety Cab' (registered 1834), hence Dickens's reference to the 'Last Cab Driver' in the title of a 'Boz' sketch (2nd series, 1836). The term 'Hackney' had been freely applied since Stuart times to any vehicle or driver offered out for hire, but often denoting the former private coach of a nobleman (cf. 'Hackney Coach Stands', *SB*). The term derived originally from the area of pasture due north of the city of London that provided spirited 'hackney' horses (thoroughbred sires, half-bred mares) for harness work. The Hackney Carriage Act (1831) established fares for coach hire, which could be charged either by distance or time: 1 shilling up to a mile, and sixpence per half mile thereafter; or 1 shilling per half hour, and sixpence per quarter thereafter. The lighter, newer cabs cost eightpence per mile, but drivers seemed to expect the fourpence change from a shilling by way of a tip. Both kinds of 'Hackney Carriage' were prohibited from plying for hire while in motion, and had to report to appointed stands. In the late 1840s Henry Mayhew recorded that there were some 5,000 cabdrivers in London, of whom 800–1,000 were unlicensed 'bucks' who picked up occasional business by relieving the 1,500 or so 'long-day men' (drivers on a 16–20 hour shift) while they rested or ate. Of the remainder, approximately 2,000 were respectable 'small masters', owning their own cabs and living respectably on 15–25 shillings per week (*London Labour and the London Poor*, 1850; see LONDON: STREETS).

In 1829 the first horse-drawn 'omnibus' (Latin, 'for all') was introduced in London, and the 'cad' was its conductor. The term probably derived from the Scots 'cadie' or 'cawdie', denoting a small servant, errand-boy, or carrier of a sedan chair. Unlike Hackneys, 'buses' were prohibited from standing still and waiting for business; instead, they followed a set route, which was carefully supervised by timekeepers and 'checks', mostly women, who were employed by proprietors to ride inside and prevent embezzlement by the cads. Drivers worked seven days a week, with only two hours off every other Sunday, according to Mayhew.

The manhandling and 'poaching' of passengers by rival companies were both uncivilized aspects of omnibus travel commented on by Dickens in *Sketches by Boz* ('Omnibuses', 'The Last Cab Driver', 'The Bloomsbury Christening'), but which gradually disappeared as the century progressed. Half in jest, he makes Boz comment at the close of another paper: 'We marked the advance of civilisation, and beheld it with a sigh' ('Scotland Yard', *SB*). 'Slang will be forgotten when civility becomes general', Dickens also predicts at the end of 'The Last Cab Driver, and the First Omnibus Cad', this time perhaps half in earnest. One of the commonest features in the writing of Dickens and fellow Victorians about transportation in their time is the fine alloy of regret and satisfaction with which they regarded technological advances. The railways not only promised temporal uniformity in their imposition of London (Greenwich) time on the provinces, but threatened cultural uniformity in the gradual erosion of local dialects and customs. Such subcultural groupings as London cabs and omnibuses, their drivers, 'cads', and associated slang, thus stood in a synecdochal relation to the wider debate over national progress—something which Dickens instinctively sensed, and gloriously improvised upon, as an author.                                    JMLD

Bovill, E. W., 'Tony Weller's Trade', *Notes and Queries*, 101–2 (1956–7).

Drew, John, 'Voyages Extraordinaires: Dickens's "Travelling Essays" and *The Uncommercial Traveller*' (2 parts), *Dickens Quarterly*, 13 (1996).

Robbins, Michael, *The Railway Age* (1962).

Wilson, Mona, 'Holidays and Travel', in G. M. Young (ed.), *Early Victorian England* (1934), 2.283–314.

**travel and exploration** expanded dramatically during the 19th century. Partly this resulted from vastly improved technologies of travel, the railway and the steamship most obviously, but also through new networks of roads (with smoother, more permanent surfaces) and canals (see TRANSPORT). Political and economic imperialism also fuelled travel, as it became a national boast and soon a reality that the sun never set upon the Union Jack. Journeys of exploration were particularly important in the popular imagination, perhaps because of the dawning realization that it was quite possible that very soon every corner of the world's uncharted realms should have been visited by indefatigable heroes like Mungo Park (Africa), Sir John Franklin (the Northwest Passage), and Charles Sturt (Australia).

Scientific exploration played a large part in global exploration as well. For example, Charles Darwin's career began in earnest when he joined the wide-ranging second voyage of *The Beagle*, only one of many such expeditions that put the talents of naval personnel and equipment to good use during peacetime. Rivers proved especially fascinating, and the extended searches for the sources of the Niger and later the Nile generated phenomenal public attention. Exploration led not only to knowledge but also the discovery of precious natural resources, sparking feverish international gold rushes like those of California in the 1840s and Australia in the 1850s.

Exploration cannot be understood without considering the larger context of imperial expansion during the Victorian era. Throughout the 19th century the exponential growth of British dominions (in the 1840s alone England annexed the Punjab and Sind, New Zealand, Hong Kong, Natal, and the Gold Coast) was underpinned by an imperialist ideology that linked a mélange of beliefs about the virtues of free trade and economic expansion, the moral imperative to civilize 'savage' and 'inferior' races, and scientific curiosity. Yet another important factor was the interest in EMIGRATION as a safety valve to relieve excess population in England, simultaneously reducing poverty and political stress at home while peopling 'empty' corners of the globe with superior Anglo-Saxon stock. (Dickens sent three of his sons abroad to pursue careers: see CHILDREN OF DICKENS; several characters in *David Copperfield* become successful colonists in Australia.) Often, these motives generated linked actions and effects: scientific exploration would pave the way for commercial exploitation, followed by the establishment of emigrant settlements, all under the protection of the Royal Navy and Army should force prove necessary to control indigenous populations (as it often did). Dickens was no great supporter of imperial expansion, arguing that domestic needs must be addressed before wasting effort civilizing savages abroad, as in the Borrioboola-Gha project in *Bleak House*; when the 'savages' rose up, however, as they did in Jamaica in 1865, he was very much in favour of teaching them a stern lesson about the superiority of British arms (see EYRE, E. J.).

Dickens wrote of exploration and its more obvious imperial correlatives directly in a number of periodical essays, and in two co-authored longer works, the Christmas story, 'The Perils of Certain English Prisoners' (inspired by the Indian Mutiny), and the play, *The FROZEN DEEP* (which comments obliquely on Franklin's last, doomed Arctic expedition). Only one novel, *Edwin Drood*, his last, explicitly addresses connections between the Empire and the metropolis. But as Britain expanded those areas of the globe that were coloured red on schoolboys' maps of the world, the Empire was increasingly embedded in the very fabric of metropolitan life. East India House is an important presence in

*Dombey and Son*, but the impact of the East India Company is felt even in such apparently minor details in Dickens's fiction as sending the scapegrace medical students Bob Sawyer and Ben Allen to be surgeons in India at the end of *Pickwick Papers*. The public imagination was also captured by displays of the 'spoils' of Empire, such as the Chinese Junk (subject of Dickens's essay of the same name, *Examiner*, 24 June 1848), of various foreign goods on show at the Great EXHIBITION OF 1851, and even of native peoples themselves (inspiring his essay 'The Noble Savage', *HW* 11 June 1853). For example, in 1862 the famed Palm House at Kew was built to house specimens from the Pacific; in that same year an immensely popular exhibition in South Kensington of Oriental art and artefacts led to a vogue for Japanese design in everything from china to fabric to wallpaper. Other vicarious experiences of foreign locales came from huge PANORAMAS and dioramas, like those visited by Mr Booley in 'Some Account of an Extraordinary Traveller' (*HW* 20 April 1850). This domestication of the exotic in turn fuelled public interest in foreign travel, travel that became much safer, faster, and more reliable as each decade of the century passed.

Thus, while voyages of exploration constituted travel at its most exalted levels, Victorian Britain also experienced an unprecedented democratization of travel, foreign and domestic. Dickens himself was throughout his career an intrepid and indefatigable traveller: witness his accounts of a winter transatlantic crossing and overland travel in the Western USA in AMERICAN NOTES and of continental travel in the coaching era in PICTURES FROM ITALY. His early novels feature travel as subject-matter, for example, *Pickwick Papers*, *Nicholas Nickleby*, and *The Old Curiosity Shop*, conveying enthusiasm for the first great wave of improved domestic travel, the speedy mail coaches and better roads of the 1820s and 1830s. But their heyday was brief, and it was the phenomenal growth of railways—key subject and theme in *Dombey and Son*—that by the mid-1840s revolutionized transport: suddenly there was no major town or city that could not be visited from any other within the span of a single day. The government in 1844 mandated the operation of at least one return journey on every rail line that would cost no more

than a penny per mile (hence 'parliamentary' trains, like the one taken by Mr Bounderby's mother in *Hard Times*), opening railway travel to the working classes. Thomas Cook began his travel business with a single rail excursion in 1845, but before long 'Cook's Tour' was a generic term for the organized tour.

Soon Cook was sending excursioners abroad as well—eventually he owned a fleet of Nile steamers. His and similar firms, assisted by the new publishing phenomenon of tourist guides (pioneered by the firm of John Murray, BYRON's publisher), brought European travel within the grasp of ordinary middle-class Britons, like the omnipresent Mr and Mrs Davis Dickens encounters in Rome in *Pictures from Italy* and the Meagles in *Little Dorrit*. To a degree, such foreign travel reflected the new prosperity of the ever-rising English bourgeoisie, but it was stimulated in turn by the more-daring exploits of explorers and the resultant taming of what had been inaccessible and even dangerous places. Thus, in Dickens's later fiction travel, exploration, and empire are not so much explicit subject-matter as they are part of the daily experience of metropolitan society. Characters journey to and from the Continent or the colonies (Arthur Clennam, Magwitch, and John Harmon among them), and the fruits of imperial power and trade (like the opium consumed by John Jasper in *Edwin Drood*) become as commonplace as the hackney cabs of *Sketches by Boz*. FSS

Brantlinger, Patrick, *Rule of Darkness: British Literature and Imperialism, 1830–1914* (1988).
Brothers, Barbara and Gergits, Julia (eds.), *British Travel Writers, 1837–1875* (1996).

**travel literature.** In chapter 4 of *David Copperfield* the young hero recalls his 'greedy relish' for reading about TRAVEL; indeed, he writes of spending days on end as 'Captain Somebody, of the Royal British Navy, in danger of being beset by savages, and resolved to sell his life at great price'. David here is a cipher for Dickens himself, who was throughout his life a voracious devourer of 'volumes of Voyages and Travels.'

The 19th century was a great age both of travel and of writing about it. Travel books were among the landmark literary events of the age: Frances TROLLOPE and George Borrow established their literary reputations with books about their experiences in America and Spain; other travel books, like those of Richard Burton on India and Arabia and David Livingstone on Africa, were runaway bestsellers. Dickens read widely in the genre: his library in 1844 contained classics like Mandeville as well as more contemporary works, many on AMERICA (background reading before his own journey to the USA in 1842), but also Russia, South America, Spain, and GERMANY. He refers to many others in 'The Long Voyage' (*HW* 31 December 1853).

Dickens was a producer of travel writing too: he wrote only two 'travel books' *per se*, AMERICAN NOTES and PICTURES OF ITALY, but many essays about travel in and out of England, including the series in the 1860s collected as The UNCOMMERCIAL TRAVELLER. More importantly, his fiction defies clear generic boundaries, incorporating features of travel writing from the very start. In his earliest tales and short essays (later collected as *Sketches by Boz*) he writes of London and its inhabitants as if they were exotic and foreign, and, as reviewers perennially observed, this element of reportage appealed to readers throughout his career. The early novels are centred on London, but locations throughout England and Wales are featured as well; from *Martin Chuzzlewit* (in which he uses to good purpose his first American journey), almost every novel involves foreign scenes too, including FRANCE in *Dombey and Son* and ITALY in *Little Dorrit*. Moreover, Dickens's writings still serve as an invaluable guide to the essence of the experience of Victorian travel: for example, there is no better account of early train travel than Mr Dombey's journey from London to Birmingham (*DS* 20). FSS

> Drew, John M. L., 'Voyages Extraordinaires: Dickens's "Travelling Essays" and *The Uncommercial Traveller*' (2 parts), *Dickens Quarterly*, 13 (1996).

**Trollope, Anthony** (1815–82), novelist, magazine editor, travel writer, and friend of Dickens. A prolific novelist best known for his Barchester and Palliser series, Trollope came to prominence in the 1860s with serials published in leading middle-class periodicals, such as the *Cornhill Magazine*. Although Trollope enjoyed Dickens's early fiction, he ranked Dickens after George ELIOT and

THACKERAY as the finest NOVELISTS of his day. In *The Warden* (1855), he satirizes Dickens as 'Mr Popular Sentiment', and Trollope, who was a civil servant in the Post Office for most of his working life, took exception to the depiction of the Circumlocution Office in *Little Dorrit*. Trollope's anger at Dickens's portrayal of the civil service is most notable in *The Three Clerks* (1857). Apart from professional interests, the two had an interesting personal connection: Trollope's brother Tom married Fanny Ternan (see TERNAN FAMILY), sister of Dickens's beloved Ellen TERNAN. MWT

**Trollope, Frances** (1780–1863), author, and mother of six children including the novelist, Anthony TROLLOPE. She wrote the first of over 40 books when she was over the age of 50, eventually achieving wealth and fame through her writing. She travelled for fifteen months in AMERICA, and published her caustic *Domestic Manners of the Americans* in 1832. It was partly the resounding success of this book which influenced Dickens's decision to visit and write about America (see AMERICAN NOTES). He introduced Ellen TERNAN's older sister, Fanny, to Frances Trollope in 1858; it was this introduction which led to the marriage of Fanny and Thomas Trollope (Anthony's brother) in 1866 (see TERNAN FAMILY). Thomas Trollope became a firm friend of Dickens, and eulogized him in his *What I Remember* (1887). SL

**True Sun** (5 March 1832–23 December 1837) was the evening paper where Dickens worked as a parliamentary reporter from March to July 1832 (see JOURNALIST, DICKENS AS). It was set up by Patrick Grant as a rival to the *Sun*, which Grant had also owned, and was radical in its political sympathies. In 1833 it was sued for libel by the government, and Grant was sentenced to six months' imprisonment. Samuel Laman BLANCHARD (1804–45), later hired by Dickens for the DAILY NEWS, was its editor until 1836. Leigh HUNT was briefly its literary critic, and John FORSTER its drama critic from 1832. KC

> Grubb, Gerald G., 'Charles Dickens's First Experience as a Parliamentary Reporter', *Dickensian*, 36 (1940).

**Tussaud, Marie.** See WAXWORKS.

# U

**Uncommercial Traveller, The** Sketches written by Dickens for *All the Year Round* between 1860 and 1869. Reflecting his lifelong admiration for the ESSAY and for TRAVEL LITERATURE as literary forms, the articles offer a 'reincarnation' of his earliest aspirations as a periodical writer (Schwarzbach 1979), and 'some of Dickens's greatest writing' (Smith 1996). Moreover, the interweaving of CHILDHOOD experiences with adult memories found in several of them foreshadows the sophisticated narrative methods which distinguish his novel of 1861, *Great Expectations*.

The first series, published in one volume without ILLUSTRATIONS by CHAPMAN AND HALL on 15 December 1860 (1861 on title-page), comprised seventeen papers. A further eleven sketches were added, with a frontispiece by G. J. Pinwell, when *The Uncommercial Traveller* was included in the Cheap Edition (1865: see EDITIONS OVER WHICH DICKENS HAD CONTROL). After Dickens's death eight more papers were collected, with illustrations by Pinwell and 'W. M.', in the Illustrated Library Edition (1874), and one more, unaccountably omitted before then, was first published in the Gadshill Edition (1898), bringing the complete series to a total of 37 sketches in all (see EDITIONS PUBLISHED AFTER DICKENS'S LIFETIME).

The original idea of an 'uncommercial' traveller seems to have been intended as a satirical response to the vigorous public debate about issues raised by the so-called Commercial Treaty signed on 20 January 1860 between Britain and France, only a few days before the first paper was published in *All the Year Round*. In a speech the previous month at a dinner in support of Commercial Travellers' Schools, a charitable cause on whose behalf he had previously spoken in 1854, Dickens had also speculated 'whether any analogy could be drawn between those travellers who diffuse the luxuries and necessities of existence' and other travellers, real and imaginary (*Hansard*, vol. 156, 24 January–5 March 1860, pp. 812 ff.; Forster 8.5; *Speeches*,

pp. 169–76 and 290). In the opening piece, 'His General Line of Business', the narrator introduces himself: 'I am both a town traveller and a country traveller, and am always on the road. Figuratively speaking, I travel for the great house of Human Interest Brothers, and have rather a large connection in the fancy goods way ... seeing many little things, and some great things, which, because they interest me, I think may interest others.'

Like a number of the most attractive pieces in *Sketches by Boz*, the *Uncommercial Traveller* sketches use a traveller's narrative, rather than plot or polemical purpose, as the organizing principle. The pieces lack the more extravagant stylistic features of his other journalism and his novels, and they are suffused with a warmly intimate tone of the Traveller's persona (see STYLE; 'BOZ'). Generalization drawn from the Traveller's observations is conspicuous by its absence but, as John Drew has observed, a 'latent purpose' is evident: 'the travel motif becomes a vehicle for social and cultural criticism, a medium for assessing that most Victorian of pre-occupations, change' (Drew 1996).

The best-known *Uncommercial* sketches take an overtly autobiographical stance. 'Dullborough Town' recounts a journey back to the town where the Traveller spent his boyhood, nostalgically evoking memories and lamenting the prosaic changes which have replaced a romantic past. 'Nurse's Stories' declares it 'agreeable to revisit ... places to which I have never been'—Robinson Crusoe's Island, the robbers' cave in *Gil Blas*—and recalls the terrors of the story of a certain Captain Murderer. In 'Travelling Abroad' he meets a 'very queer small boy' who aspires to live in the house at Gad's Hill, with its SHAKESPEAREAN associations—which 'amazed' the Traveller, 'for that house happens to be *my* house, and I have reason to believe that what he said was true' (see HOMES OF DICKENS). These pieces patently draw on Dickens's own childhood experiences, but, as Michael Slater warns (1987), they do not always accord with known facts of his life, and one must be cautious about trawling them for biographical purposes.

Some sketches deal with travelling itself—'Aboard Ship', 'The Calais Night Mail'—and the perils of travel—'The Shipwreck', 'The Great Tasmania's Cargo' (about the appalling condition of soldiers returned from the CRIMEAN WAR), 'Bound for the Great Salt Lake' (about a Mormon EMIGRANT ship). 'An Old Stage Coaching House' deals with the impact of the coming of the railway on an old coaching inn (see TRANSPORT). 'Refreshments for Travellers' and 'A Little Dinner in an Hour' consider the wretchedness of dining in English hotels and wayside restaurants.

The Traveller visits the Morgue at PARIS ('Some Recollections of Mortality'), a workhouse for women ('Wapping Workhouse'), an almshouse ('Titbull's Alms-houses'), and the East London Children's Hospital ('A Small Star in the East'). He explores hideously deprived areas ('On an Amateur Beat') and expensive shops in the West End ('Arcadian London'). He observes a school for children of the poor ('Short Timers') and reflects on pedantry in a popular children's book ('Mr Barlow'). He looks about him by night as well as by day ('Night Walks'; 'The Calais Night Mail'). He sees the City on a weekend, when it is deserted ('City of the Absent'; 'City of London Churches') and a colourful country fair ('In the French-Flemish Country'). He pays two visits to the Britannia Theatre, Hoxton, comparing the audiences and the entertainment on a Saturday night, when the show was a PANTOMIME and a MELODRAMA, and the next night, when a religious meeting was held in the theatre ('Two Views of A Cheap Theatre'; see THEATRES). Although prepared to judge ('I demand to have the Ruffian kept out of my way, and out of the way of all decent people': 'The Ruffian'), his usual posture is one of open-mindedness to everything he sees: 'I wonder at nothing concerning them, and take them as they are' ('Shy Neighbourhoods').

In their variety, acuteness of observation, humour, pathos, and geniality, *The Uncommercial Traveller* sketches reveal Dickens's skills as an essayist at their best.    PVWS

Drew, John M. L., 'Voyages Extraordinaires: Dickens's "Travelling Essays" and *The Uncommercial Traveller*' (2 parts), *Dickens Quarterly*, 13 (1996).

Hollington, Michael, 'Dickens the Flâneur', *Dickensian*, 77 (1981).

Slater, Michael, 'How Many Nurses Had Charles Dickens? *The Uncommercial Traveller* and Dickensian biography', *Prose Studies*, 10 (1987).

**Unitarianism.** A religious affiliation that denies the doctrine of the Trinity while emphasizing Christ's humanity, with which Dickens was briefly associated in the mid-1840s under the influence of his friend John FORSTER and several Unitarians he had met on his recent trip to AMERICA, notably William Ellery Channing, the eminent Boston divine.

Although there are early Christian heresies that deny the Trinity, the origins of modern Unitarianism derive from 16th-century Protestants who were influenced by Plato's faith in the unity of the divine and in reason. Although Unitarianism tends to liberalism, it has deep roots also in British Calvinism, and English Victorian Unitarians were often much less free in personal behaviour than in speculative thought. They had in this regard much in common with many liberal reformers, especially perhaps the UTILITARIANS, with whose membership theirs often overlapped, as in the case of Dickens's friends Dr Thomas Southwood Smith and W. J. Fox.

Dickens was repelled by disputes about doctrine, by ostentatious displays of piety, and by church politics in general (see RELIGION). He took strong objection to the powerful role played by the bishops of the Established Church in secular affairs. When he embarked on his American trip in 1842, the conservative thrust within the CHURCH OF ENGLAND known as the Oxford Movement was at its most influential and visible, and, repelled by this, Dickens looked to the United States with high hopes as a model of what a progressive nation might do both materially and spiritually. The issues of slavery and international COPYRIGHT (and his treatment by the American newspapers when he was outspoken about these) quickly disillusioned him on the score of his political hopes, but he was singularly impressed by the American Unitarians he met, and carried that enthusiasm back with him to England, where he took sittings in at least two Unitarian chapels for the next two or three years, including one in

Little Portland Street, presided over by the Revd Edward Tagart, who continued a close friend long after Dickens's sittings had ceased (Forster 4.1). In 1844 Dickens wrote an inscription for a tea service presented to Tagart that praises 'that religion which has sympathy for men of every creed and ventures to pass judgment on none' (*Dickensian*, 22, 1926). The easy version of the Gospels that Dickens wrote for his children in the late 1840s (posthumously published as *The* LIFE OF OUR LORD in 1934) bears a Unitarian reading, though it is doctrinally somewhat confused. But it seems clear that the attraction of Unitarianism for Dickens derived as much from what Unitarianism did not do as from what it did. It did not seek to revive ancient rituals or theological controversies; it did not seek to tell its members what to believe; it did not specify an elaborate church organization and hierarchy; and it did not seek to advance its own worldly power. In time, however, Dickens's objections to the Church of England steadily faded and, as the Unitarian Forster explicitly reports, he died quite reconciled with the Established Church (Forster 4.1).    RN

## United States of America. See AMERICA.

## Urania Cottage,

the Home for Homeless Women that Dickens set up and administered on behalf of Angela Burdett COUTTS, represented Dickens's most sustained philanthropic involvement (see CHARITY). Opened in November 1847 in a detached house in Shepherd's Bush, large enough to accommodate thirteen inmates and two superintendents, Urania Cottage operated under Dickens's surprisingly active management until his separation from his wife Catherine in 1858 led to a rift in his relations with Miss Coutts.

Dickens's first known reference to the project dates from a letter he wrote to Miss Coutts in May 1846, where he spelled out in detail his ideas for the establishment and governance of the home, as well as for recruiting inmates. The aim was to rescue fallen women by offering them an escape from PROSTITUTION or a life of CRIME, and to do this within a DOMESTIC rather than a carceral environment (hence the name Urania Cottage, which contrasts with the off-putting and humiliating names ordinarily given to such institutions: 'Urania' is one of Venus's epithets,

meaning 'celestial' as opposed to earthly, sexual love; Venus sublimated, as it were). The home would serve to separate inmates from their previous associations, provide them with EDUCATION in household duties and religion, help them develop self-discipline, and then assist them to EMIGRATE to the colonies. Throughout, the women would be '*tempted* to virtue' (via such inducements as Captain Maconochie's Marks System and the prospect of eventual marriage in the colonies), rather than punished, humiliated, or simply preached at, as happened in institutions like the Magdalen Hospital (founded in 1758).

An enumeration of Dickens's responsibilities reveals the extent of his involvement. At the outset, he gathered knowledgeable advisors (notably the PRISON governors G. L. Chesterton and Augustus Tracey); he selected the house and oversaw its preparation (a job that included selecting reading material, wall inscriptions, linens, and even 'cheerful' dresses for the inmates); he hired the superintendents and teachers; he wrote an *Appeal to Fallen Women* (1847) for distribution to potential inmates; and he visited prisons and other reformatory institutions to help find and recruit eligible candidates. Once the home was established, Dickens formed and served on an administrative commitee (which met monthly to audit accounts and review individual cases). He also dealt on his own with a wide array of problems, from discharging troublesome inmates to coping with unhelpful superintendents; and he continued to visit prisons, workhouses, and Ragged Schools to interview and recruit new inmates.

The scope of this last activity is a reminder that the home eventually extended its reach to take in homeless and destitute women, and women committed to prison for crimes other than prostitution. This change may have played a part in the alleged success of the home's reformatory efforts. According to Dickens's essay 'Home for Homeless Women' (*HW* 23 April 1853; repr. in *MP*), the home hoped to achieve success in one-third to one-half of its cases—a goal that it exceeded. By this date, 57 or 58 women had passed through the home. Of these, 30 were thought to have done well in AUSTRALIA or elsewhere. Of the remainder, seven had left the home during the probationary period, seven had run away, ten had been expelled, and three had relapsed on the passage out to Australia.

Most striking in all this is the blend of good sense, insight, and administrative capacity that Dickens brought to his work—at a time when he was extraordinarily busy in many other endeavours.                                    NP
   Collins (1962), ch. 4.

**urbanization.** When Dickens was born in 1812 LONDON—or the collection of miscellaneous cities, boroughs, and parishes that later would be grouped into the Administrative County of London—had a population of nearly 1 million. At the time of his death in 1870 its population was over 3,200,000. In that earlier year, 17 per cent of the population of England and Wales lived in cities of 20,000 or more inhabitants, of which there were fifteen; in the later year, 42 per cent lived in large cities, of which now there were no fewer than 103.

These few statistics convey well a sense of the breakneck pace of urbanization in 19th-century Britain. Indeed, the science of statistics itself emerged in the first decades of the century largely as a response to the need to comprehend the dramatic changes of the first Western society simultaneously to undergo urbanization and INDUSTRIALIZATION. The first statistical societies were founded in Manchester and London in 1833 and 1834, respectively, dedicated to what CARLYLE termed with horror 'counting-up and estimating men's motives': but how else but by enumeration and mathematical manipulation were such vast problems as overcrowded housing, poor sanitation, and resulting epidemic disease, the lack of EDUCATION, and above all the concomitant moral decay of the urban working classes to be defined, let alone solved? (See PUBLIC HEALTH.) And were they not solved promptly, the example of Paris and its revolutions of 1789, 1830, and 1848 indicated the likely result.

Cities were the ineluctable crucibles of the modern. Centres of industry, government, culture, education, trade, and communication, they engendered a new social order that looks astonishingly similar to our own. Indeed, many of the dominant technologies of contemporary urban life developed in Dickens's London: modern forms of TRANSPORT, including hansom cabs, buses, and railways—

even, in 1863, the underground railway; modern forms of communication, like the Penny Post and the telegraph; and modern forms of PUBLISHING, such as the cheap daily newspaper and the mass-circulation magazine (both of which Dickens helped to define and promote). And always there was the sheer weight of numbers, fed by massive immigration from every corner of the British Isles and, to a limited extent, the Empire: it was only in the last two decades of Dickens's life that London's growth shifted from being driven mainly by immigration to natural increase. Dickens captures effectively the shock of arrival of many newcomers to London in *Oliver Twist*, *David Copperfield*, and *Great Expectations*: like Pip, most must have found the city 'rather ugly, crooked, narrow, and dirty'.

With rapid demographic and technological change came dramatic social change as well. Robert Vaughan triumphantly proclaimed the 19th century 'The Age of Great Cities' in his optimistic 1843 book of the same title, but contemporary writers were more likely to respond with panic to the vast *terrae incognitae* of urban England. The rhetoric of contrast between city and country—vice and virtue, disease and health, misery and happiness, and so on—is as old as the establishment of the first city, but in the 1820s and following decades it became charged with urgency. Much of the impetus came from fear of revolutions, but also from the advent of new epidemic diseases, like cholera (arriving in England in 1830), and new awareness of urban mortality (in 1840 gentlemen in the West End could expect to live to 45, but mechanics in Bethnal Green only to 16; see DEATH). During the 1840s the determined efforts of sanitary reformers like Edwin CHADWICK (one of whose colleagues was Henry Austin, Dickens's brother-in-law) made the public fully aware of the presumed connection between urban waste and disease: rotting organic matter gave off emanations or miasma that, when inhaled, were the direct causes of fevers. The spread of disease in this manner is a leading plot device and thematic nexus in *Bleak House*. The theory eventually proved false, but the programme it inspired—tearing down slums, providing decent housing, and constructing underground sewers—was sound. Unfortunately, progress in applying it was painfully slow, especially in London, where the lack of central governance long impeded effective remedial action.

Horrifying revelations about slum housing conditions also shocked the public imagination (see LONDON: SLUMS). From the 1830s, exposé after exposé gave middle-class readers of government Blue Books, newspapers, pamphlets, and magazines the sordid details of overcrowded, foul, and dangerous housing. Yet, striking as were the physical problems of urban life, more so were those that contemporaries called the MORAL. The state of public education—or, more accurately, the almost complete lack of its provision, was partly to blame for what was seen as a moral crisis. But the common phrase 'moral malaria' suggests the prevailing view that physical deprivation inevitably caused moral depravity—overcrowding, ignorance, and dirt bred CRIME and PROSTITUTION as surely as they did physical disease.

No novelist is more closely associated with the rise of urban life than Dickens. From the very start of his career, Dickens's special relationship with London and with city life was regarded as part of his distinctive appeal. Walter BAGEHOT wrote in 1858 that Dickens 'describes London like a special correspondent for posterity', a judgement that seems valid in that the very adjective 'Dickensian' calls up the fog-bound, gaslit, crowded cobbled streets of the metropolis. Reviewers invariably noted his special sympathy for and effective representation of the life of the urban poor: especially after his second novel, *Oliver Twist*, it was assumed that each successive book would strike a blow for the downtrodden. In the 1850s a nonconformist preacher singled out three great social agencies of the time—the cholera, the London City Mission, and Dickens—all of which had brought needed attention to the condition of the working classes.

Dickens's influence as a reporter of urban change and urban life was great: for example, his account of the dramatic impact of the London and North West Railway on Stagg's Gardens (Camden Town) in *Dombey and Son* is unparalleled in its evocation of the physical upheaval and dislocation caused by rapid urban development. Yet perhaps more profound has been his impact upon the fictional representation of the city. Not only did Dickens report on city life with stunningly vivid accuracy, but he also both responded to and

helped to shape the contemporary sense that in Britain's teeming cities profound changes were under way in the nature of social life and even human nature itself. His earliest works, including *Sketches by Boz*, *Pickwick Papers*, and *Oliver Twist*, may be read for their focus on the quotidian—how London looked, sounded, and smelled; later works, such as *Bleak House*, *Little Dorrit*, and *Our Mutual Friend*, suggest the complex psychosocial effects of the urban milieu on the nature of community and even individual character. At the end of the Victorian age George GISSING observed that Dickens 'taught people a certain way of regarding the huge city'. We regard it still in that light. FSS

Dyos, H. J. and Wolff, Michael (eds.), *The Victorian City: Images and Realities* (1973).

Schwarzbach (1979).

Sheppard, Francis, *London 1808–1870: The Infernal Wen* (1971).

Williams, Raymond, *The Country and the City* (1973).

**utilitarianism** is a philosophical system developed by Jeremy BENTHAM and systematized in accessible form by his disciple, John Stuart MILL, in *Utilitarianism* (1863). In its pure form, utilitarianism is a system of ethics which judges human conduct in relation to the extent to which it conduces to the greatest happiness of the greatest number of people. It was deeply influential throughout the Victorian period, not merely in philosophical terms but also through its impact on many aspects of practical REFORM and, at the popular level, as a justification for sometimes inhuman practices in the workplace. Utilitarian ideas were disseminated in a number of ways, a major outlet being the quarterly periodical, the *Westminster Review*, which began publication in 1824. Inspired by Bentham, and initially paid for by him, it set itself up as the organ of the Philosophical Radicals, the proponents of Bentham's thought; Mill, and his father James, were amongst its regular contributors. The magazine campaigned consistently and successfully for reforms in the fields of legal, social, and political legislation based on the ideas of Bentham and his group. Bentham also attracted into his orbit a number of able and energetic younger men who carried his ideas into the world of public affairs. Among the most outstanding of these was Edwin CHADWICK, the author of the widely noticed *Report on the Sanitary Conditions of the Labouring Population* (1842); its descriptions of urban squalor and degradation still make powerful reading. Chadwick was also a prime mover of the Poor Law Amendment Act of 1834 which introduced a radical change into the treatment of the destitute poor through a reorganization of the workhouse system (see POOR RELIEF).

Dickens was introduced to the ideas of this movement when he became a reporter on the MORNING CHRONICLE newspaper in 1834 at the age of 22. The paper and its editor, John BLACK, with whom Dickens enjoyed a particularly warm relationship, were praised by John Stuart Mill for bringing Benthamite ideas to a wider public than that reached by the *Westminster Review*, but Dickens himself vigorously opposed these ideas even then. 'How often used Black and I to quarrel about the effect of the poor-law bill!' he recalled later (to Forster, 29 April 1841). From 1842, Dickens's brother-in-law, Henry Austin, was in direct contact with Chadwick (see BROTHERS AND SISTERS OF DICKENS), and through Austin Dickens assisted Chadwick's work in the field of public health by throwing the weight of his influence in the direction of the proposed reforms, as well as through articles in *Household Words* and in novels such as *Bleak House*.

However, despite Dickens's willingness to support Chadwick at the practical level, he was a lifelong opponent of utilitarian ideas as he understood them, and of what he regarded as its pernicious effect on many aspects of Victorian life. This antagonism entered Dickens's work in *Oliver Twist*, a savage attack on the changes brought about by the Poor Law Amendment Act of 1834, on which Chadwick had exerted a major influence through the Report which led to its passing into legislation. One of the major effects of the Act, in Dickens's view, was to make the workhouse so uncomfortable for the destitute that they would be willing to do almost anything rather than be housed there, thus reducing the poor rate exacted from the better-off as a method of supporting institutionalized charity. Dickens was particularly incensed by such features of the new system as its spartan diet, and the separation of men and women in the interest of preventing an increase in the pauper population, although this measure was applied indiscriminately, to old married couples, for example, long past the age of child-bearing. Dickens's fury never abated, and thirty years later, in his last completed novel, *Our Mutual Friend*, he returned to the attack in depicting a respectable member of the poorest segment of society, Betty Higden, preferring to die in the open rather than enter the workhouse.

But Dickens clearly saw utilitarian ideas operating through society at a level below that of philosophical theories and specific social institutions. John Stuart Mill's criticism of his mentor's system was based partly on what he called the 'incompleteness' of Bentham's mind 'as a representative of universal human nature': 'In many of the most natural and strongest feelings of human nature he had no sympathy; from many of its graver experiences he was altogether cut off, and the faculty by which one mind understands a mind different from itself, and throws itself into feelings of that other mind, was denied him by his deficiency of the Imagination.' Dickens saw this character type everywhere in society, and his satirical attacks on characters as diverse as Scrooge in *A Christmas Carol* and Gradgrind in *Hard Times* can be read as a response to utilitarianism, widely defined. But Bentham's ideas, at the popular level, could also be seen in the widespread attempt to evade the provisions of a series of FACTORY ACTS in the 1830s and 1840s which sought to soften the excesses of new forms of labour arising as a result of the Industrial Revolution, although these Acts were framed in ways that seem hardly less repressive today than the conditions they sought to ameliorate. Attempts to introduce educational provision into factory work and to fence in dangerous machinery were ignored on the grounds that they violated the principles of utility; and curbs on the hours worked by women and children were seen as an erosion of their freedom of choice. Such misuses of utilitarian doctrine were laid bare by a major article in *Household Words* of 1854, 'Ground in the Mill', by one of Dickens's most valued collaborators, Henry MORLEY.

Along with what CARLYLE called the 'cash nexus', there is little doubt that Dickens saw the application of the principle of utility in EDUCATION and employment as one of the major flaws in the social life of his period, and that he satirized it, in and out of season, in works as different as *The CHIMES* (in which Mr Filer is an attack on the utilitarians in response to a *Westminster Review* criticism of *A Christmas Carol*) and *Little Dorrit* (in which old Mr Nandy is thrown on the mercy of 'the Workhouse which was appointed by law to be the Good Samaritan of his district'). Thus, whether Dickens studied and understood utilitarianism as a philosophical system is irrelevant, since he did understand the power of debased utilitarianism to poison many areas of Victorian life. GFS

# V

**Vestris, Eliza.** See MATHEWS, CHARLES JAMES.

**Victoria and Albert Museum.** Most of the manuscripts of Dickens's novels from *The Old Curiosity Shop* onwards, together with some corrected proofs, first and early editions, letters, and other material, are in the FORSTER COLLECTION in the V&A. Dickens left this material to John FORSTER, who, following the example of his friend the Revd Alexander Dyce, bequeathed his entire library and art collections to the South Kensington Museum. This museum, at first of wide general scope, was reorganized in 1899, renamed the 'Victoria and Albert', and became a specialist museum of decorative arts. It includes the National Art Library, which administers the Dyce and Forster libraries as frozen collections. The NAL is a public library, but access to special collections is restricted and prospective readers should check in advance.

The Forster Collection contains much mid-19th-century literature that came to Forster in his profession as journalist, choicer items from his many literary friends, and material reflecting his own research interests (e.g. in SWIFT). There are published catalogues of the *Printed Books* (1888) and the *Paintings, Manuscripts and Pamphlets* (1893). Forster did not collect Dickens material systematically; nor has any attempt been made to augment the Collection with Dickens material published since his death, though a few items have come to rest in a Dyce and Forster Auxiliary Collection (no published catalogue). The catalogue of the V&A's Dickens exhibition (1970) describes much from the collection.

The survival, through Dickens's intention, of the manuscripts (with number plans and emendations) and proofs made it possible for Leslie Staples to reveal unpublished 'shavings from Dickens's workshop' in the DICKENSIAN in the 1950s, and for John Butt and Kathleen Tillotson to investigate his methods of COMPOSITION in *Dickens at Work* (1957). The manuscripts came to Forster in Dickens's bindings, and were inlaid and rebound in 1965–6. A completely new conservation programme began in 1993 (see *V&A Conservation Journal*, October 1993). APB

**Victoria, Queen.** See ROYALTY.

*Village Coquettes, The* A comic operetta, written by Dickens in 1836, with music by John Pyke HULLAH, who proposed the collaboration (?29 December 1835). 'A simple rural story', the play involves two village girls, rescued from seduction at the hands of the squire and his crony by the comic man, played by John Pitt HARLEY, and reconciled to their rustic lovers in the end. It was produced by John BRAHAM, who played Squire Norton, at the St James's Theatre, opening on 6 December 1836.

During its preparation Dickens worked hard, striving to create characters who 'would act and talk like people we see and hear of', negotiating for a publisher, and sending copies of the songs to reviewers (?29 December 1835). Hopes were high. Dickens reported that Harley made a wager that it would run for 50 nights (to Hullah, ?22 August 1836) and that Braham, who accepted the opera 'with the highest encomiums', 'express[ed] an earnest desire to be the first to introduce me to the Public, as a dramatic Writer' (to Cruikshank, ?1 February 1836; to Hullah, ?May 1836). 'I think it will tell', Dickens wrote to Catherine Hogarth (?23 January 1836). 'It *must* succeed' (to Cruikshank, ?1 February 1836).

The audience were enthusiastic on the opening night, calling for BOZ at the end, but it ran for only sixteen performances and ten revivals (Pilgrim 1.205n.). Reviewers liked the music but were hostile towards Dickens's libretto. 'I am not at all surprised to hear that the opera went off wretchedly', Dickens grumbled to Hullah afterwards. 'What is to be expected when the Theatre that has by many degrees the worst company in London, charges the highest prices?' (?14 January 1837). Dedicated to Harley, the operetta was published on 22 December 1836 by Richard BENTLEY but never collected in Dickens's lifetime. PVWS

# W

**Warren's Blacking.** A factory situated at 30 Hungerford Stairs, the Strand, where the 12-year-old Dickens was sent to work, putting covers and labels on pots of paste-blacking (used for boot polish), at a time when his parents were in the financial distress which soon landed them in the Marshalsea debtors' prison (see DICKENS, JOHN). At first he was treated as 'the young gentleman', sitting apart in a separate alcove, but after the business moved to Chandos Street, Covent Garden, he worked alongside the other boys in a window 'for the light's sake', and felt inexpressible 'grief and humiliation' when crowds—once including his father—gathered to watch him. 'I wondered how he could bear it', Dickens reflected. The employment lasted about a year (from late January–early February 1824 until late March–early April 1825), and was kept a dark secret from everyone except his wife and John FORSTER until revealed in the latter's biography (1872–4: see DIARIES AND AUTOBIOGRAPHY). Since then the experience has been widely considered the single most formative event for Dickens's later life and art (see CRITICISM, BIOGRAPHICAL; DICKENS: PRIVATE LIFE). Certainly the bitterness and outrage remained vivid years after the event; in his autobiographical fragment he noted that his mother, Elizabeth DICKENS, unsuccessfully tried to mend a quarrel between his father and George Lamert (the 'sort-of cousin' who owned the factory) which had led to his being dismissed, and concluded, 'I do not write resentfully or angrily: for I know how all these things have worked together to make me what I am, but I never afterwards forgot, I never shall forget, I never can forget, that my mother was warm for my being sent back' (Forster 1.2).

There were two Warrens, Robert and Jonathan, who had separate, rival establishments; Dickens worked for Jonathan. Robert was more famous from his extensive use of advertising jingles, which Dickens parodied in the doggerel verses composed by the poet Slum, celebrating Jarley's Waxworks (*OCS* 28). Dickens took the name of a boy who befriended him at the warehouse, Bob Fagin, for one of his most memorable villains, and recalled the rotten, rat-infested building at Hungerford Stairs when depicting his lair.

PVWS

Carlton, William J., 'In the Blacking Warehouse', *Dickensian*, 60 (1964).

**Watson, the Hon. Richard** (1800–52) and his wife **Lavinia** (1816–88), both of them of ancient aristocratic lineage, were Dickens's closest blue-blooded friends. They met in SWITZERLAND in 1846, where both families were then living, and instantly took to one another, Watson noting how 'unaffected' the great man was, and Dickens forgiving his having been an MP, High Sheriff, etc., because he had 'not the least nonsense about him' but was 'a thorough good liberal', very intelligent, 'as thoroughly good and true a man as ever lived' (?15–17 August 1846, 1 August 1852). He visited them at their impressive medieval castle, Rockingham, in Northamptonshire, organized AMATEUR THEATRICALS there, and used memories of it when creating Chesney Wold (*Bleak House*). *Copperfield* was 'Affectionately Dedicated' to them. Though rarely visiting Rockingham after Watson's death, he often referred nostalgically to 'the dear old Rockingham days' (8 April 1870), and he maintained an intimate friendship with Lavinia, seeing her in London and corresponding with her with uncommon frankness about his emotional life, but also commenting amply on political matters. He evidently regarded her as intelligent besides being sympathetic. Watson wrote warmly about Dickens in his diaries (*Dickensian*, 1951), as did Lavinia in F. G. Kitton's *Dickens by Pen and Pencil* (1890).

PC

**waxworks.** Wax effigies associated with funeral rites date from antiquity, and wax figures of British royalty were displayed for centuries in Westminster Abbey. In London there were permanent exhibitions such as Simmons's in Holborn and Mrs Salmon's in Fleet Street, to which David takes Peggotty (*DC* 33), but by far the most famous exhibitor in Dickens's lifetime was Marie Tussaud (1760–1850), who toured England in 1808–34 with an exhibition of well over 100 life-sized effigies. She advertised widely, stressing the superior quality of her show and its patrons, and after Princess Augusta visited it in Brighton in 1834, she routinely boasted of royal patronage. When she eventually settled in London, her showroom in Baker Street, Portman Square, was a short walk from Dickens's HOME, from 1839 to 1851, at Devonshire Terrace. Her large and constantly evolving collection quickly became 'more than an exhibition; it is an institution', and, relocated at Marylebone Road, remains to this day one of London's most popular AMUSEMENTS ('Our Eye-Witness in Great Company', *AYR* 2, 1860; see LONDON: ENTERTAINMENT). Dickens refers directly to Mme Tussaud in *PICTURES FROM ITALY* (3), and almost certainly thought of her when creating Mrs Jarley, the 'delight of the Nobility and Gentry' (*OCS* 27).      PVWS

Leslie, Anita and Chapman, Pauline, *Madame Tussaud, Waxworker Extraordinary* (1978).

**Webster, Benjamin** (1797–1882), a character actor with an exceptionally wide range, who managed some of the London THEATRES most frequently attended by Dickens. As manager of the Haymarket Theatre (1837–52), he employed many leading ACTORS and supported English drama, presenting plays by KNOWLES (*The Love Chase*, 1837), Boucicault (*Used Up*, 1844), BULWER-LYTTON (*Money*, 1844), READE (*Masks and Faces*, 1852, in which he played Triplet, one of his best parts), Taylor, and JERROLD. He shared the management of the Adelphi Theatre with Madame Celeste from 1844, taking over in 1853 until his retirement in 1874. He was in the original productions of BUCKSTONE's *Uncle John* and of *NO THOROUGHFARE* (1867). He presented a DRAMATIZATION of *The* CRICKET ON THE HEARTH (1845, Adelphi), successfully playing John Peerybingle, and with Dickens's sanction put on *The* HAUNTED MAN (1848–9, Haymarket) and *The Holly-Tree Inn* (1854, Adelphi) (see CHRISTMAS STORIES). Webster read *The Dead Heart* (by Watts Phillips) to Dickens in Brighton, a work set during the French Revolution, whose climactic substitution at the guillotine may have influenced *A Tale of Two Cities*. Dickens wrote to Webster on Maria Ternan's behalf, reminding him of the strong interest he took 'in her and her family' (9 September 1861: see TERNAN FAMILY). As a strong supporter of dramatic CHARITIES and President of the Dramatic College, Webster was frequently involved with Dickens, who had a very high opinion of him as both manager and friend.      JD

**Wellington, Duke of.** See POLITICS AND POLITICIANS.

**William IV.** See ROYALTY.

**Williams, Bransby** (1870–1961), actor and MUSIC-HALL performer. From 1896 he gave character-monologues with scripts adapted from Dickens's novels, so successfully that he sometimes played three theatres a night, changing costume and make-up in the cab. He became internationally famous as 'the Dickens man', and his acts later succeeded on radio and television. His most popular impersonations included Little Nell's grandfather (audiences wept), Quilp, Daniel Peggotty, Uriah Heep, Chadband, Scrooge, and Bill Sikes. He also gave similar shows based on SHAKESPEARE and other authors.      PC

**Williams, Emlyn** (1905–87), a Welsh dramatist and actor, impersonated Charles Dickens in a one-man show based on Dickens's PUBLIC READINGS at the Lyric, Hammersmith, in London in 1951, subsequently transferring to the Criterion Theatre. He also performed the show at the Duchess's Theatre, on radio, and on a world tour, visiting Boston and New York in the spring of 1952. Readings, given from behind a replica of the desk used by Dickens himself at his public readings, included extracts from *Our Mutual Friend*, *Dombey and Son*, *The Pickwick Papers*, *A Tale of Two Cities*, and the short story 'The Signalman' (*CS*). He continued to present the show up until his death.      JD

**Williams, Samuel** (1788–1853), wood engraver. From Colchester in Essex, Williams taught himself painting and wood engraving; the latter skill he then taught his brother and sister and his four sons. By the end of the 1830s he was much sought out as an artist who could translate others' designs into spirited wood engravings. He cut several of the early designs for MASTER HUMPHREY'S CLOCK, and when at the last minute neither George CATTERMOLE nor Hablot BROWNE was available to draw the tailpiece to the story of Nell and the Curiosity Shop, CHAPMAN AND HALL asked Williams to execute it. Dickens sent detailed corrections of the sketch, asking for 'a few grim, ugly articles' to be added and for the sleeping Nell to be made more childish (31 March 1840). The result pleased Dickens and the reviewer Thomas HOOD, whose notion that the artist's picture of Nell sleeping amidst the antiques was a kind of allegory Dickens elaborated in four new paragraphs inserted in the first volume edition. Williams engraved two further illustrations for *The Old Curiosity Shop* but never designed another picture for any Dickens work.          RLP

**Wills, William Henry** (1810–80) and **Dickens as editor.** W. H. (or 'Harry') Wills held the post of sub-editor of Dickens's successful journals *Household Words* and *All the Year Round* from 1849 to 1868, in which capacity he acquired a reputation for diligence, discretion, and excellent management. In the matter of literary flair, however, he has been almost inevitably overshadowed by his famous editor.

Born at Plymouth, Wills and his family moved to the working-class area of Somers Town in London in the winter of 1819–20, following the decline of his father's shipowning business. He attended a school for the sons of tradesmen in Clarendon Square, and is likely to have been studying there when the Dickens family moved to 29 Johnson Street, also in Somers Town, during the latter part of Dickens's employment in WARREN'S BLACKING factory and his attendance at Wellington House Academy (1824–7). Wills trained as a wood engraver but drifted into journalism as a means of supporting his family on the death of his father. He wrote for the *Penny* and *Saturday* magazines, McCulloch's *Geographical Dictionary*, and first became known to Dickens in 1839, when, as editor of BENTLEY'S MISCELLANY, Dickens accepted one of two stories submitted by him and wrote requesting more (Lehmann 1971, p. x). In 1841 Wills was among the original literary staff of PUNCH and for some time acted as its regular drama critic, but his strong editorial abilities were soon recognized in appointments as assistant editor of *Chambers's Edinburgh Journal* (1842–5) and in 1845, as secretary to the editor of the DAILY NEWS in London, where he worked

under Dickens for the first time. Wills seems to have recommended himself as an assistant: a week after Dickens's sudden resignation as editor, the latter was writing that he missed 'My Dear Mr Wills . . . a good deal more than I miss the Paper' (16 February 1846). Until 1849 Wills remained as a sub-editor at the *Daily News*, where colleague Joseph Crowe recollected, '[h]e was always correcting manuscript and liked nothing so much as correction' (*Reminiscences*, 1895, p. 71). Later in 1849, when an assistant editor was required to help with the establishment of *Household Words*, John FORSTER recalls that 'Mr Wills was chosen at my suggestion' (Forster 6.4).

The description of Wills's performance as sub-editor of *Household Words* and *All the Year Round* is inseparable from that of Dickens himself as editor, but generally has to be deduced at second-hand because so few of Wills's own letters on editorial matters have been preserved. Hundreds from Dickens to his sub-editor survive, however, making it possible to construct a picture of the different contributions of both men, based on the generalization that, although their duties and abilities overlapped to a surprising degree, Dickens controlled the element of 'fancy'— aesthetic balance and ideological persuasion —in the journals while Wills was responsible for the prosaic 'facts' relating to their publication. Prior to the launch of *Household Words*, Dickens was busy planning articles, canvassing for contributions, and fitting up the Wellington Street offices, while Wills set about organizing distribution rights and facilities, publicity, payment and printing procedures, collecting material for composite articles, and so forth. On technical matters such as layout, paper, and make-up they conferred, in conjunction with printers BRADBURY AND EVANS. Once publication had commenced, Dickens himself tended to dictate the selection and order of items, and also wrote or co-wrote articles in 41 of the first 52 numbers. Over the same period Wills contributed 74 papers, mostly composite articles. In addition, he handled all routine correspondence with contributors, and kept details of every item paid for, under the following heads: 'When and where inserted', 'Author's Name', 'Title of Article', 'Length in Columns', 'Price Paid', 'When Paid', and 'Memoranda'.

The ledger in which such facts were scrupulously recorded, known as the 'Household Words Office Book', is preserved as a valuable research tool in the Morris L. Parrish COLLECTION of Princeton University Library (see Lohrli 1973).

The early success of *Household Words* seems to have allowed both Wills and Dickens to establish a solid working relationship. When at home in London (or later, Kent) Dickens wrote to Wills and attended to editorial business on an unscheduled but almost daily basis; in addition, both regularly attended a weekly conference at the office, which usually ran from five o'clock on a Thursday evening until business was completed. When out of town—writing, holidaying, or engaged on PUBLIC READING tours —Dickens came to rely heavily on Wills for a range of editorial decisions, but the weekly conference was 'preserved' in the form of at least one postal exchange of packets, containing proofs for future numbers, letters, manuscripts, and so on, all of which were discussed in exhaustive detail.

Both Wills and Dickens read numerous unsolicited manuscripts, of which an astonishing 900 were received in the year 1852 alone. Of these, only 'eleven were available for [the] journal, after being entirely re-written' (C. Dickens and H. Morley, 'H.W.', *HW* 16 April 1852). The rewriting was extensive and painstaking. Dickens described on one occasion hacking and hewing a proof for four hours until it looked 'like an inky fishing net' (22 June 1856), and on another, how he had sat 'nine hours without stirring' rewriting one of Wills's papers (13 April 1851). Wills himself expended similar pains on recasting and tuning other writers' articles to the required pitch. Numerous letters to Wills make clear that Dickens objected to statements appearing in his journals that were obviously at variance with what he was known to have written elsewhere (e.g. to Wills, 10 March 1853, 6 January 1856). This left Wills with the unenviable task of interpreting or second-guessing Dickens's views on the gamut of social issues, although in due course he became remarkably adept at anticipating his editor's requirements (Spencer 1988, p. 149).

As might be expected, it was in areas of overlapping, or hazily defined, responsibility that Wills and Dickens clashed. Dickens's constant attention to the tone and spirit of the publication, and his readiness to take on all manner of editorial chores were virtues doubtless admired by Wills, but his caustic criticisms whenever the magazine failed to meet his criteria of imaginative excellence must have caused Wills discomfort. The minute revising of contributions and marking-up of proofs, for example, fell naturally to Wills as sub-editor, but if Dickens had a personal interest in an item he expected that prerogative. '[D]on't touch my articles without first consulting me', he wrote reprovingly on 12 July 1850, after finding that Wills had reinserted text deleted by him in his revision of 'The Devil's Acre' by Alexander Mackay. He also dismissed one of Wills's proposals for a title as 'the worst within the range of human understanding'. Rather than take offence, however, Wills mildly but stoutly defended his decisions by return of post, adding diplomatically that he took great precautions against anything appearing in the magazine 'which might have the slightest tendency to damage the name which appears at the top of each page' (Lehmann 1971, p. 31).

Wills's initial uncertainty about how to satisfy Dickens's demands is well expressed in a letter of 17 October 1851, when in answer to a complaint of a depressing 'want of fancy' in back issues, he pleads for more, not less, editorial involvement from Dickens, requesting that 'my own judgement . . . be brought to some corrective test', in the form of revision and final approval from Dickens: '[w]hen the number has had the benefit of your revision the touches you have given to it have improved it to a degree that has seemed to me marvellous.' Grounds for occasional dispute also arose over Wills's tendency to underpay contributors slightly (Lohrli 1973, p. 21). In the case of salaried staff writer R. H. HORNE, Wills eventually justified his claim that Horne was being overpaid for the quantity of work he produced, but at the expense of receiving a frosty letter from Dickens, complaining of his lack of willingness to 'accommodate matters' amicably with his colleague (Lehmann 1971, pp. 35–6).

Dickens may have been a difficult editor to work for, but Wills clearly had the right mixture of tact and professional firmness to hold his own. His ability to treat matters of personal disagreement in the context of shared aims and ideals seems eventually to have won Dickens's respect, even if it brought no praise for his artistic abilities. Wills, Dickens wrote privately to friends, 'has not the ghost of an idea in the imaginative way' (21 March 1850), and though a 'capital fellow for his work' was 'decidedly of the Nutmeg-Grater or Fancy-Bread-Rasper School' (12 May 1850); he had 'no genius, and is, in literary matters, sufficiently commonplace to represent a very large proportion of ... readers' (15 May 1861). Given the financial success of *Household Words* and *All the Year Round*, Dickens had no reason to be ungrateful for this very representativity in Wills, however, and clearly thought highly enough of Wills's writing to publish a large amount of it. He was, moreover, openly appreciative of Wills's devotion and friendship, writing in 1862 that he doubted 'whether any two men can have gone on more happily and smoothly, or with greater trust and confidence in one another' (2 January), and two years later, of their 'happy intercourse and a perfect confidence that have never had a break' (30 November).

For his part, Wills reciprocated the friendship and esteem, but in 1855 expressed a mild reservation to Dickens about the way his 'whole life' was dedicated to *Household Words* and 'the connexion into which it brings me with you' (11 June; Lehmann, p. 166). This followed Dickens's stern veto of Wills's plan to supplement his income by accepting the editorship of the *Civil Service Gazette*. In the end, Wills obediently turned down the proposal, accepting instead Dickens's nugatory offer of additional payments for papers of his own published in *Household Words*. On the founding of *All the Year Round* in 1859, however, Wills's salary remained at £420 p.a., but his partnership share increased from 18.75 to 25 per cent, giving annual returns of an additional £838 on average (as compared to approximately £247 p.a. from *Household Words*). In financial terms, therefore, he is unlikely to have regretted his decision to remain wholly devoted to Dickens's journals (figures derived from Patten 1978, p. 464).

During the last years of Dickens's life Wills became indispensable to Dickens not just as a superbly competent acting editor, but also as what Dickens once rather unkindly described as a 'factotum' for all his business and personal affairs (Lohrli 1973, p. 463). At Dickens's instigation, Wills had become secretary to the GUILD OF LITERATURE AND ART in 1851, and almoner-secretary to Miss COUTTS in 1855. He and his widely admired Scots wife Janet (neé Chambers, sister of the successful publisher) were frequent and welcome house guests, well known to the entire Dickens family. All this was a natural mingling of business and friendship, but after Dickens's separation from Catherine DICKENS in 1858, and during his many absences from London on reading engagements, Wills was called on for more confidential duties. He wrote private letters on Dickens's behalf, looked after his bank accounts, was authorized to make payments to his dependants, and was entrusted as a go-between in Dickens's affair with Ellen TERNAN (Ackroyd 1990, p. 1006). It was therefore a severe blow to Dickens no less than to Wills, when the latter was forced into early retirement in 1868, suffering from concussion after falling from his horse while hunting. Wills remained in close touch with the Dickens family, however—'Dickens's later life had no more intimate friend', Forster recalls, with any trace of personal jealousy carefully suppressed (Forster 6.4)—and on his death in 1880 was mourned as a hard-working, ardent, and kind-hearted man who had been 'at the heart of many of the most important literary undertakings' of his time (*Athenaeum*, 4 September). An interesting collection of his essays, parts of which were by Dickens (see Stone (ed.), *Uncollected Writings of Charles Dickens*, *passim*), was highly praised on its publication in 1860 ('Old Leaves Gathered from Household Words', *Examiner*, 21 January). JMLD

Grubb, Gerald G., 'The Editorial Policies of Charles Dickens', *PMLA* 58 (1943).

Lehmann, R. C. (ed.), *Charles Dickens as Editor: Being Letters Written by Him to William Henry Wills, His Sub-Editor* (1971; 1st edn. 1912).

Spencer, Sandra, 'The Indispensable Mr Wills', *Victorian Periodicals Review*, 21 (1988).

**Wilson, Edmund** (1895–1972), American critic. His essay 'Dickens: The Two Scrooges', originally a lecture at Bryn Mawr, first published in *New Republic* (1940) and expanded in *The Wound and the Bow: Seven Studies in Literature* (1941), is unquestionably the most influential single study of Dickens of the 20th

century. Taking his title from the two manifestations of the protagonist of *A Christmas
Carol*, the melancholy misanthrope and the
joyful embodiment of Christmas cheer, Wilson's approach was vigorously Freudian (see
CRITICISM: FREUDIAN; CRITICISM: BIOGRAPH-
ICAL). He located Dickens's primary achievement in the dark vision of the later fiction
rather than the comic ebullience of the early
works, which he rejected as stagey MELO-
DRAMA, and saw the source of Dickens's
artistry in deep personal and social mal-
adjustment, resulting from the trauma of
being sent at the age of 12 to work in WAR-
REN'S BLACKING warehouse (see DICKENS:
PRIVATE LIFE). The essay brought a new
seriousness and academic respectability to
Dickens studies—ironically, because Wilson
wrote not from an ivory tower but as a popular journalist. Wilson's perspectives redirected
critical attention away from sentiment and
festive merriment in Dickens's novels and on
to social and psychological insight. He later
wrote the Preface to Ada Nisbet's *Dickens and
Ellen TERNAN* (1952).                    PVWS

**Wilson, John** ('Christopher North')
(1785–1854), essayist and critic, presided over
the Edinburgh dinner given in 1841 to honour
Dickens (see SCOTLAND). In 1817 he took up
joint editorship with LOCKHART of *Blackwood's Magazine*, where they were known for
their personal attacks in an age of critical
savagery—COLERIDGE considered legal action
after Wilson's review of the *Biographia Liter-
aria* in 1816. The first winner of the Newdigate
Prize (1806), Wilson perhaps felt entitled to
call TENNYSON's 1832 *Poems* 'drivel'. A strong
Tory, he became the most prominent local literary figure after JEFFREY. Dickens described
him to FORSTER as 'a bright, clear-complex-
ioned, mountain-looking fellow . . . if you
could divest your mind of the actual SCOTT,
[Wilson] is just the figure you would put in
his place' ([23 June 1841]).

Considering his reputation as a Cockney-
hater, Wilson's benignity towards Dickens is
perhaps remarkable. For a contemporary representation of the meeting between Dickens
and Wilson, see *Boz's Introduction to Christopher North* (*Pilgrim* 2, frontispiece).    KC

**women and women's issues.** At the
heart of Dickens's ideology lies the image of
the domestic woman, 'made for Home, for

fireside peace and happiness' (*OT* 29), an ideal
expressed in its purest form in such contemporary works as Coventry Patmore's poem
*The Angel in the House*, John RUSKIN's essay
'Of Queens' Gardens', and the conduct books
of Sarah Stickney Ellis (see DOMESTICITY).
Dickens subscribed to the widely held belief
that women were inherently different from
men, formed for home-making and a life of
the affections. They should be invested with
the management of the household and
MORAL sway over the domestic realm, as wives
and mothers, sisters or daughters, but at the
cost of leaving the public sphere to men. The
ideal woman, pretty, chaste, and calmly
efficient, was charged with the vital function
of holding together the middle-class home,
that essential foundation of the Victorian
social structure. In promoting the image of
the 'Home Goddess' (*OMF* 2.13), Dickens was
therefore playing an influential role in the
establishment of a new set of values which
underpinned the growing power of the
middle classes. Many readers have been critical of Dickens's perfect heroines and disap-
pointingly conservative attitudes. However,
these negative views do not give enough
weight to Dickens's public involvement in
selected women's issues, and seriously underestimate the complexity of his novels and
their positioning within the ideological structures of their time.

Although the feminine ideal rose to
prominence early in Victoria's reign, many
women's issues were intensely debated
throughout the century: PROSTITUTION, low-
paid female WORK, EDUCATION, entry to the
professions, women's suffrage, divorce, and
rights within marriage. Dickens's response to
demands for reform was mixed, even hostile
at times, and *Household Words* could be
outspoken against women's rights. A leading
article by Dickens on manifestations of
'Bloomerism' adopted the jocular tone of
PUNCH cartoons to mock not simply a masculine style of female attire, but women's pretensions to the public platform and public
office, and even CHARITY work of an ostentatious kind ('Sucking Pigs', *HW* 8 November
1851). Another polemical contribution to
*Household Words* on 'Rights and Wrongs of
Women' (1 April 1854) attacked the kind
of woman who undermined the doctrine of
separate spheres by aspiring to become an

'inferior man'. The author of this piece, Eliza Lynn—herself a hard-working journalist—here adopted a discourse familiar to Dickens's readers, advocating the path of 'a noble, unpretending, redeeming, domestic, usefulness' to be taken by 'the loving, quiet wife, the good mother, the sweet, unselfish sister'. This theme is taken up through the character of Mrs Jellyby, who is heavily satirized for neglecting her own children in favour of the distant natives of Borrioboola-Gha. The reader is told in passing that Mrs Jellyby later directs her energies to a campaign that by implication is equally ridiculous, the right of women to sit in Parliament (*BH* 67). John Stuart MILL, the feminist reformer, reacted to the novel with anger, attacking Dickens's 'vulgar impudence' in ridiculing the rights of women.

Dickens did not systematically pursue this reactionary philosophy. He associated throughout his life with women from a great variety of backgrounds. His letters reveal his admiration for upper-class ladies who played a significant public role, from the formidable benefactress Angela Burdett COUTTS to society hostesses like the author Lady Blessington and the Hon. Mrs Richard WATSON. He appreciated the professionalism of women in the theatre, and encouraged women writers to contribute to his journals. He believed in a basic education for girls, provided it was biased towards the development of practical domestic skills, and he supported the cause of admitting women to Royal Academy schools. His daughter Kate, who developed a career as a painter with her father's support, attended art classes at Bedford College, one of the main institutions set up in the middle of the 19th century to improve women's education. However, with a few small exceptions, such as Helena Landless's aptitude for sharing her brother's advanced studies (*MED* 10), little of this interest in women's education emerges in his fiction.

Dickens's most notable intervention in women's issues was his share in the establishment of URANIA COTTAGE, a home for the rehabilitation of prostitutes and women at risk. He recognized harsh economic circumstances as a significant factor in tempting women onto the streets, and exposed the scandal of badly paid women's occupations in his novels and magazines. The vision sequence of *The* CHIMES uses Meg's fate to attack the iniquitous system of sewing outwork, a cause taken up in other mid-century social protest works like Thomas HOOD's famous poem 'The Song of the Shirt', and paintings of seamstresses by Richard Redgrave and Anna Elizabeth Blunden. The treatment of SERVANTS was another topical issue: during the 1860s the number of female domestic servants in England exceeded 1 million, a considerable number of them under 15 years old. Like the rest of the middle classes Dickens took the necessity of having servants for granted, but he strongly opposed their exploitation. In *The Old Curiosity Shop* the working conditions of Barbara, servant to the benevolent Garlands, are described as thoroughly enjoyable; by contrast, the nameless little skivvy working for the Brasses is little better than a slave. At a higher social level, the plight of respectable women working as governesses was highlighted in *Household Words* ('Only a Governess', *HW* 7 May 1859) and in a brief episode encapsulating Ruth Pinch's daily humiliations at her employers' hands (*MC* 36).

Dickens was openly committed to one feminist cause: the need for urgent changes in the divorce laws and dramatic improvements in the rights of married women. In *Hard Times*, published as the recommendations of a Royal Commission on Divorce were being translated into a parliamentary bill, Dickens gave unequivocal support to affordable divorce through the case of Stephen Blackpool. The novel's emphasis was on the plight of the wronged husband rather than the wife, but the episode in which Stephen's drunken wife returns home was published in the same number of *Household Words* as a pro-divorce article by Eliza Lynn based on the widely publicised case of Caroline Norton ('One of our Legal Fictions', *HW* 29 April 1854). Further references to the iniquities of a matrimonial system where the woman's person, property, and children belonged to her husband appear throughout *Household Words*: during the controversy preceding the 1857 Matrimonial Causes Act, another of Eliza Lynn's articles called the English husband an 'absolute lord' over his 'conjugal prisoner' ('Marriage Gaolers', *HW* 5 July 1856).

The heartless dealings of the middle-class marriage market, and its tragic consequences for women in particular, form a major theme of Dickens's fiction. In *Little Dorrit* Fanny and

Sparkler's nuptial carriage, 'after rolling for a few minutes smoothly over a fair pavement, had begun to jolt through a Slough of Despond, and through a long, long avenue of wrack and ruin' (2.15). In *Our Mutual Friend* Sophronia and Alfred Lammle betray each other into wedlock, though Georgiana Podsnap resists the upper-class matchmaking that treats her as part of the family furniture. The patriarch Mr Dombey tries to subjugate Edith as his 'chattel'; Edith, who wears the jewels bestowed by her marriage settlement like chains, retaliates with the harshest blow she can deliver, ruining Dombey's reputation by an apparently adulterous liaison. As an act of revenge, the unimpeachably respectable Mr Dombey strikes his daughter across her breast.

The threat of mental cruelty and physical violence to women is never far in the background of Dickens's novels. Weaker women like Clara Murdstone, Mrs Gradgrind, and the first Mrs Dombey fade away under harsh treatment. Men like Bill Sikes, Jonas Chuzzlewit, and Betsey Trotwood's husband deliver blows and worse. In *Little Dorrit*, Rigaud is accused of wife murder, Pet Meagles naively ties herself to a heartless husband, and Affery graphically describes marriage to Flintwich as 'a Smothering instead of a Wedding' (1.3). Behind the façade of the Dickensian marriage could be untold misery and even murder, and it was nearly always the woman who paid. However, Dickens did not condone flouting the moral code. In his novels there was no question of escaping the marriage trap simply by living in sin with a more congenial partner; once a mistake has been made, as in David Copperfield's marriage to Dora, death is the only release. Dickens seems to have applied rather different standards to his own friends, not least George CRUIKSHANK and Wilkie COLLINS, who both conducted two domestic establishments, and in the case of Ellen TERNAN, whom he may have kept quietly as his mistress for many years after the break-up of his own marriage. The women must have experienced more serious problems than their partners in living through the daily disadvantages of such socially unacceptable arrangements.

Dickens was no more consistent in his fiction than in his life. He deployed a range of standard images which schematically complement the angel figure: the sweet girl or playful puss with the capacity to grow into a domestic woman is at one end of the scale, balanced by the passionate or fallen woman at the other (see SEXUALITY). His old hags (like Mrs Skewton and Lady Tippins) and nagging shrews (like Mrs Weller and Mrs Snagsby), who stand out in humorous relief to his saccharine young women, are created with unmistakable misogynous relish. But there is no way of neatly categorizing Dickens's cast of some 400 female characters. Even conventional qualities can be differently apportioned, as with the pairing of wild Helena Landless and innocent Rosa Bud in *Edwin Drood*: Helena is both gypsy-like and marriageable, while Rosa is both kitten-like and surprisingly resilient. There are many strong portraits, comic and tragic, who do not fit the blueprints, from gruff Betsey Trotwood to sexy Dolly Varden, loyal Mrs Micawber to murderous Madame Defarge, wilful Caddy Jellyby to brave Lizzie Hexam.

Nor is it the case that the territory inhabited by Dickens's fictional women is limited to the domestic hearth. As in Victorian society, women in the novels are realistically shown pursuing a great range of female employment. Some are caricatured to stand for a whole profession, like the line of spinsterish schoolteachers stretching from the Misses Crumpton who keep the Minerva House establishment ('Sentiment', *SB*), to Miss Peecher and Miss Twinkleton in Dickens's last novels (*OMF*; *MED*). More memorable, though still merged with their occupations, are the drunken midwife Mrs Gamp (*MC*), the landladies Mrs Bardell (*PP*) and Mrs Crupp (*DC*), and the innkeepers, motherly Mrs Lupin (*MC*) and disciplinarian Miss Abbey Potterson (*OMF*). Other trades are followed by highly individualized characters: Rachael's factory work (*HT*), Madame Mantalini's dressmaking (*NN*), Little Em'ly's sewing for an undertaker (*DC*), Betty Higden's home laundry (*OMF*), Miss Mowcher's chiropody and hairdressing (*DC*), Jenny Wren's doll's dressmaking (*OMF*), and Fanny Dorrit's dancing (*LD*). Dedicated as he was to the work ethic, Dickens expected well-off women to wear the household keys at their belt and fulfil an active role in the creation of the bourgeois home. Nowhere do we find him idealizing the kind of heroine who merely adorns society with her light accomplishments, a lifestyle that is savagely satirized in Volumnia Dedlock (*BH*). Yet there is never any doubt that home is a woman's first priority and that her labour in the domestic arena should be disguised as far as possible to keep it within the bounds of the feminine. The paragon Agnes Wickfield, 'little housekeeper' and the emotional mainstay of the men in her circle, even makes the addition of a small girls' school to her responsibilities seem apparently effortless, commenting: 'The labour is so pleasant ... that it is scarcely grateful in me to call it by that name' (*DC* 60).

With the development of sophisticated models for the analysis of gender in literature, a strong case has been made that Dickens's fiction explores the constrictions and contradictions of women's roles rather than merely inscribing the dominant patriarchal ideology (see CRITICISM: FEMINIST). Certainly his later novels, from *Dombey and Son* onwards, demonstrate a growing interest in women's nature, often through the sensitive exploration of a female character at the centre of the text; in *Bleak House* Dickens boldly experiments with writing half the story in a woman's voice. Recent readings of 19th-century literature typically refuse to deal with gender in isolation, seeing the construction of femininity and masculinity in fiction as inextricably bound up with socio-economic structures (see DOMESTIC FICTION). Dickens's female stereotypes, at least as importantly as his individualized characters, contribute to this modern reconstruction of changing Victorian values. Special critical interest has attached to *Dombey and Son*, whose title ironically signals its focus on the patriarchal system while its text replaces a lost son with the claims on the father's—and the reader's— attention made by a daughter. In an influential book by Mary Poovey (1989), a chapter on *David Copperfield* is placed alongside the analysis of other social constructs such as law, in order to define the half-hidden ideological systems determining Victorians' view of society and their gendered selves. Such readings expose ambivalence in Dickens's fictional treatment of women that is not accommodated by dismissive emphasis on his household angels. Dickens's oeuvre, and indeed his personal beliefs, are increasingly read as evidence not of Victorian certainties but of

discontinuities and conflicts lying deep in 19th-century culture.                    EW

Baird, J. D., ' "Divorce and Matrimonial Causes": An Aspect of *Hard Times*', *Victorian Studies*, 15 (1977).

Barickman, R., MacDonald, S., and Stark, S., *Corrupt Relations: Dickens, Thackeray, Trollope, Collins, and the Victorian Sexual System* (1982), ch. 3.

Poovey, M., *Uneven Developments: The Ideological Work of Gender in Mid-Victorian England* (1989).

Slater (1983).

Welsh (1971), part 3.

**Wordsworth, William** (1770–1850), English poet. Dickens apparently met Wordsworth only once, at a dinner on 5 February 1839, where the poet was present with his son (of whom Dickens acerbically noted: 'copyrights need be hereditary, for genius isn't'). But the only poem from Wordsworth's voluminous output that we can be certain Dickens actually admired is his brief and rather morbid lyric 'We Are Seven' (a letter from David Wilkie to Mrs Ricketts, 14 October 1839 reports Dickens's 'very great admiration' for this poem). There are clear parallels between Wordsworth and early Dickens in their fascination with CHILDHOOD and innocence, and it could be argued that Dickens's novels represent an urbanization of the Wordsworthian pastoral ideal.                    AR

Hartog, Dirk den, *Dickens and Romantic Psychology* (1987).

**work** is defined in two conflicting ways in Dickens's writings: either positively, as opposed to Idleness, or more negatively, as opposed to Play (see AMUSEMENT AND RECREATION). Work as the healthy exertion of one's faculties, Dickens applauded: he lived his own life at a furious pace and quite probably died from overwork. Work as mindless, mechanical labour, the by-product of the Industrial Revolution, he deplored and attacked, notably in *Hard Times*, where he set it against 'Fancy', linking it (unfairly) with UTILITARIANISM and (more justifiably) with an EDUCATION system which imposed wearisome rote learning while starving the imagination.

The Gospel of Work was a central tenet of Victorian MORALITY, deeply embedded in the Puritanism of the rising middle classes. It reached Dickens most directly through the writings of Thomas CARLYLE, whose sayings became part of the fabric of Victorian thought, and whose comments on work are particularly memorable: 'There is endless hope in Work'; 'Work while it be called Today; for behold, the night cometh in which no man may work' (*Sartor Resartus*, 2.4, quoting John 9: 4); 'Blessed is the man who has found his work; let him ask no other blessedness' (*Past and Present*, 3.11). This overtly Puritan philosophy sits uneasily with Dickens's avowed detestation of anything smacking of Calvinism—but the glorification of work had become by the middle of the century a Broad Church Victorian preoccupation, evident in most of Dickens's contemporaries from Charles Kingsley ('Do the work that's nearest'), through Matthew Arnold (who was brought up on the precept 'WORK. Not, work at this or that—but, Work'), to Cardinal Newman ('every one who breathes, high and low, educated and ignorant ... has a mission, has a work') (all cited in W. E. Houghton, *The Victorian Frame of Mind*, 1957, pp. 257, 243, 244 respectively).

Dickens's commitment to the Gospel of Work emerges not only as a major philosophical underpinning of the novels, but also at a more practical and linguistic level. The business and the language of work are everywhere. In *Pickwick Papers*, to be sure, the four heroes, led by a retired businessman, seem to be on a perpetual holiday; however, all the subsequent novels are full of their author's fascination with the variety of ways in which people make their living. In the minor writings, there are many comical descriptions of very humble occupations. In the Christmas stories there is Doctor Marigold: 'I am a Cheap Jack ... of all the callings ill used in Great Britain, the Cheap Jack calling is the worst used. Why aint we a profession? Why aint we endowed with privileges?' *Sketches by Boz* begins with pen-portraits of such characters as the Beadle, the Schoolmaster, the Curate, the Half-pay Captain and the Broker's Man. The novels and journalism are full of comic waiters, a profession memorably summed up in *Dombey*: 'Mrs Wickam was a waiter's wife—which would seem equivalent to being any other man's widow' (*DS* 8). Dickens's most successful major characters too are often identified with their work: Mr Squeers

is a schoolmaster, Mrs Gamp a midwife, Mr Bucket the first fictional DETECTIVE in English literature. In *Bleak House* particularly, professions from highest to lowest are represented: politicians (Cuffy, Buffy, etc.), lawyers (Tulkinghorn), a stationer (Mr Snagsby) and a law-writer (Nemo), military men (the Bagnets, Trooper George), down to the poor brickmakers and, even below them, to Jo, the crossing-sweeper. Henry Mayhew's *London Labour and the London Poor* was published in 1851, in the year Dickens began work on *Bleak House*: both works give harrowing accounts of the ways in which, in the mid-century, the very poor made, or more often failed to make, their livings (see LONDON: STREETS). There is also a fascination with new methods of working, the more positive results of INDUSTRIAL-IZATION. Dickens was no Luddite. In a speech to the Manchester Athenaeum in 1843 he praised the 'stupendous engines and whirr and rattle of machinery' (*Speeches*, p. 46). Mrs Rouncewell's younger son in *Bleak House* is a prosperous ironmaster in the North of England. Mr Toodle in *Dombey and Son* has come out of the mines to become a stoker on the new London-to-Birmingham Railway during the railway boom of the 1840s (see TRANS-PORT). The characters who come in for most opprobrium are those who do no useful work—dilettantes (so much despised by Carlyle) like Henry Gowan in *Little Dorrit*; selfish aristocrats like Sir Mulberry Hawk in *Nicholas Nickleby*, or spongers like Harold Skimpole in *Bleak House*; in that novel too is shown, in Richard Carstone, the tragic fate of those who never find their true work.

The language of work is minutely detailed in the novels (see STYLE). In *Dombey*, for example, there is the boxing argot of the Game Chicken (who had been 'tapped and bunged and had received pepper and been made groggy, and had come up piping': *DS* 44), as well as the nautical metaphors of Captain Cuttle and the military slang of Major Bagstock. In that novel too, Toodle gives fatherly advice to his children in the language of his profession: 'Keep your whistles going and let's know where you are' (*DS* 38). Sissy Jupe's father in *Hard Times* despairs because of his failure in the Circus: he 'missed his tip at the banners ... and was loose in his ponging' (*HT* 1.6). Mr Lillyvick, the collector of water rates, complains at 'the way that punch was cut off'

(*NN* 15). All manner of occupations fascinate Dickens. In *Our Mutual Friend*, the 'Golden Dustman', John Harmon's father, has made a fine living out of the 'dustheaps' of refuse in the city streets; the novel also includes a taxidermist and articulator of skeletons (Mr Venus) and a crippled girl who earns her living as a dolls' dressmaker (Jenny Wren). In *A Tale of Two Cities* there is a bodysnatcher (Jerry Cruncher), and a prisoner, Dr Manette, who begs to be allowed to work and survives his incarceration by obsessively making shoes. Children like Charley Neckett in *Bleak House* are shown bravely making a living. Only near the end of his career, in *Our Mutual Friend*, can Dickens look with some sympathy on the aimlessness of the upper classes in the person of Eugene Wrayburn, who hopes to be saved by finding a worthwhile profession and is in fact saved by the daughter of perhaps the lowest of the low in terms of work, a Thames scavenger.

Many Victorians seem to have focused on work as a means of escaping the confusion and depression brought about by an era of rapid change and fading beliefs. This is the solution famously propounded by TENNYSON at the end of *Maud* and 'Locksley Hall'—poems which Dickens read and admired. Dickens betrays this impulse in his own feverish 'plunging' (one of his favourite words) into work. In the early years this might suggest the necessary channelling of the prodigious energies of a young adult who had emerged triumphantly, in full health and strength, from a sickly childhood. Dickens's first traumatic experience of work, in WARREN'S BLACKING factory at the age of 12, did not deter him from 'plunging', straight from school at the age of 16, into two stints as office boy before he found his feet as freelance shorthand reporter at Doctor's Commons. Soon he was working for John (later Sir John) EASTHOPE on the MORNING CHRONICLE as a parliamentary reporter, a job which satisfied his need both for hard work and for constant activity: 'often I have transcribed for the printer from my shorthand reports . . . writing on the palm of my hand, by the light of a dark lantern, in a post chaise and four, galloping through a wild country, all through the dead of night' (*Speeches*, p. 347). Such fierce discipline was essential to him and stood him in good stead as he met deadlines for the monthly numbers

of the novels: 'To the wholesome training of severe newspaper work, when I was a very young man, I constantly refer my first successes' (*Speeches*, p. 379). Once his writing career began, the pace grew ever fiercer. In 1836–7, when he began *Oliver Twist*, Dickens was still writing the monthly numbers of *Pickwick Papers*, completing the second series of *Sketches by Boz*, editing BENTLEY'S MISCELLANY, and was also working on two plays, IS SHE HIS WIFE? and *The* VILLAGE COQUETTES. Other years show a similar overreaching: in 1846–7 he struggled simultaneously with *Dombey* and with the new Christmas book, *The* BATTLE OF LIFE; the following year, for once admitting to being overworked, he held over the next Christmas book, *The* HAUNTED MAN, while he tussled with the later stages of *Dombey*.

Dickens's working day shows the intensity with which he both worked and played. His son Charley likened him to a city clerk in his methodical habits. His normal routine was to write from ten in the morning until two in the afternoon. He then walked until five and after dinner found time for family, friendships and his other multifarious activities (Ackroyd 1990, p. 561). This routine was, of course, disturbed by such insistent demands upon his time as AMATEUR THEATRICALS, SPEECHmaking, and later, from 1858, the PUBLIC READINGS.

The need for work, for the discipline and sense of purpose it gave him, is evident throughout Dickens's career. This has often been read as in part a reaction against a much-loved but feckless father; certainly, it was lack of application which caused him most distress in his own children, in particular in his seven sons, who seem variously (with the exception of Henry) to have shown lassitude and lack of direction, the qualities so fearfully presented in the fictional Richard Carstone (see DICKENS, JOHN; CHILDREN OF DICKENS). Shiftlessness in one member of a family is often placed in the novels against industry in another, with characters like Rob the Grinder and Tip Dorrit setting off the virtues of the parent Toodles (in *Dombey*) and Amy Dorrit. This was a pattern Dickens knew all too well: he himself helped support, not only his grown-up children, but also his father and BROTHERS. In his novels (until the ambiguities of *Our Mutual Friend*) hard work is always rewarded and idleness always condemned.

The foregoing account has concentrated on 'Work' defined as the opposite of Idleness. 'Idleness' in Dickens's letters and novels is almost always linked with 'dissipation' (see, for example, his account to FORSTER of the proposed decline of Walter Gay in *Dombey*). However, following another strand through Dickens's writings, one finds 'Work' defined as the opposite of 'Play', and here a quite different argument is in operation.

SUNDAY UNDER THREE HEADS was Dickens's second noteworthy publication, a pamphlet which came out in 1836, three months after *Pickwick* began to appear. Its immediate stimulus was proposed SABBATARIAN legislation, but the wider argument, defending the need for leisure and imaginative play to set against toil, is one that surfaces throughout Dickens's career and comes to a climax in the great polemical novel *Hard Times* in 1854. The anatomizing of Useless Toil as opposed to Healthy Work in *Sunday Under Three Heads* anticipates John RUSKIN and William Morris: 'that incessant toil which lasts from day to day and from month to month; that toil which is too often protracted until the silence of midnight, and resumed with the first stir of morning.' The substance of Dickens's attacks on the 'idle rich' is encapsulated here: 'The plebeian, who takes his pleasure on no day but Sunday, jostles the patrician, who takes his from year's end to year's end.' Even at this early stage, Dickens is fascinated by the making of livings: he invents, to support his argument, a poor man who 'has many children about him, all sent into the world at an early age to struggle for a livelihood; one is kept in a warehouse all day, with an interval of rest too short to enable him to reach home, another walks four or five miles to his employment at the docks, a third earns a few shillings weekly as an errand boy, or office messenger ...'

*Hard Times* continues the argument set out in *Sunday Under Three Heads*. It is dedicated to Thomas Carlyle, and shows how, in mid-Victorian society, fulfilling work had become mindless toil. Here, though, toil is presented not only in the 'dark satanic mills' of Coketown, but in the daily lives of Mr Gradgrind's comfortable, well-fed children. Dickens, by a daring imaginative leap, describes emotional starvation as being just as terrible as physical deprivation. Weariness of mind and heart comes to any section of society forced to undertake meaningless activity day after day without hope of remission. (There had been a foreshadowing of this theme in *Dombey*, where Little Paul is worn to death—at a school for young gentlemen.) It is in *Hard Times* that Dickens adapts a comment from one of his letters: 'I entertain a weak idea that the English people are as hard-worked as any people upon whom the sun shines. I acknowledge to this ridiculous idiosyncrasy, as a reason why I would give them a little more play' (*HT* 1.10). Against Gradgrind and the mechanization of thought and feeling he therefore sets, not Idleness, but Play—in terms very similar to those he had used nearly twenty years before in the Sunday pamphlet: in the case of factory hands, 'exactly in the ratio as they worked long and monotonously, the craving grew within them for some physical relief—some relaxation ... some recognised holiday ...' (*HT* 1.5). Ironically, the symbolic purveyors of 'play', of entertainment, are Mr Sleary's circus folk, who in fact work immensely hard at their profession, while Bounderby, the rich banker and manufacturer, is never shown working at all. The embodiment of work here is not a cruel factory-owner, but Mr Gradgrind the Utilitarian, owner of the school whose own children, just as much as the factory hands of Coketown, are presented as victims of an oppressive regime.

Dickens's journalism is often concerned with work and working conditions. In *All The Year Round* (15 June 1867) there is an article uncompromisingly called 'Slavery in England'. Readers of Dickens's weekly magazine are reminded once again of 'the sufferings of milliners and work-girls', but this time the attack is extended from city to countryside in condemning 'the employment of gangs of children on field labour [which] often means simply selling them to a gangmaster or mistress'. As always he is concerned to condemn mindless toil wherever it occurs. Dickens's speeches too contain poignant evidence of his interest in work of every sort. There are speeches to a wide variety of professions, most of them the humbler ones, from newsvendors to mechanics, from governesses to gardeners; there is also a speech in 1858 to the Playground and General Recreation Society—showing that his early concern about the need for Play had not abated: after a detailed account of the amusements of London's children, he goes on: 'I venture to assert that there can be no physical health without play; that there can be no efficient and satisfactory work without play; that there can be no sound and wholesome thought without play' (*Speeches*, p. 272).

There is, however, a point in Dickens's thinking at which Play comes close to Idleness and thence dangerously close to Dissipation; it is here that the contradictions in his character, and in his life, emerge. 'The LAZY TOUR OF TWO IDLE APPRENTICES', written in 1857, contains, in the two adjectives, an indication of Dickens's suspicion of where Play might lead. The apprentice Thomas Idle is a thinly disguised representation of Wilkie COLLINS, whose bohemian way of life seems to have represented to Dickens a dangerous mixture of idleness and playfulness which both repelled and attracted him. In the 1850s, in the years before his separation from his wife, Catherine DICKENS, and during the growth of his passion for Ellen TERNAN, he seems consciously to have turned to work to maintain his control over himself. He confessed to FORSTER, shortly after the 'Lazy Tour', 'I have now no relief but in action. I am become incapable of rest' (Forster 8.2). It was at this point that, against Forster's advice, he initiated the public readings which were ultimately to fulfil his wish, that he should 'die,

doing'. Like Dr Manette, he now seemed to need to work to retain his sanity. In 1870 he was still editing *All The Year Round* and was writing *Edwin Drood*. In the last month of his life, his thoughts returned to Carlyle: 'One can only work on, you know—work while it is day' (quoted in Ackroyd 1990, p. 1071).

The contradictions in Dickens's character, and in his writings, are shadowed forth in his attitude to work. The two definitions of Work enmeshed there might well be seen in context as representing what might be called his Regency—or at least Georgian—side, embodied in *Pickwick Papers* and harking back to the relaxed hedonism of the early years of the century, and his later Victorian, repressive, moralistic side: the tension between them was a source of energy in the novels throughout his career—for Dickens was never uncomplicatedly Victorian. Leisure, to many Victorian writers, came to be seen as simply a prelude to further exertion, part, in fact, of the necessary rhythm of work. This is never so in Dickens, where the Gospel of Play is preached as fervently as the Gospel of Work. In *Hard Times*, Dickens sets against Gradgrindery Mr Sleary and his circus. They embody a simple truth to which Dickens had been loyal throughout his writing life—though in his private life, especially in the later years when he was sad and driven, it acquired a wider relevance and poignancy: 'People mutht be amuthed. They can't be alwayth a learning, nor they can't be alwayth a working, they an't made for it' (*HT* 3.8).

VP

# Y

**Yates, Edmund** (1831–94), post office official, journalist, lecturer, and recitalist, for whom Dickens 'always had an affectionate regard', according to his family: certainly he was among the select few whom, in letters, Dickens addressed by their Christian names. Long an admirer, Yates introduced himself in 1854, trading on Dickens's old friendship with his parents, notable ACTORS: Dickens had 'a loving and faithful remembrance always' of Mrs Yates, whom he regarded as 'a beautiful part of my own youth' (23 September 1860; see YATES, FREDERICK). Yates was already a very active spare-time journalist, but did not think himself 'up to the *Household Words* standard'; Dickens, however, helped and encouraged him, publishing essays, verse, and several novels by him in the weeklies. They became friendly, and Yates well describes the domestic routines at Dickens's homes in his *Recollections and Experiences* (1884).

One of Yates's journalistic innovations was the literary gossip column. Soon after the break-up of Dickens's marriage to Catherine DICKENS, he published a defence of him against the damaging 'lies' circulating about that episode, and also an unfriendly 'sketch' of THACKERAY (*Town Talk*, 13 June 1858), a hasty effort which he later regretted. Thackeray took great—inordinate—umbrage, accusing Yates, in his hostile account of his conversational manner, of breaching the gentlemanly code of the GARRICK CLUB where alone, as a fellow-member, Yates could have heard him talk. Eventually Thackeray formally complained to the Club's committee, and a prolonged, full-blown public row ensued, into which Dickens was drawn when Yates sought his help and advice. It ended with Yates's exclusion, and Dickens's resignation, from the Club, and in lasting, fierce ill will between the two novelists. Dickens was unlucky that his loyalty to Yates involved him in an affair, out of which nobody emerged with credit, over an article which he too thought should never have been published.

A 'blackguard' and '*cochon sublime*', according to Swinburne, Yates was brash and vulgar, less talented than industrious, one of the companions of Dickens's later years whom FORSTER meant when he wrote that 'if any should assert his occasional preference for what was beneath his level over what was above it, this would be difficult to refute'. But the two men esteemed each other, personally and professionally. Just before his death, Dickens commended his 'particular friend' Yates to an American publisher, as 'the most punctual and reliable of men in the execution of his work' and his novel as 'being of great promise' (5 June 1870). Yates 'almost . . . worshipped' Dickens; often asked whether Dickens came up to expectations, and whether the man was as loveable as the author, he always replied 'Yes; wholly', and he 'always held that Dickens was an exception to the general rule of authors being so much less interesting than their books.' His *Recollections*, which has a lively chapter on Dickens, has been named his best book.

PC

**Yates, Frederick** (1795–1842), actor and manager. Yates became co-manager of the Adelphi Theatre with Daniel Terry in 1825. From 1828 to 1835 he managed the theatre jointly with Charles MATHEWS the elder, whose 'At Homes' were presented there. From 1836, as sole manager, he staged and acted in several Dickens DRAMATIZATIONS, playing Pickwick (1836–7); Mantalini in STIRLING'S *Nicholas Nickleby* (1838), which was praised by Dickens; Fagin in *Oliver Twist* (1839); and Sir John Chester and Miss Miggs in *Barnaby Rudge* (1841–2). Dickens himself advised on the Adelphi's *The Old Curiosity Shop* (1840), in which Yates played Quilp to Dickens's satisfaction. Yates married the actress Elizabeth Brunton in 1823, whom Dickens described to her son Edmund YATES on her death as 'a beautiful part of my own youth' (23 September 1860).

JD

# MAPS

Britain: Places with major Dickensian associations

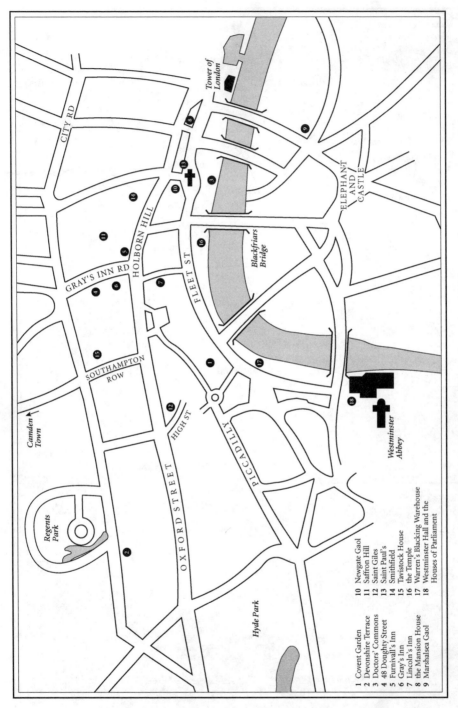

Dickens's London (based on a map of the 1850s)

1  Covent Garden
2  Devonshire Terrace
3  Doctors' Commons
4  48 Doughty Street
5  Furnivall's Inn
6  Gray's Inn
7  Lincoln's Inn
8  the Mansion House
9  Marshalsea Gaol
10  Newgate Gaol
11  Saffron Hill
12  Saint Giles
13  Saint Paul's
14  Smithfield
15  Tavistock House
16  the Temple
17  Warren's Blacking Warehouse
18  Westminster Hall and the
   Houses of Parliament

Dickens's travels in Europe

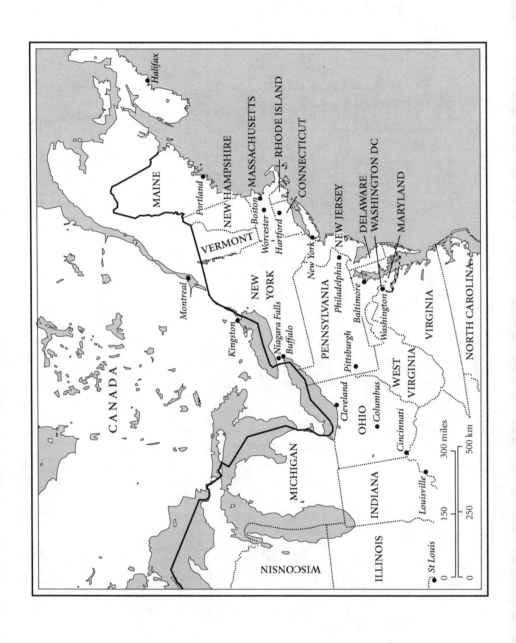

## Dickens's tours of America and Canada

**1842**

|  |  |
|---|---|
| 20 Jan | Halifax, Nova Scotia |
| 20–2 Jan | En route for Boston, aboard the *Britannia* |
| 22 Jan–5 Feb | Boston |
| 5–7 Feb | Worcester, Massachusetts |
| 7 Feb | Springfield, Massachusetts |
| 7–11 Feb | Hartford, Connecticut |
| 11–12 Feb | New Haven, Connecticut |
| 12 Feb–5 Mar | New York |
| 5–9 Mar | Philadelphia |
| 9–16 Mar | Washington |
| 17–20 Mar | Richmond, Virginia |
| 20–1 Mar | Washington |
| 21–4 Mar | Baltimore |
| 24–5 Mar | York and Harrisburg, Pennsylvania |
| 25–8 Mar | En route for Pittsburgh by canal boat |
| 28 Mar–1 Apr | Pittsburgh |
| 1–4 Apr | En route for Cincinnati by steamer, *Messenger* |
| 4–6 Apr | Cincinnati |
| 7 Apr | Louisville, Kentucky |
| 7–10 Apr | En route for St Louis by steamer, *Fulton* |
| 10–12 Apr | St Louis |
| 12 Apr | Lebanon, Missouri |
| 12–14 Apr | St Louis |
| 14–17 Apr | En route for Louisville by steamer, *Messenger* |
| 17 Apr | Louisville, Kentucky |
| 18–19 Apr | En route for Cincinnati by mail boat, *Benjamin Franklin* |
| 19–20 Apr | Cincinnati |
| 21–2 Apr | Columbus, Ohio |
| 22 Apr | Lower Sandusky, Ohio |
| 23 Apr | Sandusky, Ohio |
| 24 Apr | Cleveland, Ohio |
| 24–6 Apr | En route for Buffalo, New York, by steamer, *Constitution* |
| 26 Apr–4 May | Niagara Falls |
| 4–6 May | Toronto |
| 7–10 May | Kingston, Ontario |
| 10–11 May | En route for Montreal, by steamer and stage-coach |
| 11–30 May | Montreal |
| 30–1 May | Lake Champlain |
| 31 May–2 Jun | En route for New York by North River steamer |
| 2–3 Jun | New York |
| 3–4 Jun | Lebanon Springs, New York |
| 4–6 Jun | West Point, New York |
| 6–7 Jun | New York |

**1867–8**

|  |  |
|---|---|
| 18 Nov | Halifax, Nova Scotia |
| 19 Nov–7 Dec | Boston |
| 7–21 Dec | New York |
| 21–5 Dec | Boston |
| 25 Dec–3(?) Jan | New York |
| 3(?)–8(?) Jan | Boston |
| 8(?)–12 Jan | New York |
| 12–15 Jan | Philadelphia |
| 15–23(?) Jan | New York |
| 23(?)–25(?) Jan | Philadelphia |
| 25(?)–29(?) Jan | Baltimore |
| 29(?) Jan–1 Feb | Washington |
| 1–8 Feb | Baltimore |
| 8–12(?) Feb | Philadelphia |
| 12(?)–15(?) Feb | New York |
| 15(?)–17(?) Feb | Hartford, Connecticut |
| 17(?)–19(?) Feb | Providence, Rhode Island |
| 19(?)–22(?) Feb | Washington |
| 22(?)–25(?) Feb | Boston |
| 6–7 Mar | Albany, New York |
| 7–10 Mar | Syracuse, New York |
| 10–11 Mar | Rochester, New York |
| 11–14 Mar | Buffalo, New York |
| 14–15 Mar | Niagara Falls |
| 15–17 Mar | Rochester, New York |
| 17–18 Mar | Utica, New York |
| 18–20 Mar | Albany, New York |
| 20–2(?) Mar | Springfield, Massachusetts |
| 22–4 Mar | Worcester, Massachusetts |
| 24–5 Mar | New Haven, Connecticut |
| 25–6 Mar | Hartford, Connecticut |
| 26–7 Mar | Boston |
| 27–8 Mar | New Bedford, Massachusetts |

# GENERAL BIBLIOGRAPHY

## Works by Dickens

Only the novels, Christmas books, travel books, and collections authorized by Dickens are listed here, in chronological order. For other works see entries under their titles. Individual articles and sketches are not noted. For a comprehensive list of works and editions, see the Dickens entry by Paul Schlicke in the *Cambridge Bibliography of English Literature*, 3rd edn. (1999).

*Sketches by Boz*, first and second series (1836)
*The Pickwick Papers* (1836–7)
*Oliver Twist* (1837–9)
*Nicholas Nickleby* (1838–9)
*The Old Curiosity Shop* (1840–1)
*Barnaby Rudge* (1841)
*American Notes* (1842)
*Martin Chuzzlewit* (1843–4)
*A Christmas Carol* (1843)
*The Chimes* (1844)
*The Cricket on the Hearth* (1845)
*Pictures from Italy* (1846)
*Dombey and Son* (1846–8)
*The Battle of Life* (1846)
*The Haunted Man* (1848)
*David Copperfield* (1849–50)
*Bleak House* (1852–3)
*Hard Times* (1854)
*Little Dorrit* (1855–7)
*Reprinted Pieces* (1858)
*A Tale of Two Cities* (1859)
*Christmas Stories* (1859)
*The Uncommercial Traveller* (1860)
*Great Expectations* (1861)
*Our Mutual Friend* (1864–5)
*The Mystery of Edwin Drood* (1870)

## Reference books

Bentley, Nicolas, Slater, Michael, and Burgis, Nina, *The Dickens Index* (1988).

Chittick, Kathryn, *The Critical Reception of Charles Dickens 1833–1841* (1989).

DeVries, Duane (general ed.), The Garland Dickens Bibliographies:

Brattin, Joel J., and Bert G. Hornback, *Our Mutual Friend: An Annotated Bibliography* (1984).

DeVries, Duane. *General Studies of Charles Dickens and His Writing and Collected Editions of His Works: An Annotated Bibliography*.

Vol. 1 *Bibliographies, Catalogues, Collections, and Bibliographies and Textual Studies of Dickens's Works* (2004).

Vol. 2 *Autobiographical Writings, Letters, Obituaries, Reminiscences, Biographies and Biographical Studies* (2008).

Cox, Don Richard, *The Mystery of Edwin Drood: An Annotated Bibliography* (1998).

Dunn, Richard J., *David Copperfield: An Annotated Bibliography* (1981).

Engel, Elliot, *Pickwick Papers: An Annotated Bibliography* (1990).

Glancy, Ruth F., *Dickens's Christmas Books, Christmas Stories, and Other Short Fiction: An Annotated Bibliography* (1985).

—— *A Tale of Two Cities: An Annotated Bibliography* (1993).

Lougy, Robert E., *Martin Chuzzlewit: An Annotated Bibliography* (1990).

Litvack, Leon, *Dombey and Son: An Annotated Bibliography* (1999).

Manning, Sylvia, *Hard Times: An Annotated Bibliography* (1984).

Paroissien, David, *Oliver Twist: An Annotated Bibliography* (1986).

Rice, Thomas Jackson, *Barnaby Rudge: An Annotated Bibliography* (1987).

Schlicke, Paul, and Priscilla Schlicke, *The Old Curiosity Shop: An Annotated Bibliography* (1988).

Worth, George J., *Great Expectations: An Annotated Bibliography* (1986).

Lohrli, Anne, *Household Words: A Weekly Journal 1850–1859 Conducted by Charles Dickens* (1973).

Newlin, George, *Everyone in Dickens* (3 vols., 1995).

—— *Every Thing in Dickens* (1996).

Oppenlander, Ella Ann, Dickens' *All the Year Round: Descriptive Index and Contributor List* (1984).

Schlicke, Paul, 'Charles Dickens 1812–70', *The Cambridge Bibliography of English Literature*, ed. Joanne Shattock, *et al.* (3rd edn., 1999).

Shatto, Susan, Michael Cotsell, and David Paroissien (general eds.), The Dickens Companions:

Cotsell, Michael, *The Companion to Our Mutual Friend* (1986).

Jacobson, Wendy S., *The Companion to The Mystery of Edwin Drood* (1986).

Paroissien, David, *The Companion to Oliver Twist* (1992).

Sanders, Andrew, *The Companion to A Tale of Two Cities* (1988).

Shatto, Susan, *The Companion to Bleak House* (1988).

Simpson, Margaret, *The Companion to Hard Times* (1997).

Weinreb, Ben, and Hibbert, Christopher (eds.), *The London Encyclopaedia* (1983).

## Secondary sources (updated 2011)

Ackroyd, Peter, *Dickens* (1990).

Adrian, Arthur, *Georgina Hogarth and the Dickens Circle* (1984).

Allen, Michael, *Charles Dickens's Childhood* (1988).

Altick, R., *The English Common Reader* (1957).

Andrews, Malcolm, *Dickens and the Grown-Up Child* (1994).

—— *Charles Dickens and his Performing Selves: Dickens and Public Reading* (2006).

Axton, William F., *Circle of Fire: Dickens' Vision and Style and the Popular Victorian Theatre* (1966).

Bodenheimer, Rosemarie. *Knowing Dickens* (2007).

Bolton, H. Philip, *Dickens Dramatized* (1987)

Butt, John, and Tillotson, Kathleen, *Dickens at Work* (1957).

Chesterton, G. K., *Charles Dickens* (1906).

—— *Appreciations and Criticisms of the Works of Charles Dickens* (1911), repr. as *Chesterton on Dickens*, ed. Michael Slater (1992).

Chittick, Kathryn, *Dickens and the 1830s* (1990).

Cohen, Jane Rabb, *Charles Dickens and His Original Illustrators* (1980).

Collins, Philip, *Dickens and Crime* (1962; 3rd edn. 1994).

—— *Dickens and Education* (1963).

—— (ed.), *Dickens: the Critical Heritage* (1971).

—— (ed.), *Charles Dickens: The Public Readings* (1975).

—— (ed.), *Dickens: Interviews and Recollections* (2 vols., 1981).

Cunningham, Peter, *Handbook of London: Past and Present* (1850).

Davis, Earle, *The Flint and the Flame: The Artistry of Charles Dickens* (1964).

DeVries, Duane, *Dickens's Apprentice Years: The Making of a Novelist* (1976).

Dexter, Walter, *The London of Dickens* (1923).

Dickens, Henry, *Memories of My Father* (1928)

Eigner, E. M., *The Dickens Pantomime* (1989).

Fielding, K. J., *Charles Dickens: A Critical Introduction* (1958; 2nd edn. 1965).

—— (ed.), *The Speeches of Charles Dickens* (1960).

Ford, George, *Dickens and His Readers* (1955).

—— and Lane, Lauriat, Jr. (eds.), *The Dickens Critics* (1961).

Forster, John, *The Life of Charles Dickens* (1872–4), ed. J. W. T. Ley (1928).

Frye, Northrop, 'Dickens and the Comedy of Humors', in Ray Harvey Pearce (ed.), *Experience and the Novel* (1968).

Gilmour, Robin, *The Idea of the Gentleman in the Victorian Novel* (1981).

Gissing, George, *Critical Studies of the Works of Charles Dickens* (1924), repr. as *The Immortal Dickens*, ed. B. W. Matz (1925).

Goldberg, Michael, *Carlyle and Dickens* (1972).

Golding, Robert, *Idiolects in Dickens* (1985).

Gross, John, and Pearson, Lionel (eds.), *Dickens and the Twentieth Century* (1962).

Harvey, John, *Victorian Novelists and Their Illustrators* (1971).

House, Humphry, *The Dickens World* (1941; 2nd edn. 1942).

John, Juliet. *Dickens and Mass Culture* (2010).

Johnson, Edgar, *Charles Dickens: His Tragedy and Triumph* (2 vols., 1952).

Kaplan, Fred (ed.), *Charles Dickens's Book of Memoranda* (1981).

—— *Dickens: A Biography* (1988).

Kitton, Frederic G., *Charles Dickens by Pen and Pencil, Including Anecdotes and Reminiscences Collected by His Friends and Companions* (2 vols., 1890).

—— *Dickens and His Illustrators* (1899).

Laurence, Dan H., and Quinn, Martin (eds.), *Shaw on Dickens* (1984).

Leavis, F. R., and Leavis, Q. D., *Dickens the Novelist* (1970).

Ledger, Sally. *Dickens and the Popular Radical Imagination* (2007).

Marcus, Steven, *Dickens from Pickwick to Dombey* (1965).

Miller, J. Hillis, *Charles Dickens: The World of His Novels* (1958).

Monod, Sylvère, *Dickens the Novelist* (1968).

Moss, Sydney and Moss, Carolyn. *Charles Dickens and his Chicago Relatives* (1994).

Nayder, Lillian. *The Other Dickens: A Life of Catherine Hogarth* (2010).

Orwell, George, 'Charles Dickens', in *Inside the Whale* (1940).

Partlow, Robert B., Jr. (ed.), *Dickens the Craftsman: Strategies of Presentation* (1970).

Patten, Robert L., *Charles Dickens and His Publishers* (1978).

—— *George Cruikshank's Life, Times, and Art* (2 vols., 1992, 1996).

Pope, Norris, *Dickens and Charity* (1978).

Sanders, Andrew, *Charles Dickens Resurrectionist* (1982).

—— *Charles Dickens's London* (2010).

Schlicke, Paul, *Dickens and Popular Entertainment* (1985).

Schwarzbach, F. S., *Dickens and the City* (1979).

Slater, Michael (ed.), *Dickens 1970* (1970).

—— *Dickens and Women* (1983).

—— and John Drew (eds.) *Dickens' Journalism* (4 vols., 1994–2000).

—— *Charles Dickens: A Life Defined by Writing* (2009).

Smith, Grahame, *Dickens, Money, and Society* (1968).

—— *Charles Dickens: A Literary Life* (1996).

—— *Dickens and the Dream of Cinema* (2003).

Steig, Michael, *Dickens and Phiz* (1978).

Stone, Harry, (ed.), *Charles Dickens's Uncollected Writings from Household Words 1850–1859* (2 vols., 1968).

—— *Dickens and the Invisible World: Fairy Tales, Fantasy, and Novel-Making* (1979).

—— (ed.), *Dickens's Working Notes for His Novels* (1987).

—— *The Night Side of Dickens: Cannibalism, Passion, Necessity* (1994).

Storey, G., *Dickens and Daughter* (1939).

Sutherland, J. A., *Victorian Novelists and Publishers* (1976).

—— *Victorian Fiction, Writers, Publishers, Readers* (1996).

Thomas, Deborah A., *Dickens and the Short Story* (1982).

Thurley, Geoffrey, *The Dickens Myth: Its Genesis and Structure* (1976).

Tomalin, Claire, *The Invisible Woman. The Story of Nelly Ternan and Charles Dickens* (1990, 1991).

Van Amerongen, J. B., *The Actor in Dickens: A Study of the Histrionic and Dramatic Elements in the Novelist's Life and Works* (1926).

Van Ghent, Dorothy, 'The Dickens World: A View from Todgers'', *Sewanee Review* 58 (1950).

Walder, Dennis, *Dickens and Religion* (1981).

Welsh, Alexander, *The City of Dickens* (1971).

—— *From Copyright to Copperfield: the Identity of Dickens* (1987).

Wilson, Angus, *The World of Charles Dickens* (1970).

Wilson, Edmund, 'Dickens: The Two Scrooges', in *The Wound and the Bow* (1941).

# ALPHABETICAL LIST OF CHARACTERS

This list includes most named characters who appear in the novels, Christmas books, stories, sketches, and plays. It includes minor figures as well as main characters, and major generic figures such as Bishop, Bar, and Physician. It does NOT include characters from Dickens's journalism, characters who appear only in passing, unnamed characters, or characters who do not appear, such as Mrs Harris, Conky Chickweed, and Lady Flabella. Boodle and Buffy are listed, but not Coodle, Doodle, and Zoodle, nor Cuffy, Duffy, and Zuffy. Characters from *The Mudfog Papers, The Uncommercial Traveller,* and *Reprinted Pieces* are likewise omitted. Readers who wish to explore such arcana should consult George Newlin, *Everyone in Dickens* (1995) or Donald Hawes, *Who's Who in Dickens* (1997).

## Abbreviations to Accompany List of Characters

| | | | | |
|---|---|---|---|---|
| *Christmas Stories* | | | *SB*: B | 'The Beadle. The Parish Engine. The Schoolmaster' |
| CS: CS | 'The Child's Story' | | | |
| CS: DM | 'Doctor Marigold' | | *SB*: BC | 'The Bloomsbury Christening' |
| CS: GS | 'Going Into Society' | | *SB*: BH | 'The Boarding House' |
| CS: HH | 'The Haunted House' | | *SB*: BM | 'The Broker's Man' |
| CS: HTI | 'The Holly-Tree Inn' | | *SB*: BV | 'The Black Veil' |
| CS: MFS | 'A Message from the Sea' | | *SB*: C | 'The Curate. The Old Lady. The Half-pay Captain' |
| CS: MJ | 'Mugby Junction' | | | |
| CS: MLL | 'Mrs Lirriper's Lodgings' and 'Mrs Lirriper's Legacy' | | *SB*: CD | 'A Christmas Dinner' |
| | | | *SB*: DA | 'The Dancing Academy' |
| CS: NS | 'Nobody's Story' | | *SB*: DC | 'Doctors' Commons' |
| CS: NT | 'No Thoroughfare' | | *SB*: DD | 'The Drunkard's Death' |
| CS: PCEP | 'The Perils of Certain English Prisoners' | | *SB*: EB | 'The Election for Beadle' |
| | | | *SB*: FM | 'The First of May' |
| CS: PRS | 'The Poor Relation's Story' | | *SB*: FS | 'The Four Sisters' |
| CS: SL | 'Somebody's Luggage' | | *SB*: GWD | 'The Great Winglebury Duel' |
| CS: SPT | 'Seven Poor Travellers' | | *SB*: HCS | 'Hackney-Coach Stands' |
| CS: SS | 'The Schoolboy's Story' | | *SB*: HP | 'The Hospital Patient' |
| CS: TTG | 'Tom Tiddler's Ground' | | *SB*: HS | 'Horatio Sparkins' |
| CS: WGM | 'The Wreck of the Golden Mary' | | *SB*: LCD | 'The Last Cab Driver and the First Omnibus Cad' |
| | | | *SB*: LR | 'London Recreations' |
| GSE | 'George Silverman's Explanation' | | *SB*: LS | 'The Ladies' Societies' |
| | | | *SB*: MA | 'The Misplaced Attachment of Mr John Dounce' |
| HR | 'A Holiday Romance' | | | |
| ISHW | *Is She His Wife?* | | *SB*: MC | 'Mr Minns and His Cousin' |
| L | *The Lamplighter* | | *SB*: MEE | 'Miss Evans and the Eagle' |
| MND | *Mr Nightingale's Diary* | | *SB*: MJP | 'Mrs Joseph Porter' |
| PL | 'The Pantomime of Life' | | *SB*: MM | 'The Mistaken Milliner' |
| PLT | 'The Public Life of Mr Tulrumble' | | *SB*: MNI | 'Making a Night of It' |
| | | | *SB*: NY | 'The New Year' |
| | | | *SB*: ONN | 'Our Next-Door Neighbour' |
| *Sketches by Boz* | | | *SB*: PBS | 'The Pawnbroker's Shop' |
| *SB*: A | 'Astley's' | | *SB*: PD | 'Public Dinners' |

| | | | |
|---|---|---|---|
| Bailey, Captain | DC | Belvawney, Miss | NN |
| Balderstone, Thomas (Uncle Tom) | SB:MJP | Ben | CS:SPT |
| Balim | SYG:YLYG | Ben | OT |
| Bamber, Jack | PP | Bench | LD |
| Bangham, Mrs | LD | Benjamin | BR |
| Banks, Major | HD | Benson, Lucy | VC |
| Bantam, Angelo Cyrus | PP | Benson, Old | VC |
| Baps | DS | Benson, Young | VC |
| Baps, Mrs | DS | Benton, Miss | MHC |
| Baptista, Giovanni | TBRD | Berinthia (Berry) | DS |
| Baptiste | CS:SL | Berry (Berinthia) | DS |
| Bar | LD | Bet (Betsy) | OT |
| Barbara (Mrs Kit Nubbles) | OCS | Betley | CS:MLL |
| Barbara's Mother | OCS | Betsey | BL |
| Barbary, Miss | BH | Betsy | PP |
| Bardell, Mrs Martha | PP | Bevan | MC |
| Bardell, Tommy | PP | Bib, Julius Washington Merryweather | MC |
| Barker, Fanny | L | Biddy | GE |
| Barker, Mrs | SYG:CYG | Bigwig Family | CS:NS |
| Barker, Phil | OT | Bilberry, Lady Jemima | LD |
| Barker, William | SB:LCD | Bill | GE |
| Barkis | DC | Bill | OT |
| Barley, Clara | GE | Bill | PP |
| Barley, Old Bill | GE | Bill, Black | GE |
| Barnacle, Clarence (Barnacle, Junior) | LD | Bill, Uncle | SB:LR |
| Barnacle, Ferdinand | LD | Billikin, Mrs | MED |
| Barnacle, Lord Decimus Tite | LD | Billsmethi, Master | SB:DA |
| Barnacle, Tite | LD | Billsmethi, Miss | SB:DA |
| Barnacle, William, MP | LD | Billsmethi, Signor | SB:DA |
| Barney | OT | Bintrey | CS:NT |
| Barroneau, Madame Henri | LD | Bishop | LD |
| Barsad, John (Solomon Pross) | TTC | Bitherstone, Master | DS |
| Barton, Jacob | SB:HS | Bitzer | HT |
| Bates, Belinda | CS:HH | Black, Mrs | HR |
| Bates, Charley | OT | Blackpool, Mrs | HT |
| Bayton, Mr and Mrs | OT | Blackpool, Stephen | HT |
| Bazzard | MED | Bladud, Prince | PP |
| Beadle, Harriet ('Tattycoram') | LD | Blake, 'Warmint' | SYG:OOYG |
| Beatrice (Beatrice Tresham) | CS:MJ | Blandois (Rigaud) | LD |
| Beaver, Nat | CS:HH | Blathers | OT |
| Bebelle (Gabrielle) | CS:SL | Blight | OMF |
| Beckwith, Alfred (Meltham) | HD | Blimber, Cornelia | DS |
| Becky | OT | Blimber, Doctor | DS |
| Bedwin, Mrs | OT | Blimber, Mrs | DS |
| Begs, Mrs Ridger (Emma Micawber) | DC | Blinder, Bill | MHC |
| Belinda | MHC | Blinder, Mrs | BH |
| Bella | CS:TTG | Blockitt, Mrs | DS |
| Bella | SB:PV | Blockson, Mrs | NN |
| Belle | CC | Blogg | OMF |
| Beller, Henry | PP | Bloss, Mrs | SB:BH |
| Belling | NN | Blotton | PP |
| Bellows, Brother | LD | Blowers | BH |

| | | | |
|---|---|---|---|
| Bob | *LD* | Brogson | *SB*:MC |
| Bobbo | *CS:MLL* | Brook Dingwall, Cornelius, MP | *SB*:S |
| Bobster | *NN* | Brook Dingwall, Frederick | *SB*:S |
| Bobster, Cecilia | *NN* | Brook Dingwall, Lavinia | *SB*:S |
| Bocker, Tom | *OMF* | Brook Dingwall, Mrs Cornelius | *SB*:S |
| Boffer | *PP* | Brooker | *NN* |
| Boffin, Henrietta | *OMF* | Brooks | *NN* |
| Boffin, Nicodemus (Noddy) | *OMF* | Browdie, John | *NN* |
| Bogsby, James George | *BH* | Brown | HR |
| Bokum, Mrs | *DS* | Brown | *OCS* |
| Bolder | *NN* | Brown of Muggleton | *PP* |
| Boldheart, Captain | HR | Brown, Alice (Alice Marwood) | *DS* |
| Boldwig, Captain | *PP* | Brown, Captain John | *DS* |
| Bolo, Miss | *PP* | Brown, Emily | *SB*:GWD |
| Bolter, Morris (Noah Claypole) | *OT* | Brown, Good Mrs | *DS* |
| Bolter, Mrs (Charlotte) | *OT* | Brown, Mr and Mrs | *SYG*:FYG |
| Bonney | *NN* | Brown, the three Misses | *SB*:LS |
| Boodle, Lord | *BH* | Brownlow | *OT* |
| Boots | *OMF* | Bucket, Inspector | *BH* |
| Boots (Cobbs) | *CS*:HTI | Bucket, Mrs | *BH* |
| Boozey, William | HR | Bud, Rosa | *MED* |
| Boozle | *SYG*:TYG | Budden, Alexander Augustus | *SB*:MC |
| Borum, Mrs | *NN* | Budden, Amelia | *SB*:MC |
| Bottles | *CS*:HH | Budden, Octavius | *SB*:MC |
| Bouclet, Madame | *CS*:SL | Budger, Mrs | *PP* |
| Bounderby, Josiah | *HT* | Buffle | *CS:MLL* |
| Bounderby, Mrs (Louisa Gradgrind) | *HT* | Buffle, Mrs | *CS:MLL* |
| Bowley, Lady | *Chimes* | Buffle, Robina | *CS:MLL* |
| Bowley, Master | *Chimes* | Buffum, Oscar | *MC* |
| Bowley, Sir Joseph, MP | *Chimes* | Buffy, The Right Hon. William, MP | *BH* |
| Bowyer, The | *MHC* | Bulder, Colonel | *PP* |
| Boythorn, Lawrence | *BH* | Bulder, Mrs and Miss | *PP* |
| Brandley, Mrs | *GE* | Bule, Miss | *CS*:HH |
| Brass, Sally | *OCS* | Bullamy | *MC* |
| Brass, Sampson | *OCS* | Bulph | *NN* |
| Bravassa, Miss | *NN* | Bumble | *OT* |
| Bray, Madeline | *NN* | Bumble, Mrs (Mrs Corney) | *OT* |
| Bray, Walter | *NN* | Bumple, Michael | *SB*:DC |
| Brewer | *OMF* | Bung | *SB*:EB, BM |
| Brick, Jefferson | *MC* | Bunsby, Captain Jack | *DS* |
| Brick, Mrs | *MC* | Burton, Thomas | *PP* |
| Briggs | *DS* | Butler, Theodosius | *SB*:S |
| Briggs, Alexander | *SB*:SE | Buzfuz, Serjeant | *PP* |
| Briggs, Julia | *SB*:SE | | |
| Briggs, Kate | *SB*:SE | Calton | *SB*:BH |
| Briggs, Mr and Mrs | *SYC*:EC | Camilla | *GE* |
| Briggs, Mrs | *SB*:SE | Cape | *SB*:MJP |
| Briggs, Samuel | *SB*:SE | Capper | *SYG*:VFYG |
| Britain, Benjamin (Little Britain) | *BL* | Captain, The | *SB*:PS |
| Brittles | *OT* | Captain, The Half-pay | *SB*:HCS |
| Brobity, Miss (Ethelinda Sapsea) | *MED* | Carker, Harriet | *DS* |
| Brogley | *DS* | Carker, James | *DS* |

| | | | |
|---|---|---|---|
| Drood, Edwin | MED | Fat Boy, The (Joe) | PP |
| Drowvey, Miss | HR | Father of Marshalsea (Dorrit, William) | LD |
| Drummle, Bentley | OT | Feeder, Mr, BA | DS |
| Dubbley | PP | Feeder, The Revd Alfred, MA | DS |
| Duff | OT | Feenix, Lord (Cousin Feenix) | DS |
| Dumkins | PP | Ferdinand, Miss | MED |
| Dummins | SYG:OOYG | Fern, Lilian | Chimes |
| Dumps, Nicodemus | SB:BC | Fern, Will | Chimes |
| Dunkle, Dr Ginery | MC | Fezziwig | CC |
| Dunstable | GE | Fezziwig, Mrs and the Misses | CC |
| Durdles | MED | Fibbitson, Mrs | DC |
| | | Fielding, Emma | SYC:YC, OC |
| Edkins | SB:SE | Fielding, May | Chimes |
| Edmunds | PP | Fielding, Mrs | Chimes |
| Edmunds, John | PP | Fiercy, Captain the Hon Fitz-Whisker | PL |
| Edmunds, Mrs | PP | Filer | Chimes |
| Edson, Mr | CS:MLL | Filletoville | PP |
| Edson, Mrs Peggy | CS:MLL | Finching, Mrs Flora | LD |
| Edward | SYC:ConC | Fips | MC |
| Edwards, Miss | OCS | Fish | Chimes |
| Edwin | CS:HT | Fisher, Fanny | CS:PCEP |
| Ellis | SB:PO | Fithers | SYC:PC |
| Emile | CS:SL | Fitz Binkle, Lord and Lady | SB:PD |
| Emilia | HR | Fitz-Marshall, Captain Charles | |
| Emily | SB:PV | (Alfred Jingle) | PP |
| Em'ly, Little | DC | Fixem | SB:BM |
| Emma | CS:HT | Fizkin, Horatio | PP |
| Emma | L | Fladdock, General | MC |
| Emma | PP | Flam, The Hon Sparkins | VC |
| Emmeline | CS:HT | Flamwell | SB:HS |
| Endell, Martha | DC | Flasher, Wilkins | PP |
| Englishman, Mr The (Langley) | CS:SL | Fledgeby, 'Fascination' | OMF |
| Estella | GE | Fleetwood, Mr and Mrs | SB:SE |
| Eugene | CS:SL | Fleming, Agnes | OT |
| Evans | SB:MJP | Fleming, Rose (Maylie, Rose) | OT |
| Evans, Jemima (J'mima Ivins) | SB:MEE | Flintwich, Affery | LD |
| Evans, Mrs | SB:MEE | Flintwich, Ephraim | LD |
| Evans, Richard | OCS | Flintwich, Jeremiah | LD |
| Evans, Tilly | SB:MEE | Flite, Miss | BH |
| Evenson, John | SB:BH | Flopson | GE |
| Exchange or Barter | DC | Flowers | DS |
| Ezekiel ('The boy at Mugby') | CS:MJ | Fluggers | NN |
| | | Fogg | PP |
| F, Mr (Finching) | LD | Folair | NN |
| F's Aunt | LD | Frank, Little | CS:PRS |
| Fagin | OT | Fred | CC |
| Fairfax | SYG:CYG | | |
| Fang | OT | Gabblewig | MND |
| Fanny | CS:CS | Gabelle, Théophile | TTC |
| Fareway | GSE | Gabrielle, 'Bebelle' | CS:SL |
| Fareway, Adelina | GSE | Gallanbile, MP | NN |
| Fareway, Lady | GSE | Game Chicken, The | DS |

| | | | |
|---|---|---|---|
| Gamfield | OT | Governor, Jack | CS:HH |
| Gamp, Mrs Sarah | MC | Gowan, Henry | LD |
| Gander | MC | Gowan, Mrs | LD |
| Ganz, Dr | CS:NT | Gradgrind, Adam Smith | HT |
| Gargery, Georgiana Maria (Mrs Joe) | GE | Gradgrind, Jane | HT |
| Gargery, Joe | GE | Gradgrind, Louisa | HT |
| Garland | OCS | Gradgrind, Malthus | HT |
| Garland, Abel | OCS | Gradgrind, Mrs | HT |
| Garland, Mrs | OCS | Gradgrind, Thomas | HT |
| Gashford | BR | Gradgrind, Tom | HT |
| Gaspard | TTC | Graham, Hugh | MHC |
| Gattleton | SB:MJP | Graham, Mary | MC |
| Gattleton, the Misses | SB:MJP | Grainger | DC |
| Gattleton, Mrs | SB:MJP | Grandfather | OCS |
| Gattleton, Sempronius | SB:MJP | Grandmarina, Fairy | HR |
| Gay, Walter | DS | Granger, Edith (Edith Dombey) | DS |
| Gazingi, Miss | NN | Grannet | OT |
| General, Mrs | LD | Graymarsh | NN |
| Gentleman in Small-clothes, The | NN | Grayper, Mr and Mrs | DC |
| George | CS:HT | Green, Miss | NN |
| George | CS:MLL | Green, Tom | BR |
| George | DC | Greenwood (Joby) | CS:HH |
| George | NN | Greenwood, the Misses | SYG:CYG |
| George | OCS | Gregory | DC |
| George | PP | Gregsbury, MP | NN |
| George, Aunt and Uncle | SB:CD | Grewgious, Hiram | MED |
| George, Mrs | OCS | Grey, the Misses | SYG:DYG |
| George, Trooper (Rouncewell, George) | BH | Gride, Arthur | NN |
| Georgiana | GE | Gride, Madeline | NN |
| Ghost of Christmas Past | CC | Gridley (The Man from Shropshire) | BH |
| Ghost of Christmas Present | CC | Griffin, Miss | CS:HH |
| Ghost of Christmas Yet to Come | CC | Grig, Tom | L |
| Gibbs, Villiam | MHC | Griggins | SYG:FYG |
| Giggles, Miss | MED | Griggs family | PP |
| Gilbert, Mark | BR | Grimble, Sir Thomas | NN |
| Giles | OT | Grimmer, Miss | HR |
| Gills, Solomon | DS | Grimwig | OT |
| Gimblet, Brother | GSE | Grinder | OCS |
| Glamour, Bob | OMF | Groffin, Thomas | PP |
| Gliddery, Bob | OMF | Grogzwig, Baron | NN |
| Glubb, Old | DS | Grompus | OMF |
| Gobler | SB:BH | Groper, Colonel | MC |
| Gog and Magog | MHC | Groves, James | OCS |
| Golden Dustman, The (Nicodemus | | Grub, Gabriel | PP |
| Boffin) | OMF | Grubble, W. | BH |
| Golden Lucy (Lucy Atherfield) | CS:WGM | Grudden, Mrs | NN |
| Goldstraw, Mrs Sarah | CS:NT | Grueby, John | BR |
| Goodwin | PP | Gruff and Glum | OMF |
| Goody, Mrs | OMF | Grummer, Daniel | PP |
| Gordon, Colonel | BR | Grundy | PP |
| Gordon, Emma | HT | Gubbins | SB:C |
| Gordon, Lord George | BR | Gulpidge, Mr and Mrs | DC |

| | | | |
|---|---|---|---|
| Matthews | *NN* | Morfin | *DS* |
| Maxey, Caroline | *CS:MLL* | Mould | *MC* |
| Maxwell, Mrs | *SB:PC* | Mould, Mrs and the Misses | *MC* |
| Maylie, Harry | *OT* | Mowcher, Miss | *DC* |
| Maylie, Mrs | *OT* | Mudge, Jonas | *PP* |
| Maylie, Rose (Rose Fleming) | *OT* | Mullins, Jack | *OMF* |
| Meagles | *LD* | Mullion, John | *CS:WGM* |
| Meagles, Minnie ('Pet') | *LD* | Mullit, Professor | *MC* |
| Meagles, Mrs | *LD* | Muntle (Alfred Mantalini) | *NN* |
| 'Mealy Potatoes' | *DC* | Murdstone, Clara | *DC* |
| 'Melia | *DS* | Murdstone, Edward | *DC* |
| Mell, Charles | *DC* | Murdstone, Jane | *DC* |
| Mell, Mrs | *DC* | Murdstone, Mrs Edward the second | *DC* |
| Meltham | *HD* | Mutanhed, Lord | *PP* |
| Melvilleson, Miss M. | *BH* | Mutuel, Monsieur | *CS:SL* |
| Mercury | *BH* | Muzzle | *PP* |
| Merdle, MP | *LD* | | |
| Merdle, Mrs | *LD* | Nadgett | *MC* |
| Merrywinkle, Mr and Mrs | *SYC:CWCT* | Namby | *PP* |
| Micawber, Emma | *DC* | Nancy | *OT* |
| Micawber twins | *DC* | Nandy, John Edward | *LD* |
| Micawber, Wilkins | *DC* | Native, The | *DS* |
| Micawber, Wilkins jun. | *DC* | Neckett | *BH* |
| Michael | *CS:PRS* | Neckett, Charlotte (Charley) | *BH* |
| Miff, Mrs | *DS* | Neckett, Emma | *BH* |
| Miggs, Miss | *BR* | Neckett, Tom | *BH* |
| Mike | *GE* | Ned | *OT* |
| Miles, Owen | *MHC* | Nell, Little (Nell Trent) | *OCS* |
| Milkwash, John | *SYG:PYG* | Nemo (Hawdon, Captain) | *BH* |
| Miller | *PP* | Nettingall, the Misses | *DC* |
| Miller, Jane Ann | *CS:NT* | Newcome, Clemency | *BL* |
| Millers | *GE* | Nicholas | *SB:PS* |
| Mills | *DC* | Nickleby, Kate | *NN* |
| Mills, Julia | *DC* | Nickleby, Mrs | *NN* |
| Milvey, Margaretta | *OMF* | Nickleby, Nicholas, the elder | *NN* |
| Milvey, The Revd Frank | *OMF* | Nickleby, Nicholas, the younger | *NN* |
| Mim | *CS:DM* | Nickleby, Ralph | *NN* |
| Mincin | *SYG:VFYG* | Nightingale, Christopher | *MND* |
| Minns, Augustus | *SB:MC* | Nightingale, Christopher, jun. | *MND* |
| Mivins ('The Zephyr') | *PP* | Nightingale, Rosina | *MND* |
| Mobbs | *NN* | Niner, Margaret | *HD* |
| Moddle, Augustus | *MC* | Nipper, Susan | *DS* |
| Molly | *GE* | Nixon, Felix | *SYG:DYG* |
| 'Moloch' (Sally Tetterby) | *HM* | Nixon, Mrs | *SYG:DYG* |
| Monflathers, Miss | *OCS* | Noakes, Mrs | *SG* |
| Monks (Edward Leeford) | *OT* | Noakes, Percy | *SB:SE* |
| Montague, Julia | *SB:MM* | Nobody | *CS:NS* |
| Montague, Tigg (Montague Tigg) | *MC* | Noddy | *PP* |
| Mooney | *BH* | Noggs, Newman | *NN* |
| Mooney | *L* | Norah | *CS:HT* |
| Mopes | *CS:TTG* | Normandy | *CS:GS* |
| Mordlin, Brother | *PP* | Norris Family | *MC* |

| | |
|---|---|
| Pocket, Herbert | *GE* |
| Pocket, Jane | *GE* |
| Pocket, Joe | *GE* |
| Pocket, Matthew | *GE* |
| Pocket, Sarah | *GE* |
| Podder | *PP* |
| Poddles | *OMF* |
| Podgers, John | *MHC* |
| Podsnap, Georgiana | *OMF* |
| Podsnap, John | *OMF* |
| Podsnap, Mrs | *OMF* |
| Pogram, The Hon. Elijah | *MC* |
| Polreath, David | *CS:MFS* |
| Pordage, Mr Commissioner and Mrs | *CS:PCEP* |
| Porkenham family | *PP* |
| Porter, Emma | *SB:MJP* |
| Porter, Mrs Joseph | *SB:MJP* |
| Potkins, William | *GE* |
| Pott | *PP* |
| Pott, Mrs | *PP* |
| Potter, Thomas | *SB:MNI* |
| Potterson, Abbey | *OMF* |
| Potterson, Job | *OMF* |
| Pratchett, Mrs | *CS:SL* |
| Price | *PP* |
| Price, Matilda ('Tilda) | *NN* |
| Prig, Betsey | *MC* |
| Pross, Miss | *TTC* |
| Pross, Solomon (John Barsad) | *TTC* |
| Provis (Abel Magwitch) | *GE* |
| Pruffle | *PP* |
| Puffer, Princess | *MED* |
| Pugstyles | *NN* |
| Pumblechook, Uncle | *GE* |
| Pupford, Miss Euphemia | *CS:TTG* |
| Pupker, Sir Matthew, MP | *NN* |
| Purday, Captain | *SB:C, EB* |
| Pyke | *NN* |
| | |
| Quale | *BH* |
| Quilp, Betsey | *OCS* |
| Quilp, Daniel | *OCS* |
| Quinion | *DC* |
| | |
| Rachael | *HT* |
| Rachel, Mrs (Mrs Chadband) | *BH* |
| Raddle | *PP* |
| Raddle, Mary Ann | *PP* |
| Radfoot, George | *OMF* |
| Rainbird, Alice | *HR* |
| Rairyganoo, Sally | *CS:MLL* |

| | |
|---|---|
| Rames, William | *CS:WGM* |
| Rarx | *CS:WGM* |
| Ravender, William George | *CS:WGM* |
| Raybrock, Alfred | *CS:MFS* |
| Raybrock, Hugh | *CS:MFS* |
| Raybrock, Jorgan | *CS:MFS* |
| Raybrock, Margaret | *CS:MFS* |
| Raybrock, Mrs | *CS:MFS* |
| Raymond | *GE:* |
| Red Whisker | *DC* |
| Redburn, Jack | *MHC* |
| Redforth, Lt.-Col. Robin | *HR* |
| Redlaw | *HM* |
| Reynolds, Miss | *MED* |
| Riah ('Aaron') | *OMF* |
| Richard | *Chimes* |
| Richards (Polly Toodle) | *DS* |
| Rickitt, Miss | *MED* |
| Riderhood, Pleasant | *OMF* |
| Riderhood, Roger ('Rogue') | *OMF* |
| Rigaud (Blandois; Lagnier) | *LD* |
| Rob the Grinder (Robin Toodle) | *DS* |
| Robinson | *SB:BH* |
| Robinson | *SB:FS* |
| Robinson | *DS* |
| Robinson, Mrs | *SB:FS* |
| Rodolph, Jennings | *SB:MM* |
| Rodolph, Mrs | *SB:MM* |
| Rogers | *SB:PO* |
| Rogers, Mrs | *PP* |
| Roker, Tom | *PP* |
| Rokesmith, Bella (Bella Wilfer) | *OMF* |
| Rokesmith, John (John Harmon) | *OMF* |
| Rolland | *CS:NT* |
| Rosa | *BH* |
| Rose | *SB:BV* |
| Rose | *VC* |
| Ross, Frank | *SB:WT* |
| Rouncewell | *BH* |
| Rouncewell, George (Trooper George) | *BH* |
| Rouncewell, Mrs | *BH* |
| Rouncewell, Watt | *BH* |
| Rudge | *BR* |
| Rudge, Barnaby | *BR* |
| Rudge, Mary | *BR* |
| Rugg | *LD* |
| Rugg, Anastasia | *LD* |
| Rumty (Reginald Wilfer) | *OMF* |
| | |
| St Evremonde, Charles (Charles Darnay) | *TTC* |
| St Evremonde, Marquis, the elder | *TTC* |

# TIMECHART

Showing Dickens's life and career against the general
historical and literary background of the period

## EARLY LIFE

| Dickens Family Life | Historical and Literary Background |
|---|---|
| **1809** John Dickens, a clerk in the Royal Navy Pay Office, marries Elizabeth Barrow (13 June) at St Mary-le-Strand, London. | |
| **1810** Frances ('Fanny') Dickens born (28 Oct.) (died 1848). | |
| **1811** | Prince of Wales becomes Prince Regent owing to madness of George III. Shelley expelled from Oxford. |
| **1812** CD born (7 Feb.) Mile End Terrace, Portsmouth. Family moves to 16 Hawk Street (June). | Napoleon invades Russia. War between UK and USA. Luddite riots. Byron's *Childe Harold*, Cantos i and ii published. |
| **1813** Family moves to 39 Wish Street, Southsea (Dec.). | Battle of Leipzig between the Allies and Napoleon's forces. Jane Austen's *Pride and Prejudice* published. |
| **1814** Alfred Dickens born (Mar.; died Sept.). | Allies capture Paris. Napoleon abdicates. Jane Austen's *Mansfield Park*, Scott's *Waverley*, and Wordsworth's *The Excursion* published. |
| **1815** John Dickens posted back to London (Jan.). Family move to Norfolk Street, St Pancras. | Battle of Waterloo. Byron's *Hebrew Melodies*, Scott's *Guy Mannering*, and Wordsworth's *White Doe of Rylstone* published. |
| **1816** Letitia Dickens born (died 1893). | Coleridge settles at Highgate, publishes 'Christabel' and 'Kubla Khan'. Scott's *The Antiquary* and *Tales of My Landlord* and Jane Austen's *Emma* published. |
| **1817** John Dickens posted first to Sheerness, then (Apr.) to Chatham Dockyard. Family settles at 2 Ordnance Terrace, Chatham (Dec.). | Death of Princess Charlotte, daughter of the Prince Regent. Keats's *Poems*, Byron's *Manfred*, and Coleridge's *Biographia Literaria* published. Jane Austen dies. |
| **1818** | Keats's *Endymion*, Scott's *Heart of Midlothian*, Mary Shelley's *Frankenstein*, and Jane Austen's *Northanger Abbey* and *Persuasion* published. |
| **1819** Harriet Dickens born (died 1827). | Peterloo Massacre. Scott's *Ivanhoe*, Shelley's *The Cenci*, Byron's *Don Juan* (first two cantos) published. |
| **1820** Frederick Dickens born (died 1868). | Death of George III, accession of George IV. Shelley's *Prometheus Unbound*, Keats's *Hyperion*, and Washington Irving's *Sketch-Book* published. |
| **1821** Family moves to St Mary's Place. CD begins education at William Giles's school, | Greek War of Independence. Keats dies. De Quincey's *Confessions of an Opium Eater*, |

writes a tragedy, *Misnar, the Sultan of India.*

**1822** Alfred Dickens born (died 1860). John Dickens recalled to London (summer), settles at 16 Bayham Street, Camden Town. CD follows family to London, his schooling broken off.

**1823** Fanny Dickens becomes boarder at Royal Academy of Music (Apr.). Family moves to 4 Gower Street North (26 Dec.) where Mrs Dickens attempts to start a school but without success.

**1824** CD sent to work at Warren's Blacking Factory (late Jan./early Feb.). John Dickens arrested for debt (20 Feb.) and sent to Marshalsea Prison where Elizabeth and the younger children join him after some weeks. CD placed in lodgings with a family friend in Camden Town, subsequently in other lodgings in Lant Street, Southwark. John Dickens obtains release from the Marshalsea under the Insolvent Debtors Act (28 May). Family moves to 29 Johnson Street, Somers Town.

**1825** John Dickens retires on pension from Navy Pay Office (9 Mar.). CD removed from Blacking Factory and sent to Wellington House Academy, Hampstead Road (? late Mar./early Apr.).

**1826** John Dickens working as Parliamentary correspondent for *The British Press.*

**1827** Family evicted for non-payment of rates (Mar.). CD leaves school, becomes clerk at Ellis & Blackmore, solicitors, and then at Charles Molloy's, solicitor. Augustus Dickens born (died 1858).

**1828** John Dickens working as reporter for *The Morning Herald.*

**1829** Family move to 10 Norfolk Street, Fitzroy Square. CD, having learned shorthand, works as freelance reporter at Doctors' Commons.

Scott's *Kenilworth*, and Shelley's *Adonais* published.

Shelley dies. Byron's *Vision of Judgement* and Scott's *Fortunes of Nigel* and *Peveril of the Peak* published.

Death penalty abolished in Britain for over 100 crimes. Construction of present British Museum building begun. Mechanics' Institutes founded in London and Glasgow. Scott's *Quentin Durward* and Lamb's *Essays of Elia* published.

Death of Byron. Beethoven's Ninth Symphony performed (Vienna). British workers allowed to unionize. W. S. Landor's *Imaginary Conversations* and Mary Russell Mitford's *Our Village* published.

First passenger railway in UK (Stockton—Darlington) opened (Stephenson's 'Rocket'). Manzoni's *I promessi sposi* and Hazlitt's *Spirit of the Age* published.

University College, London, founded, also Royal Zoological Society. Mendelssohn's Overture to *A Midsummer Night's Dream*, J. F. Cooper's *Last of the Mohicans*, and Disraeli's *Vivian Grey* published.

Battle of Navarino, Turkish fleet destroyed by British, French, and Russian fleets. Deaths of Blake and Beethoven. Schubert's *Winterreise* performed. Constable paints *The Cornfield*. Heine's *Buch der Lieder* published, also the first Baedeker travel guide.

Greek independence declared. Wellington becomes Prime Minister and Andrew Jackson President of the USA. Constable paints *Salisbury Cathedral*. Death of Goya. Dumas père's *Les Trois Mousquetaires*, Scott's *Tales of a Grandfather*, and Bulwer-Lytton's *Pelham* published.

Peel establishes Metropolitan Police in London. Catholic Emancipation Act. Horse-drawn omnibuses in London. Daguerre and Niepce form partnership to develop their photographic inventions. Delacroix paints *Sardanapalus* and Turner *Ulysses Deriding Polyphemus*. Balzac's *Les Chouans* published.

## CAREER

| CD's personal Life | Writing Career | Historical and Literary Background |
|---|---|---|
| **1830** Admitted as a reader at the British Museum (Feb.). Falls in love with banker's daughter Maria Beadnell (May). | | Death of George IV, accession of William IV. 'July Revolution' in France, accession of Louis Philippe. Lyell's *Principles of Geology* begins publication. Tennyson's *Poems, Chiefly Lyrical* published. |
| **1831** Begins work as reporter for *The Mirror of Parliament* edited by his uncle, J. M. Barrow. | | Reform Bill passed by House of Commons, vetoed by the Lords. Peacock's *Crotchet Castle* and Hugo's *Notre Dame de Paris* published. |
| **1832** Parliamentary reporter on the *True Sun*. Granted audition at Covent Garden Theatre but illness prevents his attendance. | | Reform Bill passed. Darwin begins publishing *Narrative of the Surveying Voyages of H.M.S. Adventure and Beagle* and Harriet Martineau begins publishing *Illustrations of Political Economy*. Bulwer-Lytton's *Eugene Aram*, Tennyson's *Poems*, and Mrs Trollope's *Domestic Manners of the Americans* published. |
| **1833** Produces private theatricals at his parents' home in Bentinck St. Ends affair with Maria Beadnell. | CD's first story 'A Dinner at Poplar Walk' (later titled 'Mr Minns and his Cousin', *SB*) published in *The Monthly Magazine*. | First steamship crossing of the Atlantic. Slavery abolished throughout British Empire. Carlyle's *Sartor Resartus* and Lamb's *Last Essays of Elia* published. Newman, Pusey, Keble, and others begin issuing *Tracts for the Times* (beginning of the Oxford Movement in the Church of England). |
| **1834** Becomes reporter on *The Morning Chronicle* and meets Catherine Hogarth (Aug.). Takes chambers at 13 Furnival's Inn, Holborn (Dec.). | Six more stories published in *The Monthly Magazine*, also one in *Bell's Weekly Magazine*; five 'Street Sketches' published in *The Morning Chronicle*. | Poor Law Amendment Act (the New Poor Law). Transportation of 'Tolpuddle Martyrs'. Destruction by fire of old Houses of Parliament. Ainsworth's *Rookwood*, Balzac's *Père Goriot*, Lady Blessington's *Conversations with Lord Byron*, Bulwer-Lytton's *Last Days of Pompeii* and Marryat's *Peter Simple* published. Deaths of Coleridge and Lamb. |
| **1835** Becomes engaged to Catherine Hogarth. (?May) | Two more stories in *The Monthly Magazine*, twenty 'Sketches of London' in *The Evening Chronicle*, ten 'Scenes | Municipal Reform Act. Browning's *Paracelsus*, Clare's *The Rural Muse*, and Wordsworth's *Yarrow* |

and Characters' in *Bell's Life in London.*

Two more 'Scenes and Characters' in *Bell's Life*, two contributions to *The Library of Fiction* and one to *Carlton Chronicle*, four 'Sketches by Boz, New Series' in *The Morning Chronicle. Sketches by Boz, First Series* published (8 Feb.). *Pickwick Papers* begins serialization in 20 monthly numbers (31 Mar.), *Sunday Under Three Heads* (June). *The Strange Gentleman* produced at the St James's Theatre (29 Sept.) followed by *The Village Coquettes* (22 Dec.). *Sketches by Boz, Second Series* published (17 Dec.).

*Revisited, and Other Poems* published.

Chartist Movement begins. Forster's *Lives of the Statesmen of the Commonwealth* and Lockhart's *Life of Scott* begin publication; Marryat's *Mr Midshipman Easy* published.

**1836** Moves into larger chambers at 15 Furnival's Inn (Feb.). Marries Catherine Hogarth at St Luke's, Chelsea (2 Apr.). Honeymoon at Chalk (Kent). Leaves staff of *The Morning Chronicle* (Nov.).? First meeting with John Forster (Dec.).

**1837** First child (Charles) born (6 Jan.). Move to 48 Doughty Street (Apr.). Death of Mary Hogarth, CD's sister-in-law (7 May). First visit to Europe (France and Belgium—July) and first family holiday at Broadstairs (Sept.).

First number of *Bentley's Miscellany* (ed. by CD) appears (1 Jan). First of the 'Mudfog Papers' appears in it. *Oliver Twist* serialized in *Bentley's* in 24 monthly instalments from the 2nd number. *Is She His Wife?* produced at the St James's (3 Mar.). *Pickwick Papers* published in one volume (17 Nov.).

Death of William IV, accession of Victoria. Carlyle's *French Revolution* published. Death of Grimaldi, the clown.

**1838** Expedition to Yorkshire schools with H. K. Browne (Jan./Feb.), second child (Mary) born.

*Sketches of Young Gentlemen* (10 Feb.) and *Memoirs of Joseph Grimaldi* (26 Feb.). *Nicholas Nickleby* begins serialization in 20 monthly numbers (31 Mar.). *Oliver Twist* published (9 Nov.).

Anti-Corn Law League founded in Manchester. First Afghan war breaks out. Daguerre—Niepce method of photography presented to the Académies des Sciences et des Beaux Arts, Paris.

**1839** Resigns editorship of *Bentley's Miscellany* (31 Jan.). Third child (Kate) born. Moves to 1 Devonshire Place, Regent's Park.

*The Loving Ballad of Lord Bateman* published (June). *Nicholas Nickleby* published in volume form (23 Oct.).

First Opium War between Britain and China. Turner paints *The Fighting Téméraire*. Ainsworth's *Jack Sheppard* published.

**1840**

*Sketches of Young Couples* published (10 Feb.). First number of *Master Humphrey's Clock* issued (4 Apr.). *The Old Curiosity Shop* published in 40 weekly numbers in *Master Humphrey* from 25 Apr. *Master Humphrey's Clock*, vol. i published (Oct.).

Victoria marries Albert. Introduction of the Penny Post. Sir Charles Barry begins building new Houses of Parliament. Nelson's column erected in Trafalgar Square. Ainsworth's *Tower of London*, Browning's *Sordello*, Poe's *Tales of the Grotesque and Arabesque*, and Thackeray's 'A Shabby Genteel Story' (*Fraser's Magazine*) published.

**1841** Fourth child (Walter) born. CD declines invitation to be Liberal parliamentary candidate for Reading. Granted the Freedom of the City of Edinburgh (29 June).

*Barnaby Rudge* published in 42 weekly numbers in *Master Humphrey's Clock* from 13 Feb. *Master Humphrey's Clock*, vols. ii and iii published (Apr. and Dec.). Publication of *The Old Curiosity Shop* and *Barnaby Rudge*, each in one volume (15 Dec.).

Peel succeeds Melbourne as Prime Minister. John Tyler becomes tenth President of the USA. *Punch* founded. Carlyle's *On Heroes and Hero-Worship*, J. F. Cooper's *The Deerslayer*, and Poe's 'The Murders in the Rue Morgue' (*Graham's Magazine*) published.

**1842** Visits America with Catherine (Jan.–June). Visits Cornwall with Forster and other friends (Oct.–Nov.).

*American Notes* published (19 Oct.). *Martin Chuzzlewit* begins serialization in 20 monthly numbers (31 Dec.).

Weber–Ashburton Treaty between Britain and America defines Canadian frontier. Tennyson's *Poems*, Macaulay's *Lays of Ancient Rome*, and Gogol's *Dead Souls* published.

**1843** Presides at opening of the Manchester Athenaeum (5 Oct.).

*A Christmas Carol* published (19 Dec.).

Launching of SS *Great Britain*, and building of Thames Tunnel between Rotherhithe and Wapping. Carlyle's *Past and Present*, Hood's 'Song of the Shirt' (*Punch*), and vol. i of Ruskin's *Modern Painters* published.

**1844** Fifth child (Francis) born. CD breaks with Chapman and Hall; Bradbury and Evans become his publishers. Resides in Genoa from 16 July. Visits London to read *The Chimes* to his friends (30 Nov.–8 Dec.).

*Martin Chuzzlewit* published in volume form (July). *The Chimes* published (16 Dec.).

Marx meets Engels in Paris. Turner paints *Rain, Steam, and Speed*. Disraeli's *Coningsby*, Kinglake's *Eothen*, and Thackeray's *Barry Lyndon* published.

**1845** Visits Rome and Naples with Catherine, returns to London from Genoa. Directs and acts in Jonson's *Every Man in His Humour* for the Amateur Players (Sept.). Sixth child (Alfred) born.

*The Cricket on the Hearth* published (20 Dec.).

Layard begins excavations at Nineveh. Wagner's *Tannhäuser* produced in Dresden. Browning's *Dramatic Romances and Lyrics*, Disraeli's *Sybil*, and Poe's *The Raven and Other Poems* published.

**1846** Editor of *The Daily News* (21 Jan.–9 Feb.). Resides in Lausanne (11 June–16 Nov.), and then in Paris.

*Pictures from Italy* published (18 May). *Dombey and Son* begins serialization in 20 monthly numbers (30 Sept.). *The Battle of Life* published (19 Dec.).

Famine in Ireland. Repeal of Corn Laws. First Christmas card designed. Browning marries Elizabeth Barrett. Balzac's *Cousine Bette*, Lear's *Book of Nonsense*, and Thackeray's 'Snobs of England' (in *Punch*) published.

**1847** Returns from Paris (28 Feb.). Seventh child (Sydney) born. Arranges lease of house for Miss Coutts's 'Home for Homeless Women' (Urania Cottage). Performs with The Amateur Players in Manchester and Liverpool.

First Californian gold rush. First British Factory Act (restricting hours worked by women and children). Charlotte Brontë's *Jane Eyre*, Emily Brontë's *Wuthering Heights*, and Prescott's *The Conquest of Peru* published. Thackeray's *Vanity Fair* begins serialization in monthly numbers (Jan.).

| 1848 | Directs and acts in London and provincial performances by the Amateur Players (May/July). Death of CD's beloved sister Fanny. | *Dombey and Son* published in volume form (Apr.). *The Haunted Man* published (19 Dec.). | 'The Year of Revolutions' (in Paris, Berlin, Vienna, Rome, Prague, and other cities). Outbreak of cholera in London. End of the Chartist Movement. Pre-Raphaelite Brotherhood founded. Mrs Gaskell's *Mary Barton* and first two volumes of *Macaulay's History of England* published. Thackeray's *Pendennis* begins serialization in monthly numbers (Nov.). |
| --- | --- | --- | --- |
| 1849 | Eighth child (Henry) born. | *David Copperfield* begins serialization in 20 monthly numbers (30 Apr.). | Death of Poe. Dostoevsky sentenced to penal servitude in Siberia. Matthew Arnold's *The Strayed Reveller and Other Poems*, Charlotte Brontë's *Shirley*, and Ruskin's *Seven Lamps of Architecture* published. |
| 1850 | Ninth child (Dora) born. CD founds the Guild of Literature and Art with Bulwer-Lytton to help needy writers and artists. | *Household Words*, a weekly journal edited by CD, begins publication (30 Mar.). *David Copperfield* appears in volume form (Nov.). | Restoration of Catholic hierarchy in England. Wordsworth dies, Tennyson succeeds him as Poet Laureate. Millais's *Christ in the House of his Parents* exhibited (attacked by CD in *HW*). Hawthorne's *The Scarlet Letter*, Kingsley's *Alton Locke*, Tennyson's *In Memoriam*, Turgenev's *A Month in the Country*, and Wordsworth's *The Prelude* published. |
| 1851 | Amateur theatricals at Rockingham Castle. Illness of Catherine Dickens, treatment at Malvern where CD visits her. Deaths of John Dickens (31 Mar.) and baby Dora (14 Apr.). CD directs and acts in Bulwer-Lytton's *Not So Bad As We Seem* at Devonshire House (in aid of Guild of Literature and Art). Last holiday at Broadstairs. Family moves into Tavistock House (Nov.). | *Child's History of England* begins serialization in *Household Words* (Jan.). | Death of Turner. Verdi's *Rigoletto* performed. The Great Exhibition in London. Melville's *Moby Dick*, Harriet Beecher Stowe's *Uncle Tom's Cabin*, and first part of Ruskin's *Stones of Venice* published. |
| 1852 | Tenth child (Edward) born. Northern provincial tour of *Not So Bad As We Seem*. First holiday visit to Boulogne (Oct.). | *Bleak House* begins serialization in 20 monthly numbers. | Deaths of Duke of Wellington and Gogol. Holman Hunt paints *The Light of the World*. Thackeray's *Henry Esmond* and Matthew Arnold's *Empedocles on Etna and Other Poems* published. |

| | | | |
|---|---|---|---|
| **1853** | Summer holiday in Boulogne. CD visits Switzerland with Wilkie Collins and Augustus Egg. First Public Reading (of *A Christmas Carol*) in Birmingham (27 Dec.). | Publication of *Bleak House* in volume form (Sept.). Conclusion of *Child's History* in *Household Words*. | Charlotte Brontë's *Villette*, Mrs Gaskell's *Cranford*, and Thackeray's *The Newcomes* published. |
| **1854** | CD visits Preston (Jan.). Summer in Boulogne. | *Hard Times* serialized in *Household Words* (1 Apr.– 12 Aug.). | Outbreak of Crimean War: battles of Alma, Balaclava, and Inkerman. Patmore's *The Angel in the House* and Tennyson's 'Charge of the Light Brigade' published. |
| **1855** | Meets Maria Beadnell (now Mrs Winter) again (Feb.). Directs and acts in Collins's *The Lighthouse* at Tavistock House (June). Joins Administrative Reform Assoc. Dickens family resides in Paris from Oct. | *Little Dorrit* begins serialization in 20 monthly numbers (1 Dec.). | Palmerston succeeds Aberdeen as Prime Minister. Fall of Sebastopol. Kingsley's *Westward Ho!*, Longfellow's *Hiawatha*, Browning's *Men and Women*, Trollope's *The Warden*, Tennyson's *Maud*, and Whitman's *Leaves of Grass* published. |
| **1856** | Purchases Gad's Hill Place (Mar.). CD returns to England (Apr.). | | End of Crimean War. Flaubert's *Madame Bovary* published. |
| **1857** | Directs and acts in Collins's *The Frozen Deep* (Jan.). Hans Christian Andersen visits CD at Gad's Hill. CD meets Ellen Ternan, who acts, with her mother and sister, in *The Frozen Deep* at Manchester. CD holidays in Cumberland with Wilkie Collins (Sept.). | *Little Dorrit* published in volume form. 'The Lazy Tour of Two Idle Apprentices' published in *Household Words* (3–31 Oct.). | Indian Mutiny: siege and relief of Lucknow. Elizabeth Barrett Browning's *Aurora Leigh*, Baudelaire's *Les Fleurs du mal*, Thomas Hughes's *Tom Brown's Schooldays*, Thackeray's *The Virginians*, and Trollope's *Barchester Towers* published. |
| **1858** | CD's first Public Readings for his own benefit given in London (29 Apr.–22 July). Separation from Catherine (May). CD publishes personal statement about his domestic affairs in *Household Words* (12 June). First provincial Reading Tour (2 Aug.– 13 Nov.) which also takes in Ireland and Scotland. | *Reprinted Pieces* published (as vol. 8 of the Library Edition of CD's works). | Suppression of Indian Mutiny, abolition of East India Company, and establishment of Viceroyalty. Offenbach's *Orpheus in the Underworld* performed. Frith paints *Derby Day*. George Eliot's *Scenes from Clerical Life*, William Morris's *Defence of Guenevere and Other Poems*, and Carlyle's *Frederick the Great* published. |
| **1859** | Second provincial Reading Tour (10–27 Oct.). | First number of CD's new weekly journal *All the Year Round* containing the opening instalment of *A Tale of Two Cities* appears (30 Apr.). Last number of *Household Words* (28 May). 'Hunted Down' published in *The New York Ledger* (Aug./Sept.). Serialization of *A Tale of Two Cities* concluded (26 Nov.). | Gounod's *Faust* performed. Deaths of Leigh Hunt and Washington Irving. Darwin's *On the Origin of Species*, George Eliot's *Adam Bede*, Meredith's *Ordeal of Richard Feverel*, Smiles's *Self-Help*, and Tennyson's *Idylls of the King* published. |
| **1860** | Katey Dickens marries | 'The Uncommercial Traveller' | Garibaldi captures Naples |

Charles Collins. CD settles permanently at Gad's Hill.

series begins appearing in *All the Year Round* (28 Jan.). First instalment of *Great Expectations* in *All the Year Round* (1 Dec.).

and Sicily. Wilkie Collins's *The Woman in White* and George Eliot's *The Mill on the Floss* published.

**1861** Readings in London (Mar./Apr.). Third provincial Reading Tour (Oct.–Jan. 1862). Charles Dickens, Junior, marries.

*Great Expectations* published in 2 volumes (Aug.).

Death of Prince Albert. Outbreak of American Civil War (Lincoln President). Mrs Beaton's *Book of Household Management*, Turgenev's *Fathers and Sons*, Dostoevsky's *The House of the Dead*, George Eliot's *Silas Marner*, and Peacock's *Gryll Grange* published.

**1862** Readings in London (Mar./June).

Bismark Prime Minister of Prussia. Début of Sarah Bernhardt at the Comédie Française, Paris. Hugo's *Les Misérables*, Christina Rossetti's *Goblin Market*, George Eliot's *Romola*, Flaubert's *Salammbô*, and Ruskin's *Unto this Last* published.

**1863** Charity readings at the British Embassy in Paris (Jan.). Readings in London (June). Deaths of Elizabeth Dickens and CD's fourth child, Walter (in India).

Lincoln's Gettysburg Address. Work begins on London's first Underground Railway. Manet paints *Le Déjeuner sur l'herbe*. Death of Thackeray. Kingsley's *The Water Babies* published.

**1864**

*Our Mutual Friend* begins serialization in 20 monthly numbers (1 May).

First Trades Union Conference. Tennyson's *Enoch Arden* and Newman's *Apologia pro Vita Sua* published. Tolstoy's *War and Peace* begins publication.

**1865** CD and Ellen Ternan involved in serious railway accident at Staplehurst, Kent (9 June).

*Our Mutual Friend* published in volume form (Nov.). Second collection of *Uncommercial Traveller* pieces (Dec.).

Assassination of Lincoln. Death of Mrs Gaskell. Wagner's *Tristan and Isolde* performed. Matthew Arnold's *Essays in Criticism*, Lewis Carroll's *Alice in Wonderland*, and Swinburne's *Atalanta in Calydon* published.

**1866** Reading Tour in London and the provinces (Apr./June).

Dr Barnado opens home for destitute children in East London. Dostoevsky's *Crime and Punishment*, George Eliot's *Felix Holt*, and Verlaine's *Poèmes saturniens* published.

**1867** Reading Tour in England and Ireland (Jan./May). Arrives in Boston for American Reading Tour (Nov.).

Last Christmas Story (*No Thoroughfare*, written jointly with Wilkie Collins) published in *All the Year Round*.

Fenian rising in Ireland. Garibaldi invades Papal States. Wagner's *Mastersingers of Nuremberg*, Zola's *Thérèse*

*Raquin*, vol. i of Marx's *Das Kapital*, and Ibsen's *Peer Gynt* published.

**1868**   Leaves New York for England (22 Apr.). Farewell Reading Tour begins (Oct.).

'George Silverman's Explanation' published in *The Atlantic Monthly* (Jan./Mar.). 'A Holiday Romance' published in *Our Young Folks* (Jan./May).

Browning's *The Ring and The Book*, Wilkie Collins's *The Moonstone*, Louisa May Alcott's *Little Women*, Dostoevsky's *The Idiot* published.

**1869**   First public Reading of 'Sikes and Nancy' (5 Jan.). Reading Tour broken off because of CD's serious illness (22 Apr.).

Girton College for Women at Cambridge founded. Opening of Suez Canal. Arnold's *Culture and Anarchy*, Blackmore's *Lorna Doone*, W. S. Gilbert's *Bab Ballads*, Mill's *On the Subjection of Women*, Twain's *Innocents Abroad*, and Flaubert's *L'Education sentimentale* published.

**1870**   Twelve Farewell Readings in London (Jan.). CD received by Queen Victoria (9 Mar.); dies of cerebral haemorrhage at Gad's Hill (9 June); buried in Westminster Abbey (14 June).

First monthly number of *The Mystery of Edwin Drood* appears (1 Apr.): only 6 of the intended 12 numbers completed when CD died.

Franco-Prussian War. End of Second Empire in France, establishment of Third Republic. First Elementary Education Act for England and Wales.

# INDEX

*Index topics which are also headwords are listed in* SMALL CAPITALS; *topics which are not head-words are printed in ordinary typeface. Only significant references are indexed; brief allusions to persons and topics are not listed.*